# Are A Click Away

## with McGraw-Hill's Homework Management system

**COMING FALL 2009...**
The updated and enhanced version of McGraw-Hill's Homework Manager and Homework Manager Plus

Introducing...

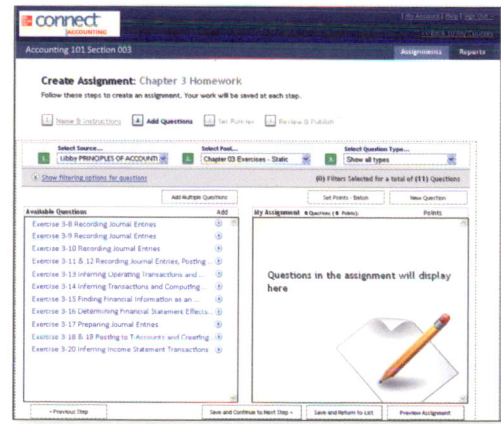

## How did we improve our online homework and testing systems with Connect Accounting and Connect Accounting Plus*?

By listening to students and instructors who told us they wanted:

- Single entry point, registration and log on
- Better reports for instructors
- Enhanced ability to export reports and grades to Blackboard and WebCT
- Enhanced question selection including the ability to sort question by AACSB and learning objective tags
- Customizable assignment policies for instructors
- Student Assignment Preview for instructors
- Local time-zone support

*Connect Plus includes an interactive, integrated version of this textbook.

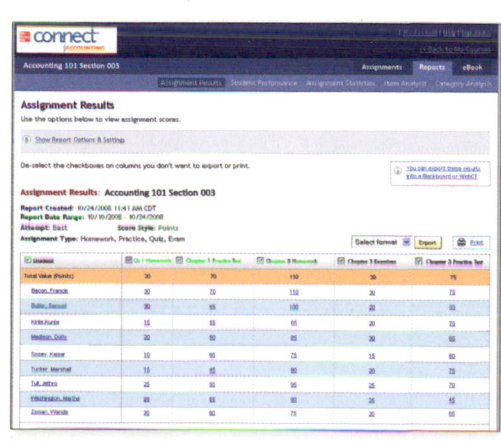

# Better Grades

**Q** Need a tutor **at midnight**?

Struggling to understand the accounting cycle?

**A**

## Accounting Cycle Tutors

- Web-based Quantum Tutors for the Accounting Cycle are like having your own personal instructor
- Answers your questions
- Helps you think of better questions to ask
- Gives you unlimited chances to practice
- Has step-by-step feedback and instruction, including animated journal entries
- Is available when you need it, day or night
- Unlimited and convenient access to help you master the most important topic in this course, the accounting cycle

**Q** Always on the run? Juggling a **hectic schedule**?

Want to **study on the go**?

**A** ## Text-specific iPod content

Download accounting videos, PowerPoints, and quizzes (see below) directly onto your iPod and take learning material with you wherever you go. Whether it's in the car, on the train, or waiting between classes – it's easy to get a quick refresher on key course information. Look for this iPod icon throughout the text. Icons connect your Media Integrated textbook with iPod study materials, making review and study time as easy as putting on headphones! Click on **www.mhhe.com/LLPW1e** to learn more about available iPod content.

## iPod content includes:

- Lecture presentations – Audio and video, audio only, video only
- Interactive self quizzes *
- Accounting videos *

*Available for certain iPod models only

Don't have an iPod? Content can be viewed on any computer! Visit **www.mhhe.com/LLPW1e** for directions.

Visit **www.mhhe.com/ipod** to view a demonstration of our iPod content.

# Are A Click Away

## with McGraw-Hill's Web-Based Study Tools

**Q.** Want an online, **searchable version** of your textbook?

Wish your textbook could be available online while you're doing your homework?

**A.** ### Connect Plus eBook

If your instructor has chosen Homework Manager Plus (or the updated version, *Connect Plus*, available fall 2009), you have an affordable and searchable online version of your book integrated with your other online homework tools.

### Connect Plus eBook offers features like:

- topic search
- adjustable text size
- jump to page number
- print by section

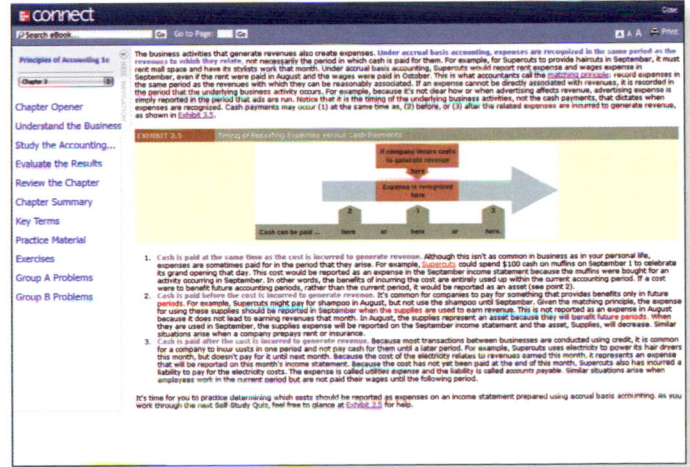

**Q.** Want to get more **value** from your textbook purchase?

Think learning accounting should be a little bit more **interesting**?

**A.** ### Check out the companion website for this textbook www.mhhe.com/LLPW1e

We put it there for you. Go online for test tips and practice problems whenever you study. The companion website for this book includes **games, quizzes, and outlines** to help you study. Get more from your textbook – use the Online Learning Center.

# PRINCIPLES OF
# Accounting

www.mhhe.com/LLPW1e

**Patricia A. Libby**
Ithaca College

**Robert Libby**
Cornell University

**Fred Phillips**
University of Saskatchewan

**Stacey Whitecotton**
Arizona State University

 **McGraw-Hill Irwin**

Boston    Burr Ridge, IL    Dubuque, IA    New York    San Francisco    St. Louis
Bangkok    Bogotá    Caracas    Kuala Lumpur    Lisbon    London    Madrid    Mexico City
Milan    Montreal    New Delhi    Santiago    Seoul    Singapore    Sydney    Taipei    Toronto

PRINCIPLES OF ACCOUNTING
Published by McGraw-Hill/Irwin, a business unit of The McGraw-Hill Companies, Inc., 1221 Avenue of the
Americas, New York, NY, 10020. Copyright © 2009 by The McGraw-Hill Companies, Inc. All rights reserved.
No part of this publication may be reproduced or distributed in any form or by any means, or stored in a
database or retrieval system, without the prior written consent of The McGraw-Hill Companies, Inc., including,
but not limited to, in any network or other electronic storage or transmission, or broadcast for distance learning.

Some ancillaries, including electronic and print components, may not be available to customers outside the
United States.

This book is printed on acid-free paper.

1 2 3 4 5 6 7 8 9 0 DOW/DOW 0 9 8

ISBN-13: 978-0-07-352684-3 (combined edition)
ISBN-10: 0-07-352684-3 (combined edition)
ISBN-13: 978-0-07-327395-2 (volume 1, chapters 1–12)
ISBN-10: 0-07-327395-3 (volume 1, chapters 1–12)
ISBN-13: 978-0-07-327396-9 (volume 2, chapters 12–25)
ISBN-10: 0-07-327396-1 (volume 2, chapters 12–25)
ISBN-13: 978-0-07-327408-9 (principles of financial accounting, chapters 1–17)
ISBN-10: 0-07-327408-9 (principles of financial accounting, chapters 1–17)

Vice president and editor-in-chief: *Brent Gordon*
Editorial director: *Stewart Mattson*
Publisher: *Tim Vertovec*
Senior sponsoring editor: *Alice Harra*
Senior developmental editor: *Kimberly D. Hooker*
Executive marketing manager: *Sankha Basu*
Manager of photo, design & publishing tools: *Mary Conzachi*
Full service project manager: *Elm Street Publishing Services*
Senior production supervisor: *Debra R. Sylvester*
Interior designer: *Pam Verros*
Senior photo research coordinator: *Jeremy Cheshareck*
Photo researcher: *Editorial Image, LLC*
Senior media project manager: *Susan Lombardi*
Cover design: *Cara Hawthorne*
Compositor: *Laserwords Private Limited*
Printer: *R. R. Donnelley*

**Library of Congress Cataloging-in-Publication Data**

Principles of accounting / Patricia A. Libby . . . [et al.].
    p. cm.
  Includes index.
  ISBN-13: 978-0-07-352684-3 (combined edition : alk. paper)
  ISBN-10: 0-07-352684-3 (combined edition : alk. paper)
  ISBN-13: 978-0-07-327395-2 (volume 1, ch. 1–12 : alk. paper)
  ISBN-10: 0-07-327395-3 (volume 1, ch 1–12 : alk. paper)
  [etc.]
  1. Accounting. 2. Accounting—Textbooks. I. Libby, Patricia A.
HF5636.P75 2009
657—dc22

                                                 2008038810

www.mhhe.com

# DEDICATION

*Herman and Doris Hargenrater,
Laura Libby, Oscar and Selma Libby.*

**–Patricia and Robert Libby**

*To the best teachers I've ever had:
my Mom and Dad, Barb, Harrison,
and Daniel.*

**–Fred Phillips**

*This book is dedicated to Mark, Riley,
and Carley Drayna. Thanks for all your
love and support.*

**–Stacey Whitecotton**

# MEET THE AUTHORS

### Patricia A. Libby

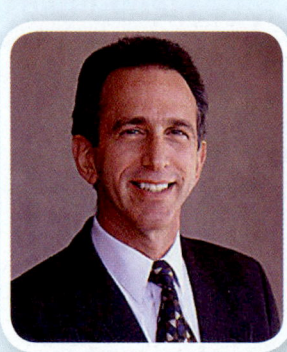

Patricia Libby is Associate Professor of Accounting at Ithaca College, where she teaches the undergraduate Principles of Accounting course. She previously taught graduate and undergraduate Principles of Accounting at Eastern Michigan University and the University of Texas. Before entering academe, she was an auditor with Price Waterhouse (now PricewaterhouseCoopers) and a financial administrator at the University of Chicago. She is also faculty adviser to Beta Alpha Psi, Ithaca College Accounting Association, and Ithaca College National Association of Black Accountants. She received her B.S. from Pennsylvania State University, her M.B.A. from DePaul University, and her Ph.D. from the University of Michigan; she is also a CPA.

Pat conducts research on using cases in the introductory course and other parts of the accounting curriculum. She has published articles in *The Accounting Review, Issues in Accounting Education*, and *The Michigan CPA*.

### Robert Libby

Robert Libby is the David A. Thomas Professor of Accounting at Cornell University, where he teaches the introductory Principles of Accounting course. He previously taught at the University of Illinois, Pennsylvania State University, the University of Texas at Austin, the University of Chicago, and the University of Michigan. He received his B.S. from Pennsylvania State University and his M.A.S. and Ph.D. from the University of Illinois; he is also a CPA.

Bob is a widely published author and researcher specializing in behavioral accounting. He was selected as the American Accounting Association (AAA) Outstanding Educator in 2000, received the AAA Outstanding Service Award in 2006, and received the AAA Notable Contributions to the Literature Award in 1985 and 1996. He is the only person to have received all three of the Association's highest awards for teaching, service, and research. He has published numerous articles in *The Accounting Review; Journal of Accounting Research; Accounting, Organizations, and Society*; and other accounting journals. He has held a variety of offices including Vice President of the American Accounting Association and is a member of the American Institute of CPAs and the editorial boards of *The Accounting Review; Accounting, Organizations, and Society; Journal of Accounting Literature*; and *Journal of Behavioral Decision Making*.

## Fred Phillips

Fred Phillips is Professor and the George C. Baxter Scholar at the University of Saskatchewan, where he teaches introductory Principles of Accounting. He also has taught introductory accounting at the University of Texas at Austin and the University of Manitoba. Fred has an undergraduate accounting degree, a professional accounting designation, and a Ph.D. from the University of Texas at Austin. He previously worked as an audit manager at KPMG.

Fred's main interest is accounting education. He has won 11 teaching awards, including three national case-writing competitions. Recently, Fred won the 2007 Alpha Kappa Psi Outstanding Professor award at The University of Texas at Austin, and in 2006 he was awarded the title Master Teacher at the University of Saskatchewan. He has published instructional cases and numerous articles in journals such as *Issues in Accounting Education, Journal of Accounting Research,* and *Organizational Behavior and Human Decision Processes.* He received the American Accounting Association Outstanding Research in Accounting Education Award in 2006 and 2007 for his articles. Fred is a past Associate Editor of *Issues in Accounting Education* and a current member of the Teaching, Learning & Curriculum and Two-Year College sections of the American Accounting Association. In his spare time, he likes to work out, play video games, and drink iced cappuccinos.

## Stacey Whitecotton

Stacey Whitecotton is Associate Professor in the School of Accountancy at Arizona State University. She received her Ph.D. and Masters of Accounting from The University of Oklahoma and her B.B.A. from Texas Tech University.

Stacey teaches managerial accounting topics at the undergraduate level and in the MBA program. She was recognized as the Outstanding Undergraduate Teacher by the School of Accountancy and Information Management in 1999 and was awarded the John W. Teets Outstanding Graduate Teacher award in 2000–2001. She is currently serving as the faculty director for the W. P. Carey Online MBA program.

Stacey's research interests center around the use of decision aids to improve the decision-making behavior of financial analysts, managers, and auditors. Her research has been published in *The Accounting Review, Organizational Behavior and Human Decision Processes, Behavioral Research in Accounting, Auditing: A Journal of Practice and Theory,* and *The Journal of Behavioral Decision Making.*

Stacey and her husband Mark enjoy traveling and the many outdoor activities Arizona has to offer with their two kids, Riley and Carley.

# What Does Pizza Have to Do with Accounting?

## Teaching challenge: Motivating students to read the book

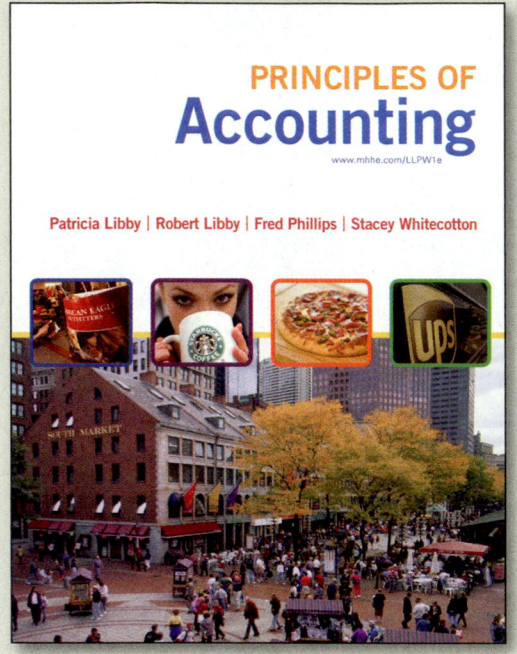

PRINCIPLES OF
**Accounting**
www.mhhe.com/LLPW1e

Patricia Libby | Robert Libby | Fred Phillips | Stacey Whitecotton

The number one challenge we hear from faculty is how to motivate students to read their textbook. Students taking Principles of Accounting don't yet know **why accounting matters** in their lives, so they aren't naturally drawn to reading their text.

However, most students do know about eating pizza, drinking Starbucks or their favorite coffee, shopping at retail stores like American Eagle, and shipping packages with UPS. Once they read about how these activities relate to accounting, they begin to see that **accounting is in their everyday lives.**

In addition, many of your students **imagine themselves starting and running a business** someday (or helping with a family business). So, our *Principles of Accounting* book opens with a novel idea: Chapters 1–4 are written around the true story of Mauricio Rosa, an immigrant from El Salvador who started Pizza Aroma, a small gourmet pizza restaurant in Ithaca, New York. Mauricio's actual experiences and decisions provide a consistent story line and create a framework for learning about accounting. In Chapter 1, Mauricio and his CPA discuss plans for starting his business, addressing topics such as choice of organizational form, accounting information needs, and financial statement reporting. In Chapter 2, Mauricio actually establishes Pizza Aroma by contributing capital, obtaining a bank loan, and investing in restaurant equipment. He learns how these activities affect Pizza Aroma's financial condition and how they are reported in the balance sheet. In Chapter 3, Pizza Aroma begins to earn revenue and incur expenses. He learns how these operating transactions affect the balance sheet and the income statement. Finally, in Chapter 4, Mauricio learns how the accounting records are adjusted prior to determining whether Pizza Aroma has been profitable.

The dialogue between Mauricio and Laurie in the first chapter invites students into a discussion like one they may have someday. Through this true story that

> *The building cover has a busy marketplace that depicts the essence of business, accounting, free enterprise, etc., and the crowd rushing off to wherever indicates that business is alive and well . . .*—Judy Daulton, Piedmont Technical College

> *The examples follow through is an excellent case of how to close the books of accounts. The classifications of accounts make sense with easy understanding for the class. The accounting cycle is clearly explained and easy to understand for the class.*—Shafi Ullah, Broward College

> *The presentation of the pizza case is awesome . . . it lends itself to a mystery and drives you to find out the ending . . . excellent. . . .*—David Laurel, South Texas College

Libby/Libby/ Phillips/Whitecotton (LLPW) is the only book to use a true story to introduce students to accounting and the accounting cycle with a running case about a pizzeria.

"Others outside your business will also need financial information about your restaurant. For example, where will the money come from to start your business?"

"I'll contribute $30,000 from personal savings. But I'll still need to ask the bank for a $20,000 loan to buy equipment. What will the bank want to know?"

continues in the entire first 4 chapters (the accounting cycle), students see the relationship between accounting and business, and they get a mini-manual for how to start their own businesses. Students get captivated by the story and may not realize they are learning accounting principles in the process.

The choice of Pizza Aroma is purposeful: Students love pizza, they connect accounting to something in their everyday lives. More important, they learn to make the connection in the first few weeks that accounting can help them be successful. **When students understand why accounting matters to them, they want to read more.**

*(Chapter One) is engaging with the interview approach. The business owner is at the same level of accounting knowledge as the students and asks the questions that are surely running through the students' minds. . . .* —Patricia Walczak, Lansing Community College

*Since many (of my students) have worked in fast-food establishments and certainly all have eaten pizza, I think this should make it more interesting and understandable to them.* —Sandra Augustine, Hilbert College

*Introducing balance sheet accounts in Chapter 2 and, exclusively, income accounts in Chapter 3 is a dynamic idea that makes sense! The focus on a proprietorship selling pizza through the first 4 chapters is a topic students can identify with.* —Marcia Sandvold, Des Moines Area Community College

# Pizza Aroma: It's a true story

Pizza Aroma, Ithaca, NY

Author Patricia Libby and Owner Mauricio Rosa

Gourmet Pizza

# How Can LLPW Ensure Students Will Master the Accounting Cycle?

## Teaching challenge: Students struggle with the accounting cycle

Faculty understand that mastering the accounting cycle is essential to success in Principles of Accounting courses. The authors agree. They believe students struggle with the accounting cycle when transaction analysis is covered in one chapter. Students are often overwhelmed when they are exposed to the accounting equation, journal entries, and T-accounts for both balance sheet and income statement accounts in a single chapter.

*Slowing down the material by **breaking transaction analysis into two chapters is an excellent idea, which I think will help students greatly.** That is one of my biggest complaints about my current text; it goes too fast.*—Amy Haas, Kingsborough Community College

The Libby/Libby/Phillips/Whitecotton approach **covers transaction analysis over two chapters** so that students have the time to master the material. In Chapter 2 of *Principles of Accounting*, students are introduced to the accounting equation and transaction analysis for investing and financing transactions that affect only balance sheet accounts. This provides students the opportunity to learn the basic structure and tools used in accounting in a simpler setting than usual. Chapter 3 introduces operating transactions that affect income statement accounts. As a result of this slower building-block approach to transaction analysis, students are better prepared to learn adjustments, financial statement preparation, and more advanced topics.

*It is presented in a very organized manner. The students are **presented the journalizing/posting information (Chapters 2 and 3) at a slower pace,** giving them the opportunity to absorb and comprehend this difficult information. Chapter 4 then wraps up the entire cycle all at once, instead of presenting adjusting entries in one chapter and then ending the accounting cycle in another. In other words, in a **more efficient and easily understandable manner.**—Carol Pace, Grayson Community College*

*The concentration and reinforcement of the basic accounting equation allow the student to **master the equation before introducing the income statement concepts. Excellent idea.**—Patricia Holmes, Des Moines Area Community College*

# LLPW is the only book offering a more patient, "building-block" approach to the accounting cycle, covering transaction analysis in 2 chapters instead of 1.

The following grid provides a detailed comparison of the Libby/Libby/Phillips/Whitecotton approach with the approach of other principles of accounting texts.

## Accounting Cycle

| Chapter | LLPW Approach | Other Approaches |
| --- | --- | --- |
| 1 | Overview of Financial Statements and Users, Transaction Analysis with Accounting Equation | Overview of Financial Statements and Users, Transaction Analysis with Accounting Equation |
| 2 | Journal Entries and T-Accounts with Transactions affecting Balance Sheet Accounts only | Journal Entries and T-Accounts with Transactions affecting both Balance Sheet and Income Statement Accounts |
| 3 | Journal Entries and T-Accounts with Transactions affecting both Balance Sheet and Income Statement Accounts | Adjusting Entries, Financial Statement Preparation |
| 4 | Adjusting Entries, Financial Statement Preparation, Closing Process, (Worksheet) | Closing Process, Worksheet, (Reversing Entries), Financial Statement Preparation |

> *First introducing income accounts in chapter 3 is great. I don't know any other text to do this.*—Jeannie Harrington, Middle Tennessee State University

Learning accounting is like learning a foreign language where practice of new terms and concepts is essential. By taking a progressive building-block approach to Chapters 2 and 3, students have more time to master transaction analysis, which is the foundation for the rest of the course. Students have more time to practice and feel less overwhelmed.

> *It caught my attention from page 1 and I wanted to read on and find out how Pizza Aroma was going to do.* The first four chapters simplify the accounting process and explain accounting on an entry level for first time accounting students. Great Job!!!—Susan Logorda, Lehigh Carbon Community College

# How Can LLPW Help Students Learn Accounting in the Context of Business?

## Teaching challenge: Many students don't have enough work experience to understand accounting in the context of business

Because many students don't have business experience, the authors teach accounting in the context of business by focusing each chapter on one well-known company and using that company as a consistent example throughout the chapter including the examples, financial statements, and data.

The authors focus every chapter of Principles of Accounting on a company that makes or provides something students use or see in their everyday lives. Chapters 1 through 4 focus on the true story of Pizza Aroma, a typical local small pizza restaurant. In Chapters 5–25, the authors profile well-known companies such as Starbucks (Chapter 21), American Eagle Outfitters (Chapter 7), Skechers (Chapter 9), Blockbuster (Chapter 25), General Mills (Chapter 14), Cedar Fair (Chapter 10), and Tombstone (Chapter 18).

> *Great explanations; fantastic use of the real world examples. . . .*—Shea Mears, Des Moines Area Community College

> *The use of Cedar Fair for (chapter 10) is great. **How fascinating this was to use roller coasters for depreciation examples.***—Jeannie Harrington, Middle Tennessee State University

> *Authors did a nice job of making it easy to read and understand. Supplemental information with real company and use of extras like the coach's tips, self-study practice and exhibits, make this a better text than I currently use.*—Larry Dragosavac, Edison CC

**LLPW is the only book that uses this unique "focus company approach" to teach accounting in the context of real business.**

# FOCUS COMPANIES

Ch 1: Introducing Accounting

Pizza Aroma

Ch 2: Balance Sheet

Pizza Aroma

Ch 3: Balance Sheet and Income Statement

Pizza Aroma

Ch 4: Adjusting and Closing the Books

Pizza Aroma

Ch 5: Accounting Systems

UPS

Ch 6: Merchandising

Wal-Mart

Ch 7: Inventories
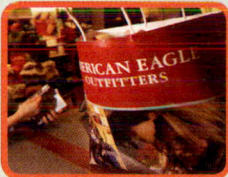
American Eagle Outfitters

Ch 8: Internal Controls
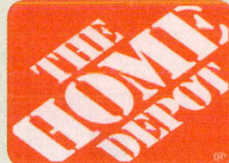
The Home Depot

Ch 9: Receivables

Skechers

Ch 10: Long-lived Assets

Cedar Fair

Ch 11: Current Liabilities

General Mills

Ch 12: Partnerships

Bloom'N Flowers

Ch 13: Corporations

Sonic Drive-In

Ch 14: Long-Term Liabilities

General Mills

Ch 15: Investments

Washington Post Companies

Ch 16: Statement of Cash Flows

Nautilus

Ch 17: Financial Statement Analysis

Lowe's

Ch 18: Managerial Accounting

Tombstone Pizza

Ch 19: Job Order Costing

Toll Brothers

Ch 20: Process Costing

CK Mondavi

Ch 21: Cost Behavior and Cost Volume Profit Analysis

Starbucks

Ch 22: Capital Budgeting

Mattel

Ch 23: Budgetary Planning

Cold Stone Creamery

Ch 24: Budgetary Control

Cold Stone Creamery

Ch 25: Standard Costing and Variance Analysis

Blockbuster

# How Can LLPW Help Students Study and Practice?

*Principles of Accounting* offers a host of pedagogical tools that complement the different ways you like to teach and the ways your students like to learn. . . .

## Coach's Tips

Every student needs encouragement, and inclusion of Coach's Tips is just one way Libby/Libby/Phillips/Whitecotton fulfills that need. Coach's Tips appear throughout the text offering tips, advice, and suggestions about how to learn principles of accounting.

If Wal-Mart takes advantage of the 2/10, n/30 discount by paying within the 10-day discount period, the discount will effectively reduce the cost of the inventory. The 2 percent discount is calculated using the initial purchase cost (2% × $100,000 = $2,000). Because the discount reduces the inventory cost, the purchaser records it as a reduction of the Inventory account, as follows:

|  | Debit | Credit |
|---|---|---|
| Accounts Payable (−L) | 100,000 | |
| Cash (−A) (98% × 100,000) | | 98,000 |
| Inventory (−A) (2% × 100,000) | | 2,000 |

| Assets | = | Liabilities | + | Owners' Equity |
|---|---|---|---|---|
| Cash −98,000 | | Accounts Payable −100,000 | | |
| Inventory −2,000 | | | | |

**Coach's Tip**
The purchase discount is calculated using the initial purchase cost times the discount percentage ($2,000 = 2% × $100,000).

## Self-Study Practice

Research shows that students learn best when they are actively engaged in the learning process. This active learning feature engages the student, provides interactivity, and promotes efficient learning. These practices ask students to pause at strategic points throughout each chapter to ensure they understand key points before moving ahead.

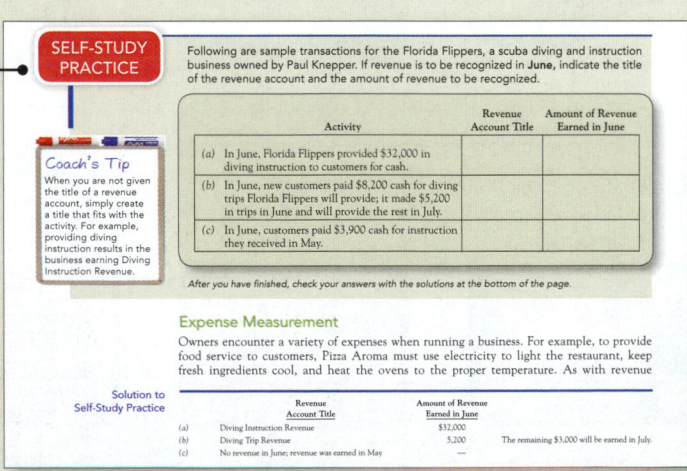

**SELF-STUDY PRACTICE**

Following are sample transactions for the Florida Flippers, a scuba diving and instruction business owned by Paul Knepper. If revenue is to be recognized in **June**, indicate the title of the revenue account and the amount of revenue to be recognized.

| Activity | Revenue Account Title | Amount of Revenue Earned in June |
|---|---|---|
| (a) In June, Florida Flippers provided $32,000 in diving instruction to customers for cash. | | |
| (b) In June, new customers paid $8,200 cash for diving trips Florida Flippers will provide; it made $5,200 in trips in June and will provide the rest in July. | | |
| (c) In June, customers paid $3,900 cash for instruction they received in May. | | |

After you have finished, check your answers with the solutions at the bottom of the page.

**Coach's Tip**
When you are not given the title of a revenue account, simply create a title that fits with the activity. For example, providing diving instruction results in the business earning Diving Instruction Revenue.

### Expense Measurement

Owners encounter a variety of expenses when running a business. For example, to provide food service to customers, Pizza Aroma must use electricity to light the restaurant, keep fresh ingredients cool, and heat the ovens to the proper temperature. As with revenue

**Solution to Self-Study Practice**

| | Revenue Account Title | Amount of Revenue Earned in June | |
|---|---|---|---|
| (a) | Diving Instruction Revenue | $32,000 | |
| (b) | Diving Trip Revenue | 5,200 | The remaining $3,000 will be earned in July. |
| (c) | No revenue in June; revenue was earned in May | — | |

## Spotlight On ETHICS

### Accounting Scandals

Accounting scandals are driven by the fear of personal failure and greed. Initially, some people may appear to benefit from fraudulent reporting. In the long run, however, fraud harms most individuals and organizations. When it is uncovered, the corporation's stock price drops dramatically. In the case involving MicroStrategy, the stock price dropped 65 percent in a single day of trading, from $243 to $86 per share. Creditors are also harmed by fraud. WorldCom's creditors recovered only 42 percent of what they were owed. They lost $36 billion. Innocent employees also are harmed by fraud. At Enron, 5,600 employees lost their jobs and many lost all of their retirement savings.

Ethical conduct is just as important for small private businesses as it is for large public companies. Laurie's advice to Mauricio and to all managers is to strive to create an ethical environment and establish a strong system of checks and controls inside the company. Do not tolerate blatant acts of fraud, such as employees making up false expenses for reimbursement, punching in a time card belonging to a fellow employee who will be late for work, or copying

# Spotlight On Ethics

This feature appears throughout the text stressing ethical issues that could be faced in relation to the chapter material and the importance of acting responsibly in business practice.

---

If Wal-Mart paid for the inventory after the 10-day discount period, it would not be eligible for the 2 percent discount. Instead, it would pay the full $100,000 owed. The payment would be recorded as a decrease in Accounts Payable (debit) and a decrease in Cash (credit) of $100,000.[2]

## Spotlight On BUSINESS DECISIONS

### To Take or Not to Take the Discount, That Is the Question

Purchasers usually pay within the discount period because the savings are much larger than they may appear to you. Although 2 percent might seem a small discount, if taken consistently on all purchases made during the year, it can add up to substantial savings. All the purchaser must do to earn the 2 percent discount is to pay the bill 20 days early (on the 10th day instead of the 30th). Over a year (365 days), this discount is equivalent to a 37 percent annual interest rate.* So even if purchasers must borrow from the bank at a high rate, such as 15 percent, they will still save a great deal by taking the discount.

# Spotlight On Business Decisions

Good decision making is essential in business whether you are preparing, using, or analyzing accounting information. Spotlight On Business Decisions helps students develop good decision-making skills by illustrating the relevance of accounting in real-world decision making.

---

## Spotlight On FINANCIAL REPORTING

### Accrued Expenses in the Millions and Billions

Accrued expenses are significant liabilities for many companies. For example, Tootsie Roll Industries recently reported the following:

**NOTE 2—ACCRUED LIABILITIES:**
Accrued liabilities are comprised of the following:

| (in thousands of dollars) | DECEMBER 31, | |
| --- | --- | --- |
| | 2006 | 2005 |
| Compensation | $ 12,923 | $ 15,756 |
| Other employee benefits | 5,631 | 5,213 |
| Taxes, other than income | 1,781 | 1,765 |
| Advertising and promotions | 17,854 | 14,701 |
| Other | 5,613 | 7,534 |
| | $ 43,802 | $ 44,969 |

The $43.8 million in total accrued liabilities represents 70 percent of Tootsie Roll's current liabilities and 27 percent of total liabilities.

Likewise, Wal-Mart Stores, Inc., reported approximately $14.7 billion in accrued liabilities, primarily from accrued wages and benefits owed to employees. This was 28 percent of current liabilities and 17 percent of total liabilities.

# Spotlight On Financial Reporting

Concepts come to life when you see how well-known businesses apply them. Spotlight On Financial Reporting helps students to apply their knowledge to relevant, real-world financial reporting issues.

# From Reading to Doing—Extensive End-of-Chapter Material to Help

## Chapter Summary

End-of-chapter summaries complement the learning objectives outlined at the beginning of the chapter.

### Chapter Summary

**LO1 Define internal control and explain why it is needed. p. 344**

- Internal control encompasses the methods an organization uses to protect against the theft of assets, to enhance the reliability of accounting information, to promote efficient and effective operations, and to ensure compliance with applicable laws and regulations.
- Internal controls are needed to ensure that people will behave in ways that benefit the organization. When internal controls operate effectively, they can improve an organization's efficiency and minimize waste, unintentional errors, and fraud.

**LO2 Explain the common principles and limitations of internal control. p. 346**

- The concept of internal control is broad. Most employees of a company will encounter five basic internal control principles: (1) establish responsibility for each task, (2) segregate duties so that one employee cannot initiate, approve, record, and handle a single transaction, (3) restrict access to assets and information to those employees who have been assigned responsibility for them, (4) document all procedures, and (5) independently verify work that has been done using information from others inside and outside the business.
- Internal controls are limited because they (1) are implemented only to the extent that their benefits exceed their costs and (2) may fail to operate effectively as a result of error and fraud.

**LO3 Apply internal control principles to cash receipts and payments. p. 348**

- When applied to cash receipts, internal control principles require that (1) cashiers be held individually responsible for the cash they receive, (2) different individuals be assigned to receive, maintain custody of, and record cash, (3) cash be stored in a locked safe until it has been securely deposited in a bank, (4) cash register receipts, cash count sheets, daily cash summary reports, and bank deposit slips be prepared to document the cash received and deposited, and (5) cash register receipts be matched to cash counts and deposits to independently verify that all cash was received and deposited.
- When applied to cash payments, internal control principles require that (1) only certain individuals or departments initiate purchase requests, (2) different individuals be assigned to order, receive, and pay for purchases, (3) access to checks and

## Key Terms

Terms, definitions, and page references are given.

### Key Terms

| | | |
|---|---|---|
| Bank Reconciliation (p. 355) | Electronic Funds Transfer (EFT) (p. 351) | Petty Cash Fund (p. 353) |
| Bonding (p. 347) | Imprest System (p. 352) | Remittance Advice (p. 351) |
| Cash (p. 360) | Internal Control (p. 344) | Sarbanes-Oxley (SOX) Act of 2002 (p. 344) |
| Cash Count Sheet (p. 350) | NSF (Not Sufficient Funds) Checks (p. 357) | |
| Cash Equivalents (p. 360) | Outstanding Check (p. 357) | Segregation of Duties (p. 346) |
| Collude (p. 348) | Override (p. 348) | Voucher (p. 352) |
| Deposits in Transit (p. 357) | | Voucher System (p. 352) |
| See complete glossary in back of text. | | |

## Questions

Each chapter includes 10–20 questions that ask students to explain and discuss terms and concepts discussed in the chapter.

### Questions

1. What are internal controls and why are they needed?
2. What aspect(s) of the Sarbanes-Oxley Act of 2002 might counteract the incentive to commit fraud?
3. What aspect(s) of the Sarbanes-Oxley Act of 2002 might reduce opportunities for fraud?
4. What aspect(s) of the Sarbanes-Oxley Act of 2002 might allow the good character of employees to prevail?
5. From the perspective of a CEO or CFO, what does internal control mean?
6. What are five common internal control principles?
7. Why is it a good idea to assign each task to only one employee?
8. Why should responsibilities for certain duties, like cash handling and cash recording, be separated? What specific responsibilities should be separated?
9. What are some of the methods for restricting access?
10. In what ways does documentation act as a control?
11. In what ways can independent verification occur?
12. In what way does a mandatory vacation policy act as a control?
13. What are the three limitations of internal control?
14. What is the primary internal control goal for cash receipts?
15. What internal control functions are performed by a cash register? How are these functions performed when cash is received by mail?
16. How is cash received in person independently verified?
17. What is the primary internal control goal for cash payments?
18. In what ways is a petty cash system similar to and different from an imprest payroll system?
19. Describe three ways in which banking services help businesses control cash.
20. What are the purposes of a bank reconciliation? What balances are reconciled?
21. Define *cash* and indicate the types of items that should be reported as cash. Define *cash equivalents* and give two examples of a cash equivalent.

## Multiple-Choice Questions

Each chapter includes 10 multiple-choice questions that let students practice basic concepts. Solutions are provided for all questions.

### Multiple Choice

1. Which of the following accounts would not appear in a closing journal entry?
   a. Interest Revenue.
   b. Accumulated Depreciation.
   c. Owner's Capital.
   d. Salary Expense.

   Quiz 4-1
   www.mhhe.com/LLPW1e

2. Which account is least likely to appear in an adjusting journal entry?
   a. Cash.
   b. Interest Receivable.
   c. Accumulated Depreciation.
   d. Salaries Payable.

# LLPW is written by best-selling authors whose books are well-known for the quality of their end-of-chapter problem material.

## Mini Exercises
Assignments illustrate and apply single learning objectives from the chapter.

## Exercises
Additional assignments illustrate and apply single and multiple learning objectives from the chapter.

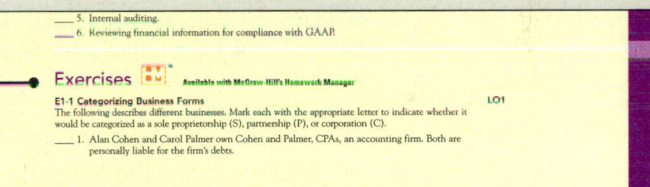

## Problems (Sets A and B)
Assignments illustrate and apply the chapter's learning objectives.

## Cases and Projects
End-of-chapter cases and projects use data from The Home Depot's and Lowe's annual reports and show students how to draw information from an annual report, providing them with a valuable perspective on how information is used in decision making.

# How Can McGraw-Hill Technology Help Students Study and Practice?

## McGraw-Hill's Homework Manager System
## Easy. Effective. Reliable.

### McGraw-Hill's Homework Manager® and Homework Manager Plus.®

*The #1 choice in web-based assessment, course management, and homework.*

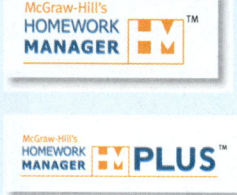

With Homework Manager and Homework Manager Plus system, instructors can create web-based assignments and assessments that can be customized to meet course needs. Assignments are based on content from the textbook, so terminology and problem styles are consistent, eliminating confusion for students.

Homework Manager and Homework Manager Plus include:

- Automatically graded homework
- Immediate student feedback
- Personalized gradebook
- Static and algorithmic exercises, problems, and select test bank questions
- Self-graded practice quizzes
- Online testbank
- Interactive, integrated eBook*

*eBook available only with McGraw-Hill's Homework Manager Plus*

### EASY.

With a simple, four-step process and intuitive interface, Homework Manager and Homework Manager Plus system allows instructors to get their course online in less than an hour!

### EFFECTIVE.

Instructors and students using McGraw-Hill's Homework Manager and Homework Manager Plus system report improved grades, greater retention, and increased student engagement.

### RELIABLE.

Stability and support are as important to our customers as they are to us. Only Homework Manager and Homework Manager Plus offer a 24-hour support line to ensure you and your students stay connected.

To connect you with your students in even better ways, we're delighted to announce the new version of Homework Manager and Homework Manager Plus called CONNECT, coming in fall 2009. . . .

As with Homework Manager, Connect Accounting lets instructors easily deliver customized assignments, quizzes and tests online.

- Students can practice important skills on their own schedule and get instant feedback.
- Instructors get automatically graded homework, personalized student feedback and gradebook, static and algorithmic exercises, problems, and test questions.
- Access to an interactive eBook is available with Connect Accounting Plus.
- Continuous improvement: Homework Manager customers will find the following enhancements with CONNECT Accounting:
  - Single entry point, registration, and sign on
  - Enhanced gradebook reporting capabilities
  - The ability to export reports and grades to WebCT and Blackboard
  - Enhanced question selection including AACSB and learning objectives
  - Customizable assignment policies
  - Integrated, interactive eBook*
  - Student Assignment Preview for instructors
  - Local time-zone support

*eBook available only with McGraw-Hill CONNECT ACCOUNTING PLUS.

### iPod Downloadable Content

*Principles of Accounting* gives students the option to download content for review and study to their Apple® iPods and most other MP3/MP4 devices. iPod icons appear throughout the text pointing students to chapter-specific audio lecture presentation slides and course-related videos.

# McGraw-Hill has leading technology products for your classroom presentations, course management, labs, and self-study.

## Carol Yacht's General Ledger and Peachtree

 From one of the most trusted names in computer accounting education, Carol Yacht, comes a general ledger package that's a perfect fit for your course no matter how you like to teach it.

Students using Carol Yacht's General Ledger (CYGL) can move from financial statements to the specific journal entries with just a click of the mouse; changing an entry updates the financial statements on the fly, allowing students to see instantly how journal entries impact financial statements.

If you want your students to practice on the same software the professionals use, the CYGL CD includes Peachtree for use on numerous problems from the text.

## Excel Templates

 If they are going to work in accounting (or business in general), students have to know Microsoft Excel. *Principles of Accounting* offers Excel templates tied to specific end-of-chapter problems and annual report cases. This allows students to experience problem solving as it truly happens in real companies. The templates are available on the text Web site www.mhhe.com/LLPW1e.

## Online Learning Center

www.mhhe.com/LLPW1e

For instructors, *Principles of Accounting*'s Online Learning Center (OLC) includes the Instructor's Resource Manual, PowerPoint slides, Solutions Manual, and Excel Template solutions tied to the end-of-chapter material. There are also links to professional resources.

For students and instructors, the OLC includes multiple-choice quizzes, Excel templates, The Home Depot and Lowe's Companies annual reports, check figures, Web links, and McGraw-Hill's Homework Manager (see below). Instructors can pull all of this material as part of another online course management system.

## ALEKS®

www.business.aleks.com

 ALEKS (Assessment and Learning in Knowledge Spaces) delivers precise, qualitative diagnostic assessments of students' knowledge, guides them in the selection of appropriate new study material, and records their progress toward mastery of curricular goals in a robust classroom management system.

ALEKS interacts with the student much as a skilled human tutor would, moving between explanation and practice as needed, correcting and analyzing errors, defining terms and chapter topics on request. By sophisticated modeling of a student's knowledge state for a given subject, ALEKS can focus clearly on what the student is most ready to learn next. When students focus on exactly what they are ready to learn, they build confidence and a learning momentum that fuels success.

ALEKS Math Prep for Accounting provides coverage of the basic math skills needed to succeed in introductory *Principles of Accounting*, while ALEKS for the Accounting Cycle provides a detailed, guided overview through every stage of the accounting cycle.

## CourseSmart

http://www.coursesmart.com

 With the CourseSmart eTextbook, students can save up to 45 percent of the cost of a print book, reduce their impact on the environment, and access powerful Web tools for learning. CourseSmart is an online eTextbook, which means users access and view their textbook online when connected to the Internet. Students can also print sections of the book for maximum portability. CourseSmart eTextbooks are available in one standard online reader with full text search, notes and highlighting, and e-mail tools for sharing notes between classmates.

## Quantum Tutors for the Accounting Cycle

*Proven to Increase Test Scores by as Much as 50 percent*

The Quantum Tutors for the Accounting Cycle help tutor students on the fundamental accounting concepts and problem-solving skills needed for principles and financial accounting courses. Just like working with an excellent instructor, students can enter their own work into the software, ask questions, and receive step-by-step feedback at a detailed level not available with any other software or homework management system. The Quantum Tutors are ideal when the student needs immediate help and the instructor is not available to answer questions. Accessed over the Internet, it offers students unlimited, convenient access day or night. It also allows them to study independently at their own pace.

We are happy to help you integrate technology into your course. Please call your local McGraw-Hill representative to learn more.

# Instructor Resources

### ☑ McGraw-Hill's Homework Manager

See page (xvi) for details.

### ☑ Instructor CD-ROM

ISBN 0073274038

This integrated CD-ROM allows you to access most of the text's ancillary materials. You no longer need to worry about the various supplements that accompany your text. Instead, almost everything is available on one convenient CD-ROM: PowerPoint slides, Solutions Manual, Instructor's Resource Manual, Test Bank, and Computerized Test Bank.

### ☑ Online Learning Center

www.mhhe.com/LLPW1e
See page (xvii) for details.

### ☑ Solutions Manual

Prepared by Patricia Libby, Robert Libby, Fred Phillips, and Stacey Whitecotton, the manual provides solutions for end-of-chapter questions, mini exercises, exercises, problems, and cases and projects. Available on the Instructor CD-ROM and text Web site.

### ☑ Test Bank

Prepared by Laura Rickett, Kent State University, and Jay Holmen, University of Wisconsin–Eau Claire, this comprehensive Test Bank includes more than 2,000 true/false and multiple-choice questions, problems, essays, and matching questions. It is available on the Instructor CD-ROM.

### ☑ Presentation Slides

Prepared by Jon Booker and Charles Caldwell at Tennessee Technological University and Susan Galbreath at David Lipscomb University, this option provides completely customized PowerPoint presentations for use in your classroom. Available on the Instructor CD-ROM and text Web site.

### ☑ Instructor's Resource Manual

Prepared by J. Lowell Mooney, Georgia Southern University, supplements, including the Financial Accounting Videos, Study Guide, and PowerPoint slides, are topically cross-referenced in the Instructor's Manual

to help instructors direct students to specific ancillaries to reinforce key concepts. Available on the Instructor CD-ROM and text Web site.

### ☑ Algorithmic-Diploma Testbank

ISBN 0073274054

This feature allows you to add and edit questions; create up to 99 versions of each chapter test; attach graphic files to questions; import and export ASCII files; and select questions based on type, level of difficulty, or learning objective. This software provides password protection for saved tests and question databases and can run on a network.

### ☑ EZ Test

McGraw-Hill's EZ Test is a flexible and easy-to-use electronic testing program that allows instructors to create tests from book-specific items. EZ Test accommodates a wide range of question types and allows instructors to add their own questions. Multiple versions of the test can be created, and any test can be exported for use with course management systems such as BlackBoard/WebCT. EZ Test Online is a new service that gives instructors a place to easily administer EZ Test–created exams and quizzes online. The program is available for Windows and Macintosh environments.

### ☑ Excel Templates

Available on the text Web site www.mhhe.com/LLPW1e, these templates are tied to selected end-of-chapter material.

### ☑ Instructor Excel Templates

This feature provides solutions to the student Excel Templates for selected end-of-chapter assignments. Available on the text Web site.

### ☑ Check Figures

Prepared by Lu Ann Bean, Florida Institute of Technology, it provides key numbers in the solutions to the problems at the end of each chapter. Available on the text Web site.

# Student Resources

## ☑ Online Learning Center

www.mhhe.com/LLPW1e
Practice what you're learning. Lots of free practice problems are online whenever you're ready. Even at 1 A.M.

## ☑ McGraw-Hill's Homework Manager

See page (xviii) for details.

## ☑ Working Papers

Volume 1 (Chapters 1–12) 007327397X
Volume 2 (Chapters 12–25) 0073273988
Prepared by Jeannie Folk at College of DuPage, these items contain all of the forms necessary for completing end-of-chapter assignments.

## ☑ Study Guide

Volume 1 (Chapters 1–12) 0073273929
Volume 2 (Chapters 12–25) 0073273937
Prepared by Jeannie Folk at College of DuPage, this outstanding learning tool gives students a deeper understanding of the course material and reinforces, step by step, what they are learning in the main text.

## ☑ Check Figures

Available on the text Web site, www.mhhe.com/LLPW1e, check figures provide key numbers in solutions to end-of-chapter material.

## ☑ iPod Downloadable Content

See below for details.

## ☑ Excel Templates

Available on the text Web site www.mhhe.com/LLPW1e, these templates are tied to selected end-of-chapter material.

## ☑ Carol Yacht's General Ledger and Peachtree

Carol Yacht's General Ledger Software is McGraw-Hill/Irwin's custom-built general ledger package. Carol Yacht's General Ledger can help you master every aspect of the general ledger, from inputting sales and cash receipts to calculating ratios for analysis or inventory valuations. Carol Yacht's General Ledger allows you to review an entire report and then double-click any single transaction to review or edit it. The report will then be updated on the fly to include the revised figures. When it comes to learning how an individual transaction affects the outcome of an entire report, no other approach matches that of Carol Yacht's General Ledger. Students can use Carol Yacht's General Ledger and Peachtree to solve numerous problems from the textbook.

## iPod Downloadable Content

You are holding a media-integrated textbook that provides students portable educational content—just right for those students who want to study when and where it's most convenient for them. *Principles of Accounting* gives students the option to download content for review and study to their Apple® iPods and most other MP3/MP4 devices. iPod icons appear throughout the text pointing students to chapter-specific audio lecture presentation slides and course-related videos.

Photo Courtesy of Apple.®

### Quick Reference to iPod Icons

| Lectured slideshow–LP3-1 | Video 3-1 | Quiz 3-1 |
|---|---|---|
| www.mhhe.com/LLPW1e | www.mhhe.com/LLPW1e | www.mhhe.com/LLPW1e |
| Lecture presentations available for download to your iPod, Zune, or MP3 device (audio and visual depending on your device) | Topical videos available for download to your iPod, Zune, or MP3 (depending on your device) | Multiple-choice quizzes available for download to your iPod, Zune, or MP3 (depending on your device) |

# Acknowledgments

Many dedicated instructors have devoted their time and effort to help us develop this text. We would like to acknowledge and thank all of our colleagues who helped guide our decisions. This text would not be what it is without the help of our dedicated contributors:

## Reviewers

Alan Applebaum, Broward Community College
Leah Arrington, Northwest Mississippi Community College
Cynthia Ash, Davenport University
Sandy Augustine, Hilbert College
Collin Battle, Broward Community College
LuAnn Bean, Florida Institute of Technology
Sarah Beauchea, Berkeley College
Lisa Bernard, Pearl River Community College
Margaret Black, San Jacinto College
David Bland, Cape Fear Community College
Linda Bolduc, Mount Wachusett Community College
Patrick Borja, Citrus College
Thomas Branton, Alvin Community College
Gregory Brookins, Santa Monica College
Pennye Brown, Austin Peay State University
William P. Burke, Neumann College
Carla Cabarle, Minot State University
Michelle Cannon, Ivy Tech Community College of Indiana
Lloyd Carroll, Borough of Manhattan Community College
Lisa Cole, Johnson County Community College
Joan Cook, Milwaukee Area Technical College
Susan Cordes, Johnson County Community College
Christine Crosby, York Technical College
Judy Daulton, Piedmont Technical College
Passard Dean, Saint Leo University
Larry Dragosavac, Edison Community College
Karla Duckworth, Hinds Community College
Rebecca Evans, Blue Ridge Community College
Mary Falkey, Prince George Community College
John Gabeleman, Columbus State Community College
Patrick Geer, Hawkeye Community College
Gloria Grayless, Sam Houston State University
Joyce Griffin, Kansas City Kansas Community College
Amy Haas, Kingsborough Community College
Betty Harper, Middle Tennessee State University
Jeannie Harrington, Middle Tennessee State University
Paul Harris, Camden Community College
Patricia Holmes, Des Moines Area Community College
Robert Holtfreter, Central Washington University
Audrey Hunter, Broward Community College
Connie Hylton, George Mason University
Phillip Imel, Northern Virginia Community College
Thomas Kam, Hawaii Pacific University
Naomi Karolinski, Monroe Community College
Randy Kidd, Longview Community College
Thomas Knight, Borough of Manhattan Community College
Jerry Krueze, Western Michigan University
David Laurel, South Texas College
Susan Logorda, Lehigh Carbon Community College

Linda Mallory, Central Virginia Community College
Robert Mandau, Piedmont Technical College
Kenneth Mark, Kansas City Kansas Community College
Cynthia McCall, Des Moines Area Community College
Kevin McFarlane, Front Range Community College
Chris McNamara, Finger Lakes Community College
Shea Mears, Des Moines Area Community College
Terri Meta, Seminole Community College
Tammy Metzke, Milwaukee Area Technical College
Norma Montague, Central Carolina Community College
Karen Mozingo, Pitt Community College
Andrea Murowski, Brookdale Community College
Seved Noorian, Wentworth Institute of Technology
Shelly Ota, Leeward Community College
Carol Pace, Grayson Community College
Susan Pallas, Southeast Community College
Gregory L. Prescott, University of South Alabama
Timothy Prindle, Des Moines Area Community College
LaVonda Ramey, Schoolcraft College
Jenny Resnick, Santa Monica College
Carla Rich, Pensacola Junior College
Eric Rothenburg, Kingsborough Community College
Gary Rupp, SUNY–Farmingdale
Marcia Sandvold, Des Moines Area Community College
Richard Sarkisian, Camden Community College
Mona Seiler, Queensborough Community College
James Shimko, Sinclair Community College
Jay Siegel, Union County College
Alice Sineath, Forsyth Technical Community College
Lois Slutsky, Broward Community College–South Campus
Daniel Small, J. Sergeant Reynolds Community College
Robert Smolin, Citrus College
Laura Solano, Pueblo Community College
Laurel Stevenson, Seminole Community College
Janice Stoudemire, Midlands Technical College
Lynette Teal, Western Wisconsin Technical College
Lynda Thompson, Massasoit Community College
Judith Toland, Buck County Community College
Shafi Ullah, Broward Community College
Ski Vanderlaan, Delta College
Patricia Walczak, Lansing Community College
Scott Wallace, Blue Mountain Community College
Shane Warrick, Southern Arkansas University
Jack Wiehler, San Joaquin Delta College
Terrence Willyard, Baker College

## TACTYC Focus Group Attendees (May 2006)

Patricia Walczak, Lansing Community College
Amy Haas, Kingsborough Community College
Mary Falkey, Prince George's Community College
Kenneth, Mark, Kansas City Kansas Community College
Allen Applebaum, Broward Community College
Audrey Hunter, Broward Community College
Scott Wallace, Blue Mountain Community College
Carla Rich, Pensacola Junior College
Marcia Sandvold, Des Moines Area Community College

## TACTYC Focus Group Attendees (May 2007)

Amy Haas, Kingsborough Community College
Mary Falkey, Prince George Community College
Scott Wallace, Blue Mountain Community College
Patricia Holmes, Des Moines Area Community College
Ski Vanderlaan, Delta College
Lisa Cole, Johnson County Community College
Marcia Sandvold, Des Moines Area Community College

## TACTYC Focus Group Attendees (May 2008)

Stanley Chapteru, Borough of Manhattan Community College
Paul Shinal, Cayuga Community College
Lois Slutsky, Broward Community College
Joan Cook, Milwaukee Area Technical College
John Gabelman, Columbus State Community College
Mary Halford, Prince George's Community College
Patty Holmes, Des Moines Area Community College
Marcia Sandvold, Des Moines Area Community College
Harvey Man, Manhattan Community College
Ron Dougherty, Tech Community College–Columbus
Natasha Librizzi, Milwaukee Area Technical College
Mary Falkey, Prince George's Community College
Melvin Williams, College of the Mainland
Carol Hutchinson, Asheville Buncombe Technical College

## Principles of Accounting Symposium Attendees (March 2008)

Beverly Beatty, Anne Arundel Community College
George Bernard, Seminole Community College
Carla Cabarle, Minot State University
Chapterris Crosby, York Technical College
Steve Doster, Shawnee State University
Robert Dunlevy, Montgomery County Community College
Richard Fredericsk, Lasell College
John Gabelman, Columbus State Community College
Gloria Grayless, Sam Houston State University
Jeannie Harrington, Middle Tennessee State University
William Herd, Springfield Technical Community College
Susan Logorda, Lehigh Carbon Community College
Cathryn Nash, Dekalb Technical College
LaVonda Ramey, Schoolcraft College
Pamela Strysick, Broward Community College
Mario Tripaldi, Hudson County Community College
David Verduzco, University of Texas at Austin

## Design Reviewers (WebEx, November 2007)

Paul Harris, Camden Community College
Audrey Hunter, Broward County Community College
Amy Haas, Kingsborough Community College
Kevin McFarlane, Front Range Community College
Patrick Geer, Hawkeye Community College
Patricia Holmes, Des Moines Area Community College
Sandra Augustine, Hilbert College

David Bland, Cape Fear Community College
David Laurel, South Texas College
Hoossein Noorian, Wentworth Institute of Technology
Margaret Black, San Jacinto College
Terri Meta, Seminole Community College
Lynda Thompson, Massasoit Community College
Jeannie Harrington, Middle Tennessee State University
John Gabelman, Columbus State Community College
Thomas Kam, Hawaii Pacific University
Tammy Metzke, Milwaukee Area Technical College
Chris McNamara, Finger Lakes Community College
Constance Hylton, George Mason University
Tom Branton, Alvin Community College
Lisa Cole, Johnson County Community College
Lois Slutksy, Broward Community College
Shane Warrick, South Arkansas University

We are grateful to the following individuals who helped develop, critique, and shape the text and ancillary package: Cheryl Bartlett, Central New Mexico Community College; Jeannie Folk, College of DuPage; Kimberly Temme, Maryville University of Saint Louis; Angela Sandberg, Jacksonville State University; Patricia Holmes, Des Moines Area Community College; LuAnn Bean, Florida Technical Institute; Beth Woods, Accuracy Counts; Laura Rickett, Kent State University; J. Lowell Mooney, Georgia Southern University; Rada Brooks, University of California–Berkeley; Jay Holmen, University of Wisconsin–Eau Claire; Susan Galbreath, David Lipscomb University; Jon Booker, Tennessee Technological University; Charles Caldwell, Tennessee Technological University; Matthew Muller, Adirondack Community College, Carol Yacht; Jack Terry, ComSource Associates, Inc.; and James Aitken, Central Michigan University.

Special thanks to Alan Cohen, Ithaca College, and John Gabelman, Columbus State Community College, and their Principles of Accounting Students, for class testing.

Last, we thank a talented group of individuals at McGraw-Hill/Irwin whose extraordinary efforts made all of this come together. We would especially like to thank our editorial director, Stewart Mattson; Tim Vertovec, our publisher; Alice Harra, our sponsoring editor; Kimberly Hooker, our developmental editor; Sankha Basu, our marketing manager; Mary Conzachi, our project manager; Martha Beyerlein, our freelance project manager; Pam Verros and Cara Hawthorne, our designers; Debra Sylvester, our production supervisor; Susan Lombardi, our media producer; Jeremy Cheshareck, our photo research coordinator; David Tietz, our photo researcher; and Marcy Lunetta, our permission researcher.

Patricia A. Libby
Robert Libby
Fred Philips
Stacey Whitecotton

# Assurance of Accuracy

Dear Colleagues,

Accuracy has always been our top priority in producing a textbook. We test every word through your eyes and those of our many professional copy editors, line editors, accuracy checkers, and contributing supplement authors. We have taken every effort to ensure the accuracy of this first edition of *Principles of Accounting* including the following:

- *Three drafts of manuscript*: We wrote and edited the entire manuscript three times, reading each other's chapters and making sure our voices, vocabulary, and pedagogy were consistent throughout.

- *Three rounds of accuracy checking*: Three professional accuracy checkers individually tested every problem at different stages of the production so that you don't have any surprises.

- *Two rounds of professional line editing*: A large investment was made to ensure consistency of voice and appropriate reading level.

- *Two hundred and sixty reviews:* Detailed reviews of every chapter from principles instructors around the country were compiled, synthesized, studied, and acted upon during each draft of our manuscript.

- *Forty* students participated in a class test of Chapters 1–4.

- *Thirty-six* members at three different conferences of Teachers of Accounting at Two-Year Colleges participated in focus groups held in 2006 (Atlanta), 2007 (Indianapolis), and 2008 (San Antonio) where we spent several hours listening to their advice that helped us shape the content and pedagogy.

- *Twenty-six* faculty attendees of McGraw-Hill's Principles of Accounting Symposium in 2008 (Las Vegas) spent several days discussing the challenges of teaching principles of accounting.

- *Twenty-five* professors served as design reviewers via WebEx to critique the design and overall visual appeal of the text and challenged us to help their students with a book that says "You can do it!" through its design.

All of our editorial advisers, reviewers, and attendees are listed on page xxii.

You and your students can be assured that our dedication and commitment to producing an error-free text has gone into every page of *Principles of Accounting*.

Patricia Libby      Robert Libby      Fred Phillips      Stacey Whitecotton

# To Our Students and Readers: Advice on How to Read Your Textbook

Dear Students,

The following advice is generated from an in-depth study of 172 undergraduate students of varying backgrounds, all of whom were enrolled in an introductory accounting course.

- **Read the chapters to learn rather than just to get through them.** Learning doesn't miraculously occur just because your eyes have skimmed all the assigned lines of the textbook. You have to think and focus while reading to ensure that you sink the material into your understanding and memory. Use the learning objectives in the text to focus on what's really important in each chapter.

- **Don't get discouraged if you initially find some material challenging to learn.** At various times, both the best and weakest students describe themselves as "confused" and "having a good grasp of the material," "anxious" and "confident," and "overwhelmed" and "comfortable." The simple fact is that learning new material can be challenging and initially confusing. Success doesn't appear to depend as much on whether you become confused as it does on what you do when you become confused.

- **Clear up confusion as it arises.** A key difference between the most and least successful students is how they respond to difficulty and confusion. When successful students are confused or anxious, they immediately try to enhance their understanding through rereading, self-testing, and seeking outside help if necessary. In contrast, unsuccessful students try to reduce anxiety by delaying further reading or by resorting to memorizing without understanding. Aim to clear up confusion when it arises because accounting in particular is a subject for which your understanding of later material depends on your understanding of earlier material.

- **Think of reading as the initial stage of studying.** Abandon the idea that "studying" occurs only during the final hours before an exam. By initially reading with the same intensity that occurs during later reviews for an exam, you can create extra time for practicing exercises and problems. This combination of concentrated reading and extensive practice is likely to contribute to better learning and superior exam scores.

To learn more about the study on which this advice is based, see B. J. Phillips and F. Phillips, "Sink or Skim: Textbook Reading Behaviors of Introductory Accounting Students," *Issues in Accounting Education* 22 (February 2007), pp. 21–44.

# Brief Table of Contents

# Table of Contents

# Chapter 4

## Completing the Accounting Cycle   144

## PIZZA AROMA   145

# Chapter 5

## Accounting Systems   202

## THE UPS STORE   203

Chapter **6**

## Merchandising Operations   260

Chapter **7**

## Inventories   302

**Chapter 14**

**Long-Term Liabilities   598**

**GENERAL MILLS, INC.   599**

**Chapter 15**

**Accounting for Investments   640**

**THE WASHINGTON POST COMPANY   641**

Chapter **16**

**Reporting and Interpreting the Statement of Cash Flows    680**

**NAUTILUS INC.    681**

Chapter **17**

**Financial Statement Analysis    728**

**LOWE'S    729**

# Chapter 18

## Managerial Accounting   764

### TOMBSTONE PIZZA   765

# Chapter 19

## Job Order Costing   798

### TOLL BROTHERS INC.   799

Chapter **20**

## Process Costing and Activity Based Costing   840

**CK MONDAVI FAMILY VINYARDS**   841

Chapter **21**

## Cost Behavior and Cost-Volume-Profit Analysis   882

**STARBUCKS COFFEE**   883

Chapter **25**

**Decentralized Performance Evaluation 1026**

**BLOCKBUSTER 1027**

# 1 The Role of Accounting in Starting a Business

*At the beginning of each chapter, you'll see a list of learning objectives that identify the key topics you need to master. You can also use the list as an outline for taking notes as you read through the chapter.*

## LEARNING OBJECTIVES

**After studying this chapter, you should be able to:**

Lectured slideshow–LP1-1
www.mhhe.com/LLPW1e

**LO1** Categorize business types and organizational forms.

**LO2** Describe accounting and its role in business decisions.

**LO3** Identify users of financial information.

**LO4** Describe the fundamental accounting equation and elements of financial statements.

**LO5** Explain the structure of basic financial statements.

**LO6** Understand the importance of ethical decisions in financial reporting and business.

**Focus Company:** PIZZA AROMA, Ithaca, NY

**"A Small Business Comes to Life"**

Have you ever walked into a local store or restaurant and thought, I'm good at this, and I can do it better? But when you thought about it further, you realized that you did not have all the knowledge you needed to start the business and monitor its success. How would you know you really could do it better? Where would you get good advice? Who else would be interested in how well your business did? In the next four chapters, you will learn about the start of a real business—one person's dream turned into reality—and two of the authors of this text are now regular customers.

About two decades ago, Mauricio Rosa and his wife emigrated from El Salvador to the United States to build a better life. While working in pizza shops in Massachusetts and New York, Mauricio perfected a gourmet pizza concept that caught the attention of a business owner in Ithaca, New York. Thinking that great gourmet pizza would be a new and exciting addition to the restaurant scene in Ithaca, the man encouraged Mauricio to start his own pizza business there.

Although the idea interested Mauricio, he had many questions to ask and decisions to make before attempting such a venture. The business owner suggested that Mauricio contact Laurie Hensley, a local CPA (certified public accountant), to ask her advice. The two met at her Ithaca office at the beginning of April.

| BUSINESS TYPES AND ORGANIZATIONAL FORMS | ACCOUNTING AND BUSINESS DECISIONS | BASIC FINANCIAL REPORTS | PROFESSIONAL STANDARDS AND ETHICAL CONDUCT |
|---|---|---|---|
| • Business Types<br>• Organizational Forms | • Accounting Defined<br>• Accounting Professionals<br>• Users of Financial Information | • The Accounting Equation<br>• Pizza Aroma Illustration<br>• Financial Statements | • Generally Accepted Accounting Principles<br>• Ethical Conduct |

*Throughout this text, we will provide you with tips to highlight explanations of selected topics. Please read them carefully.*

# BUSINESS TYPES AND ORGANIZATIONAL FORMS

**Coach's Tip**

In this chapter, the conversation between Mauricio and Laurie is important to the flow of the material. Please do not skip the dialogue.

"Hi, Laurie. I'm opening a gourmet pizza restaurant named Pizza Aroma, and I have lots of questions."

 "It's nice to meet you, Mauricio, and I'm glad to help. We should start by talking about what type of business you're establishing and how you want to organize it."

## Business Types

**Learning Objective 1**

Categorize business types and organizational forms.

Laurie explained the types of businesses. Most businesses, whether they are large like Wal-Mart or small like a pizza restaurant, exist so their owners can earn a profit. These businesses earn their profits by selling goods or services to customers for more than the cost of producing them.[1] Mauricio's pizza restaurant is a service business. **Service companies** do not make or sell goods; instead, they provide a service to customers or clients. Hilton Hotels provides lodging services, Southwest Airlines provides air transportation services, and Mauricio's restaurant will provide food service. Other companies earn profits in other ways. **Manufacturers** make products from raw inputs. For example, Dell uses various plastic, metal, and electronic components to build computers. **Merchandisers** sell the goods that manufacturers produced. Merchandisers that sell exclusively to other businesses are called wholesalers. Those that sell to customers are called retailers. Wal-Mart, Macy's, Linens 'n Things, and Best Buy are retailers.

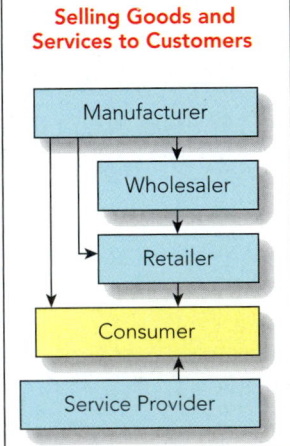

**Selling Goods and Services to Customers**

Manufacturer → Wholesaler → Retailer → Consumer ← Service Provider

## Organizational Forms

One of the first decisions Mauricio must make is to determine how to organize his business. Laurie outlined for him the three major ways that businesses can be organized, each of which has unique strengths and weaknesses.[2]

### Sole Proprietorship

A **sole proprietorship** is owned by one individual who often manages the business as well. Sole proprietorships are relatively inexpensive to form. Because they are not legally separate from their owners, all of their profits (or losses) become part of the proprietor's taxable income. The proprietor is also personally liable for all of the business's debts.

*Key terms such as sole proprietorship are printed in blue type throughout the text. Each is listed at the end of the chapter and defined at the end of the book in the glossary.*

[1] Some organizations (such as city governments, colleges, and the United Way) are considered nonprofit because the objective is to provide benefits to society rather than to earn a profit.

[2] For additional information on starting, financing, and managing a small business, go to the U.S. Small Business Association Web site at www.sba.gov.

## Partnership

A **partnership** is similar to a proprietorship, but it has two or more owners rather than one. A partnership agreement outlines how the profits (or losses) are to be shared and how the ownership of the business can change (for example, by adding a new partner, buying out an existing partner, or dissolving the partnership). As sole proprietors attempt to expand their businesses, they often add partners to obtain the resources the business needs to grow.

## Corporation

Unlike a proprietorship or partnership, a **corporation**[3] is a separate legal entity. This means that corporations are taxed separately from their owners, and their owners cannot be held

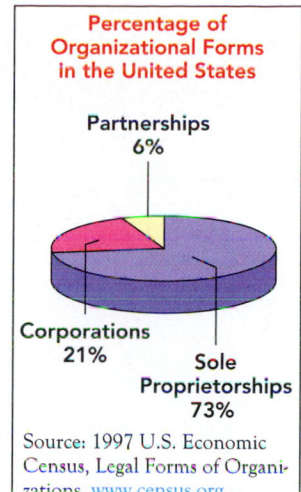

**Percentage of Organizational Forms in the United States**

Partnerships 6%
Corporations 21%
Sole Proprietorships 73%

Source: 1997 U.S. Economic Census, Legal Forms of Organizations, www.census.org.

liable for more than their investments in the corporation—a major advantage to an investor.

A corporation's ownership is divided into shares of stock. When a relatively small number of individuals own the stock, the corporation is a privately held company. Public companies, on the other hand, sell stock on the stock market to reach many more individuals.

In addition to the limited liability advantage, another major advantage of a corporation is that, at any time, stockholders can sell all or part of their shares to someone else. These advantages make it easier for a corporation to raise large amounts of money to finance its growth. A corporation's major disadvantage is the higher cost of its creation, primarily due to higher legal fees. Most of the big-name companies you are familiar with, such as Home Depot, The Gap, and Papa John's, are corporations. A share of stock is shown above.

"Although I certainly think the corporate form has its advantages, I intend to start out as a **sole proprietor.** If I decide to grow my business beyond what I can personally afford, then I'll consider changing it by adding a partner or establishing a corporation."

Coach's Tip

The best way to know whether you are reading the chapter carefully enough is to see how well you do on a short exercise. Therefore, at important points throughout each chapter, you will find an exercise that will help you to reinforce the concepts you have just learned and provide feedback on how well you learned them. We urge you not to skip these practices.

Complete this short practice exercise to make sure you understand how to categorize businesses.

**SELF-STUDY PRACTICE**

Match the following terms to the most appropriate statements. Select only one statement to describe each term.

1. _____ Corporation
2. _____ Merchandiser
3. _____ Public company
4. _____ Sole proprietorship
5. _____ Manufacturer
6. _____ Partnership
7. _____ Service provider

A. Sells goods made by manufacturers to customers.
B. Has two or more individuals who have agreed on how to share the profits.
C. Is a separate legal and accounting entity that sells stock to owners.
D. Makes products from raw inputs.
E. Provides a service to customers or clients.
F. Sells stock on the stock market.
G. Is a business owned by one individual.

*After you have finished, check your answers with the solutions at the bottom of the page.*

[3] Another form of business is a **limited liability company** or **LLC** in which a partnership can be organized as a corporation to limit liability to the partners' individual investments. However, it is taxed as a partnership with each partner paying taxes on his or her percentage of the profits.

1. C    2. A    3. F    4. G    5. D    6. B    7. E

Solution to Self-Study Practice

"Laurie, I believe passionately that I can make the best pizza around using the highest quality ingredients. I brought a copy of my menu and some samples of my pizza for you to try. What do you think?"

"Wow, Mauricio! This is awesome. I think you're going to sell a lot of pizza, and it's going to be the best in town. But the question is, can you do it at a profit? Let me explain how accounting and accounting professionals can help."

# ACCOUNTING AND BUSINESS DECISIONS

Laurie defined accounting and the role it plays in business decisions.

## Accounting Defined

To know just how successful his company will be, Mauricio will need to establish and maintain a system of financial recordkeeping—that is, an accounting system. **Accounting** is an information system designed by an organization to capture (analyze, record, and summarize) the activities affecting its financial condition and performance and then communicate the results to decision makers, both inside and outside the organization. When business owners, managers, investors, and creditors talk about business operations, they use accounting as their language, so accounting is often referred to as the **language of business.**

## Accounting Professionals

Every organization needs accountants to help its owner(s) understand the financial effects of business decisions and to assist in communicating financial information for making decisions. Accountants who are employed by a single business or nonprofit organization work in **private accounting**. Like Laurie, accountants who charge a fee for their services to businesses and nonprofit organizations work in **public accounting**. Laurie is a licensed **certified public accountant** (CPA) who has passed a rigorous exam and been in practice in public accounting. Supplement 1-A to this chapter illustrates the wide variety of career choices available to accounting professionals. Some accounting graduates start their careers in CPA firms and then decide to move into private accounting within businesses, government organizations such as the Internal Revenue Service (IRS) and the Federal Bureau of Investigation (FBI), or nonprofit organizations such as the American Red Cross. Many of them become top managers of large companies. After earning a graduate degree, some devote their careers to teaching and research.

Because today's cost of computers and accounting software such as Peachtree[4] is low, most small business owners do their own bookkeeping and hire public accountants to provide assistance and advice. Because Mauricio's business will be small, he decides to have Pizza Aroma contract with a CPA who will help him set up an accounting system for the business and advise him on key business decisions. As his business grows, Mauricio may then decide to hire a private accountant or to ask an independent CPA to review his financial records and accounting system.

"I feel confident now that there are professionals who can help me with my financial issues. How will an accounting system help me run my business?"

## Users of Financial Information

Whether focused on marketing, human resources, finance, or production and operations, all businesspeople need accounting information to understand the financial condition and performance of a business. As Exhibit 1.1 indicates, the accounting system produces two kinds of reports: managerial accounting reports and financial accounting reports.

[4] We illustrate the use of Peachtree in Chapter 5.

**Learning Objective 2**
Describe accounting and its role in business decisions.

Video 1-1
www.mhhe.com/LLPW1e

**Learning Objective 3**
Identify users of financial information.

## Exhibit 1.1    The Accounting System and Decision Makers

Managerial accounting reports include detailed financial plans and continually updated reports about the financial performance of the business. These reports are made available only to the company's managers (**internal users** of the information) so that they can make business decisions such as whether to build, buy, or rent a building; whether to continue or discontinue making particular products; how much to pay employees; and how much to borrow from creditors. **Sole proprietors** and **partners** who manage their own businesses and other **managers** who are hired by owners clearly have an interest in receiving the best, most up-to-date information for use in making these decisions.

As owner and manager of Pizza Aroma, Mauricio will regularly need managerial accounting reports to monitor the quantity of supplies on hand, evaluate the various costs associated with making and selling his gourmet pizza, and assess his employees' productivity. He will also use the information to forecast the possible effects of any changes he may consider, such as expanding his business to a second location or adding salads and desserts to the menu. Owners who do not manage their own businesses use accounting information to evaluate how effectively the managers are operating their companies.

"Others outside your business will also need financial information about your restaurant. For example, where will the money come from to start your business?"

"I'll contribute $30,000 from personal savings. But I'll still need to ask the bank for a $20,000 loan to buy equipment. What will the bank want to know?"

Laurie described **financial accounting** reports called **financial statements** that a business prepares periodically to provide information to people it does not employ. These **external financial statement users** are not given access to the company's detailed internal records, so they rely extensively on the financial statements. Creditors and investors are the two primary external user groups, but other external users also find the information helpful.

**Creditors** (anyone to whom money is owed)

- **Banks** evaluate the risk of lending money to a business based on a review of its past performance and future prospects. Because banks take a risk when they lend money, they want to receive ongoing financial reports from the business so they can monitor its progress and anticipate problems.
- **Suppliers** want to be sure that a business can pay them for the goods or services they deliver. They usually check the business's credit standing and may also ask for financial reports before entering into significant business relationships.

**Investors**

- **External investors,** unlike internal managers, do not have access to detailed internal records, but they are very interested in knowing how well the company is doing.
- Current and potential **stockholders** of corporations are a major group of external users. They need information that will help them to predict what their shares will be worth in the future and whether to buy, sell, or hold the stock.

**Other external users**

- Certain **customers** are concerned with the company's ability to provide service on its products and honor its warranties.
- Various local, state, and federal **governments** collect taxes and monitor businesses based on the financial statements.

In Pizza Aroma's case, the bank it borrows from will be interested in the overall profitability of the business and its cash flows, which help bank managers determine whether the business can make its loan payments. Mauricio will need to prepare financial information to obtain the loan from the bank, and he will need to continue to provide the bank with financial reports until the loan has been repaid. See Exhibit 1.1 for a summary of the difference between financial accounting reports such as these and the managerial accounting reports that are prepared for internal users.

---

**SELF-STUDY PRACTICE**

A.  Define *accounting*.

B.  For each of the following, indicate whether the person or entity is an internal user (I) or an external user (E) of accounting information.

1. _____ Banker     3. _____ Supplier     5. _____ Public company stockholder
2. _____ Manager    4. _____ Government   6. _____ Sole proprietor

*After you have finished, check your answers with the solutions at the bottom of the page.*

---

## BASIC FINANCIAL REPORTS

Mauricio understood everything Laurie had told him, but he had another major concern.

"I want to be knowledgeable when I talk to my accountants and bankers, but I don't know much about accounting."

 "This is a common concern for new business owners. Let's start with the most basic thing you need to know about accounting."

---

**Solution to Self-Study Practice**

A.  Accounting is an information system designed to capture a business's financial condition and financial performance and communicate it to decision makers inside and outside the organization.

B.  1. E     2. I     3. E     4. E     5. E     6. I

# The Accounting Equation

One of the keys to understanding financial reports is the concept that **what a business owns must equal what a business owes to its creditors and owners.** The business owns the **resources** it uses to generate profits, pay its creditors, and provide a return to the owners. It owes money to its creditors and owners who have **claims to the resources.** Accountants use special names for these: Resources a business owns are called **assets.** The claims it owes are called **liabilities** when they are held by creditors and **owners' equity** when they are held by investors. The result is the fundamental accounting equation that provides the structure for accounting and financial reporting.

**Learning Objective 4**

Describe the fundamental accounting equation and elements of financial statements.

Because the elements of the accounting equation (Assets = Liabilities + Owner's Equity) are fundamental to reading and understanding financial statements, let's look at each in detail.

**Coach's Tip**

When the business is a sole proprietorship with one owner, like Pizza Aroma, *owner's equity* is singular. When the business has more than one owner, claims by the owners are called *owners' equity* (plural).

## Assets

An **asset** is any resource controlled by the business that has measurable value and is expected to provide future benefits. Pizza Aroma's assets would include resources such as cash, supplies (including ingredients), and equipment such as tables, chairs, and pizza ovens. Initially, these assets would be reported in the business's financial statements at their purchase price, also called their historical cost.

However, not all valuable resources are reported as assets. For example, Mauricio's secret recipe for a specialty pizza may be a very valuable resource, but its value is difficult to measure. He created it himself rather than purchasing it from someone else (that is, the recipe has no measurable historical cost).

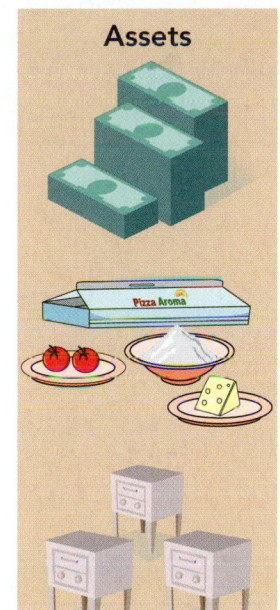

## Liabilities

A **liability** is a measurable amount that a business owes to a creditor. What would be Pizza Aroma's liabilities? If it borrows from a bank, it would owe a liability called Notes Payable. This particular name is used because banks require borrowers to sign a legal document called a *note* that describes details about the business's promise to repay the bank.

The business would also owe payments to the suppliers who deliver ingredients and other supplies to the restaurant. When a company buys goods from suppliers, it usually does so on credit by promising to pay for them at a later date. The amount that is owed, as indicated on the supplier's bill or invoice, is called Accounts Payable because purchases made using credit are said to be "on account." Pizza Aroma could also owe wages to its employees (Wages Payable) and sales taxes to the government (Taxes Payable) among other liabilities. As you may have noticed, anything with the word **payable** in its name is considered a liability.

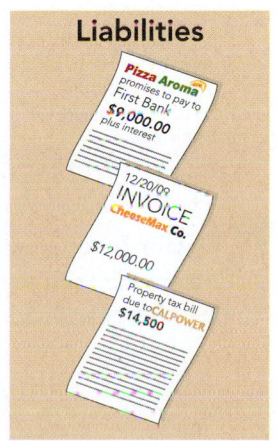

## Owner's Equity

**Owner's equity** represents the owner's claim to the business. The claim arises for two reasons:

- First, the owner has a claim on amounts he or she invested in the business by making direct contributions to the company.
- Second, the owner has a claim on the amounts the company has earned through profitable business operations.

The goal of most business owners is to generate profits because this increases owners' equity and allows owners to receive more money back from the business than they put in (a return on their investment). Mauricio's goal should be to increase his stake (his equity) in the business by making more money than he invests (generating profits).

How will Mauricio know if the business is making profits that will increase his equity? You've heard that to reap a reward, you must expend effort—"no pain, no gain." This is the

Video 1-2
www.mhhe.com/LLPW1e

same concept behind measuring the profits in a business. Profits are generated when the total amount earned from selling goods and services is more than all of the costs incurred to generate those sales. This means Pizza Aroma will be profitable if it earns more from selling its gourmet pizzas (generating revenues) than its costs to make its pizzas and run the business (incurring expenses). The difference between total revenues and expenses is sometimes loosely called **profit** or **earnings,** but the preferred term in accounting is **net income.** Thus, the fundamental accounting equation can be expanded to show the effects of revenues, expenses, and owner investments and withdrawals:

| Assets | = | Liabilities | + | Owner's Equity |
|---|---|---|---|---|

+ Owner Investments
− Owner Withdrawals
**+ Net Income = Revenues − Expenses**

### Revenues

Revenues are sales of goods or services to customers. They will be measured at the amount Pizza Aroma charges its customers for the pizza it delivers. Most restaurants receive cash and earn revenue at the time they provide the food service. If a business sells goods or services to customers "on account," then, instead of receiving cash on delivery, the company receives a different asset from the customer: a promise to pay, called Accounts Receivable.

### Expenses

Utilities expense

Expenses are all costs of doing business that are necessary to earn revenues. For Pizza Aroma, the expenses will include utilities, rent, wages to employees, advertising, insurance, repairs, and supplies used in making pizza. Some of these, such as supplies, insurance, and rent, are paid for before they are used to generate revenues. Other expenses, such as utilities and employees' wages, are paid for after they are used or owed to suppliers. Accountants say that expenses are **incurred** to generate revenues. This means that the activities giving rise to a cost (e.g., running an ad, using electricity) have occurred.

Wages expense

Supplies expense

## Pizza Aroma Illustration

"Mauricio, let me illustrate for you some common activities you can expect to undertake for Pizza Aroma to show how resources would balance with the claims to those resources made by creditors and owners."

### Coach's Tip

Unless indicated otherwise in the text and assignments, analyze all activities from the standpoint of the **business.**

Laurie explained that activities of the business are reported separately from personal activities of its owners. This is called the **separate entity assumption**. The illustrated activities are shown from the standpoint of the effects on the business Pizza Aroma. It is important to learn in this section the types of activities businesses undertake and typical terms used by businesses. The process for analyzing these activities is the focus in Chapter 2.

**1** **Obtain Investments from Owners.** The first resource any new business needs is cash. Sole proprietors often begin by contributing their personal funds. They invest in the business because they expect a return on their investment. Let's assume Mauricio will contribute $30,000 of his personal funds to start the business.

| | Assets | | = | Liabilities | + | Owner's Equity | |
|---|---|---|---|---|---|---|---|
| **1** Cash | | +30,000 | = | | | M. Rosa, Capital | +30,000 |

**2** **Borrow from Bank.** When Pizza Aroma needs more cash, it may borrow the money from a bank. The bank lends cash to the business and expects the loan to be repaid with interest. Assume Pizza Aroma obtains a $20,000 loan from a local bank.

| | Assets | = | Liabilities | + | Owner's Equity |
|---|---|---|---|---|---|
| **2** Cash | +20,000 | = | Notes Payable | +20,000 | |

**3** **Purchase Equipment.** Once the financing is complete, the business can purchase the resources necessary to run the business, such as a building, equipment, and supplies. The business can either buy these resources with cash or borrow the money from suppliers and banks. Assume Pizza Aroma buys ovens, chairs, tables, counters, a refrigerator, a computer, a cash register, and pots, all for $40,000 in cash.

| | Assets | = | Liabilities | + | Owner's Equity |
|---|---|---|---|---|---|
| **3** Equipment | +40,000 | = | No change | | |
| Cash | −40,000 | | | | |

**4** **Earn Revenues.** Now let's consider what happens if Pizza Aroma sells pizza in the first month of operations, earning revenues. Assume the business sells pizza to customers at the restaurant for $10,000 cash and delivers an additional $1,000 in pizza on account to local colleges. Selling goods and services "on account" means that Pizza Aroma will bill the colleges (customers) after delivering the pizza; it receives no cash on delivery. The customers' promise to pay the business is called Accounts Receivable.

| | Assets | = | Liabilities | + | Owner's Equity |
|---|---|---|---|---|---|
| **4** Cash | +10,000 | = | | Pizza Revenue | +11,000 |
| Accounts Receivable | + 1,000 | | | | |

**5** **Incur Expenses.** Businesses must incur many types of expenses to generate the revenues. Let's assume Pizza Aroma incurs the following expenses during the first month of operations, paying for everything in cash: Buying and using $4,000 in supplies and paying $2,000 for rent, $2,000 for wages to employees, $600 for utilities, $300 for insurance, and $100 for advertising.

| | Assets | = | Liabilities | + | Owner's Equity | |
|---|---|---|---|---|---|---|
| **5** Cash | − 9,000 | = | | Supplies Expense | − 4,000 |
| | | | | Rent Expense | − 2,000 |
| | | | | Wages Expense | − 2,000 |
| | | | | Utilities Expense | − 600 |
| | | | | Insurance Expense | − 300 |
| | | | | Advertising Expense | − 100 |

**6** **Purchase Supplies on Account.** To be ready for business the following month, assume Pizza Aroma purchases "on account" $3,000 in pizza ingredients and supplies (flour, tomatoes, cheese, napkins, pizza boxes, utensils, and cups). Purchasing goods and services on account means that suppliers will bill Pizza Aroma for them after delivery rather than expecting cash on delivery. The company's promises to pay suppliers are called Accounts Payable.

| | Assets | = | Liabilities | + | Owner's Equity | |
|---|---|---|---|---|---|---|
| **6** Supplies | +3,000 | = | Accounts Payable | | +3,000 | |

**7** **Distribute Profits to Owners.** The business can use any profits it earns to buy more assets, pay creditors, or distribute profits to the owners. Let's assume Pizza Aroma distributes $1,000 to Mauricio at the end of the first month of operations. Withdrawing a portion of profits is how Mauricio "pays" himself or "draws" from the business each month.

| | Assets | = | Liabilities | + | Owner's Equity | |
|---|---|---|---|---|---|---|
| **7** Cash | −1,000 | = | | | M. Rosa, Drawing | −1,000 |

Exhibit 1.2 summarizes these activities.

When you first begin to study accounting, among the most difficult things to grasp are the various **account titles** for the many kinds of assets, liabilities, revenues, and expenses a business can have. Laurie showed Mauricio the list of common account titles (see Exhibit 1.3) that most businesses use and suggested that he refer to it often while learning accounting.

In Exhibit 1.3, notice that "receivables" are assets and "payables" are liabilities. Also note that a "prepaid" expense account is always an asset, and an "unearned" revenue account is always a liability. When you are trying to determine what to call an account that is not on the list (the "specific type of" accounts), keep it simple. For example, when supplies are used, call the expense account Supplies Expense.

**Exhibit 1.2    Activity Summary**

| | | Assets | = | Liabilities | | + | Owner's Equity | |
|---|---|---|---|---|---|---|---|---|
| **1** | Cash | + 30,000 | = | | | | M. Rosa, Capital | + 30,000 |
| **2** | Cash | + 20,000 | = | Notes Payable | + 20,000 | | | |
| **3** | Equipment | + 40,000 | = | No Change | | | | |
| | Cash | − 40,000 | | | | | | |
| **4** | Cash | + 10,000 | = | | | | Pizza Revenue | + 11,000 |
| | Accounts Receivable | + 1,000 | | | | | | |
| | | | | | | | Supplies Expense | − 4,000 |
| | | | | | | | Rent Expense | − 2,000 |
| **5** | Cash | − 9,000 | = | | | | Wages Expense | − 2,000 |
| | | | | | | | Utilities Expense | − 600 |
| | | | | | | | Insurance Expense | − 300 |
| | | | | | | | Advertising Expense | − 100 |
| **6** | Supplies | + 3,000 | = | Accounts Payable | + 3,000 | | | |
| **7** | Cash | − 1,000 | = | | | | M. Rosa, Drawing | − 1,000 |
| | Totals | $54,000 | = | | $23,000 | + | | $31,000 |

## Exhibit 1.3   Typical Account Titles

| Assets | Liabilities | Owner's Equity |
|---|---|---|
| Cash | Accounts Payable (*to suppliers including utilities*) | "Proprietor's name," Capital |
| Short-Term Investments | | "Proprietor's name," Drawing |
| Accounts Receivable | Short-Term Notes Payable | |
| Inventory (*to be sold to customers*) | Wages Payable | **Revenues** |
| Supplies | Taxes Payable | Sales Revenue        Pizza Revenue |
| Prepaid Expenses (*rent, insurance, and advertising paid in advance*) | Interest Payable | Investment Revenue    Fee Revenue |
| | Unearned Revenues (*collections from customers before earning revenue*) | "Specific type of" revenue   Service Revenue |
| Land | | **Expenses** |
| Building | Long-Term Notes Payable | Cost of Goods Sold (*inventory sold to customers*)   Rent Expense |
| Equipment | Bonds Payable | Advertising Expense    Interest Expense |
| Long-Term Investments | "Specific type of" payable | Insurance Expense    Wages Expense |
| Intangible Assets | | "Specific type of" expense  Utilities Expense |
| "Specific type of" asset | | Supplies Expense |

Because the five financial statement elements and account titles are so important to understanding the rest of this chapter and other chapters, let's stop for a short practice exercise.

**SELF-STUDY PRACTICE**

For each of the following account titles, indicate what type of element it is. Use <u>A</u> for asset, <u>L</u> for liability, <u>OE</u> for owner's equity, <u>R</u> for revenue, and <u>E</u> for expense. Try to answer this quiz without referring to the exhibits just to see how well you have learned the terms.

1. _____ Supplies Expense
2. _____ Equipment
3. _____ M. Rosa, Capital
4. _____ Sales Revenue
5. _____ Wages Payable
6. _____ Accounts Receivable
7. _____ Fee Revenue
8. _____ Utilities Expense
9. _____ M. Rosa, Drawing
10. _____ Prepaid Rent

*After you have finished, check your answers with the solutions at the bottom of the page.*

## Financial Statements

"Okay, I think I get it, but can you tell me how all those items relate to each other and how they are reported in the financial statements?"

This was a good question. Laurie explained that before statements can be prepared, it is necessary to determine balances in accounts. She created a new table in Exhibit 1.4 that included a separate coloumn for each asset and liability and a separate section for revenues and expenses. This table shows the effects of the same seven activities on each account along with each account's ending total. The various asset, liability, owner's equity, revenue, and expense accounts appear in different financial statements. The term *financial statements* refers to four accounting reports, typically prepared in the following order:

1. Income Statement.
2. Statement of Owner's Equity.
3. Balance Sheet.
4. Statement of Cash Flows.

**Learning Objective 5**

Explain the structure of basic financial statements.

1. E   2. A   3. OE   4. R   5. L   6. A   7. R   8. E   9. OE   10. A

Solution to
Self-Study Practice

| Exhibit 1.4 | Account Balances |
| --- | --- |

| | Assets | | | | = | Liabilities | | + | Owner's Equity | |
| --- | --- | --- | --- | --- | --- | --- | --- | --- | --- | --- |
| | Cash | Accounts Receivable | Supplies | Equipment | = | Accounts Payable | Note Payable | + | M. Rosa, Capital | |
| Beg. | $    0 | $    0 | $    0 | $    0 | = | $    0 | $    0 | + | $    0 | |
| 1 | +30,000 | | | | = | | | | +30,000 | Owner investment |
| 2 | +20,000 | | | | = | | +20,000 | | | |
| 3 | −40,000 | | | +40,000 | = | No change | | | | |
| 4 | +10,000 | +1,000 | | | = | | | | +11,000 | Pizza Revenue |
| | | | | | | | | | −4,000 | Supplies Expense |
| | | | | | | | | | −2,000 | Rent Expense |
| | | | | | | | | | −2,000 | Wages expense |
| 5 | −9,000 | | | | = | | | | −600 | Utilities Expense |
| | | | | | | | | | −300 | Insurance Expense |
| | | | | | | | | | −100 | Advertising Expense |
| 6 | | +3,000 | | | = | +3,000 | | | | |
| 7 | −1,000 | | | | = | | | | −1,000 | M. Rosa, Drawing |
| Totals | $10,000 | $1,000 | $3,000 | $40,000 | = | $3,000 | $20,000 | | $31,000 | |
| | | | $54,000 | | | | $23,000 | | $31,000 | |

"I think you'll understand these relationships better if I show you how Pizza Aroma's financial reports might look at the end of the first month of operation, based on the activities I discussed earlier."

Laurie wanted Mauricio to focus at this meeting on the structure of the financial statements and how, given the illustrated activities, Pizza Aroma's financial statements would be reported. She also emphasized that the structure of the financial statements she would present is typical for any size of business.

Financial statements can be prepared at any time during the year, although they are most commonly prepared monthly, every three months (quarterly), and at the end of the year (annual reports). Businesses are allowed to choose any date for the end of their accounting (or fiscal) year. For example, the toy maker Mattel uses a December 31 year-end because this is the start of its slow business period. It sells fewer toys in January through May than in the first three weeks of December. The only U.S. professional sports team operating as a public company—the Green Bay Packers, Inc.—has chosen a fiscal year-end of March 31, the month after the season wraps up with the Pro Bowl.

## Income Statement

The income statement (also called the **statement of income** or **statement of operations**) reports a business's financial performance over a specific period. Although the term *profit* is used widely for this measure of performance, accountants prefer to use the technical term **net income** or **net earnings.** A company measures its success by selling goods and/or providing services for more than the costs to generate those revenues. Each revenue and expense account is an accumulation of activities over a period of time.

An initial look at the income statement in Exhibit 1.5 indicates a great deal about the statement's purpose and content. The heading identifies the name of the business, the title of the report, and the specified period (for the month ended May 31, 2009) covered by the statement. Larger businesses with thousands or millions of dollars in revenues and expenses add a fourth

| Exhibit 1.5 | Income Statement | | PIZZA AROMA |
|---|---|---|---|

**Pizza Aroma**
**Income Statement**
**For the Month Ended May 31, 2009**

| | | Heading |
|---|---|---|
| | | Name of the entity |
| | | Title of the statement |
| | | Accounting period |
| **Revenue** | | |
| Pizza revenue | $11,000 | Revenue earned from the sale/delivery of pizza to customers |
| Total revenues | 11,000 | ◄ Total amount earned during May |
| **Expenses** | | |
| Supplies expense | 4,000 | Cost of supplies used in making and selling pizzas |
| Wages expense | 2,000 | Amount for employees' work in May |
| Rent expense | 2,000 | Rent for the month of May |
| Utilities expense | 600 | Utilities used in May |
| Insurance expense | 300 | Insurance coverage for May |
| Advertising expense | 100 | Advertising used in May |
| Total expenses | 9,000 | ◄ Total amount incurred in May to generate revenues |
| **Net income** | **$ 2,000** | |

line under the date to indicate that the numbers have been rounded to the nearest thousand "(in thousands)" or million "(in millions)."

Notice that an income statement for Pizza Aroma would have three major captions—revenues, expenses, and net income—corresponding to the income statement equation (Revenues – Expenses = **Net Income**). Individual types of revenues and expenses would be reported under the revenues and expenses headings. For Pizza Aroma, the revenue and expense accounts shaded in yellow in Exhibit 1.4 are reported on its income statement. These accounts are typical for most businesses, whether small or large. Notice that each major caption in Exhibit 1.5 has a subtotal, and the bottom line amount for net income has a double underline to highlight it.

A dollar sign is placed at the top and bottom of the column of numbers. In accounting, we assume we can report financial information in the standard monetary denomination of the country in which the business operates, such as reporting in dollars in the United States or euros in Germany. This is called the **monetary unit assumption**.

When listing the accounts on the income statement, revenues are on top, usually with the largest, most relevant revenue listed first. Then expenses are subtracted, again usually with the largest and most relevant expense listed first.

"So does the $2,000 of net income mean that I'll have that much more in cash?"

"No. Net income is a measure of how much better off your business is, not how much cash you made."

Laurie's point is one of the key understandings about the income statement. It is quite common for a business to provide goods or services to customers in one month but not collect cash from them until a later month. Similarly, expenses for the current month's activities may actually be paid in a different month. You will learn this in more detail later, but it is worth trying to understand from the beginning that revenues do not necessarily equal cash coming in during the month and expenses do not equal cash going out during the month.

Mauricio seemed disappointed with a projected net income of $2,000 for the first month. Laurie reassured him that it is typical for new businesses like Pizza Aroma to struggle initially to generate a profit because they have lots of expenses related to advertising and employee training but relatively little revenues due to a lack of a loyal customer base.[5] As you can probably expect, Pizza Aroma's net income would likely increase in the future after the business becomes established. By selling more pizza, revenues would increase without a major increase in expenses except for the cost of ingredients and supplies used in making the additional pizzas. Expenses such as employee wages and rent would likely not increase all that much.

"I guess that's not so bad. It does make me want to watch my expenses carefully and try to boost my pizza sales quickly. What about reporting what Pizza Aroma owes to the bank? Should we talk about the balance sheet?"

"Before we look at that, I want to show you the next statement that connects the income statement to the balance sheet, so you'll understand the relationships between the reports."

## Statement of Owner's Equity

Pizza Aroma, a sole proprietorship, will report a **statement of owner's equity**. Corporations prepare a more comprehensive statement of stockholders' equity in a similar fashion. For Pizza Aroma, most changes in owner's equity will relate to generating and distributing earnings.

The heading in Exhibit 1.6 identifies the name of the entity, the title of the report, and the accounting period (for the period ended May 31, 2009). The green shaded accounts on Exhibit 1.4 along with net income are reported on the statement of owner's equity.

The statement starts with the owner's equity balance at the beginning of the period. Because Pizza Aroma is a new business, the beginning balance of owner's equity would be $0. Then it would add additional investments made by the owner during the period and the net income reported on the income statement ($2,000 in Exhibit 1.5). A **net loss** in which expenses exceed revenues would be subtracted. Finally, any withdrawals made by the owner for the period would be subtracted to determine the owner's equity balance at the end of the period. Investments by Mauricio and earning profits (net income) add to his ownership in the business, while distributing profits as withdrawals by Mauricio reduces his equity in the business. Again, notice the use of a dollar sign at the top and bottom of the column of numbers and the double underscore at the bottom.

**Coach's Tip**

Next period, the beginning balance would be $31,000, this period's ending balance.

---

[5] In fact, 50 percent of all new businesses fail or close within the first six years of opening. Not many start out with a positive net income in the first month as projected of Pizza Aroma (Exhibit 1.5). Instead, most report a net loss in which their expenses exceed their revenues. For more information on small business failures, see Brian Headd, "Redefining Business Success: Distinguishing Between Closure and Failures," *Small Business Economics*, August 21, 2003, pp. 51–61.

---

| **Exhibit 1.6** | **Statement of Owner's Equity** |  |

**Pizza Aroma**
**Statement of Owner's Equity**
**For the Month Ended May 31, 2009**

| | | | |
|---|---|---:|---|
| **M. Rosa, capital, May 1, 2009** | | $    0 | ← Last period's ending owner's equity balance |
| Add: | Investments by owner | 30,000 | Initial and/or additional resources from owner |
| | Net income | 2,000 | Reported on the income statement (Exhibit 1.5) |
| Less: | Withdrawals by owner | (1,000) | Withdrawals made by owner |
| **M. Rosa, capital, May 31, 2009** | | **$31,000** | ← This period's ending owner's equity balance |

**Heading**
  Name of the entity
  Title of the statement
  Accounting period

## Balance Sheet

The next financial report is the **balance sheet**, also known as the **statement of financial position.** The balance sheet's purpose is to report the amount of a business's assets, liabilities, and owner's equity at a specific point in time. Think of the balance sheet as a picture or snapshot of Pizza Aroma's resources and claims to its resources at the end of the day on May 31, 2009. Exhibit 1.7 shows a projected balance sheet for Pizza Aroma based on assumed activities for May, the first month of business.

Notice again that the heading specifically identifies the name of the entity and title of the statement. Unlike the other financial reports, the balance sheet is presented for a specific point in time (at May 31, 2009). The assets are listed in order of how soon they are to be used or turned into cash. Likewise, liabilities are listed in order of how soon each is to be paid or settled.

The blue shaded row at the bottom of Exhibit 1.4 provides the ending balances for the accounts on the balance sheet. It first lists the assets of the business that for Pizza Aroma total $54,000. The second section lists the business's liabilities and owner's equity balances, also totaling $54,000. The balance sheet balances because the resources equal the claims to the resources. The fundamental accounting equation reflects the business's financial position on May 31, 2009:

| Assets | = | Liabilities | + | Owner's Equity |
|--------|---|-------------|---|----------------|
| $54,000 | = | $23,000 | + | $31,000 |

In the assets section, Cash is the first asset reported. The $10,000 represents the total amount of cash expected to be on hand and in Pizza Aroma's bank account. The $1,000 reported as Accounts Receivable represents the amount that Pizza Aroma expects to collect from customers (local colleges) for prior pizza deliveries sold on credit. Pizza Aroma will allow area colleges to buy pizza for events on account by running a tab that Pizza Aroma sends as a bill after it makes the deliveries. The $3,000 reported for Supplies indicates the

**Exhibit 1.7**   Balance Sheet

### Pizza Aroma
### Balance Sheet
### At May 31, 2009

**Heading**
Name of the entity
Title of the statement
Point in time

**Assets**

| | | |
|---|---|---|
| Cash | $ 10,000 | Amount on hand and in the business's bank account |
| Accounts receivable | 1,000 | Amount owed by customers (colleges) |
| Supplies | 3,000 | Amount of food and paper supplies on hand |
| Equipment | 40,000 | Cost of ovens, tables, etc. |
| **Total assets** | **$54,000** | ← **Total amount of the business's resources** |

**Liabilities and Owner's Equity**
*Liabilities*

| | | |
|---|---|---|
| Accounts payable | $ 3,000 | Amount owed to suppliers |
| Notes payable | 20,000 | Amount of loan owed to the bank |
| Total liabilities | 23,000 | |

*Owner's Equity*

| | | |
|---|---|---|
| M. Rosa, capital | 31,000 | Amount invested plus amount earned that is retained in the business (from Exhibit 1.6) |
| **Total liabilities and owner's equity** | **$54,000** | ← **Total claims on the business's resources** |

cost of pizza supplies that are expected to remain on hand at May 31, 2009. The same is true for the $40,000 of Equipment.

Under liabilities, the $3,000 of Accounts Payable is the amount Pizza Aroma is expected to owe to suppliers for food and paper supplies purchased on account. The Notes Payable is the written promise to repay the $20,000 loan from the bank.[6] As with all liabilities, these are financial obligations of the business arising from past business activities.

Finally, owner's equity of $31,000 reflects all contributions that Mauricio would have made during the month ($30,000) plus the restaurant's expected net income ($2,000) less Mauricio's withdrawals ($1,000). It matches the ending amount for owner's equity reported on the statement of owner's equity (see Exhibit 1.6).

"So, besides monitoring my revenues and expenses, it looks like I need to make sure I have enough assets to pay liabilities."

"Sharp observation! Your creditors are most interested in your ability to pay cash to them in the future. However, not all assets can easily be turned into cash, and not all revenues and expenses are received or paid in cash. So, there is one more financial statement."

## Statement of Cash Flows

Pizza Aroma's projected income statement shows a positive net income of $2,000. However, net income does not necessarily equal cash because revenues are reported when earned and expenses are reported when incurred regardless of when cash is received or paid. The fourth financial report of interest to external users, then, is the statement of cash flows. It includes only those activities in the Cash column, reflecting changes much like a video camera with a telephoto lens focused on activities affecting only cash. See Exhibit 1.8 for Pizza Aroma's projected statement of cash flows for the month ended May 31, 2009, based on the illustrated activities. The statement of cash flows is divided into three types of business activities:

- **Operating activities.** These activities are directly related to running the business to earn profit. For Pizza Aroma, they include buying supplies, cleaning the facility, paying employees for their labor, buying advertising, renting a building, repairing ovens, and obtaining insurance.
- **Investing activities.** These activities involve buying and selling productive resources with long lives, such as buildings, land, equipment, and tools, as well as investing funds in other businesses and lending to others. Pizza Aroma is expected to purchase equipment for $40,000 cash.
- **Financing activities.** Any borrowing from banks, repaying bank loans, receiving investments from owners, or distributing business profits to owners are considered financing activities.

Many new businesses have **negative** cash flows from operations when they are just starting. In the long run, businesses need to generate positive cash flows from their operating activities to remain in business because of the limited amount of money banks and others will provide. Pizza Aroma's projected $1,000 cash flow from operating activities is lower than its net income of $2,000 but positive—better than expected of new companies.

## Notes to the Financial Statements

The four basic financial statements are incomplete without notes that help those who study the statements to understand how the amounts were measured and what other information may affect their decisions. We will discuss the notes in other chapters.

---

[6] To simplify this discussion, interest on the Notes Payable is presented in future chapters. Interest Expense is the amount incurred during the period for using the borrowed funds; Interest Payable is the amount of interest not yet paid.

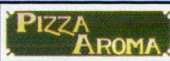

| Exhibit 1.8 | Statement of Cash Flows |
| --- | --- |

**Pizza Aroma**
**Statement of Cash Flows**
**For the Month ended May 31, 2009**

| | |
| --- | --- |
| **Cash Flows from Operating Activities** | |
| Cash from customers | $ 10,000 |
| Cash to suppliers and employees | (9,000) |
| Cash used in operating activities | **1,000** |
| **Cash Flows from Investing Activities** | |
| Purchase of equipment | (40,000) |
| Cash used in investing activities | **(40,000)** |
| **Cash Flows from Financing Activities** | |
| Investment by owner | 30,000 |
| Withdrawal by owner | (1,000) |
| Borrowing from bank | 20,000 |
| Cash provided by financing activities | **49,000** |
| Change in Cash | 10,000 |
| Beginning Cash balance, May 1, 2009 | 0 |
| Ending Cash balance, May 31, 2009 | **$ 10,000** |

**Heading**
  Name of the entity
  Title of the statement
  Accounting period

**Directly related to earning income**
  Amount of cash received from customers
  Amount of cash paid to suppliers and employees

**Related to the sale/purchase of productive assets**

**Activities with owners and banks**

**Sum of three flows ($1,000 + $[40,000] + $49,000)**

**Amount reported on the balance sheet (Exhibit 1.7)**

"How does the whole picture fit together, and what will my external users look for?"

## Relationships among the Financial Statements

Exhibit 1.9 shows how the four basic financial statements connect to one another. The arrow indicates that net income shown on the income statement is a component in determining the ending balance of owner's equity that is reported on the balance sheet. In addition, cash flows for the period added to the cash at the beginning of the period equal the cash reported on the balance sheet at the end of the period.

The financial statements are a key source of information when external users such as creditors and investors make decisions concerning a business. As you will see throughout this course, the amounts reported in the financial statements can be used to calculate percentages and ratios that reveal important insights about a company's performance. For now, however, let's consider how creditors and investors might gain valuable information simply by reading the dollar amounts reported in each financial statement.

Creditors are mainly interested in assessing two things:

1. **Is the company generating enough cash to make payments on its loan?** Answers to this question will come from the statement of cash flows. In particular, creditors would be interested in seeing whether operating activities are producing positive cash flows sufficient to make cash payments on loans. Pizza Aroma's net inflow of $1,000 cash from operating activities for the month is projected to be very good for a new business.

2. **Does the company have enough assets to cover its liabilities?** Answers to this question will come from comparing assets and liabilities reported on the balance sheet. At May 31, Pizza Aroma is expected to own slightly more than twice what it owes to creditors

**Exhibit 1.9**    Relationships among Pizza Aroma's Projected Financial Statements    PIZZA AROMA

### Pizza Aroma
### Income Statement
### For the Month Ended May 31, 2009

| | |
|---|---|
| **Revenue** | |
| Pizza revenue | $11,000 |
| Total revenues | 11,000 |
| **Expenses** | |
| Supplies expense | 4,000 |
| Wages expense | 2,000 |
| Rent expense | 2,000 |
| Utilities expense | 600 |
| Insurance expense | 300 |
| Advertising expense | 100 |
| Total expenses | 9,000 |
| **Net income** | **$ 2,000** |

### Pizza Aroma
### Statement of Owner's Equity
### For the Month Ended May 31, 2009

| | |
|---|---|
| **M. Rosa, capital, May 1, 2009** | $    0 |
| Add:   Investments by owner | 30,000 |
| Net income | 2,000 |
| Less:   Withdrawals by owner | (1,000) |
| **M. Rosa, capital, May 31, 2009** | **$31,000** |

### Pizza Aroma
### Statement of Cash Flows
### For the Month Ended May 31, 2009

| | |
|---|---|
| **Cash Flows from Operating Activities** | **$ 1,000** |
| **Cash Flows from Investing Activities** | **(40,000)** |
| **Cash Flows from Financing Activities** | **49,000** |
| Change in Cash | 10,000 |
| Beginning Cash balance, May 1, 2009 | 0 |
| Ending Cash balance, May 31, 2009 | $ 10,000 |

### Pizza Aroma
### Balance Sheet
### At May 31, 2009

| | |
|---|---|
| **Assets** | |
| Cash | $ 10,000 |
| Accounts receivable | 1,000 |
| Supplies | 3,000 |
| Equipment | 40,000 |
| Total assets | **$54,000** |
| **Liabilities and Owner's Equity** | |
| *Liabilities* | |
| Accounts payable | $  3,000 |
| Notes payable | 20,000 |
| Total liabilities | 23,000 |
| *Owner's Equity* | |
| M. Rosa, capital | 31,000 |
| Total liabilities and owner's equity | **$54,000** |

(total assets of $54,000 versus total liabilities of $23,000). With $10,000 in cash, Pizza Aroma could pay all of its accounts payable and part of its notes payable right now if needed.

Investors look for either an **immediate return** on their contributions to a company or a **long-term return** (increasing growth in owner's equity). Owner's equity is more likely to increase if a company is profitable. As a result, investors look closely at the income statement for information about the company's ability to generate profits. Pizza Aroma's expected net income of $2,000 for its first month of operations is a positive sign of future profitability, especially in light of the net losses reported by most start-up businesses.

A summary of the purposes, structures, and content of the four financial statements is provided in Exhibit 1.10.

## Exhibit 1.10    Summary of Four Basic Financial Statements

| Financial Statement | Purpose: To report | Structure | Examples of Content |
|---|---|---|---|
| **Income Statement** | The accountant's primary measure of economic performance *during the accounting period.* | Revenues<br>− Expenses<br><u>Net income</u> | Sales Revenue<br>Rent Expense<br>Wages Expense<br>Utilities Expense |
| **Statement of Owner's Equity** | The way that net income, owner investments, and owner withdrawals affected the company's financial position *during the accounting period.* | Beginning owner's equity<br>+ Additional investments<br>+ Net income (or − Net loss)<br>− Withdrawals<br><u>Ending owner's equity</u> | Net income is from the income statement |
| **Balance Sheet** | The financial position (economic resources and sources of financing) of a business *at a specific point in time.* | Assets<br>=<br>Liabilities<br>+<br>Owner's Equity | Cash, Receivables, Supplies, Equipment, Accounts Payable, Notes Payable, Owner's Capital |
| **Statement of Cash Flows** | Inflows (receipts) and outflows (payments) of cash *during the accounting period* in the operating, investing, and financing categories. | ± Cash flows from Operating Activities<br>± Cash flows from Investing Activities<br><u>± Cash flows from Financing Activities</u><br>Change in cash<br>+ Beginning cash balance<br><u>Ending cash balance</u> | Cash collected from customers, Cash paid to suppliers, Cash paid to purchase equipment, Cash borrowed from banks |

You have been introduced to new and important material. Before moving on, take a moment to complete two short exercises to make sure that you understand business activities and financial statements.

**SELF-STUDY PRACTICE A**

In the space provided, indicate the type of account (A = asset, L = liability, OE = owner's equity, R = revenue, E = expense) and whether the account is reported on the income statement (I/S) or balance sheet (B/S).

| Account Title | Type | Statement |
|---|---|---|
| 1.  Land | | |
| 2.  Wages Expense | | |
| 3.  Prepaid Insurance | | |
| 4.  Rent Revenue | | |
| 5.  S. Mattson, Capital | | |
| 6.  Note Payable | | |

*After you have finished, check your answers with the solutions at the bottom of the page.*

**Solution to Self-Study Practice A**

| | Type | Statement | | | Type | Statement |
|---|---|---|---|---|---|---|
| 1. | A | B/S | | 4. | R | I/S |
| 2. | E | I/S | | 5. | OE | B/S |
| 3. | A | B/S | | 6. | L | B/S |

**SELF-STUDY PRACTICE B**

A year ago, you formed a Web design business (called WebTech) as a sole proprietorship by making a $100,000 investment in cash. For the year ended August 31, 2009, the business had revenues of $350,000 and expenses of $270,000, and you withdrew $10,000 from the business. The business had $210,000 in assets at year-end and owed suppliers and banks $40,000. Complete all of the white areas in the following financial statements with the appropriate terms or amounts.

**WebTech**
**Income Statement**

| | |
|---|---|
| Revenues | $ 350,000 |
| Expenses | |
| | $ |

**WebTech**

**For the Year Ended August 31, 2009**

| | | |
|---|---|---|
| Beginning owner's equity | $ | 0 |
| Additional investments | | 100,000 |
| Net income | | |
| Withdrawals | | (10,000) |
| | $ | |

**WebTech**
**Balance Sheet**

| | |
|---|---|
| Assets | $ 210,000 |
| Total assets | $ |
| Liabilities | $ |
| Owner's Equity | |
| Total liabilities and owner's equity | $ |

**Coach's Tip**

**Remember:** Beginning balances for new companies are $0, and the balance sheet always balances.

**Fill in the Blank:** In the next period, beginning owner's equity would be _____ .

*After you have finished, check your answers with the solutions at the bottom of the page.*

# PROFESSIONAL STANDARDS AND ETHICAL CONDUCT

 "So, you've just seen how your financial statements should look in one month and how they relate to one another. Are you feeling okay with all this?"

"It actually makes me anxious to get started. But first, I've heard a lot about 'cooking the books.' How do users know the information they're getting is reliable and can be trusted?"

This is another important question. Laurie indicated that, to enhance the reliability of financial reporting, managers must apply accounting principles in an ethical business environment.

**Solution to Self-Study Practice B**

| WebTech Income Statement For the Year Ended 8/31/09 | | WebTech Statement of Owner's Equity For the Year Ended 8/31/09 | | WebTech Balance Sheet At 8/31/09 | |
|---|---|---|---|---|---|
| Revenues | $ 350,000 | Beginning owner's equity | $    0 | Assets | $210,000 |
| Expenses | 270,000 | Additional investments | 100,000 | Total assets | $210,000 |
| Net income | $ 80,000 | Net income | 80,000 | Liabilities | $ 40,000 |
| | | Withdrawals | (10,000) | Owner's equity | 170,000 |
| | | Ending owner's equity | $170,000 | Total liabilities and owner's equity | $210,000 |

**Solution to Coach's Tip**
$170,000

# Generally Accepted Accounting Principles

The system of financial statement reporting in use today has a long history going all the way back to a publication in 1494 by the Italian monk and mathematician Luca Pacioli. Now the primary responsibility for setting the rules of accounting rests with the **Financial Accounting Standards Board** (FASB) in the United States and the International Accounting Standards Board (IASB) in most other countries. As a group, these rules are called **generally accepted accounting principles**, or **GAAP** for short. ("GAAP" is pronounced like the name of the clothing store.)

For financial information to be useful, managers, creditors, owners, and others need to have confidence that the information is

- **Relevant** (it helps in making decisions).
- **Reliable** (it is unbiased and verifiable).
- **Comparable** (against other companies).
- **Consistent** (over time).

GAAP follow these guidelines to provide helpful information to users.

As a summary, Laurie showed Mauricio the information in Exhibit 1.11—the key concepts the FASB uses in developing new accounting principles. The concepts discussed in this chapter are highlighted in red; the rest will be introduced in later chapters. Mauricio was surprised at how many concepts he had already learned.

Many of the FASB's rules that result from following these key concepts are quite complex and apply mostly to large public companies. In future chapters, we will focus on accounting rules that have the greatest impact on financial statements at an appropriate introductory level.

> "Who is responsible for ensuring that businesses follow GAAP?"

Laurie told Mauricio that a company's **managers have primary responsibility for following GAAP and preparing fair financial statements.** To provide additional assurance, some private companies and all public companies hire independent auditors to check their financial records. Following rules approved by the **Public Company Accounting Oversight Board** (PCAOB) and other accounting bodies, these auditors report whether, beyond a reasonable doubt, the financial statements represent what they claim to represent and whether they comply with GAAP. In a sense, GAAP are to auditors and accountants what the criminal code is to lawyers and the public. The **Securities and Exchange Commission** (SEC) is the government agency that supervises the work of the FASB and the PCAOB.

 > "Overall, users expect information that is truthful, and this assumes that the company is following strong ethical business and accounting practices."

## Exhibit 1.11   Key Concepts for External Financial Reporting

**Objective of External Financial Reporting**

To provide useful economic information to external users for decision making
  Useful information is
- Relevant, Reliable, Comparable, and Consistent

**Elements to be Measured and Reported**
- Assets, Liabilities, Owner's Equity, Revenues, and Expenses

**Concepts for Measuring and Reporting Information**
- **Assumptions:** Separate Entity, Monetary Unit, Continuity, Time Period
- **Principles:** Historical Cost, Revenue Recognition, Matching, Full Disclosure
- **Exceptions:** Cost Benefit, Materiality, Conservatism, Industry Practices

**Coach's Tip**

Concepts in red are discussed in Chapters 1 and 2. Those in black will be discussed in Chapters 3 and 4.

## Ethical Conduct

Ethics refers to the standards of conduct for judging right from wrong, honest from dishonest, and fair from unfair. Intentional financial misreporting is both unethical and illegal. As you will see throughout this course, some accounting and business issues have clear answers that are either right or wrong. However, many situations require accountants, auditors, and managers to weigh the pros and cons of alternatives before making final decisions. To help ensure these decisions are made in a professional and ethical manner, the American Institute of Certified Public Accountants (AICPA) requires all its members to adhere to a Code of Professional Conduct.

Mauricio's concern about "cooking the books" likely stems from hearing about several high-profile accounting frauds that occurred a few years ago involving Enron, WorldCom (now owned by Verizon), Global Crossing, and Xerox. In response to these frauds, the U.S. Congress stepped into the crisis to create the **Sarbanes-Oxley Act of 2002.** The Act requires top managers of public companies to sign a report certifying their responsibilities for the financial statements, maintain an audited system of internal controls to ensure accuracy in the accounting reports, and maintain an independent committee to ensure that managers cooperate with auditors. As a result of the act, corporate executives now face severe consequences—20 years in prison and $5 million in fines—if they are found guilty of committing accounting fraud.

> **Coach's Tip**
>
> **Internal controls** are designed to protect assets from loss and ensure the accuracy of the accounting records. Controls you have seen include the security tags on clothing and using a bank to keep cash safe. We will discuss many internal controls throughout the text.

## Spotlight On ETHICS

### Accounting Scandals

Accounting scandals are driven by the fear of personal failure and greed. Initially, some people may appear to benefit from fraudulent reporting. In the long run, however, fraud harms most individuals and organizations. When it is uncovered, the corporation's stock price drops dramatically. In the case involving MicroStrategy, the stock price dropped 65 percent in a single day of trading, from $243 to $86 per share. Creditors are also harmed by fraud. WorldCom's creditors recovered only 42 percent of what they were owed. They lost $36 billion. Innocent employees also are harmed by fraud. At Enron, 5,600 employees lost their jobs and many lost all of their retirement savings.

Ethical conduct is just as important for small private businesses as it is for large public companies. Laurie's advice to Mauricio and to all managers is to strive to create an ethical environment and establish a strong system of checks and controls inside the company. Do not tolerate blatant acts of fraud, such as employees making up false expenses for reimbursement, punching in a time card belonging to a fellow employee who will be late for work, or copying someone's ideas and claiming them as his or her own. Also be aware that not all ethical dilemmas are clear-cut. Some situations will require you to weigh one moral principle (e.g., honesty) against another (e.g., loyalty). Advise your employees that, when faced with an ethical dilemma, they should follow a three-step process:

1. **Identify who will benefit from the situation** (often the manager or employee) and how others will be harmed (other employees, the company's reputation, owners, creditors, and the public in general).
2. **Identify the alternative courses of action.**
3. **Choose the alternative that is the most ethical**—and that you would be proud to have reported in the news.

Often, there is no one right answer to ethical dilemmas and hard choices will need to be made. In the end, however, following strong ethical practices is a key factor in business success and in ensuring good financial reporting.

As the meeting between Laurie and Mauricio concluded, Laurie made the following comments:

"I've enjoyed our meeting. For now, you don't need to worry about all the details; this is just an overview. But try to remember these points:

1. The elements of the financial reports.
2. The purpose and structure of the reports.
3. The account titles.
4. The key concepts.

If you do, the bookkeeping tasks we'll discuss later will be easier."

"Thanks, Laurie. I look forward to learning more."

## Epilogue for Pizza Aroma

Not long after Mauricio's conversation with Laurie, *The Ithaca Journal* reported his restaurant's opening:

> Mauricio Rosa was ready to become a father twice on Monday — once to a newborn and once to a (new) business . . . Pizza Aroma. . . . He wasn't even sure he'd be there to see the first lunch-hour rush of his own: Dora was home . . . and he was waiting for a phone call telling him to head to the hospital. "I can't take any more excitement," Mauricio said. . . .
>
> Mauricio has 39 pizzas on the menu and 4 more he's concocted that he hasn't had time to tell the printer about yet. . . . "I just think what people would like better," Mauricio said of his creative impulses. . . .
>
> One thing he's learned about being successful is to use fresh ingredients, never frozen, never cheap, Mauricio said. He apparently has learned the businessman's art of diplomacy, too. What's his favorite? "Actually, everything is my favorite," he said.
>
> Kenneth Aaron, "Aroma," *The Ithaca Journal*, November 9, 1999, p. 6A.

Since then, Pizza Aroma has received the "Best Pizza" award several years in a row in the *Ithaca Times* readers' poll.

The next three chapters will take you step by step through the financing, investing, and operating decisions that occurred at Pizza Aroma during its first month of operations. We will look at the way accountants collect data about business activities and process it to construct the financial statements. The key to success in this course is to **practice** the skills that are presented in this text. It is very difficult to learn accounting without doing the assignments and keeping up with the reading.

## Coach's Tip

At the end of most chapters, you will find one or more demonstration cases. These cases show you how to apply what you have learned to problems like the ones you will be asked to do as homework. It is worth your effort to treat these cases as if they are exam questions, and then check the suggested solutions.

# Demonstration Case

This introductory case reviews the structure and content of the income statement, the statement of owner's equity, and the balance sheet.

In 2006, Rich Kolasa opened Rich's Repair Shop, a new bike repair business, as a sole proprietorship. Most of the repairs that Rich's shop does are paid for in cash. Rich receives an advance from a local bike rental store in return for an agreement to repair the store's bikes as needed. He also bills a regional bike club whenever his shop repairs a member's bicycle. Within one year, the repair shop grew so busy that Rich had to hire several employees. Following is an alphabetical list of the shop's accounts and their balances for 2009. The business's year ends on December 31.

*Required:*

1.  For each account, indicate in the space provided:

    a.  The type of account it is (A = asset, L = liability, OE = owner's equity, R = revenue, or E = expense).

    b.  On which financial statement the account is found (I/S = income statement, SOE = statement of owner's equity, or B/S = balance sheet).

| Element | Statement | | |
|---|---|---|---|
| _____ | _____ | Accounts Payable | $ 7,000 |
| _____ | _____ | Accounts Receivable | 2,000 |
| _____ | _____ | Cash (balance on December 31, 2009) | 21,000 |
| _____ | _____ | Equipment | 83,000 |
| _____ | _____ | Insurance Expense | 5,000 |
| _____ | _____ | Notes Payable (due in three years) | 35,000 |
| _____ | _____ | Rent Expense | 24,000 |
| _____ | _____ | Rich Kolasa, Drawing (during the year) | 100,000 |
| _____ | _____ | Service Revenues | 311,000 |
| _____ | _____ | Supplies Expense | 12,000 |
| _____ | _____ | Supplies | 33,000 |
| _____ | _____ | Utilities Expense | 7,000 |
| _____ | _____ | Wages Expense | 120,000 |
| _____ | _____ | Wages Payable | 3,000 |

2.  At the beginning of the year, the Rich Kolasa, Capital account held $41,000. During the year, he made an additional investment of $10,000 in cash in the business. Prepare an income statement, a statement of owner's equity, and a balance sheet for the year ended December 31, 2009, following the formats of Exhibits 1.5 to 1.7.

3.  Describe the purpose of each of these statements.

4.  Did financing for Rich's Repair Shop's assets come primarily from liabilities or from owner's equity?

## Suggested Solution

1.

| Element | Statement | | |
|---|---|---|---|
| L | B/S | Accounts Payable | $ 7,000 |
| A | B/S | Accounts Receivable | 2,000 |
| A | B/S | Cash (balance on December 31, 2009) | 21,000 |
| A | B/S | Equipment | 83,000 |
| E | I/S | Insurance Expense | 5,000 |
| L | B/S | Notes Payable (due in three years) | 35,000 |
| E | I/S | Rent Expense | 24,000 |
| OE | SOE | Rich Kolasa, Drawing (during the year) | 100,000 |

| | | | |
|---|---|---|---|
| R | I/S | Service Revenues | 311,000 |
| E | I/S | Supplies Expense | 12,000 |
| A | B/S | Supplies | 33,000 |
| E | I/S | Utilities Expense | 7,000 |
| E | I/S | Wages Expense | 120,000 |
| L | B/S | Wages Payable | 3,000 |

2.

**Rich's Repair Shop**
**Income Statement**
**For the Year Ended December 31, 2009**

| | |
|---|---|
| **Revenues** | |
| Service revenues | $ 311,000 |
| Total revenues | 311,000 |
| **Expenses** | |
| Wages expense | 120,000 |
| Rent expense | 24,000 |
| Supplies expense | 12,000 |
| Utilities expense | 7,000 |
| Insurance expense | 5,000 |
| Total expenses | 168,000 |
| **Net income** | **$143,000** |

**Rich's Repair Shop**
**Balance Sheet**
**At December 31, 2009**

| | |
|---|---|
| **Assets** | |
| Cash | $  21,000 |
| Accounts receivable | 2,000 |
| Supplies | 33,000 |
| Equipment | 83,000 |
| **Total assets** | **$139,000** |
| **Liabilities and Owner's Equity** | |
| *Liabilities* | |
| Accounts payable | $   7,000 |
| Wages payable | 3,000 |
| Notes payable | 35,000 |
| Total liabilities | 45,000 |
| *Owner's Equity* | |
| Rich Kolasa, capital | 94,000 |
| Total owner's equity | 94,000 |
| **Total liabilities and owner's equity** | **$139,000** |

**Rich's Repair Shop**
**Statement of Owner's Equity**
**For the Year Ended December 31, 2009**

| | |
|---|---|
| **Rich Kolasa, capital, Jan. 1, 2009** | $  41,000 |
| Add:   Additional investments | 10,000 |
| Net income | 143,000 |
| Less:   Rich Kolasa, drawing | (100,000) |
| **Rich Kolasa, capital, Dec. 31, 2009** | **$  94,000** |

3.  The income statement reports the economic performance (net income) of a business during the period. The statement of owner's equity reports the way net income, owner investments, and owner withdrawals affect the financial position of the business during the period. The balance sheet reports the business's financial position (its assets, liabilities, and owner's equity) at a specific point in time.

4.  Financing for Rich's Repair Shop's assets is provided primarily from owner's equity ($94,000) rather than from liabilities ($45,000). Owner's equity includes a combination of owner investments, owner withdrawals, and net income over time.

# Supplement 1A

## Overview of Career Choices for Accounting Professionals

According to the government's labor department, accounting is one of the fastest growing fields with 49,000 new jobs a year expected to be added through 2014. The following summarizes the career opportunities available in private and public accounting.

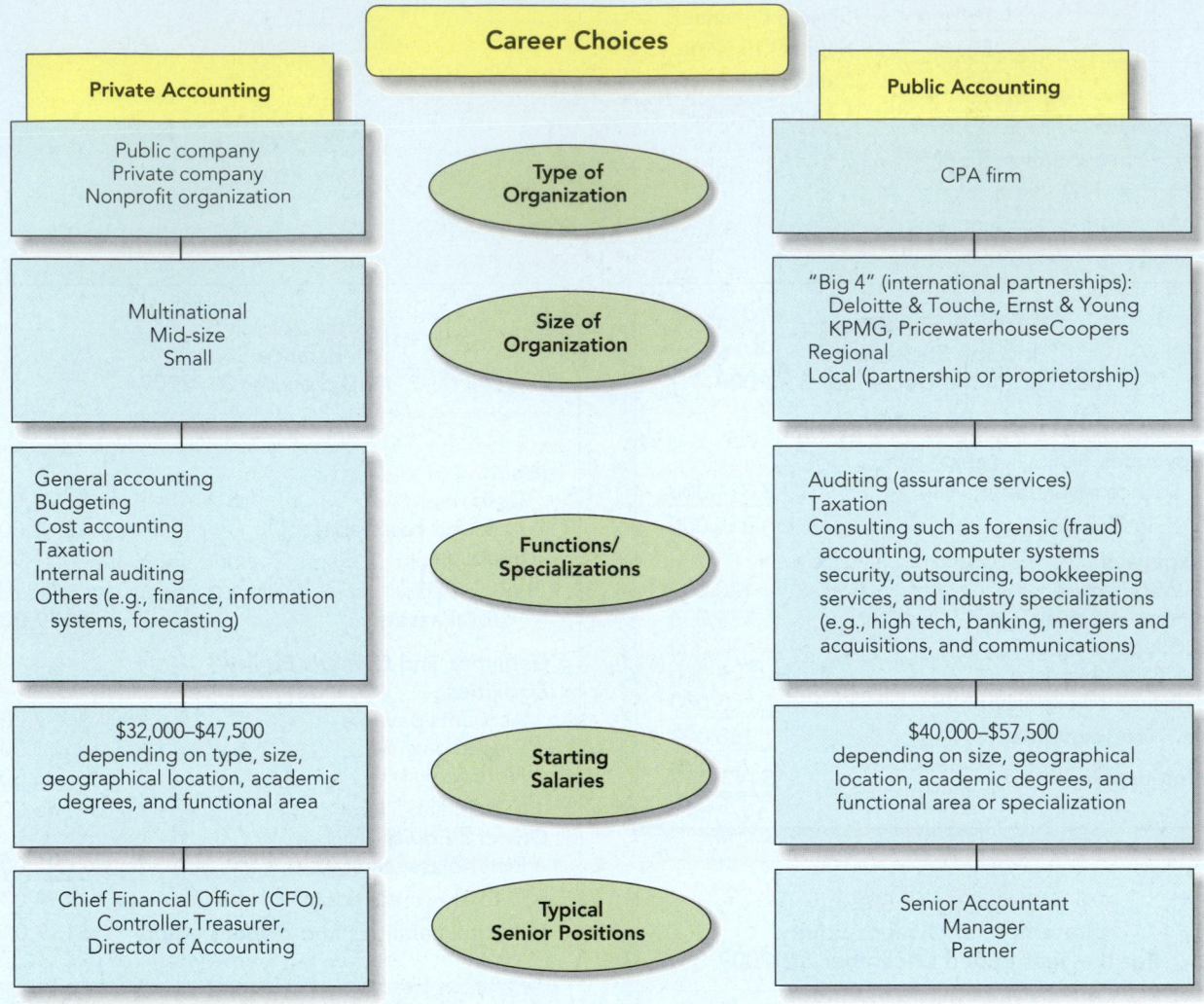

| Private Accounting | Career Choices | Public Accounting |
|---|---|---|
| Public company<br>Private company<br>Nonprofit organization | Type of Organization | CPA firm |
| Multinational<br>Mid-size<br>Small | Size of Organization | "Big 4" (international partnerships):<br>  Deloitte & Touche, Ernst & Young<br>  KPMG, PricewaterhouseCoopers<br>Regional<br>Local (partnership or proprietorship) |
| General accounting<br>Budgeting<br>Cost accounting<br>Taxation<br>Internal auditing<br>Others (e.g., finance, information<br>  systems, forecasting) | Functions/ Specializations | Auditing (assurance services)<br>Taxation<br>Consulting such as forensic (fraud)<br>  accounting, computer systems<br>  security, outsourcing, bookkeeping<br>  services, and industry specializations<br>  (e.g., high tech, banking, mergers and<br>  acquisitions, and communications) |
| $32,000–$47,500<br>depending on type, size,<br>geographical location, academic<br>degrees, and functional area | Starting Salaries | $40,000–$57,500<br>depending on size, geographical<br>location, academic degrees, and<br>functional area or specialization |
| Chief Financial Officer (CFO),<br>Controller, Treasurer,<br>Director of Accounting | Typical Senior Positions | Senior Accountant<br>Manager<br>Partner |

*Source:* 2008 Robert Half *Salary Guide*

Accountants may pursue a variety of certifications. In CPA firms, staff members become licensed certified public accountants (CPAs) when they have met the state's educational requirements, passed the certified public accounting examination, and practiced with supervision for a set period.[7] CPAs specializing in forensic accounting investigate fraud as Certified Fraud Examiners (CFE). In private accounting, accountants can earn alternative certifications, including Certified Management Accountant (CMA), Certified Internal Auditor (CIA), Certified Financial Manager (CFM), and Chartered Financial Analyst (CFA), among others. For additional information on accounting careers, certifications, salaries, and opportunities, visit www.aicpa.org, www.collegegrad.com, and www.imanet.org.

# Chapter Summary

## LO1 Categorize business types and organizational forms. p. 4

- **Business Types**
  **Manufacturing businesses** make products from raw inputs.
  **Merchandising businesses** sell manufactured goods to customers.
  **Service businesses** provide service to customers or clients; they do not make or sell products.
- **Organizational Forms**
  **Sole proprietorships** are owned by one individual, are relatively inexpensive to form, and are not legally separate from their owners. Thus, all profits or losses become part of the taxable income of the owner, who is also personally responsible for all of the business's debts.

---

[7] Each state sets its own requirements. At the time this text is being written, 44 states plus Puerto Rico, Guam, and Washington, D.C. require 150 credit hours of education to be eligible to take the CPA examination. For more information, visit the National Association of State Boards of Accountancy Web site (www.NASBA.org) and see an accounting faculty advisor.

**Partnerships** are legally similar to proprietorships, but they have two or more owners.

**Corporations** are separate legal entities (thus, they pay taxes) that sell shares of stock to investors (stockholders). Corporations are more costly to establish than sole proprietorships and partnerships. Stockholders in corporations cannot be held liable for more than their investment in the corporation. Private corporations sell stock to a few individuals; public corporations sell stock on the stock market.

## LO2  Describe accounting and its role in business decisions. p. 6

- **Accounting Defined**

  **Accounting** is an information system designed to capture and communicate a business's financial condition and performance to decision makers inside and outside the organization.

- **Accounting Professionals**

  **Private accountants** are employed by a single business or nonprofit organization. Many pursue the Certified Management Accountant certification.

  **Public accountants** charge fees for services to a variety of businesses and nonprofit organizations. Staff members of CPA firms become licensed certified public accountants.

## LO3  Identify users of financial information. p. 6

- **Users of Financial Information**

  **Internal** users (primarily managers, sole proprietors, and partners) are those inside the organization who make business decisions affecting the organization's operating, investing, and financing activities.

  - **Management accounting** is the area of accounting that produces financial information for internal users.

  **External** users (primarily bankers, suppliers, governments, and stockholders in corporations) are not directly involved in running the business.

  - **Financial accounting** is the area of accounting that produces financial information for external users.

## LO4  Describe the fundamental accounting equation and elements of financial statements. p. 9

- **The Accounting Equation**

  The **fundamental accounting equation** is Assets = Liabilities + Owner's Equity.

  The five financial statement elements are:

  - **Assets** are measurable economic resources that the business owns and are likely to provide future benefits.
  - According to the **historical cost principle,** assets are initially measured at the total cost to acquire them.
  - **Liabilities** are measurable and probable obligations that require the business to pay cash or deliver goods or services to others in the future.
  - **Owner's equity** is the difference between the assets the business owns and the liabilities it owes.
  - **Revenues** are the amounts that the business earned in delivering goods and services to customers.
  - **Expenses** are the amounts of resources an entity used to earn revenues during a period.

## LO5  Explain the structure of basic financial statements. p. 13

- **Financial Statements**

  **Income statement**

  - Its purpose is to report the performance of a business over a period of time.
  - The income statement equation is Revenues − Expenses = Net Income (or Net Loss).

  **Statement of owner's equity**

  - Its purpose is to report the changes in owner's equity for a period of time and link the income statement to the balance sheet.
  - The owner's equity equation is Beginning Owner's Equity + Additional Investments + Net Income (or − Net Loss) − Withdrawals = Ending Owner's Equity.

  **Balance sheet**

  - Its purpose is to report the amount of a business's assets, liabilities, and owner's equity at a particular point in time.
  - The balance sheet equation is Assets = Liabilities + Owner's Equity

  **Statement of cash flows**

  - The purpose is to report the cash inflows and outflows for operating, investing, and financing activities during a period of time.
  - The cash flow equation is ± Cash from Operating Activities ± Cash from Investing Activities ± Cash from Financing Activities = Change in cash during the period.
    - **Operating activities**—those activities directly related to earning profits.
    - **Investing activities**—buying and selling productive resources primarily with long lives.
    - **Financing activities**—borrowing and repaying bank loans, receiving additional investments from owners, and withdrawing profits from the business by owners.
  - According to the **monetary unit assumption,** financial information is reported in the standard monetary unit of the country in which the business operates.

Notes to the financial statements explain how amounts were measured and provide additional information that may affect users' decisions.

### LO6  Understand the importance of ethical decisions in financial reporting and business. p. 23

- **Generally Accepted Accounting Principles**

  The Financial Accounting Standards Board (FASB) sets the rules of accounting, which are the main source of **generally accepted accounting principles** (GAAP).

  Financially useful information should be **reliable, relevant, comparable,** and **consistent.**

  The Public Company Accounting Oversight Board (PCAOB) sets the rules for independent auditors.

- **Ethical Conduct**

  **Ethics** in business and accounting refers to the standards of conduct used to judge right from wrong, honest from dishonest, and fair from unfair. Ethical dilemmas harm employees, the business's reputation, the corporation's stock price, lenders, and the public in general.

  Companies need a strong system of **internal controls** to ensure the accuracy of their accounting records and to protect their assets from loss. An audit by independent auditors provides additional credibility regarding the strength of the companies' internal controls and the quality of their financial information.

  Independent auditors (CPAs) must adhere to an ethics code, the Code of Professional Conduct, when providing services to clients.

## Key Terms

Accounting (p. 6)

Asset (p. 9)

Balance Sheet (p. 17)

Certified Public Accountant (p. 6)

Code of Professional Conduct (p. 24)

Comparable (p. 23)

Consistent (p. 23)

Corporation (p. 5)

Ethics (p. 24)

Expenses (p. 10)

Financial Accounting (p. 8)

Financial Accounting Standards Board (FASB) (p. 23)

Financing Activities (p. 18)

Fundamental Accounting Equation (p. 9)

Generally Accepted Accounting Principles (GAAP) (p. 23)

Historical Cost (p. 9)

Income Statement (p. 14)

Internal Controls (p. 24)

Investing Activities (p. 18)

Liability (p. 9)

Managerial Accounting (p. 7)

Monetary Unit Assumption (p. 15)

Net Income (p. 15)

Net Loss (p. 16)

Notes (p. 18)

Operating Activities (p. 18)

Owner's Equity (p. 9)

Partnership (p. 5)

Private Accounting (p. 6)

Public Accounting (p. 6)

Public Company Accounting Oversight Board (PCAOB) (p. 23)

Relevant (p. 23)

Reliable (p. 23)

Revenues (p. 10)

Securities and Exchange Commission (SEC) (p. 23)

Separate Entity Assumption (p. 10)

Sole Proprietorship (p. 4)

Statement of Cash Flows (p. 18)

Statement of Owner's Equity (p. 16)

**See complete glossary in the back of text.**

## Questions

1. List the organizational forms for business and the primary strengths and weaknesses of each.

2. Define *accounting*.

3. Briefly distinguish
   a.  financial accounting from managerial accounting and
   b.  private accounting from public accounting.

4. The accounting process generates financial reports for both internal and external users. Describe some of the specific groups of internal and external users.

5. Write the fundamental accounting equation and define each of its elements.

6. Write the equation for the income statement and define each of its elements.

7. Briefly define *net income* and *net loss*.

8. Write the equation for the statement of owner's equity.

9. Write the equation for the statement of cash flows, and explain the three major types of activities reported on the statement.

10. Describe the purpose of the
    a.  balance sheet,
    b.  income statement,
    c.  statement of owner's equity, and
    d.  statement of cash flows.

11. What information should be included in the heading of each of the four primary financial statements?

12. What is the purpose of the notes to the financial statements?

13. Briefly describe the organizations responsible for developing accounting measurement rules (generally accepted accounting principles) in the United States.

14. What are *ethical dilemmas* in accounting, and who benefits and who is harmed by unethical behaviors?

# Multiple Choice

1. Which of the following is *not* a primary objective of external users who read a company's financial statements?

    Quiz 1-1
    www.mhhe.com/LLPW1e

    a. Understanding the company's current financial state.
    b. Assessing the company's contribution to social and environmental policies.
    c. Predicting the company's future financial performance.
    d. Evaluating the company's ability to generate cash from sales.

2. Which of the following is *not* one of the four basic financial statements?

    a. Balance sheet
    b. Audit report
    c. Income statement
    d. Statement of cash flows

3. The income statement reports

    a. Net earnings or losses for a period of time.
    b. Revenues, expenses, and liabilities.
    c. Only revenue for which cash was received at the point of sale.
    d. Financial position of a business at a specific point in time.

4. Which of the following is *false* regarding the balance sheet?

    a. The accounts shown on a balance sheet represent the basic accounting equation for a particular business.
    b. The owner's equity balance shown on the balance sheet must agree to the ending owner's equity balance shown on the statement of owner's equity.
    c. The balance sheet summarizes the net changes in specific account balances over a period of time.
    d. The balance sheet reports the amount of assets, liabilities, and owner's equity of a business at a point in time.

5. Which of the following is *not* one of the items required to be shown in the heading of a financial statement?

    a. The financial statement preparer's name.
    b. The title of the financial statement.
    c. The financial reporting date or period.
    d. The name of the business entity.

6. A company reported assets of $130,000, liabilities of $20,000, expenses of $220,000, and net income of $40,000. Revenues and owner's equity would be reported as:

    | | Revenues | Owner's Equity |
    |---|---|---|
    | a. | $110,000 | $180,000 |
    | b. | $180,000 | $110,000 |
    | c. | $260,000 | $110,000 |
    | d. | $260,000 | $150,000 |

7. Which of the following is a liability?

    a. Prepaid expense
    b. Accounts receivable
    c. Wages payable
    d. Sales revenue

8. Which of the following regarding GAAP is *true*?

    a. GAAP is an abbreviation for goodie, another accounting problem.
    b. Changes in GAAP do not affect the amount of income reported by a company.
    c. GAAP is the abbreviation for generally accepted accounting principles.
    d. Changes to GAAP must be approved by the Senate Finance Committee.

9. Which of the following is *false*?

    a. Assets are the resources the business owns.
    b. Assets = Liabilities − Owner's Equity.
    c. Ethical decisions are an important component of sound financial reporting.
    d. The primary responsibility for the information in financial statements lies with management.

10. (Supplement 1-A) Public accountants provide which of the following services for clients?

    a. Internal auditing, cost accounting, and budgeting.
    b. Assurance, forensic, and consulting.
    c. Internal auditing, taxation, and consulting.
    d. Assurance, cost accounting, and bookkeeping.

| Solutions to Multiple-Choice Questions | | | | | | |
|---|---|---|---|---|---|---|
| 1. b | 2. b | 3. a | 4. c | 5. a | 6. c | 7. c |
| 8. c | 9. b | 10. b | | | | |

# Mini Exercises     Available with McGraw-Hill's Homework Manager

## M1-1 Matching Business Types to Definitions    LO1

Match each term with its related definition by entering the appropriate letter on the blank provided.

| Term | Definition |
|---|---|
| ____ 1. Manufacturing business | A. Provides service to customers. |
| ____ 2. Merchandising business | B. Produces goods from raw inputs. |
| ____ 3. Service business | C. Sells goods produced by others to customers. |

**LO1**

### M1-2 Matching Business Forms to Definitions

Match each term with its related definition by entering the appropriate letter on the blank provided.

| Term | Definition |
|------|------------|
| ____ 1. Sole proprietorship | A. Business owned by more than one individual who are liable for the debts of the business. |
| ____ 2. Partnership | B. Business owned by one individual who pays taxes on the profits of the business. |
| ____ 3. Corporation | C. Business that pays taxes and sells shares of stock to owners. |

**LO3**

### M1-3 Identifying Users of Financial Information

1.  Who are the primary internal users of financial information, and what decisions do they make?

2.  Who are the primary external users of financial information, and what decisions do they make?

**LO4**

*P&G*

### M1-4 Identifying Elements of the Financial Statements

According to its annual report, "Procter & Gamble markets a broad range of laundry, cleaning, paper, beauty care, health care, food and beverage products in more than 140 countries around the world, with leading brands including Tide, Ariel, Crest, Crisco, Vicks and Max Factor." The following are items taken from its recent balance sheet and income statement. Mark each item in the following list with a letter(s) to indicate whether it would be reported as an asset (A), liability (L), or owners' equity (OE) account on the balance sheet or a revenue (R) or expense (E) account on the income statement.

| | | | |
|---|---|---|---|
| ____ 1. Accounts payable | | ____ 6. Interest expense | |
| ____ 2. Accounts receivable | | ____ 7. Inventories | |
| ____ 3. Cash | | ____ 8. Selling and administrative expenses | |
| ____ 4. Cost of goods sold | | ____ 9. Sales revenue | |
| ____ 5. Buildings | | ____ 10. Notes payable | |

**LO4**

**Microsoft Corporation**

### M1-5 Identifying Elements of the Financial Statements

Microsoft Corporation manufactures home entertainment devices such as Xbox, creates software such as Word, and operates networks such as MSN Hotmail. The following items were presented in the company's financial statements. Mark each item from the balance sheet as an asset (A), liability (L), or owners' equity (OE) and each item from the income statement as a revenue (R) or expense (E).

| | | | |
|---|---|---|---|
| ____ 1. Inventories | | ____ 6. Owners' capital | |
| ____ 2. Accounts payable | | ____ 7. Accounts receivable | |
| ____ 3. Sales revenue | | ____ 8. Cash | |
| ____ 4. Property and equipment | | ____ 9. Promotion expense | |
| ____ 5. Notes payable | | ____ 10. Cost of goods sold | |

**LO4**

### M1-6 Matching Financial Statement Items to the Four Basic Financial Statements

Match each element with its financial statement by entering the appropriate letter in the space provided.

| Element | Financial Statement |
|---------|---------------------|
| ____ 1. Expenses | A. Balance sheet |
| ____ 2. Cash flows from investing activities | B. Income statement |
| ____ 3. Assets | C. Statement of owner's equity |
| ____ 4. Withdrawals | D. Statement of cash flows |
| ____ 5. Revenues | |
| ____ 6. Cash flows from operating activities | |
| ____ 7. Liabilities | |
| ____ 8. Cash flows from financing activities | |

**LO5**

### M1-7 Preparing an Income Statement

The Tea Room, a sole proprietorship owned by Gerry Stayman, earned revenues of $220,000 and incurred expenses of $150,000 during its first year of operations ended December 31, 2010. At the end of the year, The Tea Room owned assets of $180,000 and owed liabilities of $30,000. Gerry invested $100,000 cash to establish the new business and withdrew $20,000 during the year. Prepare the Tea Room's income statement for 2010.

**LO5**

### M1-8 Preparing a Statement of Owner's Equity

Refer to the information in M1-7. Prepare a statement of owner's equity for 2010.

**M1-9 Preparing a Balance Sheet**                                            LO5
Refer to the information in M1-7. Prepare a balance sheet at December 31, 2010.

**M1-10 Determining the Effects of Business Activities**                      LO5
For each of the following activities, indicate what the company owns (the account and effect) and
what the company owes (the account and effect) using the fundamental accounting equation. An
example is provided. Be sure to answer from the standpoint of the business.

a.   Received $10,000 contribution from owner, Alecia Simpson.
b.   Purchased a $4,000 computer for use in the business on account.
c.   Provided $22,000 of service to customers for cash.
d.   Paid employees $15,000 cash.
e.   Withdrew $1,200 cash from the business profits.

| | Assets | = | Liabilities | + | Owner's Equity |
|---|---|---|---|---|---|
| **Example:** Borrowed $30,000 from a bank. | Cash    +30,000 | | Notes Payable    +30,000 | | |

**M1-11 Identifying Definitions with Abbreviations**                          LO6
The following is a list of important abbreviations used in the chapter and widely in business. Give the
full designation of each abbreviation. The first one is an example.

| Abbreviation | Full Designation |
|---|---|
| 1. CPA | certified public accountant |
| 2. GAAP | _____ |
| 3. FASB | _____ |
| 4. SEC | _____ |

**M1-12 Identifying Ethical Dilemmas**                                        LO6
The following is a short list of scenarios. Write a brief statement about whether you believe the
scenario is an ethical dilemma and, if so, who will be harmed by the unethical behavior.

1.   You are a tax accounting professional and a client informs you that some of the receipts used in
     preparing the tax return are falsified.
2.   A friend gives you his accounting homework assignment. You change his name to yours on the
     top of the paper and turn in the assignment as your work.
3.   You are an employee at a local clothing store. Your manager asks you to sell her a few expensive
     items priced at $1,200 but charge her only $100.

**M1-13 (Supplement 1-A) Identifying Areas of Accounting**
For each of the following job responsibilities, identify the area of accounting (private accounting, public
accounting, or both) that is most involved.

_____ 1. Preparing financial statements for external users.
_____ 2. Consulting.
_____ 3. Cost accounting.
_____ 4. Auditing by CPA.
_____ 5. Internal auditing.
_____ 6. Reviewing financial information for compliance with GAAP.

# Exercises  ™   Available with McGraw-Hill's Homework Manager

**E1-1 Categorizing Business Forms**                                          LO1
The following describes different businesses. Mark each with the appropriate letter to indicate whether it
would be categorized as a sole proprietorship (S), partnership (P), or corporation (C).

_____ 1. Alan Cohen and Carol Palmer own Cohen and Palmer, CPAs, an accounting firm. Both are
         personally liable for the firm's debts.

_____ 2. Crystal's Spa and Salon does not have separate legal existence apart from its one owner, Crystal Mullinex.

_____ 3. Gimme Coffee is divided into 12,000 shares of stock.

_____ 4. Johnson Boatyard does not pay taxes and has one owner.

**LO4**

**E1-2 Inferring Values Using the Income Statement and Balance Sheet Equations**

Review the chapter explanations of the income statement and the balance sheet equations. Apply these equations in each of the following independent cases to compute the two missing amounts for each case. Assume that it is the end of 2010, the first full year of operations for the company.

| Independent Cases | Total Revenues | Total Expenses | Net Income (Loss) | Total Assets | Total Liabilities | Owner's Equity |
|---|---|---|---|---|---|---|
| A. | $100,000 | $82,000 | $ _____ | $150,000 | $70,000 | $ _____ |
| B. | _____ | 80,000 | 12,000 | 112,000 | _____ | 60,000 |
| C. | 80,000 | 86,000 | _____ | 104,000 | 26,000 | _____ |
| D. | 50,000 | _____ | 13,000 | _____ | 22,000 | 77,000 |
| E. | _____ | 81,000 | (6,000) | _____ | 73,000 | 28,000 |

**LO4, 5**

**E1-3 Matching Financial Statement Items to the Four Basic Financial Statements**

Oakley, Inc., manufactures sunglasses, goggles, shoes, watches, footwear, and clothing. Recently, the company reported the following items in its financial statements. Indicate whether these items appeared on the balance sheet (B/S), income statement (I/S), statement of owners' equity (SOE), or statement of cash flows (SCF).

_____ 1. Total owners' equity      _____ 5. Total liabilities

_____ 2. Sales Revenue             _____ 6. Net income

_____ 3. Total assets              _____ 7. Cash flows from financing activities

_____ 4. Cash flows from operating activities

**LO4**

**E1-4 Matching Financial Statement Items to Balance Sheet and Income Statement Categories**

General Mills is a manufacturer of food products, such as Lucky Charms cereal, Pillsbury crescent rolls, and Jolly Green Giant vegetables. The following items were presented in the company's financial statements. Mark each item in the following list with letters to indicate whether it would be reported as an asset (A), liability (L), or owners' equity (OE) account on the balance sheet or a revenue (R) or expense (E) account on the income statement.

_____ 1. Inventories            _____ 6. Notes Payable

_____ 2. Accounts Payable       _____ 7. Owners' Capital

_____ 3. Income Tax Expense     _____ 8. Cost of Goods Sold

_____ 4. Equipment             _____ 9. Selling and Administrative Expenses

_____ 5. Accounts Receivable   _____ 10. Sales Revenue

**LO4**

**E1-5 Matching Financial Statement Items to Balance Sheet and Income Statement Categories**

Tootsie Roll Industries manufactures and sells candy. Major products include Tootsie Roll, Tootsie Roll Pops, Tootsie Pop Drops, Tootsie Flavor Rolls, Charms, and Blow-Pop lollipops. The following items were listed on Tootsie Roll's recent income statement and balance sheet. Mark each item in the following list with letters to indicate whether it would be reported as an asset (A), liability (L), or owners' equity (OE) account on the balance sheet or a revenue (R) or expense (E) account on the income statement.

_____ 1. Accounts Payable        _____ 7. Cash

_____ 2. Accounts Receivable     _____ 8. Machinery

_____ 3. Wages Payable           _____ 9. Promotion and Advertising Expenses

_____ 4. Owners' Capital         _____ 10. Sales Revenue

_____ 5. Income Tax Expense      _____ 11. Notes Payable to Banks

_____ 6. Inventories             _____ 12. Selling and Administrative Expenses

## E1-6 Preparing Financial Statements

John Clay organized Clay Company as a sole proprietorship on January 1, 2010. At the end of January 2010, the following monthly financial data are available:

| | |
|---|---:|
| Service Revenue | $130,000 |
| Other Expenses | 80,000 |
| Wages Expense | 15,000 |
| Cash | 30,000 |
| Accounts Receivable from Customers | 15,000 |
| Supplies | 42,000 |
| Accounts Payable (to suppliers for merchandise purchased during the month) | 26,000 |
| J. Clay, Capital | 26,000 |

John Clay made no withdrawals during January.

*Required:*

1. Using formats from the chapter, prepare an income statement, statement of owner's equity, and balance sheet for the month of January, including appropriate headings.
2. Discuss whether Clay Company will be able to pay its liabilities.

## E1-7 Reporting Amounts on the Four Basic Financial Statements

The following summary information was reported by Lucus Rock, the sole proprietor of Lucus Rock Company, for the year ending December 31, 2011. Amounts are in thousands (i.e., assets = $18,200,000).

| | | | |
|---|---:|---|---:|
| Assets | $18,200 | L. Rock, capital, December 31, 2010 | $3,500 |
| Liabilities | 13,750 | Cash flows from operating activities | 1,600 |
| Revenue | 10,500 | Cash flows from investing activities | (1,000) |
| Expenses | 9,200 | Cash flows from financing activities | (900) |
| L. Rock, drawings in 2011 | 500 | | |
| Additional investment by owner | | Cash, December 31, 2010 | 1,000 |
| during 2011 | 150 | Cash, December 31, 2011 | 700 |

*Required:*

Prepare the four basic financial statements for 2011:

    a.   Income statement.
    b.   Statement of owner's equity.
    c.   Balance sheet.
    d.   Statement of cash flows.

## E1-8 Preparing an Income Statement and Inferring Missing Values

FedEx is an industry leader in providing rapid delivery of packages and freight around the world. Its May 31, 2007, income statement contained the following items (in millions of dollars):

| | | | |
|---|---:|---|---:|
| Salaries Expense | $ 8,051 | Rent Expense | $1,598 |
| Maintenance and Repairs Expense | 1,440 | Fuel Expense | 2,946 |
| Net income | ? | Other Expenses | 7,241 |
| Delivery Revenues | 22,527 | Total Expenses | ? |

*Required:*

1. Solve for the missing amounts and prepare an income statement for the year ended May 31, 2007.
2. What is FedEx's largest expense?

## E1-9 Preparing a Balance Sheet

Dave & Buster's Inc. is a restaurant/entertainment company. Founded in 1982, Dave & Buster's provides high-quality food and beverage items and offers an extensive array of interactive entertainment attractions such as pocket billiards, shuffleboard, state-of-the-art simulators, and virtual reality and traditional carnival-style amusements and games of skill. Its February 4, 2007, balance sheet contained the following items (in millions).

| | | | |
|---|---|---|---|
| Cash | $ 10 | Property and Equipment | $317 |
| Owners' Capital | 97 | Other Assets | 167 |
| Accounts Payable | 19 | Wages Payable | 46 |
| Other Liabilities | 91 | Total Assets | 507 |
| Supplies | 13 | Total Liabilities and Owners' Equity | ? |
| Notes Payable | 254 | | |

**Required:**

1.  Prepare the balance sheet as of February 4, 2007, solving for the missing amount.
2.  Which of Dave & Buster's assets has the highest total?
3.  As of February 4, 2007, did most of the financing for assets come from creditors or owners?

**LO5**

### E1-10 Completing a Balance Sheet and Inferring Net Income

Terry Lopez organized Read More Store as a sole proprietorship, contributing $100,000 cash to start the business. The store completed its first year of operations on December 31, 2010. On that date, the following financial items for the year were determined:

| | |
|---|---|
| Cash on hand and in the bank | $ 48,900 |
| Amounts due from customers from sales of books | 26,000 |
| Equipment | 48,000 |
| Amounts owed to publishers for books purchased | 8,000 |
| One-year note payable to a local bank | 2,120 |
| Terry Lopez, Capital account balance | 112,780 |

The owner made no withdrawals during the year.

**Required:**

1.  Using typical account titles, prepare a balance sheet as of the end of 2010.
2.  Using the statement of owner's equity equation and an opening balance of $0, compute the amount of net income for the year.
3.  As of December 31, 2010, did most of the financing for assets come from creditors or owners?

**LO5**

### E1-11 Analyzing Revenues and Expenses and Computing Net Income

Assume that you are the sole proprietor of Collegiate Laundry Service that provides pick-up, cleaning, and delivery of laundry for students in local colleges. For the month of October 2010, you have the following information:

a.   The business's records in October indicated $12,000 in laundry services for cash. They also showed 20 laundry services totaling $1,000 on account (due from college students in November).

b.   You determined that the business used $800 in laundry supplies (the amount paid for the supplies) in October.

c.   According to the business's checkbook in October, it paid $3,500 for employees' wages and $500 for other expenses. However, the business has not yet paid the $600 October advertising expense for newspaper advertisements run during October.

**Required:**

On the basis of the data given, what was net income for October? Show computations.

**LO5**

### E1-12 Analyzing Revenues and Expenses and Completing an Income Statement

TNT Cleaning Service, owned by sole proprietor Kathy Terwilliger, has been operating for 20 years. The following financial items were determined for the fiscal year ended December 31, 2009:

| | |
|---|---|
| Cleaning Service Revenue (cash received in 2009) | $150,000 |
| Cleaning Service Revenue (services provided in 2009 with cash to be received in 2010) | 16,000 |
| Wages expense (2009 expense paid in 2009) | 97,000 |
| Wages expense (2009 expense to be paid in 2010) | 5,775 |
| Fuel expense | 525 |
| Advertising expense | 9,025 |
| Supplies expense | 18,500 |

*Required:*

Prepare an income statement for TNT Cleaning Service for 2009.

### E1-13 Matching Cash Flow Statement Items to Business Activity Categories

LO5

Tech Data Corporation is a leading distributor of computer peripherals and network solutions, and recently was ranked by *Fortune* as the second most admired company in its industry category. The following items were taken from its recent cash flow statement.

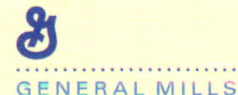

*Required:*

Indicate

1.  Whether each item is a cash flow from operating (O), investing (I), or financing (F) activities.
2.  The direction of the effect on cash (+ for cash increases and − for cash decreases).

| O, I, or F | + or − | |
| --- | --- | --- |
| _____ | _____ | A. Cash paid to suppliers and employees. |
| _____ | _____ | B. Cash collected from customers. |
| _____ | _____ | C. Cash received from borrowing long-term debt. |
| _____ | _____ | D. Cash received from owners as additional investments. |
| _____ | _____ | E. Cash paid to purchase equipment. |

### E1-14 Matching Cash Flow Statement Items to Business Activity Categories

LO5

Coca-Cola Company

The Coca-Cola Company is one of the world's leading manufacturers, marketers, and distributors of nonalcoholic beverage concentrates and syrups producing more than 300 beverage brands. The following items were taken from a recent cash flow statement.

*Required:*

Indicate

1.  Whether each item is a cash flow from operating (O), investing (I), or financing (F) activities.
2.  The direction of the effect on cash (+ for cash increases and − for cash decreases).

| O, I, or F | + or − | |
| --- | --- | --- |
| _____ | _____ | A. Cash paid for purchases of buildings and equipment. |
| _____ | _____ | B. Cash paid to owners as distributions of profits. |
| _____ | _____ | C. Cash received on sales of buildings and equipment. |
| _____ | _____ | D. Cash paid to suppliers and employees. |
| _____ | _____ | E. Cash received from owners as additional investments. |
| _____ | _____ | F. Cash received from borrowing long-term debt. |
| _____ | _____ | G. Cash received from customers. |
| _____ | _____ | H. Cash paid on long-term debt. |

### E1-15 Reporting Amounts on the Statement of Cash Flows

LO4

The following are independent cases.

a.  During a recent year, General Mills delivered breakfast cereal to customers who paid or promised to pay amounts totaling $10,506 million. During the same period, General Mills collected $6,375 million in cash from its customers.

GENERAL MILLS

Microsoft Corporation

b.  During a recent year, Microsoft delivered software to customers who paid or promised to pay amounts totaling $32.2 billion. During the same period, Microsoft collected $25.4 billion in cash from its customers.

*Required:*

1.  Indicate which of the two amounts will be shown on General Mills' cash flow statement.
2.  Indicate which of the two amounts will be shown on Microsoft's cash flow statement.

### E1-16 Determining the Effects of Business Activities

LO5

For each of the following activities, indicate what the company owns (the account and effect) and what the company owes (the account and effect) using the fundamental accounting equation. Be sure to answer from the standpoint of the business. An example is provided.

1. Purchased a building for $40,000; paid $30,000 cash and signed a note payable for the rest.
2. Purchased $1,000 of supplies on account.
3. Provided $31,000 of consulting service to customers on account.
4. Paid employees $19,000 cash.
5. Received a $600 utility bill to be paid next month.
6. Provided $6,200 of consulting service to customers for cash.
7. Purchased a new copy machine for $3,000 cash.
8. Paid $5,000 cash as a withdrawal by owner.

| | Assets | = | Liabilities + | Owner's Equity |
|---|---|---|---|---|
| **Example:** Received $100,000 contribution from owner, Carl Reyes. | Cash  +100,000 | | | C. Reyes, Capital  +100,000 |

**LO1, 2, 4, 5, 6**

### E1-17 Matching Definitions with Terms or Abbreviations

Match each definition with its related term or abbreviation by entering the appropriate letter on the blank provided.

____ 1. SEC
____ 2. Investing activities
____ 3. Private company
____ 4. Corporation
____ 5. Accounting
____ 6. Partnership
____ 7. FASB
____ 8. Financing activities
____ 9. Monetary unit
____ 10. GAAP
____ 11. Public company
____ 12. Operating activities

A. System that collects and processes financial information about an organization and reports that information to decision makers.

B. Measurement of information about a business in dollars or other national currency.

C. Unincorporated business owned by two or more persons.

D. Company that sells shares of its stock to a small number of individuals.

E. Incorporated business that issues shares of stock as evidence of ownership.

F. Purchases and disposals of long-term assets.

G. Transactions with lenders (borrowing and repaying cash) and owners (receiving additional investments from owners and providing withdrawals to owners).

H. Day-to-day activities related to a company's core business.

I. Securities and Exchange Commission.

J. Financial Accounting Standards Board.

K. Company that has its stock bought and sold by investors on established stock exchanges.

L. Generally accepted accounting principles.

## Problems—Set A

**Available with McGraw-Hill's Homework Manager**

**LO5**

### PA1-1 Preparing Financial Statements

Assume that Craig Reed is the sole proprietor of Nuclear Company. At the end of the first year of operations (December 31, 2010), the following financial data for the company are available:

| | | | |
|---|---|---|---|
| Cash | $ 25,000 | Notes Payable | $ 2,000 |
| Accounts Receivable (from customers) | 12,000 | Service Revenue | 140,000 |
| Supplies | 90,000 | Wages Expense | 60,000 |
| Equipment | 45,000 | Advertising Expense | 1,100 |
| Accounts Payable (to suppliers) | 57,370 | Other Expenses | 38,000 |

Mr. Reed invested $87,000 in cash to start up the business at the beginning of 2010. He withdrew $15,270 in cash from the business during 2010.

**Required:**

1. Prepare an income statement for the year ended December 31, 2010.
2. Prepare a statement of owner's equity for the year ended December 31, 2010.
3. Prepare a balance sheet at December 31, 2010.

### PA1-2 Preparing Financial Statements

LO5

Assume that Dr. Aaron Jones is the sole owner of Family Medicine. At the end of the first year of operations (June 30, 2009), the following financial data for the company are available:

| | |
|---|---|
| Cash | $13,500 |
| Accounts Receivable (from patients) | 9,500 |
| Supplies | 17,000 |
| Equipment | 76,000 |
| Accounts Payable (to suppliers) | 3,500 |
| Notes Payable | 21,000 |
| Medical Service Revenue | 90,000 |
| Wages Expense | 46,000 |
| Utilities Expense | 6,500 |
| Other Expenses | 2,000 |

Dr. Jones invested $62,000 in cash to start the practice at the beginning of the year and withdrew $6,000 in cash from the business during the year.

**Required:**

1. Prepare an income statement for the year ended June 30, 2009.
2. Prepare a statement of owner's equity for the year ended June 30, 2009.
3. Prepare a balance sheet at June 30, 2009.

### PA1-3 Preparing Financial Statements

LO5

www.mhhe.com/LLPW1e

**Electronic Arts**

Electronic Arts is the world's leading developer and publisher of interactive entertainment software for personal computers and advanced entertainment systems made by Sony, Nintendo, and Microsoft. Assume that the company is revising its methods for displaying its financial statements, and the controller in the accounting department has asked you to create electronic worksheets that can be used as the standard format for financial statement reporting. The controller has provided you an alphabetical list of account names with corresponding balances as of September 30. All amounts are in thousands of dollars. She has asked you to use a spreadsheet program to create two worksheets that organize the accounts into a properly formatted balance sheet and income statement. Use formulas to compute the unknown amount.

| | | | |
|---|---|---|---|
| Accounts Payable | $120,200 | Other Liabilities | $333,600 |
| Accounts Receivable | 139,300 | Owners' Capital | ? |
| Cash | 920,800 | Promotion Expense | 55,500 |
| Cost of Goods Sold (expense) | 198,900 | Property and Equipment | 307,100 |
| Inventories | 36,800 | Research and Development Expense | 22,500 |
| Notes Payable | 1,400 | Sales Revenue | 450,500 |
| Other Assets | 443,000 | Selling Expense | 98,100 |
| Other Expenses | 29,600 | | |

Not knowing quite where to start, you e-mailed your friend Billy for advice on using a spreadsheet. Billy provided this very detailed reply:

From:      BillyTheTutor@yahoo.com
To:        HairZed@hotmail.com
Subject:   Excel Help

Hey, pal. Long time, no chat. Here's the scoop on creating those worksheets with a screenshot that shows how to go. If you need more help, let me know and I'll submit an application for your position there. ☺

1. Start-up Excel to open a new spreadsheet file. You'll need only two worksheets for this assignment, so delete the third worksheet by clicking on the *Sheet3* tab at the bottom of the worksheet and selecting Edit/Delete Sheet in the pull-down menu. While you're at it, rename *Sheet1* and *Sheet2* to *Balance Sheet* and *Income Statement* by double-clicking on the worksheet tabs and typing in the new names.

2. Plan the layout for your reports. Use the first column as a blank margin, the second column for account names and their headings, and the third column for the numbers corresponding to each account name or total. If you want to apply the same format to all worksheets, begin by right-clicking on the tab at the bottom of a worksheet and choosing Select All Sheets. Next, resize the first column by clicking on the A at the top of that column, selecting Format/Column/Width. . . from the pull-down menu, and choosing a width of 2. Using this same procedure, resize columns B and C to 50 and 15, respectively.

3. Starting with cell B1, enter the company's name. Enter the report name and date in cells B2 and B3. To merge cells so these headings span more than one column, select the cells to be merged and click on ⊞. Continue with the body of the report in cell B5, entering any necessary amounts in column C.

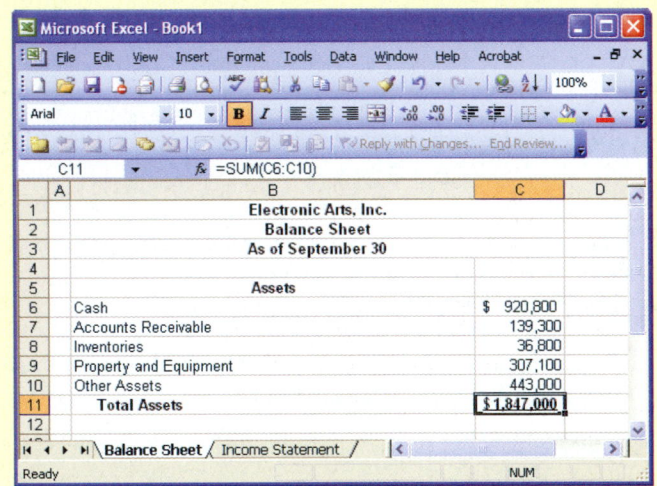

4. To use formulas to compute subtotals and totals, the equals sign = is entered first into the cell and is followed immediately by the formula. So, to subtract cell C16 from C13, enter = C16-C13. To add a series of amounts, say C6 through C10, use a formula like =SUM(C6:C10), as shown in the screenshot.

5. After you get all the data entered and totals calculated, be sure to save the file. To do this, just click on File-Save As. . . and enter the file name.

6. If you need to print the worksheets, it might be best to highlight what you want printed, then click File/Print . . . and choose Selection in the dialog box that pops up.

7. Go to it, you accounting guru!

*Required*:
Follow Billy's advice to create a balance sheet and income statement with each statement saved on a separate worksheet in a file called *meEA.xls* where the *me* part of the file name uniquely identifies you.

**LO5**    **PA1-4 Analyzing and Interpreting an Income Statement**
Three individuals organized Pest Away Company on January 1, 2011, to provide insect extermination services. At the end of 2011, the following income statement was prepared:

**PEST AWAY COMPANY**
**Income Statement**
**For the Year Ended December 31, 2011**

| | |
|---|---:|
| Revenues | |
| Sales revenue ($192,000 in cash | |
| and $24,000 in credit) | $216,000 |
| Expenses | |
| Wages expense | 84,000 |
| Supplies expense | 33,000 |
| Advertising expense | 14,000 |
| Utilities expense | 13,000 |
| Interest expense | 8,000 |
| Other expenses | 25,000 |
| Total expenses | 177,000 |
| Net income | $ 39,000 |

*Required:*
1. What was the average amount of monthly revenue?
2. What was the average amount of monthly wages expense?
3. Explain why Supplies Expense is reported as an expense.
4. Explain why Advertising Expense is reported as an expense.
5. Can you determine how much cash the company had on December 31, 2011? Answer yes or no, and explain your reasoning.

**PA1-5 Reporting Amounts on the Four Basic Financial Statements**
The following summary information was reported by Hannah Company, a sole proprietorship owned by Dan Hannah, for the quarter ending September 30, 2010.

LO5

www.mhhe.com/LLPW1e

| | | | |
|---|---|---|---|
| Assets | $79,500 | D. Hannah, Capital, June 30, 2010 | $51,000 |
| Liabilities | 18,500 | | |
| D. Hannah, Capital, September 30, 2010 | 61,000 | Cash flows from operating activities | 15,700 |
| Revenue | 32,100 | Cash flows from investing activities | (7,200) |
| Expenses | 18,950 | Cash flows from financing activities | (5,300) |
| D. Hannah, Drawings | 4,900 | | |
| Additional investment by owner | 1,750 | Cash, June 30, 2010 | 3,200 |
| | | Cash, September 30, 2010 | 6,400 |

*Required:*
Prepare the four basic financial statements for the quarter:
a. Income statement.
b. Statement of owner's equity.
c. Balance sheet.
d. Statement of cash flows.

**PA1-6 Reporting Amounts on the Four Basic Financial Statements (Challenging Problem)**
The following information for the year ended December 31, 2006, was reported by OSI Restaurant Partners, Inc., that owns and operates Outback Steakhouse and Carrabba's Italian Grill restaurants. Amounts are in millions of dollars.

LO5
OSI Restaurant
Partners, Inc.

www.mhhe.com/LLPW1e

| | | | |
|---|---|---|---|
| Accounts Payable | $ 166 | Other Liabilities | $ 330 |
| Wages and Taxes Payable | 120 | Other Revenues | 21 |
| Cash (balance on January 1, 2006) | 84 | Owners' Capital (balance on January 1, 2006) | 1,144 |
| Cash (balance on December 31, 2006) | 94 | Property, Fixtures and Equipment | 1,549 |
| Food and Supplies Expense | 1,415 | Restaurant Sales Revenue | 3,920 |
| General and Administrative Expenses | 235 | Unearned Revenue (a liability) | 187 |
| Food and Supply Inventories | 87 | Utilities and Other Expenses | 1,104 |
| Notes Payable | 235 | Wages Expense | 1,087 |
| Other Assets | 529 | | |

Other information
| | |
|---|---|
| Cash paid to purchase equipment | $ 384 |
| Cash paid to suppliers and employees | 2,578 |
| Cash received from customers | 2,946 |
| Cash received from bank borrowings | 375 |
| Repayments of bank borrowings | 294 |
| Cash received from sale of fixtures and equipment | 32 |
| Other cash outflows from financing activities | 62 |
| Other cash outflows from investing activities | 2 |
| Additional investment by owners | 16 |
| Withdrawals (distribution of profits to owners in cash) | 39 |

*Required:*
Prepare the four basic financial statements for 2006:
a. Income statement.
b. Statement of owners' equity.
c. Balance sheet.
d. Statement of cash flows.

## Problems—Set B ![HM] Available with McGraw-Hill's Homework Manager

**LO5**    **PB1-1 Preparing Financial Statements**

Assume that Marcia Waxman is the sole proprietor of the Write-r-Wrong Company. At the end of the first year of operations (April 30, 2011), the following financial data for the company are available:

| | | | |
|---|---|---|---|
| Cash | $ 39,150 | Notes Payable | $ 3,500 |
| Accounts Receivable (from customers) | 27,500 | Service Revenue | 270,000 |
| Supplies | 35,000 | Supplies Expense | 22,000 |
| Equipment | 208,000 | Wages Expense | 138,500 |
| Accounts Payable (to suppliers) | 47,800 | Other Expenses | 10,000 |

Ms. Waxman invested $186,000 in cash to start the business at the beginning of the year, May 1, 2010. She withdrew $27,150 in cash from the business during the year.

**Required:**

1. Prepare an income statement for the year ended April 30, 2011.
2. Prepare a statement of owner's equity for the year ended April 30, 2011.
3. Prepare a balance sheet at April 30, 2011.

**LO5**    **PB1-2 Preparing Financial Statements**

Assume that Elyse Rosati is the sole owner of Sweaters 'n Things Company. At the end of the first year of operations (December 31, 2012), the following financial data for the company are available:

| | | | |
|---|---|---|---|
| Cash | $ 31,500 | Notes Payable | $ 35,000 |
| Accounts Receivable (from customers) | 79,000 | Sales Revenue | 945,000 |
| Inventories | 152,000 | Cost of Goods Sold (expense) | 746,000 |
| Fixtures and Equipment | 140,000 | Utilities Expense | 42,500 |
| Accounts Payable (to suppliers) | 71,500 | Other Expenses | 2,000 |

Ms. Rosati invested $200,000 in cash to start the business at the beginning of the year and withdrew $58,500 in cash from the business during the year.

**Required:**

1. Prepare an income statement for the year ended December 31, 2012.
2. Prepare a statement of owner's equity for the year ended December 31, 2012.
3. Prepare a balance sheet at December 31, 2012.

**LO5**    **PB1-3 Preparing Financial Statements**

Best Buy Co. Inc. is a specialty retailer of consumer electronics, home-office products, entertainment software, appliances, and related services. Assume that the company is revising its methods for displaying its financial statements, and the controller in the accounting department has asked you to create electronic worksheets that can be used as the standard format for financial statement reporting. The controller has provided you an alphabetical list of account names with corresponding balances (in millions of dollars) as of December 31. He has asked you to use a spreadsheet program to create two worksheets that organize the accounts into a properly formatted balance sheet and income statement. Use formulas to compute the unknown amount.

| | | | |
|---|---|---|---|
| Accounts Payable | $ 2,824 | Other Liabilities | $ 2,063 |
| Accounts Receivable | 375 | Owners' Capital | ? |
| Cash | 470 | Promotion Expense | 1,002 |
| Cost of Goods Sold (expense) | 27,165 | Property and Equipment | 2,464 |
| Inventories | 2,851 | Research and Development Expense | 2,051 |
| Notes Payable | 958 | Sales Revenue | 35,934 |
| Other Assets | 4,134 | Selling Expense | 3,717 |
| Other Expenses | 753 | Other Revenue | 131 |

Not knowing quite where to start, you e-mailed your friend Susan for advice on using a spreadsheet. Susan provided a very detailed reply.

From:       SusanTutor@yahoo.com
To:         PaloozaJoe@hotmail.com
Subject:    Excel Help

Hey, friend. Long time, no chat. Here's the scoop on creating those worksheets with a screenshot that shows how to go. If you need more help, let me know and I'll submit an application for your position there. ☺

1. Start-up Excel to open a new spreadsheet file. You'll need only two worksheets for this assignment, so delete the third worksheet by clicking on the *Sheet3* tab at the bottom of the worksheet and selecting Edit/Delete Sheet in the pull-down menu. While you're at it, rename *Sheet1* and *Sheet2* to *Balance Sheet* and *Income Statement* by double-clicking on the worksheet tabs and typing in the new names.

2. Plan the layout for your reports. Use the first column as a blank margin, the second column for account names and their headings, and the third column for the numbers corresponding to each account name or total. If you want to apply the same format to all worksheets, begin by right-clicking on the tab at the bottom of a worksheet and choosing Select All Sheets. Next, resize the first column by clicking on the A at the top of that column, selecting Format/Column/Width. . . from the pull-down menu, and choosing a width of 2. Using this same procedure, resize columns B and C to 50 and 15, respectively.

3. Starting with cell B1, enter the company's name. Enter the report name and date in cells B2 and B3. To merge cells so these headings span more than one column, select the cells to be merged and click on 🔲. Continue with the body of the report in cell B5, entering any necessary amounts in column C.

4. To use formulas to compute subtotals and totals, the equals sign = is entered first into the cell and is followed immediately by the formula. So, to subtract cell C16 from C13, enter =C16-C13. To add a series of amounts, say C6 through C10, use a formula like =SUM(C6:C10), as shown in the screenshot.

5. After you get all the data entered and totals calculated, be sure to save the file. To do this, just click on File/Save As. . . and enter the file name.

6. If you need to print the worksheets, it might be best to highlight what you want printed, then click File/Print. . . and choose Selection in the dialog box that pops up.

7. Go to it, you accounting guru!

*Required:*

Follow Susan's advice to create a balance sheet and income statement with each statement saved on a separate worksheet in a file called *meBB.xls* where the *me* part of the file name uniquely identifies you.

## PB1-4 Analyzing and Interpreting an Income Statement                                            LO5

Lauren DiLorenzo organized Viva Lingerie Company on January 1, 2010, to manufacture undergarments with a French flair. At the end of 2010, the following income statement was prepared:

**VIVA LINGERIE COMPANY**
Income Statement
For the Year Ended December 31, 2010

| | |
|---|---:|
| Revenues | |
| Sales revenue (cash) | $276,000 |
| Sales revenue (credit) | 192,000 |
| Total revenues | 468,000 |
| Expenses | |
| Cost of goods sold | 236,000 |
| Wages expense | 148,000 |
| Advertising expense | 4,000 |
| Interest expense | 5,000 |
| Utilities expense | 12,000 |
| Other expenses | 15,000 |
| Total expenses | 420,000 |
| Net income | $ 48,000 |

*Required:*

1. What was the average amount of monthly revenue?
2. What was the average amount of monthly selling expense?
3. Explain why cost of goods sold is reported as an expense.
4. Explain why utilities expense is reported as an expense.
5. Can you determine how much cash the company had on December 31, 2010? Answer yes or no, and explain your reasoning.

**LO5**

### PB1-5 Reporting Amounts on the Four Basic Financial Statements

The following summary information was reported by Darryl Company, a sole proprietorship owned by Jane Darryl, for the year ending December 31, 2009.

| | | | |
|---|---|---|---|
| Assets | $ 97,500 | J. Darryl, Capital, January 1, 2009 | $ 7,400 |
| Liabilities | 81,500 | | |
| J. Darryl, Capital, December 31, 2009 | 16,000 | Cash flows from operating activities | 20,200 |
| Revenue | 135,600 | Cash flows from investing activities | (47,000) |
| Expenses | 128,100 | Cash flows from financing activities | 40,100 |
| Withdrawals | 4,900 | Cash, January 1, 2009 | 8,200 |
| Additional investment by owner | 6,000 | Cash, December 31, 2009 | 21,500 |

*Required:*

Prepare the four basic financial statements for 2009:

a. Income statement.
b. Statement of owner's equity.
c. Balance sheet.
d. Statement of cash flows.

**LO5**

### PB1-6 Reporting Amounts on the Four Basic Financial Statements (Challenging Problem)

The Cheesecake Factory Incorporated reported the following information for the 2006 fiscal year ended January 2, 2007. Amounts are in thousands of dollars.

| | | | |
|---|---|---|---|
| Accounts Payable | $ 45,570 | Other Assets | $ 186,453 |
| Accounts Receivable | 11,639 | Other Liabilities | 126,012 |
| Wages and Other Expenses Payable | 117,226 | Other Revenues | 8,171 |
| Cash (balance on January 3, 2006) | 31,052 | Owners' Capital (balance on | |
| Cash (balance on January 2, 2007) | 44,790 | January 3, 2006) | 646,699 |
| Food and Supplies Expense | 333,528 | Prepaid Rent | 43,870 |
| General and Administrative Expenses | 72,751 | Property and Equipment | 732,204 |
| Food and Supply Inventories | 20,775 | Restaurant Sales Revenue | 1,315,325 |
| Notes Payable | 39,381 | Utilities and Other Expenses | 414,978 |
| | | Wages Expense | 420,957 |

Other information

| | |
|---|---|
| Additional investments by owners | $    33,555 |
| Cash paid to purchase equipment | 243,211 |
| Cash paid to suppliers and employees | 1,123,353 |
| Repayments of borrowings | 170,242 |
| Cash received from customers | 1,276,008 |
| Cash received from borrowings | 175,000 |
| Cash received from sale of long-term assets | 115,975 |
| Withdrawals (payments to owners) | 49,994 |

*Required:*

Prepare the four basic financial statements for the 2006 fiscal year:

a. Income statement.
b. Statement of owners' equity.
c. Balance sheet.
d. Statement of cash flows.

# Cases and Projects

### CP1-1 Finding Financial Information

Refer to the financial statements of The Home Depot in Appendix A at the end of this book, or download the annual report from the *Cases* section of the text's Web site at www.mhhe.com/LLPW1e.

*Required:*

1. What type of business and organizational form is The Home Depot? How do you know?
2. What is the amount of net income for the most recent year reported?
3. What amount of revenue was earned for the most recent year reported?
4. How much inventory does the company have on February 3, 2008?
5. How much does The Home Depot have in cash on February 3, 2008?
6. The Home Depot's stock is traded on the New York Stock Exchange under the symbol HD. What kind of company does this make The Home Depot?

### CP1-2 Comparing Financial Information

Refer to the financial statements of The Home Depot in Appendix A and Lowe's in Appendix B at the end of this book, or download the annual reports from the *Cases* section of the text's Web site at www.mhhe.com/LLPW1e.

Lowe's

*Required:*

1. Was Lowe's net income for the most recent year greater or less than The Home Depot's?
2. Was Lowe's revenue for the most recent year greater or less than The Home Depot's?
3. Did Lowe's have more or less inventories than The Home Depot at the end of the year?
4. Did Lowe's have more or less cash than The Home Depot at the end of the year?
5. Is Lowe's the same type of business organization as The Home Depot?
6. On an overall basis, was Lowe's or The Home Depot more successful in the most recent fiscal year?

### CP1-3 Examining an Annual Report: Internet-Based Team Research

As a team, select an industry to analyze. Reuters provides lists of industries and their makeup at www.investor.reuters.com/Industries.aspx. Each group member should acquire the annual report (or Form 10-K filed with the SEC) for one publicly traded company in the industry with each member selecting a different company. (In addition to the company's own Web site, a great source is the SEC's Electronic Data Gathering, Analysis, and Retrieval (EDGAR) service. This free source is available by going to the Filings & Forms section of www.sec.gov and clicking on Search for Company Filings and then Companies & Other Filers.)

*Required:*

1. On an individual basis, each team member should write a short report that lists the following information for the business:

    *a.* What type of business organization is it?
    *b.* What types of products or services does it sell?
    *c.* On what day of the year does its fiscal year end?
    *d.* For how many years does it present complete (1) balance sheets, (2) income statements, and (3) cash flow statements?
    *e.* Are its financial statements audited by independent CPAs? If so, by whom?
    *f.* Did its total assets increase or decrease over the last year?
    *g.* Did its net income increase or decrease over the last year?

2. Then, as a team, write a short report comparing and contrasting your companies using these attributes. Discuss any patterns across the companies that you as a team observe. Provide potential explanations for any differences discovered.

### CP1-4 Making Ethical Decisions: Real-Life Example

In September 2002, John Rigas, his three sons, and another executive from Adelphia Communications were charged with defrauding investors and lenders of more than a billion dollars. John Rigas went to prison in 2007. If others are convicted, each would face more than 30 years in prison. To understand the charges, you need to first understand a bit about Adelphia's history. Adelphia started as a one-town cable company in 1952 and, at the time the fraud accusations were made public, had grown into the sixth largest cable television provider in the country. With the company starting as a family-owned business, Adelphia's operations were always a central part of the personal lives of the Rigas family members. However, the extent to which their personal lives were mixed with the business activities was never clear to stockholders—at least not nearly as clear as when they were reported in an article in the August 12, 2002, issue of *Fortune*. After the following questions, we present a table from that article, which summarizes how the Rigas family allegedly used more than $1.2 billion dollars of Adelphia's money that ultimately belonged to Adelphia's stockholders.

### Required:

1. What accounting concept is the Rigas family accused of violating?
2. Based on the information provided in the following table, can you determine which of the family's dealings are clearly inappropriate and which are clearly appropriate?
3. As a stockholder, how might you attempt to ensure that this type of behavior does not occur or, at least, does not occur without you knowing about it?
4. Aside from Adelphia's stockholders, who else might be harmed by the Rigas family's actions?

**Family Assets, Sort of**   Some of the notable ways the Rigas family used Adelphia shareholder dollars.

| On the Receiving End... | Who's Behind the Entity | How Much? |
| --- | --- | --- |
| Dobaire Designs | Adelphia paid this company, owned by Doris Rigas (John's wife), for design services. | $371,000 |
| Wending Creek Farms | Adelphia paid John Rigas's farm for lawn care and snowplowing. | $2 million |
| SongCatcher Films | Adelphia financed the production of a movie by Ellen Rigas (John's daughter). | $3 million |
| Eleni Interiors | The company made payments to a furniture store run by Doris Rigas and owned by John. | $12 million |
| The Golf Club at Wending Creek Farms | Adelphia began developing a ritzy golf club. | $13 million |
| Wending Creek 3656 | The company bought timber rights that would eventually revert to a Rigas family partnership. | $26 million |
| Praxis Capital Ventures | Adelphia funded a venture capital firm run by Ellen Rigas's husband. | $65 million |
| Niagara Frontier Hockey LP | Adelphia underwrote the Rigas' purchase of the Buffalo Sabres hockey team. | $150 million |
| Highland 2000 | Adelphia guaranteed loans to a Rigas family partnership, which used the funds to buy stock. | $1 billion |
| Total | | $1,271,371,000 |

LO6    **CP1-5 Making Ethical Decisions: A Mini-Case**

You are one of three partners who own and operate Mary's Maid Service. The company has been operating for seven years. One of the other partners has always prepared the company's annual financial statements. Recently, you proposed that the statements be audited each year because it would benefit the partners and prevent possible disagreements about the division of profits. The partner who prepares the statements proposed that his Uncle Ray, who has a lot of financial experience, do the job and at little cost. Your other partner remained silent.

### Required:

1. What position would you take on the proposal? Justify your response.
2. What would you strongly recommend? Give the basis for your recommendation.

LO5    **CP1-6 Developing a Balance Sheet and Income Statement: Critical Thinking Exercise**

On September 30, Jill and Jack started arguing about who is better off. Jack said he was better off because he had the latest PlayStation console that he bought last year for $350. Jill, on the other hand, argued that she was better off because she had $1,000 and a '75 Mustang that she bought two years ago for $800. Jack countered that Jill still owed $250 on her car and that Jack's dad promised to buy him a Porsche if he gets a great score in his accounting class. Jill pointed out that she inherited a collection of trading cards that she figured she could sell for about $250. Jack said he had $6,000 in his bank account then because he just received a $4,800 student loan. Jill knows that Jack still owes an $800 installment on this term's tuition.

Jill and Jack met again in early November. They asked how each other was doing. Jill claimed that she'd become much more successful than Jack. She had a part-time job and earned $500 per month. Jack laughed at Jill because he had won $950 on a lottery ticket he bought in October for which the "work" was standing in line for a minute. It was just what he needed because his apartment cost $450 each month. Jill, on the other hand, paid $120 for her share of the rent. Both Jill and Jack had other normal living costs that total $300 each month.

*Required:*

1. Prepare a report that compares what Jill and Jack each own and owe on September 30. Note any decisions you had to make when preparing your report. Which of the two is better off?

2. Prepare a report that compares what Jill and Jack each earned during October. Note any decisions you had to make when preparing your report. Which of the two is more successful?

# 2 Establishing a Business and the Balance Sheet

## LEARNING OBJECTIVES

**After studying this chapter, you should be able to:**

Lectured slideshow–LP2-1
www.mhhe.com/LLPW1e

**LO1** Identify what constitutes a business transaction and recognize common balance sheet account titles used in business.

**LO2** Apply transaction analysis to simple business transactions in terms of the accounting model: Assets = Liabilities + Owner's Equity.

**LO3** Determine the impact of business transactions on the balance sheet using two basic tools, journal entries and T-accounts.

**LO4** Prepare a simple classified balance sheet.

## Focus Company: PIZZA AROMA, Ithaca, NY

## "Use of Accounting Tools"

As you learned in Chapter 1, Mauricio Rosa is the owner-manager of Pizza Aroma, a gourmet pizza restaurant in Ithaca, New York. In April, after an informative discussion about the role of accounting in starting a business, Mauricio hired Laurie Hensley to provide recordkeeping services for his new venture. Laurie told him that all businesses, large or small, need systems for gathering and organizing the detailed information that she and other accountants require. What would happen, for example, if FedEx did not have a system to monitor and evaluate the use of its $12.6 billion in airplanes, facilities, and package-handling and ground-support equipment (over half of all of its resources) or to track the 6.4 million packages and $96 million in revenues the company handles every day?[1] Clearly, big companies need well-organized systems for tracking their business activities and financial results. The same is true for small businesses like Pizza Aroma.

Laurie showed Mauricio how to create an accounting system for Pizza Aroma. In Chapters 2, 3, and 4, you will look at this business as if you were a manager. You will learn about the decisions that business managers make and see how Pizza Aroma's accounting system tracks its financial results from the revenues the restaurant earns from selling pizza to the costs of equipment, rent, employee wages, and those marvelous fresh ingredients that Mauricio uses. You will see how managers and others analyze and interpret these results before making new business decisions.

In particular, this chapter will focus on the activities that establish a business so it is ready to open its doors. In Chapter 3, we will focus on the operating activities that occur after a business is established, most importantly earning revenues and incurring expenses. We will conclude our discussion of the accounting system in Chapter 4.

---

[1] http://www.fedex.com/us/investorrelations/financialinfo/2007annualreport/.

| DETERMINE THE EFFECTS OF BUSINESS ACTIVITIES | PREPARE ACCOUNTING RECORDS | PREPARE A BALANCE SHEET |
|---|---|---|
| • Nature of Business Transactions<br>• Balance Sheet Accounts<br>• Transaction Analysis<br>• Analysis of Pizza Aroma's Transactions | • The Accounting Cycle<br>• Analyzing Business Transactions<br>• Recording Transaction Effects<br>• Posting Transaction Effects<br>• Pizza Aroma's Accounting Records<br>• Preparing a Trial Balance | • Classified Balance Sheet<br>• Limitations of the Balance Sheet<br>• Summary of the Accounting Cycle |

# DETERMINE THE EFFECTS OF BUSINESS ACTIVITIES

## Nature of Business Transactions

**Learning Objective 1**

Identify what constitutes a business transaction and recognize common balance sheet account titles used in business.

As you saw in Chapter 1, Mauricio must make many decisions and undertake several activities to establish Pizza Aroma as a business. Those business activities that affect the accounting equation are called **transactions**. Which activities are accounting transactions? Transactions include two types of activities or events, external events and internal events.

- **External events** are measurable **exchanges between the business and others**—exchanges of assets and services from one entity for other assets or promises to pay from another entity. Businesses undertake these exchanges either to bring in profits or to acquire resources with the potential to bring in profits. In other words, businesses create value through exchanges. As Exhibit 2.1 shows, the external events at Pizza Aroma include:

  (1) Receiving a cash investment from Mauricio Rosa in exchange for an ownership stake in the business.

  (2) Borrowing cash from banks in exchange for Pizza Aroma's promise to repay the debt.

  (3) Acquiring equipment, ingredients, and paper supplies from suppliers in exchange for Pizza Aroma's cash payment or promise to pay.

  (4) Selling pizza to customers in exchange for their cash payments or promises to pay.

- **Internal events** include certain events that are not exchanges between the business and others but nevertheless have a direct and measurable effect on the entity. Examples

| Exhibit 2.1 | Business Exchanges |
|---|---|

(1) Owners — Business gives ownership rights / Business receives $ or assets
(2) Banks — Business gives promise to pay / Business receives $
(3) Suppliers — Business gives $ or promise to pay / Business receives assets or services
(4) Customers — Business sells goods or performs services / Business receives $ or promise to pay

include the use of supplies and the use of a building over time. When Pizza Aroma uses its ovens and supplies to make and sell pizza, those activities are internal events.

Throughout this textbook, we will use the word *transaction* in a broad sense that includes both types of events.

You should note that some important activities are *not* reflected in the financial statements either because an exchange of assets has not yet occurred or because the assets are not measurable. If Pizza Aroma orders supplies, for example, no exchange of assets or services occurs. Only the supplier's promise to deliver and Pizza Aroma's promise to pay are exchanged—**an exchange of promises is not an accounting transaction.**

# Balance Sheet Accounts

Once a transaction has been identified, names must be given to the items that have been exchanged. Companies use a standardized format called an account that is an individual record of both increases and decreases in a specific asset, liability, owner's equity, revenue, or expense. Each company establishes a **chart of accounts**—a list of all account titles and their numbers that are unique to each company. Exhibit 2.2 shows a partial chart of accounts that includes some common balance sheet account titles along with some simple account numbers. These accounts are usually organized by financial statement element with asset accounts listed first (the 100 series in the exhibit) followed by liabilities (the 200 series) and owner's equity (the 300 series). Pizza Aroma will use several of the accounts listed in Exhibit 2.2. (In Chapter 3, we will add revenue and expense accounts to the chart.) In doing assignments, if you are unsure of an account title, refer to this exhibit for help.

If you recognize some key words in an account title, you can tell what type of account it is. Recall the following points from Chapter 1:

- Accounts with **receivable** in the title are always assets; they represent amounts owed to the business by (receivable from) customers and others.
- Accounts with **payable** in the title are always liabilities; they represent amounts owed by the company to others to be paid in the future.

**Coach's Tip**

In homework problems, you will either be given the account names or expected to select appropriate names similar to the ones in Exhibit 2.2. After you have selected a name for an account, you must use that exact name in all transactions affecting that account.

**Exhibit 2.2**    Chart of Accounts (partial—balance sheet accounts only)

| Account Number | Account Name | |
|---|---|---|
| 101 | Cash | — amount of coins, paper money, and funds in the bank |
| 104 | Investments | — amount of excess cash invested in stocks, bonds, certificates of deposit, etc. |
| 106 | Accounts Receivable | — amounts owed by customers buying goods or services on account |
| 107 | Notes Receivable | — signed promises to pay by customers, employees, and others |
| 110 | Inventory | — goods to be sold |
| 115 | Supplies | — pencils, boxes, paper, etc. to be used in future periods |
| 120 | Prepaid Rent | — amount paid to rent buildings and equipment in future periods |
| 121 | Prepaid Insurance | — amount paid to receive insurance coverage in future periods |
| 122 | Prepaid Advertising | — amount paid to advertise in future periods |
| 140 | Equipment | — trucks, machinery, computers, etc., to be used in future periods |
| 145 | Buildings | — structures acquired to use in future periods |
| 160 | Land | — real estate property acquired to use in future periods |
| 180 | Intangibles | — long-term rights such as patents and trademarks |
| 201 | Accounts Payable | — amounts owed to suppliers due to buying goods or services on account |
| 205 | Wages (or Salaries) Payable | — amounts owed to employees for work in past periods |
| 210 | Notes Payable | — signed promise by the company to repay borrowed money |
| 217 | Interest Payable | — amount due on notes payable as the cost of borrowing |
| 230 | Unearned Revenue | — amount received from customers in advance of delivering goods or services to them |
| 300 | "Owner's Name," Capital | — amount of equity owner has in the business |
| 301 | "Owner's Name," Drawing | — amount withdrawn by owner from the business |

- Any account with **prepaid** in the title is an asset because it represents amounts paid to others for future benefits, such as insurance coverage and property rentals.
- Accounts with **unearned** in the title are always liabilities that represent amounts paid to the company in the past by others who expect to receive goods or services from the company in the future.

Although the account titles in Exhibit 2.2 are common ones, every company has a variation on the chart of accounts, depending on the nature of its business activities. Some companies may refer to Accounts Payable by another title, such as Trade Accounts Payable. Others may have no Unearned Revenue account. Still other companies may create account titles to fit their business activities. For example, FedEx has an account called Package Handling and Ground Support Equipment.[2]

## Transaction Analysis

Video 2-1
www.mhhe.com/LLPW1e

Now that Mauricio can identify accounting transactions and the accounts involved, what does he need to do to accumulate the effects of his transactions? For each transaction, Mauricio must perform what is called **transaction analysis.** Transaction analysis is the process of studying a transaction and its related documents to determine their effect on the business in terms of the accounting equation. Documents (also called source documents) are the sources of evidence that a business activity has occurred. Source documents include, for example, sales receipts, checks, invoices (bills) from suppliers, cash register tapes, and employee time cards.

Recall from Chapter 1 that the basic accounting equation for a business that is organized as a sole proprietorship is:

$$\text{Assets (A)} = \text{Liabilities (L)} + \text{Owner's Equity (OE)}$$

There are two rules to follow in performing transaction analysis:

- **Dual effects:** Every transaction affects at least two accounts. It is critical that you correctly identify those accounts and the direction of the effect (whether an increase or a decrease). This is what accountants have developed into a system known as *double-entry bookkeeping*.
- **Balancing the accounting equation:** The accounting equation must remain in balance after each transaction is recorded.

**To succeed in performing transaction analysis, you need a clear understanding of these principles. Slow down and think carefully as you read the following material.**

### Dual Effects

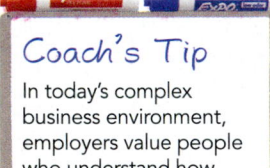
Every transaction has **at least two effects** on the basic accounting equation. Transactions with external parties involve an **exchange** through which the business entity both receives something and gives something else up. For example, suppose Pizza Aroma purchased some paper napkins for cash. In this exchange, Pizza Aroma would receive supplies (an increase in an asset) in return for giving up cash (a decrease in an asset).

| Transaction | Pizza Aroma Received | Pizza Aroma Gave |
|---|---|---|
| Purchased paper napkins for cash | Supplies (increased) | Cash (decreased) |

---

[2] The accounts you see in the financial statements of most large businesses are actually summations (or aggregations) of several specific accounts. For example, Papa John's International keeps separate accounts for equipment, buildings, and land, but combines them under one title on the balance sheet, called Property and Equipment.

In this transaction, notice that Supplies and Cash were the two accounts that were affected. As you saw in Chapter 1, however, most supplies are purchased on credit and paid for later. In that case, Pizza Aroma would engage in *two* transactions: (1) the purchase of an asset on credit and (2) the eventual payment. In the first transaction, Pizza Aroma would receive supplies (an increase in an asset) and in return give a promise to the supplier to pay later, called an **Account Payable** (an increase in a liability). In the second transaction, Pizza Aroma would give up cash (a decrease in an asset) and eliminate or receive back its promise to pay (a decrease in the Accounts Payable liability).

| Transactions | Pizza Aroma Received | Pizza Aroma Gave |
|---|---|---|
| (1) Purchased paper napkins on credit | Supplies (increased) | Accounts Payable (increased) [a promise to pay] |
| (2) Paid on its Accounts Payable | Accounts Payable (decreased) [a promise was eliminated] | Cash (decreased) |

## Balancing the Accounting Equation

The accounting equation must remain in balance after each transaction. That is, total assets (resources) must equal total liabilities and owner's equity (claims to resources). If all of the correct accounts have been identified and the appropriate direction of the effect on each account has been determined, the equation should remain in balance.

Based on these two rules, you can see that transaction analysis includes the following steps:

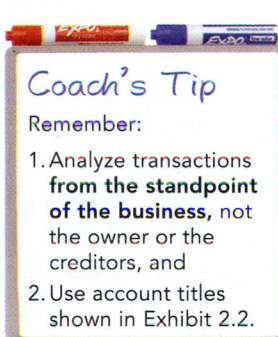

**Coach's Tip**

Remember:

1. Analyze transactions **from the standpoint of the business,** not the owner or the creditors, and

2. Use account titles shown in Exhibit 2.2.

---

**Transaction Analysis Steps**

**Step 1** : Ask yourself What did the company receive? and What did the company give in return?

- **Identify the accounts affected** (by name), making sure that at least two accounts change.
- **Classify them by the type of account** (A for asset, L for liability, and OE for owner's equity).
- **Determine the direction of the effect** (an increase [+] or a decrease [−]) on each account.

**Step 2** : **Verify that the accounting equation (A = L + OE) remains in balance.**

---

# Analysis of Pizza Aroma's Transactions

To illustrate the process of transaction analysis, let's analyze Pizza Aroma's transactions during the **first week** of May just before the restaurant began to sell pizza. Mauricio has found a store he can rent for a reasonable amount of money, but it will require some renovation as well as new equipment and furnishings. Thus, he needs to obtain cash to finance these activities. Mauricio has $30,000 of his own money to contribute, and he estimates Pizza Aroma will need to borrow $20,000 from a local bank to pay for everything Mauricio needs to do before he opens for business.

---

**(a) RECEIVE INVESTMENT BY OWNER:** To establish Pizza Aroma, a new gourmet pizza restaurant, the business receives $30,000 cash as an initial investment from owner-manager Mauricio Rosa.

**1** *Identify and classify accounts and effects:*
   **Received:** Cash (+A) $30,000        **Given:** Recognition of owner's investment,
                                                    M. Rosa, Capital (+OE) $30,000

**2** *Is the accounting equation in balance?*
   Yes. The left side increased by $30,000 and the right side increased by $30,000.

| | Assets | = | Liabilities | + | Owner's Equity |
|---|---|---|---|---|---|
| | Cash | | | | M. Rosa, Capital |
| (a) | +30,000 | = | | | +30,000 |

---

**(b) BORROW FROM BANK:** Mauricio negotiates with a local bank and signs a three-year, $20,000 note in Pizza Aroma's name (the loan is a liability of the business).

**1** *Identify and classify accounts and effects:*
   **Received:** Cash (+A) $20,000        **Given:** A written promise by the business to pay the bank,
                                                    Notes Payable (+L) $20,000

**2** *Is the accounting equation in balance?*
   Yes. The left side increased by $20,000 and the right side increased by $20,000.

| | Assets | = | Liabilities | + | Owner's Equity |
|---|---|---|---|---|---|
| | Cash | | Notes Payable | | M. Rosa, Capital |
| (a) | +30,000 | = | | | +30,000 |
| (b) | +20,000 | = | +20,000 | | |

Transactions (a) and (b) are **financing** transactions. Companies that need cash to buy or build additional facilities often seek funds from owners (investors), as in transaction (a), or from banks (creditors), as in transaction (b). Mauricio is excited; he has the cash he needs. Before he can renovate the store, however, he needs to pay rent to the building's owner.

---

**(c) PREPAY RENT:** Pizza Aroma pays $4,800 in advance to the building owner to cover rent for the store from May through October (six months).

**1** *Identify and classify accounts and effects:*
   **Received:** Prepaid Rent (+A) $4,800        **Given:** Cash (−A) $4,800

**2** *Is the accounting equation in balance?*
   Yes. The left side increased and decreased by the same amount, $4,800.

| | Assets | | = | Liabilities | + | Owner's Equity |
|---|---|---|---|---|---|---|
| | Cash | Prepaid Rent | | Notes Payable | | M. Rosa, Capital |
| (a) | +30,000 | | = | | | +30,000 |
| (b) | +20,000 | | = | +20,000 | | |
| (c) | − 4,800 | +4,800 | = | No change | | |

Recall that any account with the word *prepaid* in the title is an asset. Prepaid rent represents Pizza Aroma's right to use the store in the future. Now it is time to renovate the space. Pizza Aroma hires a construction company to renovate the store including the installation of new ovens and refrigerators, work counters, tables, chairs, a computerized cash register, and a sign at a cost of $36,000. The business pays $33,000 cash to the construction company and owes the rest on account (due in 30 days).

CHAPTER 2 Establishing a Business and the Balance Sheet 55

**(d) PURCHASE EQUIPMENT:** A construction company renovates the store and installs equipment at a cost of $36,000; Pizza Aroma pays $33,000 in cash and promises to pay the balance next month.

1. *Identify and classify accounts and effects:*
   **Received:** Equipment (+A) $36,000    **Given:** Cash (−A) $33,000 and
   a promise to pay, Accounts Payable (+L) $3,000

2. *Is the accounting equation in balance?*
   Yes. The left side increased by $3,000 ($36,000 − $33,000) and the right side increased by $3,000.

| | Cash | Prepaid Rent | Equipment | = | Accounts Payable | Notes Payable | + | M. Rosa, Capital |
|---|---|---|---|---|---|---|---|---|
| (a) | +30,000 | | | = | | | | +30,000 |
| (b) | +20,000 | | | = | | +20,000 | | |
| (c) | − 4,800 | +4,800 | | = | No change | | | |
| (d) | −33,000 | | +36,000 | = | +3,000 | | | |

*Notice that more than two accounts were affected by this transaction.*

Now Mauricio must acquire the ingredients he needs to make his dough and gourmet sauces. To serve the pizza to customers, he also needs paper and plastic supplies.

**(e) PURCHASE SUPPLIES:** Pizza Aroma orders and receives $2,000 in supplies on account from local fresh food suppliers.

1. *Identify and classify accounts and effects:*
   **Received:** Supplies (+A) $2,000    **Given:** A promise to pay, Accounts Payable (+L) $2,000

2. *Is the accounting equation in balance?*
   Yes. The left side increased by $2,000 and the right side increased by $2,000.

| | Cash | Supplies | Prepaid Rent | Equipment | = | Accounts Payable | Notes Payable | + | M. Rosa, Capital |
|---|---|---|---|---|---|---|---|---|---|
| (a) | +30,000 | | | | = | | | | +30,000 |
| (b) | +20,000 | | | | = | | +20,000 | | |
| (c) | − 4,800 | | +4,800 | | = | No change | | | |
| (d) | −33,000 | | | +36,000 | = | +3,000 | | | |
| (e) | | +2,000 | | | = | +2,000 | | | |

Mauricio gathers all of the documents that are related to the transactions that have taken place. One is a bill that he pays to one of Pizza Aroma's food suppliers.

**(f) PAY ACCOUNT OWED TO SUPPLIER:** Pizza Aroma pays $1,000 cash on account to a supplier.

1. *Identify and classify accounts and effects:*
   **Received:** A reduction in the amount owed to the supplier, Accounts Payable (−L) $1,000    **Given:** Cash (−A) $1,000

2. *Is the accounting equation in balance?*
   Yes. The left side decreased by $1,000 and the right side decreased by $1,000.

| | Cash | Supplies | Prepaid Rent | Equipment | = | Accounts Payable | Notes Payable | + | M. Rosa, Capital |
|---|---|---|---|---|---|---|---|---|---|
| (a) | +30,000 | | | | = | | | | +30,000 |
| (b) | +20,000 | | | | = | | +20,000 | | |
| (c) | − 4,800 | | +4,800 | | = | No change | | | |
| (d) | −33,000 | | | +36,000 | = | +3,000 | | | |
| (e) | | +2,000 | | | = | +2,000 | | | |
| (f) | − 1,000 | | | | = | −1,000 | | | |

After paying the supplier, Mauricio realizes that he has not used all of Pizza Aroma's cash. Because he does not think the business will need another $6,000 for several months, he decides to invest the excess money in a savings account at a local bank. The investment, opened in Pizza Aroma's name, will earn interest while the cash is idle.

---

**(g) INVEST EXCESS CASH:** Pizza Aroma puts $6,000 cash in a savings account at a bank.

1. *Identify and classify accounts and effects:*
   **Received:** Investments (+A) $6,000          **Given:** Cash (−A) $6,000

2. *Is the accounting equation in balance?*
   Yes. The left side increased and decreased by $6,000.

| | | Assets | | | = | Liabilities | | + | Owner's Equity |
|---|---|---|---|---|---|---|---|---|---|
| Cash | Investments | Supplies | Prepaid Rent | Equipment | | Accounts Payable | Notes Payable | | M. Rosa, Capital |
| (a) +30,000 | | | | | = | | | | +30,000 |
| (b) +20,000 | | | | | = | | +20,000 | | |
| (c) − 4,800 | | | +4,800 | | = | No change | | | |
| (d) −33,000 | | | | +36,000 | = | +3,000 | | | |
| (e) | | +2,000 | | | = | +2,000 | | | |
| (f) − 1,000 | | | | | = | −1,000 | | | |
| (g) − 6,000 | +6,000 | | | | = | No change | | | |
| Totals 5,200 | 6,000 | 2,000 | 4,800 | 36,000 | = | 4,000 | 20,000 | | 30,000 |

$54,000                                   $54,000

---

**SELF-STUDY PRACTICE**

Practice is the most effective way to develop your transaction analysis skills. Review the analysis of Pizza Aroma's transactions (pages 53–56); then complete the analysis of the following events. For each, identify and classify the accounts involved and the effects of the transaction on them. Then show the effects on the accounting equation at the bottom of the exercise. Repeat the steps until they become a natural part of your thought process.

1. Paul Knepper contributes $50,000 to establish a new scuba business, Florida Flippers, a sole proprietorship that offers scuba instruction and diving services.

   a. *Identify and classify accounts and effects:*
      **Received:**                          **Given:**
   b. *Is the accounting equation in balance?*

2. Florida Flippers buys a small building near the ocean for $250,000, paying $25,000 cash with Paul signing a 10-year note in Florida Flippers' name for the balance.

   a. *Identify and classify accounts and effects:*
      **Received:**                          **Given:**
   b. *Is the accounting equation in balance?*

| | Assets | | = | Liabilities | + | Owner's Equity |
|---|---|---|---|---|---|---|
| | Cash | Building | | Notes Payable | | P. Knepper, Capital |
| 1. | | | = | | | |
| 2. | | | = | | | |

*After you have finished, check your answers with the solutions at the bottom of the next page.*

# PREPARE ACCOUNTING RECORDS

## The Accounting Cycle

**Learning Objective 3**

Determine the impact of business transactions on the balance sheet using two basic tools, journal entries and T-accounts.

As you have just learned, the first step in capturing financial information is to analyze each transaction. For most organizations, however, recording the transaction effects and keeping track of account balances in this way is impractical. To process the many transactions that businesses generate every day, most companies establish computerized accounting systems. These systems follow a cycle, called the accounting cycle. Exhibit 2.3 illustrates the three steps during the period:

1. **Analyze** transactions that result in exchanges between the company and external parties.
2. **Record** the effects in chronological order in the first accounting book, called the general journal.
3. **Post** (transfer) each effect in the general journal to a specific page in another accounting book, called the general ledger, in which each page represents a separate account.

In this chapter, you will learn how these activities affect the balance sheet accounts **during the period.** You will not learn about activities that affect the income statement accounts until Chapter 3, so you will have a chance to become comfortable with the accounting process first. In Chapter 4, you will learn about activities that occur at the **end of the period,** when accountants adjust the records, prepare financial statements, and set up the records for the next cycle.

## Analyzing Business Transactions

As you saw earlier, transactions can increase or decrease assets, liabilities, and owner's equity. Now you will learn how to use the fundamental accounting equation to create a transaction analysis model that shows the **direction** of these effects—that is, whether they are increases or decreases. You can think of each individual account as looking like a T, with a left side and

| Exhibit 2.3 | The Accounting Cycle |
| --- | --- |

**DURING THE PERIOD**

**(Chapters 2 and 3)**

- Analyze transactions
- Record journal entries in the general journal
- Post amounts to the general ledger

**AT THE END OF THE PERIOD**

**(Chapter 4)**

- Adjust revenues and expenses and related balance sheet accounts
- Prepare a complete set of financial statements and disseminate it to users
- Close revenues, gains, expenses, losses and owner's withdrawals to owner's equity

Solution to
Self-Study Practice

1. a.  Received: Cash (+A) $50,000. Given: Sole ownership, P. Knepper, Capital (+OE) $50,000.
   b.  Yes. The left side increased by $50,000 and the right side increased by $50,000.
2. a.  Received: Building (+A) $250,000. Given: Cash (−A) $25,000 and Notes Payable (+L) $225,000.
   b.  Yes. The left side increased by $225,000 ($250,000 − $25,000) and the right side increased by $225,000.

| | Assets | | = | Liabilities | + | Owner's Equity |
| --- | --- | --- | --- | --- | --- | --- |
| | Cash | Building | | Notes Payable | | P. Knepper, Capital |
| a. | + 50,000 | | = | | | + 50,000 |
| b. | − 25,000 | + 250,000 | = | + 225,000 | | |

**Coach's Tip**

As you learn to perform transaction analysis, refer to this model often. **Write it out and have it in front of you as you answer homework assignments, especially in the next few chapters.**

**Exhibit 2.4    Transaction Analysis Model**

| Assets | | = | Liabilities | | + | Owner's Equity | |
|---|---|---|---|---|---|---|---|
| +<br>debit | –<br>credit | | –<br>debit | +<br>credit | | –<br>debit | +<br>credit |
| | | | | | | Withdrawals by owners | Investments by owners<br>Net income of business (Ch. 3) |

a right side (see Exhibit 2.4). Remember two important points about this model: **First and most important, the direction of the effect on a T-account depends on which side of the accounting equation's equal sign you are:**

- Because **assets** are shown on the **left** side of the equal sign in the accounting equation, an increase (+) is shown on the **left** side of the T-account.
- Because **liabilities and owner's equity** are shown on the **right** side of the equal sign in the accounting equation, an increase (+) is shown on the **right** side of the T-account.

**The second important point to remember is that there are special accounting names for the left and right sides of the accounts:**

- **Debit** is on the **left.** So, asset accounts that are on the left side of the equal sign in the accounting equation generally have debit balances. It is highly unusual for an asset account such as Inventory to have a negative (credit) balance.
- **Credit** is on the **right.** So liability and owner's equity accounts that are on the right side of the equal sign in the accounting equation generally have credit balances.

| Assets | = | Liabilities | + | Owner's Equity |
|---|---|---|---|---|
| ↑ with Debits | | ↑ with Credits | | ↑ with Credits |
| Accounts have **debit** balances | | Accounts have **credit** balances | | Accounts have **credit** balances |

Many students have trouble with accounting because they forget that debit means "left" and credit means "right." Perhaps someone once told you that you were a credit to your school or your family (a good thing). You also know that using your debit card to pay for purchases reduces the cash balance in your bank account (a bad thing). As a result, you may think that credits are good and debits are bad. Such is not the case. Just remember that **debit is the left side** of the T-account and **credit is the right side** of the T-account.

If you have identified the correct accounts and effects through transaction analysis, the accounting equation will remain in balance. Moreover, in any transaction, **the total dollar value of all debits must equal the total dollar value of all credits.** For an extra measure of assurance, add this equality check (Debits = Credits) to the transaction analysis process.

**Coach's Tip**

Why are they called "Debit" cards? From the bank's perspective, your bank account is a liability on the bank's books (the bank owes you money that you deposited at the bank) and liabilities are reduced with debits. When you use your debit card, the bank debits (reduces) your account.

# Recording Transaction Effects

You have learned that there are two types of records or books in a bookkeeping system: a general journal and a general ledger. After reviewing the business documents that support a transaction, the bookkeeper analyzes the effects of the transaction on the accounts and then enters them in the journal **in chronological order,** using a special form called the journal entry. The journal entry, then, is an accounting tool for expressing the effects of a transaction on the accounts. It is written in a debits-equal-credits format like the entries shown in the sample journal page in Exhibit 2.5.

Notice the following points about this formal handwritten way of recording journal entries:

- The first item in each entry is the date of the transaction.
- The *debited* account titles (listed in Exhibit 2.2 for Pizza Aroma) are written first (on top); the *credited* accounts are written below the debits and are indented to the right (both the words and the amounts) as a reminder to credit these accounts.

**Exhibit 2.5**    Formal Journal Page

| General Journal | | | | Page G1 |
|---|---|---|---|---|
| Date | Account Titles and Explanation | Ref. | Debit | Credit |
| May 1 | Cash | | 30,000 | |
| | M. Rosa, Capital | | | 30,000 |
| | (Investment by owner.) | | | |
| May 2 | Cash | | 20,000 | |
| | Notes Payable | | | 20,000 |
| | (Borrowed from bank.) | | | |
| May 5 | Equipment | | 36,000 | |
| | Cash | | | 33,000 |
| | Accounts Payable | | | 3,000 |
| | (Purchased equipment paying part cash and the rest on credit.) | | | |

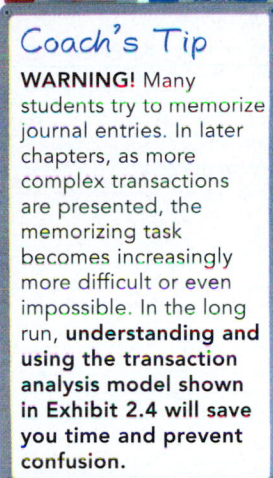

**Coach's Tip**

**WARNING!** Many students try to memorize journal entries. In later chapters, as more complex transactions are presented, the memorizing task becomes increasingly more difficult or even impossible. In the long run, **understanding and using the transaction analysis model shown in Exhibit 2.4 will save you time and prevent confusion.**

- Total debits (in the May 5 transaction, $36,000) equal total credits (in the May 5 transaction, $33,000 + $3,000).
- Because the journal is an internal record of the business, dollar signs are not necessary.
- The May 5 transaction affected three accounts. Any journal entry that affects more than two accounts is called a **compound entry.** Many transactions require a compound journal entry.
- When more than one account is debited, the order of the debited accounts does not matter. That means Buildings can be on the first line of a journal entry and Equipment can be on the second line when they are purchased, or vice versa. Likewise, the same is true for recording more than one credited account. Cash can be indented on the third line with Notes Payable indented on the fourth line when both are given to purchase buildings and equipment. Just make sure **debits are on top and the credits are on the bottom.**
- The reference column (Ref.) is used when the effects of the transactions are posted to the general ledger (the next step); it provides cross-references between the journal and the ledger. As you will soon see, the ledger page number will be the same as the account number from the chart of accounts in Exhibit 2.2.
- A description of the transaction with the necessary details is written below the debits and credits.
- A line is left blank after the description before the next journal entry begins.

In this text, we will present journal entries with slight changes to this formal way of recording entries to help you in your learning. For example, the May 5 entry in Exhibit 2.5 is the same as Transaction (d) in the Pizza Aroma illustration (page 55). The simplified journal entry we will use for Pizza Aroma is as follows:

| Event | Account Titles | Debit | Credit |
|---|---|---|---|
| (d) | Equipment (+A) | 36,000 | |
| | Cash (−A) | | 33,000 |
| | Accounts Payable (+L) | | 3,000 |

Here are the differences between the two ways of recording journal entries:

- Instead of a date, we will use a different form of reference to identify the event on which each transaction is based, such as the letter (d).
- To simplify the entry, we will omit the reference column and the description at the bottom of the entry.

- We will add the symbol A, L, or OE, along with the direction of the effect on the account (+ or −) next to each account title to clarify the effects of the transaction on the elements of the financial statements. This will help you to see that the accounting equation remains in balance.

## Posting Transaction Effects

By themselves, journal entries show the effects of transactions, but they do not provide account balances. That is why the second book, the general **ledger,** is necessary. Each page in the ledger represents an account. After the journal entries have been recorded, the bookkeeper posts (transfers) the dollar amounts to each ledger page that the transaction affected so that the account balances can be computed. The ledger page number (that is, the account number) is then entered in the reference column in the journal, and the journal page number is entered in the reference column in the ledger. In most computerized accounting systems, these cross-references are entered automatically. In the manual accounting system that some small organizations still use, the ledger is often a three-ring binder with a separate page for each account. Exhibit 2.6 shows how the May 5 journal entry is posted to the appropriate ledger pages. Notice that the

| Exhibit 2.6 | Posting from the Journal to the Ledger |
|---|---|

**General Journal**                                                                 **Page G1**

| Date | Account Titles and Explanation | Ref. | Debit | Credit |
|---|---|---|---|---|
| May 1 | Cash | 101 | 30,000 | |
| | M. Rosa, Capital | | | 30,000 |
| | (*Investment by owner.*) | | | |
| May 2 | Cash | 101 | 20,000 | |
| | Notes Payable | | | 20,000 |
| | (*Borrowed from bank.*) | | | |
| May 5 | Equipment | 140 | **36,000** | |
| | Cash | 101 | | 33,000 |
| | Accounts Payable | 201 | | 3,000 |
| | (*Purchased equipment paying part cash and the rest on credit.*) | | | |

**General Ledger**                                    **CASH**                              **101**

| Date | Explanation | Ref. | Debit | Credit | Balance |
|---|---|---|---|---|---|
| May 1 | | G1 | 30,000 | | 30,000 |
| May 2 | | G1 | 20,000 | | 50,000 |
| May 3 | | G1 | | 4,800 | 45,200 |
| May 5 | | G1 | | 33,000 | 12,200 |

**General Ledger**                                  **EQUIPMENT**                         **140**

| Date | Explanation | Ref. | Debit | Credit | Balance |
|---|---|---|---|---|---|
| May 5 | | G1 | **36,000** | | 36,000 |

**General Ledger**                              **ACCOUNTS PAYABLE**                      **201**

| Date | Explanation | Ref. | Debit | Credit | Balance |
|---|---|---|---|---|---|
| May 5 | | G1 | | 3,000 | 3,000 |

cash effects from each of the journal entries have been posted to the Cash ledger page. The right-hand column on the ledger page shows the running balance in the account.

Just as we simplified the journal entries, we will simplify the ledger pages in this text by using T-accounts. Each **T-account** represents the debit and credit columns of the ledger page. Exhibit 2.7 shows the T-accounts for Pizza Aroma's Cash, Equipment, and Accounts Payable accounts based on Transactions (*a*) through (*d*) on pages 54–55. Notice that in the T-account for the asset Cash, transactions that increase cash are shown on the left side and transactions that decrease cash are shown on the right side. For Accounts Payable, however, increases are shown on the right and decreases on the left, because Accounts Payable is a liability account.

In Exhibit 2.7, notice the following points:

- Every account starts with a beginning balance on the positive side. For balance sheet accounts, the ending balance from the prior period is the beginning balance for the current period. Because Pizza Aroma is a new business, the beginning balance in each account is zero.

- Because these are internal records, dollar signs are not necessary.

- Each line indicates the reference letter for the transaction. Thus, the effects can be traced back to the appropriate journal entry. These reference letters are very useful in finding errors that were made in posting the effects of transactions.

- To find the account balances, we can express the T-accounts as equations:

|  | Cash | Accounts Payable |
|---|---|---|
| Beginning balance | $ 0 | $ 0 |
| + "+" side | + 50,000 | + 3,000 |
| – "–" side | – 37,800 | – 0 |
| Ending balance | $ 12,200 | $ 3,000 |

This method of balancing the accounts will be useful in answering analytical questions that ask you to determine a missing value in a particular account (that is, to solve for an unknown value).

- The ending balance is indicated on the positive side and is double underlined to highlight the amount.

**Coach's Tip**

"Dr" is the shortened form of debit (left side of the T-account) and "Cr" is the shortened form of credit (right side of the T-account).

**Exhibit 2.7    Posting from a Simplified Journal Entry to T-Accounts**

| +Dr | Equipment (A) | Cr– |
|---|---|---|
| Beg. | 0 | |
| (d) | 36,000 | |
| End. | 36,000 | |

| Event | Account Titles | Debit | Credit |
|---|---|---|---|
| (d) | Equipment (+A) | 36,000 | |
|  | Cash (−A) | | 33,000 |
|  | Accounts Payable (+L) | | 3,000 |

| +Dr | Cash (A) | | Cr– |
|---|---|---|---|
| Beg. | 0 | | |
| (a) | 30,000 | 4,800 | (c) |
| (b) | 20,000 | 33,000 | (d) |
| End. | 12,200 | | |

| −Dr | Accounts Payable (L) | | Cr+ |
|---|---|---|---|
| | | 0 | Beg. |
| | | 3,000 | (d) |
| | | 3,000 | End. |

A final note on the terms *debit* and *credit*: Each word may be used as a verb, noun, and adjective. For example, you can say that Pizza Aroma's Cash account was debited (a verb) when the owner invested cash to start the business. That means that the amount was entered on the left side of the T-account. Or you can say that a credit (a noun) was entered on the right side of an account. Finally, Notes Payable may be described as a credit account (an adjective). We will use *debit* and *credit* instead of **left** and **right** throughout the rest of this textbook.

The next section illustrates the steps to follow in analyzing the effects of transactions using the transaction analysis model (Exhibit 2.4), recording those effects in journal entries (using our simplified version) and determining the account balances using T-accounts.

## Pizza Aroma's Accounting Records

Mauricio hired Laurie to prepare Pizza Aroma's accounting records. She told Mauricio to keep the documents he received with each transaction. With these documents, she would be able to analyze each transaction, record the journal entries, and post the effects to the appropriate accounts. You are about to see how Laurie created the accounting records for Pizza Aroma based on the first week of activities—transactions (*a*) through (*g*) on pages 54–56—that established the new business. Laurie followed the accounting cycle process, using the simplified journal entry and T-account formats just introduced:

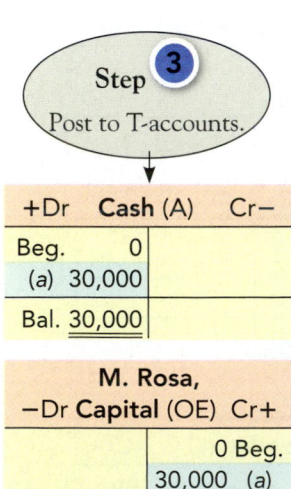

**Coach's Tip**

These critical concepts are basic to material throughout the rest of the text. The most effective way to learn it is to **practice, practice, practice—do your assigned homework!**

**Step 1**    **Analyze each transaction** by identifying and classifying accounts affected and the direction of the effects, checking to make sure that the accounting equation remains in balance and that debits equal credits in the double-entry recordkeeping system.

**Step 2**    **Record the journal entry,** reflecting the effects of the transaction on the accounting equation. Use the transaction letters (*a*) to (*g*) as references.

**Step 3**    **Post the effects** of each line of the journal entry to the appropriate T-account. Because Pizza Aroma is a new company, all beginning balances in the T-accounts (located in the margins of the following pages) will be $0.

Mauricio wanted to see what Laurie had prepared because he knew the information would help him in making future business decisions. On the morning before he opened the doors for his first day of business, Laurie explained everything to him. Just as she advised Mauricio, we urge you to **study this illustration carefully,** including the explanations of transaction analysis. Careful study is **essential** to understanding (1) the accounting model, (2) transaction analysis, (3) the dual effects of each transaction, and (4) the balancing concepts.

**Step 3**
Post to T-accounts.

| +Dr   Cash (A)   Cr− | |
|---|---|
| Beg.    0 | |
| (*a*) 30,000 | |
| Bal. 30,000 | |

| M. Rosa, −Dr Capital (OE) Cr+ | |
|---|---|
| | 0 Beg. |
| | 30,000  (*a*) |
| | 30,000 Bal. |

(*a*) **INVESTMENT BY OWNER:** To establish Pizza Aroma, a new gourmet pizza restaurant, the business receives $30,000 cash as an initial investment from owner-manager Mauricio Rosa.

**Step 2**
Record the journal entry.

| | | Debit | Credit |
|---|---|---|---|
| (*a*) | Cash (+A) | 30,000 | |
| | M. Rosa, Capital (+OE) | | 30,000 |

**Step 1**
Analyze effects.

| | Assets | = Liabilities + | Owner's Equity |
|---|---|---|---|
| (a) | Cash  +30,000 | | M. Rosa, Capital  +30,000 |

Equality checks: (1) Debits $30,000 = Credits $30,000; (2) the accounting equation is in balance. **These effects have been posted to the appropriate T-accounts** (see the shaded amounts). To post the amounts, transfer or copy the debit or credit amount on each line to the appropriate T-account. For example, the $30,000 debit is listed on the debit (increase) side of the Cash T-account.

**(b) BORROW FROM BANK:** Mauricio negotiates with a local bank and signs a three-year, $20,000 note in Pizza Aroma's name (a liability of the business).

|      |                   | Debit  | Credit |
|------|-------------------|--------|--------|
| (b)  | Cash (+A)         | 20,000 |        |
|      | Notes Payable (+L) |        | 20,000 |

| Assets | = | Liabilities | + | Owner's Equity |
|--------|---|-------------|---|----------------|
| (b) Cash  +20,000 | | Notes Payable  + 20,000 | | |

Equality checks: (1) Debits $20,000 = Credits $20,000; (2) the accounting equation is in balance.

+Dr   Cash (A)   Cr−

| | |
|---|---|
| Beg.      0 | |
| (a) 30,000 | |
| (b) 20,000 | |
| Bal. 50,000 | |

Notes
−Dr  Payable (L)  Cr+

| | |
|---|---|
| | 0 Beg. |
| | 20,000  (b) |
| | 20,000 Bal. |

**(c) PREPAY RENT:** Pizza Aroma pays $4,800 in advance to the building owner to cover rent for the store for May through October (six months).

|      |                 | Debit | Credit |
|------|-----------------|-------|--------|
| (c)  | Prepaid Rent (+A) | 4,800 |        |
|      | Cash (−A)        |       | 4,800  |

| Assets | = | Liabilities | + | Owner's Equity |
|--------|---|-------------|---|----------------|
| (c) Cash  − 4,800 | | | | |
| Prepaid Rent  + 4,800 | | | | |

Equality checks: (1) Debits $4,800 = Credits $4,800; (2) the accounting equation is in balance.

+Dr   Cash (A)   Cr−

| | |
|---|---|
| Beg.      0 | |
| (a) 30,000 | 4,800 (c) |
| (b) 20,000 | |
| Bal. 45,200 | |

Prepaid
+Dr   Rent (A)   Cr−

| | |
|---|---|
| Beg.      0 | |
| (c) 4,800 | |
| Bal.  4,800 | |

**(d) PURCHASE EQUIPMENT:** A construction company renovates the store and installs equipment at a cost of $36,000; Pizza Aroma pays $33,000 in cash and promises to pay the balance next month.

|      |                    | Debit  | Credit |
|------|--------------------|--------|--------|
| (d)  | Equipment (+A)     | 36,000 |        |
|      | Cash (−A)          |        | 33,000 |
|      | Accounts Payable (+L) |     | 3,000  |

| Assets | = | Liabilities | + | Owner's Equity |
|--------|---|-------------|---|----------------|
| (d) Equipment  + 36,000 | | Accounts Payable  + 3,000 | | |
| Cash  − 33,000 | | | | |

Equality checks: (1) Debits $36,000 = Credits $36,000; (2) the accounting equation is in balance.

+Dr   Cash (A)   Cr−

| | |
|---|---|
| Beg.      0 | |
| (a) 30,000 | 4,800  (c) |
| (b) 20,000 | 33,000 (d) |
| Bal. 12,200 | |

+Dr Equipment (A) Cr−

| | |
|---|---|
| Beg.      0 | |
| (d) 36,000 | |
| Bal. 36,000 | |

Accounts
−Dr  Payable (L)  Cr+

| | |
|---|---|
| | 0 Beg. |
| | 3,000    (d) |
| | 3,000  Bal. |

**(e) PURCHASE SUPPLIES:** Pizza Aroma orders and receives $2,000 in supplies on account from local fresh food suppliers.

|      |                    | Debit | Credit |
|------|--------------------|-------|--------|
| (e)  | Supplies (+A)      | 2,000 |        |
|      | Accounts Payable (+L) |    | 2,000  |

| Assets | = | Liabilities | + | Owner's Equity |
|--------|---|-------------|---|----------------|
| (e) Supplies  + 2,000 | | Accounts Payable  + 2,000 | | |

Equality checks: (1) Debits $2,000 = Credits $2,000; (2) the accounting equation is in balance.

+Dr  Supplies (A)  Cr−

| | |
|---|---|
| Beg.      0 | |
| (e) 2,000 | |
| Bal. 2,000 | |

Accounts
−Dr  Payable (L)  Cr+

| | |
|---|---|
| | 0 Beg. |
| | 3,000   (d) |
| | 2,000   (e) |
| | 5,000  Bal. |

| +Dr Cash (A) Cr− | |
|---|---|
| Beg. 0 | |
| (a) 30,000 | 4,800 (c) |
| (b) 20,000 | 33,000 (d) |
| | 1,000 (f) |
| Bal. 11,200 | |

| Accounts −Dr Payable (L) Cr+ | |
|---|---|
| | 0 Beg. |
| (f) 1,000 | 3,000 (d) |
| | 2,000 (e) |
| | 4,000 Bal. |

**(f) PAY ACCOUNT OWED TO SUPPLIER: Pizza Aroma pays $1,000 cash on account to a supplier.**

| | | Debit | Credit |
|---|---|---|---|
| (f) | Accounts Payable (−L) | 1,000 | |
| | Cash (−A) | | 1,000 |

| Assets | = | Liabilities | + | Owner's Equity |
|---|---|---|---|---|
| (f) Cash    − 1,000 | | Accounts Payable   −1,000 | | |

Equality checks: (1) Debits $1,000 = Credits $1,000; (2) the accounting equation is in balance.

| +Dr Cash (A) Cr− | |
|---|---|
| Beg. 0 | |
| (a) 30,000 | 4,800 (c) |
| (b) 20,000 | 33,000 (d) |
| | 1,000 (f) |
| | 6,000 (g) |
| Bal. 5,200 | |

| +Dr Investments (A) Cr− | |
|---|---|
| Beg. 0 | |
| (g) 6,000 | |
| Bal. 6,000 | |

**(g) INVEST EXCESS CASH: Pizza Aroma puts $6,000 cash in a savings account at a bank.**

| | | Debit | Credit |
|---|---|---|---|
| (g) | Investments (+A) | 6,000 | |
| | Cash (−A) | | 6,000 |

| Assets | = | Liabilities | + | Owner's Equity |
|---|---|---|---|---|
| (g) Investments    + 6,000 | | | | |
| Cash    − 6,000 | | | | |

Equality checks: (1) Debits $6,000 = Credits $6,000; (2) the accounting equation is in balance.

In addition to these transactions, two more activities took place during the first week of May:

- Mauricio hired two people to help him during the lunch and dinner hours beginning on May 8, the restaurant's opening. Because the employees have not yet worked for Pizza Aroma, the business does not yet owe them anything. The only thing that has occurred is an exchange of promises—Mauricio's promise to pay the employees and their promise to work. Hiring employees who have not yet provided any service to the business is not an accounting transaction, so nothing needs to be recorded.

- Mauricio used his personal funds to buy a larger car for his family. As you read in the epilogue of Chapter 1, he was about to expand his family, so he needed a bigger car. Under the separate entity assumption, each business must be accounted for as an individual organization, separate and apart from its owners. Therefore, this transaction does not affect Pizza Aroma.

Exhibit 2.8 summarizes the journal entries and T-accounts for transactions (a) through (g). Because this is a new company, the beginning balances in the T-accounts are $0.

## Preparing a Trial Balance

We have just used the accounting system to capture the economic events that occurred during the first week of Pizza Aroma's existence. In that week, the business obtained financing from its owner and creditors and acquired the assets necessary to run the restaurant. So what was Pizza Aroma's financial position immediately before it opened its doors? To answer this question, we need to prepare a balance sheet for the end of the first week.

| Exhibit 2.8 | Summary of Pizza Aroma Transactions: Journal Entries and T-Accounts |
| --- | --- |

**Pizza Aroma**
**Journal Entries**
**May 1–7**

| | | | Debit | Credit |
| --- | --- | --- | --- | --- |
| (a) | Cash (+A) | | 30,000 | |
| | M. Rosa, Capital (+OE) | | | 30,000 |
| (b) | Cash (+A) | | 20,000 | |
| | Notes Payable (+L) | | | 20,000 |
| (c) | Prepaid Rent (+A) | | 4,800 | |
| | Cash (−A) | | | 4,800 |
| (d) | Equipment (+A) | | 36,000 | |
| | Cash (−A) | | | 33,000 |
| | Accounts Payable (+L) | | | 3,000 |
| (e) | Supplies (+A) | | 2,000 | |
| | Accounts Payable (+L) | | | 2,000 |
| (f) | Accounts Payable (−L) | | 1,000 | |
| | Cash (−A) | | | 1,000 |
| (g) | Investments (+A) | | 6,000 | |
| | Cash (−A) | | | 6,000 |

**Pizza Aroma** T-Accounts as of May 7

| +Dr    Cash (A)    Cr− | |
| --- | --- |
| Beg.        0 | |
| (a) 30,000 | 4,800 (c) |
| (b) 20,000 | 33,000 (d) |
| | 1,000 (f) |
| | 6,000 (g) |
| Bal.  5,200 | |

| +Dr Equipment (A) Cr− | |
| --- | --- |
| Beg.        0 | |
| (d) 36,000 | |
| Bal. 36,000 | |

| +Dr Investments (A) Cr− | |
| --- | --- |
| Beg.        0 | |
| (g)  6,000 | |
| Bal.  6,000 | |

| +Dr Prepaid Rent (A) Cr− | |
| --- | --- |
| Beg.        0 | |
| (c)  4,800 | |
| Bal.  4,800 | |

| +Dr    Supplies (A)    Cr− | |
| --- | --- |
| Beg.        0 | |
| (e)  2,000 | |
| Bal.  2,000 | |

| Accounts −Dr  Payable (L)  Cr+ | |
| --- | --- |
| | 0 Beg. |
| (f)    1,000 | 3,000    (d) |
| | 2,000    (e) |
| | 4,000  Bal. |

| Notes −Dr  Payable (L)  Cr+ | |
| --- | --- |
| | 0 Beg. |
| | 20,000    (b) |
| | 20,000  Bal. |

| M. Rosa, −Dr Capital (OE)  Cr+ | |
| --- | --- |
| | 0 Beg. |
| | 30,000    (a) |
| | 30,000  Bal. |

Before the financial statements are prepared, managers usually prepare a check on the accounting system, called a **trial balance.** As Exhibit 2.9 on page 67 shows, a **trial balance** is a list of individual accounts (shown in the left column), usually in financial statement order (assets, liabilities, owner's equity, revenues, and expenses). The ending debit or credit balances from the T-accounts are shown in the next two columns. Notice that debit balances are placed in the left of the two columns and credit balances are placed in the right column. The total of these two columns provides a check on the equality of the debits and credits. The trial balance summarizes account balances for preparation of financial statements and for review and analysis for any adjustments that may be needed (as discussed in Chapter 4). And, again, as an internal document, dollar signs are not required.

**SELF-STUDY PRACTICE**

For the following events to establish Florida Flippers, a new business, analyze each transaction, record the journal entries, and then post the entries to the T-accounts at the bottom of the exercise.

(a) Paul Knepper invests $50,000 to establish a new scuba business, Florida Flippers, a sole proprietorship offering scuba instruction and diving services.

|  |  | Debit | Credit |
|---|---|---|---|
| (a) |  |  |  |
|  |  |  |  |

| Assets | = | Liabilities | + | Owner's Equity |
|---|---|---|---|---|
| (a) |  |  |  |  |

Equality checks: (1) Debits _____ = Credits _____; (2) is the accounting equation in balance? _____

(b) On behalf of Florida Flippers, Paul buys a small building near the ocean for $250,000, paying $25,000 cash and signing a note due in 10 years for the balance.

|  |  | Debit | Credit |
|---|---|---|---|
| (b) |  |  |  |
|  |  |  |  |
|  |  |  |  |

| Assets | = | Liabilities | + | Owner's Equity |
|---|---|---|---|---|
| (b) |  |  |  |  |

Equality checks: (1) Debits _____ = Credits _____; (2) is the accounting equation in balance?

| +Dr Cash (A) Cr− |  | +Dr Building (A) Cr− |  | Notes<br>−Dr Payable (L) Cr+ |  | P. Knepper,<br>−Dr Capital (OE) Cr+ |  |
|---|---|---|---|---|---|---|---|
| Beg. 0 |  | Beg. 0 |  |  | 0 Beg. |  | 0 Beg. |
| Bal. |  | Bal. |  |  | Bal. |  | Bal. |

*After you have finished, check your answers with the solutions at the bottom of the page.*

**Solution to Self-Study Practice**

**Journal Entries:**

|  |  | Debit | Credit |
|---|---|---|---|
| (a) | Cash (+A) | 50,000 |  |
|  | P. Knepper, Capital (+OE) |  | 50,000 |
| (b) | Building (+A) | 250,000 |  |
|  | Cash (−A) |  | 25,000 |
|  | Notes Payable (+L) |  | 225,000 |

**Equality Checks:**

(a) Debits $50,000 = Credits $50,000; equation is in balance.
(b) Debits $250,000 = Credits $250,000; equation is in balance.

**Transaction Analysis:**

| Assets | | = | Liabilities | | + | Owner's Equity | |
|---|---|---|---|---|---|---|---|
| (a) Cash | + 50,000 |  |  |  |  | (a) P. Knepper, Capital | + 50,000 |
| (b) Building | + 250,000 |  | (b) Notes Payable | + 225,000 |  |  |  |
| Cash | − 25,000 |  |  |  |  |  |  |

**T-Accounts:**

| +Dr Cash (A) Cr− |  |  |  | +Dr Building (A) Cr− |  |  |  | −Dr Notes Payable (L) Cr+ |  |  | −Dr P. Knepper, Capital (OE) Cr+ |  |  |
|---|---|---|---|---|---|---|---|---|---|---|---|---|---|
| Beg. | 0 |  |  | Beg. | 0 |  |  |  | 0 | Beg. |  | 0 | Beg. |
| (a) | 50,000 | 25,000 | (b) | (b) | 250,000 |  |  |  | 225,000 | (b) |  | 50,000 | (a) |
| Bal. | 25,000 |  |  | Bal. | 250,000 |  |  |  | 225,000 | Bal. |  | 50,000 | Bal. |

| Exhibit 2.9 | Trial Balance for Pizza Aroma | PIZZA AROMA |
| --- | --- | --- |

**Pizza Aroma**
**Trial Balance**
**On May 7**

| | Debit | Credit |
| --- | --- | --- |
| Cash | 5,200 | |
| Investments | 6,000 | |
| Supplies | 2,000 | |
| Prepaid Rent | 4,800 | |
| Equipment | 36,000 | |
| Accounts Payable | | 4,000 |
| Notes Payable | | 20,000 |
| M. Rosa, Capital | | 30,000 |
| **Totals** | **54,000** | **54,000** |

Ending balances in T-accounts
in Exhibit 2.8

Trial balance provides a check
on debits = credits equality

Laurie showed Mauricio the trial balance she had created for Pizza Aroma. It showed a total of $54,000 in both the debit and credit columns. Thus, the debits equaled the credits. What happens, however, when the totals do not balance?

## Locating and Correcting Errors

In a manual recordkeeping system, unequal totals may occur in a trial balance as a result of human error—that is, the type of error you might make when you are doing your homework. These errors can be traced and should be corrected before you proceed through the rest of the accounting cycle. Specifically, if the two columns are not equal, errors have occurred in one or more of the following activities:

- Totaling the debit and credit columns in the trial balance.
- Copying the ending balances (the amounts and whether a debit or credit balance) from the T-accounts (in the ledger) to the trial balance.
- Computing the ending balances in the T-accounts.
- Incorrectly posting the dollar effects of a transaction from a journal entry to the T-accounts. Examples would include (1) posting a $300 cash transaction as a debit instead of a credit to Cash and (2) posting a $330 credit as a $300 credit.
- Preparing journal entries in which the debits do not equal the credits.

To locate the error that is preventing the two columns in a trial balance from balancing, start with the first bulleted item in this list—that is, recompute the two columns. If the two columns remain unequal, proceed to the second bulleted item, and so on until you have found the error.

Certain other errors may occur in both manual and computerized recordkeeping systems, but they will not be identified by the trial balance. For example, posting $300 as a credit to Accounts Payable when it should have been a $300 credit to Cash will result in Cash being $300 too high on the debit side and Accounts Payable being $300 too high on the credit side. Because the debit and credit columns will be equal, however, this error will not show up in the trial balance.

## PREPARE A BALANCE SHEET

## Classified Balance Sheet

Now for Mauricio's first look at Pizza Aroma's financial position before selling any pizza! Exhibit 2.10 illustrates the May 7 balance sheet based on the transactions in this chapter. Notice that assets and liabilities have been separated into classifications—current and

**Learning Objective 4**

Prepare a simple classified balance sheet.

| Exhibit 2.10 | Classified Balance Sheet for Pizza Aroma | PIZZA AROMA |

**Pizza Aroma**
**Balance Sheet**
**At May 7, 2009**

**ASSETS**
*Current Assets*

| | | |
|---|---:|---|
| Cash | $ 5,200 | |
| Investments | 6,000 | |
| Supplies | 2,000 | Current assets |
| Prepaid Rent | 4,800 | |
| Total current assets | 18,000 | |
| | | |
| Equipment | 36,000 | ← Noncurrent assets |
| Total Assets | $54,000 | |

**LIABILITIES AND OWNER'S EQUITY**
*Current Liabilities*

| | | |
|---|---:|---|
| Accounts Payable | $ 4,000 | ← Current liabilities |
| Total current liabilities | 4,000 | |
| | | |
| Notes Payable | 20,000 | ← Noncurrent liabilities |
| | | |
| *Owner's Equity* | | |
| M. Rosa, Capital | 30,000 | |
| Total Liabilities and Owner's Equity | $54,000 | |

noncurrent. This creates a **classified balance sheet**. Most companies list assets **in order of liquidity,** or how soon an asset is expected to be turned into cash or used.

**Current assets** are those resources that Pizza Aroma will use or turn into cash within one year. Cash is the most liquid asset. Then investments can be turned in for cash at the business's discretion. Next Pizza Aroma will use supplies very quickly in making pizza, while Prepaid Rent will be used over six months. The only noncurrent asset for Pizza Aroma is equipment that is expected to last several years.

Just as assets are reported in order of liquidity, liabilities are listed on the balance sheet **in order of maturity,** or how soon an obligation is to be paid in cash such as Accounts Payable or settled by providing services such as Unearned Revenue. Those liabilities that Pizza Aroma will need to pay or settle within the coming year (in cash, services, or other current assets) are classified as **current liabilities**. At this point, only Accounts Payable is classified as current because most accounts payable are due within one to two months. Liabilities that are owed beyond a year are classified as noncurrent liabilities. Pizza Aroma owes notes payable to the bank in three years. Distinguishing current assets and current liabilities assists external users of the financial statements in assessing the amounts and timing of future cash flows.

## Limitations of the Balance Sheet

Some people mistakenly believe that the balance sheet reports what a business is worth. Because the balance sheet lists the company's assets and liabilities, they reason that the net difference between the two must be the company's worth. In fact, "net worth" is the term many accountants and analysts use when referring to owner's equity. So why is it wrong to think of the balance sheet as reporting what a business is worth?

The answer comes from knowing that accounting is based on recording and reporting **transactions,** as you have seen over and over in this chapter. This reliance on transactions has two significant implications for the balance sheet: (1) it affects what is (and is not) recorded, and (2) it affects the amounts assigned to recorded items.

1. **What is (and is not) recorded?**
   • Only measurable exchanges, such as a purchase of ovens, are recorded. Because Pizza Aroma's name was not acquired in an exchange, you will not see it on the balance sheet. The same is true of Mauricio's gourmet pizza recipes.

2. **What amounts are assigned to recorded items?**
   • Following the historical cost principle, assets and liabilities are first recorded at the amounts that were measurable and accurate at the time the transaction occurred. The cost principle does not allow increases in asset values (and decreases in liability values) to be recorded unless external exchanges have caused the change in value.
   • Does that mean that if an asset's value falls over time, it will continue to be reported at its original cost? The answer is no. Conservatism requires that when doubt exists about the amount at which assets and liabilities (and revenues and expenses) should be reported, the least optimistic measurement should be used. Businesses should not overstate assets and revenues or understate liabilities and expenses.

## Spotlight On FINANCIAL REPORTING

### The Competition

As in most college towns, Pizza Aroma has many competitors from other local pizza restaurants to the big chains including Pizza Hut and Papa John's. The balance sheet of Papa John's, a corporation, follows. You will notice that the structure of the balance sheet and its account titles are quite similar to Pizza Aroma's, but the amounts are significantly larger. Also, instead of ownership by a sole proprietor, approximately 30 million shareholders own Papa John's.

**Papa John's International, Inc.**
**Balance Sheet**
**At December 31, 2006**
**(In thousands)**

| | |
|---|---|
| **Assets** | |
| **Current assets** | |
| Cash | $ 12,979 |
| Accounts receivable, net | 23,326 |
| Inventories | 26,729 |
| Prepaid expenses | 7,779 |
| Other current assets | 13,730 |
| **Total current assets** | **84,543** |
| Investments | 1,254 |
| Property and equipment, net | 197,722 |
| Notes receivable, net | 12,104 |
| Intangibles | 67,357 |
| Other assets | 16,659 |
| **Total assets** | **$379,639** |
| **Liabilities and Stockholders' Equity** | |
| **Current liabilities** | |
| Accounts payable | $ 29,202 |
| Income and other taxes payable | 15,136 |
| Other current liabilities | 57,758 |
| **Total current liabilities** | **102,096** |
| Unearned fee revenue | 7,562 |
| Long-term debt | 96,511 |
| Other long-term liabilities | 27,302 |
| **Stockholders' equity** | **146,168** |
| **Total liabilities and stockholders' equity** | **$379,639** |

For perspective, cash is nearly $13 million.

Current assets

Noncurrent assets

Current liabilities

Noncurrent liabilities

## Spotlight On ETHICS

### Motivation to Be Conservative

Why are accountants conservative? It is primarily because they know that outsiders such as bankers and owners who are not active in their businesses (or investors in the case of corporations) are going to use the financial statements to make decisions, and accountants do not want to mislead them. This is a very important ethical issue to accountants. If owners invest additional amounts into their businesses after relying on financial statements with inflated amounts for assets (and revenues) and amounts for liabilities (and expenses) that are too low, they may lose their money when things go wrong in the business. So, when faced with uncertainty about the numbers, accountants take a conservative approach.

## Summary of the Accounting Cycle

Before Mauricio opens Pizza Aroma's newly painted doors for business, let's summarize the accounting cycle process in which the effects of business events move from the journal and the ledger to the company's balance sheet. Exhibit 2.11 illustrates the process for a fictitious construction company.

### Exhibit 2.11    Summary of the Accounting Cycle

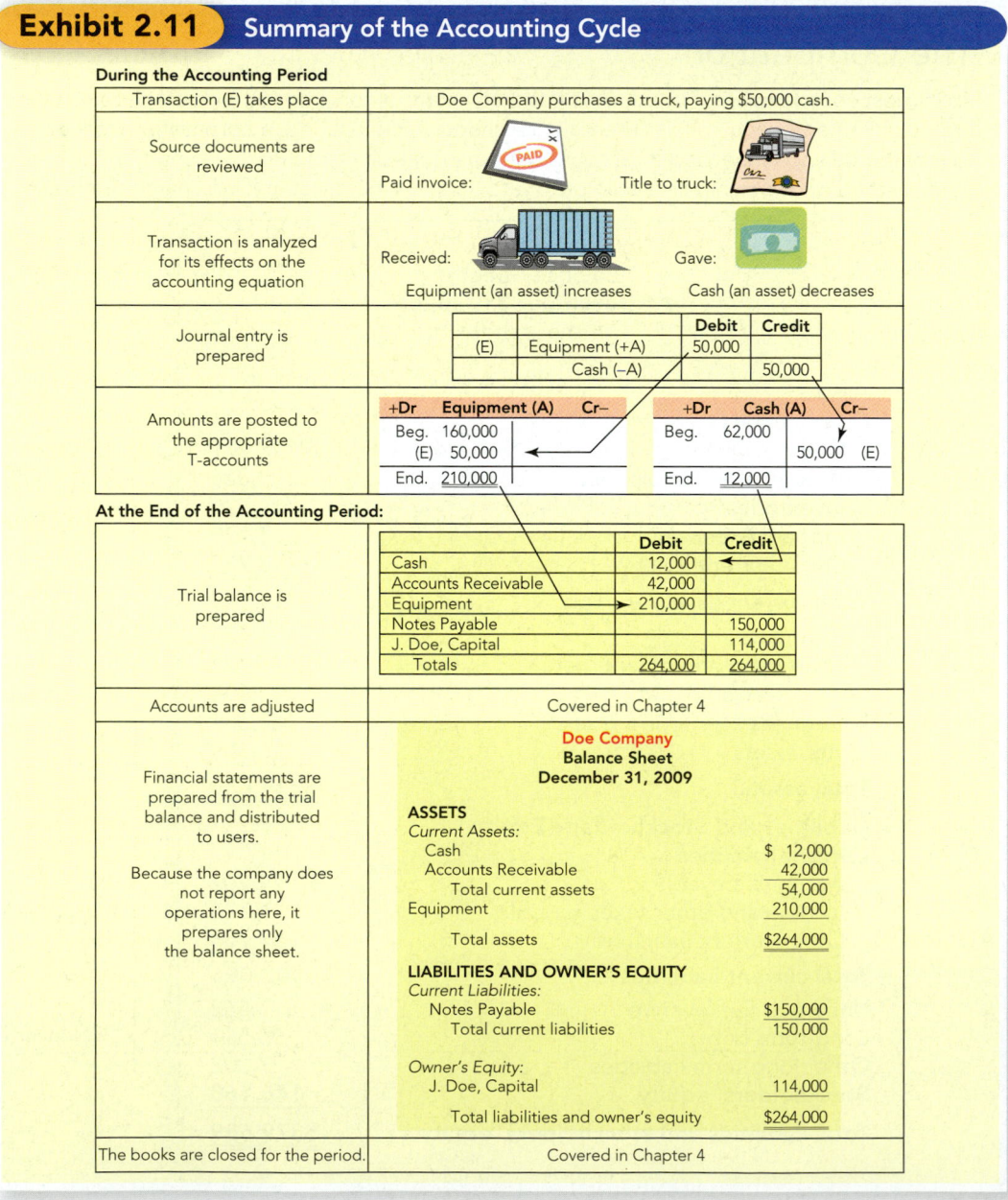

As you can see, you need to know quite a bit about accounting to interpret and use financial statements intelligently. In this chapter, we focused on the transactions that establish a business. Next, you need to learn how the accounting system handles transactions related to operating activities, and how to report the effects of those transactions in the income statement. Those topics will be the focus of Chapters 3 and 4.

## Demonstration Case

On April 1, 2010, Steve Delancey, a college student, started Goodbye Grass, a lawn care service business. Goodbye Grass's transactions to establish the business through April 30, 2010, follows:

(a) Received cash totaling $9,000 from Steve who will be the owner-manager of the business.

(b) Acquired rakes and other hand tools (equipment) for $600, paying the hardware store $200 cash and agreeing informally to pay the balance in three months.

(c) Ordered lawn mowers and edgers costing $4,000 from XYZ Lawn Supply, Inc.

(d) Purchased four acres of land for the future site of a storage garage; paid cash, $5,000.

(e) Received the mowers and edgers that had been ordered in (c), and signed a promissory note to pay XYZ Lawn Supply in full in 60 days.

(f) Sold one acre of land to the city for a park for $1,250, and accepted a note from the city indicating that Goodbye Grass will receive payment in six months.

(g) Steve borrowed $3,000 from a local bank for personal use.

### Required:

1. Analyze each event to determine its effects on the accounting equation for Goodbye Grass.
2. Prepare journal entries to record the transactions (a)–(g).
3. Set up T-accounts for Cash, Note Receivable (from the city), Equipment (hand tools and mowing equipment), Land, Accounts Payable (to hardware store), Note Payable (to the equipment supply company), and S. Delancey, Capital. Indicate the beginning balances of $0 in each T-account, and then summarize the effects of each journal entry in the appropriate T-accounts.
4. Use the amounts in the T-accounts developed in requirement 3 to prepare a *classified* balance sheet for Goodbye Grass at April 30, 2010. Show the balances for all assets, liabilities, and owner's equity accounts.
5. As of April 30, 2010, has financing for Goodbye Grass's assets come primarily from liabilities or owner's equity?

> **Coach's Tip**
>
> For possible account names, see the chart of accounts in Exhibit 2.2.

## Suggested Solution

1. Analyze transactions:

| | **Assets** | | | | = | **Liabilities** | | + | **Owner's Equity** |
|---|---|---|---|---|---|---|---|---|---|
| | Cash | Note Receivable | Equipment | Land | = | Accounts Payable | Note Payable | | S. Delancey, Capital |
| Beg. | $   0 | $   0 | $   0 | $   0 | = | $   0 | $   0 | | $   0 |
| (a) | +9,000 | | | | = | | | | +9,000 |
| (b) | − 200 | | +  600 | | = | +400 | | | |
| (c) | | | | No change* | = | No change | | | |
| (d) | −5,000 | | | +5,000 | = | No change | | | |
| (e) | | | + 4,000 | | = | | +4,000 | | |
| (f) | | +1,250 | | −1,250 | = | No change | | | |
| (g) | | | | No change* | = | No change | | | |
| Totals | $3,800 | $1,250 | $ 4,600 | $3,750 | = | $400 | $ 4,000 | | $9,000 |

$$\text{\$13,400} \quad = \quad \text{\$13,400}$$

\* Event (c) is not a considered a transaction because it involves only the exchange of promises. Event (g) is not considered a transaction of the company because the separate entity assumption (from Chapter 1) states that personal transactions of the owners are separate from transactions of the business.

2. Record journal entries:

| | | Debit | Credit |
|---|---|---|---|
| (a) | Cash (+A) | 9,000 | |
| | S. Delancey, Capital (+OE) | | 9,000 |
| (b) | Equipment (+A) | 600 | |
| | Cash (−A) | | 200 |
| | Accounts Payable (+L) | | 400 |
| (c) | This is not an accounting transaction, so a journal entry is not needed. | | |
| (d) | Land (+A) | 5,000 | |
| | Cash (−A) | | 5,000 |
| (e) | Equipment (+A) | 4,000 | |
| | Note Payable (+L) | | 4,000 |
| (f) | Note Receivable (+A) | 1,250 | |
| | Land (−A) | | 1,250 |
| (g) | This is not a transaction of the business, so a journal entry is not needed. | | |

3. Summarize journal entries in T-accounts:

**Assets = Liabilities + Owner's Equity**

+Dr Cash (A) Cr−
Beg. Bal. 0
(a) 9,000 | 200 (b)
| 5,000 (d)
End. 3,800

+Dr Equipment (A) Cr−
Beg. Bal. 0
(b) 600
(e) 4,000
End. 4,600

−Dr Accounts Payable (L) Cr+
0 Beg. Bal.
400 (b)
400 End.

S. Delancey,
−Dr Capital (OE) Cr+
0 Beg. Bal.
9,000 (a)
9,000 End.

+Dr Note Receivable (A) Cr−
Beg. Bal. 0
(f) 1,250
End. 1,250

+Dr Land (A) Cr−
Beg. Bal. 0
(d) 5,000 | 1,250 (f)
End. 3,750

−Dr Note Payable (L) Cr+
0 Beg. Bal.
4,000 (e)
4,000 End.

4. Prepare a classified balance sheet from the T-accounts:

**GOODBYE GRASS**
**Balance Sheet**
**At April 30, 2010**

| Assets | | Liabilities | |
|---|---|---|---|
| *Current Assets* | | *Current Liabilities* | |
| Cash | $ 3,800 | Accounts Payable | $   400 |
| Note Receivable | 1,250 | Note Payable | 4,000 |
| Total Current Assets | 5,050 | Total Current Liabilities | 4,400 |
| Equipment | 4,600 | | |
| Land | 3,750 | **Owner's Equity** | |
| | | S. Delancey, Capital | 9,000 |
| Total Assets | $13,400 | Total Liabilities and Owner's Equity | $13,400 |

5. The primary source of financing for Goodbye Grass's assets (totaling $13,400) has come from owner's equity ($9,000) rather than liabilities ($4,400).

# Supplement 2A
## Accounting Concepts Revisited

Recall from Chapter 1 that accounting is an information system designed to capture and communicate the results of business activities to decision makers. The word *capture* suggests the need for guidelines on how relevant business activities should be identified and measured. The word *communicate* suggests the need for guidelines on what to report and how to report it. Learning and understanding these key concepts will be helpful to you as you study because learning **how** the accounting process works will be easier if you know **why** the system works in a certain way. For a brief review of the key concepts that accountants follow in establishing **generally accepted accounting principles (GAAP),** see Exhibit 2.12.

### Objective of Financial Reporting.
The primary objective of financial reporting is to **provide useful economic information about a business in order to help external parties, primarily investors (in corporations) and creditors, to make sound financial decisions.** These external **decision makers** include, among others, current and potential owners, lenders, suppliers, customers, government agencies, and experts who provide financial advice. Certainly the bank that lends money to Pizza Aroma is a key external party that is most interested in the business's financial performance and condition. All decision makers are expected to have a reasonable understanding of accounting concepts and procedures—which may be one reason you are studying accounting.

### Qualitative Characteristics of Financial Information.
The information provided to external users of the financial statements must be **relevant.** Thus, it should be provided on a timely basis, and it should help users to assess both how well the company has met its past goals and how well it may be expected to do in the future. The information should also be **reliable.** Reliable information is not biased (that is, it does not favor any one party over another), and it can be verified (that is, others who review the evidence will arrive at the same result). Finally, information is of high quality when it is **comparable** to that of other companies and **consistent** in the use of measurement rules over time.

### Elements of the Financial Statements.
The elements of the financial statements are the categories of information to be measured and reported. On the balance sheet, the elements include assets, liabilities, and owner's equity.

**Assets** are resources with probable future benefits owned or controlled by the business as a result of past transactions. In other words, they are the resources the business can use to operate in the future.

**Liabilities** are probable debts or obligations (claims to a company's assets) that result from past transactions and will be paid for with assets or services in the future. Distinguishing between a company's current assets and current liabilities helps external users of the financial statements to assess the amount and timing of the company's future cash flows.

**Owner's equity** includes investments by the owner and the accumulated net income (or losses) from business operations (covered in Chapter 3), less any amounts withdrawn by the owner. The only investor in Pizza Aroma is Mauricio Rosa, the owner. His owner's equity account is called M. Rosa, Capital.

### Accounting Assumptions.
To measure and report the elements of the financial statements, accountants make four assumptions. Under the **separate entity assumption,** each business must be accounted for as an individual organization, separate and apart from its owners, all other persons, and other entities. Under the **monetary unit assumption,** each business accounts for and reports its financial results in terms of the national monetary unit (dollars in the United States, yen in Japan, euros in Germany).

| Exhibit 2.12 | Key Concepts for External Financial Reporting |
| --- | --- |

**Objective of External Financial Reporting**
   To provide useful economic information to external users for decision making
     Useful information is:
- Relevant, Reliable, Comparable, and Consistent

**Elements to be measured and reported**
- Assets, Liabilities, Owner's Equity, Revenues, and Expenses

**Concepts for Measuring and Reporting Information:**
- Assumptions: Separate Entity, Monetary Unit, Continuity, Time Period
- Principles: Historical Cost, Revenue Recognition, Matching, Full Disclosure
- Exceptions: Cost benefit, Materiality, Conservatism, Industry Practices

*Concepts in red are discussed in Chapters 1 and 2. Those in black will be discussed in Chapters 3 and 4.*

A third basic assumption is important in understanding the information on the balance sheet. Under the **continuity assumption** (sometimes called the **going-concern assumption**), a business is assumed to continue operating long enough to meet its contractual commitments and plans. In future chapters (unless otherwise indicated), we will assume that the businesses we are discussing, including Pizza Aroma, meet the continuity assumption. The fourth assumption, time period, is discussed in Chapter 3.

## Accounting Principles.
Four principles guide the rules for measuring and reporting accounting transactions. For assets and liabilities, the **historical cost principle** states that on the date of the acquisition, cost is measured as the cash paid plus the dollar value at that time of any assets, privileges, or rights also given in the exchange. For example, if you trade your computer plus cash for a new car, the new car's cost equals the cash paid plus the computer's market value. Thus, in most cases, cost is relatively easy to determine and can be verified. The revenue, matching, and full disclosure principles are discussed in Chapter 3.

| $15,000<br>Cash paid | | $2,000<br>Market value<br>of computer | | $17,000<br>Historical cost<br>of new car |

## Constraints.
In this chapter we introduced the constraint of **conservatism,** which requires that when doubt exists about the amount at which assets and liabilities should be reported, the least optimistic measurement should be used. If the value of an asset falls permanently below its historical cost, then the amount recorded for the asset should be reduced to that lower amount. Other constraints will be introduced in future chapters.

# Chapter Summary

**LO1   Identify what constitutes a business transaction and recognize common balance sheet account titles used in business. p. 50**

- **Nature of Business Transactions**
  Transactions include:
  *External exchanges*—measurable exchanges of assets and services from one company for other assets or promises to pay from another company, and
  *Internal events*—those that are not exchanges between the business and others, but which have a direct and measurable effect on the entity, including use of supplies and use of a building over many years.

- **Balance Sheet Accounts**
  Typical balance sheet account titles include the following:
  *Assets:* Cash, Accounts Receivable, Inventories, Supplies, Buildings, and Equipment.
  *Liabilities:* Accounts Payable and Notes Payable.
  *Owner's Equity:* "Owner's Name," Capital.

**LO2   Apply transaction analysis to simple business transactions in terms of the accounting model:  Assets = Liabilities + Owner's Equity. p. 52**

- **Transaction Analysis**
  Transaction analysis is based on dual effects and the basic accounting equation. *Dual effects* means that every transaction affects at least two accounts.
  - Transaction analysis follows a systematic approach: (1) determine whether a transaction exists; (2) examine the transaction for the accounts affected, classifying the accounts as assets, liabilities, or owner's equity and identifying the direction and amount of the effects; and (3) evaluate whether the accounting equation remains in balance.

**LO3   Determine the impact of business transactions on the balance sheet using two basic tools, journal entries and T-accounts. p. 57**

- **The Accounting Cycle**
  - During the accounting period, when a transaction occurs, it is analyzed, its effects are recorded in the general journal (using journal entries), and the amounts are posted to the general ledger (similar to T-accounts).
  - At the end of the accounting period, a trial balance is prepared; adjustments are analyzed, recorded, and posted; financial statements are prepared; and the records are closed.

- **Analyzing Business Transactions**
    - *Debit* is the left side of the T-account, and *credit* is the right side of the T-account.
    - Debits increase assets and decrease liabilities and owner's equity.
    - Credits decrease assets and increase liabilities and owner's equity.
- **Recording Transaction Effects**
  *Journal entries* express, in debit-equals-credit form, the effects of a transaction on various asset, liability, and owner's equity accounts. Journal entries are used to record financial information in the accounting system, which is later summarized by account in the ledger (T-accounts).
- **Posting Transaction Effects**
  *T-accounts* are a simplified version of the ledger, which summarizes transaction effects for each account. For assets, T-accounts show increases on the left (debit) side which are on the left side of the accounting equation, and decreases on the right (credit) side. For liabilities and owner's equity, T-accounts show increases on the right (credit) side which are on the right side of the accounting equation, and decreases on the left (debit) side.
- **Preparing a Trial Balance**
  A *trial balance* is prepared at the end of the accounting period prior to preparing the financial statements. Each account is listed along with its debit or credit balance (in separate columns). The purpose of the trial balance is to check that debits equal credits, summarize account balances, review and analyze necessary adjustments, and prepare financial statements.

## LO4  Prepare a simple classified balance sheet. p. 67

- **Classified Balance Sheet**
  A *classified balance sheet* separately classifies assets as current if they will be used up or turned into cash within one year. Liabilities are classified as current if they will be paid, settled, or fulfilled within one year.
- **Limitations of the Balance Sheet**
    - Because accounting is transaction based, the balance sheet does not necessarily represent the current value of a business.
    - Some assets are not recorded because they do not arise from transactions.
    - The amounts recorded for assets and liabilities may not represent current values because, under the cost principle, they generally are recorded at cost, using the exchange amounts established at the time of the initial transaction.
    - The concept of conservatism states that when uncertainty exists about the value of an asset or liability, care should be taken to not overstate the reported value of assets or understate the reported value of liabilities.

## Key Terms

See complete glossary in the back of text.

## Questions

1. Define the following:
   a.  Asset
   b.  Current asset
   c.  Liability
   d.  Current liability
   e.  Owner's capital
2. Define *transaction*, and give an example of each of the two types of events that are considered transactions.
3. For accounting purposes, what is an *account*? Explain why accounts are used in an accounting system.
4. What is the basic accounting equation?
5. Explain what *debit* and *credit* mean.

6. Briefly explain what *transaction analysis* means. What are the two principles underlying transaction analysis? What are the steps in performing transaction analysis?
7. What two different accounting equalities must be maintained in transaction analysis?
8. What is a *journal entry*? What is its typical format?
9. What is a *T-account*? What is its purpose?
10. What are the key features that all assets possess? What are the key features of all liabilities?
11. Explain what the following accounting terms mean:
    a.  Separate entity assumption
    b.  Conservatism

# Multiple Choice

1. Which of the following is not an asset?
   a. Cash
   b. Land
   c. Equipment
   d. Owner's Capital

Quiz 2-1
www.mhhe.com/LLPW1e

2. Which of the following statements describe transactions that would be recorded in the accounting system?
   a. An exchange of an asset for a promise to pay.
   b. An exchange of a promise for another promise.
   c. Both of the above.
   d. None of the above.

3. Total assets on a balance sheet prepared on any date must agree with which of the following?
   a. The sum of total liabilities and net income as shown on the income statement.
   b. The sum of total liabilities and owner's equity.
   c. The sum of total liabilities and cash.
   d. The sum of total liabilities, owner's equity, and net income.

4. The dual effects concept can best be described as follows:
   a. When a transaction is recorded in the accounting system, at least two effects on the basic accounting equation will result.
   b. When an exchange takes place between two parties, both parties must record the transaction.
   c. When a transaction is recorded, both the balance sheet and the income statement must be impacted.
   d. When a transaction is recorded, one account will always increase and one account will always decrease.

5. The T-account is used to summarize which of the following?
   a. Increases and decreases to a single account in the accounting system.
   b. Debits and credits to a single account in the accounting system.
   c. Changes in specific account balances over a time period.
   d. All of the above describe how accountants use T-accounts.

6. Which of the following describes how assets are listed on the balance sheet?
   a. In alphabetical order.
   b. In order of magnitude, lowest value to highest value.
   c. From most current to least current.
   d. From least current to most current.

7. A company was recently formed with $50,000 cash invested by the owner. The company then borrowed $20,000 from a bank, and bought $10,000 of supplies on account. The company also purchased $50,000 of equipment by paying $20,000 in cash and signing a note for the remainder. What is the amount of total assets to be reported on the balance sheet?
   a. $110,000
   b. $100,000
   c. $90,000
   d. None of the above

8. Which of the following is/are true regarding *debits* and *credits*?
   a. In any given transaction, the total dollar amount of the debits and the total dollar amount of the credits must be equal.
   b. Debits decrease certain accounts and credits decrease certain accounts.
   c. Liabilities and owner's equity accounts usually end in credit balances; assets usually end in debit balances.
   d. All of the above.

9. What is/are the purpose(s) of the trial balance?
   a. To check that debits equal credits.
   b. To record the effects of transactions.
   c. To accumulate effects of transactions to determine account balances.
   d. All of the above.

10. Which of the following statements is/are true regarding the balance sheet?
    a. One cannot determine the true "current value" of a company by reviewing just its balance sheet.
    b. Certain assets that are not acquired through identifiable and measurable transactions are not reported on a company's balance sheet.
    c. A balance sheet shows only the ending balances, in a summarized format, of balance sheet accounts in the accounting system as of a particular date.
    d. All of the above.

| Solutions to Multiple-Choice Questions | | | | | | |
|---|---|---|---|---|---|---|
| 1. d | 2. a | 3. b | 4. a | 5. d | 6. c | 7. a |
| 8. d | 9. a | 10. d | | | | |

---

# Mini Exercises  **HM**™   Available with McGraw-Hill's Homework Manager

**LO2**   **M2-1 Identifying Increase and Decrease Effects on Balance Sheet Accounts**
Complete the following table by entering either the word *increases* or *decreases* in each column.

| | Debit | Credit |
|---|---|---|
| Assets | _____ | _____ |
| Liabilities | _____ | _____ |
| Owner's equity | _____ | _____ |

**M2-2 Identifying Debit and Credit Effects on Balance Sheet Accounts**

LO2

Complete the following table by entering either the word *debit* or *credit* in each column.

|  | Increase | Decrease |
|---|---|---|
| Assets | _____ | _____ |
| Liabilities | _____ | _____ |
| Owner's equity | _____ | _____ |

**M2-3 Matching Terms with Definitions**

LO1, 2, 3

Match each term with its related definition by entering the appropriate letter in the space provided. There should be only one definition per term (that is, there are more definitions than terms).

| Term | Definition |
|---|---|
| ____ 1. Journal entry | A. Exchange of more than promises between a business and other parties. |
| ____ 2. A = L + OE; Debits = Credits | B. Four periodic financial statements. |
| ____ 3. Transaction | C. Two equalities in accounting that aid in providing accuracy. |
| ____ 4. Liabilities | D. Recording results of transaction analysis in debit-equals-credit format. |
| ____ 5. Assets | E. Account debited when money is borrowed from a bank. |
| ____ 6. Income statement, balance sheet, statement of owner's equity, and statement of cash flows | F. Resources owned by the business with probable future economic benefits. |
| | G. Cumulative earnings of a company that have not been withdrawn by the owners. |
| | H. At least two effects for every transaction. |
| | I. Debts or obligations to be paid with assets or fulfilled with services. |
| | J. Assignment of dollar amounts to transactions. |

**M2-4 Classifying Accounts on a Balance Sheet**

LO4

The following are a few of the accounts of Aim Delivery Service:

____ 1. Wages Payable          ____ 9. Sales Taxes Payable

____ 2. Accounts Payable       ____ 10. Equipment

____ 3. Accounts Receivable    ____ 11. Notes Payable (due in six years)

____ 4. Buildings              ____ 12. Notes Receivable (due in six months)

____ 5. Cash                   ____ 13. Prepaid Rent (for three months)

____ 6. "Owner's Name," Capital ____ 14. Investments (held for five months)

____ 7. Land                   ____ 15. Supplies

____ 8. Merchandise Inventory  ____ 16. Utilities Payable

In the space provided, classify each as it would be reported on a balance sheet. Use the following code: (CA) current asset, (CL) current liability, (OE) owner's equity, (NCA) noncurrent asset, and (NCL) noncurrent liability.

**M2-5 Identifying Accounts on a Classified Balance Sheet and Their Normal Debit or Credit Balances**

LO1, 3

Hasbro, Inc.

According to a recent report of Hasbro, Inc., the company is "a worldwide leader in children's and family games and toys." Hasbro produces items under several brands including Tonka, Milton Bradley, Playskool, and Parker Brothers. The following are several accounts from a recent balance sheet:

a. Accounts Receivable          f. Property, Plant, and Equipment

b. Short-Term Loan (payable)    g. Accounts Payable

c. "Owners" Capital             h. Cash

d. Long-Term Debt (payable)     i. Accrued Liabilities Payable (e.g., Wages Payable)

e. Income Taxes Payable         j. Inventories

*Required:*

1.  Indicate how each account normally should be categorized on a classified balance sheet. Use CA for current asset, NCA for noncurrent asset, CL for current liability, NCL for noncurrent liability, and OE for owner's equity

2.  Indicate whether the account normally has a debit or credit balance.

**LO3, 4**

**Blockbuster, Inc.**

### M2-6 Identifying Accounts on a Classified Balance Sheet and Their Normal Debit or Credit Balances

Blockbuster, Inc., is a leading global provider of rentable DVDs, videogames, and videocassettes. The following are several accounts included in a recent balance sheet:

a.  Income Taxes Payable
b.  Accounts Receivable
c.  Movie Rental Supplies
d.  "Owners'" Capital
e.  Long-Term Debt
f.  Property and Equipment
g.  Prepaid Rent

h.  Intangibles
i.  Accounts Payable
j.  Long-Term Liabilities
k.  Cash
l.  Accrued Liabilities Payable (e.g., Wages Payable)
m.  Merchandise Inventories

*Required:*

1.  Indicate how each account normally should be categorized on a classified balance sheet. Use CA for current asset, NCA for noncurrent asset, CL for current liability, NCL for noncurrent liability, and OE for owners' equity.

2.  Indicate whether the account normally has a debit or credit balance.

**LO1**

### M2-7 Identifying Events as Accounting Transactions

Do the following events result in a recordable transaction for The Toro Company? Answer yes or no for each.

____ 1.  Toro purchased robotic manufacturing equipment that it paid for by signing a note payable.
____ 2.  The Toro Company's president invested in another company.
____ 3.  The company lent $550,000 to an employee.
____ 4.  Toro ordered supplies from Office Max to be delivered next week.
____ 5.  Toro received $250,000 in cash from its owners.
____ 6.  The company borrowed $2,500,000 from a local bank.

**LO1**

### M2-8 Identifying Events as Accounting Transactions

3M Company, headquartered in St. Paul, Minnesota, manufactures Post-It Notes and Scotch Tape, among many other products. With a strong commitment to sustainability, in 2006 alone, 3M expended about $18 million for capital projects related to protecting the environment. Do the following events result in a recordable transaction for 3M? Answer yes or no for each.

____ 1.  The company sold its pharmaceuticals business in the United States, Canada, and other regions of the world.
____ 2.  The company received additional investments from investors (its corporate owners).
____ 3.  The company signed an agreement to rent a building in the United Kingdom; no cash was exchanged.
____ 4.  The company paid for renovations to add pollution control devices to manufacturing facilities in California.
____ 5.  The vice president of the company spoke at a sustainability luncheon in Indiana, which contributed to building the company's reputation as a responsible company.

**LO2**

### M2-9 Determining Financial Statement Effects of Several Transactions

Spotlighter Company, a new sole proprietorship owned and managed by Ryan Terlecki, sells lighting fixtures. For each of the following transactions for the month of January 2009 (the first month of operations), indicate the accounts, amounts, and direction of the effects on the accounting equation. A sample is provided.

a.  *(Sample)* Borrowed $3,940 from a local bank on a note due in six months.
b.  Received $4,630 in cash from Ryan Terlecki.

c. Purchased $920 in equipment, paying $190 cash and promising the rest on a note due in one year.

d. Paid $372 cash for supplies.

e. Bought $700 of supplies on account.

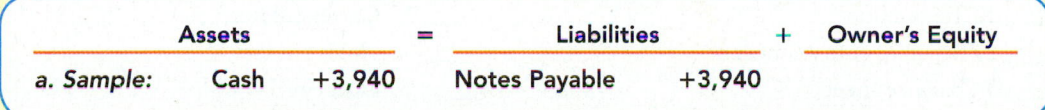

| | Assets | | = | Liabilities | | + | Owner's Equity |
|---|---|---|---|---|---|---|---|
| a. Sample: | Cash | +3,940 | | Notes Payable | +3,940 | | |

## M2-10 Preparing Journal Entries    LO3

For each of the transactions in M2–9 (including the sample), write the journal entry using the format shown in this chapter.

## M2-11 Posting to T-Accounts    LO3

For each of the transactions in M2–9 (including the sample), post the effects to the appropriate T-accounts and determine ending account balances. (*Note:* Remember to include beginning balances.)

## M2-12 Reporting a Classified Balance Sheet    LO4

Given the transactions in M2–9 (including the sample), prepare a classified balance sheet for Spotlighter Company as of January 31, 2009.

## M2-13 Preparing a Classified Balance Sheet    LO4

The following accounts are taken from the financial statements of Trump Entertainments Resorts, Inc. at year-end December 31, 2006. Amounts have been rounded to the nearest thousand.

| | | | |
|---|---|---|---|
| General Expenses | $ 279,118 | Cash | $ 127,382 |
| Salaries Payable | 28,099 | Accounts Receivable | 54,342 |
| Interest Expense | 130,144 | Inventories | 10,816 |
| Other Assets | 508,704 | Other Current Assets | 23,400 |
| Accounts Payable | 30,495 | Property and Equipment | 1,535,852 |
| Other Current Liabilities | 98,138 | Long-Term Note Payable | 1,690,996 |
| Food and Beverage Revenue | 123,091 | "Owners'" Capital | 412,768 |

*Required:*

1. Prepare a classified balance sheet at December 31, 2006. Note that some of the accounts in the list are not reported on the balance sheet.

2. Using the balance sheet, indicate whether the total assets of Trump Entertainments Resorts, Inc. at year-end were financed primarily by liabilities or owners' equity.

## Exercises H-M™    **Available with McGraw-Hill's Homework Manager**

**LO1, 2, 3**

### E2-1 Matching Terms with Definitions

Match each term with its related definition by entering the appropriate letter in the space provided. There should be only one definition per term (that is, there are more definitions than terms).

| | |
|---|---|
| ____ 1. Transaction | ____ 6. Current assets |
| ____ 2. Separate entity concept | ____ 7. Notes payable |
| ____ 3. Balance sheet | ____ 8. Dual effects |
| ____ 4. Liabilities | ____ 9. Conservatism |
| ____ 5. Assets = Liabilities + Owner's Equity | ____ 10. Debit |

A. Economic resources to be used or turned into cash within one year.

B. Reports assets, liabilities, and owner's equity.

C. Decreases assets; increases liabilities and owner's equity.

D. Increases assets; decreases liabilities and owner's equity.

E. Exchange of more than promises between a business and other parties.

F. Assumption that businesses will operate into the foreseeable future.

G. Accounts for a business separate from its owners.

H. Principle that assets should be recorded at their original cost to the company.

I. Standardized format used to accumulate data about each item reported on financial statements.

J. Basic accounting equation.

K. Two equalities in accounting that aid in providing accuracy.

L. Account credited when money is borrowed from a bank.

M. Concept that every transaction has at least two effects.

N. Debts or obligations to be paid or settled with assets or services.

O. Accounting concept that requires special care to be taken to avoid overstating assets and revenues or understating liabilities and expenses.

**LO1**

### E2-2 Identifying Account Titles

The following are independent situations.

a. A company orders and receives 10 personal computers for office use for which it signs a note promising to pay $25,000 within three months.

b. A company purchases a new delivery truck for $21,000 cash. The truck has a $24,000 list ("sticker") price.

c. A women's clothing retailer orders 30 new display stands for $300 each for future delivery.

d. A new company is formed and the owner invests $12,000 cash.

e. A company purchases a piece of land for $50,000 cash. An appraiser for the buyer valued the land at $52,500.

f. A local company's owner buys a $10,000 car for personal use. Answer from the company's point of view.

g. A company borrows $1,000 from a local bank and signs a six-month note for the loan.

h. A company pays $1,500 owed on its note payable (ignore interest).

*Required:*

1. Indicate titles of the appropriate accounts, if any, affected in each of the preceding events. Consider what the business receives and gives in the exchange.

2. At what amount would you record the delivery truck in b? The piece of land in e? What measurement principle are you applying?

3. What reasoning did you apply in c? For f, what accounting concept did you apply?

**LO1, 3**

### E2-3 Classifying Accounts and Their Usual Balances

As described in a recent annual report, Digital Diversions, Inc. (DDI) designs, develops, and distributes videogames for computers and advanced game systems such as Paystation, Y-Box, Tamecube, and Gamegirl. DDI has been operating for only one full year.

*Required:*

For each of the following accounts from DDI's recent balance sheet, complete the following table. Indicate whether the account is classified as a current asset (CA), noncurrent asset (NCA), current liability (CL), noncurrent liability (NCL), or owner's equity (OE), and whether the account usually has a debit (*dr*) or credit (*cr*) balance.

| Account | Balance Sheet Classification | Debit or Credit Balance |
|---|---|---|
| 1. Land | _____ | _____ |
| 2. Wages Payable | _____ | _____ |
| 3. Notes Payable (due in three years) | _____ | _____ |
| 4. Accounts Receivable | _____ | _____ |
| 5. Supplies | _____ | _____ |
| 6. "Owners'" Capital | _____ | _____ |
| 7. Machinery and Equipment | _____ | _____ |
| 8. Accounts Payable | _____ | _____ |
| 9. Cash | _____ | _____ |
| 10. Taxes Payable | _____ | _____ |

## E2-4 Determining Financial Statement Effects of Several Transactions                LO1, 2

The following events occurred for Favata Company:

(*a*)  Received $10,000 cash from owner, Jim Favata.

(*b*)  Borrowed $7,000 cash from a bank.

(*c*)  Purchased land for $12,000; paid $1,000 in cash and signed a note for the balance.

(*d*)  Bought $800 of supplies on account.

(*e*)  Purchased $3,000 of equipment, paying $1,000 in cash and signing a note due in six months for the rest.

*Required:*

For each of the events (*a*) through (*e*), perform transaction analysis and indicate the account, amount, and direction of the effect (+ for increase and − for decrease) on the accounting equation. Check that the accounting equation remains in balance after each transaction. Use the following headings:

| Event | Assets | = | Liabilities | + | Owner's Equity |
|---|---|---|---|---|---|
| _____ | _____ | | _____ | | _____ |

## E2-5 Determining Financial Statement Effects of Several Transactions                LO1, 2

Nike, Inc., with headquarters in Beaverton, Oregon, is one of the world's leading manufacturers of athletic shoes and sports apparel. The following activities occurred during a recent year. The amounts are presented in millions of dollars.

Nike, Inc.

(a)  Purchased $216.3 in property, plant, and equipment; paid by signing a $5.0 long-term note and fulfilling the rest with cash.

(b)  Received $21.1 in cash from investors (corporate owners).

(c)  One Nike owner personally borrowed $21.0 from a local bank.

*Required:*

1.  For each of these events, perform transaction analysis and indicate the account, amount (in millions), and direction of the effect on the accounting equation. Check that the accounting equation remains in balance after each transaction. Use the following headings:

| Event | Assets | = | Liabilities | + | Owner's Equity |
|---|---|---|---|---|---|
| _____ | _____ | | _____ | | _____ |

2.  Explain your response to transaction (*c*).

**LO3**

### E2-6 Recording Activities

Refer to E2–4.

*Required:*

For each of the events in E2–4, prepare journal entries, checking that debits equal credits.

**LO3**

### E2-7 Recording Activities

Refer to E2–5.

*Required:*

1. For each of the events in E2–5, prepare journal entries, checking that debits equal credits.
2. Explain your response to event (c).

**LO3**

### E2-8 Analyzing the Effects of Transactions in T-Accounts

Julio Estella formed Estella Consulting to provide accounting and financial consulting services to clients. The following activities occurred during the year:

- (a) Received $60,000 cash from Julio Estella to establish the sole proprietorship.
- (b) Purchased equipment for use in the business at a cost of $12,000; one-fourth was paid in cash and the company signed a note for the balance (due in six months).
- (c) Signed an agreement with a cleaning service to pay it $120 per week for cleaning the corporate offices, beginning next week.
- (d) Julio Estella borrowed $10,000 for personal use from a local bank, signing a one-year note.

*Required:*

1. Create T-accounts for the following accounts: Cash, Equipment, Notes Payable, and Julio Estella, Capital. Beginning balances are zero. For each of the preceding transactions, record its effects in the appropriate T-accounts. Include good referencing and totals for each T-account.
2. Using the balances in the T-accounts, fill in the following amounts for the accounting equation:

Assets $ _____ = Liabilities $ _____ + Owner's Equity $ _____

3. Explain your response to events (c) and (d).

**LO1**

### E2-9 Inferring Investing and Financing Transactions and Preparing a Balance Sheet

During its first week of operations, January 1–7, 2010, Home Comfort Furniture, a sole proprietorship owned by Sara Baine, completed six transactions with the dollar effects indicated in the following schedule:

|  | Assets | | | = | Liabilities | + | Owner's Equity |
|---|---|---|---|---|---|---|---|
|  | Cash | Equipment | Land | = | Notes Payable | | S. Baine, Capital |
| Beginning | $    0 | $    0 | $    0 | = | $    0 | | $    0 |
| a. | +12,000 | | | = | | | +12,000 |
| b. | +50,000 | | | = | +50,000 | | |
| c. | − 4,000 | | +12,000 | = | + 8,000 | | |
| d. | + 4,000 | | | = | + 4,000 | | |
| e. | − 7,000 | +7,000 | | = | | | |
| f. | | | + 3,000 | = | + 3,000 | | |
| Ending | | | | | | | |

*Required:*

1. Write a brief explanation of transactions (a) through (f). Explain any assumptions that you made.
2. Compute the ending balance in each account and prepare a classified balance sheet for Home Comfort Furniture on January 7, 2010.
3. As of January 7, 2010, has most of the financing for Home Comfort's assets come from liabilities or owner's equity?

**E2-10 Explaining Investing and Financing Transactions and Preparing a Balance Sheet**    LO1, 2, 3, 4

During its first month of operations, March 2011, Faye's Fashions, a sole proprietorship owned and operated by Faye Miller, completed four transactions with the dollar effects indicated in the following schedule. Parentheses around a number are negative effects.

| Accounts | DOLLAR EFFECT OF EACH OF THE FOUR TRANSACTIONS | | | | Ending Balance |
|---|---|---|---|---|---|
| | (a) | (b) | (c) | (d) | |
| Cash | $50,000 | $(4,000) | $5,000 | $(4,000) | |
| Computer Equipment | | | | 4,000 | |
| Delivery Truck | | 25,000 | | | |
| Short-Term Notes Payable | | | 5,000 | | |
| Long-Term Notes Payable | | 21,000 | | | |
| F. Miller, Capital | 50,000 | | | | |

*Required:*

1. Write a brief explanation of transactions (a) through (d). Explain any assumptions that you made.
2. Compute the ending balance in each account and prepare a *classified* balance sheet for Faye's Fashions at the end of March 2011.
3. As of March 31, 2011, has most of the financing for Faye's Fashions' assets come from liabilities or owner's equity?

**E2-11 Recording Journal Entries**    LO3

Assume that Hargett Company was organized on May 1, 2009, to compete with Stefanov Company—a company that sells office products. The following events occurred during the first month of Hargett Company's operations.

    (a) Received $60,000 cash from Megan Hargett who organized Hargett Company.
    (b) Borrowed $20,000 cash and signed a note due in two years.
    (c) Ordered computer equipment costing $16,000.
    (d) Purchased $10,000 in equipment, paying $1,000 in cash and signing a six-month note for the balance.
    (e) Received and paid for the computer equipment ordered in (c).

*Required:*

Prepare journal entries for each transaction. Be sure to use good referencing and categorize each account as an asset (A), liability (L), or owner's equity (OE). If a transaction does not require a journal entry, explain the reason.

**E2-12 Analyzing the Effects of Transactions Using T-Accounts; Preparing and Interpreting a Balance Sheet**    LO1, 2, 3, 4

Jonah Lee established Lee Delivery Company in 2010. The following transactions occurred during the year:

    (a) Received $90,000 cash from Jonah Lee, the sole owner.
    (b) Purchased land for $12,000, signing a two-year note (ignore interest).
    (c) Bought two used delivery trucks at the start of the year at a cost of $10,000 each; paid $2,000 cash and signed a note due in three years for the rest (ignore interest).
    (d) Sold one-fourth of the land for $3,000 to Birkins Moving, which signed a note agreeing to pay Lee Delivery Company in six months (ignore interest).
    (e) Paid $52,000 cash to construct a garage for the trucks.
    (f) Jonah Lee paid $122,000 cash for land for his personal use.

*Required:*

1. Analyze each item for its effects on the financial statements of Lee Delivery Company for the year ended December 31, 2010. Transaction (a) is presented as an example:

| | Assets | = | Liabilities | + | Owner's Equity |
|---|---|---|---|---|---|
| | Cash | | | | J. Lee, Capital |
| (a) | +90,000 | = | | | +90,000 |

2. Record the effects of each item into a journal entry, using the simplified journal entry format shown in the chapter.

3. Summarize the effects of the journal entries by account, using the T-account format shown in the chapter.

4. Prepare a *classified* balance sheet for Lee Delivery Company on December 31, 2010.

5. Using the balance sheet, indicate whether Lee Delivery Company's assets at year-end were financed primarily by liabilities or owner's equity.

**LO3**

### E2-13 Explaining the Effects of Transactions on Balance Sheet Accounts Using T-Accounts

Mashu Furniture Repair Service, a company owned by sole proprietor Doreen Mashu, began operations on June 1, 2009. The following T-accounts indicate the activities for the month of June.

| Cash (A) | | | Supplies (A) | | | Building (A) | |
|---|---|---|---|---|---|---|---|
| Beg. | 0 | | Beg. | 0 | | Beg. | 0 |
| (a) | 17,000 | 10,000 (b) | (c) | 1,500 | | (b) | 50,000 |
| | | 1,500 (c) | | | | | |

| Notes Payable (L) | | | D. Mashu, Capital (OE) | |
|---|---|---|---|---|
| | 0 Beg. | | | 0 Beg. |
| | 40,000 (b) | | | 17,000 (a) |

*Required:*

Explain events (a) through (c) that resulted in the entries in the T-accounts. That is, for each account what transactions made it increase and/or decrease?

**LO3**

### E2-14 Analyzing the Effects of Transactions Using T-Accounts

Ekar Company, formed by Catherine Ekar, has been operating for one year (2009). At the start of 2010, Ekar's T-account balances were as follows:

*Assets:*

| Cash | | Short-Term Investments | | Equipment | |
|---|---|---|---|---|---|
| 5,000 | | 2,000 | | 4,000 | |

*Liabilities:*

| Short-Term Notes Payable | | Long-Term Notes Payable | |
|---|---|---|---|
| | 300 | | 600 |

*Owner's Equity:*

| C. Ekar, Capital | |
|---|---|
| | 10,100 |

*Required:*

1. Using the data from these T-accounts, determine the amounts for the following on January 1, 2010:

Assets $ _____ = Liabilities $ _____ + Owner's Equity $ _____

2. Enter the following 2010 transactions in the T-accounts:
   (a) Sold $1,500 of the investments for $1,500 cash.
   (b) Sold one-fourth of the equipment for $1,000 in cash.
   (c) Borrowed $2,600 from a local bank, signing a note due in three years (ignore interest).
   (d) Paid $300 cash on a short-term note payable (ignore interest).

3. Compute ending balances in the T-accounts to determine amounts for the following on December 31, 2010:

Assets $ _____ = Liabilities $ _____ + Owner's Equity $ _____

# Problems—Set A   Available with McGraw-Hill's Homework Manager

**PA2-1 Determining Financial Statement Effects of Various Transactions**                LO1, 2
Lester's Home Healthcare Services was established on January 1, 2009, by Jennifer Lester, who invested $40,000 in the company. During the first month (January 2009), the company had the following five events:

  (a)  Collected a total of $40,000 from owner Jennifer Lester.
  (b)  Purchased a building for $65,000, equipment for $16,000, and three acres of land for $12,000; paid $13,000 in cash and signed a note for the balance that is due to be paid in 15 years. (*Note:* Five different accounts are affected.)
  (c)  Jennifer Lester personally lent $5,000 cash to another business.
  (d)  Purchased supplies for $3,000 cash.
  (e)  Sold one acre of land for $4,000 cash to another company.

**Required:**

1.  Was Lester's Home Healthcare Services organized as a sole proprietorship, partnership, or corporation? Explain the basis for your answer.
2.  During the first month, the records of the company were inadequate. You were asked to prepare the summary of the preceding transactions. To develop a quick assessment of their economic effects on Lester's Home Healthcare Services, you have decided to complete the spreadsheet that follows and to use plus (+) for increases and minus (−) for decreases for each account. Transaction (a) is presented as an example.

| | | Assets | | | | = | Liabilities | + | Owner's Equity |
|---|---|---|---|---|---|---|---|---|---|
| | Cash | Supplies | Land | Building | Equipment | | Notes Payable | | J. Lester, Capital |
| (a) | +40,000 | | | | | = | | | +40,000 |

3.  How did you handle transaction (c) between Jennifer Lester and the other business? Why?
4.  Based only on the completed spreadsheet, provide the following amounts (show computations):
  a.  Total assets at the end of the month.
  b.  Total liabilities at the end of the month.
  c.  Total owner's equity at the end of the month.
  d.  Cash balance at the end of the month.
  e.  Total current assets at the end of the month.
5.  As of January 31, 2009, has the financing for Lester's Home Healthcare Services investment in assets primarily come from liabilities or owner's equity?

**PA2-2 Recording and Posting Transactions; Preparing and Interpreting the Balance Sheet**        LO2, 3, 4
Owner-manager Nicole Cade established Athletic Performance Company as a sole proprietorship on July 1, 2010. The company's chart of accounts included the following:

| | |
|---|---|
| Accounts Payable | N. Cade, Capital |
| Building | Notes Payable |
| Cash | Supplies |
| Equipment | |

www.mhhe.com/LLPW1e

During the month of July, the company had the following activities:

  (a)  Received $200,000 cash from Nicole Cade.
  (b)  Borrowed $30,000 cash from a local bank, payable June 30, 2012.
  (c)  Bought a factory building for $141,000; paid $41,000 in cash and signed a three-year note for the balance.
  (d)  Paid cash for equipment that cost $100,000.
  (e)  Purchased supplies for $10,000 on account.

**Required:**

1.  Analyze transactions (a)–(e) to determine their effects on the accounting equation. Use the format shown in the demonstration case on page 71.

2.  Record the transaction effects determined in requirement 1 using a journal entry format.
3.  Summarize the journal entry effects from requirement 2 using T-accounts.
4.  Prepare a *classified* balance sheet at July 31, 2010.
5.  As of July 31, 2010, has the financing for Athletic Performance Company's assets primarily come from liabilities or owner's equity?

**LO2, 3, 4**

**PA2-3 Recording and Posting Transactions; Preparing and Interpreting the Balance Sheet**

Deliberate Speed Company was established as a sole proprietorship by Andrew Nguyen on July 1, 2009. The company's accounts at July 1, 2011, included the following:

| | | | |
|---|---|---|---|
| Accounts Payable | $ 10,000 | Equipment | $118,000 |
| A. Nguyen, Capital | 439,000 | Land | 200,000 |
| Cash | 26,000 | Notes Payable | 2,000 |
| Factory Building | 100,000 | Supplies | 7,000 |

During the month of July, the company had the following activities:

(a) Received $400,000 cash as an additional investment from Andrew Nguyen.
(b) Borrowed $90,000 cash from a local bank, payable June 30, 2013.
(c) Bought a factory building for $182,000; paid $82,000 in cash and signed a three-year note for the balance.
(d) Paid cash for equipment that cost $200,000.
(e) Purchased supplies for $30,000 on account.

*Required:*

1.  Analyze transactions (a)–(e) to determine their effects on the accounting equation. Use the format shown in the demonstration case on page 71.
2.  Record the transaction effects determined in requirement 1 using a journal entry format.
3.  Summarize the journal entry effects from requirement 2 using T-accounts.
4.  Prepare a *classified* balance sheet at July 31, 2011.
5.  As of July 31, 2011, has the financing for Deliberate Speed Company's assets primarily come from liabilities or owner's equity?

**LO1, 2**

**PA2-4 Determining Financial Statement Effects of Various Transactions**

Russeck Company, formed by sole proprietor Kal Russeck, is a small manufacturing business that makes model trains to sell to toy stores. It has a small service department that repairs customers' trains for a fee. The company has been in business for five years. At the end of the most recent year, 2009, the accounting records reflected total assets of $500,000 and total liabilities of $200,000. During the current year, 2010, the following summarized events occurred:

(a) Received an additional investment of $100,000 cash from owner Kal Russeck.
(b) Borrowed $120,000 cash from the bank and signed a 10-year note.
(c) Built an addition on the factory for $200,000 and paid cash to the contractor.
(d) Purchased equipment for the new addition for $30,000, paying $3,000 in cash and signing a note due in six months for the balance.
(e) Returned a $3,000 piece of equipment from (d) because it proved to be defective; received a reduction of the note payable.
(f) Purchased a delivery truck (equipment) for $10,000; paid $5,000 cash and signed a nine-month note for the remainder.
(g) Kal Russeck lent $5,000 of his personal funds to Tom Mallard, his neighbor.

*Required:*

1.  Complete the spreadsheet that follows, using plus (+) for increases and minus (−) for decreases for each account. The first transaction is used as an example.

| | Assets | | | = | Liabilities | + | Owner's Equity |
|---|---|---|---|---|---|---|---|
| | Cash | Equipment | Building | | Notes Payable | | K. Russeck, Capital |
| (a) | +100,000 | | | = | | | +100,000 |

2. Did you include event (g) in the spreadsheet? Why or why not?
3. Based on beginning balances plus the completed spreadsheet, provide the following amounts (show computations):

    a.  Total assets at the end of the year.

    b.  Total liabilities at the end of the year.

    c.  Total owner's equity at the end of the year.

4. As of December 31, 2010, has the financing for Russeck Company's assets primarily come from liabilities or owner's equity?

### PA2-5 Recording and Posting Transactions; Preparing and Interpreting the Balance Sheet

Peta Plastics Company has been operating for three years as a sole proprietorship owned and managed by James Peta. The December 31, 2009, account balances are:

LO2, 3, 4

www.mhhe.com/LLPW1e

| | | | |
|---|---|---|---|
| Cash | $ 35,000 | Land | $ 35,000 |
| Accounts Receivable | 5,000 | Factory Building | 120,000 |
| Supplies | 4,000 | Accounts Payable | 37,000 |
| Notes Receivable (due 2011) | 2,000 | Notes Payable (due 2015) | 80,000 |
| Equipment | 116,000 | J. Peta, Capital | 200,000 |

During the year 2010, the company had the following summarized activities:

  (a)  Purchased equipment that cost $20,000; paid $5,000 cash and signed a two-year note for the balance.

  (b)  Received an additional $20,000 cash investment from James Peta.

  (c)  Borrowed $30,000 cash from a local bank, payable June 30, 2015.

  (d)  Purchased $4,000 of additional supplies on account.

  (e)  Built an addition to the factory for $41,000; paid $12,000 in cash and signed a three-year note for the balance.

  (f)  Hired a new employee to start January 1, 2011, at an annual salary of $35,000.

*Required:*

1. Analyze transactions (a)–(f) to determine their effects on the accounting equation. Use the format shown in the demonstration case on page 71.
2. Record the transaction effects determined in requirement 1 using a journal entry format.
3. Summarize the journal entry effects from requirement 2 using T-accounts.
4. Explain your response to event (f).
5. Prepare a *classified* balance sheet at December 31, 2010.
6. As of December 31, 2010, has the financing for Peta Plastics Company's assets primarily come from liabilities or owner's equity?

### PA2-6 Using Technology for Analyzing Transactions and Preparing a Balance Sheet

Assume that you recently obtained a part-time accounting position at the corporate headquarters of Elizabeth Arden in Miami Lakes, Florida. Elizabeth Arden is a leading marketer and manufacturer of prestige beauty products, prominently led by the Red Door line of fragrances. The following table summarizes accounts and their balances (in thousands) reported by Elizabeth Arden in a recent September 30 balance sheet.

LO2, 3, 4

Elizabeth Arden

www.mhhe.com/LLPW1e

| | | | |
|---|---|---|---|
| Cash | $ 14,300 | Short-Term Notes Payable | $ 125,000 |
| Accounts Receivable | 285,400 | Accounts Payable | 111,800 |
| Inventories | 199,700 | Other Current Liabilities | 75,700 |
| Other Current Assets | 31,600 | Long-Term Debt | 323,600 |
| Property and Equipment | 35,800 | Other Long-Term Liabilities | 10,100 |
| Other Noncurrent Assets | 224,100 | "Owners" Capital | 144,700 |

Determine how the balance sheet of Elizabeth Arden would change if the company were to enter into the following transactions (amounts in thousands) during October:

  Oct.  2  Purchase an additional manufacturing facility at a cost of $17,000 by signing a note that becomes payable in three years.

  Oct. 10  Use $4,000 cash to repay one of the short-term loans.

Oct. 21  Receive an additional $10,000 cash from investors (corporate owners).

Oct. 28  Use cash to buy land for $5,000.

*Required:*

Elizabeth Arden's controller has asked you to create a spreadsheet in which to display:

1. The account balances at September 30.
2. The effects of the four October transactions.
3. Totals that combine the September 30 balances with the October transactions. You think you might be ready to tackle this assignment, but just to be sure, you e-mail your friend Owen for advice. Here's his reply.

---

From:      Owen@yahoo.com
To:        Helpme@hotmail.com
Cc:
Subject:   Excel Help

---

Wow, I can't believe you landed such a great job at EA. Congratulations!

- My thinking is that you'll really impress your boss if you set up the spreadsheet to look like a bunch of T-accounts, one beside another. Use two columns for each balance sheet account (with the account name spanning the two columns) to make it look just like a T-account. [To use the cell merge command to make a header span two columns, see PA1-3.] Here's a screen shot of how one part of the left-hand side of your worksheet might look just before you enter the October transactions.

- For extra spreadsheet skills, you might also try creating a balance sheet with cells that are linked to the corresponding cells in the T-accounts. To do this, open a worksheet in the same file as the T-accounts. Then click on a cell in the balance sheet worksheet where you want to import a number from the T-accounts, then type =, then click on the tab for the T-account worksheet, click on the cell with the total to be transferred, and then press enter. This links the cells so that any changes to the T-accounts automatically update the balance sheet.

- I guess the only thing that's left is to remind you that to compute the ending balances in each T-account, you have to add the increases to the beginning balance and subtract the decreases. So, to compute the totals for a particular account, your formula might look like =(SUM(C4:C9)-SUM(D5:D9)).

- Oh yeah, when you've finished, don't forget to save the file using a name that uniquely identifies you.

---

## Problems—Set B    **Available with McGraw-Hill's Homework Manager**

**LO1, 2**    **PB2-1 Determining Financial Statement Effects of Various Transactions**

Swish Watch Repair Company owned by Jacob Swish repairs expensive watches for customers. The company has been in business for three years. At the end of the most recent year, 2009, the accounting records reported total assets of $2,255,000 and total liabilities of $1,780,000. During the current year, 2010, the following summarized events occurred:

  (*a*)  Received an additional investment of $109,000 cash from Jacob Swish.

  (*b*)  Borrowed $186,000 cash from the bank and signed a 10-year note.

  (*c*)  Jacob Swish borrowed $85,000 from a local bank to acquire his summer cottage.

  (*d*)  Built an addition on the factory for $200,000 and paid cash to the construction company.

(e) Purchased equipment for the new addition for $44,000 and supplies for $18,000, paying $12,000 in cash and signing a six-month note for the balance.

(f) Returned a $4,000 piece of equipment, from (e) because it proved to be defective; received a cash refund.

**Required:**

1. Complete the spreadsheet that follows, using plus (+) for increases and minus (−) for decreases for each account. The first transaction is used as an example.

| | Assets | | | | | = | Liabilities | + | Owner's Equity |
|---|---|---|---|---|---|---|---|---|---|
| Cash | Supplies | Land | Equipment | Building | | = | Notes Payable | | J. Swish, Capital |
| (a) +109,000 | | | | | | = | | | +109,000 |

2. Did you include event (c) in the spreadsheet? Why?

3. Based on beginning balances plus the completed spreadsheet, provide the following amounts (show computations):
   a. Total assets at the end of the year.
   b. Total liabilities at the end of the year.
   c. Total owner's equity at the end of the year.

4. As of December 31, 2010, has the financing for Swish Watch Repairs' assets primarily come from liabilities or owner's equity?

**PB2-2 Recording and Posting Transactions; Preparing and Interpreting the Balance Sheet**    LO2, 3, 4

Susan Engel established Boston Bed & Breakfast as a sole proprietorship on July 1, 2009. The company's chart of accounts included the following:

| | |
|---|---|
| Accounts Payable | Notes Payable |
| Building | S. Engel, Capital |
| Cash | Supplies |
| Equipment | |

During the month of July, the company had the following activities:
   (a) Received $160,000 cash from Susan Engel.
   (b) Purchased a large existing bed and breakfast for $900,000; paid $90,000 as a down payment and signed a note payable from a local bank for the rest. The note is due on June 30, 2029.
   (c) Purchased new kitchen appliances for $16,000 cash.
   (d) Purchased supplies for $9,000 on account.
   (e) Returned a defective appliance purchased in (c) for $3,000 and received a cash refund.

**Required:**

1. Analyze transactions (a)–(e) to determine their effects on the accounting equation. Use the format shown in the demonstration case on page 71.
2. Record the transaction effects determined in requirement 1 using a journal entry format.
3. Summarize the journal entry effects from requirement 2 using T-accounts.
4. Prepare a *classified* balance sheet at July 31, 2009.
5. As of July 31, 2009, has the financing for Boston Bed & Breakfast's assets primarily come from liabilities or owner's equity?

**PB2-3 Recording and Posting Transactions; Preparing and Interpreting the Balance Sheet**    LO2, 3, 4

Ethan Allen Interiors is a leading manufacturer and retailer of home furnishings with 315 retail stores in the United States and abroad. The following is adapted from Ethan Allen's June 30, 2007, balance sheet (year-end). Dollars are in thousands.

ETHAN ALLEN

| | | | |
|---|---|---|---|
| Cash | $147,879 | Accounts Payable | $ 26,650 |
| Other Current Assets | 234,550 | Wages and Other Expenses Payable | 120,789 |
| Property, Plant, and Equipment | 322,185 | Long-Term Liabilities | 245,517 |
| Intangibles and Other Assets | 97,984 | Owners' Capital | 409,642 |

Assume that the following events occurred in the next quarter ended September 30, 2007:

(a)  Paid $1,400 cash for new intangibles and other assets.

(b)  Received $1,050 in cash as an additional investment from owners.

(c)  Purchased property, plant, and equipment; paid $1,870 in cash and signed a note payable to repay the remaining $9,300 in two years.

(d)  Sold, at cost, intangibles and other assets for $320 cash.

(e)  Conducted negotiations to purchase a sawmill that is expected to cost $36,000.

*Required:*

1.   Analyze transactions (a)–(e) to determine their effects on the accounting equation. Use the format shown in the demonstration case on page 71.

2.   Record the transaction effects determined in requirement 1 using a journal entry format.

3.   Summarize the journal entry effects from requirement 2 using T-accounts. Use the balances reported in the preceding list as the beginning balances for the quarter ended September 30, 2007.

4.   Explain your response to event (e).

5.   Prepare a *classified* balance sheet at September 30, 2007.

6.   As of September 30, 2007, has the financing for Ethan Allen's assets primarily come from liabilities or owners' equity?

**LO1, 2**

**PB2-4 Determining Financial Statement Effects of Various Transactions**

Steve Limberg established The Swimmer's Cove, a sole proprietorship selling swimming apparel and equipment, in 2006. At December 31, 2011, the accounting records reflected total assets of $850,000 and total liabilities of $375,000. During the current year, 2012, the following summarized events occurred:

(a)  Borrowed $10,000 cash from the local bank and signed a six-month note.

(b)  Purchased a warehouse for $300,000 and a delivery van for $40,000; paid cash of $50,000 and signed a 20-year note for the rest.

(c)  Ordered $150,000 in merchandise to be delivered in January 2013.

(d)  Received an additional investment of $60,000 cash from owner Steve Limberg.

(e)  Sold the delivery van to another business for $40,000; received $10,000 cash and the rest on a two-year note due from the other company.

(f)  Purchased a short-term investment for $30,000 cash.

(g)  Steve Limberg withdrew $25,000 cash from the business.

*Required:*

1.   Complete the spreadsheet that follows, using plus (+) for increases and minus (−) for decreases for each account. The first transaction is used as an example.

| | | Assets | | | = | Liabilities | + | Owner's Equity | |
|---|---|---|---|---|---|---|---|---|---|
| Cash | Short-term Investment | Notes Receivable | Equipment | Building | | Notes Payable | | S. Limberg, Capital | S. Limberg, Drawing |
| (a) +10,000 | | | | | = | +10,000 | | | |

2.   Did you include event (c) in the spreadsheet? Why or why not?

3.   Based on beginning balances plus the completed spreadsheet, provide the following amounts (show computations):

   a.   Total assets at the end of the year.

   b.   Total liabilities at the end of the year.

   c.   Total owner's equity at the end of the year.

4.   As of December 31, 2012, has the financing for The Swimmer's Cove's assets primarily come from liabilities or owner's equity?

**LO2, 3, 4**

Starbucks

**PB2-5 Recording and Posting Transactions; Preparing and Interpreting the Balance Sheet**

Starbucks is a coffee company—a big coffee company. During a 10-year period, the number of Starbucks locations increased from 165 to more than 5,800 stores—an average increase of 43 percent every year. The following is adapted from Starbucks' September 30, 2007, annual report, (Starbucks' year-end). Dollars are reported in thousands.

| | | | |
|---|---|---|---|
| Cash | $ 281,300 | Other Long-Term Assets | $ 757,000 |
| Accounts Receivable | 287,900 | Accounts Payable and Other Current Liabilities | 1,445,400 |
| Inventories | 691,700 | Short-Term Notes Payable | 710,200 |
| Other Current Assets | 435,600 | Long-Term Debt | 904,200 |
| Property, Plant, and Equipment | 2,890,400 | Owners' Capital | 2,284,100 |

Assume that the following events (dollars in thousands) occurred in the next quarter that ended December 31, 2007:

(a) Paid $10,000 cash for additional other long-term assets.

(b) Received $5,100 in cash as additional contributions (investments) from owners.

(c) Purchased property, plant, and equipment; paid $11,200 in cash and signed long-term loans for $9,500.

(d) Sold, at cost, other long-term assets for $6,000 cash.

(e) Conducted negotiations to purchase a coffee farm that is expected to cost $8,400.

**Required:**

1. Analyze transactions (a)–(e) to determine their effects on the accounting equation. Use the format shown in the demonstration case on page 71.
2. Record the transaction effects determined in requirement 1 using a journal entry format.
3. Summarize the journal entry effects from requirement 2 using T-accounts. Use the September 2007 ending balances (reported above) as the beginning balances for the October–December 2007 quarter.
4. Explain your response to event (e).
5. Prepare a *classified* balance sheet at December 31, 2007.
6. As of December 31, 2007, has the financing for Starbucks' assets primarily come from liabilities or owners' equity?

## PB2-6 Using Technology for Analyzing Transactions and Preparing a Balance Sheet

**LO2, 3, 4**

**The Estée Lauder Companies**

Assume that you recently obtained a part-time accounting position at the corporate office of Estée Lauder headquartered in New York. Estée Lauder is one of the world's leading manufacturers and marketers of quality skin care, makeup, fragrance, and hair care products including brands such as Estée Lauder, Aramis, and Clinique. The following table summarizes accounts and their balances (in millions) reported by Estée Lauder in a recent June 30 balance sheet.

| | | | |
|---|---|---|---|
| Cash | $ 369 | Accounts Payable | $ 264 |
| Accounts Receivable | 771 | Short-Term Notes Payable | 90 |
| Inventories | 766 | Other Current Liabilities | 1,084 |
| Other Current Assets | 271 | Long-Term Debt | 432 |
| Property and Equipment | 758 | Other Long-Term Liabilities | 266 |
| Other Noncurrent Assets | 849 | Owners' Capital | 1,648 |

Determine how Estée Lauder's balance sheet would change if the company were to enter into the following transactions (amounts in millions) during July:

July 5   Purchase an additional research and development facility at a cost of $25 by signing a note that becomes payable in four years.

July 11  Use $10 cash to repay one of the short-term loans.

July 25  Receive an additional $30 cash from owners.

July 27  Use cash to buy land for $13.

**Required:**

Estée Lauder's controller has asked you to create a spreadsheet in which to display:

1. The account balances at June 30.
2. The effects of the four July transactions.
3. Totals that combine the June 30 balances with the July transactions. You think you might be ready to tackle this assignment, but just to be sure, you e-mail your friend Sally for advice. Here's her reply.

From:       Sally@yahoo.com
To:         Helpme@hotmail.com
Cc:
Subject:    Excel Help

Wow, I can't believe you gave up that great job at EA. Good thing you landed another one so quickly!

- My thinking is that you'll really impress your boss if you set up the spreadsheet to look like a bunch of T-accounts, one beside another. Use two columns for each balance sheet account (with the account name spanning the two columns) to make it look just like a T-account. [To use the cell merge command to make a header span two columns, see PA1-3.] Here's a screen shot of how one part of the left-hand side of your worksheet might look just before you enter the July transactions.

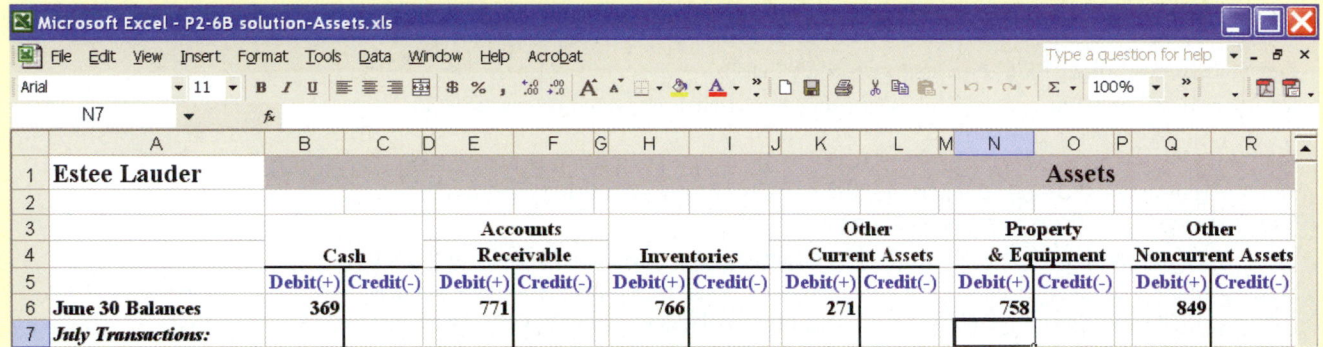

- For extra spreadsheet skills, you might also try creating a balance sheet with cells that are linked to the corresponding cells in the T-accounts. To do this, open a worksheet in the same file as the T-accounts. Then click on a cell in the balance sheet worksheet where you want to import a number from the T-accounts, then type =, then click on the tab for the T-account worksheet, click on the cell with the total to be transferred, and then press enter. This links the cells so that any changes to the T-accounts automatically update the balance sheet.

- I guess the only thing that's left is to remind you that to compute the ending balances in each T-account, you have to add the increases to the beginning balance and subtract the decreases. So, to compute the totals for a particular account, your formula might look like =(SUM(B6:B11)-SUM(C6:C11)).

- Oh yeah, when you've finished, don't forget to save the file using a name that uniquely identifies you.

# Cases and Projects

LO1, 2, 4

## CP2-1 Finding and Analyzing Financial Information

Refer to the financial statements of The Home Depot in Appendix A at the end of this book, or download the annual report from the *Cases* section of the text's Web site at www.mhhe.com/LLPW1e.

*Required:*

1. What is the company's fiscal year-end? Where did you find the exact date?
2. Use the company's balance sheet from the most recent year to determine the amounts in the accounting equation (A = L + SE).
3. What is the amount of the company's current liabilities?
4. Has financing for the company's investment in assets primarily come from liabilities or stockholders' equity?

LO1, 2, 4

## CP2-2 Comparing Financial Information

Refer to the financial statements of The Home Depot in Appendix A and Lowe's in Appendix B at the end of this book, or download the annual reports from the *Cases* section of the text's Web site at www.mhhe.com/LLPW1e.

*Required:*

Lowe's

1. Use the companies' balance sheets to determine the amounts in the accounting equation (A = L + OE) for the most recent year. Is Lowe's or The Home Depot larger in terms of total assets?

2. Does Lowe's have more or less current liabilities than The Home Depot?

3. On the balance sheet, Lowe's reports inventories of $7,611,000,000. Does this amount represent the expected selling price? Why or why not?

4. Has financing for Lowe's investment in assets primarily come from liabilities or stockholders' equity? Thinking back to Chapter 1, what does this imply about the risk assumed by Lowe's investors (corporate owners), relative to those investing in The Home Depot?

## CP2-3 Examining the Balance Sheet: Internet-Based Team Research                    LO2, 4

As a team, select an industry to analyze. Using your Web browser, each team member should acquire the annual report or 10-K for one publicly traded company in the industry, with each member selecting a different company. (See CP1-3 in Chapter 1 for a description of possible resources for these tasks.)

### Required:

1. On an individual basis, each team member should write a short report that lists the following information.
   a. The date of the balance sheet.
   b. The major noncurrent asset accounts and any significant changes in them.
   c. The major noncurrent liability accounts and any significant changes in them.
   d. Any significant changes in total owners' equity (stockholders' equity for a corporation).
   e. Whether financing for the assets primarily comes from liabilities or stockholders' (owners') equity.

2. Then, as a team, write a short report comparing and contrasting your companies using the preceding information. Discuss any similarities across the companies that you as a team observe, and provide potential explanations for any differences discovered.

## CP2-4 Examining Real-Life Fraud: Ethical Reasoning, Critical Thinking, and Communication          LO2

In the world of financial fraud, the "Ponzi scheme" is famous. Here is the story behind how the scam received its name. Charles Ponzi started the Security Exchange Company on December 26, 1919. He thought he had discovered a way to purchase American stamps in a foreign country at significantly lower amounts than they were worth in the United States. He claimed that his idea was so successful that anyone who gave money to his company would be repaid their original loan plus 50 percent interest within 90 days. Friends and family quickly offered their money to Ponzi, and they were handsomely rewarded, being repaid their original loan and the 50 percent interest within just 45 days.

Thanks to an article in *The New York Times*, word spread quickly about Ponzi's business, attracting thousands of people seeking a similar payback. He might have had a successful business had his idea actually worked. The problem, however, was that it did not. The 50 percent interest paid to early investors did not come from the profits of a successful underlying business idea (which did not even exist) but instead was obtained fraudulently from funds contributed by later lenders. Eventually, the Ponzi scheme collapsed on August 10, 1920, after an auditor examined his accounting records.

### Required:

1. Assume that on December 27, 1919, each of Ponzi's first three lenders provided $5,000 to his company. Use the basic accounting equation to show the effects of these transactions on December 27, 1919.

2. If the first two lenders are repaid their original loan amounts plus the 50 percent interest promised to them, how much cash is left in Ponzi's business to repay the third lender? Given what you discovered, how was it possible for Ponzi's company to remain in "business" for over eight months?

3. Whom did Ponzi's scheme hurt?

**Epilogue:** After taking in nearly $15 million from 40,000 people, Ponzi's company failed with just $1.5 million in total assets. Ponzi spent four years in prison before jumping bail to become involved in fraudulently selling swampland in Florida. We're not kidding.

## CP2-5 Analyzing a Mini Case: Ethical Reasoning, Critical Thinking, and Communication          LO1, 2, 4

You work as an accountant for a small land development company that desperately needs additional financing to continue in business. Your company's president is meeting with the manager of a local bank at the end of the month to try to obtain this financing. The president has approached you with two ideas to improve the company's reported financial position.

- First, he claims that because a big part of the company's value comes from its knowledgeable and dedicated employees, you should report their "intellectual abilities" as an asset on the balance sheet.
- Second, he claims that although the local economy is doing poorly and almost no one is buying land or new houses, he is optimistic that eventually things will turn around. For this reason, he asks you to continue reporting the company's land on the balance sheet at its cost rather than the much lower amount that real estate appraisers say it is really worth.

*Required:*

1. Thinking back to Chapter 1, why do you think the president is so concerned with the amount of assets reported on the balance sheet?
2. What accounting concept introduced in Chapter 2 relates to the president's first suggestion to report intellectual abilities as an asset?
3. What accounting concept introduced in Chapter 2 relates to the president's second suggestion to continue reporting land at its cost?
4. If you were to do as he asks, whom would the president's suggestions hurt? What should you do?

**LO1, 4**    **CP2-6 Evaluating the Reliability of a Balance Sheet: Financial Analysis and Critical Thinking**

Betsey Jordan asked a local bank for a $50,000 loan to expand her small company. The bank asked Betsey to submit a financial statement of the business to supplement the loan application. Betsey prepared the following balance sheet.

| Balance Sheet June 30, 2010 | |
|---|---|
| **Assets** | |
| Cash | $    9,000 |
| Inventory | 30,000 |
| Equipment | 46,000 |
| Personal residence (monthly payments, $2,800) | 300,000 |
| Remaining assets | 20,000 |
| Total assets | $405,000 |
| **Liabilities** | |
| Short-Term debt to suppliers | $  62,000 |
| Long-Term debt on equipment | 38,000 |
| Total debt | 100,000 |
| Owner's equity | 305,000 |
| Total liabilities and owner's equity | $405,000 |

*Required:*

The balance sheet has several flaws. However, there is at least one major deficiency. Identify it and explain its significance.

**LO1, 4**    **CP2-7 Preparing and Analyzing a Balance Sheet: Decision Making as a Financial Analyst**

Your best friend from home writes you a letter about an investment opportunity that has come her way. Her neighbor Josh Dewey is establishing a new business and has asked her to lend the business $20,000 (her recent inheritance from her great-aunt's estate). Your friend has never loaned money to a company before and, knowing that you are a financial analyst, asks that you look over the balance sheet and send her some advice. An *unaudited* balance sheet, in only moderately good form, is enclosed with the letter:

**Dewey, Cheetum, and Howe Services**
**Balance Sheet**
**For the Year Ending December 31, 2009**

| | |
|---|---|
| Accounts receivable | $ 8,000 |
| Cash | 1,000 |
| Inventory | 8,000 |
| Furniture and fixtures | 52,000 |
| Delivery truck | 12,000 |
| Buildings (estimated market value) | 98,000 |
| **Total assets** | **$179,000** |
| Accounts payable | $ 16,000 |
| Payroll taxes payable | 13,000 |
| Notes payable (due in three years) | 15,000 |
| Mortgage payable | 50,000 |
| **Total liabilities** | **$ 94,000** |
| J. Dewey, capital | $ 85,000 |
| **Total owners' equity** | **$ 85,000** |

The only footnote states that the building was recently purchased for $60,000 and carries a mortgage (shown in the liability section). The footnote further states that, in the company president's opinion, the building is "easily worth $98,000."

*Required:*

1. Draft a new balance sheet for your friend, correcting any errors you note. (If any of the account balances need to be corrected, you may need to adjust the owners' equity balance correspondingly.) If no errors or omissions exist, state so.

2. Write a letter to your friend explaining the changes you made to the balance sheet, if any, and offer your comments on the company's apparent financial condition based only on this information. Suggest other information your friend might want to review before coming to a final decision on whether to lend the money to the business.

# 3

# Operating a Business and the Income Statement

## LEARNING OBJECTIVES

**After studying this chapter, you should be able to:**

**LO1**  Recognize common income statement accounts.

**LO2**  Describe a typical business operating cycle and explain the necessity for the time period assumption.

**LO3**  Explain the accrual basis of accounting and apply the revenue and matching principles to measure income.

**LO4**  Apply transaction analysis to examine and record the effects of operating activities on the financial statements.

**LO5**  Understand the purpose of a trial balance and prepare a simple income statement.

Lectured slideshow–LP3-1
www.mhhe.com/LLPW1e

96

# Focus Company: PIZZA AROMA, Ithaca, NY

# "Opening the Doors"

In Chapter 2, Mauricio Rosa, owner-manager of Pizza Aroma, established his new gourmet pizza business. Using money he had contributed plus a loan from the bank, he purchased the ovens, counters, tables, chairs, and other equipment he needed to run the business. His next step was to make the critical decisions that would draw customers into the restaurant and provide them with the service that would keep them coming back—while making sure, of course, that he made a profit. What would Mauricio's operating strategy be?

Before launching into a discussion on strategy, we need to know something about the pizza business. Pizza is a global food, generating more than $32 billion[1] in sales each year. In this business, which depends heavily on human capital, companies compete through marketing and product quality. Mauricio insists on using only the highest quality, freshest ingredients, which requires an almost fanatical focus on testing ingredients and checking product quality—right down to the size of the black olives and the fat content of the meat and mozzarella.

Competition is stiff. The large pizza chains, mainly Pizza Hut, Papa John's, and Domino's, all tout the quality of their ingredients. In fact, Papa John's International, Inc., includes its motto, "Better Ingredients. Better Pizza" in its corporate logo. The big chains also use national radio and television advertising along with extensive local marketing efforts to draw in customers.

Pizza Aroma's uniqueness lies in its gourmet pizza, a niche the big chains do not emphasize. To succeed, then, Pizza Aroma needs an operating strategy that maintains quality while keeping costs low and operations simple. It also needs to advertise to the local community and colleges in novel and aggressive ways.

---

[1] http://www.pmq.com/mag/20061112/article.php?story=pizzapower2006.

For information about a business's recent financial performance—that is, the relative success of its operating activities—owners and other users of the financial statements turn to the income statement. In this chapter, we will focus on Pizza Aroma's operating activities as reflected on its income statement. To read and understand the income statement, you need to answer the following questions:

- How do business activities affect the income statement?
- How are business activities measured?
- How are business activities reported on the income statement?

## ORGANIZATION OF THE CHAPTER

| RECOGNIZE OPERATING ACTIVITIES | MEASURE OPERATING ACTIVITIES | PREPARE AN INCOME STATEMENT |
|---|---|---|
| • Income Statement Accounts<br>• Operating Cycle | • Cash-Based Measurements<br>• Accrual Basis Accounting<br>• Expanded Transaction Analysis Model<br>• Analysis of Pizza Aroma's Transactions | • Unadjusted Trial Balance<br>• Classified Income Statements<br>• Limitations of the Income Statement |

# RECOGNIZE OPERATING ACTIVITIES

## Income Statement Accounts

### Revenues

A business earns revenues when it exchanges its products or services for cash or a customer's promise to pay cash, called Accounts Receivable. When Pizza Aroma sells pizza to consumers, it has earned revenue. Pizza Aroma's primary revenue is **Pizza Revenue.**

**Revenues earned**

### Expenses

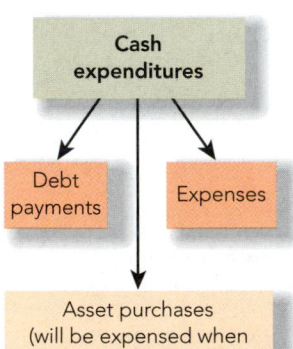

Some students confuse cash payments and **expenses.** Cash payments are outflows of money for any purpose, whether to buy equipment, pay off a bank loan, or pay a utility bill. An expense is defined more narrowly. If revenues are the positive benefits from the sale of a good or service, then expenses are the costs incurred to generate those revenues. Anything a business **uses** to generate revenues during a period is an expense, regardless of when it was or will be paid for.

What does this distinction mean for Pizza Aroma? It hires and pays employees to make and serve food. It uses electricity to operate equipment and light its facilities. It advertises its pizza and uses food ingredients and paper supplies during the course of business. All of these expenses are necessary to generate revenues. Some of them may result in cash payments at the time they are incurred; others may be incurred before or after cash is

**Expenses incurred to generate revenues**

paid. In short, not all cash payments (such as buying equipment for cash) are expenses, and expenses are necessary to generate revenues.

Account titles may vary to fit a business's specific types of revenues and expenses. When you are trying to determine the account title to use for a particular revenue or expense, think about the nature of the business and the type of activity involved. For example, when a consulting firm provides services to clients, it earns Consulting Fee Revenue or Fee Revenue—not Sales Revenue because it did not sell a product to a customer. See Exhibit 3.1 for a partial chart of accounts for a pizza restaurant.

## Operating Cycle

The long-term objective of any business is to **turn cash into more cash.** If a company is to stay in business, this excess cash must be generated from operations—that is, from the activities for which the business was established—rather than from borrowing money or selling long-lived assets.

Companies buy inventory, supplies, and services such as electricity, as well as the work of their employees. Then they sell the inventory or services to customers. The period that begins when the company pays for its inventory and services and ends when customers pay cash to the company is known as the operating (cash-to-cash) cycle. The length of time for a company to complete its operating cycle depends on the nature of the business. The graphic in Exhibit 3.2 illustrates the operating cycle for Pizza Aroma that is typical of most businesses.

Pizza Aroma's operating cycle is relatively short, from the expenditure of cash to purchase ingredients from suppliers to the sale of pizzas to customers for cash. Some companies, however, pay for inventory well before they sell it. Toys R Us, for example, builds up its inventory months before the year-end holiday season. The company borrows funds from banks to pay for the inventory and then repays the loans with interest after receiving cash from customers. Many other companies receive cash from customers well after a sale takes place. For example, furniture stores such as Ethan Allen often sell furniture to customers who make regular monthly payments over several months or years.

The operating cycle is repeated continuously until a company goes out of business. However, decision makers need to receive information about a company's financial condition and performance periodically. To measure the income for a specific period, accountants follow the time period assumption,[2] which states that the long life of a company can be reported over shorter periods, such as months, quarters, and years.

_____

[2] This is the fourth assumption accountants make as part of the key concepts for external financial reporting as shown in Exhibit 2.12 at the end of Chapter 2.

> **Learning Objective 2**
>
> Describe a typical business operating cycle and explain the necessity for the time period assumption.

| Exhibit 3.1 | Chart of Accounts (partial—income statement accounts only) |
| --- | --- |

| Account Number | Account Name |
| --- | --- |
| 401 | Pizza Revenue |
| 410 | Investment Revenue |
| 450 | Gain on Sale of Assets |
| 501 | Wages Expense |
| 503 | Supplies Expense |
| 506 | Utilities Expense |
| 507 | Telephone Service Expense |
| 510 | Rent Expense |
| 511 | Insurance Expense |
| 512 | Advertising Expense |
| 530 | Interest Expense |
| 550 | Loss on Sale of Assets |

**Coach's Tip**

Notice that the account numbers for income statement accounts start in the 400s. A full chart of accounts would start with assets (100s), liabilities (200s), and owner's equity accounts (300s) as shown in Exhibit 2.2.

| Exhibit 3.2 | Typical Business Operating Cycle |

**Typical Operating Cycle**

Purchase goods and services

Pay cash to suppliers

Sell goods and services to customers

Receive cash from customers

# MEASURE OPERATING ACTIVITIES

**Learning Objective 3**

Explain the accrual basis of accounting and apply the revenue and matching principles to measure income.

Two issues arise in reporting periodic income to users:

1. **Recognition. When** should the effects of operating activities be recognized (recorded)?
2. **Measurement. What amounts** should be recognized (recorded)?

## Cash-Based Measurements

**CASH BASIS**
**Income Measurement**

Revenues ( = cash receipts)
– Expenses ( = cash payments)

Net Income (cash basis)

How do you know if you are better off today than you were last month? You probably determine your personal financial position by looking at the cash balance in your bank account. That is, you measure your financial performance as the difference between your cash balance at the beginning of the period and your cash balance at the end of the period. If you have a higher cash balance at the end of the period than you did at the beginning, your cash receipts exceeded your cash disbursements. As long as you received and disbursed cash shortly before or after the activities that caused those cash flows, your increasing or decreasing cash balance will provide a timely measure of your financial performance. Reporting your income on this basis, called **cash basis accounting**, is usually good enough.

Cash basis accounting does not measure financial performance well when a company conducts transactions using credit rather than cash, however. Credit often introduces a significant delay between the time when an activity occurs and the time that it impacts a bank account balance. If you are paid for work once a month, for example, your hard work does not show up in your cash balance until the end of the month. Similarly, if you use a credit card to purchase groceries, those transactions will not affect your cash balance until you pay the bill the following month.

Because most businesses, including Pizza Aroma, use credit for their transactions, cash basis accounting is not likely to correspond to the business activities that actually occur during a given period. For this reason, generally accepted accounting principles do not allow cash basis accounting to be used for purposes of external reporting. Instead, generally accepted accounting principles require accrual basis accounting.

# Accrual Basis Accounting

In accrual basis accounting (accrual accounting), a business recognizes revenues and expenses when the transaction that causes them occurs, not necessarily when the business receives or is paid cash. That is, **revenues are recognized when they are earned and expenses are recognized when they are incurred** (that is, when goods or services attained from others are used). The two basic accounting principles that determine when revenues and expenses are recorded under accrual basis accounting are the **revenue principle** and the **matching principle.**

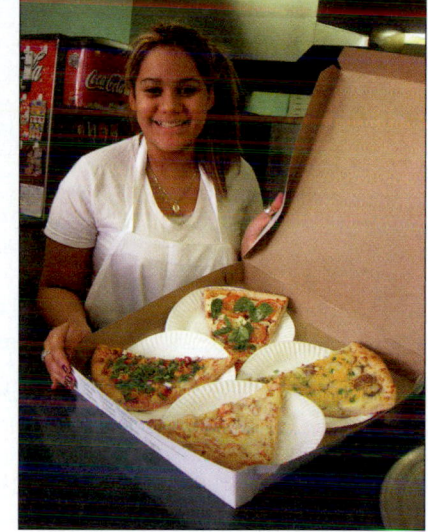

> **ACCRUAL BASIS**
> **Income Measurement**
> Revenues ( = when earned)
> − Expenses ( = when incurred)
> _____
> Net Income (accrual basis)

## Revenue Measurement

Under accrual basis accounting, a business recognizes revenues (that is, measures and records them) when it delivers goods or services to the customer. The generally accepted accounting principle that businesses use to determine when to recognize revenue is the revenue principle. This rule requires recognizing (recording and reporting) revenue in the period in which it is earned.[3] Most businesses recognize revenue at the point of delivery of goods or services—when the business transfers title, risks, and rewards of ownership to the customer. As is typical in the fast-food industry, Pizza Aroma recognizes its revenues from pizza sales **at the time it delivers its gourmet pizza to customers,** as ordered.

Although businesses expect to receive cash in exchange for their goods and services, the timing of cash receipts from customers does not dictate when businesses report revenues. Instead, the key to determining when to report revenue is whether the business has done what it promised to do. Thus, cash can be received (1) in the **same** period as, (2) in a period **before,** or (3) in a period **after** the goods or services are delivered (see Exhibit 3.3). Let's see how to handle each of these cases.

 **1**   Cash is received in the same period as the goods or services are delivered. This is the most common timing for Pizza Aroma because most customers pay cash within a few minutes of receiving their pizza. Pizza Aroma delivers the pizza to the customer as ordered, earning revenue in the process. In the exchange, Pizza Aroma receives cash from the customer.

**Coach's Tip**

When a revenue is earned, an income statement account (a revenue) and a balance sheet account are affected.

_____

[3] Under the revenue principle, four criteria or conditions must normally be met for revenue to be recognized. If *any* of these criteria is *not* met, revenue normally is *not* recognized and cannot be recorded. The four criteria are (1) the company has delivered goods or performed services (that is, the company has performed), (2) the business has persuasive evidence of an arrangement with the customer, (3) the price is fixed or determinable, and (4) the collection of cash is reasonably assured.

**Exhibit 3.3**    **Recording Revenues versus Cash Receipts**

If a business delivers goods or services *here*

TIME →

Revenue is recorded *here*

Cash is received . . . *here*   or   *here*   or   *here.*

2    1    3

**2**   **Cash is received before the goods or services are delivered.** This situation occurs, for example, when Pizza Aroma accepts a large order for an event to be held next month. Pizza Aroma requires the customer to provide a deposit when the order is placed. Cash is recorded when it is received. However, because Pizza Aroma has not yet delivered the pizza, it records no revenue. So how does Pizza Aroma account for the other half of the transaction? The promise to deliver pizza in the future creates a liability called Unearned Revenue equal to the amount of the cash deposit received in advance. When Pizza Aroma delivers the pizza next month, it will record and report Pizza Revenue on the income statement and reduce the Unearned Revenue account because the liability has been satisfied. Following the revenue principle, a business records revenue when it delivers goods or services, not when it receives cash.

**3**   **Cash is received after the goods or services are delivered.** To boost business, Pizza Aroma also arranges to deliver pizza "on account" to some customers, such as college departments. That is, the restaurant delivers pizza when it is ordered and then bills the customer at the end of the month. When a business sells goods or services on account, it earns the revenue when it delivers the goods or services. Pizza Aroma earns revenue when it delivers the pizza, even though it has not yet received cash. At that time, Pizza Aroma records both the revenue and an asset called Accounts Receivable that represents the customer's promise to pay for the deliveries in the future. When the customer pays its monthly bill, Pizza Aroma will increase its Cash account and decrease Accounts Receivable.

As you can see, under the revenue principle, a business records revenue when it earns it **regardless of when it receives the cash.** It may receive cash before, during, or after the time it earned revenue. When the business receives cash before or after earning it, it makes one entry on the date it earns revenue and another on the date it receives cash. To cement this principle in your memory, practice applying it in the following exercise.

---

## SELF-STUDY PRACTICE

Following are sample transactions for the Florida Flippers, a scuba diving and instruction business owned by Paul Knepper. If revenue is to be recognized in **June,** indicate the title of the revenue account and the amount of revenue to be recognized.

| Activity | Revenue Account Title | Amount of Revenue Earned in June |
|---|---|---|
| (a)  In June, Florida Flippers provided $32,000 in diving instruction to customers for cash. | | |
| (b)  In June, new customers paid $8,200 cash for diving trips Florida Flippers will provide; it made $5,200 in trips in June and will provide the rest in July. | | |
| (c)  In June, customers paid $3,900 cash for instruction they received in May. | | |

*After you have finished, check your answers with the solutions at the bottom of the page.*

### Coach's Tip

When you are not given the title of a revenue account, simply create a title that fits with the activity. For example, providing diving instruction results in the business earning Diving Instruction Revenue.

---

## Expense Measurement

Owners encounter a variety of expenses when running a business. For example, to provide food service to customers, Pizza Aroma must use electricity to light the restaurant, keep fresh ingredients cool, and heat the ovens to the proper temperature. As with revenue

---

**Solution to Self-Study Practice**

| | Revenue Account Title | Amount of Revenue Earned in June | |
|---|---|---|---|
| (a) | Diving Instruction Revenue | $32,000 | |
| (b) | Diving Trip Revenue | 5,200 | The remaining $3,000 will be earned in July. |
| (c) | No revenue in June; revenue was earned in May | — | |

recognition, these expenses are recorded as incurred (that is, when goods or services obtained from others are used), **regardless of when Pizza Aroma pays cash.** Under accrual basis accounting, businesses apply the matching principle, which requires that the expenses incurred to generate revenues should be recognized (that is, recorded) in the same period **to match costs with the benefits.** And as with revenue recognition, expenses may be paid for (1) at the same time as, (2) before, or (3) after they are incurred to generate revenue (see Exhibit 3.4).

**1** **Cash is paid in the same period** as the expense is incurred to generate revenue. Expenses are sometimes paid for in the period that they arise. For example, Pizza Aroma spends $50 cash now for balloons to celebrate its grand opening. It would report this cost on this month's income statement because the balloons were used for an activity occurring this month. In other words, the benefits of incurring the cost are entirely used up within the current accounting period.

**2** **Cash is paid before the expense is incurred to generate revenue.** It is common for businesses to pay for something that provides benefits only in future periods. For example, Pizza Aroma buys paper plates now but does not use them until next month. The asset Supplies is increased and Cash is decreased. Given the matching principle, the expense from using these supplies is reported next month when the supplies are used to earn revenue, not now when purchased. This month, the supplies represent an asset because they will benefit a future period. When they are used later, Supplies Expense will be reported on next month's income statement and the asset Supplies will decrease. Similar situations arise when a company prepays rent or insurance.

**3** **Cash is paid after the cost is incurred to generate revenue.** Although rent is paid and supplies are purchased before they are used, many costs are paid after receiving and using goods or services. For example, Pizza Aroma uses electricity to heat the ovens and light the restaurant this month but does not pay for its electricity usage until next month. Because the cost of the electricity relates to revenues earned now, it represents an expense that will be reported on this month's income statement. Because the cost has not yet been paid at the end of the month, a liability called Accounts Payable is created. Similar situations arise when employees work in the current period but are not paid their wages until the following period.

Now practice applying the matching principle by completing the exercise on the next page.

# Expanded Transaction Analysis Model

We have discussed the variety of business activities affecting the income statement and how to measure them. Now we will determine how to record those business activities in the accounting system and reflect them in the financial statements. To do so, we need to expand the transaction analysis model presented in Chapter 2 to include operating activities.

**Learning Objective 4**

Apply transaction analysis to examine and record the effects of operating activities on the financial statements.

Exhibit 3.4   Recording Expenses versus Cash Payments

Video 3-1
www.mhhe.com/LLPW1e

**SELF-STUDY PRACTICE**

The following sample transactions are for Florida Flippers, a scuba diving and instruction business owned by Paul Knepper. Apply the matching principle. If an expense is incurred in **June**, indicate the title of the expense account and the amount of expense to be recognized.

| Activity | Expense Account Title | Amount of Expense Incurred in June |
|---|---|---|
| (a) At the beginning of June, Florida Flippers paid a total of $6,000 cash for insurance for the months of June, July, and August. | | |
| (b) In June, Florida Flippers paid $4,000 in wages to employees who worked in June. | | |
| (c) In June, Florida Flippers paid $2,400 for electricity used in May. | | |

*After you have finished, check your answers with the solutions at the bottom of the page.*

The complete transaction model includes all five accounting elements: Assets, Liabilities, Owner's Equity, Revenues, and Expenses (see Exhibit 3.5). Recall that revenues increase owner's equity, expenses decrease owner's equity, and revenue minus expenses equals net income. That means that when net income is positive, owner's equity increases; when net income is negative, owner's equity decreases.

Before illustrating the use of the expanded transaction analysis model, we should emphasize the following points:

- Revenues increase net income, which increases owner's equity. Because owner's equity increases on the credit side of the accounting equation, revenues have **credit** balances.
- Expenses decrease net income, thus decreasing owner's equity. Therefore, expenses have **debit** balances (they are the opposite of the credit balance of owner's equity). To increase an expense, then, you debit it, which decreases net income and owner's equity. When you debit an expense account, you are adding to the expenses.
- When revenues exceed expenses, the business reports net income, increasing owner's equity. However, when expenses exceed revenues, a net loss results, decreasing owner's equity.

**Revenues**

Increase net income and owner's equity

↑ with Credits

Accounts have credit balances

**Expenses**

Decrease net income and owner's equity

↑ with Debits

Accounts have debit balances

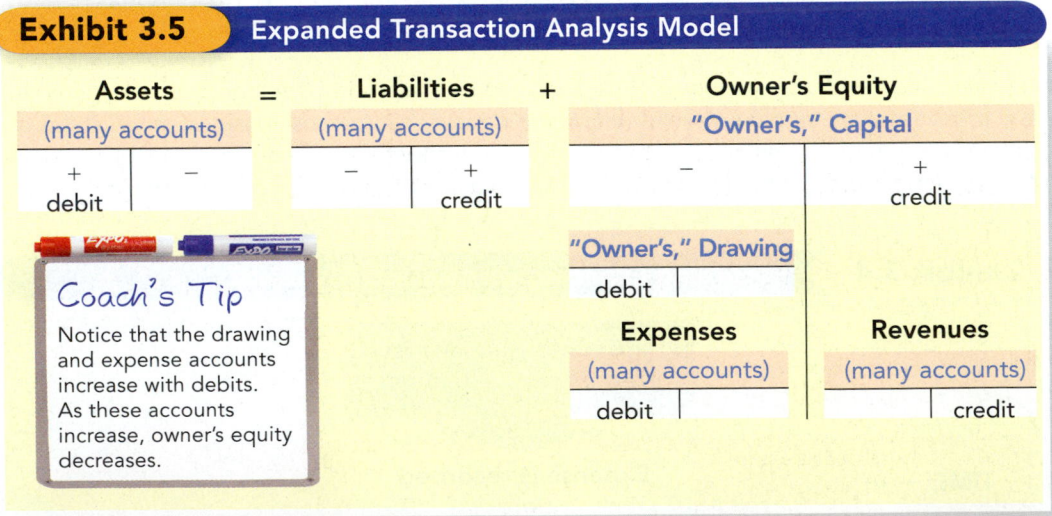

**Exhibit 3.5    Expanded Transaction Analysis Model**

**Coach's Tip**

Notice that the drawing and expense accounts increase with debits. As these accounts increase, owner's equity decreases.

**Solution to Self-Study Practice**

| | Expense Account Title | Amount of Expense Incurred in June | |
|---|---|---|---|
| (a) | Insurance Expense | $2,000 | The remaining $4,000 will be used in July and August. |
| (b) | Wages Expense | 4,000 | |
| (c) | No expense in June; expense was incurred in May | — | |

- Although the owner's drawing account is **not reported on the income statement,** it decreases owner's equity as expenses do. Therefore, the drawing account has a **debit** balance. As the owner withdraws more funds from the business, the drawing account balance increases with debits that, in turn, reduce the owner's overall stake in the business.

Furthermore, as you saw in Chapter 2, where we introduced the transaction analysis model:

1. All accounts can increase or decrease, although revenues and expenses tend to increase throughout the period. For balance sheet accounts on the left side of the accounting equation, the increase symbol + is written on the left side of the T-account. For balance sheet accounts on the right side of the accounting equation, the increase symbol + is written on the right side of the T-account.
2. Debits are written on the left side and credits on the right side of each T-account.
3. Every transaction affects at least two accounts.

Owner's Drawing Account

Decreases owner's equity

↑ with Debits

Account has a debit balance

To analyze transactions using the expanded transaction analysis model, follow these steps:

Step
- **Identify the accounts affected** by name, making sure that at least two accounts change.
- **Classify them by type of account** (A for asset, L for liability, OE for owner's equity, R for revenue, or E for expense).
- **Determine the direction of the effect** (an increase [+] or decrease [−] in each account). Include also the direction of the effect of revenues and expenses on owner's equity (e.g., [+E, −OE]).

Step
- **Verify** that the **accounting equation (A = L + OE) remains in balance.**
- **Verify** that the total dollar value of the **debits** in the transaction **equals** the total dollar value of the **credits.**

Refer to the expanded transaction analysis model shown in Exhibit 3.5 until you can construct it without assistance. **Study the exhibit carefully to make sure you understand the impact of revenues and expenses on both the balance sheet and the income statement.**

---

**SELF-STUDY PRACTICE**

For each of the following accounts, complete the table. Indicate whether:

1. The account will be reported on the balance sheet (B/S) or income statement (I/S).
2. The account is classified as a current asset (CA), noncurrent asset (NCA), current liability (CL), noncurrent liability (NCL), owner's equity (OE), revenue (R), or expense (E).
3. The account usually has a debit (Dr) or credit (Cr) balance.

| Account | (1) Balance Sheet or Income Statement | (2) Classification on Financial Statement | (3) Debit or Credit Balance |
|---|---|---|---|
| a. Interest Expense | _____ | _____ | _____ |
| b. Cost of Goods Sold | _____ | _____ | _____ |
| c. Unearned Revenue | _____ | _____ | _____ |
| d. Equipment | _____ | _____ | _____ |
| e. Wages Payable | _____ | _____ | _____ |
| f. Sales Revenue | _____ | _____ | _____ |
| g. Prepaid Insurance | _____ | _____ | _____ |
| h. Accounts Receivable | _____ | _____ | _____ |
| i. Fee Revenue | _____ | _____ | _____ |
| j. Supplies Expense | _____ | _____ | _____ |

*After you have finished, check your answers with the solutions at the bottom of the next page.*

Beginning balances in balance sheet accounts come from the May 7 trial balance in Exhibit 2.9.

↓

Postings to T-Accounts

# Analysis of Pizza Aroma's Transactions

The dough was ready; the sauce was simmering; the mushrooms, other veggies, and meats had been carefully sliced; the mozzarella had been perfectly grated; and several gourmet pizzas were in the oven when Mauricio opened the doors of Pizza Aroma on the first day of business. The restaurant had a good first month. Now let's analyze, record, and post the effects of the first month's operating activities to the T-accounts. Chapter 2 showed how to analyze transactions (a) to (g); we will continue the analysis with transaction (h).

| + | Cash (A) | − |
|---|---|---|
| Bal. | 5,200 | |
| (h) | 12,000 | |
| | 17,200 | |

**(h) During May, Pizza Aroma sells pizza to restaurant customers for $12,000 cash.**

| | | Debit | Credit |
|---|---|---|---|
| (h) | Cash (+A) | 12,000 | |
| | Pizza Revenue (+R, +OE) | | 12,000 |

| − | Pizza Revenue (R) | + |
|---|---|---|
| | | 0 Beg. |
| | | 12,000 (h) |
| | | 12,000 |

| Assets | = | Liabilities | + | Owner's Equity |
|---|---|---|---|---|
| (h) Cash    +12,000 | | | | Pizza Revenue (+R)  +12,000 |

Equality checks: (1) Debits $12,000 = Credits $12,000; (2) the accounting equation is in balance.

| + | Accounts Receivable (A) | − |
|---|---|---|
| Bal. | 0 | |
| (i) | 2,000 | |
| | 2,000 | |

**(i) Pizza Aroma delivers $2,000 in pizza on account to various college departments.**

| | | Debit | Credit |
|---|---|---|---|
| (i) | Accounts Receivable (+A) | 2,000 | |
| | Pizza Revenue (+R, +OE) | | 2,000 |

| − | Pizza Revenue (R) | + |
|---|---|---|
| | | 0 Beg |
| | | 12,000 (h) |
| | | 2,000 (i) |
| | | 14,000 |

| Assets | = | Liabilities | + | Owner's Equity |
|---|---|---|---|---|
| (i) Accounts Receivable  +2,000 | | | | Pizza Revenue (+R)  +2,000 |

Equality checks: (1) Debits $2,000 = Credits $2,000; (2) the accounting equation is in balance.

| + | Cash (A) | − |
|---|---|---|
| Bal. | 5,200 | |
| (h) | 12,000 | |
| (j) | 600 | |
| | 17,800 | |

**(j) Fraternities place large orders for end-of-May graduation events and for mid-June reunion weekend, giving Pizza Aroma $600 cash on deposit in mid-May.**

| | | Debit | Credit |
|---|---|---|---|
| (j) | Cash (+A) | 600 | |
| | Unearned Revenue (+L) | | 600 |

| − | Unearned Revenue (L) | + |
|---|---|---|
| | | 0 Beg. |
| | | 600 (j) |
| | | 600 |

| Assets | = | Liabilities | + | Owner's Equity |
|---|---|---|---|---|
| (j) Cash    +600 | | Unearned Revenue    +600 | | |

Equality checks: (1) Debits $600 = Credits $600; (2) the accounting equation is in balance.

Solution to Self-Study Practice

| | Account | Balance Sheet or Income Statement | Classification on Financial Statement | Debit or Credit Balance |
|---|---|---|---|---|
| a. | Interest Expense | I/S | E | Dr |
| b. | Cost of Goods Sold | I/S | E | Dr |
| c. | Unearned Revenue | B/S | CL | Cr |
| d. | Equipment | B/S | NCA | Dr |
| e. | Wages Payable | B/S | CL | Cr |
| f. | Sales Revenue | I/S | R | Cr |
| g. | Prepaid Insurance | B/S | CA | Dr |
| h. | Accounts Receivable | B/S | CA | Dr |
| i. | Fee Revenue | I/S | R | Cr |
| j. | Supplies Expense | I/S | E | Dr |

**(k) Pizza Aroma purchases $3,000 of additional supplies, paying $2,200 in cash and owing the rest on account.**

| (k) | | Debit | Credit |
|---|---|---|---|
| (k) | Supplies (+A) | 3,000 | |
| | Cash (−A) | | 2,200 |
| | Accounts Payable (+L) | | 800 |

| Assets | = | Liabilities | + | Owner's Equity |
|---|---|---|---|---|
| (k) Supplies +3,000 | | Accounts Payable +800 | | |
| Cash −2,200 | | | | |

Equality checks: (1) Debits $3,000 = Credits $3,000; (2) the accounting equation is in balance.

| + | Supplies (A) | − |
|---|---|---|
| Bal. 2,000 | | |
| (k) 3,000 | | |
| 5,000 | | |

| + | Cash (A) | − |
|---|---|---|
| Bal. 5,200 | | |
| (h) 12,000 | 2,200 | (k) |
| (j) 600 | | |
| 15,600 | | |

| − | Accounts Payable (L) | + |
|---|---|---|
| | 4,000 | Bal. |
| | 800 | (k) |
| | 4,800 | |

**(l) Pizza Aroma pays $800 cash for newspaper advertising during May.**

| (l) | | Debit | Credit |
|---|---|---|---|
| (l) | Advertising Expense (+E,−OE) | 800 | |
| | Cash (−A) | | 800 |

| Assets | = | Liabilities | + | Owner's Equity |
|---|---|---|---|---|
| (l) Cash −800 | | | | Advertising Expense (+E) −800 |

Equality checks: (1) Debits $800 = Credits $800; (2) the accounting equation is in balance.

| + | Cash (A) | − |
|---|---|---|
| Bal. 5,200 | | |
| (h) 12,000 | 2,200 | (k) |
| (j) 600 | 800 | (l) |
| 14,800 | | |

| | Advertising | |
|---|---|---|
| + | Expense (E) | − |
| Beg. 0 | | |
| (l) 800 | | |
| 800 | | |

**(m) Pizza Aroma pays $1,000 cash to employees for work during May.**

| (m) | | Debit | Credit |
|---|---|---|---|
| (m) | Wages Expense (+E, −OE) | 1,000 | |
| | Cash (−A) | | 1,000 |

| Assets | = | Liabilities | + | Owner's Equity |
|---|---|---|---|---|
| (m) Cash −1,000 | | | | Wages Expense (+E) −1,000 |

Equality checks: (1) Debits $1,000 = Credits $1,000; (2) the accounting equation is in balance.

| + | Cash (A) | − |
|---|---|---|
| Bal. 5,200 | | |
| (h) 12,000 | 2,200 | (k) |
| (j) 600 | 800 | (l) |
| | 1,000 | (m) |
| 13,800 | | |

| + | Wages Expense (E) | − |
|---|---|---|
| Beg 0 | | |
| (m) 1,000 | | |
| 1,000 | | |

**(n) College departments pay Pizza Aroma $1,300 cash owed on their accounts (see event [i]).**

| (n) | | Debit | Credit |
|---|---|---|---|
| (n) | Cash (+A) | 1,300 | |
| | Accounts Receivable (−A) | | 1,300 |

| Assets | = | Liabilities | + | Owner's Equity |
|---|---|---|---|---|
| (n) Cash +1,300 | | | | |
| Accounts Receivable −1,300 | | | | |

Equality checks: (1) Debits $1,300 = Credits $1,300; (2) the accounting equation is in balance.

| + | Cash (A) | − |
|---|---|---|
| Bal. 5,200 | | |
| (h) 12,000 | 2,200 | (k) |
| (j) 600 | 800 | (l) |
| (n) 1,300 | 1,000 | (m) |
| 15,100 | | |

| | Accounts | |
|---|---|---|
| + | Receivable (A) | − |
| Bal. 0 | | |
| (i) 2,000 | 1,300 | (n) |
| 700 | | |

| + | Cash (A) | – |
|---|---|---|
| Bal. 5,200 | | |
| (h) 12,000 | 2,200 | (k) |
| (j)    600 | 800 | (l) |
| (n) 1,300 | 1,000 | (m) |
| | 600 | (o) |
| 14,500 | | |

| Telephone Service | | |
|---|---|---|
| + | Expense (E) | – |
| Beg.    0 | | |
| (o)  600 | | |
| 600 | | |

**(o) Pizza Aroma receives and pays a $600 bill for telephone service in May.**

| | | Debit | Credit |
|---|---|---|---|
| (o) | Telephone Service Expense (+E, –OE) | 600 | |
| | Cash (–A) | | 600 |

| Assets | = | Liabilities | + | Owner's Equity |
|---|---|---|---|---|
| | | | | Telephone Service |
| (o) Cash    –600 | | | | Expense (+E)    –600 |

Equality checks: (1) Debits $600 = Credits $600; (2) the accounting equation is in balance.

| + | Cash (A) | – |
|---|---|---|
| Bal. 5,200 | | |
| (h) 12,000 | 2,200 | (k) |
| (j)    600 | 800 | (l) |
| (n) 1,300 | 1,000 | (m) |
| | 600 | (o) |
| | 2,400 | (p) |
| 12,100 | | |

| Prepaid | | |
|---|---|---|
| + | Insurance (A) | – |
| Bal.    0 | | |
| (p) 2,400 | | |
| 2,400 | | |

**(p) At the end of May, Pizza Aroma purchases insurance for its restaurant equipment, paying $2,400 cash to cover the months of June, July, and August.**

| | | Debit | Credit |
|---|---|---|---|
| (p) | Prepaid Insurance (+A) | 2,400 | |
| | Cash (–A) | | 2,400 |

| Assets | = | Liabilities | + | Owner's Equity |
|---|---|---|---|---|
| (p) Prepaid Insurance   +2,400 | | | | |
| Cash                    –2,400 | | | | |

Equality checks: (1) Debits $2,400 = Credits $2,400; (2) the accounting equation is in balance.

| + | Cash (A) | – |
|---|---|---|
| Bal. 5,200 | | |
| (h) 12,000 | 2,200 | (k) |
| (j)    600 | 800 | (l) |
| (n) 1,300 | 1,000 | (m) |
| | 600 | (o) |
| | 2,400 | (p) |
| | 3,000 | (q) |
| 9,100 | | |

| M. Rosa | | |
|---|---|---|
| + | Drawing (OE) | – |
| Beg.    0 | | |
| (q) 3,000 | | |
| 3,000 | | |

**(q) Owner Mauricio Rosa withdraws $3,000 in cash at the end of May.**

| | | Debit | Credit |
|---|---|---|---|
| (q) | M. Rosa, Drawing (–OE) | 3,000 | |
| | Cash (–A) | | 3,000 |

| Assets | = | Liabilities | + | Owner's Equity |
|---|---|---|---|---|
| (q) Cash    –3,000 | | | | M. Rosa, Drawing    –3,000 |

Equality checks: (1) Debits $3,000 = Credits $3,000; (2) the accounting equation is in balance.

**Coach's Tip**

**NOTICE!** The drawing account has a debit balance even though it is an owner's equity account because it reduces owner's equity. As the drawing account increases (is debited), owner's equity decreases.

See Exhibit 3.6 for a summary of the journal entries (h) through (q) and all T-accounts as of May 31.

**Exhibit 3.6**    **Summary of Pizza Aroma's Journal Entries and T-Accounts**

Pizza Aroma
Journal Entries
May 8–31

| | | Debit | Credit |
|---|---|---|---|
| (h) | Cash (+A) | 12,000 | |
| | Pizza Revenue (+R, +OE) | | 12,000 |
| (i) | Accounts Receivable (+A) | 2,000 | |
| | Pizza Revenue (+R, +OE) | | 2,000 |
| (j) | Cash (+A) | 600 | |
| | Unearned Revenue (+L) | | 600 |
| (k) | Supplies (+A) | 3,000 | |
| | Cash (−A) | | 2,200 |
| | Accounts Payable (+L) | | 800 |
| (l) | Advertising Expense (+E, −OE) | 800 | |
| | Cash (−A) | | 800 |
| (m) | Wages Expense (+E, −OE) | 1,000 | |
| | Cash (−A) | | 1,000 |
| (n) | Cash (+A) | 1,300 | |
| | Accounts Receivable (−A) | | 1,300 |
| (o) | Telephone Service Expense (+E, −OE) | 600 | |
| | Cash (−A) | | 600 |
| (p) | Prepaid Insurance (+A) | 2,400 | |
| | Cash (−A) | | 2,400 |
| (q) | M. Rosa, Drawing (−OE) | 3,000 | |
| | Cash (−A) | | 3,000 |

*(continued)*

**Exhibit 3.6** Summary of Pizza Aroma's Journal Entries and T-Accounts (*continued*)

Pizza Aroma
T-Accounts
May 31

### Assets

| + | Cash (A) | | − |
|---|---|---|---|
| Beg. | 0 | | |
| (a) | 30,000 | 4,800 | (c) |
| (b) | 20,000 | 33,000 | (d) |
| (h) | 12,000 | 1,000 | (f) |
| (j) | 600 | 6,000 | (g) |
| (n) | 1,300 | 2,200 | (k) |
| | | 800 | (l) |
| | | 1,000 | (m) |
| | | 600 | (o) |
| | | 2,400 | (p) |
| | | 3,000 | (q) |
| | 9,100 | | |

| + | Investments (A) | − |
|---|---|---|
| Beg. | 0 | |
| (g) | 6,000 | |
| | 6,000 | |

| | Accounts | |
| + | Receivable (A) | − |
|---|---|---|
| Beg. | 0 | |
| (i) | 2,000 | 1,300 (n) |
| | 700 | |

| + | Supplies (A) | − |
|---|---|---|
| Beg. | 0 | |
| (e) | 2,000 | |
| (k) | 3,000 | |
| | 5,000 | |

| + | Prepaid Rent (A) | − |
|---|---|---|
| Beg. | 0 | |
| (c) | 4,800 | |
| | 4,800 | |

| | Prepaid | |
| + | Insurance (A) | − |
|---|---|---|
| Beg. | 0 | |
| (p) | 2,400 | |
| | 2,400 | |

| + | Equipment (A) | − |
|---|---|---|
| Beg. | 0 | |
| (d) | 36,000 | |
| | 36,000 | |

### Liabilities

| − | Accounts Payable (L) | + |
|---|---|---|
| | | 0 Beg. |
| (f) 1,000 | 3,000 | (d) |
| | 2,000 | (e) |
| | 800 | (k) |
| | 4,800 | |

| − | Unearned Revenue (L) | + |
|---|---|---|
| | | 0 Beg. |
| | 600 | (j) |
| | 600 | |

| − | Notes Payable (L) | + |
|---|---|---|
| | | 0 Beg. |
| | 20,000 | (b) |
| | 20,000 | |

### Expenses

| + | Wages Expense (E) | − |
|---|---|---|
| Beg. | 0 | |
| (m) | 1,000 | |
| | 1,000 | |

| | Telephone Service | |
| + | Expense (E) | − |
|---|---|---|
| Beg. | 0 | |
| (o) | 600 | |
| | 600 | |

| | Advertising | |
| + | Expense (E) | − |
|---|---|---|
| Beg. | 0 | |
| (l) | 800 | |
| | 800 | |

### Owner's Equity

| | M. Rosa, | |
| − | Capital (OE) | + |
|---|---|---|
| | | 0 Beg. |
| | 30,000 | (a) |
| | 30,000 | |

| | M. Rosa, | |
| + | Drawing (OE) | − |
|---|---|---|
| Beg. | 0 | |
| (q) | 3,000 | |
| | 3,000 | |

### Revenues

| − | Pizza Revenue (R) | + |
|---|---|---|
| | | 0 Beg. |
| | 12,000 | (h) |
| | 2,000 | (i) |
| | 14,000 | |

Analyze each of Florida Flippers' selected transactions in **June**; then record the journal entries and post the effects to the T-accounts. Be sure to check to make sure that the accounting equation remains in balance and that debits equal credits in each journal entry.

**SELF-STUDY PRACTICE**

(a) In June, new customers paid Florida Flippers $8,200 in cash for diving trips; $5,200 was for trips made in June, and the rest is for trips that will be provided in July.

(b) In June, customers paid $3,900 in cash for instruction they received in May.

(c) At the beginning of June, Florida Flippers paid a total of $6,000 cash for insurance to cover the months of June, July, and August.

(d) In June, Florida Flippers paid $4,000 in wages to employees who worked in June.

**Coach's Tip**

- For transaction (b), a journal entry had been recorded in May for what the customers owed to Florida Flippers.
- For transaction (c), record the entry at what it represents on the date of the exchange. Because the payment is for future insurance coverage, the entire amount is an asset.

**Journal Entries**

| | Debit | Credit |
|---|---|---|
| (a) | | |
| | | |
| (b) | | |
| | | |
| (c) | | |
| | | |
| (d) | | |
| | | |

**Effects**

Assets = Liabilities + Owner's Equity

(a)

(b)

(c)

(d)

**T-Accounts**

| + Cash (A) − |
|---|
| Beg. 25,000 |

| + Accounts Receivable (A) − |
|---|
| Beg. 4,500 |

| − Unearned Revenue (L) + |
|---|
| 0  Beg. |

| − Diving Trip Revenue (R) + |
|---|
| 0  Beg. |

| + Prepaid Insurance (A) − |
|---|
| Beg. 0 |

| + Wages Expense (E) − |
|---|
| Beg. 0 |

*After you have finished, check your answers with the solutions at the bottom of the page.*

**Solution to Self-Study Practice**

**Journal Entries**

| | | Debit | Credit |
|---|---|---|---|
| (a) | Cash (+A) | 8,200 | |
| | Diving Trip Revenue (+R, +OE) | | 5,200 |
| | Unearned Revenue (+L) | | 3,000 |
| (b) | Cash (+A) | 3,900 | |
| | Accounts Receivable (−A) | | 3,900 |
| (c) | Prepaid Insurance (+A) | 6,000 | |
| | Cash (−A) | | 6,000 |
| (d) | Wages Expense (+E, −OE) | 4,000 | |
| | Cash (−A) | | 4,000 |

| Assets | | = | Liabilities | | + | Owner's Equity | |
|---|---|---|---|---|---|---|---|
| (a) Cash | +8,200 | | Unearned Revenue | +3,000 | | Diving Trip Revenue (+R) | +5,200 |
| (b) Cash | +3,900 | | | | | | |
| Accts. Rec. | −3,900 | | | | | | |
| (c) Prepd. Ins. | +6,000 | | | | | | |
| Cash | −6,000 | | | | | | |
| (d) Cash | −4,000 | | | | | Wages Expense (+E) | −4,000 |

| + | Cash (A) | − |
|---|---|---|
| Beg. | 25,000 | |
| (a) | 8,200 | 6,000 (c) |
| (b) | 3,900 | 4,000 (d) |
| | 27,100 | |

| + | Accounts Receivable (A) | − |
|---|---|---|
| Beg. | 4,500 | |
| | | 3,900 (b) |
| Bal. | 600 | |

| − | Unearned Revenue (L) | + |
|---|---|---|
| | | 0  Beg. |
| | | 3,000 (a) |
| | | 3,000 |

| − | Diving Trip Revenue (R) | + |
|---|---|---|
| | | 0  Beg. |
| | | 5,200 (a) |
| | | 5,200 |

| + | Prepaid Insurance (A) | − |
|---|---|---|
| Beg. | 0 | |
| (c) | 6,000 | |
| | 6,000 | |

| + | Wages Expense (E) | − |
|---|---|---|
| Beg. | 0 | |
| (d) | 4,000 | |
| | 4,000 | |

# PREPARE AN INCOME STATEMENT

## Unadjusted Trial Balance

Mauricio had a busy first month, and his gourmet pizzas became the rage. He was eager to find out how Pizza Aroma had performed financially. Did it make a profit, or even do better than expected? Laurie showed Mauricio the trial balance on May 31, 2009, but cautioned him that it was "unadjusted," meaning that some revenues and expenses had not yet been recorded. Mauricio needed to count the remaining supplies to determine how much the restaurant had used in May. Laurie needed to allocate the Prepaid Rent cost used in May, and she had to contact the bank to find out how much the investments had earned for the month. With that warning, Mauricio reviewed the unadjusted trial balance in Exhibit 3.7.

Based on the amounts in the trial balance, Laurie next showed Mauricio the preliminary income statement she had prepared, cautioning him again that it was unadjusted.

## Classified Income Statements

As you learned in Chapter 2, the assets and liabilities shown on the balance sheet are classified as either current or noncurrent. This classification provides useful information to external decision makers who want to assess the timing and probability of the business's future cash flows. Similarly, the revenues and expenses shown on the income statement can be classified

| Exhibit 3.7 | Unadjusted Trial Balance | | PIZZA AROMA |
|---|---|---|---|

**Pizza Aroma**
**Unadjusted Trial Balance**
**On May 31, 2009**

| | Debit | Credit |
|---|---|---|
| Cash | 9,100 | |
| Investments | 6,000 | |
| Accounts Receivable | 700 | |
| Supplies | 5,000 | |
| Prepaid Rent | 4,800 | |
| Prepaid Insurance | 2,400 | |
| Equipment | 36,000 | |
| Accounts Payable | | 4,800 |
| Unearned Revenue | | 600 |
| Notes Payable | | 20,000 |
| M. Rosa, Capital | | 30,000 |
| M. Rosa, Drawing | 3,000 | |
| Pizza Revenue | | 14,000 |
| Investment Revenue | | 0 |
| Wages Expense | 1,000 | |
| Supplies Expense | 0 | |
| Utilities Expense | 0 | |
| Telephone Service Expense | 600 | |
| Rent Expense | 0 | |
| Insurance Expense | 0 | |
| Advertising Expense | 800 | |
| Interest Expense | 0 | |
| **Totals** | **69,400** | **69,400** |

Balance sheet accounts (Cash through M. Rosa, Capital)

Income statement accounts (Pizza Revenue through Interest Expense)

**Coach's Tip**

The revenue and expense accounts will be adjusted in Chapter 4.

to create a more useful statement of financial performance. The three major classifications of amounts shown on the income statement are Operating Revenues, Operating Expenses, and Other Items.

## Operating Revenues and Expenses

Operating revenues result from the sale of goods or services—that is, from the primary or central mission of the business. Mattel earns operating revenues by manufacturing toys and games. American Eagle Outfitters earns operating revenues by selling clothing. Pizza Aroma earns operating revenues by selling pizza.

Likewise, operating expenses are the costs directly related to the generation of operating revenues. Mattel's primary operating expense is Cost of Goods Sold, which represents the inventory that Mattel "uses up" to generate revenues. Pizza Aroma's largest operating expenses are Wages Expense and Supplies Expense, as is typical in the food service industry.

## Other Items

Not all activities that affect the income statement are central to a business's operations. These **peripheral** (normal but not central) transactions are classified as Other Items on the income statement. For example, any interest or dividends that Pizza Aroma earns on its investments are stated as Investment Revenue. Because earning investment revenue is not the central focus of Pizza Aroma's business, its Investment Revenue account is classified under Other Items.

Similarly, the cost of borrowing money, called Interest Expense, is classified under Other Items. Incurring interest expense is not a central operating activity of most businesses except for financial institutions.

The separation of operating revenues and expenses from other items enables financial statement users to identify activities that should be ongoing as opposed to those that may not be. See Exhibit 3.8 for Pizza Aroma's classified income statement for May prepared using the amounts in the unadjusted trial balance.

| Exhibit 3.8 | Classified Income Statement: (from the unadjusted trial balance) | PIZZA AROMA |
|---|---|---|

### Pizza Aroma
### Income Statement (unadjusted)
### For the Month Ended May 31, 2009

| | |
|---|---:|
| **Operating Revenues** | |
| Pizza revenue | $14,000 |
| Total operating revenues | 14,000 |
| **Operating Expenses** | |
| Wages expense | 1,000 |
| Supplies expense | 0 |
| Utilities expense | 0 |
| Telephone service expense | 600 |
| Rent expense | 0 |
| Insurance expense | 0 |
| Advertising expense | 800 |
| Total operating expenses | 2,400 |
| **Operating Income** | 11,600 |
| **Other Items** | |
| Investment revenue | 0 |
| Interest expense | (0) |
| **Net Income** | $11,600 |

## Limitations of the Income Statement

There are many misconceptions about the meaning of net income. The most common one is that net income equals the amount of cash the business generated during the period. While that is the way that most of us think about our own income for a period, it is not the way to measure revenues and expenses on a company's income statement.

A second, related misconception is that a company's net income represents the change in the company's value during the period. While a company's net income is one source of value to the company, many other determinants of its value are not included in the income statement. A good example is the increase in the value of Pizza Aroma's name as its reputation for making great pizza grows.

A third common misconception is that the measurement of income involves only counting. Proper counting is critical to income measurement, but estimation also plays a role. For example, Pizza Aroma's equipment will not last forever. Instead, it will be "used up" over time to generate the company's revenue. It should therefore be expensed over the period in which it is used. Doing so requires an estimate of the period over which each category of equipment will be used. We will discuss this particular example in Chapter 4; many other examples of the role of estimates in income measurement will arise in later chapters.

## Spotlight On ETHICS

### Why All the Scandals?

You may have read about numerous accounting scandals, such as those at Enron and WorldCom (now owned by Verizon), in which managers have been accused of "cooking the books." Why did they do it? The simple answer is greed. Companies whose earnings have fallen often experience a decline in their stock prices, which usually leads to pay reductions or even job losses for senior executives. When a company is actually performing poorly, greed may lead some managers to falsify revenues and hide expenses to make it look like the company is still doing well.

While this sometimes fools people for a short time, it rarely works in the long run and often leads to very bad consequences. A few cases involving faulty revenue and expense accounting follow. As you look at these, imagine what it must have been like to be Bernie Ebbers—the person who received a 25-year prison sentence at the age of 65. It is probably just as bad as being Barry Minkow who was sentenced to 25 years in jail at the age of 21.

| The CEO | The Fraud | Conviction/Plea | The Outcome |
|---|---|---|---|
| **Bernie Ebbers,** 65 WorldCom | Recorded operating expenses as if they were assets; resulted in the largest fraud in U.S. history | Convicted July 2005 | Sentenced to 25 years |
| **Sanjay Kumar,** 44 Computer Associates | Recorded sales in the wrong accounting period | Pleaded guilty April 2006 | Sentenced to 12 years |
| **Martin Grass,** 49 Rite Aid Corporation | Recorded rebates from drug companies before they were earned | Pleaded guilty June 2003 | Sentenced to 8 years |
| **Barry Minkow,** 21 ZZZZ Best | Made up customers and sales to show profits when, in reality, the company was a sham | Convicted December 1988 | Sentenced to 25 years |

In this chapter, you learned how to measure and report revenues and expenses for the accounting period as a starting point for determining net income. The next step is to adjust the financial statements so that they will be complete and up to date at the end of the accounting period. The adjustment process is the main topic of Chapter 4, in which Laurie will help Mauricio to adjust Pizza Aroma's financial statements for May.

# Demonstration Case

This is a continuation of the Goodbye Grass case, a lawn care service business, introduced in Chapter 2. Steve Delancey established the company in April 2010 as a sole proprietorship and purchased property and equipment. The following is the April 30, 2010, balance sheet based only on the activities for establishing the business (from Chapter 2):

### GOODBYE GRASS
### Balance Sheet
### At April 30, 2010

| Assets | | Liabilities | |
|---|---|---|---|
| *Current Assets* | | *Current Liabilities* | |
| Cash | $ 3,800 | Accounts Payable | $    400 |
| Note Receivable | 1,250 | Notes Payable | 4,000 |
| Total Current Assets | 5,050 | Total Current Liabilities | 4,400 |
| Equipment | 4,600 | | |
| Land | 3,750 | **Owner's Equity** | |
| | | S. Delancey, Capital | 9,000 |
| Total Assets | $13,400 | Total Liabilities and Owner's Equity | $13,400 |

The following activities occurred during May 2010 (the next month):

a.  Purchased and used gasoline for mowers and edgers, paying $90 in cash at a local gas station.

b.  Received $1,600 cash from the city in early May in advance for lawn maintenance service for May through August ($400 each month). The entire amount is to be recorded as Unearned Revenue (a liability).

c.  Purchased in early May $300 of insurance covering six months, May through October. The entire payment is to be recorded as Prepaid Insurance (an asset).

d.  Mowed lawns for residential customers who are billed every two weeks. Earned a total of $5,200 of service in May and billed customers.

e.  Received payments of $3,500 from residential customers on their accounts.

f.  Paid wages every two weeks. Total cash paid in May was $3,900.

g.  Received a bill for $320 from the local gas station for additional gasoline purchased on account and used in May. The bill will be paid in June.

h.  Paid $40 interest (one month's interest) in mid-May on notes owed to XYZ Lawn Supply.

i.  Paid $100 on accounts payable.

j.  Steve Delancey withdrew $2,000 from the business.

### *Required:*

1.  Analyze activities (a)–(j) to determine their effects on the basic accounting equation (Assets = Liabilities + Owner's Equity).

2.  Prepare journal entries to record the transactions identified among activities (a)–(j).

3.  Summarize the effects of each transaction in the appropriate T-accounts. Before entering these effects, set up T-accounts for Cash; Accounts Receivable; Note Receivable; Prepaid Insurance; Equipment; Land; Accounts Payable; Unearned Revenue; Notes Payable; S. Delancey, Capital; S. Delancey, Drawing; Mowing Revenue; Wages Expense; Fuel Expense; and Interest Expense. The beginning balance in each T-account should be the amount shown on the preceding April 30 balance sheet or $0 if the account does not appear on the balance sheet. After posting the journal entries to the T-accounts, compute ending balances for each T-account.

4.  Use the amounts in the T-accounts to prepare an unadjusted trial balance for Goodbye Grass at May 31, 2010.

5.  Prepare a *classified* (operating revenues and expenses separated from other revenues and expenses) income statement for May 2010 based on the unadjusted trial balance.

After completing the requirements, check your answers with the following suggested solution.

## Suggested Solution

1.   Analyze transactions

| Assets | | = | Liabilities | | + | Owner's Equity | | |
|---|---|---|---|---|---|---|---|---|
| (a) Cash | − 90 | | | | | Fuel Expense (+E) | | − 90 |
| (b) Cash | + 1,600 | | Unearned Revenue | + 1,600 | | | | |
| (c) Cash | − 300 | | | | | | | |
| Prepaid Insurance | + 300 | | | | | | | |
| (d) Accounts Receivable | + 5,200 | | | | | Mowing Revenue (+R) | | + 5,200 |
| (e) Cash | + 3,500 | | | | | | | |
| Accounts Receivable | − 3,500 | | | | | | | |
| (f) Cash | − 3,900 | | | | | Wages Expense (+E) | | − 3,900 |
| (g) | | | Accounts Payable | + 320 | | Fuel Expense (+E) | | − 320 |
| (h) Cash | − 40 | | | | | Interest Expense (+E) | | − 40 |
| (i) Cash | − 100 | | Accounts Payable | − 100 | | | | |
| (j) Cash | − 2,000 | | | | | S. Delancey, Drawing | | − 2,000 |

2.   Journal entries

| | | Debit | Credit |
|---|---|---|---|
| (a) | Fuel Expense (+E, −OE) | 90 | |
| | Cash (−A) | | 90 |
| (b) | Cash (+A) | 1,600 | |
| | Unearned Revenue (+L) | | 1,600 |
| (c) | Prepaid Insurance (+A) | 300 | |
| | Cash (−A) | | 300 |
| (d) | Accounts Receivable (+A) | 5,200 | |
| | Mowing Revenue (+R, +OE) | | 5,200 |
| (e) | Cash (+A) | 3,500 | |
| | Accounts Receivable (−A) | | 3,500 |
| (f) | Wages Expense (+E, −OE) | 3,900 | |
| | Cash (−A) | | 3,900 |
| (g) | Fuel Expense (+E, −OE) | 320 | |
| | Accounts Payable (+L) | | 320 |
| (h) | Interest Expense (+E, −OE) | 40 | |
| | Cash (−A) | | 40 |
| (i) | Accounts Payable (−L) | 100 | |
| | Cash (−A) | | 100 |
| (j) | S. Delancey, Drawing (−OE) | 2,000 | |
| | Cash (−A) | | 2,000 |

3.   T-accounts

| Assets | = | Liabilities | + | Owner's Equity |

**Assets**

**+   Cash (A)   –**

| Bal. | 3,800 | | |
|---|---|---|---|
| (b) | 1,600 | 90 | (a) |
| (e) | 3,500 | 300 | (c) |
| | | 3,900 | (f) |
| | | 40 | (h) |
| | | 100 | (i) |
| | | 2,000 | (j) |
| Bal. | 2,470 | | |

**+ Accounts Receivable (A) –**

| Beg. | 0 | | |
|---|---|---|---|
| (d) | 5,200 | 3,500 | (e) |
| Bal. | 1,700 | | |

**+ Note Receivable (A) –**

| Bal. | 1,250 | |
|---|---|---|
| Bal. | 1,250 | |

**+ Prepaid Insurance (A) –**

| Beg. | 0 | |
|---|---|---|
| (c) | 300 | |
| Bal. | 300 | |

**+   Equipment (A)   –**

| Bal. | 4,600 | |
|---|---|---|
| Bal. | 4,600 | |

**+   Land (A)   –**

| Bal. | 3,750 | |
|---|---|---|
| Bal. | 3,750 | |

**Liabilities**

**– Accounts Payable (L) +**

| | | 400 | Bal. |
|---|---|---|---|
| (i) | 100 | 320 | (g) |
| | | 620 | Bal. |

**– Unearned Revenue (L) +**

| | 0 | Beg. |
|---|---|---|
| | 1,600 | (b) |
| | 1,600 | Bal. |

**– Notes Payable (L) +**

| | 4,000 | Bal. |
|---|---|---|
| | 4,000 | Bal. |

**Owner's Equity**

**S. Delancey,**
**–   Capital (OE)   +**

| | 9,000 | Bal. |
|---|---|---|
| | 9,000 | Bal. |

**S. Delancey,**
**+   Drawing (OE)   –**

| Beg. | 0 | |
|---|---|---|
| (j) | 2,000 | |
| Bal. | 2,000 | |

**Expenses**

**+  Wages Expense (E)  –**

| Beg. | 0 | |
|---|---|---|
| (f) | 3,900 | |
| Bal. | 3,900 | |

**+   Fuel Expense (E)   –**

| Beg. | 0 | |
|---|---|---|
| (a) | 90 | |
| (g) | 320 | |
| Bal. | 410 | |

**+ Interest Expense (E) –**

| Beg. | 0 | |
|---|---|---|
| (h) | 40 | |
| Bal. | 40 | |

**Revenues**

**– Mowing Revenue (R) +**

| | 0 | Beg. |
|---|---|---|
| | 5,200 | (d) |
| | 5,200 | Bal. |

4.   Unadjusted trial balance

**GOODBYE GRASS**
**Unadjusted Trial Balance**
**As of May 31, 2010**

| Account Name | Debits | Credits |
|---|---|---|
| Cash | 2,470 | |
| Accounts Receivable | 1,700 | |
| Note Receivable | 1,250 | |
| Prepaid Insurance | 300 | |
| Equipment | 4,600 | |
| Land | 3,750 | |
| Accounts Payable | | 620 |
| Unearned Revenue | | 1,600 |
| Notes Payable | | 4,000 |
| S. Delancey, Capital | | 9,000 |
| S. Delancey, Drawing | 2,000 | |
| Mowing Revenue | | 5,200 |
| Wages Expense | 3,900 | |
| Fuel Expense | 410 | |
| Interest Expense | 40 | |
| Totals | 20,420 | 20,420 |

5.  Unadjusted income statement

---

**GOODBYE GRASS**
Income Statement (unadjusted)
For the Month Ended May 31, 2010

| | |
|---|---:|
| **Operating Revenues** | |
| Mowing Revenue | $5,200 |
| Total operating revenues | 5,200 |
| **Operating Expenses** | |
| Wages Expense | 3,900 |
| Fuel Expense | 410 |
| Total operating expenses | 4,310 |
| **Operating Income** | 890 |
| **Other Items** | |
| Interest Expense | (40) |
| **Net Income** | $ 850 |

---

# Chapter Summary

### LO1  Recognize common income statement accounts. p. 98

- **Income Statement Accounts**
  The income statement reports net income that is calculated by combining:
      **Revenues.** Amounts charged to customers for sales of goods or services provided.
      **Expenses.** Costs of business activities undertaken to earn revenues.
  See Exhibit 3.1 for an expanded list of account titles.

### LO2  Describe a typical business operating cycle and explain the necessity for the time period assumption. p. 99

- **Operating Cycle**
  The process by which a company acquires and pays for goods and services and then sells goods and services to customers who pay cash to the company (the cash-to-cash cycle). The length of time to complete the cycle varies by company.

- **Cash-Based Measurements**
  Financial performance is measured as the difference between cash received and cash paid during a period. However, cash basis accounting does not measure financial performance well when transactions are conducted using credit rather than cash.

### LO3  Explain the accrual basis of accounting and apply the revenue and matching principles to measure income. p. 100

- **Accrual Basis Accounting**
  The two key concepts underlying accrual basis accounting and the income statement are:
      **Revenue principle.** Recognize (record) revenues when they are earned.
      **Matching principle.** Recognize (record) expenses when they are incurred in generating revenue.

### LO4  Apply transaction analysis to examine and record the effects of operating activities on the financial statements. p. 103

- **Expanded Transaction Analysis Model**
  The expanded transaction analysis model includes revenues, expenses, and the owner's drawing account as subcategories of owner's capital.

  - Revenues increase with credits, thus increasing owner's equity.
  - Expenses increase with debits, thus decreasing owner's equity.
  -

**LO5 Understand the purpose of a trial balance and prepare a simple income statement. p. 112**

- **Unadjusted Trial Balance**
  The unadjusted trial balance is a list of all accounts and their unadjusted balances and is used to check on the equality of recorded debits and credits.
- **Classified Income Statement**
  Revenues and expenses are classified into Operating Revenues, Operating Expenses, and Other Items on a classified income statement.
  - Operating revenues result from the sale of goods or services—the business's central mission.
  - Operating expenses are costs that are directly related to generating operating revenues in the same period.
  - Other items include revenues, expenses, gains, and losses that are not the business's primary mission. Examples include interest revenue, interest expense, and gains or losses on the sale of long-lived assets.
- **Limitations of the Income Statement**
  - Because of the application of accrual accounting concepts to measure revenues and expenses in a period, net income will **not** equal cash generated by a business during the same period. Under accrual accounting, revenues are recorded when earned and expenses are recorded when incurred regardless of the timing of the cash receipts and payments.
  - Net income is **not** the change in the value of a company during the period. Net income is one source of value, but the income statement does not include many other determinants of value change, such as the increase in value of a company's reputation for quality.
  - Estimation plays a key role in measuring income for a period.

# Key Terms

Accrual Basis Accounting (accrual accounting) (p. 101)
Cash Basis Accounting (p. 100)

Matching Principle (p. 103)
Operating (Cash-to-Cash) Cycle (p. 99)
Revenue Principle (p. 101)

Time Period Assumption (p. 99)
Unadjusted Trial Balance (p. 112)

**See complete glossary in the back of text.**

# Questions

1. Indicate the income statement equation and define each element.

2. When accounting was developed in the 14th and 15th centuries, businesses had very short lives. For instance, a business might have been created for a single shipment of goods from Europe to North America. After delivering the goods and distributing profits among those who financed the shipment, the business ceased to exist. In more recent centuries, businesses began to experience longer lives. Identify the accounting concept needed when accounting for businesses with long lives. Explain what this concept means and why it is necessary for modern-day accounting.

3. Define accrual basis accounting and contrast it with cash basis accounting.

4. Why is it appropriate to use a cash basis of accounting in your personal life but not in the business world?

5. What does it mean to "recognize" an accounting transaction?

6. When is revenue typically recognized under accrual basis accounting?

7. Explain the matching principle.

8. Explain why owner's equity increases by revenues and decreases by expenses.

9. Explain why revenues are recorded as credits and expenses as debits.

10. Complete the following table by entering either *debit* or *credit* in each cell:

| Item | Increase | Decrease |
|---|---|---|
| Revenues | | |
| Expenses | | |

11. Complete the following table by entering either *increase* or *decrease* in each cell:

| Item | Debit | Credit |
|---|---|---|
| Revenues | | |
| Expenses | | |

12. What is the difference between Accounts Receivable and Revenue?

13. What is the difference between Wages Payable and Wages Expense?

14. For each of the following situations, indicate whether it represents an accounting error and explain why it is or is

not an error. Also indicate whether a trial balance would indicate that an error exists for each situation.

a. Cash received from a customer who is paying on his or her account owed to the business was debited to Accounts Receivable and credited to Cash.

b. Revenue was recognized when a customer purchased a gift certificate for future use.

c. An expense was recorded as an asset.

d. The debit side of a journal entry was recorded in the accounts, but the credit side was not.

e. A business owner purchased a new car for personal use, but the business did not record this.

15. What are three limitations of the income statement that often lead to misconceptions?

# Multiple Choice

1. Which of the following items is **not** a specific account in a company's chart of accounts?
   a. Accounts Receivable.
   b. Net Income.
   c. Revenue.
   d. Unearned Revenue.

   Quiz 3-1
   www.mhhe.com/LLPW1e

2. Which of the following accounts normally has a debit balance?
   a. Unearned Revenue.
   b. Rent Expense.
   c. Retained Earnings.
   d. Sales Revenue.

3. The matching principle controls
   a. Where on the income statement expenses should be presented.
   b. How costs are allocated between Cost of Goods Sold (sometimes called Cost of Sales) and general and administrative expenses.
   c. The ordering of current assets and current liabilities on the balance sheet.
   d. When costs are recognized as expenses on the income statement.

4. When should businesses that sell gift certificates to customers report revenue?
   a. When the gift certificate is sold and cash is received.
   b. When the gift certificate is used by the customer.
   c. At the end of the year in which the gift certificate is sold.
   d. None of the above.

5. How will a manager's decision to record a payment as an asset rather than as an expense affect net income for the business in the current period?
   a. Net income will be higher.
   b. Net income will be lower.
   c. Net income will not be affected by this decision.
   d. The effect cannot be determined.

6. When should a company report the cost of an insurance policy as an expense?
   a. When the company first signs the policy.
   b. When the company pays for the policy.

c. When the company receives the benefits from the policy over its period of coverage.

d. When the company receives payments from the insurance company for its insurance claims.

7. When expenses exceed revenues in a given period (and there are no gains or losses),
   a. Owner's equity will not be impacted.
   b. Owner's equity will be increased.
   c. Owner's equity will be decreased.
   d. One cannot determine the impact on owner's equity without additional information.

8. Which account is *least* likely to be debited when revenue is recorded?
   a. Accounts Payable
   b. Accounts Receivable
   c. Cash
   d. Unearned Revenue

9. Webby Company reported the following amounts on its income statement: Service Revenues, $31,600; Interest Expense, $300; and Net Income, $1,600. If the only other account reported on the income statement was for "selling expenses," what is its amount?
   a. $ 2,200
   b. $29,700
   c. $30,000
   d. $30,900

10. Which of the following is the entry a law firm would record when it receives a payment from a new client that will be earned when the firm provides services in the future?
    a. *Debit* to Accounts Receivable; *credit* to Legal Services Revenue.
    b. *Debit* to Unearned Revenue; *credit* to Legal Services Revenue.
    c. *Debit* to Cash; *credit* to Unearned Revenue.
    d. *Debit* to Unearned Revenue; *credit* to Cash.

| Solutions to Multiple-Choice Questions |
| --- |
| 1. b    2. b    3. d    4. b    5. a    6. c    7. c |
| 8. a    9. b    10. c |

# Mini Exercises    Available with McGraw-Hill's Homework Manager

## M3-1 Reporting Cash Basis versus Accrual Basis Income                    LO1, 3, 5
Mostert Music Company had the following transactions in March:

- *a.* Sold music lessons to customers for $10,000; received $6,000 in cash and the rest on account.
- *b.* Paid $600 in wages for the month.
- *c.* Received a $200 bill for utilities that will be paid in April.
- *d.* Received $1,000 from customers as deposits on music lessons to be given in April.
  Complete the following statements:

| Cash Basis Income Statement | |
| --- | --- |
| **Revenues** | |
| Cash sales | $ |
| Customer deposits | |
| **Expenses** | |
| Wages paid | |
| Net income | $ |

| Accrual Basis Income Statement | |
| --- | --- |
| **Revenues** | |
| Sales to customers | $ |
| **Expenses** | |
| Wages expense | |
| Utilities expense | |
| Net income | $ |

## M3-2 Identifying Revenues                                                LO3
The following transactions are July 2011 activities of Ben's Extreme Bowling Center owned by Ben Baxter, who owns and operates several bowling centers. If revenue is to be recognized in **July,** indicate the amount. If revenue is not to be recognized in July, explain why.

| Activity | Amount or Explanation |
| --- | --- |
| *a.* Collected $12,000 from customers for games played in July. | |
| *b.* Billed a customer for $250 for a party held at the center on the last day of July. The bill is to be paid in August. | |
| *c.* Received $1,000 in July from customers who purchased bowling equipment on account in June. | |
| *d.* Received from the men's and women's bowling leagues advance payments totaling $1,500 for the fall season that starts in September. | |

## M3-3 Identifying Expenses                                                LO3
The following transactions are July 2011 activities of Ben's Extreme Bowling Center owned by Ben Baxter, who owns and operates several bowling centers. If an expense is to be recognized in **July,** indicate the amount. If an expense is not to be recognized in July, explain why.

| Activity | Amount or Explanation |
| --- | --- |
| *e.* Paid $1,500 to plumbers for repairing a broken pipe in the restrooms in July. | |
| *f.* Paid $2,000 for the June electricity bill (received and recorded as an expense at the end of June). | |
| *g.* Paid $5,475 to employees for work in July. | |
| *h.* Received the July electricity bill for $2,500 that will be paid in August. | |

**LO1, 4**    **M3-4 Recording Revenues**
For each transaction in M3-2, write the journal entry using the format shown in the chapter.

**LO1, 4**    **M3-5 Recording Expenses**
For each transaction in M3-3, write the journal entry using the format shown in the chapter.

**LO4**    **M3-6 Determining the Financial Statement Effects of Operating Activities Involving Revenues**
The following transactions are July 2011 activities of Ben's Extreme Bowling Center owned by Ben Baxter, who owns and operates several bowling centers. For each of the following transactions, complete the spreadsheet, indicating the amount and effect (+ for increase and − for decrease) of each transaction. Write NE if there is no effect. The first transaction is provided as an example.

| Transaction | BALANCE SHEET | | | INCOME STATEMENT | | |
| --- | --- | --- | --- | --- | --- | --- |
| | Assets | Liabilities | Owner's Equity | Revenues | Expenses | Net Income |
| a. Collected $12,000 from customers for games played in July. | +12,000 | NE | +12,000 | +12,000 | NE | +12,000 |
| b. Billed a customer for $250 for a party held at the center on the last day of July. The bill is to be paid in August. | | | | | | |
| c. Received $1,000 in July from customers who purchased bowling equipment on account in June. | | | | | | |
| d. Received from the men's and women's bowling leagues advance payments totaling $1,500 for the fall season that starts in September. | | | | | | |

**LO4**    **M3-7 Determining the Financial Statement Effects of Operating Activities Involving Expenses**
The following transactions are July 2011 activities of Ben's Extreme Bowling Center owned by Ben Baxter, who owns and operates several bowling centers. For each of the following transactions, complete the spreadsheet, indicating the amount and effect (+ for increase and − for decrease) of each transaction. Write NE if there is no effect. The first transaction is provided as an example.

| Transaction | BALANCE SHEET | | | INCOME STATEMENT | | |
| --- | --- | --- | --- | --- | --- | --- |
| | Assets | Liabilities | Owner's Equity | Revenues | Expenses | Net Income |
| e. Paid $1,500 to plumbers for repairing a broken pipe in the restrooms in July. | −1,500 | NE | −1,500 | NE | +1,500 | −1,500 |
| f. Paid $2,000 for the June electricity bill (received and recorded as an expense at the end of June). | | | | | | |
| g. Paid $5,475 to employees for work in July. | | | | | | |
| h. Received the July electricity bill for $2,500 that will be paid in August. | | | | | | |

**LO5**    **M3-8 Preparing an Income Statement**
Given the transactions in M3-6 and M3-7 (including the examples), prepare an income statement based on unadjusted account balances for Ben's Extreme Bowling Center for the month ended July 31, 2011.

**LO3**    **M3-9 Identifying Revenues**
The following transactions are February 2009 activities of Swing Hard, a sole proprietorship owned by Doris Heald. The business offers indoor golfing lessons. If revenue is to be recognized in February, indicate the amount. If revenue is not to be recognized in February, explain why.

| Activity | Amount or Explanation |
|---|---|
| a. Collected $15,000 from customers for lessons given in February. | _____ |
| b. Sold a gift certificate for golf lessons for $150 cash in February. | _____ |
| c. Received $4,000 from customers for services provided to them on credit in January. | _____ |
| d. Collected $2,250 in advance payments for golf lessons to start in June. | _____ |
| e. Billed a customer $125 for golf lessons given at the end of February. The customer is to pay the bill in March. | _____ |

## M3-10 Identifying Expenses                                                   LO3
The following transactions are February 2009 activities of Swing Hard, a sole proprietorship owned by Doris Heald. The business offers indoor golfing lessons. If an expense is to be recognized in February, indicate the amount. If an expense is not to be recognized in February, explain why.

| Activity | Amount or Explanation |
|---|---|
| f. Paid $1,750 for electricity used in the month of January; the bill was received and recorded at the end of January. | _____ |
| g. Received an $800 electricity bill for the month of February to be paid in March. | _____ |
| h. Paid $4,750 to its golf instructors for the month of February. | _____ |

## M3-11 Recording Revenues                                                   LO1, 4
For each transaction in M3-9, write the journal entry using the format shown in the chapter.

## M3-12 Recording Expenses                                                   LO1, 4
For each transaction in M3-10, write the journal entry using the format shown in the chapter.

## M3-13 Determining the Financial Statement Effects of Operating Activities Involving Revenues    LO4
The following transactions are February 2009 activities of Swing Hard, a sole proprietorship owned by Doris Heald. The business offers indoor golfing lessons. For each of the following transactions, complete the spreadsheet, indicating the amount and effect (+ for increase and − for decrease) of each transaction. Write NE if there is no effect. The first transaction is provided as an example.

| | BALANCE SHEET | | | INCOME STATEMENT | | |
|---|---|---|---|---|---|---|
| Transaction | Assets | Liabilities | Owner's Equity | Revenues | Expenses | Net Income |
| a. Collected $15,000 from customers for lessons given in February. | +15,000 | NE | +15,000 | +15,000 | NE | +15,000 |
| b. Sold a gift certificate for golf lessons for $150 cash in February. | | | | | | |
| c. Received $4,000 from customers for services provided to them on credit in January. | | | | | | |
| d. Collected $2,250 in advance payments for golf lessons to start in June. | | | | | | |
| e. Billed a customer $125 for golf lessons given at the end of February. The customer is to pay the bill in March. | | | | | | |

**LO4**　**M3-14 Determining the Financial Statement Effects of Operating Activities Involving Expenses**

The following transactions are February 2009 activities of Swing Hard, a sole proprietorship owned by Doris Heald. The business offers indoor golfing lessons. For each of the following transactions, complete the spreadsheet, indicating the amount and effect (+ for increase and − for decrease) of each transaction. Write NE if there is no effect. The first transaction is provided as an example.

| | BALANCE SHEET | | | INCOME STATEMENT | | |
|---|---|---|---|---|---|---|
| Transaction | Assets | Liabilities | Owner's Equity | Revenues | Expenses | Net Income |
| *f.* Paid $1,750 for electricity used in the month of January; the bill was received and recorded at the end of January. | −1,750 | −1,750 | NE | NE | NE | NE |
| *g.* Received an electricity bill for $800 for the month of February to be paid in March. | | | | | | |
| *h.* Paid $4,750 to its golf instructors for the month of February. | | | | | | |

**LO5**　**M3-15 Preparing an Income Statement**

Given the transactions in M3-13 and M3-14 (including the examples), prepare an income statement based on unadjusted account balances for Swing Hard for the month ended February 28, 2009.

**LO5**　**M3-16 Preparing an Income Statement from a Trial Balance**

The following unadjusted trial balance as of December 31, 2010, is for Buckeroo U!, a sole proprietorship owned by Tim Carey. The company specializes in horse-breaking services and rodeo lessons.

**Buckeroo U!**
**Unadjusted Trial Balance**
**As of December 31, 2010**

| Account Name | Debits | Credits |
|---|---|---|
| Cash | 59,750 | |
| Accounts Receivable | 3,300 | |
| Prepaid Insurance | 1,200 | |
| Equipment | 64,600 | |
| Land | 23,000 | |
| Accounts Payable | | 29,230 |
| Unearned Revenues | | 1,500 |
| Long-Term Notes Payable | | 74,000 |
| T. Carey, Capital | | 16,000 |
| Horse-Breaking Revenue | | 25,200 |
| Rodeo Lesson Revenue | | 10,500 |
| Wages Expense | 4,130 | |
| Maintenance Expense | 410 | |
| Interest Expense | 40 | |
| Totals | 156,430 | 156,430 |

*Required:*

Using the unadjusted trial balance provided, create a *classified* income statement for Buckeroo U! for the year ended December 31, 2010.

**M3-17 Preparing an Income Statement**

LO5

Time Warner, Inc.

The following accounts are from a recent set of financial statements of Time Warner, Inc. Dollars are in millions.

| | | | | | |
|---|---|---|---|---|---|
| Subscription Revenue | $22,222 | Accounts Receivable | $6,411 | Long-Term Debt | $20,238 |
| Other Operating Revenues | 13,818 | Interest Expense | 1,266 | Other Operating Expenses | 29,003 |
| Salaries Expense | 10,478 | Accounts Payable | 1,380 | Unearned Revenue | 1,473 |
| Cash | 4,220 | Advertising Revenue | 7,612 | Equipment | 13,676 |

*Required:*
Assume that the year ended on December 31, 2010. Prepare a *classified* income statement for the year. Note that some accounts listed are not reported on the income statement.

**M3-18 Preparing an Income Statement**

LO5

H&R Block

Henry and Richard Bloch founded H&R Block in 1955. Henry, who served as a navigator on a B-17 bomber in World War II, and Richard, who founded his first business in the 4th grade and attended Wharton at age 16, built H&R Block into the world's largest tax services company, serving more than 20 million people in 11 countries around the globe. The following accounts are from the financial statements of H&R Block at the end of a recent fiscal year. Dollars are in millions.

| | | | | | |
|---|---|---|---|---|---|
| Cost of Services (an expense) | $2,383 | Cash | $1,008 | Other Operating Expenses | $ 837 |
| Salaries Payable | 331 | Accounts Receivable | 1,000 | Long-Term Note Payable | 418 |
| Salaries Expense | 1,113 | Software Revenue | 493 | Owners' Capital | 3,492 |
| Accounts Payable | 769 | Other Operating Revenues | 917 | | |
| Service Revenue | 3,463 | Interest Expense | 49 | | |

*Required:*
Assume that the year ended on April 30, 2009. Prepare a *classified* income statement for the year. Note that some accounts are not reported on the income statement.

# Exercises  Available with McGraw-Hill's Homework Manager

**E3-1 Matching Definitions with Terms**

LO1, 3

Match each definition with its related term by entering the appropriate letter in the space provided.

| Term | Definition |
|---|---|
| _____ 1. Expenses | A. Record expenses when incurred in earning revenue. |
| _____ 2. Matching principle | B. Liability account used to record the obligation to provide future services or return cash that has been received before revenues have been earned. |
| _____ 3. Revenue principle | C. Costs that result when a company sacrifices resources to generate revenues. |
| _____ 4. Cash basis accounting | D. Record revenues when earned, not necessarily when cash is received. |
| _____ 5. Unearned Revenue | E. Record revenues when received and expenses when paid. |
| _____ 6. Accrual basis accounting | F. Type of asset account used to record the benefits obtained when cash is paid before expenses are incurred. |
| _____ 7. Prepaid Expenses | G. Record revenues when earned and expenses when incurred. |

**E3-2 Identifying Revenues**

LO1, 3

According to the revenue principle, revenues should be recognized when they are earned, which happens when the company performs acts promised to the customer. For most businesses, this condition is met at the point of delivery of goods or services. The following transactions occurred in September 2009:

    *a.*  A customer purchases 10 MP3 song files from Apple's iTunes store. The customer promises to pay $10 within three months. Answer from Apple's standpoint.

    *b.*  The Home Depot provides a carpet installation service for $2,000 cash. A comparable installation from other companies costs $3,000.

c.    AT&T is scheduled to install digital cable at 1,000 Austin-area homes next week. The installation charge is $100 per home. The terms require payment within 30 days of installation. Answer from AT&T's standpoint.

d.    AT&T completes the installations described in (c). Answer from AT&T's standpoint.

e.    AT&T receives payment from customers for the installations described in (c). Answer from AT&T's standpoint.

f.    A customer purchases a ticket from AMR Corporation's American Airlines in September for $500 cash to travel in December. Answer from American Airlines' standpoint.

**Required:**

If revenue is to be recognized in September, indicate the revenue account affected and the amount for each transaction. If revenue is not to be recognized in September, explain why.

LO1, 3    **E3-3 Identifying Revenues**

According to the revenue principle, revenues should be recognized when they are earned, which happens when the company performs acts promised to the customer. For most businesses, this condition is met at the point of delivery of goods or services. The following transactions occurred in September 2010:

a.    General Motors receives $26 million in contributions from new investors.

b.    Cal State University receives $20,000,000 cash for 80,000 five-game season football tickets. None of the games has been played.

c.    Cal State plays the first football game referred to in (b).

d.    Hall Construction signs a contract with a customer to construct a new $500,000 warehouse. At the signing, Hall receives a check for $50,000 as a deposit to be applied against amounts earned during the first phase of construction. Answer from Hall's standpoint.

e.    A popular snowboarding magazine company receives a total of $1,800 today from subscribers. The subscriptions begin in the next fiscal year. Answer from the magazine company's standpoint.

f.    T-Mobile sells a $100 cell phone plan to a customer who charges the sale on his credit card. Answer from the standpoint of T-Mobile.

**Required:**

For each of the transactions, if revenue is to be recognized in September, indicate the revenue account affected and the amount. If revenue is not to be recognized in September, explain why.

LO1, 3    **E3-4 Identifying Expenses**

Under accrual basis accounting, expenses are recognized when incurred, which means the activity giving rise to the expense has occurred. Assume the following transactions occurred in January 2010:

a.    Gateway pays its computer service technicians $90,000 in salary for the two weeks ended January 7. Answer from Gateway's standpoint.

b.    At the beginning of January, Turner Construction pays $4,500 in worker's compensation insurance for the first three months of the year.

c.    The McGraw-Hill Companies—publisher of this textbook and *BusinessWeek*—uses $1,000 worth of electricity and natural gas in January for which it has not yet been billed.

d.    Pooler's Pools receives and pays a $1,500 invoice in January from a marketing firm for services received in January.

e.    A consulting firm performs consulting services in January for a bookstore for $5,000. The terms indicate that payment is due from the bookstore within 30 days of the consultation. Answer from the bookstore's standpoint.

f.    Tawanda Canoes has its delivery van repaired in January for $280 and charges the amount on account.

**Required:**

If an expense is to be recognized in January for each transaction, indicate the expense account affected and the amount. If an expense is not to be recognized in January, indicate why.

LO1, 3    **E3-5 Identifying Expenses**

Under accrual basis accounting, expenses are recognized when incurred, which means the activity giving rise to the expense has occurred. The following transactions occurred in January 2009:

a.    American Express pays its salespersons $3,500 in commissions related to December financial advisory services sales. Answer from American Express's standpoint.

b.    On January 31, American Express determines that it will pay its salespersons $4,200 in commissions related to January sales. The payment will be made in early February. Answer from American Express's standpoint.

c.  The city of Omaha contracts with Waste Management, Inc. to provide trash collection services beginning in January. The city pays $7.2 million for the entire year. Answer from the city's standpoint.

d.  The University of Florida orders 60,000 season football tickets from its printer and pays $6,000 in advance for the custom printing. The first game will be played in September. Answer from the university's standpoint.

e.  A Houston Community College employee works eight hours at $15 per hour on January 31; payday is not until February 3. Answer from the college's point of view.

f.  Wang Consulting paid $3,600 for a fire insurance policy on January 1. The policy covers 12 months beginning on January 1. Answer from Wang's point of view.

g.  Ziegler Machines, a sole proprietorship selling farm equipment, receives a $230 phone bill at the end of January for calls made in January. The bill has not been paid to date.

*Required:*

For each transaction that is an expense to be recognized in January, indicate the expense account affected and the amount. If an expense is not to be recognized in January, indicate why.

## E3-6 Determining Financial Statement Effects of Various Transactions        LO4

The following transactions occurred during a recent year:

a.  (*Example*) Received cash investment from owner.

b.  Borrowed cash from local bank.

c.  Purchased equipment on credit.

d.  Earned revenue and collected cash.

e.  Incurred expenses, on credit.

f.  Earned revenue, on credit.

g.  Paid cash on account.

h.  Incurred expenses and paid cash.

i.  Earned revenue, collected half in cash and the balance on credit.

j.  Collected cash from customers on account.

k.  Incurred expenses, paid half in cash and the balance on credit.

l.  Paid insurance expense for the period.

*Required:*

For each transaction, complete the following table indicating its effect (+ for increase and − for decrease). Write NE if there is no effect. The first transaction is provided as an example.

| | BALANCE SHEET | | | INCOME STATEMENT | | |
|---|---|---|---|---|---|---|
| Transaction | Assets | Liabilities | Owner's Equity | Revenues | Expenses | Net Income |
| a. (*Example*) | + | NE | + | NE | NE | NE |

## E3-7 Determining Financial Statement Effects of Various Transactions        LO4

Wolverine World Wide, Inc., manufactures military, work, sport, and casual footwear and leather accessories under a variety of brand names, such as Caterpillar, Hush Puppies, Wolverine, and Steve Madden. The following transactions occurred during a recent year. Dollars are in thousands.

a.  (*Example*) Received $49,000 cash from investors.

b.  Purchased $300,000 of additional supplies on account.

c.  Borrowed $58,000, signing a long-term note.

d.  Purchased $18,600 in additional property, plant, and equipment for cash.

e.  Incurred $87,000 in selling expenses, paying two-thirds in cash and owing the rest on account.

f.  Incurred $4,700 in interest expense to be paid next year.

Wolverine World Wide, Inc.

*Required:*

For each transaction, complete the following table, indicating the effect (+ for increase and − for decrease) and amount. Write NE if there is no effect. The first transaction is provided as an example.

| | BALANCE SHEET | | | INCOME STATEMENT | | |
|---|---|---|---|---|---|---|
| Transaction | Assets | Liabilities | Owner's Equity | Revenues | Expenses | Net Income |
| a. (*Example*) | +49,000 | NE | +49,000 | NE | NE | NE |

**LO4**

**Sysco**

**E3-8 Recording Journal Entries**

Sysco, formed in 1969, is America's largest marketer and distributor of food service products, serving nearly 250,000 restaurants, hotels, schools, hospitals, and other institutions. The following transactions are typical of those that occurred in a recent year. (All amounts are rounded to the nearest thousand.)

a.  Borrowed $80,000 from a bank, signing a short-term note payable.

b.  Provided $10,000 in service to customers with $9,500 on account and the rest received in cash.

c.  Purchased plant and equipment for $130,000 in cash.

d.  Paid employee wages of $1,000.

e.  Received $410 on account from customers.

f.  Purchased and used fuel of $400,000 in delivery vehicles during the year (paid for in cash).

g.  Paid $8,200 cash on accounts payable.

h.  Incurred $20,000 in utility expenses during the year, of which $15,000 was paid in cash and the rest owed on account.

*Required:*

For each transaction, prepare journal entries. Determine whether the accounting equation remains in balance and debits equal credits after each entry.

**LO4**

**Greek Peak**

**E3-9 Recording Journal Entries**

Greek Peak is a ski resort in upstate New York. The company sells lift tickets, ski lessons, and ski equipment. It operates several restaurants and rents townhouses to vacationing skiers. The following hypothetical December 2011 transactions are typical of those that occur at the resort.

a.  Borrowed $500,000 from the bank on December 1, signing a note payable due in six months.

b.  Purchased a new snowplow for $20,000 cash on December 31.

c.  Purchased ski merchandise for $10,000 on account to sell in the ski shop.

d.  Incurred $22,000 in routine maintenance expenses for the chairlifts; paid cash.

e.  Sold $72,000 of season passes for cash. The season begins in January.

f.  Sold daily lift passes in December for a total of $76,000 cash.

g.  Received a $320 deposit on a townhouse to be rented for five days in January.

h.  Paid half the charges incurred on account in *(c)*.

i.  Paid $18,000 in wages to employees for the month of December.

*Required:*

Prepare journal entries for each transaction. Be sure to categorize each account as an asset (A), liability (L), owners' equity (OE), revenue (R), or expense (E), and check that debits equal credits for each journal entry.

**LO4**

**E3-10 Recording Journal Entries**

Rowland & Sons Air Transport Service has been in operation for three years. The following transactions occurred in February 2009:

| Feb. 1 | Paid $200 for rent of hangar space in February. |
| Feb. 2 | Purchased fuel costing $450 on account for the next flight to Dallas. |
| Feb. 4 | Received customer payment of $800 to ship several items to Philadelphia next month. |
| Feb. 7 | Flew cargo from Denver to Dallas; the customer paid $900 for the air transport. |
| Feb. 10 | Paid pilot $1,200 in wages for flying in January. |
| Feb. 14 | Paid $60 for an advertisement to run in the local paper on March 5. |
| Feb. 18 | Flew cargo for two customers from Dallas to Albuquerque for $1,700; one customer paid $500 cash and the other asked to be billed. |
| Feb. 25 | Purchased on account $1,350 in spare parts for the planes. |
| Feb. 27 | Hugh Rowland, owner, withdrew $1,800 cash from the business. |

*Required:*

Prepare journal entries for each transaction. Be sure to categorize each account as an asset (A), liability (L), owners' equity (OE), revenue (R), or expense (E).

**LO4**

**E3-11 Recording Journal Entries and Posting to T-Accounts**

Ricky's Piano Rebuilders, owned by Jon Ricky, has been operating for one year (2009). At the start of 2010, its income statement accounts had zero balances and its balance sheet account balances were as follows:

| Cash | $ 6,000 | Building | $ 22,000 |
| Accounts Receivable | 25,000 | Accounts Payable | 8,000 |
| Supplies | 1,200 | Unearned Fee Revenue (deposits) | 3,200 |
| Equipment | 8,000 | Notes Payable | 40,000 |
| Land | 6,000 | J. Ricky, Capital | 17,000 |

**Required:**

1. Create T-accounts for the balance sheet accounts and for these additional accounts: J. Ricky, Drawing; Piano Rebuilding Revenue; Rent Revenue; Wages Expense; and Utilities Expense. Enter the beginning balances.
2. Prepare journal entries for the following January 2010 transactions, using the letter of each transaction as a reference:
   a. Received a $500 deposit from a customer who wanted her piano rebuilt.
   b. Rented a part of the building to a bicycle repair shop for $300 received in January.
   c. Delivered five rebuilt pianos to customers who paid $14,500 in cash.
   d. Delivered two rebuilt pianos to customers for $7,000 charged on account.
   e. Received $6,000 from customers as payment on their accounts.
   f. Received an electric and gas utility bill for $350 for January services to be paid in February.
   g. Ordered $800 in supplies.
   h. Paid $1,700 on account in January.
   i. Paid $10,000 in wages to employees in January for work done this month.
   j. Received and paid cash for the supplies in (g).
   k. Jon Ricky withdrew $10,000 cash from the business.
3. Post the journal entries to the T-accounts. Show the unadjusted ending balances in the T-accounts.

## E3-12 Preparing an Unadjusted Trial Balance                                        LO5
Refer to E3-11.

**Required:**
Use the balances in the completed T-accounts in E3-11 to prepare an unadjusted trial balance at the end of January 2010.

## E3-13 Inferring Operating Transactions and Preparing an Unadjusted Trial Balance    LO4, 5
Virtual Golf Center, owned by Mike McCall, operates indoor golf simulators that allow individual customers and golf club members to experience courses such as Pebble Beach and Augusta without leaving their own neighborhood. Its stores are located in rented space in malls and shopping centers. During its first month of business ended April 30, 2009, Virtual Golf Center completed eight transactions with the dollar effects indicated in the following schedule:

| | Assets | | | | = | Liabilities | | + | Owner's Equity | |
| --- | --- | --- | --- | --- | --- | --- | --- | --- | --- | --- |
| | Cash | Accounts Receivable | Supplies | Equipment | | Accounts Payable | Unearned Revenue | | M. McCall, Capital | |
| Beginning Balance | 0 | 0 | 0 | 0 | | 0 | 0 | | 0 | |
| (a) | +100,000 | | | | | | | | +100,000 | |
| (b) | −30,000 | | | +30,000 | | | | | | |
| (c) | −200 | | +1,000 | | | +800 | | | | |
| (d) | +9,000 | +1,000 | | | | | | | +10,000 | Sales Revenue |
| (e) | −1,000 | | | | | | | | −1,000 | Wages Expense |
| (f) | | | | | | +1,200 | | | −1,200 | Utilities Expense |
| (g) | +2,000 | | | | | | +2,000 | | | |
| (h) | −5,000 | | | | | | | | −5,000 | M. McCall, Drawing |

*Required:*

1.  Write a brief explanation of transactions (*a*) through (*h*). Include any assumptions that you made.
2.  Compute the ending balance in each account and prepare an unadjusted trial balance for Virtual Golf Center on April 30, 2009.

**LO4**

**The Washington Post Company**

**E3-14 Inferring Transactions and Computing Effects Using T-Accounts**

The Washington Post Company is best known for publishing *The Washington Post* but also publishes *Newsweek* magazine and owns Kaplan, Inc. (admissions test preparation services among other services) and various television stations and community newspapers. A recent annual report included the following accounts. Dollars are in millions.

| +Dr Accounts Receivable (A) Cr− | | | |
|---|---|---|---|
| 1/1 | 399 | | |
| | 2,805 | ? | |
| 12/31 | 423 | | |

| +Dr Supplies (A) Cr− | | | |
|---|---|---|---|
| 1/1 | 15 | | |
| | 342 | ? | |
| 12/31 | 20 | | |

| −Dr Unearned Revenue (L) Cr+ | | | |
|---|---|---|---|
| | | 439 | 1/1 |
| | ? | 2,643 | |
| | | 509 | 12/31 |

*Required:*

1.  For each T-account, describe the typical transactions that cause it to increase and decrease.
2.  Solve for the missing amounts (in millions). (*Hint:* Express each T-account in equation format: Beginning + Increase Side − Decrease Side = Ending.)

**LO1, 3, 5**

**E3-15 Finding Financial Information as an Investor**

You are evaluating your current portfolio of investments to determine those that are not performing to your expectations. You have all of the companies' most recent annual reports.

*Required:*
For each of the following, indicate where you would locate the information in an annual report.

1.  The total cost incurred for repairs and maintenance during the year.
2.  Accounts receivable.
3.  Description of a company's revenue recognition policy.
4.  The cost of wages incurred during the year.

**LO4**

**E3-16 Determining Financial Statement Effects of Several Transactions**

Sifuentes Consulting, owned and managed by José Sifuentes, provides marketing consulting services. In January 2011, Sifuentes Consulting posted the following transactions.

a.  (*Example*) Received $9,500 cash for consulting services rendered in January.
b.  Received an additional $10,000 in cash as an investment from José Sifuentes.
c.  Purchased $12,000 of equipment, paying 25 percent in cash and owing the rest on a note due in two years.
d.  Received $7,500 cash for consulting services to be performed in February.
e.  Bought $1,000 of supplies on account.
f.  Paid $1,100 for December utility bill (recorded as expense in December 2010).
g.  Received utility bill for January for $1,250, due February 15.
h.  Consulted for customers in January for fees totaling $15,900, due in February.
i.  Received $12,000 cash for consulting services rendered in December.
j.  Paid $500 toward supplies purchased in (*e*).
k.  J. Sifuentes withdrew $3,000 cash from the business.

*Required:*
Indicate the accounts, amounts, and direction of the effects on the firm's accounting equation for each of the transactions. A sample is provided.

| | Assets | | = | Liabilities | + | Owner's Equity | |
|---|---|---|---|---|---|---|---|
| (*a*) Cash | | +9,500 | | | | Service Revenue (+R) | +9,500 |

**E3-17 Preparing Journal Entries**                                                      LO4
For each transaction in E3-16 (including the example), write the journal entry using the format shown in this chapter.

**E3-18 Posting to T-Accounts**                                                          LO4
For each transaction in E3-16 (including the example), post the effects to the appropriate T-accounts and determine ending account balances. Beginning account balances have been given. An example is provided.

| +Dr | Cash (A) | | Cr− |
|---|---|---|---|
| 1/1/11 | 10,000 | | |
| (a) | 9,500 | | |

| +Dr | Accounts Receivable (A) | | Cr− |
|---|---|---|---|
| 1/1/11 | 9,500 | | |

| +Dr | Supplies (A) | | Cr− |
|---|---|---|---|
| 1/1/11 | 800 | | |

| +Dr | Equipment (A) | | Cr− |
|---|---|---|---|
| 1/1/11 | 8,000 | | |

| −Dr | Accounts Payable (L) | | Cr+ |
|---|---|---|---|
| | | 5,000 | 1/1/11 |

| −Dr | Note Payable (L) | | Cr+ |
|---|---|---|---|
| | | 0 | 1/1/11 |

| −Dr | Unearned Revenue (L) | | Cr+ |
|---|---|---|---|
| | | 2,500 | 1/1/11 |

| −Dr | J. Sifuentes, Capital (OE) | | Cr+ |
|---|---|---|---|
| | | 20,800 | 1/1/11 |

| +Dr | J. Sifuentes, Drawing (OE) | | Cr− |
|---|---|---|---|
| 1/1/11 | 0 | | |

| −Dr | Service Revenue (R) | | Cr+ |
|---|---|---|---|
| | | 0 | 1/1/11 |
| | | 9,500 | a. |

| +Dr | Utilities Expense (E) | | Cr− |
|---|---|---|---|
| 1/1/11 | 0 | | |

**E3-19 Creating an Unadjusted Trial Balance**                                            LO5
Based on the transactions posted to T-accounts in E3-18, create an unadjusted trial balance for Sifuentes Consulting for the month ended January 31, 2011.

**E3-20 Inferring Income Statement Transactions and Creating Financial Statements**        LO4, 5
An analysis of transactions made during July 2009 by Zelkind Tech Services, an Internet service provider owned by Josh Zelkind, during its first month of operations, follows. Increases and decreases in owner's equity are explained.

| | Assets | | | | = | Liabilities | + | Owner's Equity | |
|---|---|---|---|---|---|---|---|---|---|
| | Cash | Accounts Receivable | Supplies | Equipment | | Accounts Payable | | J. Zelkind, Capital | |
| Beg. | 0 | 0 | 0 | 0 | | 0 | | 0 | |
| a. | +11,000 | | | | | | | +11,000 | Investment by owner |
| b. | | +5,000 | | | | | | +5,000 | Service Revenue |
| c. | | | | | | +710 | | −710 | Utilities Expense |
| d. | −6,000 | | | +10,000 | | +4,000 | | | |
| e. | +1,000 | | | | | | | +1,000 | Service Revenue |
| f. | | | +550 | | | +550 | | | |
| g. | −3,000 | | | | | −3,000 | | | |
| h. | −2,000 | | | | | | | −2,000 | Wage Expense |
| i. | −750 | | | | | | | −750 | Rent Expense |
| j. | +1,500 | −1,500 | | | | | | | |
| k. | −500 | | | | | | | −500 | J. Zelkind, Drawing |

*Required:*

1.  Describe the business activities that led to the accounting equation effects for each transaction (*a*)–(*k*).
2.  Prepare a *classified* income statement for July and a *classified* balance sheet as of July 31, 2009. (*Hint:* You can determine the amount for owner's equity by completing the equation: Assets = Liabilities + Owner's Equity.)

**LO1, 3, 4**

### E3-21 Determining Financial Statement Effects of Various Transactions

John "Bum" Andrews founded EZ Reader in January 2010 to provide a service in which an employee follows a student around reading assigned textbook chapters aloud so that the student will not have to. Selected transactions for EZ Readers' first month of business are as follows:

a.  Received $50,000 cash from John Andrews to establish the business.
b.  Billed customers $10,500 for services performed in January.
c.  Purchased a car for $24,500 for use in the business. Paid in cash.
d.  Purchased $2,400 of supplies on account.
e.  Received $7,500 cash from customers billed in transaction (*b*).
f.  Used $1,500 in utilities that will be paid in February.
g.  Paid employees $3,500 cash for work done in January.
h.  Paid $1,200 cash toward supplies purchased in transaction (*d*).

*Required:*

For each transaction, write (1) the name of the account being debited or credited, (2) the basic account type (A, L, OE, R, or E), (3) whether the account is increased (+) or decreased (−) due to the transaction, and (4) whether the account normally holds a debit or credit balance. Transaction (*a*) has been given as an example.

| | DEBIT SIDE OF JOURNAL ENTRY | | | | CREDIT SIDE OF JOURNAL ENTRY | | | |
|---|---|---|---|---|---|---|---|---|
| | Account Name | Account Type | Direction of Change | Normal Balance | Account Name | Account Type | Direction of Change | Normal Balance |
| *a.* | Cash | A | + | Debit | J. Andrews, Capital | OE | + | Credit |

**LO1, 3, 4, 5**

**Sigil Games Online**

### E3-22 Comprehensive Exercise

In 2002, Brad McQuaid and Jeff Butler founded Sigil Games Online, Inc. (now owned by Sony Online Entertainment) with the mission of creating massively multiplayer online (MMO) games. Its "vanguard" product has been the game *Vanguard: Saga of Heroes*, released in winter of 2007. The company intends to sell subscriptions to its game online. For the sake of this exercise, assume that Sigil has been selling subscriptions for *Vanguard* for one full year (2009) at $15 per month. At the start of 2010, its income statement accounts had zero balances, and its balance sheet account balances were as follows:

| | | | |
|---|---|---|---|
| Cash | $ 1,500,000 | Accounts Payable | $ 108,000 |
| Accounts Receivable | 150,000 | Wages Payable | 34,500 |
| Supplies | 14,700 | Unearned Revenue | 73,500 |
| Equipment | 874,500 | Notes Payable | 60,000 |
| Land | 1,200,000 | McQuaid & Butler, Capital | 3,885,200 |
| Building | 422,000 | | |

In addition to these accounts, Sigil's chart of accounts includes the following: Subscription Revenue, Licensing Revenue, Wages Expense, Advertising Expense, and Utilities Expense.

*Required:*

1.  Analyze these effect of the following January 2010 transactions on the accounting equation using the format shown in the demonstration case.
    a.  Received $50,000 cash from customers for subscriptions earned in 2009.
    b.  Received $25,000 cash from Electronic Arts, Inc., for licensing revenue earned in the month of January 2010.
    c.  Purchased 10 new computer servers for $33,500; paid $10,000 cash and signed a note for the remainder owed.

d.  Paid $10,000 for an Internet advertisement run on Yahoo! in January 2010.

e.  Sold 15,000 monthly subscriptions at $15 each for services provided during the month of January 2010. Half was collected in cash and half was sold on account.

f.  Received an electric and gas utility bill for $5,350 for January 2010 services. The bill will be paid in February.

g.  Paid $10,000 in wages to employees in January 2010 for work done in 2009. The expense was recorded in 2009.

h.  Purchased $3,000 of supplies on account.

i.  Paid $378,000 in wages to employees for work done in January 2010.

j.  Paid $3,000 cash to the supplier in (h).

2.  Prepare journal entries for the January 2010 transactions listed in requirement 1 using the letter of each transaction as a reference.

3.  Create T-accounts, enter the beginning balances shown, post the journal entries to the T-accounts, and show the unadjusted ending balances in the T-accounts.

4.  Prepare an unadjusted trial balance as of January 31, 2010.

## Problems—Set A   Available with McGraw-Hill's Homework Manager

**PA3-1 Recording Nonquantitative Journal Entries**                                   LO1, 3, 4

The following list includes a series of accounts for B-Ball Stores, a sole proprietorship owned by Ralph Ball. The business has been operating for three years. These accounts are listed alphabetically and numbered for identification. Following the accounts is a series of transactions. For each transaction, indicate the account(s) that should be debited and credited by entering the appropriate account number(s) to the right of each transaction. If no journal entry is needed, write *none* after the transaction. The first transaction is used as an example.

| Account No. | Account Title | Account No. | Account Title |
|---|---|---|---|
| 1 | Accounts Payable | 9 | R. Ball, Capital |
| 2 | Accounts Receivable | 10 | R. Ball, Drawing |
| 3 | Cash | 11 | Rent Expense |
| 4 | Equipment | 12 | Service Revenue |
| 5 | Interest Expense | 13 | Supplies Expense |
| 6 | Interest Payable | 14 | Supplies |
| 7 | Note Payable | 15 | Wages Expense |
| 8 | Prepaid Insurance | 16 | Wages Payable |

| Transactions | Debit | Credit |
|---|---|---|
| a.  (*Example:*) Purchased equipment for use in the business; paid one-third cash and signed a note payable for the balance. | 4 | 3.7 |
| b.  Received additional investment from R. Ball. | | |
| c.  Paid cash for rent this period. | | |
| d.  Collected cash for services performed this period. | | |
| e.  Collected cash on accounts receivable for services performed last period. | | |
| f.  Performed services this period on credit. | | |
| g.  Paid cash on accounts payable for expenses incurred last period. | | |
| h.  Employees worked this period but will not be paid until next period. | | |
| i.  Purchased supplies to be used later; paid cash. | | |
| j.  Paid three-fourths of the interest expense for the year; the balance will be paid next year. | | |
| k.  Ralph Ball withdrew cash from the business. | | |
| l.  On the last day of the current period, paid cash for an insurance policy covering the next two years. | | |

LO1, 3, 4

**PA3-2 Recording Nonquantitative Journal Entries**

The following is a series of accounts for Jay's Laundry Services owned and managed by Jay Lewis. The company has been operating for two years. The accounts are listed alphabetically and numbered for identification. Following the accounts is a series of transactions. For each transaction, indicate the account(s) that should be debited and credited by entering the appropriate account number(s) to the right of each transaction. If no journal entry is needed, write *none* after the transaction. The first transaction is given as an example.

| Account No. | Account Title | Account No. | Account Title |
|---|---|---|---|
| 1 | Accounts Payable | 9 | Notes Payable |
| 2 | Accounts Receivable | 10 | Prepaid Insurance |
| 3 | Advertising Expense | 11 | Service Revenue |
| 4 | Buildings | 12 | Supplies Expense |
| 5 | Cash | 13 | Supplies |
| 6 | J. Lewis, Capital | 14 | Wages Expense |
| 7 | J. Lewis, Drawing | 15 | Wages Payable |
| 8 | Land | | |

| Transactions | Debit | Credit |
|---|---|---|
| a.  (*Example*) Received cash from owner Jay Lewis. | 5 | 6 |
| b.  Performed services for customers this period on credit. | | |
| c.  Purchased on credit but did not use supplies this period. | | |
| d.  Prepaid a fire insurance policy at the end of this period to cover the next 12 months. | | |
| e.  Purchased a building this period by making a 20 percent cash down payment and signing a note payable for the balance. | | |
| f.  Collected cash this year for services that had been provided and recorded in the prior year. | | |
| g.  Paid cash this period for wages that had been earned and recorded last period. | | |
| h.  Paid cash for supplies that had been purchased on accounts payable in the prior period | | |
| i.  Paid cash for advertising expense incurred in the current period. | | |
| j.  Ran advertising in local newspaper this period to be paid next period. | | |
| k.  Collected cash for services rendered this period. | | |
| l.  This period Jay Lewis sold his summer house on the lake to another person for an amount above the original purchase price. | | |
| m.  Jay Lewis withdrew cash from the business. | | |

LO2, 3, 4

**PA3-3 Recording Journal Entries**

Ryan Olson organized MeToo, a company providing online networking management services on MySpace, Facebook, Friendster, and other electronic social networks. Ryan believes that college and high school students make up his target market. You have been hired to record the transactions occurring in the first two weeks of operations, beginning May 1, 2010.

a.  May 1  Received $30,000 cash from Ryan Olson to establish the sole proprietorship.

b.  May 1  Borrowed $50,000 from the bank to provide additional funding to begin operations; the note is due in two years.

c.  May 1  Paid $2,400 for a one-year fire insurance policy (recorded as Prepaid Insurance).

d.  May 3  Purchased furniture and fixtures for the store for $15,000 on account. The amount is due within 30 days.

e.  May 5  Placed advertisements in local college newspapers for a total of $250 cash.

f.  May 9  Sold services for $400 cash.

g.  May 14  Made full payment for the furniture and fixtures purchased on account on May 3.

**Required:**

For each transaction, prepare a journal entry. If no entry is needed, explain why. Be sure to categorize each account as an asset (A), liability (L), owner's equity (OE), revenue (R), or expense (E).

**PA3-4 Recording Journal Entries**

Robin Harrington established Time Definite Delivery on January 1, 2011. The following transactions occurred during the company's most recent quarter.

LO1, 3, 4

a.   Received $80,000 from Robin Harrington to establish the sole proprietorship.

b.   Provided delivery service to customers, receiving $72,000 in accounts receivable and $16,000 in cash.

c.   Purchased equipment costing $82,000 and signed a long-term note for the full amount.

d.   Incurred repair costs of $3,000 on account.

e.   Collected $56,000 from customers on account.

f.   Borrowed $90,000 by signing a long-term note.

g.   Prepaid $74,400 cash to rent equipment and aircraft next quarter.

h.   Paid employees $38,000 for work done during the quarter.

i.   Purchased (with cash) and used $49,000 in fuel for delivery equipment.

j.   Paid $2,000 on accounts payable.

k.   Ordered but have not yet received $700 in supplies.

l.   Robin Harrington withdrew $8,000 cash from the business.

*Required:*

For each transaction, prepare a journal entry. If no entry is needed, explain why. Be sure to categorize each account as an asset (A), liability (L), owner's equity (OE), revenue (R), or expense (E).

**PA3-5 Analyzing the Effects of Transactions Using T-Accounts and Preparing an Unadjusted Trial Balance**

Barbara Jones, a textbook editor, opened Barb's Book Fixing on February 1, 2010. The business specializes in editing accounting textbooks. You have been hired as manager. Your duties include maintaining the company's financial records. The following transactions occurred in February 2010, the first month of operations.

LO1, 3, 4, 5

a.   Received an investment of $16,000 cash from Barbara Jones to establish the sole proprietorship.

b.   Paid three months' rent for the office at $800 per month (recorded as Prepaid Rent).

c.   Purchased supplies for $300 cash.

d.   Negotiated a two-year loan at the bank, depositing $10,000 in the company's bank account.

e.   Used all of the money from (d) to purchase a computer for $2,500 and the balance for furniture and fixtures for the office.

f.   Placed an advertisement that ran the same day in the local paper for $425 cash.

g.   Made sales totaling $1,800; $1,525 was in cash and the rest on accounts receivable.

h.   Incurred and paid employee wages of $420.

i.   Collected accounts receivable of $50 from customers.

j.   Had one of the computers repaired for $120 cash.

k.   Barbara Jones withdrew $3,500 cash from the business.

*Required:*

1.   Set up appropriate T-accounts for Cash; Accounts Receivable; Supplies; Prepaid Rent; Equipment; Furniture and Fixtures; Notes Payable; B. Jones, Capital; B. Jones, Drawing; Service Revenue; Advertising Expense; Wages Expense; and Repair Expense. All accounts begin with zero balances.

2.   Record in the T-accounts the effects of each transaction for Barb's Book Fixing in February, referencing each transaction in the accounts with the transaction letter. Show the unadjusted ending balances in the T-accounts.

3.   Prepare an unadjusted trial balance at the end of February.

4.   Refer to the revenues and expenses shown on the unadjusted trial balance. Based on this information, write a short memo to Barbara offering your opinion on the results of operations during the first month of business.

**PA3-6 Analyzing the Effects of Transactions Using T-Accounts and Preparing an Unadjusted Trial Balance**

Randy Ellis established Spicewood Stables in Dripping Springs, Texas, on April 1, 2010. The company provides stables, care for animals, and grounds for riding and showing horses. You have been hired as the new assistant controller. The following transactions for April 2010 are provided for your review.

LO1, 3, 4, 5

a.   Received from Randy Ellis $200,000 in cash to establish the business as a sole proprietorship.

b.   Built a barn for $142,000. The company paid half the amount in cash on April 1 and signed a three-year note payable for the balance.

c.  Provided $15,260 in animal care services for customers, all on credit.
d.  Rented stables to customers who cared for their own animals; received cash of $13,200.
e.  Received from a customer $1,500 to board her horse in May, June, and July.
f.  Purchased hay and feed supplies on account for $3,210.
g.  Paid $840 in cash for water utilities incurred in the month.
h.  Paid $1,700 on accounts payable for previous purchases.
i.  Received $1,000 from customers on accounts receivable.
j.  Paid $4,000 in wages to employees who worked during the month.
k.  At the end of the month, prepaid a two-year insurance policy for $3,600.
l.  Received an electric utility bill for $1,200 for usage in April; the bill will be paid next month.

**Required:**

1.  Set up appropriate T-accounts. All accounts begin with zero balances.
2.  Record in the T-accounts the effects of each transaction for Spicewood Stables in April, referencing each transaction in the accounts with the transaction letter. Show the unadjusted ending balances in the T-accounts.
3.  Prepare an unadjusted trial balance as of April 30, 2010.
4.  Refer to the revenues and expenses shown on the unadjusted trial balance. Based on this information, write a short memo to Randy Ellis offering your opinion on the results of operations during the first month of business.

## Problems—Set B     Available with McGraw-Hill's Homework Manager

**LO1, 3, 4**

**Abercrombie & Fitch**

**PB3-1 Recording Nonquantitative Journal Entries**

Abercrombie & Fitch Co. is a specialty retailer of casual apparel. The company's brand was established in 1892. It was first publicly traded in 1996 and was spun off from The Limited in 1998. The following is a series of accounts for Abercrombie. They are listed alphabetically and numbered for identification. Following the accounts is a series of transactions. For each transaction, indicate the account(s) that should be debited and credited by entering the appropriate account number(s) to the right of each transaction. If no journal entry is needed, write *none* after the transaction. The first transaction is given as an example.

| Account No. | Account Title | Account No. | Account Title |
|---|---|---|---|
| 1 | Accounts Payable | 8 | Rent Expense |
| 2 | Accounts Receivable | 9 | Supplies Expense |
| 3 | Cash | 10 | Supplies |
| 4 | Equipment | 11 | Unearned Revenue |
| 5 | Interest Revenue | 12 | Wages Expense |
| 6 | Owners' Capital | 13 | Wages Payable |
| 7 | Prepaid Rent | | |

| Transactions | | Debit | Credit |
|---|---|---|---|
| a. | (*Example*) Incurred wages expense; paid cash. | 12 | 3 |
| b. | Collected cash on account. | | |
| c. | Sold gift certificates to customers; none redeemed this period. | | |
| d. | Purchased equipment, paying part in cash and charging the balance on account. | | |
| e. | Paid cash to suppliers on account. | | |
| f. | Received additional cash from owners. | | |
| g. | Paid rent to landlords for next month's use of mall space. | | |
| h. | Earned and received cash for interest on investments. | | |

**PB3-2 Recording Nonquantitative Journal Entries**                                         LO1, 3, 4

The following is a series of accounts for Cohen & Sons Consulting, owned and managed by Alan Cohen. The company has been operating for five years. The accounts are listed alphabetically and numbered for identification. Following the accounts is a series of transactions. For each transaction, indicate the account(s) that should be debited and credited by entering the appropriate account number(s) to the right of each transaction. If no journal entry is needed, write *none* after the transaction. The first transaction is given as an example.

| Account No. | Account Title | Account No. | Account Title |
|---|---|---|---|
| 1 | Accounts Payable | 10 | Interest Revenue |
| 2 | Accounts Receivable | 11 | Land |
| 3 | Advertising Expense | 12 | Notes Payable |
| 4 | A. Cohen, Capital | 13 | Prepaid Rent |
| 5 | A. Cohen, Drawing | 14 | Supplies Expense |
| 6 | Buildings | 15 | Supplies |
| 7 | Cash | 16 | Wages Expense |
| 8 | Consulting Revenue | 17 | Wages Payable |
| 9 | Equipment | | |

| Transactions | | Debit | Credit |
|---|---|---|---|
| a. | (*Example*) Received additional cash from owner Alan Cohen. | 7 | 4 |
| b. | Performed services for customers this period on credit. | | |
| c. | Purchased on credit but did not use supplies this period. | | |
| d. | Collected cash this year for services provided and recorded in the prior year. | | |
| e. | Prepaid rent on the office this period for the next six months. | | |
| f. | Purchased two cars this period, paying part cash and signing a note payable with the dealer for the balance. | | |
| g. | Paid cash for advertising expense incurred in the current period. | | |
| h. | Paid cash this period to employees for wages they had earned in the last period. | | |
| i. | Paid cash for supplies that had been purchased on accounts payable in the prior period. | | |
| j. | Ran advertising in local newspaper this period to be paid next period. | | |
| k. | This period Alan Cohen purchased a condominium in Florida for personal use. | | |
| l. | Collected cash for services rendered this period. | | |

**PB3-3 Recording Journal Entries**                                         LO1, 3, 4

Diana Mark is the president of ServicePro, a sole proprietorship that provides temporary employees for not-for-profit organizations. ServicePro has been operating for five years; its revenues are increasing with each passing year. You have been hired to help Diana in analyzing the following transactions for the first two weeks of April 2010:

a.  April 2   Purchased office supplies for $500 on account.

b.  April 5   Billed the local United Way office $1,950 for temporary services provided.

c.  April 8   Paid $250 for supplies purchased and recorded on account last period.

d.  April 8   Placed an advertisement in the local paper for $400 cash; the ad will run in May.

e.  April 9   Purchased a new computer for the office costing $2,300 cash.

f.  April 10  Paid employee wages of $1,200. Of this amount, $200 had been earned by employees in the prior period and already recorded in the Wages Payable account.

g.  April 11  Received $1,000 on account from the local United Way office (from [b] above).

h.  April 12  Purchased land as the site of a future office for $10,000. Paid $2,000 down and signed a note payable for the balance.

*i.* April 13   Received $80,000 cash as additional investment by owner Diana Mark.
*j.* April 14   Billed Family & Children's Service $2,000 for services rendered this month.
*k.* April 15   Received the April telephone bill for $245 to be paid next month.

### Required:

For each transaction, prepare a journal entry. If no entry is needed, explain why. Be sure to categorize each account as an asset (A), liability (L), owner's equity (OE), revenue (R), or expense (E).

LO1, 3, 4 **PB3-4 Recording Journal Entries**

John Cirba established Cirba Moving & Storage on April 1, 2010. The following transactions occurred during the business's most recent quarter.

*a.* Received $100,000 from John Cirba to establish the sole proprietorship.
*b.* Purchased three moving vans costing $80,000 each, paying $50,000 as a down payment and signing a long-term note for the rest.
*c.* Provided moving services to customers, receiving $23,000 in cash and billing customers for $120,000 in services on account.
*d.* Incurred $3,000 of repair costs on one of the vans; the amount is payable next quarter on account.
*e.* Paid for and used $9,000 in fuel for the moving vans.
*f.* Collected $72,000 from customers on account.
*g.* Paid $1,000 cash to a marketing firm for advertising assistance.
*h.* Purchased $12,000 in insurance coverage for the next quarter.
*i.* Ordered, but have not yet received, $3,200 in new moving pads and dollies (equipment).
*j.* Paid $2,000 on accounts payable.
*k.* Paid employees $109,000 for work done during the quarter.
*l.* John Cirba withdrew $5,000 cash from the business.

### Required:

For each transaction, prepare a journal entry. If no entry is needed, explain why. Be sure to categorize each account as an asset (A), liability (L), owner's equity (OE), revenue (R), or expense (E).

LO1, 3, 4, 5 **PB3-5 Analyzing the Effects of Transactions Using T-Accounts and Preparing an Unadjusted Trial Balance**

Jessica Pothier opened FunFlatables on June 1, 2011. The company rents out moon walks and inflatable slides for parties and corporate events. The business also has obtained the use of an abandoned ice rink located in a local shopping mall, where its rental products are displayed and available for casual hourly rental by mall patrons. The following transactions occurred during the first month of operations.

*a.* Received $50,000 cash contributions from Jessica to establish the sole proprietorship.
*b.* Purchased inflatable rides and inflation equipment, paying $20,000 cash.
*c.* Received $5,000 cash from casual hourly rentals at the mall.
*d.* Rented rides and equipment to customers for $10,000. Received cash of $2,000; the rest is due from customers.
*e.* Received $2,500 from a large corporate customer as a deposit on a party booking for July 4.
*f.* Began to prepare for the July 4 party by purchasing various party supplies on account for $600.
*g.* Paid $12,000 in cash for renting the mall space in June, July, and August.
*h.* Received $1,000 from customers on accounts receivable.
*i.* Paid $4,000 in wages to employees for work done during the month.
*j.* Paid $1,000 for running a television ad this month.
*k.* Jessica Pothier withdrew $6,000 cash from the business.

### Required:

1. Set up appropriate T-accounts for Cash; Accounts Receivable; Supplies; Prepaid Rent; Equipment; Accounts Payable; Unearned Rent Revenue; J. Pothier, Capital; J. Pothier, Drawing; Rent Revenue; Wages Expense; and Advertising Expense. All accounts begin with zero balances.
2. Record in the T-accounts the effects of each transaction for FunFlatables in June, referencing each transaction in the accounts with the transaction letter. Show the unadjusted ending balances in the T-accounts.

3.  Prepare an unadjusted trial balance for the end of June 2011.
4.  Jessica has become alarmed at how quickly the business's cash balance has fallen. Refer to the revenues and expenses shown on the unadjusted trial balance and write a short memo to her offering your opinion on the results of operations during the first month of business.

**PB3-6 Analyzing the Effects of Transactions Using T-Accounts and Preparing an Unadjusted Trial Balance**                                                                          LO1, 3, 4, 5

Margaret Foster established Body and Soul in Cortland, New York, on March 1, 2010. The company provides massage therapy and other spa services. You have been hired as the new business manager. The following transactions for March 2010 are provided for your review.

a.  Received from Margaret Foster $50,000 in cash to establish the business as a sole proprietorship.
b.  Paid $18,000 to rent store space for the business from March 1 to September 1 (six months).
c.  Purchased massage tables, towels, and other necessary equipment; paid $8,000 in cash and owed $12,000 on account.
d.  Provided spa services to customers for $20,000 cash.
e.  Received $2,400 from customers as gift certificates for future spa services (recorded as unearned revenue).
f.  Purchased spa supplies on account for $3,000.
g.  Borrowed $10,000 from a local bank to renovate additional space in the store.
h.  Paid $6,000 for a two-year insurance policy with coverage beginning on April 1, 2010.
i.  Paid $1,200 on accounts payable for previous purchases.
j.  Provided $600 in spa services to customers on account.
k.  Ordered $2,500 in spa supplies for delivery in April.
l.  Received an electric and gas utility bill for $1,500 for usage in March; the bill will be paid next month.
m.  Paid $12,000 in wages to employees who worked during the month.
n.  Margaret Foster withdrew $7,000 cash from the business.

*Required:*

1.  Set up appropriate T-accounts. All accounts begin with zero balances.
2.  Record in the T-accounts the effects of each transaction for Body and Soul in March, referencing each transaction in the accounts with the transaction letter. Show the unadjusted ending balances in the T-accounts.
3.  Prepare an unadjusted trial balance as of March 31, 2010.
4.  Refer to the revenues and expenses shown on the unadjusted trial balance. Based on this information, write a short memo to Margaret Foster offering your opinion on the results of operations during the first month of business.

# Cases and Projects

## CP3-1 Finding Financial Information                                                  LO1, 4

Refer to the financial statements of The Home Depot in Appendix A at the end of this book, or download the annual report from the *Cases* section of the text's Web site at www.mhhe.com/LLPW1e.

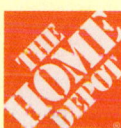

*Required:*

1.  Did The Home Depot's total revenues increase or decrease in the most recent year? By how much? Calculate this change as a percentage of the previous year's total revenues by dividing the amount of the change by the previous year's revenues and multiplying by 100.
2.  State the amount of the largest expense on the most recent income statement and describe the transaction represented by the expense. Did this expense increase or decrease from the previous year and by what percentage?

## CP3-2 Comparing Financial Information                                                LO1, 4

Refer to the financial statements of The Home Depot in Appendix A and Lowe's in Appendix B at the end of this book, or download the annual reports from the *Cases* section of the text's Web site at www.mhhe.com/LLPW1e.

Lowe's

*Required:*

1. Did Lowe's total revenues increase or decrease in the most recent year? By how much? Calculate this change as a percentage of the previous year's total revenues. Is the trend in Lowe's revenues more or less favorable than The Home Depot's?

2. State the amount of the largest expense on the most recent income statement of Lowe's and describe the transaction represented by the expense. Did this expense increase or decrease and by what percentage, as compared to the previous year? Is the trend in Lowe's largest expense more or less favorable than the trend for The Home Depot's largest expense?

**LO1, 3, 5**    **CP3-3 Examining the Income Statement: Internet-Based Team Research**

As a team, select an industry to analyze. Using your Web browser, each team member should acquire the annual report or 10-K for one publicly traded company in the industry, with each member selecting a different company. (See CP1-3 in Chapter 1 for a description of possible resources for these tasks.)

*Required:*

1. On an individual basis, each team member should write a short report that lists the following information:
   a. The major revenue and expense accounts on the most recent income statement.
   b. Description of how the company has followed the conditions of the revenue principle.
   c. The percentage of revenues that go to covering expenses and that are in excess of expenses (in other words, the percentage that remains as net income).

2. Then, as a team, write a short report comparing and contrasting your companies using these attributes. Discuss any patterns across the companies that you as a team observe. Provide potential explanations for any differences discovered.

**LO1, 3, 4**    **CP3-4 Examining a Real-Life Example: Ethical Decision Making**

Read the excerpt from a September 2, 2002, article in *Fortune* magazine and answer the questions that follow it.

> Forget about fraud. Companies don't need to lie, cheat, and steal to fool investors. Clever managers have always had, and continue to have, access to perfectly legal tricks to help make their balance sheets and income statements look better than they really are—tricks that *even today* won't jeopardize their ability to swear to the SEC that their books are on the up and up. . . . One of the most controversial of all number games—the one that got WorldCom in trouble—is to capitalize expenses. That can have a tremendous impact on the bottom line.

*Required:*

1. In this chapter, you learned that when a company incurs a cost, its accountants have to decide whether to record it as an asset or expense. When costs are recorded as an asset, they are said to be "capitalized." This builds on ideas first presented in Chapter 2, where you learned that it is appropriate to record costs as assets provided that they possess certain characteristics. What are those characteristics?

2. The author of the article argues that even with clear rules such as those referenced in requirement 1, accounting still allows managers to use "tricks" such as *capitalizing expenses*. What do you suppose the author means by the expression *capitalizing expenses*?

3. Suppose that, in the current year, a company inappropriately records a cost as an asset when it should be recorded as an expense. What is the effect of this accounting decision on the current year's net income? What is the effect of this accounting decision on the following year's net income?

4. Later in the article (not shown), the author says that the videogame industry is one in which companies frequently capitalize software development costs as assets. These costs include wages

paid to programmers, fees paid to graphic designers, and amounts paid to game testers. Evaluate whether software development costs are likely to possess the main characteristics possessed by all assets. Can you think of a situation in which software development costs might not possess these main characteristics?

5. Do you think it is always easy and straightforward to determine whether costs should be capitalized or expensed? Do you think it is always easy and straightforward to determine whether a manager is acting ethically or unethically? Give examples to illustrate your views.

## CP3-5 Analyzing a Mini-Case: Ethical Decision Making    LO1, 3, 4

Mike Lynch is the manager of an upstate New York regional office for an insurance company. As the regional manager, his pay package includes a base salary, commissions, and a bonus when the region sells new policies in excess of its quota. Lately Mike has been under enormous pressure stemming largely from two factors. First, he is experiencing mounting personal debt due to a family member's illness. Second, compounding his worries, the region's sales of new insurance policies have dipped below the normal quota for the first time in years.

You have been working for Mike for two years, and like everyone else in the office, you consider yourself lucky to work for such a supportive boss. You also feel great sympathy for his personal problems over the last few months. In your position as accountant for the regional office, you are only too aware of the drop in new policy sales and the impact this will have on Mike's bonus. While you are working on the year-end financial statements, Mike stops by your office.

Mike asks you to change the manner in which you have accounted for a new property insurance policy for a large local business. A check for the premium, substantial in amount, came in the mail on December 31, the last day of the reporting year. The premium covers a period beginning on January 5. You deposited the check and correctly debited cash and credited an *unearned revenue* account. Mike says, "Hey, we have the money this year, so why not count the revenue this year? I never did understand why you accountants are so picky about these things anyway. I'd like you to change the way you've recorded the transaction. I want you to credit a *revenue* account. And anyway, I've done favors for you in the past, and I am asking for such a small thing in return." With that, he leaves your office.

### Required:
Justify your answers to each of the following questions.

1. How should you handle this situation?
2. What are the ethical implications of Mike's request?
3. Who are the parties who would be helped or harmed if you went along with the request?
4. If you fail to comply with his request, how will you explain your position to him?

## CP3-6 Analyzing Changes in Accounts and Preparing a Trial Balance: Critical Thinking    LO1, 4, 5

Stephen Hordichuk organized Hordichuk Painting Service Company as a sole proprietorship on January 20, 2010. The following is a schedule of the cumulative account balances immediately after each of the first ten transactions ending on January 31, 2010.

### CUMULATIVE BALANCES

| Accounts | (a) | (b) | (c) | (d) | (e) | (f) | (g) | (h) | (i) | (j) |
|---|---|---|---|---|---|---|---|---|---|---|
| Cash | $ 75,000 | $ 70,000 | $ 85,000 | $ 71,000 | $ 69,000 | $ 61,000 | $ 61,000 | $ 46,000 | $ 44,000 | $ 60,000 |
| Accounts Receivable | | | 12,000 | 12,000 | 12,000 | 12,000 | 26,000 | 26,000 | 26,000 | 10,000 |
| Supplies | | | | | 5,000 | 5,000 | 5,000 | 5,000 | 5,000 | 5,000 |
| Office Fixtures | | 20,000 | 20,000 | 20,000 | 20,000 | 20,000 | 20,000 | 20,000 | 20,000 | 20,000 |
| Land | | | | 18,000 | 18,000 | 18,000 | 18,000 | 18,000 | 18,000 | 18,000 |
| Accounts Payable | | | | | 3,000 | 3,000 | 3,000 | 3,000 | 1,000 | 1,000 |
| Notes Payable | | 15,000 | 15,000 | 19,000 | 19,000 | 19,000 | 19,000 | 19,000 | 19,000 | 19,000 |
| S. Hordichuk, Capital | 75,000 | 75,000 | 75,000 | 75,000 | 75,000 | 75,000 | 75,000 | 75,000 | 75,000 | 75,000 |
| Paint Revenue | | | 27,000 | 27,000 | 27,000 | 27,000 | 41,000 | 41,000 | 41,000 | 41,000 |
| Wages Expense | | | | | | 8,000 | 8,000 | 23,000 | 23,000 | 23,000 |

*Required:*

1.  Analyze the changes in this schedule for each transaction; then explain the transaction. Transactions *(a)* and *(b)* are examples.

    a.  Cash increased $75,000, and J. Hordichuk, Capital (owner's equity) increased $75,000. Therefore, transaction *(a)* was the receipt of $75,000 cash investment from the owner to establish the business.

    b.  Cash decreased $5,000, Office Fixtures (an asset) increased $20,000, and Notes Payable (a liability) increased $15,000. Therefore, transaction *(b)* was a purchase of office fixtures that cost $20,000. Payment was made as follows: cash, $5,000; notes payable, $15,000.

2.  Based only on the preceding schedule, prepare an unadjusted trial balance.

**LO1, 4, 5**

### CP3-7 Analyzing Transactions and Preparing an Unadjusted Trial Balance

Assume you recently started a new company that rents machines for making frozen drinks such as smoothies, frozen juices, tea slush, and iced cappuccinos. For $100, your business will deliver a machine, provide supplies (straws and paper cups), set up the machine, and pick up the machine the next morning. Other businesses in your city sell drink mix and other supplies. Being a one-person operation, you are responsible for everything from purchasing to marketing to operations to accounting.

You decide that you will just write notes about what happens during the month and then do the accounting at the end of the month. You figure this will be more efficient. Your notes said the following about your first month of operations:

|   |   |   |
|---|---|---|
| a. | Oct. 2  | Received $10,000 cash investment from the owner to establish Slusher Gusher. |
| b. | Oct. 12 | Paid cash to buy three frozen drink machines on eBay at a total cost of $1,500. |
| c. | Oct. 13 | Paid cash to buy $70 of supplies. |
| d. | Oct. 16 | Received $500 cash for this past week's rentals. |
| e. | Oct. 20 | Bought $100 of supplies on account. |
| f. | Oct. 23 | Received $400 cash from customers who owe $200 more for services provided. |
| g. | Oct. 25 | Received $100 cash from one of the customers who had not paid yet. |
| h. | Oct. 26 | Ran an ad in the local paper today for $25 cash. |
| i. | Oct. 27 | Received $150 cash for a two-machine All Saints Day party to be held on November 1. |

*Required:*

Create a spreadsheet to record the effects of the October transactions and calculate end-of-month totals. Using the spreadsheet, prepare a trial balance that checks whether debits equal credits. Because you are dealing with your own business this time, you want to be extra sure that you do this just right, so you e-mail your friend Sally for advice. Her reply follows on the next page.

From:       Sally@yahoo.com
To:         Helpme@hotmail.com
Cc:
Subject:    Excel Help

Wow, you're a CEO already? I always thought you were a mover and a shaker! So you want my advice on how to set up your spreadsheet? My advice is read the last e-mail I sent *[see PB2-6]*. The main thing that's new here is that you'll need to include some columns for revenue and expenses under the owner's equity heading. Here's a screen shot of how the right-hand side of your worksheet might look just before you enter the October transactions. Notice that because expenses decrease owner's equity , the debit side is used to record expenses.

To prepare the trial balance, create three columns. In the first, copy and paste the account names (one per row). In the second column, link in each debit balance by entering = in a cell and then clicking on the debit total from the T-account. Repeat this with all accounts. Then do the same with the credit balances. At the bottom of the trial balance, use the SUM function to compute totals.

Don't forget to save the file using a name that uniquely identifies you (as my true hero).

# 4 Completing the Accounting Cycle

## LEARNING OBJECTIVES

**After studying this chapter, you should be able to:**

**LO1** Explain the purpose of adjustments at the end of the accounting cycle.

**LO2** Identify and analyze the adjustments necessary at the end of the period to update balance sheet and income statement accounts.

**LO3** Present an income statement, statement of owner's equity, and balance sheet.

**LO4** Explain the purpose and process of closing the books.

**LO5** Compute and interpret the net profit margin ratio.

Lectured slideshow—LP4-1
www.mhhe.com/LLPW1e

## Focus Company: PIZZA AROMA, Ithaca, NY

## Adjusting the Accounts, Closing the Books, and Analyzing Financial Information

In Chapter 3, you saw that Pizza Aroma sold a lot of pizza during its first month of operations—more than owner-manager Mauricio Rosa had expected. Mauricio was very curious to know how the business performed, so he made a simple computation:

- Using the preliminary income statement (in Exhibit 3.8), he found that net income was almost 83% of pizza revenue.[1] He knew that rival Papa John's usually reported a net income of only about 5% of its revenues.

Mauricio was very excited and eager to discuss these results with Laurie, his CPA.

At their meeting, Laurie congratulated Mauricio on having a good first month. However, she cautioned him that because he had been using **unadjusted amounts** in his computations, his results and comparisons were not meaningful. She emphasized that at the end of an accounting period, managers must make many evaluations and estimates (1) to update amounts already recorded in the accounting records and (2) to include events that had occurred but had not yet been recorded.

These adjustments ensure that the recognition of revenues and expenses will occur in the proper period, and that the measurement of assets and liabilities will represent their appropriate amounts. For example, this process would include updating the Supplies account to reflect the amounts used during the month, among many other adjustments. After the accounts have been adjusted, financial statements should be prepared for owners, creditors, and other users. Only then would Mauricio be able to compute and interpret useful ratios.

In this chapter, you will learn why adjustments are necessary in accrual basis accounting. Understanding the purpose of adjustments will help you to determine what adjustments

---

[1] Pizza Aroma: Net income $11,600 ÷ Pizza revenue $14,000 = 0.83, or 83%. Papa John's average from 2004 to 2006: Average net income $44.2 million ÷ Average revenues $965.2 million = 0.046, or about 5%.

are needed and how to record and summarize them. Then you will learn how to prepare Pizza Aroma's May 31 financial statements using the adjusted accounts and how to prepare its accounting records for the next period by "closing the books." Finally, you will learn a common ratio that is helpful in evaluating a business's financial performance.

## ORGANIZATION OF THE CHAPTER

| ADJUSTING REVENUES AND EXPENSES | PREPARING FINANCIAL STATEMENTS | COMPLETING THE ACCOUNTING CYCLE | ANALYZING FINANCIAL INFORMATION |
|---|---|---|---|
| • Reasons for Adjustments <br> • Types of Adjustments <br> • Analysis of Adjustments <br>   • Unearned Revenues <br>   • Accrued Revenues <br>   • Prepaid Expenses <br>   • Accrued Expenses | • Adjusted Trial Balance <br> • Relationships among Financial Statements <br> • Classified Income Statement <br> • Statement of Owner's Equity <br> • Classified Balance Sheet | • Closing the Books <br> • Preparing a Post-Closing Trial Balance | • Computing and Interpreting Key Ratios <br> • Analyzing Net Profit Margin <br> • Making Comparisons to Benchmarks |

# ADJUSTING REVENUES AND EXPENSES

Video 4-1
www.mhhe.com/LLPW1e

See Exhibit 4.1 for the basic steps in the **accounting cycle.** As you saw in Chapters 2 and 3, the accounting cycle is the process in which businesses analyze, record, and post the effects of transactions; adjust the records at the end of the period; prepare the financial statements; and then prepare the accounting records for the next accounting cycle. In this chapter, you will study the *end-of-period* phase of this cycle, which focuses primarily on adjustments made to record revenues and expenses in the proper period and to update the balance sheet accounts.

## Reasons for Adjustments

Accounting systems are designed to record most recurring daily transactions, particularly those involving cash. As cash is received or paid, it is recorded in the accounting system. In general, this focus on cash works well, especially when cash receipts and payments occur in the same period as the activities that produce revenues and expenses. However, cash is not always received in the period in which the company earns the related revenue; likewise, cash is not always paid in the period in which the company incurs the related expense.

**Exhibit 4.1    The Accounting Cycle**

**DURING THE PERIOD**
**(Chapters 2 and 3)**
- Analyze transactions
- Record journal entries in the general journal
- Post amounts to the general ledger

**AT THE END OF THE PERIOD**
**(Chapter 4)**
- Adjust revenues and expenses and related balance sheet accounts
- Prepare a complete set of financial statements and disseminate the statements to users
- Close revenues, gains, expenses, losses, and withdrawals to owner's equity

How does the accounting system record revenues and expenses when one transaction is needed to record a cash receipt or payment and another transaction is needed to record revenue when it is earned or an expense when it is incurred? The solution to the problem created by such differences in timing is to record **adjusting entries** at the end of every accounting period so that:

- Revenues are recorded when they are earned (the **revenue principle**).
- Expenses are recorded when they are incurred to generate revenue (the **matching principle**).
- **Assets** are reported at amounts that represent the probable future benefits remaining at the end of the period.
- **Liabilities** are reported at amounts that represent the probable future sacrifices of assets or services owed at the end of the period.

> **Learning Objective 2**
>
> Identify and analyze the adjustments necessary at the end of the period to update balance sheet and income statements accounts.

Companies wait until the **end of the accounting period** to adjust their accounts in this way because adjusting the records daily would be very costly and time consuming. Adjusting entries are required every time a company wants to prepare financial statements for external users. In practice, almost every account could require an adjustment. Rather than trying to memorize an endless list of specific examples, you should focus instead on learning the general types of adjustments needed and the process used to determine how to adjust the accounts.

## Types of Adjustments

There are four types of adjustments:

**Revenues**

- **Unearned Revenues** Previously recorded liabilities that were created when cash was received in advance and that must be adjusted for the amount of revenue actually earned during the period.
- **Accrued Revenues** Revenues that were earned but not yet recorded, with cash to be received in future periods.

**Expenses**

- **Prepaid Expenses** Previously recorded assets, such as Prepaid Rent, Supplies, and Equipment, that were created when cash was paid in advance and that must be adjusted for the amount of expense actually incurred during the period through use of the asset.
- **Accrued Expenses** are expenses that were incurred but not yet recorded, with cash to be paid in future periods.

Each of these types of adjustments involves two entries:

- One for the cash receipt or payment.
- One for recording the revenue or expense in the proper period (through the adjusting entry).

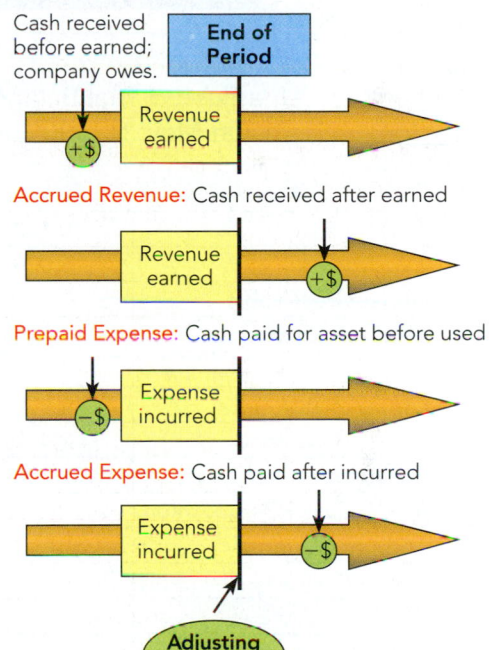

We will illustrate the process involved in analyzing and adjusting the accounts by reviewing all adjustments Laurie made for Pizza Aroma before preparing the first month's statements.

## Analysis of Adjustments

Analyzing adjustments at the end of the period involves three steps:

**Step 1** *Identify the type of adjustment.* Unearned Revenue and Prepaid Expense accounts exist at the end of the period but are overstated, and the related revenue or expense is understated. Accrued Revenues and Accrued Expenses that have occured but have not been recorded are understated, as are the related receivable and payable accounts.

**Step 2** *Determine the amount* of revenue earned or expense incurred during the period. Sometimes the amount is known, sometimes it is calculated, and sometimes it must be estimated. This will be the amount needed in the adjusting entry for the revenue or expense account.

**Step 3** *Record the adjusting journal entry* and post it to the appropriate accounts. Unearned Revenue or Prepaid Expense accounts, in which cash had previously been received

**Coach's Tip**

This section contains the topics that many people typically find the most challenging. **Read these pages carefully.**

or paid, are reduced in adjusting entries to their remaining balance. For accrued revenues, the other half of the entry increases a receivable account; for accrued expenses, the other half of the entry increases a payable account.

So what are the adjustments needed for Pizza Aroma at the end of May?

**Step ① Identify type of adjustment. Laurie showed Mauricio the unadjusted trial balance (see Exhibit 4.2) and pointed out the accounts that needed adjustment.**

As you can see, Pizza Aroma's adjustments included one unearned revenue account, one accrued revenue account, four prepaid expense accounts, and three accrued expense accounts. Let's begin with an analysis of the revenue adjustments. Note that the abbreviation *AJE* stands for adjusting journal entry.

### Unearned Revenues

When a customer pays for goods or services before the company delivers them, the company records the amount of cash received in an Unearned Revenue account. This unearned revenue

**Coach's Tip**

Remember that all adjusting entries are made at the end of the period and then are posted to appropriate accounts affected.

---

**Exhibit 4.2    Pizza Aroma's Unadjusted Trial Balance**

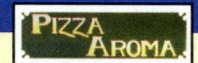

### Pizza Aroma
### Unadjusted Trial Balance
### On May 31, 2009

| | Debit | Credit | To identify where adjustments are needed: |
|---|---|---|---|
| Cash | 9,100 | | |
| Investments | 6,000 | | Determine whether any interest has been earned. If so, |
| Interest Receivable | 0 | | **Accrued Revenue** ⇒ Amount of interest earned and to be received |
| Accounts Receivable | 700 | | |
| Supplies | 5,000 | | **Prepaid Expense** ⇒ Determine amount of supplies used during period |
| Prepaid Rent | 4,800 | | **Prepaid Expense** ⇒ Determine amount of rent used during period |
| Prepaid Insurance | 2,400 | | **Prepaid Expense** ⇒ Determine amount of insurance used during period |
| Equipment | 36,000 | | **Prepaid Expense** ⇒ Determine depreciation expense |
| Accumulated Depreciation | | 0 | Represents the total amount of equipment used |
| Accounts Payable | | 4,800 | |
| Wages Payable | | 0 | **Accrued Expense** ⇒ Amount of wages incurred and owed to employees |
| Utilities Payable | | 0 | **Accrued Expense** ⇒ Amount of utilities incurred and owed for period |
| Interest Payable | | 0 | **Accrued Expense** ⇒ Amount of interest owed on debt for period |
| Unearned Revenue | | 600 | **Unearned Revenue** ⇒ Determine amount earned for deliveries during period |
| Notes Payable | | 20,000 | |
| M. Rosa, Capital | | 30,000 | |
| M. Rosa, Drawing | 3,000 | | |
| Pizza Revenue | | 14,000 | Revenue from delivering pizza sold during period |
| Investment Revenue | | 0 | Revenue on investments earned during period |
| Supplies Expense | 0 | | Expense for supplies used during period |
| Wages Expense | 1,000 | | Expense for wages incurred during period |
| Utilities Expense | 0 | | Expense for utilities used during period |
| Telephone Service Expense | 600 | | Expense for telephone service used during period |
| Rent Expense | 0 | | Expense for rent used during period |
| Insurance Expense | 0 | | Expense for insurance used during period |
| Advertising Expense | 800 | | Expense for advertising used during period |
| Depreciation Expense | 0 | | Expense for depreciation of equipment used during period |
| Interest Expense | 0 | | Expense for interest incurred on debt during period |
| **Totals** | **69,400** | **69,400** | |

is a liability representing the company's promise to perform or deliver the goods or services in the future. Recognition of (recording) the revenue is postponed (deferred) until the company meets its obligation.

**AJE 1.** During May, Pizza Aroma collected $600 in deposits from fraternities ordering pizza deliveries on upcoming graduation and reunion weekends. When received, the business recorded $600 cash as Unearned Revenue, a liability, to recognize its obligation to deliver pizzas in the future. Pizza Aroma earned no revenue when it received the cash because the company had not yet delivered the pizzas.

**Step ② Determine the amount.** By the end of May, Pizza Aroma had delivered and earned $400 of the $600 in revenue associated with the graduation events. However, that $400 is still included in the Unearned Revenue account. Because only $200 in pizza remained to be delivered in June and was therefore unearned at the end of May, the $600 balance in the Unearned Revenue account is overstated by $400.

**Step ③ Record the AJE.** An adjusting entry is therefore necessary to reduce the Unearned Revenue account by $400 and increase the Pizza Revenue account by $400. After the entry is made, its effects are posted to the appropriate T-accounts.

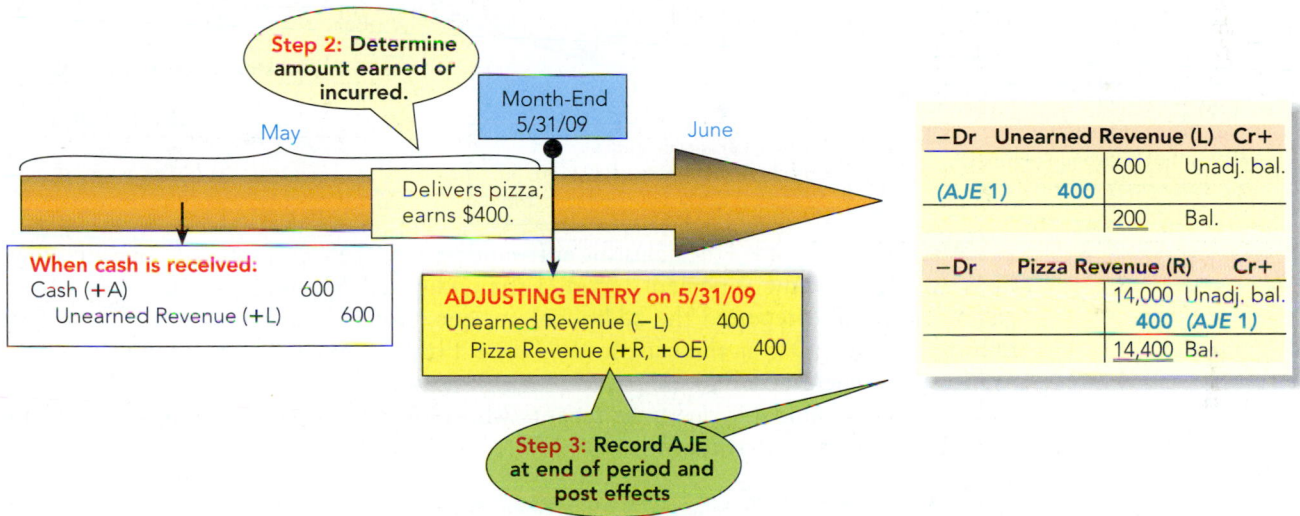

After the adjusting entry was made, the income statement reported the additional $400 of Pizza Revenue earned in May, and the balance sheet reported the remaining liability of $200 in the Unearned Revenue account.

Additional examples of unearned revenues for other companies include magazine subscriptions; season tickets to sporting events, plays, and concerts; airplane tickets sold in advance; and rent paid in advance by renters. Each of these requires an adjusting entry at the end of the accounting period to report the amount of revenue earned during the period.

## Spotlight On FINANCIAL REPORTING

### Millions, Even Billions in Unearned Revenue

In a recent year, Readers' Digest Association, producer of *Readers' Digest* magazine and 28 other magazines and numerous books, reported more than $390 million in current Unearned Revenues and $131 million in noncurrent Unearned Revenues for subscriptions sold in advance to customers. United Air Lines reported the following unearned revenues: (1) nearly $1.7 billion in Advance Ticket Sales and (2) more than $3.6 billion in unearned revenues in the account Mileage Plus Deferred Revenue representing the amount the company estimated it promised to customers for future flights under its frequent flyer program.

## Accrued Revenues

Sometimes companies perform services or provide goods (that is, earn revenue) before customers pay. Because the cash that is owed for these goods and services has not yet been received, the revenue that was earned has not been recorded. Revenues that have been earned but have not yet been recorded at the end of the accounting period are called **accrued revenues.**

**AJE 2.** Near the beginning of May, Pizza Aroma deposited $6,000 cash in a savings account at a local bank. The savings account earns investment (or interest) revenue over time, but Pizza Aroma does not receive cash until a withdrawal is made when needed in the future.

**Step 2    Amount.** The bank statement has indicated that the savings account earned $30 during May.

**Step 3    AJE.** An adjusting entry is needed at the end of May to recognize the $30 in Investment Revenue earned but not yet received. The other half of the entry is to Interest Receivable.

After Laurie recorded the adjusting entry and posted its effects to the appropriate accounts, Pizza Aroma's income statement reported the additional $30 revenue earned in May. The balance sheet also reported the additional current asset of $30, representing Pizza Aroma's right to receive $30 from the bank in the future. Pizza Aroma will make a similar adjustment at the end of each month as long as the savings account is open. Other examples of accrued revenue include amounts due from tenants who rent space from the company and interest earned on loans made to others.

## Prepaid Expenses

Businesses use many assets over time to generate revenues. At the end of every period, they must make an adjustment to record the amount of the asset that was used during the period. Let's analyze Pizza Aroma's four prepaid expenses at the end of May.

**Supplies.** Supplies are prepaid expenses that must be adjusted for the dollar amount used during the period.

**AJE 3.** During May, Pizza Aroma purchased $5,000 in supplies. On May 31, Mauricio counted that $600 worth of supplies remained on hand.

**Step 2    Amount.** The easiest way to determine the dollar amount of supplies used is to add the dollar amount of supplies available at the beginning of the period plus any purchases made during the period and then subtract the dollar amount of supplies remaining on hand at the end of the period.

| Computation of Supplies Expense | |
| --- | --- |
| Beginning balance of supplies | $    0 |
| + Supply purchases during the period | 5,000 |
| − Ending amount of supplies on hand | ( 600) |
| Supplies used during the period | $4,400 |

**Step ③ AJE.** An adjusting entry is needed to record the use of $4,400 of supplies during May.

After the adjusting entry was recorded and its effects posted to the accounts, Pizza Aroma's income statement reported $4,400 of Supplies Expense, and the balance sheet reported the remaining $600 in Supplies.

**Prepaid Rent.** Like supplies, prepaid rent is a prepaid expense that must be adjusted for the amount used during the period.

**AJE 4.** At the beginning of May, Pizza Aroma paid $4,800 in advance to rent the store for six months (May through October).

**Step ② Amount.** At the end of May, one month of the Prepaid Rent had been used to generate revenue: $4,800 \times 1/6 = \$800$ of Rent Expense in May.

**Step ③ AJE.** An adjusting entry is needed to record the amount of rent used for the month.

After the adjusting entry was recorded and its effects posted to the accounts, Pizza Aroma's income statement reported the additional $800 of Rent Expense incurred in May. The balance sheet also reported the remaining asset of $4,000, representing the unused portion of the Prepaid Rent. Pizza Aroma will make a similar adjustment at the end of each of the remaining five months.

**Prepaid Insurance.** Like rent, insurance is usually paid for before the coverage begins. At the end of May, Pizza Aroma purchased insurance for $2,400 covering June, July, and August. It recorded the asset Prepaid Insurance on that date. Because the insurance did not begin until June, none of the asset had been used by the end of May. Thus, **no adjusting entry was necessary at the end of May.** However, at the end of June, July, and August, an adjusting entry will be necessary to reduce the Prepaid Insurance account and record Insurance Expense of $800, representing one month of insurance coverage ($2,400 ÷ 3 months).

> **ADJUSTING ENTRY at the end of June, July, and August**
> Insurance Expense (+E, −OE)        800
>     Prepaid Insurance (−A)                        800

**Equipment.** Unlike supplies that are purchased and then used over a relatively short period, buildings and equipment represent prepaid expenses that will be used over many years.

Building and equipment accounts increase when the assets are **acquired** and decrease when they are **sold**. However, these assets are also **used** over time to generate revenue. Thus, a part of their cost should be expensed in the same period (the matching principle). Accountants say that buildings and equipment **depreciate** over time as they are used. Depreciation **is an allocation of an asset's cost to an expense over its estimated useful life to the company.**

It is important to keep track of the asset's historical cost. As such, the amount that has been used is not subtracted directly from the asset account. Instead, it is accumulated in a new kind of account called a **contra-account**. Contra-accounts are accounts that are directly related to another account but with an opposite balance. To identify these accounts, we will place an x in front of the type of account to which the contra-account relates. For example, the contra-account titled Accumulated Depreciation (xA) is used to accumulate the amount of historical cost used in prior periods. Because assets have debit balances, Accumulated Depreciation has a credit balance. On the balance sheet, the amount that is reported for equipment is its **net book value** (also called the book value or carrying value), which equals the ending balance in the Equipment account minus the ending balance in the Accumulated Depreciation account.

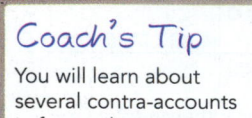

**Coach's Tip**

You will learn about several contra-accounts in future chapters. Remember: each contra-account is related to another account, but with the opposite balance.

| + Equipment (A) – | | – Accumulated Depreciation (xA) + | | |
|---|---|---|---|---|
| Beginning bal. | | | Beginning bal. | |
| Buy | Sell | | Used | |
| Ending bal. | | | Ending bal. | = Net book value |

Amount reported on the balance sheet

**AJE 5.** At the beginning of May, Pizza Aroma purchased $36,000 in equipment that is expected to be used for many years. It was used for one month to generate revenue.

**Step ❷ Amount.** Mauricio estimates that $300 is the cost allocation (depreciation) that must be adjusted to reflect the use of equipment in May. (The computations for estimating the amount of depreciation expense will be covered in detail in future chapters.)

**Step ❸ AJE.** An adjusting entry is needed to record the allocation of the cost of equipment to reflect the estimate of the amount used to generate revenue in May.

After the adjusting entry was recorded and its effects posted to the accounts, Pizza Aroma reported $300 of Depreciation Expense on the income statement and an increase in the contra-asset account Accumulated Depreciation. Notice that the Equipment account was not affected by the recording of depreciation for the month. However, the amount that was reported on the balance sheet at the end of May was $35,700, the equipment's net book value.

| Equipment | – | Accumulated Depreciation | = | Net Book Value |
|---|---|---|---|---|
| (cost) | | (used cost) | | (unused cost) |
| End of May    $36,000 | – | $300 | = | $35,700 |

Each month, the amount of cost allocated to Depreciation Expense will increase the Accumulated Depreciation account. At the end of June, for example, Accumulated Depreciation will have a $600 balance, and the balance sheet will report a net book value of $35,400.

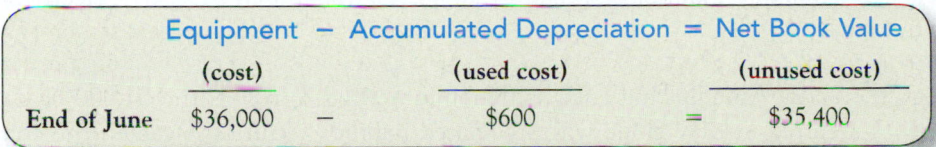

| | Equipment | − | Accumulated Depreciation | = | Net Book Value |
|---|---|---|---|---|---|
| | (cost) | | (used cost) | | (unused cost) |
| End of June | $36,000 | − | $600 | = | $35,400 |

A common misconception held by students and others unfamiliar with accounting is that depreciation as used by accountants reflects a decline in an asset's *market value* (the amount the asset could be sold for). **In accounting, depreciation is simply a cost allocation concept, not a way to report a reduction in market value.** Depreciation Expense is reported each period on the income statement and describes the portion of the asset's historical cost that is estimated to have been used up during the period.

## Accrued Expenses

Numerous expenses are incurred in the current period without being paid for until the next period. Common examples include Wages Expense for the wages owed to employees, Utilities Expense for the water, gas, and electricity used during the period, and Interest Expense incurred on debt. At the end of the period, an adjusting entry records these expenses in the proper period.

**Wages.** Businesses use the services of employees to generate revenue. Although a company may employ workers steadily, the business does not pay employees until after they work, usually at the end of the week, every two weeks, or the month. At the end of the accounting period, then, an adjusting entry records the expense for the wages owed to employees who have not yet been paid.

**AJE 6.** Pizza Aroma's employees worked the last week of May, but they will not be paid until June 1.

**Step 2 Amount.** Mauricio calculates the business incurred $100 of Wages Expense that was not recorded in May.

**Step 3 AJE.** An adjusting entry is needed to record the expense and the related liability, Wages Payable.

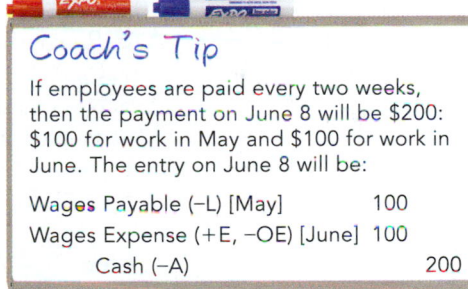

**Coach's Tip**

If employees are paid every two weeks, then the payment on June 8 will be $200: $100 for work in May and $100 for work in June. The entry on June 8 will be:

Wages Payable (−L) [May] 100
Wages Expense (+E, −OE) [June] 100
    Cash (−A) 200

After the adjusting entry was recorded and its effects posted, Pizza Aroma's income statement reported $100 of Wages Expense. The balance sheet reported a current liability of $100 in Wages Payable.

**Utilities.** Businesses use electricity, gas, and telephone service over time but the utility companies bill them at the end of the period. To reflect usage of these utility services in the proper period, an adjusting entry must be made.

**AJE 7.** Pizza Aroma used utilities to generate revenue in May, but because no bill was received by the end of the month, no entry was made to recognize the expense incurred that month.

**Step 2 Amount.** Mauricio estimates that Pizza Aroma used $1,000 of electricity and gas in May.

**Step 3 AJE.** An adjusting entry is therefore needed to record the $1,000 of Utilities Expense incurred in May along with its related liability, Utilities Payable. The company will pay the bill in June when it is received.

Similar to wages, Pizza Aroma's income statement reported $1,000 of Utilities Expense. In addition, the balance sheet reported another current liability Utilities Payable for $1,000.

**Interest.** When a company borrows funds, it must pay interest. Each day that passes, the company incurs interest expense (the cost of using borrowed funds). Most loans require payment of interest at the end of the month, quarter, or year. An adjusting entry is needed at the end of the period to record the accrual of any interest expense owed.

**AJE 8.** At the beginning of May, Pizza Aroma borrowed $20,000 from a local bank. This $20,000 is the **principal** of the loan that was recorded in Notes Payable in exchange for $20,000 cash from the bank. The loan requires Pizza Aroma to repay the principal in three years **plus interest** on May 1 each year. As each day in May passed, the company used the borrowed funds and incurred interest, but Pizza Aroma did not record any expense because no cash for the interest had yet been paid.

**Step 2 Amount.** With Laurie's assistance, Mauricio determined that $200 in interest expense was incurred during May. (The computations for determining the amount of interest expense will be covered in detail in future chapters.)

**Step 3 AJE.** At the end of May, the $20,000 principal recorded as Notes Payable remained due, so no adjustment to Notes Payable was necessary. However, one month of interest expense has been incurred. An adjusting entry is needed to record the $200 in Interest Expense for May and the related liability in Interest Payable.

After recording and posting the adjusting entry, Pizza Aroma's income statement reported Interest Expense of $200. Another current liability, Interest Payable, for $200 is reported on the balance sheet.

## Spotlight On FINANCIAL REPORTING

### Accrued Expenses in the Millions and Billions

Accrued expenses are significant liabilities for many companies. For example, Tootsie Roll Industries recently reported the following:

NOTE 2—ACCRUED LIABILITIES:
Accrued liabilities are comprised of the following:

| (in thousands of dollars) | DECEMBER 31, 2006 | 2005 |
|---|---|---|
| Compensation | $ 12,923 | $ 15,756 |
| Other employee benefits | 5,631 | 5,213 |
| Taxes, other than income | 1,781 | 1,765 |
| Advertising and promotions | 17,854 | 14,701 |
| Other | 5,613 | 7,534 |
| | $ 43,802 | $ 44,969 |

The $43.8 million in total accrued liabilities represents 70 percent of Tootsie Roll's current liabilities and 27 percent of total liabilities.

Likewise, Wal-Mart Stores, Inc., reported approximately $14.7 billion in accrued liabilities, primarily from accrued wages and benefits owed to employees. This was 28 percent of current liabilities and 17 percent of total liabilities.

Pizza Aroma's accounts have now been adjusted and all of the revenues and expenses for May properly recorded. See Exhibit 4.3 for a summary of the adjusting entries *AJE 1* through

| Exhibit 4.3 | Summary of Pizza Aroma's Adjusting Entries | | PIZZA AROMA |
|---|---|---|---|

**Pizza Aroma**
**Adjusting Journal Entries**
**May 31, 2009**

| | | Debit | Credit | |
|---|---|---|---|---|
| (AJE 1) | Unearned Revenue (−L) | 400 | | Unearned revenue |
| | Pizza Revenue (+R, +OE) | | 400 | |
| (AJE 2) | Interest Receivable (+A) | 30 | | Accrued revenue |
| | Investment Revenue (+R, +OE) | | 30 | |
| (AJE 3) | Supplies Expense (+E, −OE) | 4,400 | | |
| | Supplies (−A) | | 4,400 | |
| (AJE 4) | Rent Expense (+E, −OE) | 800 | | Prepaid expenses |
| | Prepaid Rent (−A) | | 800 | |
| (AJE 5) | Depreciation Expense (+E, −OE) | 300 | | |
| | Accumulated Depreciation (+xA, −A) | | 300 | |
| (AJE 6) | Wages Expense (+E, −OE) | 100 | | |
| | Wages Payable (+L) | | 100 | |
| (AJE 7) | Utilities Expense (+E, −OE) | 1,000 | | Accrued expenses |
| | Utilities Payable (+L) | | 1,000 | |
| (AJE 8) | Interest Expense (+E, −OE) | 200 | | |
| | Interest Payable (+L) | | 200 | |

## Exhibit 4.4   Summary of Pizza Aroma's T-Accounts after Adjustment

| Pizza Aroma | T-Accounts | May 31, 2009 |
|---|---|---|

### Assets

**+   Cash (A)   –**

| | |
|---|---|
| Bal. 9,100 | |
| Bal. 9,100 | |

**+   Investments (A)   –**

| | |
|---|---|
| Bal. 6,000 | |
| Bal. 6,000 | |

**Interest**
**+   Receivable (A)   –**

| | |
|---|---|
| Unadj. bal.   0 | |
| (AJE 2)  30 | |
| Bal.  30 | |

**Accounts**
**+   Receivable (A)   –**

| | |
|---|---|
| Bal.  700 | |
| Bal.  700 | |

**+   Supplies (A)   –**

| | |
|---|---|
| Unadj. bal.  5,000 | |
| | 4,400  (AJE 3) |
| Bal.  600 | |

**+   Prepaid Rent (A)   –**

| | |
|---|---|
| Unadj. bal.  4,800 | |
| | 800  (AJE 4) |
| Bal.  4,000 | |

**+ Prepaid Insurance (A) –**

| | |
|---|---|
| Unadj. bal.  2,400 | |
| Bal.  2,400 | |

**+   Equipment (A)   –**

| | |
|---|---|
| Bal.  36,000 | |
| Bal.  36,000 | |

**Accumulated**
**–   Depreciation (xA)   +**

| | |
|---|---|
| | Unadj.  0  bal. |
| | 300  (AJE 5) |
| | 300  Bal. |

### Liabilities

**–   Accounts Payable (L)   +**

| | |
|---|---|
| | 4,800  Bal. |
| | 4,800  Bal. |

**–   Wages Payable (L)   +**

| | |
|---|---|
| | Unadj.  0  bal. |
| | 100  (AJE 6) |
| | 100  Bal. |

**–   Utilities Payable (L)   +**

| | |
|---|---|
| | Unadj.  0  bal. |
| | 1,000  (AJE 7) |
| | 1,000  Bal. |

**–   Interest Payable (L)   +**

| | |
|---|---|
| | Unadj.  0  bal. |
| | 200  (AJE 8) |
| | 200  Bal. |

**–   Unearned Revenue (L) +**

| | |
|---|---|
| | Unadj.  600  bal. |
| (AJE 1)  400 | |
| | 200  Bal. |

**–   Notes Payable (L)   +**

| | |
|---|---|
| | 20,000  Bal. |
| | 20,000  Bal. |

### Owner's Equity

**M. Rosa,**
**–   Capital (OE)   +**

| | |
|---|---|
| | 30,000  Bal. |
| | 30,000  Bal. |

**M. Rosa,**
**+   Drawing (OE)   –**

| | |
|---|---|
| Bal.  3,000 | |
| Bal.  3,000 | |

### Expenses

**+   Supplies Expense (E)   –**

| | |
|---|---|
| Unadj. bal.  0 | |
| (AJE 3) 4,400 | |
| Bal.  4,400 | |

**+   Wages Expense (E)   –**

| | |
|---|---|
| Unadj. bal.  1,000 | |
| (AJE 6)  100 | |
| Bal.  1,100 | |

**+   Utilities Expense (E)   –**

| | |
|---|---|
| Unadj. bal.  0 | |
| (AJE 7) 1,000 | |
| Bal.  1,000 | |

**Telephone Service**
**+   Expense (E)   –**

| | |
|---|---|
| Bal.  600 | |
| Bal.  600 | |

**+   Rent Expense (E)   –**

| | |
|---|---|
| Unadj. bal.  0 | |
| (AJE 4)  800 | |
| Bal.  800 | |

**+ Advertising Expense (E) –**

| | |
|---|---|
| Bal.  800 | |
| Bal.  800 | |

**+   Interest Expense (E)   –**

| | |
|---|---|
| Unadj. bal.  0 | |
| (AJE 8)  200 | |
| Bal.  200 | |

**Depreciation**
**+   Expense (E)   –**

| | |
|---|---|
| Unadj. bal.  0 | |
| (AJE 5)  300 | |
| Bal.  300 | |

### Revenues

**–   Pizza Revenue (R)   +**

| | |
|---|---|
| | Unadj. 14,000  bal. |
| | 400  (AJE 1) |
| | 14,400  Bal. |

**Investment**
**–   Revenue (R)   +**

| | |
|---|---|
| | Unadj.  0  bal. |
| | 30  (AJE 2) |
| | 30  Bal. |

**Coach's Tip**

A T-account for Insurance Expense has not been listed here because it has a $0 balance.

AJE 8. Refer to Exhibit 4.4 for Pizza Aroma's T-accounts after the adjusting entries were made on May 31, 2009.

## Summary Exhibits

Using selected examples, Exhibit 4.5 summarizes the entries needed to adjust unearned and accrued revenues; Exhibit 4.6 summarizes those needed to adjust most prepaid and accrued expenses. Note that in both cases, the goal is to record revenues and expenses in the proper period. Note too that each adjusting entry involves one balance sheet and one income statement account and that **cash is never affected in the adjustment.**

Coach's Tip
When recording adjustments, remember: **Year-end adjustments never affect the Cash account.**

| Exhibit 4.5 | Summary Illustration of Adjusting Unearned and Accrued Revenues | |
|---|---|---|
| | | **Unearned Revenues** (for deposits on future pizza deliveries) | **Accrued Revenues** (for interest earned on investments) |
| *During the period* | Entry when **cash is received before** company earns revenue | Cash (+A) 600<br>    Unearned Revenue (+L) 600 | None |
| **End of period** | AJE needed because company has earned revenue during period | Unearned Revenue (−L) 400<br>    Pizza Revenue (+R, +OE) 400 | Interest Receivable (+A) 30<br>    Investment Revenue (+R, +OE) 30 |
| *Next period* | Entry when **cash is received after** company **earns** revenue | None | Cash (+A) 30<br>    Interest Receivable (−A) 30 |

Revenue recorded in proper period

| Exhibit 4.6 | Summary Illustration of Adjusting Prepaid and Accrued Expenses | |
|---|---|---|
| | | **Prepaid Expenses** (for renting a building) | **Accrued Expenses** (for amounts owed to workers) |
| *During the period* | Entry when **cash is paid before** company incurs expense | Prepaid Rent (+A) 4,800<br>    Cash (−A) 4,800 | None |
| **End of period** | AJE needed because company has incurred an expense during the period | Rent Expense (+E, −OE) 800<br>    Prepaid Rent (−A) 800 | Wages Expense (+E, −OE) 100<br>    Wages Payable (+L) 100 |
| *Next period* | Entry when **cash is paid after** company incurs expense | None | Wages Payable (−L) 100<br>    Cash (−A) 100 |

Expense recorded in proper period

Now it's your turn to practice adjusting accounts at the end of the period. Review Pizza Aroma's adjustments and then complete the following Self-Study Practice.

**SELF-STUDY PRACTICE**

Florida Flippers, a scuba diving and instruction business, completed its operations on December 31, 2010. Follow the three-step process for each of the following adjustments.

Step  : Identify the type of adjustment needed.

Step  : Determine the amount of the adjustment affecting a revenue or expense account.

Step **3** : Record the adjusting entries on December 31.

**AJE 1:** Florida Flippers received $6,000 from customers on November 15, 2010, for diving trips to the Bahamas in December and January. The $6,000 was recorded in Unearned Revenue on that date. By the end of December, one-third of the diving trips had been completed.

**AJE 2:** On December 30, 2010, Florida Flippers provided advanced diving instruction to 10 customers, who will pay the business $800 in January. No entry was made when the instruction was provided.

**AJE 3:** On September 1, 2010, Florida Flippers paid $24,000 for insurance for the 12 months beginning on September 1. The amount was recorded as Prepaid Insurance on September 1.

**AJE 4:** On March 1, 2010, Florida Flippers borrowed $300,000. Interest is payable each March 1 for three years. Interest incurred for the year was $20,000.

**Coach's Tip**

**Notice:** Four months have passed since purchasing insurance (September, October, November, and December).

| | ① Type of Adjustment | ② Determination of Amount of Adjustment | ③ Adjusting Journal Entry Accounts | Debit | Credit |
|---|---|---|---|---|---|
| AJE 1 | | | | | |
| AJE 2 | | | | | |
| AJE 3 | | | | | |
| AJE 4 | | | | | |

*After you have finished, check your answers with the solution at the bottom of the page.*

## Spotlight On ETHICS

### Adjustments and a Question of Ethics

When a business's financial performance lags behind expectations, managers and owners may be tempted to manipulate accounting adjustments to improve the appearance of the financial statements. For example, managers may record cash received as a revenue even though the company did not earn the revenue in the current period. Or they may fail to accrue certain expenses at year-end. Because these unethical acts cause errors in the financial statements, any ratio analysis that is based on those statements will mislead users.

*(continued)*

**Solution to Self-Study Practice**

| | Type | Amount | Adjusting Journal Entry Accounts | Debit | Credit |
|---|---|---|---|---|---|
| AJE 1 | Unearned Revenue | $6,000 × 1/3 = $2,000 earned | Unearned Revenue (−L) | 2,000 | |
| | | | Diving Trip Revenue (+R, +OE) | | 2,000 |
| AJE 2 | Accrued Revenue | $800 earned (given) | Accounts Receivable (+A) | 800 | |
| | | | Diving Instruction Revenue (+R, +OE) | | 800 |
| AJE 3 | Prepaid Expense | $24,000 × 1/12 = $2,000 per month $2,000 × 4 months = $8,000 used | Insurance Expense (+E, −OE) | 8,000 | |
| | | | Prepaid Insurance (−A) | | 8,000 |
| AJE 4 | Accrued Expense | $20,000 incurred (given) | Interest Expense (+E, −OE) | 20,000 | |
| | | | Interest Payable (+L) | | 20,000 |

**(continued)**

Let's take a look at how Pizza Aroma's financial statements would be affected by failing to record one of the adjusting entries, *AJE 7* (see Exhibit 4.3). In analyzing the effects of this error on the financial statements, follow four steps:

1. Write down the adjusting entry that should have been made.

| (AJE 7) | Utilities Expense (+E, −OE) | 1,000 | |
|---|---|---|---|
| | Utilities Payable (+L) | | 1,000 |

2. Post the effects of failing to record this entry on the following chart. Use U for understated and O for overstated. Because Utilities Expense was not recorded, expenses are understated.

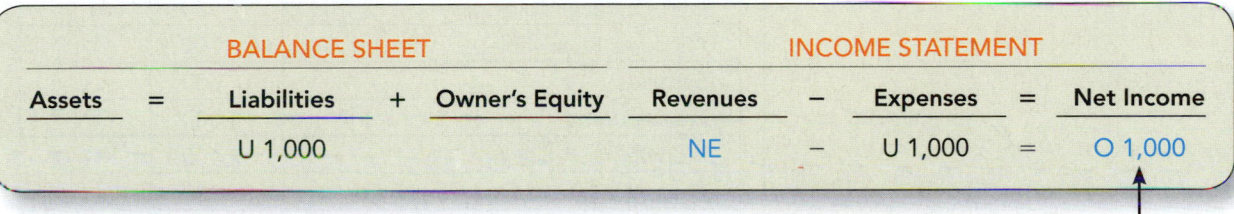

| BALANCE SHEET | | | | INCOME STATEMENT | | | |
|---|---|---|---|---|---|---|---|
| Assets | = | Liabilities | + Owner's Equity | Revenues | − Expenses | = | Net Income |
| | | U 1,000 | | | U 1,000 | | |

3. Beginning with the income statement (revenues, expenses, and net income), indicate the effects on the other elements. Use NE to indicate that there is no effect on an element.

| BALANCE SHEET | | | | INCOME STATEMENT | | | |
|---|---|---|---|---|---|---|---|
| Assets | = | Liabilities | + Owner's Equity | Revenues | − Expenses | = | Net Income |
| | | U 1,000 | | NE | − U 1,000 | = | O 1,000 |

4. Finally, because net income is part of owner's equity, the effect on net income will also be the effect on owner's equity. Complete the rest of the balance sheet elements, checking that the accounting equation remains in balance (that is, assets = liabilities + owner's equity).

**Coach's Tip**

Notice that when an expense is understated, it has the opposite effect on net income—it overstates net income. Watch the minus sign.

| BALANCE SHEET | | | | INCOME STATEMENT | | | |
|---|---|---|---|---|---|---|---|
| Assets | = | Liabilities | + Owner's Equity | Revenues | − Expenses | = | Net Income |
| NE | = | U 1,000 | + O 1,000 | NE | − U 1,000 | = | O 1,000 |

SAME EFFECT

In sum, if *AJE 7* were not recorded, Pizza Aroma's expenses and liabilities would be understated, and its net income and owner's equity would be overstated. Any ratios that are based on these totals would also be in error.

Of course, errors sometimes occur without fraudulent intent. Still, research on many companies indicates that some managers do engage in fraudulent recording of adjusting entries. These studies are borne out by enforcement actions taken by the Securities and Exchange Commission (SEC). A recent SEC study reported 227 enforcement investigations in a five-year period. Of those, "126 involved improper revenue recognition and 101 involved improper expense recognition. . . 157 resulted in charges against at least one senior manager. . . . Furthermore, . . . 57 enforcement matters resulted in charges for auditing violations. . . ."[2] In many of these cases, the businesses involved, their managers, and their auditors were penalized for their actions.

[2] These statistics are reported in the Securities and Exchange Commission's study, "Report Pursuant to Section 704 of the Sarbanes-Oxley Act of 2002," January 27, 2003, p. 47.

# PREPARING FINANCIAL STATEMENTS

## Adjusted Trial Balance

**Learning Objective 3**

Present an income statement, statement of owner's equity, and balance sheet.

Pizza Aroma's accounts are now adjusted so that all revenues and expenses for May are properly recorded. Before Laurie prepares a complete set of financial statements, however, she checks to ensure that debit balances remained equal to credit balances after the adjustments were posted to all of the accounts in the ledger.[3] Exhibit 4.7 is the adjusted trial balance based on

---

[3] For a discussion and illustration of the use of a worksheet for end-of-period adjustments, refer to Supplement 4A of this chapter.

**Exhibit 4.7**    Pizza Aroma's Adjusted Trial Balance

### Pizza Aroma
### Adjusted Trial Balance
### On May 31, 2009

| | ADJUSTED | |
| --- | --- | --- |
| | **Debit** | **Credit** |
| Cash | 9,100 | |
| Investments | 6,000 | |
| Interest Receivable | 30 | |
| Accounts Receivable | 700 | |
| Supplies | 600 | |
| Prepaid Rent | 4,000 | |
| Prepaid Insurance | 2,400 | |
| Equipment | 36,000 | |
| Accumulated Depreciation | | 300 |
| Accounts Payable | | 4,800 |
| Wages Payable | | 100 |
| Utilities Payable | | 1,000 |
| Interest Payable | | 200 |
| Unearned Revenue | | 200 |
| Notes Payable | | 20,000 |
| M. Rosa, Capital | | 30,000 |
| M. Rosa, Drawing | 3,000 | |
| Pizza Revenue | | 14,400 |
| Investment Revenue | | 30 |
| Supplies Expense | 4,400 | |
| Wages Expense | 1,100 | |
| Utilities Expense | 1,000 | |
| Telephone Service Expense | 600 | |
| Rent Expense | 800 | |
| Insurance Expense | 0 | |
| Advertising Expense | 800 | |
| Interest Expense | 200 | |
| Depreciation Expense | 300 | |
| **Totals** | **71,030** | **71,030** |

Balance sheet accounts: Cash through M. Rosa, Drawing

Income statement accounts: Pizza Revenue through Depreciation Expense the updated balances in the T-accounts in Exhibit 4.4. Because the total debits of $71,030 equaled the total credits in the adjusted trial balance, Laurie prepared Pizza Aroma's financial statements for the month of May: an income statement, a statement of owner's equity, and a balance sheet.

# Relationships among Financial Statements

As you learned in Chapter 1, the financial statements are interrelated—that is, the numbers from one statement flow into the next statement. Exhibit 4.8 illustrates the interconnections among the statements using the fundamental accounting equation. Starting on the bottom right, notice that

1. Revenue minus expenses yields net income on the **income statement.**
2. Net income, owner withdrawals, and any additional investments made by the owner during the period affect the balance in the owner's capital account on the **statement of owner's equity.**
3. The owner's capital account is a component of the **balance sheet.**

Thus, if a number on the income statement changes or is in error, it will impact the other statements.

Exhibit 4.8 also includes special labels for the accounts. Balance sheet accounts are considered **permanent,** indicating that they retain their balances from the end of one period to the beginning of the next. Revenue, expense, and the owner's drawing accounts are **temporary** accounts because their balances accumulate for a period but start with a zero balance at the beginning of the next period. These labels will be discussed in the section on *closing the books* following the presentation of Pizza Aroma's classified financial statements.

The structures of the classified financial statements as discussed in Chapters 1 through 3 are provided in summary formats in Exhibit 4.9. The connection between the income statement

**Exhibit 4.8    Relationships of the Financial Statements**

**Exhibit 4.9    Formats of the Classified Financial Statements**

and statement of owner's equity is net income. The connection between the statement of owner's equity and the balance sheet is the ending balance in owner's equity.

## Classified Income Statement

The income statement is prepared first because net income is a component of Owner's Equity. Laurie presented the following income statement for May (in Exhibit 4.10) to Mauricio for his review. Note that it is classified into operating revenue and expenses and other items (revenues and expenses not related to the central focus of the business).

Mauricio was very happy with Pizza Aroma's financial performance during its first month of operations. Before he established the business, Laurie had shown him a projected income statement for May (see Exhibit 1.5, page 15) that showed a projected revenue of $11,000. The actual revenue of $14,400 was about 31 percent higher than anticipated. Mauricio's strategy of aggressive advertising on college campuses together with word-of-mouth reports on the high quality of his gourmet pizza appears to have paid off in better-than-expected sales.

Pizza Aroma earned a net income of $5,230—more than double the $2,000 that Laurie had projected. Mauricio credits this success to his close attention to controlling costs while maintaining quality. He is greatly encouraged about the business's potential.

## Statement of Owner's Equity

To connect net income to the balance sheet, the next statement to prepare is the statement of owner's equity. The beginning balance of the account called M. Rosa, Capital is affected by the amount of net income shown on the income statement, in addition to any investments or withdrawals the owner made during the period. The result is the ending balance in the M. Rosa, Capital account, which is a component of the balance sheet.

**Exhibit 4.10**    Pizza Aroma's Classified Income Statement

### Pizza Aroma
### Income Statement
### For the Month Ended May 31, 2009

| | |
|---|---:|
| **Operating Revenues** | |
| Pizza revenue | $14,400 |
| Total operating revenues | 14,400 |
| **Operating Expenses** | |
| Supplies expense | 4,400 |
| Wages expense | 1,100 |
| Utilities expense | 1,000 |
| Telephone service expense | 600 |
| Rent expense | 800 |
| Advertising expense | 800 |
| Depreciation expense | 300 |
| Total operating expenses | 9,000 |
| **Operating Income** | 5,400 |
| **Other Items** | |
| Investment revenue | 30 |
| Interest expense | (200) |
| **Net Income** | $ 5,230 |

**Pizza Aroma**
**Statement of Owner's Equity**
**For the Month Ended May 31, 2009**

| | |
|---|---:|
| M. Rosa, capital, May 1, 2009 | $      0 |
| Additional investments | 30,000 |
| Net income | 5,230 |
| M. Rosa, drawing | (3,000) |
| M. Rosa, capital, May 31, 2009 | $32,230 |

# Classified Balance Sheet

The ending balance for M. Rosa, Capital, which is taken from the Statement of Owner's Equity, becomes the total Owner's Equity on the Balance Sheet. Note that the contra-asset account Accumulated Depreciation has been subtracted from the Equipment account to reflect the equipment's net book value (or carrying value) at month-end. Recall that assets are listed in order of their liquidity, and liabilities are listed in order of their due dates. Current assets are those that will be used or turned into cash within one year. Current liabilities are obligations that must be paid with current assets within one year.

**Pizza Aroma**
**Balance Sheet**
**May 31, 2009**

| | |
|---|---:|
| **ASSETS** | |
| *Current Assets* | |
| Cash | $ 9,100 |
| Investments | 6,000 |
| Accounts receivable | 700 |
| Interest receivable | 30 |
| Supplies | 600 |
| Prepaid rent | 4,000 |
| Prepaid insurance | 2,400 |
| Total current assets | 22,830 |
| Equipment (cost, $36,000 less accumulated depreciation, $300) | 35,700 |
| Total assets | $58,530 |
| | |
| **LIABILITIES AND OWNER'S EQUITY** | |
| *Current Liabilities* | |
| Accounts payable | $ 4,800 |
| Wages payable | 100 |
| Utilities payable | 1,000 |
| Interest payable | 200 |
| Unearned revenue | 200 |
| Total current liabilities | 6,300 |
| Notes payable | 20,000 |
| *Owner's Equity* | |
| M. Rosa, Capital | 32,230 |
| Total liabilities and owner's equity | $58,530 |

Laurie explained to Mauricio that Pizza Aroma's balance sheet shows that it is in strong financial condition. The external user of Pizza Aroma's statements, the local bank, will be pleased to see that there are sufficient current assets ($22,830) to settle the current liabilities ($6,300) that will come due in the next 12 months. Mauricio noted that he would need to purchase more supplies for the coming month, especially given the restaurant's rapid growth in sales.

Preparing the financial statements and providing them to internal and external users is an important step in the accounting communication process. However, one additional step is necessary to complete the accounting cycle: closing the books.

# COMPLETING THE ACCOUNTING CYCLE
## Closing the Books

Video 4-2
www.mhhe.com/LLPW1e

After adjusting entries have been recorded and posted, companies need to prepare the ledger accounts for the next period. This phase in the accounting cycle is called closing the books. However, only certain accounts are closed.

The ending balance in each of Pizza Aroma's asset, liability, and owner's equity accounts carries over as the beginning account balance for the next period. So the $9,100 cash balance on May 31, for example, becomes the cash balance at June 1, the beginning of the next accounting period. The balances in these permanent accounts are **not** reduced to zero (not closed) at the end of the accounting period.

In contrast, revenue, expense, and owner's drawing accounts accumulate data for the current accounting period only. As such, these accounts must begin each period with a zero balance. Therefore, the balances in these accounts, called temporary accounts, are closed (reduced to zero) at the end of each period.

The process of closing the books is simply a series of journal entries that are made for the following reasons:

1. To update the owner's capital account for (1) the net income or loss for the period and (2) any withdrawals during the period. Until the temporary accounts are closed, the owner's capital account in the ledger does not reflect the amount reported on the balance sheet.

2. To establish a zero balance in each of the temporary accounts in preparation for use in the next accounting period.

Closing entries are dated the last day of the accounting period, are entered in the journal in the usual debits-equal-credits format, and are immediately posted to the ledger (or T-accounts). **Temporary accounts with debit balances are credited and accounts with credit balances are debited.** The four closing entries (labeled CE) are:

**Coach's Tip**

Note the following:

- Only income statement accounts (revenues and expenses) are closed to Income Summary.

- Make sure you close out the temporary accounts to a zero balance; record a debit for accounts with credit balances and a credit for accounts with debit balances.

- Owner's drawing is not an expense or reported on the income statement; as such, it is **not** closed to Income Summary.

**CE ❶** All revenue accounts are closed to a new temporary account called Income Summary used only for closing the books.[4] Because revenues have credit balances, each account is debited with a credit to Income Summary for the total of the revenues.

**CE ❷** All expense accounts are closed to the Income Summary account. Because expenses have debit balances, each account is credited with a debit to Income Summary for the total of the expenses.

**CE ❸** The Income Summary account, which should be equal to net income, is closed to the Owner's Capital account.

- If revenues exceed expenses (that is, the company had net income), Income Summary will have a credit balance. To close it, debit Income Summary and credit the owner's capital account.

- If expenses exceed revenues (that is, the company had a net loss), Income Summary will have a debit balance. To close it, credit Income Summary and debit the owner's capital account.

**CE ❹** The owner's drawing account is closed to the owner's capital account.

---

[4] Some companies do not use the Income Summary account. Instead, they close revenues and expenses directly to the Owner's Capital account.

Exhibit 4.11 is a simple illustration of how to record and post closing entries to the T-accounts. Notice that all of the temporary accounts have zero balances after closing the books and that the owner's capital account in the ledger is updated to match the amount reported on the balance sheet.

Companies usually close temporary accounts at the end of the fiscal year. Because Laurie wanted Mauricio to understand the necessity and effect of closing the books, she showed Mauricio the entries she would make to close Pizza Aroma's books at the end of May if this was the end of the fiscal year. Notice that the balances in the temporary accounts are the same as the ending amounts in the T-accounts shown in Exhibit 4.4.

**Exhibit 4.11    Recording and Posting the Closing Entries (Simple Illustration)**

### Pizza Aroma
### Closing Journal Entries
### May 31, 2009

|        |                                          | Debit  | Credit |
|--------|------------------------------------------|--------|--------|
| (CE 1) | Pizza Revenue (−R, −OE)                  | 14,400 |        |
|        | Investment Revenue (−R, −OE)             | 30     |        |
|        | Income Summary (+OE)                     |        | 14,430 |
| (CE 2) | Income Summary (−OE)                     | 9,200  |        |
|        | Supplies Expense (−E, +OE)               |        | 4,400  |
|        | Wages Expense (−E, +OE)                  |        | 1,100  |
|        | Utilities Expense (−E, +OE)              |        | 1,000  |
|        | Telephone Service Expense (−E, +OE)      |        | 600    |
|        | Rent Expense (−E, +OE)                   |        | 800    |
|        | Advertising Expense (−E, +OE)            |        | 800    |
|        | Interest Expense (−E, +OE)               |        | 200    |
|        | Depreciation Expense (−E, +OE)           |        | 300    |
| (CE3)  | Income Summary (−OE)                     | 5,230  |        |
|        | M. Rosa, Capital (+OE)                   |        | 5,230  |
| (CE 4) | M. Rosa, Capital (−OE)                   | 3,000  |        |
|        | M. Rosa, Drawing (+OE)                   |        | 3,000  |

All revenue accounts

All expense accounts

Now it's your turn to practice closing accounts at the end of the period. Review the closing entries just illustrated for Pizza Aroma and then complete the following Self-Study Practice.

Florida Flippers, a scuba diving and instruction business owned by Paul Knepper, presented the following adjusted trial balance on December 31, 2010. Record all closing entries on December 31.

**Florida Flippers**
**Trial Balance**
**On December 31, 2010**

| | Adjusted | |
| --- | --- | --- |
| | Debit | Credit |
| Cash | 14,000 | |
| Accounts Receivable | 800 | |
| Supplies | 11,700 | |
| Prepaid Insurance | 6,000 | |
| Equipment | 56,000 | |
| Accumulated Depreciation | | 10,000 |
| Building | 250,000 | |
| Accumulated Depreciation | | 12,500 |
| Accounts Payable | | 6,000 |
| Interest Payable | | 20,000 |
| Unearned Revenue | | 4,000 |
| Notes Payable | | 225,000 |
| P. Knepper, Capital | | 50,000 |
| P. Knepper, Drawing | 12,000 | |
| Diving Instruction Revenue | | 81,500 |
| Diving Trip Revenue | | 30,000 |
| Wages Expense | 22,000 | |
| Supplies Expense | 3,000 | |
| Fuel Expense | 1,000 | |
| Repairs Expense | 3,000 | |
| Utilities Expense | 14,000 | |
| Advertising Expense | 3,000 | |
| Depreciation Expense | 22,500 | |
| Interest Expense | 20,000 | |
| **Totals** | **439,000** | **439,000** |

| Closing Journal Entries | Debit | Credit |
| --- | --- | --- |
| CE 1 | | |
| | | |
| | | |
| CE 2 | | |
| | | |
| | | |
| | | |
| | | |
| | | |
| | | |
| | | |
| CE 3 | | |
| | | |
| | | |
| CE 4 | | |
| | | |
| | | |

*After you have finished, check your answers with the solution at the bottom of the next page.*

# Preparing a Post-Closing Trial Balance

After Laurie completed the closing process for Pizza Aroma, all temporary accounts had a zero balance. The accounts were then ready for recording revenues and expenses in the new accounting period as well as any future withdrawals Mauricio might make. The ending balance in M. Rosa, Capital was updated and matched the balance sheet amount of $32,230. This balance was carried forward to become the beginning balance for the next period starting on June 1.

Just to make sure that all the temporary accounts have been closed and that the accounting records are still in balance, a **post-closing trial balance** should be prepared as the last step of the accounting cycle. Here is the one Laurie prepared for Pizza Aroma.

### Pizza Aroma
### Post-Closing Trial Balance
### On May 31, 2009

| | Debit | Credit |
|---|---|---|
| Cash | 9,100 | |
| Investments | 6,000 | |
| Interest Receivable | 30 | |
| Accounts Receivable | 700 | |
| Supplies | 600 | |
| Prepaid Rent | 4,000 | |
| Prepaid Insurance | 2,400 | |
| Equipment | 36,000 | |
| Accumulated Depreciation | | 300 |
| Accounts Payable | | 4,800 |
| Wages Payable | | 100 |
| Utilities Payable | | 1,000 |
| Interest Payable | | 200 |
| Unearned Revenue | | 200 |
| Notes Payable | | 20,000 |
| M. Rosa, Capital | | 32,230 |
| M. Rosa, Drawing | 0 | |
| Pizza Revenue | | 0 |
| Investment Revenue | | 0 |
| Supplies Expense | 0 | |
| Wages Expense | 0 | |
| Utilities Expense | 0 | |
| Telephone Service Expense | 0 | |
| Rent Expense | 0 | |
| Insurance Expense | 0 | |
| Advertising Expense | 0 | |
| Interest Expense | 0 | |
| Depreciation Expense | 0 | |
| **Totals** | **58,830** | **58,830** |

Permanent accounts—balances carry forward to the next period

Temporary accounts—balances begin at $0 in the next period

**Solution to Self-Study Practice**

| | Closing Journal Entries | Debit | Credit |
|---|---|---|---|
| CE 1 | Diving Instruction Revenue (−R, −OE) | 81,500 | |
| | Diving Trip Revenue (−R, −OE) | 30,000 | |
| | Income Summary (+OE) | | 111,500 |
| CE 2 | Income Summary (−OE) | 88,500 | |
| | Wages Expense (−E, +OE) | | 22,000 |
| | Supplies Expense (−E, +OE) | | 3,000 |
| | Fuel Expense (−E, +OE) | | 1,000 |
| | Repairs Expense (−E, +OE) | | 3,000 |
| | Utilities Expense (−E, +OE) | | 14,000 |
| | Advertising Expense (−E, +OE) | | 3,000 |
| | Depreciation Expense (−E, +OE) | | 22,500 |
| | Interest Expense (−E, +OE) | | 20,000 |
| CE 3 | Income Summary (−OE) | 23,000 | |
| | P. Knepper, Capital (+OE) | | 23,000 |
| CE 4 | P. Knepper, Capital (−OE) | 12,000 | |
| | P. Knepper, Drawing (+OE) | | 12,000 |

Notice that all temporary accounts have zero balances although some companies do not show accounts with zero balances. Also, note the trial balance still balances. The accounting cycle for the month of May is complete.

Managers find this last phase of the accounting cycle to be very busy. Adjusting the accounts, preparing statements, and closing the books may appear to happen on the last day of the period. However, this phase of the accounting cycle actually takes place after the end of the period, often extending over several weeks. Auditors usually conduct their audit tests and analyses at the same time. As an example of the time needed for the last phase, The Cheesecake Factory reported the date of the balance sheet as January 2, 2007, but the auditor PricewaterhouseCoopers dated the opinion February 22, 2007—a seven-week period before the accounting records were finally audited, adjusted, and closed.

**Coach's Tip**

Other examples of the timing of the end of the accounting cycle:

| Company | Statement Date | Opinion Date |
|---|---|---|
| Wal-Mart | 1/31/07 | 3/26/07 |
| Apple | 9/29/07 | 11/15/07 |
| Coca-Cola | 12/31/06 | 2/20/07 |

## ANALYZING FINANCIAL INFORMATION

### Computing and Interpreting Key Ratios

When Pizza Aroma's financial statements were complete and available for review, Laurie explained to Mauricio how to compute and interpret a key ratio that would provide information on his business's overall financial performance. Users of financial information rely on ratios in analyzing a company's past performance and financial condition as well as in predicting its future potential. Noting how ratios change over time in addition to how well they compare to competitors' ratios and to industry averages provides valuable information about a company's business decisions and strategies.

This chapter will introduce one financial ratio that was of particular interest to Mauricio in evaluating the results of Pizza Aroma's first month of business. Other ratios will be presented in later chapters of this textbook. In each instance, you will see a chart similar to the one presented below—**Accounting Decision Tools**—that summarizes the formula and its interpretation.

> **Learning Objective 5**
>
> Compute and interpret the net profit margin ratio.

### Analyzing Net Profit Margin (NPM)

The net profit margin provides information on managers' relative success at generating revenues and controlling costs.

| Accounting Decision Tools | | |
|---|---|---|
| **Name of Measure** | **Formula** | **What It Tells You** |
| Net profit margin (NPM) | $\dfrac{\text{Net Income}}{\text{Total Sales (or Operating) Revenues}} \times 100$ | • The percentage of every sales dollar generated during the period that was profit<br>• A higher ratio means that managers are more effective at generating sales and/or controlling expenses |

Using the information from Pizza Aroma's income statement presented in Exhibit 4.10, its net profit margin would be computed as follows:

$$\text{Net profit margin} = \frac{\text{Net Income}}{\text{Total Sales (or Operating) Revenues}} \times 100 = \frac{\$5,230}{\$14,400} \times 100 = 36.3\%$$

The net profit margin measures how effective management was in generating revenues and controlling costs and expenses during the period. For the first month of operation, Pizza Aroma realized 36.3 percent of net profit to revenue or $0.363 for every dollar of pizza revenue. This is less than half the 83 percent that Mauricio originally computed based on the unadjusted accounts (see the beginning of the chapter), and another demonstration of the impact of year-end adjusting entries on results. Mauricio was concerned by this information because the business's performance was not as strong as he had originally thought. Laurie assured him that Pizza Aroma was doing very well for a new business.

Because managers' sales growth strategies and cost control measures impact this ratio, a rising net profit margin signals more effective management of sales and/or control of expenses. Financial analysts expect well-run businesses to maintain or improve their net profit margins over time.

## Making Comparisons to Benchmarks

2.5%    4.8%    6.3%

2004   2005   2006

**NET PROFIT MARGIN**

Comparing a company's ratio (1) over time and (2) to its competition provides additional useful information on the effectiveness of management.

### Comparison over Time

We do not have historical data for Pizza Aroma for computing ratios over time, but we can analyze a competitor's NPM ratio over time to observe any trends. As you can see from the graphic in the margin, Papa John's has had an increasing NPM over time, more than doubling its NPM between 2004 and 2006. This suggests that its managers have become more effective at generating sales and/or controlling expenses. Pizza Aroma's ratio at 36.3 percent far surpasses the 6.3 percent net profit margin of Papa John's, a major international competitor.

### Comparison to Competition

As Exhibit 4.12 shows, Papa John's, Domino's, and Yum! Brands (owner of Pizza Hut and several other restaurants) reported for 2006 a 6.3 percent, 7.4 percent, and 8.6 percent net profit margin ratio, respectively. All three companies fell short of the restaurant industry average of 13.3 percent, which includes large restaurant chains, not just pizza restaurants.

You should also be aware that the net profit margin can vary greatly between different types of industries. Exhibit 4.12 shows that auto and truck manufacturers recently reported an average net profit margin of 8.2 percent compared to the 14.3 percent reported by footwear companies and the 17.5 percent reported by pharmaceutical companies.

With Laurie's advice and support, Mauricio was energized by the strong results of his new business and the ratio information about Pizza Aroma's major competitors. He was ready to take on the challenges of expanding his customer base and building customer loyalty—while doing so at a profit.

In this chapter, you learned the importance of adjusting the accounts to measure revenue and expenses in the proper period. You also learned how to close the books at the end of the accounting period to update the owner's capital account and prepare the temporary accounts to accumulate the next period's financial information. In the following chapter, you will learn about the accounting information system.

**Exhibit 4.12    Average Net Profit Margin Ratios by Industry**

| Restaurant Industry | | Other Industries | |
|---|---|---|---|
| Papa John's | 6.3% | Auto/Truck Manufacturers | 8.2% |
| Domino's | 7.4% | Footwear | 14.3% |
| Yum! Brands | 8.6% | Pharmaceuticals (Diversified) | 17.5% |
| All companies in industry | 13.3% | | |

Source of industry averages: www.reuters.com/finance/industries

# Demonstration Case

This final installment of the case of Goodbye Grass, the lawn care business started by Steve Delancey, covers three end-of-cycle activities: the adjustment process, financial statement preparation, and recording of closing entries. So far, no adjustments have been made to the accounts. The starting point for this process is the unadjusted trial balance as of May 31, 2010, which follows.

### GOODBYE GRASS
### Unadjusted Trial Balance
### As of May 31, 2010

| Account Name | Debits | Credits |
|---|---|---|
| Cash | 2,470 | |
| Accounts Receivable | 1,700 | |
| Note Receivable | 1,250 | |
| Prepaid Insurance | 300 | |
| Equipment | 4,600 | |
| Land | 3,750 | |
| Accounts Payable | | 620 |
| Unearned Revenue | | 1,600 |
| Notes Payable | | 4,000 |
| S. Delancey, Capital | | 9,000 |
| S. Delancey, Drawing | 2,000 | |
| Mowing Revenue | | 5,200 |
| Wages Expense | 3,900 | |
| Fuel Expense | 410 | |
| Interest Expense | 40 | |
| Totals | 20,420 | 20,420 |

In reviewing this unadjusted trial balance, you should be able to identify one unearned revenue account and two prepaid expense accounts that may need to be adjusted in addition to accruals that may be necessary regarding wages, interest expense on notes payable, and interest earned on the note receivable. The following information was determined at the end of the accounting cycle:

### Revenues

- **Unearned Revenue**

  a. One-fourth of the $1,600 cash received from the city at the beginning of May for future mowing service was earned in May. The $1,600 in Unearned Revenue represents four months of service (May through August).

- **Accrued Revenue**

  b. Interest earned and receivable on Goodbye Grass's outstanding note receivable was $25 for the month of May.

### Expenses

- **Prepaid Expenses**

  c. Insurance purchased at the beginning of May for $300 provided coverage for six months (May through October).

  d. Mowers, edgers, rakes, and hand tools (equipment) were used in May to generate revenues. The company estimates $25 in depreciation of this equipment in May.

- **Accrued Expenses**

  e. Wages were paid through the third week in May. Employees who worked the last week of May will be paid in June. Wages amount to $400.

  f. One month of interest on the $4,000 notes payable has been paid through mid-May. Another $20 of interest needs to be accrued and will be paid in June.

*Required:*

1. Analyze the effects of the required adjustments in items *a* through *f* on the basic accounting equation (Assets = Liabilities + Owner's Equity) and record the adjusting journal entries required at the end of May. Follow the steps outlined in the chapter: (1) Identify adjustments by type; (2) determine the amount of the revenue or expense to be recorded; and (3) record the adjusting entry and post the effects to the T-accounts.

2. Post the adjusting entry effects to the appropriate T-accounts. Obtain the beginning balances from the unadjusted trial balance and then calculate the adjusted May 31 balances.

3. Prepare an adjusted trial balance to ensure that debit and credit balances are equal, remembering to include all the accounts in the trial balance (not just the ones affected by the adjusting journal entries).

4. Prepare a *classified* income statement, a statement of owner's equity, and a *classified* balance sheet from the amounts in the adjusted trial balance.

5. Prepare the closing journal entries that would be required if Goodbye Grass's fiscal *year* ended May 31, 2010.

After completing requirements 1–5, check your answers with the following solution.

## Suggested Solution

### 1. Analyze and record adjusting entries

All adjusting entries are written together at the end of this requirement.

    *a.* **Unearned Revenue**

        *(1)* **Type:** Unearned Revenue
        *(2)* **Amount:** The unadjusted balance for Unearned Revenue is $1,600. One-fourth of that $1,600 ($400 = ¼ × $1,600) was earned in May.
        *(3)* **Entry:** Therefore, an adjusting entry is needed to increase the Mowing Revenue account by the $400 earned in May and reduce the Unearned Revenue liability account by $400.

    *b.* **Interest Revenue**

        *(1)* **Type:** Accrued Revenue
        *(2)* **Amount:** The business earned but has not yet recorded the $25 interest on its Note Receivable due from the city.
        *(3)* **Entry:** Therefore, an adjusting entry is needed to increase the Interest Revenue account and create an Interest Receivable account for the amount earned and due from the city.

    *c.* **Insurance**

        *(1)* **Type:** Prepaid Expense
        *(2)* **Amount:** The business received insurance coverage in May, so one month of the six-month prepaid insurance policy has been used ($300 × ⅙ = $50 used).
        *(3)* **Entry:** Therefore, an adjusting entry is needed to increase the Insurance Expense account by the $50 incurred in May and reduce the Prepaid Insurance account by $50.

    *d.* **Equipment**

        *(1)* **Type:** Prepaid Expense
        *(2)* **Amount:** The business estimates monthly depreciation on the equipment to be $25.
        *(3)* **Entry:** Therefore, an adjusting entry is needed to increase the Depreciation Expense account by the $25 incurred and increase the contra-account Accumulated Depreciation by the amount of the equipment used in May.

    *e.* **Wages**

        *(1)* **Type:** Accrued Expense
        *(2)* **Amount:** Employees who worked the last week in May will be paid in early June. The business used the employees' labor to generate revenues in May but has not yet recorded the $400 expense incurred.
        *(3)* **Entry:** Therefore, an adjusting entry is needed to increase the Wages Expense account by $400 and create a Wages Payable account for the $400 owed to the employees.

    *f.* **Interest Expense**

        *(1)* **Type:** Accrued Expense
        *(2)* **Amount:** The business owes two additional weeks of interest on the $4,000 note payable. The amount given is $20.
        *(3)* **Entry:** Therefore, an adjusting entry is needed to increase the Interest Expense account by $20 and create an Interest Payable account for the $20 due the bank by the end of May.

**Goodbye Grass**
**Adjusting Journal Entries**
**May 31, 2010**

| | | Debit | Credit |
|---|---|---|---|
| (AJE a) | Unearned Revenue (−L) | 400 | |
| | Mowing Revenue (+R, +OE) | | 400 |
| (AJE b) | Interest Receivable (+A) | 25 | |
| | Interest Revenue (+R, +OE) | | 25 |
| (AJE c) | Insurance Expense (+E, −OE) | 50 | |
| | Prepaid Insurance (−A) | | 50 |
| (AJE d) | Depreciation Expense (+E, −OE) | 25 | |
| | Accumulated Depreciation (+xA, −A) | | 25 |
| (AJE e) | Wages Expense (+E, −OE) | 400 | |
| | Wages Payable (+L) | | 400 |
| (AJE f) | Interest Expense (+E, −OE) | 20 | |
| | Interest Payable (+L) | | 20 |

2.  Post adjusting entries to T-accounts

**Assets**  =  **Liabilities**  +  **Owner's Equity**

**+   Cash (A)   −**

| | | | |
|---|---|---|---|
| Bal. | 2,470 | | |
| Bal. | 2,470 | | |

**− Accounts Payable (L) +**

| | | | |
|---|---|---|---|
| | | 620 | Bal. |
| | | 620 | Bal. |

**S. Delancey,**
**−   Capital (OE)   +**

| | | | |
|---|---|---|---|
| | | 9,000 | Bal. |
| | | 9,000 | Bal. |

**+ Accounts Receivable (A) −**

| | | | |
|---|---|---|---|
| Bal. | 1,700 | | |
| Bal. | 1,700 | | |

**− Unearned Revenue (L) +**

| | | | |
|---|---|---|---|
| | | | Unadj. |
| | | 1,600 | bal. |
| AJE a | 400 | | |
| | | 1,200 | Bal. |

**S. Delancey,**
**+   Drawing (OE)   −**

| | | | |
|---|---|---|---|
| Bal. | 2,000 | | |
| Bal. | 2,000 | | |

**+ Interest Receivable (A) −**

| | | | |
|---|---|---|---|
| Unadj. bal. | 0 | | |
| AJE b | 25 | | |
| Bal. | 25 | | |

**− Wages Payable (L) +**

| | | | |
|---|---|---|---|
| | | | Unadj. |
| | | 0 | bal. |
| | | 400 | AJE e |
| | | 400 | Bal. |

**Expenses**

**+ Wages Expense (E) −**

| | | | |
|---|---|---|---|
| Unadj. bal. | 3,900 | | |
| AJE e | 400 | | |
| Bal. | 4,300 | | |

**Revenues**

**− Mowing Revenue (R) +**

| | | | |
|---|---|---|---|
| | | | Unadj. |
| | | 5,200 | bal. |
| | | 400 | AJE a |
| | | 5,600 | Bal. |

**+ Note Receivable (A) −**

| | | | |
|---|---|---|---|
| Bal. | 1,250 | | |
| Bal. | 1,250 | | |

**− Interest Payable (L) +**

| | | | |
|---|---|---|---|
| | | | Unadj. |
| | | 0 | bal. |
| | | 20 | AJE f |
| | | 20 | Bal. |

**+ Fuel Expense (E) −**

| | | | |
|---|---|---|---|
| Bal. | 410 | | |
| Bal. | 410 | | |

**− Interest Revenue (R) +**

| | | | |
|---|---|---|---|
| | | | Unadj. |
| | | 0 | bal. |
| | | 25 | AJE b |
| | | 25 | Bal. |

**+ Prepaid Insurance (A) −**

| | | | |
|---|---|---|---|
| Unadj. bal. | 300 | | |
| | | 50 | AJE c |
| Bal. | 250 | | |

**+ Interest Expense (E) −**

| | | | |
|---|---|---|---|
| Unadj. bal. | 40 | | |
| AJE f | 20 | | |
| Bal. | 60 | | |

**+   Equipment (A)   −**

| | | | |
|---|---|---|---|
| Bal. | 4,600 | | |
| Bal. | 4,600 | | |

**− Notes Payable (L) +**

| | | | |
|---|---|---|---|
| | | 4,000 | Bal. |
| | | 4,000 | Bal. |

**+ Insurance Expense (E) −**

| | | | |
|---|---|---|---|
| Unadj. bal. | 0 | | |
| AJE c | 50 | | |
| Bal. | 50 | | |

**Accumulated**
**−   Depreciation (xA)   +**

| | | | |
|---|---|---|---|
| | | 0 | Unadj. bal. |
| | | 25 | AJE d |
| | | 25 | Bal. |

**+ Depreciation Expense (E) −**

| | | | |
|---|---|---|---|
| Unadj. bal. | 0 | | |
| AJE d | 25 | | |
| Bal. | 25 | | |

**+   Land (A)   −**

| | | | |
|---|---|---|---|
| Bal. | 3,750 | | |
| Bal. | 3,750 | | |

3.  Adjusted trial balance

### GOODBYE GRASS
### Adjusted Trial Balance
### As of May 31, 2010

| Account Name | Debits | Credits |
|---|---|---|
| Cash | 2,470 | |
| Accounts Receivable | 1,700 | |
| Interest Receivable | 25 | |
| Note Receivable | 1,250 | |
| Prepaid Insurance | 250 | |
| Equipment | 4,600 | |
| Accumulated Depreciation | | 25 |
| Land | 3,750 | |
| Accounts Payable | | 620 |
| Unearned Revenue | | 1,200 |
| Wages Payable | | 400 |
| Interest Payable | | 20 |
| Notes Payable | | 4,000 |
| S. Delancey, Capital | | 9,000 |
| S. Delancey, Drawing | 2,000 | |
| Mowing Revenue | | 5,600 |
| Interest Revenue | | 25 |
| Wages Expense | 4,300 | |
| Fuel Expense | 410 | |
| Interest Expense | 60 | |
| Insurance Expense | 50 | |
| Depreciation Expense | 25 | |
| Totals | 20,890 | 20,890 |

4. **Income statement, statement of owner's equity, and balance sheet**

### GOODBYE GRASS
### Income Statement
### For the Month Ended May 31, 2010

**Operating Revenues**

| | |
|---|---|
| Mowing revenue | $5,600 |
| Total operating revenue | 5,600 |

**Operating Expenses**

| | |
|---|---|
| Wages expense | 4,300 |
| Fuel expense | 410 |
| Insurance expense | 50 |
| Depreciation expense | 25 |
| Total operating expenses | 4,785 |
| **Operating Income** | 815 |

**Other Items**

| | |
|---|---|
| Interest revenue | 25 |
| Interest expense | (60) |
| **Net Income** | **$ 780** |

### GOODBYE GRASS
### Statement of Owner's Equity
### For the Month Ended May 31, 2010

| | |
|---|---|
| S. Delancey, Capital, May 1, 2010 | $ 9,000 |
| Add: Additional investments | 0 |
| Net income | 780 |
| Less: S. Delancey, Drawing | (2,000) |
| S. Delancey, Capital, May 31, 2010 | **$ 7,780** |

**GOODBYE GRASS**
Balance Sheet
As of May 31, 2010

| Assets | | Liabilities | |
|---|---|---|---|
| Current Assets | | Current Liabilities | |
| Cash | $ 2,470 | Accounts Payable | $    620 |
| Accounts Receivable | 1,700 | Unearned Revenue | 1,200 |
| Interest Receivable | 25 | Wages Payable | 400 |
| Note Receivable | 1,250 | Interest Payable | 20 |
| Prepaid Insurance | 250 | Notes Payable | 4,000 |
| Total Current Assets | 5,695 | Total Current Liabilities | 6,240 |
| Equipment | 4,600 | **Owner's Equity** | |
| Less: Accumulated Depreciation | (25) | S. Delancey, Capital | 7,780 |
| Land | 3,750 | | |
| **Total Assets** | **$14,020** | **Total Liabilities and Owner's Equity** | **$14,020** |

5.  Closing journal entries

**Goodbye Grass**
Closing Journal Entries
May 31, 2010

| | | Debit | Credit |
|---|---|---|---|
| (CE 1) | Mowing Revenue (−R, −OE) | 5,600 | |
| | Interest Revenue (−R, −OE) | 25 | |
| | Income Summary (+OE) | | 5,625 |
| (CE 2) | Income Summary (−OE) | 4,845 | |
| | Wages Expense (−E, +OE) | | 4,300 |
| | Fuel Expense (−E, +OE) | | 410 |
| | Interest Expense (−E, +OE) | | 60 |
| | Insurance Expense (−E, +OE) | | 50 |
| | Depreciation Expense (−E, +OE) | | 25 |
| (CE 3) | Income Summary (−OE) | 780 | |
| | S. Delancey, Capital (+OE) | | 780 |
| (CE 4) | S. Delancey, Capital (−OE) | 2,000 | |
| | S. Delancey, Drawing (+OE) | | 2,000 |

# Supplement 4A
## Using an Accounting Worksheet

An accounting worksheet may be prepared to facilitate end-of-period accounting activities. If an accounting worksheet is used, it should be prepared before recording the adjusting and closing entries. The final worksheet provides all of the data needed to complete the remaining end-of-period steps, bringing together in one place the (1) unadjusted trial balance, (2) amounts for the adjusting entries, (3) income statement, (4) statement of owner's equity, and (5) balance sheet. Closing entries can also be prepared from the information provided on the worksheet.

The following simplified case for High-Rise Apartments shows how to prepare a worksheet at the end of the accounting period. High-Rise Apartments is a sole proprietorship for the management of rental properties in Collegetown. Brooks Lape owns and operates it.

Exhibit 4.13 includes a series of transparencies that correspond to the steps needed to complete the worksheet. You can turn over each transparency as directed. To help you, each step is color coded to match the columns on the worksheet. Follow these steps to develop the worksheet:

**Step 1**    *Refer to Exhibit 4.13.* Set up the worksheet format by entering the appropriate column headings. The left-hand column shows the account titles (taken directly from the ledger). There are six separate pairs of Debit–Credit columns. Notice that the last three pairs of Debit–Credit columns show the data for the financial statements. Enter the unadjusted trial balance as of the

(continued on page 177)

## Exhibit 4.13 — Accounting Worksheet

### HIGH-RISE APARTMENTS
### Worksheet for the Year Ended December 31, 2010

| Account Titles | Unadjusted Trial Balance Debit | Unadjusted Trial Balance Credit | Adjusting Entries Debit | Adjusting Entries Credit | Adjusted Trial Balance Debit | Adjusted Trial Balance Credit | Income Statement Debit | Income Statement Credit | Owner's Equity Debit | Owner's Equity Credit | Balance Sheet Debit | Balance Sheet Credit |
|---|---|---|---|---|---|---|---|---|---|---|---|---|
| Cash | 12,297 | | | | | | | | | | | |
| Rent Revenue Receivable | | | | | | | | | | | | |
| Prepaid Insurance | 2,400 | | | | | | | | | | | |
| Maintenance Supplies | 600 | | | | | | | | | | | |
| Land | 25,000 | | | | | | | | | | | |
| Apartment Building | 360,000 | | | | | | | | | | | |
| Accumulated Depreciation-Building | | 10,000 | | | | | | | | | | |
| Unearned Rent Revenue | | 1,000 | | | | | | | | | | |
| Salaries Payable | | | | | | | | | | | | |
| Interest Payable | | | | | | | | | | | | |
| Notes Payable, Long-Term | | 30,000 | | | | | | | | | | |
| Mortgage Payable, Long-Term | | 238,037 | | | | | | | | | | |
| B. Lape, Capital (Jan. 1) | | 84,960 | | | | | | | | | | |
| B. Lape, Drawing | 12,000 | | | | | | | | | | | |
| Rent Revenue | | 127,463 | | | | | | | | | | |
| Advertising Expense | 500 | | | | | | | | | | | |
| Maintenance Supplies Expense | 3,000 | | | | | | | | | | | |
| Salary Expense | 17,400 | | | | | | | | | | | |
| Interest Expense | 19,563 | | | | | | | | | | | |
| Utilities Expense | 34,500 | | | | | | | | | | | |
| Miscellaneous Expenses | 4,200 | | | | | | | | | | | |
| Insurance Expense | | | | | | | | | | | | |
| Depreciation Expense | | | | | | | | | | | | |
| | 491,460 | 491,460 | | | | | | | | | | |

end of the accounting period directly from the ledger into the first pair of Debit–Credit columns. When all current entries for the period excluding the adjusting entries have been recorded in the journal and posted to the ledger, the amounts for the Unadjusted Trial Balance columns will equal the balances in the respective ledger accounts. Before going on to the next step, check the equality of the debits and credits by totaling each column ($491,460). Adding up the numbers in the columns in this way is called footing. When you use a worksheet, it is not necessary to develop a separate unadjusted trial balance because you can develop one on the worksheet.

**Step ②** *Refer to Exhibit 4.13a (turn over the first transparency).* Complete the second pair of Debit–Credit columns, headed Adjusting Entries, by developing and then entering the amounts of the adjusting entries directly on the worksheet. The adjustments for High-Rise Apartments that are shown in Exhibit 4.13a were entered for illustration purposes. Review each entry to be sure you can explain why it was recorded. To facilitate examination for potential errors, the adjusting entries are usually referenced as illustrated in Exhibit 4.13a. Some of the adjusting entries may need one or more account titles in addition to those of the original trial balance (see the last five account titles in Exhibit 4.13a). After the adjusting entries on the worksheet are complete, check the equality of debits and credits for those amounts by totaling the two columns ($14,200 each).

**Step ③** *Refer to Exhibit 4.13b (turn over the second transparency).* Complete the pair of Debit–Credit columns headed Adjusted Trial Balance. Although it is not essential, this pair of columns helps to ensure accuracy. The adjusted trial balance reflects the line-by-line combined amounts of the unadjusted trial balance, plus or minus the amounts entered as adjusting entries in the second pair of columns. For example, the Rent Revenue account shows a $128,463 credit balance under Unadjusted Trial Balance. Add to this amount the credit amount, $600, minus the debit amount, $500, for a combined amount of $128,563, and enter it as a credit under Adjusted Trial Balance. (Adding across rows in this way is called cross-footing.) For those accounts that were not affected by the adjusting entries, carry the unadjusted trial balance amount directly across to the Adjusted Trial Balance column. After you complete each line, check the equality of the debits and credits under Adjusted Trial Balance (column totals, $503,560).

**Step ④** *Refer to Exhibit 4.13c (turn over the third transparency).* Extend the amount on each line under Adjusted Trial Balance horizontally across the worksheet and enter it under the heading for the financial statement on which it must be reported (income statement, owner's equity, or balance sheet). Carry debit amounts across as debits and credit amounts across as credits. Note that (1) each amount that you extended across the worksheet is entered under only one of the six remaining columns, and (2) debits remain debits and credits remain credits. Enter net income as a balancing debit amount in the Income Statement column and a credit amount in the Owner's Equity column. This amount represents the closing process entry that results in a debit to Income Summary (after revenues and expenses have been closed to the Income Summary) and a credit to B. Lape, Capital. (A net loss should be entered as a credit in the Income Statement column and a debit in the owner's equity column.)

**Step ⑤** *Refer to Exhibit 4.13d (turn over the fourth transparency).* Sum the two Owner's Equity columns. The difference is the ending balance of B. Lape, Capital. Enter this amount ($109,260) as a balancing debit amount under Owner's Equity and a balancing credit under Balance Sheet (that is, an increase to owner's equity). At this point, the two Balance Sheet columns should sum to equal amounts. The continuous checking of the equality of debits and credits in each pair of Debit-Credit columns helps to ensure the correctness of the worksheet. You can prepare the financial statements for High-Rise Apartments directly from the completed worksheet in Exhibit 4.13d.

# Chapter Summary

## LO1 Explain the purpose of adjustments at the end of the accounting cycle. p. 146

- Reasons for Adjustments
  Adjustments are needed to ensure that:
    - Revenues are recorded when they are earned (the revenue principle).
    - Expenses are recorded when they are incurred to generate revenues (the matching principle).
    - Assets are reported at amounts representing the economic benefits remaining at the end of the current period.
    - Liabilities are reported at amounts owed at the end of the current period, which will require a future sacrifice of resources.

## LO2 Identify and analyze the adjustments necessary at the end of the period to update balance sheet and income statement accounts. p. 147

- Types of Adjustments
    - Unearned revenues. Cash was received before it was earned. The adjusting entry (AJE) reduces the liability and increases the revenue account.

- Accrued revenues. Cash will be received after being earned in the current period. The AJE increases the revenue account and increases a receivable account.
- Prepaid expenses. Cash was paid for an asset before it was used to generate revenue. The AJE reduces the asset (or increases its contra-account) and increases a related expense.
- Accrued expenses. Cash will be paid after the expense was incurred. The AJE increases the expense account and increases a payable account.

- Analysis of Adjustments
The process for preparing adjustments includes

Step 1   Identify the type of adjustment. Review the trial balance.
Step 2   Determine the amount of the revenue earned or expense incurred. Use of a timeline may help to determine the amount.
Step 3   Record the adjusting journal entry and post it to the appropriate T-accounts (accounts in the ledger).

Adjusting entries never affect the Cash account.

## LO3  Present an income statement, statement of owner's equity, and balance sheet. p. 160

- Relationships among Financial Statements
Net income is a component in determining ending owner's capital. Ending owner's capital is included on the balance sheet. Thus, an error on the income statement will cause the other statements to also be in error.
- Adjusted Trial Balance
An adjusted trial balance is a list of all accounts with their adjusted debit or credit balances indicated in the appropriate columns to provide a check on the equality of debits and credits.
- Classified Income Statement
Using the adjusted balances for revenues and expenses from the adjusted trial balance, a classified income statement lists operating revenues and then subtracts operating expenses to determine the operating income.
    - A revenue or expense is classified as "operating" if it is earned or incurred as part of the business's central operations (the primary focus of the business).
    - Other revenues and expenses that are not central to operations, such as interest revenue and interest expense, are added to or subtracted from operating income to determine net income.
- Statement of Owner's Equity
A statement of owner's equity connects the income statement to the balance sheet.
- Classified Balance Sheet
A classified balance sheet lists assets in order of liquidity and liabilities in order of their due dates. The ending balance of the owner's capital account on the statement of owner's equity is a component on the balance sheet.

## LO4  Explain the purpose and process of closing the books. p. 164

- Closing the Books
Closing entries are required
    - (a) To transfer net income (or loss) and owner withdrawals during the period to the owner's capital account.
    - (b) To prepare all temporary accounts (revenue, expense, and owner's drawing accounts) for the following year by establishing zero balances.
The process includes four entries:
    - CE1. Debit each revenue account and credit the total revenues to Income Summary, an account used only during the closing process. All revenues should now have zero balances.
    - CE2. Credit each expense account and debit the total expenses to Income Summary. All expenses should now have zero balances.
    - CE3. If net income is positive, then there should be a credit balance equal to the amount of net income in Income Summary. Debit Income Summary and credit the owner's capital account for the balance. Do just the opposite if there is a net loss. Income Summary should now have a zero balance.
    - CE4. Debit the owner's capital account and credit the owner's drawing account for its balance. The drawing account should now have a zero balance, and there should be no additional temporary accounts to close.
- Preparing a Post-Closing Trial Balance
A post-closing trial balance provides a final check on the equality of the accounting equation and ensures that all temporary accounts have been closed to a zero balance.

**LO5 Compute and interpret the net profit margin ratio. p. 169**

- **Computing and Interpreting Key Ratios**
  Users of financial information compute and interpret ratios in analyzing a company's past performance and financial condition and predicting future potential.

- **Analyzing Net Profit Margin (NPM)**
  A measure of how much profit management generated on every dollar of sales during the period:
  - Computation: NPM = (Net Income ÷ Sales (or operating) revenues) × 100
  - Assesses management's effectiveness at generating sales and/or controlling costs.
  - A higher ratio suggests management is more effective at generating sales and/or controlling costs.

- **Making Comparisons to Benchmarks**
  Ratios should be computed (1) for a company over time and (2) against competitors and industry averages to observe trends.

## Key Terms

Accrued Expenses (p. 147)

Accrued Revenues (p. 147)

Adjusted Trial Balance (p. 160)

Adjusting Entries (p. 147)

Closing the Books (p. 164)

Contra-account (p. 152)

Depreciation (p. 152)

Income Summary (p. 164)

Net Book Value (also called *book value* or *carrying value*) (p. 152)

Net Profit Margin (p. 169)

Permanent Accounts (p. 164)

Prepaid Expenses (p. 147)

Temporary Accounts (p. 164)

Unearned Revenues (p. 147)

See complete glossary in the back of text.

## Questions

1. Briefly explain the purposes of adjustments.
2. Explain the relationships between adjustments and (a) the time period assumption (from chapter 3), (b) the revenue principle, and (c) the matching principle.
3. List the four types of adjustments, and give an example of each type.
4. Explain the effect of adjusting journal entries on cash.
5. What is a contra-asset? Give an example of one.
6. Explain the differences between depreciation expense and accumulated depreciation.
7. What is an adjusted trial balance? What is its purpose?
8. On December 31, a company makes a $9,000 payment to rent a warehouse in January, February, and March of the following year. Show the accounting equation effects of the transaction on December 31, as well as the adjustments required on January 31, February 28, and March 31.
9. Using the information in question 8, determine the amounts and accounts that will be reported on the January 31 balance sheet and the income statement for the month ended January 31.
10. Using the information in question 8, prepare the journal entry and adjusting journal entries to be made on December 31, January 31, February 28, and March 31.
11. What is the equation for each of the following statements: (a) income statement, (b) statement of owner's equity, and (c) balance sheet?
12. Explain how the financial statements in question 11 relate to each other.
13. What is the purpose of closing journal entries?
14. How do permanent accounts differ from temporary accounts?
15. Why are the income statement accounts closed but the balance sheet accounts are not?
16. Is the owner's drawing account considered an asset, liability, or owner's equity account? Is it a permanent or temporary account? Does it normally have a debit or credit balance?
17. What is a post-closing trial balance? Is it a useful part of the accounting cycle? Explain.
18. How is a company's net profit margin computed and what does it measure?

## Multiple Choice

1. Which of the following accounts would not appear in a closing journal entry?
   a. Interest Revenue.
   b. Accumulated Depreciation.
   c. Owner's Capital.
   d. Salary Expense.

Quiz 4-1
www.mhhe.com/LLPW1e

2. Which account is least likely to appear in an adjusting journal entry?
   a. Cash.
   b. Interest Receivable.
   c. Accumulated Depreciation.
   d. Salaries Payable.

3.  When a concert promotions company collects cash for ticket sales two months in advance of the show date, which of the following accounts is affected?
    a.  Accrued Liability.
    b.  Accounts Receivable.
    c.  Prepaid Expense.
    d.  Unearned Revenue.

4.  On December 31, an adjustment is made to reduce unearned revenue and report revenue earned during the period. How many accounts will be included in this adjusting journal entry?
    a.  None.
    b.  One.
    c.  Two.
    d.  Three.

5.  An adjusting journal entry to recognize accrued salaries payable would cause which of the following?
    a.  A decrease in assets and owner's equity.
    b.  A decrease in assets and liabilities.
    c.  An increase in expenses, liabilities, and owner's equity.
    d.  An increase in expenses and liabilities and a decrease in owner's equity.

6.  An adjusted trial balance
    a.  Shows the ending balances in a "debit" and "credit" format before adjusting journal entries are posted.
    b.  Is prepared after closing entries have been posted.
    c.  Is a tool financial analysts use to review the performance of publicly traded companies.
    d.  Shows the ending balances resulting from the adjusting journal entries in a "debit" and "credit" format.

7.  Company A owns a building. Which of the following statements regarding depreciation is **false** from an accounting perspective?
    a.  As the value of the building decreases over time, it "depreciates."
    b.  Depreciation is an estimated expense to be recorded each period during the building's life.
    c.  As depreciation is recorded, owner's equity is reduced.
    d.  As depreciation is recorded, total assets are reduced.

8.  Which of the following trial balances is used as a source for preparing the income statement?
    a.  Unadjusted trial balance.
    b.  Preadjusted trial balance.
    c.  Adjusted trial balance.
    d.  Post-closing trial balance.

9.  Assume the balance in Prepaid Insurance is $2,500 but it should be $1,500. The adjusting journal entry should include which of the following?
    a.  Debit to Prepaid Insurance for $1,000.
    b.  Credit to Insurance Expense for $1,000.
    c.  Debit to Insurance Expense for $1,000.
    d.  Debit to Insurance Expense for $1,500.

10. Assume that a company receives a bill for $10,000 for advertising done during the current year. If this expense is not yet recorded by the end of the year, what will the adjusting journal entry include?
    a.  Debit to Advertising Expense of $10,000.
    b.  Credit to Advertising Expense of $10,000.
    c.  Debit to Accrued Liabilities of $10,000.
    d.  Need more information to determine.

---

Solutions to Multiple-Choice Questions

1. *b*      2. *a*      3. *d*      4. *c*      5. *d*      6. *d*      7. *a*      8. *c*      9. *c*      10. *a*

---

## Mini Exercises  ⊞⊞ ™   Available with McGraw-Hill's Homework Manager

**LO2**     **M4-1 Understanding Concepts Related to Adjustments**
Match each of the following situations to two applicable reasons that require an adjustment to be made.

____ & ____  1. Northwest Airlines provided flights this month for customers who paid cash last month for tickets.

____ & ____  2. Abercrombie & Fitch received a telephone bill for services this month, which must be paid next month.

____ & ____  3. GSD + M (an advertising firm in Austin, Texas) completed work on an advertising campaign that will be billed and collected next month.

____ & ____  4. The Tiger Woods Foundation used up some of the benefits of its 35,000-square-foot building when teaching students about forensic science, aerospace, and video production.

A. Revenue has been earned.
B. Expense has been incurred.
C. Liability has been incurred.
D. Liability has been fulfilled.
E. Asset has been created.
F. Asset has been used up.

## M4-2 Preparing an Adjusted Trial Balance                                      LO3

Macro Company has the following adjusted accounts and balances at year-end (June 30, 2010):

| | | | | | |
|---|---|---|---|---|---|
| Accounts Payable | $ 300 | Depreciation Expense | $ 110 | Prepaid Expenses | $ 40 |
| Accounts Receivable | 550 | Insurance Expense | 110 | Salaries Expense | 660 |
| Accrued Liabilities | 150 | Interest Expense | 180 | Sales Revenue | 3,600 |
| Accumulated Depreciation | 250 | Interest Payable | 30 | Supplies | 710 |
| Buildings and Equipment | 1,400 | Interest Revenue | 50 | Supplies Expense | 820 |
| Cash | 1,020 | Land | 200 | Rent Expense | 400 |
| J. Macro, Capital | 420 | Long-Term debt | 1,300 | Unearned Revenue | 100 |

*Required:*
Prepare an adjusted trial balance for Macro Company at June 30, 2010.

## M4-3 Matching Transactions with Type of Adjustment                            LO2

Match each transaction with the type of adjustment that will be required by entering the appropriate letter in the space provided.

| Transaction | Type of Adjustment |
|---|---|
| ____ 1. An expense has not yet been incurred but has been paid in advance. | A. Unearned revenue. |
| ____ 2. Rent has not yet been collected but is already earned. | B. Accrued revenue. |
| ____ 3. Office supplies on hand will be used next accounting period. | C. Prepaid expense. |
| ____ 4. An expense has been incurred but not yet paid or recorded. | D. Accrued expense. |
| ____ 5. Revenue has been collected in advance and will be earned later. | |

## M4-4 Matching Transactions with Type of Adjustment                            LO2

Match each transaction with the type of adjustment that will be required by entering the appropriate letter in the space provided.

| Transaction | Type of Adjustment |
|---|---|
| ____ 1. Supplies for office use were purchased during the year for $500, and $100 of the office supplies remained on hand (unused) at year-end. | A. Unearned revenue.<br>B. Accrued revenue.<br>C. Prepaid expense.<br>D. Accrued expense. |
| ____ 2. Interest of $250 on a note receivable was earned at year-end, although collection of the interest is not due until the following year. | |
| ____ 3. At year-end, wages payable of $3,600 had not been recorded or paid. | |
| ____ 4. At year-end, service revenue of $2,000 was collected in cash but was only partly earned. | |

## M4-5 Determining Effects of Adjustments                                       LO2

For each of the following transactions for Sky Blue Company owned by sole proprietor Anna Cerveny, give the effects amounts and direction of effect (+ for increase or − for decrease) of the adjustments required at the end of the month on December 31, 2010. Use the following form. If an element is not affected, write NE for no effect.

a.  Collected $1,200 rent for the period December 1, 2010, to February 28, 2011, that was credited to Unearned Rent Revenue on December 1, 2010.

b.  Paid $2,400 for a two-year insurance premium on December 1, 2010; debited Prepaid Insurance for that amount.

c.  Used a machine purchased on December 1, 2010, for $48,000. The company estimates *annual* depreciation of $4,800.

| | BALANCE SHEET | | | INCOME STATEMENT | | |
|---|---|---|---|---|---|---|
| Transaction | Assets | Liabilities | Owner's Equity | Revenues | Expenses | Net Income |
| a. | | | | | | |
| b. | | | | | | |
| c. | | | | | | |

**LO2    M4-6 Recording Adjusting Journal Entries**

Using the information in M4-5, for each transaction, (1) identify the type of adjustment and (2) prepare the adjusting journal entry required on December 31, 2010.

**LO2    M4-7 Determining Accounting Equation Effects of Adjustments**

For each of the following transactions for Sky Blue Company owned by sole proprietor Anna Cerveny, give the effects amounts and direction of effect (+ for increase or − for decrease) of the adjustments required at the end of the month on December 31, 2010. Use the following form. If an element is not affected, write NE for no effect.

a.  Received a $600 utility bill for electricity usage in December to be paid in January 2011.

b.  Owed wages to 10 employees who worked three days at $100 each per day at the end of December. The company will pay employees at the end of the first week of January 2011.

c.  On December 1, 2010, loaned money to an employee who agreed to repay the loan in one year along with one full year of interest equal to $1,200.

| | BALANCE SHEET | | | INCOME STATEMENT | | |
|---|---|---|---|---|---|---|
| Transaction | Assets | Liabilities | Owner's Equity | Revenues | Expenses | Net Income |
| a. | | | | | | |
| b. | | | | | | |
| c. | | | | | | |

**LO2    M4-8 Recording Adjusting Journal Entries**

Using the information in M4-7, for each transaction, (1) identify the type of adjustment and (2) prepare the adjusting journal entry required on December 31, 2010.

**LO3    M4-9 Reporting an Income Statement**

Sky Blue Company, owned by sole proprietor Anna Cerveny, provides computer technology services to customers. The company has the following adjusted accounts at December 31, 2010.

| | | | |
|---|---|---|---|
| Cash | $ 1,200 | A. Cerveny, Capital | $ 3,400 |
| Accounts Receivable | 2,000 | A. Cerveny, Drawing | 300 |
| Interest Receivable | 30 | Service Revenue | 42,000 |
| Prepaid Insurance | 2,300 | Interest Revenue | 30 |
| Notes Receivable | 3,000 | Rent Revenue | 300 |
| Equipment | 12,000 | Wages Expense | 21,600 |
| Accumulated Depreciation | 300 | Depreciation Expense | 300 |
| Accounts Payable | 1,600 | Utilities Expense | 220 |
| Wages Payable | 3,820 | Insurance Expense | 100 |
| Interest Payable | 2,900 | Rent Expense | 9,000 |
| Unearned Rent Revenue | 600 | Interest Expense | 2,900 |

Prepare a *classified* income statement for 2010.

**LO3    M4-10 Reporting a Statement of Owner's Equity**

Refer to M4-9. Prepare a statement of owner's equity for 2010. Assume that the owner did not make any investments during the year.

**LO3    M4-11 Reporting a Balance Sheet**

Refer to M4-9. Prepare a *classified* balance sheet at December 31, 2010. Are Sky Blue Company's assets financed primarily by debt or equity?

**LO4    M4-12 Recording Closing Journal Entries**

Refer to the adjusted accounts in M4-9. Prepare closing journal entries on December 31, 2010.

**LO5    M4-13 Analyzing Financial Information**

Refer to M4-9. Compute the net profit margin ratio, and interpret what the result suggests for Sky Blue Company.

**For M4-14 through M4-19, complete the following requirements:**

1.  What type of adjustment is this?
2.  Prepare the adjusting journal entry on December 31.
3.  In separate T-accounts for each account, enter the unadjusted balance, post the adjusting journal entry, and report the adjusted balance.

**M4-14 Preparing and Posting Adjusting Journal Entries**  LO2

At December 31, the unadjusted trial balance of H&R Tacks reports Supplies Expense of $0 and Supplies of $9,000, representing the beginning cost of Supplies plus the amount purchased during the year. On December 31, supplies costing $1,300 are on hand. (See requirements on prior page.)

**M4-15 Preparing and Posting Adjusting Journal Entries**  LO2

At December 31, the unadjusted trial balance of H&R Tacks reports Equipment of $38,000 and zero balances in Accumulated Depreciation and Depreciation Expense. Depreciation for the period is estimated to be $6,000. (See requirements on prior page.)

**M4-16 Preparing and Posting Adjusting Journal Entries**  LO2

At December 31, the unadjusted trial balance of H&R Tacks reports Prepaid Insurance of $7,200 and Insurance Expense of $0. The insurance was purchased on July 1 and provides coverage for 12 months. (See requirements on prior page.)

**M4-17 Preparing and Posting Adjusting Journal Entries**  LO2

At December 31, the unadjusted trial balance of H&R Tacks reports Unearned Revenue of $5,000 and Service Revenue of $33,800. One-half of the unearned revenue has been earned as of December 31. (See requirements on prior page.)

**M4-18 Preparing and Posting Adjusting Journal Entries**  LO2

At December 31, the unadjusted trial balance of H&R Tacks reports Wages Payable of $0 and Wages Expense of $20,000. Employees have been paid for work done up to December 27, but the $1,200 they have earned for December 28–31 has not yet been paid or recorded. (See requirements on prior page.)

**M4-19 Preparing and Posting Adjusting Journal Entries**  LO2

At December 31, the unadjusted trial balance of H&R Tacks reports Interest Payable of $0 and Interest Expense of $0. Interest incurred and owed in December totals $500. (See requirements on prior page.)

**M4-20 Preparing an Adjusted Trial Balance**  LO3

The following alphabetical listing is the adjusted account balances for H&R Tacks, owned and managed by Jeremy Daily.

| | | | | | |
|---|---|---|---|---|---|
| Accounts Payable | $ 400 | Insurance Expense | $ 3,600 | Prepaid Insurance | $ 3,600 |
| Accounts Receivable | 500 | Interest Expense | 500 | Service Revenue | 46,300 |
| Accumulated Depreciation | 6,000 | Interest Payable | 500 | Supplies | 1,300 |
| Cash | 5,000 | J. Daily, Capital | 27,700 | Supplies Expense | 7,700 |
| Depreciation Expense | 6,000 | J. Daily, Drawing | 200 | Unearned Revenue | 2,500 |
| Equipment | 38,000 | Notes Payable | 3,000 | Wages Expense | 21,200 |
| | | | | Wages Payable | 1,200 |

Prepare an adjusted trial balance as of December 31.

**M4-21 Closing the Books**  LO4

Refer to the adjusted account balances in M4-20. Prepare closing journal entries on December 31.

**M4-22 Computing Net Profit Margin**  LO5

Refer to the adjusted account balances in M4-20.

*Required:*

1. Compute net income.
2. Compute net profit margin for H&R Tacks.
3. What does the result of your computation suggest about H&R Tacks?

# Exercises  ™  **Available with McGraw-Hill's Homework Manager**

**E4-1 Preparing an Adjusted Trial Balance**  LO3

Gibson Consultants provides marketing research for clients in the retail industry. The company had the following adjusted balances at December 31, 2010:

| Cash | | Accumulated Depreciation | | Accrued Liabilities | |
|---|---|---|---|---|---|
| 173,000 | | | 18,100 | | 25,650 |

| Wages Expense | | Advertising Expense | | Supplies | |
|---|---|---|---|---|---|
| 1,590,000 | | 320,050 | | 12,200 | |

| Accounts Receivable | | Prepaid Expenses | | Interest Expense | |
|---|---|---|---|---|---|
| 225,400 | | 10,200 | | 17,200 | |

| Interest Payable | | Consulting Fees Revenue | | P. Gibson, Capital | |
|---|---|---|---|---|---|
| | 2,030 | | 2,577,200 | | ? |

| Utilities Expense | | Travel Expense | | Building and Equipment | |
|---|---|---|---|---|---|
| 25,230 | | 23,990 | | 323,040 | |

| Investment Revenue | | P. Gibson, Drawing | | Unearned Consulting Fees | |
|---|---|---|---|---|---|
| | 7,800 | 5,000 | | | 32,500 |

| Training Expenses | | Accounts Payable | | Land | |
|---|---|---|---|---|---|
| 188,000 | | 86,830 | | 60,000 | |

| Notes Payable | | Depreciation Expense | | Investments | |
|---|---|---|---|---|---|
| | 160,000 | 18,600 | | 145,000 | |

| Rent Expense | |
|---|---|
| 152,080 | |

*Required:*

1. Prepare an adjusted trial balance for Gibson Consultants at December 31, 2010. Solve for the '?' in the P. Gibson, Capital account (*Hint:* Remember: Assets = Liabilities + Owner's Equity.)
2. Assume that no investments were made by P. Gibson during the year. Does the P. Gibson, Capital balance determined in 1 represent the balance at December 31, 2010, or December 31, 2009? Explain.

**LO2**

**Coach, Inc.**

**E4-2 Identifying Adjustments by Scanning a Trial Balance**

Coach, Inc.—the maker of handbags and other women's and men's accessories—was owned by Sara Lee Corporation until April 2001, when Coach was spun off as a separate company. Assume the following adjusted balances were reported in Coach's trial balance and were used to prepare its July 2, 2009, year-end financial statements.

**COACH INCORPORATED**
**Adjusted Trial Balance**
**At July 2, 2009**
**(millions of dollars)**

| | Debit | Credit |
|---|---|---|
| Cash | 154,556 | |
| Accounts Receivable | 65,399 | |
| Inventories | 184,419 | |
| Prepaid Expenses | 25,671 | |
| Property and Equipment | 203,862 | |
| Other Assets | 713,215 | |
| Accounts Payable | | 64,985 |
| Wages Payable | | 185,502 |
| Interest Payable | | 2,851 |
| Notes Payable | | 3,270 |
| Other Liabilities | | 57,748 |
| Owners' Capital | | 644,114 |
| Sales Revenue | | 1,710,423 |
| Cost of Sales (used up inventory) | 399,652 | |
| Selling, General, and Administrative Expenses | 688,961 | |
| Interest Expense | 13,641 | |
| Interest Revenue | | 15,760 |
| Other Expenses | 235,277 | |
| | 2,684,653 | 2,684,653 |

*Required:*

1. Based on the information in the trial balance, identify any accounts that likely were unearned revenues or prepaid expenses requiring an adjusting entry as of July 2 (no computations are necessary).
2. Based on the information in the trial balance, identify any accounts that likely were accrued revenues or accrued expenses requiring an adjusting entry as of July 2 (no computations are necessary).

## E4-3 Determining Adjustments and Accounting Equation Effects

LO1, 2

MoBo, a wireless phone carrier owned by sole proprietor Morris Bonner, completed its first year of operations on December 31, 2011. All of the 2011 entries have been recorded except for the following:

    a.  At year-end, employees earned wages of $6,000 that will be paid on the next payroll date, January 6, 2012.

    b.  At year-end, the company had earned interest revenue of $3,000. It will be collected March 1, 2012.

*Required:*

1. What is the annual reporting period for this company?
2. Identify whether each required adjustment is an unearned revenue, accrued revenue, prepaid expense, or accrued expense.
3. Show the accounting equation effects (amounts and direction of effects) of each required adjustment. Use + for increase, − for decrease, or NE for no effect. Complete the following schedule:

| | BALANCE SHEET | | | INCOME STATEMENT | | |
|---|---|---|---|---|---|---|
| Transaction | Assets | Liabilities | Owner's Equity | Revenues | Expenses | Net Income |
| a. | | | | | | |
| b. | | | | | | |

4. Why are these adjustments needed?

## E4-4 Recording Adjusting Journal Entries

LO2

Refer to E4-3.

*Required:*

Record the required adjusting journal entries for transactions *a* and *b*.

## E4-5 Determining Adjustments and Accounting Equation Effects

LO1, 2

Mary Fes, owner of Fes Company, has hired you to help with the accounting entries at the end of the year on December 31, 2009. In developing information for the adjusting journal entries, you learned the following:

    a.  A two-year insurance premium of $7,200 was paid on January 1, 2009, for coverage beginning on that date. As of December 31, 2009, the unadjusted balances were $7,200 for Prepaid Insurance and $0 for Insurance Expense.

    b.  At December 31, 2009, you obtained the following data relating to shipping supplies.

| | |
|---|---|
| Balance in Shipping Supplies on December 31, 2008 | $15,000 |
| Shipping supplies purchased in 2009 | 72,000 |
| Shipping supplies on hand, counted on December 31, 2009 | 10,000 |

*Required:*

1. Of the $7,200 paid for insurance, what amount should be reported on the 2009 income statement as Insurance Expense? What amount should be reported on the December 31, 2009, balance sheet as Prepaid Insurance?
2. What amount should be reported on the 2009 income statement as Shipping Supplies Expense? What amount should be reported on the December 31, 2009, balance sheet as Shipping Supplies?
3. Using the following format, indicate the accounting equation effects (amounts and direction of effects) of the adjustment required for (*a*) insurance and (*b*) shipping supplies. Use + for increase, − for decrease, or NE for no effect.

| | BALANCE SHEET | | | INCOME STATEMENT | | |
|---|---|---|---|---|---|---|
| Transaction | Assets | Liabilities | Owner's Equity | Revenues | Expenses | Net Income |
| a. | | | | | | |
| b. | | | | | | |

**LO2**

### E4-6 Recording Adjusting Journal Entries

Refer to E4-5.

*Required:*

Prepare adjusting journal entries at December 31, 2009, for (*a*) insurance and (*b*) shipping supplies.

**LO2**

### E4-7 Recording Adjusting Journal Entries

Jaworski's Ski Store is completing the accounting process for its first year ended December 31, 2010. The transactions during 2010 have been journalized and posted. The following data are available to determine adjusting journal entries:

a.   The balance in Office Supplies was $50 at December 31, 2009. Jaworski's purchased $800 of supplies during 2010. The unadjusted balance in Supplies Expense was $0 at December 31, 2010. A year-end count showed $100 of supplies on hand.

b.   Wages earned by employees during December 2010, unpaid and unrecorded at December 31, 2010, amounted to $3,700. The last paychecks were issued December 28; the next payments will be made on January 6, 2011. The unadjusted balance in Wages Expense was $40,000 at December 31, 2010.

c.   Jaworski's rents a portion of the store's basement for $1,100 per month to K. Frey. On November 1, 2010, the store collected six months' rent in the amount of $6,600 in advance from Frey. It was credited in full to Unearned Rent Revenue when collected. The unadjusted balance in Rent Revenue was $0 at December 31, 2010.

d.   The store purchased delivery equipment at the beginning of the year 2010. The estimated depreciation for 2010 is $3,000, although none has been recorded yet.

e.   On December 31, 2010, the unadjusted balance in Prepaid Insurance was $4,800. This was the amount paid in the middle of the year for a two-year insurance policy with coverage beginning on July 1, 2010. The unadjusted balance in Insurance Expense was $800, which was the cost of insurance from January 1 to June 30, 2010.

f.   Jaworski's operates a repair shop doing some work for Frey. At the end of December 31, 2010, Frey had not paid for completed work amounting to $750. This amount has not yet been recorded as Repair Shop Revenue. Collection is expected during January 2011.

*Required:*

For each of the preceding items,

1.   Identify the type of adjustment.

2.   Prepare the adjusting journal entry that should be recorded at December 31, 2010.

3.   Indicate the account names and adjusted balances that should be reported on Jaworski's year-end balance sheet and income statement.

**LO2**

### E4-8 Determining Financial Statement Effects of Adjusting Journal Entries

Refer to E4-7.

*Required:*

For each transaction in E4-7, indicate the amount and direction of effects of the adjusting journal entry on the elements of the balance sheet and income statement. Use the following format: + for increase, − for decrease, and NE for no effect.

| | BALANCE SHEET | | | INCOME STATEMENT | | |
|---|---|---|---|---|---|---|
| Transaction | Assets | Liabilities | Owner's Equity | Revenues | Expenses | Net Income |
| a. | | | | | | |
| b. | | | | | | |
| etc. | | | | | | |

**LO2, 4**

### E4-9 Recording Transactions Including Adjusting and Closing Journal Entries

Cooper Paving, owned by Chuck Cooper, uses the following accounts:

| Codes | Accounts | Codes | Accounts |
|-------|----------|-------|----------|
| A | Accounts Receivable | J | Notes Payable |
| B | Accumulated Depreciation | K | Paving Equipment |
| C | Cash | L | Service Revenue |
| D | C. Cooper, Capital | M | Supplies |
| E | C. Cooper, Drawing | N | Supplies Expense |
| F | Depreciation Expense | O | Unearned Service Revenue |
| G | Income Summary | P | Wages Expense |
| H | Interest Expense | Q | Wages Payable |
| I | Interest Payable | R | None of the above |

**Required:**

For each of the following independent situations, give the journal entry by entering the appropriate code(s) and amount(s). The first one is an example.

| | Independent Situations | DEBIT Code | DEBIT Amount | CREDIT Code | CREDIT Amount |
|---|---|---|---|---|---|
| a. | (*Example*) Accrued wages, unrecorded and unpaid at year-end, $400. | P | 400 | Q | 400 |
| b. | Service revenue collected in advance, $600. | | | | |
| c. | Amounts withdrawn by the owner during year, $900. | | | | |
| d. | Depreciation expense for year, $1,000. | | | | |
| e. | Service revenue earned but not yet collected at year-end, $1,000. | | | | |
| f. | Balance in supplies account, $400; supplies on hand at year-end, $150. | | | | |
| g. | At year-end, interest on notes payable not yet recorded or paid, $220. | | | | |
| h. | Balance at year-end in Service Revenue account, $75,000. Give the journal entry to close this one account at year-end. | | | | |
| i. | Balance at year-end in Interest Expense account, $420. Give the journal entry to close this one account at year-end. | | | | |

## E4-10 Inferring Transactions from Accrual Accounts

**LO2**

**Deere & Company**

Deere & Company was incorporated in 1868 and today is the world's leading producer of agricultural equipment. The company also provides credit, managed health care plans, and insurance products for businesses and the general public. The following information is taken from a recent annual report (in millions of dollars):

| Wages and Benefits Payable | | |
|---|---|---|
| | Beg. bal. | 981 |
| 2,261 | (a) | ? |
| | End. bal. | 1,060 |

| Product Warranties Payable | | |
|---|---|---|
| | Beg. bal. | 507 |
| (b) ? | | 565 |
| | End. bal. | 549 |

| Interest Payable | | |
|---|---|---|
| | Beg. bal. | 129 |
| 1,140 | (c) | ? |
| | End. bal. | 140 |

**Required:**

1.  For each accrued liability account, describe the typical transactions that cause it to increase and decrease.

2.  Solve for the missing amounts for (*a*), (*b*), and (*c*) (in millions).

## E4-11 Analyzing the Effects of Adjusting Journal Entries on the Income Statement and Balance Sheet

**LO2, 3**

On December 31, 2009, Laura's Pie Company, owned by Laura Anne, prepared an income statement and balance sheet, but the bookkeeper accidentally failed to take into account four adjusting journal entries. The income statement, prepared on this incorrect basis, reported income of $30,000. The balance sheet reflected total assets, $90,000; total liabilities, $40,000; and owner's equity, $50,000. The data for the four adjusting journal entries follow:

a.   Depreciation of $8,000 for the year on equipment was not recorded.

b.   Wages amounting to $17,000 for the last three days of December 2009 were not paid and not recorded (the next payroll will be on January 10, 2010).

c.   Rent revenue of $4,800 was collected on December 1, 2009, for office space for the three-month period December 1, 2009, to February 28, 2010. The $4,800 was credited in full to Unearned Rent Revenue when collected.

d.   The company borrowed $10,000 from a local bank on January 1, 2009. The note principal is due in three years but requires payment of $1,500 interest every January 1 with the next payment due on January 1, 2010. No interest has been paid or recorded for 2009.

**Required:**
Complete the following table to show the effects of the four adjusting journal entries (indicate deductions with parentheses):

| Items | Net Income | Total Assets | Total Liabilities | Owner's Equity |
|---|---|---|---|---|
| Amounts reported | $30,000 | $90,000 | $40,000 | $50,000 |
| Effect of depreciation | | | | |
| Effect of wages | | | | |
| Effect of rent revenue | | | | |
| Effect of interest | | | | |
| Correct amounts | | | | |

**LO1, 2, 3**   **E4-12 Reporting an Adjusted Income Statement**
Dyer Rental Store, a sole proprietorship owned by Jessica Dyer, completed its first year of operations on December 31, 2010. Because this is the end of the annual accounting period, the business's bookkeeper prepared the following tentative income statement:

| Income Statement, 2010 (amounts are unadjusted) | |
|---|---|
| Rental Revenue | $114,000 |
| Expenses | |
| Salaries and Wages Expense | 28,500 |
| Supplies Expense | 12,000 |
| Rent Expense | 9,000 |
| Utilities Expense | 4,000 |
| Gas and Oil Expense | 3,000 |
| Other Operating Expenses | 1,000 |
| Total expenses | 57,500 |
| Income | $ 56,500 |

You are an independent CPA hired by the business to audit its accounting systems and financial statements. In your audit, you developed additional data as follows:

a.   Salaries and wages for the last three days of December amounting to $310 were not recorded or paid.

b.   The $400 telephone bill for December 2010 has not been recorded or paid.

c.   Depreciation on vans amounting to $23,000 for 2010 was not recorded.

d.   Interest of $500 was not recorded on the note payable by Dyer Rental.

e.   The Unearned Rental Revenue account includes $4,000 revenue earned in 2010.

f.   Supplies costing $600 were used during 2010, but this has not yet been recorded.

*Required:*

1. Explain why adjusting entries are necessary.
2. For each item *a* through *f*, indicate the type of adjustment and then prepare the adjusting journal entry that should be recorded at December 31, 2010. If none is required, explain why.
3. Prepare a *classified* income statement for 2010 using adjusted amounts.

**E4-13 Recording Adjusting Entries and Preparing an Adjusted Trial Balance**          LO2, 3

Ninja Sockeye Star, owned by Johnny Chen, had the following unadjusted accounts at the end of its second year of operations ending December 31, 2009. The accounts have normal debit or credit balances.

| Cash | $12,000 | Wages Payable | $ 0 |
|---|---|---|---|
| Accounts Receivable | 6,000 | J. Chen, Capital | 31,900 |
| Prepaid Rent | 2,400 | Commissions Revenue | 45,000 |
| Equipment | 21,000 | Wages Expense | 25,000 |
| Accumulated Depreciation | 1,000 | Utilities Expense | 12,500 |
| Accounts Payable | 1,000 | Rent Expense | 0 |
| Utilities Payable | 0 | Depreciation Expense | 0 |

Other data not yet recorded at December 31, 2009, follow:

*a.* Rent used during 2009, $1,200.
*b.* Depreciation expense for 2009, $1,000.
*c.* Utilities used in 2009 but not yet paid, $9,000.
*d.* Wages earned by employees in 2009 but not yet paid, $800.

*Required:*

1. Create T-accounts based on the accounts titles and balances at December 31, 2009.
2. Using the steps outlined in the chapter, (1) identify the type of adjustment of (*a*) through (*d*), (2) determine the amount, and (3) prepare the adjusting journal entries required at December 31, 2009.
3. Post the effects of the adjusting journal entries to the T-accounts and prepare an adjusted trial balance as of December 31, 2009.

**E4-14 Recording Adjusting Entries and Preparing an Adjusted Trial Balance**          LO2, 3

Mint Cleaning, owned by Kat Slifer, had the following unadjusted accounts at the end of its second year of operations ending December 31, 2010. To simplify this exercise, the amounts given are in thousands of dollars and have normal debit or credit balances.

| Cash | $38 | Unearned Service Revenue | $ 27 |
|---|---|---|---|
| Accounts Receivable | 9 | K. Slifer, Capital | 80 |
| Prepaid Insurance | 16 | K. Slifer, Drawing | 16 |
| Equipment | 90 | Service Revenue | 179 |
| Accumulated Depreciation | 4 | Supplies Expense | 26 |
| Accounts Payable | 25 | Wages Expense | 120 |
| Wages Payable | 0 | | |

Other data not yet recorded at December 31, 2010, follow:

*a.* One-fourth of the Prepaid Insurance expired during 2010.
*b.* Depreciation expense for 2010, $4.
*c.* Wages earned by employees but not yet paid in 2010, $7.
*d.* One-third of the Unearned Service Revenue was earned in 2010.

*Required:*

1. Create T-accounts based on the account titles and balances at December 31, 2010.
2. Using the steps outlined in the chapter, (1) identify the type of adjustment of *a* through *d*, (2) determine the amount, and (3) prepare the adjusting journal entries required at December 31, 2010.

3.  Post the effects of the adjusting journal entries to the T-accounts and prepare an adjusted trial balance as of December 31, 2010.

**LO3**

### E4-15 Reporting an Income Statement, Statement of Owner's Equity, and Balance Sheet
Refer to E4-14.

*Required:*

Using the adjusted balances in E4-14, prepare a *classified* income statement, statement of owner's equity, and *classified* balance sheet for 2010.

**LO4**

### E4-16 Recording Closing Entries
Refer to E4-14.

*Required:*

1.  Using the adjusted balances in E4-14, give the closing journal entries for 2010.
2.  What is the purpose of closing the books at the end of the accounting period?

**LO5**

### E4-17 Analyzing Financial Information Using Net Profit Margin
Refer to the financial statements created in E4-15.

*Required:*

Compute and interpret the net profit margin ratio for Mint Cleaning for 2010.

**LO1, 2**

### E4-18 Recording Initial Transactions and Subsequent Adjustments
During the month of September, Texas Go-Kart Company had the following business activities:

a.  Paid rent on September 1 on the track facility for six months at a total cost of $12,000.
b.  Sold season tickets on September 1 for 12-month admission to the race track. Season ticket sales totaled $60,000.
c.  Reserved the race track on September 1 for a private organization that will use the track one day per month beginning on September 15 for $2,000, to be paid in the following month.
d.  Hired a new manager on September 1 at a monthly salary of $3,000 to be paid the first Monday following the end of the month. The manager started on September 2.

*Required:*

Using the following table, prepare

1.  The journal entry, if any, required to record each of the initial business activities on September 1.
2.  The adjusting journal entry, if any, required on September 30.

| Ref / Date | Journal Entries and Adjusting Journal Entries | DEBIT | CREDIT |
|---|---|---|---|
| (a) Sept 1 | | | |
| Sept 30 | | | |
| (b) Sept 1 | | | |
| Sept 30 | | | |
| (c) Sept 1 | | | |
| Sept 30 | | | |
| (d) Sept 1 | | | |
| Sept 30 | | | |

### E4-19 Completing a Worksheet Starting with an Unadjusted Trial Balance (Chapter Supplement)
Fairbanks Company is completing its annual accounting information processing cycle at December 31, 2011. The following worksheet has been started.

**Fairbanks Company**
**Unadjusted Trial Balance**
**December 31, 2011**
**(dollars in thousands)**

| Account No. | Account Titles | Debit | Credit |
|---|---|---|---|
| 101 | Cash | 38 | |
| 102 | Accounts Receivable | 40 | |
| 103 | Supplies | 21 | |
| 104 | Prepaid Insurance | 4 | |
| 110 | Equipment | 80 | |
| 111 | Accumulated Depreciation, Equipment | | 8 |
| 119 | Accounts Payable | | 12 |
| 120 | Wages Payable | | |
| 121 | Interest Payable | | |
| 122 | Unearned Revenue | | 10 |
| 123 | Note Payable (due 2014) | | 25 |
| 130 | K. Fairbanks, Capital | | 89 |
| 145 | Service Revenue | | 108 |
| 146 | Wages Expense | 69 | |
| 147 | Insurance Expense | | |
| 148 | Depreciation Expense | | |
| 150 | Interest Expense | | |
| | | 252 | 252 |

Data not yet recorded for 2011:

a.   Half of Prepaid Insurance was used in 2011.
b.   Depreciation expense, $8.
c.   Wages earned by employees; not yet paid, $1.
d.   Revenue collected by Fairbanks; not yet earned, $6.
e.   Interest expense incurred; not yet paid, $3.

**Required:**
Complete the worksheet. Set up additional column headings for Adjusting Entries, Adjusted Trial Balance, Income Statement, Owner's Equity, and Balance Sheet.

## Problems—Set A  Available with McGraw-Hill's Homework Manager

**PA4-1 Recording Adjusting Journal Entries**                                                    LO2
Jordan Company's annual accounting year ends on December 31. Jordan Broome owns and manages the company. It is now December 31, 2009, and all of the 2009 entries have been made except for the following:

a.   The company owes interest of $400 on a bank loan taken out on October 1, 2009. The interest will be paid when the loan is repaid on September 30, 2010.
b.   On September 1, 2009, Jordan collected six months' rent of $4,800 on storage space. At that date, Jordan debited Cash and credited Unearned Rent Revenue for $4,800.
c.   The company earned service revenue of $3,000 on a special job completed December 29, 2009. Collection will be made during January 2010. No entry has been recorded.
d.   On November 1, 2009, Jordan paid a $4,200, one-year premium for property insurance for coverage starting on that date. Prepaid Insurance was debited and Cash was credited for this amount.

e.  At December 31, 2009, wages earned by employees totaled $1,100. The employees will be paid on the next payroll date, January 15, 2010.

f.  Depreciation of $1,000 must be recognized on a service truck purchased this year.

g.  On December 27, 2009, the company received a tax bill of $400 from the city for 2009 property taxes on land. The tax bill is payable during January 2010.

**Required:**
Following the steps outlined in the chapter, for each transaction:

1.  Identify the type of adjustment (unearned revenue, accrued revenue, prepaid expense, or accrued expense).

2.  Determine the amount of revenue or expense to be recorded.

3.  Record the adjusting journal entry at December 31, 2009.

**LO2**

**PA4-2 Determining Financial Statement Effects of Adjusting Journal Entries**
Refer to PA4-1.

**Required:**
Using the following headings, indicate the effect of each adjusting journal entry and the amount of the effect. Use + for increase, − for decrease, and NE for no effect.

| | BALANCE SHEET | | | INCOME STATEMENT | | |
|---|---|---|---|---|---|---|
| Transaction | Assets | Liabilities | Owner's Equity | Revenues | Expenses | Net Income |
| a. | | | | | | |
| b. | | | | | | |
| etc. | | | | | | |

**LO3, 4**

www.mhhe.com/LLPW1e

**PA4-3 Preparing an Adjusted Trial Balance, Closing Journal Entries, and Post-Closing Trial Balance**
Dell is the world's largest computer systems company selling directly to customers. The following is a list of adjusted accounts and amounts reported for a recent fiscal year ended February 3. The accounts have normal debit or credit balances and the dollars are rounded to the nearest million.

| | | | |
|---|---|---|---|
| Accounts Payable | $ 9,840 | Long-Term Debt | $   504 |
| Accounts Receivable | 5,452 | Other Assets | 14,635 |
| Accrued Liabilities | 6,087 | Other Expenses | 1,002 |
| Accumulated Depreciation | 749 | Other Liabilities | 2,549 |
| Cash | 9,807 | Property, Plant, and Equipment | 2,005 |
| Cost of Goods Sold (inventory used) | 45,958 | Research and Development Expense | 463 |
| Dell Owners' Capital | 9,174 | Sales Revenue | 55,908 |
| Interest Revenue | 227 | Selling, General, and | |
| Inventories | 576 | Administrative Expenses | 5,140 |

**Required:**

1.  Prepare an adjusted trial balance at February 3, 2009. Is the Dell Owners' Capital balance of $9,174 the amount that would be reported on the balance sheet as of February 3, 2009?

2.  Prepare the closing entries required at February 3, 2009.

3.  Prepare a post-closing trial balance at February 3, 2009.

**LO4, 5**

**Starbucks Corporation**

www.mhhe.com/LLPW1e

**PA4-4 Preparing Closing Entries and Computing and Analyzing Net Profit Margin**
Starbucks Corporation purchases and roasts high-quality whole bean coffees and sells them along with fresh-brewed coffees, its exclusive line of Frappucino blended beverages, Italian-style espresso beverages, and premium teas. The following is a simplified list of accounts and amounts reported in its accounting records. The accounts have normal debit or credit balances, and the dollars are rounded to the nearest million. Assume that the year ended on September 30, 2010.

| | | | |
|---|---|---|---|
| Accounts Payable | $ 221 | Long-Term Debt | $ 196 |
| Accounts Receivable | 191 | Other Current Assets | 71 |
| Accrued Liabilities | 354 | Other Long-Lived Assets | 461 |
| Accumulated Depreciation | 300 | Other Expenses | 499 |
| Cash | 307 | Prepaid Expenses | 94 |
| Cost of Sales (an expense for inventory sold) | 2,605 | Property, Plant, and Equipment | 2,142 |
| Depreciation Expense | 340 | Service Revenues | 6,369 |
| General and Administrative Expenses | 357 | Short-Term Bank Debt | 476 |
| Interest Revenue | 92 | Starbucks Owners' Capital | 1,596 |
| Inventories | 546 | Store Operating Expenses | 2,166 |
| | | Unearned Revenue | 175 |

*Required:*

1. Prepare the closing entries required at September 30, 2010.
2. Compute net profit margin for the year ended September 30, 2010.
3. In the year ended September 30, 2009, assume that Starbucks had an 8.6% net profit margin and that the industry ratio was 10.5%. What does this information suggest to you about Starbucks?

**PA4-5 Recording Transactions (including adjusting journal entries), Preparing Financial Statements, Closing the Books, and Analyzing a Key Ratio: Comprehensive Review Problem (Chapters 2, 3, and 4)**

LO1, 2, 3, 4, 5

www.mhhe.com/LLPW1e

Harry Hermann began operations of his machine shop (H-H Tool) on January 1, 2009. The annual reporting period ends December 31. The trial balance on January 1, 2011, follows (the amounts are rounded to thousands of dollars to simplify):

**H-H Tool**
**Trial Balance**
**On January 1, 2011**
**(in thousands)**

| Account Titles | Debit | Credit | Account Titles | Debit | Credit |
|---|---|---|---|---|---|
| Cash | 3 | | Utilities Payable | | 0 |
| Accounts Receivable | 5 | | H. Hermann, Capital | | 73 |
| Supplies | 12 | | H. Hermann, Drawing | 0 | |
| Land | 0 | | Service Revenue | | 0 |
| Equipment | 60 | | Depreciation Expense | 0 | |
| Accumulated Depreciation | | 6 | Wages Expense | 0 | |
| Other Assets | 4 | | Interest Expense | 0 | |
| Accounts Payable | | 5 | Supplies Expense | 0 | |
| Notes Payable | | 0 | Utilities Expense | 0 | |
| Wages Payable | | 0 | Other Operating Expenses | 0 | |
| Interest Payable | | 0 | | 84 | 84 |

*(continued)*

Transactions during 2011 (summarized in thousands of dollars) follow:

    *a.* Borrowed $12 cash on a short-term note payable dated March 1, 2011.

    *b.* Purchased land for future building site, paid cash, $9.

    *c.* Earned $160 in Service Revenue for 2011, including $40 on credit and $120 collected in cash.

    *d.* Received an additional $3 investment by H. Hermann.

    *e.* Recognized $70 in Wages Expense for 2011, paid in cash, and $15 of Other Operating Expenses on credit.

    *f.* Collected accounts receivable from customers, $24.

    *g.* Purchased other assets, $10 cash.

        *h.* Paid accounts payable, $13.
        *i.* Purchased supplies on account for future use, $18.
        *j.* Signed a $25 service contract to start February 1, 2012.
        *k.* Paid $17 cash to H. Hermann on his drawing account.

Data for adjusting journal entries follow:

        *l.* Supplies counted on December 31, 2011, $10.
        *m.* Depreciation for the year on the equipment, $6.
        *n.* Accrued interest on notes payable, $1.
        *o.* Wages earned by employees since the December 24 payroll not yet paid, $12.
        *p.* Utility bill of $8 for December usage was received on December 31, 2011. It will be paid in 2012.

**Required:**

1. Set up T-accounts for the accounts on the trial balance and enter beginning balances.
2. Record journal entries for transactions (*a*) through (*k*) and post them to the T-accounts.
3. Prepare an unadjusted trial balance.
4. Record and post the adjusting journal entries (*l*) through (*p*).
5. Prepare an adjusted trial balance.
6. Prepare a classified income statement, statement of owner's equity, and classified balance sheet.
7. Prepare and post the closing journal entries.
8. Prepare a post-closing trial balance.
9. How much net income did H-H Tool generate during 2011? Is the company financed primarily by debt or equity?
10. Compute and interpret the net profit margin for H-H Tool for the year ended December 31, 2011.

**PA4-6 Completing a Worksheet and Preparing Closing Entries** (Chapter Supplement)
Anderson Plumbing Supply has partially completed the following worksheet for the year ended December 31, 2010:

| Account Titles | UNADJUSTED TRIAL BALANCE Debit | UNADJUSTED TRIAL BALANCE Credit | ADJUSTING ENTRIES Debit | ADJUSTING ENTRIES Credit |
|---|---|---|---|---|
| Cash | 13,000 | | | |
| Accounts Receivable | 22,000 | | | |
| Supplies | 1,200 | | | (*a*)     600 |
| Interest Receivable | | | (*b*)    300 | |
| Long-Term Note Receivable | 9,000 | | | |
| Equipment | 80,000 | | | |
| Accumulated Depreciation | | 35,000 | | (*c*) 10,000 |
| Accounts Payable | | 10,000 | | |
| Short-Term Note Payable | | 12,000 | | |
| Interest Payable | | | | (*d*)     720 |
| Accrued Liabilities Payable | | | | (*e*)   3,620 |
| J. Anderson, Capital | | 55,000 | | |
| J. Anderson, Drawing | 20,000 | | | |
| Service Revenue | | 72,000 | | |
| Interest Revenue | | | | (*b*)     300 |
| Expenses (not detailed) | 38,800 | | (*a*)     600 | |
| Depreciation Expense | | | (*c*) 10,000 | |
| Interest Expense | | | (*d*)     720 | |
| Other Operating Expenses | | | (*e*)   3,620 | |
| Totals | 184,000 | 184,000 | 15,240 | 15,240 |

*Required:*

1. Use additional columns for Adjusted Trial Balance, Income Statement, Owner's Equity, and Balance Sheet to complete the worksheet.

2. Explain each of the adjustments.

3. Give the closing entries.

4. Why are the adjusting and closing entries journalized and posted?

## Problems—Set B 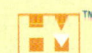    Available with McGraw-Hill's Homework Manager

### PB4-1 Recording Adjusting Journal Entries                          LO2

Greenly Company's annual accounting year ends on June 30. It is June 30, 2010, and all of the 2010 entries except the following adjusting journal entries have been made:

a. The company earned service revenue of $2,000 on a special job that was completed June 29, 2010. Collection will be made during July 2010; no entry has been recorded.

b. On March 30, 2010, Greenly paid a $3,200, six-month premium for property insurance for coverage starting on that date. Cash was credited and Prepaid Insurance was debited for this amount.

c. At June 30, 2010, wages of $900 earned by employees were not yet paid. The employees will be paid on the next payroll date, July 15, 2010.

d. On June 1, 2010, Greenly collected two months' maintenance revenue of $450. At that date, Greenly debited Cash and credited Unearned Maintenance Revenue for $450.

e. Depreciation of $1,500 must be recognized on a service truck purchased on July 1, 2007.

f. Cash of $4,200 was collected on May 1, 2010, for services to be rendered evenly over the next year beginning on May 1. Unearned Service Revenue was credited when the cash was received.

g. The company owes $600 interest on a bank loan taken out on February 1, 2010. The interest will be paid when the loan is repaid on January 31, 2011.

*Required:*

Following the steps outlined in the chapter, for each transaction:

1. Identify the type of adjustment (unearned revenue, accrued revenue, prepaid expense, or accrued expense).

2. Determine the amount of revenue or expense to be recorded.

3. Record the adjusting journal entry at June 30, 2010.

### PB4-2 Determining Financial Statement Effects of Adjusting Journal Entries          LO2
Refer to PB4-1.

*Required:*

Using the following headings, indicate the effect of each adjusting journal entry and the amount of the effect. Use + for increase, − for decrease, and NE for no effect.

| | BALANCE SHEET | | | INCOME STATEMENT | | |
|---|---|---|---|---|---|---|
| Transaction | Assets | Liabilities | Owner's Equity | Revenues | Expenses | Net Income |
| a. | | | | | | |
| b. | | | | | | |
| etc. | | | | | | |

**Pacific Sunwear of California**

### PB4-3 Preparing an Adjusted Trial Balance, Closing Journal Entries, and Post-Closing Trial Balance

Pacific Sunwear of California operates three chains of retail stores under the names Pacific Sunwear (also known as PacSun), Pacific Sunwear (PacSun) Outlet, and d.e.m.o. The following is a simplified list of adjusted accounts and amounts reported in the company's records for a recent year ended January 28. Dollars are in thousands.

| | | | |
|---|---:|---|---:|
| Accounts Payable | $ 47,550 | Inventories | $ 215,140 |
| Accounts Receivable | 12,679 | Long-Term Liabilities | 138,300 |
| Accrued Liabilities | 33,649 | Sales Revenue | 1,391,473 |
| Accumulated Depreciation | 247,140 | Other Current Assets | 81,357 |
| Cash | 95,185 | Other Current Liabilities | 14,896 |
| Cost of Goods Sold (used inventory) | 884,982 | Other Long-Lived Assets | 332,893 |
| Depreciation Expense | 74,617 | Other Operating Expenses | 76,734 |
| Selling, General, and | | PacSun Owners' Capital | 534,513 |
|    Administrative Expenses | 309,218 | Prepaid Expenses | 22,360 |
| Interest Expense | 7,269 | Property, Plant, and Equipment | 295,087 |

*Required:*

1. Prepare an adjusted trial balance at January 28, 2009. Is the PacSun Owners' Capital balance of $534,513 the amount that would be reported on the balance sheet as of January 28, 2009?

2. Prepare the closing entries required at January 28, 2009.

3. Prepare a post-closing trial balance at January 28, 2009.

**Federal Express Corporation**

### PB4-4 Preparing Closing Entries and Computing and Analyzing Net Profit Margin

Federal Express Corporation delivers packages and freight to over 220 countries via air and land routes. The company also owns FedEx Kinko's. The following is a simplified list of adjusted accounts and amounts reported in its accounting records. The accounts have normal debit or credit balances, and the dollars are rounded to the nearest million. Assume that the year ended on May 31, 2011.

| | | | |
|---|---:|---|---:|
| Accounts Payable | $1,594 | Long-Term Debt | $ 3,778 |
| Accounts Receivable | 1,429 | Other Current Assets | 836 |
| Accrued Expenses Payable | 1,755 | Other Long-Lived Assets | 5,199 |
| Accumulated Depreciation | 8,988 | Other Expenses | 8,009 |
| Cash | 257 | Prepaid Expenses | 125 |
| Salary and Benefits Expense | 8,051 | Property and Equipment | 16,905 |
| Depreciation Expense | 845 | Service Revenues | 22,527 |
| Interest Expense | 40 | FedEx Owners' Capital | 8,905 |
| Interest Revenue | 213 | Landing Fees Expense | 1,598 |
| Spare Parts and Supplies | 269 | Fuel Expense | 2,946 |

*Required:*

1. Prepare the closing entries required at May 31, 2011.

2. Compute net profit margin for the year ended May 31, 2011.

3. In the year ended May 31, 2010, assume that FedEx had a net profit margin of 5.1% and that the industry ratio was 11.7%. What does this information suggest to you about FedEx?

### PB4-5 Recording Transactions (including adjusting entries), Preparing Financial Statements, Closing the Books, and Analyzing a Key Ratio Comprehensive Review Problem (Chapters 2, 3, and 4)

Alison Renny began operations of her furniture repair shop (Lazy Sofa Furniture) on January 1, 2010. The annual reporting period ends December 31. The trial balance on January 1, 2011, was as follows (the amounts are rounded to thousands of dollars to simplify):

**Lazy Sofa Furniture**
**Trial Balance**
**On January 1, 2011**
**(in thousands)**

| Account Titles | Debit | Credit | Account Titles | Debit | Credit |
|---|---|---|---|---|---|
| Cash | 5 | | Utilities Payable | | 0 |
| Accounts Receivable | 4 | | Unearned Revenue | | 0 |
| Supplies | 2 | | A. Renny, Capital | | 19 |
| Small Tools | 6 | | A. Renny, Drawing | 0 | |
| Equipment | 0 | | Service Revenue | | 0 |
| Accumulated Depreciation | | 0 | Depreciation Expense | | 0 |
| Other Assets | 9 | | Wages Expense | | 0 |
| Accounts Payable | | 7 | Interest Expense | | 0 |
| Notes Payable | | 0 | Supplies Expense | | 0 |
| Wages Payable | | 0 | Utilities Expense | | 0 |
| Interest Payable | | 0 | Other Operating Expenses | 0 | 0 |
| | | | | 26 | 26 |

*(continued)*

Transactions during 2011 (summarized in thousands of dollars) follow:

a. Borrowed $21 cash on July 1, 2011, signing a short-term note payable.
b. Purchased equipment for $18 cash on July 1, 2011.
c. Received $5 cash as an additional investment from owner A. Renny.
d. Earned $65 in Service Revenue in 2011, including $9 on credit and $56 received in cash.
e. Recognized $28 in Wages Expense for 2011, paid in cash, and $7 of Other Operating Expenses on credit.
f. Purchased additional small tools, $3 cash.
g. Collected accounts receivable, $8.
h. Paid accounts payable, $11.
i. Purchased on account supplies for future use, $10.
j. Received a $3 deposit on work to start January 15, 2012.
k. Paid $10 cash to A. Renny on her drawing account.

Data for adjusting journal entries:

l. Supplies of $4 were counted on December 31, 2011.
m. Depreciation for 2011, $2.
n. Accrued interest on notes payable of $1.
o. Wages earned since the December 24 payroll not yet paid, $3.
p. Utility bill for $4 for December utility usage was received on December 31, 2011. It will be paid in 2012.

*Required:*

1. Set up T-accounts for the accounts on the trial balance and enter beginning balances.
2. Record journal entries for transactions (a) through (k) and post them to the T-accounts.
3. Prepare an unadjusted trial balance.
4. Record and post the adjusting journal entries (l) through (p).
5. Prepare an adjusted trial balance.
6. Prepare a classified income statement, statement of owner's equity, and classified balance sheet.
7. Prepare and post the closing journal entries.
8. Prepare a post-closing trial balance.

9. How much net income did Lazy Sofa Furniture generate during 2011? Is the company financed primarily by debt or equity?

10. Compute and interpret the net profit margin ratio for Lazy Sofa Furniture for the year ended December 31, 2011.

**PB4-6 Completing a Worksheet and Preparing Closing Entries** (Chapter Supplement)

Marine Pool Service & Repair, a sole proprietorship owned by Robert Horn, has been in operation for several years. Revenues have increased gradually from both the pool cleaning and repair services. The annual financial statements prepared in the past have not conformed to GAAP. The newly employed president decided that a balance sheet, income statement, and statement of owner's equity should be prepared in conformity with GAAP. The first step was to employ a full-time bookkeeper and engage a local CPA firm. It is now December 31, 2009, the end of the current accounting year. The bookkeeper has developed a trial balance from the ledger. A member of the staff of the CPA firm will advise and assist the bookkeeper in completing the accounting information processing cycle for the first time. The unadjusted trial balance at December 31, 2009, follows.

### Marine Pool Service & Repair
#### Unadjusted Trial Balance
#### December 31, 2009

| Debits | | Credits | |
|---|---|---|---|
| Cash | 27,500 | Accumulated Depreciation | 24,000 |
| Accounts Receivable | 2,080 | Accounts Payable | 8,000 |
| Supplies | 820 | Wages Payable | 0 |
| Prepaid Insurance | 800 | Interest Payable | 0 |
| Land (for future building site-not in use) | 5,000 | Unearned Cleaning Revenue | 4,000 |
| Equipment | 72,000 | Note Payable | 20,000 |
| Remaining Assets (not detailed) | 22,000 | R. Horn, Capital | 37,800 |
| R. Horn, Drawing | 3,000 | Repair Revenue | 72,000 |
| Wages Expense | 60,000 | Cleaning Revenue | 34,000 |
| Advertising Expense | 2,000 | | |
| Utilities Expense | 1,400 | | |
| Maintenance Expense | 3,200 | | |
| Supplies Expense | 0 | | |
| Insurance Expense | 0 | | |
| Depreciation Expense | 0 | | |
| Interest Expense | 0 | | |
| | 199,800 | | 199,800 |

Examination of the records and related documents provided the following additional information that should be considered for adjusting entries:

a. A physical count of office supplies inventory at December 31, 2009, reflected $70 on hand.

b. On July 1, 2009, a two-year insurance premium was paid amounting to $800; it was debited to Prepaid Insurance.

c. The equipment cost $72,000 when acquired. Annual depreciation expense is $12,000.

d. Unpaid and unrecorded wages earned by employees at December 31, 2009, amounted to $900.

e. The one-year, $20,000 note payable was signed on October 1, 2009. Interest of $600 is owed and will be paid in 2010. No entry has yet been made for the interest.

f. All but $1,000 of the Unearned Cleaning Revenue had been earned by December 31, 2009.

g. Gasoline, oil, and fuel purchased for the vehicles and used during the last two weeks of December 2009 amounting to $200 have not been paid for or recorded (this is considered maintenance expense).

*Required:*

1. Create and complete a worksheet.
2. Give the closing entries.

**Additional problems are available at www.mhhe.com/LLPW1e. Click on Chapter 4 and select Additional Problems (PC4-1 through PC4-7).**

# Cases and Projects

### CP4-1 Finding Financial Information

LO3

Refer to the financial statements of The Home Depot in Appendix A at the end of this book, or download the annual report from the *Cases* section of the text's Web site at www.mhhe.com/LLPW1e.

*Required:*

1. The company's Prepaid Advertising Expenses arc included in the balance sheet under Other Current Assets. Refer to the notes to the financial statements to determine the amount of the Prepaid Advertising Expenses as of February 3, 2008.

2. How much did The Home Depot owe for salaries and related expenses at the end of the more recent year? Was this an increase or decrease from the previous year?

3. In which line of the balance sheet does The Home Depot include its intangible assets and what kinds of intangible assets does the company have?

### CP4-2 Comparing Financial Information

LO2, 3

Lowe's

Refer to the financial statements of The Home Depot in Appendix A and Lowe's in Appendix B at the end of this book, or download the annual reports from the *Cases* section of the text's Web site at www.mhhe.com/LLPW1e.

*Required:*

1. Refer to the notes to the financial statements to determine how much The Home Depot and Lowe's each spent on advertising expenses in the most recent fiscal year.

2. How much did The Home Depot and Lowe's each owe for salaries and wages at the end of the most recent year? Provide one reason that would explain the difference between the two companies' accrued payroll liabilities.

### CP4-3 Examining Adjustments: Internet-Based Team Research

LO2, 3, 5

As a team, select an industry to analyze. Using your Web browser, each team member should acquire the annual report or 10-K for one publicly traded company in the industry with each member selecting a different company. (See CP1-3 in Chapter 1 for a description of possible resources for these tasks.)

*Required:*

1. On an individual basis, each team member should write a short report listing the following:

   a. The company's total assets and total liabilities at the end of each year.

   b. The company's prepaid expenses and accrued liabilities at the end of each year.

   c. The percentage of prepaid expenses to total assets and the percentage of accrued liabilities to total liabilities.

   d. Describe and explain the types of accrued liabilities reported in the notes to the financial statements.

   e. Compute the company's net profit margin ratio for the most recent year and the prior year. What does this suggest to you about the company?

2. Discuss any patterns that you as a team observe. Then, as a team, write a short report comparing and contrasting your companies according to the preceding attributes. Provide potential explanations for any differences discovered.

### CP4-4 Ethical Decision Making: A Real-Life Example

LO2

On December 12, 2002, the SEC filed a lawsuit against four executives of Safety-Kleen Corp., one of the country's leading providers of industrial waste collection and disposal services. The primary issue was that the executives had directed others in the company to record improper adjustments in 1999 and 2000, which had the effect of overstating net income during those periods. The following table was included in the SEC's court documents to demonstrate the (combined) effect of proper and improper adjustments on net income. (All amounts are in millions.)

| | YEAR (QUARTER) | | | | |
| --- | --- | --- | --- | --- | --- |
| | 1999(Q1) | 1999(Q2) | 1999(Q3) | 1999(Q4) | 2000(Q1) |
| Net income before adjustments | $ 90.9 | $ 76.7 | $ 47.9 | $ 57.3 | $ 47.0 |
| Effect of improper adjustments | 36.6 | 30.9 | 75.5 | 53.1 | 69.8 |
| Net income after adjustments | $127.5 | $107.6 | $123.4 | $110.4 | $116.8 |

The following excerpts from the SEC's complaint describe two of the allegedly improper adjustments:

### Improper Capitalization of Operating Expenses

26. As part of the fraudulent accounting scheme, [three top executives] improperly recorded several adjusting entries to capitalize certain operating expenses. These adjustments caused the company to materially overstate both its assets and its earnings. For example, at the end of the third quarter of fiscal 1999, they improperly capitalized approximately $4.6 million of payroll expenses relating to certain marketing and start-up activities.

### Improper Treatment of Accruals

33. During the fourth quarter of fiscal 1999, [the CFO] created additional fictitious income by directing [other accounting executives] to eliminate a $7.6 million accrual that had been established to provide for management bonuses that had been earned in fiscal 1999, but were to be paid the following quarter. Humphreys' action suggested that no bonuses were going to be paid for that year. In fact, the bonuses for 1999 were paid as scheduled.

*Required:*

1.  Discuss whether large adjustments, such as those included by Safety-Kleen in 1999 and 2000, necessarily indicate improper accounting procedures.

2.  What does the SEC's document mean in paragraph 26 when it says three top executives "improperly recorded several adjusting entries to *capitalize* certain operating expenses" (emphasis added). Drawing on concepts presented in Chapters 2 and 3, explain why it is improper to record payroll expenses for marketing personnel as assets.

3.  Assume the $7.6 million in bonuses referred to in paragraph 33 were recorded in the third quarter of 1999. What journal entry would have been used to record this accrual? Assume this accrual was eliminated in the fourth quarter of 1999. What adjusting journal entry would have been recorded to eliminate (remove) the previous accrual? What journal entry would have been used to record the $7.6 million in bonuses paid in the first quarter of 2000 (assuming the accrual had been removed in the fourth quarter of 1999)? What accounting concept is violated by recording an expense for management bonuses when they are paid rather than when they are earned by managers?

*Epilogue:*

In April 2005, a federal judge found the company's former CEO and CFO liable for $200 million for their role in the fraud.

**LO3**

**Escalade, Inc.**

### CP4-5 Aggregating Accounts on an Adjusted Trial Balance to Prepare an Income Statement, Statement of Owner's Equity, and Balance Sheet

Assume that you recently were hired for a job in Evansville, Indiana, at the head office of Escalade, Inc., which makes Goalrilla™ and Goaliath basketball systems and is the exclusive supplier of Ping Pong and Stiga equipment for table tennis. Your first assignment is to review the company's lengthy adjusted trial balance to determine the accounts that can be combined ("aggregated") into single line items that will be reported on the financial statements. By querying the accounting system, you were able to obtain the following alphabetical list of accounts and their adjusted balances (in thousands) as of December 31. Accounts have normal debit or credit balances.

| | | | | | |
|---|---|---|---|---|---|
| Accounts Payable | $ 2,792 | Interest Receivable | $ 415 | Packaging Expenses | $ 1,010 |
| Accounts Receivable | 34,141 | Inventory of Finished Goods | 10,263 | Prepaid Insurance | 108 |
| Accrued Interest Payable | 42 | Inventory of Goods Being Made | 4,536 | Prepaid Rent | 434 |
| Accrued Wages Payable | 5,856 | Inventory of Supplies and Materials | 5,750 | Rent Expense | 7,350 |
| Accrued Warranties Payable | 1,324 | Long-Term Bank Loan | 14,000 | Salaries Expense | 3,582 |
| Accumulated Depreciation | 26,198 | Long-Term Contract Payable | 1,837 | Sales Commissions Expense | 3,349 |
| Cash | 3,370 | Long-Term Note Payable | 2,700 | Sales of Basketball Systems | 98,998 |
| Cost of Goods Sold | 111,164 | Manufacturing Equipment | 12,962 | Sales of Other Products | 28,710 |
| Depreciation Expense | 862 | Notes Payable (current) | 11,390 | Sales of Ping Pong Tables | 27,746 |
| Escalade Owners' Capital | 34,736 | Notes Receivable | 400 | Shipping Expenses | 1,448 |
| Factory Buildings | 7,070 | Office Building | 2,301 | Transport Equipment | 7,560 |
| Income Tax Expense | 5,804 | Office Equipment | 2,363 | Unearned Revenue | 8,144 |
| Income Tax Payable | 1,189 | Office Supplies Expense | 69 | Utilities Expense | 2,111 |
| Insurance Expense | 2,368 | Other Accrued Liabilities | 1,638 | Wages Expense | 3,024 |
| Interest Expense | 950 | Other Long-Term Assets | 28,310 | Warehouse Buildings | 3,000 |
| | | | | Warranties Expense | 1,226 |

*Required:*

1. With the preceding account names and balances, prepare an adjusted trial balance using a spreadsheet.

2. Prepare an income statement, statement of owners' equity, and balance sheet that import their numbers from the adjusted trial balance or from the other statements where appropriate. If similar accounts can be aggregated into a single line item for each financial statement, use a formula to compute the aggregated amount. To be sure that you understand how to import numbers from other parts of a spreadsheet, you e-mail your friend Owen for advice. Here's his reply.

From:     Owen@yahoo.com
To:       Helpme@hotmail.com
Cc:
Subject:  Excel Help

Hey, pal. You're bouncing from job to job like one of those ping-pong balls that your company sells. Okay, to import a number from another spreadsheet, you first click on the cell where you want the number to appear. For example, if you want to enter the Cash balance in the balance sheet, click on the cell in the balance sheet where the cash number is supposed to appear. Enter the equals sign (=) and then click on the tab that takes you to the worksheet containing the adjusted trial balance. In that worksheet, click on the cell that contains the amount you want to import into the balance sheet and then press enter. This will create a link from the adjusted trial balance cell to the balance sheet cell. At the end of this message, I've pasted a screen shot showing the formula I would enter on the balance sheet to import the total of three related inventory accounts from the adjusted trial balance. Don't forget to save the file using a name that indicates who you are.

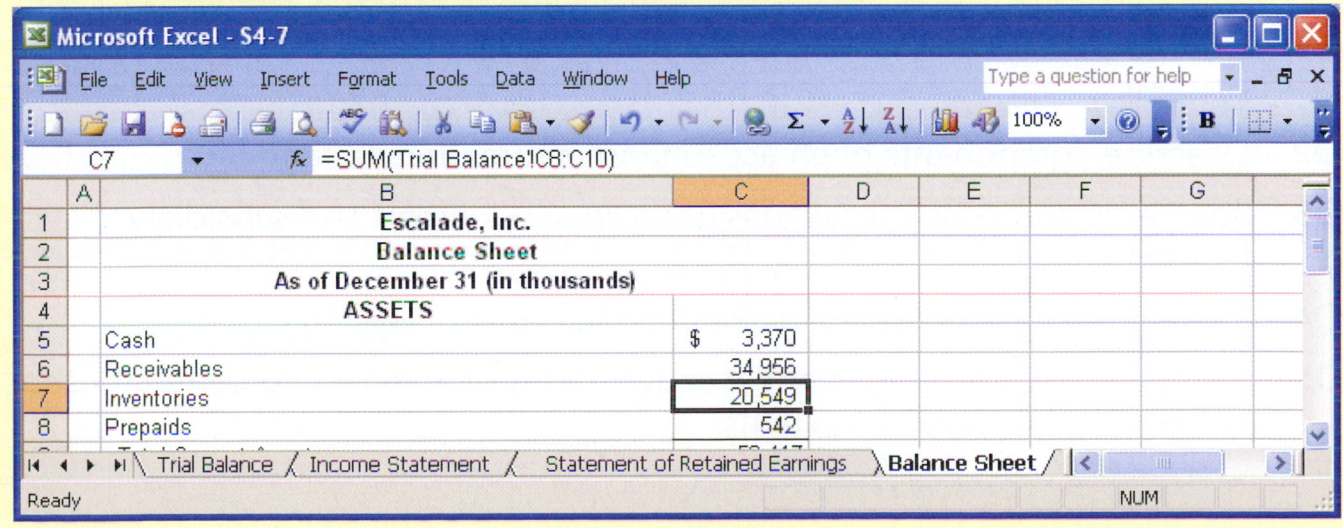

# 5 Accounting Systems

## LEARNING OBJECTIVES

**After completing this chapter, you should be able to:**

**LO1** Describe processing methods of accounting information systems.

**LO2** Describe components of an accounting information system.

**LO3** Journalize and post transactions using special journals and subsidiary ledgers.

**LO4** Explain the basic theory of accounting information systems.

**LO5** Compare the advantages and disadvantages of manual and computerized accounting information systems.

Lectured slideshow–LP5-1
www.mhhe.com/LLPW1e

# Focus Company: THE UPS STORE®

## Retail Packing, Shipping, Postal & Business Services

www.theupsstore.com/index.html

Just as universities and colleges have seen a huge demand for one-time photocopy services, United Parcel Service (UPS) has noticed considerable demand from individuals and small businesses for photocopy services as well as binding, laminating, collating, faxing, packaging, and shipping. In response to this demand, UPS created an opportunity for aspiring business managers to start their own full-service packaging and shipping stores under the familiar UPS Store name. Each UPS Store is independently owned and operated to provide packaging, copying, and shipping services to a variety of customers.

This chapter explains the methods that a UPS Store uses to track the amounts owed by customers. It also explains how the store tracks its own purchases of services and supplies and the payments it makes on account to creditors. We illustrate the tracking process first using a manual accounting system and then using a well-known computerized system.

**MANUAL VERSUS COMPUTERIZED ACCOUNTING INFORMATION SYSTEMS**

**COMPONENTS OF AN ACCOUNTING INFORMATION SYSTEM**

- Accounts Receivable Subsidiary Ledger
- Accounts Payable Subsidiary Ledger

**SPECIAL JOURNALS AND POSTING OF TRANSACTIONS**

- Revenue Journal
- Cash Receipts Journal
- Purchases Journal
- Cash Payments Journal
- Use of the General Journal
- Summary of the Recording Process

**BASIC THEORY OF ACCOUNTING INFORMATION SYSTEMS**

- Underlying Assumptions
- Developmental Phases

**COMPUTERIZED ACCOUNTING INFORMATION SYSTEMS**

- Advantages and Disadvantages
- Peachtree Complete 2008—An Illustration

# MANUAL VERSUS COMPUTERIZED ACCOUNTING INFORMATION SYSTEMS

**Learning Objective 1**

Describe processing methods of accounting information systems.

The term accounting information system (AIS) refers to everything involved in collecting, processing, and distributing accounting information for managers to use internally or creditors and investors to use externally. Chapters 1–4 presented the basic elements of an accounting system. In reality, however, most businesses need a more detailed system than the one illustrated in those chapters. For example, The UPS Store needs to know more than the fact that together, customers owe $6,476. Rather, the store needs to know which specific customers owe which particular amounts. To provide this extra detail, an accounting information system must include some additional tools for tracking transactions as well as a certain degree of computerization.

Although a few small businesses still use a manual accounting information system that records and processes all financial information by hand on paper, today most accounting information systems are computerized. A computerized accounting information system uses a software program to perform basic bookkeeping functions. The program journalizes and posts transactions, prepares trial balances, and generates financial statements, all electronically. See Exhibit 5.1 for the features of computerized accounting systems, compared to manual systems.

**Exhibit 5.1** Comparison of Features of Manual and Computerized Accounting Systems

| | Manual System | Computerized System |
|---|---|---|
| Journalizing and posting | • Performed by hand<br>• Extremely time consuming | • Performed by computer<br>• Quick and easy |
| Handling of errors | • Error prone<br>• Finding and correcting errors can be time consuming | • Virtually error free<br>• Program identifies journal entries that are out of balance and will not record them until the error is corrected |
| Financial statement preparation | • Prepared by hand<br>• Extremely time consuming | • Prepared by computer<br>• Quick and easy |
| Accountant's responsibilities | • Mainly bookkeeping tasks | • Bookkeeping<br>• Ensuring that all transactions and adjustments have been recorded |

Although a computerized accounting system automates the basic bookkeeping functions, it does not eliminate the need for an accountant. Instead, it frees the accountant to focus on more important functions, such as:

- Ensuring that all transactions have been entered into the system.
- Making necessary adjustments at the end of each accounting period.

Because computerized accounting systems simplify the bookkeeping process, you might think they are easier to understand as well. As Exhibit 5.2 shows, however, that is not the case. The process of double-entry bookkeeping is easy to see and trace in a manual accounting system because every transaction results in recording both debits and credits in the same place and at the same time using the same journal entry. That is often not the case for a computerized system, which may use one computer module to record one part of a transaction and a different module to record other parts of the same transaction. In summarizing the results of the transaction, the program later combines information from the various modules.

**Exhibit 5.2    Understanding Manual versus Computerized Accounting Systems**

| Manual Accounting System | Computerized Accounting System |
|---|---|
| **Easier to Understand** because transactions are: | **More Difficult to Understand** because some parts of a transaction are |
| • Processed by hand<br>• Easily traced back to specific journal entries<br>• Easily traced to corresponding postings in the ledger accounts | • Processed by different parts of the software<br>• Often accessible only by specific program modules<br>• Processed behind the scenes, making transactions difficult if not impossible to trace |

The differences in Exhibit 5.2 explain why, in Chapters 1–4, you learned to process all steps in the accounting cycle by hand. As with any automated technology (such as spreadsheets and electronic calculators), you need to understand what the technology can do for you before you can use it properly. Because a manual system is easier to understand than a computerized system, we use it here to introduce the extra tools businesses need to track their accounting transactions. Later in this chapter, when we illustrate the computerized accounting program Peachtree Complete 2008, you will better appreciate what such programs can do for you.

---

**SELF-STUDY PRACTICE**

Indicate whether each of the following statements represents a characteristic of a manual (M) or computerized (C) accounting information system.

1. The accountant performs mainly bookkeeping tasks. _____
2. Journalizing, posting, and financial statement preparation are performed quickly and easily. _____
3. Debits and credits are recorded in the same place and at the same time using the same journal entry. _____
4. It frees the accountant to ensure that all transactions have been entered into the system and to make the necessary adjustments at the end of each accounting period. _____
5. Some transactions are difficult to trace because they are performed behind the scenes.

   _____

*After you have finished, check your answers with the solution at the bottom of the page.*

---

1. M      2. C      3. M      4. C      5. C

Solution to
Self-Study Practice

# COMPONENTS OF AN ACCOUNTING INFORMATION SYSTEM

The accounting steps illustrated in Chapters 1–4 involved recording transactions in the general journal, posting them to the general ledger accounts (sometimes represented by T-accounts), and summarizing the results in the financial statements. At the end of the accounting period, you could easily determine the total balance in any account by looking at either the financial statements or the general ledger accounts. But what if the following happens?

- A specific customer wants to know how much he owes The UPS Store on June 10 of the current year.
- The UPS Store needs to pay the accounts payable owed to a supplier on October 18.

General ledger account balances are not useful for supplying this type of detailed information because they report totals, not amounts pertaining to specific individuals or businesses.

To accomplish these tasks, businesses use subsidiary ledgers. A subsidiary ledger is used to group accounts that share a common feature. Two of the most frequently used subsidiary ledgers are:

1. The accounts receivable subsidiary ledger used to track accounts receivable transactions and balances for individual customers.
2. The accounts payable subsidiary ledger used to track accounts payable transactions and balances for individual creditors.

## Accounts Receivable Subsidiary Ledger

Keeping detailed records for each individual customer is a massive undertaking, so The UPS Store uses an accounts receivable subsidiary ledger to manage the task. Assume that on September 30, The UPS Store has a total of $6,476 in Accounts Receivable as shown in the general ledger in the top portion of Exhibit 5.3. This balance consists of various amounts owed by individual customers. The accounts receivable subsidiary ledger contains the details of each customer's account, as shown in the bottom portion of Exhibit 5.3.

You can think of a general ledger account as a large file drawer and the accounts receivable subsidiary ledger as a collection of file folders for the various customers, arranged in alphabetical order. Each file folder contains the following information:

- The customer's name.
- A chronological record of the services charged to the customer's account.
- A chronological record of the payments the customer has made on the account.
- An up-to-date balance indicating the amount the customer currently owes.

If you examine the bottom portion of Exhibit 5.3 closely, you will see all four of these elements in the subsidiary ledger. Thus, The UPS Store has an up-to-date balance for each customer at all times.

The individual customer accounts in the accounts receivable subsidiary ledger and the Accounts Receivable general ledger account serve complementary purposes.

- The subsidiary ledger accounts capture and report a detailed transaction history for each customer.
- The general ledger account captures and reports the same information but in a highly summarized form.

Because the same information is captured in different places, accountants can use the Accounts Receivable general ledger account as a way to double-check the information recorded in the subsidiary ledger accounts. To use the general ledger account in this way, as a control account, the total of the subsidiary ledger accounts is computed at the end of each month. A list called a schedule of accounts receivable is prepared by listing each customer account name and balance as shown in Exhibit 5.4. Notice that the total of these balances in Exhibit 5.4 ($6,476) matches the ending balance in the Accounts Receivable control account (shown in the top of Exhibit 5.3), as it should if no errors are made.

**Exhibit 5.3**   **Accounts Receivable Account and Accounts Receivable Subsidiary Ledger**

### General Ledger

| | Accounts Receivable | | | Acct. No. 110 |
|---|---|---|---|---|
| Date | Item | Debit | Credit | Balance |
| Aug. 31 | Bal. | | | 5,416 |
| Sep. 30 | | 7,300 | | 12,716 |
| Sep. 30 | | | 6,240 | 6,476 |

### Accounts Receivable Subsidiary Ledger

**Downtown Dental Services**

| Date | Item | Debit | Credit | Balance |
|---|---|---|---|---|
| Aug. 31 | Bal. | | | 2,410 |
| Sep. 1 | | 1,389 | | 3,799 |
| Sep. 18 | | | 2,410 | 1,389 |

**Gallegos Gift Shop**

| Date | Item | Debit | Credit | Balance |
|---|---|---|---|---|
| Aug. 31 | Bal. | | | 886 |
| Sep. 12 | | 1,825 | | 2,711 |
| Sep. 29 | | | 1,000 | 1,711 |

**Keays Optical**

| Date | Item | Debit | Credit | Balance |
|---|---|---|---|---|
| Aug. 31 | Bal. | | | 1,277 |
| Sep. 20 | | 2,298 | | 3,575 |
| Sep. 22 | | | 1,987 | 1,588 |

**Matthews Custom Computers**

| Date | Item | Debit | Credit | Balance |
|---|---|---|---|---|
| Aug. 31 | Bal. | | | 843 |
| Sep. 21 | | 1,788 | | 2,631 |
| Sep. 28 | | | 843 | 1,788 |

**Coach's Tip**
The total of the individual balances in the accounts receivable subsidiary ledger must equal the total for the Accounts Receivable account in the general ledger ($1,389 + $1,711 + $1,588 + $1,788 = $6,476).

**Exhibit 5.4**   **Schedule of Accounts Receivable**

| | |
|---|---|
| Downtown Dental Services | $ 1,389 |
| Gallegos Gift Shop | 1,711 |
| Keays Optical | 1,588 |
| Matthews Custom Computers | 1,788 |
| Total | $ 6,476 |

When using an accounts receivable subsidiary ledger, a company must record any transactions with customers on account in both the subsidiary ledger and the Accounts Receivable account. This requires that journal entries include the customers' names. For example, Exhibit 5.5 shows the journal entry to record services provided on account to Downtown Dental Services. Notice that the first line of the journal entry indicates the control account name (Accounts Receivable) as well as the subsidiary ledger account name (Downtown Dental Services). Both parts are needed because **transactions with customers on account are posted to both the**

| Exhibit 5.5 | General Journal Entry Involving a Subsidiary Ledger Account | | | |

| Date | Account Titles | Ref. | Debit | Credit |
|---|---|---|---|---|
| Sep. 1 | Accounts Receivable—Downtown Dental Services | 110/✔ | 1,389 | |
| | Fees Earned | 410 | | 1,389 |

control account and a subsidiary ledger account to ensure the control account balance equals the total of the subsidiary accounts.

When the debit to the Accounts Receivable control account and the related subsidiary account (Downtown Dental Services) is posted, the Ref. column (in Exhibit 5.5) indicates the account number (110) for the control account and a checkmark (✔) for the subsidiary account. A slash ( / ) separates the references to indicate that the debit has been posted in these two separate locations.

# Accounts Payable Subsidiary Ledger

Much like the accounts receivable subsidiary ledger, the accounts payable subsidiary ledger provides detailed information on all purchases and payments that The UPS Store has made on account as well as the current balance owed to each individual creditor. Collectively, these balances add to the outstanding balance in the Accounts Payable account in the general ledger.

The accounts payable subsidiary ledger looks exactly like the accounts receivable subsidiary ledger. The only difference is that it tracks creditor transactions rather than customer transactions. At the end of the month, the accountant compiles a schedule of accounts payable to verify that the individual balances in the subsidiary ledger equal the balance in the Accounts Payable account in the general ledger. The procedures for recording transactions in the accounts payable subsidiary ledger are virtually identical to those for the accounts receivable subsidiary ledger.

## Advantages of Subsidiary Ledgers

At this point, you may be thinking that subsidiary ledgers require a lot of extra work. In the long run, subsidiary ledgers actually save time and effort and simplify the accounting process. See Exhibit 5.6 for a summary of the many advantages of using subsidiary ledgers.

| Exhibit 5.6 | Advantages of Using Subsidiary Ledgers |

- **Provides dedicated accounts for individual customers and creditors**
  Each customer or creditor has an individual account in which all transactions for that customer or creditor are recorded. Thus, the company can maintain accurate, up-to-date account balances for individual customers and creditors.

- **Reduces unnecessary detail in the general ledger accounts**
  Because the details of each transaction are entered into the subsidiary ledger accounts, only a summary entry must be made in the general ledger. This arrangement, which requires far fewer entries, reduces labor.

- **Makes locating errors in individual customer and creditor accounts easier**
  Because all details for individual customers or creditors are located only in the subsidiary ledgers, the potential for errors is reduced.

- **Allows for division of labor**
  If all accounts are located in one place, the work of maintaining them cannot be divided among several individuals. Because the accounts receivable and accounts payable subsidiary ledgers are updated separately from the general ledger, the three ledgers can be maintained by three different individuals, which reduces the risk of undetected errors.

To make sure you understand how subsidiary and control accounts work, take a moment to try the following Self-Study Practice.

**SELF-STUDY PRACTICE**

Indicate whether each of the following is a true (T) or false (F) statement regarding the components of an accounting information system.

1. Subsidiary ledgers can be used only for accounts receivable and accounts payable transactions. _____
2. A schedule of accounts receivable is a list of all transactions in the Accounts Receivable account in the general ledger. _____
3. One advantage of using subsidiary ledgers is that they make locating errors in individual customer and creditor accounts easier. _____
4. Another name for a subsidiary ledger account is a control account. _____
5. A checkmark in the Ref. column of the general journal indicates that the amount has been posted to the general ledger. _____

*After you have finished, check your answers with the solution at the bottom of the page.*

# SPECIAL JOURNALS AND POSTING OF TRANSACTIONS

**Learning Objective 3**

Journalize and post transactions using special journals and subsidiary ledgers.

Imagine how many times a day companies such as The UPS Store collect money from customers and make payments to creditors. If accountants were to record a general journal entry each time Cash was debited or credited, they would be exhausted after only a few hours. Reading through earlier chapters, you yourself may have thought, "There must be an easier way to do this—I am writing Cash and Accounts Receivable over and over again!"

In this section, we introduce special journals, which provide an efficient way to account for repetitive, frequent transactions. By aggregating similar journal entries in one special journal, accountants can greatly reduce the amount of time and effort needed to journalize and post transactions. **Special journals do not eliminate the need for a general journal,** but they do allow the general journal to be used only for transactions that cannot be recorded efficiently in special journals.

Several types of special journals can be tailored to the needs of a particular business, but we limit our discussion to the four most common ones: the revenue journal, cash receipts journal, purchases journal, and cash payments journal.

## Revenue Journal

Assume The UPS Store recorded the general journal entries shown in Exhibit 5.7.

Ordinarily, these four transactions would require you to perform the following tasks:

- Prepare the four journal entries shown.
- Post eight times to the general ledger accounts.
- Post four more times to the individual subsidiary ledger accounts.

Considering that the average UPS Store probably makes hundreds of such entries each day, it should be clear that no one has enough time to record them all in a general journal. Instead, accountants have created the revenue journal for recording these transactions efficiently. A revenue journal is used only for recording revenues earned on account, such as those in Exhibit 5.7. If a revenue journal were used instead of a general journal, those four transactions would be recorded as in Exhibit 5.8.

The five columns in the revenue journal in Exhibit 5.8 serve the following purposes:

1. **Date.** This column indicates the date on which a customer is billed for services provided on account. The bill is commonly called an invoice and may take the form of a sales slip or billing statement given to a customer at the time the services are provided.

1. F—Subsidiary ledgers can be used for any group of accounts that share a common feature such as inventory or fixed assets.
2. F—It is a listing of individual customer account balances at the end of an accounting period.
3. T—This is one of many advantages of using subsidiary ledgers.
4. F—A control account is another name for a general ledger account that is supported by a subsidiary ledger.
5. F—A checkmark indicates that the amount has been posted to the subsidiary ledger.

Solution to
Self-Study Practice

## Exhibit 5.7    General Journal

| Date | Account Titles | Ref. | Debit | Credit |
|---|---|---|---|---|
| Sep. 1 | Accounts Receivable—Downtown Dental Services | 110/✓ | 1,389 | |
| | Fees Earned | 410 | | 1,389 |
| | | | | |
| 12 | Accounts Receivable—Gallegos Gift Shop | 110/✓ | 1,825 | |
| | Fees Earned | 410 | | 1,825 |
| | | | | |
| 20 | Accounts Receivable—Keays Optical | 110/✓ | 2,298 | |
| | Fees Earned | 410 | | 2,298 |
| | | | | |
| 29 | Accounts Receivable—Matthews Custom Computers | 110/✓ | 1,788 | |
| | Fees Earned | 410 | | 1,788 |

2. **Invoice No.**  All invoices are sequentially numbered, and the invoice number is shown in the Invoice No. column to ensure that all invoices have been accounted for at the end of the month. Thus, even if an invoice has been voided, it must be recorded as on the September 10 line of Exhibit 5.8.

3. **Account Debited.**  The Account Debited column indicates the specific subsidiary account (customer) that is debited. Because all transactions in the revenue journal are debited to Accounts Receivable, indicating the name of the control account in this column is not needed.

4. **Ref.**  This column is used to indicate whether an invoice has been recorded in a customer's account in the subsidiary ledger. For example, the checkmark in Exhibit 5.8 for Downtown Dental Services is placed in the Ref. column when the fees charged on account for Downtown Dental Services ($1,389) are debited to that customer's subsidiary ledger account. **Postings to the subsidiary ledger are done daily** to ensure that customer balances are always up to date.

5. **Accounts Receivable Dr. Fees Earned Cr.**  This column lists the individual amounts charged to each customer, which have been recorded in the subsidiary ledger each day. These amounts have not been recorded in the general ledger, so they are totaled at the end of the month and recorded as a single entry in the Accounts Receivable control account and the Fees Earned revenue account in the general ledger. The total in this column of the revenue journal actually represents a journal entry, so it is posted to the ledger accounts just like any other journal entry. The debit is recorded first followed by the credit as indicated by the account numbers (110/410) in Exhibit 5.8. A benefit of using the revenue journal is that **postings to the general ledger are made at the end of the accounting period,** which saves time and makes the posting process more efficient.

> **Coach's Tip**
>
> Individual transactions are posted to customer accounts in the accounts receivable subsidiary ledger each day, but their total is posted only at the end of each month to the Accounts Receivable control account in the general ledger.

## Exhibit 5.8    Revenue Journal

| | | Revenue Journal | | Page 2 |
|---|---|---|---|---|
| Date | Invoice No. | Account Debited | Ref. | Accts Receivable Dr. Fees Earned Cr. |
| Sep. 1 | 820 | Downtown Dental Services | ✓ | 1,389 |
| 10 | 821 | VOID | — | — |
| 12 | 822 | Gallegos Gift Shop | ✓ | 1,825 |
| 20 | 823 | Keays Optical | ✓ | 2,298 |
| 29 | 824 | Matthews Custom Computers | ✓ | 1,788 |
| | | Total | | 7,300 |
| | | | | (110 / 410) |

See Exhibit 5.9 for a summary of postings from the revenue journal to the subsidiary ledger and general ledger accounts.

**Exhibit 5.9** — Summary of Postings from the Revenue Journal

# Cash Receipts Journal

Until now, we have recorded individual cash receipts with a general journal entry such as the one in Exhibit 5.10. For a company such as The UPS Store, many transactions involve the Cash account. Given the heavy use of the Cash account, most companies prefer to use two special journals, the cash receipts journal and the cash payments journal, to record their cash transactions.

Just as the revenue journal simplifies recording numerous revenue transactions on account, the cash receipts journal simplifies the recording of numerous cash receipts. The cash receipts journal is used to record any transaction that requires a debit to Cash. Because the Cash account is debited for a variety of reasons, the cash receipts journal includes several columns to accommodate all accounts that might be credited when Cash is debited. Consequently, this special journal appears more complex than the revenue journal, but it functions the same way.

Refer to Exhibit 5.11 for a cash receipts journal similar to one that The UPS Store would use to record its cash receipts. Each line in the journal represents a separate journal entry consisting of at least one debit and at least one credit. The first entry includes a debit to Cash and a credit to Fees Earned for $820. You may have to look carefully to see the debit to Cash, which is shown in the last column. This column of the cash receipts journal will have an amount on every line because every transaction recorded in the journal includes a debit to Cash.

An all-encompassing cash receipts journal would contain a separate column for every possible credit. In practice, however, a business would require hundreds, if not thousands, of columns to accommodate all of the many possibilities. Consequently, most businesses set up specific columns only for those accounts that are credited frequently when Cash is received. At The UPS Store, Cash is debited most frequently when accounts receivable are collected or when fees are earned by providing services. To record the credit part of these transactions, Exhibit 5.11 includes two dedicated coloums. To accommodate all other possible credits, another column, called Other Accounts Cr., is included. This column is used to record amounts credited to any account that does not have a dedicated column.

Let's go through the cash receipts journal in Exhibit 5.11 column by column.

**Coach's Tip**

Postings from the Other Accounts Cr. column are typically made on a daily basis. Postings to the Accounts Receivable control account, Fees Earned, and Cash accounts must be done on a monthly basis.

1. **Account Credited.** This column indicates the specific customer in the subsidiary ledger whose account will be credited for the transaction. This column is also used to indicate the account name of any general ledger account affected by amounts in the Other Accounts Cr. column. In some cases (September 15 and 30), this column will be blank because a dedicated column (Fees Earned) exists for the credits.

2. **Other Accounts Cr.** When no column heading exists for an account that is being credited, the amount is placed in the Other Accounts Cr. column. For example, the transaction on September 20 relates to interest revenue. Because no column exists for Interest Revenue, that amount is recorded in the Other Accounts Cr. column. The name of the account credited must be identified in the Account Credited column, and the account number (710) is recorded in the Ref. column when the amount is posted.

3. **Accounts Receivable Cr.** This column is used for recording the dollar amount of receipts from customers on account. The specific customer's account is listed in the

| Exhibit 5.10 | General Journal |
| --- | --- |

| Date | Account Titles | Ref. | Debit | Credit |
| --- | --- | --- | --- | --- |
| Sep. 18 | Cash | 105 | 2,410 | |
| | Accounts Receivable—Downtown Dental Services | 110/✓ | | 2,410 |

**Exhibit 5.11**   Cash Receipts Journal

| | Cash Receipts Journal | | | | | Page 3 |
|---|---|---|---|---|---|---|
| Date | Account Credited | Ref. | Other Accounts Cr. | Accounts Receivable Cr. | Fees Earned Cr. | Cash Dr. |
| Sep. 15 | | | | | 820 | 820 |
| 18 | Downtown Dental Services | ✓ | | 2,410 | | 2,410 |
| 20 | Interest Revenue | 710 | 80 | | | 80 |
| 22 | Keays Optical | ✓ | | 1,987 | | 1,987 |
| 28 | Matthews Custom Computers | ✓ | | 843 | | 843 |
| 29 | Gallegos Gift Shop | ✓ | | 1,000 | | 1,000 |
| 30 | | | | | 890 | 890 |
| | Totals | | 80 | 6,240 | 1,710 | 8,030 |
| | | | (✓) | (110) | (410) | (105) |

Account Credited column. For example, the entry on September 18 illustrates a cash receipt of $2,410 on account from Downtown Dental Services. The ✓ indicates that the amount was posted to the accounts receivable subsidiary ledger. Subsidiary ledger postings are made on a daily basis.

4. **Fees Earned Cr.**   This column is used for recording cash received from customers at the time services are provided.

5. **Cash Dr.** This column is used for recording the amount of each debit to Cash.

## Posting to the General Ledger

The accounts receivable subsidiary ledger will be completely up to date on September 30 because all transactions involving individual customer accounts have been posted daily. However, in most cases, cash transactions involving the general ledger accounts are not posted from the cash receipts journal until the end of the month. So, at the end of the period, the columns in the cash receipts journal must be totaled and the totals posted to the general ledger accounts. Totaling the numbers in a column in this manner is to **foot** the column. These end-of-month totals are posted to the appropriate general ledger account as in the CR3 postings in Exhibit 5.12.

You must also **crossfoot the columns** in a multiple-column journal at the end of the accounting period. Doing so means verifying that debits equal credits for the footed totals in the journal. Look at the cash receipts journal in Exhibit 5.11. Notice that:

- The amounts in the credit columns ($80 + $6,240 + $1,710) add to a total of $8,030 and
- The total amount debited to Cash is $8,030.

Because the columns on this journal page crossfoot, we can be confident that the entry is in balance (that is, debits equal credits).

When footed column totals are posted to the general ledger accounts, the account number is shown beneath the total. The Other Accounts Cr. column is one exception to this procedure. The total in this column is not posted anywhere as a single total because postings from this column are made to the general ledger on a daily basis. The checkmark (✓) under the column total in Exhibit 5.11 indicates that the amounts in this column were posted individually. The totals in the remaining columns must be posted to the general ledger accounts as shown in Exhibit 5.12.

**Exhibit 5.12**    **End-of-Month Posting to the General Ledger**

Cash    Acct. No. 105

| Date | Item | Ref. | Debit | Credit | Balance |
|------|------|------|-------|--------|---------|
| Aug. 31 | Bal. | | | | 4,220 |
| Sep. 30 | | CR3 | 8,030 | | 12,250 |

Accounts Receivable    Acct. No. 110

| Date | Item | Ref. | Debit | Credit | Balance |
|------|------|------|-------|--------|---------|
| Aug. 31 | Bal. | | | | 5,416 |
| Sep. 30 | | R2 | 7,300 | | 12,716 |
| Sep. 30 | | CR3 | | 6,240 | 6,476 |

Fees Earned    Acct. No. 410

| Date | Item | Ref. | Debit | Credit | Balance |
|------|------|------|-------|--------|---------|
| Aug. 31 | Bal. | | | | 54,080 |
| Sep. 30 | | R2 | | 7,300 | 61,380 |
| Sep. 30 | | CR3 | | 1,710 | 63,090 |

The Ref. columns of the Cash, Accounts Receivable, and Fees Earned accounts in the general ledger (Exhibit 5.12) indicate the journal page on which each entry originated. The abbreviation CR stands for cash receipts. Therefore, the abbreviation CR3 in the Ref. column of the Cash account indicates that the underlying details of this entry can be found on page 3 of the cash receipts journal.

## Preparation of the Schedule of Accounts Receivable

Although the accounts receivable subsidiary ledger is updated daily, the Accounts Receivable control account is updated only at the end of the month. Throughout the month, the balances in the control account and the subsidiary accounts differ. To determine whether errors were made in updating these records, the Accounts Receivable general ledger control account is reconciled to the accounts receivable subsidiary ledger at the end of the month. Exhibit 5.13 shows that the September balances in the subsidiary ledger accounts equal the $6,476 general ledger balance in Exhibit 5.12, so no errors had been made.

Exhibit 5.14 (page 215) summarizes the postings from the cash receipts journal. Some of the detail in the general ledger accounts and subsidiary ledger accounts has been eliminated to save space.

**Coach's Tip**

In adding up the individual balances in the accounts receivable subsidiary ledger, it is not necessary to list those customers whose accounts currently have a zero balance.

**Exhibit 5.13**    **Preparing the Schedule of Accounts Receivable**

Schedule of Accounts Receivable

| | |
|------|------|
| Downtown Dental Services | $1,389 |
| Gallegos Gift Shop | 1,711 |
| Keays Optical | 1,588 |
| Matthews Custom Computers | 1,788 |
| Total | $6,476 |

**Exhibit 5.14**    Summary of Postings from Cash Receipts Journal

### Cash Receipts Journal — Page 3

| Date | Account Credited | Ref. | Other Accounts Cr. | Accounts Receivable Cr. | Fees Earned Cr. | Cash Dr. |
|---|---|---|---|---|---|---|
| Sep. 15 | | | | | 820 | 820 |
| 18 | Downtown Dental Services | ✓ | | 2,410 | | 2,410 |
| 20 | Interest Revenue | 710 | 80 | | | 80 |
| 22 | Keays Optical | ✓ | | 1,987 | | 1,987 |
| 28 | Matthews Custom Computers | ✓ | | 843 | | 843 |
| 29 | Gallegos Gift Shop | ✓ | | 1,000 | | 1,000 |
| 30 | | | | | 890 | 890 |
| | Totals | | 80 | 6,240 | 1,710 | 8,030 |
| | | | (✓) | (110) | (410) | (105) |

### ACCOUNTS RECEIVABLE SUBSIDIARY LEDGER

**Downtown Dental Services**

| Date | Ref. | Debit | Credit | Balance |
|---|---|---|---|---|
| Aug. 31 | | | | 2,410 |
| Sep. 1 | R2 | 1,389 | | 3,799 |
| Sep. 18 | CR3 | | 2,410 | 1,389 |

**Gallegos Gift Shop**

| Date | Ref. | Debit | Credit | Balance |
|---|---|---|---|---|
| Aug. 31 | | | | 886 |
| Sep. 12 | R2 | 1,825 | | 2,711 |
| Sep. 29 | CR3 | | 1,000 | 1,711 |

**Keays Optical**

| Date | Ref. | Debit | Credit | Balance |
|---|---|---|---|---|
| Aug. 31 | | | | 1,277 |
| Sep. 20 | R2 | 2,298 | | 3,575 |
| Sep. 22 | CR3 | | 1,987 | 1,588 |

**Matthews Custom Computers**

| Date | Ref. | Debit | Credit | Balance |
|---|---|---|---|---|
| Aug. 31 | | | | 843 |
| Sep. 21 | R2 | 1,788 | | 2,631 |
| Sep. 28 | CR3 | | 843 | 1,788 |

**Cash    Acct. No. 105**

| Date | Ref. | Debit | Credit | Balance |
|---|---|---|---|---|
| Aug. 31 | | | | 4,220 |
| Sep. 30 | CR3 | 8,030 | | 12,250 |

**Accounts Receivable    Acct. No. 110**

| Date | Ref. | Debit | Credit | Balance |
|---|---|---|---|---|
| Aug. 31 | | | | 5,416 |
| Sep. 30 | R2 | 7,300 | | 12,716 |
| Sep. 30 | CR3 | | 6,240 | 6,476 |

**Fees Earned    Acct. No. 410**

| Date | Ref. | Debit | Credit | Balance |
|---|---|---|---|---|
| Aug. 31 | | | | 54,080 |
| Sep. 30 | R2 | | 7,300 | 61,380 |
| Sep. 30 | CR3 | | 1,710 | 63,090 |

**Interest Revenue    Acct. No. 710**

| Date | Ref. | Debit | Credit | Balance |
|---|---|---|---|---|
| Aug. 31 | | | | 0 |
| Sep. 30 | CR3 | | 80 | 80 |

To make sure you understand how to use the revenue journal and the cash receipts journal, try the following Self-Study Practice.

**SELF-STUDY PRACTICE**

Indicate whether each of the following is a true (T) or false (F) statement regarding the use of special journals.

1. The revenue journal is used to record all transactions involving a credit to the Fees Earned account. _____
2. The Invoice No. column does not serve any useful purpose in the revenue journal. _____
3. Posting from the cash receipts journal and the revenue journal to the subsidiary ledger accounts is done at the end of the month. _____
4. Footing is the act of adding up a row of numbers to ensure that debits equal credits. _____
5. The notation (110/510) beneath a column of numbers in a journal indicates the date and time when a posting was made. _____

*After you have finished, check your answers with the solution at the bottom of the page.*

## Purchases Journal

**Coach's Tip**

The purchases journal (below) has two different Ref. columns. The one on the left is used only to show the posting to the individual creditors for the Accounts Payable Cr. Column. The one on the right is used to identify the specific general ledger account that is debited when something is recorded in the Other Accounts Dr. column.

The **purchases journal** is used only to record purchases made and expenses incurred on account. Several columns are needed in this journal because the number of accounts that could be debited when Accounts Payable is credited is nearly limitless. The UPS Store, for example, might purchase any of the following items on account: store equipment, advertising, shipping supplies, and so on. The purchases journal must be able to accommodate each of them. Exhibit 5.15 is a page from a typical purchases journal.

Notice that some of the columns in the purchases journal are identical to those in the cash receipts journal (see Exhibit 5.11, page 213). Because of space considerations, we limit this analysis to those columns not discussed in connection with the cash receipts journal.

1. **Account Credited.**    Because the purchases journal is used for recording all purchases made and expenses incurred on account, every transaction involves a creditor in the accounts payable subsidiary ledger. This column is used to identify the creditor whose subsidiary account is increased by each transaction.
2. **Accounts Payable Cr.**    This column is used for recording the dollar amount of the credit to Accounts Payable.

**Exhibit 5.15    Purchases Journal**

Purchases Journal — Page 4

| Date | Account Credited | Ref. | Accounts Payable Cr. | Shipping Supplies Dr. | Other Accounts Dr. Accounts | Ref. | Amount |
|---|---|---|---|---|---|---|---|
| Sep. 11 | XYZ Suppliers | ✓ | 1,418 | 1,418 | | | |
| 18 | Carlson Equipment | ✓ | 2,000 | | Store Equipment | 170 | 2,000 |
| 29 | EmilRado Advertising Co. | ✓ | 715 | | Advertising Expense | 520 | 715 |
| 30 | XYZ Suppliers | ✓ | 500 | 500 | | | |
| | Totals | | 4,633 | 1,918 | | | 2,715 |
| | | | (210) | (115) | | | (✓) |

Solution to
Self-Study Practice

1. F—The revenue journal can be used only to record revenue transactions on account.
2. F—Keeping track of every invoice is important in the event an invoice is lost, misplaced, or otherwise unaccounted for.
3. F—Posting to the subsidiary ledger is performed on a daily basis.
4. F—Footing is adding up a column of numbers.
5. F—The 110 and 510 indicate that account 110 has been debited for the amount in the column and that a credit for the same amount has been placed into account 510.

3. **Shipping Supplies Dr.**   When an account is used often (for example, the Shipping Supplies account at The UPS Store), a column should be created for it in the purchases journal. The number of Debit columns and the accounts they represent differs depending on the business. Commonly used debit columns in a purchases journal include Office Supplies, Equipment, and Inventory.

4. **Other Accounts Dr.**   This column is used for identifying the name of any account being debited for which the purchases journal has no dedicated column.

Because the purchases journal has multiple columns, its columns must be footed and crossfooted like the ones in the cash receipts journal. Once the equality of debits and credits has been verified, the amounts can be posted. Remember that a checkmark (✓) below a column total indicates that the total should not be posted anywhere because the individual amounts were posted daily. After posting transactions from the purchases journal, selected general ledger accounts (illustrating an asset, liability, and expense) would appear as in Exhibit 5.16.

## Cash Payments Journal

Just as the cash receipts journal is used to record all cash received by a business, a **cash payments journal** like the one in Exhibit 5.17 is used for recording all transactions involving cash payments.

1. **Check No.**   All cash payments are made with sequentially numbered checks so that every check can be tracked. To ensure that every check has been accounted for, even voided checks are listed in the Cash Payments Journal as in Exhibit 5.17.

2. **Account Debited.**   This column is for the name of the creditor whose account is being debited in the accounts payable subsidiary ledger or the specific general ledger account that is being debited in the Other Accounts Dr. column.

3. **Other Accounts Dr.**   The dollar amounts recorded in this column are posted to general ledger accounts other than Cash and Accounts Payable. These accounts are identified by name in the Account Debited column.

4. **Accounts Payable Dr.**   This is the dollar amount of those transactions that will be posted individually to the accounts payable subsidiary ledger and in total to the Accounts Payable general ledger account.

Because the cash payments journal is a multiple-column journal, its columns must be footed and cross-footed. If the column totals do not crossfoot, one or more errors have been made.

> **Coach's Tip**
>
> A separate column (Other Accounts Dr.) is required for any account that is debited but does not have a dedicated column. The additional column is required because the Account Credited column is used only to identify the specific subsidiary account being charged.

### Exhibit 5.16   Posting to the General Ledger

**Shipping Supplies**   Acct. No. 115

| Date | Item | Ref. | Debit | Credit | Balance |
|------|------|------|-------|--------|---------|
| Aug. 31 | Bal. | | | | 285 |
| Sep. 30 | | P4 | 1,918 | | 2,203 |

**Accounts Payable**   Acct. No. 210

| Date | Item | Ref. | Debit | Credit | Balance |
|------|------|------|-------|--------|---------|
| Aug. 31 | Bal. | | | | 3,113 |
| Sep. 30 | | P4 | | 4,633 | 7,746 |

**Advertising Expense**   Acct. No. 520

| Date | Item | Ref. | Debit | Credit | Balance |
|------|------|------|-------|--------|---------|
| Aug. 31 | Bal. | | | | 1,768 |
| Sep. 29 | | P4 | 715 | | 2,483 |

**Coach's Tip**

Amounts in the Other Accounts Dr. column must be posted daily. Amounts in the Accounts Payable Dr. column are posted daily to the subsidiary ledger and the total is posted at the end of the period to the Accounts Payable control account.

## Exhibit 5.17    Cash Payments Journal

**Cash Payments Journal** — Page 8

| Date | Check No. | Account Debited | Ref. | Other Accounts Dr. | Accounts Payable Dr. | Cash Cr. |
|------|-----------|------------------|------|---------------------|----------------------|----------|
| Sep. 1 | 5601 | Carlson Equipment | ✓ | | 1,228 | 1,228 |
| 2 | 5602 | Advertising Expense | 520 | 645 | | 645 |
| 11 | 5603 | VOID | | | | |
| 12 | 5604 | EmilRado Advertising Co. | ✓ | | 365 | 365 |
| 26 | 5605 | XYZ Suppliers | ✓ | | 1,538 | 1,538 |
| 29 | 5606 | Shipping Supplies | 115 | 325 | | 325 |
| 30 | 5607 | Salaries Expense | 510 | 850 | | 850 |
| | Totals | | | 1,820 | 3,131 | 4,951 |
| | | | | (✓) | (210) | (105) |

As in earlier examples, the column totals in the cash payments journal must be posted to the appropriate general ledger accounts. See Exhibit 5.18 for selected general ledger accounts after the end-of-month postings have been made. The abbreviation used for all cash payment postings is CP8, indicating that the amounts recorded came from page 8 of the cash payments journal. **Notice that an entire month's worth of transactions has been recorded in the Cash account with nothing more than one debit and one credit.** This is the beauty (and ease) of using special journals.

A final step is required because the accounts payable subsidiary ledger has been updated continuously while the Accounts Payable control account was updated only at the end of the month. Thus, the Accounts Payable account in the general ledger must be reconciled with the related subsidiary ledger accounts through a schedule of accounts payable, as in Exhibit 5.19.

## Use of the General Journal

Every business uses a general journal—even when it uses special journals—because certain transactions cannot be recorded in any of the special journals. Assume, for example, that The UPS Store purchased $4,000 of store equipment by issuing a note payable to Carlson

## Exhibit 5.18    General Ledger after End-of-Month Postings

**Cash** — Acct. No. 105

| Date | Item | Ref. | Debit | Credit | Balance |
|------|------|------|-------|--------|---------|
| Aug. 31 | Bal. | | | | 4,220 |
| Sep. 30 | | CR3 | 8,030 | | 12,250 |
| Sep. 30 | | CP8 | | 4,951 | 7,299 |

**Accounts Payable** — Acct. No. 210

| Date | Item | Ref. | Debit | Credit | Balance |
|------|------|------|-------|--------|---------|
| Aug. 31 | Bal. | | | | 3,113 |
| Sep. 30 | | P4 | | 4,633 | 7,746 |
| Sep. 30 | | CP8 | 3,131 | | 4,615 |

**Exhibit 5.19**    Accounts Payable Control Account and Schedule of Accounts Payable

| | | | Accounts Payable | | Acct. No. 210 |
|---|---|---|---|---|---|
| Date | Item | Ref. | Debit | Credit | Balance |
| Aug. 31 | Bal. | | | | 3,113 |
| Sep. 30 | | P4 | | 4,633 | 7,746 |
| Sep. 30 | | CP8 | 3,131 | | 4,615 |

**Schedule of Accounts Payable**

| | |
|---|---|
| Carlson Equipment | $ 2,000 |
| EmilRado Advertising Co. | 715 |
| XYZ Suppliers | 1,900 |
| Total | $ 4,615 |

Equipment. Initially, you might be tempted to record this entry in the purchases journal. However, the purchases journal can be used only for purchases made on account, and a note payable is not the same as an account payable. If this entry were recorded in the purchases journal, the note payable would never be recorded, and the balance in Accounts Payable would be $4,000 more than it should be. The proper treatment of this transaction is to record it in the general journal as in Exhibit 5.20.

In addition to this type of entry, the general journal is used to record all correcting entries, adjusting entries, and closing entries. So even though the general journal is used less often when special journals are used, it cannot be eliminated.

## Summary of the Recording Process

See Exhibit 5.21 for an overview of the process for recording transactions when special journals and subsidiary ledgers are used.

Four points are worth emphasizing:

1. Transactions are entered into either the general journal or one of the four special journals, but not both.
2. Entries involving Accounts Receivable or Accounts Payable that are recorded in a special journal or in the general journal must be posted to **both** the subsidiary ledger account **and** the related general ledger control account.
3. Each month the subsidiary ledger accounts must be reconciled to the related control account in the general ledger (as indicated by the dotted line in Exhibit 5.21).
4. Information for preparing the financial statements must still be obtained from the general ledger.

See Exhibit 5.22 for a summary of the frequency of posting required for each of the journals.

**Coach's Tip**

Transactions posted from a special journal should never be entered again into the general journal. To do so would be to journalize and post the transaction twice because special journals do in fact represent journal entries.

**Exhibit 5.20**    Recording Unusual Transactions in the General Journal

| Date | Account Titles and Explanation | Ref. | Debit | Credit |
|---|---|---|---|---|
| Sep. 1 | Store Equipment | 170 | 4,000 | |
| | Notes Payable | 250 | | 4,000 |
| | (Purchased equipment by issuing a note payable) | | | |

**Exhibit 5.21**    Summary of the Recording Process for Special Journals and Subsidiary Ledgers

**Exhibit 5.22**    Frequency of Posting from Journals

| Journal | Item | Posting Frequency |
|---|---|---|
| Revenue journal | Subsidiary Accounts Dr. (customers) | Daily |
| | Column totals to general ledger (GL) | Monthly |
| Cash receipts journal | Subsidiary Accounts Cr. (customers) | Daily |
| | Other Accounts Cr. items to GL | Daily |
| | Column totals (except Other) to GL | Monthly |
| Purchases journal | Subsidiary Accounts Cr. (creditors) | Daily |
| | Other Accounts Dr. items to GL | Daily |
| | Column totals (except Other) to GL | Monthly |
| Cash payments journal | Subsidiary Accounts Dr. (creditors) | Daily |
| | Other Accounts Dr. items to GL | Daily |
| | Column totals (except Other) to GL | Monthly |
| General journal | Subsidiary Accounts Dr./Cr. (all) | Daily |
| | General ledger accounts (all) | Daily |

To make sure you understand how to use special journals, try the following Self-Study Practice.

**SELF-STUDY PRACTICE**

Indicate whether Legal Ease should use the revenue journal (R), cash receipts journal (CR), purchases journal (P), cash payments journal (CP), or general journal (G) to record each of the following events.

1. A check is written to Agro's Advertising for an advertisement in the local paper. _____

2. Cash is collected from a customer for a previous balance owed. _____
3. Legal Ease bought office supplies on account from Office Outlet, Inc. _____
4. Legal Ease prepared a legal brief on account for Superior Roofing. _____
5. End-of-period closing entries are made for Legal Ease. _____

*After you have finished, check your answers with the solution at the bottom of the page.*

Solution to
Self-Study Practice

1. CP—All checks are essentially cash payments and, therefore, are recorded in the cash payments journal.
2. CR—Cash collections of any kind are recorded in the cash receipts journal.
3. P—Any purchases made on account are recorded in the purchases journal.
4. R—Services performed on account are recorded in the revenue journal.
5. G—Transactions that cannot be recorded in any of the special journals are recorded in the general journal.

# BASIC THEORY OF ACCOUNTING INFORMATION SYSTEMS

In Chapters 2–4, you learned how to journalize and post daily transactions in the general ledger, prepare adjusting and closing entries, and generate end-of-period financial statements. During this process, you generated three different types of journal entries, three trial balances, and a set of general-purpose financial statements. This chapter has presented some additional tools for collecting and processing financial data efficiently and effectively.

The entire process described in Chapters 2–4 and in this chapter, along with the distribution of the resulting financial information to creditors and investors, is referred to as the accounting information system. An accounting information system includes the source documents used in preparing transactions (receipts, bills, checks) as well as the trial balances, journals, ledger accounts, schedules, and financial statements that are the end result of the process. In this section, we discuss some of the assumptions behind such systems and sketch the process of developing one from scratch.

## Underlying Assumptions

The most effective accounting information systems have three basic features: usefulness, cost effectiveness, and flexibility.

1. **Usefulness.** An accounting information system must adequately meet the needs of a variety of different users whether they work in accounting, marketing, or production.
2. **Cost effectiveness.** As tempting as it might be to create the Rolls Royce of accounting systems, the benefits of an accounting system must be balanced against the costs of implementing and maintaining it.
3. **Flexibility.** An accounting information system must have the capacity to expand or shrink with a business's information needs.

How do you create an accounting information system that is useful, cost effective, and flexible? Achieving these goals requires a time-consuming development process.

## Developmental Phases

The development of an accounting information system has four phases: analysis, design, implementation, and feedback.

1. **Analysis.** This first phase identifies the needs of both internal and external users. Internal users need to keep track of transactions with customers and creditors; investors need to assess the company's profitability; the bank needs to determine the likelihood that its loan will be repaid. A good accounting information system should adequately meet all these needs.
2. **Design.** In the second phase, design, planners create a cost-effective system that will meet the needs identified during the first phase. This step may require nothing more than selecting a suitable general ledger software program, or it may require creating a complex system that professional systems designers must implement. This phase of development must answer the critical question of whether the system will be manual or computerized.
3. **Implementation.** Proper implementation of the new system is critical to its success (or failure). A design that works "on paper" must be transformed into a workable, effective, and efficient system.
4. **Feedback.** A new accounting information system is likely to require occasional tweaking as certain aspects of its design prove unmanageable. In some cases, the business may even outgrow the system and require a more sophisticated design. Replacing an old design often involves switching from a manual to a computerized system.

Exhibit 5.23 summarizes the four phases in the development of an accounting information system.

In the next section, we examine a computerized accounting information system, the general ledger package Peachtree Complete 2008. But first, make sure you understand the

**Exhibit 5.23**    Development of an Accounting Information System

basic theory of accounting information systems by completing the following Self-Study Practice.

**SELF-STUDY PRACTICE**

Indicate whether each of the following statements regarding the basic theory of accounting information systems is true (T) or false (F).

1. Most accounting information systems are manual or computerized. _____

2. The underlying assumptions of accounting information systems are usefulness, flexibility, and design. _____

3. The correct order of the developmental phases of an accounting information system is design, analysis, implementation, and feedback. _____

4. A critical question that must be answered during the implementation phase of developing an accounting information system is whether the system will be manual or computerized. _____

5. A popular general ledger software package is Peachtree Complete 2008. _____

*After you have finished, check your answers with the solution at the bottom of the page.*

**Learning Objective 5**

Compare the advantages and disadvantages of manual and computerized accounting information systems.

# COMPUTERIZED ACCOUNTING INFORMATION SYSTEMS

The use of computerized accounting information systems has become quite common, even by small businesses. Substantial declines in the cost of general ledger software packages and computer hardware are partly responsible for their increased use combined with an increase in user-friendly commercial general ledger software programs, such as Peachtree Complete 2008. What are the pros and cons of using such systems?

## Advantages and Disadvantages

Computerized accounting information systems have three primary advantages:

1. **Fewer recording errors.**   Computerized programs calculate invoice totals and account balances virtually without error.

Solution to
Self-Study Practice

1. T.
2. F — The underlying assumptions of an accounting information system are usefulness, cost effectiveness, and flexibility.
3. F — The correct order of the development phases is analysis, design, implementation, and feedback.
4. F — This question is answered during the design phase of developing an accounting information system.
5. T.

2. **Simplified recordkeeping.** The information entered on a customer's invoice or creditor's bill is posted simultaneously to all subsidiary and general ledger accounts.
3. **Up-to-date balances.** Because account balances are always current, trial balances and/ or financial statements can be generated at any time.

Compared to these advantages, computerized accounting systems have few disadvantages. These systems can create unexpected problems, however, such as:

1. **Information input errors.** That is, human errors can be made while inputting information into the system. Computers cannot distinguish between good information and bad information and will process both with dizzying speed.
2. **Lack of control over some accounting procedures.** Because much of the accounting process is performed internally in these programs, tracking down errors can be difficult.
3. **Ease of altering records.** Although changes and corrections are easier to make electronically than by hand, criminals also find it easier to commit fraud and/or engage in illegal activities electronically.

# Peachtree Complete 2008—An Illustration

Assume managers at a local UPS Store recently analyzed their manual accounting information system. Based on projected growth of the business, managerial reporting requirements, and additional information requested by creditors, managers decided to convert to a computerized accounting information system. Because The UPS Store is a small service business with no complex reporting requirements, the managers agreed that the general ledger software package Peachtree Complete 2008 would easily accommodate both their managerial requirements and the information needs of any external users.

In this section, we examine various reports generated by Peachtree Complete 2008. This short example shows how the software generates and displays accounting reports similar to those shown earlier in this chapter using a manual system. The following reports are generated for The UPS Store:

1. **Sales Journal.** Peachtree Complete 2008 does not use a revenue journal. Instead, it prepares a sales journal. The major difference between the two is that a sales journal can be used by businesses that provide services as well as by those that sell goods (inventory). Unlike a manual accounting system, the sales journal contains both debit and credit columns. Compare the sales journal in Exhibit 5.24 to the Revenue Journal in Exhibit 5.8 (page 210).
2. **Cash receipts journal.** See Exhibit 5.25 for a cash receipts journal generated by Peachtree Complete 2008. Notice that it has only two columns containing the dollar amounts for debit and credit compared to the multiple columns in the manual version in Exhibit 5.11 (page 213).

## Exhibit 5.24 Sales Journal

**The UPS Store**
**Sales Journal**
**For the Period from Sep. 1, 2008 to Sep. 30, 2008**

Filter criteria includes: Report order is by check date. Report is printed in detail format.

| Date | Account ID | Invoice/CM # | Line Description | Debit Amnt | Credit Amnt |
|---|---|---|---|---|---|
| 9/1/08 | 410 | 820 | Shipping Fees Earned | | 1,389.00 |
| | 110 | | Downtown Dental Services | 1,389.00 | |
| 9/10/08 | 110 | 821 | Cash Customer | | |
| 9/10/08 | 110 | 821V | Cash Customer | | |
| 9/12/08 | 410 | 822 | Shipping Fees Earned | | 1825.00 |
| | 110 | | Gallegos Gift Shop | 1825.00 | |
| 9/20/08 | 410 | 823 | Shipping Fees Earned | | 2,298.00 |
| | 110 | | Keays Optical | 2,298.00 | |
| 9/21/08 | 410 | 824 | Shipping Fees Earned | | 1,788.00 |
| | 110 | | Matthews Custom Computers | 1,788.00 | |
| | | Total | | 7,300.00 | 7,300.00 |

## Exhibit 5.25 Cash Receipts Journal

**The UPS Store**
**Cash Receipts Journal**
**For the Period from Sep. 1, 2008 to Sep. 30, 2008**

Filter criteria includes: Report order is by check date. Report is printed in detail format.

| Date | Account ID | Transaction Ref | Line Description | Debit Amnt | Credit Amnt |
|------|-----------|-----------------|------------------|-----------:|------------:|
| 9/15/08 | 410 | 101 | Shipping Fees Earned | | 820.00 |
| | 105 | | Cash Customer | 820.00 | |
| 9/18/08 | 110 | 2 | Invoice: 757 | | 2,410.00 |
| | 105 | | Downtown Dental Services | 2,410.00 | |
| 9/20/08 | 710 | Int | Interest Earned | | 80.00 |
| | 105 | | Albuquerque City Bank | 80.00 | |
| 9/22/08 | 110 | 4 | Invoice: 776 | | 1,277.00 |
| | 110 | | Invoice: 823 | | 710.00 |
| | 105 | | Keays Optical | 1,987.00 | |
| 9/28/08 | 110 | 5 | Invoice: 743 | | 843.00 |
| | 105 | | Matthews Custom Computers | 843.00 | |
| 9/29/08 | 110 | 6 | Invoice: 755 | | 886.00 |
| | 110 | | Invoice: 822 | | 114.00 |
| | 105 | | Gallegos Gift Shop | 1,000.00 | |
| 9/30/08 | 410 | 102 | Shipping Fees Earned | | 890.00 |
| | 105 | | Cash Customer | 890.00 | |
| | | | | **8,030.00** | **8,030.00** |

3. **Customer ledgers.** Peachtree Complete 2008 refers to the accounts receivable subsidiary ledger simply as Customer Ledgers, as shown in Exhibit 5.26. Compare it to the accounts receivable subsidiary ledger in Exhibits 5.3 (page 207) and 5.14 (page 215).

4. **General ledger accounts.** See Exhibit 5.27 for the Accounts Receivable account in the general ledger as Peachtree Complete 2008 presented it. Note that the balance in the control account is the same as the balance in the customer ledgers. The transactions are not summarized as they are in a manual system. Instead they are very detailed because, unlike you and me, the computer does not get tired of posting. Note too that the references to the special journals (in the column labeled **Jrnl**) are SJ (sales journal) and CRJ (cash receipts journal).

### Coach's Tip

Notice that the customer balances in the Balance column of Exhibit 5.26 are identical to those calculated manually in Exhibits 5.3 and 5.14. The only difference between manual and computerized accounting information systems is how the information is processed and displayed. The end result is the same using either process.

## Exhibit 5.26 Customer Ledgers

**The UPS Store**
**Customer Ledgers**
**For the Period from Aug. 31, 2008 to Sep. 30, 2008**

Filter criteria includes: Report order is by ID. Report is printed in detail format.

| Customer ID / Customer | Date | Trans No | Type | Debit Amt | Credit Amt | Balance |
|------------------------|------|----------|------|----------:|-----------:|--------:|
| 11 | 9/10/08 | 821 | SJ | | | 0.00 |
| Cash Customer | 9/10/08 | 821V | SJ | | | 0.00 |
| | 9/15/08 | 101 | CRJ | 820.00 | 820.00 | 0.00 |
| | 9/30/08 | 102 | CRJ | 890.00 | 890.00 | 0.00 |
| 12 | 9/20/08 | Int | CRJ | 80.00 | 80.00 | 0.00 |
| Albuquerque City Bank | | | | | | |
| 22 | 8/31/08 | 757 | SJ | 2,410.00 | | 2,410.00 |
| Downtown Dental Services | 9/1/08 | 820 | SJ | 1,389.00 | | 3,799.00 |
| | 9/18/08 | 2 | CRJ | | 2,410.00 | 1,389.00 |
| 34 | 8/31/08 | 755 | SJ | 886.00 | | 886.00 |
| Gallegos Gift Shop | 9/12/08 | 822 | SJ | 1,825.00 | | 2,711.00 |
| | 9/29/08 | 6 | CRJ | | 1,000.00 | 1,711.00 |
| 57 | 8/31/08 | 776 | SJ | 1,277.00 | | 1,277.00 |
| Keays Optical | 9/20/08 | 823 | SJ | 2,298.00 | | 3,575.00 |
| | 9/22/08 | 4 | CRJ | | 1,987.00 | 1,588.00 |
| 66 | 8/31/08 | 743 | SJ | 843.00 | | 843.00 |
| Matthews Custom Computers | 9/21/08 | 824 | SJ | 1,788.00 | | 2,631.00 |
| | 9/28/08 | 5 | CRJ | | 843.00 | 1,788.00 |
| **Report Total** | | | | **14,506.00** | **8,030.00** | **6,476.00** |

| Exhibit 5.27 | General Ledger Accounts—Accounts Receivable |
|---|---|

**The UPS Store**
**General Ledger**
**For the Period from Sep. 1, 2008 to Sep. 30, 2008**

Filter criteria includes: IDs: 110. Report order is by ID. Report is printed with shortened descriptions and with hide period subtotals.

| Account ID Account Description | Date | Reference | Jrnl | Trans Description | Debit Amt | Credit Amt | Balance |
|---|---|---|---|---|---|---|---|
| 110 | 9/1/08 | | | Beginning Balance | | | 5,416.00 |
| Accounts Receivable | 9/1/08 | 820 | SJ | Downtown Dental | 1,389.00 | | |
| | 9/12/08 | 822 | SJ | Gallegos Gift Shop | 1,825.00 | | |
| | 9/18/08 | 3 | CRJ | Downtown Dental | | 2,410.00 | |
| | 9/20/08 | 823 | SJ | Keays Optical | 2,298.00 | | |
| | 9/21/08 | 824 | SJ | Matthews Custom | 1,788.00 | | |
| | 9/22/08 | 5 | CRJ | Keays Optical - Inv | | 710.00 | |
| | 9/22/08 | 5 | CRJ | Keays Optical - Inv | | 1,277.00 | |
| | 9/28/08 | 1 | CRJ | Matthews Custom | | 843.00 | |
| | 9/29/08 | 6 | CRJ | Gallegos Gift Shop | | 114.00 | |
| | 9/29/08 | 6 | CRJ | Gallegos Gift Shop | | 886.00 | |
| | | | | Change | 7,300.00 | 6,240.00 | 1,060.00 |
| | 9/30/08 | | | **Ending Balance** | | | **6,476.00** |

Clearly, the accumulation, presentation, and control of information is much easier, faster, and more accurate in a computerized accounting information system than in a manual system. However, users of a computerized system must take extra care to prevent both intentional misstatements and unintentional human errors.

Before you close this chapter, take a moment to complete the following Self-Study Practice.

**SELF-STUDY PRACTICE**

Indicate whether each of the following is an advantage of a computerized accounting system (C) or a manual accounting system (M).

1. Virtually all postings are error free. _____
2. Financial statement preparation takes relatively little time. _____
3. The process of double-entry accounting can be easily seen and traced. _____
4. The accountant has more time to spend on critical accounting issues. _____

*After you have finished, check your answers with the solution at the bottom of the page.*

# Demonstration Case

Selected transactions of Miller Accounting, Inc., for the month of August, the first month of operations, are as follows:

Aug.  1    Issued Check 5280 for August office rent of $1,800.
     3    Received $1,600 cash from Camel Enterprises for accounting services rendered today.
     9    Issued Check 5281 for $850 of office supplies purchased today from Office Emporium.
    12    Provided accounting services worth $2,500 on account to Willoby Warner (Invoice 201).
    14    Purchased $6,000 of office equipment on account from Eli's Equipment.
    16    Received $100 cash for office supplies sold to employees at cost.
    21    Received $2,000 from Willoby Warner in payment of services provided on August 12.
    23    Purchased $400 of office supplies on account from Rudy's Supplies.
    27    Issued Check 5282 for $6,000 to Eli's Equipment as payment for August 14 purchase.
    30    Purchased $20,000 office equipment from Rudy's Supplies by issuing a note payable.

**Solution to Self-Study Practice**

1.  C—Because computers perform the postings, virtually no errors occur.
2.  C—Computerized accounting systems are relatively efficient, whereas financial statements in a manual system must be prepared by hand and take a great deal of time.
3.  M—Manual performance of all financial functions makes the double-entry process easier to see and trace.
4.  C—Because performing tedious accounting functions takes less time, the accountant has more time to spend on important accounting issues.

Miller uses the following journals: a Revenue Journal, Cash Receipts Journal, Purchases Journal, Cash Payments Journal, and General Journal. Use the following account numbers where applicable: Office Supplies—115, Office Equipment—180, Notes Payable—250, and Rent Expense—615.

**Required:**

1. For each of the August transactions, indicate the journal in which to record the transaction.
2. Indicate whether the accounts receivable subsidiary ledger or the accounts payable subsidiary ledger would be affected by each transaction. If so, indicate the subsidiary ledger that would be affected. If not, write No effect.
3. Journalize all transactions for August in the appropriate journal. Post only to the subsidiary ledgers. However, record items in the Ref. column as if the daily postings to the general ledger accounts have been made.

## Suggested Solution

1. Journal used to record transaction:

| | | | | | |
|---|---|---|---|---|---|
| Aug. | 1 | Cash payments journal | Aug. | 16 | Cash receipts journal |
| | 3 | Cash receipts journal | | 21 | Cash receipts journal |
| | 9 | Cash payments journal | | 23 | Purchases journal |
| | 12 | Revenue journal | | 27 | Cash payments journal |
| | 14 | Purchases journal | | 30 | General journal |

You may have placed the August 3 transaction in the revenue journal because it involved a customer. However, customers can charge services or simply pay for them at the time services are rendered. In this case, payment was made when the services were performed, requiring the use of the cash receipts journal. The same logic explains why the August 9 transaction is recorded in the cash payments journal rather than the purchases journal.

2. Subsidiary ledger affected:

| | | | | | |
|---|---|---|---|---|---|
| Aug. | 1 | No effect | Aug. | 16 | No effect |
| | 3 | No effect | | 21 | Accounts receivable subsidiary ledger |
| | 9 | No effect | | 23 | Accounts payable subsidiary ledger |
| | 12 | Accounts receivable subsidiary ledger | | 27 | Accounts payable subsidiary ledger |
| | 14 | Accounts payable subsidiary ledger | | 30 | No effect |

The transaction on August 3 has no impact on the accounts receivable subsidiary ledger because the customer paid cash for services rendered (this was not a collection on account). The same logic applies to the August 9 cash payment for office supplies.

3. Journalize transactions in the appropriate journal:

**Revenue Journal**     Page 1

| Date | Invoice No. | Account Debited | Ref. | Accts Receivable Dr. Fees Earned Cr. |
|---|---|---|---|---|
| Aug. 12 | 201 | Willoby Warner | ✓ | 2,500 |

**Cash Receipts Journal**     Page 1

| Date | Account Credited | Ref. | Other Accounts Cr. | Accounts Receivable Cr. | Fees Earned Cr. | Cash Dr. |
|---|---|---|---|---|---|---|
| Aug. 3 | | | | | 1,600 | 1,600 |
| 16 | Office Supplies | 115 | 100 | | | 100 |
| 21 | Willoby Warner | ✓ | | 2,000 | | 2,000 |

| Purchases Journal | | | | | | | Page 1 |
|---|---|---|---|---|---|---|---|
| Date | Account Credited | Ref. | Accounts Payable Cr. | Office Supplies Dr. | Other Accounts Dr. | | |
| | | | | | Accounts | Ref. | Amount |
| Aug. 14 | Eli's Equipment | ✓ | 6,000 | | Office Equipment | 180 | 6,000 |
| 23 | Rudy's Supplies | ✓ | 400 | 400 | | | |

The columns in this purchases journal differ somewhat from those used for The UPS Store. Special journals can be modified to meet the specific needs of each company, so be aware of the column headings the business uses.

| Cash Payments Journal | | | | | | | Page 1 |
|---|---|---|---|---|---|---|---|
| Date | Check No. | Account Debited | Ref. | Other Accounts Dr. | Accounts Payable Dr. | Cash Cr. |
| Aug. 1 | 5280 | Rent Expense | 615 | 1,800 | | 1,800 |
| 9 | 5281 | Office Supplies | 115 | 850 | | 850 |
| 27 | 5282 | Eli's Equipment | ✓ | | 6,000 | 6,000 |

| General Journal | | | | Page 1 |
|---|---|---|---|---|
| Date | Account Titles and Explanations | Ref. | Debit | Credit |
| Aug. 30 | Office Equipment | 180 | 20,000 | |
| | Notes Payable | 250 | | 20,000 |
| | (Equipment purchased on a Note Payable) | | | |

This transaction involves a Note Payable rather than an Account Payable, so it is not entered in the purchases journal, which is reserved for purchases and charges made on account. If it were recorded in the purchases journal, the $20,000 would be credited erroneously to Accounts Payable rather than Notes Payable at the end of the accounting period.

### ACCOUNTS RECEIVABLE SUBSIDIARY LEDGER

**Willoby Warner**

| Date | Ref. | Debit | Credit | Balance |
|---|---|---|---|---|
| Aug. 12 | R1 | 2,500 | | 2,500 |
| 21 | CR1 | | 2,000 | 500 |

Note that the transaction with Camel Enterprises on August 3 has no impact on the accounts receivable subsidiary ledger.

### ACCOUNTS PAYABLE SUBSIDIARY LEDGER

**Eli's Equipment**

| Date | Ref. | Debit | Credit | Balance |
|---|---|---|---|---|
| Aug. 14 | P1 | | 6,000 | 6,000 |
| 27 | CP1 | 6,000 | | 0 |

**Rudy's Supplies**

| Date | Ref. | Debit | Credit | Balance |
|---|---|---|---|---|
| Aug. 23 | P1 | | 400 | 400 |

Note that the transaction with Rudy's Supplies on August 30 has no impact on the accounts payable subsidiary ledger.

# Chapter Summary

### LO1 Describe processing methods of accounting information systems. p. 204

- Two different methods are used for processing accounting information.
    - Manual: all transactions are recorded and posted using paper and pen.
    - Computerized: all transactions are journalized and posted using proprietary software.
- Computerized accounting information systems can make the accounting function easier to perform, but the difficulty of following transactions through the system can make these systems more difficult to understand.

### LO2 Describe components of an accounting information system. p. 206

- Accounts receivable subsidiary ledger: collects and maintains individual customer records for transactions made on account.
- Accounts payable subsidiary ledger: collects and maintains individual creditor records for transactions made on account.
- Advantages of using subsidiary ledgers:
    - Dedicated accounts for individual customers.
    - Omission of unnecessary detail from the general ledger accounts.
    - Ease of locating errors in individual customer and creditor accounts.
    - Division of labor.
- Control account—general ledger account that summarizes all transactions in the related subsidiary ledger.

### LO3 Journalize and post transactions using special journals and subsidiary ledgers. p. 209

- Use the revenue journal to record all revenues earned from customers on account.
- Use the cash receipts journal to record all collections of cash (regardless of the purpose).
- Use the purchases journal to record all purchases or expenses recorded on account with creditors.
- Use the cash payments journal to record all payments of cash (regardless of the purpose).
- Use the general journal to record unusual, correcting, adjusting, and closing entries even if the business uses special journals.

### LO4 Explain the basic theory of accounting information systems. p. 221

- The underlying assumptions of accounting information systems (AIS) are:
    - Usefulness: to adequately serve users, the AIS should be reliable, relevant, and accurate.
    - Cost effective: the usefulness of the AIS must be balanced against the cost of implementing it.
    - Flexibility: the AIS should meet the changing needs of a growing company.
- The developmental phases of an accounting system are:
    - Analysis: identify the needs of internal and external users.
    - Design: create a system that meets users' needs and determine whether it should be manual or computerized.
    - Implementation: transform a design on paper into a workable, effective, and efficient system.
    - Feedback: monitor the system periodically to ensure that needs are being met as planned.

### LO5 Compare the advantages and disadvantages of manual and computerized accounting information systems. p. 222

- The advantages of using a computerized accounting information system include:
    - Fewer errors.
    - Simplified recordkeeping.
    - Up-to-date balances.
- The disadvantages of using a computerized accounting information system include:
    - Human errors made inputting information.
    - Loss of control over portions of the accounting process.
    - Ease of altering records and the potential for fraud.

# Key Terms

Accounting Information System (AIS) (p. 204)

Accounts Payable Subsidiary Ledger (p. 206)

Accounts Receivable Subsidiary Ledger (p. 206)

Cash Payments Journal (p. 217)

Cash Receipts Journal (p. 212)

Computerized Accounting Information System (p. 204)

Control Account (p. 206)

Crossfoot the Columns (p. 213)

Foot (p. 213)

Manual Accounting Information System (p. 204)

Purchases Journal (p. 216)

Revenue Journal (p. 209)

Special Journal (p. 209)

Subsidiary Ledger (p. 206)

See complete glossary in back of text.

# Questions

1. What is an accounting information system?
2. What is the key difference between manual and computerized accounting information systems?
3. Is it easier or more difficult to find errors in a computerized accounting information system? Why or why not?
4. Which is easier to understand: How a computerized accounting system functions or how a manual accounting system functions? Explain.
5. What is a subsidiary ledger? What type of information is contained in an accounts receivable subsidiary ledger?
6. What is a schedule of accounts receivable? Why is it necessary? When is it generated?
7. What are two advantages of using subsidiary ledgers?
8. Explain what a control account is. Describe each of the two control accounts illustrated in the chapter.
9. When subsidiary accounts are used without special journals, the Ref. column of the general journal will include a checkmark (✓) and an account number (210). What is the purpose of each?
10. What is a special journal? List the four special journals illustrated in the chapter.
11. What is the purpose of the revenue journal? How often are transactions posted to the general ledger Accounts Receivable account from this journal?
12. What is the purpose of the cash receipts journal? What types of transactions are recorded in this journal?
13. What types of transactions are recorded in the purchases journal?
14. What is the purpose of a cash payments journal? Are all cash payments recorded here? Why or why not?
15. Subsidiary ledger postings are made daily regardless of the special journal from which they are posted. Discuss the validity of this statement.
16. What does the following notation in the Ref. column of a special journal mean? CP4
17. Define the terms foot and crossfoot.
18. Is there a need for a general journal when special journals are used by a business? Why or why not?
19. What are the three underlying assumptions of accounting information systems?
20. Briefly describe the four developmental phases of an accounting information system.
21. List two advantages and two disadvantages of using a computerized accounting information system.

# Multiple Choice

1. All individual transactions with customers on account are tracked in the
   a. Accounts payable control account
   b. Accounts payable subsidiary ledger
   c. Accounts receivable control account
   d. Accounts receivable subsidiary ledger

   Quiz 5-1
   www.mhhe.com/LLPW1e

2. A ✓ in the Ref. column of a special journal indicates that
   a. The transaction was posted to the applicable control account.
   b. The transaction was posted to the applicable general ledger account.
   c. The transaction was posted to the applicable subsidiary ledger.
   d. The transaction was not posted.

3. Which of the following is a true statement regarding special journals?
   a. The revenue journal is used for recording cash revenues.
   b. Posting to the subsidiary ledgers is done daily from all special journals and the general journal.
   c. The purchases journal is used for recording cash payments for purchases on account.
   d. In some cases the general journal will be used to record cash receipts.

4. Which of the following statements is false?
   a. The sum of the individual subsidiary accounts balances and the balance in the corresponding control account will not be equal until the end of the accounting period.

   b. Special journals are used to record repetitive, frequent transactions.
   c. Single column special journals must be crossfooted.
   d. The use of the general journal is not eliminated by the use of special journals.

5. In recording transactions to the subsidiary ledger and the control account, which of the following is a true statement?
   a. Transactions are posted daily to the subsidiary ledger and at the end of the accounting period to the control account.
   b. A transaction should be posted only to the subsidiary ledger or the control account; otherwise the transactions will be recorded twice.
   c. Both the control account and the subsidiary ledger should have identical balances at all times.
   d. All of these are true statements regarding the control account and subsidiary ledger.

6. Which of the following is a true statement regarding the use of subsidiary ledgers and special journals?
   a. The use of subsidiary ledgers reduces the number of transactions recorded in the control account.
   b. The use of subsidiary ledgers greatly increases individual efforts because everything is recorded twice.
   c. Special journals contain specific column headings that cannot be changed regardless of the type of business using them.
   d. A general journal is not required when special journals are used.

7. Which of the following is a true statement regarding the use of special journals?

    a. Crossfooting the revenue journal is a useful step that helps ensure errors are detected before amounts are posted to ledger accounts.

    b. Cash transactions can be recorded in any of the four special journals.

    c. All special journals contain at least two amount columns, one for the account debited and one for the account credited.

    d. A separate column is required when specific accounts are impacted that do not have a dedicated column in the special journal.

8. All of the following are true statements regarding posting from special journals except

    a. Postings to the subsidiary ledgers are made on a daily basis from the special journals.

    b. Postings to the control accounts are made at the end of the accounting period from the special journals.

    c. Postings to the subsidiary ledgers and control accounts are made on a daily basis from the general journal.

    d. Postings to the general ledger accounts are made at the end of the accounting period from the Other Accounts column of the special journals.

9. Which of the following is not a step in the development of an accounting information system?

    a. Implementation

    b. Flexibility

    c. Feedback

    d. Analysis

10. Which of the following is not an advantage of using a computerized accounting information system?

    a. Fewer transaction posting errors.

    b. Information input errors.

    c. Up-to-date balances in the subsidiary ledgers and general ledger at all times.

    d. Simplification of recordkeeping.

---

**Solutions to Multiple-Choice Questions**

1. d    2. c    3. b    4. c    5. a    6. a    7. d    8. d    9. b    10. b

---

# Mini Exercises  Available with McGraw-Hill's Homework Manager

**LO2**

**M5-1 Identifying Appropriate Ledger for Specific Accounts**

Identify whether each of the following items would be found in the general ledger or a subsidiary ledger.

1. Accounts Payable—D & E Electric
2. Interest Earned
3. Office Supplies
4. Interest Receivable
5. Salaries Expense
6. Notes Payable
7. Accounts Receivable—Blaugrund
8. Notes Receivable

**LO2**

**M5-2 Determining Balance in Accounts Receivable Control Account**

Determine the balance in the Accounts Receivable control account (No. 110) as of August 31, 2009, by posting the following information about the revenues and receipts on account for Joy, Inc. during August 2009. Assume a balance of $2,000 in Accounts Receivable at July 31, 2009, all owed from Silky Somethings. You may omit any posting references.

|  | Revenues | Receipts |
|---|---|---|
| Lady-Like Apparel | $ 800 | $ 200 |
| Uptown Clothiers | 147 | 147 |
| Silky Somethings | 675 | 375 |
| Luxury Lingerie | 950 | 950 |
| Totals | $ 2,572 | $ 1,672 |

**LO2**

**M5-3 Determining Balance in Accounts Payable Control Account**

Determine the balance in the Accounts Payable control account (No. 210) as of June 30, 2009, by posting the following purchases and payments made on account during June 2009. Assume a balance of $315 in Accounts Payable at May 31, 2009, all due to Midtown Suppliers. You may omit any posting references.

|  | Purchases | Payments |
|---|---|---|
| Classy Supplies, Inc. | $ 215 | $ 112 |
| Indigo Enterprises | 52 | 52 |
| Midtown Suppliers | 410 | 515 |
| Wholesale Suppliers Inc. | 300 | 300 |
| Totals | $ 977 | $ 979 |

## M5-4 Identifying Posting References in a Revenue Journal

LO3

Using the revenue journal below, identify the appropriate posting reference for each of the letters (a – f) shown, as either:

1. An amount posted to the subsidiary ledger.
2. An amount posted to a general ledger account.
3. An amount not posted.

### Revenue Journal                                          Page 6

| Date | Invoice No. | Account Debited | Ref. | Accts Receivable Dr. Fees Earned Cr. |
|---|---|---|---|---|
| Mar. 1 | 255 | Koala Child Care | a | 4,251 |
| 4 | 256 | Blue Bird Day Care | b | 2,795 |
| 15 | 257 | Kindra Care | c | 968 |
| 23 | 258 | Leaning Tree Child Care | d | 10,643 |
| 31 | 259 | Creative Child Care | e | 3,447 |
|  |  |  |  | 22,104 |
|  |  |  |  | f |

## M5-5 Identifying Posting References in a Cash Receipts Journal

LO3

Using the following cash receipts journal, identify the appropriate posting reference for each of the letters (a – j) shown, as either:

1. An amount posted to the subsidiary ledger.
2. An amount posted to a general ledger account.
3. An amount not posted.

### Cash Receipts Journal                                              Page 9

| Date | Account Credited | Ref. | Other Accounts Cr. | Accounts Receivable Cr. | Fees Earned Cr. | Cash Dr. |
|---|---|---|---|---|---|---|
| Mar. 3 | Koala Child Care | a |  | 4,251 |  | 4,251 |
| 9 | Blue Bird Day Care | b |  | 1,000 |  | 1,000 |
| 15 |  | c |  |  | 2,741 | 2,741 |
| 18 | Kindra Care | d |  | 968 |  | 968 |
| 25 | Interest Revenue | e | 222 |  |  | 222 |
| 30 | Leaning Tree Child Care | f |  | 8,643 |  | 8,643 |
|  |  |  | 222 | 14,862 | 2,741 | 17,825 |
|  |  |  | g | h | i | j |

## M5-6 Posting to the Accounts Receivable Control Account

LO2, 3

Using the special journals presented in M5-4 and M5-5, determine the ending balance in the Accounts Receivable control account by posting the appropriate amounts into the following ledger account.

| | Accounts Receivable | | | | Acct. No. 110 |
| --- | --- | --- | --- | --- | --- |
| Date | Item | Ref. | Debit | Credit | Balance |
| Feb 28 | Balance | | | | 0 |
| | | | | | |
| | | | | | |

**LO2, 3**

**M5-7 Posting to the Accounts Receivable Subsidiary Ledger and Preparing a Schedule of Accounts Receivable**

Using the special journals from M5-4 and M5-5, perform the following tasks:

1. Assuming there are no balances in any of the customer accounts at February 28, post the necessary information to each of the customer accounts in the accounts receivable subsidiary ledger and determine the ending balance in each account.
2. Prepare a schedule of accounts receivable.

**LO3**

**M5-8 Identifying the Appropriate Journal for Recording Transactions**

Identify the appropriate journal that would be used to record each of the following transactions:

1. Cash paid for rent
2. Owner contribution of cash to business
3. Purchase of office supplies on account
4. Office supplies returned to supplier on account
5. Cash received for services rendered
6. Owner contribution of furniture to business
7. Cash payments to creditors on account
8. Revenue earned on account
9. Cash received from customers on account
10. Office supplies returned to supplier for cash

**LO3**

**M5-9 Identifying the Appropriate Journal for Recording Transactions**

Identify the appropriate journal that would be used to record each of the following transactions:

1. Revenue earned on account
2. Sales supplies returned to supplier for cash
3. Owner contribution of an automobile to the business
4. Cash payments to creditors on account
5. Purchase of sales supplies on account
6. Cash received for services rendered
7. Sales supplies returned to supplier on account
8. Cash received from customers on account
9. Owner contribution of cash to the business
10. Cash paid for annual fire insurance policy

**LO3**

**M5-10 Identifying the Frequency of Posting from Various Journals**

Freeburrow, Inc., uses a revenue journal, purchases journal, cash receipts journal, cash payments journal, and general journal for recording transactions. For each column of a special journal described below, indicate how often amounts in the column should be posted using the following: (The first one has been done for you.)

D—Daily only

T—In total only at the end of the accounting period

B—Both daily and in total at the end of the accounting period

| Special Journal Column | Frequency of Posting |
| --- | --- |
| 1. Cash column of a cash payments journal | T—In total only at the end of the accounting period |
| 2. Other Accounts column of a cash receipts journal | |
| 3. Column in a single column revenue journal | |
| 4. Cash column of a cash receipts journal | |
| 5. Fees Earned column of a cash receipts journal | |
| 6. Accounts Payable column of a cash payments journal | |
| 7. Other Accounts column of a cash payments journal | |
| 8. All amounts recorded in a general journal | |
| 9. Accounts Receivable column of a cash receipts journal | |
| 10. Other Accounts column of a purchases journal | |

## M5-11 Identifying Columns in Special Journals

LO3

Identify the special journal in which you would find the following column headings. (Note: Some column headings may be found in more than one special journal.)

1. Accounts Receivable Cr.
2. Accounts Payable Cr.
3. Ref.
4. Accts Receivable Dr./Fees Earned Cr.
5. Cash Cr.

6. Cash Dr.
7. Other Accounts Dr.
8. Accounts Payable Dr.
9. Other Accounts Cr.
10. Fees Earned Cr.

## M5-12 Identifying the Underlying Assumptions of Accounting Information Systems

LO4

Indicate whether each of the following statements regarding accounting information systems is true or false.

1. Flexibility in an accounting system is not realistic because accounting information systems are built to meet a specific need and any attempt to alter the system will render it unable to meet these needs.
2. An accounting information system must meet the needs of various users in a sufficient manner.
3. The underlying assumptions of accounting information systems require that an adequate system must be: Cost effective, flexible, and useful.
4. Accounting information systems can be manual or computerized.

## M5-13 Matching Each Developmental Phase of an Accounting Information System with its Description

LO4

Match each developmental phase with the related description by entering the appropriate letter in the space provided.

| Phase | Description |
| --- | --- |
| 1. Implementation | A. Determining whether the company will use a manual or computerized system. |
| 2. Analysis | B. Identifying the needs of internal and external users of the system. |
| 3. Feedback | C. Tweaking the system when portions of the system are unmanageable. |
| 4. Design | D. Transforming the design into a workable, effective, and efficient system. |

## M5-14 Identifying Advantages and Disadvantages of Computerized Accounting Information Systems

LO5

Indicate whether each of the following items is an advantage or disadvantage of using a computerized accounting information system:

| Answer | Phase |
| --- | --- |
| _____ | 1. Lack of control over portions of the accounting procedures |
| _____ | 2. Simplification of recordkeeping |
| _____ | 3. Up-to-date balances in the general ledger and subsidiary ledgers |
| _____ | 4. Ease of altering records |
| _____ | 5. Information input errors |
| _____ | 6. Fewer posting errors |

## Exercises  Available with McGraw-Hill's Homework Manager

### E5-1 Determining Account Balance in Accounts Receivable Control Account and Explaining How Items are Posted from Special Journals

LO2, 3

Cluney Company uses the four special journals described in this chapter. On October 31, the balance in the Accounts Receivable control account was $50,000.

After footing and crossfooting the special journals for November, the following column totals were obtained from the special journals:

| | |
|---|---|
| Revenue journal | $710,000 |
| Cash receipts journal (Accounts Receivable Cr. column) | 652,000 |

**Required:**

1. Determine the balance in the Accounts Receivable control account as of November 30 after all special journal postings have been made.
2. The total amount from the revenue journal of $710,000 is posted to which account(s) in the general ledger?

**LO2, 3**

**E5-2 Determining Account Balance in Accounts Payable Control Account and Explaining How Items are Posted from Special Journals**

Georgy Company uses the four special journals described in this chapter. On January 31, the balance in the Accounts Payable control account was $84,000.

After footing and crossfooting the special journals for February, the following column totals were obtained from the special journals:

| | |
|---|---|
| Purchases journal (Accounts Payable column) | $ 278,000 |
| Cash payments journal (Accounts Payable column) | 283,000 |

**Required:**

1. Determine the balance in the Accounts Payable control account as of February 28 after all special journal postings have been made.
2. The total amount from the Accounts Payable column in the cash payments journal of $283,000 is posted to which account(s) in the general ledger?

**LO2, 3**

**E5-3 Identifying Transactions in Accounts Receivable and Accounts Payable Ledgers**

Various debit and credit transactions are presented in the following subsidiary ledger accounts:

*Example 1:*

Crystal Products, Inc.

| Date | Account | Ref. | Debit | Credit | Balance |
|---|---|---|---|---|---|
| Jul. 31 | Bal. | | | | 30,000 |
| Aug. 31 | (a) | CR5 | | 30,000 | 0 |
| Aug. 31 | (b) | R2 | 27,000 | | 27,000 |

*Example 2:*

Superior Supplies, Inc.

| Date | Account | Ref. | Debit | Credit | Balance |
|---|---|---|---|---|---|
| Jul. 31 | Bal. | | | | 16,000 |
| Aug.  8 | (c) | P4 | | 21,500 | 37,500 |
| Aug. 19 | (d) | G1 | 1,500 | | 36,000 |
| Aug. 30 | (e) | CP9 | 16,000 | | 20,000 |

**Required:**

1. Identify the source of each transaction (a)–(e).
2. Describe each transaction (a)–(e).
3. Based on your responses for requirements 1 and 2, indicate whether Example 1 is taken from an accounts receivable subsidiary ledger or an accounts payable subsidiary ledger.

4.  Based on your responses for requirements 1 and 2, indicate whether Example 2 is taken from an accounts receivable subsidiary ledger or an accounts payable subsidiary ledger.

**E5-4 Identifying Proper Posting Treatment for Transactions in the Cash Payments Journal**   LO2, 3
The following cash payments journal was taken from the records of Lemski Corporation for the month of February:

| | | Cash Payments Journal | | | | Page 1 |
|---|---|---|---|---|---|---|
| Date | Check No. | Account Debited | Ref. | Other Accounts Dr. | Accounts Payable Dr. | Cash Cr. |
| Feb. 8 | 361 | Sales Supplies | (a) | 900 | | 900 |
| 14 | 362 | Utilities Expense | (b) | 1,450 | | 1,450 |
| 21 | 363 | Craig Company | (c) | | 12,000 | 12,000 |
| 25 | 364 | Rent Expense | (d) | 4,800 | | 4,800 |
| 28 | 365 | Wages Expense | (e) | 2,400 | | 2,400 |
| | | Totals | | 9,550 | 12,000 | 21,550 |
| | | | | (f) | (g) | (h) |

*Required:*
For each of the posting references (a)–(h), identify which of the  following is the appropriate treatment of the item:

1.  A posting to a general ledger account.
2.  A posting to a subsidiary ledger account.
3.  No posting is required.

**E5-5 Matching Transactions to Revenue, Cash Receipts, and General Journals**   LO3
Indicate the journal in which each of the following transactions would be recorded by writing the letter of the appropriate journal in the space provided.

| Transaction | Journal |
|---|---|
| ___ 1.  Provided services on account. | A.  Revenue journal |
| ___ 2.  Investment of cash by the owner. | B.  Cash receipts journal |
| ___ 3.  Received cash from customer on account. | C.  General journal |
| ___ 4.  Provided services for cash. | |
| ___ 5.  Received cash from customer for services not yet rendered. | |
| ___ 6.  Recorded depreciation at the end of the accounting period. | |

**E5-6 Matching Transactions to Purchases, Cash Payments, and General Journals**   LO3
Indicate the journal in which each of the following transactions would be recorded by writing the letter of the appropriate journal in the space provided.

| Transaction | Journal |
|---|---|
| ___ 1.  Recorded office supplies used at the end of the accounting period. | A.  Purchases journal |
| ___ 2.  Purchased office furniture with a promissory note. | B.  Cash payments journal |
| ___ 3.  Paid Rent for three months in advance. | C.  General journal |
| ___ 4.  Paid for supplies purchased on account. | |
| ___ 5.  Purchased supplies on account. | |
| ___ 6.  Paid a one-year insurance policy in advance. | |

**LO3**

**E5-7 Matching Transactions to Appropriate Journal for Revenue- and Purchase-Related Transactions**

Indicate the journal in which each of the following transactions would be recorded by writing the letter of the appropriate journal in the space provided.

| Transaction | Journal |
|---|---|
| _____ 1. Paid for office equipment purchased on account. | A. Revenue journal |
| _____ 2. Provided services for customer for cash. | B. Cash receipts journal |
| _____ 3. Returned office supplies purchased on account. | C. Purchases journal |
| _____ 4. Accrued salaries for the month of December. | D. Cash payments journal |
| _____ 5. Collected cash from customers on account. | E. General journal |
| _____ 6. Provided services for customer on account. | |
| _____ 7. Recorded depreciation on office equipment. | |
| _____ 8. Purchased office supplies on account. | |

**LO3**

**E5-8 Recording Transactions in the Revenue Journal**

Revenue-related transactions for King Enterprises are presented for the month of June, 2009.

Jun.  1  Issued invoice No. 101 to Rice Company; $1,600.

    8  Issued invoice No. 102 to Barney's Bakes; $2,100.

   11  Received cash from Rice Corporation on account; $1,444.

   17  Issued invoice No. 103 to Lola, Inc.; $5,600.

   20  Issued invoice No. 104 to Tony Company; $3,300.

*Required:*

Prepare a revenue journal with one column for dollar amounts. Assume no postings have been made to any subsidiary or general ledger accounts.

**LO3**

**E5-9 Recording Transactions in the Revenue Journal**

Revenue-related transactions for Prince Ltd. are presented for the month of August, 2009.

Aug. 5  Issued invoice No. 520 to Duke Company; $3,900.

    9  Issued invoice No. 521 to Princess Rakes; $5,700.

   12  Issued invoice No. 522 to Joker Corporation; $2,200.

   20  Received cash from Duke Company on account; $3,900.

   25  Issued invoice No. 523 to Knave Company; $4,100.

*Required:*

Prepare a revenue journal with one column for dollar amounts. Assume no postings have been made to any subsidiary or general ledger accounts.

**LO2, 3**

**E5-10 Posting from the Revenue Journal to Control and Subsidiary Accounts**

The revenue journal for Jungle Fever, Inc. is presented for the month of March 2009.

| Revenue Journal | | | | Page 12 |
|---|---|---|---|---|
| Date | Invoice No. | Account Debited | Ref. | Accts Receivable Dr. Fees Earned Cr. |
| Mar. 5 | 1001 | Macaw Incorporated | | 10,200 |
| 9 | 1002 | Boa, Ltd. | | 9,400 |
| 18 | 1003 | Macaw Incorporated | | 13,600 |
| 22 | 1004 | Chimply Awesome, Inc. | | 1,500 |
| 31 | 1005 | Boa, Ltd. | | 18,000 |
| | | Total | | |

*Required:*

1. Complete the revenue journal with a total.
2. Post the transactions in Jungle Fever's revenue journal to the Accounts Receivable control account (No. 110) and the related subsidiary ledger for the month of March. Use appropriate references, dates, and frequency of posting rules described in the chapter. Assume there was no previous balance in Accounts Receivable.

## E5-11 Recording Transactions in the Cash Receipts Journal          LO3

Transactions involving cash receipts for Percy Enterprises are presented for the month of July 2008.

Jul.  8   Received cash from Starrburst, Inc., for services rendered; $5,800.
     11   Received cash from Haute Tamales Corporation on account; $1,950.
     24   Received cash from Rollo Company on account; $200.
     29   Received cash from Blow Popps Enterprises for services rendered; $350.
     31   Received cash for supplies sold to employees at cost; $25.

*Required:*
Prepare a cash receipts journal for these transactions. The cash receipts journal should contain the following headings: Date; Account Credited; Ref.; Other Accounts Cr.; Accounts Receivable Cr.; Fees Earned Cr.; and Cash Dr. Assume no postings have been made to any subsidiary or general ledger accounts.

## E5-12 Recording Transactions in the Cash Receipts Journal          LO3

Transactions involving cash receipts for Prog Company are presented for the month of April 2008.

Apr.  2   Received cash from Gorm, Inc., on account; $2,800.
      6   Received cash from Slock Corporation for services rendered; $400.
     12   Received cash for supplies sold to employees at cost; $15.
     22   Received cash from Tring Company on account; $3,600.
     27   Received cash from Drong Enterprises for services rendered; $750.

*Required:*
Prepare a cash receipts journal for these transactions. The cash receipts journal should contain the following headings: Date; Account Credited; Ref.; Other Accounts Cr.; Accounts Receivable Cr.; Fees Earned Cr.; and Cash Dr. Assume no postings have been made to any subsidiary or general ledger accounts.

## E5-13 Posting from the Cash Receipts Journal to Control Account and Subsidiary Ledger          LO2, 3

The cash receipts journal for Jewel Company is presented for the month of November 2008.

| | Cash Receipts Journal | | | | | Page 9 |
|---|---|---|---|---|---|---|
| Date | Account Credited | Ref. | Other Accounts Cr. | Accounts Receivable Cr. | Fees Earned Cr. | Cash Dr. |
| Nov. 3 | Sapphire Enterprises | | | 800 | | 800 |
| 10 | Diamond Corporation | | | 1,300 | | 1,300 |
| 17 | | | | | 15,800 | 15,800 |
| 21 | Sapphire Enterprises | | | 1,600 | | 1,600 |
| 28 | Interest Revenue | | 180 | | | 180 |
| 30 | Diamond Corporation | | | 7,700 | | 7,700 |
| | Totals | | | | | |

*Required:*

1. Complete the cash receipts journal with totals.
2. Post the transactions shown in Jewel Company's cash receipts journal to the subsidiary ledger accounts, as well as the affected general ledger accounts for the month of November. Use appropriate references, dates, and frequency of posting rules described in the chapter. October 31

balances: Diamond Corporation—$12,200 and Sapphire Enterprises—$3,400. Use the following general ledger accounts and balances:

| Account No. | Account Title | Oct. 31 Balance | Account No. | Account Title | Oct. 31 Balance |
|---|---|---|---|---|---|
| 105 | Cash | $12,000 | 410 | Fees Earned | $2,400 |
| 110 | Accounts Receivable | 15,600 | 710 | Interest Revenue | 800 |

**LO3**

**E5-14 Recording Transactions in the Revenue and Cash Receipts Journals**

Revenue-related transactions for Foods Enterprises are presented for the month of January, 2008.

Jan. 1   Issued invoice No. 601 to Cheese Company; $1,600.
     4   Received cash from Angus, Inc., for services rendered; $800.
    12   Issued invoice No. 602 to Rogers Steaks; $2,100.
    16   Received cash from Cheese Company on account; $1,444.
    20   Issued invoice No. 603 to Bean, Inc.; $5,600.
    23   Issued invoice No. 604 to Noodle Company; $3,300.
    26   Received cash from Noodle Company on account; $600.
    31   Received cash for supplies sold to employees at cost; $30.

*Required:*

Prepare a revenue journal and a cash receipts journal for these transactions. The cash receipts journal should contain the following headings: Date; Account Credited; Ref.; Other Accounts Cr.; Accounts Receivable Cr.; Fees Earned Cr.; and Cash Dr. Assume no postings have been made to any subsidiary or general ledger accounts.

**LO3**

**E5-15 Recording Transactions in the Revenue and Cash Receipts Journals**

Revenue-related transactions for Spot Enterprises are presented for the month of September 2009.

Sep. 2   Received cash from Angrila Corporation for services rendered; $60.
     4   Issued invoice No. 421 to Rice Company; $2,500.
    11   Issued invoice No. 422 to Barney's Bakes; $1,400.
    16   Received cash from Holt, Inc., for services rendered; $1,100.
    19   Issued invoice No. 423 to Lola, Inc.; $4,200.
    22   Issued invoice No. 424 to Tony Company; $2,200.
    24   Received cash for supplies sold to employees at cost; $40.
    30   Received cash from Tony Company on account; $1,000.

*Required:*

Prepare a revenue journal and a cash receipts journal for these transactions. The cash receipts journal should contain the following headings: Date; Account Credited; Ref.; Other Accounts Cr.; Accounts Receivable Cr.; Fees Earned Cr.; and Cash Dr. Assume no postings have been made to any subsidiary or general ledger accounts.

**LO3**

**E5-16 Recording Transactions in the Purchases Journal**

Purchase-related transactions for Topo Company are presented for the month of February 2009.

Feb. 1   Received a bill from Rob's Rentals for February rent; $2,400.
     2   Purchased office equipment on account from Eddie's Equipment; $6,000.
     9   Received a bill from Irma's Insurance for a one-year flood insurance policy; $4,000.
    10   Purchased office supplies on account from Otto's Supplies; $360.
    16   Received a bill for cleaning services from Jane's Janitorial; $300.
    22   Received a bill for office supplies from Office Mart; $225.

*Required:*

Prepare a purchases journal for these transactions. The purchases journal should contain the following headings: Date; Account Credited; Ref.; Accounts Payable Cr.; Office Supplies Dr.; Other Accounts Dr.; Ref.; and Amount. Assume no postings have been made to any subsidiary or general ledger accounts.

**E5-17 Recording Transactions in the Purchases Journal**                                    LO3

Purchase-related transactions for Gigio Company are presented for the month of May 2009.

May.  2    Received a bill from State Barn Insurance for a two-year fire insurance policy; $4,980.
       7    Purchased store supplies on account from Supplies R Us; $250.
      12    Received a bill from Mary Maids for cleaning services; $400.
      25    Received a bill for advertising from The Daily Grind; $600.
      30    Purchased store equipment on account from Equipment Wholesalers; $5,000.
      31    Received a bill from Alice's Archives for advertising placed in their magazine; $1,200.

*Required:*

Prepare a purchases journal for these transactions. The purchases journal should contain the following headings: Date; Account Credited; Ref.; Accounts Payable Cr.; Advertising Expense Dr.; Other Accounts Dr.; Ref.; and Amount. Use appropriate references and dates, and assume no postings have been made to any subsidiary or general ledger accounts.

**E5-18 Posting from the Purchases Journal to Control Account and Subsidiary Ledger**       LO2, 3

The Purchases Journal for Crown Company is presented for the month of August 2009.

Purchases Journal                                                        Page 3

| Date | Account Credited | Ref. | Accounts Payable Cr. | Delivery Expense Dr. | Other Accounts Dr. Accounts | Ref. | Amount |
|------|------------------|------|----------------------|----------------------|-----------------------------|------|--------|
| Aug. 1 | Rent and Insurance, Inc. | | 3,500 | | Prepaid Insurance | | 3,500 |
| 8 | Danny's Deliveries | | 145 | 145 | | | |
| 17 | Super Supplies | | 200 | | Office Supplies | | 200 |
| 24 | The Daily Herald | | 350 | | Advertising Expense | | 350 |
| 29 | Danny's Deliveries | | 475 | 475 | | | |
| 30 | Rent and Insurance, Inc. | | 2,500 | — | Rent Expense | | 2,500 |
| | Totals | | 7,170 | | | | |

*Required:*

1.  Complete the purchases journal with totals.

2.  Post the transactions shown in Crown Company's purchases journal to the subsidiary ledger, as well as any affected general ledger accounts for the month of August. Assume no beginning balances in any accounts. Use appropriate references, dates, and frequency of posting rules described in the chapter. Use the following accounts: 115—Office Supplies; 140—Prepaid Insurance; 210—Accounts Payable; 520—Advertising Expense; 525—Delivery Expense; 615—Rent Expense.

**E5-19 Recording Transactions in the Cash Payments Journal**                                LO3

Transactions involving cash payments for Klink Corporation are presented for the month of November 2009.

Nov.  5    Issued check No. 330 to Supply Outfitters on account; $450.
      10    Issued check No. 331 to Southern Utilities for gas and electric; $725.
      19    Issued check No. 332 to Phisher Company on account; $650.
      26    Issued check No. 333 to Season's Deal on account; $1,400.
      29    Issued check No. 334 to secretary for November wages; $1,200.
      30    Issued check No. 335 to Allgreat Insurance for a one-year fire insurance policy; $2,400.

*Required:*

Prepare a cash payments journal for these transactions. The cash payments journal should contain the following headings: Date; Check No.; Account Debited; Ref.; Other Accounts Dr.; Accounts Payable Dr.; and Cash Cr. Assume no postings have been made to any subsidiary or general ledger accounts.

**LO3**    **E5-20 Recording Transactions in the Cash Payments Journal**

Transactions involving cash payments for Housin Company are presented for the month of January 2009.

Jan.  2    Issued check No. 801 to Mutual of Omaha for a one-year insurance policy; $1,600.
     10    Issued check No. 802 to Sliver Enterprises on account; $950.
     17    Issued check No. 803 to Digger Company on account; $1,100.
     23    Issued check No. 804 to Northern Utilities for gas and electric; $820.
     27    Issued check No. 805 to Wholesale Sellers on account; $5,000.
     30    Issued check No. 806 to secretary for January wages; $1,800.

*Required:*

Prepare a cash payments journal for these transactions. The cash payments journal should contain the following headings: Date; Check No.; Account Debited; Ref.; Other Accounts Dr.; Accounts Payable Dr.; and Cash Cr. Assume no postings have been made to any subsidiary or general ledger accounts.

**LO2, 3**    **E5-21 Posting from the Cash Payments Journal to Control Account and Subsidiary Ledger**

The cash payments journal for Shrimp Enterprises is presented for the month of April 2009.

### Cash Payments Journal                                                                                 Page 6

| Date | Check No. | Account Debited | Ref. | Other Accounts Dr. | Accounts Payable Dr. | Cash Cr. |
|------|-----------|-----------------|------|--------------------|----------------------|----------|
| Apr.  2 | 521 | Store Supplies | | 500 | | 500 |
| 8 | 522 | Crayfish Corporation | | | 750 | 750 |
| 13 | 523 | Fishing Suppliers, Inc. | | | 2,100 | 2,100 |
| 20 | 524 | Advertising Expense | | 260 | | 260 |
| 26 | 525 | Lobsters, Ltd. | | | 825 | 825 |
| 29 | 526 | Wages Expense | | 910 | | 910 |
| | | Totals | | | | |

*Required:*

1. Complete the cash payments journal with totals.
2. Post the transactions shown in Shrimp Enterprises cash payments journal to the subsidiary ledger accounts, as well as the affected general ledger accounts for the month of April. Use appropriate references, dates, and frequency of posting rules described in the chapter. March 31 balances: Crayfish Corporation—$1,750; Fishing Suppliers, Inc.—$2,100; and Lobsters, Ltd.—$1,000. Use the following general ledger accounts and balances:

| Account No. | Account Title | Mar. 31 Balance | Account No. | Account Title | Mar. 31 Balance |
|-------------|---------------|-----------------|-------------|---------------|-----------------|
| 105 | Cash | $9,000 | 510 | Wages Expense | $2,400 |
| 115 | Store Supplies | 250 | 520 | Advertising Expense | 800 |
| 210 | Accounts Payable | 4,850 | | | |

**LO2, 3**    **E5-22 Recording Transactions in the Purchases and Cash Payments Journals**

Transactions for Twilight Company are presented for the month of October 2009.

Oct.  3    Purchased postage meters on account from Potter's Postage Equipment; $1,000.
     8    Issued check No. 1101 to Everything Postal for packaging supplies; $120.
    12    Purchased bubble wrap on account from Everything Postal; $160.
    18    Issued check No. 1102 to Southern Utilities for gas and electric; $155.
    20    Received a bill for packaging supplies from Postal Suppliers; $80.
    25    Received a bill for advertising charges from The Daily Post; $75.
    31    Issued check No. 1103 to Everything Postal on account; $100.

*Required:*

Prepare a purchases journal and a cash payments journal for these transactions. The purchases journal should contain the following headings: Date; Account Credited; Ref.; Accounts Payable Cr.; Packaging Supplies Dr.; Other Accounts Dr.; Ref.; and Amount. The cash payments journal should contain the following headings: Date; Check No.; Account Debited; Ref.; Other Accounts Dr.; Accounts Payable Dr.; and Cash Cr. Assume no postings have been made to any subsidiary or general ledger accounts.

**E5-23 Recording Transactions in the Purchases and Cash Payments Journals**    LO3

Purchase-related transactions for Tofflet Enterprises are presented for the month of February 2009.

Feb. 1   Issued check No. 651 to Rentals R Us for February rent; $3,400.
  6   Purchased supplies on account from Sophie's Sundries; $200.
  11   Received a bill for advertising from The Daily Bugle; $150.
  15   Purchased equipment from Office Suppliers on account; $2,150.
  21   Issued check No. 652 to Sophie's Sundries for supplies; $95.
  24   Received a bill from Public Gas and Oil for gas bill; $400.
  28   Issued check No. 653 to Office Suppliers on account; $1,000.

*Required:*

Prepare a purchases journal and a cash payments journal for these transactions. The purchases journal should contain the following headings: Date; Account Credited; Ref.; Accounts Payable Cr.; General Supplies Dr.; Other Accounts Dr.; Ref.; and Amount. The cash payments journal should contain the following headings: Date; Check No.; Account Debited; Ref.; Other Accounts Dr.; Accounts Payable Dr.; and Cash Cr. Assume no postings have been made to any subsidiary or general ledger accounts.

**E5-24 Recording Transactions in the General Journal**    LO3

Various purchase-related transactions for GenaFlynn, Inc., are presented for the month of December 2009.

Dec. 2   Returned supplies to Suppliers Incorporated on account; $30.
  9   Received a credit from The Daily Journal for an advertising billing error; $40.
  16   Purchased a delivery truck by issuing a note payable to Dodgge, Inc.; $40,000.
  19   Received a check from The Supply Hut for amount overpaid on account; $15.

*Required:*

Prepare a general journal for these transactions. Assume no postings have been made to any subsidiary or general ledger accounts. If a transaction would not be recorded in the general journal, indicate which special journal it should be recorded in (if any).

**E5-25 Recording Transactions in the General Journal**    LO3

Purchase-related transactions for Cryogelf Limited are presented for the month of January 2009.

Jan. 6   Purchased office equipment by issuing a $10,000 note payable to Equipers, Inc.
  12   Returned office supplies to Total Office on account; $50.
  22   Received a credit from Delivery Enterprises for error on delivery bill; $25.
  31   Received a check from the National Inquiry for an amount that Cryogelf overpaid on account; $20.

*Required:*

Prepare a general journal for these transactions. Assume no postings have been made to any subsidiary or general ledger accounts. If a transaction would not be recorded in the general journal, indicate which special journal it should be recorded in (if any).

**E5-26 Posting from the General Journal to Control Account and Subsidiary Ledger**    LO3

Purchase-related transactions for Katanga Company are presented for the month of July 2009.

**General Journal**    Page 1

| Date | Account Titles | Ref. | Debit | Credit |
|---|---|---|---|---|
| Jul. 8 | Accounts Payable—All Country Insurance | | 400 | |
| | Insurance Expense | | | 400 |
| | | | | |
| 16 | Furniture and Fixtures | | 6,000 | |
| | Notes Payable | | | 6,000 |
| | | | | |
| 29 | Accounts Payable—Store Suppliers, Inc. | | 12 | |
| | Store Supplies | | | 12 |

*Required:*

Post the transactions shown in Katanga Company's general journal to the subsidiary ledger accounts, as well as the affected general ledger accounts for the month of July. Use appropriate references, dates, and frequency of posting rules described in the chapter. June 30 balances: All Country Insurance—$1,000 and Store Suppliers, Inc.—$140. Use the following general ledger accounts and balances:

| Account No. | Account Tittle | June 30 Balance | Account No. | Account Tittle | June 30 Balance |
|---|---|---|---|---|---|
| 115 | Store Supplies | $ 450 | 250 | Notes Payable | $2,400 |
| 160 | Furniture and Fixtures | 4,000 | 650 | Insurance Expense | 2,100 |
| 210 | Accounts Payable | 1,140 | | | |

**LO2, 3**    **E5-27 Correcting Errors in Accounts Payable Subsidiary Ledger**

After all end-of-period postings were made, the accounts payable subsidiary ledger and the Accounts Payable control account for Kramar Enterprises did not agree. After investigating the problem, it was determined that the control account balance of $178,230 was correct. Use the accounts payable subsidiary ledger that follows to perform each of the requirements.

*Required:*

1. As the new accounts payable clerk for Kramar Enterprises, you have been asked to find the errors made by the previous clerk and identify any corrections that should be made. Write a brief memo to Mary Cliff, the head bookkeeper, listing the errors that were made.

2. After listing the corrections necessary, prove that the accounts payable subsidiary ledger agrees with the Accounts Payable control account by preparing a schedule of accounts payable.

## ACCOUNTS PAYABLE SUBSIDIARY LEDGER

**Dean Disposables**

| Date | Item | Ref. | Debit | Credit | Balance |
|---|---|---|---|---|---|
| Jul. 31 | Bal. | | | | 14,000 |
| Aug. 1 | | CP8 | 14,000 | | 28,000 |
| 18 | | P4 | | 65,000 | 93,000 |

**Office Suppliers**

| Date | Item | Ref. | Debit | Credit | Balance |
|---|---|---|---|---|---|
| Jul. 31 | Bal. | | | | 30,110 |
| Aug. 10 | | CP8 | 30,110 | | 60,220 |
| 30 | | P4 | | 25,000 | 35,220 |

**Nolan Consulting Services**

| Date | Item | Ref. | Debit | Credit | Balance |
|---|---|---|---|---|---|
| Jul. 31 | Bal. | | | | 9,555 |
| Aug. 12 | | CP8 | 9,555 | | 0 |
| 29 | | P4 | | 35,010 | 35,010 |

**Reliable Equipment**

| Date | Item | Ref. | Debit | Credit | Balance |
|------|------|------|-------|--------|---------|
| Jul. 31 | Bal. | | | | 72,220 |
| Aug. 11 | | P4 | | 41,000 | 51,220 |
| 26 | | CP8 | 60,000 | | 111,220 |

**Specialists Inc.**

| Date | Item | Ref. | Debit | Credit | Balance |
|------|------|------|-------|--------|---------|
| Jul. 31 | Bal. | | | | 6,000 |
| Aug. 11 | | P4 | | 33,000 | 39,000 |
| 26 | | CP6 | 39,000 | | 0 |

# Problems—Set A  Available with McGraw-Hill's Homework Manager

## PA5-1 Matching Terminology with Definitions LO1, 2, 3, 4

Following are the terms and definitions covered in Chapter 5. Match each term with its definition by entering the appropriate letter in the space provided. Use one letter for each blank.

| Terms | Definitions |
|-------|-------------|
| ____ 1. Crossfoot | A. A general ledger account that summarizes all transactions occurring in its related subsidiary account. |
| ____ 2. Special journal | |
| ____ 3. Accounts receivable subsidiary ledger | B. Used to record services rendered to customers on account. |
| ____ 4. Manual accounting information system | C. Used to record all correcting, adjusting, closing, and unusual entries that cannot be recorded elsewhere. |
| ____ 5. Revenue journal | D. The steps in the accounting cycle are performed with the aid of general ledger software. |
| ____ 6. Accounting information system | E. Used to record all cash collections in a business, regardless of the reason for the collection. |
| ____ 7. Control account | F. Individual transactions with creditors on account are collected and maintained. |
| ____ 8. General ledger | G. A collection of all accounts used in a business. |
| ____ 9. Foot | H. Collect, classify, summarize, and report the financial information about a business to interested parties. |
| ____ 10. Cash payments journal | |
| ____ 11. Computerized accounting system | I. Used to record all transactions involving the disbursement of cash from a business. |
| | J. Used to record similar types of transactions in one convenient place. |
| ____ 12. Purchases journal | K. Verifies that the total amounts of the debit columns equal the total amounts of the credit columns in a special journal. |
| ____ 13. Accounts payable subsidiary ledger | L. Used to record all purchases or expenses that are made on account. |
| ____ 14. General journal | M. Individual transactions with customers on account are collected and maintained. |
| ____ 15. Cash receipts journal | N. The steps in the accounting cycle are performed by hand. |
| | O. Adding up the dollar amounts in a column. |

LO2, 3

**PA5-2 Journalizing Transactions in the Cash Receipts Journal; Posting to Control Account and Subsidiary Ledger**

Purple Pirates (owned by George Sparrow) performs magic tricks and other entertainment at children's birthday parties. The following selected accounts are taken from the chart of accounts.

| | | | | |
|---|---|---|---|---|
| 105 | Cash | | 310 | George Sparrow, Capital |
| 110 | Accounts Receivable | | 410 | Fees Earned |
| 115 | Supplies | | | |

On September 30, 2009, the accounts receivable subsidiary ledger had the following balances: G. Bridger $200; T. Mato $1,000; H. Potter $800; and JB Rabitt $600. The following transactions occurred during October:

Oct.  2   Received cash from JB Rabitt as payment in full on his account.

    4   Received check from T. Mato for $700 as partial payment on his account.

    10   George Sparrow invested an additional $6,000 into the business.

    16   Performed party services for a client and received immediate cash payment of $500.

    20   Received check from H. Potter as payment in full on his account.

    25   Received check from G. Bridger for $100 as partial payment on her account.

    30   Received cash refund for supplies returned to supplier for $65 because they were defective. (Hint: Reduce the Supplies account for the cost of the returned supplies.)

***Required:***

1.   Journalize the transactions for October in a four-column cash receipts journal using the following column headings: Date; Account Credited; Ref.; Other Accounts Cr.; Accounts Receivable Cr.; Fees Earned Cr.; and Cash Dr.

2.   Set up the Accounts Receivable control account and the individual accounts receivable subsidiary ledger accounts by placing the September 30 balances in them.

3.   Post the October transactions to the control account and the subsidiary ledger accounts in the manner described in the chapter.

4.   Prepare a schedule that proves that the balances in the control account and the subsidiary ledger accounts are equal.

LO2, 3

**PA5-3 Journalizing Transactions in the Cash Payments Journal; Posting to Control Account and Subsidiary Ledger**

Sally's Sewing does alterations and creates custom fashions for its customers. The following selected accounts were taken from its chart of accounts.

| | | | | |
|---|---|---|---|---|
| 105 | Cash | | 210 | Accounts Payable |
| 115 | Sewing Supplies | | 311 | Sally Sartoria, Drawing |
| 145 | Prepaid Rent | | 510 | Salaries Expense |
| 160 | Furniture & Fixtures | | | |

On January 31, 2009, the accounts payable subsidiary ledger had the following balances: Lacey Gayne $300; Ted Knee $800; Lars Pyn $1,100; and Tammy Seem $2,100. The following transactions occurred during February:

Feb.  3   Paid Ted Knee balance due on account, using check #103.

    4   Bought needles, pins, seam rippers, etc. from Tammy Seem for $230, using check #104.

    11   Purchased a new sofa for her lobby; $1,800, using check #105.

    13   Paid Lars Pyn balance due on account, using check #106.

    16   Paid Lacey Gayne balance due on account, using check #107.

    17   Sally Sartoria withdrew $2,000 cash for her personal use, using check #108.

    20   Paid Tammy Seem $400 as a partial payment on the account, using check #109.

    28   Paid monthly salary to her employee—Suzee Seemstress; $1,200, using check #110.

    28   Paid four months' rent in advance; $4,000, using check #111.

*Required:*

1. Journalize the transactions for February in a cash payments journal using the following column headings: Date; Check No.; Account Debited; Ref.; Other Accounts Dr.; Accounts Payable Dr.; and Cash Cr.

2. Set up the Accounts Payable control account and the individual accounts payable subsidiary ledger accounts by placing the January 31 balances in them.

3. Post the February transactions to the control account and the subsidiary ledger accounts in the manner described in the chapter.

4. Prepare a schedule that proves that the balances in the control account and the subsidiary ledger accounts are equal.

**PA5-4 Posting Accounts Receivable and Accounts Payable Transactions and Preparing Schedules of Accounts Receivable and Accounts Payable**

LO2, 3

www.mhhe.com/LLPW1e

The Accounts Receivable control account for the Dupree Company as of December 31, 2008, was $10,284, consisting of the following balances: $8,652 from Doe, Inc., and $1,632 from Dosey, Inc. The Accounts Payable control account as of December 31, 2008, was $3,658, consisting of the following balance: $3,658 Redhouse, Inc. Dupree Company's revenue journal, cash receipts journal, purchases journal, and cash payments journal for January 2009 are as follows:

### Revenue Journal                                                                 Page 2

| Date | Invoice No. | Account Debited | Ref. | Accts Receivable Dr. Fees Earned Cr. |
|------|-------------|-----------------|------|--------------------------------------|
| Jan. 1 | 165 | Ella Company | | 4,176 |
| 10 | 166 | Doe, Inc. | | 9,410 |
| 14 | 167 | Mand Company | | 1,400 |
| 23 | 168 | Promenade Company | | 7,823 |
| 31 | 169 | Dosey, Inc. | | 2,011 |

### Cash Receipts Journal                                                           Page 7

| Date | Account Credited | Ref. | Other Accounts Cr. | Accounts Receivable Cr. | Fees Earned Cr. | Cash Dr. |
|------|------------------|------|--------------------|-------------------------|-----------------|----------|
| Jan. 5 | Dosey, Inc. | | | 1,632 | | 1,632 |
| 12 | Ella Company | | | 4,176 | | 4,176 |
| 16 | Doe, Inc. | | | 8,652 | | 8,652 |
| 25 | Mand Company | | | 1,400 | | 1,400 |
| 30 | Promenade Company | | | 3,000 | | 3,000 |

### Purchases Journal                                                               Page 1

| Date | Account Credited | Ref. | Accounts Payable Cr. | Supplies Dr. | Other Accounts Dr. Accounts | Ref. | Amount |
|------|------------------|------|----------------------|--------------|-----------------------------|------|--------|
| Jan. 1 | Gonzales Co. | | 1,140 | | Advertising Expense | | 1,140 |
| 1 | Simms Company | | 2,388 | | Rent Expense | | 2,388 |
| 3 | Nguyen Inc. | | 654 | 654 | | | |
| 8 | Tidwell Enterprises | | 3,858 | | Furniture & Fixtures | | 3,858 |
| 20 | Redhouse Inc. | | 295 | 295 | | | |

### Cash Payments Journal                                                        Page 1

| Date | Check No. | Account Debited | Ref. | Other Accounts Dr. | Accounts Payable Dr. | Cash Cr. |
|------|-----------|-----------------|------|--------------------|----------------------|----------|
| Jan. 1 | 101 | Prepaid Insurance | | 6,000 | | 6,000 |
| 2 | 102 | Rent Expense | | 3,450 | | 3,450 |
| 18 | 103 | Simms Company | | | 2,388 | 2,388 |
| 20 | 104 | Tidwell Enterprises | | | 3,858 | 3,858 |
| 29 | 105 | Gallagher, Drawing | | 2,000 | | 2,000 |
| 31 | 106 | Nguyen, Inc. | | | 654 | 654 |

*Required:*

1. Set up the Accounts Receivable (No. 110) and Accounts Payable (No. 210) control accounts as well as the corresponding individual subsidiary ledger accounts by placing the December 31 balances in them.

2. Foot and crossfoot the four special journals and post the appropriate information into the subsidiary ledger accounts and control accounts for Accounts Receivable and Accounts Payable in the manner described in the chapter. Do not post to any other general ledger accounts.

3. Prepare schedules of accounts receivable and accounts payable for Dupree Company as of January 31, 2009.

**LO2, 3**

www.mhhe.com/LLPW1e

**PA5-5 Journalizing Transactions in the Revenue Journal, Purchases Journal, and General Journal; Posting to Subsidiary Ledgers and Control Accounts**

The following selected accounts were taken from the chart of accounts for Lionel Corporation.

| | | | | |
|---|---|---|---|---|
| 110 | Accounts Receivable | 210 | Accounts Payable |
| 115 | Office Supplies | 410 | Fees Earned |
| 160 | Furniture & Fixtures | 520 | Advertising Expense |

The following selected transactions occurred in July. All purchases and revenues were on account, unless otherwise indicated.

July  1  Provided services to Talin Jenkins in the amount of $850; invoice #650.

7  Purchased office supplies from Office Emporium; $230.

9  Purchased a new desk for the office from The Furniture Factory; $1,800.

10  Returned office supplies to the Office Emporium that were defective; $30. (Hint: Reduce the Office Supplies account.)

12  Provided services to Franklin Jones in the amount of $390; invoice #651.

17  Received bill from Avian Advertising; $630.

19  Purchased bookcases for $2,420 from The Furniture Factory.

21  Provided services to Ross Butler in the amount of $1,620; invoice #652.

29  Purchased office supplies from Office Emporium; $180.

*Required:*

1. Journalize the transactions for July in a revenue journal, a purchases journal, and a general journal. Use the following column heading for the purchases journal: Date; Account Credited; Ref.; Accounts Payable Cr.; Office Supplies Dr.; Other Accounts Dr.; Ref. and Amount.

2. Post to the general ledger and subsidiary ledger accounts. (Assume all general ledger accounts and subsidiary ledger accounts have no beginning balances.)

3. Prepare schedules that prove that the balances in the control accounts and the subsidiary ledger accounts are equal.

**PA5-6 Journalize Transactions in the Special Journals and General Journal**     LO2, 3

Selected accounts from the chart of accounts of Doyle Company are shown below:

| | | | |
|---|---|---|---|
| 105 | Cash | 210 | Accounts Payable |
| 110 | Accounts Receivable | 410 | Fees Earned |
| 115 | Office Supplies | 510 | Salaries Expense |
| 180 | Office Equipment | 630 | Utilities Expense |

The following selected transactions occurred in August. All purchases and revenues were on account, unless otherwise indicated. Doyle Company uses the following journals: revenue journal; purchases journal; cash receipts journal; cash payments journal; and general journal.

Aug. 4   Purchased office supplies on account from Supply Emporium; $150.

6   Purchased office equipment on account from Rose Co.; $1,800.

7   Returned $25 of office supplies purchased on August 4 from Supply Emporium because they were defective. (Hint: Reduce the Office Supplies account.)

12   Fees earned on account from Gorgeous George's; $2,100, invoice #601.

15   Paid salaries to employees $12,300; check #851.

20   Fees earned from cash customers for the week; $1,735.

24   Received $1,000 payment from Gorgeous George's.

28   Paid Supply Emporium the amount owed; check #852.

31   Purchased office supplies from Office Suppliers, Inc. with check #853; $325.

31   Fees earned on account from Little Lola's; $2,600, invoice #602.

31   Received bill for utilities from State Utilities for the month of August; $600.

*Required:*

1.   Record the August transactions in a revenue journal, a purchases journal, a cash receipts journal, a cash payments journal, and a general journal. Use the following headings for the special journals:

Cash receipts journal: Date; Account Credited; Ref.; Other Accounts Cr.; Accounts Receivable Cr.; Fees Earned Cr.; Cash Dr.

Purchases journal: Date; Account Credited; Ref.; Accounts Payable Cr.; Office Supplies Dr.; Other Accounts Dr.; Ref.; and Amount.

Cash payments journal: Date; Check No.; Account Debited; Ref.; Other Accounts Dr.; Accounts Payable Dr.; Cash Cr.

2.   Foot and crossfoot all special journals as necessary.

3.   Using the methods shown in the chapter, show the posting references that would be made if amounts were posted to the general ledger and subsidiary ledgers (actual posting to the ledger accounts is not required for this problem).

**PA5-7 Journalizing Transactions in Revenue and Cash Receipts Journals; Posting; Preparing a**     LO2, 3
**Trial Balance; Reconciling Control and Subsidiary Accounts; Preparing a Trial Balance**

Shown below are the purchases and cash payments journals for Pepperine for its first month of operations, October 2008:

Purchases Journal                                                                      Page 1

| Date | Account Credited | Ref. | Accounts Payable Cr. | Supplies Dr. | Other Accounts Dr. | | |
|---|---|---|---|---|---|---|---|
| | | | | | Accounts | Ref. | Amount |
| Oct. 2 | Bitterling, Inc. | | 2,280 | | Rent Expense | | 2,280 |
| 2 | Aloha Company | | 1,428 | | Advertising Expense | | 1,428 |
| 4 | Norris Inc. | | 841 | 841 | | | |
| 9 | Simple Enterprises | | 1,620 | | Furniture & Fixtures | | 1,620 |
| 21 | Bitterling, Inc. | | 967 | 967 | | | |
| | Totals | | 7,136 | 1,808 | | | 5,328 |

**Cash Payments Journal**                                    Page 1

| Date | Check No. | Account Debited | Ref. | Other Accounts Dr. | Accounts Payable Dr. | Cash Cr. |
|---|---|---|---|---|---|---|
| Oct. 2 | 810 | Prepaid Insurance | | 3,500 | | 3,500 |
| 3 | 811 | Salaries Expense | | 1,250 | | 1,250 |
| 19 | 812 | Aloha Company | | | 1,428 | 1,428 |
| 21 | 813 | Simple Enterprises | | | 1,620 | 1,620 |
| 30 | 814 | Pepperine, Drawing | | 1,500 | | 1,500 |
| 31 | 815 | Norris, Inc. | | — | 841 | 841 |
| | | Totals | | 6,250 | 3,889 | 10,139 |

Additionally, the following transactions have not been journalized for October.

Oct. 1  The owner, Sal Pepperine, invests $95,000 in cash.

4  Revenues earned on account, K. Witkowski, $4,895; invoice #460.

5  Cash revenues total $6,100.

7  Revenues earned on account, M. Romero, $2,670; invoice #461.

9  Revenues earned on account, J. DiVincenzo, $1,100; invoice #462.

20  Received payment in full from K. Witkowski.

22  Received payment in full from J. DiVincenzo.

24  Provided services to B. Arredondo for $3,000 on account; invoice #463.

27  Received payment in full from M. Romero.

31  Cash revenues total $5,995.

***Required:***

1.  Open the following accounts in the general ledger:

| | | | |
|---|---|---|---|
| 105 | Cash | 310 | Pepperine, Capital |
| 110 | Accounts Receivable | 311 | Pepperine, Drawing |
| 115 | Supplies | 410 | Fees Earned |
| 140 | Prepaid Insurance | 510 | Salaries Expense |
| 160 | Furniture & Fixtures | 520 | Advertising Expense |
| 210 | Accounts Payable | 615 | Rent Expense |

2.  Journalize the transactions that have not been journalized by preparing a revenue journal and a cash receipts journal. Use the following headings for the cash receipts journal: Date; Account Credited; Ref.; Other Accounts Cr.; Accounts Receivable Cr.; Fees Earned Cr.; Cash Dr.

3.  Foot and crossfoot the revenue and cash receipts journals.

4.  Post from *all journals* to the accounts receivable and accounts payable subsidiary ledgers. Complete any other daily and month-end postings that are needed in the order that transactions are presented in the problem.

5.  Prepare a trial balance at October 31, 2008.

6.  Use the methods described in the chapter to verify that the subsidiary ledgers agree with the control accounts in the general ledger.

LO2, 3    **PA5-8 Journalizing in Special Journals; Posting; Preparing a Trial Balance**
The post-closing trial balance for Ken Flammer—Attorney at Law is as follows:

**Ken Flammer—Attorney at Law**
**Post-Closing Trial Balance**
**December 31, 2008**

| | Debit | Credit |
|---|---|---|
| Cash | 16,500 | |
| Accounts Receivable | 5,350 | |
| Notes Receivable | 6,000 | |
| Office Equipment | 32,000 | |
| Accumulated Depreciation—Office Equipment | | 4,000 |
| Accounts Payable | | 9,500 |
| K. Flammer, Capital | | 46,350 |
| **Totals** | **59,850** | **59,850** |

The following detail is contained in the subsidiary ledgers:

- Accounts receivable—B. Baily $1,460; N. Hite $2,320; W. Price $1,570.
- Accounts payable—G. Clump $3,000; P. Dormond $2,800; O. Kadhi $3,700.

The following transactions occurred in January of 2009.

| | | |
|---|---|---|
| Jan. | 1 | Paid $14,400 rent for the year; check #500. |
| | 1 | Received $4,000 as an advance payment for four months of legal representation. |
| | 5 | Provided services on account to B. Baily; invoice #201 for $1,100. |
| | 6 | Paid O. Kadhi amount owed in full; check #501. |
| | 8 | Received partial payment on account of $1,000 from N. Hite. |
| | 11 | Purchased office supplies from P. Dormond on account $520. |
| | 14 | Returned office supplies to P. Dormond of $60 because they were defective. (Hint: Reduce the Office Supplies account.) |
| | 18 | Paid secretary for two weeks' wages; $1,600; check #502. |
| | 20 | Purchased office equipment with a note payable to G. Clump; $25,000. |
| | 21 | Paid for advertisements in the local newspaper; check #503 for $220. |
| | 25 | Provided services on account to W. Price; invoice #202 for $850. |
| | 28 | Paid P. Dormond $2,800 on account; check #504. |
| | 30 | Received payment on account of $1,460 from B. Baily. |
| | 31 | Provided services on account to N. Hite; invoice #203 for $2,300. |
| | 31 | Recorded cash revenues earned for the month of $6,000. |
| | 31 | Ken Flammer withdrew $4,000 from the business for personal use; check #505. |

**Required:**

1.  Open general ledger accounts and subsidiary ledger accounts for each of the following:

| | | | | |
|---|---|---|---|---|
| 105 | Cash | | 250 | Notes Payable |
| 110 | Accounts Receivable | | 260 | Unearned Legal Fees |
| 112 | Notes Receivable | | 310 | K. Flammer, Capital |
| 115 | Office Supplies | | 311 | K. Flammer, Drawing |
| 145 | Prepaid Rent | | 410 | Legal Fees Earned |
| 180 | Office Equipment | | 510 | Salaries Expense |
| 181 | Accumulated Depreciation, Office Equipment | | 520 | Advertising Expense |
| 210 | Accounts Payable | | | |

2. Record the January transactions in the revenue journal, cash receipts journal, purchases journal, cash payments journal, and general journal. Use the following headings for the journals:

Cash receipts journal: Date; Account Credited; Ref.; Other Accounts Cr.; Accounts Receivable Cr.; Fees Earned Cr.; Cash Dr.

Purchases journal: Date; Account Credited; Ref.; Accounts Payable Cr.; Office Supplies Dr.; Other Accounts Dr.; Ref.; and Amount.

Cash payments journal: Date; Check No.; Account Debited; Ref.; Other Accounts Dr.; Accounts Payable Dr.; Cash Cr.

3. Post to the general ledger and subsidiary ledger accounts as appropriate.
4. Prepare a trial balance at January 31, 2009.
5. Use the methods described in the chapter to verify that the subsidiary ledgers agree with the control accounts in the general ledger.

## Problems—Set B      Available with McGraw-Hill's Homework Manager

**LO1, 2, 3, 4**    **PB5-1 Matching Terminology with Definitions**
Following are the terms and definitions covered in Chapter 5. Match each term with its definition by entering the appropriate letter in the space provided. Use one letter for each blank.

| Terms | Definitions |
|---|---|
| ____ 1. General journal | A. This may require nothing more than selecting a suitable general ledger software program for a business. |
| ____ 2. Special journal | B. Each line represents a separate journal entry consisting of at least one debit to cash and at least one credit to another account. |
| ____ 3. Monthly posting | |
| ____ 4. Implementation phase | |
| ____ 5. Cash receipts journal | C. Would be used to record the payment to a creditor on account. |
| ____ 6. Accounting information system | D. Provides the accountant with more time to ensure that all transactions and adjustments have been recorded. |
| ____ 7. Control account | E. Presents the same information as a detailed transaction history, but in a highly summarized form. |
| ____ 8. Purchases journal | F. A critical factor in the ultimate success or failure of an accounting information system. |
| ____ 9. Analysis phase | |
| ____ 10. Cash payments journal | G. Several columns are needed because a nearly limitless number and variety of accounts could be debited when accounts payable is credited. |
| ____ 11. Feedback phase | |
| ____ 12. Computerized accounting system | |
| ____ 13. Design phase | H. Used for recording repetitive, frequent transactions. |
| ____ 14. Daily posting | I. Required for subsidiary ledger accounts because balances must be kept up to date at all times. |
| ____ 15. Subsidiary ledger | J. This must be useful, cost effective, and flexible. |
| | K. Will always be utilized by every business even if special journals are used. |
| | L. Provides detailed history of transactions on account with each individual or business. |
| | M. Control accounts in the general ledger normally only need to be updated when financial statements are prepared. |
| | N. Changes are made to a new information system when problems are discovered. |
| | O. Internal and external user needs are identified. |

**PB5-2 Journalizing Transactions in the Cash Receipts Journal; Posting to Control Account and Subsidiary Ledger**    LO2, 3

Dave's Dentistry, DDS (owned by David Mastic) provides basic dental care (cleanings, fillings, etc.). The following selected accounts are taken from its chart of accounts.

| | | | | |
|---|---|---|---|---|
| 105 | Cash | 310 | David Mastic, Capital |
| 110 | Accounts Receivable | 410 | Dental Fees Earned |
| 115 | Dental Supplies | 710 | Interest Revenue |

On February 28, 2009, the accounts receivable subsidiary ledger had the following balances: R. Cannell $600; Dee Kaye $2,700; Moe Larr $1,400; and Ginger Vytis $3,000. The following transactions occurred during March:

Mar. 4    Received a check from Ginger Vytis as payment in full on her account.

6    Received a check from Moe Larr for $500 as partial payment on his account.

12    David Mastic invested an additional $10,000 into the business.

18    Performed a root canal for Dee Kaye and received immediate cash payment of $2,000.

22    Received check from R. Cannell as payment in full on his account.

27    Received check from Dee Kaye for $1,200 as partial payment on her account.

31    Received a cash refund for dental supplies returned to the supplier for $140 because they were defective. (Hint: Reduce the Dental Supplies account.)

### Required:

1.    Journalize the transactions for March in a four-column cash receipts journal using the following column headings: Date; Account Credited; Ref.; Other Accounts Cr.; Accounts Receivable Cr.; Dental Fees Earned Cr.; and Cash Dr.

2.    Set up the Accounts Receivable control account and the individual accounts receivable subsidiary ledger accounts by placing the February 28 balances in them.

3.    Post the March transactions to the control account and the subsidiary ledger accounts in the manner described in the chapter.

4.    Prepare a schedule that proves that the balances in the control account and the subsidiary ledger accounts are equal.

**PB5-3 Journalizing Transactions in the Cash Payments Journal; Posting to Control Account and Subsidiary Ledger**    LO2, 3

Pete's Packaging packages and ships items worldwide. The following selected accounts were taken from its chart of accounts.

| | | | | |
|---|---|---|---|---|
| 105 | Cash | 210 | Accounts Payable |
| 115 | Packaging Supplies | 311 | Pete Zelin, Drawing |
| 140 | Prepaid Insurance | 510 | Salaries Expense |
| 190 | Delivery Truck | | |

On May 31, the Accounts Payable subsidiary ledger had the following balances: Charlie's Corrugated Boxes $510; Ev'ry Kinda Envelope $950; Packaging Plus $600; Speedy Labels $450. The following transactions occurred during June:

June 4    Paid Speedy Labels the balance due on account, using check #840.

6    Bought mailing tape, black markers, etc. from Ev'ry Kinda Envelope, using check #841; $380.

10    Purchased a new delivery truck $30,000, using check #842.

15    Paid Packaging Plus balance due on account, using check #843.

18    Paid Charlie's Corrugated Boxes balance due on account, using check #844.

19    Pete Zelin withdrew $1,000 cash for his personal use, using check #845.

22    Paid Ev'ry Kinda Envelope $300 as partial payment on the balance due, using check #846.

28    Paid monthly salary to his employee—Yupee Ess, $900, using check #847.

30    Paid annual premium on insurance policy, $10,800, using check #848.

*Required:*

1. Journalize the transactions for June in a cash payments journal using the following column headings: Date; Check No.; Account Debited; Ref.; Other Accounts Dr.; Accounts Payable Dr.; and Cash Cr.

2. Set up the Accounts Payable control account and the individual accounts payable subsidiary ledger accounts by placing the May 31 balances in them.

3. Post the June transactions to the control account and the subsidiary ledger accounts in the manner described in the chapter.

4. Prepare a schedule that proves that the balances in the control account and the subsidiary ledger accounts are equal.

**LO2, 3**    **PB5-4 Posting Accounts Receivable and Accounts Payable Transactions and Preparing Schedules of Accounts Receivable and Accounts Payable**

The Accounts Receivable control account for Grate Plains, Inc., as of April 30, 2009, was $16,500 consisting of the following balances: $5,500 from Pomegranate Company and $11,000 from Star, Inc. The Accounts Payable control account as of April 30, 2009, was $3,000 consisting of the following balances: $2,000 from Fennel Company and $1,000 from Thyme, Inc. The revenue journal, cash receipts journal, purchases journal, and cash payments journal for Grate Plains for May 2009 follow:

### Revenue Journal    Page 2

| Date | Invoice No. | Account Debited | Ref. | Accts Receivable Dr. Fees Earned Cr. |
|---|---|---|---|---|
| May  2 | 451 | Mango Company | | 3,816 |
| 12 | 452 | Persimmon, Inc. | | 8,320 |
| 16 | 453 | Papaya Company | | 2,600 |
| 25 | 454 | Pomegranate Company | | 6,914 |
| 30 | 455 | Star, Inc. | | 3,140 |

### Cash Receipts Journal    Page 7

| Date | Account Credited | Ref. | Other Accounts Cr. | Accounts Receivable Cr. | Fees Earned Cr. | Cash Dr. |
|---|---|---|---|---|---|---|
| May  7 | Star, Inc. | | | 10,000 | | 10,000 |
| 14 | Mango Company | | | 3,816 | | 3,816 |
| 18 | Persimmon, Inc. | | | 6,320 | | 6,320 |
| 27 | Papaya Company | | | 2,600 | | 2,600 |
| 31 | Pomegranate Company | | | 5,500 | | 5,500 |

### Purchases Journal    Page 5

| Date | Account Credited | Ref. | Accounts Payable Cr. | Supplies Dr. | Other Accounts Dr. Accounts | Ref. | Amount |
|---|---|---|---|---|---|---|---|
| May  2 | Fennel Company | | 800 | 800 | | | |
| 9 | Parsley Parties | | 1,900 | | Rent Expense | | 1,900 |
| 17 | Tarragon Ltd. | | 200 | 200 | | | |
| 18 | Cilantro Sisters, Inc. | | 6,500 | | Office Equipment | | 6,500 |
| 24 | Basil Company | | 2,200 | | Furniture & Fixtures | | 2,200 |
| 28 | Cilantro Sisters, Inc. | | 3,600 | | Prepaid Insurance | | 3,600 |

## Cash Payments Journal                                        Page 9

| Date | Check No. | Account Debited | Ref. | Other Accounts Dr. | Accounts Payable Dr. | Cash Cr. |
|------|-----------|-----------------|------|--------------------|----------------------|----------|
| May 1 | 655 | Thyme, Inc. | | | 1,000 | 1,000 |
| 1 | 656 | Fennel Company | | | 2,000 | 2,000 |
| 20 | 657 | Parsley Parties | | | 1,200 | 1,200 |
| 29 | 658 | Cilantro Sisters, Inc. | | | 3,500 | 3,500 |
| 31 | 659 | Tarragon Ltd. | | | 200 | 200 |

**Required:**

1. Set up the Accounts Receivable (No. 110) and Accounts Payable (No. 210) control accounts as well as the corresponding individual subsidiary ledger accounts by placing the April 30 balances in them.
2. Foot and crossfoot the four special journals, post the appropriate information into the subsidiary accounts and control accounts for Accounts Receivable and Accounts Payable in the manner described in the chapter. Do not post to any other general ledger accounts.
3. Prepare schedules of accounts receivable and accounts payable for Grate Plains, Inc., as of May 31, 2009.

**PB5-5 Journalizing Transactions in the Revenue Journal, Purchases Journal, and General Journal; Posting to Subsidiary Ledgers and Control Accounts**                LO2, 3

The following selected accounts were taken from the chart of accounts for Cewlio Corporation.

| | | | | |
|---|---|---|---|---|
| 110 | Accounts Receivable | | 210 | Accounts Payable |
| 115 | Store Supplies | | 410 | Fees Earned |
| 170 | Store Equipment | | 630 | Utilities Expense |

The following selected transactions occurred in December. All purchases and revenues were on account, unless otherwise indicated.

Dec. 2  Provided services to Judy Crowder in the amount of $1,800; invoice #100.
   8  Purchased store supplies from The Store House; $900.
   10  Purchased a cash register from Registers R Us; $3,700.
   13  Returned store supplies to The Store House that were defective; $100. (Hint: Reduce the Store Supplies account.)
   16  Provided services to Gawain Aster in the amount of $925; invoice #101.
   18  Received bill from State Gas & Electric; $1,160.
   20  Purchased two more cash registers for $7,000 from Registers R Us.
   23  Provided services to Scarlet Els in the amount of $640; invoice #102.
   30  Purchased store supplies from The Store House; $245.

**Required:**

1. Journalize the transactions for December in a revenue journal, a purchases journal, and a general journal. Use the following column headings for the purchases journal: Date; Account Credited; Ref.; Accounts Payable Cr.; Store Supplies Dr.; Other Accounts Dr., Ref. and Amount.
2. Post to the general ledger and subsidiary ledger accounts. (Assume all general ledger accounts and subsidiary ledger accounts have zero beginning balances.)
3. Prepare schedules that prove that the balances in the control accounts and the subsidiary ledger accounts are equal.

**LO2, 3**

**PB5-6 Journalizing Transactions in Special Journals and the General Journal**

Selected accounts from the chart of accounts of Clover Company are shown below:

| | | | |
|---|---|---|---|
| 105 | Cash | 210 | Accounts Payable |
| 110 | Accounts Receivable | 410 | Fees Earned |
| 115 | Office Supplies | 510 | Salaries Expense |
| 180 | Office Equipment | 630 | Utilities Expense |

The following selected transactions occurred in May. All purchases and revenues were on account unless otherwise indicated.

May  3  Purchased office supplies on account from Office Emporium; $225.

  7  Purchased office equipment on account from Furniture Liquidators; $3,000.

  8  Returned $50 of office supplies purchased on May 3 because they were defective. (Hint: Reduce the Office Supplies account.)

  13  Fees earned on account from Peterson Plumbing; $4,000, invoice #630.

  16  Paid salaries to employees; $8,500, using check #405.

  21  Fees earned from cash customers for the week; $6,200.

  25  Received $2,500 payment from Peterson Plumbing.

  28  Paid Office Emporium the amount owed using check #406.

  29  Purchased office supplies from Office Emporium for cash; $410, using check #407.

  31  Fees earned on account from Magna Carta; $4,100, invoice #631.

  31  Received bill for utilities from City Utilities for the month of May; $550.

*Required:*

1.  Record the May transactions in a revenue journal, a cash receipts journal, a purchases journal, a cash payments journal, and a general journal. Use the following headings for the special journals:

Cash receipts journal: Date; Account Credited; Ref.; Other Accounts Cr.; Accounts Receivable Cr.; Fees Earned Cr.; Cash Dr.

Purchases journal: Date; Account Credited; Ref.; Accounts Payable Cr.; Office Supplies Dr.; Other Accounts Dr.; Ref.; and Amount.

Cash payments journal: Date; Check No.; Account Debited; Ref.; Other Accounts Dr.; Accounts Payable Dr.; Cash Cr.

2.  Foot and crossfoot all special journals.

3.  Using the methods shown in the chapter, show the posting references that would be made if amounts were posted to the subsidiary ledgers and general ledger (actual posting to the ledger accounts is not required for this problem).

**LO2, 3**

**PB5-7 Journalizing Transactions in Revenue and Cash Receipts Journals; Posting; Preparing a Trial Balance; Reconciling Control and Subsidiary Accounts; Preparing a Trial Balance**

Shown below are the purchases and cash payments journals for Solara Corporation for April 2009, its first month of operations:

**Purchases Journal**                                                                 Page 1

| Date | Account Credited | Ref. | Accounts Payable Cr. | Supplies Dr. | Other Accounts Dr. | | |
|---|---|---|---|---|---|---|---|
| | | | | | Accounts | Ref. | Amount |
| Apr.  1 | Gilliland Co. | | 300 | 300 | | | |
| 1 | Rivera Company | | 4,000 | | Advertising Expense | | 4,000 |
| 4 | Hawthorne, Inc. | | 1,310 | 1,310 | | | |
| 9 | Orbon Enterprises | | 6,146 | | Furniture & Fixtures | | 6,146 |
| 22 | Doan Ltd. | | 1,244 | 1,244 | | | |
| | Totals | | 13,000 | 2,854 | | | 10,146 |

**Cash Payments Journal** Page 1

| Date | Check No. | Account Debited | Ref. | Other Accounts Dr. | Accounts Payable Dr. | Cash Cr. |
|---|---|---|---|---|---|---|
| Apr. 1 | 1001 | Prepaid Insurance | | 2,000 | | 2,000 |
| 2 | 1002 | Rent Expense | | 3,600 | | 3,600 |
| 20 | 1003 | Rivera Company | | | 4,000 | 4,000 |
| 23 | 1004 | Orbon Enterprises | | | 6,146 | 6,146 |
| 28 | 1005 | Solara, Drawing | | 1,200 | | 1,200 |
| 30 | 1006 | Hawthorne, Inc. | | | 1,310 | 1,310 |
| | | Totals | | 6,800 | 11,456 | 18,256 |

Additionally, the following transactions have not been journalized for April.

Apr. 1 The owner, Luz Solara, invests $70,000 in cash.
6 Revenues earned on account, V. Long, $2,220; invoice #261.
7 Cash revenues total $4,300.
9 Revenues earned on account, C. Lara, $3,325; invoice #262.
11 Revenues earned on account, L. Begay, $2,500; invoice #263.
21 Received payment in full from V. Long.
24 Received payment in full from L. Begay.
26 Provided services to S. Lutheran for $4,300 on account; invoice #264.
29 Received payment in full from C. Lara.
30 Cash revenues total $6,294.

*Required:*

1. Open the following accounts in the general ledger:

| | | | |
|---|---|---|---|
| 105 | Cash | 310 | Solara, Capital |
| 110 | Accounts Receivable | 311 | Solara, Drawing |
| 115 | Supplies | 410 | Fees Earned |
| 140 | Prepaid Insurance | 520 | Advertising Expense |
| 160 | Furniture & Fixtures | 615 | Rent Expense |
| 210 | Accounts Payable | | |

2. Journalize the transactions that have not been journalized in the revenue journal and cash receipts journal. Use the following headings for the cash receipts journal: Date; Account Credited; Ref.; Other Accounts Cr.; Accounts Receivable Cr.; Fees Earned Cr.; Cash Dr.
3. Post to the accounts receivable and accounts payable subsidiary ledgers in the order that transactions are presented in the problem.
4. Post entries to the general ledger.
5. Prepare a trial balance at April 30, 2009.
6. Use the methods described in the chapter to verify that the subsidiary ledgers agree with the control accounts in the general ledger.

**PB5-8 Journalizing in Special Journals; Posting; Preparing a Trial Balance** LO2, 3
The post-closing trial balance for Joe's Accounting Services is as follows:

**Joe's Accounting Services**
**Post-Closing Trial Balance**
**December 31, 2009**

|  | Debit | Credit |
|---|---|---|
| Cash | 23,300 |  |
| Accounts Receivable | 6,500 |  |
| Notes Receivable | 2,000 |  |
| Office Equipment | 16,000 |  |
| Accumulated Depreciation—Office Equipment |  | 3,200 |
| Accounts Payable |  | 5,000 |
| J. Bency, Capital |  | 39,600 |
| Totals | **47,800** | **47,800** |

The following detail is contained in the subsidiary ledgers:

- Accounts receivable—N. Bonham $2,150; H. Giahi $1,300; J. Teak $3,050.
- Accounts payable—J. Bright $1,050; S. Cutler $950; J. Storer $3,000.

The following transactions occurred in January of 2010.

Jan.  1  Paid $23,400 rent for the year; check #800.
   1  Received $3,000 as an advance payment for three months of accounting services.
   5  Provided services on account to J. Teak; invoice #501 for $2,350.
   8  Paid J. Storer amount owed in full; check #801.
   8  Received partial payment on account of $2,000 from J. Teak.
   13  Purchased office supplies from S. Cutler on account; $150.
   14  Returned office supplies costing $15 to S. Cutler because they were defective. (Hint: Reduce the Office Supplies account.)
   20  Paid secretary for two weeks' wages; $1,900; check #802.
   22  Purchased office equipment with a Note Payable to J. Romero; $10,000.
   23  Paid for advertisements in the local newspaper; check #803 for $195.
   25  Provided services on account to H. Giahi; invoice #502 for $1,600.
   27  Paid S. Cutler $950 on account; check #804.
   30  Received payment on account of $1,300 from H. Giahi.
   31  Provided services on account to N. Bonham; invoice #503 for $4,400.
   31  Recorded cash revenues earned for the month of $8,500.
   31  Joe Bency withdrew $2,500 from the business for personal use; check #805.

*Required:*

1. Open general ledger accounts and subsidiary ledger accounts for each of the following:

| 105 | Cash | 250 | Notes Payable |
|---|---|---|---|
| 110 | Accounts Receivable | 260 | Unearned Accounting Fees |
| 112 | Notes Receivable | 310 | J. Bency, Capital |
| 115 | Office Supplies | 311 | J. Bency, Drawing |
| 145 | Prepaid Rent | 410 | Accounting Fees Earned |
| 180 | Office Equipment | 510 | Salaries Expense |
| 181 | Accumulated Depreciation, Office Equipment | 520 | Advertising Expense |
| 210 | Accounts Payable |  |  |

2.  Record the January transactions in the revenue journal, cash receipts journal, purchases journal, cash payments journal, and general journal. Use the following headings for the journals:

Cash receipts journal: Date; Account Credited; Ref.; Other Accounts Cr.; Accounts Receivable Cr.; Fees Earned Cr.; Cash Dr.

Purchases journal: Date; Account Credited; Ref.; Accounts Payable Cr.; Office Supplies Dr.; Other Accounts Dr.; Ref.; and Amount.

Cash payments journal: Date; Check No.; Account Debited; Ref.; Other Accounts Dr.; Accounts Payable Dr.; Cash Cr.

3.  Post to the general ledger and subsidiary ledger accounts as appropriate.
4.  Prepare a trial balance at January 31, 2010, and determine whether the subsidiary ledgers agree with the control accounts in the general ledger.
5.  Use the methods described in the chapter to verify that the subsidiary ledgers agree with the control accounts in the general ledger.

# Cases and Projects

## CP5-1 Financial Reporting Project: Mini Practice Set                                      LO1, 2, 3, 4

Young Co. established the following chart of accounts.

| | | | | | |
|---|---|---|---|---|---|
| 105 | Cash | 211 | Salaries Payable | 510 | Salaries Expense |
| 110 | Accounts Receivable | 212 | Interest Payable | 515 | Rent Expense |
| 115 | Store Supplies | 250 | Notes Payable | 516 | Utilities Expense |
| 140 | Prepaid Insurance | 310 | Shawna Young, Capital | 518 | Store Supplies Expense |
| 170 | Store Equipment | 311 | Shawna Young, Drawing | 620 | Depreciation Expense |
| 171 | Accumulated Depreciation | 315 | Income Summary | 650 | Insurance Expense |
| 210 | Accounts Payable | 410 | Fees Earned | 810 | Interest Expense |

Young Co. uses both an accounts receivable and an accounts payable subsidiary ledger. The transactions for Young Co. for the first month of business, March 2009, are presented below.

March 1   The owner, Shawna Young, contributed $25,000 to the business.
1   Received store supplies and an invoice from Farnswood Co. for $1,300.
1   Borrowed $10,000 by giving Second State Bank a long-term promissory note.
1   Paid $1,200 for insurance for one year using check #650.
1   Paid March rent of $2,900 using check #651.
2   Purchased store equipment on account for $10,000 from Nelson, Inc.
5   Earned $3,600 on account from Zachary Makey, Invoice #275.
5   Returned $200 of damaged supplies received from Farnswood Co. on March 1. (Hint: Reduce the Store Supplies account.)
6   The owner, Shawna Young, gave store equipment to the business valued at $3,000.
6   Earned $4,900 on account from John Dilbert, Invoice #276.
7   Earned $4,300 on account from Edward Solano, Invoice #277.
11   Sent check #652 to Farnswood Co. in payment of its March 1 invoice.
12   Purchased store supplies on credit from Corsair Co. $440.
15   Cash fees earned for the first half of the month were $7,340.
15   Paid salaries of $7,950 using check #653.
19   Received payment from Zachary Makey for the March 5 transaction.
22   Received payment from Edward Solano for the March 7 transaction.
25   Issued check #654 to Corsair Co. for the March 12 transaction.

26    Earned $6,220 on account from John Dilbert, Invoice #278.

27    Issued check #655 for $2,000 to Nelson, Inc., for partial payment of March 2 transaction.

28    Earned $4,440 on account from Sydney Locke, Invoice #279.

29    Purchased store supplies on credit from Corsair Co., $510.

31    Cash fees earned for the last half of the month were $2,345.

31    Received the utility bill from Texas Utilities for the month of March, $2,400.

31    The owner, Shawna Young, withdrew $2,500 for personal use using check #656.

**Required:**

1. Record the March transactions in a revenue journal, a cash receipts journal, a purchases journal, a cash payments journal, and a general journal.

2. Complete all necessary daily and end-of-month postings.

3. Prepare an unadjusted trial balance at March 31, 2009.

4. Use the following information to prepare and post adjusting entries, and prepare an adjusted trial balance.
   Adjustment data at March 31, 2009.

   a. Store supplies on hand totaled $185.

   b. Depreciation is $120 on the store equipment.

   c. Interest of $50 is accrued on notes payable at March 31.

   d. Salaries of $2,000 are accrued and unpaid at March 31.

   e. One month insurance has expired.

5. Prepare an Income Statement, an Owner's Equity Statement, and a classified Balance Sheet for March 2009.
   (Note: Young Co. must pay $2,000 on the Notes Payable in the coming year.)

6. Prepare and post closing entries.

7. Prepare a post-closing trial balance.

## CP5-2 Implementing a Computerized Accounting Information System: Critical Thinking

Bessie Jacobs is the founder and sole manager of Bessie's Flowers. The business has been operating for nearly 15 years and has developed a loyal customer base consisting of individuals and businesses. Individuals typically purchase flowers on the spur of the moment using cash, whereas most businesses purchase flowers on credit. Bessie has promised to deliver flowers to business customers each week. Bessie's business expenses are modest with her greatest expenses being for flower purchases from several southern states and greenhouses in the Pacific Northwest. Bessie also incurs substantial transportation costs to have her purchases flown in to her shop. Until this year, Bessie has tracked the majority of her business transactions manually. The only computerized application in her business has been the automated cash register. Bessie has come to you for advice on implementing a computerized accounting information system.

**Required:**

Write a report that advises Bessie about implementing a computerized accounting system. In your report, describe some of the factors she should consider when deciding whether to implement such a system. Also, based on your preliminary understanding of Bessie's business, describe the components that should be included in the system and what information each component would capture.

# 6 Merchandising Operations

## LEARNING OBJECTIVES

**After completing this chapter, you should be able to:**

**LO1** Distinguish among service, merchandising, and manufacturing operations.

**LO2** Explain the use of perpetual and periodic inventory systems and their role in inventory control.

**LO3** Analyze merchandise purchases under a perpetual inventory system.

**LO4** Analyze merchandise sales under a perpetual inventory system.

**LO5** Prepare a merchandiser's multistep income statement.

**LO6** Analyze the gross profit percentage.

Lectured slideshow–LP6-1
www.mhhe.com/LLPW1e

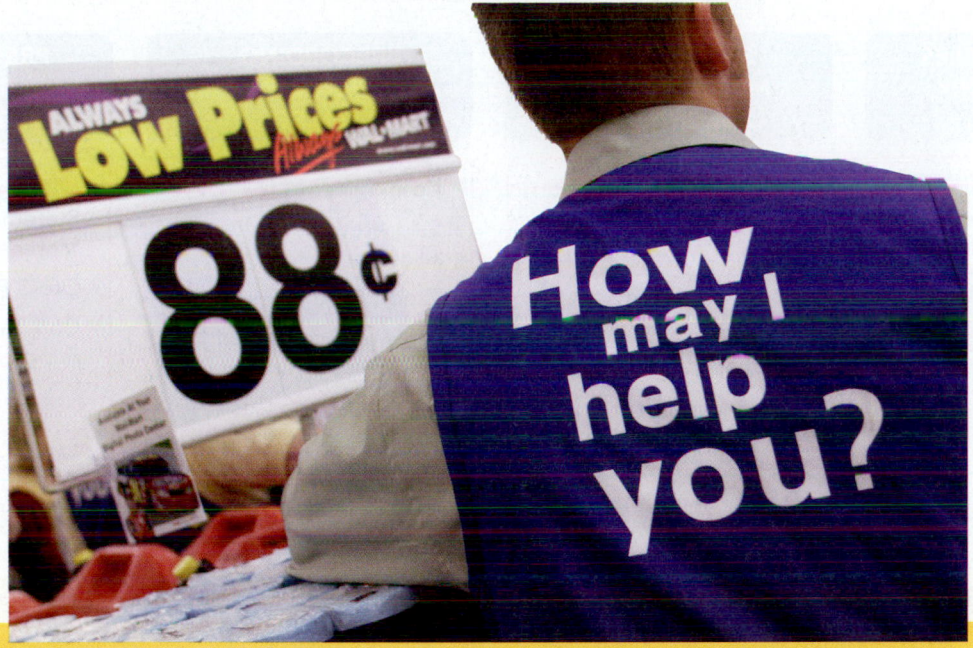

## Focus Company: WAL-MART

## "Every Day Low Prices" and Modern Supply-Chain Management Change the World.

www.walmart.com

If you compare your grandparents' first car or TV to the one you own now, you can see how improvements in technology have changed the products you use in daily life. Less obvious are the changes that have taken place in the way we shop for these products. From Bentonville, Arkansas, to Beijing, China, "big-box" stores have changed the world of retailing. Just five of these giants—Wal-Mart, Kmart, Target, Costco, and Sears—account for nearly 60 percent of general merchandise sales in the United States. The leader, Wal-Mart, has done as much as any high-tech company to change American lifestyles over the last 40 years.

Seventeen years after the company was founded, Wal-Mart rang up yearly sales of $1 billion. Fourteen years later, it sold that much in a week. Today, Wal-Mart's sales are approaching $1 billion a day. Wal-Mart's trucks transport goods purchased from hundreds of thousands of suppliers. The store's greeters welcome more than 100 million customers every week in more than 6,100 locations worldwide. To track its huge inventory purchases and sales and ensure that each store is properly stocked and each transaction properly recorded, Wal-Mart needs state-of-the-art accounting systems.

Chapters 1–5 illustrate accounting for the operations of two small companies: Pizza Aroma and a UPS Store. In this chapter, we demonstrate that the same accounting principles apply to much larger companies such as Wal-Mart. The operating activities of Pizza Aroma and a UPS Store also relate to the provision of services rather than to the sale of goods. This chapter focuses on companies such as Wal-Mart that sell merchandise to customers and the way they control and report the unique aspects of their operating activities. You will also learn what to look for in a merchandiser's financial statements.

| OPERATING CYCLES AND INVENTORY SYSTEMS | RECORDING MERCHANDISE PURCHASES | RECORDING MERCHANDISE SALES | PREPARING AND ANALYZING THE INCOME STATEMENT |
|---|---|---|---|
| • Operating Cycles: Service, Merchandising, and Manufacturing Cos.<br>• Inventory Systems: Perpetual and Periodic | • Purchases on Account<br>• Transportation Cost (Freight-In)<br>• Purchase Returns and Allowances<br>• Purchase Discounts<br>• Summary of Purchase-Related Transactions | • Cash Sales<br>• Sales Returns and Allowances<br>• Credit Card Sales<br>• Sales on Account and Sales Discounts<br>• Transportation Cost (Freight-Out)<br>• Summary of Sales-Related Transactions<br>• Comparison of Sales and Purchases Accounting | • Multistep Income Statement for Merchandisers<br>• Gross Profit Percentage<br>• Comparison to Benchmarks |

# OPERATING CYCLES AND INVENTORY SYSTEMS

## Operating Cycles

**Learning Objective 1**

Distinguish among service, merchandising, and manufacturing operations.

An **operating cycle** is the series of activities that a company undertakes to generate sales and, ultimately, cash. Based on their operating cycle, businesses can be classified into three types: (1) service companies, (2) merchandising companies, and (3) manufacturing companies. As in Exhibit 6.1 the operating cycle for service companies such as Pizza Aroma and The UPS Store is simple: They use cash to provide services to customers and then collect cash from those customers. The operating cycle for merchandising companies has an additional step: These companies use cash to buy inventory, sell the inventory to customers, and then collect cash from customers. Like merchandising companies, manufacturing companies such as Ford and Mattel sell physical products, but instead of acquiring ready-to-sell merchandise, they make their own products from raw materials.

This chapter focuses on merchandising companies. In turn, merchandising companies can be classified in two specific subgroups. One group, **retail** merchandising companies, includes companies such as Wal-Mart and American Eagle Outfitters, which sell directly to consumers. Another group, **wholesale** merchandising companies, includes companies such as SYSCO, that sell only to retail businesses for resale to consumers. This chapter applies equally to both retail and wholesale merchandisers.

As the figure in Exhibit 6.1 suggests, the accounting processes that you learned in earlier chapters also apply to merchandising companies. The difference is that merchandising companies must account for the purchase and sale of products. Unlike services, which cannot be stored for future sale, products can be acquired for sale in the future. These stored products, which are called Inventory, present some new accounting issues that you will learn about in this chapter. We begin with a discussion of inventory systems and how they work.

## Inventory Systems

Video 6-1
www.mhhe.com/LLPW1e

Because inventory management is vital to merchandising operations, companies spend a great deal of time and money tracking their inventory transactions. A strong accounting system plays three roles in this process:

- It provides up-to-date information on inventory quantities and costs so that managers can make informed decisions.
- It provides accurate information for preparing financial statements. Until inventory is sold, it is reported as an asset on the balance sheet. After its sale, it is removed from the

**Learning Objective 2**

Explain the use of perpetual and periodic inventory systems and their role in inventory control.

| Exhibit 6.1 | Operating Cycles for Service, Merchandising, and Manufacturing Companies |

**Service companies**
(Gold's Gym, UPS, Southwest Airlines)

Sell services → Receive cash → Incur operating expenses → (back to Sell services)

**Merchandising companies**
(Wal-Mart, Sears, GAP)

Buy products → Sell products → Receive cash → Incur operating expenses → Buy products

**Manufacturing companies**
(Ford, Dell, Nike)

Make products → Sell products → Receive cash → Incur operating expenses → Buy raw materials → Make products

balance sheet and reported on the income statement as an expense, called Cost of Goods Sold.

- It provides information that controls inventory and helps to prevent theft.

To perform these functions, companies can use either of two types of inventory accounting system: perpetual or periodic.

## Perpetual Inventory System

A **perpetual inventory system** updates inventory records every time an item is bought, sold, or returned. You may not realize it, but the bar code readers at Wal-Mart's checkouts serve two purposes: (1) they calculate and record the sales revenue for each product you buy and (2) they remove the product and its cost from Wal-Mart's inventory records. Similar scanners are used in the "employees only" part of the store, where products are unloaded from the trucks or returned to suppliers. As a result of this continuous, or "perpetual," updating, the balances in Wal-Mart's Inventory and Cost of Goods Sold accounts are always up to date.

## Periodic Inventory System

A **periodic inventory system** differs from a perpetual system in several ways, which are described in detail later in this chapter. The main difference is that rather than updating the inventory records immediately after each purchase and sale (as in a perpetual system), a periodic system updates the inventory records only at the end of the period. Most of the time, then, accurate records of the inventory on hand and the inventory that has been sold are unavailable. To determine these amounts, employees must physically count the inventory, which they do at the end of the period, when the store is "closed for inventory." The resulting inventory count is then used to adjust the balances for Inventory and Cost of Goods Sold.

## Inventory Control

A perpetual inventory system's continuous tracking of transactions allows companies to keep just the right quantity of products on the shelves for just the right amount of time. Doing so saves companies a great deal of money in financing and storage charges. It also benefits consumers, who pay less for the products they buy. When companies use less money or labor to produce a product or service, the productivity of our entire economy goes up. From 1995 to 1999, Wal-Mart's perpetual inventory system accounted for more than 50 percent of U.S. productivity gains in general merchandising.[1] This amazing performance is likely to continue as the company adopts new microchip technologies that transmit data automatically from every inventory item that enters, moves within, and exits its stores.

Another benefit of a perpetual inventory system is that it allows managers to estimate **shrinkage,** the politically correct term for loss of inventory from theft, fraud, and error. How can companies estimate how much of their inventory is missing? They do it by monitoring the transactions that are recorded in their inventory accounts. Here is the procedure:

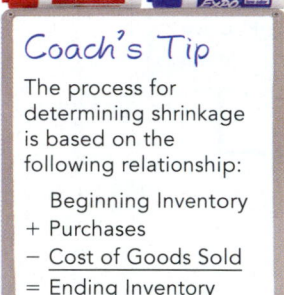

**Coach's Tip**

The process for determining shrinkage is based on the following relationship:

Beginning Inventory
+ Purchases
− Cost of Goods Sold
= Ending Inventory

1. **Determine how much inventory is on hand at the beginning of the period.**
2. **Monitor every piece of inventory that enters and exits the inventory during the period.**
   a. Add any purchases.
   b. Subtract any goods that are sold.

   If items are tracked in this way, the inventory records should exactly match the quantity of inventory on hand—unless some items have been wrongfully removed.

3. **Count the inventory to determine what is actually there.** If the records say that more inventory is on hand than what was counted, the difference is the amount of shrinkage—that is, the number of items that have been removed from inventory without permission.

   **Shrinkage =**

   Notice that you cannot do this kind of detective work with a periodic inventory system, because it does not provide an up-to-date record of the inventory that should be on hand when you count it. Even if you are using a perpetual inventory system, you still need to count the inventory occasionally (at least once a year) to ensure that the accounting records are accurate and that any shrinkage has been detected.

---

[1] "Retail: The Wal-Mart Effect," *The McKinsey Quarterly,* no. 1 (2002).

Until recently, perpetual inventory systems were too costly for most merchandisers to implement. Today, however, computerized inventory systems have become so cheap that most merchandisers use a perpetual system. Accordingly, this chapter focuses on the accounting process that perpetual systems use. Because you may still encounter a periodic system, particularly in small companies or large ones that have been slow to switch, Supplement 6A at the end of this chapter discusses the accounting process for periodic systems.

## Spotlight On ETHICS

### Sources of Inventory Shrinkage

Independent verification of inventory quantities is important. A recent study suggests that more than $37 billion of inventory goes missing from U.S. retailers each year.* Although shoplifting is a major cause of shrinkage (accounting for 33 percent of lost units), an even larger portion (47 percent) results from employee theft. To avoid hiring dishonest employees, companies screen job applicants using employment and criminal background checks. To deter and detect employee theft, they use security tags, closed-circuit TV, and complex computer programs that monitor cash registers.

\* Richard Hollinger, "2005 National Retail Security Survey," University of Florida, 2006.

## RECORDING MERCHANDISE PURCHASES

### Purchases on Account

> **Learning Objective 3**
>
> Analyze merchandise purchases under a perpetual inventory system.

Inventory purchases should be recorded at the point at which ownership is transferred. Most purchase and sales agreements specify one of two possible times:

- When the goods leave the seller's shipping department, known as the **FOB (free on board) shipping point**.
- When the goods reach the customer at their destination point, known as the **FOB destination**.

In a perpetual system, all purchases of merchandise inventory are recorded directly into the Inventory account. Because most companies use credit rather than cash to purchase goods, Accounts Payable is usually the other account that is affected. If Wal-Mart purchased $5,000 of DVDs on account, the transaction would be recorded as follows:

> **Coach's Tip**
>
> Inventory includes only merchandise purchased for sale. Other purchases, such as supplies for internal use, are recorded in different accounts.

| | Debit | Credit |
|---|---|---|
| Inventory (+A) | 5,000 | |
| Accounts Payable (+L) | | 5,000 |

| Assets | = | Liabilities | + | Owners' Equity |
|---|---|---|---|---|
| Inventory +5,000 | | Accounts Payable +5,000 | | |

### Transportation Cost (Freight-In)

The inventory that Wal-Mart purchases does not magically appear in its stores. It must be shipped from the supplier to Wal-Mart. If the terms are **FOB shipping point,** the purchaser pays for the shipping. If the terms are **FOB destination,** the seller pays for the shipping. When the purchaser pays for the shipping, the additional cost of transporting the goods (called **freight-in**) is added to the Inventory account.

> **Coach's Tip**
>
> When the purchaser incurs the transportation cost (**freight-in**), the amount is added to the purchaser's cost of inventory. When the seller incurs the transportation cost (**freight-out**), it is an operating expense to the seller.

Assume that Wal-Mart pays $300 cash to a trucker who delivers goods to one of its stores. Wal-Mart would account for this transaction as follows:

|  | Debit | Credit |
|---|---|---|
| Inventory (+A) | 300 | |
| Cash (−A) | | 300 |

| Assets | = | Liabilities | + | Owners' Equity |
|---|---|---|---|---|
| Inventory +300 | | | | |
| Cash −300 | | | | |

In general, a purchaser should include in the Inventory account any costs needed to get the inventory ready for sale. Costs that are incurred after the inventory has been made ready for sale, such as freight-out to deliver goods to customers, should be treated as selling expenses.

## Purchase Returns and Allowances

When goods purchased from a supplier arrive in damaged condition or fail to meet specifications, the buyer can (1) return them for a full refund or (2) keep them and ask for a cost reduction, called an allowance. **Purchase returns** and **purchase allowances** are accounted for either by reducing the cost of the inventory and recording a cash refund or by reducing the liability owed to the supplier.

Assume, for example, that Wal-Mart returned merchandise to a supplier and received a $400 reduction in the balance owed. This transaction would be analyzed and recorded as follows:

|  | Debit | Credit |
|---|---|---|
| Accounts Payable (−L) | 400 | |
| Inventory (−A) | | 400 |

| Assets | = | Liabilities | + | Owners' Equity |
|---|---|---|---|---|
| Inventory −400 | | Accounts Payable −400 | | |

## Purchase Discounts

When merchandise is bought on credit, terms such as "2/10, n/30" are sometimes specified. The "2/10" means that if the purchaser pays within 10 days of the date of purchase, a 2 percent **purchase discount** will be deducted from the cost. The "n/30" implies that if payment is not made within the 10-day discount period, the full amount will be due 30 days after the purchase date. If a purchaser fails to pay by the end of that period, interest will be charged. (In the future, the seller may deny credit because of a purchaser's failure to pay on time, and the seller may hire a collection agency to collect the amount owed.) See Exhibit 6.2 for an illustration of a 2/10, n/30 purchase that occurred on November 1.

When offered a purchase discount at the time of purchase, the purchaser accounts for it in two stages. Initially, the purchase is accounted for at **full cost** because it is not clear whether the

**Exhibit 6.2**   **Interpreting Credit Terms**

company will take advantage of the discount. Later, by making payment within the discount period, the purchaser reduces the Inventory account by the amount of the discount because it effectively reduces the cost of the inventory.

Assume, for example, that Wal-Mart receives a shipment of LCD televisions bought from Sony. How would a $100,000 purchase with terms of 2/10, n/30 affect Wal-Mart's accounting records? Initially, the purchase would be recorded as follows:

|  | Debit | Credit |
|---|---|---|
| Inventory (+A) | 100,000 | |
|     Accounts Payable (+L) | | 100,000 |

| Assets | = | Liabilities | + | Owners' Equity |
|---|---|---|---|---|
| Inventory   +100,000 | | Accounts Payable   +100,000 | | |

If Wal-Mart takes advantage of the 2/10, n/30 discount by paying within the 10-day discount period, the discount will effectively reduce the cost of the inventory. The 2 percent discount is calculated using the initial purchase cost (2% × $100,000 = $2,000). Because the discount reduces the inventory cost, the purchaser records it as a reduction of the Inventory account, as follows:

**Coach's Tip**

The purchase discount is calculated using the initial purchase cost times the discount percentage ($2,000 = 2% × $100,000).

|  | Debit | Credit |
|---|---|---|
| Accounts Payable (−L) | 100,000 | |
|     Cash (−A) (98% × 100,000) | | 98,000 |
|     Inventory (−A) (2% × 100,000) | | 2,000 |

| Assets | = | Liabilities | + | Owners' Equity |
|---|---|---|---|---|
| Cash          −98,000 | | Accounts Payable   −100,000 | | |
| Inventory   −2,000 | | | | |

If Wal-Mart paid for the inventory after the 10-day discount period, it would not be eligible for the 2 percent discount. Instead, it would pay the full $100,000 owed. The payment would be recorded as a decrease in Accounts Payable (debit) and a decrease in Cash (credit) of $100,000.[2]

## Spotlight On BUSINESS DECISIONS

### To Take or Not to Take the Discount, That Is the Question

Purchasers usually pay within the discount period because the savings are much larger than they may appear to you. Although 2 percent might seem a small discount, if taken consistently on all purchases made during the year, it can add up to substantial savings. All the purchaser must do to earn the 2 percent discount is to pay the bill 20 days early (on the 10th day instead of the 30th). Over a year (365 days), this discount is equivalent to a 37 percent annual interest rate.* So even if purchasers must borrow from the bank at a high rate, such as 15 percent, they will still save a great deal by taking the discount.

## Summary of Purchase-Related Transactions

You have now seen how several types of purchase-related transactions besides the initial purchase affect the Inventory account on the balance sheet. Before you move on to accounting for merchandise sales, make sure you understand how each of these purchase-related transactions affects Inventory. Cost of Goods Sold is recorded as part of the sales transactions described in the next section. See Exhibit 6.3 for a summary of the effects of the purchase transactions discussed in this section assuming beginning inventory was $75,000.

| Exhibit 6.3 | Effects of Purchase-Related Transactions on the Inventory Account |
| --- | --- |

| | |
| --- | --- |
| Beginning inventory | $ 75,000 |
| Add: Purchases* | 105,000 |
| Add: Freight-in | 300 |
| Less: Purchase returns and allowances | (400) |
| Less: Purchase discounts | (2,000) |
| Cost of goods available for sale | 177,900 |
| Less: Cost of goods sold | ? |
| Ending inventory | $       ? |

{ *Recorded as part of the sales transactions described in the next section.* }

*Purchased inventory includes ($105,000 = $5,000 + $100,000).

---

[2] An alternative approach to accounting for purchase discounts (called the net method) exists, but we leave that topic for discussion in intermediate accounting textbooks.

* To calculate the annual interest rate, first compute the interest rate for the discount period. When taking the 2 percent discount, the customer pays only 98 percent of the gross sales price. For example, on a $100 sale with terms 2/10, n/30, the customer woulds save $2 and pay $98 twenty days early.

The interest rate for the 20-day discount period is computed as follows:

$$\frac{\text{Amount Saved}}{\text{Amount Paid}} = \text{Interest Rate for 20 Days}$$

$$\frac{\$2}{\$98} = 2.04\% \text{ for 20 Days}$$

The annual interest rate is:

$$\text{Interest rate for 20 Days} \times \frac{365 \text{ Days}}{20 \text{ Days}} = \text{Annual Interest Rate}$$

$$2.04\% \times \frac{365 \text{ Days}}{20 \text{ Days}} = 37.23\% \text{ Annual Interest Rate}$$

## Spotlight On FINANCIAL REPORTING

### Summary of Significant Accounting Policies

Companies must describe how they account for the major items reported on their financial statements in the first note to their financial statements. This note is normally called the Summary of Significant Accounting Policies. Wal-Mart explains the costs included in the cost of sales when the goods are sold as follows:

*Cost of Sales*

Cost of sales includes actual product cost, change in inventory, the cost of transportation to the Company's warehouses from suppliers, the cost of transportation from the Company's warehouses to the stores and clubs. . . . Substantially all allowances are accounted for as a reduction of purchases. . . .

This description exactly matches the manner in which we have just accounted for purchased inventory.

---

**SELF-STUDY PRACTICE**

How would each of the following independent transactions be recorded in the accounting records?

1. Wal-Mart returns to a supplier damaged boots that cost $1,000. Wal-Mart has not paid for the boots.

| | Debit | Credit |
|---|---|---|
| | | |
| | | |

Assets = Liabilities + Owners' Equity

2. Wal-Mart purchases DVD players with an invoice price of $20,000 and payment terms of 2/10, n/30. It then makes the payment within the discount period. Record the purchase and the subsequent payment.

| | Debit | Credit |
|---|---|---|
| | | |
| | | |
| | | |
| | | |

Assets = Liabilities + Owners' Equity

*After you have finished, check your answers with the solutions at the bottom of the next page.*

# RECORDING MERCHANDISE SALES

Merchandisers (the sellers) generally record the sale (and the customer records the purchase) at the point at which ownership is transferred to the customer. For a retail merchandiser like Wal-Mart, the transfer occurs when a customer buys and takes possession of the goods at checkout. For a wholesale merchandiser, the transfer of ownership occurs at the time stated in the written sales agreement—either **FOB shipping point** or **FOB destination.**

**A perpetual system records two effects when inventory is sold:**

1. An increase in Sales Revenue and a corresponding increase in either Cash (for a cash sale) or Accounts Receivable (for a credit sale).

2. A decrease in Inventory and a corresponding increase in Cost of Goods Sold (CGS), an expense account for the cost of inventory sold.

## Cash Sales

Assume that Wal-Mart sells a Schwinn mountain bike for $225 cash. The bike's cost to Wal-Mart was $175. Exhibit 6.4 illustrates this transaction.

Notice that Wal-Mart records **the sale of inventory as two transactions.** The first journal entry, which increases Cash and Sales Revenue, is recorded at the selling price ($225). The second part, which increases Cost of Goods Sold and decreases Inventory, is recorded at Wal-Mart's cost ($175). The $50 difference between the selling price and the cost ($225 − 175) is the gross profit. **Gross profit is not recorded directly in an account.** Rather, it is a subtotal that is produced by subtracting the cost of goods sold from the selling price.

| **Exhibit 6.4** | **Sale of Merchandise in a Perpetual System** |
| --- | --- |

(a) $225 Sales Revenue

(b) $175 Cost of Goods Sold

| | Debit | Credit |
| --- | --- | --- |
| (a) Cash (+A) | 225 | |
| Sales Revenue (+R, +OE) | | 225 |
| (b) Cost of Goods Sold (+E, −OE) | 175 | |
| Inventory (−A) | | 175 |

| **Assets** | **= Liabilities +** | **Owners' Equity** |
| --- | --- | --- |
| (a) Cash      +225 | | Sales Revenue (+R)      +225 |
| (b) Inventory −175 | | Cost of Goods Sold (+E) −175 |

---

**Solution to Self-Study Practice**

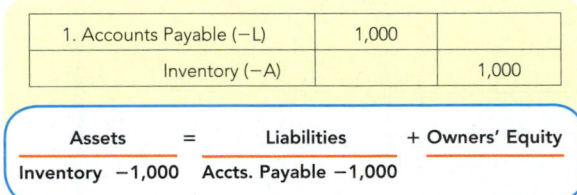

| 1. Accounts Payable (−L) | 1,000 | |
| --- | --- | --- |
| Inventory (−A) | | 1,000 |

| **Assets** | **=** | **Liabilities** | **+ Owners' Equity** |
| --- | --- | --- | --- |
| Inventory −1,000 | | Accts. Payable −1,000 | |

| 2. Inventory (+A) | 20,000 | |
| --- | --- | --- |
| Accounts Payable (+L) | | 20,000 |
| Accounts Payable (−L) | 20,000 | |
| Inventory (−A) (2% × $20,000) | | 400 |
| Cash (−A) (98% × $20,000) | | 19,600 |

| **Assets** | **=** | **Liabilities** | **+ Owners' Equity** |
| --- | --- | --- | --- |
| Inventory +20,000 | | Accts. Payable +20,000 | |
| Inventory   −400 | | Accts. Payable −20,000 | |
| Cash    −19,600 | | | |

# Sales Returns and Allowances

**Sales returns and allowances** are the same as purchase returns and allowances except that they are recorded from the seller's perspective rather than the purchaser's. Suppose that after Wal-Mart sold the Schwinn mountain bike, the customer returned it to Wal-Mart. Assuming that the bike's condition was still like new, Wal-Mart would refund the purchase price of $225 to the customer.

To account for this transaction, Wal-Mart would make two entries to basically reverse the entries recorded when the bike was sold. We say "basically" because there is one catch: Wal-Mart does not directly reduce its Sales Revenue account. Instead, the company tracks sales returns and allowances in a contra-revenue account that is deducted from total sales revenue.

Just as a contra-asset account such as Accumulated Depreciation reduces the total in an asset account such as Plant and Equipment, a contra-revenue account such as Sales Returns and Allowances reduces the total in a revenue account such as Sales Revenues. **Using a contra-revenue account instead of directly reducing the Sales account allows Wal-Mart to track the value of goods returned,** an indication of whether customers are happy with Wal-Mart's products.[3] Sales returns are recorded as follows:

|  | Debit | Credit |
|---|---|---|
| Sales Returns & Allowances (+xR, −OE) | 225 | |
|     Cash (−A) | | 225 |
| Inventory (+A) | 175 | |
|     Cost of Goods Sold (−E, +OE) | | 175 |

| Assets | = | Liabilities | + | Owners' Equity | |
|---|---|---|---|---|---|
| Cash       −225 | | | | Sales Returns & Allowances (+xR) | −225 |
| Inventory  +175 | | | | Cost of Goods Sold (−E) | +175 |

**Coach's Tip**

To indicate that an increase in a contra-revenue account reduces revenues, which reduces owner's equity, use (+xR, −OE).

# Credit Card Sales

In addition to cash, Wal-Mart accepts credit card payments. Wal-Mart's managers decided to accept credit cards—mainly Visa, Mastercard, and American Express—for a variety of reasons:

1. To increase customer traffic.
2. To avoid the costs of providing credit directly to customers, including credit checks, recordkeeping, and collections.
3. To receive payments faster (credit card receipts can be deposited directly into the seller's bank account).

Credit card companies charge a fee for the service they provide. When Wal-Mart deposits its credit card receipts, it might receive only 99 percent of the sales price. To account for these transactions, the company records the full sales price as sales revenue and then records the 1 percent credit card fee as an expense.

---

[3] We have assumed that the return occurs in the same period as the sale. When significant returns are likely to occur after the period of sale, the seller records an estimate of those expected returns using methods similar to those described in Chapter 9. We also have assumed the returned bike was as good as new.

Assume, for example, Wal-Mart sold an LCD TV for $500 and received $495 (= 99% × $500) from the credit card company. If the TV cost Wal-Mart $350, the company's accountant would make the following two entries:

| | Debit | Credit |
|---|---|---|
| Cash (+A) (99% × $500) | 495 | |
| Credit Card Fees (+E, −OE) (1% × $500) | 5 | |
|     Sales Revenue (+R, +OE) | | 500 |
| Cost of Goods Sold (+E, −OE) | 350 | |
|     Inventory (−A) | | 350 |

| Assets | | = | Liabilities | + | Owners' Equity | |
|---|---|---|---|---|---|---|
| Cash | +495 | | | | Sales Revenue (+R) | +500 |
| | | | | | Credit Card Fees (+E) | −5 |
| Inventory | −350 | | | | Cost of Goods Sold (+E) | −350 |

Sales using a retailer-issued credit card (such as Saks) are treated like any sale on account.

## Sales on Account and Sales Discounts

You already know that buyers sometimes receive purchase discounts to encourage them to pay promptly for the purchases they make on account. From the seller's point of view, these discounts are called **sales discounts**. As with purchase discounts, sales discounts involve two transactions: (1) the initial sale and (2) the discount given for prompt payment.

Assume Wal-Mart's warehouse store (Sam's Club) sells $1,000 of printer paper on account to a local business with payment terms of 2/10, n/30. The paper cost Sam's Club $670. Wal-Mart records this sale as follows:

| | Debit | Credit |
|---|---|---|
| Accounts Receivable (+A) | 1,000 | |
|     Sales Revenue (+R, +OE) | | 1,000 |
| Cost of Goods Sold (+E, −OE) | 670 | |
|     Inventory (−A) | | 670 |

| Assets | | = | Liabilities | + | Owners' Equity | |
|---|---|---|---|---|---|---|
| Accounts Receivable | +1,000 | | | | Sales Revenue (+R) | +1,000 |
| Inventory | −670 | | | | Cost of Goods Sold (+E) | −670 |

If the customer pays Wal-Mart within the 10-day discount period, it will receive a $20 discount (2% × $1,000). Wal-Mart accounts for the transaction as follows:

### Coach's Tip
Sales discounts are calculated after taking into account any sales returns and allowances.

| | Debit | Credit |
|---|---|---|
| Cash (+A) (98% × $1,000) | 980 | |
| Sales Discounts (+xR, −OE) (2% × $1,000) | 20 | |
|     Accounts Receivable (−A) | | 1,000 |

| Assets | | = | Liabilities | + | Owners' Equity | |
|---|---|---|---|---|---|---|
| Cash | +980 | | | | Sales Discounts (+xR) | −20 |
| Accounts Receivable | −1,000 | | | | | |

| Exhibit 6.5 | Effects of Sales-Related Transactions on Net Sales |

| | |
|---|---|
| Sales revenue | $1,725* |
| Less: Sales returns and allowances | (225) |
| Sales discounts | (20) |
| Net sales (reported on the income statement) | $1,480 |

\* Sales revenue totaled ($1,725 = $225 + $500 + $1,000).

If the customer does not pay by the end of the discount period, Wal-Mart will not allow the customer to take the discount for early payment. Instead, the customer will have to pay the full $1,000. Wal-Mart would record this payment as an increase in Cash (debit) and a decrease in Accounts Receivable (credit). (What if the customer does not pay at all? We will discuss that issue in detail in Chapter 9.)

Before leaving the topic of sales discounts, we should clear up a common misconception. Sales discounts differ from the discount you get as a consumer buying clearance items at a reduced price. The sales discounts discussed in this chapter are given only in business-to-business (B2B) transactions in return for prompt payment. We are sorry to say that as a consumer, you are not likely to be offered this type of discount.

## Transportation Cost (Freight-Out)

If Wal-Mart pays to have the printer paper delivered to the business that bought it, its accountant will record the shipping cost (called **freight-out**) as a Delivery Expense. To illustrate, assume Wal-Mart pays UPS $50 cash to deliver the printer paper to the business. Wal-Mart records the cost of transporting the goods to the customer as follows:

| | Debit | Credit |
|---|---|---|
| Delivery Expense (+E, −OE) | 50 | |
| Cash (−A) | | 50 |

| Assets | = | Liabilities | + | Owners' Equity | |
|---|---|---|---|---|---|
| Cash −50 | | | | Delivery Expense (+E) | −50 |

## Summary of Sales-Related Transactions

The sales returns and allowances and sales discounts introduced in this section were recorded using contra-revenue accounts. Exhibit 6.5 summarizes their effects on sales reporting.

Note that **credit card fees** and **freight-out** were recorded as an expense. Normally, both of these transactions would be included in the category **selling, general, and administrative expenses** or **operating expenses**.

## Spotlight On FINANCIAL REPORTING

### The Makeup of Net Sales

As you have seen, the documentation procedure involving contra-revenue accounts allows managers to monitor and control how sales discounts, returns, and allowances affect the company's revenues. For example, frequent returns of defective products would show up as an increase in the Sales Returns and Allowances account. In response to such an increase, Wal-Mart's managers might decide to discontinue the product or find a new supplier.

Detailed information relating to sales discounts and returns is a key part of a merchandiser's business operations. To avoid revealing these secrets to competitors, most companies report these contra-accounts only on their internal financial statements as in Exhibit 6.5. Externally reported income statements almost never include contra-revenue accounts. Instead, like the one for Wal-Mart, the income statements begin with **Net Sales**.

**SELF-STUDY PRACTICE**

1. Assume that Wal-Mart's warehouse store (Sam's Club) sells tables on account to a local business for $500 with payment terms of 2/10, n/30. The tables cost Wal-Mart $270. Analyze and record this sale.

|  | Debit | Credit |
|---|---|---|
|  |  |  |
|  |  |  |
|  |  |  |

Assets    =    Liabilities    +    Owners' Equity

2. The customer pays Wal-Mart for the purchase within the discount period.

|  | Debit | Credit |
|---|---|---|
|  |  |  |
|  |  |  |
|  |  |  |

Assets    =    Liabilities    +    Owners' Equity

*After you have finished, check your answers with the solutions at the bottom of the page.*

## Comparison of Sales and Purchases Accounting

You may have noticed that when one business sells products to another, the resulting transactions affect the books of both seller and purchaser. An example should clarify these relationships. In the examples just given, Wal-Mart was both the purchaser and the seller of the merchandise. Assume instead that the computer maker HP is the **seller** and Wal-Mart the **purchaser.** Furthermore:

1. HP sold 1,000 notebook computers to Wal-Mart for $500,000 on terms of 3/10, n/30. The computers had an inventory cost to HP of $300,000.

**Solution to Self-Study Practice**

| 1. Accounts Receivable (+A) | 500 |  |
|---|---|---|
| Sales Revenue (+R, +OE) |  | 500 |
| Cost of Goods Sold (+E, −OE) | 270 |  |
| Inventory (−A) |  | 270 |

| Assets | = | Liabilities | + | Owners' Equity | |
|---|---|---|---|---|---|
| Accts. Rec.  +500 |  |  |  | Sales Revenue (+R) | +500 |
| Inventory   −270 |  |  |  | Cost of Goods Sold (+E) | −270 |

| 2. Cash (+A) (98% × $500) | 490 |  |
|---|---|---|
| Sales Discounts (+xR, −OE) (2% × $500) | 10 |  |
| Accounts Receivable (−A) |  | 500 |

| Assets | = | Liabilities | + | Owners' Equity | |
|---|---|---|---|---|---|
| Cash | +490 |  |  | Sales Discounts (+xR) | −10 |
| Accts. Rec. | −500 |  |  |  |  |

| HP (Seller) | | |
|---|---|---|
| Accounts Receivable (+A) | 500,000 | |
| Sales Revenue (+R, +OE) | | 500,000 |
| Cost of Goods Sold (+E, −OE) | 300,000 | |
| Inventory (−A) | | 300,000 |

| Wal-Mart (Purchaser) | | |
|---|---|---|
| Inventory (+A) | 500,000 | |
| Accounts Payable (+L) | | 500,000 |

2. Wal-Mart returned 200 of those computers, for which the total purchase price was $100,000 (HP's cost was $60,000).

| HP (Seller) | | |
|---|---|---|
| Sales Returns and Allowances (+xR, −OE) | 100,000 | |
| Accounts Receivable (−A) | | 100,000 |
| Inventory (+A) | 60,000 | |
| Cost of Goods Sold (−E, +OE) | | 60,000 |

| Wal-Mart (Purchaser) | | |
|---|---|---|
| Accounts Payable (−L) | 100,000 | |
| Inventory (−A) | | 100,000 |

3. Wal-Mart paid HP for the remaining computers within the discount period.

| HP (Seller) | | |
|---|---|---|
| Cash (+A) | 388,000 | |
| Sales Discounts (+xR, −OE) | 12,000* | |
| Accounts Receivable (−A) | | 400,000 |
| *($12,000 = $400,000 × 3%) | | |

| Wal-Mart (Purchaser) | | |
|---|---|---|
| Accounts Payable (−L) | 400,000 | |
| Cash (−A) | | 388,000 |
| Inventory (−A) | | 12,000 |

Note that the 3 percent discount is applied to the amount owed after considering the return ($400,000 = $500,000 − $100,000).

As indicated earlier, the terms of sale (**FOB shipping point** or **FOB destination**) determine when the sale and purchase should be recorded. **The same terms indicate which party pays for the shipping.** The purchaser pays for shipping if the terms are FOB shipping point; the seller pays if the terms are FOB destination.

> **Coach's Tip**
>
> Note that **Net Sales** for the seller equals the total cost of the **Inventory** recorded by the purchaser:
>
> $500,000
> −100,000
> − 12,000
> $388,000

| HP (Seller) | | |
|---|---|---|
| If HP paid the $1,000 transportation cost on the shipment, it would record the freight–out on its books as a delivery expense: | | |
| Delivery Expense (+E, −OE) | 1,000 | |
| Cash (−A) | | 1,000 |

OR

| Wal-Mart (Purchaser) | | |
|---|---|---|
| If Wal-Mart paid the $1,000 transportation cost on the shipment, the freight–in would be recorded on its books as part of inventory: | | |
| Inventory (+A) | 1,000 | |
| Cash (−A) | | 1,000 |

The terms of the sales contract are usually stated in the invoice the seller sends to the buyer. Exhibit 6.6 shows a facsimile of an invoice for the transaction just analyzed with terms 3/10, n/30 and FOB destination (transportation paid by customer).

**Exhibit 6.6**     Invoice Sent by HP (the seller) to Wal-Mart (the buyer)

Invoice No. 2389

# HP

**3000 Hanover Street**
**Palo Alto, CA 94304**

Sold to:
Wal-Mart
Bentonville, Arkansas 33302

| Date: 07/02/2010 | Terms: 3/10, n/30 | | | Freight: Paid by Customer |
|---|---|---|---|---|

| Item Number | Description | Quantity | Price | Total |
|---|---|---|---|---|
| DV6000T | Notebook computer | 1,000 | $500.00 | $500,000 |
| Returns period: 30 days | | | Total: | $500,000 |

**Learning Objective 5**

Prepare a merchandiser's multistep income statement.

# PREPARING AND ANALYZING THE INCOME STATEMENT

## Multistep Income Statement for Merchandisers

One of the basic facts of merchandising is that to survive, a merchandiser must sell goods for more than their purchase cost. That is the only way companies such as Wal-Mart or Best Buy can generate enough money to cover their operating expenses. To help financial statement users to see how much income merchandising companies earned from product sales, merchandisers often present their income statements in a multistep format.

The multistep format separates revenues and expenses related to core operations from all other items that affect net income. We use the multistep format to prepare the income statement throughout this text. Because the amount of profit earned after deducting the cost of goods sold is a key measure for merchandisers, their multistep income statement also separates the Cost of Goods Sold from other expenses. As Exhibit 6.7 shows, this extra step produces a subtotal called Gross Profit (Gross Margin), or the amount the company earned from selling goods over and above the cost of those goods. If you buy something for $70 and sell it for $100, you will have a gross profit of $30.

Notice that after the gross profit line, the multistep income statement in Exhibit 6.7 presents other items in much the same format as that used by Pizza Aroma in Chapter 4. The category **Selling, General, and Administrative Expenses** (or Operating Expenses) represents a variety of expenses including wages, utilities, advertising, and rent. Those expenses are subtracted from the Gross Profit to yield **Operating Income,** a measure of the company's income from regular operating activities.

Revenues, expenses, gains, and losses from transactions that are not central to ongoing operations (that is, nonoperating items) are added and subtracted next. Typical items in this category include:

1. Interest revenue.
2. Interest expense.
3. Gains on the sale of investments and equipment.
4. Losses on the sale of investments and equipment.

| Exhibit 6.7 | Sample Multistep Income Statement |
|---|---|

**Wal-Mart Stores, Inc.**
Income Statements
Fiscal Years Ended January 31
(amounts in millions)

|  | 2006 | 2005 | 2004 |
|---|---|---|---|
| Net sales | $ 312,427 | $ 285,222 | $ 256,329 |
| Cost of goods sold | 240,391 | 219,793 | 198,747 |
| Gross profit | 72,036 | 65,429 | 57,582 |
| Selling, general, and administrative expenses | 53,506 | 48,338 | 42,557 |
| Operating income | 18,530 | 17,091 | 15,025 |
| Other revenue and expense, net | 1,172 | 986 | 832 |
| Income before income taxes | 17,358 | 16,105 | 14,193 |
| Income tax expense | 6,127 | 5,838 | 5,139 |
| Net income | $  11,231 | $  10,267 | $   9,054 |

The first and third of these items increase net income; the second and fourth decrease it. Thus, this line on the statement is called **Other Revenue and Expense, Net.** The term **net** refers to the fact that the amount reported combines amounts that both increase and decrease net income.

Wal-Mart's income statement includes one more subtotal and expense that we did not discuss in Chapter 4. We noted earlier that like many small businesses, Pizza Aroma is organized as a sole proprietorship. In contrast, most large companies are organized as corporations. Because a corporation is a separate legal entity, its owners cannot be held liable for more than their investment in the corporation—a major advantage to investors. Corporations are also taxed separately from their owners, so they normally list the subtotal **Income before Income Taxes** next. Then they subtract the account **Income Tax Expense** to arrive at the "bottom line," **Net Income.** This basic format is used by most merchandising and manufacturing companies.

**Coach's Tip**

The term **net** included in an account title listed on a financial statement means that positive and negative amounts have been combined.

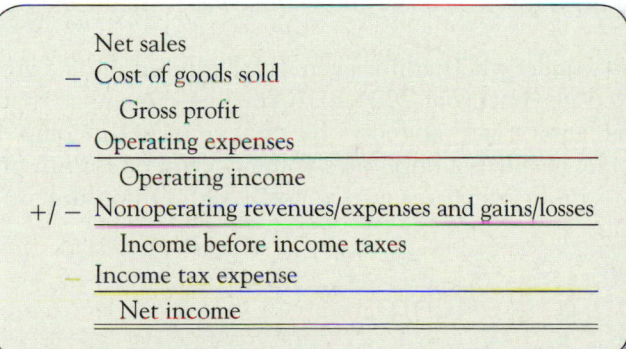

```
          Net sales
        − Cost of goods sold
          Gross profit
        − Operating expenses
          Operating income
      +/ − Nonoperating revenues/expenses and gains/losses
          Income before income taxes
        − Income tax expense
          Net income
```

# Gross Profit Percentage

Let's focus again on the gross profit line on the income statement in Exhibit 6.7. Although the dollar amount of gross profit can be impressive—Wal-Mart really did generate more than $72 billion of gross profit in 2006—by itself, this number is difficult to interpret. According to Exhibit 6.7, Wal-Mart's gross profit increased from 2004 to 2005 to 2006. The problem is that Wal-Mart also increased its sales over those three years, so we do not know whether the increase in gross profit arose because Wal-Mart increased its sales volume or because it

**Learning Objective 6**

Analyze the gross profit percentage.

generated more profit per sale. To determine the amount of gross profit included in each dollar of sales, analysts typically evaluate the **gross profit percentage.**

| Accounting Decision Tools | | |
| --- | --- | --- |
| **Name of Measure** | **Formula** | **What It Tells You** |
| Gross profit percentage | $\dfrac{(\text{Net Sales} - \text{CGS})}{\text{Net Sales}} \times 100$ | • The percentage of profit earned on each dollar of sales after considering the cost of products sold<br>• A higher ratio means that more profit is available to cover operating and other expenses |

The **gross profit percentage** measures the percentage of profit earned on each dollar of sales. Using the numbers from Wal-Mart's income statement in Exhibit 6.7, Wal-Mart's 2006 gross profit percentage would be computed as follows:

$$\text{Gross Profit Percentage} = \frac{(\text{Net Sales} - \text{CGS})}{\text{Net Sales}} \times 100 = \frac{(\$312{,}427 - \$240{,}391)}{\$312{,}427} \times 100 = 23.1\%$$

This ratio is used (1) to analyze changes in the company's operations over time, (2) to compare one company with another, and (3) to determine whether a company is earning enough revenue on each sale to cover its operating expenses. A higher gross profit percentage means that the company is selling products for a larger markup over their cost.

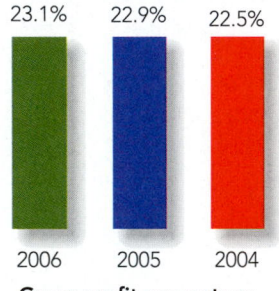

23.1%    22.9%    22.5%

2006    2005    2004

**Gross profit percentage**

**Wal-Mart**

As the bar graph in the margin shows, Wal-Mart's gross profit percentage increased ever so slightly from 2004 through 2006. In 2006, each dollar of sales included 23.1 cents of gross profit compared with 22.9 or 22.5 cents of gross profit in the prior two years, respectively. So not only did Wal-Mart sell more in 2006 than in the prior two years but it also generated more profit per sale. How was that possible? To find out, you could read the Management's Discussion and Analysis section of Wal-Mart's annual report. You would find that Wal-Mart was able to reduce inventory shrinkage and markdowns, which yields more profit per dollar of sales.

You might also wonder whether it is even worth talking about a gross profit percentage increase of only 0.6 percent from 2004 to 2006. Just remember that a small change in the gross profit percentage can produce a big change in net income. In Wal-Mart's case, because the company has such a huge sales volume, even one-tenth of a percentage point increase in its gross profit translates into almost half a billion dollars. Yes, that is billion with a **b.**

## Comparison to Benchmarks

Be aware that gross profit percentages can vary greatly among different types of companies. Wal-Mart's 23.1 percent is characteristic of its business strategy, which is to sell at "Low Prices, Always." In contrast, Saks' high-end department stores carry fashions with high-end prices, producing a 37.5 percent gross profit percentage. These two companies represent the extremes of merchandising; the typical department store earns a gross profit percentage of 28.1 percent.

Gross profit percentages can vary across industries as well (see Exhibit 6.8). Pharmaceutical companies recently reported an average gross profit percentage of 74.2 percent compared to the 15.2 percent automakers reported. Of course, these cross-industry differences are to be expected. Drug companies need a higher gross profit percentage than carmakers do because their research and development expenses are much higher.

**Exhibit 6.8**　　**Average Gross Profit Percentages by Industry Sector**

Merchandising sector
- Wal-Mart　23.1%
- Other department stores　28.1%
- Saks　37.5%

Manufacturing sector
- Automotive manufacturing　15.2%
- Pharmaceutical and medicine manufacturing　74.2%

*Source:* Retrieved October 17, 2006 from Industry Center n.d., http://www.investor.reuters.com/ (October 17, 2006).

## Demonstration Case A

Assume that Apple Inc. sold iPods costing $137,200 on account to Best Buy for $405,000 at terms 2/10, n/30. Because some of the merchandise differed from Best Buy's order, the manager returned the merchandise, which had a total purchase price of $5,000 (and a $1,500 cost to Apple). Best Buy satisfied the remaining balance (of $400,000) by paying within the discount period.

*Required:*

1. Assuming that both companies use a perpetual inventory system, prepare the journal entries that Apple and Best Buy would make to record the following transactions:

   a. Apple's sale to Best Buy.
   b. Best Buy's return of goods to Apple.
   c. Best Buy's payment made to Apple.

2. Compute Apple's Net Sales, assuming that Sales Returns and Allowances and Sales Discounts are treated as contra-revenues.
3. Compute Apple's Gross Profit from this sale.

## Suggested Solution

1. Journal entries:
   a. Apple's sale to Best Buy:

| Apple (Seller) | | |
|---|---|---|
| Accounts Receivable (+A) | 405,000 | |
| Sales Revenue (+R, +OE) | | 405,000 |
| Cost of Goods Sold (+E, −OE) | 137,200 | |
| Inventory (−A) | | 137,200 |

| Best Buy (Purchaser) | | |
|---|---|---|
| Inventory (+A) | 405,000 | |
| Accounts Payable (+L) | | 405,000 |

b.    **Best Buy's return of goods to Apple:**

| Apple (Seller) | | |
|---|---|---|
| Sales Returns and | | |
|     Allowances (+xR, −OE) | 5,000 | |
|     Accounts Receivable (−A) | | 5,000 |
| Inventory (+A) | 1,500 | |
|     Cost of Goods Sold (−E, +OE) | | 1,500 |

| Best Buy (Purchaser) | | |
|---|---|---|
| Accounts Payable (−L) | 5,000 | |
|     Inventory (−A) | | 5,000 |

c.    **Best Buy's payment made to Apple:**

| Apple (Seller) | | |
|---|---|---|
| Cash (+A) | 392,000 | |
| Sales Discounts (+xR, −OE) | 8,000* | |
|     Accounts Receivable (−A) | | 400,000 |
| *[$8,000 = ($405,000 − $5,000) × 2%] | | |

| Best Buy (Purchaser) | | |
|---|---|---|
| Accounts Payable (−L) | 400,000 | |
|     Cash (−A) | | 392,000 |
|     Inventory (−A) | | 8,000 |

2.    **To compute Net Sales, subtract Sales Returns and Allowances and Sales Discounts from Sales Revenue:**

| | | |
|---|---|---|
| Sales revenue | | $405,000 |
| Less:    Sales returns and allowances | | 5,000 |
|         Sales discounts [0.02 × ($405,000 − $5,000)] | | 8,000 |
|         Net sales | | $392,000 |

3.    **To compute Gross Profit, subtract Cost of Goods Sold from Net Sales:**

| | |
|---|---|
| Net sales | $392,000 |
| Cost of goods sold ($137,200 − $1,500) | 135,700 |
| Gross profit | $256,300 |

# Demonstration Case B

Among membership warehouse stores, Costco Wholesale Corporation is Sam's Club's major competitor. Costco's income statement for the year ended September 3, 2006, included the following revenues and expenses (presented in alphabetical order, in millions of dollars):

| | |
|---|---|
| Cost of merchandise sold | $ 52,745 |
| Other income and expense, net | +125 |
| Net sales | 60,151 |
| Income tax expense | 648 |
| Selling, general, and administrative expenses | 5,780 |

*Required:*

1. Prepare Costco's income statement for the year ended September 3, 2006, using the multistep format presented in this chapter.
2. Compute Costco's gross profit percentage for the year. What does it tell you about the company?

## Suggested Solution

1. **Multistep income statement:**

**Costco Wholesale Corporation**
Income Statement
Fiscal Year Ended September 3, 2006
(in millions)

| | |
|---|---:|
| Net sales | $ 60,151 |
| Cost of merchandise sold | 52,745 |
| Gross profit | 7,406 |
| Selling, general, and administrative expenses | 5,780 |
| Operating income | 1,626 |
| Other income and expense, net | 125 |
| Income before income taxes | 1,751 |
| Income tax expense | 648 |
| Net income | $ 1,103 |

2. **Gross profit percentage:**

$$\left(\frac{(\text{Net Sales} - \text{CGS})}{\text{Net Sales}}\right) \times 100$$

$$\frac{(\$60,151 - \$52,745)}{\$60,151} \times 100 = 12.3\%$$

This percentage means that each dollar of sales in 2006 included 12.3 cents of gross profit.

# Supplement 6A
## Periodic Inventory Records

As you have learned in this chapter, businesses using a periodic inventory system update inventory records only at the end of the accounting period. Unlike a perpetual inventory system, a periodic system does not track the cost of goods sold during the accounting period.

This supplement illustrates some typical journal entries made when using a periodic inventory system. The table that follows contrasts those entries with the entries that would be recorded using a perpetual inventory system. A summary of the effects of the journal entries on the accounting equation follows them. Note that the total effects and the resulting financial statements are identical. Only the timing and nature of the entries differ.

Assume for the purposes of this illustration only that a local cell phone dealer stocks and sells just one item, the MOTORAZR phone and that only the following events occurred in 2010:

| | | |
|---|---|---|
| Jan. | 1 | Beginning inventory: 800 units at a unit cost of $50. |
| Apr. | 14 | Purchased 1,100 additional units on account at a unit cost of $50. |
| Nov. | 30 | Sold 1,300 units on account at a unit sales price of $83. |
| Dec. | 31 | Counted 600 units at a unit cost of $50. |

| Periodic Records | Perpetual Records |
|---|---|

**A. Record purchases:**

April 14, 2010:

| Purchases (+A) (1,100 units at $50) | 55,000 | |
|---|---|---|
| Accounts Payable (+L) | | 55,000 |

**B. Record sales (but not cost of goods sold):**

November 30, 2010:

| Accounts Receivable (+A) | 107,900 | |
|---|---|---|
| Sales Revenue (+R, +OE) (1,300 units at $83) | | 107,900 |

No cost of goods sold entry

**C. Record end-of-period adjustments:**

  a. Count the number of units on hand.
  b. Compute the dollar valuation of the ending inventory.
  c. Compute and record the cost of goods sold.

| Beginning inventory (last period's ending) (800 units at $50) | $40,000 |
|---|---|
| Add: Net purchases | 55,000 |
| Cost of goods available for sale | 95,000 |
| Deduct Ending inventory (physical count—600 units at $50) | 30,000 |
| Cost of goods sold | $65,000 |

December 31, 2010:

**Transfer beginning inventory and net purchases to cost of goods sold:** (act as if all goods were sold)

| Cost of Goods Sold (+E, −OE) | 95,000 | |
|---|---|---|
| Inventory (−A) (beginning) | | 40,000 |
| Purchases (−A) | | 55,000 |

**Adjust the cost of goods sold by subtracting the amount of ending inventory still on hand** (recognize that not all goods were sold):

| Inventory (+A) (ending) | 30,000 | |
|---|---|---|
| Cost of Goods Sold (−E, +OE) | | 30,000 |

---

**A. Record purchases:**

April 14, 2010:

| Inventory (+A) (1,100 units at $50) | 55,000 | |
|---|---|---|
| Accounts Payable (+L) | | 55,000 |

**B. Record sales and cost of goods sold:**

November 30, 2010:

| Accounts Receivable (+A) | 107,900 | |
|---|---|---|
| Sales Revenue (+R, +OE) (1,300 units at $83) | | 107,900 |

| Cost of Goods Sold (+E, −OE) | 65,000 | |
|---|---|---|
| Inventory (−A) (1,300 units at $50) | | 65,000 |

**C. Record end-of-period adjustments:**

At the end of the accounting period, the balance in the Cost of Goods Sold account is reported on the income statement. Computing the cost of goods sold is not necessary because the **Cost of Goods Sold** account is up to date. Also, the **Inventory** account shows the ending inventory amount reported on the balance sheet. A physical inventory count is still necessary to assess the accuracy of the perpetual records and identify theft and other forms of shrinkage. Any shrinkage would be recorded by reducing the **Inventory** account and increasing an expense account (such as **Inventory Shrinkage** or **Cost of Goods Sold**). This illustration assumes that no shrinkage has been detected.

No entry

---

### Periodic (Totals table)

| Assets | | = | Liabilities | + | Owners' Equity | |
|---|---|---|---|---|---|---|
| Purchases | +55,000 | | Accounts Payable +55,000 | | | |
| Accts. Rec. | +107,900 | | | | Sales Revenue (R) | +107,900 |
| Inventory | −40,000 | | | | Cost of Goods Sold (E) | −95,000 |
| Purchases | −55,000 | | | | | |
| Inventory | +30,000 | | | | Cost of Goods Sold (E) | +30,000 |
| **Totals** | **+97,900** | | **+55,000** | | | **+42,900** |

### Perpetual (Totals table)

| Assets | | = | Liabilities | + | Owners' Equity | |
|---|---|---|---|---|---|---|
| Inventory | +55,000 | | Accounts Payable +55,000 | | | |
| Accts. Rec. | +107,900 | | | | Sales Revenue (R) | +107,900 |
| Inventory | −65,000 | | | | Cost of Goods Sold (E) | −65,000 |
| **Totals** | **+97,900** | | **+55,000** | | | **+42,900** |

# Supplement 6B

## Closing Entries for a Merchandiser

Like service companies, merchandisers must close their temporary accounts. The process is very similar to that followed by a service company. Assume for the purposes of this illustration only that a local cell phone dealer's preclosing trial balance included the following revenues, contra-revenues, and expenses at the end of 2010. The owner, John T. Lyon, organized his business as a sole proprietorship and uses a perpetual inventory system.

| | Debit | Credit |
|---|---|---|
| Sales Revenue | | 175,000 |
| Cost of Goods Sold | 92,000 | |
| Salaries Expense | 28,000 | |
| Rent Expense | 24,000 | |
| Shipping Expense (Freight-Out) | 2,000 | |
| Interest Income | | 2,400 |
| Depreciation Expense | 3,200 | |
| Sales Returns and Allowances | 1,200 | |
| Sales Discounts | 600 | |

The company would make the following closing entries:

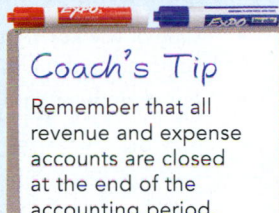

**Coach's Tip**

Remember that all revenue and expense accounts are closed at the end of the accounting period.

| | Debit | Credit |
|---|---|---|
| Sales Revenue (−R, −OE) | 175,000 | |
| Interest Income (−R, −OE) | 2,400 | |
|     Income Summary (+OE) | | 177,400 |

| | Debit | Credit |
|---|---|---|
| Income Summary (−OE) | 151,000 | |
|     Cost of Goods Sold (−E, +OE) | | 92,000 |
|     Salaries Expense (−E, +OE) | | 28,000 |
|     Rent Expense (−E, +OE) | | 24,000 |
|     Shipping Expense (Freight–Out) (−E, +OE) | | 2,000 |
|     Depreciation Expense (−E, +OE) | | 3,200 |
|     Sales Returns and Allowances (−xR, +OE) | | 1,200 |
|     Sales Discounts (−xR, +OE) | | 600 |

| | Debit | Credit |
|---|---|---|
| Income Summary (−OE) | 26,400 | |
|     John T. Lyon, Capital (+OE) | | 26,400 |

Note that the major differences between this merchandising example and the service company examples in Chapter 4 are that the Cost of Goods Sold and the contra-revenue accounts, Sales Returns and Allowances and Sales Discounts, must also be closed to the Income Summary.

# Chapter Summary

## LO1 Distinguish among service, merchandising, and manufacturing operations. p. 262

- Service companies sell services rather than physical goods; consequently, their income statements show the cost of services rather than the cost of goods sold.
- Merchandise companies sell goods that have been obtained from a supplier. Retail merchandise companies sell directly to consumers. Wholesale merchandise companies sell to retail companies.
- Manufacturing companies sell goods that they have made themselves.

**LO2 Explain the use of perpetual and periodic inventory systems and their role in inventory control. p. 262**

- A perpetual inventory system updates inventory records every time an item is bought, sold, or returned.
- Rather than update inventory records immediately after each purchase and sale, a periodic system updates inventory records only at the end of the accounting period.

**LO3 Analyze merchandise purchases under a perpetual inventory system. p. 265**

- The Inventory account should include the purchase price and any costs, such as freight-in, that are needed to prepare the inventory for sale.
- The Inventory account is decreased whenever the purchaser returns goods to the supplier or receives a discount for prompt payment.

**LO4 Analyze merchandise sales under a perpetual inventory system. p. 270**

- Two entries are made every time inventory is sold: One entry records the sale (and a corresponding debit to Cash or Accounts Receivable) and the other entry records the cost of goods sold (and a corresponding credit to Inventory).
- Sales discounts and sales returns and allowances are reported as contra-revenues, which reduce net sales.
- Credit card discounts and freight-out are recorded as operating expenses.

**LO5 Prepare a merchandiser's multistep income statement. p. 276**

- One of the key items in a merchandiser's multistep income statement is Gross Profit, which is a subtotal calculated by subtracting the Cost of Goods Sold from Net Sales.
- For both merchandisers and manufacturers, the basic format for the multistep income statement is:

|  | Net sales |
| − | Cost of goods sold |
|  | Gross profit |
| − | Operating expenses |
|  | Operating income |
| +/− | Nonoperating revenues/expenses and gains/losses |
|  | Income before income taxes |
| − | Income tax expense |
|  | Net income |

**LO6 Analyze the gross profit percentage. p. 277**

- The gross profit percentage is calculated by dividing the amount of Gross Profit (which is Net Sales minus Cost of Goods Sold) by the Net Sales amount. This measure indicates the amount of gross profit that is included in each dollar of sales.

## Financial Analysis Tools

| Name of Measure | Formula | What It Tells You |
|---|---|---|
| Gross profit percentage | $\dfrac{(\text{Net Sales} - \text{CGS})}{\text{Net Sales}} \times 100$ | • The percentage of profit earned on each dollar of sales after considering the cost of products sold<br>• A higher ratio means that more profit is available to cover operating and other expenses |

# Key Terms

See complete glossary in back of text.

# Questions

1. What is the distinction between service and merchandising companies? What is the distinction between merchandising and manufacturing companies? What is the distinction between retail and wholesale merchandising companies?

2. What is the main distinction between perpetual and periodic inventory systems? Which type of system provides better internal control over inventory? Explain why.

3. Why is a physical count of inventory necessary in a periodic inventory system? Why is it still necessary in a perpetual system?

4. Describe how transportation costs to obtain inventory (freight-in) are accounted for by a merchandising company using a perpetual inventory system. Explain the reasoning behind this accounting treatment.

5. What is the distinction between purchase returns and allowances and purchase discounts?

6. What is a purchase discount? Use 1/10, n/30 in your explanation.

7. Describe in words the journal entries that are made in a perpetual inventory system when inventory is sold on credit.

8. What is a credit card fee? How does it affect amounts reported on the income statement?

9. What is a sales discount? Use 1/10, n/30 in your explanation.

10. What is the distinction between sales allowances and sales discounts?

11. Is the amount of sales discount taken recorded (a) at the time the sale is recorded or (b) at the time the collection of the account is recorded?

12. Explain the difference between sales revenue and net sales.

13. Why are contra-revenue accounts used for sales discounts and sales returns and allowances rather than direct deductions from the sales account?

14. What is gross profit? How is the gross profit percentage computed? Illustrate its calculation and interpretation assuming net sales revenue is $100,000 and cost of goods sold is $60,000.

# Multiple Choice

1. Mountain Gear, Inc., buys bikes, tents, and climbing supplies from Rugged Rock Corporation for sale to consumers. What type of company is Mountain Gear, Inc.?

   Quiz 6-1
   www.mhhe.com/LLPW1e

   a. Service.
   b. Retail merchandiser.
   c. Wholesale merchandiser.
   d. Manufacturer.

2. Which of the following is false regarding a perpetual inventory system?

   a. Physical counts are never needed since records are maintained on a transaction-by-transaction basis.
   b. The balance in the inventory account is updated with each inventory purchase and sale transaction.
   c. Cost of goods sold is increased as sales are recorded.
   d. The account Purchases is not used as inventory is acquired.

3. Purchase discounts with terms 2/10, n/30 mean:

   a. 10 percent discount for payment within 30 days.
   b. 2 percent discount for payment within 10 days or the full amount (less returns) is due within 30 days.
   c. Two-tenths of a percent discount for payment within 30 days.
   d. None of the above.

4. Which of the following describes how payments to suppliers made within the purchase discount period are recorded in a perpetual inventory system (using the method shown in the chapter)?

   a. Reduce Cash, reduce Accounts Payable.
   b. Reduce Cash, reduce Accounts Payable, reduce Inventory.

   c. Reduce Cash, reduce Accounts Payable, increase Purchase Discounts.
   d. Reduce Cash, reduce Accounts Payable, decrease Purchase Discounts.

5. What is the best description of a credit card fee?

   a. The discount offered by a seller to a consumer for using a national credit card such as VISA.
   b. The fee charged by a seller to a consumer for the right to use a credit card, calculated as a percentage of total revenue for the sale.
   c. The discount offered by a seller to a customer for early payment of an account receivable.
   d. The percentage fee charged by a credit card company to a seller.

6. Sales discounts with terms 2/10, n/30 mean:

   a. 10 percent discount for payment within 30 days.
   b. 2 percent discount for payment within 10 days or the full amount (less returns) is due within 30 days.
   c. Two-tenths of a percent discount for payment within 30 days.
   d. None of the above.

7. Which of the following describes proper accounting for the costs of transporting purchased goods from the seller to the purchaser (freight-in) that is paid for by the purchaser?

   a. The amount is included in the cost of inventory by the purchaser.
   b. The amount is recorded as an other operating expense by the purchaser.

c. The amount is recorded as part of cost of goods sold by the seller.

d. None of the above.

8. Which of the following is not a component of net sales?

a. Sales returns and allowances.   c. Cost of goods sold.

b. Sales discounts.                d. Sales revenue.

9. A $1,000 sale is made on May 1 with terms 2/10, n/30. Items with a $100 selling price are returned on May 3. What amount, if received on May 9, will be considered payment in full?

a. $700

b. $800

c. $882

d. $880

10. Earlier this year, your company negotiated larger purchase discounts when paying for its merchandise inventory, which it has consistently taken throughout the year. What effect will this factor have on the company's gross profit percentage this year, in comparison to last year's percentage?

a. The ratio will not change.

b. The ratio will increase.

c. The ratio will decrease.

d. Either b or c.

| Solutions to Multiple-Choice Questions | | | | |
|---|---|---|---|---|
| 1. b | 2. a | 3. b | 4. b | 5. d |
| 6. b | 7. a | 8. c | 9. c | 10. b |

## Mini Exercises   ™    Available with McGraw-Hill's Homework Manager

**LO1**

**M6-1 Distinguishing Among Operating Cycles**

Identify the type of business as service (S), retail merchandiser (RM), wholesale merchandiser (WM), or manufacturer (M) for each of the following.

1. The company reports no inventory on its balance sheet.

2. The company's customers have been slow in paying their accounts because their own customers have been slow in paying.

3. Approximately one-third of the company's inventory requires further work before it will be ready for sale.

**LO2**

Nordstrom, Inc.

**M6-2 Choosing between a Perpetual and a Periodic Inventory System**

Nordstrom, Inc., started in business in 1901. It only took 100 years, but eventually the company changed from a periodic inventory system to a perpetual inventory system (in 2002). Write a brief report describing how this change is likely to improve the company's inventory control.

**LO2**

**M6-3 Calculating Shrinkage in a Perpetual Inventory System**

Corey's Campus Store has $50,000 of inventory on hand at the beginning of the month. During the month, the company buys $8,000 of merchandise and sells merchandise that had cost $30,000. At the end of the month, $25,000 of inventory is on hand. How much "shrinkage" occurred during the month?

**LO3**

**M6-4 Preparing Journal Entries for Purchases, Purchase Discounts, and Purchase Returns Using a Perpetual System**

Assume Anderson's General Store bought, on credit, a truckload of merchandise from American Wholesaling costing $23,000. The company was charged $650 in transportation cost by National Trucking, immediately returned goods to American Wholesaling costing $1,200, and then took advantage of a 2/10, n/30 purchase discount. Prepare journal entries to record the inventory transactions, assuming Anderson's uses a perpetual inventory system.

**LO3**

**M6-5 Determining Inventory Cost in a Perpetual System**

Using the information in M6-4, how much should Anderson's report as the cost of inventory?

**LO4**

**M6-6 Preparing Journal Entries for Credit Card Sales**

Credit card sales were $8,000 (credit card fee 3 percent). The goods sold had cost the company $3,500. Prepare journal entries to record these transactions.

**LO2, 3, 4, 5**

**M6-7 Preparing Journal Entries for Purchases and Sales Using a Perpetual Inventory System**

Inventory at the beginning of the year cost $13,400. During the year, the company purchased (on account) inventory costing $54,000. Inventory that had cost $60,000 was sold on account for $75,000. At the end of the year, inventory was counted and its cost was determined to be $7,400. (a) Prepare journal entries to record these transactions, assuming a perpetual inventory system is used. (*b*) What was the gross profit? (*c*) Was there any shrinkage?

**M6-8 Recording Journal Entries for Sales and Sales Discounts**    LO4

Merchandise costing $1,500 is sold for $2,000 on terms 2/10, n/30. The company uses a perpetual inventory system. Prepare the journal entries needed at the time of sale and collection, assuming that the buyer pays within the discount period.

**M6-9 Reporting Net Sales and Gross Profit with Sales Discounts**    LO4, 5

Using the information in M6-8, what amount will be reported on the income statement as net sales and as gross profit?

**M6-10 Journal Entries to Record Sales Discounts**    LO4

Inventory that cost $500 is sold for $700, with terms of 2/10, n/30. Give the journal entries to record (*a*) the sale of merchandise and (*b*) collection of the accounts receivable assuming that it occurs during the discount period. (Use the method shown in the chapter for recording sales discounts.)

**M6-11 Preparing a Multistep Income Statement**    LO5

Sellall Department Stores reported the following amounts in its adjusted trial balance prepared as of its December 31, 2010, fiscal year-end: Administrative Expenses, $2,400; Cost of Goods Sold, $22,728; Income Tax Expense, $3,000; Interest Expense, $1,600; Interest Revenue, $200; Operating Expenses, $2,600; Sales Revenue, $42,000; Sales Discounts, $2,200; Sales Returns and Allowances, $1,920; and Delivery (freight-out) Expense, $300. Prepare a multistep income statement for distribution to external financial statement users.

**M6-12 Computing and Interpreting the Gross Profit Percentage**    LO6

Using the information in M6-11, calculate the gross profit percentage for 2010. Evaluate the company's performance using Exhibit 6.8 as a benchmark.

**M6-13 Computing and Interpreting the Gross Profit Percentage**    LO6

Ziehart Pharmaceuticals reported net sales of $178,000 and cost of goods sold of $58,000. Candy Electronics Corp. reported net sales of $36,000 and cost of goods sold of $26,200. Calculate the gross profit percentage for both companies. From these calculations, can you determine which company is more successful? Explain.

**M6-14 Evaluating the Effect of Discounts and Returns on Gross Profit**    LO4, 5, 6

One of the few companies to report the extent of sales discounts and returns is sunglass maker Oakley, Inc. In the Management's Discussion and Analysis section of its 2005 annual report, Oakley reports the following information about its sales discounts and returns.

| | Year ended December 31, (in thousands) | | |
|---|---|---|---|
| | 2005 | 2004 | 2003 |
| Gross sales | $693,342 | $621,652 | $567,077 |
| Discounts and returns | (45,211) | (36,184) | (39,043) |
| Net sales | 648,131 | 585,468 | 528,034 |
| Cost of goods sold | 277,230 | 262,483 | 245,578 |
| Gross profit | 370,901 | 322,985 | 282,456 |

*Required:*

1. For each year, calculate the percentage of sales discounts and returns by dividing discounts and returns by gross sales and multiplying by 100. Based on these percentages, explain whether sales discounts and returns have a greater impact in 2005 or 2004.

2. For each year, calculate the gross profit percentage using the formula shown in this chapter (i.e., using net sales).

# Exercises

**Available with McGraw-Hill's Homework Manager**

**LO2**    **E6-1 Inferring Shrinkage Using a Perpetual Inventory System**

Calculate the amount of shrinkage for each of the following independent cases:

| Cases | Beginning Inventory | Purchases | Cost of Goods Sold | Ending Inventory (as counted) | Shrinkage |
|---|---|---|---|---|---|
| A | $100 | $700 | $300 | $420 | $ ? |
| B | 200 | 800 | 850 | 150 | ? |
| C | 150 | 500 | 200 | 440 | ? |
| D | 260 | 600 | 650 | 200 | ? |

**LO2**    **E6-2 Inferring Shrinkage Using a Perpetual Inventory System**

**JCPenney**    JCPenney Company, Inc., is a major retailer with department stores in all 50 states. The main part of the company's business consists of providing merchandise and services to consumers through department stores. In 2006 JCPenney reported cost of goods sold of $11,405 million, ending inventory for the current year of $3,234 million, and ending inventory for the previous year (2005) of $3,167 million.

*Required:*

If you knew that the cost of inventory purchases was $11,474 million, could you estimate the cost of shrinkage during the year? If so, prepare the estimate and, if not, explain why.

**LO3**    **E6-3 Recording the Cost of Purchases for a Merchandiser**

Apparel.com purchased 80 new shirts and recorded a total cost of $3,015 determined as follows:

| | |
|---|---|
| Invoice cost | $2,600 |
| Transportation cost (freight-in) | 165 |
| Estimated cost of shipping to customers | 250 |
| | $3,015 |

*Required:*

Calculate the correct inventory cost.

**LO3**    **E6-4 Recording Journal Entries for Purchases and Purchase Discounts Using a Perpetual Inventory System**

During the months of January and February, Axe Corporation purchased goods from three suppliers. The sequence of events was as follows:

Jan.  6  Purchased goods for $1,200 from Green with terms 2/10, n/30.
     6  Purchased goods from Munoz for $900 with terms 2/10, n/30.
    14  Paid Green in full.
Feb.  2  Paid Munoz in full.
    28  Purchased goods for $350 from Reynolds with terms 2/10, n/45.

*Required:*

Assume Axe uses a perpetual inventory system. The company had no inventory on hand at the beginning of January, and no sales were made during January and February. Prepare journal entries to record the transactions.

**LO3**    **E6-5 Reporting Purchases and Purchase Discounts Using a Perpetual Inventory System**

Using the information in E6-4, calculate the cost of inventory as of February 28.

**E6-6 Recording Journal Entries for Purchases, Purchase Discounts, and Purchase Returns Using a Perpetual Inventory System**   **LO3**

During the month of June, Ace Incorporated purchased goods from two suppliers. The sequence of events was as follows:

June   3   Purchased goods for $3,200 from Diamond Ltd. with terms 2/10, n/30.
      5   Returned goods costing $1,100 to Diamond Ltd. for full credit.
      6   Purchased goods from Club Corp. for $1,000 with terms 2/10, n/30.
   11   Paid the balance owed to Diamond.
   22   Paid Club Corp. in full.

**Required:**

Assume Ace uses a perpetual inventory system and that the company had no inventory on hand at the beginning of the month. Prepare journal entries to record the transactions.

**E6-7 Reporting Purchases, Purchase Discounts, and Purchase Returns Using a Perpetual Inventory System**   **LO3**

Using the information in E6-6, calculate the cost of inventory as of June 30.

**E6-8 Recording Journal Entries for Net Sales with Credit Sales and Sales Discounts**   **LO4**

During the months of January and February, Solitare Corporation sold goods to three customers. The sequence of events was as follows:

Jan.   6   Sold goods for $100 to Wizard Inc. with terms 2/10, n/30. The goods cost Solitare $70.
      6   Sold goods to SpyderCorp for $80 with terms 2/10, n/30. The goods cost Solitare $60.
   14   Collected cash due from Wizard Inc.
Feb.   2   Collected cash due from SpyderCorp.
   28   Sold goods for $50 to Bridges with terms 2/10, n/45. The goods cost Solitare $30.

**Required:**

Assume Solitare uses a perpetual inventory system and that sales discounts are reported as a contra-revenue. Prepare journal entries to record the transactions.

**E6-9 Reporting Net Sales with Credit Sales and Sales Discounts**   **LO4**

Using the information in E6-8, compute net sales for the two months ended February 28.

**E6-10 Recording Journal Entries for Net Sales with Credit Sales and Sales Discounts**   **LO4**

The following transactions were selected from the records of Evergreen Company:

July 12   Sold merchandise to Wally Butler, who paid for the $1,000 purchase with cash. The goods cost Evergreen Company $600.
   15   Sold merchandise to Claudio's Chair Company at a selling price of $5,000 on terms 3/10, n/30. The goods cost Evergreen Company $3,500.
   20   Sold merchandise to Otto's Ottomans at a selling price of $3,000 on terms 3/10, n/30. The goods cost Evergreen Company $1,900.
   23   Collected payment from Claudio's Chair Company from the July 15 sale.
Aug. 25   Collected payment from Otto's Ottomans from the July 20 sale.

**Required:**

Assume Evergreen Company uses a perpetual inventory system and that sales discounts are reported as a contra-revenue. Prepare journal entries to record the transactions.

**E6-11 Reporting Net Sales with Credit Sales and Sales Discounts**   **LO4**

Using the information in E6-10, compute net sales for the two months ended August 31.

**E6-12 Recording Journal Entries for Net Sales with Credit Card Sales, Credit Sales, Sales Discounts, and Sales Returns**   **LO4**

The following transactions were selected from among those completed by Bear's Retail Store in 2010:

Nov. 20   Sold two items of merchandise to Cheryl Jahn, who charged the $400 sales price on her Visa credit card. Visa charges Bear's a 2 percent credit card fee. The goods cost Bear's $300.

25    Sold 20 items of merchandise to Vasko Athletics at a selling price of $4,000 (total); terms 3/10, n/30. The goods cost Bear's $2,500.

28    Sold 10 identical items of merchandise to Nancy's Gym at a selling price of $6,000 (total); terms 3/10, n/30. The goods cost Bear's $4,000.

29    Nancy's Gym returned one of the items purchased on the 28th. The item was in perfect condition, and credit was given to the customer.

Dec.   6    Nancy's Gym paid the account balance in full.

30    Vasko Athletics paid in full the invoice of November 25, 2010.

**Required:**

Assume Bear's Retail Store uses a perpetual inventory system and that sales returns and sales discounts are reported as contra-revenues. Prepare journal entries to record the transactions.

**LO4**   **E6-13 Reporting Net Sales with Credit Card Sales, Credit Sales, Sales Discounts, and Sales Returns**

Using the information in E6-12, compute net sales for the two months ended December 31, 2010.

**LO4, 5**   **E6-14 Determining the Effects of Credit Sales, Sales Discounts, and Sales Returns and Allowances on Income Statement Categories**

Rockland Shoe Company records sales returns and allowances and sales discounts as contra-revenues. Complete the following table for Rockland, indicating the amount and direction of effect (+ for increase, − for decrease, and NE for no effect) of each transaction on each item listed below.

July 12    Rockland sold merchandise to Kristina Zee at its factory store. Kristina paid for the $300 purchase in cash. The goods cost Rockland $160.

July 15    Sold merchandise to Shoe Express at a selling price of $5,000, with terms 3/10, n/30. Rockland's cost was $3,000.

July 20    Collected cash due from Shoe Express.

July 21    Sold merchandise to Fleet Foot Co. at a selling price of $2,000, with terms 2/10, n/30. Rockland's cost was $1,200.

July 23    Fleet Foot Co. returned $1,000 of shoes, and promised to pay for the remaining goods in August. The returned shoes were in perfect condition and had cost Rockland $600.

| Transaction | July 12 | July 15 | July 20 | July 21 | July 23 |
|---|---|---|---|---|---|
| Sales Revenue | | | | | |
| Sales Returns and Allowances | | | | | |
| Sales Discounts | | | | | |
| Net Sales | | | | | |
| Cost of Goods Sold | | | | | |
| Gross Profit | | | | | |

**LO3, 4**   **E6-15 Recording Sales and Purchases with Discounts**

Cycle Wholesaling sells merchandise on credit terms of 2/10, n/30. A sale for $800 (cost of goods sold of $500) was made to Sarah's Cycles on February 1, 2010. On March 4, 2010, Cycle Wholesaling purchased bicycles from a supplier on credit, invoiced at $8,000 with terms 1/15, n/30. Assume Cycle Wholesaling uses a perpetual inventory system.

**Required:**

Sales Transactions:

1.   Give the journal entry Cycle Wholesaling would make to record the sale to Sarah's Cycles.

2.   Give the journal entry to record the collection of the account, assuming it was collected in full on February 9, 2010.

3.   Give the journal entry, assuming instead that the account was collected in full on March 2, 2010.

Purchase Transactions:

4.   Give the journal entry to record the purchase on credit.

5.   Give the journal entry to record the payment of Cycle Wholesaling's account, assuming it was paid in full on March 12, 2010.

6.   Give the journal entry, assuming instead that the account was paid in full on March 28, 2010.

**E6-16 Analyzing Sales and Purchases with Discounts and the Gross Profit Percentage**    LO3, 4, 6

Refer to the information in E6-15.

*Required:*

1.  Calculate the gross profit percentage for the sale to Sarah's Cycles, assuming the account was collected in full on February 9, 2010.
2.  At what cost will the bicycles purchased on March 4 be reported, assuming they are paid for on March 12, 2010?

**E6-17 Inferring Missing Amounts Based on Income Statement Relationships**    LO5

Supply the missing dollar amounts for the 2010 income statement of Williamson Company for each of the following independent cases:

|  | Case A | Case B | Case C |
|---|---|---|---|
| Sales revenue | $ 8,000 | $ 6,000 | $ ? |
| Sales returns and allowances | 150 | ? | 275 |
| Net sales revenue | ? | ? | 5,920 |
| Cost of goods sold | 5,750 | 4,050 | 5,400 |
| Gross profit | ? | 1,450 | ? |

**E6-18 Inferring Missing Amounts Based on Income Statement Relationships**    LO5

Supply the missing dollar amounts for the 2010 income statement of Lewis Retailers for each of the following independent cases:

| Cases | Sales Revenue | Beginning Inventory | Purchases | Cost of Goods Sold | Cost of Ending Inventory | Gross Profit |
|---|---|---|---|---|---|---|
| A | $ 650 | $100 | $700 | $300 | ? | $ ? |
| B | 900 | 200 | 800 | ? | 150 | ? |
| C | ? | 150 | ? | 200 | 300 | 400 |
| D | 800 | ? | 600 | 650 | 250 | ? |
| E | 1,000 | 50 | 900 | ? | ? | 500 |

**E6-19 Analyzing Gross Profit Percentage on the Basis of a Multistep Income Statement**    LO5, 6

The following summarized data were provided by the records of Mystery Incorporated for the year ended December 31, 2010:

| | |
|---|---|
| Sales of merchandise for cash | $240,000 |
| Sales of merchandise on credit | 42,000 |
| Cost of goods sold | 165,000 |
| Selling expense | 40,200 |
| Administrative expense | 19,000 |
| Sales returns and allowances | 7,000 |
| Income tax expense | 17,600 |

*Required:*

1.  Based on these data, prepare a multistep income statement (showing gross sales, net sales, gross profit, and all other appropriate subtotals).
2.  What was the amount of gross profit? What was the gross profit percentage? Explain what these two amounts mean.
3.  Evaluate the 2010 results in light of the 38 percent gross profit percentage in 2009.

**LO5, 6**

*Wolverine World Wide*

### E6-20 Analyzing Gross Profit Percentage on the Basis of an Income Statement

Wolverine World Wide prides itself as being the "world's leading marketer of U.S. branded non-athletic footwear." The following data (in thousands) were taken from its annual report for the year ended 2005:

| | |
|---|---:|
| Sales of merchandise | $1,060,999 |
| Income taxes | 36,780 |
| Cash dividends paid | 14,814 |
| Selling and administrative expense | 291,891 |
| Cost of products sold | 655,800 |
| Interest expense | 3,647 |
| Other revenues | 1,736 |

*Required:*

1. Based on these data, prepare a multistep income statement.
2. How much was the gross profit? What was the gross profit percentage (rounded to the nearest tenth of a percent)? Explain what these two amounts mean.
3. Evaluate the 2005 results in light of the 37.7 percent gross profit percentage in 2004.
4. Compare Wolverine's gross profit percentage to Wal-Mart's average gross profit percentage of 23.1 percent. From this information, can you determine which company is more successful? Why or why not?

**LO5, 6**

*Circuit City*

### E6-21 Comparing Multistep Income Statements

Abbreviated income statements for Circuit City and Best Buy are shown below (in millions) for the year ended February 28, 2006.

| | Best Buy | Circuit City |
|---|---:|---:|
| Net sales | $ 30,848 | $ 11,598 |
| Cost of goods sold | 23,122 | 8,767 |
| Gross profit | 7,726 | 2,831 |
| Operating expenses | 6,082 | 2,611 |
| Income from operations | 1,644 | 220 |
| Other income and expenses | 77 | 19 |
| Income before income taxes | 1,721 | 239 |
| Income tax expense | 581 | 88 |
| Net income | $ 1,140 | $ 151 |

*Required:*

1. Which company generated more net income and gross profit?
2. Which company generated a higher gross profit percentage? Show calculations.
3. Interpret your findings from 1 and 2.

### E6-22 (Supplement A) Recording Purchases and Sales Using Perpetual and Periodic Inventory Systems

Kangaroo Jim Company reported beginning inventory of 100 units at a per unit cost of $25. It had the following purchase and sales transactions during 2010:

Jan. 14   Sold 25 units at a unit sales price of $45 on account.
Apr. 9   Purchased 15 additional units at a per unit cost of $25 on account.
Sep. 2   Sold 50 units at a unit sales price of $50 on account.
Dec. 31   Counted inventory and determined 40 units were still on hand.

*Required:*

Record each transaction, assuming that Kangaroo Jim Company uses (*a*) a perpetual inventory system and (*b*) a periodic inventory system.

### E6-23 (Supplement B) Closing Entries for a Merchandiser

Koala Joe's preclosing trial balance included the following amounts (among others):

|  | Debit | Credit |
|---|---|---|
| Sales revenue |  | 75,000 |
| Cost of goods sold | 42,000 |  |
| Sales returns and allowances | 1,500 |  |
| Sales discounts | 500 |  |

Prepare any entries necessary to close these accounts to the Income Summary account.

## Problems—Set A     Available with McGraw-Hill's Homework Manager

### PA6-1 Journalizing Sales and Purchase Transactions between Wholesale and Retail Merchandisers with Sales/Purchase Allowances and Sales/Purchase Discounts Using Perpetual Inventory Systems

LO3, 4

The transactions listed below are typical of those involving New Books and Readers' Corner. New Books is a wholesale merchandiser and Readers' Corner is a retail merchandiser. Assume the following transactions between the two companies occurred in the order listed during the year ended August 31, 2010. Assume all sales of merchandise from New Books to Readers' Corner are made with terms 2/10, n/30, and that the two companies use perpetual inventory systems.

Transactions during the year ended August 31, 2010 are as follows:

a.  New Books sold merchandise to Readers' Corner at a selling price of $550,000. The merchandise had cost New Books $415,000.

b.  Two days later, Readers' Corner complained to New Books that some of the merchandise differed from what Readers' Corner had ordered. New Books agreed to give an allowance of $10,000 to Readers' Corner.

c.  Just three days later, Readers' Corner paid New Books, which settled all amounts owed.

*Required:*

1.  Prepare the journal entries that New Books would record, and show any computations.
2.  Prepare the journal entries that Readers' Corner would record, and show any computations.

### PA6-2 Reporting Sales and Purchase Transactions between Wholesale and Retail Merchandisers, with Sales/Purchase Allowances and Sales/Purchase Discounts Using Perpetual Inventory Systems

LO3, 4, 5

Use the information presented in PA6-1 to complete the following requirements.

*Required:*

1.  For each of the events *a* through *c*, indicate the amount and direction of the effect (+ for increase, − for decrease, and NE for no effect) on New Books in terms of the following items.

| Sales Revenues | Sales Returns and Allowances | Sales Discounts | Net Sales | Cost of Goods Sold | Gross Profit |
|---|---|---|---|---|---|

2.  Which of the above items are likely to be reported on New Books' external financial statements?
3.  Indicate the effect (direction and amount) of each transaction on the balance in Readers' Corner's inventory account.

LO3, 4, 5, 6

www.mhhe.com/LLPW1e

**PA6-3 Recording Sales and Purchases with Discounts, Returns, and Credit Card Fees and Computing the Gross Profit Percentage**

Hair World Inc. is a wholesaler of hair supplies. Hair World uses a perpetual inventory system. The following transactions (summarized) have been selected from 2010:

| | | |
|---|---|---:|
| a. | Sold merchandise for cash (cost of merchandise $18,600). | $31,200 |
| b. | Received merchandise returned by customers as unsatisfactory, for cash refund (original cost of merchandise $360). | 600 |
| c. | Sold merchandise to customers who charged the sales on their credit cards (cost of merchandise $12,000). The credit card fee is 3 percent. | 20,000 |
| d. | Purchased merchandise from Cari's Comb Company with terms 3/10, n/30. | 1,000 |
| e. | Purchased merchandise from other suppliers with terms 3/10, n/30. | 24,000 |
| f. | Purchased equipment for use in the store; paid cash. | 400 |
| g. | Purchased office supplies for future use in the store; paid cash. | 140 |
| h. | Freight on merchandise purchased; paid cash. | 100 |
| i. | Paid Cari's Comb Company after the discount period. | 1,000 |
| j. | Paid other suppliers (see part e) within the 3 percent discount period. | 23,280 |

*Required:*

1. Prepare journal entries for transactions *a–j*.
2. Assume that Hair World had inventory on hand at the beginning of the period at a cost of $100,000. At what amount should inventory be reported at the end of the period?
3. Compute gross profit and the gross profit percentage for sales this period.

LO4, 5, 6

www.mhhe.com/LLPW1e

**PA6-4 Preparing a Multistep Income Statement with Sales Discounts and Sales Returns and Allowances and Computing the Gross Profit Percentage**

Big Tommy Corporation is a local grocery store organized seven years ago as a corporation. The store is in an excellent location, and sales have increased each year. At the end of 2010, the bookkeeper prepared the following statement (assume that all amounts are correct, but note the incorrect terminology and format):

**BIG TOMMY CORPORATION**
Profit and Loss
December 31, 2010

| | Debit | Credit |
|---|---:|---:|
| Sales | | $420,000 |
| Cost of goods sold | $279,000 | |
| Sales returns and allowances | 10,000 | |
| Sales discounts | 6,000 | |
| Selling expense | 58,000 | |
| Administrative expense | 16,000 | |
| General expenses | 1,000 | |
| Income tax expense | 15,000 | |
| Net profit | 35,000 | |
| Totals | $420,000 | $420,000 |

*Required:*

1. Compute net sales. Treat sales discounts and sales returns and allowances as contra-revenues.
2. Prepare a multistep income statement, beginning with the amount for net sales.
3. Compute the gross profit percentage and explain its meaning.

**PA6-5 (Supplement A) Journalizing Sales and Purchase Transactions between Wholesale and Retail Merchandisers Using Periodic Inventory Systems**

Use the information presented in PA6-1 and transaction *a* (only) to complete the following requirements, except assume that both companies use periodic inventory systems.

*Required:*

1. Prepare the journal entries that New Books would record for transaction *a* only.
2. Prepare the journal entries that Readers' Corner would record for transaction *a* only.
3. Assume that, during the year, Readers' Corner sold merchandise on credit for $250,000. Prepare the journal entries that Readers' Corner would record.
4. Assume that, at the end of the year, Readers' Corner counted the inventory it had purchased from New Books and determined that its cost was $135,000. There was no beginning inventory. Prepare any adjusting entries that Readers' Corner would record, and show any computations.

**PA6-6 (Supplement B) Closing Entries for a Merchandiser**

R. Gupta Chemical's preclosing trial balance included the following amounts (among others):

| | Debit | Credit |
|---|---|---|
| Sales Revenue | | 615,000 |
| Interest Expense | 12,500 | |
| Sales Returns and Allowances | 53,200 | |
| Sales Discounts | 14,600 | |
| Cost of Goods Sold | 376,000 | |
| Selling Expense | 23,000 | |
| Rental Expense | 27,000 | |
| Shipping Expense (Freight-out) | 5,200 | |
| Depreciation Expense | 18,000 | |

*Required:*

Prepare the entries necessary to close these accounts.

# Problems—Set B   Available with McGraw-Hill's Homework Manager

**PB6-1 Journalizing Sales and Purchase Transactions between Wholesale and Retail Merchandisers with Sales/Purchase Allowances and Sales/Purchase Discounts Using Perpetual Inventory Systems**

LO3, 4

The transactions listed below are typical of those involving Southern Sporting Goods and Sports R Us. Southern Sporting Goods is a wholesale merchandiser and Sports R Us is a retail merchandiser. Assume the following transactions between the two companies occurred in the order listed during the year ended December 31, 2010. Assume all sales of merchandise from Southern Sporting Goods to Sports R Us are made with terms 2/10, n/30, and that the two companies use perpetual inventory systems.

Transactions during 2010:

a. Southern Sporting Goods sold merchandise to Sports R Us at a selling price of $125,000. The merchandise had cost Southern Sporting Goods $94,000.
b. Two days later, Sports R Us complained to Southern Sporting Goods that some of the merchandise differed from what Sports R Us had ordered. Southern Sporting Goods agreed to give an allowance of $3,000 to Sports R Us.
c. Just three days later Sports R Us paid Southern Sporting Goods, which settled all amounts owed.

*Required:*

1. Prepare the journal entries that Southern Sporting Goods would record, and show any computations.
2. Prepare the journal entries that Sports R Us would record, and show any computations.

**LO3, 4, 5**

**PB6-2 Reporting Sales and Purchase Transactions between Wholesale and Retail Merchandisers with Sales/Purchase Allowances and Sales/Purchase Discounts Using Perpetual Inventory Systems**

Use the information presented in PB 6-1 to complete the following requirements.

*Required:*

1. For each of the events *a* through *c*, indicate the amount and direction of the effect (+ for increase, − for decrease, and NE for no effect) on Southern Sporting Goods in terms of the following items.

| Sales Revenues | Sales Returns and Allowances | Sales Discounts | Net Sales | Cost of Goods Sold | Gross Profit |
|---|---|---|---|---|---|

2. Which of the above items is likely to be reported on Southern Sporting Goods' external financial statements.
3. Indicate the effect (direction and amount) of each transaction on the balance in Sports R Us's inventory account.

**LO3, 4, 5, 6**

**PB6-3 Recording Sales and Purchases with Discounts, Returns, and Credit Card Fees and Computing the Gross Profit Percentage**

Larry's Hardware, Incorporated, is a locally owned and operated hardware store. Larry's Hardware uses a perpetual inventory system. The following transactions (summarized) have been selected from 2010:

| | | |
|---|---|---|
| *a.* | Sold merchandise for cash (cost of merchandise $285,000). | $400,000 |
| *b.* | Received merchandise returned by customers as unsatisfactory, for cash refund (original cost of merchandise $1,900). | 3,000 |
| *c.* | Sold merchandise to customers who charged the sales on their credit cards (cost of merchandise $60,000). The credit card fee is 2 percent. | 100,000 |
| *d.* | Purchased merchandise from Do It Yourself Company with terms 3/10, n/30. | 27,000 |
| *e.* | Purchased merchandise from other suppliers with terms 3/10, n/30. | 237,000 |
| *f.* | Purchased equipment for use in store; paid cash. | 5,000 |
| *g.* | Purchased office supplies for future use in the store; paid cash. | 400 |
| *h.* | Freight on merchandise purchased; paid cash. | 350 |
| *i.* | Paid Do It Yourself Company after the discount period. | 27,000 |
| *j.* | Paid other suppliers (see transaction *e*) within the discount period. | 229,890 |

*Required:*

1. Prepare journal entries for transactions *a–j*.
2. Assume that Larry's Hardware had inventory on hand at the beginning of the period at a cost of $350,000. At what amount should inventory be reported at the end of the period?
3. Compute gross profit and the gross profit percentage for sales this period.

**LO4, 5, 6**

**PB6-4 Preparing a Multistep Income Statement with Sales Discounts and Sales Returns and Allowances, and Computing the Gross Profit Percentage**

Emily's Greenhouse Corporation is a local greenhouse organized 10 years ago as a corporation. The greenhouse is in an excellent location, and sales have increased each year. At the end of 2010, the bookkeeper prepared the following statement (assume that all amounts are correct, but note the incorrect terminology and format):

**EMILY'S GREENHOUSE CORPORATION**
Profit and Loss
December 31, 2010

|  | Debit | Credit |
|---|---|---|
| Sales |  | $504,000 |
| Cost of goods sold | $311,000 |  |
| Sales returns and allowances | 11,000 |  |
| Sales discounts | 8,000 |  |
| Selling expense | 61,000 |  |
| Administrative expense | 13,000 |  |
| General expenses | 3,000 |  |
| Income tax expense | 18,000 |  |
| Net profit | 79,000 |  |
| Totals | $504,000 | $504,000 |

*Required:*

1. Compute net sales. Treat sales discounts and sales returns and allowances as contra-revenues.
2. Prepare a multistep income statement, beginning with the amount for net sales.
3. Compute the gross profit percentage and explain its meaning.

**PB6-5 (Supplement A) Journalizing Sales and Purchase Transactions between Wholesale and Retail Merchandisers Using Periodic Inventory Systems**

Use the information presented in PB6-1 and transaction *a* (only) to complete the following requirements, except assume that both companies use periodic inventory systems.

*Required:*

1. Prepare the journal entries that Southern Sporting Goods would record for transaction *a* only.
2. Prepare the journal entries that Sports R Us would record for transaction *a* only.
3. Assume that, during the year, Sports R Us sold merchandise on credit for $97,000. Prepare the journal entries that Sports R Us would record.
4. Assume that, at the end of the year, Sports R Us counted the inventory it had purchased from Southern Sporting Goods and determined that its cost was $43,000. There was no beginning inventory. Prepare any adjusting entries that Sports R Us would record, and show any computations.

**PB6-6 (Supplement B) Closing Entries for a Merchandiser**

Paul Ethan's Skateboard Shop's preclosing trial balance included the following amounts (among others):

|  | Debit | Credit |
|---|---|---|
| Sales Revenue |  | 65,000 |
| Other Income |  | 12,500 |
| Wage Expense | 13,000 |  |
| Rental Expense | 5,000 |  |
| Shipping Expense (Freight-out) | 500 |  |
| Sales Discounts | 1,600 |  |
| Sales Returns and Allowances | 5,200 |  |
| Cost of Goods Sold | 31,000 |  |
| Interest Expense | 800 |  |

*Required:*

Prepare the entries necessary to close these accounts.

# Cases and Projects

LO2, 5, 6

### CP6-1 Finding Financial Information

Refer to the financial statements of The Home Depot in Appendix A at the end of this book, or download the annual report from the *Cases* section of the text's Web site at www.mhhe.com/LLPW1e.

*Required:*

1. What amount of Net Sales does the company report during the current year?

2. Assuming that Cost of Sales is the same thing as Cost of Goods Sold, compute the company's gross profit percentage for the most recent two years. Has it risen or fallen? Explain the meaning of the change.

3. Assume that The Home Depot experienced no shrinkage in the most current year. Using the balance sheet and income statement, estimate the amount of purchases in the most recent year. (Hint: Use the cost of goods sold equation to solve for purchases.)

LO4, 5, 6

Lowe's

### CP6-2 Comparing Financial Information

Refer to the financial statements of The Home Depot in Appendix A and Lowe's in Appendix B at the end of this book, or download the annual reports from the *Cases* section of the text's Web site at www.mhhe.com/LLPW1e.

1. Does Lowe's report higher or lower Net Sales than The Home Depot during the current year?

2. Assuming that Cost of Sales is the same thing as Cost of Goods Sold, compute Lowe's gross profit percentage for the most recent two years. Is it greater or less than The Home Depot's?

3. Assume that Lowe's and The Home Depot experienced no shrinkage in the most recent year. Using the balance sheet and income statement, estimate the amount of purchases in the most recent year. How much greater (or less) were Lowe's purchases than The Home Depot's for the most recent year? (Hint: Use the cost of goods sold equation to solve for purchases.)

LO1, 6

### CP6-3 Examining an Annual Report: Internet-Based Team Research

As a team, select an industry to analyze. Using your Web browser, each team member should acquire the annual report or 10-K for one publicly traded company in the industry, with each member selecting a different company. (See CP1-3 in Chapter 1 for a description of possible resources for these tasks.)

*Required:*

1. On an individual basis, each team member should write a short report that incorporates the following:

   *a.* Describe the company's business in sufficient detail to be able to classify it as a service, merchandising, or manufacturing company. What products or services does the company provide?

   *b.* Calculate the gross profit percentage at the end of the current and prior year, and explain any change between the two years.

2. Then, as a team, write a short report comparing and contrasting your companies using these attributes. Discuss any patterns across the companies that you as a team observe. Provide potential explanations for any differences discovered.

LO5, 6

### CP6-4 Making Ethical Decisions: A Mini Case

Assume you work as an accountant in the merchandising division of a large public company that makes and sells athletic clothing. To encourage the merchandising division to earn as much profit on each individual sale as possible, the division manager's pay is based, in part, on the division's gross profit percentage. To encourage control over the division's operating expenses, the manager's pay also is based on the division's net income.

You are currently preparing the division's financial statements. The division had a good year, with sales of $100,000, cost of goods sold of $50,000, sales returns and allowances of $6,000, sales discounts of $4,000, and other selling expenses of $30,000. (Assume the division does not report income taxes.) The division manager stresses that "it would be in your personal interest" to classify sales returns and allowances, and sales discounts as selling expenses rather than as contra-revenues on the division's income statement. He justifies this "friendly advice" by saying that he is not asking you to fake the numbers—he just believes that those items are more accurately reported as expenses. Plus, he claims, being a division of a larger company, you do not have to follow GAAP.

**Required:**

1. Prepare an income statement for the division using the classifications advised by the manager. Using this income statement, calculate the division's gross profit percentage.

2. Prepare an income statement for the division using the classifications shown in this chapter. Using this income statement, calculate the division's gross profit percentage.

3. What reason (other than reporting "more accurately") do you think is motivating the manager's advice to you?

4. Do you agree with the manager's statement that he "is not asking you to fake the numbers"?

5. Do you agree with the manager's statement about not having to follow GAAP?

6. How should you respond to the division manager's "friendly advice"?

## CP6-5 Preparing Multistep Income Statements and Calculating Gross Profit Percentage          LO5, 6

Assume that you have been hired by Big Sky Corporation as a summer intern. The company is in the process of preparing their annual financial statements. To help in the process, you are asked to prepare an income statement for internal reporting purposes and an income statement for external reporting purposes. Your boss has also requested that you determine the company's gross profit percentage based on the statements that you are to prepare. The following adjusted trial balance was created from the general ledger accounts on May 31, 2010.

| Account Titles | Debit | Credit |
|---|---|---|
| Cash | $ 57,000 | |
| Accounts receivable | 67,000 | |
| Inventory | 103,000 | |
| Property and equipment | 252,000 | |
| Accumulated depreciation | | $ 103,000 |
| Liabilities | | 75,000 |
| Owners' equity, June 1, 2009 | | 265,900 |
| Sales revenue | | 369,000 |
| Sales returns and allowances | 9,500 | |
| Sales discounts | 14,000 | |
| Cost of goods sold | 248,000 | |
| Selling expense | 19,000 | |
| Administrative expense | 23,000 | |
| General expenses | 5,000 | |
| Income tax expense | 15,400 | |
| Totals | $ 812,900 | $ 812,900 |

Your boss wants you to create the spreadsheet in a way that automatically recalculates net sales and any other related amounts whenever changes are made to the contra-revenue accounts. To do this, you know that you will have to use formulas throughout the worksheets and even import or link cells from one worksheet to another. Once again, your friend Owen is willing to help.

From:        Owen@yahoo.com
To:          Helpme@hotmail.com
Cc:
Subject:     Excel Help

Sounds like you are going to get some great experience this summer. Okay, to import a number from another spreadsheet, you first click on the cell where you want the number to appear. For example, if you want to enter the Net Sales balance in the external income statement, click on the cell in the external income statement where the net sales number is supposed to appear. Enter the equals sign (=) and then click on the tab that takes you to the worksheet containing the internal income statement. In that worksheet, click on the cell that contains the amount you want to import into the external income statement and then press enter. This will create a link from the internal income statement cell to the external income statement cell. Here is a screen shot showing the formula that will appear after you import the number.

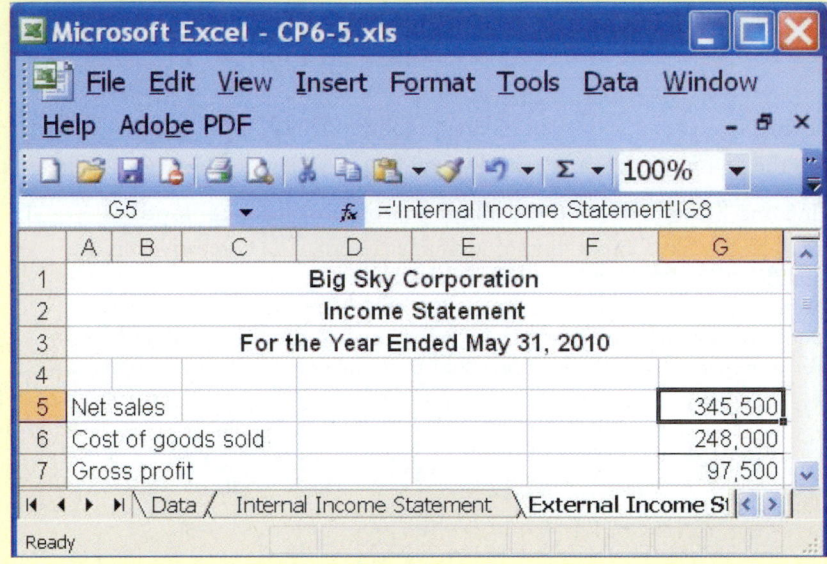

Do not forget to save the file using a name that indicates who you are.

***Required:***

Enter the trial balance information into a spreadsheet and complete the following:

1. Prepare a multistep income statement that would be used for internal reporting purposes. Classify sales returns and allowances and sales discounts as contra-revenue accounts.

2. Prepare a multistep income statement that would be used for external reporting purposes, beginning with the amount for net sales.

3. Compute the gross profit percentage.

# 7 Inventories

## LEARNING OBJECTIVES

**After completing this chapter, you should be able to:**

Lectured slideshow–LP7-1
www.mhhe.com/LLPW1e

**LO1** Explain how to report inventory and cost of goods sold.

**LO2** Explain the cost of goods sold equation.

**LO3** Compute inventory costs using four inventory costing methods.

**LO4** Report inventory at the lower of cost or market.

**LO5** Determine the effects of inventory errors on the income statement and balance sheet.

**LO6** Compute and interpret the inventory turnover ratio.

# Focus Company: AMERICAN EAGLE OUTFITTERS

## "Relentless Customer Focus Leads to Record Profitability"

www.ae.com

Whether you are shopping for gasoline, groceries, or a new flat-screen TV, prices always seem to be changing. The political situation in oil-producing nations can cause a stunning increase in prices at the pump. A late freeze in Florida can hike the price of orange juice. Increasing competition can dramatically lower the cost of that new TV.

Companies face similar price changes when they purchase or produce the goods they sell. Increases in demand can cause the cost of inventory to increase over time; technological innovation can cause it to decrease. Either way, inventory is likely to include some items that were acquired at a lower unit cost and others that were acquired at a higher unit cost.

Suppose American Eagle Outfitters, the clothing retailer, purchases three batches of its AE Springweight Track Jackets at a cost of $40 per jacket for the first batch, $50 per jacket for the second batch, and $60 per jacket for the third. How would you account for this inventory? Fortunately, there are specific rules to follow in determining the cost of inventory on hand and the cost of inventory sold. The tricky part is that these rules allow accountants to use several different methods, each of which leads to a different number. This flexibility allows managers to choose the method that best fits their business environment. But it also means that you must know which method managers are using and how it works. That is our focus in this chapter.

## ORGANIZATION OF THE CHAPTER

| REPORTING INVENTORY AND COST OF GOODS SOLD | CHOOSING AMONG INVENTORY COSTING METHODS | REPORTING INVENTORY AT THE LOWER OF COST OR MARKET | IDENTIFYING THE EFFECTS OF INVENTORY ERRORS | EVALUATING INVENTORY MANAGEMENT |
|---|---|---|---|---|
| • Balance Sheet and Income Statement Reporting<br>• Cost of Goods Sold Equation | • Cost Flow Methods under a Perpetual Inventory System<br>• First-In, First-Out (FIFO)<br>• Last-In, First-Out (LIFO)<br>• Weighted Average Cost<br>• Financial Statement Effects of Inventory Costing Methods | | • Income Statement Effects<br>• Balance Sheet Effects | • Inventory Turnover Analysis<br>• Comparison to Benchmarks |

# REPORTING INVENTORY AND COST OF GOODS SOLD

The generic term **inventory** includes both goods that are held for sale in the normal course of business and goods that are used to produce other goods. Merchandisers such as American Eagle Outfitters hold merchandise inventory, which they usually acquire in finished condition, ready for sale without further processing. Manufacturers often hold three types of inventory, each of which represents a different stage in the manufacturing process. For purposes of this chapter, we focus on merchandise inventory, but be aware that the concepts discussed in this chapter apply to both merchandise and manufacturing inventories.

## Balance Sheet and Income Statement Reporting

**Learning Objective 1**

Explain how to report inventory and cost of goods sold.

**AMERICAN EAGLE OUTFITTERS**
ae.com

Because inventory will be used or converted into cash within one year, it is reported on the balance sheet as a current asset. Goods placed in inventory are initially recorded at cost, which is the amount paid to acquire the asset and prepare it for sale. See Exhibit 7.1 for the way American Eagle's partial balance sheet reports inventory.

**Exhibit 7.1**    Reporting Inventory on the Balance Sheet (Partial)

### American Eagle Outfitters, Inc.
### Consolidated Balance Sheets
### At January 31, 2007 and 2006

| (in millions) | 2007 | 2006 |
|---|---|---|
| **Assets** | | |
| Current assets | | |
|     Cash and cash equivalents | $ 60 | $131 |
|     Short-term investments | 767 | 621 |
|     Merchandise inventory | 264 | 211 |
|     Accounts and note receivable | 26 | 29 |
|     Prepaid expenses and other | 34 | 30 |

| Exhibit 7.2 | Reporting Cost of Goods Sold on the Income Statement (Partial) |
|---|---|

**AMERICAN EAGLE OUTFITTERS**
ae.com

**American Eagle Outfitters, Inc.**
**Consolidated Income Statements**
**For the Years Ended January 31, 2007, 2006, and 2005**

| (in millions) | 2007 | 2006 | 2005 |
|---|---|---|---|
| Net sales | $2,794 | $2,322 | $1,890 |
| Cost of goods sold | 1,454 | 1,244 | 1,009 |
| Gross profit | 1,340 | 1,078 | 881 |

When a company sells goods, it removes their cost from the Inventory account and reports the cost on the income statement as the expense Cost of Goods Sold. See Exhibit 7.2 for how American Eagle reports the Cost of Goods Sold (CGS) on its partial income statement. Notice that it follows directly after net sales. The difference between these two line items is a subtotal called gross profit.

## COST OF GOODS SOLD EQUATION

Although the cost of inventory and the cost of goods sold are reported on different financial statements, they are related. A company starts each accounting period with a stock of inventory called **beginning inventory (BI).** During the accounting period, new **purchases (P)** are added to the beginning inventory. As in Exhibit 7.3, the sum of these two amounts (BI + P) becomes the cost of goods available for sale during the period.

Some of the goods available for sale will be sold during the period; some will not. The portion that is sold is reported as the cost of goods sold on the income statement. The portion that remains unsold at the end of the period is reported as the **ending inventory (EI)** on the balance sheet. The ending inventory for one accounting period then becomes the beginning

> **Learning Objective 2**
> Explain the cost of goods sold equation.

| Exhibit 7.3 | Relationship between Inventory and Cost of Goods Sold |
|---|---|

inventory for the next period. The cost of goods sold (CGS) equation summarizes the relationships between these inventory amounts:

$$BI + P - CGS = EI$$

To illustrate the CGS equation, assume that, as in Exhibit 7.3, American Eagle Outfitters began the period with $40,000 of Springweight Track Jackets in beginning inventory. During the period, the company purchased more of these jackets for $55,000. The cost of goods sold for the period is $60,000. At the end of the period, $35,000 of jackets was left in inventory. These amounts can be represented in the cost of goods sold equation or by the inventory T-account:

**Cost of Goods Sold Calculation**

| | |
|---|---:|
| Beginning inventory | $40,000 |
| + Purchases of merchandise during the period | + 55,000 |
| Goods available for sale | 95,000 |
| − Cost of goods sold | − 60,000 |
| Ending inventory | 35,000 |

**+ Merchandise Inventory (A) −**

| | | | |
|---|---:|---:|---|
| Beginning Inventory | 40,000 | | |
| Purchases of Inventory | 55,000 | 60,000 | Cost of Goods Sold |
| Ending Inventory | 35,000 | | |

If one of these values is unknown, you can use either the cost of goods sold equation or the inventory T-account to solve for the missing value. See for yourself in the following Self-Study Practice.

**SELF-STUDY PRACTICE**

Assume the following facts for the AE Eyelet Ts product line for the year 2008:

**Beginning inventory (BI) held 500 units at a unit cost of $10.**

**Purchases (P) of inventory equaled 1,200 units at a unit cost of $10.**

**Sales equaled 1,100 units at a sales price of $12 (and a unit cost of $10).**

Using the cost of goods sold equation or a T-account, compute the dollar amount of Eyelet Ts in inventory at the end of the period.

| | |
|---|---|
| Beginning inventory (BI) | $ 5,000 |
| + Purchases of merchandise during the year | _____ |
| − Cost of goods sold (CGS) | _____ |
| = Ending inventory (EI) | $ _____ |

**+ Merchandise Inventory (A) −**

| | | | |
|---|---|---|---|
| BI | _____ | | |
| P | _____ | _____ | CGS |
| EI | _____ | | |

*After you have finished, check your answers with the solutions at the bottom of the page.*

# CHOOSING AMONG INVENTORY COSTING METHODS

In the example presented in the Self-Study Practice, the cost of all units of the item was the same—$10. If inventory costs normally remained constant, our discussion would end here. But just as you notice every time you fill up your car with gas, the cost of goods does not always

**Solution to Self-Study Practice**

| | |
|---|---|
| BI = 500 × $10 = $5,000 | BI + P − CGS = EI |
| P = 1,200 × $10 = $12,000 | 5,000 + 12,000 − 11,000 = EI |
| CGS = 1,100 × $10 = $11,000 | 6,000 = EI |

stay the same. In recent years, the costs of many items have risen moderately. In other cases, such as LCD TVs, costs have dropped dramatically.

When the costs of inventory change over time, it is not obvious how to determine the cost of goods sold (and the cost of remaining inventory). To see why, think about the following simple example for a new company:

Learning Objective 3

Compute inventory costs using four inventory costing methods.

> May 3   Purchased 1 unit of Product A for **$70**.
> May 5   Purchased 1 unit of Product A for **$75**.
> May 6   Purchased 1 unit of Product A for **$95**.
> May 8   Sold 2 units of Product A for $125 each.

Video 7-1
www.mhhe.com/LLPW1e

The sale on May 8 of two units for $125 each would generate sales revenue of $250 ($125 × 2), but what amount would be considered the cost of goods sold? Because the cost of Product A increased, the answer depends on which goods are assumed to have been sold.

Four generally accepted inventory costing methods are available for determining the cost of goods sold and the cost of goods remaining in ending inventory. Any one of these four methods is acceptable under GAAP in the United States. The specific identification method individually identifies and records the cost of each item sold as part of cost of goods sold. This method requires accountants to keep track of the purchase cost of each item. In the example just given, if the items sold were identified as the ones that cost $70 and $95, the total cost of those items ($70 + 95 = $165) would be reported as the cost of goods sold. The cost of the remaining item ($75) would be reported as inventory on the balance sheet at the end of the period. The specific identification method is used primarily to account for individually expensive and unique items. Toll Brothers, the country's leading builder of luxury homes, reports the costs of home construction using the specific identification method.

Because each unit in a product line is identical, American Eagle Outfitters does not use the specific identification method. Like most companies, American Eagle uses one of the three cost flow methods to account for inventory items. These three other inventory costing methods are **not based on the physical flow** of goods on and off the shelves. Instead, these methods are based on **assumptions** that accountants make about the flow of inventory costs. These three cost flow assumptions are applied to our simple three-unit example in Exhibit 7.4.

*Coach's Tip*

Remember that generally accepted accounting principles do **not** require a company to use a cost flow assumption that mirrors the physical flow of goods.

1. **First-in, first-out (FIFO)** assumes that the inventory costs flow out in the order the goods are received. As in Exhibit 7.4, the earliest items received, the $70 and $75 units received on May 3 and 5, become the $145 cost of goods sold on the income statement and the remaining $95 unit received on May 6 becomes ending inventory on the balance sheet.

2. **Last-in, first-out (LIFO)** assumes that the inventory costs flow out in the opposite of the order the goods are received. As in Exhibit 7.4, the latest items received, the $95 and $75 units received on May 6 and 5, become the $170 cost of goods sold on the income statement, and the remaining $70 unit received on May 3 becomes ending inventory on the balance sheet.

3. **Weighted average** uses the weighted average of the costs of goods available for sale for both the cost of each item sold and those remaining in inventory. As in Exhibit 7.4, the average of the costs [($70 + 75 + 95) ÷ 3 = $80] is assigned to the two items sold totaling $160 cost of goods sold and the one item totaling $80 ending inventory.

As Exhibit 7.4 illustrates, the choice of cost flow assumption can have a major effect on gross profit on the income statement and inventory on the balance sheet. By one estimate, the combined effect of this decision on the profits of large U.S. corporations exceeds $60 billion a year.[1] Now that you have seen how cost flow assumptions work and why they make a difference in a company's reported results, you are ready for a more complex example.

---
[1] "Big Oil's Accounting Methods Fuel Criticism," *The Wall Street Journal*, August 8, 2006, C1.

## Exhibit 7.4     FIFO, LIFO, and Weighted Average Cost Flow Assumptions

The following sections apply the three cost flow assumptions using a perpetual inventory system. Supplement 7A applies the cost flow assumptions using a periodic inventory system. Your instructor may assign either one or both of these sections.

# Cost Flow Methods under a Perpetual Inventory System

In this section, we will apply the cost flow methods using what is called a **perpetual inventory system that records all inventory purchases, sales, and cost of goods sold in sequence as they occur.** Assume American Eagle engaged in the following transactions for its AE Alpine Bomber Jacket product line during the month of January and that all sales were for $150 per unit.

| Date | Description | Units | Unit Cost | Total Cost | Balance in Units |
|------|-------------|-------|-----------|-----------|------------------|
| Jan 1 | Beginning inventory | 20 | $ 70 | $1,400 | 20 |
| 12 | Purchase | 60 | 80 | 4,800 | 80 |
| 17 | Sale | 50 | | | 30 |
| 19 | Purchase | 20 | 100 | 2,000 | 50 |
| 26 | Sale | 32 | | | 18 |
| | | | | $8,200 | |

# First-In, First-Out (FIFO)

The **first-in, first-out method (FIFO)** assumes that the oldest goods (the first ones into inventory) are the first ones sold (the first ones out of inventory). So you **use the costs of the** oldest goods as of the date of sale to calculate the cost of goods sold. **The costs of the newer goods become the costs of the ending inventory.** As in Exhibit 7.5,

- The cost of the 50 units sold on January 17 include the 20 units costing $70 from beginning inventory and 30 of the $80 units from the January 12 purchase (the oldest units). The remaining 30 of the $80 units (the newest units) become ending inventory.
- The 32 items sold on January 26 include the 30 remaining $80 units and 2 of the $100 units (the oldest units). The remaining 18 of the $100 units (the newest units) become ending inventory.

> **Coach's Tip**
> FIFO allocates the oldest unit costs to the cost of goods sold and the newest unit costs to the ending inventory.

## Last-In, First-Out (LIFO)

The **last-in, first-out method (LIFO)** assumes that the newest goods (the last ones into inventory) are the first ones sold (the first ones out of inventory). So you **use the costs of the newest goods as of the date of sale to calculate the cost of goods sold. The costs of the older goods become the costs of the ending inventory.** As in Exhibit 7.6,

- The cost of the 50 units sold on January 17 include 50 of the $80 units from the most recent January 12 purchase (the newest units). The remaining 10 of the $80 units and the 20 units costing $70 from beginning inventory (the oldest units) become ending inventory.

> **Coach's Tip**
> LIFO allocates the newest unit costs to the cost of goods sold and the oldest unit costs to the ending inventory.

### Exhibit 7.5 | FIFO Computations—Perpetual Inventory

| | | PURCHASES | | | COST OF GOODS SOLD | | | INVENTORY BALANCE | | |
|---|---|---|---|---|---|---|---|---|---|---|
| **FIFO Perpetual Calculations** | | Units | Unit Cost | Total Cost | Units | Unit Cost | Total Cost | Units | Unit Cost | Total Cost |
| Date | Description | | | | | | | | | |
| Jan 1 | Beginning inventory | | | | | | | 20 | $ 70 | $1,400 |
| 12 | Purchase | 60 | $ 80 | $4,800 | | | | 60 | 80 | 4,800 |
| 17 | Sale | | | | 20 | $ 70 | $1,400 | | | |
| | | | | | 30 | 80 | 2,400 | 30 | 80 | 2,400 |
| 19 | Purchase | 20 | 100 | 2,000 | | | | 20 | 100 | 2,000 |
| 26 | Sale | | | | 30 | 80 | 2,400 | | | |
| | | | | | 2 | 100 | 200 | 18 | 100 | 1,800 |
| | Total | 80 | | $6,800 | 82 | | $6,400 | 18 | | $1,800 |

### Exhibit 7.6 | LIFO Computations—Perpetual Inventory

| | | PURCHASES | | | COST OF GOODS SOLD | | | INVENTORY BALANCE | | |
|---|---|---|---|---|---|---|---|---|---|---|
| **LIFO Perpetual Calculations** | | Units | Unit Cost | Total Cost | Units | Unit Cost | Total Cost | Units | Unit Cost | Total Cost |
| Date | Description | | | | | | | | | |
| Jan 1 | Beginning inventory | | | | | | | 20 | $ 70 | $1,400 |
| 12 | Purchase | 60 | $ 80 | $4,800 | | | | 60 | 80 | 4,800 |
| 17 | Sale | | | | 50 | $ 80 | $4,000 | 20 | $ 70 | 1,400 |
| | | | | | | | | 10 | 80 | 800 |
| 19 | Purchase | 20 | 100 | 2,000 | | | | 20 | 100 | 2,000 |
| 26 | Sale | | | | 20 | 100 | 2,000 | | | |
| | | | | | 10 | 80 | 800 | | | |
| | | | | | 2 | 70 | 140 | 18 | 70 | 1,260 |
| | Total | 80 | | $6,800 | 82 | | $6,940 | 18 | | $1,260 |

- The cost of the 32 items sold on January 26 include the 20 most recently purchased $100 units from the January 19 purchase, the remaining 10 of the $80 units, and 2 of the $70 units (the newest units). The remaining 18 of the $70 units from beginning inventory (the oldest units) become ending inventory.

## Weighted Average Cost

**Coach's Tip**

In calculating the weighted average cost, be sure to **weight** the costs by the number of units purchased at each cost. Do not just average the unit costs (e.g., $70, $80, $100) without considering the number of units purchased at each cost.

In the **weighted average cost method,** you calculate the **weighted average cost per unit of the goods available for sale as of the date of sale.** You add the total cost of beginning inventory and purchases before the date of sale to get the total cost of goods available for sale. As in Exhibit 7.7, you then divide this amount by the number of units available for sale to compute the weighted average cost and assign that cost to all units sold and in ending inventory.

- For the January 17 sale, the cost of goods available for sale is computed by adding the $1,400 cost of the beginning inventory and the $4,800 cost of the January 12 purchase and dividing by the 80 total units available ($6,200 ÷ 80 = $77.50). This $77.50 average cost per unit is then assigned to the 50 units sold ($77.50 × 50 = $3,875) and the 30 units that remain in ending inventory ($77.50 × 30 = $2,325).
- For the January 26 sale, the cost of goods available for sale is computed by adding the $2,325 cost of the units remaining after the January 17 sale and the $2,000 cost of the January 19 purchase and dividing by the 50 total units available ($4,325 ÷ 50 = $86.50). This $86.50 average cost per unit is then assigned to the 32 units sold ($86.50 × 32 = $2,768) and the 18 units that remain in ending inventory ($86.50 × 18 = $1,557).

## Financial Statement Effects of Inventory Costing Methods

Exhibit 7.8 illustrates the journal entries that would have been made under each method for the purchases and sales transactions assuming that all sales were for $150 cash per unit. Note that the purchases and sales revenue entries are identical across the methods. **For the cost of goods sold entries, the accounts affected are the same, but the amounts are different.**

Exhibit 7.9 summarizes the financial statement effects of the FIFO, LIFO, and weighted average cost methods. Remember that these methods differ only in the way they split the cost of goods available for sale between the cost of goods sold and the ending inventory. Because a cost that goes into ending inventory cannot also go into the cost of goods sold, the method that assigns the highest cost to ending inventory will assign the lowest cost to the cost of goods sold and vice versa.

---

**Exhibit 7.7    Weighted Average Computations—Perpetual Inventory**

| Weighted Average Perpetual Calculations | | PURCHASES | | | COST OF GOODS SOLD | | | INVENTORY BALANCE | | | |
|---|---|---|---|---|---|---|---|---|---|---|---|
| Date | Description | Units | Unit Cost | Total Cost | Units | Unit Cost | Total Cost | Units | Unit Cost | Total Cost | |
| Jan 1 | Beginning inventory | | | | | | | 20 | $70.00 | $1,400 | $6,200÷80=$77.50 per unit |
| 12 | Purchase | 60 | $ 80 | $4,800 | | | | 60 | 80.00 | 4,800 | |
| 17 | Sale | | | | 50 | $77.50 | $3,875 | 30 | 77.50 | 2,325 | $4,325÷50=$86.50 per unit |
| 19 | Purchase | 20 | 100 | 2,000 | | | | 20 | 100.00 | 2,000 | |
| 26 | Sale | | | | 32 | 86.50 | 2,768 | 18 | 86.50 | 1,557 | |
| | Total | 80 | | $6,800 | 82 | | $6,643 | 18 | | $1,557 | |

| Exhibit 7.8 | Journal Entries—Perpetual Inventory |
|---|---|

|  |  | FIFO | | LIFO | | WEIGHTED AVERAGE | |
|---|---|---|---|---|---|---|---|
|  |  | Debit | Credit | Debit | Credit | Debit | Credit |
| Jan 12 | Inventory (+A) | 4,800 |  | 4,800 |  | 4,800 |  |
|  | Accounts Payable (+L) |  | 4,800 |  | 4,800 |  | 4,800 |
| Jan 17 | Cash (+A) (50 × $150) | 7,500 |  | 7,500 |  | 7,500 |  |
|  | Sales Revenue (+R, +OE) |  | 7,500 |  | 7,500 |  | 7,500 |
|  | Cost of Goods Sold (+E, −OE) | 3,800 |  | 4,000 |  | 3,875 |  |
|  | Inventory (−A) |  | 3,800 |  | 4,000 |  | 3,875 |
| Jan 19 | Inventory (+A) | 2,000 |  | 2,000 |  | 2,000 |  |
|  | Accounts Payable (+L) |  | 2,000 |  | 2,000 |  | 2,000 |
| Jan 26 | Cash (+A) (32 × $150) | 4,800 |  | 4,800 |  | 4,800 |  |
|  | Sales Revenue (+R, +OE) |  | 4,800 |  | 4,800 |  | 4,800 |
|  | Cost of Goods Sold (+E, −OE) | 2,600 |  | 2,940 |  | 2,768 |  |
|  | Inventory (−A) |  | 2,600 |  | 2,940 |  | 2,768 |

| Exhibit 7.9 | Financial Statement Effects of Inventory Costing Methods |
|---|---|

|  | FIFO | LIFO | Weighted Average |
|---|---|---|---|
| **Effect on the Income Statement** |  |  |  |
| Sales | $12,300 | $12,300 | $12,300 |
| Cost of goods sold | 6,400 | 6,940 | 6,643 |
| Gross profit | 5,900 | 5,360 | 5,657 |
| **Effect on the Balance Sheet** |  |  |  |
| Inventory | $1,800 | $1,260 | $1,557 |

Depending on whether costs are rising or falling, different methods have different effects on the financial statements. **When costs are rising,** as they are in our example, FIFO produces a higher inventory value (making the balance sheet **appear** to be stronger) and a lower cost of goods sold (resulting in a higher gross profit, which makes the company **look** more profitable). **When costs are falling,** these effects are reversed; FIFO produces a lower ending inventory value and a higher cost of goods sold—a double whammy. These are not "real" economic effects, however, because the same number of units is sold or held in ending inventory under either method. The following table summarizes the effects:

| **Effects of Increasing Costs on the Financial Statements** |  |  |
|---|---|---|
|  | FIFO | LIFO |
| Inventory on balance sheet | Higher | Lower |
| Cost of goods sold on income statement | Lower | Higher |
| **Effects of Decreasing Costs on the Financial Statements** |  |  |
|  | FIFO | LIFO |
| Inventory on balance sheet | Lower | Higher |
| Cost of goods sold on income statement | Higher | Lower |

## Spotlight On BUSINESS DECISIONS

### Choosing Inventory Costing Methods

Given the effects of different inventory costing methods, you might wonder why a company would ever choose a method that produces a lower inventory value and a higher cost of goods sold. American Eagle, like Wal-Mart and the rest of the companies discussed in this text, is a corporation, and corporations must pay income taxes. Faced with increasing costs per unit as in our example, a company that uses FIFO will incur a higher income tax expense. That tax effect is a real economic cost in the sense that the higher income tax will reduce the company's cash. So most companies that face a rising per unit inventory cost choose LIFO. Companies choosing LIFO for their tax returns must also use LIFO on their financial statements.*

**Increasing cost companies using LIFO:** Harley-Davidson, Ford, General Motors, Exxon.

————
* In other cases such as choosing depreciation methods, companies may use one method on their tax return and a different method on their financial statements.

A common question that people ask is whether managers are free to choose LIFO one period, FIFO the next, and then LIFO again, depending on whether unit costs are rising or falling at the time. Because doing so would make it difficult to compare financial results across periods, accounting rules require that costing methods be applied consistently. A change in inventory costing method is allowed only if it will improve the accuracy with which a company's financial results and financial position are reported, and that does not happen often. Companies can use different inventory costing methods for different product lines, however, as long as they do so consistently over time.

## Spotlight On ETHICS

### Just Who Are You Working For?

Given a choice between FIFO and LIFO, most stockholders would want managers to use the method that results in the lowest income taxes. Managers, on the other hand, might prefer the method that produces the highest net income, particularly if they receive a bonus based on reported profits. Clearly, a manager who selected an accounting method that is less than optimal for the company solely to increase his or her own pay would be engaging in questionable ethical behavior.

---

**SELF-STUDY PRACTICE**

Assume that a firm had the following inventory purchases and sales during January. Compute the cost of goods sold and the ending inventory using the LIFO method.

| | |
|---|---|
| Beginning inventory | 20 units at $6 each |
| Purchase January 5 | 30 units at $8 each |
| Sale January 8 | 36 units |
| Purchase January 28 | 16 units at $9 each |

*After you have finished, check your answers with the solutions at the bottom of the next page.*

---

**Learning Objective 4**

Report inventory at the lower of cost or market.

## REPORTING INVENTORY AT THE LOWER OF COST OR MARKET

For two reasons, the value of inventory can sometimes fall below its recorded cost: (1) It can be easily replaced by identical goods at a lower cost or (2) it has become outdated or damaged. The first case typically involves high-tech goods such as cell phones. As companies become more efficient at making these cutting-edge products, they become cheaper to make. The second case commonly occurs with fad items or seasonal goods such as American Eagle's winter coats, which tend to drop in value at the end of the season.

In either instance, when the value of inventory falls below its recorded cost, GAAP requires that the amount that was originally recorded for inventory be written down to its lower market value. This rule is known as reporting inventories at the **lower of cost or market (LCM)**. It is based on the **conservatism** concept, which ensures that inventory assets are not reported at more than they are worth.

Let's look at how the inventory write-down is determined and recorded. Assume that American Eagle's ending inventory includes two items whose replacement costs have recently changed: leather coats and fleece hoodies.[2] The replacement costs of these items can be used as estimates of market value and compared to the original recorded cost per unit. You then take the lower of those two amounts (the lower of cost or market) and multiply it by the number of units on hand. The result is the amount at which the inventory should be reported after all adjustments have been made:

| Item | Quantity | Cost per Item | Replacement Cost (Market) per Item | LCM per Item | Total Lower of Cost or Market |
|---|---|---|---|---|---|
| Leather coats | 1,000 | $165 | $150 | $150 | 1,000 × $150 = $150,000 |
| Fleece hoodies | 400 | 20 | 25 | 20 | 400 × $ 20 = 8,000 |

Because the market value of the 1,000 leather coats ($150) is **lower** than the recorded cost ($165), the recorded amount for ending inventory should be written down by $15 per unit ($165 − $150). If American Eagle has 1,000 units in inventory, the total write-down should be $15,000 ($15 × 1,000). The effect of this write-down on the accounting equation and the journal entry to record it would be:

| | Debit | Credit |
|---|---|---|
| Cost of Goods Sold (+E, −OE) | 15,000 | |
| Inventory (−A) | | 15,000 |

| Assets | = | Liabilities | + | Owners' Equity |
|---|---|---|---|---|
| Inventory −15,000 | | | | Cost of Goods Sold (+E) −15,000 |

**Solution to Self-Study Practice**

| LIFO Perpetual Calculations | | PURCHASES | | | COST OF GOODS SOLD | | | INVENTORY BALANCE | | |
|---|---|---|---|---|---|---|---|---|---|---|
| Date | Description | Units | Unit Cost | Total Cost | Units | Unit Cost | Total Cost | Units | Unit Cost | Total Cost |
| Jan 1 | Beginning inventory | | | | | | | 20 | $6 | $120 |
| 5 | Purchase | 30 | 8 | $240 | | | | 30 | 8 | 240 |
| 8 | Sale | | | | 30 | $8 | $240 | | | |
| | | | | | 6 | 6 | 36 | 14 | 6 | 84 |
| 28 | Purchase | 16 | 9 | 144 | | | | 16 | 9 | 144 |
| | Total | 46 | | $384 | 36 | | $276 | 30 | | $228 |

Cost of goods sold is $276; ending inventory is $228.

---

[2] We apply lower of cost or market on an item basis. It also may be applied on a category or total inventory basis.

Because the market value of the fleece hoodies ($25) is higher than the original cost ($20), no write-down is necessary. The fleece hoodies should remain on the books at their original cost of $20 per unit ($8,000 in total). Their value should not be increased based on the higher replacement cost because GAAP requires that they be reported at the **lower** of cost or market.

## Spotlight On FINANCIAL REPORTING

### Using Lower of Cost or Market in Practice

**AMERICAN EAGLE OUTFITTERS**
ae.com

American Eagle explains the use of the LCM rule in Note 2 to its financial statements.

> **American Eagle Outfitters, Inc.**
> **Notes to the Consolidated Financial Statements**
>
> . . . . . . .
> **2. Summary of Significant Accounting Policies**
> *Merchandise Inventory*
> Merchandise inventory is valued at the lower of average cost or market. . . .

## IDENTIFYING THE EFFECTS OF INVENTORY ERRORS

Errors in inventory valuations can significantly affect both the balance sheet and the income statement. As the cost of goods sold equation indicates, there is a direct relationship between ending inventory and the cost of goods sold: Items that are not in the ending inventory are assumed to have been sold. Thus, any errors in ending inventory affect both the balance sheet (current assets) and the income statement (cost of goods sold, gross profit, and net income). Furthermore, the effects of inventory errors impact more than one year because the ending inventory for one year becomes the beginning inventory for the next.

### Income Statement Effects

To determine the effects of inventory errors on the financial statements in both the current and following years, you use the cost of goods sold equation. Assume, for example, that ending inventory was overstated by $10,000 due to an error that was not discovered until the following year. This error would have the following effects in the current year:

| Current Year | |
| --- | --- |
| Beginning inventory | Accurate |
| + Purchases of merchandise during the year | Accurate |
| Goods available for sale | Accurate |
| − Ending inventory (balance sheet) | Overstated $10,000 |
| = Cost of goods sold (income statement) | Understated $10,000 |

Because the cost of goods sold was understated in the current year, gross profit and net income would be overstated by $10,000 in the same year (ignoring taxes).

The current year's ending inventory becomes next year's beginning inventory. So, the $10,000 overstatement of ending inventory in the current year would have the following effects next year (assuming that ending inventory is calculated correctly that year):

| Next Year | |
|---|---|
| Beginning inventory | Overstated $10,000 |
| + Purchases of merchandise during the year | Accurate |
| Goods available for sale | Overstated $10,000 |
| − Ending inventory (balance sheet) | Accurate |
| = Cost of goods sold (income statement) | Overstated $10,000 |

Because the cost of goods sold, which is an expense, is overstated in the next year, gross profit and net income are understated by $10,000 in the same year.

Exhibit 7.10 shows the effects of these errors on net income in each of the two years (ignoring income taxes). Notice that the cost of goods sold is understated in the first year and overstated in the second year. Over the two years, these errors would offset each other. However, inventory errors will "self-correct" in this way only if the ending inventory is calculated accurately at the end of the following year and adjusted to the correct amount.

## Balance Sheet Effects

Errors in ending inventory affect two balance sheet accounts. First, the amount used as ending inventory in the cost of goods sold equation becomes the value of the current asset inventory shown on the balance sheet. Second, the cost of goods sold affects the value of owners' equity when it is closed to that account.

Exhibit 7.11 shows both of these effects. Note that they will offset each other over the two years only if the value of the ending inventory is calculated accurately at the end of the second year and adjusted to the correct amount.

### Exhibit 7.10  Two-Year Effects of an Inventory Error on the Income Statement

| | CURRENT YEAR | | NEXT YEAR | |
|---|---|---|---|---|
| | With an Error | Without an Error | With an Error | Without an Error |
| Sales | $120,000 | $120,000 | $110,000 | $110,000 |
| Beginning inventory | $ 50,000 | $ 50,000 | $ 45,000 | $ 35,000 |
| Purchases | 75,000 | 75,000 | 70,000 | 70,000 |
| Cost of goods available for sale | 125,000 | 125,000 | 115,000 | 105,000 |
| Ending inventory | 45,000 | 35,000 | 20,000 | 20,000 |
| Cost of goods sold | 80,000 | 90,000 | 95,000 | 85,000 |
| Gross profit | 40,000 | 30,000 | 15,000 | 25,000 |
| Operating expenses | 10,000 | 10,000 | 10,000 | 10,000 |
| Net income | $ 30,000 | $ 20,000 | $ 5,000 | $ 15,000 |

Net income overstated by $10,000 → Cancels out ← Net income understated by $10,000

**Exhibit 7.11    Two-Year Effects of an Inventory Error on the Balance Sheet**

| Year | Ending Inventory Error | Assets | Owners' Equity |
|---|---|---|---|
| Current year | Overstated $10,000 | Overstated $10,000 | Overstated $10,000 |
| Next year | Accurate | Accurate | Accurate |

# EVALUATING INVENTORY MANAGEMENT

## Inventory Turnover Analysis

**Learning Objective 6**

Compute and interpret the inventory turnover ratio.

If a company's inventory balance increases from $100,000 in one period to $130,000 in the next, is that good news or bad news? If the increase occurs because management is building up stock in anticipation of higher sales, it could be good news. But if it results from an accumulation of old inventory items that nobody wants, it is probably bad news. Those who work inside the company can easily determine whether the change is good or bad news by talking with the sales managers. But if you are looking at the company's financial statements from the outside, how can you tell?

The method most analysts use to evaluate such changes is called **inventory turnover analysis.** Exhibit 7.12 illustrates the idea behind inventory turnover analysis. As a company buys goods, its inventory balance goes up; as it sells goods, its inventory balance goes down. This process of buying and selling, which is called **inventory turnover,** is repeated over and over during each accounting period for each line of products.

Analysts can assess how many times, on average, inventory has been bought and sold during the period by calculating the inventory turnover ratio. A higher ratio indicates that inventory moves more quickly from purchase to sale, reducing storage and obsolescence costs. Because less money is tied up in inventory, the excess can be invested to earn interest or reduce borrowing, which reduces interest expense. More efficient purchasing and production techniques as well as high product demand will boost this ratio. A sudden decline in the inventory turnover ratio may signal an unexpected drop in demand for the company's products or poor inventory management.

Rather than evaluate the **number of times** inventory turns over during the year, some analysts prefer to think in terms of the **length of time** (in days) required to sell inventory. Converting the inventory turnover ratio to the number of days needed to sell the inventory is easy. You simply divide 365 days by the inventory turnover ratio to get the **days to sell.** This measure does not tell analysts anything different about a company's ability to buy and sell inventory; it is just a little easier to interpret than the inventory turnover ratio. In terms of Exhibit 7.12, the inventory turnover ratio indicates the number of loops in a given period; days to sell indicates the average number of days between loops.

Inventory turnover analysis can be applied to merchandisers as well as manufacturers. For manufacturers, inventory turnover refers to the production and delivery of inventory to customers. For merchandisers, it refers to the buying and selling of goods to customers.

**Exhibit 7.12    Inventory Turnover Analysis**

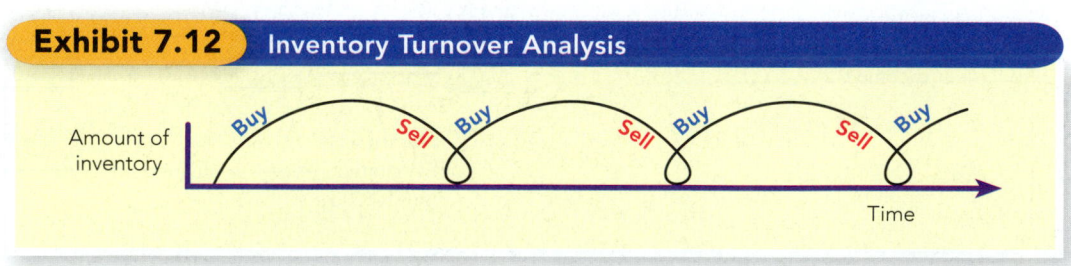

## Financial Analysis Tools

| Name of Measure | Formula | What It Tells You |
|---|---|---|
| Inventory Turnover Ratio | $\dfrac{\text{Cost of Goods Sold}}{\text{Average Inventory}}$ | • The number of times inventory turns over during the period<br>• A higher ratio means faster turnover |
| Days to Sell | $\dfrac{365}{\text{Inventory Turnover Ratio}}$ | • The average number of days from purchase to sale<br>• A higher number means a longer time to sell |

American Eagle's turnover ratio and days to sell would be computed as follows:

$$\frac{\text{Inventory}}{\text{Turnover Ratio}} = \frac{\text{Cost of Goods Sold}}{\text{Average Inventory}} = \frac{\$1,454}{\$(264 + 211)/2} = 6.1 \text{ times}$$

$$\text{Days to Sell} = \frac{365}{\text{Inventory Turnover Ratio}} = \frac{365 \text{ days}}{6.1 \text{ times}} = 59.8 \text{ days}$$

**Coach's Tip**

The average inventory balance outstanding over the entire year is used in the bottom of the receivables turnover ratio. It is computed as (Beginning Balance + Ending Balance)/2.

## Comparison to Benchmarks

Inventory turnover ratios and the number of days to sell can be helpful in comparing different companies' inventory management practices. You should use them cautiously, however, because these measures can vary significantly from one industry to another. As in Exhibit 7.13, Ruby Tuesday had a turnover ratio of 30.0 in 2006, meaning that it took about 12 days to sell its entire food inventory (including the contents of its freezers). Harley-Davidson took more time to produce and sell its motorcycles—as its inventory turnover ratio of 14.0 indicates, about 26 days. American Eagle's inventory turned over only 6.1 times during the year, or just once every 59.8 days.

Given this wide range in ratios among industries and companies, it is usually more useful to compare a company's inventory turnover with its own results in prior periods or to similar (competitor) companies. For practice in computing these measures and comparing them to a competitor, try the following Self-Study Practice, which asks you to calculate the inventory turnover ratio and days to sell.

---

**SELF-STUDY PRACTICE**

a.  Urban Outfitters reported cost of goods sold of $773 and beginning and ending inventories of $140 and $154 (all in millions) for 2006. Calculate its inventory turnover and days to sell in 2006.

b.  Compare its inventory turnover and days to sell to that of American Eagle. How would you interpret the difference?

| 2006 Inventory Turnover | 2006 Days to Sell |
|---|---|
| $\dfrac{\rule{1cm}{0.4pt}}{(\rule{0.8cm}{0.4pt} + \rule{0.8cm}{0.4pt})/2} = \rule{0.5cm}{0.4pt} = $ times<br>times | $\dfrac{365 \text{ days}}{\rule{0.8cm}{0.4pt} \text{ times}} = \rule{0.5cm}{0.4pt} $ days |

*When you have finished, check your answers with the solutions at the bottom of the page.*

---

Solution to
Self-Study Practice

a.  $\dfrac{773}{(140 + 154)/2} = 5.3$ times

$365 \div 5.3 = 68.9$ days

b.  Urban Outfitters' inventory turnover was lower and days to sell was higher, indicating less efficient inventory management.

| Exhibit 7.13 | Inventory Turnover Analysis for Three Different Companies |
| --- | --- |

| Company | 2006 Inventory Turnover | 2006 Days to Sell |
| --- | --- | --- |
| American Eagle | 6.1 | 59.8 days |
| Harley-Davidson | 14.0 | 26.1 days |
| RubyTuesday | 30.0 | 12.2 days |

## Spotlight On FINANCIAL REPORTING

### Impact of Inventory Costing Methods

As you saw in Exhibit 7.4, different cost flow assumptions often yield different amounts for inventory and cost of goods sold. Accounting rules require that any company that chooses to use LIFO must report in the notes to the financial statements what the inventory balance would have been had it used FIFO instead. Deere & Company, the manufacturer of John Deere farm, lawn, and construction equipment, disclosed this information as follows.

**Deere & Company**
**Notes to the Consolidated Financial Statements**

**Note 13—Inventories**

Most inventories owned by Deere & Company and its United States equipment subsidiaries are valued at cost, on the "last-in, first-out" (LIFO) basis. If all inventories had been valued on a FIFO basis, estimated inventories at October 31 in millions of dollars would have been as follows:

|  | 2006 | 2005 |
| --- | --- | --- |
| Total FIFO value | $ 3,097 | $ 3,267 |
| Adjustment to LIFO basis | 1,140 | 1,132 |
| Inventories | $ 1,957 | $ 2,135 |

Deere & Company

Notice that the cost of inventory under the FIFO assumption ($3,097 in 2006) was more than 1.5 times higher than the cost of inventory under the LIFO assumption ($1,957 in 2006). The lesson here is that in analyzing a company's inventory or cost of goods sold, you should compare that company's results only to its own results in prior periods or to those of another company that uses the same cost flow assumption.

## Demonstration Case

Ebert Electronics distributes consumer electronics. One product has been selected for use in this case. Assume the completion of the following summarized transactions during the month of March 2008 in the order given. All transactions involved cash.

|  | Units | Unit Cost |
| --- | --- | --- |
| Beginning inventory (March 1) | 11 | $200 |
| New inventory purchases (March 15) | 5 | 208 |
| Sales (March 19) (selling price, $420) | 12 | — |
| New inventory purchases (March 21) | 9 | 220 |

**Required:**

1. Compute the following amounts using the FIFO, LIFO, and weighted average cost methods applied on a perpetual basis:

| | ENDING INVENTORY | | COST OF GOODS SOLD | |
|---|---|---|---|---|
| | Units | Dollars | Units | Dollars |
| FIFO | | | | |
| LIFO | | | | |
| Weighted average | | | | |

2. Assuming the company's inventory costs are expected to follow the trend for this particular product and Ebert Electronics wants to minimize its income taxes, which inventory costing method would you recommend that the company use to account for inventory? Explain your answer.

3. If Ebert's ending inventory were overstated by $100 at the end of March 2008, how would this affect its cost of goods sold for the month of March 2008?

## Suggested Solution

1.

| | ENDING INVENTORY | | COST OF GOODS SOLD | |
|---|---|---|---|---|
| | Units | Dollars | Units | Dollars |
| FIFO | 13 | $2,812 | 12 | $2,408 |
| LIFO | 13 | 2,780 | 12 | 2,440 |
| Weighted average | 13 | 2,790 | 12 | 2,430 |

| FIFO Perpetual Calculations | | PURCHASES | | | COST OF GOODS SOLD | | | INVENTORY BALANCE | | |
|---|---|---|---|---|---|---|---|---|---|---|
| Date | Description | Units | Unit Cost | Total Cost | Units | Unit Cost | Total Cost | Units | Unit Cost | Total Cost |
| Mar 1 | Beginning inventory | | | | | | | 11 | $200 | $2,200 |
| 15 | Purchase | 5 | $208 | $1,040 | | | | 5 | 208 | 1,040 |
| 19 | Sale | | | | 11 | $200 | $2,200 | | | |
| | | | | | 1 | 208 | 208 | 4 | 208 | 832 |
| 21 | Purchase | 9 | 220 | 1,980 | | | | 9 | 220 | 1,980 |
| | Total | 14 | | $3,020 | 12 | | $2,408 | 13 | | $2,812 |

| LIFO Perpetual Calculations | | PURCHASES | | | COST OF GOODS SOLD | | | INVENTORY BALANCE | | |
|---|---|---|---|---|---|---|---|---|---|---|
| Date | Description | Units | Unit Cost | Total Cost | Units | Unit Cost | Total Cost | Units | Unit Cost | Total Cost |
| Mar 1 | Beginning inventory | | | | | | | 11 | $200 | $2,200 |
| 15 | Purchase | 5 | $208 | $1,040 | | | | 5 | 208 | 1,040 |
| 19 | Sale | | | | 5 | $208 | $1,040 | | | |
| | | | | | 7 | 200 | 1,400 | 4 | 200 | 800 |
| 21 | Purchase | 9 | 220 | 1,980 | | | | 9 | 220 | 1,980 |
| | Total | 14 | | $3,020 | 12 | | $2,440 | 13 | | $2,780 |

| Weighted Average Perpetual Calculations | | PURCHASES | | | COST OF GOODS SOLD | | | INVENTORY BALANCE | | |
|---|---|---|---|---|---|---|---|---|---|---|
| Date | Description | Units | Unit Cost | Total Cost | Units | Unit Cost | Total Cost | Units | Unit Cost | Total Cost |
| Mar 1 | Beginning inventory | | | | | | | 11 | $200.00 | $2,200 |
| 15 | Purchase | 5 | $208 | $1,040 | | | | 5 | 208.00 | 1,040 |
| 19 | Sale | | | | 12 | $202.50 | $2,430 | 4 | 202.50 | 810 |
| 21 | Purchase | 9 | 220 | 1,980 | | | | 9 | 220.00 | 1,980 |
| | Total | 14 | | $3,020 | 12 | | $2,430 | 13 | | $2,790 |

$3,240 ÷ 16 = $202.50 per unit

$2,790

2. LIFO should be selected. Because costs are rising, LIFO produces a higher cost of goods sold, a lower income before income taxes, and lower income taxes.

3. If ending inventory were overstated by $100 at the end of March 2008, cost of goods sold would be understated by the same amount.

# Supplement 7A
## Cost Flow Methods under a Periodic Inventory System

In this section, we apply the cost flow methods using what is called a **periodic inventory system that makes the computations as if all purchases made during the period take place before any sales or cost of goods sold are recorded.** Assume that American Eagle engaged in the following transactions for its AE Alpine Bomber Jacket product line during the month of January and that all sales were for $150 per unit.

| Date | Description | Units | Unit Cost | Total Cost |
|---|---|---|---|---|
| Jan 1 | Beginning inventory | 20 | $70 | $1,400 |
| 12 | Purchase | 60 | 80 | 4,800 |
| 19 | Purchase | 20 | 100 | 2,000 |
| | Sales during the month | (82) | | |
| | | | | $8,200 |

Remember that a periodic inventory system records merchandise purchases as they occur but updates the inventory account and records cost of goods sold only at the end of the period. Ending inventory is determined by taking a physical count, and cost of goods sold is computed using the cost of goods sold equation in the following form:

$$BI + P - EI = CGS$$

**Coach's Tip**

FIFO allocates the oldest unit costs to the cost of goods sold and the newest unit costs to the ending inventory.

### First-In, First-Out Method (FIFO)

The first-in, first-out method (FIFO) assumes that the oldest goods (the first ones into the inventory) are the first ones sold (the first ones out of the inventory). So you use the costs of the **oldest goods to calculate the cost of goods sold** (the 20 units at $70 plus the 60 units at $80 plus 2 units at $100 = $6,400). The **costs of the newer goods become the costs of the ending inventory** (the 18 units at $100 = $1,800).

**Cost of Goods Sold and Ending Inventory Calculation (FIFO)**

| | | |
|---|---|---|
| Beginning inventory | (20 units at $70 each) | $1,400 |
| + Purchases | (60 units at $80 each) | 4,800 |
| | (20 units at $100 each) | 2,000 |
| Goods available for sale | | 8,200 |
| − Ending inventory (18 × $100) | | 1,800 |
| Cost of goods sold (20 × $70) + (60 × $80) + (2 × $100) | | $6,400 |

## Last-In, First-Out Method (LIFO)

The last-in, first-out method (LIFO) assumes that the **newest** goods (the **last** ones into the inventory) are the first ones sold (the first ones out of the inventory). So you use the **costs of the newest goods to calculate the cost of goods sold** (20 units at $100 plus 60 units at $80 plus 2 units at $70). The **costs of the older costs become the costs of the ending inventory** (18 units at $70).

**Coach's Tip**

LIFO allocates the newest unit costs to the cost of goods sold and the oldest unit costs to the ending inventory.

**Cost of Goods Sold and Ending Inventory Calculation (LIFO)**

| | | |
|---|---|---|
| Beginning inventory | (20 units at $70 each) | $1,400 |
| + Purchases | (60 units at $80 each) | 4,800 |
| | (20 units at $100 each) | 2,000 |
| Goods available for sale | | 8,200 |
| − Ending inventory (18 × $70) | | 1,260 |
| Cost of goods sold (20 × $100) + (60 × $80) + (2 × $70) | | $6,940 |

## Weighted Average Cost Method

The **weighted average cost method** calculates the weighted average cost per unit of the goods available for sale. The first step is to calculate the total cost of the goods available for sale. You multiply the number of units purchased at each cost by the cost per unit and then add to get the total cost:

**Coach's Tip**

In calculating the weighted average cost, be sure to **weight** the costs by the number of units purchased at each cost. Do not just average the unit costs ($100, $80, $70) without considering the number of units purchased at each cost.

| | | |
|---|---|---|
| Beginning inventory | (20 units at $70 each) | $1,400 |
| + Purchases | (60 units at $80 each) | 4,800 |
| | (20 units at $100 each) | 2,000 |
| Goods available for sale | (100 units) | $8,200 |

Then you calculate the weighted average cost per unit using the following formula:

$$\frac{\text{Weighted}}{\text{Average Cost}} = \frac{\text{Cost of Goods Available for Sale}}{\text{Number of Units Available for Sale}} = \frac{\$8,200}{100 \text{ Units}} = \frac{\$82}{\text{per unit}}$$

Cost of goods sold and ending inventory are both calculated using the same weighted average cost per unit, $82.

### Cost of Goods Sold and Ending Inventory Calculation (Average Cost)

| | | |
|---|---|---:|
| Beginning inventory | (20 units at $70 each) | $1,400 |
| + Purchases | (60 units at $80 each) | 4,800 |
| | (20 units at $100 each) | 2,000 |
| Goods available for sale | | $8,200 |
| − Ending inventory | (18 units at $82 average cost each) | 1,476 |
| Cost of goods sold | (82 units at $82 average cost each) | $6,724 |

## Financial Statement Effects of Inventory Costing Methods

Exhibit 7A.1 summarizes the financial statement effects of the FIFO, LIFO, and weighted average cost methods. Remember that these methods differ only in the way they split the cost of goods available for sale between the cost of goods sold and the ending inventory. Because a cost that goes into ending inventory cannot also go into the cost of goods sold, the method that assigns the highest cost to ending inventory assigns the lowest cost to the cost of goods sold and vice versa.

Depending on whether costs are rising or falling, different methods have different effects on the financial statements. **When costs are rising,** as they are in our example, FIFO produces a higher inventory value (making the balance sheet **appear** to be stronger) and a lower cost of goods sold (resulting in a higher gross profit, which makes the company **look** more profitable). **When costs are falling,** these effects are reversed; FIFO produces a lower ending inventory value and a higher cost of goods sold—a double whammy. These are not "real" economic effects, however, because the same number of units is sold or held in ending inventory under either method. The following table summarizes the effects:

**Effects of Increasing Costs on the Financial Statements**

| | FIFO | LIFO |
|---|---|---|
| Inventory on balance sheet | Higher | Lower |
| Cost of goods sold on income statement | Lower | Higher |

**Effects of Decreasing Costs on the Financial Statements**

| | FIFO | LIFO |
|---|---|---|
| Inventory on balance sheet | Lower | Higher |
| Cost of goods sold on income statement | Higher | Lower |

**Exhibit 7A.1** **Financial Statement Effects of Inventory Costing Methods**

| | FIFO | LIFO | Weighted Average |
|---|---:|---:|---:|
| **Effect on the Income Statement** | | | |
| Sales | $12,300 | $12,300 | $12,300 |
| Cost of goods sold | 6,400 | 6,940 | 6,724 |
| Gross profit | 5,900 | 5,360 | 5,576 |
| **Effect on the Balance Sheet** | | | |
| Inventory | $1,800 | $1,260 | $1,476 |

# Supplement 7B
## Estimating Inventory

### Gross Profit Method

When perpetual records and a physical inventory count are unavailable, the cost of goods sold and ending inventory may be estimated using one of two methods. The first, the **gross profit method,** relies on an estimate of the gross profit percentage (discussed in Chapter 6):

$$\text{Gross Profit Percentage} = \frac{(\text{Net Sales} - \text{CGS})}{\text{Net Sales}} \times 100$$

To illustrate, assume the company's accounting records indicate the following:

| | |
|---|---:|
| Beginning inventory | $14,000 |
| Purchases | 48,000 |
| Net sales | 75,000 |
| Estimated gross profit percentage | 40% |

The gross profit method involves two steps:

1. Compute the cost of goods sold using the following formula:

   (100% − Gross Profit Percentage) × Net Sales = Cost of Goods Sold
   (100% − 40%) × $75,000 = $45,000

2. Compute the ending inventory using the cost of goods sold equation:

| | |
|---|---:|
| Beginning inventory | $14,000 |
| + Purchases of merchandise during the year | 48,000 |
| Goods available for sale | 62,000 |
| − Estimated cost of goods sold | 45,000 |
| Estimated ending inventory | $17,000 |

### Retail Inventory Method

When a retailer maintains a record of the retail price of its entire inventory, the **retail inventory method** may be used. This method relies on an estimate of the ratio of cost to the retail price. To illustrate, assume the company's accounting records indicate the following:

| | Cost | Retail |
|---|---:|---:|
| Beginning inventory | $24,000 | $ 40,000 |
| Purchases | 48,000 | 80,000 |
| Goods available for sale | $72,000 | $120,000 |
| Sales | | $100,000 |

The retail method involves three steps:

1. Compute the ratio of cost to retail using the following formula:

$$\text{Ratio of Cost to Retail} = \frac{\text{Goods Available for Sale at Cost}}{\text{Goods Available for Sale at Retail}} = \frac{\$72,000}{\$120,000} = 0.6$$

2. Compute the ending inventory at retail:

| | |
|---|---:|
| Goods available for sale | $120,000 |
| Sales | 100,000 |
| Ending inventory at retail | $ 20,000 |

3. Compute the ending inventory at estimated cost:

Ending Inventory at Retail × Ratio of Cost to Retail = Ending Inventory at Cost
$20,000 × 0.6 = $12,000

# Chapter Summary

### LO1  Explain how to report inventory and cost of goods sold. p. 304

- Goods held in inventory are recorded initially at cost, which is the amount given up to acquire the assets and prepare them for sale.
- When the goods are sold, their cost is removed from the inventory account and reported on the income statement as an expense called Cost of Goods Sold.

### LO2  Explain the cost of goods sold equation. p. 305

$$
\begin{array}{l}
\text{Beginning inventory} \\
\underline{+ \text{ Purchases of merchandise made during the year}} \\
= \text{Goods available for sale} \\
\underline{- \text{ Ending inventory}} \\
= \text{Cost of goods sold}
\end{array}
$$

### LO3  Compute inventory costs using four inventory costing methods. p. 307

- Any of four generally accepted methods can be used to allocate the cost of inventory available for sale between goods that have been sold and goods that remain on hand at the end of the accounting period.
- The specific identification method assigns costs to ending inventory and the cost of goods sold by identifying and tracking specific inventory items.
- The FIFO method assigns the costs of the goods first in to the cost of goods sold and the costs of the goods last in (the most recent) to the ending inventory.
- The LIFO method assigns the costs of the goods last in to the cost of goods sold and the costs of the goods first in (the oldest) to the ending inventory.
- The weighted average cost method assigns the weighted average cost per unit of inventory to both the cost of goods sold and the ending inventory.

### LO4  Report inventory at the lower of cost or market. p. 312

- The LCM rule ensures that inventory assets are not reported at more than they are worth.

### LO5  Determine the effects of inventory errors on the income statement and balance sheet. p. 320

- An overstatement of ending inventory results in an understatement of the cost of goods sold in the current year and an overstatement of the cost of goods sold in the following year.
- An understatement of ending inventory has the opposite effects.

### LO6  Compute and interpret the inventory turnover ratio. p. 316

- The inventory turnover ratio is calculated by dividing the cost of goods sold by average inventory. It indicates how many times average inventory was acquired and sold during the period and reflects the efficiency of inventory management.
- Days to sell is computed by dividing 365 by the inventory turnover ratio. It indicates the average number of days from purchase to sale.

## Financial Analysis Tools

| Name of Measure | Formula | What It Tells You |
|---|---|---|
| Inventory Turnover Ratio | $\dfrac{\text{Cost of Goods Sold}}{\text{Average Inventory}}$ | • The number of times inventory turns over during the period<br>• A higher ratio means faster turnover ☺ |
| Days to Sell | $\dfrac{365}{\text{Inventory Turnover Ratio}}$ | • The average number of days from purchase to sale<br>• A higher number means a longer time to sell ☹ |

# Key Terms

Cost of Goods Sold (CGS) Equation (p. 306)   Last-In, First-Out (LIFO) (p. 307)   Specific Identification (p. 307)
First-In, First-Out (FIFO) (p. 307)   Lower of Cost or Market   Weighted Average (p. 307)
Goods Available for Sale (p. 305)   (LCM) (p. 313)

See complete glossary in back of text.

# Questions

1. Define goods available for sale. How does it differ from cost of goods sold?
2. Define beginning inventory and ending inventory.
3. The chapter discussed four inventory costing methods. List the four methods and briefly explain each.
4. Where possible, the inventory costing method should mimic actual product flows. Do you agree? Explain.
5. Contrast the effects of LIFO versus FIFO on ending inventory when (a) costs are rising and (b) costs are falling.
6. Contrast the income statement effect of LIFO versus FIFO (on cost of goods sold and gross profit) when (a) costs are rising and (b) costs are falling.

7. Explain briefly the application of the LCM rule to ending inventory. Describe its effect on the balance sheet and income statement when market is lower than cost.
8. Explain why an error in ending inventory in one period affects the following period.
9. How is the inventory turnover ratio computed?
10. (Supplement A) Distinguish perpetual inventory systems from periodic inventory systems by describing when and how cost of goods sold is calculated.

# Multiple Choice

1. How many of the following statements is/are true regarding cost of goods sold?

    Quiz 7-1
    www.mhhe.com/LLPW1e

    - Cost of goods sold represents the cost that a company incurred to purchase or produce inventory in the current period.
    - Cost of goods sold is an expense on the income statement.
    - Cost of goods sold is affected by the inventory method selected by a company (FIFO, LIFO, etc.).

    a. None.          c. Two.
    b. One.           d. Three.

2. The inventory costing method selected by a company can affect
    a. The balance sheet.
    b. The income statement.
    c. Neither statement.
    d. Both statements.

3. An overstatement of ending inventory will affect reported net income in which periods?
    a. The period of the overstatement.
    b. The subsequent period.
    c. The period of the overstatement and the subsequent period.
    d. None of the above.

4. In each period, the cost of goods available for sale is allocated between
    a. Assets and liabilities.
    b. Assets and expenses.
    c. Assets and revenues.
    d. Expenses and liabilities.

5. A New York bridal dress retailer purchased three units of the same dress as follows: January 4: $170, January 12: $180, January 18: $190. It sold one dress on January 21 and

one on January 29. What was cost of goods sold during the month of January using FIFO, LIFO, and weighted average costing methods?
    a. FIFO: $370, LIFO: $350, weighted average: $360.
    b. FIFO: $170, LIFO: $190, weighted average: $180.
    c. FIFO: $350, LIFO: $370, weighted average: $360.
    d. None of the above.

6. If costs are rising, which of the following will be true?
    a. The cost of goods sold will be higher if LIFO is used rather than weighted average.
    b. The cost of ending inventory will be higher if FIFO is used rather than LIFO.
    c. The gross profit will be higher if FIFO is used rather than LIFO.
    d. All of the above are true.

7. Which inventory method provides a better matching of current costs with sales revenue on the income statement but also results in older values being reported for inventory on the balance sheet?
    a. FIFO.            c. LIFO.
    b. Weighted average.  d. Specific identification.

8. Assume ending inventory included the following items, and the lower of cost or market rule for inventory was applied. What amount would be reported as ending inventory?

    |      |        | Units | Cost | Market |
    |------|--------|-------|------|--------|
    | i.   | Item A | 20    | $35  | $25    |
    | ii.  | Item B | 50    | $40  | $42    |

    a. $2,600.
    b. $2,700.
    c. $2,500.
    d. None of the above.

9.  An increasing inventory turnover ratio
    a.  Indicates a longer time span between ordering and receiving inventory.
    b.  Indicates a shorter time span between ordering and receiving inventory.
    c.  Indicates a shorter time span between the purchase and sale of inventory.
    d.  Indicates a longer time span between the purchase and sale of inventory.

10. Which of the following is true regarding companies that report their inventories on a LIFO basis?
    a.  They will always have a higher income tax expense.
    b.  They will always have a higher inventory balance.
    c.  Both of the above.
    d.  None of the above.

---

Solutions to Multiple-Choice Questions

1. c    2. d    3. c    4. b    5. c    6. d    7. c    8. c    9. c    10. d

---

# Mini Exercises   Available with McGraw-Hill's Homework Manager

**LO2**

**Dillard's**

**M7-1 Inferring Purchases Using the Cost of Goods Sold Equation**

Dillard's, Inc., operates 330 department stores located in 29 states primarily in the Southwest, Southeast, and Midwest. In its annual report for the year ended January 28, 2006, the company reported cost of goods sold of $5,014 million, ending inventory for the current year of $1,803 million, and ending inventory for the previous year of $1,733 million. Is it possible to develop a reasonable estimate of the merchandise purchases for the year? If so, prepare the estimate. If not, explain why.

**LO3**

**M7-2 Matching Financial Statement Effects to Inventory Costing Methods**

Complete the following table by indicating which inventory costing method (FIFO or LIFO) would lead to the effects noted in the rows for each of the circumstances described in the columns.

|                            | 1. Rising Costs | 2. Declining Costs |
|----------------------------|-----------------|--------------------|
| a. Lowest net income       |                 |                    |
| b. Lowest ending inventory |                 |                    |

**LO3**

**M7-3 Matching Inventory Costing Method Choices to Company Circumstances**

Indicate whether a company interested in minimizing its income taxes should choose the FIFO or LIFO inventory costing method under each of the following circumstances.

    a.  Declining costs    _____
    b.  Rising costs       _____

**LO3**

**M7-4 Calculating Cost of Goods Sold and Ending Inventory under FIFO, LIFO, and Weighted Average (Perpetual Inventory)**

Given the following information, calculate sales, cost of goods sold, and gross profit, under (a) FIFO, (b) LIFO, and (c) weighted average. Assume a perpetual inventory system is used.

|         |                     | Units  | Unit Cost | Unit Selling Price |
|---------|---------------------|--------|-----------|--------------------|
| July 1  | Beginning inventory | 100    | $10       |                    |
| July 13 | Purchase            | 500    | 13        |                    |
| July 25 | Sold                | (200)  |           | $15                |
| July 31 | Ending inventory    | 400    |           |                    |

**M7-5 Calculating Cost of Ending Inventory and Cost of Goods Sold under FIFO, LIFO, and**   LO3
**Weighted Average (Perpetual Inventory)**

Scrappers Supplies uses a perpetual inventory system. At the end of January, its inventory records showed the following:

| Transactions | Units | Unit Cost |
|---|---|---|
| Beginning inventory, January 1, 2008 | 200 | $30 |
| Transactions: | | |
| a. Purchase, January 15 | 300 | 32 |
| b. Sale, January 19 ($46 each) | (350) | |
| c. Purchase, January 24 | 250 | 36 |

*Required:*

1. Calculate the cost of the 350 units sold under the (a) FIFO, (b) LIFO, and (c) weighted average cost methods.
2. Calculate the cost of ending inventory using the (a) FIFO, (b) LIFO, and (c) weighted average cost methods.

**M7-6 Calculating Cost of Ending Inventory and Cost of Goods Sold under FIFO, LIFO, and**   LO3
**Weighted Average (Perpetual Inventory)**

Assume Oahu Kiki's uses a perpetual inventory system that shows the following for the month of January. (Round weighted average cost per unit to the nearest cent.)

| | Date | Units | Unit Cost | Total Cost |
|---|---|---|---|---|
| Beginning Inventory | January 1 | 120 | $ 8 | $ 960 |
| Purchase | January 15 | 380 | 9 | 3,420 |
| Sale | January 19 | 240 | | |
| Purchase | January 24 | 200 | 11 | 2,200 |
| Total | | | | $6,580 |

*Required:*

1. Calculate the cost of the 240 units sold under the (a) FIFO, (b) LIFO, and (c) weighted average cost methods.
2. Calculate the cost of ending inventory using the (a) FIFO, (b) LIFO, and (c) weighted average cost methods.

**M7-7 Reporting Inventory under Lower of Cost or Market**   LO4

The Jewel Fool had the following inventory items on hand at the end of the year.

| | Quantity | Cost per Item | Replacement Cost per Item |
|---|---|---|---|
| Necklaces | 50 | $75 | $70 |
| Bracelets | 25 | 60 | 50 |

Determine the lower of cost or market per unit and the total amount that should be reported on the balance sheet for each item of inventory.

**LO5**

**M7-8 Determining the Financial Statement Effects of Inventory Errors**

Assume the 2007 ending inventory of Shea's Shrimp Shack was understated by $10,000. Explain how this error would affect the amounts reported for cost of goods sold and gross profit for 2007 and 2008.

**LO5**

**M7-9 Determining the Financial Statement Effects of Inventory Errors**

Repeat M7-8, except assume the 2007 ending inventory was overstated by $100,000.

**LO6**

Dillard's
Macy's

**M7-10 Calculating the Inventory Turnover Ratio and Days to Sell**

Using the data in M7-1, calculate to one decimal place the inventory turnover ratio and days to sell for Dillard's. In a recent year, Macy's reported an inventory turnover ratio of 2.6. Which company's inventory turnover is faster?

**M7-11 (Supplement A) Calculating Cost of Goods Sold and Ending Inventory under FIFO, LIFO, and Weighted Average (Periodic Inventory)**

Complete the requirements in M7-5 assuming a periodic inventory system is used under FIFO, LIFO, and weighted average cost.

**M7-12 (Supplement A) Calculating Cost of Goods Sold and Ending Inventory under FIFO, LIFO, and Weighted Average (Periodic Inventory)**

Complete the requirements in M7-6, except assume that the company uses a periodic inventory system.

**M7-13 (Supplement B) Estimating Inventory Using the Gross Profit Method**

Net sales were $150,000 and the estimated gross profit percentage was 40 percent. Estimate cost of goods sold using the gross profit method.

**M7-14 (Supplement B) Estimating Inventory Using the Retail Inventory Method**

Net sales were $200,000 and goods available for sale were $250,000 at retail and $150,000 at cost. Compute ending inventory at cost.

# Exercises  Available with McGraw-Hill's Homework Manager

**LO2**

**E7-1 Inferring Missing Amounts Based on Income Statement Relationships**

Supply the missing dollar amounts for the 2008 income statement of Lewis Retailers for each of the following independent cases:

| Case | Sales Revenue | Beginning Inventory | Purchases | Total Available | Ending Inventory | Cost of Goods Sold | Gross Profit | Operating Expenses | Income from Operations |
|------|---------------|---------------------|-----------|-----------------|------------------|--------------------|--------------|--------------------|------------------------|
| A | $800 | $100 | $700 | $ ? | $500 | $  ? | $  ? | $200 | $  ? |
| B | 900 | 200 | 700 | ? | ? | ? | ? | 150 | 0 |
| C | ? | 150 | ? | ? | 250 | 200 | 400 | 100 | ? |
| D | 800 | ? | 600 | ? | 250 | ? | ? | 250 | 100 |

**LO2**

The Gap

**E7-2 Inferring Merchandise Purchases**

The Gap, Inc., is a specialty retailer that operates stores selling clothes under the trade names Gap, Forth and Towne, Banana Republic, and Old Navy. Assume you are employed as a stock analyst and your boss has just completed a review of the Gap annual report for the year ended January 28, 2006. She provided you with her notes, but they are missing some information that you need. Her notes show that the ending inventory for Gap in the current year was $1,696,000,000 and in the previous year was $1,814,000,000. Net sales for the current year were $16,023,000,000. Gross profit was $5,869,000,000 and net income was $1,113,000,000. For your analysis, you determine that you need to know the amount of purchases and cost of goods sold for the year.

*Required:*

Do you need to ask your boss for her copy of the annual report, or can you develop the information from her notes? Explain and show calculations.

### E7-3 Calculating Cost of Goods Sold and Ending Inventory under FIFO, LIFO, and Weighted Average (Perpetual Inventory)

LO3

Given the following information, calculate the cost of ending inventory and cost of goods sold, assuming a perpetual inventory system is used in combination with (a) FIFO, (b) LIFO, and (c) weighted average cost. (Round weighted average cost per unit to the nearest tenth of a cent; three decimal places.)

|  |  | Units | Unit Cost |
|---|---|---|---|
| July 1 | Beginning Inventory | 2,000 | $ 20.60 |
| July 5 | Sold | 1,000 | |
| July 13 | Purchased | 6,000 | 22.00 |
| July 17 | Sold | 3,000 | |
| July 25 | Purchased | 8,000 | 25.10 |
| July 27 | Sold | 5,000 | |

### E7-4 Calculating Cost of Goods Sold and Ending Inventory under FIFO, LIFO, and Weighted Average (Perpetual Inventory)

LO3

In its first month of operations, Literacy for the Illiterate opened a new bookstore and bought merchandise in the following order: (1) 300 units at $7 on January 1, (2) 450 units at $8 on January 8, and (3) 750 units at $9 on January 29. Assuming the company sold 350 units on January 12 and 550 units on January 30, calculate the cost of goods sold and ending inventory on January 31 under the (a) FIFO, (b) LIFO, and (c) weighted average cost flow assumptions. Assume a perpetual inventory system is used. (Round weighted average cost per unit to the nearest tenth of a cent; three decimal places.)

### E7-5 Evaluating the Effects of Three Inventory Methods on Income from Operations, Income Taxes, and Net Income (Perpetual Inventory)

LO3

Courtney Company uses a perpetual inventory system. Data for 2009: beginning merchandise inventory (December 31, 2008), 1,000 units at $35; purchases include 2,000 units at $38 on March 22 and 3,000 units at $40 on July 1; operating expenses (excluding income taxes), $71,000; sales for the year include 1,500 units sold on April 14 and 3,500 sold on September 30; sales price per unit, $70; and income tax expense is 30 percent of income from operations.

*Required:*

1.  Compute cost of goods sold under the FIFO, LIFO, and weighted average costing methods using a format similar to Exhibits 7.5, 7.6, and 7.7. (Round weighted average cost per unit to the nearest tenth of a cent; three decimal places.) Then prepare income statements for each method using a format similar to the following:

|  | INVENTORY COSTING METHOD | | |
|---|---|---|---|
|  | FIFO | LIFO | Weighted Average |
| **Income Statement** | | | |
| Sales revenue | $ | $ | $ |
| Cost of goods sold | | | |
| Gross profit | | | |
| Operating expenses | | | |
| Income from operations | | | |
| Income tax expense | | | |
| Net income | | | |

2. Between FIFO and LIFO, which method is preferable in terms of (*a*) maximizing operating income or (*b*) minimizing income taxes? Explain.

3. What would be your answer to requirement 2 if costs were falling? Explain.

**LO3**

**E7-6 Evaluating the Effects of Three Inventory Methods on Income from Operations, Income Taxes, and Net Income (Perpetual Inventory)**

Following is partial information for the cost of goods sold calculation and income statement of Timber Company under three different inventory costing methods, assuming the use of a perpetual inventory system:

**Transactions**

Beginning inventory (330 units @ $34) on Jan. 1
Purchases:
    Jan. 10—175 units purchased at $36
    Jan. 25—300 units purchased at $37
Sales:
    Jan. 12 — 200 units sold at $50 per unit
    Jan. 28 — 95 units sold at $50 per unit
Operating expences: $1,600

**Required:**

1. Compute cost of goods sold under the FIFO, LIFO, and weighted average inventory costing methods. (Round weighted average cost per unit to the nearest tenth of a cent; three decimal places.)

2. Prepare an income statement (up to income before income taxes) that compares each method.

3. Rank the three methods in order of highest income before income taxes.

4. Calculate income tax expense under each of the three methods, assuming income tax expense equal to 30 percent of income before income taxes.

5. Rank the three methods in order of lowest income taxes.

**LO3**

**E7-7 Choosing LIFO versus FIFO When Costs Are Rising and Falling**

Use the following information to complete this exercise: sales, 550 units for $12,500; beginning inventory on January 1 of 300 units; purchases of 100 units on February 18, and 300 units on September 14; sales of 300 units on June 5, and 250 units on October 22; and operating expenses of $4,000. Begin by setting up the following table and then complete the requirements that follow.

|  | COSTS RISING | | COSTS FALLING | |
|---|---|---|---|---|
|  | SITUATION A | SITUATION B | SITUATION C | SITUATION D |
|  | FIFO | LIFO | FIFO | LIFO |
| Sales revenue | $12,500 | $12,500 | $12,500 | $12,500 |
| Cost of goods sold | _____ | _____ | _____ | _____ |
| Gross profit |  |  |  |  |
| Operating expenses | 4,000 | 4,000 | 4,000 | 4,000 |
| Income before income taxes |  |  |  |  |
| Income tax expense (30%) | _____ | _____ | _____ | _____ |
| Net income | _____ | _____ | _____ | _____ |

**Required:**

1. First use the included information to calculate the cost of goods sold in Situations A through D, and then complete the table for each situation. In Situations A and B (costs rising), assume the following: beginning inventory, 300 units at $12 = $3,600; February and September purchases

were made at $13. In Situations C and D (costs falling), assume the opposite; that is, beginning inventory, 300 units at $13 = $3,900; subsequent purchases were made at $12. Use perpetual inventory procedures.

2. Describe the relative effects on income from operations as demonstrated by requirement 1 when costs are rising and when costs are falling.

3. Describe the relative effects on income taxes for each situation.

4. Would you recommend FIFO or LIFO? Explain.

### E7-8 Reporting Inventory at Lower of Cost or Market                     LO4

Peterson Furniture Designs is preparing the annual financial statements dated December 31, 2009. Ending inventory information about the five major items stocked for regular sale follows:

| | | ENDING INVENTORY, 2007 | | | |
|---|---|---|---|---|---|
| Item | Quantity on Hand | Unit Cost When Acquired (FIFO) | Replacement Cost (Market) at Year-End | LCM per Item | Total LCM |
| Alligator armoires | 50 | $15 | $12 | _____ | _____ |
| Bear bureaus | 75 | 40 | 40 | _____ | _____ |
| Cougar beds | 10 | 50 | 52 | _____ | _____ |
| Dingo cribs | 30 | 30 | 30 | _____ | _____ |
| Elephant dressers | 400 | 10 | 6 | _____ | _____ |
| Total | | | | | _____ |

**Required:**

Complete the final two columns of the table and then compute the amount that should be reported for the 2009 ending inventory using the LCM rule applied to each item.

### E7-9 Reporting Inventory at Lower of Cost or Market                     LO4

Sandals Company was formed on January 1, 2008, and is preparing the annual financial statements dated December 31, 2008. Ending inventory information about the four major items stocked for regular sale follows:

| | | ENDING INVENTORY, 2008 | |
|---|---|---|---|
| Product Line | Quantity on Hand | Unit Cost When Acquired (FIFO) | Replacement Cost (Market) at Year-End |
| Air flow | 20 | $12 | $ 14 |
| Blister buster | 75 | 40 | 38 |
| Coolonite | 35 | 55 | 50 |
| Dudesly | 10 | 30 | 35 |

**Required:**

1. Compute the amount that should be reported for the 2008 ending inventory using the LCM rule applied to each item.

2. How will the write-down of inventory to lower of cost or market affect the cost of goods sold reported for the year ended December 31, 2008?

### E7-10 Preparing the Journal Entry to Record Lower of Cost or Market (LCM) Adjustments     LO 4

RadioShack Corporation (RadioShack) sells consumer electronic goods and services through its 4,972 stores and 777 kiosks. In its annual report filed with the SEC for a recent year, the company reported that it wrote down inventory by approximately $62,000,000 because its cost exceeded its market value. Show the journal entry that the company would have made to record this adjustment as well as the effects on the accounting equation.

**LO5**

### E7-11 Analyzing and Interpreting the Impact of an Inventory Error

Dallas Corporation prepared the following two income statements:

|  | First Quarter 2009 | | Second Quarter 2009 | |
|---|---|---|---|---|
| Sales revenue |  | $15,000 |  | $18,000 |
| Cost of goods sold |  |  |  |  |
| Beginning inventory | $ 3,000 |  | $ 4,000 |  |
| Purchases | 7,000 |  | 12,000 |  |
| Goods available for sale | 10,000 |  | 16,000 |  |
| Ending inventory | 4,000 |  | 9,000 |  |
| Cost of goods sold |  | 6,000 |  | 7,000 |
| Gross profit |  | 9,000 |  | 11,000 |
| Operating expenses |  | 5,000 |  | 6,000 |
| Operating income |  | $ 4,000 |  | $ 5,000 |

During the third quarter, the company's internal auditors discovered that the ending inventory for the first quarter should have been $4,400. The ending inventory for the second quarter was correct.

*Required:*

1. What effect would the error have on the total operating income for the two quarters combined? Explain.
2. What effect would the error have on the operating income for each of the two quarters? Explain.
3. Prepare corrected income statements for each quarter.

**LO5**

### E7-12 Analyzing and Interpreting the Impact of an Inventory Error

Houston Corporation prepared the same two income statements presented in E7-11. During the third quarter, the company's internal auditors discovered that the ending inventory for the first quarter should have been $3,600. The ending inventory for the second quarter was correct.

*Required:*

1. What effect would the error have on the total operating income for the two quarters combined? Explain.
2. What effect would the error have on the operating income for each of the two quarters? Explain.
3. Prepare corrected income statements for each quarter.

**LO6**

**Polaris Industries**

### E7-13 Analyzing and Interpreting the Inventory Turnover Ratio

Polaris Industries Inc. is the biggest snowmobile manufacturer in the world. It reported the following amounts in its recent financial statements (in millions):

|  | Current Year | Prior Year |
|---|---|---|
| Net sales revenue | $1,870 | $1,773 |
| Cost of sales | 1,452 | 1,349 |
| Average inventory | 188 | 179 |

*Required:*

1. Calculate to one decimal place the inventory turnover ratio and average days to sell inventory for the current and prior years.

2. Comment on any trends, and compare the effectiveness of inventory managers at Polaris to inventory managers at its main competitor, Arctic Cat, where inventory turns over 7.5 times per year (48.7 days to sell). Both companies use the same inventory costing method (FIFO).

**E7-14 (Supplement A) Calculating Cost of Ending Inventory and Cost of Goods Sold under Periodic FIFO, LIFO and Weighted-Average**

Refer to the information in E7-3. Assume the company uses a periodic inventory system. Calculate the cost of goods sold and the cost of ending inventory using the FIFO, LIFO, and weighted average cost methods (Round weighted average cost per unit to the nearest tenth of a cent; three decimal places.)

**E7-15 (Supplement A) Calculating Cost of Ending Inventory and Cost of Goods Sold under Periodic FIFO, LIFO, and Weighted Average**

Refer to the information in E7-4. Assume the company uses a periodic inventory system. Calculate the cost of ending inventory and the cost of goods sold using the FIFO, LIFO, and weighted average cost methods. (Round weighted average cost per unit to the nearest tenth of a cent; three decimal places.)

**E7-16 (Supplement B) Estimating Inventory Using the Gross Profit Method**

Hartman Co.'s accounting records contained the following information related to the month of November:

| | |
|---|---|
| Beginning inventory | $16,000 |
| Purchases | 52,000 |
| Net sales | 75,000 |
| Estimated gross profit percentage | 30% |

Estimate cost of goods sold for the month and ending inventory at month-end using the gross profit method.

**E7-17 (Supplement B) Estimating Inventory Using the Retail Inventory Method**

Ralph's Clothing's accounting records indicated the following at the end of the quarter:

| | Cost | Retail |
|---|---|---|
| Beginning inventory | $26,000 | $ 41,600 |
| Purchases | 48,000 | 76,800 |
| Goods available for sale | 74,000 | 118,400 |
| Sales | | 100,400 |

Compute ending inventory at cost using the retail method.

# Problems—Set A    Available with McGraw-Hill's Homework Manager

**PA7-1 Analyzing the Effects of Four Alternative Inventory Methods in a Perpetual Inventory System**   LO3

Gladstone Company uses a perpetual inventory system. At the end of the annual accounting period, December 31, 2007, the accounting records for the most popular item in inventory showed the following:

| Transactions | Units | Unit Cost |
|---|---|---|
| Beginning inventory, January 1, 2007 | 1,800 | $5.00 |
| Transactions during 2007: | | |
| Purchase, January 30 | 2,500 | 6.20 |
| Sale, March 14 ($10 each) | (1,450) | |
| Purchase, May 1 | 1,200 | 8.00 |
| Sale, August 31 ($10 each) | (1,900) | |

*Required:*

1. Compute the ending inventory and cost of goods sold at December 31, 2007, under each of the following inventory costing methods:

   a. First-in, first-out.

   b. Last-in, first-out.

   c. Weighted average cost. (Round weighted average cost per unit to the nearest tenth of a cent; three decimal places.)

   d. Specific identification, assuming that the March 14, 2007, sale was comprised of 580 units from the beginning inventory and 870 units from the purchase of January 30, 2007. Assume that the sale of August 31, 2007, was comprised of 1,220 units from beginning inventory, and 680 units from the purchase of May 1, 2007.

2. Of the four methods, which will result in the highest gross profit? Which will result in the lowest income taxes?

**LO3**

www.mhhe.com/LLPW1e

**PA7-2 Analyzing and Interpreting the Financial Statement Effects of FIFO, LIFO, and Weighted Average (Perpetual Inventory)**

Orion Iron Corp. uses a perpetual inventory system. At the end of the annual accounting period, December 31, 2009, the accounting records provided the following information:

| Transactions | Units | Unit Cost |
|---|---|---|
| Inventory, December 31, 2008 | 2,000 | $ 8.00 |
| For the year 2009: | | |
| Purchase, April 11 | 10,000 | 10.40 |
| Sale, May 1 (sold for $40 per unit) | 2,000 | |
| Purchase, June 1 | 8,000 | 12.25 |
| Sale, July 3 (sold for $40 per unit) | 6,000 | |
| Operating expenses (excluding income tax expense), $195,000 | | |

*Required:*

1. Compute the cost of goods sold under (*a*) FIFO, (*b*) LIFO, and (*c*) weighted average. (Round weighted average cost per unit to the nearest tenth of a cent; three decimal places.)

2. Prepare an income statement that shows 2009 amounts for the FIFO method in one column, the LIFO method in another column, and the weighted average method in a final column. Include the following line items in the income statement: sales revenue, cost of goods sold, gross profit, operating expenses, and income from operations.

3. Compare the income from operations and the ending inventory amounts that would be reported under the three methods. Explain the similarities and differences.

4. Which inventory costing method may be preferred by Orion Iron Corp. for income tax purposes? Explain.

**LO4**

www.mhhe.com/LLPW1e

**PA7-3 Evaluating the Income Statement and Income Tax Effects of Lower of Cost or Market**

Springer Anderson Gymnastics prepared its annual financial statements dated December 31, 2009. The company used the FIFO inventory costing method, but it failed to apply LCM to the ending inventory. The preliminary 2009 income statement follows:

| | | |
|---|---:|---:|
| Sales revenue | | $140,000 |
| Cost of goods sold | | |
|   Beginning inventory | $ 15,000 | |
|   Purchases | 91,000 | |
|     Goods available for sale | 106,000 | |
|   Ending inventory (FIFO cost) | 22,000 | |
|     Cost of goods sold | | 84,000 |
| Gross profit | | 56,000 |
| Operating expenses | | 31,000 |
| Income before income taxes | | 25,000 |
|   Income tax expense (30%) | | 7,500 |
| Net income | | $ 17,500 |

Assume you have been asked to restate the 2009 financial statements to incorporate LCM. You have developed the following data relating to the 2009 ending inventory:

| Item | Quantity | ACQUISITION COST | | CURRENT REPLACEMENT UNIT COST |
| | | Per Unit | Total | Market |
| --- | --- | --- | --- | --- |
| A | 1,500 | $3 | $ 4,500 | $4 |
| B | 750 | 4 | 3,000 | 2 |
| C | 3,500 | 2 | 7,000 | 1 |
| D | 1,500 | 5 | 7,500 | 3 |
| | | | $22,000 | |

**Required:**

1. Restate the income statement to reflect LCM valuation of the 2009 ending inventory. Apply LCM on an item-by-item basis and show computations.
2. Compare and explain the LCM effect on each amount that was changed in requirement 1.
3. What is the conceptual basis for applying LCM to merchandise inventories?

## PA7-4 Analyzing and Interpreting the Effects of Inventory Errors

LO5

www.mhhe.com/LLPW1e

The income statement for Sherwood Company summarized for a four-year period shows the following:

| | 2005 | 2006 | 2007 | 2008 |
| --- | --- | --- | --- | --- |
| Sales revenue | $2,000,000 | $2,400,000 | $2,500,000 | $3,000,000 |
| Cost of goods sold | 1,400,000 | 1,660,000 | 1,770,000 | 2,100,000 |
| Gross profit | $ 600,000 | $ 740,000 | $ 730,000 | $ 900,000 |

An audit revealed that in determining these amounts, the ending inventory for 2006 was overstated by $20,000. The inventory balance on December 31, 2007, was accurately stated.

**Required:**

1. Restate the income statements to reflect the correct amounts after fixing the inventory error.
2. Compute the gross profit percentage for each year (*a*) before the correction and (*b*) after the correction. Do the results lend confidence to your corrected amounts? Explain.

## PA7-5 Calculating and Interpreting the Inventory Turnover Ratio and Days to Sell

LO6

**H** Harman International
Boston Acoustics

Harman International Industries is a world leading producer of loudspeakers and other electronics products, which are sold under brand names like JBL, Infinity, and Harman/Kardon. The company reported the following amounts in its financial statements (in millions):

| | Current Year | Previous Year |
| --- | --- | --- |
| Net sales revenue | $3,248 | $3,031 |
| Cost of sales | 2,095 | 1,999 |
| Beginning inventory | 312 | 292 |
| Ending inventory | 345 | 312 |

**Required:**

1. Determine the inventory turnover ratio and average days to sell inventory for the current and previous years.
2. Comment on any changes in these measures, and compare the effectiveness of inventory managers at Harmon to inventory managers at Boston Acoustics, where inventory turns over 3.7 times per year (99 days to sell). Both companies use the same inventory costing method (FIFO).

**PA7-6 (Supplement A) Analyzing the Effects of the LIFO Inventory Method in a Periodic Inventory System**

Using the information in PA7-1, calculate the cost of goods sold and ending inventory under (*a*) FIFO, (*b*) LIFO, and (*c*) weighted average in combination with a periodic inventory system. (Round the weighted average cost to the nearest tenth of a cent; three decimal places.). Which method will result in the highest gross profit? Which method will result in the lowest taxes?

**PA7-7 (Supplement B) Estimating Inventory Using the Gross Profit Method**

Bunky's Business Solutions uses the gross profit method to estimate cost of goods sold and ending inventory for its quarterly financial statements. Last year, net sales were $750,000 and cost of goods sold were $540,000. The accounting records for the current quarter contained the following information:

| | |
|---|---|
| Beginning inventory | $ 40,000 |
| Purchases | 112,000 |
| Net sales | 181,000 |

*Required:*

1. Compute the gross profit percentage for last year.
2. Estimate cost of goods sold for the quarter and ending inventory at quarter-end using the gross profit method.

**PA7-8 (Supplement B) Estimating Inventory Using the Retail Inventory Method**

Fleming Enterprises' accounting records indicated the following at the end of the quarter:

| | Cost | Retail |
|---|---|---|
| Beginning inventory | $ 84,000 | $112,000 |
| Purchases | 318,000 | 424,000 |
| Goods available for sale | $402,000 | $536,000 |
| Sales | | $468,000 |

*Required:*

1. Compute ending inventory at cost using the retail method.
2. Compute cost of goods sold using the answer to requirement 1.

# Problems—Set B    **Available with McGraw-Hill's Homework Manager**

LO3    **PB7-1 Analyzing the Effects of Four Alternative Inventory Methods in a Perpetual Inventory System**

Mojo Industries uses a perpetual inventory system. At the end of the accounting period, January 31, 2009, the inventory records showed the following for an item that sold at $9 per unit:

| Transactions | Unit Cost | Units | Total Cost |
|---|---|---|---|
| Inventory, January 1, 2009 | $2.50 | 250 | $625 |
| Sale, January 10 | | (200) | |
| Purchase, January 12 | 3.00 | 300 | 900 |
| Sale, January 17 | | (150) | |
| Purchase, January 26 | 4.00 | 80 | 320 |

*Required:*

1. Compute the ending inventory and cost of goods sold at January 31, 2009, under each of the following inventory costing methods:
   *a.* First-in, first-out.
   *b.* Last-in, first-out.

 c.  Weighted average cost (Round weighted average unit cost to the nearest tenth of a cent; three decimal places.)
 d.  Specific identification, assuming that the January 10 sale was from the beginning inventory and the January 17 sale was from the January 12 purchase.

2.  Of the four methods, which will result in the highest gross profit? Which will result in the lowest income taxes?

## PB7-2 Analyzing and Interpreting the Financial Statement Effects of FIFO, LIFO, and Weighted Average (Perpetual Inventory)    LO3

Scoresby Inc. uses a perpetual inventory system. At the end of the annual accounting period, December 31, 2008, the accounting records provided the following information:

| Transactions | Units | Unit Cost |
|---|---|---|
| Inventory, December 31, 2007 | 3,000 | $7.90 |
| For the year 2008: | | |
| Purchase, March 5 | 8,000 | 9.00 |
| Sale, April 15 (sold for $29 per unit) | 4,000 | |
| Purchase, September 19 | 5,000 | 11.82 |
| Sale, October 31 (sold for $31 per unit) | 8,000 | |
| Operating expenses (excluding income tax expense), $240,000 | | |

### Required:

1.  Compute the cost of goods sold under (a) FIFO, (b) LIFO, and (c) weighted average. (Round weighted average cost per unit to the nearest tenth of a cent; three decimal places.)
2.  Prepare an income statement that shows 2008 amounts for the FIFO method in one column, the LIFO method in another column, and the weighted average method in a final column. Include the following line items in the income statement: sales revenue, cost of goods sold, gross profit, operating expenses, and income from operations.
3.  Compare the income from operations and the ending inventory amounts that would be reported under the two methods. Explain the similarities and differences.
4.  Which inventory costing method may be preferred by Scoresby for income tax purposes? Explain.

## PB7-3 Evaluating the Income Statement and Income Tax Effects of Lower of Cost or Market    LO4

Mondetta Clothing prepared its annual financial statements dated December 31, 2008. The company used the FIFO inventory costing method, but it failed to apply LCM to the ending inventory. The preliminary 2008 income statement follows:

| | | |
|---|---:|---:|
| Sales revenue | | $420,000 |
| Cost of goods sold | | |
| Beginning inventory | $ 45,000 | |
| Purchases | 273,000 | |
| Goods available for sale | 318,000 | |
| Ending inventory (FIFO cost) | 66,000 | |
| Cost of goods sold | | 252,000 |
| Gross profit | | 168,000 |
| Operating expenses | | 93,000 |
| Income before income taxes | | 75,000 |
| Income tax expense (30%) | | 22,500 |
| Net income | | $ 52,500 |

Assume you have been asked to restate the 2008 financial statements to incorporate LCM. You have developed the following data relating to the 2008 ending inventory:

| | | ACQUISITION COST | | CURRENT REPLACEMENT UNIT COST |
|---|---|---|---|---|
| Item | Quantity | Per Unit | Total | Market |
| A | 3,000 | $4.50 | $13,500 | $6.00 |
| B | 1,500 | 6.00 | 9,000 | 3.00 |
| C | 7,000 | 3.00 | 21,000 | 6.00 |
| D | 3,000 | 7.50 | 22,500 | 4.50 |
| | | | $66,000 | |

*Required:*

1. Restate the income statement to reflect LCM valuation of the 2008 ending inventory. Apply LCM on an item-by-item basis and show computations.
2. Compare and explain the LCM effect on each amount that was changed in requirement 1.
3. What is the conceptual basis for applying LCM to merchandise inventories?

**LO5**

**PB7-4 Analyzing and Interpreting the Effects of Inventory Errors**

"Oops, I Did It Again" was the song being sung by the accountants at Spears & Cantrell when they announced inventory had been overstated by $30 (million) at the end of the second quarter. The error was not discovered and corrected in the company's periodic inventory system until after the end of the third quarter. The following table shows the amounts (in millions) that were originally reported by the company.

| | Q1 | Q2 | Q3 |
|---|---|---|---|
| Sales revenue | $3,000 | $3,600 | $3,750 |
| Cost of goods sold | 2,100 | 2,490 | 2,655 |
| Gross profit | $ 900 | $1,110 | $1,095 |

*Required:*

1. Restate the income statements to reflect the correct amounts, after fixing the inventory error.
2. Compute the gross profit percentage for each quarter (*a*) before the correction and (*b*) after the correction. Do the results lend confidence to your corrected amounts? Explain.

**LO6**

**amazon**.com

**Borders**

**PB7-5 Calculating and Interpreting the Inventory Turnover Ratio and Days to Sell**

Amazon.com reported the following amounts in its financial statements (in millions):

| | Current Year | Prior Year |
|---|---|---|
| Net sales revenue | $8,490 | $6,921 |
| Cost of sales | 6,451 | 5,319 |
| Beginning inventory | 480 | 294 |
| Ending inventory | 566 | 480 |

*Required:*

1. Determine the inventory turnover ratio and average days to sell inventory for the current and prior years.
2. Comment on any changes in these measures and compare the inventory turnover at Amazon.com to inventory turnover at Borders, where inventory turned over 2.2 times during the current year

(166 days to sell). Based on your own experience, what is the key difference between Amazon.com and Borders that leads one company's results to be the picture of efficiency and the other to seem like a library?

**PB7-6 (Supplement A) Analyzing the Effects of Three Inventory Methods in a Periodic Inventory System**

Using the information in PB7-1, calculate the cost of goods sold and ending inventory under (*a*) FIFO, (*b*) LIFO, and (*c*) weighted average in combination with a periodic inventory system. (Round the weighted-average cost to the nearest tenth of a cent; three decimal places.) Which method will result in the highest gross profit? Which method will result in the lowest taxes?

**PB7-7 (Supplement B) Estimating Inventory Using the Gross Profit Method**

Greeley & Morgan, LLP uses the gross profit method to estimate cost of goods sold and ending inventory for its quarterly financial statements. Last year, net sales were $328,125 and cost of goods sold were $210,000. Its accounting records for the current quarter contained the following information:

| | |
|---|---|
| Beginning inventory | $ 9,000 |
| Purchases | 52,000 |
| Net sales | 85,000 |

*Required:*

1. Compute the gross profit percentage for last year.
2. Estimate cost of goods sold for the quarter and ending inventory at quarter-end using the gross profit method.

**PB7-8 (Supplement B) Estimating Inventory Using the Retail Inventory Method**

Indieser, Inc.'s accounting records indicated the following at the end of the quarter:

| | Cost | Retail |
|---|---|---|
| Beginning inventory | $252,000 | $ 315,000 |
| Purchases | 676,000 | 845,000 |
| Goods available for sale | 928,000 | 1,160,000 |
| Sales | | 980,000 |

*Required:*

1. Compute ending inventory at cost using the retail method.
2. Compute cost of goods sold using the answer to requirement 1.

# Cases and Projects

**CP7-1 Finding Financial Information**                                    LO1, 2, 6

Refer to the financial statements of The Home Depot in Appendix A at the end of this book, or download the annual report from the *Cases* section of the text's Web site at www.mhhe.com/LLPW1e.

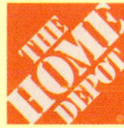

1. How much inventory does the company hold at the end of the most recent year? Does this represent an increase or decrease in comparison to the prior year?
2. What method(s) does the company use to determine the cost of its inventory? Describe where you found this information.
3. Compute to one decimal place the company's inventory turnover ratio and days to sell for the most recent year.

**CP7-2 Comparing Financial Information**                                    LO1, 2, 6

Refer to the financial statements of The Home Depot in Appendix A and Lowe's in Appendix B at the end of this book, or download the annual reports from the *Cases* section of the text's Web site at www.mhhe.com/LLPW1e.

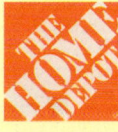

1. Does Lowe's hold more or less inventory than The Home Depot at the end of the most recent year?
2. What method does Lowe's use to determine the cost of its inventory? Comment on how this affects comparisons you might make between Lowe's and The Home Depot's inventory turnover ratios.

Lowe's

3. Compute to one decimal place Lowe's inventory turnover ratio and days to sell for the most recent year and compare to The Home Depot's. What does this analysis suggest to you?

**LO1, 2, 3, 4, 5, 6**

**CP7-3 Examining an Annual Report: Internet-Based Team Research**

As a team, select an industry to analyze. Using your Web browser, each team member should acquire the annual report or 10-K for one publicly traded company in the industry, with each member selecting a different company. (See CP1-3 in Chapter 1 for a description of possible resources for these tasks.)

*Required:*

1. On an individual basis, each team member should write a short report that incorporates the following:

   a. Describe the types of inventory held by the company. Does the company indicate its inventory management goals anywhere in its annual report?

   b. Describe the inventory costing method that it used. Why do you think the company chose this method rather than the other acceptable methods? Do you think its inventory costs are rising or falling?

   c. Calculate the inventory turnover ratio for the current and prior year, and explain any change between the two years. (To obtain the beginning inventory number for the prior year, you will need the prior year's annual report.)

   d. Search the 10-K for information about the company's approach for applying the LCM rule to inventory. Did the company report the amount of inventory written down during the year?

2. Then, as a team, write a short report comparing and contrasting your companies using these attributes. Discuss any patterns across the companies that you as a team observe. Provide potential explanations for any differences discovered.

**LO3**

**CP7-4 Making Ethical Decisions: A Mini Case**

David Exler is the CEO of AquaGear Enterprises, a seven-year-old manufacturer of boats. After many long months of debate with the company's board of directors, David obtained the board's approval to expand into water ski sales. David firmly believed that AquaGear could generate significant profits in this market, despite recent increases in the cost of skis. A board meeting will be held later this month for David to present the financial results for the first quarter of ski sales. As AquaGear's corporate controller, you reported to David that the results were not great. Although sales were better than expected at $165,000 (3,000 units at $55 per unit), the cost of goods sold was $147,500. This left a gross profit of $17,500. David knew this amount would not please the board. Desperate to save the ski division, David asks you to "take another look at the cost calculations to see if there's any way to reduce the cost of goods sold. I know you accountants have different methods for figuring things out, so maybe you can do your magic now when I need it most." You dig out your summary of inventory purchases for the quarter to recheck your calculations, using the LIFO method that has always been used for the company's inventory of boats.

|  | Date | Units | Unit Cost | Total Cost |
|---|---|---|---|---|
| Beginning inventory of water skis | January 1 | 0 | — | — |
| Purchases | January 15 | 1,500 | $ 30 | $ 45,000 |
| Purchases | February 18 | 2,000 | 45 | 90,000 |
| Purchases | February 27 | 2,500 | 50 | 125,000 |

*Required:*

1. Calculate cost of goods sold using the LIFO method. (Assume all sales took place in March.) Does this confirm the statement you made to David about the gross profit earned on water ski sales in the first quarter?

2. Without doing any calculations, is it likely that any alternative inventory costing method will produce a lower cost of goods sold?

3. Calculate cost of goods sold using the FIFO method. Would use of this method solve David's current dilemma?

4. Is it acceptable within GAAP to report the water skis using one inventory costing method and the boats using a different method?

5. Do you see any problems with using the FIFO numbers for purposes of David's meeting with the board?

**LO4**

*Perfumania*

**CP7-5 Calculating and Recording the Effects of Lower of Cost or Market (LCM) on Ending Inventory**

Assume you recently obtained a job in the Miami head office of Perfumania, the largest specialty retailer of discounted fragrances in the United States. Your job is to estimate the amount of write-down required to value inventory at the lower of cost or market. The cost of inventory is calculated using the weighted average cost method and, at approximately $70 million, it represents the company's largest and most important asset. Assume the corporate controller asked you to prepare a spreadsheet that can be used to determine the amount of LCM write-down for the current year. The controller provides the following hypothetical numbers for you to use in the spreadsheet.

| Product Line | Quantity on Hand | Weighted Average Unit Cost | Replacement Cost (Market) at Year-End |
|---|---|---|---|
| Alfred Sung Shi | 80 | $ 22 | $ 20 |
| Animale | 75 | 15 | 16 |
| Azzaro | 50 | 10 | 10 |
| Mambo | 30 | 16 | 17 |
| OP Juice | 400 | 8 | 7 |

You realize that you will need to multiply the quantity of each item by the lower of cost or market per unit, but you cannot figure out how to get the spreadsheet to choose the lower number. You e-mailed your friend Billy for help, and here is his reply.

From: Billy@yahoo.com
To: Helpme@hotmail.com
Cc:
Subject: Excel Help

You can do this several different ways, but the easiest is to use the MIN command. Set up your spreadsheet similar to the table you sent me, and then add two new columns. In the first new column, enter the command "=MIN(costcell, marketcell)" where costcell is the cell containing the cost per unit and marketcell is the cell containing the market value per unit. Next, in the second new column, multiply the quantity by the LCM per unit. Here is a screenshot of what this will probably look like in your spreadsheet.

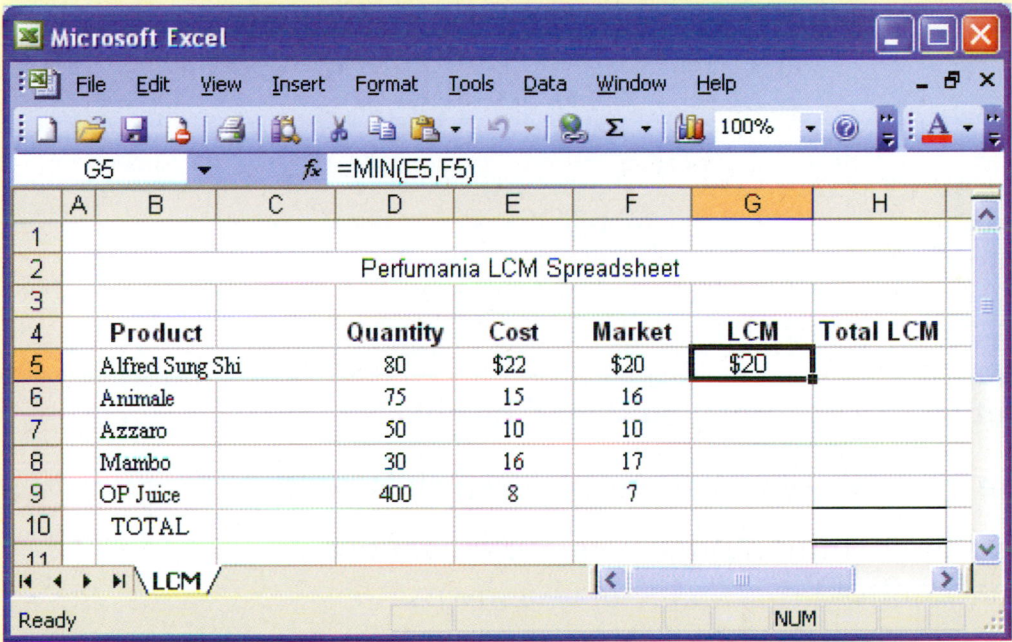

Be sure to enter a formula to sum down the Total LCM column for all the products so that this grand total can be subtracted from the cost presently recorded in the inventory accounting records to determine the write-down.

**Required:**

1. Prepare a spreadsheet that calculates total LCM for inventory, applied on an item-by-item basis.
2. Prepare a journal entry to record the write-down needed for the five products in this problem.

# 8 Internal Control and Cash

## LEARNING OBJECTIVES

**After completing this chapter, you should be able to:**

**LO1** Define internal control and explain why it is needed.

**LO2** Explain the common principles and limitations of internal control.

**LO3** Apply internal control principles to cash receipts and payments.

**LO4** Describe the operation of voucher and petty cash systems.

**LO5** Prepare a bank reconciliation.

**LO6** Describe the reporting of cash and cash equivalents.

Lectured slideshow—LP8-1
www.mhhe.com/LLPW1e

# Focus Company: THE HOME DEPOT

## "You Can Do It. We Can Help."

ir.homedepot.com

The Home Depot's business code of conduct and ethics states that the company's success depends on doing the right thing each and every day for the benefit of employees, customers, vendors, suppliers, and the communities the company serves. A clerk who was working at a Home Depot store in New York recently took these words to heart and provided a phone tip that led to the discovery of "the largest, most remarkable, most extraordinary theft" from a school system in U.S. history. The clerk had become suspicious of a customer who used a school district's Home Depot credit card to buy construction materials for delivery far outside the school district. The clerk's tip prompted an audit and later a criminal investigation, which ultimately revealed an embezzlement of more than $11 million. It turned out that the customer, who was the son of the school's assistant superintendent, had given 74 unauthorized cards to friends and family to use for personal purchases. Other misdeeds and attempted cover-ups involving the school's superintendent, assistant superintendent, auditor, and others resulted in jail terms of up to 12 years and fines ranging from $780,000 to $4.3 million. According to a report issued by the State of New York, the embezzlement was possible because the school district's "internal control weaknesses created an environment that was conducive to fraud and abuse."[1]

You are not likely to find these kinds of internal control problems at The Home Depot. As you will see in this chapter, The Home Depot takes internal control seriously. In fact, the company recently ranked among the top 10 companies in the United States for internal control and other governance practices.[2]

---

[1] "Roslyn Union Free School District: Anatomy of a Scandal," n.d., http://www.osc.state.ny.us/localgov/audits/2005/schools/roslyn2.pdf, February 25, 2007.

[2] "Corporate Governance Quotient: Benchmarking Your Governance Against Your Peers," n.d., http://www.isscorporate-services.com/ratings/cgqtop10.html, February 25, 2007.

**INTERNAL CONTROL**

- Definition and Purpose
- Sarbanes-Oxley Act of 2002
- Common Control Principles
- Control Limitations

**INTERNAL CONTROL OF CASH**

- Cash Receipts
- Cash Payments
- Bank Procedures and Reconciliation

**FINANCIAL REPORTING OF CASH**

- Cash and Cash Equivalents

# INTERNAL CONTROL

## Definition and Purpose

All businesses have one thing in common: To be successful, they must control their operations. They must hire the right people, pay them the right amount of wages, order and receive the right products, pay suppliers the right amounts at the right times, set the right prices, collect and deposit the right amount of cash, and so on.

To achieve this state of control, each company establishes and follows specific procedures and policies that describe how the business is to be run. These procedures and policies are internal controls. In your personal life, internal controls include basic precautions, such as locking your car door and checking the accuracy of your bank statement. In business, **internal control** is defined as the methods an organization uses to protect against the theft of assets, enhance the reliability of accounting information, promote efficient and effective operations, and ensure compliance with applicable laws, regulations, and codes of ethical conduct.

The ideas behind internal control, which have been around for more than 5,000 years,[3] apply to all government, not-for-profit, and business organizations, both large and small. In simple terms, internal controls are needed to help ensure that people will act in ways that benefit the organization. When internal controls operate effectively, they can improve efficiency and minimize waste, unintentional errors, and fraud. In fact, one group of researchers found companies that emphasized internal control and an ethical culture grew their revenues four times faster and increased their stock prices 12 times as much as companies without those practices.[4] It is little wonder, then, that The Home Depot owes much of its success to the internal controls in place at its 1,500 store locations, which ensure that the 1.3 billion transactions processed by the company each year are completed with consistency, efficiency, accuracy, and honesty.

## Sarbanes-Oxley Act of 2002

Although internal control is essential to businesses of all sizes, it has become one of the most important issues facing public companies today. The first decade of this century brought several high-profile accounting scandals involving Enron, WorldCom, and a number of other publicly owned companies. To restore investor confidence and improve the quality of financial reporting in the United States, the U.S. Congress passed the Sarbanes-Oxley (SOX) Act of 2002. This new act has led public companies to strengthen their internal controls and to better inform financial statement users of their effectiveness in producing accurate financial statements and preventing fraud. In this section, we explain some of the key features of SOX as summarized in Exhibit 8.1.[5]

---

[3] See T. A. Lee, "The Historical Development of Internal Control from the Earliest Times to the End of the Seventeenth Century," *Journal of Accounting Research*, Spring 1971, pp. 150–57.

[4] J. P. Kotter and J. L. Heskett, 1992, *Corporate Culture and Performance* (New York: Maxwell MacMillan International).

[5] The triangle in Exhibit 8.1 corresponds to what fraud investigators call the "fraud triangle," meaning the convergence of (1) the opportunity, (2) the incentive, and (3) the unscrupulous character that enables individuals to commit, rationalize, and conceal fraud.

| Exhibit 8.1 | Significant Changes Introduced by the Sarbanes-Oxley Act of 2002 |

**Reduce opportunities for error and fraud**
- Internal control report from management
- Stronger oversight by directors
- Internal control audit by external auditors

**Encourage good character**
- Anonymous tip lines
- Whistle-blower protection
- Code of ethics

**Counteract incentives for fraud**
- Stiffer fines and prison terms

## Reduce Opportunities for Error and Fraud

A primary goal of SOX is improved internal controls, particularly in relation to financial reporting. SOX aims to achieve this goal in three ways:

1. **Internal control report from management.**   Every year managers must review their company's internal controls and issue a report that indicates whether controls over financial reporting were effective. This new requirement means that most marketing managers, for example, now have some accounting responsibilities, such as determining whether their staff members submit accurate sales and expense reports.

2. **Stronger oversight by directors.**   Each company must establish an independent audit committee to oversee the company's financial matters. One of the main roles of this committee is to hire external auditors and ensure that they perform their work effectively as described in the following paragraph.

3. **Internal control audit by external auditors.**   The company's external auditors must test the effectiveness of the company's internal controls and issue a report that gives an opinion about the effectiveness of the company's internal controls over financial reporting. As was the case before SOX, external auditors must also examine the company's financial statements and report whether they were prepared using GAAP.

## Counteract Incentives for Committing Fraud

Under SOX, those who intentionally misstate a company's financial results face much stiffer penalties than before. They must repay any money obtained via fraud and can be assessed additional fines of up to $5 million. Executives cannot avoid these penalties by declaring personal bankruptcy, which explains why a former sales director at Computer Associates will be giving 15 percent of every paycheck he earns for the rest of his life to a fraud restitution fund. SOX also increased the maximum jail sentence for fraudulent financial reporting to 20 years, which can add up because federal sentencing guidelines allow judges to declare consecutive jail terms for each violation.

## Encourage Good Character in Employees

Admittedly, it is difficult for a law to make people act appropriately, but SOX introduces new rules that should help employees of good character to confront those of questionable character. For example, audit committees are now required to create tip lines that allow employees to secretly submit concerns they may have about suspicious accounting or auditing practices. SOX gives these "whistle-blowers" legal protection from retaliation by those charged with fraud. That is, if you tattle on your boss for submitting a fraudulent expense claim, you cannot be fired for doing so. Finally, to reinforce good character, public companies must adopt a code of ethics for senior financial officers.

Identify whether each of the following actions is most likely to increase (+) or decrease (−) the risk of error or fraud arising from opportunities (O), incentives (I), or an individual's character (C).

|  | + / − | I/O/C |
|---|---|---|
| 1. **Enron** implemented a "rank-and-yank" practice that involved ranking the financial performance of each business unit and then firing managers in the lowest 20 percent. | _____ | _____ |
| 2. **Microsoft Corporation** invites anonymous or confidential submission of questionable accounting or auditing matters to msft.buscond@alertline.com. | _____ | _____ |
| 3. The **H. J. Heinz Company**'s board of directors is one of the strongest boards in the United States, according to Institutional Shareholder Services. | _____ | _____ |

*After you have finished, check your answers with the solution at the bottom of this page.*

## Common Control Principles

From the perspective of a company's chief executive officer (CEO), chief financial officer (CFO), and board of directors, internal control is a broad concept that includes more than accounting. It includes setting strategic objectives, identifying risks the company faces, hiring good employees, instilling ethical principles in them, motivating them to achieve the company's objectives, and providing the resources and information they need to fulfill those objectives. Rather than overwhelm you with the list of 20 control principles that senior executives must think about,[6] we focus on just five basic principles that you are likely to see in your own work. We want you to understand why certain types of control exist so that when you encounter them during your career, you will appreciate them and ensure that others respect them.

All good systems of internal control are based on these five common principles, which are summarized in Exhibit 8.2. These principles are typically applied to all aspects of a company's business activities, including human resource management, finance, marketing, and general business operations. Our focus here, however, is on their relationship to accounting, as follows.

1. **Establish responsibility.** Whenever possible, assign each task to only one employee. Doing so will allow you to determine who caused any errors or thefts that may have occurred. Thus, The Home Depot assigns a separate cash register drawer to each employee at the beginning of a shift. If two cashiers were to use the same drawer, determining which cashier caused the drawer to be short of cash would not be possible. With just one person responsible for adding and removing money from the drawer, however, no doubt exists about who is responsible for a cash shortage.

2. **Segregate duties.** Segregation of duties involves assigning responsibilities so that one employee cannot make a mistake or commit a dishonest act without someone else discovering it. This principle is the reason that cashiers at The Home Depot need a manager's approval for price changes at the checkout counter. Without this control, cashiers could lower the price for a friend or relative. Segregation of duties is most effective when a company assigns the responsibilities for related activities to two or more people and assigns recordkeeping responsibilities to people who do not handle the assets

---

[6] These 20 principles are outlined in "Internal Control for Financial Reporting—Guidance for Smaller Public Companies," published June 2006 at www.coso.org by The Committee of Sponsoring Organizations (COSO).

1. + / I (increased pressure to report stronger financial results)
2. − / C (less likelihood that unethical behavior will go unreported)
3. − / O (strong oversight by directors)

| Exhibit 8.2 | Five Common Principles of Internal Control |
| --- | --- |

| Principle | Explanation | Example | |
| --- | --- | --- | --- |
| 1. Establish responsibility. | Assign each task to only one employee. | Each Home Depot cashier uses a different cash drawer. |  |
| 2. Segregate duties. | Do not make one employee responsible for all parts of a transaction. | Home Depot cashiers, who ring up cash sales, do not also approve price changes. | |
| 3. Restrict access. | Do not provide access to assets or information unless it is needed to fulfill assigned responsibilities. | Home Depot secures valuable assets such as cash and access to its computer systems. | |
| 4. Document procedures. | Prepare documents to show activities that have occurred. | Home Depot pays suppliers using prenumbered checks. |  |
| 5. Independently verify. | Check others' work. | Home Depot compares the cash balances in its records to the cash balances reported by its bank and accounts for any differences. | |

for which they are accounting. A single employee should not initiate, approve, record, and access the items involved in the same transaction.

3. **Restrict access.**   Some controls involve rather obvious steps such as physically locking up valuable assets and electronically securing access to other assets and information. The Home Depot restricts access to check-signing equipment, requires a password to open cash registers, and protects computer systems with firewalls. The company provides access to important assets and valuable information on an as-needed basis. If employees do not need assets or information to fulfill their assigned responsibilities, they are denied access.

4. **Document procedures.**   Digital and paper documents are such common features of business that you may not realize they represent an internal control. By documenting each business activity, a company creates a record of whether goods were shipped, customers were billed, cash was received, and so on. Without these documents, a company would not know what transactions have been or need to be entered into the accounting system. To enhance this control, most companies assign sequential numbers to their documents and then check at the end of every accounting period to make sure that each document number corresponds to one and only one accounting entry. The Home Depot's computer system automatically assigns sequential numbers to cash sales so that the accounting staff can ensure that every sale has been recorded.

5. **Independently verify.**   A business can perform independent verification in various ways. The most obvious is to hire someone (an internal auditor) to check that the work done by others within the company is appropriate and is supported by documentation. Independent verification can also be made part of a person's job. For example, before The Home Depot issues a check to pay for a truckload of lumber, a clerk first verifies that the bill relates to goods that were actually received and that it has been calculated correctly. A third form of independent verification involves comparing the company's accounting information to

# Spotlight On CONTROLS

## Is That a Control, Too?

The five principles covered in this section do not represent all possible forms of internal control. Many other policies and procedures exist, some of which you might not recognize as contributing to internal control. For example, most businesses establish a mandatory vacation policy for employees who handle cash because it is difficult for them to cover prior thefts while they are away from the business. Another simple control is an anonymous hotline that allows anyone to tip off independent auditors about suspected fraud. The Association of Certified Fraud Examiners claims that more than 45 percent of workplace fraud cases are identified in this way. A final example of a control that can limit losses from theft is **bonding** employees, which involves obtaining an insurance policy that partially reimburses the organization for losses caused by employee fraud.

information kept by an independent third party, such as a bank. For example, the company may compare internal cash records to a statement of account issued by the bank. The next section of this chapter demonstrates this procedure, called a bank reconciliation.

## Control Limitations

Internal controls can never completely prevent and detect errors and fraud for two reasons. First, an organization will implement internal controls only to the extent that their benefits exceed their costs. The Home Depot could nearly eliminate shoplifting by body searching every customer who leaves the store, but such an irritating policy would soon drive customers away. The cost of the lost sales would far exceed the benefits of reduced shoplifting. Second, internal controls can fail as a result of human error or fraud. People do make simple mistakes in performing control procedures, especially if they are tired, careless, or confused. Finally, criminally minded employees have been known to override (disarm) internal controls or collude (work together) to get around them.

**SELF-STUDY PRACTICE**

Identify the internal control principles suggested in the following diagram. Some principles may appear more than once.

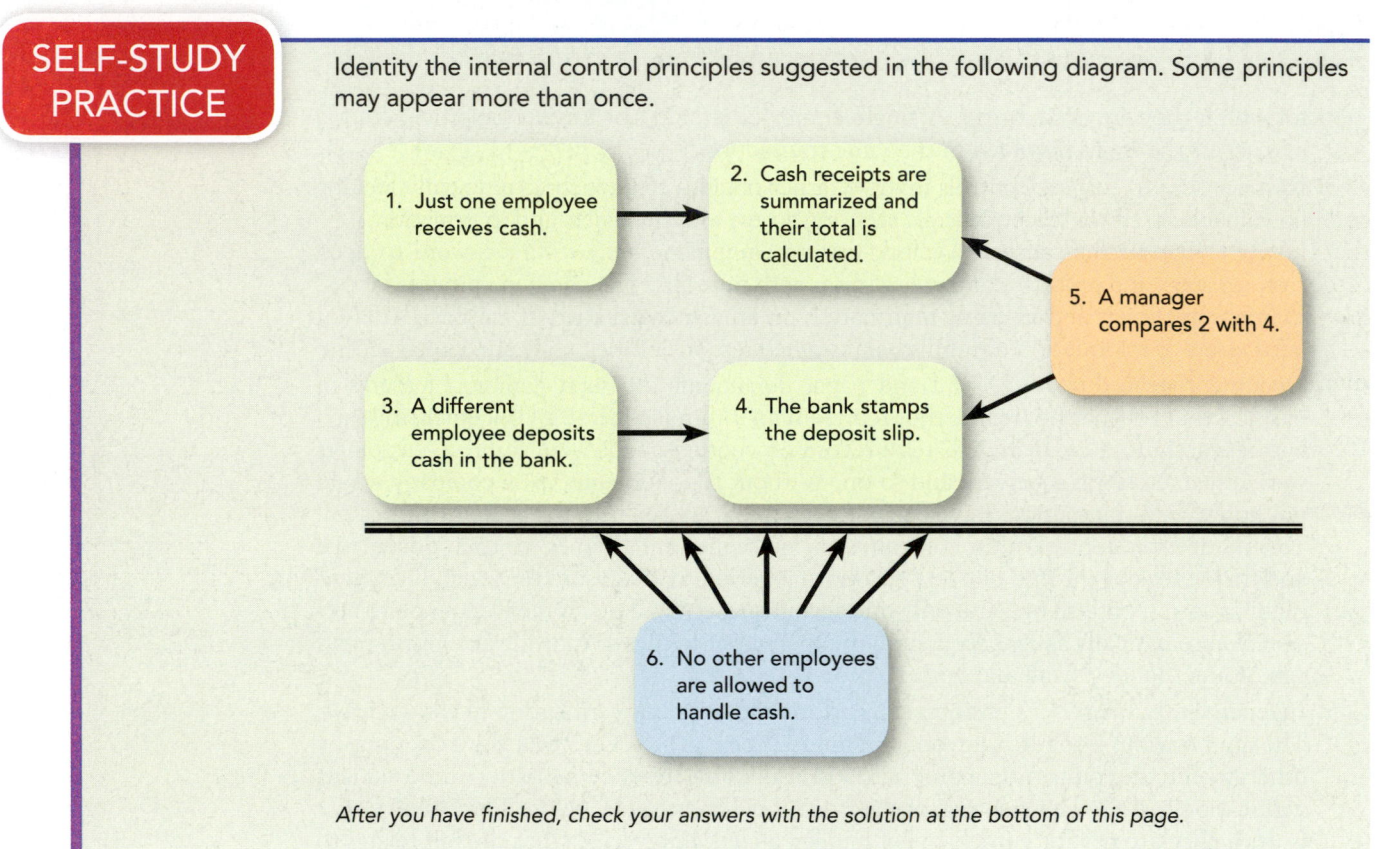

*After you have finished, check your answers with the solution at the bottom of this page.*

## INTERNAL CONTROL OF CASH

**Learning Objective 3**

Apply internal control principles to cash receipts and payments.

Internal control of cash is important to any organization for two main reasons. First, because the volume of transactions affecting cash is enormous, any errors that are made in handling cash can quickly add up. By our estimates, The Home Depot received about $78 billion from customers in 2007 and paid $72 billion for inventory, wages, and other operating expenses. Second, because cash is valuable, portable, and difficult to specifically identify, thieves often target it. The Association of Certified Fraud Examiners reports that 93 percent of all known

**Solution to Self-Study Practice**

1. Establish responsibility.
2. Document procedures.
3. Segregate duties.
4. Document procedures.
5. Independently verify.
6. Restrict access.

asset thefts involve cash. The following discussion describes common applications of internal control principles to cash receipts and cash payments.

# Cash Receipts

Businesses can receive cash in two different ways. They can receive it **in person** at the time of a sale, or they can receive it **from a remote source** as payment on an account. Most businesses, including The Home Depot, receive cash either physically, in the form of dollars, coins, and checks payable to the business, or through electronic transactions involving credit cards, debit cards, and electronic funds transfers. Generally speaking, The Home Depot applies similar controls to cash received in both these forms, so in the following discussion, we do not distinguish between them. Regardless of the way or form in which a business receives cash, **the primary internal control goal for cash receipts is to ensure that the business receives the appropriate amount of cash and safely deposits it in the bank.**

## Cash Received in Person

To properly segregate duties involving cash receipts, specific responsibilities are usually assigned to three different employees. First, a cashier is responsible for collecting cash and issuing a receipt at the point of sale. Second, a supervisor is responsible for taking custody of the cash at the end of each cashier's shift and depositing it in the bank. Third, members of the accounting staff are responsible for ensuring that the receipts from cash sales are properly recorded in the accounting system. If this segregation of duties did not exist, employees could steal the cash and cover up the theft by changing the accounting records. Segregating the duties ensures that those who handle the cash (the cashiers and supervisor) do not have access to those who record it (the accounting staff). Exhibit 8.3 illustrates the steps involved in carrying out these duties, which we explain in the context of The Home Depot's internal control procedures.

As Exhibit 8.3 shows, the control process begins at the cash register. The register performs three important functions: (1) it restricts access to cash, (2) it documents the amount charged for each item sold, and (3) it summarizes the total cash sales. By restricting access, the cash register

## Exhibit 8.3    Processing Cash Received in Person

## Exhibit 8.4    Sample Cash Count Sheet and Daily Cash Receipts Summary

**Count Sheet – Cashier 101**

Accounting for Cash

| | |
|---|---:|
| Beginning cash in drawer | $  50.00 |
| + Cash Sales (per register) | 3,515.70 |
| = Cash to account for | 3,565.70 |
| −/+ Cash (short) over | (5.00) |
| = Actual cash on hand (per count) | $3,560.70 |

Distribution of Cash

| | |
|---|---:|
| Cash for deposit | $3,510.70 |
| Ending cash in drawer | 50.00 |
| Actual cash on hand | $3,560.70 |

Ben Stiller
Supervisor

Jessica Simpson
Cashier

**Daily Cash Receipts Summary**                    4/27/09

| Cashier | 101 | 102 | Total |
|---|---:|---:|---:|
| Register sales | $3,515.70 | $2,585.30 | $6,101.00 |
| (Short) over | (5.00) | 1.00 | (4.00) |
| Cash deposit | $3,510.70 | $2,586.30 | $6,097.00 |

Prepared by:

Ben Stiller
Supervisor

reduces the risk of cash being lost or stolen. In documenting each item sold (both on screen and on a paper receipt), the cash register reduces errors by allowing customers to dispute overcharges should they occur. By summarizing the total cash sales, the cash register provides an independent record of the amount of cash the cashier should have collected and passed on for deposit at the bank. This record is securely forwarded to the accounting department (see the **black arrow** in Exhibit 8.3). The cashier also uses it to complete a cash count sheet (see the red arrow in Exhibit 8.3).

Each cashier prepares a cash count sheet, shown in detail in Exhibit 8.4, at the end of each shift to determine the amount of cash available for deposit at the bank. The cash count sheet documents the amount of cash the cashier received and determines any cash short or over that occurred during the shift. The supervisor independently verifies and signs each cashier's count sheet (as in Exhibit 8.3). The supervisor then uses each cashier's cash count sheet to prepare a daily cash receipts summary and sends one copy to the accounting department (see the blue arrow in Exhibit 8.3). The supervisor is also responsible for placing the cash in a locked safe until the end of the day at which time it is taken to the bank for deposit. At that time, a deposit slip listing the amounts included in the deposit is prepared and presented to the bank for a teller to verify. After verifying and receiving the funds, the bank teller stamps the deposit slip, which is then forwarded to the company's accounting department. The green arrows in Exhibit 8.3 indicate this process.

The accounting department compares the record of cash sales maintained by the cash register with the count sheet prepared by the cashier, the daily cash receipts summary prepared by the supervisor and the stamped bank deposit slip returned by the bank (see Exhibit 8.3). This comparison provides independent verification that the amount of cash rung up at the time of sale was deposited into the bank account. Based on this information, a journal entry is prepared to record Sales Revenue at the amount rung up by the cash register and Cash at the amount deposited in the bank. Any difference between the two amounts is recorded in a Cash Shortage (or Overage) account, which is reported on the income statement as a miscellaneous expense (or revenue). In our example, the daily cash receipts summary in Exhibit 8.4 shows that Cashier 101 had a $5 shortage and Cashier 102 was over by $1, for a net cash shortage of $4. This shortage would be recorded using the following journal entry.

| Account Titles | Debit | Credit |
|---|---:|---:|
| Cash (+A) | 6,097 | |
| Cash Shortage (+E,−OE) | 4 | |
| Sales Revenue (+R, +OE) | | 6,101 |

| Assets | = | Liabilities | + | Owners' Equity | |
|---|---|---|---|---|---|
| Cash          +6,097 | | | | Sales Revenue (+R) | +6,101 |
| | | | | Cash Shortage (+E) | −4 |

## Cash Received from a Remote Source

**Cash Received by Mail.** Businesses receive checks in the mail when customers pay on account. The Home Depot, for example, allows approved businesses to buy on account and pay their account balances using checks or money orders mailed to The Home Depot's credit division in Nevada. Because this cash is not received in the form of currency and coins, the Nevada office does not have a cashier enter these amounts into a cash register. Instead, the clerk who opens the mail performs this function. In fact, to visualize the following description, you need only glance back at Exhibit 8.3 and replace the cash register with a mail clerk.

Like a cash register, the mail clerk lists all amounts received on the cash receipt list, which also includes the customers' names and the purpose of each payment. The customer typically explains the purpose of the payment using a remittance advice, which is a tear-off portion of the monthly bill that the customer includes with the payment. Ideally, someone supervises the clerk who opens the mail to ensure that he or she takes no cash receipts for personal use. As evidence of this supervision, both the mail clerk and the supervisor sign the completed cash receipts list. To ensure that no one diverts the checks for personal use, the clerk stamps each check "For Deposit Only," which instructs the bank to deposit the check in the company's account rather than exchange it for cash.

After these steps have been completed, the cash received is separated from the record of cash received, and each follows a separate route similar to the routes shown in Exhibit 8.3 (page 349). Checks and money orders are given to the person who prepares the bank deposit whereas the cash receipts list and remittance advices are sent to the accounting department. The accounting department then independently verifies that all cash received by mail was deposited in the bank by ensuring that the total on the cash receipts list equals the stamped deposit slip received from the bank. The accounting department then uses the cash receipts list to record the journal entries that debit Cash and credit Accounts Receivable from each customer.

**Cash Received Electronically.** Businesses also receive payments from customers via electronic funds transfer (EFT). An EFT occurs when a customer electronically transfers funds from its bank account to the company's bank account. The Home Depot encourages customers to use EFTs because they speed The Home Depot's collections. The company may not receive mailed payments for five to seven days, but it receives EFTs immediately. And because these payments are deposited directly into the company's bank account without ever passing through the hands of a Home Depot employee, EFTs eliminate the need for some internal controls. To process an EFT, The Home Depot's accounting department merely records journal entries to debit Cash and credit each customer's account receivable. The Home Depot receives EFT notices from its bank every afternoon and records them in customers' accounts the same day.

# Cash Payments

For a business, cash payments usually occur in three situations: (1) writing a check to a supplier for goods or services purchased on account, (2) paying employees via EFT, and (3) reimbursing cash paid by employees for minor business expenses. Regardless of the situation, **the primary goal of internal controls for cash payments is to ensure that the business pays only for properly authorized transactions.** These payments should be made efficiently to minimize the cost to the organization and take advantage of discounts when possible. Internal control is generally more effective and efficient when payments are made using prenumbered checks or EFTs rather than cash.

## Cash Paid by Check for Purchases on Account

Most businesses purchase goods and services on account and pay for them later by check. Purchases and payments cause increases and decreases in Accounts Payable, so they are closely controlled for financial reporting reasons. Control over purchases and payments is also important to avoid inefficiency and fraud. Because companies incur substantial internal costs to process each transaction with a supplier, controls that promote efficiency can significantly improve a company's profits. Companies can also avoid or reduce losses due to fraud by having strong internal controls. A 2006 report by the Association of Certified Fraud Examiners estimated that fraudulent purchases and payments cost small businesses—defined as those with fewer than 100 employees—an average of $150,000 per year.

> **Coach's Tip**
> Because payments must be credited to each customer's account, it is important that the cash receipt list include the customer's name and payment purpose.

> **Learning Objective 4**
> Describe the operation of voucher and petty cash systems.

Most companies rely on a voucher system to control these transactions. A **voucher system** is a process for approving and documenting all purchases and payments made on account. The **voucher** includes the documents prepared at each step in the system. See Exhibit 8.5 for the typical steps involved in obtaining goods or services from a supplier and the documentation prepared at each step. Exhibit 8.5 also gives some examples of the related cash controls. **Study this exhibit in detail,** noticing how at each step employee responsibilities are limited to specific tasks that occur only after obtaining and documenting proper authorization in the prior step. The purchasing, receiving, and bill payment duties are segregated to ensure that the company obtains and pays only for the goods or services that have been properly authorized.

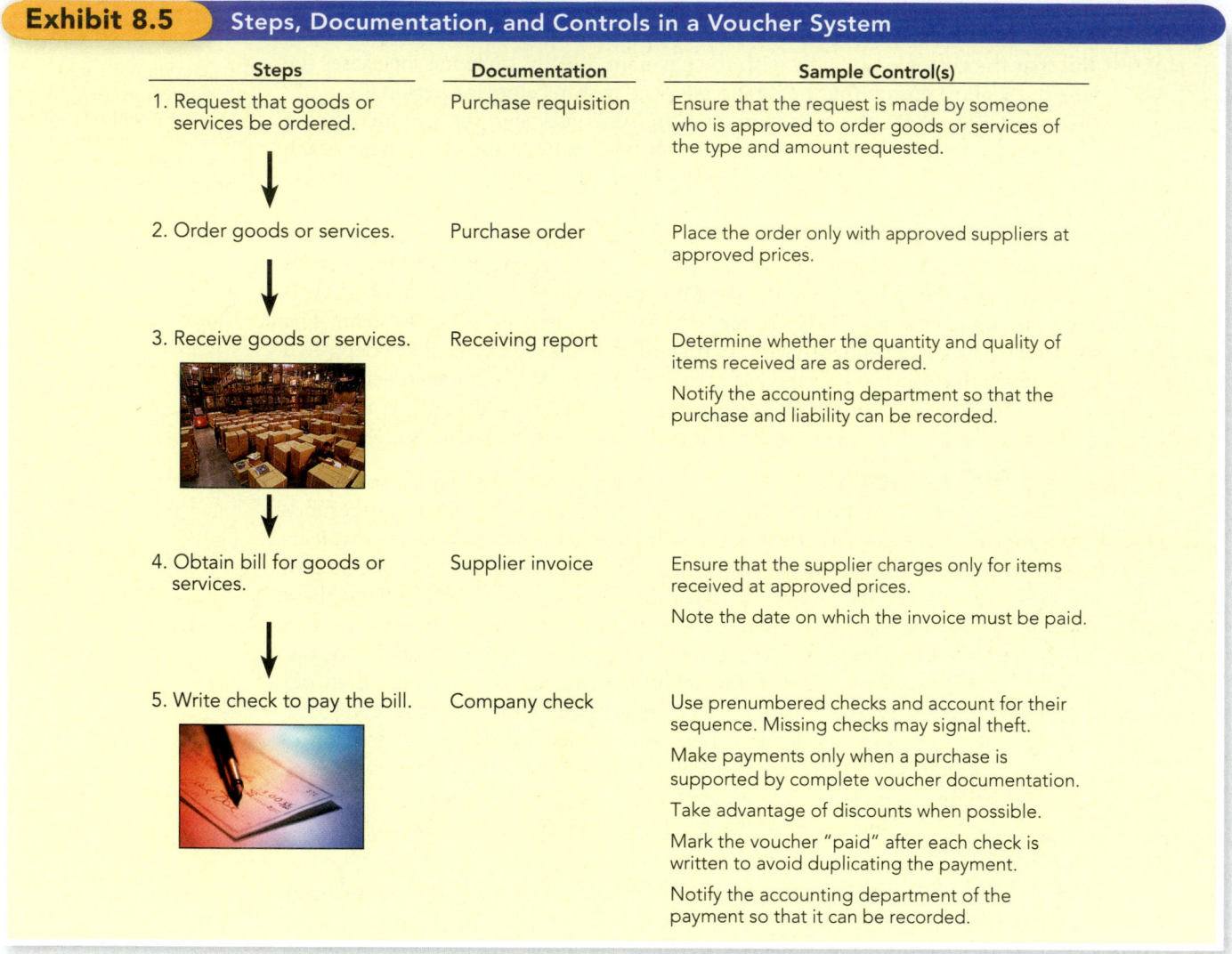

**Exhibit 8.5**    **Steps, Documentation, and Controls in a Voucher System**

| Steps | Documentation | Sample Control(s) |
|---|---|---|
| 1. Request that goods or services be ordered. | Purchase requisition | Ensure that the request is made by someone who is approved to order goods or services of the type and amount requested. |
| 2. Order goods or services. | Purchase order | Place the order only with approved suppliers at approved prices. |
| 3. Receive goods or services. | Receiving report | Determine whether the quantity and quality of items received are as ordered. Notify the accounting department so that the purchase and liability can be recorded. |
| 4. Obtain bill for goods or services. | Supplier invoice | Ensure that the supplier charges only for items received at approved prices. Note the date on which the invoice must be paid. |
| 5. Write check to pay the bill. | Company check | Use prenumbered checks and account for their sequence. Missing checks may signal theft. Make payments only when a purchase is supported by complete voucher documentation. Take advantage of discounts when possible. Mark the voucher "paid" after each check is written to avoid duplicating the payment. Notify the accounting department of the payment so that it can be recorded. |

## Cash Paid to Employees via Electronic Funds Transfer

Most companies pay cash to their employees through EFTs, which are known by employees as **direct deposits.** The company initiates the EFT when it instructs its bank to transfer the net pay due each employee directly from the company's bank account to each employee's checking account. This system is convenient and efficient for the employer because it eliminates the tasks of physically writing and distributing the checks and for the employee who has access to the funds without having to deposit a check. One risk, however, is that the bank might accidentally overpay or underpay an employee by transfering the wrong amount of money out of the company's bank account.

To avoid this risk, many companies use an imprest system for paying employees. An **imprest system** restricts the total amount paid to others by limiting the amount of money available to be transferred. Using an imprest payroll system, the company instructs the bank to transfer the total net pay of all employees for the pay period out of the company's general bank account and into a special payroll account established for that purpose. Then the bank transfers the individual amounts from the payroll account to the employees' checking accounts. If the transfers occur without error, the special payroll account equals zero after all employees have been paid. If the account is overdrawn or a balance remains, the company knows that an error has occurred.

## Cash Paid to Reimburse Employees (Petty Cash)

To avoid the time and cost of writing checks for business expenses that are small in amount, most organizations use a petty cash fund. A **petty cash fund** is a system used to reimburse employees for expenditures they have made on behalf of the organization. Like the imprest payroll account described in the last section, a petty cash fund acts as a control by establishing a limited amount of cash to use for specific types of expenses. The main difference between the two is that rather than transfer funds from a general bank account to another special account at the bank, the company removes cash from its general bank account to hold at its premises in a locked cash box. An employee with the title petty cash custodian is responsible for operating the petty cash fund as follows.

1. **Put money into the fund.**   The company establishes the fund by writing a check to the petty cash custodian. The amount of the check equals the total estimated payments to be made from the fund over a fairly short period, such as a month or quarter. The custodian cashes the check and places the funds in the locked cash box. At this time, the petty cash still belongs to the company, so it represents an asset that must be recorded in the accounting system. The following journal entry is recorded to establish a $100 petty cash fund.

| Account Titles | Debit | Credit |
|---|---|---|
| Petty Cash (+A) | 100 | |
|     Cash (−A) | | 100 |

| Assets | = | Liabilities | + | Owners' Equity |
|---|---|---|---|---|
| Petty Cash   +100 | | | | |
| Cash   −100 | | | | |

**Coach's Tip**

Journal entries affect the Petty Cash account only when a petty cash fund is established or when its approved total increases or decreases.

2. **Pay money out of the fund.**   The custodian determines when to make payments out of the cash box following policies established by the company's managers. Usually, these policies limit the size and nature of payments to items such as postage, taxi fares, and low-cost supplies. Petty cash policies require that payments be documented using a petty cash receipt signed by both the custodian and the payee as in the following example. The custodian attaches any related documents, such as a bill of sale or an invoice, to the petty cash receipt and places it in the cash box. Documents such as these act as controls to ensure that petty cash payments are made only for approved purchases.

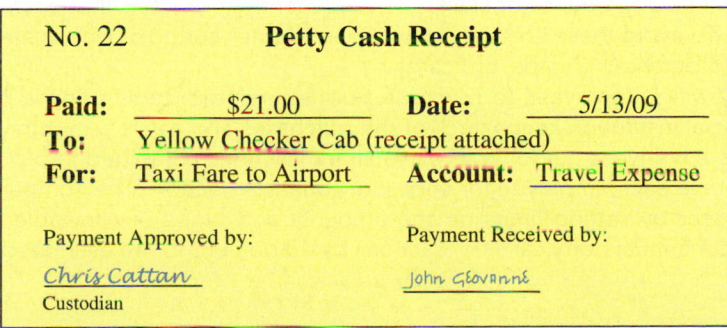

No. 22              **Petty Cash Receipt**

**Paid:**        $21.00        **Date:**        5/13/09

**To:**    Yellow Checker Cab (receipt attached)

**For:**    Taxi Fare to Airport     **Account:**  Travel Expense

Payment Approved by:              Payment Received by:

Chris Cattan                      John Giovanni

Custodian

Because these receipts involve such small amounts, **payments out of petty cash are not recorded in the accounting system until the fund is replenished.** To ensure that the fund is operating appropriately, however, most companies require that an internal auditor or manager conduct surprise audits of the fund. At any point, the sum of the petty cash receipts and the funds in the cash box should equal the fund's total when it was established.

3. **Replenish the fund.** When the amount of cash in the cash box runs low, the petty cash custodian asks that the fund be replenished. To support this request, the petty cash custodian presents a summary of payments and all supporting petty cash receipts to the accounting department. After reviewing these items, the accounting department marks the receipts "paid" and issues a check to the custodian for the total amount spent. The amount of the check is recorded as a reduction in Cash (with a credit), and the various items that were paid are recorded in their corresponding accounts (with debits). For example, if the custodian requested a check for $67 to replenish the fund after payments were made for supplies ($40), travel ($21), and a dozen Krispy Kreme donuts awarded to the employee of the month ($6), the following journal entry would be recorded.

| Account Titles | Debit | Credit |
|---|---|---|
| Supplies (+A) | 40 | |
| Travel Expense (+E, −OE) | 21 | |
| Office Expense (+E, −OE) | 6 | |
| Cash (−A) | | 67 |

| Assets | | = | Liabilities | + | Owners' Equity | |
|---|---|---|---|---|---|---|
| Cash | −67 | | | | Travel Expense (+E) | −21 |
| Supplies | +40 | | | | Office Expense (+E) | −6 |

Because petty cash transactions are recorded only when the fund is replenished, some companies have a policy of replenishing all petty cash funds at the end of each accounting period so that the expenses are recorded in the appropriate period. Other companies do not observe this policy on the grounds that unrecorded petty cash transactions are "immaterial" (too small to affect the decisions of financial statement users).

# Spotlight On CONTROLS

## Pcards: Efficient Control of Small-Dollar Transactions

Until recently, the administrative costs of processing small-dollar purchases often exceeded the cost of the items themselves. For example, a consultant to the City Council of Dallas, Texas, recently estimated that each petty cash transaction costs the city $60 to process. To avoid these costs and implement tighter controls over small-dollar purchases, many organizations have turned to purchasing cards, or Pcards.

Pcards work like a credit card by allowing employees to purchase business-related items using a plastic card issued by a financial institution. The financial institution keeps track of the purchases and sends a monthly bill to the company for all purchases the company's employees made. With all small transactions combined into one monthly bill, the company avoids having to reimburse each employee for each individual transaction. The company can also tighten controls before the purchases occur by setting limits on the amounts and types of allowable purchases. Pcards have helped the City of Dallas to cut annual petty cash transactions by 40 percent for an estimated savings of $1.1 million.*

* www.dallascityhall.com/council_briefings/briefings0806/20060802_P-Card.pdf, n.d., June 20, 2007.

The following transactions occurred during the month. Indicate whether a voucher system (V) or a petty cash system (PC) would be used for each transaction. Then show the journal entry and accounting equation effects when the petty cash fund is replenished after only these transactions.

_____ 1. A $3,000 check is written for inventory purchased from a manufacturer.
_____ 2. A $30 cash payment is made to FedEx for delivery of goods to a customer.
_____ 3. A $300 check is written for supplies purchased from Office Depot.
_____ 4. A $60 cash payment is made to Pizza Hut for an employee luncheon.

*After you have finished, check your answers with the solution at the bottom of this page.*

# Bank Procedures and Reconciliation

Banks provide important services to individuals and businesses. They accept deposits, process payments to others, and provide statements that account for these and other transactions. Their services help businesses to control cash in several ways:

**Learning Objective 5**

Prepare a bank reconciliation.

1. **Safeguarding.**   Because banks provide a secure place to deposit cash, businesses need to keep only a limited amount of cash on hand, which reduces the risk that it will be stolen or misplaced.
2. **Improving efficiency and effectiveness.**   By processing payments made by check or EFT, banks facilitate business transactions.
3. **Independently verifying.**   Company accountants can use the statement of account prepared by the bank to double-check the accuracy of the cash records. By comparing these two sets of records and investigating any differences, they can verify that the company's records are accurate or identify necessary adjustments.

The process of comparing two sets of records is **reconciling.** Thus, the internal accounting report that compares the company's cash records with the bank's is a **bank reconciliation**. A bank reconciliation is a key internal control because it provides independent verification of all cash transactions that the bank has processed for the company. This document is prepared monthly, ideally by a company employee whose duties are segregated from recording and handling cash. To prepare a bank reconciliation, you must first understand the items on the bank's statement of account.

## Bank Statement

Large businesses such as The Home Depot can have many bank accounts. For each account a business opens, the bank generates a monthly statement of account that it either mails to the business or makes available online. The format varies from bank to bank, but the statement in Exhibit 8.6 is typical. This statement, prepared by Texas Commerce Bank for one of the accounts opened by Habitat Design (HD), provides an overall summary of the activity in the account (labeled ① in Exhibit 8.6). The summary is followed by a list of specific transactions posted to the account (labeled ② through ④) and a running balance in the account (labeled ⑤). In the following section, we explain the transactions that caused changes in the account's balance.

Solution to
Self-Study Practice

1. V    2. PC    3. V    4. PC

| Account Titles | Debit | Credit |
|---|---|---|
| Delivery Expense (+E, −OE) | 30 | |
| Office Expense (+E, −OE) | 60 | |
| Cash (−A) | | 90 |

| Assets | | = | Liabilities | + | Owners' Equity | |
|---|---|---|---|---|---|---|
| Cash | −90 | | | | Delivery Expense (+E) | −30 |
| | | | | | Office Expense (+E) | −60 |

**Exhibit 8.6**    Sample Bank Statement

**Checks Cleared.**  You may not have thought much about what happens after a check is written. The payee to whom the check is written usually presents the check to a financial institution for deposit or cash. That financial institution contacts the check writer's bank, which in turn withdraws the amount of the check from the check writer's account and reports it as a deduction on the bank statement. The check is then said to have **cleared the bank.**

Checks are listed on the bank statement in the order in which they clear the bank. Look closely at column ② in Exhibit 8.6 and you will see that four checks cleared the bank in June. Because HD's checks are used in their prenumbered order, the bank statement provides a hint that check 103 did not clear the bank this month. (This fact will be important later when we prepare the bank reconciliation.)

**Deposits Made.**  Deposits are listed on the bank statement in the order in which the bank processes them. If you make a deposit after the bank closes (using an ATM or a night deposit chute), it will not appear on the bank statement until the bank processes it the following business day. Knowing this detail will help you to prepare the bank reconciliation.

**Other Debits and Credits.**  The balance in a bank account can change for a variety of reasons other than checks and deposits. For example, the account balance increases when the account earns interest and when funds are transferred into the account electronically. The account balance decreases when the bank charges a service fee or transfers funds out of the account electronically.

To understand how these items are reported on a bank statement, it is important to realize that **the bank statement is presented from the bank's point of view.** The amounts in a

**Coach's Tip**

Bank statements often refer to checks as **debits** and deposits as **credits.** This apparent flipping of debit and credit rules occurs because the bank reports from its perspective, not yours. To the bank, your account is a liability that decreases when you take money out (debit the liability) and increases when you deposit money (credit the liability).

company's bank account are liabilities to the bank because they will eventually be used by or returned to the company. As with all liabilities, increases are reported as credits on the bank statement. Amounts that are removed from a bank account reduce the bank's liability, so they are reported as debits on the bank statement. Banks typically explain the reasons for these increases (credits) and decreases (debits) with symbols or in a short memo, appropriately called a credit or debit memo.

## Need for Reconciliation

A bank reconciliation involves comparing the company's records to the bank's statement of account to determine whether they agree. The company's records can differ from the bank's records for two basic reasons: (1) the company has recorded some items that the bank does not know about at the time it prepares the statement of account or (2) the bank has recorded some items that the company does not know about until the bank statement arrives. Exhibit 8.7 lists specific causes of these differences, which we discuss below.

1. **Bank errors.**   Bank errors happen in real life, just as they do in Monopoly. If you discover a bank error, you should ask the bank to correct its records, but you should not change yours.

2. **Time lags.** Time lags are common. A time lag occurs, for example, when you make a deposit after the bank's normal business hours. *You* know you made the deposit, but your bank does not know until it processes the deposit the next day. Time lags involving deposits are called **deposits in transit**. Another common time lag is an **outstanding check**. This lag occurs when you write and mail a check to a company, but your bank does not find out about it until that company deposits the check in its own bank, which then notifies your bank. As you will see later, although deposits in transit and outstanding checks may be a significant part of a bank reconciliation, they do not require any further action on your part.

3. **Interest deposited.**   You may know that your bank pays interest, but you probably do not know exactly how much interest you will receive because it varies depending on the average balance in your account. When you read your bank statement, you will see how much interest to add to your records.

4. **Electronic funds transfer (EFT).**   It does not happen every day, but occasionally funds may be transferred into or out of your account without your knowing about it. If you discover these electronic transfers on your bank statement, you will need to adjust your records.

5. **Service charges.**   These are the amounts the bank charges for processing your transactions. Rather than send you a bill and wait for you to pay it, the bank just takes the amount directly out of your account. You will need to reduce the Cash balance in your accounting records for these charges.

6. **NSF checks.**   Checks that were deposited in the bank but were later rejected ("bounced") because of insufficient funds in the check writer's account are referred to as **NSF (not sufficient funds) checks**. Because the bank increased the account when the check was deposited, it decreases the account when it discovers that the deposit was not valid. You will need to reduce your Cash balance by the amount of these bounced checks (and any additional bank charges), and you will have to try to collect these amounts from the check writer.

7. **Your errors.**   You may have made mistakes or forgotten to record some amounts in your checkbook. If so, you will need to adjust your records for these items.

**Exhibit 8.7**     **Reconciling Differences between the Bank Statement and Company Records**

| Your Bank May Not Know About | You May Not Know About |
|---|---|
| 1. Errors made by the bank | 3. Interest the bank has put into your account |
| 2. Time lags | 4. EFTs |
|    *a.* Deposits that you made recently | 5. Service charges taken out of your account |
|    *b.* Checks that you wrote recently | 6. Customer checks you deposited but that bounced |
| | 7. Errors you made |

## Bank Reconciliation

The ending cash balance shown on the bank statement does not usually agree with the ending cash balance in the company's Cash account. For example, HD's Cash account at the end of June might contain the information shown in this T-account.

| + | Cash (A) | | − |
|---|---|---|---|
| June 1 balance | 7,762.40 | | |
| June 6 deposit | 3,000.00 | 500.00 | Check 100 written June 4 |
| June 23 deposit | 500.00 | 55.00 | Check 101 written June 17 |
| June 30 deposit | 1,800.00 | 100.00 | Check 102 written June 20 |
| | | 145.00 | Check 103 written June 24 |
| | | 56.00 | Check 104 written June 30 |
| | | 815.00 | Check 105 written June 30 |
| Ending balance | 11,391.40 | | |

**Coach's Tip**

You will need to adjust your cash records for items that appear only on the right-hand side of Exhibit 8.8.

Notice that HD's ending cash balance of $11,391.40 differs from the $10,638.40 ending cash balance shown on the bank statement in Exhibit 8.6 (page 356). To determine the appropriate cash balance, these balances must be reconciled.

Exhibit 8.8 presents the bank reconciliation prepared by HD for the month of June. The completed reconciliation shows that the up-to-date cash balance is $11,478.40—an amount that differs from both the bank statement and HD's accounting records. This balance is the amount that HD will report as Cash on its balance sheet after adjusting its records (we discuss the adjusting entries later).

To prepare the bank reconciliation in Exhibit 8.8, HD compared the entries in the Cash account to the bank statement in Exhibit 8.6 with the following goals:

1. **Identify the deposits in transit.**   A comparison of HD's recorded deposits with those listed on the bank statement revealed that the bank statement did not list a deposit of $1,800 made on June 30. More than likely, the bank did not process this deposit until July 1. HD did not need to change its records for this item because it was already in HD's books on June 30. Instead, HD entered the amount on the bank reconciliation as an addition to update the bank's records.

2. **Identify the outstanding checks.**   A comparison of HD's record of written checks with the checks listed on the bank statement revealed that Checks 103 and 105 were still outstanding at the end of June (that is, they had not cleared the bank). They were entered on the reconciliation as a deduction from the bank account because the bank will reduce the account balance when the checks eventually clear the bank. (HD had already deducted Checks 103 and 105 from its cash records.)

3. **Record other transactions reported on the bank statement.**

   a. **Interest received** from the bank, $20—this amount was entered on the bank reconciliation as an addition to the company's balance because it was included in the bank balance but had not yet been recorded in the company's books.

---

**Exhibit 8.8**   **Sample Bank Reconciliation**

| Updates to Bank Statement | | | Updates to Company's Books | | |
|---|---|---|---|---|---|
| Ending cash balance per bank statement | | $10,638.40 | Ending cash balance per books | | $11,391.40 |
| Additions | | | Additions | | |
| (1) Deposit in transit | | 1,800.00 | (3a) Interest received from the bank | $ 20.00 | |
| | | 12,438.40 | (3b) EFT received from customer | 100.00 | 120.00 |
| | | | | | 11,511.40 |
| Deductions | | | Deductions | | |
| (2) Outstanding checks: | | | (3c) NSF check of R. Smith | 18.00 | |
| 103 | $145.00 | | (3d) Bank service charges | 6.00 | |
| 105 | 815.00 | 960.00 | (4) Error in recording check no. 104 | 9.00 | 33.00 |
| Up-to-date ending cash balance | | $11,478.40 | Up-to-date ending cash balance | | $11,478.40 |

b. **Electronic funds transfer** received from customer, $100—this amount was entered on the bank reconciliation as an addition to the company's balance because it was included in the bank balance but had not yet been recorded in the company's books.

c. **NSF check** rejected, $18—this amount was entered on the bank reconciliation as a deduction from the company's balance because it was deducted from the bank balance but had not yet been deducted from the company's records.

d. **Service charges,** $6—this amount was entered on the bank reconciliation as a deduction from the company's balance because it had been deducted from the bank balance but had not yet been removed from the company's Cash account.

4. **Determine the impact of errors.** After performing the three steps just listed, HD's accountant found that the reconciliation was still out of balance by $9. In checking the journal entries made during the month, the accountant found that Check 104 had been recorded as $56 when in fact it had been written for $65 (in payment of an account payable). As Exhibit 8.6 (page 356) shows, the bank correctly processed this check on June 30 for $65. To correct the company's error, HD's accountant deducted $9 (= $65 − $56) from the company's side of the bank reconciliation.

> **Coach's Tip**
>
> This example involves the company's error in recording the amount of the check. In other cases, the bank errs if it processes the check at the wrong amount. In all instances, the amount written on the check is the correct amount at which the transaction should be recorded.

Now that we know that the up-to-date ending balance in the Cash account should be $11,478.40, we need to prepare journal entries that will bring the Cash account to that balance. The entries on the Bank Statement side of the bank reconciliation (the deposit in transit and the two outstanding checks) do not require entries because they will work out automatically when the bank processes them next month. **Only the items on the Company's Books side of the bank reconciliation need to be recorded in the company's records** using the following journal entries:

| | Account Titles and Explanations | Debit | Credit |
|---|---|---|---|
| (3a) | Cash (+A) | 20 | |
| | Interest Revenue (+R, +OE) | | 20 |
| | (To record interest received from the bank.) | | |
| | | | |
| (3b) | Cash (+A) | 100 | |
| | Accounts Receivable (−A) | | 100 |
| | (To record EFT received from customer.) | | |
| | | | |
| (3c) | Accounts Receivable (+A) | 18 | |
| | Cash (−A) | | 18 |
| | (To record NSF check rejected by bank and still owed by customer.) | | |
| | | | |
| (3d) | Office Expense (+E, −OE) | 6 | |
| | Cash (−A) | | 6 |
| | (To record service charges deducted by bank.) | | |
| | | | |
| (3e) | Accounts Payable (−L) | 9 | |
| | Cash (−A) | | 9 |
| | (To correct company error on a check paid to a creditor.) | | |

> **Coach's Tip**
>
> Notice that the changes in Cash correspond to amounts on the right-hand side of the bank reconciliation in Exhibit 8.8.

| Assets | = | Liabilities | + | Owners' Equity | |
|---|---|---|---|---|---|
| Cash                          +87* | | Accounts Payable  −9 | | Interest Revenue (+R) | +20 |
| Accounts Receivable −82⁺ | | | | Office Expense (+E)    | − 6 |

*20 + 100 − 18 − 6 − 9 = 87
⁺− 100 + 18 = −82

**SELF-STUDY PRACTICE**

Indicate which of the following items discovered during preparation of a bank reconciliation for Nordstrom will need to be recorded in the Cash account on the company's books.

1. Outstanding checks.
2. Deposits in transit.
3. Bank service charges.
4. NSF checks that were deposited.

*After you have finished, check your answers with the solution at the bottom of this page.*

## Spotlight On CONTROLS

### Granny Does Time

Grandmothers seem so trustworthy. In one well-known case, however, a granny stole nearly half a million dollars from the small company where she worked as a bookkeeper. It was easy to do. Because the owner knew very little about accounting, he gave her responsibility for all of the company's accounting and never independently verified her work. Granny realized that this lack of internal control gave her unlimited opportunity, so she wrote checks to herself and recorded them as inventory purchases. Then, when she did the bank reconciliation, she destroyed the checks to cover her tracks. Granny kept this fraud going for eight years until she confessed after becoming overwhelmed by guilt.

## FINANCIAL REPORTING OF CASH
### Cash and Cash Equivalents

**Learning Objective 6**

Describe the reporting of cash and cash equivalents.

For the purposes of external financial statement reporting, cash includes **cash** deposited with banks, petty cash, and cash equivalents. **Cash equivalents** are short-term, highly liquid investments obtained within three months of maturity. They are combined with cash and reported as current assets because they are readily convertible to known amounts of cash and are so near to maturity that there is little risk that their value will change. In your personal life, cash equivalents could include checks you have received but not yet deposited into your bank account as well as certificates of deposit (CDs) you purchased within three months of maturity.

The Home Depot held $445 million of Cash and Cash Equivalents at the end of January 2008, only a portion of which was held as cash. In fact, the first note to the financial statements explained that the company held various cash equivalents including money market funds and financial instruments issued by investment-grade companies and the U.S. government.

**Solution to Self-Study Practice**

1 and 2 represent time lags between the bank's and company's records. Nordstrom does not need to record them because the company recorded them when it wrote the checks and made the deposits.

3. Bank service charges are deducted from the company's bank account, so Nordstrom must reduce Cash and record an expense.

4. When checks are deposited, Nordstrom records them on the books as increases in the Cash account. When the bank later rejects a check as NSF, Nordstrom must decrease Cash and increase the related account receivable.

# Demonstration Case A

In June, a local Amtrak office established a petty cash fund with Terrell Noman as its custodian. Terrell received and cashed a company check of $175 to establish the fund. During that month, Terrell paid cash from the fund for supplies ($30), delivery charges ($80), and other minor office expenses ($40). On July 10, he received a company check for $150 to replenish the fund.

*Required:*

1. Prepare the journal entry required in June.
2. Prepare the journal entry required in July.
3. Explain why it may be appropriate or inappropriate to wait until July to record the payments from the petty cash fund.

## Suggested Solution

1.

| | Debit | Credit |
|---|---|---|
| Petty Cash (+A) | 175 | |
| Cash (−A) | | 175 |

| Assets | = | Liabilities | + | Owners' Equity |
|---|---|---|---|---|
| Petty Cash +175 | | | | |
| Cash −175 | | | | |

2.

| | Debit | Credit |
|---|---|---|
| Supplies (+A) | 30 | |
| Delivery Expense (+E, −OE) | 80 | |
| Office Expense (+E, −OE) | 40 | |
| Cash (−A) | | 150 |

| Assets | = | Liabilities | + | Owners' Equity | |
|---|---|---|---|---|---|
| Cash −150 | | | | Delivery Expense (+E) | −80 |
| Supplies + 30 | | | | Office Expense (+E) | −40 |

3. Waiting until July to record payments from the fund may be inappropriate because the expenses occurred in June, and the matching principle suggests that they should therefore be recorded in June—not in July, when the fund is replenished. However, waiting until July may be appropriate because the unrecorded amounts are immaterial—that is, too small to influence the decisions of those who use Amtrak's records.

# Demonstration Case B

Kat Bardash, a student at a small state college, has just received her first checking account statement for the month ended September 30. This is her first chance to attempt a bank reconciliation. The bank's statement of account shows the following information:

| | |
|---|---|
| Bank balance, September 1 | $1,150 |
| Deposits during September | 650 |
| Checks cleared during September | 900 |
| Bank service charge | 25 |
| Interest earned | 5 |
| Bank balance, September 30 | 880 |

Kat is surprised that her bank has not yet reported the $50 deposit that she made on September 29 and pleased that her $200 rent check has not yet cleared her account. Her September 30 checkbook balance is $750.

*Required:*

1. Complete Kat's bank reconciliation. What adjustments, if any, does she need to make in her checkbook?
2. Why is it important for individuals and businesses to prepare a bank reconciliation each month?

## Suggested Solution

1. **Kat's bank reconciliation:**

| Updates to Bank Statement | | Updates to Kat's Books | |
|---|---|---|---|
| September 30 cash balance | $880 | September 30 cash balance | $750 |
| Additions | | Additions | |
| Deposit in transit | 50 | Interest earned | 5 |
| Deductions | | Deductions | |
| Outstanding check | (200) | Bank service charge | (25) |
| Up-to-date cash balance | $730 | Up-to-date cash balance | $730 |

Kat should increase her checkbook balance by $5 for the interest earned and reduce her checkbook balance by $25 for the service charges.

2. Bank statements, whether personal or business, should be reconciled each month to ensure that the depositor's books reflect a correct balance. Failure to reconcile a bank statement increases the chance that an error will not be discovered and may result in writing NSF checks. Businesses reconcile their bank statements for an additional reason: They report the up-to-date balance calculated during reconciliation on the balance sheet.

## Chapter Summary

**LO1 Define internal control and explain why it is needed. p. 344**

- Internal control encompasses the methods an organization uses to protect against the theft of assets, to enhance the reliability of accounting information, to promote efficient and effective operations, and to ensure compliance with applicable laws and regulations.
- Internal controls are needed to ensure that people will behave in ways that benefit the organization. When internal controls operate effectively, they can improve an organization's efficiency and minimize waste, unintentional errors, and fraud.

**LO2 Explain the common principles and limitations of internal control. p. 346**

- The concept of internal control is broad. Most employees of a company will encounter five basic internal control principles: (1) establish responsibility for each task, (2) segregate duties so that one employee cannot initiate, approve, record, and handle a single transaction, (3) restrict access to assets and information to those employees who have been assigned responsibility for them, (4) document all procedures, and (5) independently verify work that has been done using information from others inside and outside the business.
- Internal controls are limited because they (1) are implemented only to the extent that their benefits exceed their costs and (2) may fail to operate effectively as a result of error and fraud.

**LO3 Apply internal control principles to cash receipts and payments. p. 348**

- When applied to cash receipts, internal control principles require that (1) cashiers be held individually responsible for the cash they receive, (2) different individuals be assigned to receive, maintain custody of, and record cash, (3) cash be stored in a locked safe until it has been securely deposited in a bank, (4) cash register receipts, cash count sheets, daily cash summary reports, and bank deposit slips be prepared to document the cash received and deposited, and (5) cash register receipts be matched to cash counts and deposits to independently verify that all cash was received and deposited.
- When applied to cash payments, internal control principles require that (1) only certain individuals or departments initiate purchase requests, (2) different individuals be assigned to order, receive, and pay for purchases, (3) access to checks and

valuable property be restricted, (4) purchase requisitions, purchase orders, receiving reports, and prenumbered checks be used to document the work done, and (5) each step in the payment process occur only after the preceding step has been independently verified using the documents listed in (4).

### LO4  Describe the operation of voucher and petty cash systems. p. 351

- A voucher system is used to record most purchases of goods and services. The voucher includes documentation for each step in requesting, ordering, receiving, and paying for goods or services from a supplier. These documents are used for independent verification, which helps to ensure that each step proceeds only after an authorized individual or department has completed the previous steps.
- A petty cash system is used to reimburse employees for relatively small business-related expenditures. The petty cash custodian is involved in establishing, making payments from, and replenishing the fund.

### LO5  Prepare a bank reconciliation. p. 355

- Preparing a bank reconciliation involves identifying items in two categories: (1) those that have been recorded in the company's books but not in the bank's statement of account and (2) those that have been reported in the bank's statement of account but not in the company's books. Items in the second category provide the data needed to adjust the cash account to the balance reported on the balance sheet.

### LO6  Describe the reporting of cash and cash equivalents. p. 360

- Cash (including petty cash and reconciled bank account balances) and cash equivalents are reported as a current asset on the balance sheet. Cash equivalents are short-term, highly liquid investments acquired within three months of maturity.

## Key Terms

Bank Reconciliation (p. 355)
Bonding (p. 347)
Cash (p. 360)
Cash Count Sheet (p. 350)
Cash Equivalents (p. 360)
Collude (p. 348)
Deposits in Transit (p. 357)

Electronic Funds Transfer (EFT) (p. 351)
Imprest System (p. 352)
Internal Control (p. 344)
NSF (Not Sufficient Funds) Checks (p. 357)
Outstanding Check (p. 357)
Override (p. 348)

Petty Cash Fund (p. 353)
Remittance Advice (p. 351)
Sarbanes-Oxley (SOX) Act of 2002 (p. 344)
Segregation of Duties (p. 346)
Voucher (p. 352)
Voucher System (p. 352)

**See complete glossary in back of text.**

## Questions

1. What are internal controls and why are they needed?
2. What aspect(s) of the Sarbanes-Oxley Act of 2002 might counteract the incentive to commit fraud?
3. What aspect(s) of the Sarbanes-Oxley Act of 2002 might reduce opportunities for fraud?
4. What aspect(s) of the Sarbanes-Oxley Act of 2002 might allow the good character of employees to prevail?
5. From the perspective of a CEO or CFO, what does internal control mean?
6. What are five common internal control principles?
7. Why is it a good idea to assign each task to only one employee?
8. Why should responsibilities for certain duties, like cash handling and cash recording, be separated? What specific responsibilities should be separated?
9. What are some of the methods for restricting access?
10. In what ways does documentation act as a control?
11. In what ways can independent verification occur?
12. In what way does a mandatory vacation policy act as a control?
13. What are the three limitations of internal control?
14. What is the primary internal control goal for cash receipts?
15. What internal control functions are performed by a cash register? How are these functions performed when cash is received by mail?
16. How is cash received in person independently verified?
17. What is the primary internal control goal for cash payments?
18. In what ways is a petty cash system similar to and different from an imprest payroll system?
19. Describe three ways in which banking services help businesses control cash.
20. What are the purposes of a bank reconciliation? What balances are reconciled?
21. Define *cash* and indicate the types of items that should be reported as cash. Define *cash equivalents* and give two examples of a cash equivalent.

# Multiple Choice

1. Which of the following was required of publicly traded companies prior to the laws arising from SOX?

   **Quiz 8-1**
   www.mhhe.com/LLPW1e

   a. Internal control report from management.
   b. Internal control audit by external auditors.
   c. Financial statement audit by external auditors.
   d. Tip lines for anonymously submitting concerns about accounting or auditing practices.

2. Which of the following does not enhance internal control?
   a. Assigning different duties to different employees.
   b. Ensuring adequate documentation is maintained.
   c. Allowing access only when required to complete assigned duties.
   d. None of the above—all enhance internal control.

3. Which of the following internal control principles is best exemplified by hiring internal auditors?
   a. Segregate duties.
   b. Establish responsibility.
   c. Restrict access.
   d. Independently verify.

4. Which of the following internal control principles underlies the requirement that all customers be given a sales receipt?
   a. Segregate duties.
   b. Establish responsibility.
   c. Restrict access.
   d. Document procedures.

5. At most movie theaters, one employee collects cash and issues a receipt, and another employee collects the tear-away portion of that receipt. Which of the following internal control principles does this description best illustrate?
   a. Segregate duties.
   b. Establish responsibility.
   c. Restrict access.
   d. Document procedures.

6. Which of the following documents is least likely to be included in a voucher?
   a. Purchase order.
   b. Invoice.
   c. Purchase requisition.
   d. Remittance advice.

7. Which of the following explains why almost all businesses use banking services?
   a. Banking services allow the business to keep only a minimal amount of cash on hand.
   b. Banking services make it easier for the business to transact with other businesses.

c. Banking services enable the business to independently verify the accuracy of its cash records.
d. All of the above.

8. Upon review of your company's bank statement, you discover that you recently deposited a check from a customer that was rejected by your bank as NSF. Which of the following describes the actions to be taken when preparing your company's bank reconciliation?

| Balance per Bank | Balance per Books |
|---|---|
| a. Decrease | No change |
| b. Increase | Decrease |
| c. No change | Decrease |
| d. Decrease | Increase |

9. Upon review of the most recent bank statement, you discover that a check made out to your supplier for $86 was recorded in your Cash and Accounts Payable accounts as $68. Which of the following describes the actions to be taken when preparing your bank reconciliation?

| Balance per Bank | Balance per Books |
|---|---|
| a. Decrease | No change |
| b. Increase | No change |
| c. No change | Decrease |
| d. Decrease | Increase |

10. Assume a business has $2,000 cash in its checking account on August 1. On August 2, the business writes a check to establish a $100 petty cash fund. Later in the month, cash payments totaling $20 are made out of the fund and checks totaling $350 are written (including a check to replenish the petty cash fund). If all checks except for one in the amount of $10 clear the bank in August, what amount would the business report as Cash and Cash Equivalents at the end of August? Assume there are no other items affecting cash and cash equivalents.
    a. $1,650.
    b. $1,630.
    c. $1,550.
    d. $1,530.

---

**Solutions to Multiple-Choice Questions**

| 1. c | 2. d | 3. d | 4. d | 5. a | 6. d |
|---|---|---|---|---|---|
| 7. d | 8. c | 9. c | 10. a | | |

# Mini Exercises  Available with McGraw-Hill's Homework Manager

**M8-1 Classifying Sarbanes-Oxley (SOX) Objectives and Requirements**                LO1
Match each of the following SOX requirements to the corresponding objective by entering the appropriate letter in the space provided.

____ 1. Establish a tip line for employees
       to report questionable acts.

____ 2. Increase maximum fines to $5 million.

____ 3. Require management to report on
       effectiveness of internal controls.

____ 4. Legislate whistle-blower protections.

____ 5. Require external auditors' report on internal
       control effectiveness.

A. Counteract incentives for fraud.
B. Reduce opportunities for error and fraud.
C. Encourage good character.

**M8-2 Identifying Internal Control Procedures and Principles**                LO2
Fox Erasing has a system of internal control with the following procedures. Match the procedure to the corresponding internal control principle.

| Procedure | Internal Control Principle |
|---|---|
| ____ 1. The treasurer signs checks. | A. Establish responsibility. |
| ____ 2. The treasurer is not allowed to make bank deposits. | B. Segregate duties. |
| ____ 3. The company's checks are prenumbered. | C. Restrict access. |
| ____ 4. Unused checks are stored in the vault. | D. Document procedures. |
| ____ 5. A bank reconciliation is prepared each month. | E. Independently verify. |

**M8-3 Identifying Internal Control Principles Applied by a Merchandiser**                LO2, 4
Identify the internal control principle represented by each point in the following diagram.

**LO3**

### M8-4 Matching Cash Receipt Processes to Internal Control Principles

Match each of the following cash receipt activities to the internal control principle to which it best relates, by entering the appropriate letter in the space provided.

____ 1. A list of checks received in the mail is prepared.

____ 2. Total cash receipts are compared to the amount on the bank deposit slip.

____ 3. A password is required to open the cash register.

____ 4. Price changes at the checkout require a manager's approval.

____ 5. Each cashier is assigned a separate cash drawer.

A. Establish responsibility.
B. Segregate duties.
C. Restrict access.
D. Document procedures.
E. Independently verify.

**LO3**

### M8-5 Identifying Internal Control Weaknesses in Descriptions of Cash Receipts Process

Each situation below describes an internal control weakness in the cash receipts process. Identify which of the five internal control principles is violated, explain the weakness, and then suggest a change that would improve internal control.

1) Cashiers prepare a cash count summary, attach tapes from the cash register showing total receipts, and then prepare a bank deposit slip, which they take to the bank for deposit. After the deposit is made, all documents are forwarded to the accounting department for review and recording.

2) Each cash register is password protected but, for convenience, the password is written on a note stuck to the side of the cash register.

3) The receptionist opens the mail each morning, sorts it into piles, and then gives checks received from customers to the mail clerk for delivery to the accounting department, where a cash receipts list is prepared.

4) The accounting department receives cash register totals each day and promptly files them by cash register number. The accounting department also receives cash count sheets from cashiers each day and files them by employee number. The accounting department receives stamped bank deposit slips the morning after the bank deposit is made, prepares the journal entry, and files the deposit slips by date.

5) To avoid boredom, the employee who works the cash register at the movie theater trades off with either the employee who collects the tickets or an employee who works at the concessions stand.

6) To enhance efficiency, cashiers are assigned the responsibility of authorizing price changes at the cash register.

**LO3**

### M8-6 Matching Cash Payment Processes to Internal Control Principles

Match each of the following cash payment activities to the internal control principle to which it best relates by entering the appropriate letter in the space provided.

____ 1. The business manager has the only key to the check signing equipment.

____ 2. The purchasing manager orders all goods and services for the business.

____ 3. A bank reconciliation is prepared monthly.

____ 4. Prenumbered checks are used for all payments.

____ 5. The company asks suppliers to deliver their merchandise to the warehouse but mail their invoices to the accounting department.

A. Establish responsibility.
B. Segregate duties.
C. Restrict access.
D. Document procedures.
E. Independently verify.

**LO3, 4**

### M8-7 Identifying Internal Control Weaknesses in Descriptions of Cash Payment Processes

Each situation below describes an internal control weakness in the cash payments process. Identify which of the five internal control principles is violated, explain the weakness, and then suggest a change that would improve internal control.

1) The warehouse clerk is responsible for ordering inventory when levels become low, and advising the accounting department to issue a payment to the supplier when ordered goods are received.

2) For each purchase, the accountant compares the purchase order (prepared by the purchasing manager) to the receiving report (prepared by warehouse employees), and then attaches these documents to the corresponding supplier invoice and files them by supplier name. The accountant then prepares a check, which the owner merrily signs and sends to the mail clerk for mailing.

3) The petty cash custodian prepared a template for petty cash receipts using Microsoft Word and e-mailed a copy of it to employees in his department for them to use when submitting their reimbursement claims.

4) The check-signing machine is stored with a supply of blank checks in the lunch room closet.

5) Purchase orders can be approved by the purchasing manager, accountant, or warehouse supervisor, depending on who is least busy.

6) The petty cash custodian assists the assistant controller by preparing the monthly bank reconciliation.

**M8-8 Recognizing Voucher and Petty Cash Systems**　　　　　　　　　　　　　　　　　LO4
The following transactions occurred during the month. Indicate whether a voucher (V) or petty cash (PC) system would be used to process each transaction.

\_\_\_\_ 1. A $10 cash payment is made to Starbucks to purchase coffee for a business client.

\_\_\_\_ 2. A $40 cash payment is made for supplies purchased from Office Depot.

\_\_\_\_ 3. A $30 cash payment is made to UPS to deliver goods to a customer.

\_\_\_\_ 4. A $300 check is written for supplies purchased on account from Office Max.

**M8-9 Accounting for Petty Cash Transactions**　　　　　　　　　　　　　　　　　　　　LO4
Refer to M8-8. Prepare the journal entry that would be recorded to replenish the petty cash fund.

**M8-10 Accounting for Petty Cash Transactions**　　　　　　　　　　　　　　　　　　　LO4
On September 30, Hector's petty cash fund of $100 is replenished. At the time, the cash box contained $18 cash and receipts for taxi fares ($40), delivery charges ($12), and office supplies ($30). Prepare the journal entry to record the replenishment of the fund.

**M8-11 Organizing Items on the Bank Reconciliation**　　　　　　　　　　　　　　　　LO5
Indicate whether the following items would be added (+) to or subtracted (−) from the company's books or the bank statement side of a bank reconciliation.

| Reconciling Item | Bank Statement | Company's Books |
| --- | --- | --- |
| 1. Outstanding checks of $12,000 | | |
| 2. Bank service charge of $15 | | |
| 3. Deposit in transit of $2,300 | | |
| 4. Interest earned of $5 | | |

**M8-12 Preparing Journal Entries after a Bank Reconciliation**　　　　　　　　　　　LO5
Using the information in M8-11, prepare any journal entries needed to adjust the company's books.

**M8-13 Preparing a Bank Reconciliation**　　　　　　　　　　　　　　　　　　　　　　LO5
Prepare a bank reconciliation for Trigger Company, using the following information at June 30, 2009.

| | |
| --- | --- |
| Balance per bank | $10,000 |
| Balance per company | 9,030 |
| Bank service charges | 80 |
| Bank interest earned | 50 |
| Deposit in transit | 3,000 |
| Outstanding checks | 4,000 |

**M8-14 Preparing Journal Entries after a Bank Reconciliation**　　　　　　　　　　LO5
Refer to M8-13. Prepare any journal entries needed to adjust the company's books.

**M8-15 Reporting Cash and Cash Equivalents**　　　　　　　　　　　　　　　　　　　LO6
Indicate (Yes or No) whether each of the following would be properly included as Cash and Cash Equivalents.

\_\_\_\_ 1. $10,000 of government Treasury bills purchased 10 days prior to their maturity.

\_\_\_\_ 2. $5,000 of stock in Zoogle—a private company that operates a lost pet search business.

\_\_\_\_ 3. $20,000 of cash owed by customers on sales made within 20 days of year-end.

\_\_\_\_ 4. $1,000 of cash in the petty cash custodian's locked cash box.

## Exercises HM

Available with McGraw-Hill's Homework Manager

**LO1, 2**

### E8-1 Identifying Internal Control Principles

At most movie theaters, one employee sells tickets and another employee collects them. One night when you are at the movies, your friend comments that this is a waste of the theater's money.

*Required:*

1. Identify the control principle to which this situation relates.
2. Explain to your friend what could happen if the same person did both jobs.

**LO2**

### E8-2 Identifying Internal Control Principles

Your student club recently volunteered to go door-to-door collecting cash donations on behalf of a local charity. The charity's accountant went berserk when you said you wrote receipts only for donors who asked for one.

*Required:*

Identify the control principle that you violated, and explain why the accountant reacted so strongly. What controls might be appropriate to use in the future?

**LO3**

### E8-3 Identifying Internal Control Principles in Cash Receipt Processes

Locker Rentals Corp. (LRC) operates locker rental services at several locations throughout the city including the airport, bus depot, shopping malls, and athletics facilities. Unlike some of the old mechanical lockers that charge a fixed amount per use, LRC's lockers operate electronically and are able to charge based on hours of use. The locker system transmits a daily message to LRC's office indicating the number of hours that lockers have been used, which the office manager uses to determine when cash should be picked up at each location. LRC's cash receipts system is described below.

a. Two employees ("cash collection clerks") are responsible for collecting cash from the lockers. Based on instructions from the office manager, one clerk collects cash from specific locations on the west side of the city and the other collects from specific locations on the east side.

b. When each cash collection clerk returns the cash, a supervisor counts the cash and prepares a cash count sheet.

c. The supervisor summarizes the cash count sheets in a prenumbered daily cash summary and files the prenumbered cash count sheets by date.

d. The supervisor places the cash in a locked cash box until it is taken to the bank for deposit.

e. The supervisor, not the cash collection clerks, takes the cash to the bank for deposit.

f. The supervisor prepares a duplicate deposit slip, which the bank stamps after the deposit is made, to indicate the date and amount of the deposit.

g. The supervisor sends the stamped bank deposit slip and daily cash summary to the accountant, who compares them before preparing a journal entry debiting Cash and crediting Locker Rental Revenue.

*Required:*

1. For each statement a–g, identify the internal control principle being applied.
2. Prepare a diagram similar to Exhibit 8.3 showing the flow of information and materials. In what two ways does LRC's system differ from Exhibit 8.3?
3. After several months, LRC's supervisor is arrested for stealing nearly $10,000 from the company. Identify the internal control weakness that allowed this theft to occur.
4. After the theft, LRC hired an external auditor to evaluate the company's cash receipts system. One of the auditor's recommendations was for LRC's accountant to verify that the cash collection clerks were returning all the cash received at each locker location. Explain how the accountant could use the electronic information transmitted by each locker location to verify that the cash collection clerks were not stealing from the company.

**LO3, 4**

### E8-4 Identifying Internal Control Principles in Cash Payment Processes

Home Repair Corp. (HRC) operates a building maintenance and repair business. The business has three office employees—a sales manager, a materials/crew manager, and an accountant. HRC's cash payments system is described below.

a. After a contract is signed with a customer, the sales manager prepares a prenumbered purchase requisition form that indicates the materials needed for the work at the repair site.

b. Based on the purchase requisition form, the materials/crew manager prepares and sends a prenumbered purchase order to suppliers of materials, advising them of the specific materials needed and the repair site to which they should be delivered.

c.  The materials/crew manager is the only employee authorized to order goods.

d.  Upon receiving a supplier's invoice, the accountant compares it to terms indicated on the purchase order, noting in particular the prices charged and quantity ordered.

e.  If these documents are in agreement, the accountant prepares a prenumbered check, stamps the invoice "paid," and prepares a journal entry to record the payment. The journal entry explanation references the sequential number on the purchase order.

f.  HRC's owner prepares a monthly bank reconciliation and reviews checks returned with the bank statement to ensure they have been issued to valid suppliers.

**Required:**

1.  For each statement a–f, identify the internal control principle being applied.

2.  Using the above description, prepare a list of steps and documentation similar to Exhibit 8.5. Which document in Exhibit 8.5 is excluded from the above description?

3.  After several months, HRC's materials/crew manager is arrested for having $20,000 of materials delivered to his home, but charged to the company. Identify the internal control weakness that allowed this theft to occur.

**E8-5 Recording Petty Cash Transactions**                                           LO4

Mountain Air Company established a $200 petty cash fund on January 1. From January 2 through 15, payments were made from the fund, as listed below. On January 17, the fund was replenished with a check for $172.

a.  January 3—Paid cash to courier for deliveries to customers—$43.

b.  January 8—Paid cash to restaurant for catering lunch—$83.

c.  January 10—Paid cash for postage—$14.

d.  January 15—Paid cash for office supplies—$32.

**Required:**

1.  Prepare the journal entry, if any, required on January 1.

2.  Prepare the journal entries, if any, required on January 2 through 15.

3.  Prepare the journal entries, if any, required on January 17.

**E8-6 Recording Petty Cash Transactions**                                           LO4

Sunshine Health established a $100 petty cash fund on January 1. From January 2 through 10, payments were made from the fund, as listed below. On January 12, the fund had only $10 remaining; a check was written to replenish the fund.

a.  January 2—Paid cash to courier for deliveries to customers—$23.

b.  January 7—Paid cash for taxi fares—$50.

c.  January 10—Paid cash for postage—$13.

**Required:**

1.  Prepare the journal entry, if any, required on January 1.

2.  Prepare the journal entries, if any, required on January 2 through 10.

3.  Prepare the journal entries, if any, required on January 12.

(**Tip:** The Coach's Tip on page 354 explains how to account for cash shortages when a fund is replenished.)

**E8-7 Preparing a Bank Reconciliation and Journal Entries and Reporting Cash**       LO5, 6

Hills Company's June 30, 2009, bank statement and the June ledger account for cash are summarized here:

### BANK STATEMENT

|  | Checks | Deposits | Other | Balance |
|---|---|---|---|---|
| Balance, June 1, 2009 |  |  |  | $ 7,200 |
| Deposits during June |  | $18,000 |  | 25,200 |
| Checks cleared during June | $19,100 |  |  | 6,100 |
| Bank service charges |  |  | $30 | 6,070 |
| Balance, June 30, 2009 |  |  |  | 6,070 |

| | + | Cash (A) | – | | |
|---|---|---|---|---|---|
| June 1 | Balance | 6,800 | | | |
| June | Deposits | 19,000 | June | Checks written | 19,400 |
| June 30 | Balance | 6,400 | | | |

*Required:*

1. Prepare a bank reconciliation. A comparison of the checks written with the checks that have cleared the bank shows outstanding checks of $700. Some of the checks that cleared in June had been written prior to June. No deposits in transit were noted in May, but a deposit is in transit at the end of June.

2. Give any journal entries that should be made as a result of the bank reconciliation.

3. What is the balance in the Cash account after the reconciliation entries?

4. In addition to the balance in its bank account, Hills Company also has $300 of Petty Cash, which is recorded in a separate account. What is the total amount of Cash and Cash Equivalents that should be reported on the balance sheet at June 30?

**LO5, 6**

**E8-8 Preparing a Bank Reconciliation and Journal Entries and Reporting Cash**

The September 30, 2009, bank statement for Cadieux Company and the September ledger account for cash are summarized here:

### BANK STATEMENT

| | Checks | | Deposits | Other | Balance |
|---|---|---|---|---|---|
| Balance, September 1, 2009 | | | | | $ 2,000 |
| September 7 | | | | NSF $100 | 1,900 |
| September 11 | | | $3,000 | | 4,900 |
| September 12 | #101 | $ 800 | | | 4,100 |
| September 17 | #102 | 1,700 | | | 2,400 |
| September 26 | #103 | 2,300 | | | 100 |
| September 29 | | | | EFT 150 | 250 |
| September 30 | | | | Service 20 | 230 |

| | | + | Cash (A) | – | |
|---|---|---|---|---|---|
| Sept 1 | Balance | 2,000 | | | |
| Sept 10 | | 3,000 | 800 | Sept 10 | 101 |
| Sept 30 | | 2,500 | 1,700 | Sept 15 | 102 |
| | | | 2,300 | Sept 22 | 103 |
| | | | 50 | Sept 28 | 104 |
| Sept 30 | Balance | 2,650 | | | |

No outstanding checks and no deposits in transit were noted in August. However, there were deposits in transit and checks outstanding at the end of September. The NSF check and electronic funds transfer (EFT) involved transactions with Cadieux Company's customers.

*Required:*

1. Prepare a bank reconciliation.

2. Give any journal entries that should be made as a result of the bank reconciliation.

3. What should the balance in the Cash account be after recording the journal entries in requirement 2?

4. If the company also has $400 in a Petty Cash account, what total amount of Cash and Cash Equivalents should the company report on the September 30 balance sheet?

# Problems—Set A     Available with McGraw-Hill's Homework Manager

### PA8-1 Evaluating Internal Control Strengths and Weaknesses in Cash Receipts and Disbursements

LO2, 3, 4

The following procedures are used by Richardson Light Works.

a.  When customers pay cash for lighting products, it is placed in a cash register and a receipt is issued to the customer.

b.  At the end of each day, the cash is counted by the cashier and a cash count sheet is prepared.

c.  The manager checks the accuracy of the cash count sheet before taking it to the bank for deposit.

d.  The journal entry to record cash sales is prepared using the cash count sheet.

e.  Disbursements from the petty cash fund are made for postage, office supplies, and small loans to fellow employees.

f.  Checks are written to suppliers immediately after supplier invoices are received.

g.  Receiving reports are prepared to indicate the quantity and condition of goods received from suppliers based on inspections made by warehouse personnel.

*Required:*

1.  Indicate whether each procedure represents a strength or weakness. Explain your reasons.

2.  For each weakness, describe a change in procedures that would address the weakness.

### PA8-2 Controlling and Accounting for Petty Cash Disbursements

LO3, 4

Superior Cabinets maintains a petty cash fund for minor business expenditures. The petty cash custodian, Mo Smith, describes the events that occurred during the last two months:

a.  I established the fund by cashing a Superior Cabinets' check for $300 made payable to me.

b.  Liz Clay provided a receipt for $50 for various office supplies. I paid $50 cash to her.

c.  James Flyer provided a $70 taxi receipt, so I paid $70 cash to him.

d.  Ricky Ricota claimed to have photocopied brochures for Superior Cabinets at The UPS Store for $97, but had misplaced the receipt. I took him at his word and paid $97 cash to him.

e.  On the last day of the month, I prepared a summary of expenditures and requested the fund be replenished. I received and cashed a Superior Cabinets' check for $217, placing the cash into the locked cash box.

f.  James Flyer provided receipts for taxi costs ($65) and airport Internet connection fees ($10), so I paid $75 cash to him.

g.  Woo Riun provided a $147 receipt from a local delivery company for an expedited delivery to a customer. I paid her $147 cash.

h.  Ricky Ricota claimed to have purchased $20 of envelopes, which were used to mail brochures to potential customers, but again he had misplaced the receipt. He did provide a receipt for $15 of postage, so I paid him $35 cash.

i.  On the last day of the month, I prepared a summary of expenditures and discovered that the petty cash fund was $2 short. After requesting that the fund be replenished, I received and cashed a Superior Cabinets' check for $259, placing the cash into the locked cash box.

j.  After suggesting that the petty cash fund be increased, I received and cashed a Superior Cabinets' check for $100 cash, which I placed in the locked cash box.

*Required:*

1.  Prepare journal entries where required.

2.  From the description of events, identify one control strength and one control weakness.

### PA8-3 Preparing a Bank Reconciliation and Journal Entries and Reporting Cash

LO5, 6

Martin Company's bank reconciliation at the end of April 2009 showed a reconciled cash balance of $18,800. No deposits were in transit at the end of April, but a deposit was in transit at the end of May. The bookkeeper at Martin Company has asked you to prepare a bank reconciliation as of May 31, 2009. The May 31, 2009, bank statement and the May T-account for Cash showed the following (summarized):

## BANK STATEMENT

| | Checks | Deposits | Other | | Balance |
|---|---|---|---|---|---|
| Balance, May 1, 2009 | | | | | $18,800 |
| May 2 | | $ 8,000 | | | 26,800 |
| May 5 | #301 $11,000 | | | | 15,800 |
| May 7 | #302  6,000 | | | | 9,800 |
| May 8 | | 10,000 | | | 19,800 |
| May 14 | #303  500 | | | | 19,300 |
| May 17 | | | Interest | $120 | 19,420 |
| May 22 | | | NSF | 280 | 19,140 |
| May 27 | #304  4,600 | | | | 14,540 |
| May 31 | | | Service charge | 60 | 14,480 |
| Balance, May 31, 2009 | | | | | 14,480 |

| + Cash (A) − | | | |
|---|---|---|---|
| May 1 Balance | 18,800 | | |
| May 1 | 8,000 | 11,000 | 301 May 2 |
| May 7 | 10,000 | 6,000 | 302 May 4 |
| May 29 | 4,000 | 500 | 303 May 11 |
| | | 4,600 | 304 May 23 |
| | | 1,300 | 305 May 29 |
| May 31 Balance | 17,400 | | |

*Required:*

1.  Prepare a bank reconciliation for May.
2.  Prepare any journal entries required as a result of the bank reconciliation. Why are they necessary?
3.  After the reconciliation journal entries are posted, what balance will be reflected in the Cash account in the ledger?
4.  If the company also has $50 of petty cash and $10,000 in government T-bills, which are recorded in different accounts, what total amount of Cash and Cash Equivalents should be reported on the balance sheet at the end of May?

**LO5, 6**  **PA8-4 Identifying Outstanding Checks and Deposits in Transit and Preparing a Bank Reconciliation and Journal Entries**
The December 2009 bank statement and Cash T-account for Stewart Company follow:

## BANK STATEMENT

| Date | Checks | Deposits | Other | | Balance |
|---|---|---|---|---|---|
| Dec. 1 | | | | | $48,000 |
| 2 | $500 | | | | 47,500 |
| 4 | 7,000 | | | | 40,500 |
| 6 | 120 | | | | 40,380 |
| 11 | 550 | $28,000 | | | 67,830 |
| 13 | 1,900 | | | | 65,930 |
| 17 | 12,000 | | | | 53,930 |
| 23 | 60 | 36,000 | | | 89,870 |
| 26 | 900 | | | | 88,970 |
| 28 | 2,200 | | | | 86,770 |
| 30 | 17,000 | 19,000 | NSF* | $300 | 88,470 |
| 31 | 1,650 | | Interest earned | 50 | 86,870 |
| 31 | | | Service charge | 150 | 86,720 |

* NSF check from J. Left, a customer.

| + Cash (A) − | | | |
|---|---|---|---|
| Dec. 1 Balance | 48,000 | Checks written during December: | |
| Deposits | | | |
| Dec. 11 | 28,000 | 500 | 60 |
| 23 | 36,000 | 7,000 | 900 |
| 30 | 19,000 | 120 | 150 |
| 31 | 13,000 | 550 | 17,000 |
| | | 1,900 | 3,500 |
| | | 12,000 | 1,650 |
| | | 2,200 | |
| Dec. 31 Balance | 96,470 | | |

There were no deposits in transit or outstanding checks at November 30.

**Required:**

1. Identify and list the deposits in transit at the end of December.
2. Identify and list the outstanding checks at the end of December.
3. Prepare a bank reconciliation for December.
4. Give any journal entries that the company should make as a result of the bank reconciliation. Why are they necessary?
5. After the reconciliation journal entries are posted, what balance will be reflected in the Cash account in the ledger?
6. The company also has $300 of petty cash, $1,000 of government T-bills, and a $20,000 investment in a small privately owned company, each of which is recorded in a different account. What total amount of Cash and Cash Equivalents should be reported on the December 31, 2009, balance sheet?

**PA8-5 Preparing a Bank Reconciliation and Journal Entries Including Petty Cash Transactions**   LO4, 5, 6
The August 2009 bank statement for Martha Company and the Cash T-account for August 2009 follow:

## BANK STATEMENT

| Date | Checks | Deposits | Other | Balance |
|---|---|---|---|---|
| Aug. 1 | | | | $17,470 |
| 2 | $300 | | | 17,170 |
| 3 | | $12,000 | | 29,170 |
| 4 | 400 | | | 28,770 |
| 5 | 250 | | | 28,520 |
| 9 | 890 | | | 27,630 |
| 10 | 310 | | | 27,320 |
| 15 | | 4,000 | | 31,320 |
| 21 | 400 | | | 30,920 |
| 24 | 21,000 | | | 9,920 |
| 25 | | 7,000 | | 16,920 |
| 30 | 800 | | | 16,120 |
| 30 | | | Interest earned $20 | 16,140 |
| 31 | | | Service charge   10 | 16,130 |

| + Cash (A) − | | | |
|---|---|---|---|
| Aug. 1 Balance | 17,470 | Checks written | |
| Deposits | | | |
| Aug. 2 | 12,000 | 300 | Aug. 1 |
| 12 | 4,000 | 400 | 2 |
| 24 | 7,000 | 250 | 3 |
| 31 | 5,000 | 310 | 4 |
| | | 890 | 5 |
| | | 290 | 15 |
| | | 550 | 17 |
| | | 800 | 18 |
| | | 400 | 19 |
| | | 21,000 | 23 |
| Aug. 31 Balance | 20,280 | | |

No deposits were in transit and no checks were outstanding at the end of July.

*Required:*

1. Identify and list the deposits in transit at the end of August.
2. Identify and list the outstanding checks at the end of August.
3. Prepare a bank reconciliation for August.
4. Give any journal entries that the company should make as a result of the bank reconciliation. Why are they necessary?
5. After the reconciliation journal entries are posted, what balance will be reflected in the Cash account in the ledger?
6. The company also has a petty cash fund of $300, which was established several months ago. The fund was replenished on August 31, 2009, with a payment of $125 to cover office supplies ($50), taxi fares ($60), and postage costs ($15) paid out of the fund. Give any journal entries the company should make when the fund is replenished.
7. If the company also has $5,000 of government T-bills recorded in a different account, what total amount of Cash and Cash Equivalents should be reported on the August 31, 2009, balance sheet?

## Problems—Set B  Available with McGraw-Hill's Homework Manager

**LO2, 3, 4**

### PB8-1 Evaluating Internal Control Strengths and Weaknesses in Cash Receipts and Disbursements

The following procedures are used by The Taco Shop.

a. Customers pay cash for all food orders. Cash is placed in a cash register and a receipt is issued upon request by the customer.
b. At the end of each day, the cashier counts the cash, prepares a cash count sheet, and has the manager review and sign the cash count sheet.
c. At three times during the day, excess cash is removed from the cash register and placed in a vault until it is taken for night deposit at the local bank.
d. Orders for drink cups, straws, condiments, and other supplies are written on prenumbered purchase order forms and are approved by the manager before being sent to an authorized supplier.
e. When supplies are received, they are stacked just inside the back door to the kitchen, which is left unlocked because part-time employees frequently arrive and leave at various times during the day.
f. Rather than maintain a formal petty cash system, reimbursement for minor business expenses are paid using cash in the cash register. Employees show a receipt to the cashier on duty, who then files the receipt in a cardboard box under the counter.

*Required:*

1. Indicate whether each procedure represents a strength or weakness. Explain your reasons.
2. For each weakness, describe a change in procedures that would address the weakness.

### PB8-2 Controlling and Accounting for Petty Cash Disbursements

LO3, 4

Harristown Hockey Club (HHC) maintains a petty cash fund for minor club expenditures. The petty cash custodian, Wayne Crosby, describes the events that occurred during the last two months:

a.  I established the fund by cashing a check from HHC for $250 made payable to me.

b.  Tom Canuck provided a $70 receipt for repairs to the club's computer, so I paid $70 cash to him.

c.  Kim Harra provided a receipt for $50 for various supplies she had used to decorate the arena last month. I paid $50 cash to her.

d.  Trainer Jim bought a bag of pucks that the club intends to use for the next few years. He gave me the receipt and I paid him $80.

e.  On the last day of the month, I prepared a summary of expenditures and requested the fund be replenished. I received and cashed a check from HHC for $200, placing the cash into a locked cash box.

f.  Wendy Wignes provided receipts for chips and sodas purchased for the club's entertainment event. I paid $125 cash to her.

g.  Destiny Hook provided a phone bill showing she had paid $30 for calls made to contact referees for the annual tournament. I paid her $30 cash.

h.  Gutty McTavish submitted a receipt for $35 for a haircut he received. I did not pay him.

i.  I could not make it to the bank in time to take out money for the weekend, so I borrowed $50 from the petty cash box and will repay it next month.

j.  On the last day of the month, I prepared a summary of expenditures and discovered that the petty cash fund was $10 short. After requesting that the fund be replenished, I received and cashed a check from HHC for $215, placing the cash into the locked cash box.

*Required:*

1.  Prepare journal entries where required.

2.  From the description of events, identify one control strength and one control weakness.

### PB8-3 Preparing a Bank Reconciliation and Journal Entries and Reporting Cash

LO5, 6

The April 30, 2010, bank statement for KMaxx Company and the April ledger account for Cash are summarized here:

#### BANK STATEMENT

|  | Checks | | Deposits | Other | | Balance |
|---|---|---|---|---|---|---|
| Balance, April 1, 2010 | | | | | | $6,000 |
| April 5 | #101 | $700 | | | | 5,300 |
| April 9 | | | $2,500 | | | 7,800 |
| April 12 | #102 | 200 | | | | 7,600 |
| April 19 | #103 | 500 | | | | 7,100 |
| April 22 | #104 | 1,000 | | | | 6,100 |
| April 27 | | | | EFT | $200 | 5,900 |
| April 30 | | | | Service charge | 25 | 5,875 |

|  | + Cash (A) − | | | |
|---|---|---|---|---|
| Apr 1 Balance | 6,000 | | | |
| Apr 8 | 2,500 | 700 | Apr 2 | 101 |
| Apr 28 | 500 | 200 | Apr 10 | 102 |
| | | 500 | Apr 15 | 103 |
| | | 1,100 | Apr 20 | 104 |
| | | 300 | Apr 29 | 105 |
| Apr 30 Balance | 6,200 | | | |

No outstanding checks and no deposits in transit were noted in March. However, there are deposits in transit and checks outstanding at the end of April. The electronic funds transfer (EFT) involved an automatic monthly payment to one of KMaxx's creditors. Check 104 was written for $1,100.

*Required:*

1.  Prepare a bank reconciliation for April.
2.  Give any journal entries that should be made as a result of the bank reconciliation.
3.  What should the balance in the Cash account be after recording the journal entries in requirement 2?
4.  If the company also has $500 of petty cash and $10,000 worth of 60-day government treasury bills (T-bills) purchased last month, what total amount of Cash and Cash Equivalents should the company report on the April 30 balance sheet?

LO5, 6    **PB8-4 Preparing a Bank Reconciliation and Journal Entries and Reporting Cash**
The bookkeeper at Tony Company has asked you to prepare a bank reconciliation as of February 29, 2010. The February 29, 2010, bank statement and the February T-account for Cash showed the following (summarized):

## BANK STATEMENT

|  | | Checks | Deposits | Other | | Balance |
|---|---|---|---|---|---|---|
| Balance, February 1, 2010 | | | | | | $49,400 |
| February 2 | 101 | $15,000 | | | | 34,400 |
| February 4 | | | $ 7,000 | | | 41,400 |
| February 5 | | | | NSF | $320 | 41,080 |
| February 9 | 102 | 11,000 | | | | 30,080 |
| February 12 | 103 | 7,500 | | | | 22,580 |
| February 14 | | | 9,500 | | | 32,080 |
| February 19 | 104 | 9,000 | | | | 23,080 |
| February 23 | | | 14,150 | | | 37,230 |
| February 26 | 105 | 6,700 | | | | 30,530 |
| February 28 | | | | Interest | 150 | 30,680 |
| February 29 | | | | Service charge | 40 | 30,640 |

| + | Cash (A) | − | |
|---|---|---|---|
| Feb 1 Balance | 49,400 | | |
| Feb 2 | 7,000 | 15,000 | Feb 1   101 |
| Feb 13 | 9,500 | 11,000 | Feb 7   102 |
| Feb 21 | 14,150 | 7,500 | Feb 11 103 |
| Feb 28 | 7,800 | 9,000 | Feb 17 104 |
| | | 6,700 | Feb 25 105 |
| | | 1,200 | Feb 29 106 |
| Feb 29 Balance | 37,450 | | |

Tony Company's bank reconciliation at the end of January 2010 showed no outstanding checks. No deposits were in transit at the end of January, but a deposit was in transit at the end of February.

*Required:*

1.  Prepare a bank reconciliation for February.
2.  Prepare any journal entries required as a result of the bank reconciliation. Why are they necessary?
3.  After the reconciliation journal entries are posted, what balance will be reflected in the Cash account in the ledger?
4.  The company also has $400 of petty cash, $2,000 of government T-bills, and a $20,000 investment in a small privately owned company, each of which is recorded in a different account. What total amount of Cash and Cash Equivalents should be reported on the February 29, 2010, balance sheet?

**PB8-5 Identifying Outstanding Checks and Deposits in Transit and Preparing a Bank Reconciliation and Journal Entries Including Petty Cash**

LO4, 5, 6

The September 2010 bank statement for Terrick Company and the Cash T-account for September 2010 follow:

### BANK STATEMENT

| Date | Checks | Deposits | Other | | Balance |
|---|---|---|---|---|---|
| Sept. 1 | | | | | $ 75,900 |
| 2 | $620 | | | | 75,280 |
| 4 | 2,000 | | | | 73,280 |
| 6 | 1,500 | | | | 71,780 |
| 11 | 300 | 14,000 | | | 85,480 |
| 13 | 650 | | | | 84,830 |
| 17 | 10,000 | | | | 74,830 |
| 23 | 90 | 27,000 | | | 101,740 |
| 26 | 700 | | | | 101,040 |
| 28 | 8,000 | | | | 93,040 |
| 29 | 730 | 17,000 | NSF* | $500 | 108,810 |
| 30 | 400 | | Interest earned | 60 | 108,470 |
| 30 | | | Service charge | 40 | 108,430 |

\* NSF check from B. Frank, a customer.

| + Cash (A) − | | | |
|---|---|---|---|
| Sept.  1 Balance | 75,900 | Checks written during September | |
| Deposits | | 620 | 8,000 |
| Sept. 11 | 14,000 | 2,000 | 730 |
| 23 | 27,000 | 1,500 | 400 |
| 29 | 17,000 | 300 | 500 |
| 30 | 21,000 | 650 | 6,000 |
| | | 10,000 | 90 |
| | | 700 | |
| Sept. 30 Balance | 123,410 | | |

There were no deposits in transit or outstanding checks at August 31.

*Required:*

1. Identify and list the deposits in transit at the end of September.
2. Identify and list the outstanding checks at the end of September.
3. Prepare a bank reconciliation for September.
4. Give any journal entries that the company should make as a result of the bank reconciliation. Why are they necessary?
5. After the reconciliation journal entries are posted, what balance will be reflected in the Cash account in the ledger?
6. The company also has a petty cash fund of $300, which was established several months ago. The fund was replenished on September 30, 2010, with a payment of $175 to cover office supplies ($60), selling expenses ($90), and courier fees ($25) paid out of the fund. Give any journal entries the company should make when the fund is replenished.
7. The company also acquired 60-day government treasury bills (T-bills) last month, now valued at $4,000. What total amount of Cash and Cash Equivalents should be reported on the September 30, 2010, balance sheet?

# Cases and Projects

LO6

## CP8-1 Finding Financial Information

Refer to the financial statements of The Home Depot in Appendix A at the end of this book, or download the annual report from the Cases and Projects section of the text's Web site at www.mhhe.com/ LLPW1e. How much cash (including cash equivalents) does the company report at February 3, 2008? According to the company's management and external auditors, were internal controls over financial reporting effective at that time?

LO6

Lowe's

## CP8-2 Comparing Financial Information

Refer to the financial statements of The Home Depot in Appendix A and Lowe's in Appendix B at the end of this book, or download the annual reports from the Cases section of the text's Web site at www.mhhe.com/ LLPW1e. Does Lowe's report more or less cash (including cash equivalents) than The Home Depot in February 2008? According to the company's management and external auditors, were internal controls over financial reporting effective at that time?

LO1, 6

## CP8-3 Examining an Annual Report: Internet-Based Team Research

As a team, select an industry to analyze. Using your Web browser, each team member should access the annual report or 10-K for one publicly traded company in the industry, with each member selecting a different company. (See CP1–3 in Chapter 1 for a description of possible resources for these tasks.)

*Required:*

1. On an individual basis, each team member should write a short report that incorporates the following:

   *a.* Read management's report on internal control effectiveness. Did any material weaknesses or deficiencies exist during the year? Did the external auditors agree with management's assessment?

   *b.* How much did the company report in total Cash and Cash Equivalents? Does the company present sufficient information to determine the proportion of Cash versus Cash Equivalents?

2. Then, as a team, write a short report comparing and contrasting your companies using these attributes. Discuss any patterns across the companies that you as a team observe. Provide potential explanations for any differences discovered.

LO2

Famous Footwear

## CP8-4 Making Ethical Decisions: A Real-Life Example

When some people think about inventory theft, they imagine a shoplifter running out of a store with goods stuffed inside a jacket or bag. But that's not what the managers at the Famous Footwear store on Chicago's Madison Street thought. No, they suspected their own employees were the main cause of their unusually high shrinkage. One scam involved dishonest cashiers who would let their friends take a pair of Skechers without paying for them. To make it look like the shoes had been bought, cashiers would ring up a sale, but instead of charging $50 for shoes, they would charge only $2 for a bottle of shoe polish. When the company's managers saw a drop in gross profit, they decided to put the accounting system to work. In just two years, the company cut its Madison Street inventory losses in half. Here's how a newspaper described the store's improvements:

---

**Retailers Crack Down on Employee Theft**
*SouthCoast Today*, September 10, 2000, Chicago
By Calmetta Coleman, *Wall Street Journal* Staff Writer

. . . Famous Footwear installed a chainwide register-monitoring system to sniff out suspicious transactions, such as unusually large numbers of refunds or voids, or repeated sales of cheap goods.

. . . [B]efore an employee can issue a cash refund, a second worker must be present to see the customer and inspect the merchandise.

. . . [T]he chain has set up a toll-free hotline for employees to use to report suspicions about co-workers.

These improvements in inventory control came as welcome news for investors and creditors of Brown Shoe Company, the company that owns Famous Footwear. Although these improvements helped the Chicago store, Brown Shoe has been forced to shut down operations in other cities.

Brown Shoe
Company

**Required:**

1. Explain how the register-monitoring system would allow Famous Footwear to cut down on employee theft.

2. What is the name of the control that is addressed by Famous Footwear's new cash refund procedure?

3. Think of and describe at least four different parties that are harmed by the type of inventory theft described in this case.

## CP8-5 Making Ethical Decisions: A Mini Case

LO1, 6

You are an assistant in the accounting department of Hasher Electronics, a small electronics retailer. Hasher has a loan that requires the company to maintain a minimum cash balance of $125,000, as reported on its year-end balance sheet. Although Hasher has struggled in recent years, as of yesterday it looked as though Hasher would be able to meet this requirement. The cash balance in Hasher's general ledger was $130,000 and the company's credit manager was expecting to receive a $30,000 electronic funds transfer that day on account from your biggest customer. Your department supervisor had been worried about meeting the loan requirement, so she had delayed making payments to Hasher's suppliers for several days. But in anticipation of receiving the EFT, she decided yesterday to issue checks to suppliers totaling $15,000.

It is now the last day of the fiscal year and your supervisor approaches you with a problem. Your big customer had backed out at the last minute, indicating it had "some financial issues to sort out" before it can transfer money to Hasher. The supervisor says the only way Hasher can meet its loan requirement is to put the $15,000 back into the Cash account and pretend as if the supplier checks were not issued until after year-end. You questioned whether this would be ethical. Her reply was, "Well, we don't really have a choice. Either we do this, or we violate the terms of the loan agreement and possibly be forced to repay the loan immediately. That could put us out of business. Think of all the people who would lose their jobs! Just make a journal entry today to increase Cash and Accounts Payable. Then tomorrow we can reduce Cash and Accounts Payable—probably before many of our suppliers even get the checks we have written to them."

**Required:**

1. Who might suffer in the short term if you go along with your supervisor's request? What might happen in the future if you go along with her request this time? If you do not go along, who might suffer in the short term and what could be the long-term consequences?

2. You want to be loyal to your supervisor but honest to others who rely on your work. As an accounting assistant, which of these concerns should be most important? Why?

3. What alternative courses of action can you take? Which of these is "best" given the circumstances?

## CP8-6 Analyzing Internal Control Weaknesses: Critical Thinking

LO1, 2, 3

Snake Creek Company has one trusted employee who, as the owner said, "handles all of the bookkeeping and paperwork for the company." This employee is responsible for counting, verifying, and recording cash receipts and payments, making the weekly bank deposit, preparing checks for major expenditures (signed by the owner), making small expenditures from the cash register for daily expenses, and collecting accounts receivable. The owners asked the local bank for a $20,000 loan. The bank asked that an audit be performed covering the year just ended. The independent auditor (a local CPA), in a private conference with the owner, presented some evidence of the following activities of the trusted employee during the past year:

a. Cash sales sometimes were not entered in the cash register, and the trusted employee pocketed approximately $50 per month.

b. Cash taken from the cash register (and pocketed by the trusted employee) was replaced with expense memos with fictitious signatures (approximately $12 per day).

**Required:**

1. What was the approximate amount stolen during the past year?

2. What would be your recommendations to the owner?

# 9 Receivables

## LEARNING OBJECTIVES

**After completing this chapter, you should be able to:**

**LO1**   Identify the different types of receivables.

**LO2**   Account for and report the effects of uncollectible accounts.

**LO3**   Use two different methods to estimate uncollectible accounts.

**LO4**   Compute and report interest on notes receivable.

**LO5**   Compute and interpret the receivables turnover ratio.

Lectured slideshow—LP9-1
www.mhhe.com/LLPW1e

## Focus Company: SKECHERS

## "Global Leader in the Lifestyle Footwear Industry"

www.skechers.com

One of the most challenging parts of your academic and professional career will be managing events that you cannot completely control. Think, for example, about a group project that you must complete this term. You may believe that in theory the project should take only six days from start to finish. You know from experience, however, that someone in your group is likely to be late in completing the assigned work or may fail to complete it at all. The problem is that you do not know who it will be or how long the delay will take; these matters are largely beyond your control. To allow for the possibility that someone may be late, you might set a shorter period (say, four days) to complete the work. Establishing a two-day margin of safety will give you a realistic basis for planning and successfully completing the project.

This situation is similar to one faced by many companies, including Skechers, a shoe manufacturer that sells to retailers such as Foot Locker. Skechers' managers know from experience that some of their customers will not pay their bills. The problem is that at the time the sales are made, they cannot identify those customers. In this chapter, you will learn a method of accounting for such uncertainties—one that is similar to the approach you took with your group project. This method allows Skechers to report in a timely manner how much money the company is likely to collect from customers. In doing so, the company provides financial statement users a realistic basis for decision making.

Also in this chapter, you will learn about accounting for receivables, which arise either from selling to customers or from lending to others. As of December 31, 2006, receivables accounted for more than 25 percent of Skechers' total assets. If the company is to be successful, then, it must manage those assets effectively. You will see exactly how companies such as Skechers extend credit to others. Then you will confront the interesting accounting issues that arise when businesses decide to do so.

| TYPES OF RECEIVABLES | ACCOUNTS RECEIVABLE | NOTES RECEIVABLE AND INTEREST REVENUE | EVALUATING RECEIVABLES MANAGEMENT |
|---|---|---|---|
| | • Accounting for Bad Debts: The Allowance Method<br>• Recording Estimated Bad Debt Expense<br>• Methods for Estimating Bad Debts<br>• Other Issues | • Calculating Interest<br>• Recording Notes Receivable and Interest Revenue | • Receivables Turnover Analysis<br>• Comparison to Benchmarks |

# TYPES OF RECEIVABLES

**Learning Objective 1**

Identify the different types of receivables.

Receivables may be classified in three common ways. First, they may be classified as either an account receivable or a note receivable. A credit sale on an open account creates an **account receivable**. For example, an account receivable is created when Skechers sells shoes on open account to Fontana Shoes in Ithaca, New York, or a large chain such as Foot Locker.

A **note receivable** is a promise made in writing (that is, a formal document) to pay (1) a specified amount of money called the **principal** at a definite future date known as the **maturity date** and (2) a specified amount of **interest** on one or more future dates. The interest is the amount that is charged for use of the principal. Legally, notes receivable are viewed as stronger claims than accounts receivable. Because a new note must be created for every transaction, however, notes receivable are used less frequently than accounts receivable, typically only for expensive items such as vehicles or for transactions with borrowers who do not have an established credit history.

Second, receivables may be classified as trade or nontrade receivables (see Exhibit 9.1). A **trade receivable** is created in the normal course of business when a sale of merchandise or services is made on credit. A **nontrade receivable** arises from transactions other than the normal sale of merchandise or services. If Skechers were to lend money to an employee to finance a home at a new job location, for example, the loan would be classified as a nontrade receivable.

Third, on a classified balance sheet, receivables are classified as either **current** or **noncurrent** (that is, short term or long term), depending on when the company expects to collect cash. Like many companies, Skechers reports Trade Accounts Receivable (from customers) as well as Other Receivables and classifies both as current assets because they are expected to be paid within one year (see Exhibit 9.1).

**Exhibit 9.1**    **Classification of Accounts Receivable on the Balance Sheet**

Skechers, Inc.

### Skechers U.S.A., Inc.
**Partial Consolidated Balance Sheets** (in thousands)

| | December 31, 2006 | December 31, 2005 |
|---|---|---|
| **ASSETS** | | |
| Current assets | | |
| Cash and cash equivalents | $220,485 | $197,007 |
| Trade accounts receivable, less allowances of $10,558 in 2006 and $7,196 in 2005 | 177,740 | 134,600 |
| Other receivables | 8,035 | 6,888 |
| Total receivables | 185,775 | 141,488 |
| Inventories | 200,877 | 136,171 |
| Prepaid expenses and other current assets | 15,321 | 11,628 |
| Deferred tax assets | 9,490 | 5,755 |
| Total current assets | 631,948 | 492,049 |

# ACCOUNTS RECEIVABLE

## Accounting for Bad Debts: The Allowance Method

You already know from earlier chapters that **accounts receivable** arise from the sale of goods or services on credit. What you may not know is that some accounts receivable are never collected. In fact, a recent study estimated the cost of bad debts to be as high as 5 percent of the net incomes of all U.S. corporations.[1] Like that "friend" of yours who says he will pay you later but for one reason or another never gets around to it, some customers just do not pay their bills.

For billing and collection purposes, Skechers keeps a separate accounts receivable account (called a **subsidiary account**) for each of the retail stores that carries its footwear and apparel. On the balance sheet, the amount for Accounts Receivable represents the total of these individual customer accounts. When Skechers extends credit to these commercial customers, managers know that some of these customers will not pay their debts. If a customer does not pay the bill on time, Skechers first rebills the customer and then attempts to contact the customer to determine the reason for nonpayment. If these measures do not work, Skechers turns the account over to a collection agency.

Managers may not learn which customers will not pay until the **next** accounting period, however. At the end of the period of sale, then, they normally do not know which accounts receivable represent bad debts. To solve this problem and to satisfy both the **matching** principle and the **conservatism** principle, they use the allowance method to measure bad debt expense. The allowance method is based on estimates of the expected amount of bad debts relative to a period's sales. The two major steps in employing the allowance method are:

1. Make an end-of-period adjusting entry to record the **estimated** bad debt expense in the period in which the sale took place.
2. Write off (remove) specific customer balances during the period when they are determined to be uncollectible.

## Recording Estimated Bad Debt Expense

Bad debt expense (also called **uncollectible accounts expense**) is the expense associated with estimated uncollectible accounts receivable. **At the end of the accounting period,** accountants will make an **adjusting journal entry** to record the bad debt estimate. For the year ended December 31, 2006, for example, if Skechers estimated bad debt expense to be $4,591 (expressed in thousands of dollars), accountants would make the following adjusting entry to record the expense:

|  | Debit | Credit |
|---|---|---|
| Bad Debt Expense (+E, −OE) | 4,591 | |
| Allowance for Doubtful Accounts (+xA, −A) | | 4,591 |

| Assets | = | Liabilities | + | Owners' Equity | |
|---|---|---|---|---|---|
| Allowance for Doubtful Accounts (+xA)  −4,591 | | | | Bad Debt Expense (+E)  −4,591 | |

On the income statement, Bad Debt Expense is included under operating expenses. It decreases net income and owners' equity.

Why not credit Accounts Receivable in the adjusting entry? The answer is that at this point, there is no way to know which customers' accounts receivable are involved, and thus which subsidiary ledger accounts to reduce. The credit is made instead to the contra-asset account Allowance for Doubtful Accounts. (**Allowance for Bad Debts** and **Allowance for Uncollectible Accounts** are other common names for this account.) As with other contra-assets, the balance in Allowance for Doubtful Accounts is always subtracted from the balance of the asset Accounts Receivable. Thus, the entry decreases the net book value of Accounts Receivable and total assets. But because the estimated uncollectible portion is not taken

[1] PriceWaterhouse Coopers National Economic Consulting, *Value of Third-Party Debt Collection to the U.S. Economy: Survey and Analysis* (June 27, 2006).

### Learning Objective 2

Account for and report the effects of uncollectible accounts.

Video 9-1
www.mhhe.com/LLPW1e

### Coach's Tip

On their financial statements, companies use the terms **bad debt, uncollectible account,** and **doubtful account** interchangeably.

**Coach's Tip**

Accounts Receivable, net of allowance ("Trade accounts receivable, less allowances" in Exhibit 9.1) is not a separate account. It is a subtotal that is computed by subtracting the contra-asset account Allowance for Doubtful Accounts from the asset account Accounts Receivable.

directly out of Accounts Receivable, Skechers can still track the customers who owe money—even those who are believed to be unlikely to pay.

Of course, like all contra-asset accounts, the Allowance for Doubtful Accounts is a permanent account, so its balance carries forward from one accounting period to the next. The balance of Bad Debt Expense, which is a temporary account, is reduced to zero at the end of each accounting period. Consequently, the balance in the Allowance for Doubtful Accounts equals the balance in Bad Debt Expense only during the first year the Allowance for Doubtful Accounts is established.

### Removing (Writing Off) Specific Customer Balances

Throughout the year, whenever it becomes clear that a particular customer will not pay, Skechers removes the customer's account from the accounts receivable records. After removing the receivable, Skechers no longer needs to make an allowance for it, so the company removes the corresponding amount from the Allowance for Doubtful Accounts. Removing the uncollectible account and its corresponding allowance is called a **write off**. In the 2006 annual report, if Skechers stated that it had written off customer accounts totaling $1,229 (in thousands), the effects of these write-offs and the journal entry to record them were as follows:

|  | Debit | Credit |
|---|---|---|
| Allowance for Doubtful Accounts (−xA, +A) | 1,229 | |
| Accounts Receivable (−A) | | 1,229 |

| Assets | = | Liabilities | + | Owners' Equity |
|---|---|---|---|---|
| Allowance for Doubtful Accounts (−xA)    +1,229 | | | | |
| Accounts Receivable    −1,229 | | | | |

Note that **a write-off does not affect the income statement accounts.** The estimated bad debt expense related to these uncollectible accounts was recorded with an adjusting entry in the period when the sale was recorded. Therefore, no additional expense is incurred when the account is finally written off. Notice too that the decrease in Accounts Receivable offsets the decrease in Allowance for Doubtful Accounts so that the write-off does not affect the Net Accounts Receivable subtotal on the balance sheet.

### Summary of the Allowance Method

Here is a quick summary of the two main steps in the allowance method:

| Step | Timing | Journal Entry | Financial Statement Effects | | | | |
|---|---|---|---|---|---|---|---|
| | | | **Balance Sheet** | | **Income Statement** | | |
| 1. Record adjustment for estimated bad debts | End of the period in which sales are made | Bad Debt Expense (+E, −OE)<br>　Allowance for Doubtful<br>　　Accounts (+xA, −A) | Accounts receivable<br>　Less: **Allowance**<br>Net accounts receivable | No effect<br>⇧<br>⇩ | Revenues<br>Expenses<br>　Bad debt expense<br>Net income | | No effect<br><br>⇧<br>⇩ |
| 2. Identify and write off actual bad debts | As accounts are determined uncollectible | Allowance for Doubtful<br>　Accounts (−xA, +A)<br>Accounts Receivable (−A) | Accounts receivable<br>　Less: **Allowance**<br>Net accounts receivable | ⇩<br>⇩<br>No effect | Revenues<br>Expenses<br>　Bad debt expense<br>Net income | | No effect<br><br>No effect<br>No effect |

The effects of these two steps on Skechers' 2006 balance sheet can be summarized in terms of the following changes in the related T-accounts:

| Accounts Receivable (A) | | | | Allow. for Doubtful Accts (xA) | | | |
|---|---|---|---|---|---|---|---|
| Unadj. Bal. 189,527 | | | | | | 7,196 | Beg. Bal. |
| | | 1,229 | Write-offs | Write-offs | 1,229 | 4,591 | Estimate |
| End. Bal 188,298 | | | | | | 10,558 | End. Bal. |

**Ending Balances December 31, 2006**

| | |
|---|---|
| Accounts Receivable | $188,298 |
| −Allowance for Doubtful Accounts | 10,558 |
| Accounts Receivable (Net) | 177,740 |

## Spotlight On CONTROLS

### Segregating Collections and Write-Offs

One way to control accounts receivable is to ensure that the same person does not both receive collections from customers and write off account balances. This segregation of duties helps to prevent errors and fraud. Without adequate segregation between these duties, a single dishonest employee could divert customer payments to his or her own bank account and then cover up the theft by writing off the customer's balance.

### SELF-STUDY PRACTICE

Indicate the effect (+ / − / No Effect) of each of the following on net income and total assets.

|  | Net Income | Total Assets |
|---|---|---|

1. Polaris Industries recorded an increase in estimated bad debts on December 31, 2008.
2. Kellogg's wrote off 12 customer account balances during 2008.

*After you have finished, check your answers with the solution at the bottom of the page.*

## Methods for Estimating Bad Debts

In the examples given so far, we simply stated the estimated amount of uncollectibles to record. In the real world, companies must estimate the amount that they record in the end-of-period adjusting entry for bad debt expense. Such estimates may be based on either (1) a percentage of total credit sales for the period or (2) an "aging" of accounts receivable. Both methods are acceptable under GAAP and are used widely. The percentage of credit sales method is simpler to apply, but the aging method is generally more accurate. Some companies use the simpler method on a weekly or monthly basis and the more accurate method on a monthly or quarterly basis to check the accuracy of earlier estimates. In our example, both methods produce exactly the same estimate—a result that rarely occurs in the real world.

**Learning Objective 3**
Use two different methods to estimate uncollectible accounts.

Solution to Self-Study Practice

| | Net Income | Total Assets |
|---|---|---|
| 1. | − | − |
| 2. | NE | NE* |

*The decrease in Accounts Receivable is offset by the decrease in Allowance for Doubtful Accounts.

## Percentage of Credit Sales Method

**Coach's Tip**

In multiplying to compute the bad debt expense, be sure to convert the bad debt percentage from percentage to decimal format (from ¼% to 0.0025).

The allowance method of accounting for bad debts requires estimating and recording bad debts in the same period as the sale to which they relate. The **percentage of credit sales method** estimates bad debt expense by multiplying the historical percentage of bad debt losses by the current year's credit sales. Assume, for example, that Skechers has experienced bad debt losses of ¼ of 1 percent of credit sales in past years. If credit sales in the current year total $1,836,400, Skechers could estimate the current year's bad debt expense as:

| | |
|---|---:|
| Credit sales this year | $1,836,400 |
| × Bad debt loss rate (0.25%) | × 0.0025 |
| Bad debt expense this year | $    4,591 |

This estimate would be recorded using the following journal entry, which you first saw on page 383:

| | Debit | Credit |
|---|---|---|
| Bad Debt Expense (+E, −OE) | 4,591 | |
|     Allowance for Doubtful Accounts (+xA, −A) | | 4,591 |

## Accounts Receivable Methods

While the percentage of sales method computes the estimated Bad Debt Expense for the period, accounts receivable methods compute the estimated ending balance in the Allowance for Doubtful Accounts. To find the ending balance, managers must first determine the percentage of the total accounts receivable that is likely to be uncollectible. This method is often called the **percentage of accounts receivable method**.

A related, more commonly used and accurate approach for estimating uncollectible amounts is called the **aging of accounts receivable method**. This method gets its name because it is based on the "age" of each amount in accounts receivable. The older and more overdue an account receivable becomes, the less likely it is to be collectible. For example, a receivable that was due in 30 days but has not been paid after 45 days is more likely to be collected than a similar receivable that remains unpaid after 120 days. Based on prior experience, a company can estimate what portion of receivables of a specific age will not be paid.

The aging of accounts receivable method includes three steps as summarized in Exhibit 9.2:

1. **Prepare an aged listing of accounts receivable** with totals for each age category. Most accounting software will produce this report automatically.
2. **Estimate bad debt loss percentages for each category.** The percentage each company uses varies according to its circumstances. Generally, the longer an amount remains unpaid, the less likely it is to be collected. Therefore, a higher percentage is applied to amounts uncollected after 120 days than to those uncollected after 30 days.
3. **Compute the total estimate by multiplying the totals in Step 1 by the percentages in Step 2 and then summing across all categories.** The total across all aging categories ($1,000 + $2,121 + $5,317 + $2,120 = $10,558) equals the balance to which the Allowance for Doubtful Accounts will need to be adjusted at the end of the period.

**The amount computed in Step 3 is the desired balance in the Allowance for Doubtful Accounts, not the amount of the adjustment.** To compute the amount of the adjustment, you must subtract the existing, unadjusted balance from the desired adjusted balance computed in Step 3. Skechers had a beginning balance in the Allowance for Doubtful Accounts of $7,196 and had written off $1,229 in bad debts during the period, so its unadjusted credit balance would be $5,967 ($7,196 − $1,229). The desired credit balance computed in Exhibit 9.2 was $10,558, so an adjustment of $4,591 (= $10,558 − $5,967) needs to be recorded as a credit to the account. A corresponding amount is debited to Bad Debt Expense.

**Exhibit 9.2**    Estimating Uncollectible Amounts with an Aging of Accounts Receivable

| Customer | Total | NUMBER OF DAYS UNPAID | | | | |
|---|---|---|---|---|---|---|
| | | 0–30 | 31–60 | 61–90 | Over 90 | |
| Adam's Sports Stores | $   648 | $   405 | $   198 | $   45 | — | ⎫ |
| Backyard Shoe Company | 2,345 | — | — | — | $2,345 | ⎬ ←Step 1—Age |
| Other customers | 185,305 | 91,388 | 52,822 | 37,935 | 3,160 | ⎭ |
| **Total receivables** | $188,298 | $ 91,793 | $53,020 | $37,980 | $5,505 | |
| × Estimated bad debt percentages | | 1% | 4% | 14% | 40% | ←Step 2—Estimate |
| = **Estimated uncollectible** | $ 10,558 | $   918 | $ 2,121 | $ 5,317 | $2,202 | ←Step 3—Compute |

| | | | |
|---|---|---|---|
| Desired balance | $ 10,558 Credit | Beginning balance | $7,196 |
| −Unadjusted **credit** balance ($7,196 − $1,229) | 5,967 Credit ← | −Write-offs | 1,229 |
| **Required adjustment** | $  4,591 Credit | Unadjusted balance | $5,967 Credit (Debit if negative) |

| | Debit | Credit |
|---|---|---|
| Bad Debt Expense (+E, −OE) | 4,591 | |
|     Allowance for Doubtful Accounts (+xA, −A) | | 4,591 |

Although the Allowance for Doubtful Accounts normally has a credit balance, it may have a **debit balance** before it is adjusted for uncollectible accounts. This situation occurs when a company has recorded write-offs that exceed previous estimates of uncollectible accounts. If so, you can still calculate the amount of the adjustment needed to reach the desired balance under the aging of accounts receivable method. The only difference is that to reach the desired balance, you need to record an amount equal to the desired balance **plus** the existing debit balance. For example, if the unadjusted balance was a debit of $1,000, the amount of the entry is computed as follows:

| | | |
|---|---|---|
| Desired balance | $ 10,558 | Credit |
| +Unadjusted **debit** balance | 1,000 | Debit |
| **Required adjustment** | $11,558 | Credit |

## Comparison of Methods

**Students often fail to recognize that the approach to estimating bad debt expense using the percentage of credit sales method is different from that for the aging method.** The difference in the approaches is illustrated in the following two T-accounts:

| Allowance for Doubtful Accts (xA) | | |
|---|---|---|
| | 7,196 | Beg. Bal. |
| Write-offs   1,229 | 4,591 | **Estimate** |
| | 10,558 | End. Bal. |

{ *Percent of credit sales estimate*

| Allowance for Doubtful Accts (xA) | | |
|---|---|---|
| | 7,196 | Beg. Bal. |
| Write-offs   1,229 | 4,591 | **Estimate** |
| | 10,558 | End. Bal. |

{ *Desired balance from aging*

- **Percentage of credit sales.** Directly compute the amount to be recorded as **Bad Debt Expense** on the **income statement** for the period in the adjusting journal entry.
- **Aging.** Compute the **desired ending balance** you would like to have in the **Allowance for Doubtful Accounts** on the **balance sheet** after you make the necessary adjusting entry. The difference between the current balance in the account and the desired balance is recorded as the adjusting entry for Bad Debt Expense for the period.

In either case, the balance sheet presentation for 2006 would show Accounts Receivable less Allowance for Doubtful Accounts of $177,740 ($188,298 − $10,558).

**SELF-STUDY PRACTICE**

In a previous year, Mad Catz reported a beginning balance in the Allowance for Doubtful Accounts of $5,971. It also recorded write-offs of bad accounts amounting to $3,979 (all numbers are expressed in thousands of dollars).

1. Assume that Mad Catz used the percentage of sales method and had estimated its bad debt loss rate to be 2 percent. Its credit sales for the year were $216,850. Compute Bad Debt Expense for the period and the ending balance in the Allowance for Doubtful Accounts.

2. Assume instead that Mad Catz used the aging method. The aging of accounts receivable produced a desired balance of $6,329. Compute Bad Debt Expense for the period and the ending balance in the Allowance for Doubtful Accounts. Use either the following equation or T-account to solve for the missing value.

| | |
|---|---|
| Desired balance | Credit |
| −Unadjusted **credit** balance _____ | Credit |
| **Required adjustment** | Credit |

| − Allowance for Doubtful Accts (xA) + | |
|---|---|
| | 5,971    Beg. Bal. |

*After you have finished, check your answers with the solution at the bottom of the next page.*

## Spotlight On FINANCIAL REPORTING

### Bad Debt Policies

Skechers, Inc.

Companies must take action both to minimize the costs of bad debts and to accurately estimate those debts. Skechers described its policies regarding bad debts in its annual report, as follows:

> We provide a reserve against our receivables for estimated losses that may result from our customers' inability to pay. To minimize the likelihood of uncollectibility, customers' credit-worthiness is reviewed periodically based on external credit reporting services and our experience with the account, and it is adjusted accordingly. Should a customer's account become past due, we generally place a hold on the account and discontinue further shipments to that customer, minimizing further risk of loss. We determine the amount of the reserve by analyzing known uncollectible accounts, aged receivables, economic conditions in the customers' country or industry, historical losses and our customers' credit-worthiness. Amounts later determined and specifically identified to be uncollectible are charged or written off against this reserve.

## Other Issues

### Revising Estimates

Unless managers can see into the future, bad debt estimates always differ from the amounts that are later written off. Rather than go back and revise the initial estimates, companies are required to revise their bad debt estimates for the current period. That is, they correct overestimates in prior periods by lowering estimates in the current period; they correct underestimates in prior periods by raising estimates in the current period.

### Account Recoveries

In the same way that someone you have written off as a friend might do something to win you back, a customer might pay an account balance that has been written off. The collection of a previously written off account, called a **recovery,** is accounted for in two parts. First, you put the receivable back on the books by reversing the write-off. Second, you record the collection of the account. To illustrate, let's assume that Skechers collects $50 on an account previously written off. The recovery would be recorded with the following journal entries:

|   |   | Debit | Credit |
|---|---|---|---|
| 1. | Accounts Receivable (+A) | 50 | |
|   | Allowance for Doubtful Accounts (+xA, −A) | | 50 |
| 2. | Cash (+A) | 50 | |
|   | Accounts Receivable (−A) | | 50 |

} Reverse the write-off

} Record the collection

Look closely at these journal entries and you will see that Accounts Receivable is first debited and then credited for $50. Although it is tempting to cancel out these two amounts, doing so would create an inaccurate credit history for the customer. After all is said and done, the customer's balance was removed because it was collected, not written off, and the accounting records should reflect that fact.

**Coach's Tip**

Like the initial write-off, a recovery does not affect net income.

### Direct Write-Off Method

You should be aware that some small companies do not use the allowance method. Instead, they use an alternative approach called the **direct write-off method**. Using this single-step approach, these companies record bad debt expense only when they write off specific accounts. Although this alternative method is easier to use, it violates both the conservatism and matching principles. Thus, it is not considered a generally accepted accounting method. However, the Internal Revenue Service (IRS) accepts the use of this method for tax purposes, so we demonstrate it in Supplement 9A at the end of this chapter.

---

## Spotlight On **BUSINESS DECISIONS**

### Deciding Whether to Grant Credit

Given the costs of granting credit (recordkeeping, collections, bad debts), why do so many companies grant credit? As in most business decisions, the expected benefits of granting credit outweigh the costs. Consider the following example:

Nutware Productions Inc. generated sales of $30,000 and gross profit of $10,000 last year. The company estimates that it would have generated sales of $60,000 and gross profit of $20,000 by extending credit but would have incurred additional costs totaling $11,000 for recordkeeping, collections, and bad debts. Should the company have extended credit?

| | |
|---|---|
| Benefits (extra gross profit) ($20,000 − $10,000) | $10,000 |
| Costs (additional recordkeeping, collections & bad debts) | 11,000 |
| Gain (Loss) from granting credit | $ (1,000) |

In this example, the costs outweigh the benefits, so Nutware was better off by forgoing the additional sales that the company would have generated by granting credit. If the benefits had exceeded the costs, granting credit would have been the right decision.

---

**Solution to Self-Study Practice**

1.

| Credit sales this year | $216,850 |
|---|---|
| × Bad debt loss rate (2%) | × 0.02 |
| Bad debt expense this year | $ 4,337 |

| Allowance for Doubtful Accts | | |
|---|---|---|
| | 5,971 | Beg. Bal |
| Write-offs  3,979 | 4,337 | Estimate |
| | 6,329 | End. Bal. |

2.

| Desired balance | 6,329 | Credit |
|---|---|---|
| −Unadjusted **credit** balance* | 1,992 | Credit |
| **Required adjustment** | **4,337** | Credit |

*Beginning − Write-offs = Unadjusted Balance
$5,971 − $3,979 = $1,992

| Allowance for Doubtful Accts | | |
|---|---|---|
| | 5,971 | Beg. Bal |
| Write-offs  3,979 | 4,337 | Estimate |
| | 6,329 | End. Bal. |

Beginning + Bad Debt Estimate − Write-offs = Ending
$5,971 +      X      −  $3,979 = $6,329; X = $4,337

# NOTES RECEIVABLE AND INTEREST REVENUE

The accounting issues for notes receivable are similar to those for accounts receivable with one exception. Unlike accounts receivable, which do not normally incur interest until they become overdue, notes receivable start incurring interest the day they are created. Let's look at how to calculate the interest.

## Calculating Interest

To calculate interest, you need to consider three variables: (1) the **principal,** which is simply the amount of the note receivable, (2) the **interest rate** charged on the note, and (3) the **time** period covered in the interest calculation. Because **interest rates are always stated as an annual percentage even if the note is for less than a year,** the time period is the portion of a year for which the interest is calculated. Ask yourself how many months out of 12 or how many days out of 365 the interest period covers. Then use the following interest formula to calculate the interest:

$$\text{Interest (I)} = \text{Principal (P)} \times \text{Interest Rate (R)} \times \text{Time (T)}$$

*Coach's Tip*

When computing interest for partial years, be sure to multiply by the time period (number of months out of 12).

Many financial institutions use the number of days out of 365 to compute interest. In doing homework assignments, assume that the time is measured in terms of number of months out of 12. See Exhibit 9.3 for the computation of interest for three different notes, 6, 8, and 10 percent.

## Recording Notes Receivable and Interest Revenue

The four key events that occur with any note are (1) establishing the note, (2) accruing interest earned but not received, (3) recording interest payments received, and (4) recording principal payments received. Assume that on November 1, 2009, Skechers lent $100,000 to an inventor by creating a note that required the inventor to pay Skechers 6 percent interest and the $100,000 principal on October 31, 2010. Skechers prepared year-end financial statements as of December 31, 2009, but made no other adjustments for interest during the year.

### Establishing a Note Receivable

The $100,000 loan that created the note receivable has the following accounting equation effects, which Skechers would record using the following journal entry:

| | Debit | Credit |
|---|---|---|
| Note Receivable (+A) | 100,000 | |
| Cash (−A) | | 100,000 |

| Assets | | = | Liabilities | + | Owners' Equity |
|---|---|---|---|---|---|
| Note Receivable | +100,000 | | | | |
| Cash | −100,000 | | | | |

*Coach's Tip*

In multiplying to compute the interest, be sure to convert the interest rate from percentage to decimal format (from 6% to .06).

**Exhibit 9.3**　　Sample Interest Computations

| | | | INTEREST FORMULA | | | | |
|---|---|---|---|---|---|---|---|
| Terms | Principal | × | Interest Rate | × | Time | = | Interest |
| $6,000, 6%, 1 month | $6,000 | × | 6% | × | 1/12 | = | $ 30 |
| 7,000, 8%, 6 months | 7,000 | × | 8% | × | 6/12 | = | 280 |
| 9,000, 10%, 1 year | 9,000 | × | 10% | × | 1 | = | 900 |

**Exhibit 9.4**   Use of a Timeline to Keep Track of Interest Periods

## Accruing Interest Earned

Although a note receivable earns interest each day, interest payments might be made only once or twice a year. Thus, a company with a note receivable needs to accrue interest revenue and interest receivable at the end of each accounting period (unless it happens to receive an interest payment on the last day of the period).

The timeline in Exhibit 9.4 shows how Skechers should account for the interest revenue earned from the note over its one-year term. Note that between the date of the note's creation (November 1, 2009) and the year-end (December 31, 2009), Skechers earned two months of interest revenue (the yellow portion of the time line) because the note was outstanding for all of November and December 2009. As you learned in Chapter 4, when a company has earned interest in the current period but has not yet recorded the interest, the company must make an adjusting entry at the end of the current period to accrue the interest earned. The amount of interest to record for the two months of 2009 is computed as follows:

$$\text{Interest (I)} = \text{Principal (P)} \times \text{Interest Rate (I)} \times \text{Time (T)}$$
$$\$1,000 = \$100,000 \times 6\% \times 2/12$$

The effect of this adjustment, along with the adjusting journal entry to record the $1,000 of interest revenue receivable on December 31, 2009, is as follows.

| | Debit | Credit |
|---|---|---|
| Interest Receivable (+A) | 1,000 | |
| Interest Revenue (+R, +OE) | | 1,000 |

| Assets | = | Liabilities | + | Owners' Equity | |
|---|---|---|---|---|---|
| Interest Receivable    +1,000 | | | | Interest Revenue (+R)    +1,000 | |

**Coach's Tip**

Except for banks, interest is considered a peripheral source of revenue, so it is reported on the income statement immediately following the Income from Operations subtotal.

## Recording Interest Received

The timeline in Exhibit 9.4 indicates that on October 31, 2010, Skechers received a cash interest payment of $6,000 (= $100,000 × 6% × 12/12). This interest payment included the $1,000 accrued as interest receivable on December 31, 2009, plus the $5,000 earned during the 10-month period from January 1 to October 31, 2010, which had yet to be recorded. When Skechers received this interest, the company's accountant recorded the receipt of $6,000 in cash. Of that amount, $1,000 reduced the Interest Receivable, and the remaining of $5,000 was recorded as Interest Revenue for 2010.

|  | Debit | Credit |
|---|---|---|
| Cash (+A) | 6,000 | |
|     Interest Receivable (−A) | | 1,000 |
|     Interest Revenue (+R, +OE) | | 5,000 |

| Assets | | = Liabilities + | Owners' Equity | |
|---|---|---|---|---|
| Cash | +6,000 | | Interest Revenue (+R) | +5,000 |
| Interest Receivable | −1,000 | | | |

### Recording Principal Received

A company accounts for the collection of a note receivable just as it does the collection of an account receivable. Assuming that Skechers received the $100,000 principal that was due on October 31, 2010, the journal entry would be:

|  | Debit | Credit |
|---|---|---|
| Cash (+A) | 100,000 | |
|     Note Receivable (−A) | | 100,000 |

| Assets | | = | Liabilities | + | Owners' Equity |
|---|---|---|---|---|---|
| Cash | +100,000 | | | | |
| Note Receivable | −100,000 | | | | |

### Accounting for Uncollectible Notes

Just as a customer might fail to pay an accounts receivable balance, some companies might fail to pay the principal (and interest) owed on a note receivable. When a note receivable's collectibility is in doubt, the company should record an allowance for doubtful accounts against the note receivable, just as it records an allowance for doubtful accounts against accounts receivable.

---

**SELF-STUDY PRACTICE**

Assume that Mad Catz lent $12,000 to an employee on October 1, 2008, by creating a note that required that the employee pay the principal and 8 percent interest on September 30, 2009. Assume that the company makes adjusting entries only at year-end on December 31.

1. Record the creation of the note.
2. Record any necessary end-of-period adjusting entry to be made at the end of 2008.
3. Record the receipt of interest and principal on September 30, 2009.

*After you have finished, check your answers with the solution at the bottom of the page.*

**Solution to Self-Study Practice**

| | | Debit | Credit |
|---|---|---|---|
| 1. | Note Receivable (+A) | 12,000 | |
| |     Cash (−A) | | 12,000 |
| 2. | Interest Receivable (+A) ($12,000 × 8% × 3/12) | 240 | |
| |     Interest Revenue (+R, +OE) | | 240 |
| 3. | Cash (+A) ($12,000 × 8% × 12/12) | 960 | |
| |     Interest Receivable (−A) ($12,000 × 8% × 3/12) | | 240 |
| |     Interest Revenue (+R, +OE) ($12,000 × 8% × 9/12) | | 720 |
| | Cash (+A) | 12,000 | |
| |     Note Receivable (−A) | | 12,000 |

### Resetting the Clock

Earlier in this chapter you saw that as customer balances grow older, the Allowance for Doubtful Accounts should be increased. Because increases in the Allowance for Doubtful Accounts require increases in Bad Debt Expense, the result of an increase in the age of customer accounts should be a decrease in net income.

Managers at MCI knew about these accounting effects. To avoid reducing net income, they "reset the clock" on the amounts customers owed. They did so by making loans to customers, who then used the money to pay off their account balances. By replacing old accounts receivable with new notes receivable, managers avoided recording approximately $70 million in bad debts. Their scheme did not last for long, though. After the fraud was revealed, the managers involved spent several years in prison and are now working to pay off more than $10 million in fines.

# EVALUATING RECEIVABLES MANAGEMENT

## Receivables Turnover Analysis

Managers, directors, investors, and creditors can evaluate the effectiveness of a company's credit-granting and collection activities by performing a receivables turnover analysis. The idea behind the analysis is simple. When a company sells goods or services on credit, the receivables balance goes up; when the company collects from customers, the receivables balance goes down. This process of selling and collecting, called **receivables turnover,** is repeated over and over during each accounting period for each customer as in the following diagram.

**Learning Objective 5**

Compute and interpret the receivables turnover ratio.

**Receivables Turnover Analysis**

The receivables turnover ratio indicates how many times, on average, this process of selling and collecting is repeated during the period. The higher the ratio, the faster the collection of receivables. A low turnover ratio can be a warning sign, suggesting that the company is allowing too long a time for customers to pay. As you learned earlier in this chapter, the longer an account goes without being collected, the higher is the risk that it will never be collected. Analysts watch for changes in the receivables turnover ratio because a sudden decline may mean that a company is recording sales of merchandise that customers are likely to return later. It also may mean that the company is allowing customers more time to pay their accounts to entice them to buy as much as possible—a practice known as **channel stuffing.**

Rather than evaluate the **number** of times that accounts receivable turn over during the year, some people find it easier to think in terms of the **length** of time (in days) needed to collect accounts receivable (called **days to collect**). Converting the year's receivables turnover ratio into the average days to collect is easy. Simply divide 365 by the receivables turnover ratio. This alternative measure does not tell analysts anything more about the company's ability to collect receivables than the receivables turnover ratio does.

**Coach's Tip**

Days to collect is also called days sales outstanding.

| Financial Analysis Tools | | |
| --- | --- | --- |
| Name of Measure | Formula | What It Tells You |
| Receivables Turnover Ratio | $\dfrac{\text{Net Sales Revenue}}{\text{Average Net Receivables}}$ | • Number of times receivables turn over during the period<br>• A higher ratio means faster turnover |
| Days to Collect | $\dfrac{365}{\text{Receivables Turnover Ratio}}$ | • Average number of days from sale on account to collection<br>• A higher number means a longer time to collect |

Skechers' receivables turnover ratio and days to collect would be computed as follows:

$$\text{Receivables Turnover Ratio} = \frac{\text{Net Sales Revenue}}{\text{Average Net Receivables}} = \frac{\$1,205}{(\$177.7 + \$134.6)/2} = 7.7 \text{ times}$$

$$\text{Days to Collect} = \frac{365}{\text{Receivables Turnover Ratio}} = \frac{365 \text{ days}}{7.7 \text{ times}} = 47.4 \text{ days}$$

## Comparison to Benchmarks

### To Stated Credit Terms

By calculating the days to collect, you can compare a company's collection performance to its stated collections policy. You might recall from Chapter 6 that when companies sell on account, they specify the length of the credit period (as well as any discounts for prompt payment). By comparing the number of days to collect to the length of the credit period, you can gain a sense of whether customers are complying with the stated policy. Managers inside a company watch this measure closely, and so do investors and creditors on the outside. Why? If customers appear to be disregarding the stated credit period, they may be dissatisfied with the product or service they bought.

## Spotlight On FINANCIAL REPORTING

### Comparing Days to Collect with Stated Credit Terms          Kellogg

Kellogg is one of the rare companies that provides information about its normal credit policies in its annual report. In the notes to the financial statements, Kellogg indicates that the stated policy is to require payment from customers 11 to 16 days after making a sale. The company's collection period of 18 to 19 days suggests that customers are generally willing to comply.

> In the United States, the Company generally has required payment for goods sold eleven or sixteen days subsequent to the date of invoice as 2%,10 / net 11 or 1%,15 / net 16, and days sales outstanding (DSO) averages 18–19 days.

### To Other Companies or Prior Periods

Receivables turnover ratios and number of days to collect often vary across industries. Compare the ratios for Skechers, Boeing (an airplane manufacturer), and Deere & Co. (a farm implements company) in Exhibit 9.5. As the exhibit shows, Skechers turned its receivables over 7.7 times, or once every 47 days. Boeing had a turnover ratio of 11.7, which translates to a jet-fast collection period of about 31 days. Deere & Co. trailed behind with a ratio of 6.5, or about 56 days to collect.

Given the wide range in ratios among industries, a company's receivables turnover should be compared only to those of other companies in the same industry or to the company's own ratio from prior periods. For practice at computing these ratios and comparing them to those from prior periods, try the following Self-Study Practice, which asks you to calculate Skechers' receivables turnover ratio and days to collect in 2005.

**SELF-STUDY PRACTICE**

Skechers reported net accounts receivable of $134.6 on December 31, 2005, and $120.4 on December 31, 2004. Credit sales were $1,006 during 2005. (All numbers are in millions.) Use this information to calculate Skechers' receivables turnover and days to collect in 2005.

| 2005 Receivables Turnover | 2005 Days to Collect |
|---|---|
| $$\frac{\underline{\hspace{3cm}}}{(\underline{\hspace{2cm}} + \underline{\hspace{2cm}})/2} = \underline{\hspace{1cm}} \text{ times}$$ | $$\frac{365 \text{ days}}{\underline{\hspace{2cm}} \text{ times}} = \underline{\hspace{1cm}} \text{ days}$$ |

*When you have finished, check your answers with the solutions at the bottom of the next page.*

**Exhibit 9.5**    Receivables Turnover in Three Different Industries

| Company | Relevant Information (in millions) | | | 2006 Accounts Receivable Turnover Calculation | 2006 Days to Collect Calculation |
|---|---|---|---|---|---|
| | | 2006 | 2005 | | |
| **Skechers, Inc.** | Net sales | $1,205 | $1,006 | $\dfrac{\$1,205}{(\$177.7 + \$134.6)/2} = 7.7$ times | $\dfrac{365 \text{ days}}{7.7 \text{ times}} = 47.4$ days |
| | Net accounts receivable | $177.7 | $134.6 | | |
| | | 2006 | 2005 | | |
| **BOEING** | Net sales | $61,530 | $54,845 | $\dfrac{\$61,530}{(\$5,285 + \$5,246)/2} = 11.7$ times | $\dfrac{365 \text{ days}}{11.7 \text{ times}} = 31.2$ days |
| | Net accounts receivable | $ 5,285 | $ 5,246 | | |
| | | 2006 | 2005 | | |
| **Deere & Co.** | Net sales | $19,884 | $19,401 | $\dfrac{\$19,884}{(\$3,038 + \$3,118)/2} = 6.5$ times | $\dfrac{365 \text{ days}}{6.5 \text{ times}} = 56.2$ days |
| | Net accounts receivable | $ 3,038 | $ 3,118 | | |

## Spotlight On BUSINESS DECISIONS

### Factoring Receivables

To generate the cash needed to pay for a company's business activities, managers must ensure that the company collects receivables on a timely basis. You might wonder what managers can do to speed up sluggish collections. One approach is to sell outstanding accounts receivable to another company, called a **factor**. In this factoring arrangement, your company receives cash for the receivables it sells to the factor (minus a factoring fee), and the factor receives the right to collect the outstanding amounts your customers owe. In the same way that you can get cash immediately for any check you bring to a local Checks Cashed store, factoring is a fast and easy way for your company to get cash for receivables. This service does come at a cost, however. The factoring fee can amount to as much as 3 percent of the receivables sold.

## Demonstration Case A

Shooby Dooby Shoes (SDS) sold $950,000 in merchandise on credit during 2009. During the same year, SDS determined that a $500 account balance owed by a deceased customer (R. Cutler) was uncollectible.

*Required:*

1. Prepare the journal entry to record the write-off of R. Cutler's account receivable.
2. Assume that SDS uses the aging of accounts receivable method and has collected the information presented in the aging schedule that follows. As of December 31, 2009, the Allowance for

Solution to Self-Study Practice

$\dfrac{1,006}{\$(134.6 + 120.4)/2} = 7.9$ times    $365 \div 7.9 = 46.2$ days

Doubtful Accounts had an unadjusted credit balance of $3,000. Compute the desired balance for uncollectible accounts and prepare a journal entry to record the bad debt expense.

|  | Total | NUMBER OF DAYS UNPAID | | | |
|---|---|---|---|---|---|
|  |  | 0–30 | 31–60 | 61–90 | >90 |
| Total receivables | $171,000 | $50,000 | $80,000 | $40,000 | $1,000 |
| × Estimated bad debt % |  | × 1% | × 5% | × 15% | × 50% |
| = Estimated uncollectible |  |  |  |  |  |

3.  Assume SDS reported net accounts receivable of $160,000 on December 31, 2009, and $167,586 on December 31, 2008. Calculate the receivables turnover ratio for 2009.

4.  If the receivables turnover ratio was 6.4 in 2008, what was the number of days to collect in 2008? Given your calculations in requirement 3, were SDS collections in 2009 faster or slower than collections in 2008?

5.  Assume that SDS uses the percentage of credit sales method (rather than the aging of accounts receivable method) for estimating bad debt expense. If SDS estimates that 1 percent of credit sales will become bad debts, prepare the journal entry to record those effects.

## Suggested Solution

1.

| Allowance for Doubtful Accounts (−xA, +A) | 500 |  |
|---|---|---|
| Accounts Receivable (−A) |  | 500 |

2.  Using the aging of accounts receivable method, you first determine the desired balance in the Allowance for Doubtful Accounts ($11,000) and then subtract its unadjusted balance ($3,000) to determine the amount of the adjustment ($8,000 = $11,000 − 3,000).

|  | Total | NUMBER OF DAYS UNPAID | | | |
|---|---|---|---|---|---|
|  |  | 0–30 | 31–60 | 61–90 | >90 |
| Total receivable | $171,000 | $50,000 | $80,000 | $40,000 | $1,000 |
| × Estimated bad debt % |  | × 1% | × 5% | × 15% | × 50% |
| = Estimated uncollectible | $11,000 | $500 | $4,000 | $6,000 | $500 |

| Bad Debt Expense (+E, −OE) | 8,000 |  |
|---|---|---|
| Allowance for Doubtful Accounts (+xA, −A) |  | 8,000 |

3.  The receivables turnover ratio is calculated as Net Sales ÷ Average Accounts Receivable. The average accounts receivable in 2009 was $163,793 (= ($160,000 + $167,586)/2), so the receivables turnover ratio for 2009 was 5.8 (= $950,000 ÷ $163,793).

4.  Days to collect is calculated as 365 ÷ Receivables Turnover Ratio. The 6.4 turnover in 2008 equates to (365 ÷ 6.4 =) 57 days (and the 5.8 turnover in 2009 equates to 63 days). Collections were slower in 2009 than in 2008.

5.  In the percentage of credit sales method, you multiply historical bad debt losses (1%) by this period's credit sales ($950,000) to directly estimate the amount of bad debt expense to record ($9,500 = 1% × $950,000).

| Bad Debt Expense (+E, −OE) (0.01 × $950,000) | 9,500 |  |
|---|---|---|
| Allowance for Doubtful Accounts (+xA, −A) |  | 9,500 |

# Demonstration Case B

On March 1 of a recent year, Rocky Mountain Chocolate Factory, Inc. (RMCF) reported that the company had issued $120,000 of notes receivable at an annual interest rate of 10 percent. As a public company, RMCF prepares financial statements every quarter: on May 31, August 31, November 30, and February 28. Assume the notes were created on March 1, 2009, when RMCF lent money to another company and RMCF receives interest payments semiannually on July 31 and January 31.

**Required:**

1. Calculate the amount of interest that RMCF earned each month after issuing the notes on March 1.
2. Calculate the amount of the interest payments that RMCF will receive on July 31, 2009, and January 31, 2010.
3. Prepare a timeline showing the amount of interest earned and received during each period.
4. Prepare journal entries to record the note's issuance, the interest earned, and the interest payments received on each given date.

## Suggested Solution

1. Interest earned = Principal × Interest Rate × Time
   = $120,000 × 10% × 1/12 = $1,000 per month.

2. The period from March 1 to July 31 is five months. The period from August 1 to January 31 is six months.

   Interest Payment = Principal × Interest Rate × Time
   = $120,000 × 10% × 5/12 = $5,000 on July 31

   Interest Payment = Principal × Interest Rate × Time
   = $120,000 × 10% × 6/12 = $6,000 on January 31

3. Timeline

4. Journal Entries

March 1, 2009 (Notes Issued)

| | | |
|---|---|---|
| Notes Receivable (+A) | 120,000 | |
| Cash (−A) | | 120,000 |

May 31, 2009 (Interest Accrued)

| | | |
|---|---|---|
| Interest Receivable (+A) | 3,000 | |
| Interest Revenue (+R, +OE) | | 3,000 |

July 31, 2009 (Interest Payment Received)

| | | |
|---|---|---|
| Cash (+A) | 5,000 | |
| Interest Receivable (−A) | | 3,000 |
| Interest Revenue (+R, +OE) | | 2,000 |

August 31, 2009 (Interest Accrued)

| | | |
|---|---|---|
| Interest Receivable (+A) | 1,000 | |
| Interest Revenue (+R, +OE) | | 1,000 |

November 30, 2009 (Interest Accrued)

| | Debit | Credit |
|---|---|---|
| Interest Receivable (+A) | 3,000 | |
| Interest Revenue (+R, +OE) | | 3,000 |

January 31, 2010 (Interest Payment Received)

| | Debit | Credit |
|---|---|---|
| Cash (+A) | 6,000 | |
| Interest Receivable (−A) | | 4,000 |
| Interest Revenue (+R, +OE) | | 2,000 |

February 28, 2010 (Interest Accrued)

| | Debit | Credit |
|---|---|---|
| Interest Receivable (+A) | 1,000 | |
| Interest Revenue (+R, +OE) | | 1,000 |

## Supplement 9A

### Direct Write-Off Method

As noted earlier in this chapter, **the direct write-off method** is an alternative method of accounting for uncollectible accounts. This alternative approach does not estimate bad debts or use an allowance for doubtful accounts. Instead, you report sales when they occur and bad debt expense when you discover it. Again, although this method is acceptable for use on federal income tax returns, it is not acceptable for the preparation of financial statements under generally accepted accounting principles (GAAP).

The reason that the direct write-off method is not acceptable under GAAP is that it ignores both the conservatism concept and the matching principle. It violates the concept of conservatism by reporting accounts receivable at the total amount owed by customers (an overly optimistic amount) rather than at the smaller amount estimated to be collectible (a more realistic amount). It violates the matching principle by recording bad debt expense in the period when customer accounts are determined to be bad rather than in the period when the credit sales are actually made. The failure to match bad debt expense to sales distorts net income both in the period of the sale and in later periods when bad debts are discovered.

The direct write-off method makes no journal entries until the discovery of a bad debt. The journal entry used to record bad debt expense when a $1,000 customer account is determined to be uncollectible would be:

| | Debit | Credit |
|---|---|---|
| Bad Debt Expense (+E, −OE) | 1,000 | |
| Accounts Receivable (−A) | | 1,000 |

| Assets | | = | Liabilities | + | Owners' Equity | |
|---|---|---|---|---|---|---|
| Accounts Receivable | −1,000 | | | | Bad Debt Expense (+E) | −1,000 |

## Chapter Summary

### LO1  Identify the different types of receivables. p. 382

- A credit sale on open account creates an account receivable. A note receivable is a promise in writing (a formal document) to pay (1) a specified amount of money, called the principal, on a definite future date known as the maturity date and (2) a specified amount of interest on one or more future dates.

- A sale of merchandise or services on credit in the normal course of business creates a trade receivable. A nontrade receivable arises from transactions other than the normal sale of merchandise or services.
- Receivables are classified as either current or noncurrent (short term or long term), depending on when cash is expected to be collected.

## LO2  Account for and report the effects of uncollectible accounts. p. 383

- Under generally accepted accounting principles, companies must use the allowance method to account for uncollectibles. This method involves two steps:
    1. Estimate and record uncollectibles with an end-of-period adjusting entry that increases Bad Debt Expense (debit) and increases the Allowance for Doubtful Accounts (credit).
    2. Identify and write off specific customer balances in the period when they are determined to be uncollectible by decreasing the specific customer Account Receivable (credit) and decreasing the Allowance for Doubtful Accounts (debit).
- The adjusting entry (in 1) reduces net income as well as net accounts receivable. The write-off (in 2) affects neither.

## LO3  Use two different methods to estimate uncollectible accounts. p. 385

- The percentage of credit sales method estimates bad debt expense by multiplying the historical percentage of bad debt losses by the current year's credit sales.

$$\begin{array}{r} \text{Credit sales this year} \\ \times\ \text{Bad debt loss rate} \\ \hline \text{Bad debt expense this year} \end{array}$$

- The aging of accounts receivable method estimates bad debts based on the "age" of each amount in accounts receivable. The older and more overdue accounts receivable become, the less likely they are to be collected. Therefore, for each age category, we multiply an estimated bad debt loss percentage by the amount of the accounts receivable in that category. The total amount is the desired ending balance in the Allowance for Doubtful Accounts.

## LO4  Compute and report interest on notes receivable. p. 390

- Calculate interest on a note receivable by multiplying the principal, the interest rate, and the time period (the number of months out of 12). As time passes and interest is earned on the note, accountants record an adjusting entry to accrue the interest revenue receivable on the note.

## LO5  Compute and interpret the receivables turnover ratio. p. 393

- The receivables turnover ratio measures the effectiveness of credit-granting and collection activities. It reflects how many times, on average, a company recorded and collected trade receivables during the period.
- Analysts and creditors watch this ratio because a sudden decline may mean that a company is extending payment deadlines in an attempt to prop up lagging sales. Or it may mean that the company is recording sales of merchandise that customers are likely to return later.

### Financial Analysis Tools

| Name of Measure | Formula | What It Tells You |
|---|---|---|
| Receivables Turnover Ratio | $\dfrac{\text{Net Sales Revenue}}{\text{Average Net Receivables}}$ | • The number of times receivables turn over during the period<br>• A higher ratio means faster turnover ☺ |
| Days to Collect | $\dfrac{365}{\text{Receivables Turnover Ratio}}$ | • Average number of days from sale on account to collection<br>• A higher number means a longer time to collect ☹ |

## Key Terms

Account Receivable (p. 382)

Aging of Accounts Receivable Method (p. 386)

Allowance for Doubtful Accounts (p. 383)

Allowance Method (p. 383)

Bad Debt Expense (p. 383)

Direct Write-Off Method (p. 389)

Interest Formula (p. 390)

Note Receivable (p. 382)

Percentage of Accounts Receivable Method (p. 386)

Percentage of Credit Sales Method (p. 386)

Write-Off (p. 384)

See complete glossary in back of text.

# Questions

1. What determines whether receivables are current or noncurrent assets?

2. Which basic accounting principles does the allowance method of accounting for bad debts satisfy?

3. Using the allowance method, is bad debt expense recognized in the period in which (*a*) sales related to the uncollectible account were made or (*b*) the seller learns that the customer is unable to pay?

4. What is the effect of the write-off of uncollectible accounts (using the allowance method) on (*a*) net income and (*b*) net accounts receivable?

5. What is the primary difference between accounts receivable and notes receivable?

6. What are the three components of the interest formula? Explain how this formula adjusts for interest periods that are less than a full year.

7. Are interest revenues most appropriately recognized in the period in which (*a*) a note receivable has remained unpaid or (*b*) the company receives a cash payment for the interest?

8. Does an increase in the receivables turnover ratio generally indicate faster or slower collection of receivables? Explain.

9. What two approaches can managers take to speed up sluggish collections of receivables? List one advantage and one disadvantage for each approach.

10. (Supplement) Describe how (and when) the direct write-off method accounts for uncollectible accounts. What are the disadvantages of this method?

# Multiple Choice

1. When a company using the allowance method writes off a specific customer's account receivable from the accounting system, how many of the following are true?

   Quiz 9-1
   www.mhhe.com/LLPW1e

   - Total owners' equity remains the same.
   - Total assets remain the same.
   - Total expenses remain the same.

   a. None.          c. Two.
   b. One.           d. Three.

2. When using the allowance method, as bad debt expense is recorded,
   a. Total assets remain the same and owners' equity remains the same.
   b. Total assets decrease and owners' equity decreases.
   c. Total assets increase and owners' equity decreases.
   d. Total liabilities increase and owners' equity decreases.

3. You have determined that Carefree Company estimates bad debt expense using the aging of accounts receivable method. Generally, its estimate of uncollectible receivables resulting from the aging analysis equals:
   a. Bad debt expense for the current period.
   b. The ending balance in the Allowance for Doubtful Accounts for the period.
   c. The change in the Allowance for Doubtful Accounts for the period.
   d. None of the above.

4. Which of the following best describes the proper presentation of Accounts Receivable in the financial statements?
   a. Gross Accounts Receivable plus the Allowance for Doubtful Accounts in the asset section of the balance sheet.

   b. Gross Accounts Receivable in the asset section of the balance sheet and the Allowance for Doubtful Accounts in the expense section of the income statement.
   c. Gross Accounts Receivable less Bad Debt Expense in the asset section of the balance sheet.
   d. Gross Accounts Receivable less the Allowance for Doubtful Accounts in the asset section of the balance sheet.

5. If the Allowance for Doubtful Accounts had a beginning balance of $10,000, included write-offs of $5,000 (with no recoveries) during the period, and had a desired ending balance based on aging of $20,000, what was the amount of bad debt expense?
   a. $5,000.
   b. $10,000.
   c. $15,000.
   d. $20,000.

6. When an account receivable that has been written off is "recovered"
   a. Total assets increase.     c. Owners' equity increases.
   b. Total assets decrease.     d. None of the above.

7. If a 10 percent note receivable for $10,000 is created on January 1, 2006, and it has a maturity date of December 31, 2010,
   a. No interest revenue will be recorded in 2006.
   b. The note receivable will be classified as a current asset.
   c. Interest revenue of $1,000 will be recorded in 2006.
   d. None of the above.

8.  If a 12 percent note receivable for $20,000 is created on December 1, 2009, and interest and principal are due on November 30, 2010, what amount of interest revenue would be reported for the year ended December 31, 2009?
    a.  $2,400.              c.  $2,200.
    b.  $200.               d.  None of the above.

9.  If the receivables turnover ratio decreased during the year,
    a.  The days to collect also decreased.
    b.  Receivables collections slowed down.
    c.  Sales revenues increased at a faster rate than receivables increased.
    d.  None of the above.

10. In a recent year, Coca-Cola Company had a receivables turnover ratio of 10.2. Which of the following would cause the ratio to decrease?
    a.  Write off additional customer accounts receivable.
    b.  Increase the percentages used to estimate bad debts.
    c.  Lengthen credit terms from 30 to 60 days.
    d.  None of the above.

| Solutions to Multiple-Choice Questions |
| --- |
| 1. d    2. b    3. b    4. d    5. c    6. d    7. c |
| 8. b    9. b    10. c |

# Mini Exercises  Available with McGraw-Hill's Homework Manager

### M9-1 Recording Write-Offs and Bad Debt Expense Using the Allowance Method          LO2
Prepare journal entries for each transaction listed.

  a.  During the period, customer balances in the amount of $17,000 are written off.
  b.  At the end of the period, bad debt expense is estimated to be $14,000.

### M9-2 Determining Financial Statement Effects of Write-Offs and Bad Debt Expense Using the Allowance Method          LO2
Using the following categories, indicate the effects of the following transactions. Use + for increase and − for decrease and indicate the accounts affected and the amounts.

  a.  During the period, customer balances in the amount of $8,000 are written off.
  b.  At the end of the period, bad debt expense is estimated to be $10,000.

| Assets | = | Liabilities | + | Owners' Equity |
| --- | --- | --- | --- | --- |
| | | | | |

### M9-3 Reporting Accounts Receivable and Recording Write-Offs Using the Allowance Method          LO2
At the end of 2008, Extreme Fitness has adjusted balances of $800,000 in Accounts Receivable and $55,000 in the Allowance for Doubtful Accounts. On January 2, 2009, the company learns that certain customer accounts are not collectible, so management authorizes a write-off of these accounts totaling $5,000.

  a.  Show how the company would have reported its receivable accounts on December 31, 2008. As of that date, what amount did Extreme Fitness expect to collect?
  b.  Prepare the journal entry to write off the accounts on January 2, 2009.
  c.  Assuming no other transactions occurred between December 31, 2008, and January 3, 2009, show how Extreme Fitness would have reported its receivable accounts on January 3, 2009. As of that date, what amount did Extreme Fitness expect to collect? Has this changed from December 31, 2008? Explain why or why not.

### M9-4 Recording Recoveries Using the Allowance Method          LO2
Let's go a bit further with the example from M9-3. Assume that on February 2, 2009, Extreme Fitness received a payment of $500 from one of the customers whose balance had been written off. Prepare the journal entries to record this transaction.

### M9-5 Estimating Bad Debts Using the Percentage of Credit Sales Method          LO3
Assume Simple Co. had credit sales of $250,000 and cost of goods sold of $150,000 for the period. Simple uses the percentage of credit sales method and estimates that ½ percent of credit sales would result in uncollectible accounts. The balance in the Allowance for Doubtful Accounts before the end-of-period adjustment is made is $250. What amount of bad debt expense would the company record as an end-of-period adjustment?

**LO3**

**M9-6 Estimating Bad Debts Using the Aging Method**

Assume that Simple Co. had credit sales of $250,000 and cost of goods sold of $150,000 for the period. Simple uses the aging method and estimates that the appropriate ending balance in the Allowance for Doubtful Accounts is $1,500. The balance in the Allowance for Doubtful Accounts before the end-of-period adjustment is made is $250. What amount of bad debt expense would the company record as an end-of-period adjustment?

**LO4**

**M9-7 Using the Interest Formula to Compute Interest**

Complete the following table by computing the missing amounts (?) for the following independent cases.

| Principal Amount on Note Receivable | Annual Interest Rate | Time Period | Interest Earned |
|---|---|---|---|
| a. $ 100,000 | 10% | 6 months | ? |
| b.          ? | 10% | 12 months | $ 4,000 |
| c. $  50,000 | ? | 9 months | $ 3,000 |

**LO4**

**M9-8 Recording Note Receivable Transactions**

Scotia Corporation hired a new corporate controller and agreed to provide her with a $20,000 relocation loan on a six-month, 7 percent note. Prepare journal entries to record the following transactions for Scotia Corporation. Rather than using letters to refer to each transaction, use the date of the transaction.

    *a.*    The company loans the money on January 1, 2008.

    *b.*    The new employee pays Scotia the full principal and interest on its maturity date.

**LO4**

**M9-9 Recording Note Receivable Transactions**

RecRoom Equipment Company received an $8,000, six-month, 6 percent note to settle an $8,000 unpaid balance owed by a customer. Prepare journal entries to record the following transactions for RecRoom. Rather than using letters to reference each transaction, use the date of the transaction.

    *a.*    The note is accepted by RecRoom on November 1, 2008, causing the company to increase its notes receivable and decrease its accounts receivable.

    *b.*    RecRoom adjusts its records for interest earned to December 31, 2008.

    *c.*    RecRoom receives the principal and interest on the note's maturity date.

**LO5**

**M9-10 Determining the Effects of Credit Policy Changes on Receivables Turnover Ratio and Days to Collect**

Indicate the most likely effect of the following changes in credit policy on the receivables turnover ratio and days to collect (+ for increase, − for decrease, and NE for no effect).

    *a.*    Granted credit with shorter payment deadlines.

    *b.*    Increased effectiveness of collection methods.

    *c.*    Granted credit to less creditworthy customers.

**LO5**

**M9-11 Evaluating the Effect of Factoring on the Receivables Turnover Ratio and Computing the Cost of Factoring**

After noting that its receivables turnover ratio had declined, Imperative Company decided to sell $500,000 of receivables to a factoring company. The factor charges a factoring fee of 3 percent of the receivables sold. All else equal, how will this affect Imperative's receivables turnover ratio in the future? How much cash does Imperative receive on the sale? Calculate the factoring fee and describe how it is reported by Imperative Company.

**LO2**

**CATERPILLAR®**

**M9-12 Preparing Financial Statements**

Caterpillar, Inc., reported the following accounts and amounts (in millions) in its December 31, 2005, year-end financial statements. Prepare the current assets section of a classified balance sheet. Assume that the Allowance for Doubtful Accounts relates to Accounts Receivable rather than Notes Receivable.

| | | | |
|---|---|---|---|
| Accounts Payable | $3,471 | Long-Term Debt | $19,545 |
| Accounts Receivable | 7,828 | Long-Term Notes Receivable | 10,301 |
| Allowance for Doubtful Accounts | 302 | Notes Receivable—Current | 6,442 |
| Cash and Cash Equivalents | 1,108 | Other Current Assets | 2,490 |
| Inventories | 5,224 | Other Current Liabilities | 9,952 |
| Loans Payable—Current | 5,569 | Other Noncurrent Assets | 5,990 |
| | | Property, Plant, and Equipment, net | 7,888 |

### M9-13 (Supplement) Recording Write-Offs and Reporting Accounts Receivable Using the Direct Write-off Method

Complete all requirements of M9-3, except assume that Extreme Fitness uses the direct write-off method. Note that this means Extreme does not have an Allowance for Doubtful Accounts balance.

## Exercises  Available with McGraw-Hill's Homework Manager

### E9-1 Recording Bad Debt Expense Estimates and Write-Offs                                          LO2

During 2008, Blackhorse Productions, Inc., estimated bad debt losses of $9,750.

*Required:*

Prepare journal entries for each transaction.

   a.  On October 31, 2008, an account receivable for $1,000 from March 2008 was determined to be uncollectible and was written off.

   b.  The appropriate bad debt expense adjustment was recorded for the year 2008.

### E9-2 Determining Financial Statement Effects of Bad Debt Expense Estimates and Write-Offs                                          LO2

Using the following categories, indicate the effects of the transactions in E9-1. Use + for increase and − for decrease and indicate the accounts affected and the amounts.

| Assets | = | Liabilities | + | Owners' Equity |
|---|---|---|---|---|
| | | | | |

### E9-3 Recording and Determining the Effects of Write-Offs, Recoveries, and Bad Debt Expense Estimates on the Balance Sheet and Income Statement (Percentage of Sales Method)                                          LO2, 3

Academic Dishonesty Investigations Ltd. operates a plagiarism detection service for universities and community colleges. While most of its customers reliably pay amounts owed, the company has historically experienced a 2 percent rate of bad debts on credit sales. The company estimates bad debts with the percentage of credit sales method.

*Required:*

1. Prepare journal entries for each transaction below.

   a.  On March 31, 2008, 10 customers were billed for detection services totaling $25,000.

   b.  On October 31, 2008, a customer balance for $1,500 from a prior year was determined to be uncollectible and was written off.

   c.  On December 15, 2008, a customer paid an old balance of $900, which had been written off in a prior year.

   d.  On December 31, 2008, the appropriate bad debt expense adjustment was recorded for the year 2008.

2. Complete the following table, indicating the amount and effect (+ for increase, − for decrease, and NE for no effect) of each transaction.

| Transaction | Net Receivables | Net Sales | Income from Operations |
|---|---|---|---|
| *a.* | | | |
| *b.* | | | |
| *c.* | | | |
| *d.* | | | |

**LO2, 3**

### E9-4 Recording, Reporting, and Evaluating a Bad Debt Estimate (Percentage of Credit Sales Method)

During the year ended December 31, 2007, Kelly's Camera Shop had sales revenue of $170,000, of which $85,000 was on credit. At the start of 2007, Accounts Receivable showed a $10,000 debit balance, and the Allowance for Doubtful Accounts showed an $800 credit balance. Collections of accounts receivable during 2007 amounted to $68,000.

Data during 2007 follows:

a. On December 10, 2007, a customer balance of $1,500 from a prior year was determined to be uncollectible, so it was written off.

b. On December 31, 2007, a decision was made to continue the accounting policy of basing estimated bad debt losses on 2 percent of credit sales for the year.

*Required:*

1. Give the required journal entries for the two events in December 2007.
2. Show how the amounts related to Accounts Receivable and Bad Debt Expense would be reported on the income statement and balance sheet for 2007.
3. On the basis of the data available, does the 2 percent rate appear to be reasonable? Explain.

**LO2, 3**

### E9-5 Recording Write-Offs, Recoveries, and Bad Debt Expense Estimates (Aging Method)

Prior to recording the following, Elite Electronics, Incorporated had a credit balance of $2,000 in its allowance for doubtful accounts.

*Required:*

Prepare journal entries for each transaction.

a. On August 31, 2008, a customer balance for $300 from a prior year sale was determined to be uncollectible and was written off.

b. On December 15, 2008, the customer balance for $300 written off on August 31, 2008, was collected in full.

c. Based on an aging of accounts receivable, the company determined that the December 31 balance in the Allowance for Doubtful Accounts should be $5,600. On December 31, 2008, the appropriate bad debt adjustment was recorded.

**LO2, 3**

### E9-6 Determining Financial Statement Effects of Write-Offs, Recoveries, and Bad Debt Expense Estimates (Aging Method)

Using the following categories, indicate the effects of the transactions in E9-5.

Use + for increase and − for decrease and indicate the accounts affected and the amounts.

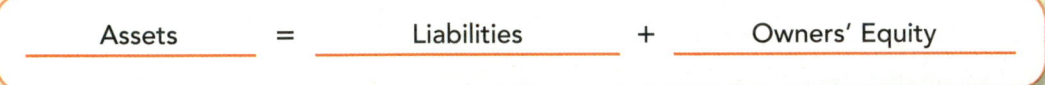

| Assets | = | Liabilities | + | Owners' Equity |
|---|---|---|---|---|

**LO2, 3**

### E9-7 Computing Bad Debt Expense Using Aging of Accounts Receivable Method

Young and Old Corporation (YOC) uses two aging categories to estimate uncollectible accounts. Accounts less than 60 days outstanding are considered young and have a 5 percent uncollectible rate. Accounts more than 60 days outstanding are considered old and have a 35 percent uncollectible rate.

*Required:*

1. If YOC has $10,000 of young accounts and $40,000 of old accounts, how much should be reported in the Allowance for Doubtful Accounts?
2. If YOC's Allowance for Doubtful Accounts currently has an unadjusted credit balance of $4,000, how much should be credited to the account?

3.  If YOC's Allowance for Doubtful Accounts has an unadjusted debit balance of $500, how much should be credited to the account?

4.  Explain how YOC's Allowance for Doubtful Accounts could have a debit balance.

### E9-8 Computing Bad Debt Expense Using Aging of Accounts Receivable Method    LO2, 3

Brown Cow Dairy uses the aging approach to estimate bad debt expense. The balance of each account receivable is aged on the basis of three time periods as follows: (1) 1–30 days old, $12,000, (2) 31–90 days old, $5,000, and (3) more than 90 days old, $3,000. Experience has shown that for each age group, the average loss rate on the amount of the receivable due to uncollectibility is (1) 3 percent, (2) 15 percent, and (3) 30 percent, respectively. At December 31, 2008 (end of the current year), the Allowance for Doubtful Accounts balance was $800 (credit) before the end-of-period adjusting entry is made.

#### Required:

1.  Prepare an aging schedule to estimate an appropriate year-end balance for the Allowance for Doubtful Accounts.

2.  What amount should be recorded as Bad Debt Expense for the current year?

3.  If the unadjusted balance in the Allowance for Doubtful Accounts was a $600 debit balance, what would be the amount of Bad Debt Expense in 2008?

### E9-9 Recording and Reporting Allowance for Doubtful Accounts Using Aging of Accounts Receivable Method    LO2, 3

InnovativeTech, Inc. uses the aging approach to estimate bad debt expense. The balance of each account receivable is aged on the basis of three time periods as follows: (1) 1–30 days old, $75,000, (2) 31–90 days old, $10,000, and (3) more than 90 days old, $4,000. Experience has shown that for each age group, the average loss rate on the amount of the receivable due to uncollectibility is (1) 1 percent, (2) 15 percent, and (3) 40 percent, respectively. At December 31, 2009 (end of the current year), the Allowance for Doubtful Accounts balance was $100 (credit) before the end-of-period adjusting entry is made.

#### Required:

1.  Prepare an aging schedule to estimate an appropriate year-end balance for the Allowance for Doubtful Accounts.

2.  Prepare the appropriate bad debt expense adjusting entry for the year 2009.

3.  Show how the various accounts related to accounts receivable should be shown on the December 31, 2009, balance sheet.

### E9-10 Comprehensive Recording and Reporting of Credit Sales and Bad Debts Using Aging    LO2, 3

Okay Optical, Inc. (OOI) began operations in January 2008 selling inexpensive sunglasses to large retailers like Walgreens and other smaller stores. Assume the following transactions occurred during its first six months of operations.

| January | 4 | Sold merchandise to Walgreens for $20,000; the cost of these goods to OOI was $12,000. |
| February | 2 | Received payment in full from Walgreens. |
| March | 9 | Sold merchandise to Tony's Pharmacy on account for $3,000; the cost of these goods to OOI was $1,400. |
| April | 22 | Sold merchandise to Travis Pharmaco on account for $8,000. The cost to OOI was $4,400. |
| May | 30 | Sold merchandise to Anjuli Stores on account for $2,000; the cost to OOI was $1,200. |
| June | 15 | Received $6,500 on account from Travis Pharmaco. |

#### Required:

1.  Complete the following aged listing of customer accounts as of June 30, 2008.

| Customer | Total Balance | June (1 month) | May (2 months) | April (3 months) | March (>3 months) |
|---|---|---|---|---|---|
| Anjuli Stores | $2,000 | | | | |
| Tony's Pharmacy | 3,000 | | | | |
| Travis Pharmaco | | | | | |
| Walgreens | | | | | |

2. Estimate the Allowance for Doubtful Accounts required at June 30, 2008, assuming the following uncollectible rates: one month, 1 percent; two months, 5 percent; three months, 20 percent; more than three months, 40 percent.

3. Show how OOI would report its accounts receivable on its June 30 balance sheet. What amounts would be reported on an income statement prepared for the six-month period ended June 30, 2008?

4. Bonus Question: In July 2008, OOI collected the balance due from Tony's Pharmacy but discovered that the balance due from Travis Pharmaco needed to be written off. Using this information, determine how accurate OOI was in estimating the Allowance for Doubtful Accounts needed for each of these two customers and in total.

**LO4**

### E9-11 Recording Note Receivable Transactions, Including Accrual Adjustment for Interest

The following transactions took place for Smart Solutions Ltd.

| 2007 | July 1 | Loaned $70,000 to an employee of the company and received back a one-year, 10 percent note. |
| | Dec. 31 | Accrued interest on the note. |
| 2008 | July 1 | Received interest and principal on the note. (No interest has been accrued since December 31.) |

*Required:*

Prepare the journal entries that Smart Solutions Ltd. would record for the above transactions.

**LO4**

### E9-12 Recording Note Receivable Transactions, Including Accrual Adjustment for Interest

The following transactions took place for Parker's Grocery.

| 2008 | Jan. 1 | Loaned $50,000 to a cashier of the company and received back a one-year, 7 percent note. |
| | June 30 | Accrued interest on the note. |
| | Dec. 31 | Received interest and principal on the note. (No interest has been accrued since June 30.) |

*Required:*

Prepare the journal entries that Parker's Grocery would record for the above transactions.

**LO4**

### E9-13 Recording Note Receivable Transactions, Including Accrual Adjustment for Interest

To attract retailers to its shopping center, the Marketplace Mall will lend money to tenants under formal contracts, provided that they use it to renovate their store space. On November 1, 2008, the company loaned $100,000 to a new tenant on a one-year note with a stated annual interest rate of 6 percent. Interest is to be received by Marketplace Mall on April 30, 2009, and at maturity on October 31, 2009.

*Required:*

Prepare journal entries that Marketplace Mall would record related to this note on the following dates: (*a*) November 1, 2008; (*b*) December 31, 2008 (Marketplace Mall's fiscal year-end); (*c*) April 30, 2009; and (*d*) October 31, 2009.

**LO2, 5**

Microsoft

### E9-14 Using Financial Statement Disclosures to Infer Write-Offs and Bad Debt Expense and to Calculate the Receivables Turnover Ratio

Microsoft develops, produces, and markets a wide range of computer software including the Windows operating system. Microsoft reported the following information about net sales revenue and accounts receivable (in millions).

| | June 30, Current Year | June 30, Prior Year |
|---|---|---|
| Accounts receivable, net of allowances of $142 and $171 | $ 9,316 | $ 7,180 |
| Net revenues | 44,282 | 39,788 |

According to its Form 10-K, Microsoft recorded bad debt expense of $40 and did not recover any previously written off accounts during the current year.

*Required:*

1. What amount of accounts receivable was written off during the current year? (Hint: Construct the T-account for the Allowance for Doubtful Accounts and solve for the missing number.)
2. What was Microsoft's receivables turnover ratio for the current year?

**E9-15 Using Financial Statement Disclosures to Infer Bad Debt Expense**    LO2

The annual report for Sears Holding Corporation contained the following information (in millions):    Sears

|  | Prior Year | Current Year |
|---|---|---|
| Accounts receivable | $686 | $846 |
| Allowance for doubtful accounts | (40) | (35) |
| Accounts receivable, net | $646 | $811 |

A footnote to the financial statements disclosed that accounts receivable write-offs amounted to $92 during the current year. Assume Sears did not record any recoveries.

*Required:*

Determine the bad debt expense for the current year based on the above facts. (Hint: Construct the T-account for the Allowance for Doubtful Accounts and solve for the missing number.)

**E9-16 Determining the Effects of Uncollectible Accounts on the Receivables Turnover Ratio**    LO2, 5

Complete the following table indicating the direction of the effect (+ for increase, – for decrease, and NE for no effect) of each transaction during 2009:

| Transaction | Net Credit Sales | Average Net Accounts Receivable | Receivables Turnover Ratio |
|---|---|---|---|
| a. Writing off of $92,000,000 in uncollectible accounts. | | | |
| b. Recording bad debt expense. | | | |

**E9-17 Analyzing and Interpreting Receivables Turnover Ratio and Days to Collect**    LO5

A recent annual report for FedEx Corporation contained the following data (in millions):    FedEx

| | MAY 31, | |
|---|---|---|
| | Current Year | Prior Year |
| Accounts receivable | $3,660 | $3,422 |
| Less: Allowance for doubtful accounts | 144 | 125 |
| Net accounts receivable | $3,516 | $3,297 |
| Net sales (assume all on credit) | $32,294 | |

*Required:*

1. Determine the accounts receivable turnover ratio and days to collect for the current year.
2. Explain the meaning of each number.

**LO2, 5**

### E9-18 Determining the Effects of Bad Debts on Receivables Turnover Ratio

During 2008, Jesse Enterprises Corporation recorded credit sales of $650,000. Based on prior experience, the company estimates a 1 percent bad debt rate on credit sales. At the beginning of the year, the balance in Net Trade Accounts Receivable was $50,000. At the end of the year, but *before* the bad debt expense adjustment was recorded and before any bad debts had been written off, the balance in Net Trade Accounts Receivable was $55,500.

**Required:**

1.  Assume that on December 31, 2008, the appropriate bad debt expense adjustment was recorded for the year 2008, and accounts receivable totaling $6,000 for the year were determined to be uncollectible and written off. What was the receivables turnover ratio for 2008?
2.  Assume instead that on December 31, 2008, the appropriate bad debt expense adjustment was recorded for the year 2008, and $7,000 of accounts receivable was determined to be uncollectible and written off. What was the receivables turnover ratio for 2008?
3.  Explain why the answers to requirements 1 and 2 differ or do not differ.

### E9-19 (Supplement) Recording Write-Offs and Reporting Accounts Receivable Using the Direct Write-Off Method

Trevorson Electronics is a small company privately owned by Jon Trevorson, an electrician who installs wiring in new homes. Because the company's financial statements are prepared only for tax purposes, Jon uses the direct write-off method. During 2007, its first year of operations, Trevorson Electronics sold $30,000 of services on account. The company collected $26,000 of these receivables during the year, and Jon believed that the remaining $4,000 was fully collectible. In 2008, Jon discovered that none of the $4,000 would be collected, so he wrote off the entire amount. To make matters worse, Jon sold only $5,000 of services during the year.

**Required:**

1.  Prepare journal entries to record the transactions in 2007 and 2008.
2.  Using only the information provided (ignore other operating expenses), prepare comparative income statements for 2007 and 2008. Was 2007 really as profitable as indicated by its income statement? Was 2008 quite as bad as indicated by its income statement? What should Jon do if he wants better information for assessing his company's ability to generate profit?

## Problems—Set A     Available with McGraw-Hill's Homework Manager

**LO2, 3**

**Kraft Foods**

### PA9-1 Recording Accounts Receivable Transactions Using the Allowance Method

Kraft Foods Inc. is the second-largest food and beverage company in the world. Assume the company recently reported the following amounts in its unadjusted trial balance as of December 31, 2007 (all amounts in millions):

|  | Debits | Credits |
| --- | --- | --- |
| Accounts Receivable | $3,900 | |
| Allowance for Doubtful Accounts | | $    110 |
| Sales | | 32,010 |

**Required:**

1.  Assume Kraft uses the aging of accounts receivable method and estimates that $233 of accounts receivable will be uncollectible. Prepare the adjusting journal entry required at December 31, 2007, for recording bad debt expense.
2.  Repeat requirement 1, except this time assume the unadjusted balance in Kraft's Allowance for Doubtful Accounts at December 31, 2007, was a debit balance of $20.
3.  If one of Kraft's main customers declared bankruptcy in 2008, what journal entry would be used to write off its $15 balance?

4. Assume Kraft uses ½ of 1 percent of sales to estimate its bad debt expense for the year. If you also assume that no bad debt expense has been recorded for 2007, what adjusting journal entry would be required at December 31, 2007, for bad debt expense?

## PA9-2 Interpreting Disclosure of Allowance for Doubtful Accounts

LO2

Stride Rite, Corp., designs, develops, and markets performance-oriented athletic footwear, athletic apparel, and casual leather footwear. It recently disclosed the following information concerning the Allowance for Doubtful Accounts.

**Stride Rite**

### VALUATION AND QUALIFYING ACCOUNTS (DOLLARS IN THOUSANDS)

| Allowance for Doubtful Accounts | Balance at Beginning of Year | Additions Charged to Bad Debt Expense | Deductions from Allowance | Balance at End of Year |
|---|---|---|---|---|
| | $1,547 | $1,400 | $1,638 | $1,309 |

*Required:*

1. Record summary journal entries for the year related to (*a*) estimating bad debt expense and (*b*) writing off specific balances.
2. Create a T-account for the Allowance for Doubtful Accounts and enter into it the amounts from the above schedule. Then write the T-account in equation format to prove that the above items account for the changes in the account.
3. If Stride Rite had written off an additional $200 of accounts receivable during the year, how would net receivables have been affected? How would net income have been affected? Explain why.

## PA9-3 Recording Notes Receivable Transactions

LO4

C&S Marketing (CSM) recently hired a new marketing director, Jeff Otos, for its downtown Minneapolis office. As part of the arrangement, CSM agreed on February 28, 2007, to advance Jeff $50,000 on a one-year, 8 percent note, with interest to be paid at maturity on February 28, 2008. CSM prepares financial statements on June 30 and December 31.

www.mhhe.com/LLPW1e

*Required:*

1. Prepare the journal entry that CSM will make to record the establishment of the note.
2. Prepare the journal entries that CSM will make to accrue interest on June 30 and December 31.
3. Prepare the journal entry that CSM will make to record the interest and principal payments on February 28, 2008.

## PA9-4 Recording and Reporting Accounts Receivable and Notes Receivable Transactions

LO2, 4

Merle Adventures, Inc., is a distributor of kayaks, kayaking equipment, and kayaking accessories. The company ships mainly to retail stores in the northeastern United States. Most of its sales are made on account, but some particularly large orders are sold in exchange for notes receivable. Merle Adventures reported the following balances in its December 31, 2008, unadjusted trial balance:

www.mhhe.com/LLPW1e

| | Debit | Credit |
|---|---|---|
| Accounts Receivable | $2,700,000 | |
| Allowance for Doubtful Accounts | | $ 11,000 |
| Bad Debt Expense | 0 | |
| Interest Receivable | 0 | |
| Interest Revenue | | 0 |
| Notes Receivable | 20,000 | |

Notes Receivable consists of principal owed by a customer on a two-year, 6 percent note accepted on November 1, 2008. The note requires the customer to make annual interest payments on October 31, 2009 and 2010. Merle Adventures has no concerns about the collectibility of this note. Merle Adventures estimates that $25,000 of its accounts receivable will be uncollectible.

*Required:*

1. Prepare the December 31, 2008, adjusting journal entries related to Accounts Receivable and Notes Receivable.
2. Show how the adjusted balances for the above balance sheet accounts will be reported on Merle Adventures' classified balance sheet as of December 31, 2008.

**LO2, 5**

Coca-Cola
PepsiCo

www.mhhe.com/LLPW1e

### PA9-5 Analyzing Allowance for Doubtful Accounts, Receivables Turnover Ratio, and Days to Collect

Coca-Cola and PepsiCo are two of the largest and most successful beverage companies in the world in terms of the products that they sell and in terms of their receivables management practices. To evaluate their ability to collect on credit sales, consider the following information reported in their 2005, 2004, and 2003 annual reports (amounts in millions).

|  | COCA-COLA | | | PEPSICO | | |
|---|---|---|---|---|---|---|
| Fiscal Year Ended | 2005 | 2004 | 2003 | 2005 | 2004 | 2003 |
| Net sales | $23,104 | $21,742 | $20,857 | $32,562 | $29,261 | $26,971 |
| Accounts receivable | $ 2,353 | $ 2,313 | $ 2,152 | $ 3,261 | $ 2,999 | $ 2,830 |
| Allowance for doubtful accounts | 72 | 69 | 61 | 105 | 116 | 121 |
| Accounts receivable, net of allowance | $ 2,281 | $ 2,244 | $ 2,091 | $ 3,156 | $ 2,883 | $ 2,709 |

*Required:*

Calculate the receivables turnover ratios and days to collect for Coca-Cola and PepsiCo for 2005 and 2004. (Round to one decimal place.) Which of the companies is quicker to convert its receivables into cash?

## Problems—Set B     **Available with McGraw-Hill's Homework Manager**

**LO2, 3**

### PB9-1 Recording Accounts Receivable Transactions Using the Allowance Method

Intel Corporation is a well-known supplier of computer chips, boards, systems, and software building blocks. Assume the company recently reported the following amounts in its unadjusted trial balance as of December 31, 2008 (all amounts in millions):

|  | Debits | Credits |
|---|---|---|
| Accounts Receivable | $3,300 | |
| Allowance for Doubtful Accounts | | $    65 |
| Sales | | 32,404 |

*Required:*

1. Assume Intel uses the aging of accounts receivable method and estimates that $200 of accounts receivable will be uncollectible. Prepare the adjusting journal entry required at December 31, 2008, for recording bad debt expense.
2. Repeat requirement 1, except this time assume the unadjusted balance in Intel's Allowance for Doubtful Accounts at December 31, 2008, was a debit balance of $20.
3. If one of Intel's main customers declared bankruptcy in 2009, what journal entry would be used to write off its $15 balance?
4. Assume Intel uses ¼ of 1 percent of sales to estimate its bad debt expense for the year. If you also assume that no bad debt expense has been recorded for 2008, what adjusting journal entry would be required at December 31, 2008, for bad debt expense?

**LO2**

xerox

### PB9-2 Interpreting Disclosure of Allowance for Doubtful Accounts

Xerox Corporation is the company that made the photocopier popular, although it now describes itself as a technology and services enterprise that helps businesses deploy document management strategies and improve productivity. It recently disclosed the following information concerning the Allowance for Doubtful Accounts.

### VALUATION AND QUALIFYING ACCOUNTS (DOLLARS IN MILLIONS)

| Allowance for Doubtful Accounts | Balance at Beginning of Year | Additions Charged to Bad Debt Expense | Deductions from Allowance | Balance at End of Year |
|---|---|---|---|---|
| | $459 | $72 | $166 | $365 |

*Required:*

1. Record summary journal entries for the year related to (*a*) estimating bad debt expense and (*b*) writing off specific balances.
2. Create a T-account for the Allowance for Doubtful Accounts and enter into it the amounts from the above schedule. Then, write the T-account in equation format to prove that the above items account for the changes in the account.
3. If Xerox had written off an additional $20 of accounts receivable during the year, how would net accounts receivable have been affected? How would net income have been affected? Explain why.

### PB9-3 Recording Notes Receivable Transactions

LO4

Stinson Company recently agreed to loan an employee $100,000 for the purchase of a new house. The loan was established on May 31, 2007, and is a one-year, 6 percent note, with interest payments required on November 30, 2007, and May 31, 2008. Stinson Co. issues quarterly financial statements on March 31, June 30, September 30, and December 31.

*Required:*

1. Prepare the journal entry that Stinson Co. will make to record the establishment of the note.
2. Prepare the journal entries that Stinson Co. will make to record the interest accruals at each quarter-end and interest payments at each payment date.
2. Prepare the journal entry that Stinson Co. will make to record the principal payment at the maturity date.

### PB9-4 Recording and Reporting Accounts Receivable and Notes Receivable Transactions

LO2, 4

Tractors-R-Us is a supplier of garden tractors. Most of its sales are made on account, but some particularly large orders are sold in exchange for notes receivable. Tractors-R-Us reported the following balances in its December 31, 2007, unadjusted trial balance:

| | Debit | Credit |
|---|---|---|
| Accounts Receivable | $1,650,000 | |
| Allowance for Doubtful Accounts | | $ 16,000 |
| Bad Debt Expense | 0 | |
| Interest Receivable | 0 | |
| Interest Revenue | | 0 |
| Notes Receivable | 115,000 | |

Notes receivable consists of principal owed by a customer on a two-year, 5 percent note accepted on July 1, 2007. The note requires the customer to make annual interest payments on June 30, 2008 and 2009. Tractors-R-Us has no concerns about the collectibility of this note. Tractors-R-Us does estimate, however, that $25,000 of its accounts receivable will be uncollectible.

*Required:*

1. Prepare the December 31, 2007, adjusting journal entries related to accounts receivable and notes receivable.
2. Show how the adjusted balances for the above balance sheet accounts will be reported on Tractors-R-Us's classified balance sheet as of December 31, 2007.

**LO2, 5**
Wal-Mart
Target

**PB9-5 Analyzing Allowance for Doubtful Accounts, Receivables Turnover Ratio, and Days to Collect**

Wal-Mart and Target are two of the largest and most successful retail chains in the world. To evaluate their ability to collect on credit sales, consider the following information reported in their 2005 and 2004 annual reports (amounts in millions).

| Fiscal Year Ended | WAL-MART | | | TARGET | | |
|---|---|---|---|---|---|---|
| | 2005 | 2004 | 2003 | 2005 | 2004 | 2003 |
| Net sales | $312,427 | $285,222 | $256,329 | $52,620 | $46,839 | $42,025 |
| Gross accounts receivable | $ 2,662 | $ 1,715 | $ 1,254 | $ 6,117 | $ 5,456 | $ 4,973 |
| Allowance for doubtful accounts | 186 | 129 | 90 | 451 | 387 | 352 |
| Accounts receivable, net of allowance | $ 2,476 | $ 1,586 | $ 1,164 | $ 5,666 | $ 5,069 | $ 4,621 |

*Required:*

Calculate the receivables turnover ratios and days to collect for Wal-Mart and Target for 2005 and 2004. (Round to one decimal place.) Which of the companies is quicker to convert its receivables into cash?

# Cases and Projects

**LO2, 5**

**CP9-1 Finding Financial Information**

Refer to the financial statements of The Home Depot in Appendix A at the end of this book, or download the annual report from the *Cases* section of the text's Web site at www.mhhe.com/LLPW1e.

1.  Does the company report an Allowance for Doubtful Accounts on the balance sheet or in the notes? Explain why it does or does not. (*Hint:* The company refers to its Allowance for Doubtful Accounts as a "Valuation Reserve" related to Accounts Receivable.)

2.  Compute the company's receivables turnover ratio and days to collect for the most recent year.

**LO2, 5**
Lowe's

**CP9-2 Comparing Financial Information**

Refer to the financial statements of Lowe's in Appendix B at the end of this book, or download the annual report from the *Cases* section of the text's Web site at www.mhhe.com/LLPW1e.

1.  Does the company report Accounts Receivable or an Allowance for Doubtful Accounts in its financial statements? Explain why it does or does not.

2.  Based on your observations for requirement 1, describe the usefulness of the receivables turnover ratio and days to collect analyses for companies that are involved in home improvement retail sales.

**LO1, 2, 5**

**CP9-3 Internet-Based Team Research: Examining an Annual Report**

As a team, select an industry to analyze. Using your Web browser, each team member should acquire the annual report or 10-K for one publicly traded company in the industry, with each member selecting a different company. (See CP1-3 in Chapter 1 for a description of possible resources for these tasks.)

*Required:*

1.  On an individual basis, each team member should write a short report that incorporates the following:

    a.  Calculate the receivables turnover ratio for the current and prior years, and explain any change between the two years. (To obtain the beginning accounts receivable number for the prior year, you will need the prior year's annual report.)

    b.  Look in the 10-K for the Schedule II analysis of "Valuation and Qualifying Accounts," which provides additional disclosures concerning the allowance for doubtful accounts. From this schedule, determine the level of bad debt expense, as a percentage of sales, for the current and prior years.

2.  Then, as a team, write a short report comparing and contrasting your companies using these attributes. Discuss any patterns across the companies that you as a team observe. Provide potential explanations for any differences discovered.

**CP9-4 Ethical Decision Making: A Mini-Case**                    LO2, 3, 5

Having just graduated with a business degree, you are excited to begin working as a junior accountant at Clear Optics, Inc. The company supplies lenses, frames, and sunglasses to opticians and retailers throughout the country. Clear Optics is currently in the process of finalizing its third quarter (Q3) operating results. All Q3 adjusting entries have been made, except for bad debt expense. The preliminary income statement for Q3 is shown below, along with reported results for Q2 and Q1.

**Clear Optics, Inc.**
**Quarterly Income Statements**
**(amounts in thousands of U.S. dollars)**

|  | Q3 (preliminary) | Q2 (as reported) | Q1 (as reported) |
|---|---|---|---|
| Net sales | $ 135,800 | $ 135,460 | $ 130,100 |
| Cost of goods sold | 58,400 | 58,250 | 55,990 |
| Gross profit | 77,400 | 77,210 | 74,110 |
| Selling, general, and administrative expenses | 56,560 | 53,975 | 53,690 |
| Bad debt expense | — | 6,050 | 4,200 |
| Income before income taxes | 20,840 | 17,185 | 16,220 |
| Income tax expense | 5,620 | 5,155 | 5,020 |
| Net income | $ 15,220 | $ 12,030 | $ 11,200 |

The corporate controller has asked you to examine the Allowance for Doubtful Accounts and use the aged listing of accounts receivable to determine the adjustment needed to record estimated bad debts for the quarter. The controller states, "Although our customers are somewhat slower in paying this quarter, we can't afford to increase the Allowance for Doubtful Accounts. If anything, we need to decrease it—an adjusted balance of about $8,000 is what I'd like to see. Play around with our estimated bad debt loss rates until you get it to work."

You were somewhat confused by what the controller had told you, but you chalked it up to your lack of experience and decided to analyze the Allowance for Doubtful Accounts. You summarized the transactions recorded in the Allowance for Doubtful Accounts using the T-account below:

**Allowance for Doubtful Accounts (xA)**

|  |  |  |  |
|---|---|---|---|
|  |  | 7,900 | January 1 bal. fwd. |
| Q1 Write-offs | 4,110 | 4,200 | Q1 Bad debts estimate |
|  |  | 7,990 | March 31 adjusted |
| Q2 Write-offs | 4,120 | 6,050 | Q2 Bad debts estimate |
|  |  | 9,920 | June 30 adjusted |
| Q3 Write-offs | 4,030 | — |  |
|  |  | 5,890 | September 30 unadjusted |

**Required:**

1.  What bad debts estimate for Q3 will produce the $8,000 balance that the controller would like to see?
2.  Prepare the adjusting journal entry that would be required to record this estimate.
3.  If the entry in requirement 2 is made, what does it do to the Q3 income and the trend in earnings? (Assume that income tax expense does not change.)
4.  Reconsider the statement the controller made to you. Is his suggestion a logical way to use the aging method to estimate bad debts?
5.  What would be the Q3 net income if the bad debt expense estimate was the average of bad debt expense in Q2 and Q1? What would this do to the trend in net income across the three quarters? (Assume that income tax expense does not change.)
6.  Is there any evidence of unethical behavior in this case? Explain your answer.

LO3     **CP9-5 Using an Aging Schedule to Estimate Bad Debts and Improve Collections from Customers**

Assume you were recently hired by Caffe D'Amore, the company that formulated the world's first flavored instant cappuccino and now manufactures several lines of flavored cappuccino mixes. The company recently has experienced tremendous growth in its sales to retailers, given that there are an estimated 8 million weekly drinkers of iced cappuccino nationwide. Given its tremendous sales growth, Caffe D'Amore's receivables also have grown. Your job is to evaluate and improve collections of the company's receivables.

By analyzing collections of accounts receivable over the past five years, you were able to estimate bad debt loss rates for balances of varying ages. To estimate this year's uncollectible accounts, you jotted down the historical loss rates on the last page of a recent aged listing of outstanding customer balances (see below).

| Customer | Total | NUMBER OF DAYS UNPAID | | | | |
|---|---|---|---|---|---|---|
| | | 1–30 | 31–60 | 61–90 | 91–120 | Over 120 |
| Subtotal from previous page | $280,000 | $150,000 | $60,000 | $40,000 | $20,000 | $10,000 |
| Jumpy Jim's Coffee | 1,000 | | | | | 1,000 |
| Pasadena Coffee Company | 24,500 | 14,500 | 8,000 | 2,000 | | |
| Phillips Blender House | 17,000 | 12,000 | 4,000 | | 1,000 | |
| Pugsly's Trading Post | 26,600 | 19,600 | 7,000 | | | |
| Q-Coffee | 12,400 | 8,400 | 3,000 | 1,000 | | |
| Special Sips | 10,000 | 6,000 | 4,000 | | | |
| Uneasy Isaac's | 3,500 | 500 | | | | 3,000 |
| Total accounts receivable | 375,000 | 211,000 | 86,000 | 43,000 | 21,000 | 14,000 |
| Bad debt loss rates | | 1% | 5% | 10% | 15% | 30% |

***Required:***

1.  With a spreadsheet, use the above information to calculate the total estimated uncollectible accounts.

2.  Prepare the year-end adjusting journal entry to adjust the Allowance for Doubtful Accounts to the balance you calculated above. Assume the allowance account has an unadjusted credit balance of $8,000.

3.  Of the customer account balances shown above on the last page of the aged listing, which should be your highest priority for contacting and pursuing collection?

4.  Assume Jumpy Jim's Coffee account is determined to be uncollectible. Prepare the journal entry to write off the entire account balance.

# 10 Long-Lived Tangible and Intangible Assets

## LEARNING OBJECTIVES

**After completing this chapter, you should be able to:**

**LO1** Define, classify, and explain the nature of long-lived assets.

Lectured slideshow–LP10-1
www.mhhe.com/LLPW1e

**LO2** Apply the cost principle to the acquisition of long-lived assets.

**LO3** Apply various depreciation methods as economic benefits are used up over time.

**LO4** Explain the effect of asset impairment on the financial statements.

**LO5** Account for the disposal of long-lived tangible assets that are discarded or sold.

**LO6** Account for the acquisition, use, and disposal of long-lived intangible assets.

**LO7** Interpret the fixed asset turnover ratio.

**LO8** Describe the factors to consider when comparing long-lived assets across companies.

## Focus Company: CEDAR FAIR

### Owner of the "Best Amusement Park in the World"

www.cedarfair.com

Most people agonize over how much money to spend on a house or which car to buy. After all, they will own these expensive items for many years to come. The same concerns exist when companies acquire long-lived assets. One of the major challenges business managers face is determining the right amount to invest in long-lived assets.

The task is especially challenging for companies such as Disney, Six Flags, and Cedar Fair, which operate amusement parks. Unlike merchandising companies, an amusement park cannot build up an inventory of unused seats to be sold sometime in the future. If managers build more rides than needed to satisfy park-goers, some rides will run with empty seats. Although the company will still incur all the costs of running the rides, it will generate only a fraction of the potential revenue. On the other hand, amusement parks can also run into trouble if they have too few rides to satisfy patrons. Who wants to stand in line for an hour or more? Because most people want to ride the newest, most exciting rides they can find, amusement park managers are always having to decide whether to buy new rides.

In this chapter, by studying specific long-lived asset decisions at Cedar Fair, you will see the significant effect that long-lived assets can have on a company's financial statements. Although manufacturing companies, retailers, and even airlines must deal with the same issues as Cedar Fair, the impact on this amusement park company is particularly significant because it relies almost exclusively on long-lived assets. As of December 31, 2007, in fact, Cedar Fair's rides, hotels, and other long-lived assets accounted for more than 97 percent of its total assets.

| DEFINITION AND CLASSIFICATION | TANGIBLE ASSETS: ACQUISITION, USE, IMPAIRMENT, AND DISPOSAL | INTANGIBLE ASSETS: TYPES, ACQUISITION, USE, AND DISPOSAL | EVALUATION OF LONG-LIVED ASSET USE |
|---|---|---|---|
| • Tangible Assets<br>• Intangible Assets | • Acquisition of Tangible Assets<br>• Use of Tangible Assets<br>• Impairment of Tangible Assets<br>• Disposal and Exchange of Tangible Assets | • Types of Intangible Assets<br>• Acquisition, Use, and Disposal of Intangible Assets | • Turnover Analysis<br>• Impact of Differences in Depreciation |

# DEFINITION AND CLASSIFICATION

**Learning Objective 1**

Define, classify, and explain the nature of long-lived assets.

Long-lived assets are business assets acquired for use over one or more years. These assets are not intended for resale. Instead, they are considered "productive" assets in the sense that they enable the business to produce the goods or services that the business then sells to customers. Examples include the ovens in which Pizza Aroma bakes pizza, the stores where Wal-Mart sells merchandise, and the legal rights that restrict use of The UPS Store logo to companies authorized by UPS. So when you hear the term "long-lived assets," think more broadly than just rusty old equipment. This class of assets includes two major types: tangible and intangible.[1]

## Tangible Assets

Tangible assets are long-lived assets with physical substance—that is, you can see, touch, or kick them. The most prominent examples of tangible assets are land, buildings, factories, machinery, vehicles, office equipment, and furniture and fixtures. On the balance sheet, these assets are often grouped in the single line item Property, Plant, and Equipment. Because many long-lived tangible assets are fixed in place, these assets are also known as fixed assets. Cedar Fair's tangible assets include roller coasters, hotels, and nearly 5,000 acres of land in the western, midwestern, and northeastern United States.

## Intangible Assets

Long-lived intangible assets have special rights but no physical substance. The existence of most intangible assets is indicated only by legal documents that describe their rights. Compared to the tangible assets that you see in daily life, such as store buildings and cash registers, intangible assets are probably less familiar to you. For this reason, we describe the various types of intangible assets in detail later in this chapter. For now, you can think of this category as including brand names, trademarks, and licensing rights such as the ones that allow Cedar Fair to use PEANUTS characters throughout its amusement parks.

See Exhibit 10.1 for the way Cedar Fair reported long-lived assets on its 2007 balance sheet. Looking at this exhibit, you can see how important tangible and intangible assets are to Cedar Fair. Of the $2.4 billion in assets Cedar Fair owned that year, long-lived assets comprised more than $2.3 billion ($1,933,562 + $422,358 = $2,355,920, in thousands).

In the next section, you will see how to account for tangible long-lived assets. The section that follows that one covers intangible assets.

---

[1] A third type of long-lived asset, one that includes assets that are depleted over time, such as oil wells or gold mines, is common in natural resource industries. Supplement 10A explains how to account for natural resource assets.

| Exhibit 10.1 | Cedar Fair's Assets | | Cedar fair. L.P. |
|---|---|---|---|

| | (in thousands) | |
|---|---|---|
| December 31, | 2007 | 2006 |
| **Assets** | | |
| Current assets | | |
| Cash | $    5,501 | $    30,203 |
| Receivables | 16,516 | 21,796 |
| Inventories | 26,884 | 26,377 |
| Prepaids | 13,847 | 26,132 |
| Total current assets | 62,748 | 104,508 |
| Property and equipment | | |
| Land | 344,688 | 325,617 |
| Land improvements | 317,811 | 315,406 |
| Buildings | 582,654 | 580,588 |
| Rides and equipment | 1,270,852 | 1,237,790 |
| Construction in progress | 33,997 | 25,288 |
| | 2,550,002 | 2,484,689 |
| Less: Accumulated depreciation | (616,440) | (498,980) |
| | 1,933,562 | 1,985,709 |
| Intangible assets | 422,358 | 420,704 |
| Total assets | $2,418,668 | $2,510,921 |

# TANGIBLE ASSETS: ACQUISITION, USE, IMPAIRMENT, AND DISPOSAL

**Learning Objective 2**

Apply the cost principle to the acquisition of long-lived assets.

Most companies own a variety of tangible assets. Earlier chapters introduced you to the most common examples: land, buildings, equipment, and automobiles. Other, less common examples include land improvements and construction in progress—both of which Cedar Fair reported on its balance sheet in Exhibit 10.1. Land improvements differ from land in that they deteriorate over time, whereas land is assumed to last forever. Land improvements include the sidewalks, pavement, landscaping, and trees that are added to improve the usefulness of land. Construction in progress includes the costs of constructing new buildings and equipment. When construction is finished, these costs are moved from this account into the building or equipment account to which they relate.

## Acquisition of Tangible Assets

The general rule for accounting for tangible assets under the cost principle is that **all reasonable and necessary costs to acquire and prepare an asset for use should be recorded as a cost of the asset.** Accountants say costs have been capitalized when they are recorded as assets (rather than as expenses).

Deciding whether a cost is a reasonable and necessary cost of acquiring or preparing tangible assets for use can involve a great deal of judgment. Because capitalizing costs has a significant impact on both the balance sheet (it increases assets) and the income statement (it decreases expenses), some dishonest accountants and managers have exploited the judgment involved by capitalizing costs that should have been expensed. A well-known example of this tactic is described in the following Spotlight on Ethics feature. As you read the feature and the next couple of pages, focus on distinguishing between what types of costs should be capitalized and what types should be expensed.

The illustration that follows shows the types of cost that should be capitalized when a tangible asset is acquired. All are necessary for acquiring and preparing tangible assets for use. Notice that they are not limited to the amounts paid to purchase or construct the assets. For example, the Land account at Cedar Fair would include legal fees for title searches, fees for land surveys, and commissions paid to brokers when purchasing the land on Ohio's Sandusky Bay shown in the photograph on the left. Take a moment right now to read the lists of costs that should be capitalized when buildings (middle) and equipment (right) are acquired.

**Land**

Purchase cost
Legal fees
Survey fees
Broker's commissions

**Equipment**

Purchase/Construction cost
Sales taxes
Transportation costs
Installation costs

**Buildings**

Purchase/Construction cost
Legal fees
Appraisal fees
Architect fees

If a company buys land, a building, or a piece of used equipment and incurs demolition, renovation, or repair costs before it can be used, the company would capitalize the additional costs as a cost of the land, building, or equipment. These costs are capitalized because they are needed to prepare the asset for use. Cedar Fair spent $10 million in 2006 to relocate its X-Flight roller coaster from Cleveland to Cincinnati. The full cost of the move was capitalized to its Rides and Equipment account.

In some cases, land, buildings, and equipment are purchased together. On June 30, 2006, Cedar Fair bought five amusement parks from Paramount Parks for $1.24 billion. When this type of "basket purchase" occurs, the total cost is split among the assets in proportion to the market value of the assets as a whole. For example, if Cedar Fair were to pay $10 million for a hotel and the land surrounding it, based on an appraisal that estimates that the land contributes 40 percent of the property's value and the building contributes 60 percent, Cedar Fair would record 40 percent of the total cost as land ($4 million) and the other 60 percent as buildings ($6 million). Splitting the total purchase price among individual assets is necessary because the cost of different asset types may be depreciated over different periods. Land is not depreciated, so any costs assigned to Land will remain in that account until Cedar Fair sells the land.

To illustrate how the costs of tangible assets are recorded, consider the Top Thrill Dragster ride, which Cedar Fair purchased in 2002 from Intamin, a Swiss roller-coaster manufacturer.

When it was purchased, the Top Thrill Dragster was the biggest, fastest roller coaster in the world. Some of its specs are shown in the accompanying graphic.

| Top Thrill Dragster | |
|---|---|
| Ride Height: | 42 stories |
| Vertical Drop: | 400 ft. |
| Track Length: | 2,800 ft. |
| Ride Time: | 17 seconds |
| Angle of Descent: | 90 degrees |
| Angle of Twist: | 270 degrees |
| Launch Speed: | 120 mph in 4 seconds |
| Ride Capacity: | 1,500 riders per hour |

Assume the list price for the roller coaster (including sales tax) was $26 million but that Cedar Fair received a $1 million discount. In other words, the roller coaster's net purchase price to Cedar Fair was $25 million. Assume too that Cedar Fair paid $125,000 to have the roller coaster delivered and another $625,000 to have it assembled and prepared for use. Cedar Fair would calculate the costs to be capitalized for this asset as follows:

| | |
|---|---:|
| Invoice price | $26,000,000 |
| Less: Discount | 1,000,000 |
| Net cash invoice price | 25,000,000 |
| Add: Transportation costs paid by Cedar Fair | 125,000 |
| Installation costs paid by Cedar Fair | 625,000 |
| Total cost of the roller coaster | $25,750,000 |

The total $25,750,000 cost would be the amount Cedar Fair recorded in the Rides and Equipment account regardless of how the company paid for or financed the roller coaster. As you will see next, the method of payment or financing affects only whether the purchase reduces cash, increases liabilities, or both.

## Cash Purchase

Assuming that Cedar Fair paid cash for the roller coaster and related transportation and installation costs, the company would record the transaction as follows:

| | Debit | Credit |
|---|---|---|
| Rides and Equipment (+A) | 25,750,000 | |
| Cash (−A) | | 25,750,000 |

| Assets | | = | Liabilities | + | Owners' Equity |
|---|---|---|---|---|---|
| Cash | −25,750,000 | | | | |
| Rides and Equipment | +25,750,000 | | | | |

You may find it hard to believe that Cedar Fair would pay cash for assets that cost more than $25 million, but that is not unusual. Companies often pay with cash generated from operations or with cash that has been borrowed. In addition, the seller may extend credit to the buyer, a situation we examine next.

## Credit Purchase

If we assume Cedar Fair signed a note payable for the new roller coaster and paid cash for the transportation and installation costs, the journal entry to record the purchase would be:

| | Debit | Credit |
|---|---|---|
| Rides and Equipment (+A) | 25,750,000 | |
| Cash (−A) | | 750,000 |
| Note Payable (+L) | | 25,000,000 |

| Assets | = | Liabilities | + | Owners' Equity |
|---|---|---|---|---|
| Cash            −750,000 | | Note Payable  +25,000,000 | | |
| Rides and | | | | |
| Equipment  +25,750,000 | | | | |

**SELF-STUDY PRACTICE**

In a recent year, the New Bakery Company of Ohio opened a new baking plant that can make 3 million hamburger buns a day. The equipment cost $21,000,000. Assume New Bakery financed the purchase cost using a note payable and paid in cash $800,000 of sales taxes, $70,000 of transportation costs, and $50,000 of installation costs before the equipment could be used.

1. What amount should be recorded as the total acquisition cost of the equipment?

   _____

2. Complete the following journal entry to record the acquisition.

| | Debit | Credit |
|---|---|---|
| | | |
| | | |
| | | |

*After you have finished, check your answers with the solution at the bottom of the page.*

Before we leave this section, we should mention that not all fixed asset costs are capitalized. The cost of some fixed assets, such as staplers and hole punches, is such a small amount that it is not worth the trouble of recording and tracking as a fixed asset. Outback Steakhouse, for example, reports in the notes to its financial statements that the company expenses all expenditures of less than $1,000 when incurred. Such policies are acceptable because immaterial (relatively small) amounts will not affect users' analysis of the financial statements. **Other costs that are expensed when incurred include insurance for fixed assets, interest on loans obtained to purchase fixed assets, and—as discussed in the next section—ordinary repairs and maintenance.**

Solution to
Self-Study Practice

1. $21,000,000 + $800,000 + $70,000 + $50,000 = $21,920,000

2.

| | Debit | Credit |
|---|---|---|
| Equipment (+A) | 21,920,000 | |
| Cash (−A) | | 920,000 |
| Note Payable (+L) | | 21,000,000 |

| Assets | = | Liabilities | + | Owners' Equity |
|---|---|---|---|---|
| Equipment  +21,920,000 | | Note Payable   +21,000,000 | | |
| Cash          −920,000 | | | | |

# Use of Tangible Assets

## Maintenance Costs Incurred during Use

Most tangible assets require substantial expenditures over the course of their lives to maintain or enhance their operation. Maintenance is extremely important in the roller-coaster industry where safety is vital. Despite the tremendous stress created by the frequent use and ultra-fast speeds of the rides, surprisingly few accidents occur at amusement parks. According to some estimates, the odds of a serious injury occurring at an amusement park are 1 in 23 million. In fact, you are 38 times more likely to get hit by lightning than you are to be injured at an amusement park.[2] The companies that run the parks have achieved this high level of safety by spending a lot of money on two types of maintenance: (1) ordinary repairs and maintenance and (2) extraordinary repairs and maintenance.

**Ordinary Repairs and Maintenance.** Ordinary repairs and maintenance are expenditures for the routine maintenance and upkeep of long-lived assets. Like an oil change for your car, these are recurring, relatively small expenditures that do not directly lengthen an asset's useful life. Because they are made to maintain the asset's productive capacity for a short time, they are recorded as expenses in the current period. Because expenses are matched to revenues, ordinary repairs and maintenance costs are sometimes called revenue expenditures.

In Cedar Fair's case, ordinary repairs and maintenance would include greasing the tracks on the Steel Venom roller coaster at Valleyfair in Minnesota. It would also include replacing the lights on the eight-story Ferris wheel at Michigan's Adventure and tightening the seams on a water slide at Knott's Soak City in California.

**Extraordinary Repairs, Replacements, and Additions.** In contrast to ordinary repairs and maintenance, extraordinary repairs occur infrequently, involve large expenditures, and increase an asset's economic usefulness through enhanced efficiency, capacity, or lifespan. Examples include additions, major overhauls, complete reconditioning, and major replacements and improvements, such as the complete replacement of the passenger train on a roller coaster. Because these costs increase the usefulness of tangible assets beyond their original condition, they are added to the appropriate long-lived asset accounts. And because doing so means capitalizing these costs, extraordinary repairs, replacements, and additions are sometimes called capital expenditures.

---

[2] "Newtonian Nightmare Rack-and-Pinion Inversions and Pneumatic Accelerators: This Is Fun?" *Forbes*, July 23, 2001, p. 112.

## Spotlight On FINANCIAL REPORTING

### Accounting for Ordinary and Extraordinary Repairs

Cedar Fair L.P.

Companies are required to describe the policies they use to account for any significant expenditures on property, plant, and equipment. In the notes to the financial statements, Cedar Fair clearly indicates that accounting for ordinary repairs differs from that for expenditures on improvements and upgrades (extraordinary repairs).

> **Cedar Fair**
> **Notes to the Financial Statements**
> *Key Accounting Policies*
>
> Expenditures made to maintain assets in their original operating condition are expensed as incurred, and improvements and upgrades are capitalized.

**SELF-STUDY PRACTICE**

As you know from living in a house, apartment, or dormitory, buildings require continuous maintenance and repair. Indicate whether each of the following expenditures should be expensed in the current period or capitalized as part of the cost of the building.

> **Expense or Capitalize?**
>
> 1. Replacing electrical wiring and plumbing throughout the building.
> 2. Repairing the hinge on the front door of the building.
> 3. Cleaning the building's air conditioning filters once every year.
> 4. Making major structural improvements to a clubhouse.

*After you have finished, check your answers with the solution at the bottom of the page.*

## Depreciation Expense

In addition to repairs and maintenance expense, a company reports depreciation expense every period that a tangible asset is used. This expense does not involve new payments for use of the asset. Instead, depreciation is the allocation of existing costs that have already been recorded as a long-lived tangible asset. The idea is that the cost of a long-lived tangible asset is essentially a prepaid cost representing future benefits. Because these benefits are used up when the asset is used, **following the matching principle, a portion of the asset's cost is removed from the balance sheet and reported on the income statement as an expense in the period when the asset is used to generate revenue.** Cedar Fair earns revenues when the rides are open to customers, so depreciation expense is recorded at that time to show the allocated cost of the tangible assets used to generate revenues.

Depreciation is recorded in two accounts. First, the income statement account Depreciation Expense reports the amount of depreciation for the current period. Second, the balance sheet reports a contra-asset account, Accumulated Depreciation, which includes the current period depreciation as well as the depreciation accumulated from all prior periods since the asset was first used. Accumulated Depreciation is subtracted from the cost of related assets to compute their book values, or carrying values. The book (or carrying) value of a long-lived asset is its acquisition cost less the accumulated depreciation from the acquisition date to the balance sheet date.

To see how Cedar Fair reported these items on the balance sheet, take a quick look at Exhibit 10.1 on page 419. You should see that at the end of 2007, Cedar Fair's total cost of property and equipment (in thousands) was $2,550,002. Accumulated depreciation was $616,440 and the book (or carrying) value was $1,933,562 ($2,550,002 − $616,440). In Cedar Fair's 2007 income statement (not shown), depreciation expense of $55,765 was included. Although some companies report depreciation expense as a separate operating expense, many (including Cedar Fair) combine it with other operating expenses for external reporting purposes.

To calculate depreciation expense, you need three amounts:

1. **Asset cost.** The asset cost includes all of the asset's capitalized costs—for example, the purchase cost, sales tax, legal fees, and other costs needed to acquire and prepare the asset for use.

2. **Residual value.** Residual (or salvage or scrap) value is an estimate of the amount the company will receive when it disposes of the asset. Cedar Fair will recover some of the cost of its roller coasters when it disposes of them either by selling them "as is" to local amusement companies or by dismantling them and selling the parts to other roller coaster or scrap metal companies.

3. **Useful life.** Useful life is an estimate of the asset's useful economic life to the company (rather than its economic life to all potential users). It may be expressed in terms of years or units of asset capacity, such as the number of units it can produce or the number

**Solution to Self-Study Practice**

1. Capitalize—extends life.
2. Expense.
3. Expense.
4. Capitalize—extends life.

of miles it will travel. **Land is the only tangible asset that is assumed to have an unlimited (indefinite) useful life. Thus, land is not depreciated.**

The basic idea behind depreciation is to match the dollar amount of the asset that will be used up (the asset cost minus the residual value) to the periods in which the asset will be used to generate revenue (the useful life). Residual value is considered when calculating depreciation because we want to leave a little of the asset's cost in the accounts after we have finished depreciating it. We do so because when we dispose of the asset, we are likely to get back some of the money we initially paid for it. So the amount to be depreciated over the asset's useful life is the difference between its cost and its residual value, an amount called the depreciable cost. A company should record depreciation each year of an asset's useful life until the total accumulated depreciation equals the depreciable cost. After that, the company should report no additional depreciation even if the company continues to use the asset.

If every company used the same techniques to calculate depreciation, we would stop right here. Because companies own different assets and use them differently, however, accountants have not been able to agree on a single best method of depreciation. As a result, managers are allowed to choose from several different methods based on how well they match the cost of using the assets to the revenues those assets generate over time. These alternative depreciation methods produce different numbers for depreciation. To interpret such differences, you need to understand how the methods work.

Water structures and facilities such as the Hoover Dam are depreciated over periods extending to 100 years.

*Source:* U.S. Department of the Interior, Bureau of Reclamation, 2005 annual report.

## Depreciation Methods

In this section, we discuss three common depreciation methods:

- Straight line.
- Units of production.
- Declining balance.

Because these methods assume different patterns of depreciation over an asset's useful life, they use different methods to calculate depreciation. Regardless of the method, however, the calculated amount of depreciation should be recorded with the same journal entry you learned in Chapter 4. For example, the journal entry to record $20,000 of depreciation for a given period would be:

|  | Debit | Credit |
|---|---|---|
| Depreciation Expense (+E, −OE) | 20,000 | |
| Accumulated Depreciation (+xA, −A) | | 20,000 |

| Assets | = | Liabilities | + | Owners' Equity | |
|---|---|---|---|---|---|
| Accumulated Depreciation (+xA) −20,000 | | | | Depreciation Expense (+E) | −20,000 |

**Learning Objective 3**

Apply various depreciation methods as economic benefits are used up over time.

**Coach's Tip**

Depreciation has two effects: (1) it is reported as an expense of the current period on the income statement and (2) it accumulates with depreciation from prior periods on the balance sheet in a contra-asset account that is subtracted from the asset's cost.

To demonstrate how each depreciation method works, we assume that Cedar Fair acquired a new go-cart ride on January 1, 2009. See Exhibit 10.2 for the relevant information.

### Exhibit 10.2    Information for Depreciation Computations

**Cedar Fair—Acquisition of a New Go-Cart Ride**

| | |
|---|---|
| Cost, purchased on January 1, 2009 | $62,500 |
| Estimated residual value | $ 2,500 |
| Estimated useful life | 3 years; 100,000 miles |

### Straight-Line Method.
The straight-line depreciation method reports an equal amount of depreciation in each period of the asset's estimated useful life. The straight-line formula for estimating annual depreciation expense is:

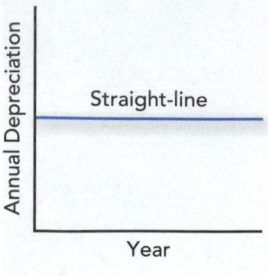

**Straight-Line Formula**

$$(\text{Cost} - \text{Residual Value}) \times \frac{1}{\text{Useful Life}} = \text{Depreciation Expense}$$

In the straight-line formula, Cost − Residual Value is the total amount to be depreciated (the depreciable cost). The depreciation rate is 1/Useful Life. Using the information in Exhibit 10.2, the depreciation expense for Cedar Fair's new ride is $20,000 per year, calculated in the following depreciation schedule:

**Straight-line**
(Cost − Residual Value) × (1/Useful Life)

|  |  | Income Statement | Balance Sheet | | |
|---|---|---|---|---|---|
| Year | Yearly Computation | Depreciation Expense | Cost | Accumulated Depreciation | Book Value |
| At acquisition |  |  | $62,500 | $    0 | $62,500 |
| 2009 | ($62,500 − $2,500) × (1/3) | $20,000 | 62,500 | 20,000 | 42,500 |
| 2010 | ($62,500 − $2,500) × (1/3) | 20,000 | 62,500 | 40,000 | 22,500 |
| 2011 | ($62,500 − $2,500) × (1/3) | 20,000 | 62,500 | 60,000 | 2,500 |
|  | Total | $60,000 |  |  |  |

Take a moment to study the straight-line depreciation schedule. Notice that as the name straight line suggests,

1. Depreciation expense is a constant amount each year.
2. Accumulated depreciation increases by an equal amount each year.
3. Book value decreases by the same equal amount each year.

Notice too that at the end of the asset's life, accumulated depreciation ($60,000) equals the asset's depreciable cost ($62,500 − $2,500), and book value ($2,500) equals residual value.

As you will see with other depreciation methods, the amount of depreciation depends on estimates of an asset's useful life and residual value at the end of that life. A question people often ask is: **How do accountants estimate useful lives and residual values?** While some of this information can be obtained from the asset's supplier or from other sources such as reseller databases or insurance companies, the simple answer is that professional judgment is required. Because useful lives and residual values are difficult to estimate with precision, accountants are encouraged to update their calculations regularly (see Supplement 10B at the end of this chapter).

### Units-of-Production Method.
Whereas the straight-line method bases depreciation on the amount of time that has passed, the units-of-production depreciation method bases it on the amount of asset production. An asset's production is defined in terms of miles, products, or machine-hours. The units-of-production formula for estimating depreciation expense is:

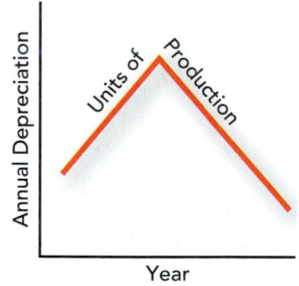

**Units-of-Production Formula**

$$(\text{Cost} - \text{Residual Value}) \times \frac{\text{Actual Production this Period}}{\text{Estimated Total Production}} = \frac{\text{Depreciation}}{\text{Expense}}$$

If the go-cart in Exhibit 10.2 was driven 30,000 miles in 2009, 50,000 miles in 2010, and 20,000 miles in 2011, the units-of-production method would calculate depreciation in each year of the asset's life as follows:

| | | Income Statement | Balance Sheet | | |
|---|---|---|---|---|---|
| **Units-of-production** (Cost − Residual Value) × (Actual/Estimated Total Production) | | | | | |
| Year | Yearly Computation | Depreciation Expense | Cost | Accumulated Depreciation | Book Value |
| At acquisition | | | $62,500 | $    0 | $62,500 |
| 2009 | ($62,500 − $2,500) × (30,000/100,000 miles) | $18,000 | 62,500 | 18,000 | 44,500 |
| 2010 | ($62,500 − $2,500) × (50,000/100,000 miles) | 30,000 | 62,500 | 48,000 | 14,500 |
| 2011 | ($62,500 − $2,500) × (20,000/100,000 miles) | 12,000 | 62,500 | 60,000 | 2,500 |
| | Total | $60,000 | | | |

Notice that **under the units-of-production method, the depreciation expense, accumulated depreciation, and book value vary from period to period, depending on the number of units produced.**

## Declining-Balance Method.

Under the declining-balance depreciation method, depreciation expense is higher in the early years of an asset's life and lower in the later years. That is why this method is sometimes called an accelerated depreciation method. Although accelerated methods are used infrequently for financial reporting purposes in the United States, they are used commonly in financial reporting in other countries, such as Japan and Canada, as well as in tax reporting in the United States (a point we discuss in greater detail later).

The declining-balance method applies a depreciation rate to the book value of the asset at the beginning of each accounting period. Notice that the following formula uses book value (Cost − Accumulated Depreciation) rather than depreciable cost (Cost − Residual Value). This slight difference in the formula produces declining amounts of depreciation as the asset ages. Because the 2/Useful Life rate used in the formula is double the straight-line rate, this particular version of the declining-balance method is called the double-declining-balance depreciation method.

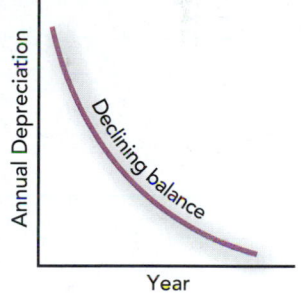

> **Double-Declining-Balance Formula**
>
> $$(\text{Cost} - \text{Accumulated Depreciation}) \times \frac{2}{\text{Useful Life}} = \text{Depreciation Expense}$$

This formula uses the accumulated depreciation balance at the beginning of each year. In the first year of an asset's life, the beginning balance in Accumulated Depreciation is zero. However, with each passing year as additional depreciation is recorded, the Accumulated Depreciation balance increases, causing the amount of double-declining depreciation expense to decline over time.

Because **residual value is not included in the formula for the declining-balance method of computing depreciation expense,** you must take extra care to ensure that an asset's book value is not depreciated beyond its residual value. If the calculated amount of depreciation for the year would reduce the book value below the asset's residual value, you must record a lower amount of depreciation so that the book value will equal the residual value. The following depreciation schedule illustrates this point.

**Coach's Tip**

Remember that the declining-balance formula does not include an asset's residual value, so you must consider it separately.

| | | Income Statement | | Balance Sheet | |
|---|---|---|---|---|---|
| **Double-declining-balance** | | | | | |
| (Cost − Residual Value) × (2/Useful Life) | | | | Accumulated | |
| **Year** | **Yearly Computation** | **Depreciation Expense** | **Cost** | **Depreciation** | **Book Value** |
| At acquisition | | | $62,500 | $    0 | $62,500 |
| 2009 | ($62,500 − $0      ) × (2/3) | $41,667 | 62,500 | 41,667 | 20,833 |
| 2010 | ($62,500 − $41,667) × (2/3) | 13,889 | 62,500 | 55,556 | 6,944 |
| 2011 | ($62,500 − $55,556) × (2/3) | ~~4,629~~ | 62,500 | ~~60,185~~ | ~~2,315~~ |
| | | 4,444 | 62,500 | 60,000 | 2,500 |
| | Total | $60,000 | | | |

Notice that the calculated depreciation expense for 2011 ($4,629) has not been recorded because it would cause the asset's book value to fall below its residual value. Instead, in the final year of the asset's life, just enough depreciation ($4,444) is recorded to make the book value of the asset equal its residual value of $2,500.

**Summary of Depreciation Methods.**  See Exhibit 10.3 for a summary of the depreciation expense that would be reported in each year of our example under the three alternative depreciation methods. Notice that **the amount of depreciation expense recorded in each year of an asset's life depends on the method that is used. That means that the amount of net income that is reported can vary, depending on the depreciation method used.** At the end of an asset's life, after it has been fully depreciated, the total amount of depreciation will equal the asset's depreciable cost regardless of the depreciation method used.

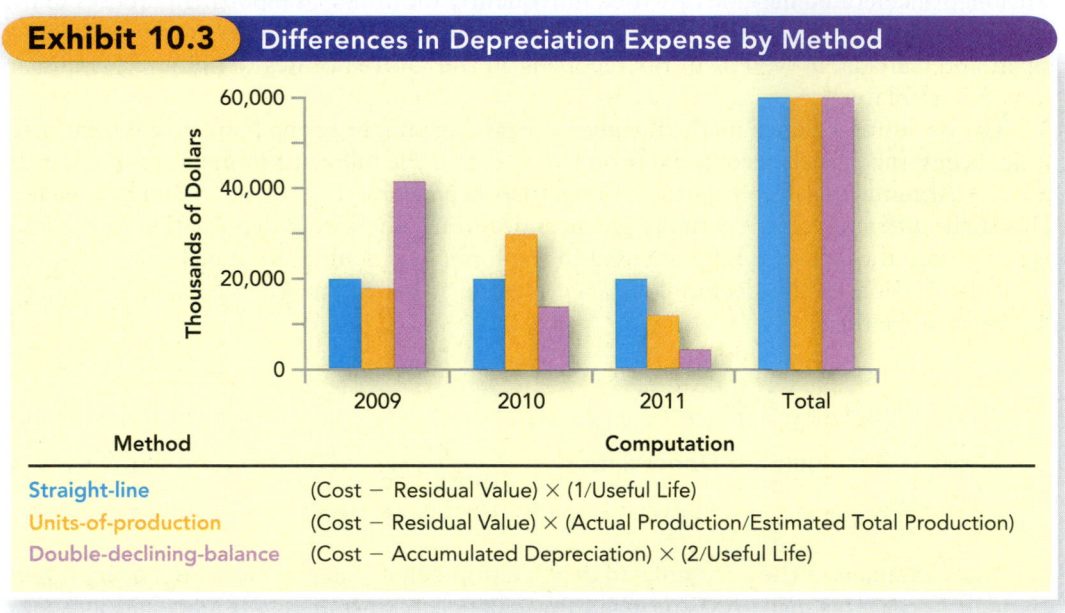

**Exhibit 10.3**    Differences in Depreciation Expense by Method

| Method | Computation |
|---|---|
| Straight-line | (Cost − Residual Value) × (1/Useful Life) |
| Units-of-production | (Cost − Residual Value) × (Actual Production/Estimated Total Production) |
| Double-declining-balance | (Cost − Accumulated Depreciation) × (2/Useful Life) |

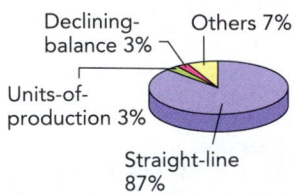

Managers may use any rational and systematic depreciation method provided that the company describes it in the notes to the financial statements. Because tangible assets are not identical, different depreciation methods can be used for different classes of assets provided they are used consistently over time so that financial statement users can compare results across periods. The methods that companies use most frequently are shown in the margin. The straight-line method is the preferred choice because it is the easiest to use and understand, and it does a good job of matching depreciation expense to revenues when assets are used evenly over their useful lives. The units-of-production method is the typical choice when asset use fluctuates significantly from period to period. Declining-balance methods apply best to assets that are most productive when they are new but quickly lose their usefulness as they get older.

Assume that Cedar Fair has acquired new equipment at a cost of $24,000. The equipment has an estimated useful life of six years, an estimated operating life of 5,000 hours, and an estimated residual value of $3,000. Determine the depreciation expense for the second year under each of the following methods:

1. Straight-line method.

$$(\$24{,}000 - \$\underline{\hspace{1cm}}) \times (\underline{\hspace{1cm}}/6) = \$\underline{\hspace{1cm}}$$

2. Units-of-production method (assume that the equipment ran for 800 hours in Year 2).

$$(\$\underline{\hspace{1cm}} - \$\underline{\hspace{1cm}}) \times (\underline{\hspace{1cm}}/5{,}000) = \$\underline{\hspace{1cm}}$$

3. Double-declining-balance method.

Year 1: $(\$24{,}000 - \$\underline{\hspace{1cm}}) \times (\underline{\hspace{1cm}}/\underline{\hspace{1cm}}) = \$\underline{\hspace{1cm}}$

Year 2: $(\$24{,}000 - \$\underline{\hspace{1cm}}) \times (\underline{\hspace{1cm}}/\underline{\hspace{1cm}}) = \$\underline{\hspace{1cm}}$

*After you have finished, check your answers with the solution at the bottom of the page.*

## Partial-Year Depreciation Calculations.

Purchases of long-lived assets seldom occur on the first or last day of the accounting period. Consequently, the need arises to calculate depreciation for periods shorter than a year. **Under the straight-line and declining-balance methods, the annual depreciation is multiplied by the fraction of the year for which depreciation is being calculated.**

For purposes of these calculations, accountants typically assume that assets were purchased at the beginning of the month nearest to the actual purchase date. For example, if Cedar Fair purchased the go-cart ride on October 7, 2009, it would have owned the asset for about three months during the year ended December 31, 2009. Thus, the depreciation for the ride in 2009 would be calculated by multiplying the annual straight-line depreciation of $20,000 by $3 \div 12$, representing the 3 months of 12 that Cedar Fair owned it. Similarly, if an asset is disposed of during the year, the annual depreciation is multiplied by the fraction of the year during which the asset was owned. **These partial-year modifications are not required in the units-of-production method because that method is based on actual production for the period.** If the accounting period is shorter than a year, the level of actual production already reflects that shorter period.

## Tax Depreciation.

Before we leave the topic of depreciation, we should note that if a business is operated as a corporation, it may use one method of depreciation for reporting to owners and a second method for determining the income taxes that a corporation must pay. Keeping two sets of accounting records is both ethical and legal because the objective of GAAP differs from that of the Internal Revenue Code.

| Financial Reporting (GAAP) | Tax Reporting (Internal Revenue Code) |
| --- | --- |
| The objective of financial reporting is to provide economic information about a business that is useful in projecting future cash flows of the business. | The objective of the Internal Revenue Code is to raise sufficient revenues to pay for the expenditures of the federal government and to encourage certain social and economic behaviors. |

One of the behaviors the government wants to encourage is economic renewal and growth. Thus, the IRS allows companies to deduct larger amounts of tax depreciation than GAAP

---

1. $(\$24{,}000 - \$3{,}000) \times (1/6) = \$3{,}500$
2. $(\$24{,}000 - \$3{,}000) \times (800/5{,}000) = \$3{,}360$
3. Year 1: $(\$24{,}000 - \$0) \times (2/6) = \$8{,}000$
   Year 2: $(\$24{,}000 - \$8{,}000) \times (2/6) = \$5{,}333$

allows.[3] The larger tax deduction reduces the company's income taxes significantly in the years immediately following the purchase of a long-lived asset.

Although the IRS allows super-sized deductions in the early years of an asset's life, it does not allow a company to depreciate more than an asset's depreciable cost over its life. So the tax savings that companies enjoy in the early years of an asset's life will eventually be returned to the government in later years of that asset's life. The amount of tax that is put off (deferred) as a result of taking large tax deductions for depreciation is reported as a long-term liability, Deferred Income Taxes. Although the deferral delays the payment of taxes only temporarily, it can be worth the effort of keeping two sets of records. The following companies report that they deferred significant tax obligations in recent years by choosing different depreciation methods for tax and financial reporting purposes.

| Company | Deferred Tax Liabilities | Percentage due to Applying Different Depreciation Methods |
|---|---|---|
| AT&T Corp. | $27,406 million | 77% |
| Southwest Airlines | 2,104 million | 87 |
| Revlon, Inc. | 27 million | 99 |

This table shows that like most individuals, companies follow an economic rule called the **least and the latest rule.** All taxpayers want to pay the least tax that is legally permitted, at the latest possible date. If you had the choice of paying $1,000 to the federal government at the end of this year or at the end of next year, you would choose the end of next year. Doing so would allow you to invest the money for an extra year and earn a significant return on your investment.

# Impairment of Tangible Assets

**Coach's Tip**

Under current U.S. accounting rules, if long-lived tangible assets increase in value, the accounting records are not adjusted to write up their value.

As a result of recording depreciation, an asset's book value declines as it ages. However, because **depreciation is not intended to report an asset at its current value,** an asset's book value could exceed its current value, particularly if the asset becomes impaired. **Impairment** occurs when events or changed circumstances cause the estimated future cash flows from a long-lived asset to fall below its book value. If an asset's estimated future cash flows are less than its book value, the book value should be written down to what the asset is worth (called fair value) with the amount of the write-down reported as an impairment loss. Impairment losses are typically included with Other Expenses and Losses, which is reported below the Operating Income line near the bottom of the income statement.

Cedar Fair recorded a write-down in 2002 after a rare engineering phenomenon called "vortex shedding" reportedly caused a steel support tower in a VertiGo slingshot ride to snap during the off-season. Even though only one ride was affected, Cedar Fair dismantled and removed both its VertiGo rides.[4] To see how this bizarre event would be accounted for, assume that the book value of Cedar Fair's VertiGo rides was $8 million. If the fair value of the rides was estimated to be $4.8 million—an amount that represents what other amusement park companies and scrap dealers might be expected to pay for the rides' parts—then the impairment loss would be calculated as $8 million minus $4.8 million. The resulting $3.2 million impairment loss would be recorded using the following journal entry:

| | Debit | Credit |
|---|---|---|
| Loss Due to Impairment of Assets (+E, −OE) | 3,200,000 | |
| Rides and Equipment (−A) | | 3,200,000 |

| Assets | = | Liabilities | + | Owners' Equity |
|---|---|---|---|---|
| Rides and Equipment   −3,200,000 | | | | Loss Due to Impairment (+E) −3,200,000 |

[3] Most corporations use the IRS-approved Modified Accelerated Cost Recovery System (MACRS) to calculate depreciation expense on their tax returns. MACRS is similar to the declining-balance method and is applied over relatively short asset lives set by the IRS to yield high tax deductions for depreciation expense in the early years.

[4] "Insurer Refuses Damage Payment to Sandusky, Ohio-Based Amusement Park Company," Knight Ridder/Tribune Business News, February 11, 2003.

## Exhibit 10.4    Financial Statement Note Describing Impairment

**Impairment of Long-Lived Assets**  During the first quarter . . . , we removed certain fixed assets from service at our parks, and recorded a provision of $3.2 million for the estimated portion of the net book value of these assets that may not be recoverable.

When Cedar Fair reported this loss on the income statement, it caused a huge reduction in net income. Because the loss was so large and unusual in nature, it was reported as the separate line item Nonrecurring Loss. Cedar Fair also described the impairment loss and asset write-down in the notes to its financial statements (see Exhibit 10.4).

# Disposal and Exchange of Tangible Assets

> **Learning Objective 5**
>
> Account for the disposal of long-lived tangible assets that are discarded or sold.

In some cases, a business may voluntarily decide not to hold a long-term asset for its entire life. For example, your local gym might decide to replace its treadmills with elliptical trainers. Or, if a company discontinues a product, it may sell the equipment that was used to make the product. To get rid of used assets, companies do just what you do: They discard them in a junkyard, sell them on eBay, or exchange them as a trade-in on a new asset.

Regardless of how a depreciable asset is disposed of, two accounting adjustments are required:

1. **Update the Depreciation Expense and Accumulated Depreciation accounts.**    If a long-lived asset is disposed of during the year, it should be depreciated to the date of disposal using the partial-year calculations discussed on page 429.

2. **Record the disposal.**    All disposals of long-lived assets require that you account for (1) the book value of the items given up, (2) the market value of the items received, and (3) any difference between the two amounts, which reflects a gain or loss on the disposal. Because the disposal of a long-lived asset is not a core part of a company's operations, any gains or losses on the disposal should be reported as Nonoperating Gains and Losses below the Operating Income line on the income statement (see Exhibit 6.7 on page 277, for example).[5] The specific journal entries to record disposals of long-lived assets depend on whether the asset is discarded, sold, or exchanged as a trade-in. In this section, we illustrate the entries for assets that are discarded or sold. Supplement 10C at the end of this chapter discusses exchanges of assets.

## Discarding Assets

Long-lived assets are discarded when they are no longer useful to the company. For example, in May 2005, Cedar Fair discarded its White Water Landing ride, which was acquired in 1982 for $3,400,000. If we assume that this asset was fully depreciated—meaning that the accumulated depreciation equaled the asset's cost—then Cedar Fair would record the following journal entry.

|  | Debit | Credit |
|---|---|---|
| Accumulated Depreciation—Rides (−xA, +A) | 3,400,000 |  |
| Rides and Equipment (−A) |  | 3,400,000 |

| Assets | = | Liabilities | + | Owners' Equity |
|---|---|---|---|---|
| Rides and Equipment          −3,400,000 |  |  |  |  |
| Accumulated Depreciation (−xA)  +3,400,000 |  |  |  |  |

[5] One exception to reporting gains or losses on the income statement involves asset exchanges that lack commercial substance. This exception is discussed in intermediate accounting.

Notice that **both the cost of the asset and any related accumulated depreciation are removed from the accounting records.** Because the book value of the ride was zero and Cedar Fair received nothing when it discarded the asset, the company recorded no gain or loss.

## Selling Assets

To illustrate how companies account for assets that are disposed of through a sale, assume that Cedar Fair sold its Demon Drop ride on December 31, 2008. The ride cost Cedar Fair $2,500,000, and on December 31, 2008, had accumulated depreciation of $2,200,000. In other words, at the time of sale, it had a net book value of $300,000 ($2,500,000 − $2,200,000). If Cedar Fair had sold the ride for more than $300,000, Cedar Fair would record a gain. If the ride were sold for less than $300,000, Cedar Fair would record a loss. Both cases are shown here.

**Gain on Sale.** If Cedar Fair sold the Demon Drop ride for $350,000 cash, the company would receive an asset (cash) with a value ($350,000) more than the ride's book value ($300,000). In other words, Cedar Fair would receive a gain of $50,000. The required journal entry would be:

|  | Debit | Credit |
|---|---|---|
| Cash (+A) | 350,000 |  |
| Accumulated Depreciation—Rides (−xA, +A) | 2,200,000 |  |
|     Rides and Equipment (−A) |  | 2,500,000 |
|     Gain on Sale of Rides and Equipment (+R, +OE) |  | 50,000 |

| Assets | | = Liabilities + | Owners' Equity | |
|---|---|---|---|---|
| Cash | + 350,000 | | Gain on Sale of Rides and | |
| Rides and Equipment | −2,500,000 | | Equipment (+R) | + 50,000 |
| Accumulated Depreciation—Rides (−xA) | +2,200,000 | | | |

## Coach's Tip

When you record the disposal of a depreciable asset, remember to remove both the cost of the asset and its accumulated depreciation.

**Loss on Sale.** If the Demon Drop ride were sold for $200,000 cash, Cedar Fair would receive an asset (cash) with a value ($200,000) that is less than the ride's book value ($300,000). A $100,000 loss would result. The required journal entry would be:

|  | Debit | Credit |
|---|---|---|
| Cash (+A) | 200,000 |  |
| Loss on Sale of Rides and Equipment (+E, −OE) | 100,000 |  |
| Accumulated Depreciation—Rides (−xA, +A) | 2,200,000 |  |
|     Rides and Equipment (−A) |  | 2,500,000 |

| Assets | | = Liabilities + | Owners' Equity | |
|---|---|---|---|---|
| Cash | + 200,000 | | Loss on Sale of Rides and | |
| Rides and Equipment | −2,500,000 | | Equipment (+E) | −100,000 |
| Accumulated Depreciation —Rides (−xA) | +2,200,000 | | | |

Assume Cedar Fair sold a hotel on March 31, 2009. The hotel, which had an original cost of $21 million, had been depreciated using the straight-line method with an estimated residual value of $1 million and an estimated useful life of 20 years. Depreciation recorded on December 31, 2008, brought the Accumulated Depreciation balance to $16 million. No depreciation has been recorded since then.

1. What is the hotel's annual amount of straight-line depreciation? What amount of depreciation should be recorded for the hotel on March 31, 2009? To what balance would this adjustment bring the Accumulated Depreciation account?
2. What would be the journal entry if Cedar Fair sold the hotel for $3 million cash?
3. What would be the journal entry if Cedar Fair sold the hotel for $5 million cash?

*After you have finished, check your answers with the solution at the bottom of the page.*

# INTANGIBLE ASSETS: TYPES, ACQUISITION, USE, AND DISPOSAL

Intangible assets are long-lived assets that lack physical substance. Their existence is usually indicated by legal documents of the types described in the following section.

## Types of Intangible Assets

### Trademarks

A **trademark** is a special name, image, or slogan identified with a product or company, such as the name Kleenex or the image of McDonald's golden arches. The symbol ® signifies a trademark that has been registered with the U.S. Patent and Trademark Office. The symbol™ indicates an unregistered trademark. Both types of trademark are considered intangible assets.

**Learning Objective 6**

Account for the acquisition, use, and disposal of long-lived intangible assets.

**Solution to Self-Study Practice**

1. Annual depreciation: (Cost − Residual Value) × (1/Life) = ($21 − $1) × (1/20) = $1 million per year.
   January 1–March 31 = 3 months out of 12; $1 million × (3/12) = $250,000.
   Accumulated Depreciation on March 31 = $16,000,000 + $250,000 = $16,250,000.

2.

| | | Debit | Credit |
|---|---|---|---|
| March 31 | Cash (+A) | 3,000,000 | |
| | Loss on Sale of Assets (+E, −OE) | 1,750,000 | |
| | Accumulated Depreciation (−xA, +A) | 16,250,000 | |
| | Buildings (−A) | | 21,000,000 |

| Assets | | = | Liabilities | + | Owners' Equity | |
|---|---|---|---|---|---|---|
| Cash | + 3,000,000 | | | | | |
| Buildings | −21,000,000 | | | | Loss on Sale of Assets (+E) | −1,750,000 |
| Acc. Depn. (−xA) | +16,250,000 | | | | | |

3.

| | | Debit | Credit |
|---|---|---|---|
| March 31 | Cash (+A) | 5,000,000 | |
| | Accumulated Depreciation (−xA, +A) | 16,250,000 | |
| | Buildings (−A) | | 21,000,000 |
| | Gain on Sale of Assets (+R, +OE) | | 250,000 |

| Assets | | = | Liabilities | + | Owners' Equity | |
|---|---|---|---|---|---|---|
| Cash | + 5,000,000 | | | | | |
| Buildings | −21,000,000 | | | | Gain on Sale of Assets (+R) | +250,000 |
| Acc. Depn. (−xA) | +16,250,000 | | | | | |

### Copyrights

A copyright gives the owner the exclusive right to publish, use, and sell a literary, musical, artistic, or dramatic work for a period not exceeding 70 years after the author's death. The book you are reading is copyrighted. It is illegal, therefore, for an instructor to copy several chapters from this book and hand them out in class without first obtaining permission from the copyright owner.

### Patents

A patent is an exclusive right granted by the federal government for a period of 20 years, typically to whoever invents a new product or discovers a new process. The patent declares the owner to be the only person who can use, manufacture, or sell the patented item. This protection is intended to encourage people to be inventive because it prevents others from simply copying an innovation until after the inventor has had time to profit from the new product or process. One of the first roller-coaster patents was granted in 1884 for what was then called a "gravity pleasure road."

### Licensing Rights

Licensing rights are limited permissions to use something according to specific terms and conditions. Your university or college has likely obtained the licensing right to make certain computer programs available for use on your campus network. A licensing right also allows Cedar Fair to showcase the PEANUTS character Snoopy at its parks.

### Franchises

A franchise is a contractual right to sell certain products or services, use certain trademarks, or perform certain activities in a specific geographical region. For example, a business can buy franchise rights that allow it to use the Krispy Kreme name, store format, recipes, and ingredients by paying an up-front fee ranging from $20,000 to $50,000 per store plus ongoing fees of 4.5 to 6.0 percent of store sales.[6]

### Goodwill

Goodwill tops the charts as the most frequently reported intangible asset. This asset can encompass a favorable location, an established customer base, a great reputation, and successful business operations. Although many companies have probably built up their own goodwill, GAAP does not allow it to be reported as an intangible asset on the balance sheet unless it has been purchased from another company. To understand the reasons for this rule, keep reading; we explain them in the next section.

# Acquisition, Use, and Disposal of Intangible Assets

## Acquisition of Intangible Assets

**The costs of intangible assets are recorded as assets only if they have been purchased.** If an intangible asset was developed internally, its costs are reported as research and development expenses. The primary reason that the cost of internally developed intangibles is reported as an expense rather than an asset is that it is easy for managers to claim they developed a valuable (but invisible) intangible asset. To believe the claim, you need to see some evidence that the asset is actually worth what they say it is worth. That evidence is created only when someone gives up hard-earned cash to buy the asset. At that time, the purchaser records the intangible asset at its acquisition cost. This general rule applies to trademarks, copyrights, patents, licensing rights, franchises, and goodwill.

Goodwill is a particularly interesting type of intangible asset because it represents the value paid for another business's unidentifiable assets. You might wonder how anyone can put a value on something that cannot be identified, but it is possible. When one company buys another business, the purchase price is often more than the value of all of the business's net assets. Why would a company pay more for a business as a whole than it would for

---

[6] Krispy Kreme 2007 Form 10-K annual report.

the individual assets? The answer is to obtain the business's goodwill. You could easily buy equipment to produce and sell generic chocolate sandwich cookies, but that strategy probably would not be as successful as acquiring the goodwill associated with Oreos. That is part of the reason that Kraft Foods paid $40 billion more than the value of Nabisco's net assets: to acquire the goodwill associated with Nabisco's Oreo and Ritz snacks.

For accounting purposes, goodwill is defined as the difference between the purchase price of a company as a whole and the fair value of its net assets:

> Purchase price
> − Fair value of identifiable assets, net of liabilities
> = Goodwill to be reported

Both parties to the sale estimate an acceptable amount for the goodwill of the business and add it to the appraised value of the business's net assets. Then they negotiate the sales price of the business. Based on the cost principle, the resulting goodwill is recorded as an intangible asset (but only when it has been purchased at a measurable cost).

## Use of Intangible Assets

The rules of accounting for intangible assets after they have been purchased depend on whether the intangible asset has a limited or an unlimited life.

**Limited Life.** The cost of intangible assets with a limited life (such as copyrights, patents, licensing rights, and franchises) is spread over each period of useful life in a process called amortization, which is similar to straight-line depreciation. Most companies do not estimate a residual value for their intangible assets because unlike tangible assets that can be sold as scrap, most intangibles have no value at the end of their useful lives. Amortization is reported as an expense on the income statement each period. It is also subtracted directly from the applicable intangible asset accounts on the balance sheet.[7]

To illustrate, assume that Cedar Fair purchased a patent for an uphill water coaster for $800,000. The company intends to use it for 20 years. Each year, the company would record $40,000 in patent amortization expense ($800,000 ÷ 20 years). The journal entry to record this amortization follows.

|  | Debit | Credit |
|---|---|---|
| Amortization Expense (+E, −OE) | 40,000 |  |
|     Patents (−A) |  | 40,000 |

| Assets | = | Liabilities | + | Owners' Equity |
|---|---|---|---|---|
| Patents   −40,000 |  |  |  | Amortization Expense (+E)  −40,000 |

**Unlimited Life.** Intangibles with unlimited (or indefinite) lives, such as goodwill and trademarks, are not amortized. However, they are tested for possible impairment, just like other long-lived assets. If an intangible asset is impaired, its book value is written down (decreased) to its fair value.

## Disposal of Intangible Assets

As with disposals of long-lived tangible assets, disposals of intangible assets result in gains (or losses) if the amounts received on disposal are more than (or less than) their book values.

Exhibit 10.5 summarizes and compares the accounting rules for long-lived tangible and intangible assets.

---

[7] As in the procedure for recording accumulated depreciation, a company may use an Accumulated Amortization account. In practice, however, most companies reduce the intangible asset account directly.

**Exhibit 10.5** | **Accounting Rules for Long-Lived Tangible and Intangible Assets**

| Stage | Subject | Tangible Assets | Intangible Assets |
|---|---|---|---|
| Acquire | **Purchased asset** | Capitalize all related costs | Capitalize all related costs |
| Use | **Repairs and maintenance** | | |
| | Ordinary | Expense related costs | Not applicable |
| | Extraordinary | Capitalize related costs | Not applicable |
| | **Depreciation/amortization** | | |
| | Limited life | One of several methods:<br>• Straight line<br>• Units of production<br>• Declining balance | Straight-line method |
| | Unlimited life | Do not depreciate (e.g., land) | Do not amortize (e.g., goodwill) |
| | **Impairment test** | Write down if necessary | Write down if necessary |
| Dispose | **Report gain (loss) when . . .** | Receive more (less) on disposal than book value | Receive more (less) on disposal than book value |

# EVALUATION OF LONG-LIVED ASSET USE

## Turnover Analysis

**Learning Objective 7**

Interpret the fixed asset turnover ratio.

A primary goal of financial analysts is to evaluate how well management uses long-lived tangible assets to generate revenues. The fixed asset turnover ratio provides a good measure of this aspect of managerial performance. It is calculated as shown in the table that follows. The denominator uses the value of **average** net fixed assets over the same period as the revenues in the numerator. You can calculate the average net fixed assets by summing the beginning and ending balances in fixed assets (net of accumulated depreciation) and dividing by 2.

### Accounting Decision Tools

| Name of Measure | Formula | What It Tells You |
|---|---|---|
| Fixed Asset Turnover Ratio | $\dfrac{\text{Net Sales Revenue}}{\text{Average Net Fixed Assets}}$ | • Indicates dollars of sales generated for each dollar invested in fixed assets (long-lived tangible assets)<br>• A higher ratio implies greater efficiency |

The fixed asset turnover ratio measures the sales dollars generated by each dollar invested in (tangible) fixed assets. Just as the number of miles per gallon provides a measure of a car's fuel efficiency, the fixed asset turnover ratio provides a measure of fixed asset operating efficiency. Generally speaking, a high or increasing turnover ratio relative to the industry average suggests better than average use of fixed assets in the sense that each dollar of fixed assets is generating higher than average sales.

Be aware that fixed asset turnover ratios can vary across industries because capital intensity—the need for tangible assets—also varies widely. A company such as Yahoo!, for example, needs fewer fixed assets than most companies to generate revenues. So Yahoo! is likely to have a high turnover ratio compared to companies such as Cedar Fair and Six Flags, which must invest considerable money in fixed assets to attract customers. Exhibit 10.6 shows the fixed asset turnover ratios for the three companies in 2007. Practice computing this ratio and comparing it to prior periods by trying the Self-Study Practice that follows Exhibit 10.6.

| Exhibit 10.6 | Summary of Fixed Asset Turnover Ratio Analyses |

| Company | Relevant Information (in millions) | | | 2007 Fixed Asset Turnover Calculation |
|---|---|---|---|---|
| | | 2007 | 2006 | |
| Cedar fair, L.P. | Sales | $ 987.0 | $ 831.4 | $\dfrac{\$987.0}{(\$1,933.6 + \$1,985.7) \div 2} = 0.50$ |
| | Net fixed assets | $1,933.6 | $1,985.7 | |
| Six Flags | Sales | $ 972.8 | $ 945.7 | $\dfrac{\$972.8}{(\$1,641.1 + \$1,661.6) \div 2} = 0.59$ |
| | Net fixed assets | $1,641.1 | $1,661.6 | |
| YAHOO! | Sales | $6,969.3 | $6,425.7 | $\dfrac{\$6,969.3}{(\$1,101.4 + \$1,331.6) \div 2} = 5.73$ |
| | Net fixed assets | $1,101.4 | $1,331.6 | |

**SELF-STUDY PRACTICE**

Cedar Fair reported net fixed assets of $967.3 (million) on December 31, 2005.

1. Use this information and that in Exhibit 10.6 to calculate Cedar Fair's fixed asset turnover ratio in 2006.

$$\text{2006 Fixed Asset Turnover}$$

$$\frac{\overline{\phantom{xxxx}}}{(\underline{\phantom{x}} + \underline{\phantom{x}}) \div 2} = \underline{\phantom{xxx}}$$

2. Did Cedar Fair's fixed asset turnover improve or decline in 2007 compared to 2006?

*When you have finished, check your answers with the solution at the bottom of the page.*

## Impact of Differences in Depreciation

Just as differences in the nature of business operations affect financial analyses and the conclusions you draw from them, so too do differences in depreciation. Depreciation varies from one company to the next as a result of differences in depreciation methods, estimated useful lives, and estimated residual values. In this section, we present a simple example to show how different depreciation methods can affect financial analysis throughout the life of a long-lived asset. Do not be fooled by the simplicity of the example. Differences in depreciation can have a significant impact in the real world.

Assume that Cedar Fair and Six Flags each acquired a new roller coaster at the beginning of the year for $15.5 million. The two companies estimate that the roller coasters will have residual values of $1.5 million at the end of their seven-year useful lives. Assume too that

**Learning Objective 8**

Describe the factors to consider when comparing long-lived assets across companies.

Solution to Self-Study Practice

1. $\dfrac{\$831.4}{(\$1,985.7 + \$967.3) \div 2} = 0.56$

2. Cedar Fair's fixed asset turnover declined from 0.56 in 2006 to 0.50 in 2007.

## Exhibit 10.7    Straight-Line versus Double-Declining-Balance Depreciation Schedules

| Cedar Fair (Straight line) | | | | Six Flags (Double-declining balance) | | |
| Depreciation Expense | Accumulated Depreciation | Book Value | Year | Depreciation Expense | Accumulated Depreciation | Book Value |
|---|---|---|---|---|---|---|
| $2,000,000 | $ 2,000,000 | $13,500,000 | 1 | $4,429,000 | $ 4,429,000 | $11,071,000 |
| 2,000,000 | 4,000,000 | 11,500,000 | 2 | 3,163,000 | 7,592,000 | 7,908,000 |
| 2,000,000 | 6,000,000 | 9,500,000 | 3 | 2,259,000 | 9,851,000 | 5,649,000 |
| 2,000,000 | 8,000,000 | 7,500,000 | 4 | 1,614,000 | 11,465,000 | 4,035,000 |
| 2,000,000 | 10,000,000 | 5,500,000 | 5 | 1,153,000 | 12,618,000 | 2,882,000 |
| 2,000,000 | 12,000,000 | 3,500,000 | 6 | 823,000 | 13,441,000 | 2,059,000 |
| 2,000,000 | 14,000,000 | 1,500,000 | 7 | 559,000 | 14,000,000 | 1,500,000 |

**Coach's Tip**

For tips and practice involving the calculations in Exhibit 10.7, try CP10-7 at the end of this chapter.

everything about the roller coasters is identical. However, Cedar Fair uses the straight-line depreciation method and Six Flags uses the double-declining-balance method. Exhibit 10.7 shows the yearly depreciation reported by the two companies. Notice that early in the asset's life, before year 4, the straight-line depreciation expense reported by Cedar Fair is less than the declining-balance depreciation expense reported by Six Flags. Thus, even if the two companies attract exactly the same number of customers and earn exactly the same total revenues, their reported net incomes will differ each year simply because they use two different (but equally acceptable) methods of depreciation. This example shows why a user of financial statements needs to understand the accounting methods companies use.

These differences in depreciation affect more than just depreciation expense, however. Taking this example one step further, assume that the two companies sell the roller coasters at the end of year 4 for $6,000,000. Because the disposal occurs on the last day of the year, the companies will record a full year of depreciation prior to the disposal. Thus, at the time of disposal, Cedar Fair's roller coaster will have a book value of $7,500,000, but Six Flags' roller coaster will have a book value of $4,035,000 (see the highlighted line in Exhibit 10.7). To account for the disposal at the end of year 4, the companies record what they received, remove what they gave up (the book value of the asset), and recognize a gain or loss for the difference between what was received and what was given up. Exhibit 10.8 shows the calculations for the two companies.

Based on the information in Exhibit 10.8, which company appears to be better managed? Someone who does not understand accounting is likely to say that Six Flags is better managed because it reported a gain on disposal whereas Cedar Fair reported a loss. You know that cannot be right, however, because both companies experienced exactly the same events. They bought the same asset at the same cost ($15.5 million) and sold it for the same amount of money ($6 million). The only difference between them is that Cedar Fair reported less depreciation over the years leading up to the disposal, so its roller coaster had a larger book value at the time of disposal. Six Flags reported more depreciation, so its roller coaster had a smaller book

## Exhibit 10.8    Calculation of Gain/Loss on Disposal, Straight-Line versus Double-Declining-Balance Depreciation

| | Cedar Fair | Six Flags |
|---|---|---|
| Selling price | $ 6,000,000 | $ 6,000,000 |
| Book value (see Exhibit 10.7) | (7,500,000) | (4,035,000) |
| Gain (loss) on disposal | $(1,500,000) | $ 1,965,000 |

value at the time of disposal. As a financial statement user, you should realize that any gain or loss on disposal that is reported on the income statement tells you as much about the method used to depreciate the asset as about management's apparent ability to successfully negotiate the sale of long-lived assets.

Although the previous example concerned different depreciation methods, the same effects can occur for two companies that use the same depreciation method but different estimated useful lives or residual values. Useful lives can vary for several reasons including differences in (1) the type of equipment each company used, (2) the frequency of repairs and maintenance, (3) the frequency and duration of use, and (4) the degree of conservatism in management's estimates. How large can these differences be? Even within the same industry, sizable differences can occur. The notes to the financial statements of various companies in the airline industry, for example, reveal the following differences in the estimated useful lives of airplanes and other flight equipment:

| Company | Estimated Life (in years) |
| --- | --- |
| US Airways | Up to 30 |
| Southwest Airlines | Up to 25 |
| Alaska Airlines | Up to 20 |
| Singapore Airlines | Up to 15 |

Some analysts try to sidestep such differences in depreciation calculations by focusing on financial measures that exclude the effects of depreciation. One popular measure is called **EBITDA** (pronounced something like *'e bit, duh*), which stands for "earnings before interest, taxes, depreciation, and amortization." Analysts calculate EBITDA by starting with net income and then adding back depreciation and amortization expense (as well as nonoperating expenses such as interest and taxes). The idea is that this measure allows analysts to conduct financial analyses without having to deal with possible differences in depreciation and amortization.

## Demonstration Case

Diversified Industries (DI) began operations as a home construction company but recently expanded into heavy construction, ready-mix concrete, sand and gravel, construction supplies, and earth-moving services. The company completed the following transactions during 2009. Amounts have been simplified.

July   1   Management decided to buy a 10-year-old building for $175,000 and, for $130,000, the land on which it was built. DI paid $100,000 in cash and signed a note payable for the rest.

July   3   DI paid $38,000 in cash for renovations to the building prior to its use.

Oct. 10   DI paid $1,200 cash for ordinary repairs on the building.

Dec. 31   DI considered the following information to determine year-end adjustments:

(a)  The building will be depreciated on a straight-line basis over an estimated useful life of 30 years. Its estimated residual value is $33,000.

(b)  DI purchased another company several years ago at $100,000 more than the fair values of the net assets acquired. The goodwill has an unlimited life.

(c)  At the beginning of the year, DI owned equipment with a cost of $650,000 and accumulated depreciation of $150,000. The equipment is being depreciated using the double-declining-balance method with a useful life of 20 years and no residual value.

(d)  At year-end, DI tested its long-lived assets for possible impairment of their value. Included in its equipment was a piece of old excavation equipment with a cost of $156,000 and a book value of $120,000 after the adjustment made in (c). Due to its small size and lack of safety features, the old equipment has limited use. Its future cash flows and fair value are expected to be $35,000. Goodwill was found not to be impaired.

December 31, 2009, is the end of the annual accounting period.

*Required:*

1.  Prepare the journal entries to record each event that occurred during the year and the adjusting journal entries required on December 31. After each entry, show the effects on the accounting equation and explain any supporting decisions or calculations.

2.  Show the December 31, 2009, balance sheet classification and amount for each of the following items:
    Fixed assets—land, building, and equipment.
    Intangible asset—goodwill.

3.  Assuming that the company had sales of $1,000,000 for the year and a book value of $500,000 for fixed assets at the beginning of the year, compute the fixed asset turnover ratio. Explain its meaning.

## Suggested Solution

1.  **Journal entries for events during the year:**

<u>July 1, 2009</u>

|  | Debit | Credit |
|---|---|---|
| Land (+A) | 130,000 | |
| Building (+A) | 175,000 | |
|     Cash (−A) | | 100,000 |
|     Note Payable (+L) | | 205,000 |

| Assets | | = | Liabilities | | + | Owners' Equity |
|---|---|---|---|---|---|---|
| Cash | −100,000 | | Note Payable | +205,000 | | |
| Land | +130,000 | | | | | |
| Building | +175,000 | | | | | |

<u>July 3, 2009</u>

|  | Debit | Credit |
|---|---|---|
| Building (+A) | 38,000 | |
|     Cash (−A) | | 38,000 |

| Assets | | = | Liabilities | + | Owners' Equity |
|---|---|---|---|---|---|
| Cash | −38,000 | | | | |
| Building | +38,000 | | | | |

The $38,000 expenditure is capitalized because it is necessary to prepare the asset for use.

<u>October 10, 2009</u>

|  | Debit | Credit |
|---|---|---|
| Repairs Expense (+E, −OE) | 1,200 | |
|     Cash (−A) | | 1,200 |

| Assets | | = | Liabilities | + | Owners' Equity | |
|---|---|---|---|---|---|---|
| Cash | −1,200 | | | | Repairs Expense (+E) | −1,200 |

This is an ordinary repair that should be expensed.

<u>December 31, 2009 (adjusting journal entries)</u>

(*a*) **See page 441 for the calculation of this adjusting journal entry.**

|  | Debit | Credit |
|---|---|---|
| Depreciation Expense (+E, −OE) | 3,000 | |
| Accumulated Depreciation (+xA, −A) | | 3,000 |

| Assets | = | Liabilities | + | Owners' Equity |
|---|---|---|---|---|
| Accumulated Depreciation (+xA)  −3,000 | | | | Depreciation Expense (+E)  −3,000 |

**Cost of Building**
| | |
|---|---|
| Initial payment | $175,000 |
| Renovations prior to use | 38,000 |
| Acquisition cost | $213,000 |

**Straight-Line Depreciation**
($213,000 cost − $33,000 residual value) ×
(1/30) years = $6,000 annual depreciation
$6,000 × (6/12) = $3,000

(b) No adjusting journal entry is required because goodwill is assumed to have an unlimited (or indefinite) life. Goodwill is tested for impairment annually, but as described in the case, it was found not to be impaired.

(c) **Double-declining-balance depreciation**
($650,000 cost − $150,000 accumulated depreciation) × (2/20) years = $50,000 annual depreciation

|  | Debit | Credit |
|---|---|---|
| Depreciation Expense (+E, −OE) | 50,000 | |
| Accumulated Depreciation (+xA, −A) | | 50,000 |

| Assets | = | Liabilities | + | Owners' Equity |
|---|---|---|---|---|
| Accumulated Depreciation (+xA)  −50,000 | | | | Depreciation Expense (+E)  −50,000 |

(d) **Asset impairment test**
The book value of the old equipment ($120,000) exceeds its expected future cash flows ($35,000). The asset has become impaired, so it should be written down to its fair value.

**Impairment loss**
| | |
|---|---|
| Book value | $120,000 |
| Less: Fair value | − 35,000 |
| Loss due to impairment | $ 85,000 |

|  | Debit | Credit |
|---|---|---|
| Loss Due to Asset Impairment (+E, −OE) | 85,000 | |
| Equipment (−A) | | 85,000 |

| Assets | = | Liabilities | + | Owners' Equity |
|---|---|---|---|---|
| Equipment  −85,000 | | | | Loss Due to Asset Impairment (+E)  −85,000 |

2.  **Partial balance sheet, December 31, 2009:**

|  |  | Assets |  |  |
|---|---|---|---|---|
| **Fixed assets** | | | | |
| Land | | | | $130,000 |
| Building | | | $213,000 | |
| Less: Accumulated depreciation | | | 3,000 | 210,000 |
| | | | | |
| Equipment ($650,000 − $85,000) | | | 565,000 | |
| Less: Accumulated depreciation ($150,000 + $50,000) | | | 200,000 | 365,000 |
| Total fixed assets | | | | 705,000 |
| **Intangible asset** | | | | |
| Goodwill | | | | 100,000 |

3.  **Fixed asset turnover ratio:**

$$\frac{\text{Net Sales Revenue}}{(\text{Beginning Net Fixed Asset Balance} + \text{Ending Net Fixed Asset Balance}) \div 2} = \frac{\$1,000,000}{(\$500,000 + \$705,000) \div 2} = 1.66$$

This construction company is capital intensive. The fixed asset turnover ratio measures management's efficiency at using the company's investment in property, plant, and equipment to generate sales. On average, approximately $1.66 of sales were generated for each dollar of fixed assets.

# Supplement 10A
## Natural Resources

Industries such as oil and gas, mining, and timber harvesting rely on a third category of long-lived assets called **natural resources.** These natural resources, whether in the form of oil wells, mineral deposits, or timber tracts, provide the raw materials for products sold by companies such as ExxonMobil and International Paper.

When a company first acquires or develops a natural resource, the cost is recorded in conformity with the **cost principle.** As the natural resource is used up, this cost must be split among the periods in which revenues are earned in conformity with the **matching principle.** The term **depletion** describes this process of allocating a natural resource's cost over the period of its extraction or harvesting. Depletion is often computed using the units-of-production method.

With one important exception, depletion is similar to the concepts of depreciation and amortization discussed in connection with tangible and intangible assets. When a natural resource such as timberland is depleted, the company obtains **inventory.** For example, a timber company obtains an inventory of logs. Because depletion of the natural resource is necessary to obtain the inventory, the depletion that is computed during a period is **added** to the cost of the inventory, not expensed in the period. For example, if a timber tract costing $530,000 is depleted over its estimated cutting life based on a cutting rate of approximately 20 percent per year, it would be depleted by $106,000 each year. The yearly depletion would be recorded with the following journal entry.

| | Debit | Credit |
|---|---|---|
| Timber Inventory (+A) | 106,000 | |
| Timber Tract (−A) | | 106,000 |

| Assets | | = | Liabilities | + | Owners' Equity |
|---|---|---|---|---|---|
| Timber Inventory | +106,000 | | | | |
| Timber Tract | −106,000 | | | | |

# Supplement 10B
## Changes in Depreciation

Depreciation is based on two estimates, useful life and residual value, that are made at the time a depreciable asset is acquired. As time goes by, one or both of these estimates may need to be revised. In addition, extraordinary repairs and additions may be added to the original acquisition cost at some time during the asset's use. When it is clear that either estimate should be revised significantly or that the asset's cost has changed, the undepreciated asset balance (less any residual value estimated at that date) should be assigned to the remaining years of estimated life using a new amount of depreciation.

To compute the new depreciation expense, you substitute the book value for the original acquisition cost, the new residual value for the original residual value, and the estimated remaining life for the original useful life. The revised formula to use with the straight-line method is:

<u>Original</u>

$$(\text{Cost} - \text{Residual Value}) \times \frac{1}{\text{Useful Life}} = \text{Depreciation Expense}$$

<u>Revised</u>

$$(\text{Book Value} - \text{New Residual Value}) \times \frac{1}{\text{Remaining Life}} = \text{Depreciation Expense}$$

Assume Cedar Fair purchased the largest, fastest roller coaster in the world for $60,000,000. The equipment had an estimated useful life of 20 years and an estimated residual value of $3,000,000. Shortly after the start of year 5, Cedar Fair changed the estimated total life to 25 years and lowered the estimated residual value to $2,400,000. At the end of year 5, the computation of the new amount of depreciation expense would be as follows:

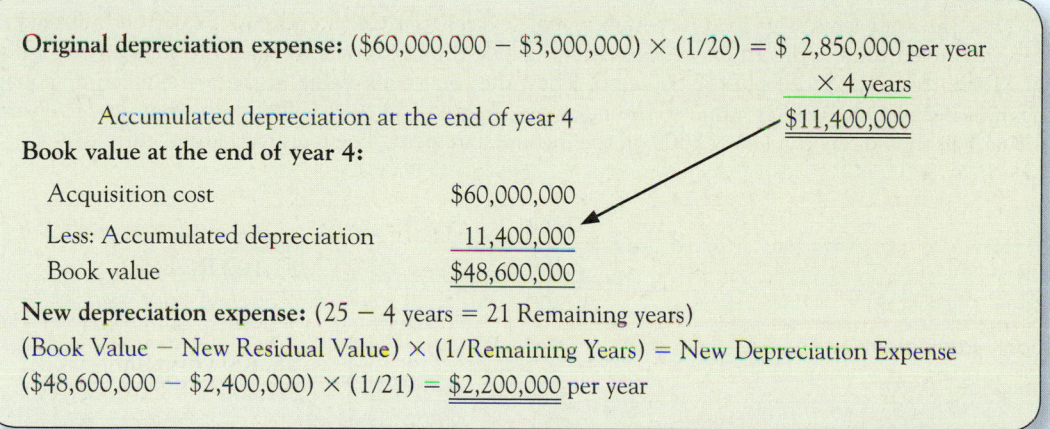

**Original depreciation expense:** ($60,000,000 − $3,000,000) × (1/20) = $2,850,000 per year

× 4 years

Accumulated depreciation at the end of year 4      $11,400,000

**Book value at the end of year 4:**

| | |
|---|---|
| Acquisition cost | $60,000,000 |
| Less: Accumulated depreciation | 11,400,000 |
| Book value | $48,600,000 |

**New depreciation expense:** (25 − 4 years = 21 Remaining years)

(Book Value − New Residual Value) × (1/Remaining Years) = New Depreciation Expense

($48,600,000 − $2,400,000) × (1/21) = $2,200,000 per year

Companies may also change their depreciation method (for example, from declining balance to straight line). Such a change requires significantly more disclosure as described in intermediate accounting textbooks. GAAP requires changes in accounting estimates and depreciation methods to be made only when a new estimate or accounting method better measures the periodic income of the business.

# Supplement 10C
## Exchanging Assets

In the same way that you may trade in an old car when buying a new one, companies can trade in their used fixed assets when acquiring new ones. Until recently, accounting rules required that these asset exchanges be recorded one way for losses and a different way for gains. Fortunately, that distinction no longer exists for most commercial asset exchanges.

Accounting for an asset exchange is similar to accounting for an asset sale. There are only two small differences: (1) rather than receive cash, you give up cash and (2) rather than simply dispose of the old asset, you also receive a new asset. If the new asset you receive has a market value that is more than the total book value of the cash and old asset that you gave up, you should report a gain on the income statement. You report a loss if the market value of the new asset is less than the total book value of the cash and old asset given up.

Assume, for example, that Cedar Fair trades in a cotton candy machine costing $2,200 with accumulated depreciation of $800 for a new machine worth $3,100. In the first case that follows (a gain), Cedar Fair also pays $1,000 cash as part of the deal.

## Gain on Commercial Asset Exchange

The assets given up by Cedar Fair include the cotton candy machine with a book value of $1,400 ($2,200 – $800) and $1,000 cash. Thus, the total book value of the assets given up equals $2,400. Because the market value of the machine acquired ($3,100) is higher than what was given up, Cedar Fair should report a $700 gain on the income statement. The required journal entry is:

| | Debit | Credit | |
|---|---|---|---|
| Equipment (new machine)  (+A) | 3,100 | | $3,100 Received |
| Accumulated Depreciation—Equipment  (−xA, +A) | 800 | | |
| Equipment (old machine)  (−A) | | 2,200 | $2,400 Given up |
| Cash  (−A) | | 1,000 | ($2,200 − $800 + $1,000) |
| Gain on Exchange of Assets  (+R, +OE) | | 700 | |

| Assets | | = | Liabilities | + | Owners' Equity | |
|---|---|---|---|---|---|---|
| Cash | −1,000 | | | | Gain on Exchange of Assets (+R) | +700 |
| Equipment (+3,100 − 2,200) | + 900 | | | | | |
| Accumulated Depreciation— Equipment (−xA) | + 800 | | | | | |

## Loss on Commercial Asset Exchange

Assume the same facts as in the preceding example except that Cedar Fair pays $2,000 cash instead of $1,000. Given these terms, the assets given up include the cotton candy machine with a book value of $1,400 ($2,200 – $800) plus $2,000 cash. Thus, the total book value of the assets given up equals $3,400. Because the market value of the machine acquired ($3,100) is less than what was given up, Cedar Fair should report a loss of $300 on the income statement. The required journal entry is:

| | Debit | Credit | |
|---|---|---|---|
| Equipment (new machine)  (+A) | 3,100 | | $3,100 Received |
| Loss on Exchange of Assets  (+E, −OE) | 300 | | |
| Accumulated Depreciation—Equipment  (−xA, +A) | 800 | | |
| Equipment (old machine)  (−A) | | 2,200 | $3,400 Given up |
| Cash  (−A) | | 2,000 | ($2,200 − $800 + $2,000) |

| Assets | | = | Liabilities | + | Owners' Equity | |
|---|---|---|---|---|---|---|
| Cash | −2,000 | | | | Loss on Exchange of Assets (+E) | −300 |
| Equipment (+3,100 − 2,200) | + 900 | | | | | |
| Accumulated Depreciation— Equipment (−xA) | + 800 | | | | | |

# Chapter Summary

**LO1  Define, classify, and explain the nature of long-lived assets. p. 418**

- Long-lived assets are those that a business retains for long periods for use in the course of normal operations rather than for sale. They may be divided into tangible assets (land, buildings, and equipment) and intangible assets (including goodwill, patents, and franchises).

**LO2  Apply the cost principle to the acquisition of long-lived assets. p. 419**

- The acquisition cost of property, plant, and equipment is the cash-equivalent purchase price plus all reasonable and necessary expenditures made to acquire and prepare the asset for its intended use.

- Expenditures made after the asset is in use are expensed if they recur frequently, involve relatively small amounts, and do not directly lengthen the asset's useful life. These expenditures are considered ordinary repairs and maintenance expense.
- Expenditures made after the asset is in use are capitalized as a cost of the asset if they provide benefits for one or more accounting periods beyond the current period. This category includes extraordinary repairs, replacements, and additions.

## LO3  Apply various depreciation methods as economic benefits are used up over time. p. 425

- In conformity with the matching principle, the cost of long-lived tangible assets (less any estimated residual value) is allocated to depreciation expense over each period benefited by the assets.
- Depreciation is reported as an expense on the income statement and is accumulated on the balance sheet in the contra-asset account Accumulated Depreciation, which is subtracted from the cost of the long-lived tangible assets to which it relates.
- Common depreciation methods include straight line (a constant amount over time), units of production (a variable amount over time), and double declining balance (a decreasing amount over time).

## LO4  Explain the effect of asset impairment on the financial statements. p. 430

- When events or changes in circumstances reduce the estimated future cash flows of a long-lived asset below book value, the book value should be written down and the amount of the write-down reported as an impairment loss.

## LO5  Account for the disposal of long-lived tangible assets that are discarded or sold. p. 431

- Disposals occur when assets are discarded or sold; they involve the following adjustments:
  - Record additional depreciation arising since the last depreciation adjustment.
  - Remove the cost of the old asset and its related accumulated depreciation.
  - Recognize the cash proceeds (if any).
  - Recognize a gain (or loss) equal to the amount by which the cash received is more (less) than the asset's book value (cost less accumulated depreciation).

## LO6  Account for the acquisition, use, and disposal of long-lived intangible assets. p. 433

- Intangible assets are recorded at cost but only when they are purchased. The costs of most internally developed intangible assets are expensed when they are incurred as research and development costs.
- Intangibles are reported at book value on the balance sheet.
- Amortization is calculated for intangibles with limited useful lives using the straight-line method.
- Intangibles with unlimited useful lives, including goodwill, are not amortized but are reviewed for impairment.

## LO7  Interpret the fixed asset turnover ratio. p. 436

- The fixed asset turnover ratio measures management's efficiency in using the company's investments in property, plant, and equipment to generate sales. Higher turnover ratios imply greater efficiency.

## LO8  Describe the factors to consider when comparing long-lived assets across companies. p. 437

- Companies in different industries require different levels of investment in long-lived assets. Beyond that, you should consider whether differences exist in depreciation methods, estimated useful lives, and estimated residual values. Such differences can affect the book value of long-lived assets as well as the ratios that are calculated using those book values and any gains or losses reported at the time of an asset's disposal.

### Financial Analysis Tools

| Name of Measure | Formula | What It Tells You |
|---|---|---|
| Fixed Asset Turnover Ratio | $\dfrac{\text{Net Sales Revenue}}{\text{Average Net Fixed Assets}}$ | - Indicates dollars of sales generated for each dollar invested in fixed assets (long-lived tangible assets)<br>- A higher ratio implies greater efficiency |

## Key Terms

Amortization (p. 435)
Book (or Carrying) Value (p. 424)
Capital Expenditure (p. 423)
Capitalize (p. 419)
Construction in Progress (p. 419)
Copyright (p. 434)
Declining-Balance Depreciation Method (p. 427)
Depreciable Cost (p. 425)
Depreciation (p. 424)
Double-Declining-Balance Depreciation Method (p. 427)
EBITDA (p. 439)
Extraordinary Repairs (p. 423)
Fixed Assets (p. 418)

446     CHAPTER 10     Long-Lived Tangible and Intangible Assets

See complete glossary in back of text.

## Questions

1. Define long-lived assets. Identify and describe each of the two common categories of long-lived asset.

2. Under the cost principle, what amounts should be recorded as a cost of a long-lived asset?

3. What is the term for recording costs as assets rather than as expenses? Describe how the decision to record costs as assets rather than expenses affects the balance sheet and income statement.

4. Distinguish between ordinary repairs and extraordinary repairs. How do you account for each?

5. Describe the relationship between the matching principle and accounting for long-lived assets.

6. Why are different depreciation methods allowed?

7. In computing depreciation, three values must be known or estimated. Identify and describe each.

8. What type of depreciation expense pattern is used under each of the following methods, and when is its use appropriate?
   a. The straight-line method.
   b. The units-of-production method.
   c. The double-declining-balance method.

9. What is an *asset impairment*? How do you account for it?

10. What is book value? When equipment is sold for more than book value, how is the transaction recorded? How is it recorded when the selling price is less than book value?

11. Distinguish between depreciation and amortization.

12. Define *goodwill*. When is it appropriate to record goodwill as an intangible asset?

13. How is the fixed asset turnover ratio computed? Explain its meaning.

14. (Supplement 10A) How does depletion affect the balance sheet and income statement? Why is depletion accounted for in a manner that differs from depreciation and amortization?

15. (Supplement 10B) Over what period should an addition to an existing long-lived asset be depreciated? Explain.

16. (Supplement 10C) In what two ways does the disposal of an asset through exchange differ from disposal through discarding or selling the asset?

## Multiple Choice

1. Which of the following should be capitalized when a piece of production equipment is acquired for a factory?

   Quiz 10-1
   www.mhhe.com/LLPW1e
   a. Sales taxes.
   b. Transportation costs.
   c. Installation costs.
   d. All of the above.

2. When recording depreciation, which of the following statements is true?
   a. Total assets increase and owners' equity increases.
   b. Total assets decrease and total liabilities increase.
   c. Total assets decrease and owners' equity increases.
   d. None of the above is true.

3. Under what depreciation method(s) is an asset's book value used to calculate depreciation each year?
   a. Straight-line method.
   b. Units-of-production method.
   c. Declining-balance method.
   d. All of the above.

4. Which of the following decisions will result in a higher net income in the year fixed assets are acquired?
   a. Using MACRS depreciation rates prescribed by the IRS rather than straight-line depreciation.
   b. Using long estimated useful lives.
   c. Using lower estimated residual values.
   d. Using the double-declining-balance method rather than the straight-line method.

5. Barber, Inc., followed the practice of depreciating its building on a straight-line basis. Barber purchased a building on January 1, 2010, that had an estimated useful life of 20 years and a residual value of $20,000. The company's depreciation expense for 2010 was $20,000 on the building. What was the original cost of the building?
   a. $360,000.
   b. $380,000.
   c. $400,000.
   d. $420,000.

6. Under which depreciation method is partial-year depreciation not calculated by multiplying the annual depreciation by the fraction of the year for which the asset has been used?
   a. Straight line.
   b. Units of production.
   c. Declining balance.
   d. None of the above—partial-year depreciation always is calculated by multiplying the annual depreciation by the fraction of the year for which the asset has been used.

7. ACME, Inc., uses straight-line depreciation for all of its depreciable assets. ACME sold a used piece of machinery on December 31, 2010, that it had purchased on January 1, 2009, for $10,000. The asset had a five-year life, zero residual value, and Accumulated Depreciation as of December 31, 2009, of $2,000. If the sales price of the used machine was $7,500, the resulting gain or loss on disposal was which of the following amounts?
   a. Loss of $3,500.
   b. Gain of $3,500.
   c. Loss of $1,500.
   d. Gain of $1,500.

8. What assets should be amortized using the straight-line method?
   a. Land.
   b. Intangible assets with limited useful lives.
   c. Intangible assets with unlimited (or indefinite) lives.
   d. All of the above.

9. How many of the following statements regarding goodwill are true?
   • Goodwill is not reported unless purchased in an exchange.
   • Goodwill must be reviewed annually for possible impairment.
   • Impairment of goodwill results in a decrease in net income.
   a. None.                    c. Two.
   b. One.                     d. Three.

10. The Simon Company and the Allen Company each bought a new delivery truck on January 1, 2009. Both companies paid exactly the same cost, $30,000, for their respective vehicles. As of December 31, 2010, the book value of Simon's truck was less than the Allen Company's book value for the same vehicle. Which of the following are acceptable explanations for the difference in book value?
   a. Both companies elected straight-line depreciation, but the Simon Company used a longer estimated life.
   b. The Simon Company estimated a lower residual value, but both estimated the same useful life and both elected straight-line depreciation.
   c. Because GAAP specifies rigid guidelines regarding the calculation of depreciation, this situation is not possible.
   d. None of the above explains the difference in book value.

---

Solutions to Multiple-Choice Questions

1. d    2. d    3. c    4. b    5. d    6. b    7. d
8. b    9. d    10. b

---

# Mini Exercises    Available with McGraw-Hill's Homework Manager

## M10-1 Classifying Long-Lived Assets and Related Cost Allocation Concepts    LO1, 3, 6

For each of the following long-lived assets, indicate its nature and related cost allocation concept. Use the abbreviations shown on the right:

| Asset | Nature | Cost Allocation | Nature |
|---|---|---|---|
| 1. Operating license | | | L  Land |
| 2. Property | | | B  Building |
| 3. New engine for old machine | | | E  Equipment |
| 4. Delivery vans | | | I  Intangible |
| 5. Production plant | | | |
| 6. Warehouse | | | **Cost Allocation** |
| 7. Copyright | | | D  Depreciation |
| 8. Trademark | | | A  Amortization |
| 9. Computers | | | NO  No cost allocation |

## M10-2 Deciding Whether to Capitalize or Expense    LO2, 6

American Golf Corporation operates over 170 golf courses throughout the country. For each of the following items, enter the correct letter to show whether the cost should be capitalized (C) or expensed (E).

**American Golf Corporation**

*Transactions*

____ 1. Purchased a golf course in Orange County, California.

____ 2. Paid a landscaping company to clear 100 acres of land on which to build a new course.

____ 3. Paid a landscaping company to apply fertilizer to the fairways on its Coyote Hills Golf Course.

____ 4. Hired a building maintenance company to build a 2,000 square-foot addition on a clubhouse.

____ 5. Hired a building maintenance company to replace the locks on a clubhouse and equipment shed.

____ 6. Paid an advertising company to create a campaign to build goodwill.

**LO2, 6**

### M10-3 Deciding Whether to Capitalize an Expense

For each of the following items, enter the correct letter to the left to show whether the expenditure should be capitalized (C) or expensed (E).

*Transactions*

____ 1. Paid $600 for ordinary repairs.

____ 2. Paid $16,000 for extraordinary repairs.

____ 3. Paid cash, $200,000, for addition to old building.

____ 4. Paid for routine maintenance, $250, on credit.

____ 5. Purchased a machine, $70,000; gave long-term note.

____ 6. Purchased a patent, $45,300 cash.

____ 7. Paid $20,000 for monthly salaries.

**LO3**

### M10-4 Computing Book Value (Straight-Line Depreciation)

Calculate the book value of a two-year-old machine that cost $200,000, has an estimated residual value of $40,000, and has an estimated useful life of four years. The company uses straight-line depreciation.

**LO3**

### M10-5 Computing Book Value (Units-of-Production Depreciation)

Calculate the book value of a two-year-old machine that cost $200,000, has an estimated residual value of $40,000, and has an estimated useful life of 20,000 machine hours. The company uses units-of-production depreciation and ran the machine 3,000 hours in year 1 and 8,000 hours in year 2.

**LO3**

### M10-6 Computing Book Value (Double-Declining-Balance Depreciation)

Calculate the book value of a two-year-old machine that cost $200,000, has an estimated residual value of $40,000, and has an estimated useful life of four years. The company uses double-declining-balance depreciation. Round to the nearest dollar.

**LO3**

### M10-7 Computing and Recording Partial-Year Straight-Line Depreciation

Calculate the amount of straight-line depreciation to report during the year ended December 31, 2009, for a machine that was purchased at a cost of $33,000 on September 1, 2009. The machine has an estimated residual value of $3,000, and has an estimated useful life of five years. Round to the nearest dollar. Prepare the journal entry to record the depreciation.

**LO3**

### M10-8 Computing and Recording Partial-Year Double-Declining-Balance Depreciation

Calculate the amount of double-declining-balance depreciation to report during the year ended December 31, 2009, for a machine that was purchased at a cost of $33,000 on September 1, 2009. The machine has an estimated residual value of $3,000, and has an estimated useful life of five years. Round to the nearest dollar. Prepare the journal entry to record the depreciation.

**LO4**

### M10-9 Identifying Asset Impairment

For each of the following impaired assets, indicate the amount of impairment loss to report.

|  | Book Value | Fair Value | Amount of Loss |
|---|---|---|---|
| *a.* Machine | $ 17,000 | $ 9,000 | |
| *b.* Copyright | 41,000 | 39,000 | |
| *c.* Factory building | 60,000 | 30,000 | |
| *d.* Building | 250,000 | 210,000 | |

**M10-10 Recording the Disposal of a Long-Lived Asset through Sale**    LO5

Prepare journal entries to record these transactions: (a) Morrell Corporation disposed of computer equipment at the end of its useful life. The computer equipment had cost $4,800 and its Accumulated Depreciation balance was $4,800. No residual value was received. (b) Assume the same information as (a) except that Accumulated Depreciation, updated to the date of disposal, was $3,600.

**M10-11 Reporting and Recording the Disposal of a Long-Lived Asset through Sale (Straight-Line Depreciation)**    LO5

As part of a major renovation at the beginning of the year, Hauser Pharmaceuticals, Inc., sold shelving units (store fixtures) that were 10 years old for $1,000 cash. The shelves originally cost $6,400 and had been depreciated on a straight-line basis over an estimated useful life of 10 years with an estimated residual value of $400. Assuming that depreciation has already been recorded to the date of sale, prepare the journal entry to record the sale of the shelving units and show the effects of the disposal on the accounting equation.

**M10-12 Capitalizing versus Expensing Intangible Asset Costs**    LO6

Most highly visible companies spend significant amounts of money to protect their intellectual property, ensuring that no one uses this property without direct permission. For example, to include logos throughout this book, we had to obtain written permission from each company—a process that stretched over nearly a year and often resulted in requests being denied. Discuss whether companies should capitalize or expense the money paid to employees who evaluate requests for use of their logos and who search for instances where the companies' intellectual property has been used without permission. Draw an analogy to similar costs incurred for employees responsible for the use and upkeep of tangible assets.

**M10-13 Computing Goodwill and Patents**    LO6

Taste-T Company has been in business for 30 years and has developed a large group of loyal restaurant customers. Down Home Foods made an offer to buy Taste-T Company for $6,000,000. The market value of Taste-T's recorded assets, net of liabilities, on the date of the offer is $5,600,000. Taste-T also holds a patent for a fluting machine that the company invented (the patent with a market value of $200,000 was never recorded by Taste-T because it was developed internally). How much has Down Home Foods included for intangibles in its offer of $6,000,000? Assuming Taste-T accepts this offer, which company will report goodwill on its balance sheet?

**M10-14 Computing and Evaluating the Fixed Asset Turnover Ratio**    LO7

The following information was reported by Amuse Yourself Parks (AYP) for 2009:

| | |
|---|---|
| Net fixed assets (beginning of year) | $8,450,000 |
| Net fixed assets (end of year) | 8,250,000 |
| Net sales for the year | 4,175,000 |
| Net income for the year | 1,700,000 |

Compute the company's fixed asset turnover ratio for the year. What can you say about AYP's fixed asset turnover ratio when compared to Cedar Fair's 2007 ratio in Exhibit 10.6?

**M10-15 (Supplement 10A) Recording Depletion for a Natural Resource**

Saskatchewan Forestry Company purchased a timber tract for $600,000, and estimates that it will be depleted evenly over its 10-year useful life with no residual value. Show the journal entry that would be recorded if 10 percent of the total timber is cut and placed into inventory during the current year.

**M10-16 (Supplement 10B) Computing Revised Depreciation after Change in Cost and Estimated Life**

Thornton Industries purchased a machine for $45,000 and is depreciating it with the straight-line method over a life of 10 years, using a residual value of $3,000. At the beginning of the sixth year, an extraordinary repair was made costing $5,000, the estimated useful life was extended to 13 years, and no change was made to the estimated residual value. Calculate depreciation expense for year 6, rounded to the nearest dollar.

### M10-17 (Supplement 10C) Recording the Exchange of Assets

Crosstown Motors acquired a new piece of hydraulic equipment worth $60,000, by paying $50,000 cash and trading in its old equipment. The old equipment had a cost of $40,000 and accumulated depreciation of $35,000. Calculate the amount of the gain or loss that arises from this transaction and prepare the journal entry to record the exchange of assets.

### M10-18 (Supplement 10C) Recording the Exchange of Assets

Assume the same facts as M10-17, except that the old equipment has accumulated depreciation of $24,000 at the time of the transaction. Calculate the amount of the gain or loss that arises from the transaction and prepare the journal entry to record the exchange of assets.

## Exercises  Available with McGraw-Hill's Homework Manager

**LO1**

Hasbro, Inc.

### E10-1 Preparing a Classified Balance Sheet

The following is a list of account titles and amounts (in millions) reported at December 31, 2006, by Hasbro, Inc., a leading manufacturer of games, toys, and interactive entertainment software for children and families:

| | | | |
|---|---|---|---|
| Buildings and Improvements | $186 | Goodwill | $470 |
| Prepaids and Other Current Assets | 243 | Machinery and Equipment | 368 |
| Allowance for Doubtful Accounts | 28 | Accumulated Depreciation | 379 |
| Other Noncurrent Assets | 195 | Inventories | 203 |
| Cash and Cash Equivalents | 715 | Other Intangibles, Net | 532 |
| Accounts Receivable | 584 | Land and Improvements | 7 |

*Required:*

Prepare the asset section of a classified balance sheet for Hasbro, Inc.

**LO2, 3**

### E10-2 Computing and Recording a Basket Purchase and Straight-Line Depreciation

Bridge City Consulting bought a building and the land on which it is located for $182,000 cash. The land is estimated to represent 70 percent of the purchase price. The company also paid renovation costs on the building of $22,000.

*Required:*

1. Explain how to account for the renovation costs.
2. Give the journal entry to record all expenditures. Assume that all transactions were for cash and they occurred at the start of the year.
3. Compute straight-line depreciation on the building at the end of one year, assuming an estimated 12-year useful life and a $4,600 estimated residual value.
4. What should be the book value of the land and building at the end of year 2?

**LO2, 3**

### E10-3 Recording Asset Acquisition Costs and Straight-Line Depreciation

Conover Company ordered equipment on January 1, 2009, at a purchase price of $30,000. On date of delivery, January 2, 2009, the company paid $8,000 for the equipment and signed a note payable for the balance. On January 3, 2009, it paid $250 for freight on the equipment. On January 5, Conover paid $1,500 cash for installation costs relating to the equipment. On December 31, 2009 (the end of the accounting period), Conover recorded depreciation on the equipment using the straight-line method with an estimated useful life of 10 years and an estimated residual value of $2,750.

*Required:*

1. Record journal entries, if any, that would be required on January 1, 2, 3, and 5.
2. Compute the acquisition cost of the equipment.
3. Compute the depreciation expense to be reported for 2009, and show the journal entry to record it.
4. What should be the book value of the equipment at the end of 2010?

## E10-4 Recording Straight-Line Depreciation and Repairs    LO2, 3

Wiater Company operates a small manufacturing facility. At the beginning of 2010, an asset account for the company showed the following balances:

| | |
|---|---|
| Manufacturing equipment | $160,000 |
| Accumulated depreciation through 2009 | 110,000 |

During 2010, the following cash expenditures were made for repairs and maintenance:

| | |
|---|---|
| Routine maintenance and repairs on the equipment | $ 1,850 |
| Major overhaul of the equipment that improved efficiency | 21,000 |

The equipment is being depreciated on a straight-line basis over an estimated life of 15 years with a $10,000 estimated residual value. The annual accounting period ends on December 31.

**Required:**

1. Give the adjusting journal entry that would have been made at the end of 2009 for depreciation on the manufacturing equipment.
2. Give the journal entries to record the two expenditures for repairs and maintenance during 2010.

## E10-5 Determining Financial Statement Effects of Straight-Line Depreciation and Repairs    LO2, 3

Refer to E10-4.

**Required:**

Indicate the effects (accounts, amounts, and + or −) of the following items on the accounting equation, using the headings shown below.

1. The adjustment for depreciation made at the end of 2009.
2. The two expenditures for repairs and maintenance during 2010.

| Item | Assets | = | Liabilities | + | Owners' Equity |
|------|--------|---|-------------|---|----------------|

## E10-6 Computing Depreciation under Alternative Methods    LO3

PlasticWorks Corporation bought a machine at the beginning of the year at a cost of $12,000. The estimated useful life was five years, and the residual value was $2,000. Assume that the estimated productive life of the machine is 10,000 units. Expected annual production was 3,000 units in year 1; 3,000 units in year 2; 2,000 units in year 3; 1,000 units in year 4; and 1,000 units in year 5.

**Required:**

1. Complete a depreciation schedule for each of the alternative methods using a format similar to the one that follows.

   a. Straight line.
   b. Units of production.
   c. Double-declining balance.

| | | INCOME STATEMENT | | BALANCE SHEET | |
|------|-------------|----------------------|------|--------------------------|------------|
| Year | Computation | Depreciation Expense | Cost | Accumulated Depreciation | Book Value |
| At acquisition | | | | | |
| 1 | | | | | |

2. Which method will result in the highest net income in year 2? Does this higher net income mean the machine was used more efficiently under this depreciation method?

**LO3**

**Sonic Corp.**

**E10-7 Computing Depreciation under Alternative Methods**

Sonic Corp. purchased and installed electronic payment equipment at its drive-in restaurants in San Marcos, Texas, at a cost of $27,000. The equipment has an estimated residual value of $1,500. The equipment is expected to process 255,000 payments over its three-year useful life. Per year, expected payment transactions are 61,200 in year 1; 140,250 in year 2; and 53,550 in year 3.

*Required:*

Complete a depreciation schedule for each of the alternative methods using a format similar to the one that follows.

1.    Straight line.
2.    Units of production.
3.    Double declining balance.

| | | INCOME STATEMENT | | BALANCE SHEET | |
|---|---|---|---|---|---|
| Year | Computation | Depreciation Expense | Cost | Accumulated Depreciation | Book Value |
| At acquisition | | | | | |
| 1 | | | | | |

**LO3**

**E10-8 Computing Partial-Year Depreciation under Alternative Methods**

A vehicle was purchased on July 1, 2009, at a cost of $50,000. The vehicle had an estimated useful life of five years and a residual value of $5,000. The company's fiscal year ends on December 31. The vehicle was expected to be driven 30,000 miles in 2009, 40,000 miles in 2010, and 10,000 miles in each of years 2011, 2012, and 2013.

*Required:*

Compute depreciation for 2009 and 2010, under the following methods.

1.    Straight line.
2.    Units of production.
3.    Double declining balance.

**LO3**

**E10-9 Recording Partial-Year Depreciation under Alternative Methods**

Refer to E10-8.

*Required:*

Prepare journal entries for 2009 and 2010, for each of the alternative methods.

1.    Straight line.
2.    Units of production.
3.    Double declining balance.

**LO3**

**FedEx Corporation**

**E10-10 Interpreting Management's Choice of Different Depreciation Methods for Tax and Financial Reporting**

The annual report for FedEx Corporation includes the following information:

> For financial reporting purposes, we record depreciation and amortization of property and equipment on a straight-line basis over the asset's service life. For income tax purposes, depreciation is generally computed using accelerated methods.

*Required:*

Explain why FedEx uses different methods of depreciation for financial reporting and tax purposes.

**E10-11 Inferring Asset Age from Straight-Line Depreciation**                    LO3

On January 1, 2009, the records of Tuff Turf Corporation (TTC) showed the following regarding production equipment:

| | |
|---|---|
| Equipment (estimated residual value, $4,000) | $14,000 |
| Accumulated depreciation (straight line, one year) | 2,000 |

*Required:*
Based on the data given, compute the estimated useful life of the equipment.

**E10-12 Exploring Financial Statement Effects of Asset Impairment**              LO4

Refer to E10-11.

*Required:*
If TTC's management estimated that the equipment had future cash flows and a fair value of only $6,800 at December 31, 2009, how would this affect TTC's balance sheet and income statement? Explain.

**E10-13 Demonstrating the Effect of Book Value on Reporting an Asset Disposal through Sale**    LO5

FedEx is the world's leading express-distribution company. In addition to the world's largest fleet of all-cargo aircraft, the company has more than 46,400 ground vehicles that pick up and deliver packages. Assume that FedEx sold a delivery truck for $16,000. FedEx had originally purchased the truck for $28,000 and had recorded depreciation for three years.                    FedEx

*Required:*

1.  Give the journal entry for the disposal of the truck, assuming that
    a.  The accumulated depreciation was $12,000.
    b.  The accumulated depreciation was $10,000.
    c.  The accumulated depreciation was $15,000.

2.  Based on the three preceding situations, explain how the amount of depreciation recorded up to the time of disposal affects the amount of gain or loss on disposal.

**E10-14 Demonstrating the Effect of Book Value on Recording an Asset Disposal through Sale**    LO5

Refer to E10–13.

*Required:*

1.  Calculate the amount of gain or loss on disposal, assuming that
    a.  The accumulated depreciation was $12,000.
    b.  The accumulated depreciation was $10,000.
    c.  The accumulated depreciation was $15,000.

2.  Based on the three preceding situations, explain how the amount of depreciation recorded up to the time of disposal affects the amount of gain or loss on disposal.

**E10-15 Computing and Reporting the Acquisition and Amortization of Three Different Intangible Assets**    LO 6

Kreiser Company had three intangible assets at the end of 2009 (end of the accounting year):

a.  A patent purchased from J. Miller on January 1, 2009, for a cash cost of $5,640. Miller had registered the patent with the U.S. Patent Office five years ago.
b.  A trademark was registered with the federal government for $10,000. Management estimated that the trademark could be worth as much as $200,000 because it has an indefinite life.
c.  Computer licensing rights were purchased on January 1, 2008, for $60,000. The rights are expected to have a four-year useful life to the company.

*Required:*

1.  Compute the acquisition cost of each intangible asset.
2.  Compute the amortization of each intangible asset for the year ended December 31, 2009.
3.  Show how these assets and any related expenses should be reported on the balance sheet and income statement for 2009.

**LO4, 6**

**Nutek, Inc.**

**E10-16 Recording the Purchase, Amortization, and Impairment of a Patent**

Nutek, Inc., holds a patent for the Full Service handi-plate, which the company described in its annual report as "a patented plastic buffet plate that allows the user to hold both a plate and cup in one hand" and that "has a multitude of uses including social gatherings such as backyard barbecues, buffets, picnics, tailgate and parties of any kind." (No, we are not making this up.) Nutek also purchased a patent for $1,000,000 for "a specialty line of patented switch plate covers and outlet plate covers specifically designed to light up automatically when the power fails." Assume the switch plate patent was purchased January 1, 2009, and it is being amortized over a period of 10 years. Assume Nutek does not use an Accumulated Amortization account but instead charges amortization directly against the intangible asset account.

*Required:*

1. Describe the effects of the purchase and amortization of the switch plate patent on the 2009 balance sheet and income statement.
2. Give the journal entries to record the purchase and amortization of the switch plate patent in 2009.
3. After many months of unsuccessful attempts to manufacture the switch plate covers, Nutek determined the patent was significantly impaired and its book value on January 1, 2010, was written off. Show the journal entry and the accounting effects of recording the asset impairment.

**LO7**

**Apple Inc.**

**E10-17 Computing and Interpreting the Fixed Asset Turnover Ratio from a Financial Analyst's Perspective**

The following data were included in a recent Apple Inc. annual report (in millions):

| | 2007 | 2006 | 2005 | 2004 | 2003 | 2002 | 2001 |
|---|---|---|---|---|---|---|---|
| Net sales | $24,006 | $19,315 | $13,931 | $8,279 | $6,207 | $5,742 | $5,363 |
| Net property, plant, and equipment | 1,832 | 1,281 | 817 | 707 | 669 | 669 | 564 |

*Required:*

1. Compute Apple's fixed asset turnover ratio for 2002, 2004, and 2006 (the even years). Round your answers to one decimal place.
2. If you were a financial analyst, what would you say about the results of your analyses?

**LO3, 7**

**E10-18 Computing Depreciation and Book Value for Two Years Using Alternative Depreciation Methods and Interpreting the Impact on the Fixed Asset Turnover Ratio**

Torge Company bought a machine for $65,000 cash. The estimated useful life was five years, and the estimated residual value was $5,000. Assume that the estimated useful life in productive units is 150,000. Units actually produced were 40,000 in year 1 and 45,000 in year 2.

*Required:*

1. Determine the appropriate amounts to complete the following schedule. Show computations.

| | DEPRECIATION EXPENSE FOR | | BOOK VALUE AT THE END OF | |
|---|---|---|---|---|
| Method of Depreciation | Year 1 | Year 2 | Year 1 | Year 2 |
| Straight line | | | | |
| Units of production | | | | |
| Double-declining balance | | | | |

2.   Which method would result in the lowest net income for year 1? For year 2?
3.   Which method would result in the lowest fixed asset turnover ratio for year 1? Why?

### E10-19 Accounting for Operating Activities (Including Depreciation) and Preparing Financial Statements (Comprehensive Exercise)

LO2, 3

Grid Iron Prep Inc. (GIPI) is a sole proprietorship created in January 2009 to provide personal training for athletes aspiring to play college football. The following transactions occurred during the year ended December 31, 2009.

(a)  Gerry Ingalls contributed $90,000 cash to start his sole proprietorship.
(b)  GIPI purchased a gymnasium building and gym equipment at the beginning of the year for $50,000, 80 percent of which related to the gymnasium and 20 percent to the equipment.
(c)  GIPI paid $250 cash to have the gym equipment refurbished before it could be used.
(d)  GIPI collected $36,000 cash in training fees during the year, of which $2,000 was for customer deposits to be earned in 2010.
(e)  GIPI paid $23,000 of wages and $7,000 in utilities.
(f)  GIPI provided $3,000 in training during the final month of the year and expected collection in 2010.
(g)  GIPI will depreciate the gymnasium building using the double-declining-balance method over 20 years. Gym equipment will be depreciated using the straight-line method, with an estimated residual value of $2,250 at the end of its four-year useful life.
(h)  GIPI received a bill for $350 of advertising done during December. The bill has not been paid or recorded.
(i)  GIPI will record an estimated 5 percent of its accounts receivable as not collectible.

*Required:*
1.   Prepare journal entries to record the transactions and adjustments listed in *a* through *i*.
2.   Prepare GIPI's 2009 income statement, statement of owners' equity, and classified balance sheet.

### E10-20 (Supplement 10A) Calculating and Reporting Depletion

Louisiana Oil Company (LOC) paid $3,000,000 for an oil reserve estimated to hold 50,000 barrels of oil. Oil production is expected to be 10,000 barrels in year 1, 30,000 barrels in year 2, and 10,000 barrels in year 3. LOC expects to begin selling barrels from its oil inventory in year 2.

*Required:*
Assuming these estimates are accurate, describe the amounts, financial statements, and classifications that would be used for the oil reserves and oil inventory at the end of year 1.

### E10-21 (Supplement 10B) Recording a Change in Estimate

Refer to E10-4.

*Required:*
Give the adjusting entry that should be made at the end of 2010 for depreciation of the manufacturing equipment, assuming no change in the original estimated total life or residual value. Show computations.

### E10-22 (Supplement 10C) Comparing Exchange of Assets under Two Depreciation Methods

Scrimshaw Industries acquired a new dump truck worth $120,000 on December 31, 2010, by paying $70,000 cash and trading in its used dump truck, which had been purchased three years ago at a cost of $100,000. The old truck had an estimated useful life of five years and a residual value of $20,000.

*Required:*
1.   Calculate the amount of depreciation recorded on the old dump truck on December 31, 2008, 2009, and 2010, assuming (a) straight-line depreciation and (b) double-declining-balance depreciation.
2.   Give the journal entry to record the exchange of assets on December 31, 2010, assuming depreciation has already been recorded in 2010 using (a) straight-line and (b) double-declining-balance methods.
3.   Does the amount recorded as the cost of the new dump truck differ for situations (a) and (b)? Does the amount recorded as a gain or loss on disposal of the old dump truck differ for situations (a) and (b)? What is responsible for producing any differences between (a) and (b)?

## Problems—Set A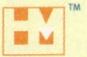

**Available with McGraw-Hill's Homework Manager**

LO1, 2, 3, 4, 5, 6

### PA10-1 Recording Transactions and Adjustments for Tangible and Intangible Assets

The following transactions and adjusting entries were completed by a paper-packaging company called Gravure Graphics International. The company uses straight-line depreciation for trucks and other vehicles, double-declining-balance depreciation for buildings, and straight-line amortization for patents.

| | |
|---|---|
| January 2, 2009 | Paid $95,000 cash to purchase storage shed components. |
| January 3, 2009 | Paid $5,000 cash to have the storage shed erected. The storage shed has an estimated life of 10 years, and a residual value of $10,000. |
| April 1, 2009 | Paid $38,000 cash to purchase a pickup truck for use in the business. The truck has an estimated useful life of five years, and a residual value of $8,000. |
| May 13, 2009 | Paid $250 cash for repairs to the pickup truck. |
| July 1, 2009 | Paid $20,000 cash to purchase patent rights on a new paper bag manufacturing process. The patent is estimated to have a remaining useful life of five years. |
| December 31, 2009 | Recorded depreciation and amortization on the pickup truck, storage shed, and patent. |
| June 30, 2010 | Sold the pickup truck for $33,000 cash. (Record the depreciation on the truck prior to recording its disposal.) |
| December 31, 2010 | Recorded depreciation on the storage shed. Determined that the patent was impaired and wrote off its remaining book value (i.e., wrote down the book value to zero). |

*Required:*

Give the journal entries required on each of the above dates.

LO2, 3

### PA10-2 Computing Acquisition Cost and Recording Depreciation under Three Alternative Methods

At the beginning of the year, Chemical Control Corporation bought three used machines from Radial Compression Incorporated. The machines immediately were overhauled, installed, and started operating. Because the machines were different, each was recorded separately in the accounts.

| | Machine A | Machine B | Machine C |
|---|---|---|---|
| Cost of the asset | $10,000 | $31,500 | $22,000 |
| Installation costs | 1,600 | 2,100 | 800 |
| Renovation costs prior to use | 600 | 1,400 | 1,600 |
| Repairs after production began | 500 | 400 | 700 |

By the end of the first year, each machine had been operating 7,000 hours.

*Required:*

1. Compute the cost of each machine. Explain the rationale for capitalizing or expensing the various costs.

2. Give the journal entry to record depreciation expense at the end of year 1, assuming the following:

| | | ESTIMATES | |
|---|---|---|---|
| Machine | Life | Residual Value | Depreciation Method |
| A | 4 years | $1,000 | Straight line |
| B | 33,000 hours | 2,000 | Units of production |
| C | 5 years | 1,400 | Double-declining balance |

## PA10-3 Recording and Interpreting the Disposal of Long-Lived Assets Sold and Discarded　LO5

During 2009, Ly Company disposed of two different assets. On January 1, 2009, prior to their disposal, the accounts reflected the following:

| Asset | Original Cost | Residual Value | Estimated Life | Accumulated Depreciation (straight line) |
|---|---|---|---|---|
| Machine A | $24,000 | $2,000 | 5 years | $17,600 (4 years) |
| Machine B | 59,200 | 3,200 | 14 years | 48,000 (12 years) |

The machines were disposed of in the following ways:

a. Machine A: Sold on January 1, 2009, for $7,000 cash.

b. Machine B: On January 1, 2009, this machine suffered irreparable damage from an accident and was removed immediately by a salvage company at no cost.

### Required:

1. Give the journal entries related to the disposal of each machine at the beginning of 2009.
2. Explain the accounting rationale for the way that you recorded each disposal.

## PA10-4 Determining Financial Statement Effects of Activities Related to Intangible Assets　LO6

Norton Pharmaceuticals entered into the following transactions that potentially affect intangible assets:

(a) On January 1, 2009, the company spent $18,600 cash to buy a patent that expires in 15 years.

(b) During 2009, the company spent $25,480 working on a new drug that will be submitted for FDA testing in 2010.

(c) Norton Pharmaceuticals purchased the assets of another business in 2009 for a cash lump-sum payment of $650,000. Included in the purchase price was "Goodwill, $75,000."

### Required:

1. Give the journal entry for each of these transactions.
2. For each of the intangible assets, compute amortization for the year ended December 31, 2009.

## PA10-5 (Supplement 10B) Analyzing and Recording Entries Related to a Change in Estimated Life and Residual Value

Reader's Digest is a global publisher of magazines, books, and music and video collections, and is one of the world's leading direct-mail marketers. Many direct-mail marketers use high-speed Didde press equipment to print their advertisements. These presses can cost more than $1 million. Assume that Reader's Digest owns a Didde press acquired at an original cost of $600,000. It is being depreciated on a straight-line basis over a 20-year estimated useful life and has a $75,000 estimated residual value. At the end of 2009, the press had been depreciated for a full eight years. In January 2010, a decision was made, on the basis of improved maintenance procedures, that a total estimated useful life of 25 years and a residual value of $109,500 would be more realistic. The accounting period ends December 31.

**Reader's Digest**

### Required:

1. Compute (a) the amount of depreciation expense recorded in 2009, and (b) the book value of the printing press at the end of 2009.
2. Compute the amount of depreciation that should be recorded in 2010. Show computations.
3. Give the adjusting entry for depreciation at December 31, 2010.

## Problems—Set B

### PB10-1 Recording Transactions and Adjustments for Tangible and Intangible Assets　LO1, 2, 3, 4, 5, 6

The following transactions and adjusting entries were completed by a local delivery company called Super Swift. The company uses straight-line depreciation for delivery vehicles, double-declining-balance depreciation for buildings, and straight-line amortization for franchise rights.

January 2, 2010　Paid $75,000 cash to purchase a small warehouse building near the airport. The building has an estimated life of 20 years, and a residual value of $15,000.

| | |
|---|---|
| July 1, 2010 | Paid $40,000 cash to purchase a delivery van. The van has an estimated useful life of five years, and a residual value of $8,000. |
| October 2, 2010 | Paid $400 cash to paint a small office in the warehouse building. |
| October 13, 2010 | Paid $150 cash to get the oil changed in the delivery van. |
| December 1, 2010 | Paid $60,000 cash to UPS to begin operating Super Swift business as a franchise using the name The UPS Store. This franchise right expires in five years. |
| December 31, 2010 | Recorded depreciation and amortization on the delivery van, warehouse building, and franchise right. |
| June 30, 2011 | Sold the warehouse building for $64,000 cash. (Record the depreciation on the building prior to recording its disposal.) |
| December 31, 2011 | Recorded depreciation on the delivery van and amortization on the franchise right. Determined that the franchise right was not impaired in value. |

*Required:*
Give the journal entries required on each of the above dates.

LO2, 3

**PB10-2 Computing Acquisition Cost and Recording Depreciation under Three Alternative Methods**

At the beginning of the year, Oakmont Company bought three used machines from American Manufacturing, Inc. The machines immediately were overhauled, installed, and started operating. Because the machines were different, each was recorded separately in the accounts.

| | Machine A | Machine B | Machine C |
|---|---|---|---|
| Amount paid for asset | $19,600 | $10,100 | $9,800 |
| Installation costs | 300 | 500 | 200 |
| Renovation costs prior to use | 100 | 300 | 600 |
| Repairs after production began | 220 | 900 | 480 |

By the end of the first year, each machine had been operating 4,000 hours.

*Required:*

1.  Compute the cost of each machine. Explain the rationale for capitalizing or expensing the various costs.

2.  Give the journal entry to record depreciation expense at the end of year 1, assuming the following:

| | ESTIMATES | | |
|---|---|---|---|
| Machine | Life | Residual Value | Depreciation Method |
| A | 7 years | $1,100 | Straight line |
| B | 40,000 hours | 900 | Units of production |
| C | 4 years | 2,000 | Double-declining balance |

LO5

**PB10-3 Recording and Interpreting the Disposal of Long-Lived Assets Sold and Discarded**

During 2009, Rayon Corporation disposed of two different assets. On January 1, 2009, prior to their disposal, the accounts reflected the following:

| Asset | Original Cost | Residual Value | Estimated Life | Accumulated Depreciation (straight line) |
|---|---|---|---|---|
| Machine A | $60,000 | $11,000 | 7 years | $28,000 (4 years) |
| Machine B | 14,200 | 1,925 | 5 years | 7,365 (3 years) |

The machines were disposed of in the following ways:

a.   Machine A: Sold on January 2, 2009, for $33,500 cash.
b.   Machine B: On January 2, 2009, this machine suffered irreparable damage from an accident and was removed immediately by a salvage company at no cost.

**Required:**

1.   Give the journal entries related to the disposal of each machine at the beginning of 2009.
2.   Explain the accounting rationale for the way that you recorded each disposal.

## PB10-4 Determining Financial Statement Effects of Activities Related to Intangible Assets    LO6

Pandey Company entered into the following transactions that potentially affect intangible assets:

(a)   Soon after Pandey Company started business, in January 2008, it purchased the assets of another business for a cash lump-sum payment of $400,000. Included in the purchase price was "Goodwill, $60,000." The account balance has not changed in two years.

(b)   The company purchased a patent at a cash cost of $54,600 on January 1, 2009. The patent has an estimated useful life of 13 years.

(c)   In 2009, Pandey hired a director of brand development to create a marketable identity for the company's products. The director devoted the entire year to this work, at a cost to the company of $125,000.

**Required:**

1.   Give the journal entries required in 2009.
2.   For each of the intangible assets, compute amortization for the year ended December 31, 2009.

## PB10-5 (Supplement 10C) Analyzing and Recording Entries Related to an Exchange of Assets

The following transactions and adjusting entries were completed by a glass-cutting company. The company uses straight-line depreciation.

| | |
|---|---|
| June 30, 2009 | Paid $10,000 cash to purchase waterjet cutting equipment. The equipment has an estimated life of three years and residual value of $1,300. |
| July 1, 2009 | Paid $300 cash to have the waterjet cutter installed in the production facility. |
| December 31, 2009 | Recorded depreciation on the waterjet cutting equipment. |
| April 1, 2010 | Paid $10,000 cash and traded in the waterjet cutting equipment to acquire a $19,000 plasmacutter, which will allow the company to cut at higher levels of precision. (Record the depreciation on the old equipment prior to recording its exchange.) The new plasmacutter has an estimated useful life of four years, and a residual value of $1,000. |
| December 31, 2010 | Recorded depreciation on the plasmacutter. |

**Required:**

1.   Compute the amount of depreciation expense recorded (a) in 2009, and (b) for the three months up to April 1, 2010
2.   Indicate the (a) cost of the new equipment acquired April 1, 2010, and (b) depreciation on the new equipment for the nine months from April 1 through December 31, 2010. Show computations.
3.   Give the journal entries required on each of the above dates.

# Cases and Projects

## CP10-1 Finding Financial Information    LO2, 3, 6, 7

Refer to the financial statements of The Home Depot in Appendix A at the end of this book, or download the annual report from the Cases and Projects section of the text's Web site at www.mhhe.com/ LLPW1e.

**Required:**

1.   What method of depreciation does the company use?
2.   What is the amount of Accumulated Depreciation at February 3, 2008? What percentage is this of the total cost of property and equipment?

3.  For depreciation purposes, what is the range of estimated useful lives for the buildings?

4.  What amount of depreciation and amortization expense was reported for the current year? What percentage of net sales is it?

5.  What is the fixed asset turnover ratio for the current year?

6.  For each of the preceding questions, where did you locate the information?

**LO2, 3, 6, 7**

Lowe's

### CP10-2 Comparing Financial Information

Refer to the financial statements of The Home Depot in Appendix A and Lowe's Companies in Appendix B at the end of this book, or download the annual reports from the Cases section of the text's Web site at www.mhhe.com/ LLPW1e.

*Required:*

1.  What method of depreciation does the company use?

2.  What is the amount of Accumulated Depreciation at February 1, 2008? What percentage is this of the total cost of property and equipment? Is this a larger (or smaller) percentage of the total cost of property and equipment than for The Home Depot (in CP10-1)? What does it suggest to you about the length of time the assets have been depreciated?

3.  Lowe's estimated useful life of buildings differs from that estimated by The Home Depot. How will this affect the fixed asset turnover ratios of the two companies?

4.  What amount of depreciation expense was reported on the income statement for the current year? What percentage of net sales is it? Compare this percentage to that of The Home Depot and describe what this implies about the two companies' operations.

5.  What is the fixed asset turnover ratio for the current year? Compare this ratio to that of The Home Depot and describe what it implies about the operations of the two companies.

**LO1, 3, 6, 7**

### CP10-3 Examining an Annual Report: Internet-Based Team Research

As a team, select an industry to analyze. Using your Web browser, each team member should acquire the annual report or 10-K for one publicly traded company in the industry, with each member selecting a different company. (See CP1-3 in Chapter 1 for a description of possible resources for these tasks.)

*Required:*

1.  On an individual basis, each team member should write a short report that incorporates the following:

    *a.* Describe the depreciation methods used.

    *b.* Compute the percentage of fixed asset cost that has been depreciated. What does this imply about the length of time the assets have been depreciated?

    *c.* Compute the fixed asset turnover ratios for the current and prior years. What does this tell you about the efficiency of the company's asset use?

    *d.* Describe the kinds of intangible assets, if any, that the company reports on the balance sheet.

2.  Then, as a team, write a short report comparing and contrasting your companies using these attributes. Discuss any patterns across the companies that you as a team observe. Provide potential explanations for any differences discovered.

**LO2, 7**

### CP10-4 Making Ethical Decisions : A Real-Life Example

Assume you work as a staff member in a large accounting department for a multinational public company. Your job requires you to review documents relating to the company's equipment purchases. Upon verifying that purchases are properly approved, you prepare journal entries to record the equipment purchases in the accounting system. Typically, you handle equipment purchases costing $100,000 or less.

This morning, you were contacted by the executive assistant to the Chief Financial Officer (CFO). She says that the CFO has asked to see you immediately in his office. Although your boss's boss has attended a few meetings where the CFO was present, you have never met the CFO during your three years with the company. Needless to say, you are anxious about the meeting.

Upon entering the CFO's office, you are warmly greeted with a smile and friendly handshake. The CFO compliments you on the great work that you have been doing for the company. You soon feel a little more comfortable, particularly when the CFO mentions that he has a special project for you. He states that he and the CEO have negotiated significant new arrangements with the company's equipment suppliers, which require the company to make advance payments for equipment to be purchased in the future. The CFO says that, for various reasons that he did not want to discuss, he will be processing the payments through the operating division of the company rather than the equipment accounting group. Given that the payments will be made through the operating division, they will initially be classified as operating expenses of the company. He indicates clearly that these advance payments for property and equipment should "obviously" be recorded as assets, so he will be contacting you at the end of every quarter to make an adjusting journal entry to capitalize the amounts inappropriately classified as operating expenses. He advises you that a new account, called Prepaid Equipment, has been established for this purpose. He quickly wraps up the meeting by telling you that it is important that you not talk about the special project with anyone. You assume he does not want others to become jealous of your new important responsibility.

A few weeks later, at the end of the first quarter, you receive a voice mail from the CFO stating, "The adjustment that we discussed is $771,000,000 for this quarter." Before deleting the message, you replay it to make sure you heard it right. Your company generates over $8 billion in revenues and incurs $6 billion in operating expenses every quarter, but you have never made a journal entry for that much money. So, just to be sure there is not a mistake, you send an e-mail to the CFO confirming the amount. He phones you back immediately to abruptly inform you, "There is no mistake. That is the number." Feeling embarrassed that you may have annoyed the CFO, you quietly make the adjusting journal entry.

For each of the remaining three quarters in that year and for the first quarter in the following year, you continue to make these end-of-quarter adjustments. The "magic number" as the CFO liked to call it was $560,000,000 for Q2, $742,745,000 for Q3, $941,000,000 for Q4, and $818,204,000 for Q1 of the following year. During this time, you have had several meetings and lunches with the CFO where he provides you the magic number, sometimes supported with nothing more than a Post-it note with the number written on it. He frequently compliments you on your good work and promises that you will soon be in line for a big promotion.

Despite the CFO's compliments and promises, you are growing increasingly uncomfortable with the journal entries that you have been making. Typically, whenever an ordinary equipment purchase involves an advance payment, the purchase is completed a few weeks later. At that time, the amount of the advance is removed from an Equipment Deposit account and transferred to the appropriate equipment account. This has not been the case with the CFO's special project. Instead, the Prepaid Equipment account has continued to grow, now standing at over $3.8 billion. There has been no discussion about how or when this balance will be reduced, and no depreciation has been recorded for it.

Just as you begin to reflect on the effect the adjustments have had on your company's fixed assets, operating expenses, and operating income, you receive a call from the vice president for internal audit. She needs to talk with you this afternoon about "a peculiar trend in the company's fixed asset turnover ratio and some suspicious journal entries that you have been making."

*Required:*

1. Complete the following table to determine what the company's accounting records would have looked like had you not made the journal entries as part of the CFO's special project. Comment on how the decision to capitalize amounts, which were initially recorded as operating expenses, has affected the level of operating income in each quarter.

| (amounts in millions of U.S. dollars) | Q1 Year 1 (March 31) With the Entries | Q1 Year 1 Without the Entries | Q2 Year 1 (June 30) With the Entries | Q2 Year 1 Without the Entries | Q3 Year 1 (September 30) With the Entries | Q3 Year 1 Without the Entries | Q4 Year 1 (December 31) With the Entries | Q4 Year 1 Without the Entries | Q1 Year 2 (March 31) With the Entries | Q1 Year 2 Without the Entries |
|---|---|---|---|---|---|---|---|---|---|---|
| Property and equipment, net | $38,614 | $ | $35,982 | $ | $38,151 | $ | $38,809 | $ | $39,155 | $ |
| Sales revenues | 8,825 | 8,825 | 8,910 | 8,910 | 8,966 | 8,966 | 8,478 | 8,478 | 8,120 | 8,120 |
| Operating expenses | 7,628 | | 8,526 | | 7,786 | | 7,725 | | 7,277 | |
| Operating income | 1,197 | | 384 | | 1,180 | | 753 | | 843 | |

2. Using the numbers that include the special journal entries that you recorded, compute the fixed asset turnover ratio for the periods ended Q2 through Q4 of year 1 and Q1 of year 2. What does the trend in this ratio suggest to you? Is this consistent with the changes in operating income reported by the company?

3. Before your meeting with the vice president for internal audit, you think about the above computations and the variety of peculiar circumstances surrounding the "special project" for the CFO. What in particular might have raised your suspicion about the real nature of your work?

4. Your meeting with internal audit was short and unpleasant. The vice president indicated that she had discussed her findings with the CFO before meeting with you. The CFO claimed that he too had noticed the peculiar trend in the fixed assets turnover ratio, but that he had not had a chance to investigate it further. He urged internal audit to get to the bottom of things, suggesting that perhaps someone might be making unapproved journal entries. Internal audit had identified you as the source of the journal entries and had been unable to find any documents that approved or substantiated the entries. She ended the meeting by advising you to find a good lawyer. Given your current circumstances, describe how you would have acted earlier had you been able to foresee where it might lead you.

5. In the real case on which this one is based, the internal auditors agonized over the question of whether they had actually uncovered a fraud or whether they were jumping to the wrong conclusion. *The Wall Street Journal* mentioned this on October 30, 2002, by stating, "it was clear . . . that their findings would be devastating for the company. They worried about whether their revelations would result in layoffs. Plus, they feared that they would somehow end up being blamed for the mess." Beyond the personal consequences mentioned in this quote, describe other potential ways in which the findings of the internal auditors would likely be devastating for the publicly traded company and those associated with it.

*Epilogue:*

World Com
Verizon

This case is based on a fraud committed at WorldCom (now owned by Verizon). The case draws its numbers, the nature of the unsupported journal entries, and the CFO's role in carrying out the fraud from a report issued by WorldCom's bankruptcy examiner. Year 1 in this case was actually 2001 and year 2 was 2002. This case excludes other fraudulent activities that contributed to WorldCom's $11 billion fraud. The 63-year-old CEO was sentenced to 25 years in prison for planning and executing the biggest fraud in the history of American business. The CFO, who cooperated in the investigation of the CEO, was sentenced to five years in prison.

LO3    **CP10-5 Making Ethical Decisions: A Mini Case**

Assume you are one of three members of the accounting staff working for a small, private company. At the beginning of this year, the company expanded into a new industry by acquiring equipment that will be used to make several new lines of products. The owner and general manager of the company has indicated that, as one of the conditions for providing financing for the new equipment, the company's bank will receive a copy of the company's annual financial statements. Another condition of the loan is that the company's total assets cannot fall below $250,000. Violation of this condition gives the bank the option to demand immediate repayment of the loan. Before making the adjustment for this year's depreciation, the company's total assets are reported at $255,000. The owner has asked you to take a look at the facts regarding the new equipment and "work with the numbers to make sure everything stays onside with the bank."

A depreciation method has yet not been adopted for the new equipment. Equipment used in other parts of the company is depreciated using the double-declining-balance method. The cost of the new equipment was $35,000 and the manager estimates it will be worth "at least $7,000" at the end of its four-year useful life. Because the products made with the new equipment are only beginning to catch on with consumers, the company used the equipment to produce just 4,000 units this year. It is expected that, over all four years of its useful life, the new equipment will make a total of 28,000 units.

*Required:*

1. Calculate the depreciation that would be reported this year under each of the three methods shown in this chapter. Which of the methods would meet the owner's objective?

2. Evaluate whether it is ethical to recommend that the company use the method identified in requirement 1. What two parties are most directly affected by this recommendation? How would each party be benefited or harmed by the recommendation? Does the recommendation violate any laws or applicable rules? Are there any other factors that you would consider before making a recommendation?

### CP10-6 Thinking Critically: Analyzing the Effects of Depreciation Policies on Income         LO3, 5, 8

As an aspiring financial analyst, you have applied to a major Wall Street firm for a summer job. To screen potential applicants, the firm provides them a short case study and asks them to evaluate the financial success of two hypothetical companies that started operations on January 1, 2008. Both companies operate in the same industry, use very similar assets, and have very similar customer bases. Among the additional information provided about the companies are the following comparative income statements.

|  | FAST CORPORATION | | SLOW CORPORATION | |
|---|---|---|---|---|
|  | 2009 | 2008 | 2009 | 2008 |
| Net sales | $60,000 | $60,000 | $60,000 | $60,000 |
| Cost of goods sold | 20,000 | 20,000 | 20,000 | 20,000 |
| Gross profit | 40,000 | 40,000 | 40,000 | 40,000 |
| Selling, general, and administrative expenses | 19,000 | 19,000 | 19,000 | 19,000 |
| Depreciation expense | 3,555 | 10,667 | 5,000 | 5,000 |
| Operating income | 17,445 | 10,333 | 16,000 | 16,000 |
| Other gains (losses) | 2,222 | — | (2,000) | — |
| Income before income taxes | $19,667 | $10,333 | $14,000 | $16,000 |

*Required:*

Prepare an analysis of the two companies with the goal of determining which company is better managed. If you could request two additional pieces of information from these companies' financial statements, describe specifically what they would be and explain how they would help you to make a decision.

### CP10-7 Preparing Depreciation Schedules for Straight-Line and Double-Declining-Balance Methods         LO3

To make some extra money, you have started preparing templates of business forms and schedules for others to download from the Internet (for a small fee). After relevant information is entered into each template, it automatically performs calculations using formulas you have entered into the template. For the depreciation template, you decide to produce two worksheets—one that calculates depreciation and book value under the straight-line method and another that calculates these amounts using the double-declining-balance method. The templates perform straightforward calculations of depreciation and book value, when given the cost of an asset, its estimated useful life, and its estimated residual value. These particular templates will not handle disposals or changes in estimates—you plan to create a deluxe version for those functions. To illustrate that your templates actually work, you enter the information used to produce the depreciation schedules shown in Exhibit 10.7, with Cedar Fair and Six Flags as examples.

Although you are confident you can use appropriate formulas in the spreadsheet to create a template for the straight-line method, you are a little uncertain about how to make the double-declining-balance method work. You e-mail your friend Sally for advice. Here is what she said:

From:        Sally@yahoo.com
To:          Helpme@hotmail.com
Cc:
Subject:     Excel Help

I wish I had thought of charging money for showing how to do ordinary accounting activities. You would have made me rich by now. ☺ Here is how to set up your worksheets. Begin by creating an "input values" section. This section will allow someone to enter the asset cost, residual value, and estimated life in an area removed from the actual depreciation schedule. You do not want someone accidentally entering amounts over formulas that you have entered into the schedule.

The cells from the input values section will be referenced by other cells in the depreciation schedule. You will want to enter formulas in the cells for the first year row, and then copy and paste them to rows for the other years. When doing this, you will need to use what is called an "absolute reference," which means that the cell reference does not change when one row is copied and pasted to a different row. Unlike an ordinary cell reference that has a format of A1, an absolute reference has the format of $A$1, which prevents the spreadsheet from changing either the column (A) or row (1) when copying the cell to other cells. You may find this useful when preparing both the straight-line and double-declining-balance schedules.

To create the depreciation schedules, use five columns labeled: (1) year, (2) beginning of year accumulated depreciation, (3) depreciation, (4) end-of-year accumulated depreciation, and (5) end-of-year book value.

The double-declining-balance template will be the trickiest to create because you need to be concerned that the book value is not depreciated below the residual value in the last year of the asset's life. To force the template to automatically watch for this, you will need to use the IF function. Here's a screenshot of a template I created, using the IF function to properly calculate depreciation for all years of the asset's life. Notice the formula bar at the top.

*Required:*

Create the spreadsheet templates to calculate depreciation and book value using the straight-line and double-declining-balance methods. Demonstrate that the template works by reproducing the schedules in Exhibit 10.7.

**Tip:** To switch between displaying cell formulas and their values, press CTRL and ~ (tilde) at the same time.

# 11 Current Liabilities and Payroll

## LEARNING OBJECTIVES

**After completing this chapter, you should be able to:**

**LO1** Explain how to report the major types of liabilities.

**LO2** Calculate and interpret the current ratio.

**LO3** Demonstrate how to account for notes payable and the current portion of long-term debt.

**LO4** Demonstrate how to account for sales taxes and unearned revenues.

**LO5** Demonstrate how to account for warranties and other contingent liabilities.

**LO6** Calculate and record payroll including employer payroll taxes.

Lectured slideshow–LP11-1
www.mhhe.com/LLPW1e

**GENERAL MILLS**

## Focus Company: GENERAL MILLS, INC.

### Maker of Pillsbury, Green Giant, Cheerios, and More

**www.generalmills.com**

f you are like most people, you probably owe money to someone. Maybe you used your credit card to buy some new shoes or you took out a student loan to pay your tuition. Whatever the reason, you should make sure you can pay those liabilities when they become due. Americans spend about $14 billion each year just for late fees on their overdue credit card balances. When you consider the interest that is charged on an overdue balance, you can see why the failure to pay liabilities on time is a leading cause of personal bankruptcy. For businesses, too, paying liabilities is a big issue.

General Mills knows the importance of paying its liabilities on time. The cereal and grocery maker buys on account from thousands of suppliers, so the company cannot afford to slip up in paying its liabilities. General Mills also employs more than 28,000 workers to whom at one time or another General Mills will owe salaries and wages. Needless to say, those employees expect General Mills to pay their salaries and wages on time. In this chapter, you will learn how the Big G (Wall Street's nickname for General Mills) accounts for payroll and other short-term liabilities. Later, in Chapter 14, you will learn how the company accounts for long-term liabilities.

**REPORTING LIABILITIES**

- Measuring Liabilities
- Classifying Liabilities
- Calculating and Interpreting the Current Ratio

**ACCOUNTING FOR CURRENT LIABILITIES**

- Accounts Payable
- Notes Payable
- Current Portion of Long-Term Debt
- Other Current Liabilities

**PAYROLL ACCOUNTING**

- Calculating the Payroll
- Recording the Payroll
- Applying Internal Control Principles

# REPORTING LIABILITIES

**Learning Objective 1**

Explain how to report the major types of liabilities.

Video 11-1
www.mhhe.com/LLPW1e

Businesses record liabilities when they become obligated to pay cash or to provide services in the future. These obligations arise in several ways: from acquiring goods or services on credit with a promise to pay in the future, from borrowing cash with a promise to repay in the future, or from receiving cash before providing future services. In each of these cases, the business records a liability on the date it becomes obligated to pay cash or provide future services. Later, when the cash has been paid or the services have been provided, the business reduces the liability.

Two questions arise when recording liabilities:

1. At what amount should they be measured?
2. Should they be classified as current or long term?

## Measuring Liabilities

A business must record a liability whenever a transaction or event obligates the company to give up assets or provide services in the future. The dollar amount that is reported for a liability depends on three considerations:

1. **The initial amount of the liability.** Initially, the business records a liability at its **cash equivalent**, which is the amount of cash a creditor would accept to settle the liability immediately after the transaction or event.
2. **Additional amounts owed to the creditor.** The business increases liabilities whenever additional obligations arise, by purchasing goods and services or incurring interest charges over time.
3. **Payments or services provided to the creditor.** The business reduces liabilities whenever the company makes a payment or provides services to the creditor.

Notice that a liability is first recorded at a cash-equivalent amount, which excludes interest charges. This practice makes sense; if you borrowed $10 from a friend and paid it back a split-second later, you would not need to pay interest. Because interest arises only with the passage of time, it is recorded as a liability only after time has passed.

## Classifying Liabilities

Most businesses have liabilities that are to be settled on various dates. General Mills, for example, reports not only accounts payable that must be paid within 30 to 60 days but also loans that are not due to be repaid until the year 2078. To help financial statement users evaluate whether a business will be able to pay its liabilities as they come due, liabilities on the balance sheet are usually classified as either current or long term. Current liabilities are short-term obligations that will be paid with current assets within the business's current operating cycle or one year after the balance sheet date, whichever is longer. Because most companies have an operating cycle that is shorter than one year, the definition of current liabilities can be simplified as liabilities due within one year.

Refer to Exhibit 11.1 for an excerpt from the 2007 balance sheet for General Mills. You can see that the company owed more than $11.7 billion. That may sound like a lot to owe,

## Exhibit 11.1    General Mills' Liabilities

GENERAL MILLS

### LIABILITIES

| (in millions) | 2007 | 2006 |
|---|---|---|
| **Current liabilities** | | |
| Accounts payable | $ 778 | $ 673 |
| Notes payable | 1,254 | 1,503 |
| Current portion of long-term debt | 1,734 | 2,131 |
| Other current liabilities | 2,079 | 1,831 |
| Total current liabilities | 5,845 | 6,138 |
| Long-term debt | 3,218 | 2,415 |
| Other liabilities | 2,663 | 2,614 |
| Total liabilities | 11,726 | 11,167 |

but only half of it ($5.8 billion) was payable in the coming year. And General Mills had many current assets to use in satisfying its current liabilities as we will see shortly.

## Calculating and Interpreting the Current Ratio

The **current ratio** is a financial measure used to evaluate **liquidity**, which is a concept representing a company's ability to pay the amounts it currently owes. The current ratio indicates whether a business has enough current assets to pay its current liabilities. Generally speaking, a high current ratio suggests good liquidity. An old rule of thumb was that companies should have a current ratio of between 1.0 and 2.0. Today, however, many successful companies use financial management techniques that minimize their current assets. As a result, those companies have current ratios that are less than 1.0.

**Learning Objective 2**

Calculate and interpret the current ratio.

| Financial Analysis Tools | | |
|---|---|---|
| Name of Measure | Formula | What It Tells You |
| Current Ratio | $\dfrac{\text{Current Assets}}{\text{Current Liabilities}}$ | • Whether current assets are sufficient to pay current liabilities<br>• A higher ratio means better ability to pay |

At the time General Mills owed $5.8 billion in current liabilities (see Exhibit 11.1), the company owned $3.1 billion in current assets. Therefore, its current ratio was calculated as:

$$\frac{\text{Current}}{\text{Ratio}} = \frac{\text{Current Assets}}{\text{Current Liabilities}} = \frac{\$3.1\text{ billion}}{\$5.8\text{ billion}} = 0.53$$

A current ratio of 0.53 indicates that a company's current assets are only 53 percent as large as its current liabilities. For many companies, a ratio of less than 1.0 (100 percent) would be a significant concern. However, it is not as much of a concern to General Mills because, as the notes to the company's financial statements explain, operating activities generate nearly $5 million in cash each day. In addition, General Mills has arranged a **line of credit**—basically a preapproved bank loan—that the company can use at any time as needed. This arrangement gives General Mills the freedom to invest its cash in assets that generate more income than the interest that is typically paid on cash sitting in a checking account. If General Mills ever has too little cash to pay its current liabilities, the company can borrow more immediately via the line of credit.

# ACCOUNTING FOR CURRENT LIABILITIES

## Accounts Payable

Most companies purchase goods and services on credit from other companies. Typically, these transactions involve three stages: (1) order the goods or services, (2) receive the goods or services, and (3) pay for the goods or services. Accountants record liabilities at the stage that "obligates the company to give up assets or services." When do you think Big G becomes obligated to pay for the grain it buys for making Wheaties and Cheerios?

If a grain order were never filled, General Mills would not be expected to pay for it. So the point at which the liability is created and recorded is the receipt of goods or services, not the order. Like Big G, most companies call this liability Accounts Payable. According to Exhibit 11.1, General Mills owed $778 million in Accounts Payable at the end of 2007. The great advantage of using accounts payable to buy goods and services is that suppliers do not charge interest on the unpaid balances unless they are overdue.

## Notes Payable

The next liability reported by General Mills in Exhibit 11.1 is Notes Payable. This liability represents the amount the company owes to others as a result of issuing promissory notes. A **promissory note** is a written document outlining the terms and conditions according to which one company will repay another. In this section, we illustrate an **interest-bearing** note, which requires payment of the borrowed amount (the principal) plus interest calculated using the interest rate stated in the note. In Chapter 14, we illustrate a different type of promissory note, called a discounted note, which does not explicitly state an interest rate.

Chapter 9 showed how a company records Notes Receivable to account for promissory notes created when the company lends money. This section presents the other side of the transaction—the Notes Payable that are created when a company borrows money by issuing promissory notes. Assume that on November 1, 2009, General Mills negotiated an agreement to borrow $100,000 cash on a one-year note. The note specified that General Mills would pay 6 percent interest one year later on October 31, 2010. The principal was also to be repaid on the maturity date (October 31, 2010). See Exhibit 11.2 for a summary of these events assuming that General Mills adjusts its accounting records on December 31, 2009.

The arrows in Exhibit 11.2 point to three aspects of the note to be accounted for. First, General Mills will need to increase Cash when the company creates the note. Next, **under the matching principle, General Mills will need to adjust its records to account for the interest incurred each accounting period.** In reality, General Mills would make this kind of adjustment every month or quarter, but for simplicity, we have assumed it occurs only once (on December 31, 2009). Finally, the company will decrease Cash when interest and principal are paid. The following discussion addresses these three elements that exist for any promissory note.

1. **The note is issued and cash is received.** When General Mills receives $100,000 cash on November 1, 2009, it becomes obligated to repay that amount. This transaction would be recorded as follows:

|  | Debit | Credit |
|---|---|---|
| Cash (+A) | 100,000 |  |
| Notes Payable (+L) |  | 100,000 |

| Assets | = | Liabilities | + | Owners' Equity |
|---|---|---|---|---|
| Cash    +100,000 |  | Notes Payable    +100,000 |  |  |

2. **Interest is owed at the end of the accounting period.** Interest is like rent for the privilege of using someone else's money. Although interest becomes payable with each day that passes, it is not paid nearly that often. Typically, interest is paid monthly or in some cases once or twice a year. Rather than record the unpaid interest on a daily basis,

Video 11-2
www.mhhe.com/LLPW1e

**Learning Objective 3**

Demonstrate how to account for notes payable and the current portion of long-term debt.

*Coach's Tip*

This example shows how to account for the note from the borrower's perspective. The same example is presented from the lender's perspective on page 390.

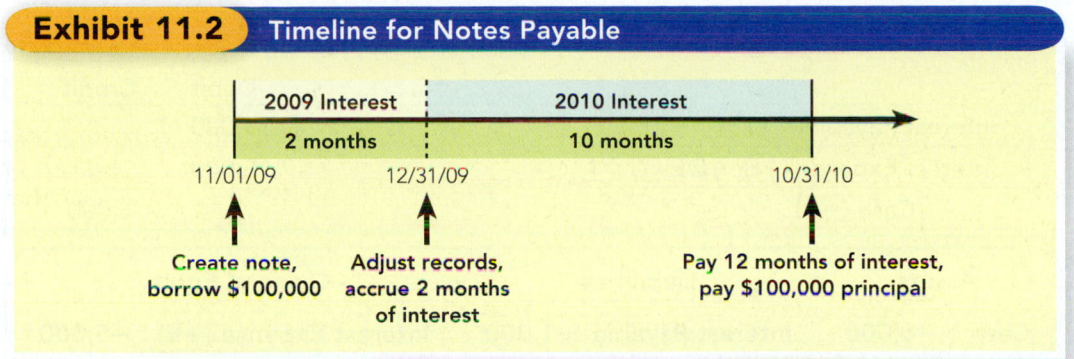

**Exhibit 11.2**  **Timeline for Notes Payable**

most companies record it at the end of the accounting period. For interest-bearing notes, the interest obligations are recorded in the current liability account Interest Payable.

When General Mills adjusts its records on December 31, 2009, it records the amount of interest incurred but not paid during the period. This period is represented by the light yellow shading in Exhibit 11.2. As you may recall from Chapter 9, interest is calculated using the following formula:

$$\text{Interest} = \text{Principal} \times \text{Interest Rate} \times \text{Time}$$

As of December 31, the General Mills note has existed for two months, but no interest has been paid, so the unpaid interest is $1,000 (= $100,000 × 6% × 2/12). Notice in this calculation that the principal is the amount owed at the beginning of the interest period, which is equal to the amount of the liability recorded in the Notes Payable account on November 1. The interest rate is the 6 percent annual rate stated on the note, and the time component is the fraction of the year for which the interest is being calculated (2 months out of 12).

The adjusting entry to accrue interest from November 1 to December 31 is as follows.

**Coach's Tip**
The "time" component refers to the portion of a year for which interest is calculated, not the portion of the note's entire life. A 2-month interest calculation on a 3-year note has a time component of 2/12, not 2/36.

|  | Debit | Credit |
|---|---|---|
| Interest Expense (+E, −OE) | 1,000 | |
| Interest Payable (+L) | | 1,000 |

| Assets | = | Liabilities | + | Owners' Equity |
|---|---|---|---|---|
| | | Interest Payable  +1,000 | | Interest Expense (+E)  −1,000 |

3. **Payments are made to the lender.**  General Mills will pay both the principal and the interest on the October 31, 2010, maturity date. Although the company is likely to pay both amounts with a single check, it is instructive to consider these payments separately. We begin with the interest payment. This payment covers the full year from the time the note was signed until the time it matures on October 31. The total interest payment is $6,000 (= $100,000 × 6% × 12/12). As the following timeline shows, this interest payment includes 2 months of interest recorded as an expense and a liability in 2009 ($1,000) plus 10 months of interest expense related to the period from January 1 to October 31, 2010 ($5,000 = $100,000 × 6% × 10/12).

The $6,000 interest payment is recorded as follows:

| | Debit | Credit |
|---|---|---|
| Interest Payable (−L) | 1,000 | |
| Interest Expense (+E, −OE) | 5,000 | |
| Cash (−A) | | 6,000 |

| Assets | = | Liabilities | + | Owners' Equity |
|---|---|---|---|---|
| Cash   −6,000 | | Interest Payable   −1,000 | | Interest Expense (+E)   −5,000 |

The principal payment of $100,000 made on October 31, 2010, is recorded as:

| | Debit | Credit |
|---|---|---|
| Notes Payable (−L) | 100,000 | |
| Cash (−A) | | 100,000 |

| Assets | = | Liabilities | + | Owners' Equity |
|---|---|---|---|---|
| Cash         −100,000 | | Notes Payable      −100,000 | | |

**SELF-STUDY PRACTICE**

Assume Starbucks issues a $12,000 note on December 1 with interest due annually at a rate of 5 percent. Record (1) this transaction and (2) the December 31 interest adjustment.

1.

| | Debit | Credit |
|---|---|---|
| | | |
| | | |

| Assets | = | Liabilities | + | Owners' Equity |
|---|---|---|---|---|
| | | | | |

2.

| | Debit | Credit |
|---|---|---|
| | | |
| | | |

| Assets | = | Liabilities | + | Owners' Equity |
|---|---|---|---|---|
| | | | | |

*After you have finished, check your answers with the solution at the bottom of the next page.*

## Current Portion of Long-Term Debt

Remember when you were in the ninth grade and it seemed as if it would be forever before you would graduate from high school? At that time, graduation was something that would happen in the long term. Later, when you became a senior, graduation became a current event—one that was less than a year away. A similar progression occurs with long-term debt.

If a company borrows money with the promise to repay it in two years, the loan is classified as a long-term debt. The company reports only the accrued interest on the loan as a current liability on that year's balance sheet. After a year has passed, however, the loan becomes a current liability (just as your graduation became a current event when you reached your senior year). When that happens, the borrower must report the loan in the Current Liabilities section of the balance sheet. Rather than create a different account, accountants simply remove the amount of principal to be repaid in the upcoming year from the total long-term debt and report it as a current liability, Current Portion of Long-Term Debt.

The third line item in the Current Liabilities section of the General Mills balance sheet (see Exhibit 11.1, page 469) provides an example. Notice that in 2007, General Mills reported a current liability for the $1.7 billion of long-term debt that was expected to be paid in 2008. Similarly, in 2006, current liabilities included $2.1 billion of long-term debt expected to be paid in 2007. This reclassification of long-term debt to a current liability is needed so that the balance sheet will accurately report the dollar amount of liabilities that Big G will pay in the upcoming year.

**SELF-STUDY PRACTICE**

Assume that on December 31, 2009, Blockbuster borrowed $10,000, a portion of which was to be repaid each year on November 30. Specifically, Blockbuster will make the following principal payments: $1,000 in 2010, $2,000 in 2011, $3,000 in 2012, and $4,000 in 2013. Show how this loan will be reported on the balance sheets on December 31, 2010 and 2009, assuming that the principal payments will be made when required.

|  | AS OF DECEMBER 31 | |
| --- | --- | --- |
|  | 2010 | 2009 |
| Current liabilities: |  |  |
| Current portion of long-term debt | $ | $ |
| Long-term debt |  |  |
| Total liabilities | $ 9,000 | $ 10,000 |

*After you have finished, check your answers with the solutions at the bottom of the next page.*

# Other Current Liabilities

**Learning Objective 4**

Demonstrate how to account for sales taxes and unearned revenues.

Because of the nature of General Mills' business, the company does not report certain current liabilities that are common to other companies. In this section, we examine a few of those liabilities.

**Solution to Self-Study Practice**

1.

| | Debit | Credit |
| --- | --- | --- |
| Cash (+A) | 12,000 | |
| Notes Payable (+L) | | 12,000 |

| Assets | = | Liabilities | + | Owners' Equity |
| --- | --- | --- | --- | --- |
| Cash +12,000 | | Notes Payable +12,000 | | |

2. $12,000 \times 5\% \times 1/12 = \$50$

| | Debit | Credit |
| --- | --- | --- |
| Interest Expense (+E, −OE) | 50 | |
| Interest Payable (+L) | | 50 |

| Assets | = | Liabilities | + | Owners' Equity |
| --- | --- | --- | --- | --- |
| | | Interest Payable +50 | | Interest Expense (+E) −50 |

## Sales Tax Payable

Retail companies are required to charge a sales tax in all but five states (Alaska, Delaware, Montana, New Hampshire, and Oregon). Retailers collect sales tax from consumers at the time of sale and forward it to the state government. They report the taxes they collect as a current liability until they forward them to the government. Sales tax is not an expense to the retailer because it is simply collected and passed on to the government. So if Best Buy sold a television for $1,000 cash plus 5 percent sales tax, Best Buy would earn $1,000 in sales revenue and recognize a $50 liability (= 5% × $1,000) for the sales tax collected. The sale would be recorded as follows.

|  | Debit | Credit |
|---|---|---|
| Cash (+A) | 1,050 | |
| Sales Tax Payable (+L) ($1,000 × 0.05) | | 50 |
| Sales Revenue (+R, +OE) | | 1,000 |

| Assets | = | Liabilities | + | Owners' Equity |
|---|---|---|---|---|
| Cash +1,050 | | Sales Tax Payable +50 | | Sales Revenue (+R) +1,000 |

When Best Buy pays the sales tax to the state government, its accountants will reduce Sales Tax Payable (with a debit) and reduce Cash (with a credit).

## Unearned Revenue

In Chapter 4, you learned that some companies receive cash before they provide goods or services to customers. IAC, the owner of Ticketmaster and Match.com, provides a great example of this type of liability. Consider what happens when IAC receives cash for subscription services to Match.com. Because IAC receives cash before providing the subscription services, accountants initially record a liability in the account Unearned Revenue. As the subscription services are provided, IAC reduces the liability and reports the subscription fees earned as revenue.

Assume, for example, that on October 1, IAC received cash for a three-month subscription paid in advance at a rate of $10 per month ($30 in total). IAC records this transaction in two steps:

**1. Receive cash and create a liability** (on October 1):

|  | Debit | Credit |
|---|---|---|
| Cash (+A) | 30 | |
| Unearned Revenue (+L) | | 30 |

| Assets | = | Liabilities | + | Owners' Equity |
|---|---|---|---|---|
| Cash +30 | | Unearned Revenue +30 | | |

**Solution to Self-Study Practice**

|  | AS OF DECEMBER 31 | |
|---|---|---|
|  | 2010 | 2009 |
| Current liabilities | | |
| Current portion of long-term debt | $2,000 | $ 1,000 |
| Long-term debt | 7,000 | 9,000 |
| Total liabilities | $9,000 | $10,000 |

**2. Fulfill part of the liability and earn revenue** (on October 31):

| | Debit | Credit |
|---|---|---|
| Unearned Revenue (−L) | 10 | |
|     Subscription Revenue (+R, +OE) | | 10 |

| Assets | = | Liabilities | + | Owners' Equity |
|---|---|---|---|---|
| | | Unearned Revenue   −10 | | Subscription Revenue (+R)   +10 |

As each month passes, IAC would make another adjustment like the one in Step 2 to show that it has continued to fulfill its obligation and to earn subscription revenue. Do not let the small amounts in this example fool you; unearned revenues can be huge. For IAC, they total more than $199 million.

## Warranties Payable

Most companies that sell physical items, such as watches and computers, provide a warranty that obligates the company to repair defective products for a limited time. Because the warranty applies to each product that is sold, it is considered a cost of making the sale. **According to the matching principle, warranty costs should be reported as an expense when the sale is recorded.**

Because the company does not pay these costs at the time of the sale, the company records a liability. Like other liabilities discussed in this chapter, the liability for warranty costs requires the company to give up resources in the future. Unlike other current liabilities, however, the precise amount to be given up is not known. Instead, it must be estimated based on the company's history of product repairs and any recent changes in product quality.

To understand how to estimate and record warranty costs, consider the following example. In the second quarter of 2007, Gateway sold 1 million computers. Managers estimated that warranty repairs on the computers would cost $16 million. To come up with the $16 million figure, they estimated both the percentage of computers they expected would require warranty repairs and the average cost of the repairs. Assuming that 10 percent of the computers were expected to require warranty repairs at an average cost of $160 per unit, the managers calculated total estimated warranty repair costs as follows.

| | |
|---|---|
| Total unit sales in this period | 1,000,000 |
| Percent requiring warranty repair | ×    10% |
| Units requiring warranty repair | 100,000 |
| Average warranty repair cost | ×  $160 |
| Estimated cost of warranty repairs | $16,000,000 |

> Based on this estimate, Gateway could record an estimated warranty repair cost each time it sold a computer, but that would be inefficient. Instead, accountants make an adjusting entry to record estimated warranty repair costs at the end of each accounting period. Warranty Expense is reported as a selling expense on the income statement. If the warranty repairs are likely to occur within a year, Warranty Liability is classified as a current liability on the balance sheet.

| | Debit | Credit |
|---|---|---|
| Warranty Expense (+E, −OE) | 16,000,000 | |
|     Warranty Liability (+L) | | 16,000,000 |

| Assets | = | Liabilities | + | Owners' Equity |
|---|---|---|---|---|
| | | Warranty Liability +16,000,000 | | Warranty Expense (+E) −16,000,000 |

**Learning Objective 5**

Demonstrate how to account for warranties and other contingent liabilities.

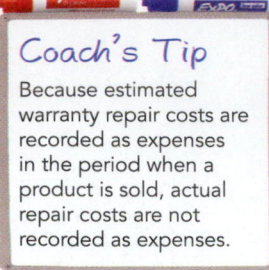

**Coach's Tip**

Because estimated warranty repair costs are recorded as expenses in the period when a product is sold, actual repair costs are not recorded as expenses.

Later, when Gateway actually repairs a computer under warranty, the repair costs will be recorded as a reduction in the Warranty Liability account. For example, if Gateway used $300 of parts to repair a computer under warranty, the accountant makes the following journal entry.

|  | Debit | Credit |
|---|---|---|
| Warranty Liability (−L) | 300 | |
| Computer Parts (−A) | | 300 |

| Assets | = | Liabilities | + | Owners' Equity |
|---|---|---|---|---|
| Computer Parts −300 | | Warranty Liability −300 | | |

Other repair costs are handled in a similar way. For example, most manufacturers outsource much of their repair work. If Gateway paid a company $2,000 to repair 20 computers under warranty, the accountant makes the following journal entry.

|  | Debit | Credit |
|---|---|---|
| Warranty Liability (−L) | 2,000 | |
| Cash (−A) | | 2,000 |

| Assets | = | Liabilities | + | Owners' Equity |
|---|---|---|---|---|
| Cash −2,000 | | Warranty Liability −2,000 | | |

At the end of the accounting period, Gateway would evaluate whether the balance in the Warranty Liability account is adequate to cover the work likely to be done in future periods. If the balance is judged to be too low, managers will increase it; if the balance is too high, they will decrease it.

## Other Contingent Liabilities

A warranty is one example of a special type of liability called contingent liabilities. **Contingent liabilities** are potential liabilities that arise as a result of past transactions or events, but their ultimate resolution depends (is contingent) on a future event. Gateway's Warranty Liability arises from the warranty promised when the company sells computers, but the exact amount of the liability depends on the extent of repairs that may be required in the future. As is often the case, the challenge for accountants is to anticipate what is likely to happen in the future so that it can be reported now if appropriate.

Many other types of contingent liability exist. The most common is a lawsuit against the company. Unlike warranties, for which future costs can usually be estimated, the cost of a lawsuit is difficult to predict. Some suits will be defended successfully; others may result in huge fines or penalties. Given such uncertainties, accounting rules require the company to evaluate whether it is likely to be found liable and, if so, whether the amount of the liability is estimable. As Exhibit 11.3 indicates, if a contingent liability is possible but not probable or its amount cannot be estimated, a liability should not be recorded. Instead, the potential liability should be described in a note to the financial statements.

**Exhibit 11.3** Accounting for Contingent Liabilities

## Spotlight On FINANCIAL REPORTING

### Disclosure of Contingent Liabilities

Gateway

To forewarn financial statement users of potential liabilities related to existing lawsuits, computer maker Gateway provided the following disclosure in its 2006 annual report:

> Gateway is a party to various lawsuits, claims, including assertions of patent infringements, investigations and administrative proceedings that arise in connection with its business, including **Lucent Technologies, Inc. v. Gateway, Inc.** . . . asserting that Gateway infringes seven patents owned by Lucent Technologies, Inc. . . . Gateway reserves for a legal liability when it is both probable that a liability has been incurred and the amount of the loss can be reasonably estimated. At least quarterly Gateway reviews and adjusts these reserves to reflect the impacts of negotiations, settlements, rulings, advice of legal counsel and other information and events pertaining to a particular case. The ultimate outcome of such matters cannot presently be determined or estimated.

## PAYROLL ACCOUNTING

**Payroll** refers to the processes followed to pay employees for their work. For large companies, payroll can be a huge and difficult undertaking. At one time, General Mills was managing eight different payroll systems at 47 different production plants. Even small companies can find payroll challenging because all employers are required by law to maintain certain payroll records and to calculate payroll in particular ways. And of course, employees expect this task to be done on time without error.

Payroll costs can be significant in terms of their impact on both current liabilities and operating expenses. At the end of 2007, for example, General Mills owed more than $1.3 billion to employees (included in Other current liabilities in Exhibit 11.1), and payroll expenses for the year totaled many times that amount. Typical payroll costs include salaries, wages, bonuses, employer payroll taxes, and employee benefits. **Salaries** are fixed amounts that are paid monthly, typically to managerial, sales, and administrative personnel. **Wages** are based on a rate per hour or per unit of production and are typically paid to clerks, factory workers, and part-time employees. Bonuses are extra amounts paid to employees for outstanding performance. It is not unusual for executive-level employees to receive more in bonuses than in salary as was the case in 2007, when General Mills' chief executive officer received $2.5 million in bonuses and $1.3 million in salary. Employer payroll taxes also add significant costs, as we show later in detail. Finally, employee benefits include amounts employers paid on behalf of employees for health insurance,

**Learning Objective 6**

Calculate and record payroll including employer payroll taxes.

retirement pensions, and vacation, illness, and family leaves. The methods used to account for employee benefits are discussed in Supplement 11A.

## Calculating the Payroll

As illustrated in Exhibit 11.4, payroll calculations involve three steps: (1) computing gross earnings, (2) determining payroll deductions, and (3) subtracting payroll deductions from gross earnings to compute net pay—the amount actually paid to employees. As the arrows in Exhibit 11.4 indicate, each of these steps provides information that the business must account for, as we explain in the following sections.

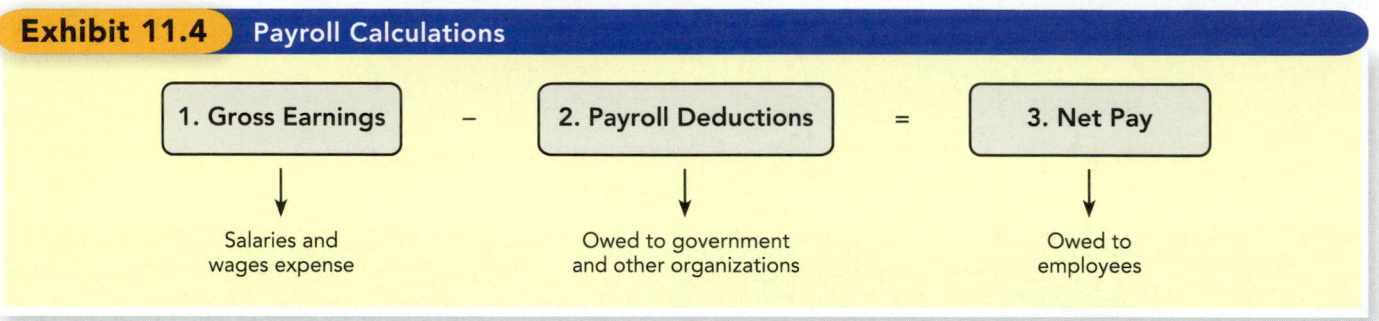

| Exhibit 11.4 | Payroll Calculations |
|---|---|

| 1. Gross Earnings | – | 2. Payroll Deductions | = | 3. Net Pay |
|---|---|---|---|---|
| ↓ | | ↓ | | ↓ |
| Salaries and wages expense | | Owed to government and other organizations | | Owed to employees |

### Gross Earnings

**Gross earnings** represents the amount employees earn as compensation for the work they do. From the employer's point of view, this is an expense called Salaries and Wages Expense. Employers and employees determine salaries and wage rates by agreement. An employee who agrees to a yearly salary of $60,000 would be entitled to $5,000 of gross earnings for each month of work (= $60,000 ÷ 12). An employee who agrees to an hourly wage rate of $10 would be entitled to gross earnings of $400 for 40 hours of work (= 40 × $10).

Most employers are required by law to pay an overtime premium to hourly employees who work more than 8 hours per day or 40 hours per week. Overtime pay is typically calculated as "time and a half," which means $1\frac{1}{2}$ times the regular pay rate. Some employers pay an even higher overtime premium ("double time") to employees who work on weekends or holidays. Assume Nigel Lithgow earns a regular pay rate of $10 per hour for the first 40 hours per week and time and a half for anything over 40 hours. If Nigel works 54 hours during the first week of the year, his gross earnings will be $610, calculated as follows:

|  | Pay Rate | × | Hours | = | Gross Earnings |
|---|---|---|---|---|---|
| Regular | $10 | | 40 | | $ 400 |
| Overtime | ($10 × 1½) | | 14 | | 210 |
| Total | | | 54 | | $ 610 |

### Payroll Deductions

**Payroll deductions** are amounts a company subtracts from each employee's gross earnings. The employer does not keep these deductions but rather pays ("remits") them to another organization or government agency on behalf of employees. Some deductions are required by law; others are made on a voluntary basis as a service to employees. Deductions required by law, such as those for income taxes and FICA taxes (commonly referred to as Social Security taxes), are calculated according to specific rules. Voluntary deductions are amounts for charitable donations, retirement savings, union dues, medical and dental plans, life insurance, parking fees, and so on.

From the employer's perspective, payroll deductions create liabilities, not expenses. They are not expenses because they do not directly increase the employer's salary and wage costs. Instead, they simply redirect part of the salary and wage payments to a government agency or other organization rather than to employees.

**Income Taxes.**    At a minimum, federal income tax must be deducted ("withheld") from each employee's pay. In addition, deductions may be required for state, county, and city income taxes depending on where employees live. These additional income taxes are often specified as a percentage of federal income tax. To avoid complicating our examples, we assume no state, county, or city income taxes.

The Internal Revenue Service (IRS) explains the methods employers can use to determine the federal income tax deduction for each employee. The simplest method is to look up the amount of the deduction in the tax bracket tables the IRS provides. These tables take into account the employee's gross earnings for a given pay period (as calculated by the employer), as well as "allowances" for other personal factors, such as marital status and number of children and dependents (as each employee indicates on a W-4 Form). Exhibit 11.5 is an excerpt from a tax bracket table. According to this table, the employer should deduct $58 income tax from Nigel Lithgow's pay assuming that he earned $610 during the week, that he is single, and he claimed two allowances.

**FICA Taxes.**    To support Medicare and Social Security, the Federal Insurance Contributions Act requires employees to pay FICA taxes to the government through employee payroll deductions. In 2008, employers were required to deduct 1.45 percent from each employee's earnings for Medicare and 6.2 percent (on earnings of up to $102,000) for Social Security. To simplify calculations, we will assume a total FICA rate of 8 percent. At that rate, Nigel's $610 of gross earnings requires a deduction of $48.80 for FICA taxes (= $610 × 0.08).

**Voluntary Deductions.**    Each employee should approve in writing the amount to be withheld from his or her earnings for voluntary deductions. Just like income tax and FICA tax deductions, the company records voluntary deductions as a liability until the business pays them to the designated charity, savings plan, union, or other organization.

## Net Pay

As Exhibit 11.4 showed, net pay is calculated by subtracting payroll deductions from gross earnings. Nigel Lithgow's net pay is calculated as follows, assuming a voluntary deduction of $10 for a United Way contribution.

| | | |
|---|---|---|
| Gross earnings | | $ 610.00 |
| Payroll deductions: | | |
| Federal income tax | $ 58.00 | |
| FICA taxes | 48.80 | |
| United Way | 10.00 | 116.80 |
| **Net pay** | | **$ 493.20** |

> **Coach's Tip**
> Always think from the company's perspective, not your own personal perspective. Although payroll deductions seem to be expenses to you on a personal basis, they create liabilities, not expenses, for the employer.

---

**Exhibit 11.5    Table for Determining Income Tax Deductions**

SINGLE Persons—WEEKLY Payroll Period

| If the wages are— | | And the number of withholding allowances claimed is— | | | | | | | | | | |
|---|---|---|---|---|---|---|---|---|---|---|---|---|
| At least | But less than | 0 | 1 | 2 | 3 | 4 | 5 | 6 | 7 | 8 | 9 | 10 |
| | | The amount of income tax to be withheld is— | | | | | | | | | | |
| $600 | $610 | $76 | $66 | $58 | $47 | $37 | $27 | $17 | $10 | $3 | $0 | $0 |
| 610 | 620 | 77 | 68 | 58 | 48 | 38 | 28 | 19 | 11 | 4 | 0 | 0 |
| 620 | 630 | 79 | 69 | 59 | 50 | 40 | 30 | 20 | 12 | 5 | 0 | 0 |
| 630 | 640 | 80 | 71 | 61 | 51 | 41 | 31 | 22 | 13 | 6 | 0 | 0 |
| 640 | 650 | 82 | 72 | 62 | 53 | 43 | 33 | 23 | 14 | 7 | 1 | 0 |

**SELF-STUDY PRACTICE**

Mia Miller worked 42 hours this week. Her regular wage rate is $14 per hour, and the overtime rate is 1½ times the regular pay rate. Her employer pays Mia weekly. She is single, claims three allowances, pays no state, county, or city income tax, and has requested a voluntary deduction of $5 per week for a charity. Using the tax bracket table in Exhibit 11.5 and assuming total FICA taxes of 8 percent, calculate Mia's gross earnings, payroll deductions, and net pay.

1. Gross earnings:

| | Pay Rate | Hours | Gross Earnings |
|---|---|---|---|
| Regular | | | |
| Overtime | | | |
| Total | | | |

2. Payroll deductions:
   Federal income tax
   FICA taxes
   Charitable contribution
   Total

3. Net pay:
   Gross earnings
   Payroll deductions
   Net pay

*After you have finished, check your answers with the solution at the bottom of the next page.*

## Recording the Payroll

The system for recording payroll transactions is designed to achieve two objectives: (1) to comply with state and federal laws requiring a cumulative record of each employee's gross earnings, deductions, and net pay and (2) to summarize those amounts to enable the business to record journal entries.

### Employee Earnings Records

Payroll computations for each employee are captured each pay period in an **employee earnings record**. See Exhibit 11.6 for excerpts from Nigel Lithgow's employee earnings record for the year ended December 31, 2009. The calculations for Nigel's first pay period are highlighted in red.

The employee earnings record is used in three ways. First, it is used to determine whether the employee has reached the maximum earnings that are subject to the full FICA tax rate. The Cumulative column in Exhibit 11.6 shows that at no point during the year did Nigel's total earnings exceed the $102,000 FICA limit, so the full FICA rate is applied to all his earnings.

**Exhibit 11.6    Employee Earnings Record**

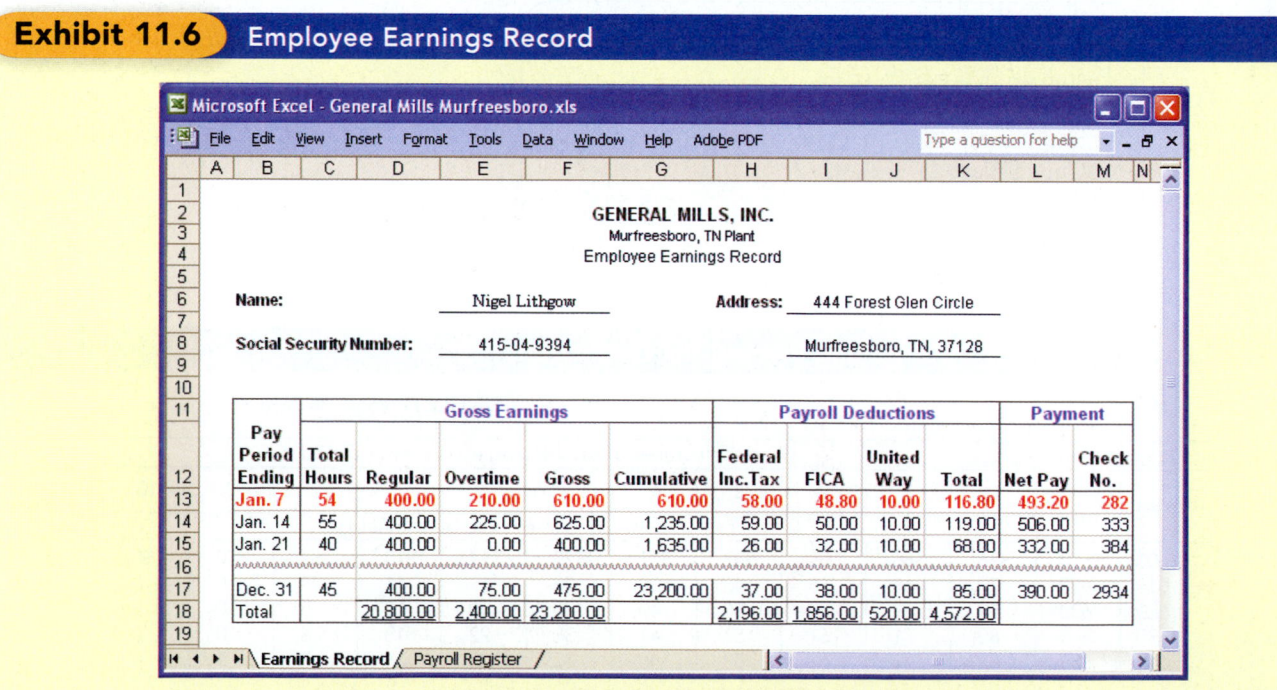

The second function of the employee earnings record is to accumulate information for employees' use in tracking their gross pay, payroll deductions, and net pay. This information is typically conveyed by a statement of earnings, which is either attached to each paycheck or distributed separately. Exhibit 11.7 provides an example. Because this example is for the first pay period of the year, the year-to-date numbers equal the amounts for the current period.

**Exhibit 11.7   Paycheck with Detachable Statement of Earnings**

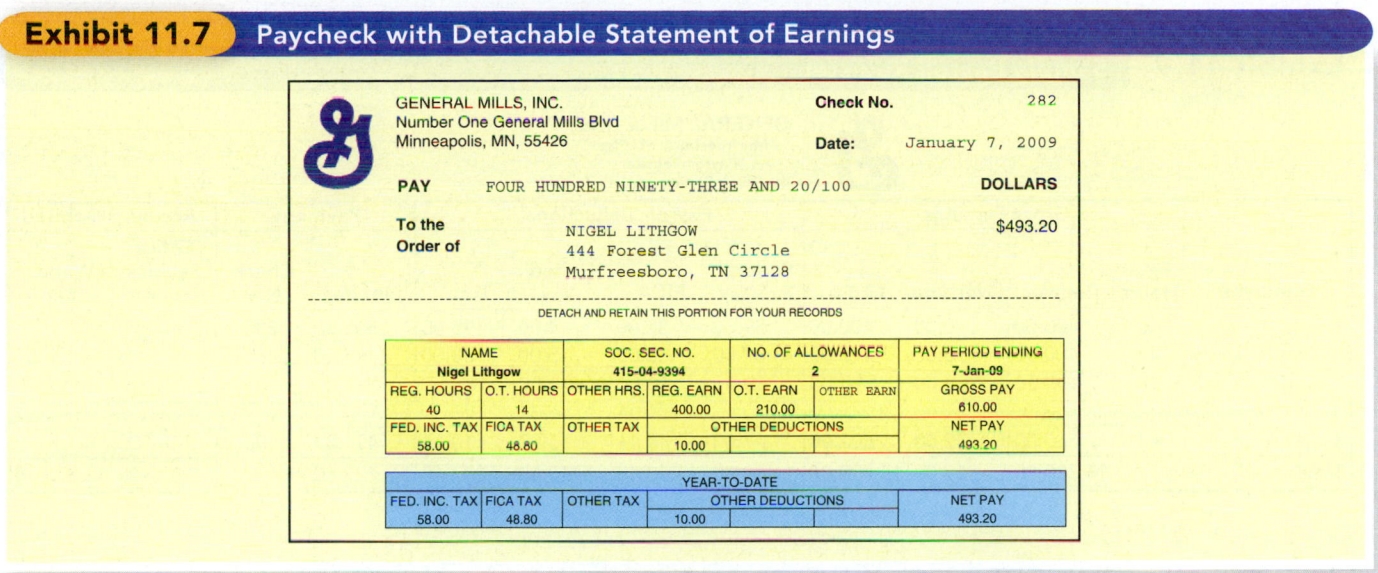

The third function of the employee earnings record is to provide information for preparing quarterly and annual reports for tax, insurance, and other purposes. For example, by January 31 of the following year, employers must prepare for each employee a year-end Wage and Tax Statement (Form W-2) similar to the one in Exhibit 11.8. The employer provides a copy of Form W-2 to each employee for use in preparing personal income taxes. The employer submits another copy to the Social Security Administration, which relays the income information to the IRS.

**Exhibit 11.8   Sample Wage and Tax Statement (Form W-2)**

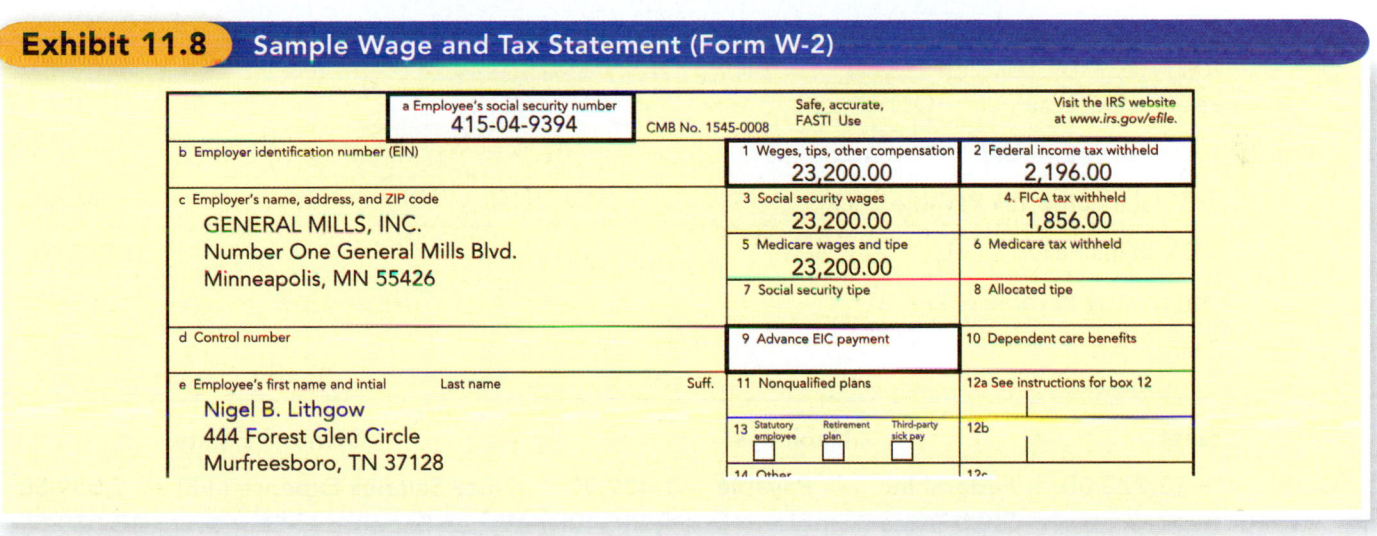

Solution to
Self-Study Practice

**1. Gross earnings:**

| | Pay Rate | Hours | Gross Earnings |
|---|---|---|---|
| Regular | $14 | 40 | $ 560 |
| Overtime | ($14 × 1½) | 2 | 42 |
| Total | | 42 | $ 602 |

**2. Payroll deductions**

| | |
|---|---|
| Federal income tax | $ 47.00 |
| FICA taxes ($602 × 0.08) | 48.16 |
| Charitable contribution | 5.00 |
| Total | $100.16 |

**3. Net pay:**

| | |
|---|---|
| Gross earnings | $602.00 |
| Payroll deductions | 100.16 |
| Net pay | $501.84 |

## Payroll Register

In addition to computing and reporting payroll information for each employee, the employer's payroll system must summarize the information across all employees so that total payroll costs and liabilities can be recorded in the accounting system. Typically, a **payroll register** like the one shown in Exhibit 11.9 serves this purpose.

**Exhibit 11.9** **Sample Payroll Register**

**GENERAL MILLS, INC.**
Murfreesboro, TN Plant
Payroll Register
For the Week Ending January 7, 2009

| Employee | Total Hours | Gross Earnings | | | Payroll Deductions | | | | Payment | | Accounts Debited | |
| | | Regular | Overtime | Gross | Federal Inc. Tax | FICA | United Way | Total | Net Pay | Check No. | Office Salaries Expense | Wages Expense |
|---|---|---|---|---|---|---|---|---|---|---|---|---|
| Arent, Jason | 40 | 400.00 | 0.00 | 400.00 | 59.00 | 32.00 | 4.00 | 95.00 | 305.00 | 280 | 400.00 | |
| Caldwell, Nancy | 45 | 400.00 | 75.00 | 475.00 | 37.00 | 38.00 | 5.00 | 80.00 | 395.00 | 281 | | 475.00 |
| Lithgow, Nigel | 54 | 400.00 | 210.00 | 610.00 | 58.00 | 48.80 | 10.00 | 116.80 | 493.20 | 282 | | 610.00 |
| Zvinakis, Kris | 42 | 560.00 | 42.00 | 602.00 | 47.00 | 48.16 | 15.00 | 110.16 | 491.84 | 308 | 602.00 | |
| Total | | 14,780.00 | 950.00 | 15,730.00 | 1,489.00 | 1,258.40 | 260.00 | 3,007.40 | 12,722.60 | | 2,359.50 | 13,370.50 |

Reading the payroll register in Exhibit 11.9 from left to right, we see the company incurred $15,730 of gross salaries and wages during the first week of January. From this, payroll deductions were withheld for income tax ($1,489), FICA ($1,258.40), and United Way ($260), leaving net pay of $12,722.60. Of the gross pay, $2,359.50 was for office salaries and $13,370.50 was for wages. General Mills would make the following journal entry to record this payroll information for the pay period ended January 7, 2009.

| | Debit | Credit |
|---|---|---|
| Office Salaries Expense (+E, −OE) | 2,359.50 | |
| Wages Expense (+E, −OE) | 13,370.50 | |
|    Federal Income Tax Payable (+L) | | 1,489.00 |
|    FICA Taxes Payable (+L) | | 1,258.40 |
|    United Way Payable (+L) | | 260.00 |
|    Cash (−A) | | 12,722.60 |

| Assets | = | Liabilities | + | Owners' Equity | |
|---|---|---|---|---|---|
| Cash −12,722.60 | | Federal Inc. Tax Payable +1,489.00 | | Office Salaries Expense (+E) − | 2,359.50 |
| | | FICA Taxes Payable +1,258.40 | | Wages Expense (+E) | −13,370.50 |
| | | United Way Payable + 260.00 | | | |

Note that the third-to-last column in the payroll register shows that employees were paid on January 7 using checks numbered 280–308. Had those checks not been prepared until later in the month, the company would have recorded the expenses and liabilities shown in the journal entry just given, but the credit for $12,722.60 would have been recorded to Salaries and Wages Payable (+L) instead of to Cash (−A).

## Employer Payroll Taxes

Salaries and wages are not the only payroll expenses that businesses incur. Like their employees, employers are required to pay FICA taxes. In addition, employers are required to pay unemployment taxes at both the federal and state levels. Employer FICA and unemployment taxes, known generally as **employer payroll taxes**, are calculated and recorded using the methods that follow.

**FICA Taxes.**   Employers are required to match each employee's FICA contribution. In other words, the company's required FICA tax contribution is equal to the total of all employees' contributions. The payroll register shown in Exhibit 11.9 indicates that **employee** FICA contributions totaled $1,258.40. This total implies that the **employer's** FICA contribution for the period was an additional $1,258.40. Until it has been paid, this liability is recorded in the same FICA Taxes Payable account as the amount that is withheld from employees.

**Unemployment Taxes.**   Employers are charged unemployment taxes through the Federal Unemployment Tax Act (FUTA) and state unemployment tax acts (SUTA). This legislation provides limited financial support to employees who lose their jobs through no fault of their own. Typically, federal tax calculations give employers credit for unemployment taxes paid at the state level, so we begin by calculating the state unemployment tax.

An employer calculates the amount of the state unemployment tax by multiplying a tax rate by a specified amount of wages paid to employees during the calendar year. Because the rate and specified amount of wages vary by state, industry, and number of company employees receiving unemployment benefits in prior years, it is difficult to cover all possibilities here.[1] We illustrate the calculation of the tax by assuming a basic rate of 5.4 percent, which is applied to just the first $7,000 of wages. (Unless you are instructed otherwise, use this same assumption in all homework exercises and assignments.) The payroll register in Exhibit 11.9 shows that as of January 7, no employee had earned more than $7,000, so the 5.4 percent tax rate applies to all employees in this pay period. Thus, state unemployment taxes for the week ended January 7 are calculated by multiplying the 5.4 percent rate by the total wages of $15,730.00, yielding $849.42 (= $15,730.00 × 0.054) in state unemployment tax.

The FUTA specifies a federal tax rate of 6.2 percent on taxable wages up to the first $7,000 for each employee. However, if the employer has a good payment history, the tax rate can be reduced by unemployment taxes paid at the state level. The maximum credit for state taxes is 5.4 percent of taxable wages. Assuming that General Mills receives this credit, its federal tax rate would be lowered to 0.8 percent (= 6.2 − 5.4) of taxable wages. Applying this rate to the taxable wages for the week ended January 7 (shown in Exhibit 11.9 as $15,730.00), we find that General Mills owes $125.84 (= 0.008 × $15,730.00) in federal unemployment taxes.

These three employer payroll taxes represent additional costs the employer incurs beyond the costs of salaries and wages. The business therefore reports these costs as an expense on the income statement. Until they have been paid, these three taxes are recorded as current liabilities using separate accounts as shown in the following journal entry:

> **Coach's Tip**
>
> The company records its liabilities for FICA and unemployment taxes in separate accounts because they are payable to different government agencies.

| | Debit | Credit |
|---|---|---|
| Payroll Tax Expense (+E, −OE) | 2,233.66 | |
| FICA Taxes Payable (+L) | | 1,258.40 |
| State Unemployment Taxes Payable (+L) | | 849.42 |
| Federal Unemployment Taxes Payable (+L) | | 125.84 |

| Assets | = | Liabilities | | + | Owners' Equity | |
|---|---|---|---|---|---|---|
| | | FICA Taxes Payable | +1,258.40 | | Payroll Tax Expense (+E) | −2,233.66 |
| | | State Unemployment Taxes Payable | +849.42 | | | |
| | | Federal Unemployment Taxes Payable | +125.84 | | | |

---

[1] Tax rates and specific wage limitations by state are available from the Department of Labor Employment and Training Administration Web site at www.doleta.gov.

**SELF-STUDY PRACTICE**

The payroll register for the two weeks ended October 31, 2008, indicates the following:

| | | | |
|---|---|---|---|
| Gross salaries | $14,000 | United Way contributions | $400 |
| Federal income tax deductions | 1,093 | State unemployment taxes | 756 |
| FICA tax deductions | 1,120 | Federal unemployment taxes | 112 |

Assuming that employees received their net pay on October 31 but no other payments were made for payroll, prepare journal entries to record (1) salaries and wages and (2) employer payroll taxes. Also show the accounting equation effects.

*After you have finished, check your answers with the solution at the bottom of the page.*

## Applying Internal Control Principles

Employers apply to payroll the same internal control principles used for cash receipts and payments. These controls focus on **establishing responsibilities** for: tracking the work done by each employee, approving pay rates, calculating deductions, and distributing net pay. These **duties are segregated** so that an employee cannot both authorize and pay oneself. **Restricted access** to timecards, pay rate files, and check-signing equipment limits the risk of unauthorized activities. Payroll staff members **document procedures** performed using internal records, such as the payroll register, as well as external reports, such as Form W-2. **Independent verification** by each employee helps prevent underpayments, and the imprest payroll system discussed in Chapter 8 (page 352) helps prevent overpayments.

## Spotlight On CONTROLS

### Biometric Time Tracking: A Replacement for Timecards

Biometric time tracking is quickly replacing time clocks as the internal control method used to track employee work hours. Palm scanners, fingerprint scanners, voice recognition systems, and retinal scanners are all examples of biometric time-tracking devices that record when an employee enters and exits the workplace. Biometric systems can eliminate administrative time spent with timecard records calculating the number of hours worked. They can also reduce theft caused by employees punching in for tardy or absent co-workers and eliminate human error from timecard processing. Studies by the American Payroll Association indicate that such inefficiencies and problems can cost organizations up to 8 percent of their annual gross payroll.

### Solution to Self-Study Practice

| | Debit | Credit | | Debit | Credit |
|---|---|---|---|---|---|
| 1. Salaries Expense (+E, −OE) | 14,000 | | 2. Payroll Tax Expense (+E, −OE) | 1,988 | |
| Federal Income Tax Payable (+L) | | 1,093 | FICA Taxes Payable (+L) | | 1,120 |
| FICA Taxes Payable (+L) | | 1,120 | State Unemployment Taxes Payable (+L) | | 756 |
| United Way Payable (+L) | | 400 | Federal Unemployment Taxes Payable (+L) | | 112 |
| Cash (−A) | | 11,387 | | | |

| Assets | = | Liabilities | | + | Owners' Equity | |
|---|---|---|---|---|---|---|
| 1. Cash   −11,387 | | Federal Income Tax Payable | +1,093 | | Salaries Expense (+E) | −14,000 |
| | | FICA Taxes Payable | +1,120 | | | |
| | | United Way Payable | + 400 | | | |
| 2. | | FICA Taxes Payable | +1,120 | | Payroll Tax Expense (+E) | − 1,988 |
| | | State Unemployment Taxes Payable | + 756 | | | |
| | | Federal Unemployment Taxes Payable | + 112 | | | |

# Demonstration Case A

## Notes Payable, the Current Ratio, and Warranty Liabilities

On June 30, 2006, Caterpillar Inc. reported $24.3 billion in current assets and $21.1 billion in current liabilities. On August 3, 2006, Caterpillar received $500 million from an issue of promissory notes that will mature in 2016. The notes pay interest on February 15 at an annual rate of 6.05 percent. Caterpillar's fiscal year ends on December 31.

**CATERPILLAR®**

*Required:*

1. Explain which sections of Caterpillar's classified balance sheet the new promissory notes affect.
2. Give the journal entry on August 3, 2006, to record the issue of notes payable.
3. Give the journal entry on December 31, 2006, to record interest expense, assuming that none had been accrued prior to that date. Calculate interest assuming the notes had been outstanding for five full months.
4. Give the journal entry on February 15, 2007, to record the first interest payment. Calculate the interest payment using a period of 6.5 months.
5. Compute Caterpillar's current ratio on June 30, 2006.
6. Assume that as of December 31, 2006, Caterpillar had not yet used the cash obtained from the issue of notes on August 3, 2006. What is the effect, if any, of the note issue on the company's current ratio at the end of the fiscal year?
7. On January 1, 2007, Caterpillar had accrued product warranty liabilities totaling $953 million. From January 1 to September 30, 2007, the company paid $677 million under existing warranty agreements and accrued $754 million for additional warranties arising from sales made in 2007. Give the journal entries to record the total payment and accrual made during 2007. What is the balance in warranty liability at September 30, 2007?

## Suggested Solution

1. Issuing of the notes increases Caterpillar's cash (a current asset) and notes payable (a long-term liability) by $500 million.
2. August 3, 2006 (issue date):

| | Debit | Credit |
|---|---|---|
| Cash (+A) | 500,000,000 | |
|     Notes Payable (+L) | | 500,000,000 |

3. December 31, 2006 (accrual of interest expense for five months):

| | Debit | Credit |
|---|---|---|
| Interest Expense (+E, −OE) ($500,000,000 × 6.05% × 5/12) | 12,604,167 | |
|     Interest Payable (+L) | | 12,604,167 |

4. February 15, 2007 (first interest payment date):

| | Debit | Credit |
|---|---|---|
| Interest Expense (+E, −OE) ($500,000,000 × 6.05% × 1.5/12) | 3,781,250 | |
| Interest Payable (−L) | 12,604,167 | |
|     Cash (−A) ($500,000,000 × 6.05% × 6.5/12) | | 16,385,417 |

5. June 30 current ratio:
$$\frac{\text{Current Assets}}{\text{Current Liabilities}} = \frac{\$24,300,000,000}{\$21,100,000,000} = 1.15$$

6. December current ratio:
$$\frac{\text{Current Assets}}{\text{Current Liabilities}} = \frac{(\$24,300,000,000 + \$500,000,000)}{(\$21,100,000,000 + \$12,604,167)} = 1.17$$

Issuing the notes increases the current ratio because cash from the notes increased current assets by $500 million, but the only increase in current liabilities was a relatively small amount of interest payable. The $500 million in notes payable increased long-term liabilities.

7.  Warranty Payments

|  | Debit | Credit |
|---|---|---|
| Warranty Liabilities (−L) | 677,000,000 | |
| Cash (−A) | | 677,000,000 |

Warranty Accrual

|  | Debit | Credit |
|---|---|---|
| Warranty Expense (+E, −OE) | 754,000,000 | |
| Warranty Liabilities (+L) | | 754,000,000 |

Warranty Liabilities (Jan. 1) − Payments (Jan.–Sept) + Additional Accrual (Jan.–Sept.)
= Warranty Liabilities (Sept. 30) = \$953 − \$677 + \$754 = \$1,030 (million)

# Demonstration Case B
## Unearned Revenue

Online Games, Inc., reported that it received $120,000 in annual subscription payments during the year ended December 31, 2009. The company will earn these subscription payments equally throughout each month of 2010.

*Required:*

1.  Explain how Online Games should report the 2009 subscription payments on the balance sheet and income statement on (a) December 31, 2009, and (b) January 31, 2010.
2.  Give the journal entries for (a) the receipt of annual subscription payments in December 2009 and (b) any required adjustments for the subscription payments on January 31, 2010.

## Suggested Solution

1.  (a)  On December 31, 2009, the $120,000 of advanced subscription payments would be reported on the balance sheet as the current liability Unearned Revenue. No amounts related to 2009 subscription payments would be reported on the 2009 income statement.

    (b)  On January 31, 2010, one month of subscription services would be earned, so the Unearned Revenue account on the balance sheet would be reduced by $10,000 (= $120,000 × 1/12), and the Subscription Revenue account on the income statement would be increased by $10,000.

2.  (a)  December 2009 (receipt of 2009 subscription payments)

|  | Debit | Credit |
|---|---|---|
| Cash (+A) | 120,000 | |
| Unearned Revenue (+L) | | 120,000 |

| Assets | = | Liabilities | + | Owners' Equity |
|---|---|---|---|---|
| Cash +120,000 | | Unearned Revenue +120,000 | | |

(b)  January 31, 2010 (earned one month of 2010 subscriptions)

|  | Debit | Credit |
|---|---|---|
| Unearned Revenue (−L) | 10,000 | |
| Subscription Revenue (+R, +OE) | | 10,000 |

| Assets | = | Liabilities | + | Owners' Equity | |
|---|---|---|---|---|---|
| | | Unearned Revenue    −1,000 | | Subscription Revenue (+R) | +1,000 |

# Demonstration Case C
## Payroll

Bexco Industries reported the following information in its accounting records on December 31, 2009 related to the December 26 to December 31 payroll.

| | |
|---|---|
| Gross salaries earned by employees | $3,600 |
| Income taxes withheld from employees | 550 |
| FICA taxes withheld from employees | 210 |
| Net payment to employees | 2,840 |
| State unemployment taxes | 194 |
| Federal unemployment taxes | 29 |

Bexco paid employees $2,840 on December 31, 2009 but did not remit the withholdings. Bexco has not recorded employer payroll taxes for the period from December 26 to December 31.

*Required:*

1.  Compute the total payroll costs related to the period from December 26 to December 31, 2009.

2.  Give the journal entry on December 31, 2009, to record payroll related to the period from December 26 to December 31, 2009. Separate the journal entry for the employer's payroll expenses from the entry for salaries and wages expense, and show the effects of each on the accounting equation.

## Suggested Solution

1.   **Computation of total payroll costs**

| | | |
|---|---|---|
| Salaries and wages | | $3,600 |
| Employer payroll taxes | | |
|    FICA taxes (matching contribution) | $210 | |
|    State unemployment taxes | 194 | |
|    Federal unemployment taxes | 29 | 433 |
| Total payroll costs | | $4,033 |

2. **Employee-related payroll costs**

|  | Debit | Credit |
|---|---|---|
| Salaries and Wages Expense (+E, −OE) | 3,600 | |
| Federal Income Tax Payable (+L) | | 550 |
| FICA Taxes Payable (+L) | | 210 |
| Cash (−A) | | 2,840 |

| Assets | = | Liabilities | | + | Owners' Equity | |
|---|---|---|---|---|---|---|
| Cash    −2,840 | | Federal Income Tax Payable | +550 | | Salaries and Wages Expense (+E) | −3,600 |
| | | FICA Taxes Payable | +210 | | | |

**Employer-related payroll costs**

|  | Debit | Credit |
|---|---|---|
| Payroll Tax Expense (+E, −OE) | 433 | |
| FICA Taxes Payable (+L) | | 210 |
| State Unemployment Taxes Payable (+L) | | 194 |
| Federal Unemployment Taxes Payable (+L) | | 29 |

| Assets | = | Liabilities | | + | Owners' Equity | |
|---|---|---|---|---|---|---|
| | | FICA Taxes Payable | +210 | | Payroll Tax Expense (+E) | −433 |
| | | State Unemployment Taxes Payable | +194 | | | |
| | | Federal Unemployment Taxes Payable | +29 | | | |

# Supplement 11A
## Employee Benefits

Employees earn salaries and wages as direct compensation for their work. They may also receive additional benefits, such as paid leaves and post-retirement benefits. The general principle of accounting for employee benefits is based on the **matching principle.** That is, the employer should record an expense for employee benefits when the employees have earned benefits, not when the employer pays them.

### Paid Leaves

Most businesses give employees the opportunity to take paid leaves from work for short periods. General Mills, for example, provides illness, childbirth, adoption, and military leaves to many employees. One of the most common paid leaves is vacation pay, which allows an employee to leave work for a period (several days or weeks) and still be paid.

Why does this topic require special discussion apart from ordinary salaries and wages? Unlike salaries and wages, which are earned and paid within a short time, such as a week or month, vacation pay is often earned over a longer period (a year). In fact, depending on its terms, vacation pay may accumulate and be paid out a long time after it has been earned. Some employers allow vacation pay to accumulate from one year to the next, resulting in a huge payment when the employee leaves the company.

To ensure that vacation pay is properly recorded in the period in which the employee earns it, the company should record a liability (and expense) for the estimated cost of paid vacations that employees will take. For example, if the estimated vacation time earned but not taken by employees in the current pay period is $1,000, it should be recorded as follows:

| | Debit | Credit |
|---|---|---|
| Vacation Benefits Expense (+E, −OE) | 1,000 | |
| Vacation Benefits Payable (+L) | | 1,000 |

| Assets | = | Liabilities | | + | Owners' Equity | |
|---|---|---|---|---|---|---|
| | | Vacation Benefits Payable | +1,000 | | Vacation Benefits Expense (+E) | −1,000 |

Later, when employees use the vacation time, the liability Vacation Benefits Payable should be reduced (with a debit).

## Post-Employment Benefits

Post-employment benefits are benefits that employees receive after they retire as part of the total compensation they earned while working for the company. As the matching principle requires, the cost of post-employment benefits is recorded as an expense in the period when the employees work for the company. Because these costs are paid after employees leave the company, the employer must record a liability as the costs are incurred.

Several benefits may be provided after retirement including pensions and medical and life insurance. In this section, we focus on pensions, which operate differently depending on whether they involve defined benefits or defined contributions. In a defined benefit pension, the employer promises to pay specified amounts (benefits) to employees after they retire. It is up to the employer to ensure that sufficient funds are invested in the pension plan to cover the promised benefits. In a defined contribution pension, the employer is responsible only for making specified contributions to the plan, not for the amounts that are ultimately paid out as pensions. Instead, the amount paid out depends on how much the pension investments earn. On balance, defined benefit plans involve more uncertainty for the employer and much more complex accounting than defined contribution plans. We illustrate accounting for only defined contribution plans because these plans are the most common type of pension plans you will encounter.

The most popular type of defined contribution plan is a 401(k), which gets its name from the section of the Internal Revenue Code that explains how it works. The basic idea is that employees contribute amounts into the plan, and the employer makes matching contributions. The money in the plan is then invested, and any income it generates is accumulated in the plan without being taxed. Employees are not taxed until later when they near retirement and can withdraw amounts from the plan. This deferral of tax and the matching employer contribution are what make this plan so popular.

The matching contribution is the only part of the plan that the employer records in the accounting records. If the employer is required to make a matching contribution of $10,000, the following journal entry should be recorded:

| | Debit | Credit |
|---|---|---|
| Pension Expense (+E, −OE) | 10,000 | |
| Pension Liability (+L) | | 10,000 |

| Assets | = | Liabilities | | + | Owners' Equity | |
|---|---|---|---|---|---|---|
| | | Pension Liability | +10,000 | | Pension Expense (+E) | −10,000 |

When the employer pays the matching contribution to the pension plan, the Pension Liability should be reduced (with a debit) and Cash should be reduced (with a credit).

# Chapter Summary

## LO1 Explain how to report the major types of liabilities. p. 468

- Liabilities represent probable future sacrifices of economic benefits that arise from past transactions.
- Liabilities are classified as current if they are due to be paid with current assets within the current operating cycle or within one year of the balance sheet date, whichever is longer. All other liabilities are considered long term.

**LO2  Calculate and interpret the current ratio. p. 469**

- The current ratio is calculated by dividing current assets by current liabilities. A higher ratio suggests greater liquidity, a concept that represents the company's ability to pay current liabilities using current assets.

**LO3  Demonstrate how to account for notes payable and the current portion of long-term debt. p. 470**

- Notes payable are initially reported at their cash-equivalent value, which is the amount of cash received when the notes are signed. Interest expense is recorded as time passes; if it is not paid, the liability Interest Payable should be recorded.
- If any principal is owed on long-term debt in the upcoming year (or operating cycle), that amount should be classified as a current liability called Current Portion of Long-term Debt.

**LO4  Demonstrate how to account for sales taxes and unearned revenues. p. 473**

- Most states require retailers to charge sales tax on the selling price of products. Until they pay the tax, retailers should record sales tax as a current liability.
- Unearned revenues represent cash a business receives before it is earned. Because unearned revenues require the business to provide future services (or return the cash), unearned revenues are reported as current liabilities.

**LO5  Demonstrate how to account for warranties and other contingent liabilities. p. 475**

- Warranties are promises companies make to provide future repair services on any product sold during the current period. A warranty is considered a contingent liability because the cost of a future repair will not be known until a future event (the repair) occurs. Accounting rules require that estimable costs be recorded as a liability (Warranty Payable) and an expense in the period of sale. Actual repair costs then reduce the Warranty Payable account.
- Similarly, other contingent liabilities that are probable and estimable are recorded in the period when they arise. Contingent liabilities that are possible but not probable or are not estimable are disclosed in the notes to the financial statements.

**LO6  Calculate and record payroll including employer payroll taxes. p. 477**

- Calculating the payroll involves calculating gross earnings (based on the amount of work done by employees), payroll deductions (as required by law or requested voluntarily by employees), and net pay, which is the amount paid to employees.
- In addition to the cost of salaries and wages, employers incur additional payroll expenses related to FICA taxes and state and federal unemployment taxes.

### Financial Analysis Tools

| Name of Measure | Formula | What It Tells You |
|---|---|---|
| Current Ratio | $\dfrac{\text{Current Assets}}{\text{Current Liabilities}}$ | • Whether current assets are sufficient to pay current liabilities<br>• A higher ratio means better ability to pay |

## Key Terms

Cash Equivalent (p. 468)
Contingent Liabilities (p. 476)
Current Liabilities (p. 468)
Current Ratio (p. 469)
Employee Earnings Record (p. 480)

Employer Payroll Taxes (p. 483)
Gross Earnings (p. 478)
Line of Credit (p. 469)
Liquidity (p. 469)
Payroll (p. 477)
Payroll Deductions (p. 478)

Payroll Register (p. 482)
Promissory Note (p. 470)
Salaries (p. 477)
Wages (p. 477)

See complete glossary in back of text.

## Questions

1. Define *liability*. What is the difference between a current liability and a long-term liability?
2. What three factors influence the dollar amount reported for liabilities?
3. What is the current ratio? How is it related to the classification of liabilities?
4. What is a line of credit? Does a line of credit affect the amount of cash that a company needs to have available to pay current liabilities?
5. Why is the "time" factor included in the formula to compute interest?

6. If a company has a long-term loan that has only two years remaining until it matures, how is it reported on the balance sheet (a) this year and (b) next year?

7. Why are sales taxes considered liabilities?

8. Why is unearned revenue considered a liability?

9. Why are warranty repair costs estimated and recorded in the period of sale rather than simply recorded when they are provided for customers?

10. How is the liability for warranties similar to and different from liabilities for sales taxes and accounts payable?

11. What is a contingent liability? How is a contingent liability reported?

12. Why are payroll deductions considered current liabilities?

13. Why do you think the federal government requires employers to deduct income taxes from employees' pay? How does this benefit the government? How might it benefit employees?

14. If a company maintains employee earnings records for each employee, is there additional value in maintaining a payroll register?

15. (Supplement 11A) If a company records and pays salaries each month, why is it necessary to estimate and record paid vacations too?

16. (Supplement 11A) Why should employees participate in a 401 (k) plan? Is this a defined contribution or defined benefit plan?

## Multiple Choice

1. Which of the following does not create a current liability?

Quiz 11-1
www.mhhe.com/LLPW1e

   a. Cash is received from customers but not yet earned.
   b. Sales taxes are collected but not remitted.
   c. Amounts are withheld from employee wages but not yet remitted.
   d. None of the above—all create current liabilities.

2. Which of the following statements about the current ratio is true?
   a. The current ratio is always more than or equal to 1.0.
   b. The current ratio decreases when a company fulfills its obligation for unearned revenues.
   c. The higher the current ratio, the greater the risk the business will not be able to pay current liabilities.
   d. None of the above—all are false.

3. Assume that Warnaco Group Inc., the makers of Calvin Klein underwear, borrowed $100,000 from the bank to be repaid over the next five years with principal payments beginning next month. Which of the following best describes the presentation of this debt in the balance sheet as of today (the date of borrowing)?
   a. $100,000 in the Long-Term Liability section.
   b. $100,000 plus the interest to be paid over the five-year period in the Long-Term Liability section.
   c. A portion of the $100,000 in the Current Liability section and the remainder of the principal in the Long-Term Liability section.
   d. A portion of the $100,000 plus interest in the Current Liability Section and the remainder of the principal plus interest in the Long-Term Liability section.

4. Assume Speedo International received $400,000 for promissory notes that it issued on November 1. The notes pay interest on April 30 and October 31 at the annual rate

of 6 percent. Which of the following journal entries must Speedo make at December 31?

   a. Interest Expense          4,000
         Interest Payable                4,000

   b. Interest Expense          4,000
         Cash                            4,000

   c. Interest Expense          4,000
      Interest Payable          8,000
         Cash                           12,000

   d. Interest Expense          8,000
      Interest Payable          4,000
         Cash                           12,000

5. As of February 28, 2007, American Greetings Corporation had 9,400 full-time and 19,500 part-time employees. Assume that in the last pay period of the year, the company paid $8,000,000 to employees after deducting $2,000,000 for employee income taxes, $612,000 for FICA taxes, and $700,000 of voluntary deductions. The company had made no payments to the government or other organizations relating to these payroll deductions. Which of the following statements is true regarding this pay period?
   a. FICA taxes payable is $612,000.
   b. FICA taxes payable is $1,224,000.
   c. Salaries and wages expense is $4,688,000.
   d. None of the above is true.

6. Which of the following is true when a retailer sells a computer for $1,000 cash and collects a 5 percent sales tax?
   a. Sales Revenue is $1,000.
   b. Sales Taxes Payable is $50.
   c. Cash collected totals $1,050.
   d. All of the above are true.

7. Which of the following accounts is debited when a company pays cash to have its products repaired under warranty?
   a. Warranty Expense.
   b. Cash.
   c. Warranty Liability.
   d. Repairs and Maintenance Expense.

8. Big Hitter Corp. is facing a class-action lawsuit in the upcoming year. It is possible, but not probable, that the company will have to pay a settlement of approximately $2,000,000. How would this fact be reported, if at all, in the financial statements to be issued at the end of the current month?
   a. Report $2,000,000 as a current liability.
   b. Report $2,000,000 as a long-term liability.
   c. Report the potential liability in the notes to the financial statements.
   d. Reporting is not required in this case.

9. Lucinda Perez worked 50 hours this week. She earns $10 for the first 40 hours and $15 for any overtime work. She had $75 in payroll deductions. What is her gross earnings?
   a. $550.    c. $475.
   b. $665.    d. $590.

10. The payroll records for Coolo Ice Cream Company showed gross employee earnings of $10,000 as well as payroll deductions of $1,200 for income tax, $800 for FICA taxes, and $500 for voluntary deductions. If the company owes $80 in federal unemployment taxes and $540 for state unemployment taxes, what is the total cost for payroll?
   a. $8,120.    c. $10,620.
   b. $8,920.    d. $11,420.

---

**Solutions to Multiple-Choice Questions**

| 1. d | 2. d | 3. c | 4. a | 5. b | 6. d | 7. c |
| 8. c | 9. a | 10. d | | | | |

---

## Mini Exercises  Available with McGraw-Hill's Homework Manager

**LO1**

### M11-1 Reporting Liabilities in a Classified Balance Sheet

Prepare the liabilities sections of a classified balance sheet for Electronic Games Inc. using the following balances reported at March 31, 2009: Unearned Revenue of $23,000; Accrued Salaries and Employee benefits of $35,670; Accounts Payable of $180,330; Short-Term Notes Payable of $50,000; Long-Term Debt of $100,000 (including current portion of long-term debt equal to $20,000); and Sales Taxes and Other Current Liabilities of $1,000.

**LO2**

### M11-2 Computing and Interpreting the Current Ratio

Refer to M11-1. Compute the Electronic Games current ratio to two decimal places assuming current assets totaled $487,500 at March 31, 2009. Knowing the current ratio was 1.15 on March 31, 2008, would you say the company's liquidity improved or deteriorated in 2009?

**LO2**

### M11-3 Computing and Interpreting the Current Ratio

The balance sheet for Shaver Corporation reported the following: total assets, $250,000; noncurrent assets, $150,000; current liabilities, $40,000; total owners' equity, $90,000; net income, $3,320; interest expense, $4,400; and income before income taxes, $5,280. Compute Shaver's current ratio. Based on this ratio alone, does it appear Shaver will be able to meet its obligations to pay current liabilities as they become due?

**LO2**

### M11-4 Analyzing the Impact of Transactions on the Current Ratio

BSO, Inc., has a current ratio of 2.0  (= $1,000,000 ÷ $500,000). For each of the following transactions, determine whether the current ratio will increase, decrease, or remain the same.

   (a) Purchased $20,000 of new inventory on credit.
   (b) Paid accounts payable in the amount of $50,000.
   (c) Recorded accrued salaries in the amount of $100,000.
   (d) Borrowed $250,000 from a local bank to be repaid in 90 days.

**LO3**

### M11-5 Reporting Current and Noncurrent Portions of Long-Term Debt

Assume that on December 1, 2008, your company borrowed $14,000, a portion of which is to be repaid each year on November 30. Specifically, your company will make the following principal payments: 2009, $2,000; 2010, $3,000; 2011, $4,000; and 2012, $5,000. Show how this loan will be reported in the December 31, 2009 and 2008, balance sheets, assuming that principal payments will be made when required.

## M11-6 Recording a Note Payable

LO3

Greener Pastures Corporation borrowed $1,000,000 on November 1, 2008. The note carried a 6 percent interest rate with the principal and interest payable on June 1, 2009. Prepare the journal entries and show the accounting equation effects for (a) the note issued on November 1, (b) the interest accrual on December 31, and (c) the interest and principal payments on June 1, 2009.

## M11-7 Reporting Interest and Long-Term Debt, Including Current Portion

LO3

Barton Chocolates used a promissory note to borrow $1,000,000 on July 1, 2009, at an annual interest rate of 6 percent. The note is to be repaid in yearly installments of $200,000, plus accrued interest, on June 30 of every year until the note is paid in full (on June 30, 2014). Show how the results of this transaction would be reported in a classified balance sheet prepared as of December 31, 2009.

## M11-8 Recording Sales and State Sales Tax on Services

LO4

Ahlers Clocks sells and repairs wall clocks, mantles, and grandfather clocks and is located in the Empire Mall in Sioux Falls, South Dakota. Assume that a grandfather clock was repaired for $50 cash plus 4 percent sales tax. Prepare the journal entry and show the accounting equation effects related to this transaction.

## M11-9 Recording Sales, State Sales Tax, and Cost of Goods Sold

LO4

Assume Ahlers Clock sold a grandfather clock for $5,000 cash plus 4 percent sales tax. Prepare the journal entry and show the accounting equation effects related to this transaction. As part of this transaction, include the cost of goods sold using a perpetual inventory system and assuming the clock cost Ahlers $3,000.

## M11-10 Recording Unearned Revenues

LO4

A local theater company sells 1,500 season ticket packages at a price of $250 per package. The first show in the five-show season starts this week. Prepare the journal entries and show the related accounting equation effects arising from (a) the sale of the season tickets before the first show and (b) the revenue earned after the first show.

## M11-11 Accounting for Warranty Liabilities

LO5

Hugo Watch Company, based in Livingston, Montana, sold $10,000 of watches in January under a six-month warranty. The cost of warranty repairs is estimated to be 5 percent of the sales price. In February and March, customers returned watches for repair under warranty. Hugo paid $480 for a repair company to perform this work. Prepare the journal entries and show the related accounting equation effects related to (a) the estimated liability for warranty costs and (b) the payment for watch repairs. Does the warranty cost estimate appear accurate? If not, what should Hugo Watch do?

## M11-12 Reporting a Contingent Liability

LO5

Buzz Coffee Shops is famous for its large servings of hot coffee. After a famous case involving McDonald's, the lawyer for Buzz warned management (during 2007) that it could be sued if someone were to spill hot coffee and be burned. "With the temperature of your coffee, I can guarantee it's just a matter of time before you're sued for $1,000,000." Unfortunately, in 2008, the prediction came true when a customer filed suit. The case went to trial in 2009, and the jury awarded the customer $400,000 in damages, which the company immediately appealed. The company's lawyers believed the lawsuit would be overturned on appeal. During 2010, the customer and the company settled their dispute for $150,000. What is the proper reporting of this liability each year?

## M11-13 Calculating Gross Earnings

LO6

Dan Carotene earns a regular pay rate of $20 per hour for the first 40 hours per week and time and a half for anything over 40 hours. If Dan works 50 hours during the first week of the year, what is his gross earnings for the week?

## M11-14 Calculating Net Pay

LO6

Lightning Electronics is a mid-size manufacturer of lithium batteries. The company's payroll records for the November 1–14 pay period show that employees earned wages totaling $100,000 but that federal income taxes totaling $14,000 and FICA taxes totaling $5,250 were withheld from this amount. There were no voluntary deductions. The net pay was directly deposited into the employees' bank accounts. What was the amount of net pay? If the company incurs $90 for federal unemployment taxes and $608 for state unemployment taxes, what is the total payroll cost (including employer payroll taxes) for this period?

## M11-15 Recording Net Pay

LO6

Refer to M11-14. Prepare the journal entry or entries that Lightning Electronics would use to record the payroll. Include both employee and employer taxes.

## Exercises     Available with McGraw-Hill's Homework Manager

**LO2**

**Kraft Foods Inc.**

### E11-1 Calculating and Interpreting the Current Ratio

According to its Web site, Kraft Foods Inc. sells enough Kool-Aid mix to make 1,000 gallons of the drink every minute during the summer and over 560 million gallons each year. At December 31, 2006, the company reported the following amounts (in millions) in its financial statements:

|  | 2005 | 2006 |
| --- | --- | --- |
| Total current assets | $ 8,153 | $ 8,254 |
| Total current liabilities | 8,724 | 10,473 |

*Required:*

1. Compute the current ratio (to two decimal places) for 2005 and 2006.
2. Did Kraft appear to have increased or decreased its ability to pay current liabilities as they become due?

**LO2, 3**

### E11-2 Determining the Impact of Current Liability Transactions Including Analysis of the Current Ratio

Bryant Company sells a wide range of inventories that are initially purchased on accounts payable. Occasionally, a short-term note payable is used to obtain cash for current use. The following transactions were selected from those occurring during 2009:

> (*a*) On January 10, 2009, purchased merchandise on credit for $18,000. The company uses a perpetual inventory system.
> (*b*) On March 1, 2009, borrowed $40,000 cash from City Bank and gave a $40,000 interest-bearing note payable due in six months plus interest stated an annual rate of 8 percent payable at maturity.

*Required:*

1. Show the journal entry and accounting equation effects on January 10 and March 1.
2. Describe the impact of each transaction on the current ratio. (Assume Bryant Company's current assets have always been more than its current liabilities.)
3. What amount of cash is paid on the maturity date of the note?

**LO3**

**Target Corporation**

### E11-3 Journalizing Transactions Involving Notes Payable

Many businesses borrow money during periods of increased business activity to finance inventory and accounts receivable. Target Corporation is one of America's largest general merchandise retailers. Each Christmas, Target builds up its inventory to meet the needs of Christmas shoppers. A large portion of Christmas sales are on credit. As a result, Target often collects cash from the sales several months after Christmas. Assume that on November 1, 2009, Target borrowed $6 million cash from Metropolitan Bank and signed a promissory note that matures in six months. The interest rate was 7.5 percent payable at maturity. The accounting period ends December 31.

*Required:*

1. Give the journal entry to record the note on November 1, 2009.
2. Give any adjusting entry required on December 31, 2009.
3. Give the journal entry to record payment of the note and interest on the maturity date, April 30, 2010, assuming that interest has not been recorded since December 31, 2009.
4. If Target needs extra cash during every Christmas season, should management borrow money on a long-term basis to avoid the necessity of negotiating a new short-term loan each year? Why or why not?

**LO3**

### E11-4 Journalizing Transactions Involving Notes Payable

Assume that on November 1, 2009, Tops Bakery negotiated an agreement to borrow $200,000 cash on a one-year note. The note specified that Tops would pay 6 percent interest one year later, on October 31, 2010. The principal was also to be repaid on the maturity date (October 31, 2010).

*Required:*

1. Depict these events on a timeline similar to the one in Exhibit 11.2. How many months of interest are included in the payment on October 31, 2010? How many of these months relate to 2009 versus 2010?
2. Give the journal entry to record the note on November 1, 2009.

3. Give any adjusting entry required on December 31, 2009.
4. Give the journal entry to record payment of the note and interest on the maturity date, October 31, 2010, assuming that interest has not been recorded since December 31, 2009.

## E11-5 Journalizing and Reporting Transactions Involving Sales Taxes

LO2, 4

The Ferrer School (TFS) provides services to customers and collects a 5 percent state sales tax. The business entered into the following transactions.

    *a.* During January 2009, TFS sold $12,000 worth of services to customers and collected $12,600 cash.

    *b.* On February 1, 2009, TFS made a sales tax remittance for sales taxes collected during January 2009.

### Required:

1. Give the journal entries to record these events.
2. Describe the impact of these events on the current ratio assuming current assets were $200,000 and current liabilities were $100,000 on January 1, 2009.

## E11-6 Determining and Recording the Financial Statement Effects of Unearned Subscription Revenue

LO4

Reader's Digest

Reader's Digest Association is a publisher of magazines, books, and music collections. The following note is from its June 30 annual report:

**Revenues**

Sales of our magazine subscriptions, less estimated collections, are deferred (as unearned revenue) and recognized as revenues proportionately over the subscription period.

Assume that Reader's Digest collected $394 million in 2008 for magazines that will be delivered in future years. During the 2009 fiscal year, the company delivered $190 million worth of magazines on those subscriptions.

### Required:

1. Using the information given above, prepare the journal entries that would be recorded in each year.
2. Using your answers to requirement 1, compute the amount of subscription services that Reader's Digest received in 2008 but must still provide in 2010 and beyond.

## E11-7 Journalizing Transactions Involving Warranties

LO5

During 2008, Bull Manufacturing Inc. (BMI) sold 30,000 lawnmowers with a two-year warranty. The company's production manager estimated that 5 percent of the lawnmowers would require warranty repairs at an average cost of $100 per unit. BMI outsources the warranty work to repair companies and incurred $100,000 in repair costs during 2008, all of which were paid in cash.

### Required:

1. What is the total estimated cost of warranty repairs for sales made during 2008?
2. Give the journal entries to record these events.
3. If BMI's estimate is accurate, what total repair cost is yet to be incurred for the lawnmowers sold in 2008?

## E11-8 Journalizing Transactions Involving Warranties

LO5

Paloma Group sells tankless water heaters that come with a 10-year warranty against defects. Assume that during the years ended December 31, 2008 and 2009, the company sold 50,000 and 60,000 units. At the time of sale, the company's engineers estimated that only 1 percent would be returned for repair under warranty. Paloma intends to perform all of its own repair work at an estimated cost of $100 per repair. During 2008, Paloma used parts and supplies costing $5,000 for warranty repairs. In 2009, parts and supplies costing $11,000 were used. (Ignore the associated labor cost.)

### Required:

1. What is the total estimated cost of warranty repairs for sales made during 2008? 2009?
2. What was the actual cost of warranty repairs in 2008? 2009?
3. Give the journal entries to record the 2008 and 2009 transactions involving warranties.
4. Does it appear that Paloma's initial estimate of total repair costs was accurate? Explain.

**LO6**

### E11-9 Recording Payroll Costs with Discussion

McLoyd Company completed the salary and wage payroll for March 2009. The payroll provided the following details:

| | | | |
|---|---|---|---|
| Salaries and wages earned | $230,000 | Withholdings for United Way | $ 6,000 |
| Federal income taxes withheld | 50,200 | Federal unemployment tax | 1,840 |
| FICA taxes withheld | 16,445 | State unemployment tax | 12,880 |

*Required:*

1. Considering employer payroll taxes, calculate the total labor cost for the company.
2. Prepare the journal entry to record the payroll for March including employee deductions (but excluding employer payroll taxes).
3. Prepare the journal entry to record the employer's payroll taxes.

**LO6**

### E11-10 Calculating and Recording Net Pay

Assume that Nora Jones worked 46 hours this week. Her regular wage rate is $13 per hour, and the overtime rate is 1½ times the regular pay rate. She is single, paid weekly, claims three allowances, pays federal but no state, county, or city income tax, and requested voluntary deductions of $8 each week for WWF (a charitable organization).

*Required:*

1. Using the tax bracket table in Exhibit 11.5 and assuming total FICA taxes equal to 8 percent, calculate (a) gross earnings, (b) payroll deductions, and (c) net pay. If necessary, round to the nearest penny.
2. Prepare the journal entry to record this payroll assuming Nora is paid by check but the payroll deductions have not been remitted. (Ignore employer payroll taxes.)

**LO6**

### E11-11 Recording Net Pay and Payroll Taxes

The payroll register for the two weeks ended October 31, 2008, indicates the following:

| | | | |
|---|---|---|---|
| Gross salaries | $140,000 | United Way contributions | $3,000 |
| Federal income tax deductions | 10,093 | State unemployment taxes | 7,560 |
| FICA tax deductions | 11,120 | Federal unemployment taxes | 1,120 |

*Required:*

1. Calculate net pay.
2. Assuming that employees were paid their net pay on October 31 but no other payments were made for payroll, prepare journal entries to record (a) salaries and wages and (b) employer payroll taxes.

**LO6**

### E11-12 Calculating and Recording Payroll Taxes

The payroll register for Great Southern Hospitality Corp. is shown below. No employees have earned more than $7,000 to date.

**GREAT SOUTHERN HOSPITALITY CORP.**
Payroll Register
For the Week Ending January 7, 2009

| | | Gross Earnings | | | Payroll Deductions | | | | Payment | | Accounts Debited | |
|---|---|---|---|---|---|---|---|---|---|---|---|---|
| Employee | Total Hours | Regular | Overtime | Gross | Federal Inc. Tax | FICA | United Way | Total | Net Pay | Check No. | Office Salaries Expense | Wages Expense |
| Ashworth, Jay | 40 | 400.00 | 0.00 | 400.00 | 59.00 | 32.00 | 4.00 | 95.00 | 305.00 | 280 | 400.00 | |
| Cabot, Noreen | 45 | 400.00 | 75.00 | 475.00 | 37.00 | 38.00 | 5.00 | 80.00 | 395.00 | 281 | | 475.00 |
| Zuvin, Katy | 42 | 560.00 | 42.00 | 602.00 | 47.00 | 48.16 | 15.00 | 110.16 | 491.84 | 308 | 602.00 | |
| Total | | 13,302.00 | 698.00 | 14,000.00 | 1,340.00 | 1,120.00 | 290.00 | 2,750.00 | 11,250.00 | | 2,100.00 | 11,900.00 |

*Required:*

1. Calculate state unemployment taxes, assuming a 5.4 percent rate. If necessary, round to the nearest cent.
2. Calculate federal unemployment taxes assuming a 6.2 percent rate and a full credit for state unemployment taxes. If necessary, round to the nearest cent.
3. Using information in the payroll register and your answers to requirements 1 and 2, prepare journal entries that would be used to record (a) salaries and wages and (b) employer payroll taxes.

## E11-13 Recording Payroll Costs with and without Withholdings    LO6

Assume an employee of Rocco Rock Company earns $1,000 of gross wages during the current pay period and is required to remit to the government $100 for income tax and $50 for FICA. Consider the following two procedures for paying the employee. (Ignore unemployment taxes.)

| Procedure 1 (withholdings) | Procedure 2 (no withholdings) |
| --- | --- |
| Rocco Rock Company pays the employee net wages of $850 and will remit income taxes and FICA on behalf of the employee. | Rocco Rock Company pays the employee gross wages of $1,000 and the employee is responsible for remitting income taxes and FICA. |

*Required:*

1. Ignoring employer payroll taxes, under each procedure calculate (a) the total labor cost for the company and (b) the amount by which the employee's cash will increase after satisfying all responsibilities to the government.
2. Explain why procedure 1 (withholdings) is the approach preferred by the government.
3. Considering that employers are responsible for matching the employee's FICA contributions, explain why employers might also prefer procedure 1 over procedure 2.
4. Prepare the journal entries required by the employer under procedure 1 assuming the employee is paid in cash but the withholdings and matching employer FICA contribution have not been paid.

## E11-14 (Supplement) Employee Benefits

Heara Whisper Electronics (HWE) is a maker of assistive hearing devices. To attract employees, the company offers three-week paid vacations, which can be used up each year or accumulated over successive years and then paid out in cash. The company also has a defined contribution pension plan to which the company will make contributions that match 100 percent of the contributions made by employees. During 2009, Victor Ree accumulated $1,500 of vacation time, and he contributed $1,000 to the pension plan. The company expects to make cash payments in 2010 totaling $2,500 related to these transactions.

*Required:*

1. In what year should HWE record these items? Explain.
2. Prepare journal entries that HWE should make to record the effect of these transactions on the company.

# Problems—Set A  ™    Available with McGraw-Hill's Homework Manager

## PA11-1 Journalizing Transactions, Evaluating Current Ratio Effects, and Reporting Liabilities    LO1, 2, 3, 4

Jack Hammer Company completed the following transactions during 2009. The annual accounting period ends December 31, 2009.

Apr. 30   Received $550,000 from Commerce Bank after signing a 2-year, 6 percent interest-bearing note payable.

June  6   Purchased merchandise on account at a cost of $75,000.

July  15   Paid for the June 6 purchase.

Aug. 31   Signed contract to provide security service to a small apartment complex and collected six months' fees in advance amounting to $12,000. (Use the account Unearned Service Revenue.)

*Required:*

1.  Prepare journal entries for each of the transactions and for adjustments required at year-end.
2.  For each transaction, state whether the current ratio is increased, decreased, or remains the same. (Assume Jack Hammer's current assets have always been higher than its current liabilities.)
3.  Show how all of the liabilities arising from these transactions are reported on the classified balance sheet at December 31, 2009.

**LO1, 2, 3, 5**

www.mhhe.com/LLPW1e

**PA11-2 Recording Notes Payable, Warranties, and Evaluating Impact on Current Ratio**

On June 30, 2009, Sideways Movers had $243,000 in current assets and $211,000 in current liabilities. On August 1, 2009, Sideways received $50,000 from an issue of promissory notes that will mature in 2012. The notes pay interest on February 1 at an annual rate of 6 percent. Sideways' fiscal year ends on December 31.

*Required:*

1.  Explain which sections of Sideways' classified balance sheet are affected by the new promissory notes.
2.  Give the journal entry on August 1, 2009, to record the issue of notes payable.
3.  Give the journal entry on December 31, 2009, to record interest expense assuming that none had been recorded prior to that date.
4.  Give the journal entry on February 1, 2010, to record the first interest payment.
5.  Compute Sideways' current ratio on June 30, 2009.
6.  Assume that as of December 31, 2009, Sideways had not yet used the cash obtained from the issue of notes on August 1, 2009. What is the effect, if any, of the note issue on the company's current ratio at the end of the fiscal year?
7.  On January 1, 2010, Sideways had accrued product warranty liabilities totaling $9,530. From January 1 to December 31, 2010, the company paid $6,770 under existing warranty agreements and accrued $7,540 for additional warranties arising from sales made in 2010. Give the journal entries to record the total payment and accrual made during 2010. What is the balance in Warranty Liability at December 31, 2010?

**LO1, 4, 6**

www.mhhe.com/LLPW1e

**PA11-3 Recording and Reporting Unearned Revenue and Payroll**

On December 1, 2009, Lakeview Company collected rent of $3,600 for office space rented to another business. The rent collected was for two months from December 1, 2009, to January 31, 2010. Lakeview also reported the following information in its accounting records on December 31, 2009, for the December 22 to December 31 payroll.

| | |
|---|---:|
| Gross salaries earned by employees | 7,200 |
| Federal income tax withheld from employees | 1,100 |
| FICA taxes withheld from employees | 420 |
| State unemployment taxes | 388 |
| Federal unemployment taxes | 58 |

Employees were paid $5,680 on December 31, 2009, but the withholdings have not yet been remitted. No employer payroll taxes have been recorded for the period from December 22 to December 31.

*Required:*

1.  Give the journal entries to record (a) the collection of rent on December 1, 2009, and (b) the adjustment for rent on December 31, 2009.
2.  Compute the total payroll costs related to the period from December 22 to December 31, 2009.
3.  Give the journal entry on December 31, 2009, to record payroll related to the period from December 22 to December 31, 2009. Separate the journal entry for the employer's payroll expenses from the entry for salaries and wages expense.
4.  Show how any liabilities related to these transactions should be reported on the company's balance sheet at December 31, 2009.

**LO5**

Macromedia, Inc.

**PA11-4 Determining Financial Statement Reporting of Contingent Liabilities**

Macromedia, Inc., is the original maker of shockwave and flash technologies. Its 2002 annual report indicated that a lawsuit had been filed in 2000 against the company and five of its former officers for securities fraud in connection with allegedly making false or misleading statements about its financial results. The lawsuit was settled on January 9, 2002, as described in the following note:

> **Legal**
>
> The settlement amount was $48.0 million, of which approximately $19.5 million was paid by insurance. As a result, the Company recorded a $28.5 million charge as a component of other income (expense) in its consolidated statements of operations during fiscal year 2002.

**Required:**

Explain why Macromedia did not record a contingent liability in 2000 when the lawsuit was filed.

**PA11-5 Journalizing Transactions, Evaluating Current Ratio Effects, and Reporting Liabilities (Comprehensive Problem)**

LO2, 3, 4, 5, 6

www.mhhe.com/LLPW1e

Jinx Hair Salon in Iowa City completed the following transactions.

(a) Provided hair styling services and received $9,450, which included $450 in sales taxes.

(b) Received $200 for gift cards to be redeemed for future services.

(c) Prepared to expand the salon by borrowing $40,000, which was placed in the company's bank account. Signed a 9-month promissory note on February 1, with interest payable at maturity on October 31, 2009, calculated using a 5 percent annual interest rate.

(d) Provided hair styling services, which were paid for using gift cards. The total charge of $105 included $5 of sales taxes.

(e) Received a letter alleging that a Jinx stylist had ruined a customer's wedding by providing inferior hair care services. The customer was seeking $100,000 to compensate for her anguish. Jinx's lawyer believes the pending lawsuit is without merit.

(f) Paid stylists net wages of $5,500. Withheld but did not yet remit $725 for federal income tax, $315 for FICA taxes, and $20 for United Way contributions. Employer payroll costs for FICA, state unemployment taxes ($297), and federal unemployment taxes ($44) have not yet been remitted.

(g) Paid interest on the note on October 31, 2009.

(h) Paid principal on the note on October 31, 2009.

**Required:**

1. Prepare journal entries for each of the transactions and for adjustments required at year-end.
2. Indicate the independent effect of each transaction on the current ratio (increase, decrease, no change). When determining the effects, assume Jinx's current ratio at the beginning of the period was 1.1 (= $176,000 ÷ $160,000).

# Problems—Set B  Available with McGraw-Hill's Homework Manager

**PB11-1 Journalizing Transactions, Evaluating Current Ratio Effects, and Reporting Liabilities**

LO1, 2, 3, 4

Tiger Company completed the following transactions during 2009. The annual accounting period ends December 31, 2009.

Jan. 3  Purchased merchandise on account at a cost of $24,000. (Assume a perpetual inventory system.)

    27  Paid for the January 3 purchase.

Apr. 1  Received $80,000 from Atlantic Bank after signing a 12-month, 5 percent interest-bearing note payable.

Aug. 1  Rented out a small office in a building owned by Tiger Company and collected eight months' rent in advance amounting to $8,000. (Use the account Unearned Rent Revenue.)

**Required:**

1. Prepare journal entries for each of the transactions and for adjustments required at year-end.
2. For each transaction, state whether the current ratio is increased, decreased, or remains the same. (Assume Tiger Company's current assets have always been higher than its current liabilities.)
3. Show how all of the liabilities arising from these transactions are reported on the balance sheet at December 31, 2009.

**LO1, 2, 3, 5**

### PB11-2 Recording Notes Payable, Warranties, and Evaluating Impact on Current Ratio

On January 31, 2009, Dry Ice Inc. (DII) had $486,000 in current assets and $405,000 in current liabilities. On February 1, 2009, DII received $100,000 from an issue of promissory notes that will mature in 2011. The notes pay interest on January 31 at an annual rate of 6 percent. DII's fiscal year ends on December 31.

*Required:*

1.  Explain which sections of DII's classified balance sheet are affected by the new promissory notes.
2.  Give the journal entry on February 1, 2009, to record the issue of notes payable.
3.  Compute DII's current ratio on January 31, 2009. What would be the effect, if any, of the February 1 note issuance on the company's current ratio?
4.  Give the journal entry on December 31, 2009, to record interest expense assuming that none had been recorded prior to that date.
5.  Give the journal entry on January 31, 2010, to record the first interest payment.
6.  On January 1, 2010, DII had accrued product warranty liabilities totaling $10,000. From January 1 to December 31, 2010, the company paid $9,000 under existing warranty agreements and accrued $12,000 for additional warranties arising from sales made in 2010. Give the journal entries to record the total payment and accrual made during 2010. What is the balance in Warranty Liability at December 31, 2011?

**LO1, 4, 6**

### PB11-3 Recording and Reporting Unearned Revenue and Payroll

On December 1, 2009, Sandler Company collected rent of $3,600, for office space rented to another business. The rent collected was for three months from December 1, 2009, to February 28, 2010. Sandler also reported the following information in its accounting records on December 31, 2009, for the December 17 to December 31 payroll.

| | |
|---|---:|
| Gross salaries earned by employees | 18,000 |
| Federal income tax withheld from employees | 2,750 |
| FICA taxes withheld from employees | 1,050 |
| State unemployment taxes | 970 |
| Federal unemployment taxes | 145 |

Employees were paid $14,200 on December 31, 2009, but the withholdings have not yet been remitted. No employer payroll taxes have been recorded for the period from December 17 to December 31.

*Required:*

1.  Give the journal entries to record (a) the collection of rent on December 1, 2009, and (b) the adjustment for rent on December 31, 2009.
2.  Compute the total payroll costs related to the period from December 17 to December 31, 2009.
3.  Give the journal entry on December 31, 2009, to record payroll related to the period from December 17 to December 31, 2009. Separate the journal entry for the employer's payroll expenses from the entry for salaries and wages expense.
4.  Show how any liabilities related to these transactions should be reported on the company's balance sheet at December 31, 2009.

**LO5**

**Brunswick Corporation**

### PB11-4 Determining Financial Statement Reporting of Contingent Liabilities

Brunswick Corporation is a multinational company that manufactures and sells marine and recreational products. A prior annual report contained the following information:

> **Litigation**
>
> A jury awarded $44.4 million in damages in a suit brought by Independent Boat Builders, Inc., a buying group of boat manufacturers and its 22 members. Under the antitrust laws, the damage award has been tripled, and the plaintiffs will be entitled to their attorney's fees and interest. The Company has filed an appeal contending the verdict was erroneous as a matter of law, both as to liability and damages.

*Required:*

What are the alternative ways in which Brunswick could account for the loss related to this litigation?

**PB11-5 Journalizing Transactions, Evaluating Current Ratio Effects, and Reporting Liabilities (Comprehensive Problem)**   LO2, 3, 4, 5, 6

The Rosa Shell Tennis Center completed the following transactions in August 2009.

- (*a*) On August 1, sold 12-month memberships and received $128,400, which included $8,400 in sales taxes required on taxable services.
- (*b*) On August 1, purchased a new ball machine for $10,000, which was financed by signing a nine-month promissory note with interest payable at maturity on April 30, 2010, calculated using a 6 percent annual interest rate.
- (*c*) Received a letter indicating that the center was being sued by a member for failing to display signs about wet court surfaces. The member was seeking $20,000 to cover medical expenses and mental hardship arising from a sprained ankle. The tennis center's lawyer believes the pending lawsuit is without merit.
- (*d*) Paid net wages of $11,000 to staff in the pro shop. Withheld but did not yet remit $1,450 for federal income tax, $630 for FICA taxes, and $40 for Salvation Army contributions. Employer payroll costs for FICA, state unemployment taxes ($594), and federal unemployment taxes ($88) have not yet been remitted.
- (*e*) Made month-end adjustments for membership revenues earned and interest expense incurred.

*Required:*

1. Prepare journal entries for each of the transactions and month-end adjustments.
2. Indicate the independent effect of each transaction or event on the current ratio (increase, decrease, no change). When determining the effects, assume the tennis center's current ratio at the beginning of the period was 1.5 (= $150,000 ÷ $100,000).

# Cases and Projects

### CP11-1 Finding Financial Information   LO2

Refer to the financial statements of The Home Depot in Appendix A at the end of this book, or download the annual report from the Cases and Projects section of the text's Web site at www.mhhe.com/LLPW1e.

*Required:*

Calculate, to two decimal places, the company's current ratio at February 3, 2008. Does this ratio cause you any concern about the company's ability to pay its current liabilities?

### CP11-2 Comparing Financial Information   LO2, 5

Refer to the financial statements of The Home Depot in Appendix A and Lowe's Companies in Appendix B at the end of this book, or download the annual reports from the Cases section of the text's Web site at www.mhhe.com/LLPW1e.

*Required:*

1. Calculate, to two decimal places, the company's current ratio at February 1, 2008. Does this ratio cause you any concern about the company's ability to pay its current liabilities? Based on your analyses of the current ratio, does Lowe's or The Home Depot appear to be better able to pay its current liabilities?
2. According to Note 1 of the financial statements, what caused reductions and increases in the company's liability for extended warranty claims? Is this liability reported as a current or noncurrent liability?

Lowe's

### CP11-3 Examining an Annual Report: Internet-Based Team Research   LO1, 2, 5

As a team, select an industry to analyze. Using your Web browser, each team member should acquire the annual report or 10-K for one publicly traded company in the industry with each member selecting a different company. (See CP1-3 in Chapter 1 for a description of possible resources for these tasks.)

*Required:*

1. On an individual basis, each team member should write a short report that incorporates the following:
   - *a.* What are the most significant types of current liabilities owed by the company?
   - *b.* Read the company's financial statement note regarding contingencies. Does the company have any potentially significant liabilities that have not yet been recorded?
   - *c.* Compute and analyze the current ratio.

2.  Then, as a team, write a short report comparing and contrasting your companies using these attributes. Discuss any patterns across the companies that you as a team observe. Provide potential explanations for any differences discovered.

**LO2**

### CP11-4 Making Ethical Decisions: A Real-Life Example

A few months ago, you were approached by a charming, young entrepreneur named Barry who had dreams of creating the world's largest carpet cleaning company. He said his business had really taken off, which he backed up with financial statements that showed sales growth from $1,240,524 to $4,845,347 and gross profit growth from $663,830 to $2,794,568 in just one short year. To finance this rapid growth, he had borrowed more than $780,000 using short-term promissory notes, but now he needed new investors. Excerpts from the balance sheets are presented in the following table.

|  | Year 1 | Year 2 |
| --- | --- | --- |
| **ASSETS** |  |  |
| Current assets |  |  |
| Cash | $ 30,321 | $    87,014 |
| Accounts receivable | 0 | 693,773 |
| Other | 76,775 | 947,186 |
| Total current assets | 107,096 | 1,727,973 |
|  |  |  |
| **LIABILITIES** |  |  |
| Current liabilities |  |  |
| Notes payable | $       0 | $ 780,507 |
| Taxes payable | 0 | 28,027 |
| Other | 2,930 | 959,901 |
| Total current liabilities | 2,930 | 1,768,435 |

*Required:*

1.  Calculate, to two decimal places, the current ratios at the end of year 1 and year 2.

2.  Does the size of the current ratio in year 2 cause you any concern? Does the change in the ratio cause you concern? Is the change consistent with a company that has reportedly quadrupled its sales and gross profits in just one year? What questions would you ask before investing in his business?

**ZZZZ Best**

Note: This case is based on the financial statements of ZZZZ Best in 1985 and 1986 as reported in an article by Joseph T. Wells ("Irrational Ratios," *Journal of Accountancy*, August 2001, retrieved on January 17, 2008 from http://www.aicpa.org/PUBS/jofa/aug2001/wells.htm). The founder of ZZZZ Best was convicted of defrauding investors in many different ways, including overstating current assets by accruing accounts receivable for fictitious sales on account.

**LO1, 2**

### CP11-5 Making Ethical Decisions: A Mini Case

Upon reviewing your company's accounting records, you discovered that several customer accounts have credit balances instead of debit balances. Your investigation revealed that these customers had paid their balances but later were dissatisfied with the services your company had provided. Your company's sales staff agreed to fully refund amounts charged to the customers. Being a little short on cash, your company's accounting department decided to apply the refund against future purchases made by these customers, rather than issue a check for the refund. At the end of the year, your company reported total current liabilities of $9,500 and total current assets of $19,000. Included in Accounts Receivable were credit balances totaling $1,000.

*Required:*

1.  Calculate the current ratio using the totals reported by your company.

2.  If dissatisfied customers do not make future purchases from your company, they could legitimately ask to be paid the credit balances owed to them. In light of this possibility, the credit balances should be reclassified from Accounts Receivable to Accounts Payable. Recalculate the current ratio after taking into account this reclassification.

3. Your company's accountant has argued that the dollar amount of credit balances is so small that their reclassification is unnecessary. Do you agree? What if your company's bank has the right to a higher interest rate if your company's current ratio falls below 2.0?

## CP11-6 Evaluating Effects on Current Ratio: Critical Thinking                                                 LO2

Assume you work as an assistant to the chief financial officer (CFO) of Fashions First, Inc. The CFO reminds you that the fiscal year-end is only two weeks away and that he is looking to you to ensure the company complies with its loan covenant to maintain a current ratio of 1.25 or higher. A review of the general ledger indicates that current assets total $690,000 and current liabilities are $570,000. Your company has an excess of cash ($300,000) and an equally large balance in Accounts Payable ($270,000), although none of the accounts payable are due until next month.

### Required:

1. Determine whether the company is currently in compliance with its loan covenant.
2. Assuming the level of current assets and current liabilities remains unchanged until the last day of the fiscal year, evaluate whether Fashions First should pay down $90,000 of its accounts payable on the last day of the year before the accounts payable become due.

# 12 Partnerships

## LEARNING OBJECTIVES

**After completing this chapter, you should be able to:**

**LO1** Compare the partnership form of business with other forms.

**LO2** Demonstrate how to account for partnerships.

**LO3** Demonstrate the proper treatment for changes of ownership in a partnership.

**LO4** Demonstrate the proper treatment for the liquidation of a partnership.

**LO5** Calculate and interpret the partner return on equity ratio.

Lectured presentations–12-1
www.mhhe.com/LLPW1e

# Focus Company:  BLOOM 'N FLOWERS

## Fabulously Fresh Flowers.

Perhaps the single most important decision the owners of a new business face is determining the appropriate form of the business. At one time, owners could choose from only three basic forms of business: corporation, general partnership, and sole proprietorship. These forms of business are still used today, but numerous others are now available. As a result, choosing the proper business form has become an increasingly complex decision requiring future owners to wade through mountains of information. Enlisting the services of a CPA or knowledgeable attorney in making this decision is highly advisable.

In this chapter, we investigate the advantages and disadvantages of two forms of business, the general partnership and a newer form called the limited liability company (LLC). We do so by following the story of Hal Flowers and Dawn Bloom, two friends who decided to start a business together.

Hal Flowers and Dawn Bloom both sold flowers to individuals and businesses in their respective neighborhoods. They wished to expand their customer base by moving their business into a large mall located in the center of the city. Because neither had the resources or the time to run a business this large by themselves, they decided to combine their resources and form a new business—Bloom 'N Flowers. The new business would serve more customers and carry a larger inventory of fresh cut flowers than was previously possible when operating separately as sole proprietors.

Hal and Dawn knew that their most important decision would be the form of business they chose for their enterprise. After doing a bit of research, they narrowed the choice to three possibilities: the general partnership, the limited liability company, and the S-corporation.

| PARTNERSHIPS COMPARED TO SIMILAR ORGANIZATIONS | ACCOUNTING FOR PARTNERSHIPS | CHANGES OF OWNERSHIP IN A PARTNERSHIP | LIQUIDATION OF A PARTNERSHIP | RATIO ANALYSIS |
|---|---|---|---|---|
| • Characteristics of Partnerships<br>• Similar Forms of Business | • Formation: Recording Cash and Noncash Contributions<br>• Division of Income (or Loss): Four Methods<br>• Preparation of Financial Statements | • Admission of a Partner<br>• Withdrawal of a Partner<br>• Death of a Partner | • No Capital Deficiency<br>• Capital Deficiency | • Partner Return on Equity |

# PARTNERSHIPS COMPARED TO SIMILAR ORGANIZATIONS

**Learning Objective 1**

Compare the partnership form of business with other forms.

Because Hal and Dawn had little or no knowledge of the options available to them, they did some quick research. The two learned that each form of business has specific characteristics.

## Characteristics of Partnerships

The Uniform Partnership Act defines **partnership** as "the association of two or more persons to carry on as co-owners of a business for profit, whether or not the persons intend to form a partnership." Because partnerships are so easy to form—no formal contract is required—this form of business has the greatest potential for disputes and lawsuits. **To prevent misunderstandings among partners, having a formal partnership agreement, preferably drafted by a lawyer, is advisable.**

Hal and Dawn decided to evaluate the partnership by listing its advantages and disadvantages. Later, they would weigh them against the advantages and disadvantages of other forms of business before deciding on the appropriate form for their own business.

### Advantages of the Partnership

- **Pass-through taxation.** Profits from the business flow directly through to the partners' personal tax returns rather than being taxed first at the partnership level.
- **Ease of formation.** Partnerships are relatively easy and inexpensive to establish. In fact, some partnerships may be formed inadvertently through a handshake or a simple "OK."
- **Simplified recordkeeping.** No annual meetings are required and there are few recordkeeping requirements.
- **Favorable taxation.** Most small business partnerships receive favorable tax treatment and often do not have to pay the minimum taxes required of other business forms.
- **Increased ability to raise funds.** Generally, the more people involved in a business, the greater their collective ability to raise funds.

### Disadvantages of the Partnership

- **Unlimited liability.** Business partners (both individually and as a group) are liable for all legal and financial obligations of the partnership.
- **Co-ownership of property.** Profits must be shared with the other partners.
- **Limited life.** A partnership ends when a partner dies or withdraws from the business.
- **Mutual agency.** Individual partners bear responsibility for the actions of all other partners.
- **Partner disagreements.** Poorly organized partnerships and those formed orally are susceptible to disputes among owners.

Clearly, a partnership has both significant benefits and serious drawbacks. The unlimited personal liability that each general partner bears for the legal and financial obligations of the business is especially important. Hal and Dawn realized that if they chose to form a partnership, they would need to develop a formal partnership agreement. Exhibit 12.1 lists the most important concerns to address in a partnership agreement.

| Exhibit 12.1 | Essential Elements of a Partnership Agreement |
| --- | --- |

- Type of business
- Amount of equity invested by each partner
- Method for sharing profits and losses
- Partners' pay/compensation
- Distribution of assets on dissolution
- Provisions for changes to or dissolution of the partnership
- Provisions for settlement of disputes
- Settlement on death or incapacitation of partners
- Restrictions on partners' authority and expenditures
- Length of partnership's life

# Similar Forms of Business

After the two friends gained a good understanding of the advantages and disadvantages of partnerships, they were ready to consider the other forms of business that interested them. They decided to look at one of the newest forms of business, the limited liability company.

## Limited Liability Companies

The limited liability company (LLC) is a relatively new form of business organization created by state legislatures. Because this form of business is primarily state controlled, the laws regarding its formation, fees, and so on vary from state to state.

The LLC combines the most attractive features of a corporation with the best features of the partnership, creating a kind of hybrid business form. As the name suggests, it offers protection to members (owners of the LLC) against personal liability for company debts and other obligations. However, its formation is more complex and formal than that of a general partnership. The primary characteristics of the LLC follow.

> **Coach's Tip**
> Although some people mistakenly refer to an LLC as a limited liability corporation, the correct term is limited liability company.

### Advantages of the Limited Liability Company

- **Limited liability.** If the LLC is properly structured and managed, each member's personal assets will be protected from lawsuits and judgments against the business. Thus, each member's liability is limited to the assets he or she has invested in the company. This statement is true even for owners who participate in the LLC's management.
- **Ease of formation.** An LLC is easier to form than a corporation. Rules regarding the formation of an LLC differ from state to state, but setting one up typically requires only one or two documents. First, every state requires the LLC to file its articles of organization and pay any required fees. The articles of organization set out important details such as the business name, purpose, and operating structure. Because of its importance, this document should be drawn up by a lawyer. A few states require a second document, an operating agreement. It helps to define the LLC's ownership, member responsibilities, and profit sharing. Much like a partnership agreement, it can be invaluable in the event of disagreements among members and is strongly recommended even if the state does not require it.
- **Simplified recordkeeping.** LLCs are not required to hold an annual meeting, keep formal minutes, record resolutions, or observe many other formalities required of corporations. However, they do require more paperwork than partnerships.
- **Favorable taxation.** If an LLC has only one member, the IRS automatically treats it as a sole proprietorship. Similarly, an LLC with multiple members is taxed by default as a partnership. Normal business expenses may be deducted from an LLC's profits before profits are allocated to members for tax purposes. Members report their share of the LLC's profits and losses on their personal tax returns. This arrangement, referred to as pass-through taxation, allows the business to avoid the double taxation to which

corporations are subject. (Double taxation occurs when a corporation pays taxes on its corporate profits and then the individual owners pay taxes on any corporate profits distributed to them in the form of dividends. That is, the same profits are taxed twice, once at the corporate level and again at the personal level.)

- **Flexibility of operations.** An LLC allows members to allocate profits and losses as they see fit, to have great flexibility regarding the number of members, to elect to be managed as a partnership or as a corporation, and to admit new members or modify its membership and investment structure with ease.

### Disadvantages of the Limited Liability Company

- **Limited corporate characteristics.** LLCs must not have more than two of the four favorable characteristics that define corporations, or they risk being taxed as a corporation. These characteristics are (1) owners' liability limited to business assets, (2) continuity of life, (3) centralization of (nonowner) management, and (4) free transferability of ownership interests.
- **Limited life.** LLCs dissolve with the death, incapacitation, bankruptcy, retirement, resignation, or expulsion of any member.
- **Lack of legal precedents.** Predicting how an LLC will be treated in the courts may be difficult. To date, relatively few legal cases have involved LLCs. However, as time goes on and LLCs become increasingly common, this disadvantage will become less significant.

Because of its long list of advantages and relatively few disadvantages, the LLC form has become a favorite choice among businesses that meet the following criteria:

- The business has one to three members.
- All members are active participants in a small local business.
- The business has no plans for significant growth.
- The business has no foreseeable need to raise significant amounts of capital.

## S-Corporations

An **S-corporation** is a corporation with 1 to 100 shareholders that passes income (or loss) to shareholders, who are taxed at the individual shareholder level. This is a significant difference from a regular corporation, which is subject to double taxation. S-corporations enjoy many of the benefits of partnerships and LLCs, but the state requirements for forming a corporation, electing to be taxed as an S-corporation, and completing annual filings are complex and time consuming. Because of these complexities and required formalities, Dawn and Hal quickly discarded this form of business as a viable option. To compare the features of the two remaining forms of business, they set up the table in Exhibit 12.2.

**Exhibit 12.2**    **Characteristics of Partnerships and LLCs**

| Characteristic | Partnership | Limited Liability Company |
|---|---|---|
| Ease of formation and recordkeeping | Less difficult | More difficult |
| Setup costs | Medium to high | High |
| Limited liability | No, unless limited partnership | Yes |
| Annual meetings | Recommended, not required | Recommended, not required |
| Limited life | Yes* | Yes |
| Corporate tax treatment permitted | No | Yes |
| Partnership tax treatment permitted | Yes, automatic | Yes, when there are two or more members |
| Annual state filings and fees | Almost never | Yes |
| Uniform state laws governing entity | Very little variation in laws | Moderate variation in laws |

\* Partnerships can appear to achieve unlimited lives if new partners are admitted as old partners exit, but technically these changes cause the dissolution of the existing partnership.

After careful consideration, the two friends decided to form a general partnership. Although the features of an LLC sounded great, they did not think they could limit themselves to only two of the four characteristics of a corporation, and they did not want to invest a lot of time and money in forming their business.

Indicate whether each of the following is a true (T) or false (F) statement regarding partnerships and other forms of business.

1. The partnership agreement is a required document; you will be unable to register your partnership without a properly documented partnership agreement. _____

2. A limited liability company must not have more than three of the four characteristics that define corporations, or it risks being taxed as a corporation. _____

3. One disadvantage of both partnerships and LLCs is pass-through taxation. _____

4. Because of its long list of disadvantages and relatively few advantages, the LLC is rarely the business form of choice for new businesses. _____

5. One disadvantage of the LLC is that it is subject to double taxation. _____

*After you have finished, check your answers with the solution at the bottom of the page.*

# ACCOUNTING FOR PARTNERSHIPS

Because a partnership is a pass-through entity, each partner reports his or her share of the partnership's income (or loss) as an individual. In this respect, the accounting treatment is very much like that of a sole proprietorship. The only real difference is that the partners must determine how to divide the partnership's income (or loss) among themselves. To keep track of this information, accounting for a partnership requires:

1. A capital account for each partner.
2. A drawing account for each partner.
3. The allocation of the partnership's income (or loss) to each partner according to the terms of the partnership agreement.

> **Learning Objective 2**
>
> Demonstrate how to account for partnerships.

As we noted earlier, any new partnership is strongly encouraged to create a formal partnership agreement. Hal and Dawn took this recommendation seriously and asked a lawyer to draw up their partnership agreement. While they were discussing the agreement, the attorney spoke with them about some other matters including how to account for the formation of their partnership, how to allocate the partnership's income (or loss), and how to prepare the partnership's financial statements.

## Formation: Recording Cash and Noncash Contributions

When a partnership is formed, the partners can invest any combination of assets and/or liabilities in it. Because both Hal and Dawn had sole proprietorships before forming their partnership, each contributed assets from the "proprietorships" as well as cash. Hal's entire investment in the partnership consisted of cash and accounts receivable; Dawn's included cash and equipment. The partnership did not take on liabilities from the sole proprietorships.

When a partner invests cash in a partnership, that partner's capital account is credited for the amount invested. Other investments are recorded at the fair market value of the assets on the date of transfer to the partnership. Each partner must agree to these assigned values. With

1. F—although partnerships may be fraught with disagreements among partners, having a partnership agreement is not required for forming a partnership.
2. F—a limited liability company must not have more than two of the four characteristics that define corporations.
3. F—pass-through taxation is a major advantage of the LLC and partnership forms of business.
4. F—the LLC is often the business form of choice for new businesses because of its long list of advantages and relatively few disadvantages.
5. F—the LLC form of business allows members to avoid double taxation.

| Exhibit 12.3 | Valuation of Contributed Assets |
|---|---|

|  | BOOK VALUE | | MARKET VALUE | |
|---|---|---|---|---|
|  | Hal Flowers | Dawn Bloom | Hal Flowers | Dawn Bloom |
| Cash | $10,000 | $ 9,000 | $10,000 | $ 9,000 |
| Accounts receivable | 3,800 |  | 3,800 |  |
| Allowance for doubtful accounts |  |  | (800) |  |
| Store equipment |  | 10,000 |  | 8,000 |
| Accumulated depreciation |  | (1,000) |  |  |
|  | $13,800 | $18,000 | $13,000 | $17,000 |

**Coach's Tip**

To record owner contributions of non-cash assets, use the market value of the assets rather than the book value.

the attorney's help, Hal and Dawn determined and agreed to the market values shown in the two right-hand columns of Exhibit 12.3. Although the table provides both the book values and market values of the contributed assets, **only the market values are used to record the investments.**

Note that the accounts receivable were brought into the partnership at net realizable value (the net amount of cash the partnership expects to collect) by establishing an allowance for doubtful accounts. This account is needed because no one knows which particular customer accounts will not be collected, but experience shows that some portion of the receivables would not be collected. Consequently, the estimated uncollectible portion was deducted from Hal's investment. Finally, note that Dawn's contribution of store equipment did not include the accumulated depreciation from her old business. Instead, its fair market value was used in recording her contribution to the partnership. In essence, the equipment contribution was treated as if the partnership purchased used equipment.

The following journal entries were made to record Hal and Dawn's investments. Once the partners' investments were recorded, the assets were treated just as any other business asset. The receivables were collected, and any uncollectible accounts were written off. At the end of the accounting period, the allowance account was re-evaluated and adjusted accordingly. The equipment was depreciated over its useful life using the method chosen by the partnership.

|  | Debit | Credit |
|---|---|---|
| Cash (+A) ($10,000 + $9,000) | 19,000 |  |
| Accounts Receivable (+A) | 3,800 |  |
| Store Equipment (+A) | 8,000 |  |
|     Allowance for Doubtful Accounts (+xA, −A) |  | 800 |
|     Hal Flowers, Capital (+OE) |  | 13,000 |
|     Dawn Bloom, Capital (+OE) |  | 17,000 |

| Assets | | = Liabilities + | Owners' Equity | |
|---|---|---|---|---|
| Cash ($10,000 + $9,000) | +19,000 |  | Hal Flowers, Capital | +13,000 |
| Accounts Receivable | +3,800 |  | Dawn Bloom, Capital | +17,000 |
| Allowance for Doubtful Accounts (+xA) | −800 |  |  |  |
| Store Equipment | +8,000 |  |  |  |

# Division of Income (or Loss): Four Methods

A partnership's income (or loss) is divided according to the partnership agreement. Unfortunately, partners do not always draw up an agreement before forming their business. In such situations, the assumption is that the partners intend to share all profits and losses equally regardless of any oral agreements they may have made. To be legally enforceable, profit and loss allocations must be made in writing. When Hal and Dawn met with their attorney, he told them partners can use one of four methods to allocate income or loss among themselves.

1. **The fixed-ratio method** is often used when partners' initial financial contributions are the same or relatively close. This method bases income and loss allocations primarily on the amount of time each partner expects to devote to the business on a regular basis. For example, if partners expect to work equally, they may agree to split profits and losses equally. In this case, the fixed ratio can be stated in three ways: as a percentage (50 percent to 50 percent), as a proportion (1:1), or as a fraction (½ to ½).

2. **The interest on partners' capital balances method** may appeal to partners who wish to earn a specific return on their investments. This method sets a stated rate of interest partners will receive on their capital account balances; any remaining amounts are allocated on a fixed-ratio basis. This method is especially useful to partners who have invested large sums of cash in the partnership but have very little involvement in the business's day-to-day operations. Essentially, their entire return from the partnership hinges on the balances in their capital accounts.

3. **The salaries to partners method** appeals to partners who spend a great deal of time running the business on a daily basis and the partnership is their primary source of personal income. This method requires that the partners' salaries be distributed first; any remaining income (or loss) is allocated on a fixed-ratio basis.

4. **The salaries to partners and interest on partners' capital balances method** is the most complicated method. It is appropriate when the partners' needs, financial contributions, and time contributions are so diverse that some combination of each of the previous methods is necessary. With this method, the partners receive salaries and earn interest on their capital account balances. Any remaining amounts are allocated to them on a fixed-ratio basis.

Hal and Dawn asked the attorney to show them examples of each of these four allocation methods. The attorney was happy to oblige. **The following examples assume that Hal and Dawn's partnership earned a profit of $10,000 for the year and that Hal withdrew $2,600 from the partnership and Dawn withdrew $1,400.**

## Fixed-Ratio Method

Assume that Hal and Dawn decided to share the $10,000 profit according to the fixed proportions of 8:2 (that is, $8 for Hal to every $2 for Dawn). These proportions are based on the relative time and effort each partner planned to contribute to the partnership. When you use proportions as the allocation basis, each partner's individual portion is divided by the total of the partners' numbers (8 + 2 = 10).

| | |
|---|---|
| Hal's portion of the profit [$10,000 × (8 ÷ 10)] | $ 8,000 |
| Dawn's portion of the profit [$10,000 × (2 ÷ 10)] | 2,000 |
| Total profit allocated | $10,000 |

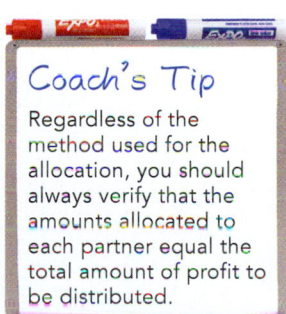

**Coach's Tip**

Regardless of the method used for the allocation, you should always verify that the amounts allocated to each partner equal the total amount of profit to be distributed.

Regardless of the allocation method used, the partners' capital accounts do not reflect the allocated amounts until the closing entries for the period have been made. The closing process for a partnership is nearly identical to that shown for a sole proprietorship in Chapter 4 on page 164. In this chapter, we assume that all revenues and expenses have been closed and that the net profit (or loss) of the business is now in the Income Summary account. In our example, the partnership had a $10,000 profit, so the Income Summary account needs to be debited and each individual partner's capital account credited for the amount of profit allocated to him or her. The entry to allocate the partnership profits to each partner under the fixed-ratio method follows.

|  | Debit | Credit |
|---|---|---|
| Income Summary (−OE) | 10,000 | |
| Hal Flowers, Capital (+OE) | | 8,000 |
| Dawn Bloom, Capital (+OE) | | 2,000 |

| Assets | = | Liabilities | + | Owners' Equity | |
|---|---|---|---|---|---|
| | | | | Income Summary | −10,000 |
| | | | | Hal Flowers, Capital | +8,000 |
| | | | | Dawn Bloom, Capital | +2,000 |

Next the partners' drawing accounts must be closed. The balance in each partner's drawing account is credited with corresponding debits to the capital accounts. Because this entry remains the same regardless of the allocation method used, it is presented only once. However, recognize that this entry would be made for each of the allocation methods presented. The entry to close the partners' drawing accounts would be:

|  | Debit | Credit |
|---|---|---|
| Hal Flowers, Capital (−OE) | 2,600 | |
| Dawn Bloom, Capital (−OE) | 1,400 | |
| Hal Flowers, Drawing (+OE) | | 2,600 |
| Dawn Bloom, Drawing (+OE) | | 1,400 |

| Assets | = | Liabilities | + | Owners' Equity | |
|---|---|---|---|---|---|
| | | | | Hal Flowers, Capital | −2,600 |
| | | | | Dawn Bloom, Capital | −1,400 |
| | | | | Hal Flowers, Drawing | +2,600 |
| | | | | Dawn Bloom, Drawing | +1,400 |

**Coach's Tip**

Do not confuse the allocation of income with the partners' withdrawals. The allocation represents how much profit each partner has **earned** from the business. The withdrawal represents how much of the partners' income has actually been taken out of the business (usually as cash).

## Interest on Partners' Capital Balances Method

To illustrate this method, we will use Hal and Dawn's original capital contributions, $13,000 and $17,000, respectively. We also assume both Hal and Dawn wanted to earn 12 percent on their beginning capital balances. Under the interest on partners' capital balances method, **the interest must first be allocated to the partners.** Then, the remaining profit is allocated according to a fixed ratio. For this example, we will use a fixed ratio of 80 percent to Hal and 20 percent to Dawn. See Exhibit 12.4 for the way this method allocates the profit.

**Exhibit 12.4** Allocation of Income with Interest on Partners' Capital Balances

| | Hal Flowers | Dawn Bloom | Total Allocated | Remainder to Allocate |
|---|---|---|---|---|
| Net income to allocate | | | | $10,000 |
| Interest | | | | |
| Hal:   $13,000 × 12% | $1,560 | | $ 1,560 | (1,560) |
| Dawn: $17,000 × 12% | | $2,040 | 2,040 | (2,040) |
| Remainder (allocate on a fixed ratio) | | | | 6,400 |
| Hal:   $6,400 × 80% | 5,120 | | 5,120 | (5,120) |
| Dawn: $6,400 × 20% | | 1,280 | 1,280 | (1,280) |
| Total | $6,680 | $3,320 | $10,000 | $ 0 |

When the partners' contributions of time and/or money differ significantly, this method or one of the remaining ones may be used to ensure that income allocation is based fairly on the individual partners' contributions of time and/or assets. The following entry records each partner's share of the partnership's income using the interest on partners' capital balances method.

| | Debit | Credit |
|---|---|---|
| Income Summary (−OE) | 10,000 | |
| Hal Flowers, Capital (+OE) | | 6,680 |
| Dawn Bloom, Capital (+OE) | | 3,320 |

| Assets | = | Liabilities | + | Owners' Equity | |
|---|---|---|---|---|---|
| | | | | Income Summary | −10,000 |
| | | | | Hal Flowers, Capital | +6,680 |
| | | | | Dawn Bloom, Capital | +3,320 |

**SELF-STUDY PRACTICE**

Jack Clumsy and Jill Mimic began the Hill Partnership on January 1, 2009. On December 31, 2009, the partnership has $18,000 of profit to allocate. Determine the amount of profit to be allocated to each partner under each of the following independent situations.

1. Fixed ratio of 3:6 to Jack and Jill, respectively.
2. Interest on capital balances of 12 percent with the remainder on a ratio of 3:6. Assume capital balances of $2,000 for Jack and $8,000 for Jill.

*After you have finished, check your answers with the solution at the bottom of the page.*

## Salaries to Partners Method

The salaries to partners method allocates income first to cover the partners' salaries and then the remainder of the income according to a fixed ratio. Assume Hal and Dawn agreed to the following salaries and fixed ratios:

| | Salaries | Fixed Ratio |
|---|---|---|
| Hal Flowers | $6,000 | 80% |
| Dawn Bloom | 2,000 | 20 |

See Exhibit 12.5 for the allocation of the partnership's net income of $10,000.

Solution to
Self-Study Practice

1. Jack receives $6,000 (=$18,000 × 3/9), and Jill receives $12,000 (=$18,000 × 6/9).
2. Jack and Jill receive the following:

| | Jack | Jill | Total Allocated | Remainder to Allocate |
|---|---|---|---|---|
| Net income to allocate | | | | $ 18,000 |
| Interest | $2,000 × 12% = $ 240 | $8,000 × 12% = $ 960 | $ 1,200 | (1,200) |
| | | | | 16,800 |
| Remainder (allocate on a fixed ratio) | $16,800 × 3/9 = 5,600 | $16,800 × 6/9 = 11,200 | 16,800 | (16,800) |
| Total allocation | $ 5,840 | $ 12,160 | $18,000 | $ 0 |

## Exhibit 12.5  Allocation of Income with Salaries to Partners

|  | Hal Flowers | Dawn Bloom | Total Allocated | Remainder to Allocate |
|---|---|---|---|---|
| Net income to allocate |  |  |  | $10,000 |
| Salary allocations | $6,000 | $2,000 | $8,000 | (8,000) |
| Remainder (allocate on a fixed ratio) |  |  |  | 2,000 |
|    Hal:  $2,000 × 80% | 1,600 |  | 1,600 | (1,600) |
|    Dawn: $2,000 × 20% |  | 400 | 400 | ( 400) |
| Total | $7,600 | $2,400 | $10,000 | $       0 |

**Coach's Tip**

Partner salaries (if any) must *always be* allocated first.

**Whenever salaries are allocated to the partners, they must be taken out of the partnership's income before any other allocations can be made.** Once again, always verify that the total of the amounts allocated to each partner equals the total partnership income (or loss). The following journal entry would be used to allocate income under this method.

|  | Debit | Credit |
|---|---|---|
| Income Summary (−OE) | 10,000 |  |
|    Hal Flowers, Capital (+OE) |  | 7,600 |
|    Dawn Bloom, Capital (+OE) |  | 2,400 |

| Assets | = | Liabilities | + | Owners' Equity | |
|---|---|---|---|---|---|
|  |  |  |  | Income Summary | −10,000 |
|  |  |  |  | Hal Flowers, Capital | +7,600 |
|  |  |  |  | Dawn Bloom, Capital | +2,400 |

### Salaries to Partners and Interest on Partners' Capital Balances Method

The salaries to partners and interest on partners' capital balances method allocates income first to the partners' salaries and second to the interest on the partners' capital accounts. Any remaining income is allocated according to a fixed ratio. Assume the following salaries, interest rate, and fixed ratios:

|  | Salaries | Interest | Fixed Ratio |
|---|---|---|---|
| Hal Flowers | $6,000 | 12% | 80% |
| Dawn Bloom | 2,000 | 12 | 20 |

See Exhibit 12.6 for the allocation of the partnership's $10,000 net income under this method. Study it carefully; it is tricky. Needless to say, this example illustrates why a proof of the allocation is so important. Sometimes allocating profit (or loss) according to the partnership agreement creates a situation in which the partnership's income is insufficient to give each partner the salaries and interest required in the partnership agreement. Nevertheless, **these amounts must be allocated** even if doing so results in the allocation of a negative amount. Any negative amount is allocated using the fixed ratio.

## Exhibit 12.6 — Allocation of Income under the Salaries to Partners and Interest on Partners' Capital Balances Method

| | Hal Flowers | Dawn Bloom | Total Allocated | Remainder to Allocate |
|---|---|---|---|---|
| Net income to allocate | | | | $10,000 |
| Salary allocations | $6,000 | $2,000 | $ 8,000 | (8,000) |
| Remaining after salary allocations | | | | 2,000 |
| Interest | | | | |
|   Hal:   $13,000 × 12% | $1,560 | | 1,560 | (1,560) |
|   Dawn: $17,000 × 12% | | $2,040 | 2,040 | (2,040) |
| Remainder (overallocated) | | | | (1,600) |
|   Hal:   ($1,600) × 80% | (1,280) | | (1,280) | 1,280 |
|   Dawn: ($1,600) × 20% | | (320) | (320) | 320 |
| Total | $6,280 | $3,720 | $10,000 | $    0 |

The entry to record the allocation of income under this method would be:

| | Debit | Credit |
|---|---|---|
| Income Summary (−OE) | 10,000 | |
|   Hal Flowers, Capital (+OE) | | 6,280 |
|   Dawn Bloom, Capital (+OE) | | 3,720 |

| Assets | = | Liabilities | + | Owners' Equity | |
|---|---|---|---|---|---|
| | | | | Income Summary | −10,000 |
| | | | | Hal Flowers, Capital | +6,280 |
| | | | | Dawn Bloom, Capital | +3,720 |

**Coach's Tip**
A fixed ratio is used to allocate the remainder amount for every allocation method. So, it is important to select a fixed ratio for each partner even when the fixed ratio method is not used for allocating profit.

**SELF-STUDY PRACTICE**

Jack and Jill began the Hill Partnership on January 1, 2009. On December 31, 2009, the partnership has $18,000 profit to allocate. Determine the amount of profit to be allocated to each partner under the salaries to partners and interest on capital balances method using the following.

| | Salaries | Interest | Capital | Fixed Ratio |
|---|---|---|---|---|
| Jack | $ 7,800 | 12% | $2,000 | 3 |
| Jill | 13,500 | 12 | 8,000 | 6 |

After you have finished, check your answers with the solution at the bottom of the page.

Solution to Self-Study Practice

| | Jack | | Jill | | Total Allocated | Remainder to Allocate |
|---|---|---|---|---|---|---|
| Net income to allocate | | | | | | $18,000 |
| Salary | | $ 7,800 | | $13,500 | $21,300 | (21,300) |
| Interest | $2,000 × 12% = | 240 | $8,000 × 12% = | 960 | 1,200 | (1,200) |
| | | | | | | (4,500) |
| Remainder (overallocated) | ($4,500) × 3/9 = | (1,500) | ($4,500) × 6/9 = | (3,000) | (4,500) | 4,500 |
| Total/proof | | $ 6,540 | | $11,460 | $18,000 | $    0 |

After listening intently to their attorney's advice and carefully considering their options for allocating the partnership's income, Hal and Dawn asked the attorney to allocate all income (or loss) using the salaries to partners method (method 3). They chose this method because Hal agreed to take on more managerial responsibilities than Dawn, and this method rewards him for his commitment of additional time.

## Preparation of Financial Statements

The financial statements of a partnership are very similar to those of a sole proprietorship. There are only three differences: (1) net income is allocated among the partners, (2) the balance sheet shows a capital account for each partner, and (3) the partners' capital statement replaces the owner's equity statement.

Net income on the partnership's income statement is calculated and reported in exactly the same way as for a sole proprietorship. The allocation of this net income to each partner's capital account is reported on the **partners' capital statement**. This statement begins with each partner's beginning capital account balance, which is increased by the portion of income allocated to each partner and reduced by withdrawals made by each partner. An illustration of this statement is shown in Exhibit 12.7, given the following assumptions.

| | Capital Contributions | Net Income (allocated) | Partner Drawings |
|---|---|---|---|
| Hal Flowers | $13,000 | $7,600 | $2,600 |
| Dawn Bloom | 17,000 | 2,400 | 1,400 |

**Exhibit 12.7    Partners' Capital Statement**

### Bloom 'N Flowers
### Partners' Capital Statement
### December 31, 2008

| | Hal Flowers | Dawn Bloom | Total |
|---|---|---|---|
| Capital, January 1, 2008 | $      0 | $      0 | $      0 |
| Add: Partner capital contributions | 13,000 | 17,000 | 30,000 |
| Net income | 7,600 | 2,400 | 10,000 |
| | 20,600 | 19,400 | 40,000 |
| Less: Partner drawings | 2,600 | 1,400 | 4,000 |
| Capital, December 31, 2008 | $18,000 | $18,000 | $36,000 |

After the partners' capital statement is complete, the balance sheet can be prepared. See Exhibit 12.8 for the owners' equity section of the balance sheet for Bloom 'N Flowers partnership. Notice that the capital account balances in Exhibits 12.7 and 12.8 are equal.

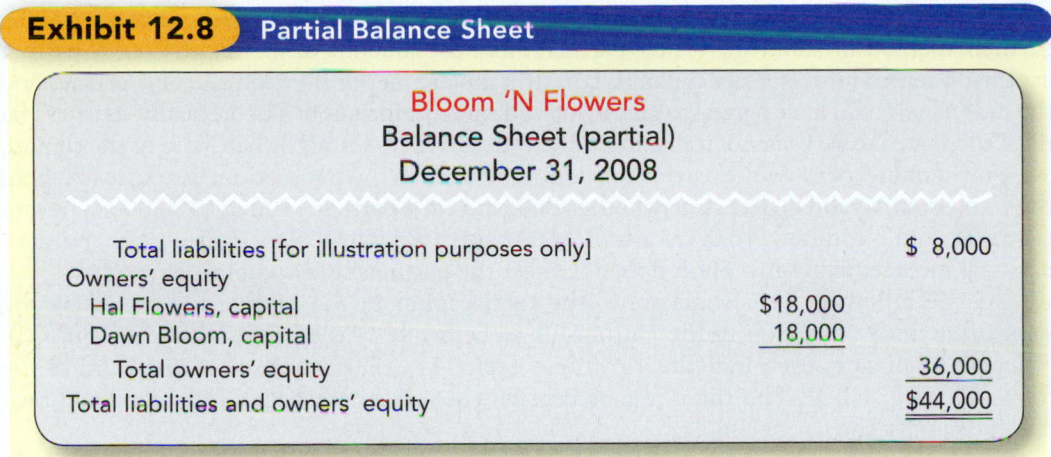

**Exhibit 12.8**    Partial Balance Sheet

Bloom 'N Flowers
Balance Sheet (partial)
December 31, 2008

| | | |
|---|---|---|
| Total liabilities [for illustration purposes only] | | $ 8,000 |
| Owners' equity | | |
|   Hal Flowers, capital | $18,000 | |
|   Dawn Bloom, capital | 18,000 | |
|     Total owners' equity | | 36,000 |
| Total liabilities and owners' equity | | $44,000 |

# CHANGES OF OWNERSHIP IN A PARTNERSHIP

Hal and Dawn later toyed with the idea of admitting another partner to their business. Hal had a friend, Bud Green, who specialized in marketing—a field with which Hal and Dawn have little experience. The two partners knew that marketing would be critical to the success of their business, however.

**Learning Objective 3**

Demonstrate the proper treatment for changes of ownership in a partnership.

## Admission of a Partner

The lawyer was pleased that Hal and Dawn had brought up the idea of admitting a new partner **before** actually going through with it. Although adding a new partner has little economic impact on a partnership, it does have a major legal effect called **partnership dissolution**. Specifically, adding a partner causes the dissolution of the existing partnership (consisting of the old partners) and the creation of a new partnership (consisting of the new partners).

Of course, additional capital and drawing accounts would need to be created for the new partner. Then the existing partners would need to decide how to complete the admission of the new partner. Legally, a new partner cannot be admitted into a partnership unless all existing partners agree to it. Assuming all current partners have agreed to admit a new partner, the new partner can be admitted in two ways: through a purchase made among partners or by the investment of additional assets.

### Purchase among Partners

A purchase among partners transfers a portion of one or more existing partners' capital account balances to the new partner's capital account. This transaction is a **personal** transaction involving **only** those individuals involved in the purchase. The only impact on the partnership is that a journal entry is required to transfer amounts from the existing partners' capital accounts to the new partner's capital account.

Assume that on January 1, 2009, Bud was admitted to the partnership with a $33\frac{1}{3}$ percent ownership. Bud agreed to pay each partner $8,000 in exchange for 1/3 of each partner's capital account balance ($18,000 \times 1/3 = $6,000). The following journal entry was made to record Bud's admission to the partnership, based on the capital balances on the balance sheet as of December 31, 2008 (see Exhibit 12.8).

| | Debit | Credit |
|---|---|---|
| Hal Flowers, Capital (−OE) | 6,000 | |
| Dawn Bloom, Capital (−OE) | 6,000 | |
|   Bud Green, Capital (+OE) | | 12,000 |

| Assets | = | Liabilities | + | Owners' Equity | |
|---|---|---|---|---|---|
| | | | | Hal Flowers, Capital | −6,000 |
| | | | | Dawn Bloom, Capital | −6,000 |
| | | | | Bud Green, Capital | +12,000 |

Hal and Dawn's attorney explained some important features of the purchase among partners method of admitting a new partner. First, the amount of money that each partner accepts in return for his or her capital is strictly a private matter between the new partner and the individuals who have agreed to give up a portion of their capital. Theoretically, neither Hal nor Dawn need to be aware of the amount the other receives for his or her share of the capital.

Furthermore, because the partnership is not involved in the transaction, the entry to record the transaction would be the same whether Bud paid each partner $100 or $100,000. The fact that Bud paid a total of $16,000 for a $12,000 capital account balance affects the partners' personal income tax returns but it does not affect the partnership's accounting records.

As the following T-accounts show, the **total** capital in the partnership would be the same **after** Bud's admission to the partnership as **before** he was admitted (that is, $36,000). After his admission, each **individual** partner's capital is $12,000 or exactly one-third of the total ($36,000 × 1/3). The three friends become equal partners, each of whom would own $33\frac{1}{3}$ percent of the partnership.

| Hal Flowers, Capital | |
|---|---|
| | Bal. 18,000 |
| Jan.1  6,000 | |
| | 12,000 |

| Dawn Bloom, Capital | |
|---|---|
| | Bal. 18,000 |
| Jan.1  6,000 | |
| | 12,000 |

| Bud Green, Capital | |
|---|---|
| | Bal.        0 |
| | Jan. 1 12,000 |
| | 12,000 |

## Investment of Additional Assets

The other way to admit a new partner is for the incoming partner to invest new assets into the partnership. Unlike the purchase among partners method, the investment method alters the partnership's assets.

Assume that Bud was admitted to Hal and Dawn's partnership as a new partner. Hal and Dawn's original capital balances did not change. They were still $18,000 each, or $36,000 in total. Bud invested $18,000 of additional cash in the partnership.

Under the investment of additional assets method, Bud's contribution affected only the partnership's net assets (cash) and Bud's capital account. The existing partners' capital accounts were unaffected. The journal entry made to record the admission of the new partner follows.

| | Debit | Credit |
|---|---|---|
| Cash (+A) | 18,000 | |
| Bud Green, Capital (+OE) | | 18,000 |

| Assets | | = | Liabilities | + | Owners' Equity | |
|---|---|---|---|---|---|---|
| Cash | +18,000 | | | | Bud Green, Capital | +18,000 |

After Bud's investment, the partners' capital accounts had the following balances:

| Hal Flowers, Capital | |
|---|---|
| | Bal. 18,000 |

| Dawn Bloom, Capital | |
|---|---|
| | Bal. 18,000 |

| Bud Green, Capital | |
|---|---|
| | Bal.        0 |
| | Jan. 1 18,000 |
| | 18,000 |

Bud's ownership of one-third of the partnership would not necessarily entitle him to one-third of the profits. Once again, the partnership agreement would dictate how to allocate profits (or losses) to the partners. The original partners may or may not have agreed to give him an equal share of the profits. If no written agreement exists, the profits would be allocated equally among all the partners whether or not that was their intention.

The example we have just presented assumed that the new partner's contribution **exactly equaled** his or her share of the partnership's total equity. Sometimes, however, the new partner contributes **more** or **less** than that amount. Let's see how these variations in the new partner's contribution affect the existing partners.

**Bonus to the Existing Partners.** In some situations, the existing partners require an extra contribution from the new partner in return for admission to the partnership. This situation is common when the fair market value of the partnership's assets is higher than the asset book value. When paying more than the book value of the assets he or she is acquiring, the new partner is effectively giving the existing partners a bonus.

Instead of contributing $18,000 to the partnership, let's assume that Bud contributed $24,000 in exchange for one-third of the partnership capital. The steps to determine the appropriate journal entry follow.

1. **Calculate the total capital in the partnership after the new partner's contribution.**

| | |
|---|---:|
| Total partnership capital before contribution | $36,000 |
| New partner's contribution | 24,000 |
| Partnership capital after contribution | $60,000 |

2. **Calculate the amount of the new partner's capital account.** Multiply the result from Step 1 by the portion of the partnership that the new partner is purchasing.

| | |
|---|---:|
| Result from Step 1 | $60,000 |
| New partner's ownership portion | × 1/3 |
| New partner's capital account balance | $20,000 |

3. **Calculate the total bonus to the existing partners.**

The total bonus to the existing partners is the difference between the amount contributed by the new partner and the amount of capital the new partner received.

| | |
|---|---:|
| Amount contributed by new partner | $24,000 |
| Amount of capital given to the new partner | (20,000) |
| Total bonus to the existing partners | $ 4,000 |

4. **Allocate the bonus to the existing partners using their fixed ratios.** The existing partners' fixed ratios (after salaries) were 80 percent to Hal and 20 percent to Dawn. Therefore, the bonus allocation was as follows:

| | |
|---|---:|
| Hal's portion of the bonus ($4,000 × 80%) | $ 3,200 |
| Dawn's portion of the bonus ($4,000 × 20%) | 800 |
| Total bonus allocated | $ 4,000 |

The following journal entry would be made to record the transaction.

| | Debit | Credit |
|---|---:|---:|
| Cash (+A) | 24,000 | |
|     Bud Green, Capital (+OE) | | 20,000 |
|     Hal Flowers, Capital (+OE) | | 3,200 |
|     Dawn Bloom, Capital (+OE) | | 800 |

| Assets | = | Liabilities | + | Owners' Equity | |
|---|---|---|---|---|---|
| Cash     +24,000 | | | | Bud Green, Capital | +20,000 |
| | | | | Hal Flowers, Capital | +3,200 |
| | | | | Dawn Bloom, Capital | +800 |

**Bonus to the New Partner.** Sometimes the opposite situation occurs: The new partner may receive a capital account balance that exceeds the amount he or she invests in the partnership. This situation results in a bonus to the new partner. It can arise when the partnership desperately needs cash or the new partner has knowledge or skills that the original partners are eager to obtain. For example, Hal and Dawn may have needed Bud's marketing expertise so much that they were willing to give him a capital account that was **more** than his cash contribution.

To illustrate this situation, we assume that Bud contributed $9,000 (instead of $24,000) to the partnership in exchange for a one-third ownership interest. The steps required to determine the resulting journal entry are:

1. **Calculate the total capital in the partnership after the new partner's contribution.**

| | |
|---|---:|
| Total partnership capital before contribution | $36,000 |
| New partner's contribution | 9,000 |
| Partnership capital after contribution | $45,000 |

2. **Calculate the amount of the new partner's capital account.** Multiply the result from Step 1 by the portion of the partnership that the new partner is purchasing.

| | |
|---|---:|
| Result from Step 1 | $45,000 |
| New partner's ownership portion | × 1/3 |
| New partner's capital account balance | $15,000 |

3. **Calculate the total bonus to the new partner.** The total bonus to the new partner is the difference between the amount of capital the new partner received and the amount the new partner contributed.

| | |
|---|---:|
| Amount of capital given to the new partner | $15,000 |
| Amount contributed by the new partner | (9,000) |
| Total bonus given by the existing partners | $ 6,000 |

4. **Allocate the bonus to the new partner using the fixed ratios.** The existing partners' fixed ratios (after their salaries) were 80 percent to Hal and 20 percent to Dawn. Therefore, the bonus given by the existing partners was allocated as follows:

| | |
|---|---:|
| Hal's portion of the bonus ($6,000 × 80%) | $4,800 |
| Dawn's portion of the bonus ($6,000 × 20%) | 1,200 |
| Total bonus allocated | $6,000 |

In this case, the $6,000 bonus to the new partner was accomplished by removing a portion of the existing partners' capital balances. The entry that would be made to record the transaction is:

| | Debit | Credit |
|---|---|---|
| Cash (+A) | 9,000 | |
| Hal Flowers, Capital (−OE) | 4,800 | |
| Dawn Bloom, Capital (−OE) | 1,200 | |
| Bud Green, Capital (+OE) | | 15,000 |

| Assets | = | Liabilities | + | Owners' Equity | |
|---|---|---|---|---|---|
| Cash   +9,000 | | | | Hal Flowers, Capital | −4,800 |
| | | | | Dawn Bloom, Capital | −1,200 |
| | | | | Bud Green, Capital | +15,000 |

After Hal and Dawn's attorney had explained the ins and outs of admitting a new partner, the two friends decided to admit Bud in return for an $18,000 cash investment to the partnership. Following Bud's admission, each partner had a capital balance of $18,000, and each owned one-third of the partnership. The new partnership agreement specified that Hal, Dawn, and Bud would share the profits and losses according to a fixed ratio of 40 percent to 40 percent to 20 percent, respectively.

SELF-STUDY PRACTICE

Billie, Mandie, and Grimm agree to allow Crustie into their partnership and to give him a 25 percent ownership interest in the partnership on January 1, 2009. Prior to Crustie's entry, the following information was available.

| | Capital | Fixed Ratio |
|---|---|---|
| Billie | $20,000 | 10% |
| Mandie | 50,000 | 60 |
| Grimm | 30,000 | 30 |

1. Assume Crustie pays the partnership $30,000 for 25 percent of the partnership capital. Calculate the bonus to the new partner and the amounts that will be debited to the capital account for each of the existing partners.
2. Assume Crustie pays the partnership $40,000 for 25 percent of the partnership capital. Calculate the bonus to the existing partners and the amount that will be credited to Crustie's capital account.

*After you have finished, check your answers with the solution at the bottom of the next page.*

## Withdrawal of a Partner

After his admission, Bud joined Hal and Dawn in all meetings with their attorney because he was a full partner. During one visit, Dawn asked the attorney to explain what would happen if one of the partners withdrew from the partnership. The attorney replied that as with the addition of a new partner, the withdrawal of a partner causes the immediate dissolution of the partnership. After dissolution, the remaining partners may carry on the business, but the partnership is legally new and different.

A partner can withdraw from a partnership in two ways: (1) voluntarily through the sale of his or her interest in the partnership to the remaining partner(s) or (2) involuntarily for one of several reasons. Death, insanity, mandatory retirement, and removal by the remaining partners (an unusual occurrence) can cause a partner's involuntary withdrawal from the partnership.

A properly prepared partnership agreement should cover the procedures, terms, and conditions for a partner's withdrawal. Similar to the admission of a new partner, certain options are available to the partners when a partner withdraws. Specifically, the remaining partners can purchase the exiting partner's capital account in one of two ways: They can pay the exiting partner with their own personal assets or with the partnership's assets. As we discuss in the following sections, the first option involves the partnership only insofar as a journal entry must be made to record the transfer of capital from the exiting partner to the remaining partner(s). The second option, in which the partnership uses its own assets to buy out the exiting partner, is more complicated.

## Purchase among Partners

When partners use their own personal assets to pay the exiting partner, the partnership does nothing more than make a journal entry to transfer the balance in the exiting partner's capital account to the remaining partners' capital accounts. The dollar amount of the purchase and all other particulars are treated as personal transactions among the partners; the partnership itself is not involved.

Assume, for example, that on January 1, 2011 (after the partnership had been operating for several years), Dawn Bloom voluntarily withdrew from the partnership. At that time, each partner had a capital account balance of $30,000 (or a total of $90,000 for the partnership). Hal and Bud each agreed to purchase half of Dawn's interest in the partnership for $20,000. The entry made to record Dawn's withdrawal in this example follows:

| | Debit | Credit |
|---|---|---|
| Dawn Bloom, Capital (−OE) | 30,000 | |
|     Hal Flowers, Capital (+OE) | | 15,000 |
|     Bud Green, Capital (+OE) | | 15,000 |

| Assets | = | Liabilities | + | Owners' Equity | |
|---|---|---|---|---|---|
| | | | | Dawn Bloom, Capital | −30,000 |
| | | | | Hal Flowers, Capital | +15,000 |
| | | | | Bud Green, Capital | +15,000 |

In this case, the amount Dawn accepted for her capital account balance was strictly a private matter between her and the other partners. Theoretically, as in the admission of a new partner, each of the remaining partners may have been unaware of the amount the other paid

Solution to Self-Study Practice

1.

| | Step 1 | Capital before contribution ($20,000 + $50,000 + $30,000) | $100,000 |
|---|---|---|---|
| | | Crustie's contribution | 30,000 |
| | | New partnership capital | $130,000 |
| | 2 | New partner's capital account balance ($130,000 × 25%) | $ 32,500 |
| | 3 | Bonus to new partner ($32,500 − $30,000) | $ 2,500 |
| | 4 | Allocate bonus of new partner to existing partners | |
| | |     Billie: $2,500 × 10% = $250 | |
| | |     Mandie: $2,500 × 60% = $1,500 | |
| | |     Grimm: $2,500 × 30% = $750 | |

2.

| | Step 1 | Capital before contribution ($20,000 + $50,000 + $30,000) | $100,000 |
|---|---|---|---|
| | | Crustie's contribution | 40,000 |
| | | New partnership capital | $140,000 |
| | 2 | New partner's capital account balance ($140,000 × 25%) | $ 35,000 |
| | 3 | Bonus to existing partners ($40,000 − $35,000) | $ 5,000 |
| | 4 | Allocate bonus to existing partners | |
| | |     Billie: $5,000 × 10% = $500 | |
| | |     Mandie: $5,000 × 60% = $3,000 | |
| | |     Grimm: $5,000 × 30% = $1,500 | |

for his half of Dawn's capital account balance. The financial impact of the transaction, if any, is handled by the partners on their individual income tax returns, not by the partnership.

As the following T-accounts show, the **total** capital in the partnership was the same **before and after** Dawn's withdrawal from the partnership ($90,000). After the withdrawal, each **remaining** partner's capital was worth $45,000—exactly half the total ($90,000 × ½). The two remaining partners each own 50 percent of the partnership's net assets.

| Hal Flowers, Capital | | Dawn Bloom, Capital | | Bud Green, Capital | |
|---|---|---|---|---|---|
| | Bal.   30,000 | | Bal. 30,000 | | Bal.   30,000 |
| | Jan. 1 15,000 | Jan. 1 30,000 | | | Jan. 1 15,000 |
| | 45,000 | | 0 | | 45,000 |

Although each remaining partner owns one-half the partnership's net assets, that does not necessarily mean that each is entitled to half the partnership's profits. The allocation of the partnership's profit (or loss) is determined by the partnership agreement. The agreement may or may not state that profits will be split 50–50 after a partner exits. If no written agreement exists, the profits would be allocated equally among the partners whether or not that was their intention.

## Withdrawal of Assets

The other means of a partner's withdrawal is to use the partnership's assets (usually cash) to purchase the exiting partner's capital account. Unlike the purchase among partners method, this method has an obvious impact on the partnership.

We assume, as before, that when Dawn withdrew from the partnership, all three partners had a capital account balance of $30,000. In this case, however, Dawn received $30,000 in cash from the partnership in return for her voluntary withdrawal. Under this method, only the partnership's net assets (cash) and Dawn's capital account were affected by her exit. The remaining partners' capital accounts were unaffected. The entry that would be made to record Dawn's withdrawal from the partnership follows.

| | Debit | Credit |
|---|---|---|
| Dawn Bloom, Capital (−OE) | 30,000 | |
|     Cash (−A) | | 30,000 |

| Assets | = | Liabilities | + | Owners' Equity | |
|---|---|---|---|---|---|
| Cash        −30,000 | | | | Dawn Bloom, Capital | −30,000 |

After the $30,000 payment to Dawn, the remaining partners' capital accounts had the following balances:

| Hal Flowers, Capital | | Dawn Bloom, Capital | | Bud Green, Capital | |
|---|---|---|---|---|---|
| | Bal.   30,000 | | Bal.   30,000 | | Bal.   30,000 |
| | | Jan. 1   30,000 | | | |
| | | | 0 | | |

As before, the remaining partners then owned 50 percent of the partnership's net assets except that those net assets have decreased by $30,000. Before Dawn's withdrawal, the partnership's net assets (Assets − Liabilities = Owners' Equity) were $90,000 (= $30,000 + $30,000 + $30,000). After her withdrawal, its net assets were $60,000 (= $30,000 + $30,000).

In this case, we assumed that the partnership paid Dawn the exact amount of her capital account—that is, one-third of the partnership's total capital. In some cases, however, the partnership may pay the exiting partner **more or less** than his or her capital account balance. In the following sections, we consider both possibilities.

**Bonus to the Remaining Partners.** Sometimes the cash payment to the exiting partner is less than that partner's capital balance. A reduced payment is possible for several reasons. The fair market value of the partnership's assets may be less than their book value, or the exiting partner may wish to leave the partnership as quickly as possible, no matter what payment is offered. Whatever the reason, the remaining partners effectively receive a bonus from the withdrawing partner.

Assume that instead of receiving $30,000 for her interest in the partnership, Dawn received only $24,000. The steps to follow in determining the journal entry to record the transaction are:

1. **Calculate the total bonus to the remaining partners.** The total bonus to the remaining partners is the difference between the amount in the exiting partner's capital account and the amount the exiting partner receives at withdrawal from the partnership.

| | |
|---|---|
| Amount in exiting partner's capital account | $30,000 |
| Amount of cash paid to the exiting partner | 24,000 |
| Total bonus to the remaining partners | $ 6,000 |

2. **Allocate the bonus to the remaining partners using their fixed ratios.** Referring to the partnership agreement that was drawn up after Bud's admission to the partnership, the fixed ratios for Hal, Dawn, and Bud were 40 percent, 40 percent, and 20 percent, respectively. With Dawn's withdrawal, the allocation was based on the remaining percentages, 40 percent and 20 percent.

Because the remaining percentages total 60 percent (= 40 percent + 20 percent), allocations were made on that basis. Therefore, the bonus was allocated as follows:

| | |
|---|---|
| Hal's portion of the bonus [$6,000 × 40/60] | $4,000 |
| Bud's portion of the bonus [$6,000 × 20/60] | 2,000 |
| Total bonus allocated | $6,000 |

The entry to record this transaction would be:

| | Debit | Credit |
|---|---|---|
| Dawn Bloom, Capital (−OE) | 30,000 | |
| Cash (−A) | | 24,000 |
| Hal Flowers, Capital (+OE) | | 4,000 |
| Bud Green, Capital (+OE) | | 2,000 |

| Assets | = | Liabilities | + | Owners' Equity |
|---|---|---|---|---|
| Cash    −24,000 | | | | Dawn Bloom, Capital −30,000 |
| | | | | Hal Flowers, Capital  + 4,000 |
| | | | | Bud Green, Capital   + 2,000 |

**Bonus to the Exiting Partner.** Now let's examine the reverse situation. In this case, the partnership paid the exiting partner **more** than her capital account balance such that she received a bonus. This situation may occur for several reasons. The other partners may have been eager to see Dawn leave, the fair market value of the partnership's assets may have been higher than their book value, or the partnership may have enjoyed exceptional earnings and/or generated goodwill within the partnership.

To illustrate, assume that the partnership paid Dawn $33,000 (instead of $24,000) in exchange for her interest in the partnership. The procedure to account for this transaction is as follows:

1. **Calculate the bonus to the exiting partner.** The bonus to Dawn is the difference between the amount of cash she receives from the partnership and the balance in her capital account at the time of her withdrawal.

| | |
|---|---:|
| Amount of cash paid to the exiting partner | $33,000 |
| Capital account balance of exiting partner | 30,000 |
| Total bonus to the exiting partner | $ 3,000 |

2. **Allocate the exiting partner's bonus to the remaining partners using their fixed ratios.** The remaining partner's fixed income ratios are the same as those shown in the last example. Therefore, the bonus would have been allocated as follows:

| | |
|---|---:|
| Hal's portion of the bonus [$3,000 × (40/60)] | $2,000 |
| Bud's portion of the bonus [$3,000 × (20/60)] | 1,000 |
| Total bonus allocated | $3,000 |

The $3,000 bonus to the exiting partner came out of the remaining partners' capital accounts. The assumption is that the remaining partners are willing to give up some of their own capital account balances to obtain the exiting partner's withdrawal. The following entry would have been made to record this transaction.

| | Debit | Credit |
|---|---:|---:|
| Dawn Bloom, Capital (−OE) | 30,000 | |
| Hal Flowers, Capital (−OE) | 2,000 | |
| Bud Green, Capital (−OE) | 1,000 | |
| Cash (−A) | | 33,000 |

| Assets | = | Liabilities | + | Owners' Equity | |
|---|---|---|---|---|---|
| Cash −33,000 | | | | Dawn Bloom, Capital | −30,000 |
| | | | | Hal Flowers, Capital | −2,000 |
| | | | | Bud Green, Capital | −1,000 |

# Death of a Partner

Although the death of a partner is not something most partners want to consider, the sobering fact is that no one knows when a partner's death might occur. When a partner dies, the existing partnership is dissolved. Because the partner's equity in the partnership will pass to his or her estate after death, the partnership agreement should include provisions for a settlement with the estate.

To determine the balance in the deceased partner's equity account on the date of death, the partnership is required to (1) calculate the partnership's net income up to the date of death, (2) close the books, and (3) prepare financial statements. If the partnership agreement requires it, the partnership's net assets may be restated at their fair market value, and an audit of the accounting records may be required.

In some cases, the remaining partners personally purchase the deceased partner's interest in the partnership. In other cases, the partnership's assets may be used to finance the buyout. Because a profitable and successful partnership can be worth hundreds of thousands, if not millions, of dollars, many partnerships purchase life insurance policies on all general partners to cover the potential cost of a buyout.

**SELF-STUDY PRACTICE**

Klock voluntarily withdraws from the 4K partnership on January 1, 2009. Prior to Klock's withdrawal, the following information is available.

|  | Capital | Fixed Ratio |
|---|---|---|
| Kharge | $15,000 | 10% |
| Klock | 20,000 | 20 |
| Knot | 25,000 | 30 |
| Katt | 60,000 | 40 |

1. Assume the partnership pays Klock $18,000 for the balance in her capital account. Calculate the bonus allocated to each of the remaining partners.
2. Assume the partnership pays Klock $23,000 for the balance in her capital account. Calculate the bonus to her and the amount that will be debited to the capital accounts of each of the remaining partners.

*After you have finished, check your answers with the solution at the bottom of the page.*

# LIQUIDATION OF A PARTNERSHIP

**Learning Objective 4**

Demonstrate the proper treatment for the liquidation of a partnership.

Although Hal, Dawn, and Bud's partnership had been successful for many years (Dawn never actually withdrew from the partnership), the three friends became weary of the time required and the stress involved in running a business. Increasingly, they talked of dissolving their partnership. As a result, they decided to meet with their attorney again to discuss the possibility of a dissolution—the process that ultimately ends in the liquidation and distribution of partnership assets.

A **partnership liquidation** may be caused by the death of a partner, the imminent bankruptcy of the partnership, or by mutual agreement among all partners. The attorney informed the three friends that when a partnership is liquidated, the assets are sold (for cash), any outstanding debts and liabilities are paid, and the remaining cash, if any, is distributed to the partners. Before the process begins, however, the accounting cycle should be completed. That is, adjustments should be made, financial statements prepared, and closing entries recorded and posted. At that point, only the permanent accounts reported on the balance sheet should contain balances.

**Solution to Self-Study Practice**

1.
| | |
|---|---|
| Amount of Klock's capital account | $20,000 |
| Cash paid to Klock | 18,000 |
| Bonus to remaining partners | $ 2,000 |

Kharge: $2,000 × [10/(10 + 30 + 40)] = $250

Knot: $2,000 × [30/(10 + 30 + 40)] = $750

Katt: $2,000 × [40/(10 + 30 + 40)] = $1,000

2.
| | |
|---|---|
| Amount paid to Klock | $23,000 |
| Capital balance of Klock | 20,000 |
| Bonus to Klock | $ 3,000 |

Kharge: $3,000 × [10/(10 + 30 + 40)] = $375

Knot: $3,000 × [30/(10 + 30 + 40)] = $1,125

Katt: $3,000 × [40/(10 + 30 + 40)] = $1,500

The four steps in the liquidation process follow.

1. **Sell.** All assets (except cash) must be sold for cash and the resulting gain or loss recognized.
2. **Allocate.** After all assets have been liquidated (that is, converted to cash), the gain or loss calculated in Step 1 must be allocated among the partners according to their fixed ratios.
3. **Pay.** The partnership's cash is then used to pay all of the partnership's liabilities.
4. **Distribute.** Any remaining cash can then be distributed to the partners according to their fixed ratios.

The attorney advised the partners that

- **These four steps must be performed in order.** Executing them in any other order could result in serious financial consequences to the partners.
- A journal entry must be recorded for each and every step in the liquidation process.
- All liabilities, debts, and/or other obligations **must** be paid before the partners receive anything.

After the business has been operating for several years, partners' capital account balances will differ from one another for several reasons. The partners may have received different percentages of the profit (or loss), or their drawings may have varied. Over the years, these additions and/or withdrawals may have greatly impacted their capital accounts. Two possibilities exist with regard to the partners' capital accounts: (1) no capital deficiency—that is, every partner has a credit balance in his or her capital account and (2) a capital deficiency—that is, one or more partners have a debit balance (deficit) in his or her capital account. These different situations dramatically affect the partnership liquidation process, as we show in the following examples.

Assume that after many years of successful operations, Hal, Dawn, and Bud decided to liquidate their partnership. Exhibit 12.9 shows the partnership's account balances just before liquidation. In the following sections, we investigate how the existence or nonexistence of a capital deficiency affects the liquidation of a partnership.

## No Capital Deficiency

After deciding to liquidate the partnership, Hal, Dawn, and Bud followed their lawyer's instructions to the letter. They completed the four steps in the liquidation process in order, as follows.

1. **Sell the partnership's assets (except cash).** The partners accepted an offer from Plantland, Inc., to purchase the partnership's assets (except cash) for $240,000. The book value of these assets at the time of the transaction is $229,000 (=$94,000 − $8,000 + $85,000 + $105,000 − $47,000).

| Exhibit 12.9 | Partnership Account Balances before Liquidation |
|---|---|

| Assets | | Liabilities and Owners' Equity | |
|---|---|---|---|
| Cash | $ 51,000 | Accounts payable | $ 79,000 |
| Accounts receivable | 94,000 | Notes payable | 118,000 |
| Allowance for doubtful accounts | (8,000) | | |
| Inventory | 85,000 | Hal Flowers, capital | 47,000 |
| Store equipment | 105,000 | Dawn Bloom, capital | 31,000 |
| Accumulated depreciation | (47,000) | Bud Green, capital | 5,000 |
| | $280,000 | | $280,000 |

The entry to record the resulting $11,000 gain on the sale of the assets ($240,000 − $229,000) was:

| | Debit | Credit |
|---|---|---|
| Cash (+A) | 240,000 | |
| Allowance for Doubtful Accounts (−xA, +A) | 8,000 | |
| Accumulated Depreciation (−xA, +A) | 47,000 | |
|     Accounts Receivable (−A) | | 94,000 |
|     Inventory (−A) | | 85,000 |
|     Store Equipment (−A) | | 105,000 |
|     Gain on Liquidation (+OE) | | 11,000 |

| Assets | | = | Liabilities | + | Owners' Equity | |
|---|---|---|---|---|---|---|
| Cash | +240,000 | | | | Gain on Liquidation | +11,000 |
| Allowance for Doubtful Accounts (−xA) | +8,000 | | | | | |
| Accumulated Depreciation (−xA) | +47,000 | | | | | |
| Accounts Receivable | −94,000 | | | | | |
| Inventory | −85,000 | | | | | |
| Store Equipment | −105,000 | | | | | |

2. **Allocate any gain or loss from the sale of the assets to the partners.** The partners allocated the $11,000 gain from Step 1 according to the partners' fixed ratios: 40 percent to Hal, 40 percent to Dawn, and 20 percent to Bud.

| | |
|---|---|
| Hal's portion of the gain ($11,000 × 40%) | $ 4,400 |
| Dawn's portion of the gain ($11,000 × 40%) | 4,400 |
| Bud's portion of the gain ($11,000 × 20%) | 2,200 |
| Total gain allocated | $11,000 |

The entry to record the allocation of the gain was:

| | Debit | Credit |
|---|---|---|
| Gain on Liquidation (−OE) | 11,000 | |
|     Hal Flowers, Capital (+OE) | | 4,400 |
|     Dawn Bloom, Capital (+OE) | | 4,400 |
|     Bud Green, Capital (+OE) | | 2,200 |

| Assets | = | Liabilities | + | Owners' Equity | |
|---|---|---|---|---|---|
| | | | | Hal Flowers, Capital | + 4,400 |
| | | | | Dawn Bloom, Capital | + 4,400 |
| | | | | Bud Green, Capital | + 2,200 |
| | | | | Gain on Liquidation | −11,000 |

After posting the entry to allocate the gain, the partners' capital accounts appeared as follows.

| Hal Flowers, Capital | | Dawn Bloom, Capital | | Bud Green, Capital | |
|---|---|---|---|---|---|
| | Bal. 47,000 | | Bal. 31,000 | | Bal. 5,000 |
| | (2) 4,400 | | (2) 4,400 | | (2) 2,200 |
| | 51,400 | | 35,400 | | 7,200 |

3. **Pay all outstanding liabilities.** After the sale of assets, the partnership had $291,000 in cash ($51,000 + $240,000). This cash was used to pay the outstanding liabilities. The following entry was made to record the payment.

|  | Debit | Credit |
|---|---|---|
| Accounts Payable (–L) | 79,000 | |
| Notes Payable (–L) | 118,000 | |
| Cash (–A) | | 197,000 |

| Assets | = | Liabilities | + | Owners' Equity |
|---|---|---|---|---|
| Cash  −197,000 | | Accounts Payable  −79,000 | | |
| | | Notes Payable  −118,000 | | |

4. **Distribute the remaining cash to the partners.** After paying all outstanding debts, the partnership had $94,000 cash remaining to distribute to the partners ($51,000 + $240,000 − $197,000). Because the partners completed each of the steps in the liquidation process properly and in sequence, the total balance in their capital accounts exactly equaled the amount of cash available for distribution ($51,400 + $35,400 + $7,200 = $94,000). The distribution of cash to the partners is shown in the following journal entry. After posting the entry, the balances in the capital accounts equaled zero, cash was zero, and the liquidation was complete.

|  | Debit | Credit |
|---|---|---|
| Hal Flowers, Capital (–OE) | 51,400 | |
| Dawn Bloom, Capital (–OE) | 35,400 | |
| Bud Green, Capital (–OE) | 7,200 | |
| Cash (–A) | | 94,000 |

| Assets | = | Liabilities | + | Owners' Equity |
|---|---|---|---|---|
| Cash  −94,000 | | | | Hal Flowers, Capital  −51,400 |
| | | | | Dawn Bloom, Capital −35,400 |
| | | | | Bud Green, Capital  −7,200 |

**Coach's Tip**

A word of caution: Do not attempt to allocate cash to the partners on the basis of fixed ratios. It is not an appropriate basis for a final distribution of cash.

# Capital Deficiency

The liquidation process is not always smooth. Sometimes one or more partners do not have a large enough balance in their capital accounts to cover all transactions the liquidation requires. This situation can occur when the partnership has suffered numerous losses over its life. It can also occur when one or more partners have made disproportionately large withdrawals or when the partnership incurs large losses in the liquidation process. The procedure for dealing with this situation is as follows.

1. **Sell the partnership's assets (except cash).** Assume that Hal, Dawn, and Bud could not find a buyer for the business's assets and were forced to auction them off for far less than their fair market value. In total, the partnership collected $150,000 for assets (except cash) whose book value was $229,000 (= $94,000 − $8,000 + $85,000 + $105,000 − $47,000). Because the partnership received only $150,000 for assets recorded on the books for $229,000, it incurred a loss on liquidation of $79,000 ($229,000 − $150,000). The following entry was made to record the loss and the sale of the assets.

| | Debit | Credit |
|---|---|---|
| Cash (+A) | 150,000 | |
| Allowance for Doubtful Accounts (−xA, +A) | 8,000 | |
| Accumulated Depreciation (−xA, +A) | 47,000 | |
| Loss on Liquidation (−OE) | 79,000 | |
|     Accounts Receivable (−A) | | 94,000 |
|     Inventory (−A) | | 85,000 |
|     Store Equipment (−A) | | 105,000 |

| Assets | | = | Liabilities | + | Owners' Equity | |
|---|---|---|---|---|---|---|
| Cash | +150,000 | | | | Loss on Liquidation | −79,000 |
| Allowance for Doubtful Accounts (−xA) | +8,000 | | | | | |
| Accumulated Depreciation (−xA) | +47,000 | | | | | |
| Accounts Receivable | −94,000 | | | | | |
| Inventory | −85,000 | | | | | |
| Store Equipment | −105,000 | | | | | |

2. **Allocate any gain or loss from the sale of assets to the partners.** The loss was allocated according to the partners' fixed income ratios: 40 percent to Hal, 40 percent to Dawn, and 20 percent to Bud.

| | |
|---|---|
| Hal's portion of the loss ($79,000 × 40%) | $ 31,600 |
| Dawn's portion of the loss ($79,000 × 40%) | 31,600 |
| Bud's portion of the loss ($79,000 × 20%) | 15,800 |
|     Total loss allocated | $ 79,000 |

This entry was made to record allocation of the loss.

| | Debit | Credit |
|---|---|---|
| Hal Flowers, Capital (−OE) | 31,600 | |
| Dawn Bloom, Capital (−OE) | 31,600 | |
| Bud Green, Capital (−OE) | 15,800 | |
|     Loss on Liquidation (+OE) | | 79,000 |

| Assets | = | Liabilities | + | Owners' Equity | |
|---|---|---|---|---|---|
| | | | | Hal Flowers, Capital | −31,600 |
| | | | | Dawn Bloom, Capital | −31,600 |
| | | | | Bud Green, Capital | −15,800 |
| | | | | Loss on Liquidation | +79,000 |

3. **Pay the partnership's outstanding liabilities.** After selling the assets, the partnership had cash of $201,000 (= $51,000 + $150,000). This cash was used to pay the outstanding liabilities. The following entry was made to record the payment.

| | Debit | Credit |
|---|---|---|
| Accounts Payable (−L) | 79,000 | |
| Notes Payable (−L) | 118,000 | |
| Cash (−A) | | 197,000 |

| Assets | | = | Liabilities | | + | Owners' Equity |
|---|---|---|---|---|---|---|
| Cash | −197,000 | | Accounts Payable | −79,000 | | |
| | | | Notes Payable | −118,000 | | |

4. **Distribute the remaining cash to the partners.** After paying all outstanding debts, the partnership had $4,000 cash (= $51,000 + $150,000 − $197,000) remaining to distribute to the partners. Normally, the partners receive the balances in their capital accounts after the first three transactions have been posted. However, as the debit balances in the following capital accounts show, both Bud and Dawn had a **capital deficiency**. Dawn owed the partnership $600, and Bud owed $10,800.

| Hal Flowers, Capital | | | Dawn Bloom, Capital | | | Bud Green, Capital | |
|---|---|---|---|---|---|---|---|
| | Bal. 47,000 | | | Bal. 31,000 | | | Bal. 5,000 |
| (2) 31,600 | | (2) 31,600 | | (2) 15,800 | |
| | 15,400 | | 600 | | | 10,800 | |

The three friends realize that this was exactly the type of situation that a limited liability company (LLC) is formed to avoid. In a general partnership, each partner bears unlimited liability for the partnership's debts. So legally, Hal had an enforceable claim against both Dawn and Bud for the deficient funds. Hal could even have accessed their personal assets in an attempt to collect the deficiencies. Alternatively, Hal could have collected **the combined deficiency of both partners' capital accounts from just one of the two partners.** Often one partner has a great deal of personal wealth and another has very little. If Hal wanted, he could try to collect the entire amount from the wealthy partner. This ability to collect from any or all partners is called **joint** (all partners) **and several** (any partner) **liability.**

A capital deficiency can be resolved during the liquidation of a partnership in two ways: (1) the partner pays the deficiency and (2) the partner fails to pay the deficiency.

## Deficiency Paid by Partner

Assume that Dawn decided to pay her $600 capital deficiency. The following entry was made to record the payment.

| | Debit | Credit |
|---|---|---|
| Cash (+A) | 600 | |
| Dawn Bloom, Capital (+OE) | | 600 |

| Assets | | = | Liabilities | + | Owners' Equity | |
|---|---|---|---|---|---|---|
| Cash | +600 | | | | Dawn Bloom, Capital | +600 |

As the following T-accounts show, after the entry was posted, Dawn's capital account had a zero balance. She received no cash when the final distribution was made, but she owed nothing more. The partnership's Cash account then had increased to $4,600 (= $4,000 + $600).

| Hal Flowers, Capital | | | Dawn Bloom, Capital | | | Bud Green, Capital | |
|---|---|---|---|---|---|---|---|
| | Bal. 47,000 | | | Bal. 31,000 | | | Bal. 5,000 |
| (2) 31,600 | | (2) 31,600 | (4a) 600 | (2) 15,800 | |
| | 15,400 | | | 0 | | 10,800 | |

## Deficiency Not Paid by Partner

Suppose that Bud could not pay his $10,800 capital deficiency. When a partner cannot pay the deficit in a capital account, the partners who have credit balances in their capital accounts must absorb the deficit. Normally, the partnership's fixed ratio would be used to allocate the deficit, but because Hal was the only partner with a credit balance, he had to absorb the entire deficit. The following entry was made to record the absorption of the deficit by the remaining partner.

| | Debit | Credit |
|---|---|---|
| Hal Flowers, Capital (−OE) | 10,800 | |
| Bud Green, Capital (+OE) | | 10,800 |

| Assets | = | Liabilities | + | Owners' Equity | |
|---|---|---|---|---|---|
| | | | | Hal Flowers, Capital | −10,800 |
| | | | | Bud Green, Capital | +10,800 |

With the deficit resolved, the partners' capital accounts had the following balances after the entry was posted.

| Hal Flowers, Capital | | | | Dawn Bloom, Capital | | | | Bud Green, Capital | | |
|---|---|---|---|---|---|---|---|---|---|---|
| | | Bal. 47,000 | | | | Bal. 31,000 | | | | Bal. 5,000 |
| (2) | 31,600 | | (2) | 31,600 | (4a) | 600 | (2) | 15,800 | (4b) | 10,800 |
| (4b) | 10,800 | | | | | 0 | | | | 0 |
| | | 4,600 | | | | | | | | |

The partnership had $4,600 cash, including the $600 that Dawn paid to resolve her deficit. Note that Hal's capital account **also** had a $4,600 balance. The final distribution to Hal could then be made. The final entry in the partnership liquidation was:

| | Debit | Credit |
|---|---|---|
| Hal Flowers, Capital (−OE) | 4,600 | |
| Cash (−A) | | 4,600 |

| Assets | | = | Liabilities | + | Owners' Equity | |
|---|---|---|---|---|---|---|
| Cash | −4,600 | | | | Hal Flowers, Capital | −4,600 |

Even then, neither Bud nor Dawn was completely free of obligation to Hal. Hal had the right to collect the remaining $10,800 that he was owed from **either or both of them.** So even though Dawn may have thought she was in the clear because she paid her deficit, she still had unlimited liability.

**SELF-STUDY PRACTICE**

At the time of liquidation, AB Partners reported $2,000 in cash, $5,000 in other assets, $4,000 in liabilities, $2,600 in Ali Augo's capital account, and $400 in Bradyn Bad's capital account. For the following two independent cases, determine (a) the amount of cash available after the assets are sold and liabilities paid, and (b) the total balances in the partners' capital accounts after any gain (or loss) is allocated 50-50 between partners.

1. The assets (other than cash) are sold for $7,500.
2. The assets (other than cash) are sold for $3,000.

*After you have finished, check your answers with the solution at the bottom of the next page.*

# RATIO ANALYSIS
## Partner Return on Equity

In our scenario, the partners certainly received their money's worth from their attorney, who gave them one last bit of information free of charge. He offered to provide the three partners a financial analysis tool called the **partner return on equity.**

Of the numerous financial measures used to analyze a business's performance, the **partner return on equity** is of particular interest to partnerships. An informative measure of profitability and managerial performance in a partnership, partner return on equity is calculated and interpreted as follows:

| Financial Analysis Tools | | |
| --- | --- | --- |
| Name of Measure | Formula | What It Tells You |
| Partner Return on Equity Ratio | $\dfrac{\text{Net Income}}{\text{Average Partner Equity}}$ | • Measures a company's efficiency at generating profits from every dollar of equity invested (or retained) in the partnership.<br>• A higher ratio indicates a greater efficiency. |

Take Hal, Dawn, and Bud's partnership, for example:

| | Total | Hal Flowers | Dawn Bloom | Bud Green |
| --- | --- | --- | --- | --- |
| Balance 1/1/2009 | $54,000 | $18,000 | $18,000 | $18,000 |
| Net income | 15,000 | 6,000 | 6,000 | 3,000 |
| Drawings | (12,000) | (2,000) | (3,000) | (7,000) |
| Balance 12/31/2009 | $57,000 | $22,000 | $21,000 | $ 14,000 |
| **Partner Return on Equity:** | | | | |
| $\dfrac{\text{Net Income}}{\text{Average Partner Equity}}$ | $\dfrac{\$15,000}{(\$54,000+\$57,000)/2}$ | $\dfrac{\$6,000}{(\$18,000+\$22,000)/2}$ | $\dfrac{\$6,000}{(\$18,000+\$21,000)/2}$ | $\dfrac{\$3,000}{(\$18,000+\$14,000)/2}$ |
| = | 0.270 or 27.0% | 0.300 or 30.0% | 0.308 or 30.8% | 0.188 or 18.8% |

Notice that the partnership's return on equity (in the Total column) is vastly different from the individual return on equity (ROE) calculated for each partner. Bud's ROE, in particular, appears relatively low when compared to the others. This should not be a surprise, though, because Bud receives a smaller income allocation than the other partners.

Solution to
Self-Study Practice

1. (a)  Cash = $2,000 + $7,500 − $4,000   = $5,500
   (b)  Gain = $7,500 − $5,000 = $2,500 ($1,250 to Ali, $1,250 to Bradyn)
       A. Augo, Capital = $2,600 + $1,250 = $3,850
       B. Bad, Capital =  $  400 + $1,250 =  1,650
           Total                            $5,500

2. (a)  Cash = $2,000 + $3,000 − $4,000   = $1,000
   (b)  Gain (loss) = $3,000 − $5,000 = ($2,000) ($1,000 to Ali, $1,000 to Bradyn)
       A. Augo, Capital = $2,600 − $1,000  = $1,600
       B. Bad, Capital =  $  400 − $1,000 =   (600)
           Total                            $1,000

In practice, very few businesses have a consistent return on equity of more than 30 percent. Moreover, maintaining ROE in a partnership at the same level over time is nearly impossible. That is because income is closed to the partners' equity accounts. Assuming the partners leave most of their earnings in the partnership to encourage its growth, the business's capital keeps increasing. To keep the partner ROE ratio high, then, income must also increase continually.

Another thing to watch for in relation to ROE is debt because a partnership can increase its ROE by relying more on debt. Assume, for example, that our partnership's beginning capital balance of $54,000 was made up entirely of partner contributions. Had the partnership instead borrowed $30,000 and required that much less in partner contributions, beginning capital would have been $24,000 rather than $54,000. In that situation, the ROE would have been a staggering 58.8%—[= $15,000/($24,000 + 27,000)/2]. But would you really want to take on all that debt just to achieve a high ROE? For this reason, the ROE should not be the only financial measure used to evaluate a business.

**SELF-STUDY PRACTICE**

Indicate whether each of the following is a true (T) or false (F) statement regarding partner return on equity.

1. Partner return on equity calculation is: Average Partner Equity ÷ Partner Net Income. _____

2. Each individual partner's ROE can vary substantially from the ROE of the partnership as a whole. _____

3. The ROE for most partnerships consistently exceeds 30 percent._____

4. Assume a partner begins the year with $20,000 in partner equity and ends the year with $35,000. Her allocated net income for the year is $34,000. In this case, her ROE is 123.6 percent. _____

5. Replacing capital with debt can increase the ROE. _____

*After you have finished, check your answers with the solution at the bottom of the page.*

## Demonstration Case A
### Division of Partnership Income

Alwin and Teddy Ernest formed a partnership to provide accounting services. Assume that their partnership net income was $600,000, and other relevant information (immediately prior to allocating partnership net income) follows.

| Partner | Capital Account Balances | Salaries | Interest | Fixed Ratio |
|---|---|---|---|---|
| Alwin Ernest | $200,000 | $100,000 | 6% | 1/3 |
| Teddy Ernest | $300,000 | $140,000 | 6% | 2/3 |

**Solution to Self-Study Practice**

1. F—ROE is calculated as Partner Net Income ÷ Average Partner Equity.
2. T—Each partner's capital balance and allocated net income may be greater or less than others in the partnership.
3. F—It is rare for a partnership to consistently maintain an ROE in excess of 30 percent.
4. T—$34,000 / [($20,000 + $35,000) / 2] = 123.6%.
5. T—This reduces the bottom number in the ROE formula.

***Required:***

Allocate net income to each partner under the following four independent assumptions:

1.  Fixed ratio.
2.  Interest on partners' capital balances.
3.  Salaries to partners.
4.  Salaries to partners and interest on partners' capital balances.

## Suggested Solution

1.  Alwin Ernest:   $600,000 × 1/3 = $200,000
    Teddy Ernest:   $600,000 × 2/3 = $400,000

2.

| | Alwin | Teddy | Total Allocated | Remainder to Allocate |
|---|---|---|---|---|
| Net income to allocate | | | | $600,000 |
| Interest: | | | | |
|     Alwin Ernest: $200,000 × 6% | $ 12,000 | | $ 12,000 | (12,000) |
|     Teddy Ernest: $300,000 × 6% | | $ 18,000 | 18,000 | (18,000) |
| Remainder (allocate on a fixed ratio): | | | | 570,000 |
|     Alwin Ernest: $570,000 × 1/3 | 190,000 | | 190,000 | (190,000) |
|     Teddy Ernest: $570,000 × 2/3 | | 380,000 | 380,000 | (380,000) |
| Total | $202,000 | $398,000 | $600,000 | $          0 |

3.

| | Alwin | Teddy | Total Allocated | Remainder to Allocate |
|---|---|---|---|---|
| Net income to allocate | | | | $600,000 |
| Salaries | $100,000 | $140,000 | $240,000 | (240,000) |
| Remainder (allocate on a fixed ratio): | | | | 360,000 |
|     Alwin Ernest: $360,000 × 1/3 | 120,000 | | 120,000 | (120,000) |
|     Teddy Ernest: $360,000 × 2/3 | | 240,000 | 240,000 | (240,000) |
| Total | $220,000 | $380,000 | $600,000 | $          0 |

4.

| | Alwin | Teddy | Total Allocated | Remainder to Allocate |
|---|---|---|---|---|
| Net income to allocate | | | | $600,000 |
| Salaries | $100,000 | $140,000 | $240,000 | (240,000) |
| Remainder | | | | 360,000 |
| Interest: | | | | |
|     Alwin Ernest: $200,000 × 6% | 12,000 | | 12,000 | (12,000) |
|     Teddy Ernest: $300,000 × 6% | | 18,000 | 18,000 | (18,000) |
| Remainder (allocate on a fixed ratio): | | | | 330,000 |
|     Alwin Ernest: $330,000 × 1/3 | 110,000 | | 110,000 | (110,000) |
|     Teddy Ernest: $330,000 × 2/3 | | 220,000 | 220,000 | (220,000) |
| Total | $222,000 | $378,000 | $600,000 | $          0 |

# Demonstration Case B
## Admission and Withdrawal of Partners

In the year following Case A, Ernest & Ernest admits two new partners. Fred Whiney is admitted as an equal partner by purchasing half of Teddy's partnership interest. At the time, Teddy's capital account balance was $400,000 and Alwin's was $200,000. At the end of the year, Arthur Yong is admitted as an equal partner by investing $280,000 cash in the partnership and receiving a 25% partnership interest. At the time of Arthur's admission, the accounting records and partnership agreement contain the following information.

| Partner | Capital Account Balances | Fixed Ratio |
|---|---|---|
| Alwin Ernest | $220,000 | 1/3 |
| Teddy Ernest | 250,000 | 1/3 |
| Fred Whiney | 250,000 | 1/3 |
| Total | $720,000 | |

In the following year, Teddy Ernest retires and the partnership pays him $190,000 for his partnership interest. At the time, his capital account balance was $250,000.

**Required:**
Prepare the journal entry to record:

1. Admission of Fred Whiney.
2. Admission of Arthur Yong.
3. Withdrawal of Teddy Ernest.

# Suggested Solution

1. Because Fred Whiney is admitted by a purchase among partners, the journal entry must only reallocate the existing balances in capital accounts. The total in the capital accounts was $600,000 ($400,000 + $200,000). Equal partnership implies 1/3 of this amount for each partner, or $200,000 (= $600,000 × 1/3). Alwin's capital account balance already equals $200,000, so a portion of only Teddy's account is reallocated.

| | | |
|---|---|---|
| Teddy Ernest, Capital (−OE) | 200,000 | |
|     Fred Whiney, Capital (+OE) | | 200,000 |

2. Arthur Yong is admitted by an investment of additional assets ($280,000 cash). The journal entry must record this additional investment, and account for any bonus to the new partner or to the existing partners.

   **Step 1**  Calculate the total partnership capital after Arthur's investment.

   | | |
   |---|---|
   | Total partnership capital before contribution | $ 720,000 |
   | Arthur Yong's contribution | 280,000 |
   | Partnership capital after contribution | $1,000,000 |

   **Step 2**  Calculate the amount of Arthur's capital account.

   | | |
   |---|---|
   | Total partnership capital after contribution | $1,000,000 |
   | Arthur's ownership portion | × 25% |
   | Arthur's capital account balance | $ 250,000 |

**Step 3    Calculate the total bonus to existing partners.**

| | |
|---|---:|
| Amount contributed by Arthur | $280,000 |
| Amount of capital given to Arthur | (250,000) |
| Total bonus to existing partners | $ 30,000 |

**Step 4    Allocate the bonus to existing partners.**

| | |
|---|---:|
| Alwin's portion ($30,000 × 1/3) | $10,000 |
| Teddy's portion ($30,000 × 1/3) | 10,000 |
| Fred's portion ($30,000 × 1/3) | 10,000 |
| Total bonus to existing partners | $30,000 |

| | | |
|---|---:|---:|
| Cash (+A) | 280,000 | |
|     Alwin Ernest, Capital (+OE) | | 10,000 |
|     Teddy Ernest, Capital (+OE) | | 10,000 |
|     Fred Whiney, Capital (+OE) | | 10,000 |
|     Arthur Yong, Capital (+OE) | | 250,000 |

3.    Upon his retirement, Teddy Ernest withdraws $190,000 of partnership assets (cash). The journal entry must record this asset distribution, and account for any bonus to the exiting partner or to the remaining partners.

**Step 1    Calculate the total bonus to the remaining partners.**

| | |
|---|---:|
| Amount in Teddy Ernest's capital account | $ 250,000 |
| Amount of cash paid to Teddy Ernest | (190,000) |
| Total bonus to remaining partners | $ 60,000 |

**Step 2    Allocate the bonus to remaining partners.**

| | |
|---|---:|
| Alwin Ernest's portion ($60,000 × 1/3) | $20,000 |
| Fred Whiney's portion ($60,000 × 1/3) | 20,000 |
| Arthur Yong's portion ($60,000 × 1/3) | 20,000 |
| Total bonus to existing partners | $60,000 |

| | | |
|---|---:|---:|
| Teddy Ernest, Capital (−OE) | 250,000 | |
|     Alwin Ernest, Capital (+OE) | | 20,000 |
|     Fred Whiney, Capital (+OE) | | 20,000 |
|     Arthur Yong, Capital (+OE) | | 20,000 |
|     Cash (−A) | | 190,000 |

## Demonstration Case C
### Liquidation of Partnership

After many years of success, the partnership of Ernest, Whiney, & Yong is dissolved and liquidated. The partnership sold its assets (other than cash) to a competitor for $1,710,000, then paid its liabilities in full, and distributed the remaining cash to its three partners. The partnership reported the following book values at the time of liquidation.

| Assets | | Liabilities and Owners' Equity | |
|---|---|---|---|
| Cash | $    50,000 | Accounts payable | $    80,000 |
| Supplies | 10,000 | Alwin Ernest, Capital | 450,000 |
| Equipment | 1,800,000 | Fred Whiney, Capital | 490,000 |
| Accumulated depreciation | (400,000) | Arthur Yong, Capital | 440,000 |
| | $1,460,000 | | $1,460,000 |

*Required:*
Prepare journal entries for the partnership to record the:

1.  Sale of assets.
2.  Allocation of gain on sale. (Assume partners' fixed ratios remain at 1/3 each.)
3.  Payment of liabilities.
4.  Final cash distribution to partners.

## Suggested Solution

1.  **Sale of assets.** The partnership received $1,710,000 for assets with a total book value of $1,410,000, resulting in a gain on liquidation equal to $300,000 ($1,710,000 − $1,410,000). (The book value of assets sold includes supplies and equipment less accumulated depreciation, calculated as $10,000 + $1,800,000 − $400,000 = $1,410,000.) The journal entry to record the cash received, assets sold, and gain follows.

| | | |
|---|---|---|
| Cash (+A) | 1,710,000 | |
| Accumulated Depreciation (−xA, +A) | 400,000 | |
| Supplies (−A) | | 10,000 |
| Equipment (−A) | | 1,800,000 |
| Gain on Liquidation (+OE) | | 300,000 |

2.  **Allocation of gain.** With a 1/3 fixed ratio for each partner, the $300,000 gain is allocated as $100,000 per partner (= $300,000 × 1/3).

| | | |
|---|---|---|
| Gain on Liquidation (−OE) | 300,000 | |
| Alwin Ernest, Capital (+OE) | | 100,000 |
| Fred Whiney, Capital (+OE) | | 100,000 |
| Arthur Yong, Capital (+OE) | | 100,000 |

3.  **Payment of liabilities.** The journal entry to record payment for $80,000 of accounts payable follows.

| | | |
|---|---|---|
| Accounts Payable (−L) | 80,000 | |
| Cash (−A) | | 80,000 |

4. **Final cash distribution to partners.** The new balance in Cash, after receiving $1,710,000 (in step 1) and paying $80,000 (in step 3) is $1,680,000 (= $50,000 + $1,710,000 − $80,000). The new balances in the capital accounts (after step 2) include Alwin $550,000 (= $450,000 + $100,000), Fred $590,000 (= $490,000 + $100,000), and Arthur $540,000 (= $440,000 + $100,000), for a total of $1,680,000 (= $550,000 + $590,000 + $540,000). The journal entry to record the final cash distribution and liquidation of capital account balances follows.

| | | |
|---|---|---|
| Alwin Ernest, Capital (−OE) | 550,000 | |
| Fred Whiney, Capital (−OE) | 590,000 | |
| Arthur Yong, Capital (−OE) | 540,000 | |
| Cash (−A) | | 1,680,000 |

# Demonstration Case D
## Partner Return on Equity

Refer to Demonstration Case A. Assume partnership income is allocated using the fixed ratio method, and the partners did not make withdrawals or contributions during the year.

*Required:*
Calculate and interpret the return on equity (ROE) for the partnership as a whole and for each individual partner.

## Suggested Solution

Remember to calculate the average balance in the Capital accounts using the beginning balances (provided in Case A) and the ending balances (after taking into account the allocated partnership income determined in Case A).

$$\text{ROE formula:} \quad \frac{\text{Net income}}{[\text{Beginning capital} + \text{Ending capital}]/2}$$

$$\text{Partnership:} \quad \frac{\$600,000}{[\$500,000 + (\$500,000 + \$600,000)]/2} = 0.750 \text{ or } 75.0\%$$

$$\text{Alwin:} \quad \frac{\$200,000}{[\$200,000 + (\$200,000 + \$200,000)]/2} = 0.667 \text{ or } 66.7\%$$

$$\text{Teddy:} \quad \frac{\$400,000}{[\$300,000 + (\$300,000 + \$400,000)]/2} = 0.800 \text{ or } 80.0\%$$

Because minimal amounts of cash and other assets are needed to start an accounting firm, the amount invested in the partnership is small relative to the amount of income generated. The very high ROEs are consistent with this. The ROE for Teddy is greater than for Alwin because Teddy receives twice as much partnership income as Alwin (2/3 versus 1/3), but Teddy did not contribute twice the amount of capital ($300,000 versus $200,000).

# Chapter Summary

### LO1 Compare the partnership form of business with other forms. p. 506

- A partnership is the association of two or more persons to carry on as co-owners of a business for profit, whether or not the persons intend to form a partnership.
- Advantages of partnerships include pass-through taxation, ease of formation, simplified recordkeeping, favorable taxation, and increased ability to raise funds.
- Disadvantages of partnerships include unlimited liability, co-ownership of property, limited life, mutual agency, and partner disagreements.

- The fees and procedures for forming a limited liability company (LLC) vary among states.
- Advantages of the LLC include limited liability, ease of formation, simplified recordkeeping, favorable taxation, and flexibility of operations.
- Disadvantages of LLCs include limited life, lack of legal precedents, limited corporate characteristics—no more than two of the following four corporate characteristics: (1) owners' liability limited to business assets, (2) continuity of life, (3) centralization of management, and (4) free transferability of assets.
- An S-Corporation is a corporation with 1 to 100 shareholders that enjoys pass-through taxation of profits. The formation requirements, annual filings, and required elections are complex and time consuming.

### LO2  Demonstrate how to account for partnerships p. 509

- Partnership accounting requires a capital account for each partner, a drawing account for each partner, and an allocation of the partnership's income (or loss) to each partner based on the partnership agreement.
- Partner cash contributions are recorded at the amount of the cash contributed; noncash assets are recorded at the asset's market value. The contributing partner's capital account is credited for the net assets contributed.
- Partnership income (or loss) is allocated to the partners using one of four methods: (1) fixed-ratio method, (2) interest on partners' capital balances method, (3) salaries to partners method, or (4) salaries to partners and interest on partners' capital balances method.
- Closing entries must be made to transfer the allocated amounts of income (or loss) to each partner's capital account.
- The procedures for preparing financial statements is the same as for a proprietorship except a partnership (1) allocates net income among the partners, (2) shows a capital account on the balance sheet for each partner, and (3) replaces the owner's equity statement with the partners' capital statement.

### LO3  Demonstrate the proper treatment for changes of ownership in a partnership. p. 517

- The admission of a new partner legally requires that all existing partners agree to it and causes the dissolution of the existing partnership and the creation of a new partnership.
- A new partner can be admitted in two ways: (1) a purchase among partners or (2) the investment of additional assets by the new partner. A purchase among partners is a personal transaction between individuals resulting in a journal entry made to transfer amounts from the original partners' capital accounts to the new partner's capital account. The investment of additional assets can result in a bonus to the new partner (or a bonus to existing partners) if the additional investment is less (or more) than the value of the partnership interest received.
- The withdrawal of a partner can also be accomplished in two ways: (1) a purchase among partners or (2) the withdrawal of assets. A purchase among partners is a personal transaction between individuals resulting in a journal entry made to transfer amounts from the exiting partner's capital account to the remaining partners' capital accounts. The withdrawal of assets can result in a bonus to the exiting partner (or the remaining partners) if the withdrawal is greater (or less) than the balance in the exiting partner's capital account.

### LO4  Demonstrate the proper treatment for the liquidation of a partnership. p. 526

- The liquidation of a partnership may result from the death of a partner, the partnership's imminent bankruptcy, or mutual agreement among all partners.
- The four steps in the liquidation process that must be performed in sequence are (1) selling all assets (except cash) for cash and recognizing the resulting gain or loss, (2) allocating this gain or loss among the partners according to their fixed ratios, (3) using the cash in the partnership to pay off all partnership liabilities, (4) distributing any remaining cash according to the partners' fixed income ratios.
- The balance in the partners' capital accounts just before liquidation may have either no capital deficiency or a capital deficiency.
- If, after posting any gain or loss on the sale of the partnership assets, no capital deficiency exists in any of the partners' capital accounts, the outstanding debts of the partnership are paid. With the remaining cash, each partner receives a distribution equal to the balance in his or her capital account.
- If, after posting any gain or loss on the sale of the partnership assets, a capital deficiency exists in any of the partners' capital accounts, two possibilities exist: (1) that partner pays the deficiency or (2) that partner fails to pay the deficiency. When the partner pays the deficiency, the partnership has sufficient cash to pay the capital account balances of other partners. When the partner is unable to pay the capital deficiency, the partners who have credit balances in their capital accounts must absorb the deficit; the allocation of the deficit is based on the partners' fixed ratio.

### LO5  Calculate and interpret the partner return on equity ratio. p. 533

- The partner return on equity ratio measures the profitability and managerial performance for each individual partner in a partnership.

| Financial Analysis Tools | | |
|---|---|---|
| **Name of Measure** | **Formula** | **What It Tells You** |
| Partner Return on Equity Ratio | $\dfrac{\text{Net Income}}{\text{Average Partner Equity}}$ | • Measures a company's efficiency at generating profits from every dollar of equity invested (or retained) in the partnership.<br>• A higher ratio indicates a greater efficiency. |

## Key Terms

Articles of Organization (p. 507)
Capital Deficiency (p. 531)
Limited Liability Company (LLC) (p. 507)
Operating Agreement (p. 507)

Partner Return on Equity (p. 533)
Partners' Capital Statement (p. 516)
Partnership (p. 506)
Partnership Agreement. (p. 506)

Partnership Dissolution (p. 517)
Partnership Liquidation (p. 526)
Pass-Through Taxation (p. 507)
S-Corporation (p. 508)

See complete glossary in back of text.

## Questions

1. What is a partnership?
2. List at least two advantages and at least two disadvantages of a partnership.
3. Define unlimited liability and limited liability. Which would you prefer if you were starting a new business? Explain.
4. What is mutual agency? Is it considered an advantage or disadvantage of a partnership? Why?
5. What are the essential elements of a partnership agreement? Is this a required document? Why or why not?
6. Define limited liability company (LLC). Why is this new form of business so popular?
7. List the two documents often required to form a limited liability company (LLC). Which is always a requirement and which is often simply a recommended document?
8. What is double taxation? Which form of business is subject to double taxation?
9. List the four characteristics of a corporation used to evaluate a limited liability company (LLC). What is the maximum number of these characteristics that a limited liability company can possess without risking its status as an LLC? Explain.
10. List the three things necessary for partnership accounting.
11. What amount is used to record partner investments into the partnership?
12. List three ways that the fixed ratio for dividing partnership profits and losses can be expressed.
13. When a new partner is admitted using the purchase among partners method, who is (are) the other party(ies) to the transaction?
14. When a new partner is admitted using the investment of additional assets method and the existing partners' capital accounts are debited, do the existing partners or the new partner receive a bonus?
15. When a partner withdraws, why might the partnership give a bonus to the withdrawing partner?
16. A dissolution is the same as a liquidation. Do you agree with this statement? Why or why not?
17. What are the four steps in the liquidation process?
18. If a capital deficiency exists upon the liquidation of a partnership, what are two possible resolutions to the situation?
19. What is one thing that can cause partner ROE to increase?

## Multiple Choice

1. Which of the following is not a disadvantage of the partnership form of business?
   a. Mutual agency.
   b. Pass-through taxation.
   c. Unlimited liability.
   d. Limited life.

Quiz 12-1
www.mhhe.com/LLPW1e

2. Which of the following is a disadvantage of the limited liability company form of business?
   a. Ease of formation.
   b. Limited liability.
   c. Simplified recordkeeping.
   d. Limited corporate characteristics.

3. The limited liability company (LLC) has become a favorite entity choice of businesses meeting all of the following criteria except:
   a. The business has plans for significant growth.
   b. All members are active participants in a small local business.
   c. The business will have one to three members.
   d. All of the above.

4. To accurately keep track of income and/or loss for individual partners, which of the following is not required for partnership accounting?
   a. Provisions for the addition or withdrawal of a partner.
   b. A drawings account for each partner.
   c. A capital account for each partner.
   d. An allocation of the partnership income/loss to each partner, according to the terms of the partnership agreement.

5. Which of the following is not a true statement regarding partnership formation?
   a. The partner's capital account is credited for the amount of assets invested.
   b. Partners can invest any combination of assets and/or liabilities into the partnership.
   c. Partnership investments are recorded at the book value of the assets on the date they are transferred into the partnership.
   d. Partnerships may be formed through a handshake.

6. A partnership has four partners who share income/loss on an 8:4:3:1 ratio according to the partnership agreement. Assuming the partnership has net income of $20,000, how much will be allocated to each partner, respectively?
   a. $8,000, $4,000, $3,000, and $1,000.
   b. $10,000, $5,000, $3,750, and $1,250.
   c. $12,000, $4,000, $3,000, and $1,000.
   d. None of the above is the correct allocation of net income.

7. Joe is admitted into a partnership with Jack and Jill. Joe invests $25,000 into the partnership in exchange for a $22,000 capital account balance. This transaction is referred to as:
   a. A purchase among partners with a bonus to the new partner.
   b. A purchase among partners with a bonus to the original partners.
   c. An investment of assets into the partnership with a bonus to the new partner.
   d. An investment of assets into the partnership with a bonus to the original partners.

8. Stan withdraws from the partnership of Stan, Lee, and Brick and the partnership pays him $54,000. Assuming the balance in his capital account at that time is $50,000, which of the following is true?
   a. There is no bonus because this transaction is personal between the withdrawing partner and each individual remaining partner.
   b. A bonus of $4,000 is allocated to Stan, Lee, and Brick.
   c. A bonus of $4,000 is allocated to Lee and Brick.
   d. A bonus of $4,000 goes to Stan.

9. Which of the following is not a true statement regarding a partnership liquidation?
   a. All liabilities, debts, and/or other obligations of the partnership must be paid before the partners receive anything.
   b. The steps in the liquidation process can be performed in any sequence.
   c. Liquidation may result from the death of a partner, partnership bankruptcy, or agreement among the partners.
   d. A journal entry must be recorded for each step in the liquidation process.

10. What is the partner return on equity for Greg assuming his average partnership equity is $62,800 and his allocated net income from the partnership is $24,000?
    a. 76.4 percent.
    b. 38.2 percent.
    c. 261.7 percent.
    d. Cannot be calculated without ending capital.

| Multiple-Choice Solutions | | | | | | |
|---|---|---|---|---|---|---|
| 1. b | 2. d | 3. a | 4. a | 5. c | 6. b | 7. d |
| 8. d | 9. b | 10. b | | | | |

## Mini Exercises   Available with McGraw-Hill's Homework Manager

**LO1, 2**    **M12-1 Journalizing Partnership Formation**

Prepare the journal entry that would be made for the formation of the DL Partnership given the following information: Doe invests $10,000 cash and equipment with a book value of $7,000 (cost $9,000). Lee invests $12,000 cash and inventory with a cost of $6,000 to the partnership. Fair market values of the equipment and inventory are $6,500 and $4,500, respectively.

**LO2**    **M12-2 Dividing and Journalizing Income with Fixed Ratio**

Tram and Quyen share income and loss based on a fixed ratio of 5/8 and 3/8, respectively. Net income for the current year is $24,000. Determine the amount of net income allocated to each partner and prepare the corresponding journal entry to record the allocation.

## M12-3 Dividing of Income with Salaries, Interest, and Fixed Ratio

**LO2**

Blaine Partnership earned $20,000 this year. The partnership agreement states that income should be allocated to Romine and Roach using the salaries to partners and interest on capital balances method. Calculate the amount of Blaine's net income that will be allocated to each partner, assuming the following for each partner.

|                        | Romine   | Roach    |
|------------------------|----------|----------|
| Salary                 | $ 8,000  | $ 4,000  |
| Interest               | 10%      | 10%      |
| Fixed ratio            | 60%      | 40%      |
| Capital account balance| $15,000  | $22,000  |

## M12-4 Dividing Income When Allocation Exceeds Net Income

**LO2**

Use the same facts as in M12-3 except that Blaine Partnership earned $14,000 this year. Calculate the amount of Blaine's net income that will be allocated to each partner.

## M12-5 Journalizing the Division of Income (Various Situations)

**LO2**

Perform the following tasks:

1. Prepare the journal entry to record the division of income made in M12-3.
2. Prepare the journal entry to record the division of income made in M12-4.

## M12-6 Preparing Partners' Capital Statement

**LO2**

A. Jel and O. Tin are partners in the Jel N Tin Partnership. Using the following information, prepare a partners' capital statement on December 31, 2009.

|         | Capital 1/1/09 | Capital Contributions | Net Income (allocated) | Partner Drawings |
|---------|----------------|-----------------------|------------------------|------------------|
| A. Jel  | $39,000        | $8,000                | $14,900                | $16,400          |
| O. Tin  | 27,000         | 6,000                 | 11,200                 | 7,700            |

## M12-7 Journalizing Admission of Partner as a Purchase among Partners

**LO3**

Dot and Dash are equal partners in the DD partnership. They agree to admit Dee into the partnership. It is agreed that Dee will pay Dot and Dash $40,000 each in exchange for one-third of each partner's current capital balance. Currently, Dot and Dash each has a capital balance of $90,000. Prepare the journal entry to admit Dee as a partner.

## M12-8 Admitting a Partner by Investment with Bonus to the Existing Partners

**LO3**

Calculate the bonus to each of the existing partners with the admission of a new partner in the following situation: Juniper, Pine, and Fir are equal partners in a partnership. They agree to admit Pinion into the partnership. Pinion invests $35,000 in the partnership in exchange for a 25 percent partnership interest. The partnership agreement stipulates that bonuses be allocated on the basis of the fixed ratios prior to the admission of a new partner. The following information is available prior to the admission of Pinion.

|                  | Juniper | Pine    | Fir     |
|------------------|---------|---------|---------|
| Capital balances | $25,000 | $35,000 | $40,000 |
| Fixed ratio      | 30%     | 30%     | 40%     |

## M12-9 Admitting a Partner by Investment with Bonus to the New Partner

**LO3**

Calculate the bonus to each of the existing partners with the admission of a new partner in the following situation: Juniper, Pine, and Fir are equal partners in a partnership. They agree to admit Pinion into the partnership. Pinion invests $20,000 into the partnership in exchange for a 25 percent partnership interest. The partnership agreement stipulates that bonuses be allocated on the basis of the fixed ratios prior to the admission of a new partner. The following information is available prior to the admission of Pinion.

| | Juniper | Pine | Fir |
|---|---|---|---|
| Capital balances | $25,000 | $35,000 | $40,000 |
| Fixed ratio | 30% | 30% | 40% |

**LO3**

**M12-10 Journalizing the Admission of a Partner (Various Situations)**

Perform the following tasks:

1. Prepare the journal entry to record the admission of the partner as calculated in M12-8.
2. Prepare the journal entry to record the admission of the partner as calculated in M12-9.

**LO3**

**M12-11 Calculating Bonus to Remaining Partners upon Withdrawal of Partner (Payment from Partnership)**

Calculate the bonus allocated to each remaining partner upon the withdrawal of a partner in the following situation: Ima, Owda, and Hier are equal partners in a partnership. Owda decides to withdraw from the partnership and is very eager to leave. The partnership agrees to pay Owda $76,000 for her partnership interest. The partnership agreement requires that bonuses be allocated on the basis of the partners' fixed ratios prior to the withdrawal. The following information is available prior to Owda's withdrawal:

| | Ima | Owda | Hier |
|---|---|---|---|
| Capital balances | $96,000 | $84,000 | $108,000 |
| Fixed ratio | 25% | 20% | 55% |

**LO3**

**M12-12 Calculating Bonus to Exiting Partner upon Withdrawal of Partner (Payment from Partnership)**

Assume the same facts as in M12-11 except that the partnership agrees to pay Owda $90,400 for her partnership interest. Calculate the bonus allocated to each remaining partner.

**LO3**

**M12-13 Journalizing the Withdrawal of a Partner (Various Situations)**

Perform the following tasks:

1. Prepare the journal entry to record the withdrawal of the partner as calculated in M12-11.
2. Prepare the journal entry to record the withdrawal of the partner as calculated in M12-12.

**LO4**

**M12-14 Liquidating Partnership with No Capital Deficiency**

For the liquidation of DDT partnership, calculate the final distribution to each partner. The partnership's net assets have been sold, and the gain/loss has been recorded. Assume the following information:

| Assets | | Liabilities and Owners' Equity | |
|---|---|---|---|
| Cash | $ 57,000 | Notes payable | $ 40,000 |
| | | Doun, capital | 9,000 |
| | | Da, capital | 6,000 |
| | | Toobes, capital | 2,000 |
| | $ 57,000 | | $ 57,000 |

**LO4**

**M12-15 Liquidating Partnership with Capital Deficiency**

For the liquidation of DDT partnership, calculate the final distribution to each partner. The partnership's net assets have been sold, and the gain/loss has been recorded. Assume the following information and that Toobes does not pay the deficiency.

| Assets | | Liabilities and Owners' Equity | |
|---|---|---|---|
| Cash | $ 57,000 | Notes payable | $ 40,000 |
| | | Doun, capital (fixed ratio: 20%) | 12,000 |
| | | Da, capital (fixed ratio: 30%) | 9,000 |
| | | Toobes, capital (fixed ratio: 50%) | (4,000) |
| | $ 57,000 | | $ 57,000 |

### M12-16 Journalizing the Liquidation of a Partnership (Various Situations)          LO4

Perform the following tasks:

1. Prepare the journal entry to record the final payments to the partners of DDT partnership assuming the liquidation scenario in M12-14.
2. Prepare the journal entries to record the allocation of deficit and the final payments to the partners of DDT partnership assuming the liquidation scenario in M12-15.

### M12-17 Calculating Partnership Return on Equity          LO5

Using the information in the following table, calculate the ROE for each partner.

|        | Capital 1/1/09 | Capital Contributions | Net Income | Partner Drawings | Capital 12/31/09 |
|--------|---------------|----------------------|-----------|------------------|------------------|
| A. Jel | $39,000       | $8,000               | $14,900   | $16,400          | $45,500          |
| O. Tin | 27,000        | 6,000                | 11,200    | 7,700            | 36,500           |

## Exercises  Available with McGraw-Hill's Homework Manager

### E12-1 Identifying Advantages and Disadvantages of a Partnership          LO1

The following are characteristics of a partnership. Determine whether each characteristic is an advantage (A) or a disadvantage (B).

| Partnership Characteristic | Advantage or Disadvantage |
|----------------------------|---------------------------|
| ___ 1.  Limited life. | A.  Advantage |
| ___ 2.  Co-ownership of property. | B.  Disadvantage |
| ___ 3.  Mutual agency. | |
| ___ 4.  Ability to raise funds. | |
| ___ 5.  Partner disagreements. | |
| ___ 6.  Ease of formation. | |
| ___ 7.  Simplified recordkeeping. | |
| ___ 8.  Pass-through taxation. | |

### E12-2 Identifying Advantages and Disadvantages of a Limited Liability Company (LLC)          LO1

Following are characteristics of a limited liability company. Determine whether each characteristic is an advantage (A) or a disadvantage (B).

| Limited Liability Company Characteristic | Advantage or Disadvantage |
|------------------------------------------|---------------------------|
| ___ 1.  Limited liability. | A.  Advantage |
| ___ 2.  Limited life. | B.  Disadvantage |
| ___ 3.  Ease of formation. | |
| ___ 4.  Limited corporate characteristics. | |
| ___ 5.  Flexible profit and loss allocations. | |
| ___ 6.  Limited legal precedents. | |

### E12-3 Journalizing Partnership Formation—Cash and Noncash Contributions          LO2

Georgy Cloon and Alfred Nunley form a partnership. The book and fair market values of the contributed assets follow:

|  | BOOK VALUE | | FAIR MARKET VALUE | |
| --- | --- | --- | --- | --- |
|  | G. Cloon | A. Nunley | G. Cloon | A. Nunley |
| Cash | $11,000 | $20,000 | $11,000 | $20,000 |
| Accounts receivable |  | 36,000 |  | 34,000 |
| Allowance for doubtful accounts |  | (2,000) |  | (3,000) |
| Furniture and fixtures | 54,000 |  | 42,000 |  |
| Accumulated depreciation | (5,000) |  |  |  |
|  | $60,000 | $54,000 | $53,000 | $51,000 |

**Required:**
Based on the information presented, prepare the journal entry to record the contributions made by each partner to the partnership.

**LO2**    **E12-4 Journalizing Division of Income—Various Allocations**

Crane, Del, and Egbert are partners in the CDE partnership. Partnership net income for the current year is $70,000. Other relevant information appears in the following table.

|  | Capital Balance | Salary | Interest | Fixed Ratio |
| --- | --- | --- | --- | --- |
| Crane | $65,000 | $20,000 | 9% | 5/8 |
| Del | 82,000 | 25,000 | 9 | 2/8 |
| Egbert | 53,000 | 18,000 | 9 | 1/8 |

**Required:**
Determine the allocation of net income to each partner under each of the following three independent assumptions:

1. Fixed-ratio method.
2. Interest on partners' capital balances and any remaining amounts on a fixed ratio.
3. Salaries to partners, interest on partners' capital balances, and any remaining on a fixed ratio.

**LO2**    **E12-5 Dividing Income and Preparing Partners' Capital Statement**

L. Len, S. Squigg, and S. Shirl are partners in the Shirl Len Squigg partnership. Partnership net income for the current year is $23,652. Other relevant information appears in the following table.

|  | Capital 1/1/08 | Capital Contributions | Fixed Ratio | Partner Drawings |
| --- | --- | --- | --- | --- |
| L. Len | $4,000 | $2,500 | 1/6 | $4,650 |
| S. Squigg | 5,000 | 1,500 | 2/6 | 5,200 |
| S. Shirl | 6,000 | 3,500 | 3/6 | 5,000 |

**Required:**

1. Allocate the net income to the partners using the fixed ratio method.
2. Prepare the partners' capital statement at December 31, 2008.

**LO3**    **E12-6 Journalizing Admission of a Partner—Investment with Bonus to Existing Partners**

Click and Clack are partners in the CC partnership. They agree to admit Cluck into the partnership. Cluck invests $45,000 into the partnership in exchange for a one-third interest in the partnership. Assume any bonuses will be allocated on the basis of the fixed ratios prior to the admission of the new partner.

Additional information prior to the admission of Cluck:

|                         | Click    | Clack    |
|-------------------------|----------|----------|
| Capital account balance | $48,000  | $21,000  |
| Fixed ratio             | 70%      | 30%      |

**Required:**

1. Determine the capital account balance for each partner after the new partner is admitted.
2. Prepare the journal entry to admit the new partner.

## E12-7 Journalizing Admission of a Partner—Investment with Bonus to New Partner    LO3

Assume the same facts as in E12-6 except that Cluck invests $31,950.

**Required:**

1. Determine the capital account balance for each partner after the new partner is admitted.
2. Prepare the journal entry to admit the new partner.

## E12-8 Journalizing Withdrawal of Partner—Payment from Partnership with Bonus to Remaining Partners    LO3

Wallice, Gromett, Victer, and Warerabbit are partners in the Gromwell partnership. Warerabbit decides to withdraw from the partnership. Additional information available prior to the withdrawal follows:

|                  | Wallice   | Gromett   | Victer    | Warerabbit |
|------------------|-----------|-----------|-----------|------------|
| Capital balances | $105,000  | $122,000  | $136,000  | 140,000    |
| Fixed ratio      | 21%       | 28%       | 35%       | 14%        |

**Required:**

According to the partnership agreement, any bonuses resulting from a partner's withdrawal from the partnership should be allocated on the basis of fixed ratios prior to the withdrawal. Assuming the partnership pays Warerabbit $124,280 for his partnership interest,

1. Calculate the amount of the bonus allocated to each of the remaining partners.
2. Prepare the journal entry to record Warerabbit's withdrawal.
3. Determine the capital account balance for each remaining partner after the withdrawal.

## E12-9 Journalizing Withdrawal of Partner—Payment from Partnership with Bonus to Exiting Partner    LO3

Assume the facts in E12-8.

**Required:**

According to the partnership agreement, any bonuses resulting from a partner's withdrawal from the partnership should be allocated on the basis of fixed ratios prior to the withdrawal. Assume the partnership pays Warerabbit $146,000 for his partnership interest.

1. Calculate the amount of the bonus allocated to each of the remaining partners.
2. Prepare the journal entry to record Warerabbit's withdrawal.
3. Determine the capital account balance for each remaining partner after the withdrawal.

## E12-10 Journalizing Admission and Withdrawal of a Partner—Among Partners    LO3

Frey, Dones, and Bance are partners in the FDB partnership. Additional information available prior to the admission or withdrawal of any partners follows:

|                  | Frey     | Dones    | Bance    |
|------------------|----------|----------|----------|
| Capital balances | $10,000  | $20,000  | $30,000  |
| Fixed ratio      | 16%      | 39%      | 45%      |

*Required:*

Each of the following is an independent transaction.

1.  Prepare the journal entry to admit a new partner given the following assumptions: Amos is admitted to the partnership with a 25 percent partnership interest and agrees to pay each partner $7,000 in exchange for receiving 25 percent of the capital account balances of Frey, Dones, and Bance.

2.  Prepare the journal entry for the withdrawal of Frey assuming the following: Using the original information (i.e., assuming Amos was not admitted to the partnership), Frey decides to withdraw from the partnership. Dones and Bance agree to purchase one-half of Frey's capital account balance for $4,000 each.

**LO4**

### E12-11 Liquidating a Partnership—No Capital Deficiency

The partnership of Law Dee Daw liquidates, and the account balances before liquidation follow.

| Assets | | Liabilities and Owners' Equity | |
|---|---|---|---|
| Cash | $ 6,000 | Accounts payable | $19,000 |
| Other partnership assets (net) | 44,000 | Notes payable | 8,000 |
| | | L. Law, capital (3/5 fixed ratio) | 4,000 |
| | | D. Dee capital (1/5 fixed ratio) | 7,000 |
| | | D. Daw, capital (1/5 fixed ratio) | 12,000 |
| | $50,000 | | $50,000 |

Assume the assets of Law Dee Daw partnership (except cash) are sold for $40,000.

*Required:*

Determine the amount of cash to be distributed to the partners upon liquidation.

**LO4**

### E12-12 Liquidating a Partnership—Capital Deficiency (payment by partner)

Refer to E12-11.

Assume the same facts except that the assets of Law Dee Daw partnership (except cash) are sold for $28,000.

*Required:*

Determine the amount of cash to be distributed to the remaining partners upon liquidation. Assume any capital deficiencies are paid to the partnership.

**LO4**

### E12-13 Liquidating a Partnership—Capital Deficiency (nonpayment by partner)

Refer to E12-11.

Assume the same facts except that the assets of Law Dee Daw partnership (except cash) are sold for $28,000.

*Required:*

Determine the amount of cash to be distributed to the remaining partners upon liquidation. Assume any capital deficiencies are not paid but rather are absorbed by other partners.

**LO5**

### E12-14 Calculating Partnership Return on Equity

Assume the following information for the partnership of Domee and Gleegal.

| | Capital 1/1/08 | Capital Contributions | Net Income | Partner Drawings |
|---|---|---|---|---|
| Domee | $28,000 | $ 5,000 | $16,500 | $10,500 |
| Gleegal | 32,000 | 7,000 | 9,400 | 12,000 |
| Total | $60,000 | $12,000 | $25,900 | $22,500 |

*Required:*

1.  Calculate the ending capital balance for each partner.
2.  Calculate the return on equity (ROE) for each partner.
3.  Explain the primary cause of any differences in the partners' ROE.

# Problems—Set A     Available with McGraw-Hill's Homework Manager

## PA12-1 Identifying Characteristics of Partnerships and Limited Liability Companies (LLCs)    LO1

Following are various characteristics of partnerships and LLCs discussed in the chapter. For each characteristic, indicate the form(s) of business, partnership (A) or limited liability company (B), the characteristic describes. Some characteristics may describe more than one form of business.

| Characteristic | Form of Business |
|---|---|
| ___ 1. Ability to raise funds | A. Partnership |
| ___ 2. Ease of formation | B. Limited Liability Company (LLC) |
| ___ 3. Favorable tax treatment | |
| ___ 4. Few legal precedents | |
| ___ 5. Flexible profit/loss allocations | |
| ___ 6. Limited corporate characteristics | |
| ___ 7. Limited liabilities | |
| ___ 8. Limited life | |
| ___ 9. Pass-through taxation | |
| ___ 10. Simplified recordedkeeping | |
| ___ 11. Unlimited liability | |

## PA12-2 Forming a Partnership—Cash and Noncash Contributions, Making Journal Entries, and Creating Owners' Equity Section of the Balance Sheet    LO2

M. Arsee, P. Ann, and G. Tsosi form the MAT partnership on January 8, 2009. The book and fair market values of the contributed assets follow.

| | BOOK VALUE | | | FAIR MARKET VALUE | | |
|---|---|---|---|---|---|---|
| | M. Arsee | P. Ann | G. Tsosi | M. Arsee | P. Ann | G. Tsosi |
| Cash | $ 9,000 | $ 6,000 | $17,000 | $ 9,000 | $ 6,000 | $17,000 |
| Accounts receivable | | | 19,000 | | | 18,000 |
| Allowance for doubtful accounts | | | (900) | | | (1,000) |
| Inventory | 26,000 | | | 25,000 | | |
| Furniture and fixtures | | 45,000 | | | 35,000 | |
| Accumulated depreciation | | (8,000) | | | | |
| Notes payable | | (7,000) | | | (7,000) | |
| Net assets contributed | $35,000 | $36,000 | $35,100 | $34,000 | $34,000 | $34,000 |

### Required:

1. Based on the information presented, prepare the journal entry to record the contributions each partner made to the partnership.
2. Prepare the Liabilities and Owners' Equity section of the partnership balance sheet immediately following the partner contributions on January 8, 2009.

## PA12-3 Dividing Income—All Four Methods    LO2

Mills and Cross are partners in the MC partnership. Partnership net income for the current year is $52,200. Other relevant information follows.

www.mhhe.com/LLPW1e

| | Capital Balances | Salaries | Interest | Fixed Ratio |
|---|---|---|---|---|
| Mills | $18,000 | $21,000 | 7% | 3/4 |
| Cross | 32,000 | 30,000 | 7 | 1/4 |

*Required:*

Determine the allocation of net income to each of the partners under each of the following four independent assumptions:

1. Fixed ratio.
2. Interest on partners' capital balances and any remaining amounts on a fixed ratio.
3. Salaries to partners and any remaining amounts on a fixed ratio.
4. Salaries to partners, interest on partners' capital balances, and any remaining amounts on a fixed ratio.

**LO2**

**PA12-4 Dividing Income, Journalizing, and Preparing Partners' Capital Statement**

A. Batt, B. Robbin, and F. Catt are partners in the Batt R Catt partnership. Partnership net income for 2009 is $46,000. Other relevant information follows:

|  | Capital 1/1/09 | Capital Contributions | Fixed Ratio | Partner Drawings |
|---|---|---|---|---|
| A. Batt | $ 7,000 | $4,400 | 25% | $4,000 |
| B. Robbin | 12,000 | 3,300 | 30 | 7,000 |
| F. Catt | 15,000 | 2,200 | 45 | 6,000 |

*Required:*

1. Allocate the net income to the partners based on fixed ratios.
2. Prepare the partners' capital statement at December 31, 2009.

**LO3**

www.mhhe.com/LLPW1e

**PA12-5 Admitting a Partner—Journalizing Purchase and Investment Situations**

Dick and Jane are partners in the DJ partnership. They agree to admit Spot into the partnership. According to the partnership agreement, any bonuses will be allocated on the basis of the fixed ratio prior to the admission of the new partner. Additional information available prior to Spot's admission follows.

|  | Dick | Jane |
|---|---|---|
| Capital account balance | $61,000 | $57,000 |
| Fixed ratio | 58% | 42% |

*Required:*

Prepare journal entries to record the admission of Spot, under each of the following independent assumptions.

1. Spot pays Dick and Jane $19,000 each. In exchange he receives 30 percent of each partner's capital account balance.
2. Spot invests $25,000 into the partnership in exchange for a 25 percent interest in the partnership.
3. Spot invests $62,000 into the partnership in exchange for a 30 percent interest in the partnership.

**LO2**

**PA12-6 Journalizing Partner Withdrawals**

Carrtman, Kennie, and Kile are partners in the Southe Parke partnership. Kennie's death required his withdrawal from the partnership. According to the partnership agreement, any bonuses will be allocated on the basis of fixed ratios prior to the withdrawal. Additional information available prior to the withdrawal follows.

|  | Carrtman | Kennie | Kile |
|---|---|---|---|
| Capital account balance | $54,000 | $64,000 | $42,000 |
| Fixed ratio | 42% | 30% | 28% |

*Required:*

Prepare journal entries to record the withdrawal of Kennie, under each of the following independent assumptions.

1. Carrtman and Kile agree to purchase ½ of Kennie's capital account balance for $40,000 each.
2. The partnership pays Kennie's estate $80,000 for his partnership interest.
3. The partnership pays Kennie's estate $59,000 for his partnership interest.

## PA12-7 Liquidating a Partnership with No Capital Deficiency and Making Journal Entries

LO4

www.mhhe.com/LLPW1e

Assume when the partnership of Shasta, Sheba, Sheeva liquidates, account balances before liquidation are as follows.

| Assets | | Liabilities and Owners' Equity | |
|---|---|---|---|
| Cash | $ 4,000 | Accounts payable | $ 3,000 |
| Inventory | 8,000 | Notes payable | 8,000 |
| Furniture and fixtures | 16,000 | Shasta, capital (35% fixed ratio) | 2,000 |
| Accumulated depreciation | (4,000) | Sheba capital (13% fixed ratio) | 5,000 |
| | | Sheeva, capital (52% fixed ratio) | 6,000 |
| | $24,000 | | $24,000 |

*Required:*
Assume the Shasta, Sheba, and Sheeva partnership sold its assets (except cash) for $18,000. Record the following entries:

1. Sale of the partnership assets (except cash).
2. Allocation of gain or loss to each of the partners.
3. Payment of outstanding partnership liabilities.
4. Distribution of remaining cash to partners.

## PA12-8 Liquidating a Partnership with Capital Deficiency (payment and nonpayment by partner) and Making Journal Entries

LO4

Assume the same facts as in PA12-7.

*Required:*
Assume the Shasta, Sheba, and Sheeva partnership sold its assets (except cash) for $12,000. Record the following entries:

1. Sale of the partnership assets (except cash).
2. Allocation of gain or loss to each of the partners.
3. Payment of outstanding liabilities of partnership.
4. Distribution of remaining cash to partners assuming Shasta pays the deficiency.
5. Distribution of remaining cash to partners assuming Shasta does not pay the deficiency.

## PA12-9 Calculating Partner Return on Equity (ROE)

LO5

Gren, Bare, and Rett are partners in the GBR partnership. Information related to the partners follows.

| | Total | Gren | Bare | Rett |
|---|---|---|---|---|
| Balance 1/1/2008 | $71,000 | $20,000 | $30,000 | $21,000 |
| Contributions | 20,000 | 10,000 | 5,000 | 5,000 |
| Net Income | 33,000 | 11,000 | 11,000 | 11,000 |
| Drawings | (30,000) | (2,000) | (20,000) | (8,000) |
| Balance 12/31/2008 | $94,000 | $39,000 | $26,000 | $29,000 |

*Required:*

1. Calculate the partnership ROE.
2. Calculate the ROE for each partner.
3. Which partner has the best ROE? Why?

# Problems—Set B     Available with McGraw-Hill's Homework Manager

### PB12-1 Matching Terminology with Definitions

**LO1**   Following are the terms and definitions covered in Chapter 12. Match each term with its definition by entering the appropriate letter in the space provided. Use one letter for each blank.

| Terms | Definitions |
|---|---|
| ___  1.  Mutual agency | A.  Lack of sufficient capital in a partner's capital account to absorb losses resulting from the liquidation of a partnership. |
| ___  2.  Partners' capital statement | B.  Document recommended when an LLC is formed to address potential problem areas in the LLC. |
| ___  3.  Capital deficiency | C.  Association of two or more persons to carry on as co-owners of a business for profit. |
| ___  4.  Partnership agreement | D.  Allows profits from a business to flow directly to the owners avoiding taxation at the business level. |
| ___  5.  S-corporation | E.  Document recommended when a partnership is formed to address potential problem areas in the partnership. |
| ___  6.  Partner return on equity | F.  Business form that offers its members limited liability protection and pass-through taxation. |
| ___  7.  Partnership dissolution | G.  Process of selling assets of the partnership, paying liabilities and distributing remaining cash to the partners. |
| ___  8.  Articles of organization | H.  Sufficient capital in a partner's capital account to absorb losses resulting from the liquidation of a partnership. |
| ___  9.  Partnership | I.  Shows all changes to capital for each partner in a partnership and replaces the owner's equity statement. |
| ___  10.  Operating agreement | J.  Occurs when a partner voluntarily or involuntarily leaves a partnership. |
| ___  11.  Partnership liquidation | K.  Corporation that allows profits to pass to the owners' personal income tax returns and provides owners limited liability. |
| ___  12.  Pass-through taxation | L.  Partnership characteristic that holds each partner accountable for the actions of all partners in the partnership. |
| ___  13.  Limited liability company | M.  Document required in states to form an LLC; provides important information about its operations and structure. |
| ___  14.  No capital deficiency | N.  Measures a company's efficiency in generating profits from every dollar of equity invested or retained by partners. |

**LO2**   ### PB12-2 Forming a Partnership—Cash and Noncash Contributions, Making Journal Entries, and Creating Owners' Equity Section of the Balance Sheet

R. Tex, T. Ark, and L. Ana form the TexArkAna partnership on November 16, 2009. The book and fair market values of the contributed assets follow.

| | BOOK VALUE | | | FAIR MARKET VALUE | | |
|---|---|---|---|---|---|---|
| | R. Tex | T. Ark | L. Ana | R. Tex | T. Ark | L. Ana |
| Cash | $ 13,500 | $ 9,000 | $25,500 | $13,500 | $ 9,000 | $25,500 |
| Accounts receivable | | | 28,500 | | | 27,000 |
| Allowance for doubtful accounts | | | (1,350) | | | (1,500) |
| Inventory | 39,000 | | | 37,500 | | |
| Furniture and fixtures | | 67,500 | | | 52,500 | |
| Accumulated depreciation | | (12,000) | | | | |
| Notes payable | | (10,500) | | | (10,500) | |
| Net assets contributed | $ 52,500 | $54,000 | $52,650 | $51,000 | $51,000 | $51,000 |

**Required:**

1. Based on the information presented, prepare the journal entry to record the contributions each partner made to the partnership.
2. Prepare the Liabilities and Owners' Equity section of the partnership balance sheet immediately following the partner contributions on November 16, 2009.

## PB12-3 Dividing Income—All Four Methods                                      LO2

Toffee and Bonnie are partners in the Toffnie partnership. Partnership net income for the current year is $81,000. Other relevant information follows.

| | Capital Balances | Salaries | Interest | Fixed Ratio |
|---|---|---|---|---|
| Toffee | $27,000 | $31,500 | 10% | 1/3 |
| Bonnie | 48,000 | 45,000 | 10 | 2/3 |

**Required:**
Determine the allocation of net income to each of the partners under each of the following four independent assumptions:

1. Fixed Ratio.
2. Interest on partners' capital balances and any remaining amounts on a fixed ratio.
3. Salaries to partners and any remaining amounts on a fixed ratio.
4. Salaries to partners, interest on partners' capital balances and any remaining amounts on a fixed ratio.

## PB12-4 Dividing Income, Journalizing, and Preparing Partners' Capital Statement            LO2

C. Crow, R. Beare, and K. Marin are partners in the CRM partnership. Partnership net income for 2009 is $59,000. Other relevant information follows.

| | Capital 1/1/09 | Capital Contributions | Fixed Ratio | Partner Drawings |
|---|---|---|---|---|
| C. Crow | $10,500 | $6,000 | 32% | $ 8,000 |
| R. Beare | 18,000 | 4,500 | 17 | 7,000 |
| K. Marin | 22,500 | 3,000 | 51 | 10,000 |

**Required:**

1. Allocate the net income to the partners based on the fixed ratio.
2. Prepare the partners' capital statement at December 31, 2009.

**LO3**

**PB12-5 Admitting a Partner—Journalizing Purchase and Investment Situations**

Dott and Latta are partners in the DL partnership. They agree to admit Caspar into the partnership. Assume any bonuses will be allocated on the basis of the fixed ratio prior to the admission of the new partner. Additional information available prior to Caspar's admission follows.

|  | Dott | Latta |
|---|---|---|
| Capital account balance | $ 91,500 | $ 85,500 |
| Fixed ratio | 60% | 40% |

*Required:*

Prepare journal entries to record the admission of Caspar, under each of the following independent assumptions.

1. Caspar pays Dott and Latta $28,500 each. In exchange he receives 25% of each partner's capital account balance.
2. Caspar invests $40,000 into the partnership in exchange for a 20% interest in the partnership.
3. Caspar invests $90,000 into the partnership in exchange for a 30% interest in the partnership.

**LO3**

**PB12-6 Journalizing Partner Withdrawals**

Pinkey, Brainne, and Snobal are partners in the Take Over partnership. Snobal decides to withdraw from the partnership. According to the partnership agreement, any bonuses will be allocated on the basis of fixed ratios prior to the withdrawal. Additional information available prior to the withdrawal follows.

|  | Pinkey | Brainne | Snobal |
|---|---|---|---|
| Capital account balance | $40,500 | $48,000 | $31,500 |
| Fixed ratio | 35% | 45% | 20% |

*Required:*

Prepare journal entries to record the withdrawal of Snobal, under each of the following independent assumptions.

1. Pinkey and Brainne agree to purchase 50 percent of Snobal's capital account balance for $17,000 each.
2. The partnership pays Snobal $29,500 for his partnership interest.
3. The partnership pays Snobal $35,100 for his partnership interest.

**LO4**

**PB12-7 Liquidating a Partnership with No Capital Deficiency and Making Journal Entries**

Assume when the partnership of Flour, Rice, and Salt liquidates, account balances before liquidation are as follows.

| Assets | | Liabilities and Owners' Equity | |
|---|---|---|---|
| Cash | $ 16,000 | Accounts payable | $ 12,000 |
| Inventory | 32,000 | Notes payable | 48,000 |
| Furniture and fixtures | 64,000 | Flour, capital (30% fixed ratio) | 5,000 |
| Accumulated depreciation | (12,000) | Rice, capital (15% fixed ratio) | 15,000 |
| | | Salt, capital (55% fixed ratio) | 20,000 |
| | $100,000 | | $100,000 |

*Required:*

Assume the Flour, Rice, and Salt partnership sold its assets (except cash) for $80,000. Record the following entries:

1. Sale of the partnership assets (except cash).
2. Allocation of gain or loss to each of the partners.
3. Payment of outstanding partnership liabilities.
4. Distribution of remaining cash to partners.

## PB12-8 Liquidating a Partnership with Capital Deficiency (Payment and Nonpayment by Partner) and Making Journal Entries

LO4

Assume the same facts as in PB12-7, except that the fixed ratios for Flour, Rice, and Salt are 25%, 30%, and 45%, respectively.

**Required:**

Assume the assets of Flour, Rice, and Salt partnership sold all assets (except cash) for $60,000. Record the following entries:

1. Sale of the partnership assets (except cash).
2. Allocation of gain or loss to each of the partners.
3. Payment of outstanding liabilities of partnership
4. Distribution of remaining cash to partners assuming Flour pays the deficiency.
5. Distribution of the remaining cash to partners assuming Flour does not pay the deficiency.

## PB12-9 Calculating Partner Return on Equity (ROE)

LO5

Preppen, Somme, and Allison are partners in the PSA partnership. Information related to the partners follows.

|                   | Total    | Preppen  | Somme    | Allison  |
|-------------------|----------|----------|----------|----------|
| Balance 1/1/2008  | $40,000  | $5,000   | $10,000  | $25,000  |
| Contributions     | 6,000    | 2,000    | 2,000    | 2,000    |
| Net income        | 25,000   | 8,000    | 10,000   | 7,000    |
| Drawings          | (18,000) | (6,000)  | (9,000)  | (3,000)  |
| Balance 12/31/2008| $53,000  | $9,000   | $13,000  | $31,000  |

**Required:**

1. Calculate the partnership ROE.
2. Calculate the ROE for each partner.
3. Which partner has the best ROE? Why?

# Cases and Projects

## CP12-1 Making Key Partnership Decisions

LO1, 2

Harrison and Daniel are two brothers who have been developing video games for several years as a hobby. Their games have proven to be very popular, so they recently decided to turn their hobby into a business venture. Harrison—the older and more responsible brother—has accumulated $30,000 to contribute to the business to get it started. Daniel, on the other hand, has relatively little capital to contribute ($3,000), but he has tremendous creativity and energy. After the business is established, Harrison is likely to work 20 hours per week developing games for the business and Daniel will work 40 hours per week. The brothers get along well, and do not anticipate any problems working together, however their oldest brother Tiger claims that eventually relationships change so they should plan for that possibility. Tiger claims that someday he might even be interested in joining them in running the business, or helping their kids to take over the business. Harrison and Daniel do not want to invest a lot of time or energy establishing the new business, so they have come to you for advice.

**Required:**

1. Should Harrison and Daniel form a partnership or limited liability company? List the differences between these two forms of business and then make a recommendation based on the facts you know about Harrison and Daniel.
2. Assume Harrison and Daniel decide to form a partnership. Explain the elements they should include in the partnership agreement. Provide specific advice for the division of profits and losses, taking into account the different contributions of capital and time that they plan to make.

## CP12-2 Resolving Inequitable Partnership Contributions

LO2

Last year, Mick and Sayesha entered into a partnership to establish and run a local music promotions business called MuSick Promos (MSP). Both partners contributed $2,000 to the business to get MSP off the ground. They had verbally agreed to contribute their own special talents to MSP in approximately equal proportions. Mick was in his final year as a marketing major at a local university and Sayesha was a struggling musician who had many contacts in the local music scene. For that first year, Sayesha worked about 20 hours a week finding bands to represent and promoting to clubs and other venues in the city. Mick spent an equal amount of time building relationships with local clubs that would hire bands to play at weekend events. Both Mick and Sayesha succeeded in their efforts. Mick had found about 15 clubs that regularly hired the artists promoted by MSP, and Sayesha had signed an equal number of bands to represent.

As MSP entered its second year of operations, Mick and Sayesha started having problems. Sayesha complained that now that Mick had graduated and taken a full-time sales job with a newspaper company, he spent only a few hours a week on MSP business, yet she still spent about 15 hours a week drumming up bands to represent. Mick responded by explaining that his hard work during the first year had led to long-lasting relationships with the clubs, so he had little to do except occasionally keep in touch with the clubs' managers. In contrast, the bands signed by Sayesha frequently broke up or moved to other cities as their popularity fell or grew. Mick tried to further justify his situation by saying that his new job allowed him to leave his share of MSP's profits in the business. In contrast, he complained, Sayesha had withdrawn most of her share to pay her rent and other living costs. Mick said this imbalance in capital account balances caused differences in the partners' return on equity ratios, which were unfair to him.

***Required:***

1. Evaluate the validity of each argument expressed by Mick and Sayesha. Are these arguments reasonable and equally valid? With whom would you side if you were asked to reconcile their situation?

2. Could the conflict have been avoided? How? Can something be done now to improve the partners' future relations?

**LO5**

### CP12-3 Making Ethical Decisions: A Mini-Case

Frank was recently hired as an accountant for the TMM Partnership. When the partnership published its quarterly figures, Frank noticed the return on equity figures seemed odd. After asking a few co-workers, he found that the figures were artificially and intentionally inflated each quarter. This type of reporting seemed to be a recurring event that co-workers questioned but accepted because they resulted in higher bonuses and "nobody" was hurt by it. The published results became a water cooler topic that Frank's co-workers were laughing about all the way to the bank. Frank saw the funding that the partnership was receiving based on the figures and realized that it was providing him and his co-workers with a great deal of job security. Frank thought, Who is it hurting anyway? Why should I put all of these benefits in jeopardy by saying something? With this reasoning, Frank decided to do nothing.

***Required:***

1. Describe the ethical dilemma that Frank faces.
2. Who benefits and who is harmed by reporting inflated ROE figures?
3. Do you think Frank handled the situation correctly? Would you have handled it differently?

**LO1**

### CP12-4 Forming a Partnership or Limited Liability Company

Assume you are considering forming a general partnership or a limited liability company (LLC) in your state. Search the Internet for the required documents and forms needed to establish such business forms in your state. A good starting place for this search is the Web site smallbusiness.findlaw.com.

***Required:***

1. Prepare a checklist of key steps to follow when starting a partnership.
2. Locate and provide copies of any forms that must be filed to form a limited liability company (LLC).

# 13 Accounting for Corporations

## LEARNING OBJECTIVES

**After completing this chapter, you should be able to:**

**LO1** Describe the characteristics of corporations.

Lectured presentations—13-1
www.mhhe.com/LLPW1e

**LO2** Demonstrate how to account for transactions involving common stock, preferred stock, and treasury stock.

**LO3** Demonstrate how to account for cash dividends, stock dividends, and stock splits.

**LO4** Analyze the earnings per share (EPS) and price/earnings (P/E) ratios.

News about shares of stock is everywhere. You can read it in the *Wall Street Journal,* listen to it on MSNBC, or search for it at Yahoo!Finance. Behind this fascination with stock is a dream many people share: taking a small amount of money and turning it into a fortune.

That is what Sonic Corp.—America's largest drive-in restaurant chain—has managed to do. When Sonic first started operations as a hamburger and root beer stand about 35 years ago, the company was selling 100 shares of stock to store owners for $100. As the company grew larger and more profitable, the value of its stock increased. By 1995, Sonic was selling 100 shares to investors for $2,125. Since then, those shares have split five times, causing 100 shares to multiply into 760 shares. Sonic is now buying back its stock at over $19 a share. That is more than $14,400 for the 100 shares bought in 1995, or an increase of nearly 700 percent in little more than a decade!

In this chapter, you will see how companies such as Sonic Corp. account for various stock transactions, including stock issues, stock splits, and stock dividends. Soon you'll understand many of the stock terms used in the financial news.

| CHARACTERISTICS OF THE CORPORATE FORM | ACCOUNTING FOR STOCK TRANSACTIONS | ACCOUNTING FOR DIVIDENDS AND SPLITS | FINANCIAL RATIO ANALYSIS |
|---|---|---|---|
| • Ownership<br>• Laws and Taxes<br>• Formation<br>• Financing | • Common and Preferred Stock<br>• Treasury Stock<br>• Financial Statement Reporting | • Cash Dividends on Common Stock<br>• Cash Dividends on Preferred Stock<br>• Stock Dividends<br>• Stock Splits<br>• Statement of Retained Earnings | • Earnings per Share (EPS)<br>• Price/Earnings (P/E) Ratio |

# CHARACTERISTICS OF THE CORPORATE FORM

**Learning Objective 1**

Describe the characteristics of corporations.

Video 13-1
www.mhhe.com/LLPW1e

If you were to write down the names of 50 familiar businesses, probably all of them would be corporations. According to Bizstats.com, corporations account for 85 percent of the total sales reported by U.S. businesses. Furthermore, many people own shares in corporations, either directly or indirectly, through a mutual fund or pension program. You probably recall from Chapter 1 that the act of creating a corporation is costly. Why, then, is the corporate form so popular?

## Ownership

The secret to the popularity of the corporate form is that investors both large and small can easily participate in a corporation's ownership. This widespread participation gives corporations one critical advantage over sole proprietorships and partnerships: They can raise large amounts of money. Several factors encourage investors to participate in corporate ownership:

1. **Shares of stock can be purchased in small amounts.** According to Yahoo!Finance, on January 21, 2008, you could have become one of Sonic Corp.'s owners by buying a single share of the company's stock for just $19. Owners of corporations are called stockholders or shareholders.

2. **Ownership interests are transferable.** Shares of a company's stock can be bought and sold, allowing new investors to become owners and existing owners to leave the business. If a corporation is a public company, any member of the public can buy or sell the company's shares through a stock market, such as the New York Stock Exchange. Sonic is a public company, but not all corporations are public companies. Chick-fil-A and Cargill, for example, are private companies whose shares are bought and sold privately.

3. **Stockholders are not liable for the corporation's debts.** Creditors have no legal claim on stockholders' personal assets as they do on the personal assets of those who own sole proprietorships and partnerships. So, if you owned stock in the old Montgomery Ward department store, which went bankrupt and was liquidated in 2000, you could lose only what you paid to buy the stock. You would not be liable for the hundreds of millions of dollars of debt that the company could not pay back.

## Laws and Taxes

The law recognizes a corporation as a separate legal entity. It may own assets, incur liabilities, expand and contract in size, sue others and be sued, and enter into contracts independently of its owners. Because a corporation exists separate and apart from its owners, it does not die when its owners die. Thomas Edison died in 1931, but the company he founded—General Electric—continues in existence today.

As a separate legal entity, a corporation is obligated to pay taxes on the net income it generates. This obligation is reported on the balance sheet as the current liability Income Taxes

Payable. Because income taxes are a necessary cost of being a corporation, they are reported as an expense on the income statement.

## Formation

To protect everyone's rights, the law tightly regulates the creation and oversight of corporations. Owners create corporations by submitting an application to a state government (not the federal government). Because laws vary from state to state, you might decide to create a corporation in a state that differs from the one(s) where it operates. Although Sonic has its headquarters in Oklahoma City, it was actually incorporated in Delaware. More than half of the largest corporations in the United States are incorporated in Delaware because it has some of the most favorable laws for establishing corporations. If the application is approved, the state issues a charter, which specifies the corporation's name and address, the nature of its business, and the type and number of shares that the corporation can issue.

The type and number of shares can vary greatly from one corporation to the next. In its most basic form, a corporation must have one type of share, appropriately called **common stock**. Owners of common stock usually enjoy the following benefits:

- **Voting rights.** For each share you own, you get one vote on major issues, such as which accounting firm will audit the company's books and who will serve on the board of directors. As Exhibit 13.1 illustrates, the board of directors appoints the corporation's executive officers and governs top management.
- **Dividends.** Dividends can be declared as a way of distributing the corporation's profits to its stockholders.
- **Residual claim.** If a corporation ceases to operate, stockholders share in any remaining assets after the company has paid all of its debts.
- **Preemptive rights.** Existing stockholders may be given the first chance to buy newly issued stock before it is offered to others.

In addition to common stock, corporations can issue **preferred stock** to a select group of investors. This special form of stock differs from common stock, typically in the following ways:

1. **Preferred stock generally does not include voting rights.** As a result, preferred stock does not appeal to investors who want some control over a company's operations. However, it does appeal to existing common stockholders because the company can sell preferred stock to raise funds without reducing common stockholders' voting control.

**Exhibit 13.1** Typical Organizational Structure of a Corporation

2. **Dividends on preferred stock, if any, are paid at a fixed rate,** specified as either a dollar amount or a percentage per share. For example, if dividends are declared on "6 percent preferred stock," the dividend will equal 6 percent of the stock's par value. A fixed dividend can be attractive to certain investors, such as retirees or company founders, who seek a stable income from their investments.

3. **Preferred stock carries priority over common stock.** Preferred stockholders have higher priority than common stockholders if a corporation distributes assets to its owners through dividends or at liquidation. That is, any dividends the corporation declares must be paid to preferred stockholders before they can be paid to common stockholders. Also, if the corporation goes out of business, its assets will be sold and used to pay creditors and then preferred stockholders. Common stockholders are paid last from whatever assets remain after paying preferred stockholders.

## Financing

Whenever a corporation needs a large amount of long-term financing, its executives must decide whether to obtain it by issuing new stock to investors (equity financing) or by borrowing money from lenders (debt financing). Both these forms of financing have certain advantages as listed in Exhibit 13.2.

| Exhibit 13.2 | Advantages of Equity versus Debt Financing |
|---|---|
| **Advantages of Equity Financing** | **Advantages of Debt Financing** |
| 1. Equity does not have to be repaid. Debt must be repaid or refinanced. | 1. Interest on debt is tax deductible. Dividends on stock are not tax deductible. |
| 2. Dividends are optional. Interest must be paid on debt. | 2. Debt does not change stockholder control. In contrast, a stock issue gives new stockholders the right to vote and share in the earnings, diluting existing stockholders' control. |

These relative advantages play a significant role in determining whether equity or debt financing is more appropriate for a particular corporation. One corporation's officers might be concerned primarily with the impact of financing on corporate income taxes. Thus, they might decide to rely on debt financing because interest payments are tax deductible. Another corporation's executives might be so concerned about the company's ability to pay off existing liabilities that they decide not to take on additional debt. By using equity financing, which does not need to be repaid, they can obtain the financing the company needs. Ultimately, the decision to pursue additional equity or debt financing depends on a company's circumstances.

## ACCOUNTING FOR STOCK TRANSACTIONS

We should mention at the outset that **all transactions between a corporation and its stockholders affect only balance sheet accounts.** In addition, you should be pleased to know that nearly everything you learned about accounting for sole proprietorships applies to corporations as well. The main differences involve owner's equity.

See Exhibit 13.3 for a summary of how accounting for corporations differs from accounting for sole proprietorships. One difference is that corporations replace the label owner's equity with stockholders' equity to indicate that stockholders own the business. Another difference is that unlike sole proprietorships, which use just one capital account to accumulate all of the owner's investments and withdrawals and the company's net income, corporations use at least two types of capital account. Contributions that are made directly to the corporation by stockholders are referred to as Contributed Capital. The net income that the corporation generates each year through profitable operations is accumulated in a separate account,

**Exhibit 13.3**   Accounting Differences for Sole Proprietorships and Corporations

| Sole Proprietorships | | | | | | | |
|---|---|---|---|---|---|---|---|
| **Owner's Equity** | | | | | | | |
| Joe Smith, Capital | = | Contributions | + | Net Income | − | Withdrawals | |
| **Corporations** | | | | | | | |
| **Stockholders' Equity** | | | | | | | |
| Contributed Capital | = | Contributions | | | | | |
| Retained Earnings | = | | | Net Income | − | Dividends | |

**Retained Earnings.** Unlike a sole proprietor, who may take money out of the business in the form of withdrawals, stockholders must rely on dividends. Dividends are subtracted from Retained Earnings as shown in Exhibit 13.3.

In the following section, we look more closely at transactions that affect Contributed Capital. Those transactions include issues of common stock and preferred stock and the repurchase of shares in the form of treasury stock.

# Common and Preferred Stock

## Stock Authorization

The corporate charter authorizes and defines the specific rights and characteristics of a corporation's stock. This authorization does not directly affect the accounting records, but it does establish certain characteristics that will later affect how to account for the stock.

One characteristic of importance is the stock's **par value**. Oddly enough, par value has little meaning today. It was originally introduced to prevent stockholders from removing their contributed capital after discovering that the business was going bankrupt. Today, stronger laws and regulations prevent that from happening, so the concept of par value is no longer critical to this aspect of the business.

Many states still require corporations to specify a par value for their stock. Typically, they set par value at a minimal amount, such as $0.01 per share, as Sonic did with its common stock. Other states have dropped the requirement to specify a par value and instead allow corporations to issue no-par value stock. **No-par value stock** is just like stock with par value except that it does not have a specified legal value per share. Although par value is a legal concept that is not related in any way to the share's market value, it does affect how to account for stock as you will see in the next section.

## Stock Issues

**Par Value Common Stock Issued for Cash.** The sale of stock from the corporation to an investor is called a stock issue. In most cases, these sales are cash transactions. To see how to account for an issue of par value stock, assume that during the next fiscal year, Sonic receives cash for 100,000 shares of its $0.01 par value common stock issued when the market price is $30 per share. This stock issue would be accounted for as follows:

**Coach's Tip**

For corporations, use the abbreviation SE (rather than OE) for accounts related to stockholders' equity.

| | Debit | Credit |
|---|---|---|
| Cash (+A) (100,000 × $30) | 3,000,000 | |
| Common Stock (+SE) (100,000 × $0.01) | | 1,000 |
| Additional Paid-In Capital (+SE) ($3,000,000 − $1,000) | | 2,999,000 |

| Assets | = | Liabilities | + | Stockholders' Equity | |
|---|---|---|---|---|---|
| Cash   +3,000,000 | | | | Common Stock | +1,000 |
| | | | | Additional Paid-In Capital | +2,999,000 |

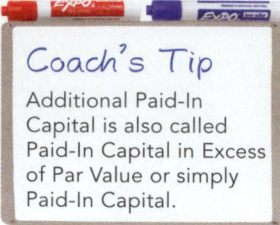

Notice that the account Common Stock is used to indicate the type of stock issued. The increase in the Common Stock account is the number of shares sold times the par value per share (100,000 × $0.01). Any amount received in excess of the par value is recorded in a separate account appropriately named Additional Paid-In Capital. These two accounts are reported in the Stockholders' Equity section of the balance sheet; together, they represent Contributed Capital.

**No-Par Value Common Stock Issued for Cash.** If the corporate charter does not specify a par value for the stock, the total cash received from the sale of stock is entered in the Common Stock account. For example, if 100,000 shares of no-par common stock were issued for $30 per share, the journal entry would be:

|  | Debit | Credit |
|---|---|---|
| Cash (+A) (100,000 × $30) | 3,000,000 | |
|    Common Stock (+SE) (100,000 × $30) | | 3,000,000 |

| Assets | = | Liabilities | + | Stockholders' Equity |
|---|---|---|---|---|
| Cash    +3,000,000 | | | | Common Stock +3,000,000 |

**Common Stock Issued for Noncash Assets.** In some cases, a corporation might receive items other than cash in exchange for its shares. This situation occurs most often when someone starts a private company and contributes land, buildings, or equipment to the corporation.

Noncash transactions such as this are accounted for using the value of the items contributed to or given up by the corporation, whichever is easier to determine. Typically, the value of a private company's stock is difficult to determine because it is bought and sold infrequently. So usually the transaction is recorded using the value of the items contributed to the corporation. For example, if equipment valued at $50,000 were contributed to a private company in exchange for 10,000 common shares with a par value of $0.01 per share, the transaction would be recorded as:

|  | Debit | Credit |
|---|---|---|
| Equipment (+A) | 50,000 | |
|    Common Stock (+SE) (10,000 × $0.01) | | 100 |
|    Additional Paid-In Capital (+SE) ($50,000 − $100) | | 49,900 |

| Assets | = | Liabilities | + | Stockholders' Equity |
|---|---|---|---|---|
| Equipment    +50,000 | | | | Common Stock    +100 |
| | | | | Additional Paid-In Capital    +49,900 |

**Preferred Stock.** Just like common stock, preferred stock may be designated par value or no-par value and may be issued for cash or noncash assets. If preferred stock specifies a par value, any contributions in excess of par value are recorded as "Additional Paid-In Capital (APIC)—Preferred" to distinguish it from Additional Paid-In Capital related to common stock. In all other respects, **preferred stock issues are accounted for in the same way as common stock issues.** To illustrate, if Sonic issued 10,000 shares of $0.01 par value preferred stock for $40 per share, the company records the following journal entry:

| | Debit | Credit |
|---|---|---|
| Cash (+A) (10,000 × $40) | 400,000 | |
| Preferred Stock (+SE) (10,000 × $0.01) | | 100 |
| Additional Paid-In Capital—<br>Preferred (+SE) ($400,000 − $100) | | 399,900 |

| Assets | = | Liabilities | + | Stockholders' Equity | |
|---|---|---|---|---|---|
| Cash    +400,000 | | | | Preferred Stock | +100 |
| | | | | APIC—Preferred | +399,900 |

**Stock Sold between Investors.** When a company issues stock to an investor, the transaction is between the issuing corporation and the investor so it is recorded by the corporation. After the initial sale, investors can sell shares to other investors without directly affecting the corporation or its accounting records.

Assume, for example, that investor Aaron Cadieux sold 1,000 shares of Sonic stock to Tara Rink. Aaron received cash for the shares he sold, and Tara received shares for the cash she paid, but Sonic did not receive or pay anything. Following the separate entity assumption (see Chapter 1), Sonic would not record a journal entry on its books because the transaction involved only the stock's owners, not the corporation itself. (Think of an auto dealer who records the sale of a car to a customer but does nothing when the customer later sells the car to someone else.)

**Stock Used to Compensate Employees.** To encourage employees to work hard, many corporations offer a combination of base pay, cash bonuses, and stock options. Stock options allow employees to buy company stock at a predetermined price during a specified period. The idea is that if employees work hard to meet the company's goals, the stock price is likely to increase. If it increases before the options expire, employees can exercise their right to buy stock at the lower price and then sell it at the higher market price for an immediate profit. If the stock price declines, employees have not lost anything. Accounting rules require that when granting stock options, a company must report an expense for the estimated cost associated with stock options. The procedures for doing so are complex, so they are discussed in intermediate accounting courses.

## Spotlight On ETHICS

### Stock Options Motivate, but at Whose Expense?

Some critics claim that stock options, which are intended to give senior executives of a company the same goals as stockholders, are often granted at the expense of existing stockholders. When senior executives exercise their stock options to buy new stock, existing stockholders lose voting power because their percentage of ownership in the company is diluted. Furthermore, critics contend that stock options encourage senior executives to overstate financial results in an attempt to increase the company's stock price so they can reap huge personal gains.

## Treasury Stock

Although corporations are never obligated to buy back their own stock, some companies find it desirable to do so. A corporation may repurchase its own stock (1) to signal to investors that the company believes its stock is worth purchasing, (2) to obtain shares that can be reissued as payment for purchases of other companies, or (3) to obtain shares to reissue to employees as part of stock option plans. When a corporation buys its own stock back from stockholders, the stock is called **treasury stock**. While the corporation holds these shares, they do not offer voting, dividend, or other stockholder rights.

## Acquisition of Treasury Stock

Most companies record the purchase of treasury stock based on the cost of the shares that are purchased. This approach is called the cost method. If a company bought 50,000 shares of its common stock at a market price of $25 per share, the total cost of $1,250,000 (= 50,000 shares × $25) would be recorded as follows:

| | Debit | Credit |
|---|---|---|
| Treasury Stock (+xSE, −SE) | 1,250,000 | |
| Cash (−A) | | 1,250,000 |

| Assets | = | Liabilities | + | Stockholders' Equity | |
|---|---|---|---|---|---|
| Cash −1,250,000 | | | | Treasury Stock (+xSE) | −1,250,000 |

**Coach's Tip**

Treasury stock is not reported as an asset because it does not differ in substance from unissued stock certificates.

**Treasury stock is recorded in a contra stockholders' equity account,** which we indicate using the abbreviation xSE. Treasury Stock is subtracted from total stockholders' equity on the balance sheet as shown in the example in Exhibit 13.4.

## Reissue of Treasury Stock

When a corporation reissues shares of treasury stock, the company receives cash. The amount of cash received may be more or less than the amount the company initially paid to acquire it, depending on the market price for the stock. The accounting effects depend on whether treasury stock is reissued above or below its initial cost.

**Reissue above Cost.** To illustrate this case, we extend the example in which the treasury stock was acquired at a cost of $25 per share. If the company resold 5,000 shares of the

---

**Exhibit 13.4**　Excerpt from Sonic Corp.'s Balance Sheet　SONIC DRIVE-IN

**Sonic Corp.**
**Partial Balance Sheet**
**November 30, 2006**
**(dollars in thousands)**

**STOCKHOLDERS' EQUITY**

Contributed Capital

Common Stock, Par Value $0.01 per share

　Authorized: 245,000,000 Shares

　Issued: 115,183,800 Shares ............................................... $  1,152

Additional Paid-In Capital .................................................... 178,115

Preferred Stock, Par Value $0.01 per share; none outstanding ... —

Retained Earnings ............................................................... 491,980

Other ................................................................................ (4,035)

　　　　　　　　　　　　　　　　　　　　　　　　　　　　667,212

Treasury Stock, at cost 47,171,602 Common Shares ............... (666,584)

Total Stockholders' Equity .................................................. $　628 treasury stock for $27 per share, the required journal entry is:

| | Debit | Credit |
|---|---|---|
| Cash (+A) (5,000 × $27) | 135,000 | |
| Treasury Stock (−xSE,+SE) (5,000 × $25) | | 125,000 |
| Additional Paid-In Capital—Treasury (+SE) [5,000 × ($27 − $25)] | | 10,000 |

| Assets | = | Liabilities | + | Stockholders' Equity | |
|---|---|---|---|---|---|
| Cash  +135,000 | | | | Treasury Stock (−xSE) | +125,000 |
| | | | | APIC—Treasury | +10,000 |

**Reissue below Cost.** Assume the company resold 5,000 shares of treasury stock for $24 per share. Again, the company initially paid $25 per share to repurchase the stock. In this case, the required journal entry is:

| | Debit | Credit |
|---|---|---|
| Cash (+A) (5,000 × $24) | 120,000 | |
| Additional Paid-In Capital—Treasury (−SE) [5,000 × ($25 − $24)] | 5,000 | |
| Treasury Stock (−xSE,+SE) (5,000 × $25) | | 125,000 |

| Assets | = | Liabilities | + | Stockholders' Equity | |
|---|---|---|---|---|---|
| Cash  +120,000 | | | | Treasury Stock (−xSE) | +125,000 |
| | | | | APIC—Treasury | −5,000 |

If a company fully depletes its balance in Additional Paid-In Capital—Treasury, any excess should be debited to Retained Earnings.

## Financial Statement Reporting

In addition to reporting the dollar amounts for common stock, preferred stock, and treasury stock, corporations must disclose the number of shares related to those amounts. Most companies report this information on the balance sheet, as in Exhibit 13.4. Note in the exhibit that the **authorized** number of shares was 245 million common shares, but only 115,183,800 common shares had actually been **issued**. Unless the company buys them back, these shares will be owned forever by one investor or another. As you can see in the next-to-last line of Exhibit 13.4, Sonic held 47,171,602 shares of treasury stock that had been repurchased from the previously issued common shares.

Shares that have been issued but the corporation has not bought back are called **outstanding shares**. Based on Exhibit 13.4, you should be able to compute the number of Sonic shares still outstanding. As Exhibit 13.5 shows, of the 115,183,800 common shares issued, 47,171,602

**Exhibit 13.5**  Authorized, Issued, Outstanding, and Treasury Stock

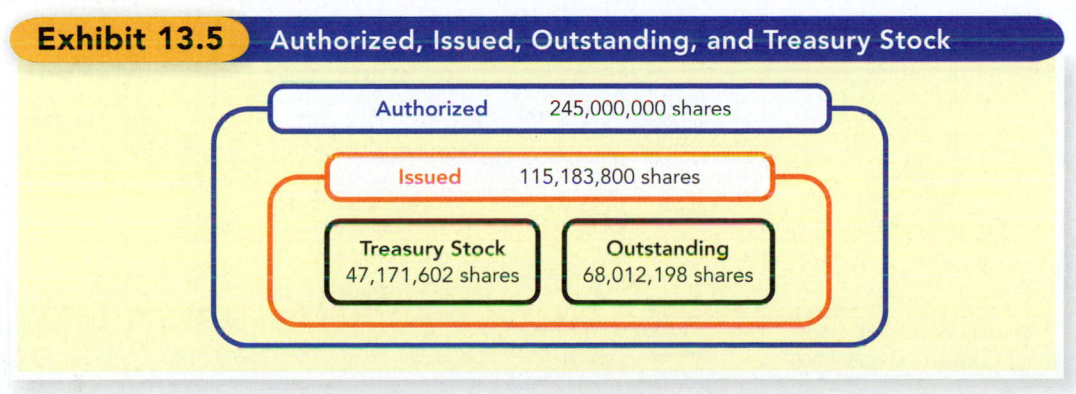

were repurchased, which means that 68,012,198 (= 115,183,800 − 47,171,602) were still outstanding. This number is important to financial analysts who need to express certain dollar amounts on a per share basis. Earnings per share (EPS)—a key financial ratio discussed later in this chapter—is expressed in terms of the number of outstanding shares.

**SELF-STUDY PRACTICE**

1. Assume that Aéropostale, Inc. issued 1,000 shares of its common stock, par value $0.01, for $21,900. Show the journal entry to record this transaction.

| | Debit | Credit |
|---|---|---|
| | | |
| | | |
| | | |

2. Assume that Aéropostale, Inc. repurchased 500 of its common shares when the stock was selling for $20 per share. Show the journal entry to record this transaction at cost.

| | Debit | Credit |
|---|---|---|
| | | |
| | | |
| | | |

3. Assume that Aéropostale, Inc. reissued 100 shares of its treasury stock at a market value of $25 per share. Show the journal entry to record this transaction.

| | Debit | Credit |
|---|---|---|
| | | |
| | | |
| | | |

*After you have finished, check your answers with the solution at the bottom of the page.*

# ACCOUNTING FOR DIVIDENDS AND SPLITS
## Cash Dividends on Common Stock

**Learning Objective 3**
Demonstrate how to account for cash dividends, stock dividends, and stock splits.

Investors buy common stock because they expect a return on their investment. That return can come in two forms: dividends and increases in the stock price. Some investors prefer to buy stocks that pay little or no dividends (called "growth stocks") because companies that reinvest most of their earnings tend to increase their future earnings potential as well as their

**Solution to Self-Study Practice**

1.

| | Debit | Credit |
|---|---|---|
| Cash (+A) | 21,900 | |
| Common Stock (+SE) (1,000 × $0.01) | | 10 |
| Additional Paid-In Capital (+SE) | | 21,890 |

2.

| | Debit | Credit |
|---|---|---|
| Treasury Stock (+xSE, −SE) | 10,000 | |
| Cash (−A) ($20 × 500) | | 10,000 |

3.

| | Debit | Credit |
|---|---|---|
| Cash (+A) ($25 × 100) | 2,500 | |
| Treasury Stock (−xSE, +SE) | | 2,000 |
| Additional Paid-In Capital—Treasury (+SE) | | 500 |

$2,000 = 100 shares × $20
$ 500 = 100 shares × ($25 − $20)

stock prices. Dell Corporation, for example, has never paid a dividend, yet if you had bought 100 shares in Dell when they were first issued on June 22, 1988, for $850, your investment would have been worth about $200,000 when this chapter was written. Other investors, such as retired people who need a steady income, prefer to receive their return in the form of dividends. These people often seek stocks that pay dividends consistently (called "income stocks"), such as Coca-Cola, which has paid cash dividends each year since 1893.

A corporation does not have a legal obligation to pay dividends. The board of directors makes the decision each time a dividend is to be paid. Whenever the board of directors formally declares a dividend, a liability is created.

## Dividend Dates

If Sonic were to declare a dividend, its press release would contain three important dates. In the following announcement, note the declaration date (May 20), the date of record (June 14), and the date of payment (July 1).

> **Sonic Corp. Announces Cash Dividend**
>
> Oklahoma City, Okla., May 20, 2008—Sonic Corp. (Nasdaq: SONC) announced today that the Company's Board of Directors declared a cash dividend of $.02 per common share, payable on or about July 1, 2008 to stockholders of record as of June 14, 2008.

**Declaration Date.** The declaration date (in this case, May 20) is the date on which the board of directors officially approves the dividend. As soon as the board makes the declaration, the company records an increase in its liabilities and a corresponding decrease in Retained Earnings. **Dividends are distributions of a company's accumulated prior earnings,** so they are reported as a reduction in Retained Earnings on the balance sheet. **Dividends are not reported on the income statement because they are not expenses.**

With over 68 million common shares outstanding, the $0.02 dividend per share would equal $1,360,244 (= $0.02 × 68,012,198). The journal entry to record them is:

|  | Debit | Credit |
|---|---|---|
| Retained Earnings (−SE) | 1,360,244 | |
|     Dividends Payable (+L) | | 1,360,244 |

| Assets | = | Liabilities | + | Stockholders' Equity |
|---|---|---|---|---|
| | | Dividends Payable   +1,360,244 | | Retained Earnings   −1,360,244 |

**Date of Record.** The next date, the record date (here, June 14), is the date on which the corporation prepares the list of current stockholders based on its records. The dividend is payable only to those names listed on the record date. Sonic makes no journal entry on this date.

**Date of Payment.** The third date, the payment date (July 1 in this example), is the date on which Sonic disburses cash to pay the dividend liability. When the dividend is paid and the liability is satisfied on July 1, the journal entry is:

|  | Debit | Credit |
|---|---|---|
| Dividends Payable (−L) | 1,360,244 | |
|     Cash (−A) | | 1,360,244 |

| Assets | = | Liabilities | + | Stockholders' Equity |
|---|---|---|---|---|
| Cash   −1,360,244 | | Dividends Payable   −1,360,244 | | |

Video 13-2
www.mhhe.com/LLPW1e

SONIC DRIVE-IN

**Exhibit 13.6** — **Dividend Timeline: Declaration Date, Date of Record, and Date of Payment**

| May 20 | June 14 | July 1 |
|---|---|---|
| Dividend declared | Date of record | Date of payment |

Balance sheet effects:

| Increase Dividends Payable  Decrease Retained Earnings | No effect | Decrease Cash  Decrease Dividends Payable |
|---|---|---|

The timeline in Exhibit 13.6 summarizes these three dates and the corresponding balance sheet effects.

### Dividend Requirements

Notice in Exhibit 13.6 that the declaration of a cash dividend decreases Retained Earnings. Notice too that payment of the cash dividend later reduces the Cash account by the same amount. These two observations explain the **two fundamental requirements for payment of a cash dividend:** sufficient retained earnings and sufficient cash.

**Coach's Tip**

A lender imposes dividend restrictions because it does not want to lend money to a corporation and then have the corporation give it to stockholders via dividends rather than use it to grow the business.

**Sufficient Retained Earnings.** The corporation must have accumulated a sufficient amount of retained earnings to cover the amount of the dividend. State laws often restrict cash dividends to the balance in the Retained Earnings account. The company may be further restricted by clauses in loan agreements that require an even larger minimum balance in Retained Earnings. If the company were to violate such a clause, a lender could demand immediate repayment of outstanding loans. Because such a restriction can severely limit a company's ability to pay dividends, accounting rules require that companies disclose it in their notes to the financial statements.

**Sufficient Cash.** The corporation must have sufficient cash to pay the dividend. The company can use cash for a variety of purposes other than just paying dividends. Sonic may use cash to install new debit machines at its drive-ins or to pay down some of its debt. So in addition to considering the balance in Retained Earnings, corporations must ensure that they have sufficient cash available to pay any dividends that are declared.

**SELF-STUDY PRACTICE**

Answer the following questions concerning dividends:

1. On which dividend date is a liability created?
2. A cash outflow occurs on which dividend date?
3. What are the two fundamental requirements for paying a cash dividend?

*After you have finished, check your answers with the solution at the bottom of the page.*

## Cash Dividends on Preferred Stock

Because purchasers of preferred stock give up the voting rights available to owners of common stock, preferred stock offers them dividend preferences in return. The two most common dividend preferences are called current and cumulative preferences.

### Current Dividend Preference

A current dividend preference requires preferred dividends to be paid before paying any dividends to holders of common stock. This preference is a feature of all preferred stock. After

Solution to
Self-Study Practice

1.  Declaration date.
2.  Date of payment.
3.  Dividends can be paid only if both sufficient retained earnings and sufficient cash are available.

the current dividend preference has been met, and if no other preference exists, dividends may be paid to the common stockholders.

When a company declares dividends, the current preferred dividend preference must be met first; then any remaining declared dividends go to common stockholders. Consider the following example:

> ### Checker Company
>
> Preferred stock outstanding, 6%, par $20; 2,000 shares
> Common stock outstanding, par $10; 5,000 shares

Assume the preferred stock carries only a current dividend preference and Checker declared dividends totaling $8,000 and $10,000 in 2009 and 2010, respectively. In each year, a portion of the total dividends would go first to the preferred stockholders; the remaining amount would go to the common stockholders, as follows.

| Year | Total Dividends Declared | Dividends on 6% Preferred Stock* | Dividends on Common Stock† |
|------|------|------|------|
| 2009 | $ 8,000 | $2,400 | $5,600 |
| 2010 | 10,000 | 2,400 | 7,600 |

\* Dividends on Preferred Stock = 2,000 Shares × $20 Par Value × 6% Dividend = $2,400
† Dividends on Common Stock = Total Dividends Declared − Dividends on Preferred Stock

If Checker Company did not declare dividends in 2009, preferred stockholders would have been entitled to dividends of $2,400 in 2010 only. The current dividend preference does not carry over to later years unless the preferred stock is designated as cumulative, as we discuss next.

## Cumulative Dividend Preference

A **cumulative dividend preference** states that if a company does not pay all or part of the current dividend in full, the cumulative unpaid amount, known as **dividends in arrears**, must be paid in the future before any other dividends may be paid. To illustrate, assume Checker Company has the same amount of stock outstanding as in the previous example but dividends have been in arrears for two years. In this case, when Checker declares dividends in 2009, preferred stockholders first receive $4,800 for the dividends in arrears (2 years × $2,400) and then they receive $2,400 for the current year (2009). Any remaining dividend goes to common stockholders:

| Year | Total Dividends Declared | DIVIDENDS ON 6% PREFERRED STOCK In Arrears* | Current† | Dividends on Common Stock‡ |
|------|------|------|------|------|
| 2009 | $ 8,000 | $4,800 | $2,400 | $ 800 |
| 2010 | 10,000 | — | 2,400 | 7,600 |

\* Dividends in Arrears Preference = 2,000 Shares × $20 Par Value × 6% Dividend × 2 Years = $4,800
† Current Dividend Preference = 2,000 Shares × $20 Par Value × 6% Dividend = $2,400
‡ Dividends on Common Stock = Total Dividends Declared − Total Dividends on Preferred Stock

Notice that after the dividends in arrears have been satisfied (in 2009), the dividend preference reverts back to just a current dividend preference (in 2010).

## Spotlight On FINANCIAL REPORTING

### Dividends in Arrears

American Skiing

Because dividends do not represent a liability until the board of directors declares them, dividends in arrears are not reported on the balance sheet. Instead, they are disclosed in the notes to the financial statements. The following note from American Skiing, a company that operates ski, snowboard, and golf resorts throughout the United States, is typical:

> Cumulative dividends in arrears totaled approximately $23.7 million and $109.3 million for the Series C-1 Preferred Stock and Series C-2 Preferred Stock, respectively.

## Stock Dividends

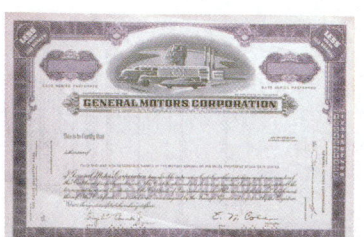

The term dividend, when used alone with no adjectives, implies a cash dividend. However, some dividends are not paid in cash but in additional shares of stock. These dividends, called **stock dividends**, are distributed to a corporation's stockholders on a pro rata basis at no cost to the stockholder. The phrase "pro rata basis" means that each stockholder receives additional shares based on the percentage of shares held. A stockholder who owns 10 percent of the outstanding shares would receive 10 percent of any additional shares issued as a stock dividend.

The value assigned to a stock dividend depends on whether it is large or small. If a stock dividend equals more than 20 to 25 percent of the currently outstanding shares, it is considered a large stock dividend and is recorded at the par value of the stock to be issued. If the stock dividend equals less than 20 to 25 percent of the outstanding shares, it is considered a small stock dividend and is recorded at the market value of the stock.

To illustrate, assume that on January 30, 2008, Sonic declared a 10 percent (small) stock dividend on its 68,012,198 shares of $0.01 par value common stock for stockholders of record on February 10, 2008. The dividend was distributed on February 21, 2008. **On the declaration date** (January 30), Sonic would record this small stock dividend at the shares' market value. Assuming that the stock price is $30 per share, the value of the dividend would be $204,036,594 (=$30 per share × 68,012,198 shares × 10% dividend). The par value of the stock to be issued would be $68,012 (=$0.01 per share × 68,012,198 shares × 10% dividend).

Until the stock is actually distributed, this amount would be recorded in the stockholders' equity account Common Stock Dividend Distributable. The difference between the total market value and the par value of the stock to be issued ($204,036,594 − $68,012 = $203,968,582) would be recorded as Additional Paid-In Capital, as follows:

| | Debit | Credit |
|---|---|---|
| Retained Earnings (−SE) | 204,036,594 | |
| Common Stock Dividend Distributable (+SE) | | 68,012 |
| Additional Paid-In Capital (+SE) | | 203,968,582 |

| Assets | = | Liabilities | + | Stockholders' Equity | |
|---|---|---|---|---|---|
| | | | | Retained Earnings | −204,036,594 |
| | | | | Common Stock | |
| | | | | Dividend Distributable | +68,012 |
| | | | | Additional Paid-In Capital | +203,968,582 |

Along with Common Stock, Additional Paid-In Capital, and Retained Earnings, Common Stock Dividend Distributable is reported in the Stockholders' Equity section of the balance sheet. It is not reported as a liability because assets will not be used to pay the dividend. Notice in the accounting equation effects shown that the stock dividend does not change total stockholders' equity. It changes only the balances in some of the accounts that make up stockholders' equity.

**On the date of record** (February 10), no journal entry would be made. **On the date of distribution** (February 21), the following journal entry would be made:

| | Debit | Credit |
|---|---|---|
| Common Stock Dividend Distributable (−SE) | 68,012 | |
| Common Stock (+SE) | | 68,012 |

| Assets | = | Liabilities | + | Stockholders' Equity | |
|---|---|---|---|---|---|
| | | | | Common Stock | +68,012 |
| | | | | Common Stock Dividend Distributable | −68,012 |

Large stock dividends (greater than 20 to 25 percent of the outstanding shares) are accounted for in the same way as small stock dividends, except that they are recorded at the stock's par value rather than its market value. Consequently, the Additional Paid-In Capital account is not affected when a large stock dividend is declared.

# Stock Splits

Stock splits are not dividends. They are similar to a stock dividend, but they are quite different in terms of how they occur and how they affect the stockholders' equity accounts. With a stock split, the corporation increases the total number of authorized shares by a specified amount, such as 2 for 1. In this example, the corporation calls in each share and issues two new shares in its place. At the same time, the par value of each share decreases, so the total par value of the shares remains unchanged. For example, if a company with 1 million shares outstanding of $0.01 par value stock executes a 2-for-1 stock split, it decreases the par value of its stock from $0.01 to $0.005 and doubles the number of shares outstanding. (Think of taking a four-piece pizza and cutting each piece into two halves.)

Because the decrease in par value per share offsets the increase in the number of shares, the company's financial position does not change, and **no journal entry is needed when stock is split.** Similarly, the market price of each share will decrease to offset the increase in the number of shares, so investors are no wealthier after the split than they were before.

| | Before a 2-for-1 Stock Split | After a 2-for-1 Stock Split |
|---|---|---|
| Number of shares outstanding | 1,000,000 | 2,000,000 |
| Par value per share | $      0.01 | $      0.005 |
| Total par value outstanding | $    10,000 | $    10,000 |

If you are like most new financial managers, you are probably wondering how a company's board of directors chooses between a 2-for-1 stock split and a "large" 100 percent stock dividend when both have the same effect—that of doubling the number of shares outstanding

**Exhibit 13.7**    Comparison of a 2-for 1 Stock Split, a 100 percent Stock Dividend, and a Cash Dividend

| | BEFORE | AFTER | | |
| Stockholders' Equity | | 2-for-1 Stock Split | 100% Stock Dividend | $10,000 Cash Dividend |
|---|---|---|---|---|
| Contributed capital | | | | |
|   Number of common shares | | | | |
|     outstanding | 1,000,000 | 2,000,000 | 2,000,000 | 1,000,000 |
|     Par value per common share | $    0.01 | $    0.005 | $    0.01 | $    0.01 |
| Common stock, at par | $    10,000 | $    10,000 | $    20,000 | $    10,000 |
| Additional paid-in capital | 30,000 | 30,000 | 30,000 | 30,000 |
| Retained earnings | 650,000 | 650,000 | 640,000 | 640,000 |
|   Total stockholders' equity | $  690,000 | $  690,000 | $  690,000 | $  680,000 |

and reducing the per share market price. The answer, it seems, is closely related to the method of accounting for stock dividends and splits. A stock dividend causes a reduction in Retained Earnings, whereas a stock split does not (see Exhibit 13.7).

By itself, this accounting difference might not mean much. Remember, though, that to declare a cash dividend, a company must maintain an adequate balance in Retained Earnings. If you are managing a company that you expect will struggle financially in the future, you will prefer a 2-for-1 stock split rather than a 100 percent stock dividend because the stock split does not reduce Retained Earnings, so it does not reduce your ability to declare cash dividends in the future. On the other hand, if you expect your company to be financially successful in the near future, you will not care that a stock dividend reduces Retained Earnings because future earnings will rebuild that account to allow cash dividends to be declared. In fact, you will probably **want** to declare a stock dividend to show how confident you are of your company's financial outlook. This reasoning suggests that **a company's board of directors may declare a stock dividend rather than a stock split to signal to financial statement users that the company expects to be sufficiently profitable to replenish the reduction in Retained Earnings caused by the stock dividend.**

## SELF-STUDY PRACTICE

To reduce the market price of its stock, which was $50 per share, Vandalay Industries declared a 10 percent (small) stock dividend on its 1,000,000 outstanding shares of common stock (par value $10).

1. Prepare the journal entry that Vandalay would use to record this transaction.
2. What journal entry would be required if the transaction instead involved a 2-for-1 split? Theoretically, what would be the new stock price after the split?

*After you have finished, check your answers with the solution at the bottom of the page.*

## Statement of Retained Earnings

Retained Earnings represents the total earnings retained in the company after distributing dividends to stockholders. You have already seen that whenever the corporation declares a cash dividend or stock dividend, the balance in Retained Earnings decreases. Its balance increases each year the company reports net income, as you will see next.

Solution to Self-Study Practice

1.

| | | |
|---|---|---|
| Retained Earnings (−SE) | 5,000,000 | |
| Common Stock Dividend Distributable (+SE) | | 1,000,000 |
| Additional Paid-in Capital (+SE) | | 4,000,000 |
| ($5,000,000 = 1,000,000 × 10% × $50; $1,000,000 = 1,000,000 × 10% × $10) | | |

2. No journal entry is required in the case of a stock split. Theoretically, the new price would be one-half of what it was before the split ($50 × ½ = $25).

Assume, for example, Sonic determined it had $78 million of net income after closing revenues and expenses to the Income Summary account. Sonic records the following journal entry to transfer that amount to Retained Earnings:

|  | Debit | Credit |
|---|---|---|
| Income Summary (−SE) | 78,000,000 |  |
| Retained Earnings (+SE) |  | 78,000,000 |

| Assets | = | Liabilities | + | Stockholders' Equity | |
|---|---|---|---|---|---|
|  |  |  |  | Income Summary | −78,000,000 |
|  |  |  |  | Retained Earnings | +78,000,000 |

To report the causes of increases and decreases in Retained Earnings, a Statement of Retained Earnings is prepared each accounting period.[1] (This report replaces the Statement of Owner's Equity that is prepared for sole proprietorships.) Exhibit 13.8 shows an example of this statement for Sonic, assuming a net income of $78 million, cash dividends on common stock of $1,360,244, stock dividends on common stock of $204,036,594, no cash dividends or stock dividends on preferred stock, and a beginning balance in Retained Earnings of $476 million.

**Exhibit 13.8   Statement of Retained Earnings     SONIC DRIVE-IN**

Sonic Corp.
Statement of Retained Earnings
For the Year Ended August 31, 2010
(in thousands of dollars)

| Retained Earnings, August 31, 2009 | $476,000 |
|---|---|
| Net Income | 78,000 |
| Cash Dividends on Common Stock | (1,360) |
| Stock Dividends on Common Stock | (204,037) |
| Retained Earnings, August 31, 2010 | $348,603 |

**Coach's Tip**

Like all permanent accounts, Retained Earnings carries its balance forward from one year to the next. In Exhibit 13.8, we have assumed an opening balance of $476 million for the sake of illustration.

# FINANCIAL RATIO ANALYSIS

You have seen how, on the inside, a corporation accounts for stockholders' equity transactions. Now it is time to consider two ratios that outsiders use to evaluate how well a company has used its capital to generate returns for the company and its stockholders.

## Financial Analysis Tools

| Name of Measure | Formula | What It Tells You |
|---|---|---|
| Earnings per share (EPS) | $\dfrac{\text{Net Income} - \text{Preferred Dividends}}{\text{Average Number of Common Shares Outstanding}}$ | • The amount of income generated for each share of common stock owned by stockholders<br>• The higher the number, the greater the profitability |
| Price/Earnings (P/E) ratio | $\dfrac{\text{Current Stock Price (per share)}}{\text{Earnings per Share (annual)}}$ | • How many times more than the current year's earnings investors are willing to pay for a company's stock<br>• The higher the number, the more investors anticipate an improvement in the company's future results |

---

[1] A more comprehensive Statement of Stockholders' Equity may be presented instead of the Statement of Retained Earnings. A Statement of Stockholders' Equity shows the causes of increases and decreases in each stockholders' equity account, not just Retained Earnings. Preparing this statement is beyond the scope of this course.

# Earnings Per Share (EPS)

The most famous of all financial ratios, earnings per share (EPS), reports how much profit is earned for each share of common stock outstanding. The calculation of EPS can involve many details and intricacies that are appropriately discussed in detail in intermediate accounting courses. In its basic form, EPS is computed by dividing net income by the average number of common shares outstanding. (If the company has declared dividends on preferred stock, they are first subtracted from net income.) Most companies report EPS on the income statement immediately below Net Income or in the notes to the financial statements.

You may be wondering why earnings per share is such a popular measure when dividends and stock prices ultimately determine the return to stockholders. The reason is that current earnings can predict future dividends and stock prices. If a company generates increased earnings in the current year, it will be able to pay higher dividends in future years. In other words, current EPS influences expectations about future dividends, which investors factor into the current stock price. That explains why Sonic Corp.'s stock price increased nearly 4 percent on January 4, 2008, immediately after the company announced that its EPS for the quarter was higher than in the preceding year.

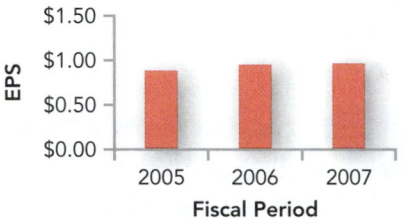

Another reason that EPS is such a popular measure is that it allows investors to make quick comparisons over time. Net income stated in dollars is more difficult to interpret. For example, in fiscal year 2007, Sonic earned a net income of $64 million compared to $78 million in the preceding year. It is hard to know whether that decrease was bad for stockholders because the decrease in Sonic's net income may have been accompanied by a decrease in the number of shares outstanding. By converting earnings to a per share basis, we adjust for the effect of any repurchased stock which gives a clearer picture of what decreased earnings might mean for each investor. As you can see from the accompanying graph, the decrease in net income in 2007 actually translated into higher EPS, from $0.91 to $0.94 per share, because fewer shares were outstanding.

Exhibit 13.9 shows how to calculate EPS for Sonic and a much larger fast food competitor, McDonald's Corporation. We should caution you to resist the temptation of comparing different companies' EPS ratios. The number of shares outstanding for one company can differ dramatically from the number of shares outstanding for a different company simply because

---

**Exhibit 13.9  Earnings per Share (EPS) and Price/Earnings (P/E) Ratios**

| Company | Relevant Information (in millions) | | | 2007 EPS | 2007 P/E |
|---|---|---|---|---|---|
| | | 2007 | 2006 | | |
| Sonic America's Drive·In | Net income | $64.2 | $78.7 | | |
| | Preferred dividends | 0.0 | 0.0 | $\dfrac{\$64.2-0}{68.3}$ | $\dfrac{\$24.59}{\$0.94}$ |
| | Average number of shares | 68.3 | 86.5 | $=\$0.94$ | $=26.2$ |
| | Stock price | $24.59 | $22.65 | | |
| | | 2007 | 2006 | | |
| McDonald's | Net income | $2,395.1 | $3,544.2 | | |
| | Preferred dividends | 0.0 | 0.0 | $\dfrac{\$2,395.1-0}{1,188.3}$ | $\dfrac{\$56.00}{\$2.02}$ |
| | Average number of shares | 1,188.3 | 1,234.0 | $=\$2.02$ | $=27.7$ |
| | Stock price | $56.00 | $46.00 | | |

one chooses to issue or repurchase more shares than the other. Also, as you have seen in earlier chapters, net income can be affected by more than just operating performance. Accounting differences in assigning inventory costs (Chapter 7), estimating bad debts (Chapter 9) and contingent liabilities (Chapter 11), and depreciating long-lived assets (Chapter 10) can reduce its comparability between companies. So while the EPS ratio is a useful measure for evaluating one company's performance over time, it is not appropriate for cross-company comparisons.

## Price/Earnings (P/E) Ratio

The EPS ratio is useful for evaluating a company's ability to generate profits for stockholders, but it does not help investors determine a reasonable price for a company's stock. Advanced finance courses teach sophisticated techniques for valuing a company, but you will likely find it helpful to start with a much simpler tool. The price/earnings (P/E) ratio is the most basic way of determining the value investors place on a company's common stock. This ratio measures how many times more than the current year's earnings investors are willing to pay for a company's stock. The more they value the company, the more they will pay for its stock relative to the earnings the company generated. The P/E ratio is calculated by dividing a company's stock price by its earnings per share for the year (see Exhibit 13.9).

Generally, a relatively high P/E ratio means that investors expect the company to increase its profits in the future and they have factored those future earnings into the current stock price. A relatively low P/E ratio typically means that investors do not expect strong performance in the future. Because P/E ratios can vary significantly across industries, they are most meaningful when used to compare a company's performance over time or to compare competitors in the same industry. In 2007, Sonic's P/E ratio of 26.2 was similar to both McDonald's P/E ratio (27.7) and the overall industry average (24.6 according to Yahoo!Finance), suggesting that investors anticipated that Sonic would be at least as successful as other fast food restaurants.

> **SELF-STUDY PRACTICE**
>
> 1. Use the information in Exhibit 13.9 to calculate Sonic's earnings per share (EPS) and price/earnings (P/E) ratio for 2006.
>
> | 2006 EPS | 2006 P/E |
> |----------|----------|
> |          |          |
>
> 2. Did Sonic's EPS improve or decline from 2006 (calculated in part 1) to 2007 (shown in Exhibit 13.9)? Does Sonic's 2006 P/E ratio suggest that investors anticipated the changes that occurred in 2007? As a point of reference, the average P/E ratio for the industry was 19.5 in 2006.
>
> *After you have finished, check your answers with the solution at the bottom of the page.*

## Demonstration Case A

### Stock Issue, Repurchase, and Financial Statement Reporting

This case focuses on selected transactions from the first year of operations of Zoogle Corporation, a lost-pet search business that became a public company on January 1, 2009. Zoogle's charter authorized it to issue the following:

Common stock, $0.10 par value; 20,000 shares.
Preferred stock, 5 percent cumulative, $100 par value; 5,000 shares.

**Solution to Self-Study Practice**

1. EPS: $78.7 / 86.5 = $0.91
   P/E: $22.65 / $0.91 = 24.9

2. Sonic's EPS improved, increasing from $0.91 in 2006 to $0.94 in 2007. Investors appeared to anticipate the improved performance because they were willing to pay 24.9 times earnings to buy a share of Sonic in 2006 when they were willing to pay only 19.5 times earnings for other companies in the industry.

The following transactions, selected from 2009, were completed on the dates indicated:

(a) Jan.  1   Issued a total of 8,000 shares of $0.10 par value common stock for cash at $50 per share.

(b) Feb.  1   Sold 2,000 shares of preferred stock at $100 per share; cash collected in full.

(c) July  1   Purchased 400 shares of common stock that had been issued earlier. Zoogle paid the stockholders $54 per share for the stock and currently holds the shares in treasury.

(d) Aug. 1   Sold 30 shares of the common treasury stock at $56 per share.

(e) Dec. 31   The board decided not to declare any dividends for the current year.

*Required:*

1.   Give the appropriate journal entries; show your calculations for each transaction.

2.   Prepare the Stockholders' Equity section of the balance sheet for Zoogle Corporation on December 31, 2009. Assume that the Retained Earnings account on that date totaled $31,000.

## Suggested Solution

1.   **Journal entries:**

| | | | Debit | Credit |
|---|---|---|---:|---:|
| (a) | Jan. 1, 2009 | Cash (+A) ($50 × 8,000 shares) | 400,000 | |
| | | Common Stock (+SE) ($0.10 × 8,000 shares) | | 800 |
| | | Additional Paid-In Capital—Common (+SE) | | 399,200 |
| (b) | Feb. 1, 2009 | Cash (+A) ($100 × 2,000 shares) | 200,000 | |
| | | Preferred Stock (+SE) ($100 par × 2,000 shares) | | 200,000 |
| (c) | July 1, 2009 | Treasury Stock (+xSE, −SE) | 21,600 | |
| | | Cash (−A) (400 shares × $54) | | 21,600 |
| (d) | Aug. 1, 2009 | Cash (+A) (30 × $56) | 1,680 | |
| | | Treasury Stock (−xSE, +SE) (30 shares × $54) | | 1,620 |
| | | Additional Paid-In Capital—Treasury (+SE) ($1,680 − $1,620) | | 60 |
| (e) | Dec. 31, 2009 | No journal entry is required. Dividends in arrears from the current year (2,000 shares × $100 × 5% = $10,000) would be reported in the notes to Zoogle's financial statements. | | |

2.   **Stockholders' equity section of the balance sheet:**

### Zoogle Corporation
### Partial Balance Sheet
### At December 31, 2009

**Stockholders' Equity**

**Contributed capital**

| | |
|---|---:|
| Common stock ($0.10 par value; authorized 20,000 shares, issued 8,000 shares of which 370 shares are held as treasury stock) | $      800 |
| Additional paid-in capital, common stock | 399,200 |
| Additional paid-in capital, treasury stock | 60 |
| Preferred stock, 5% cumulative (par value $100; 5,000 authorized shares, 2,000 issued and outstanding shares) | 200,000 |
| **Total contributed capital** | $600,060 |
| **Retained earnings** | 31,000 |
| **Treasury stock,** at cost, 370 common shares | (19,980) |
| Total stockholders' equity | $611,080 |

# Demonstration Case B

## Dividends, Stock Split, and Retained Earnings

This case extends Demonstration Case A by focusing on dividends and other stock transactions that occurred during Zoogle Corporation's second year. The following transactions selected from 2010 were completed on the dates indicated:

- (a) Nov. 1  The board declared a cash dividend on the preferred stock for the current year as well as payment of the prior year's dividends in arrears, payable on November 22 to stockholders of record as of November 15.
- (b) Dec. 1  The board declared a 10 percent stock dividend on the outstanding common stock, distributable on December 18 to shareholders of record as of December 16. The stock price was $60 per share.
- (c) Dec. 21  Zoogle Corporation completed a 2-for-1 stock split on its common stock.
- (d) Dec. 31  The $50,000 balance in the Income Summary account was closed to Retained Earnings.

*Required:*

1. Give the appropriate journal entries; show your calculations for each transaction.
2. Prepare a Statement of Retained Earnings for the year ended December 31, 2010.

## Suggested Solution

1.

| | | | Debit | Credit |
|---|---|---|---|---|
| (a) | Nov. 1, 2010 | Retained Earnings (−SE) | 20,000 | |
| | | Dividends Payable (+L) | | 20,000 |
| | | (2,000 preferred shares × $100 par × 5% dividend rate × 2 years) | | |
| | Nov. 15, 2010 | No journal entry is required on the date of record. | | |
| | Nov. 22, 2010 | Dividends Payable (−L) | 20,000 | |
| | | Cash (−A) | | 20,000 |
| (b) | Dec. 1, 2010 | Retained Earnings (−SE) | 45,780 | |
| | | Common Stock Dividend Distributable (+SE) | | 76 |
| | | Additional Paid-In Capital (+SE) | | 45,704 |
| | | $45,780 = (8,000 common shares issued − 370 in treasury) × 10% × $60 | | |
| | | $76 = (8,000 common shares issued − 370 in treasury) × 10% × $0.10 | | |
| | | $45,704 = $45,780 − $76 | | |
| | Dec. 16, 2010 | No journal entry is required on the date of record. | | |
| | Dec. 18, 2010 | Common Stock Dividend Distributable (−SE) | 8 | |
| | | Common Stock (+SE) | | 8 |
| (c) | Dec. 21, 2010 | No journal entry is required to record a stock split. | | |
| (d) | Dec. 31, 2010 | Income Summary (−SE) | 50,000 | |
| | | Retained Earnings (+SE) | | 50,000 |

2.

**Zoogle Corporation**
**Statement of Retained Earnings**
**For the Year Ended December 31, 2010**

| | |
|---|---|
| Retained earnings, December 31, 2009 | $31,000 |
| Net income | 50,000 |
| Cash dividends on preferred stock | (20,000) |
| Stock dividends on common stock | (45,780) |
| Retained earnings, December 31, 2010 | $15,220 |

# Chapter Summary

### LO1 Describe the characteristics of corporations. p. 560

- The law recognizes corporations as separate legal entities. Owners invest in a corporation and receive capital stock that can be bought from and sold to other investors.
- Common stock provides a number of rights, including the rights to vote, to receive dividends, to share in the corporation's residual assets at liquidation, and to preempt others from purchasing newly issued stock.
- Preferred stock gives investors certain advantages, including current dividend preferences and preference in asset distributions if the corporation is liquidated. If preferred stock carries cumulative dividend rights, any part of a current dividend that is not paid (dividends in arrears) must be paid in full before any additional dividends can be paid.

### LO2 Demonstrate how to account for transactions involving common stock, preferred stock, and treasury stock. p. 562

- All transactions involving common stock, preferred stock, and treasury stock affect only the balance sheet. Corporations do not report income from gains or losses on transactions involving their own stock.
- If a stock specifies a par value, any amounts received in excess of par value are recorded in the stockholders' equity account Additional Paid-In Capital.
- If the corporation repurchases a stock, it is called treasury stock. The cost method records treasury stock at the cost to reacquire it in a contra-account that is subtracted from the Stockholders' Equity section on the balance sheet. If treasury stock is reissued, the treasury stock account is decreased by the cost of the treasury stock, and any excess amount received on reissue is recorded as Additional Paid-In Capital—Treasury.

### LO3 Demonstrate how to account for cash dividends, stock dividends, and stock splits. p. 568

- Cash dividends reduce stockholders' equity (Retained Earnings) and create a liability (Dividends Payable) when the board of directors declares them. The liability is reduced when the dividends are paid.
- Stock dividends are pro rata distributions of a company's stock to existing owners. If the stock dividend is a small proportion of the outstanding stock, the transaction is accounted for by reducing Retained Earnings by the market value of the distributed stock, increasing Common Stock by the par value of the distributed stock, and increasing Additional Paid-In Capital for the excess of market value over par value. If the stock dividend is large (more than 20 to 25 percent), it is recorded at the par value of the stock.
- A stock split also involves the distribution of additional shares to owners, but no additional amount is transferred to Common Stock. Instead, the per share par value of the stock is reduced.

### LO4 Analyze the earnings per share (EPS) and price/earnings (P/E) ratios. p. 576

- The earnings per share (EPS) ratio is calculated by dividing net income (less any dividends on preferred stock) by the average number of shares of common stock outstanding during the year. This ratio is helpful in comparing a corporation's earnings over time. It does not allow reliable comparisons across companies because it does not adjust for likely differences in the number of outstanding shares in each company and in the accounting methods used by each company.
- The price-earnings (P/E) ratio relates the corporation's current stock price to its most recent annual earnings per share. It indicates the value that investors place on the company's stock.

| Financial Analysis Tools | | |
|---|---|---|
| Name of Measure | Formula | What It Tells You |
| Earnings per share (EPS) | $\dfrac{\text{Net Income} - \text{Preferred Dividends}}{\text{Average Number of Common Shares Outstanding}}$ | • The amount of income generated for each share of common stock owned by stockholders<br>• The higher the number, the greater the profitability |
| Price/Earnings (P/E) ratio | $\dfrac{\text{Current Stock Price (per share)}}{\text{Earnings per Share (annual)}}$ | • How many times more than the current year's earnings investors are willing to pay for a company's stock<br>• The higher the number, the more investors anticipate an improvement in the company's future results |

# Key Terms

**See complete glossary in the back of text.**

## Questions

1. Identify the primary advantages of the corporate form of business.

2. What four benefits do owners of common stock usually enjoy?

3. What are the differences between common stock and preferred stock?

4. What are the usual characteristics of preferred stock?

5. What are the relative advantages of equity versus debt financing?

6. In what ways does owner's equity differ for proprietorships and for corporations?

7. Explain each of the following terms: (a) authorized common stock, (b) issued common stock, and (c) outstanding common stock.

8. What is the distinction between par value and no-par value capital stock?

9. What is treasury stock? Why do corporations acquire treasury stock?

10. How is treasury stock reported on the balance sheet? How do the financial statements report the "gain or loss" on treasury stock reissued above or below cost?

11. What three dates are significant for dividends? What changes are made to the financial statement accounts on each of these three dates?

12. What are the two basic requirements to support the declaration of a cash dividend? What are the effects of a cash dividend on assets and stockholders' equity?

13. What is unique about cumulative preferred stock?

14. What is a stock dividend? How does a stock dividend differ from a cash dividend?

15. Why might a corporation's board declare a stock dividend rather than a stock split?

16. Why is the EPS number so popular? What are its limitations?

17. How do stock repurchases affect the EPS ratio?

18. Generally speaking, what does a high P/E ratio suggest?

## Multiple Choice

Quiz 13-1
www.mhhe.com/LLPW1e

1. Which feature is not applicable to common stock ownership?
   a. Right to receive dividends before preferred stock shareholders.
   b. Right to vote on appointment of external auditor.
   c. Right to receive residual assets of the company should it cease operations.
   d. None of the above (all are applicable to common stock ownership).

2. Which statement regarding treasury stock is false?
   a. Treasury stock is considered to be issued but not outstanding.
   b. Treasury stock has no voting, dividend, or liquidation rights.
   c. Treasury stock reduces total stockholders' equity on the balance sheet.
   d. None of the above.

3. Which of the following statements about stock dividends is true?
   a. Stock dividends are reported on the income statement.
   b. Stock dividends increase total stockholders' equity.
   c. Stock dividends decrease total stockholders' equity.
   d. None of the above.

4. Which of the following is ordered from the largest number of shares to the smallest number of shares?
   a. Shares authorized, shares issued, shares outstanding.
   b. Shares issued, shares outstanding, shares authorized.
   c. Shares outstanding, shares issued, shares authorized.
   d. Shares in treasury, shares outstanding, shares issued.

5. Which of the following statements about the relative advantages of equity and debt financing is false?
   a. An advantage of equity financing is that it does not have to be repaid.
   b. An advantage of equity financing is that dividends are optional.
   c. An advantage of equity financing is that new stockholders get to vote and share in the earnings of the company.
   d. An advantage of debt financing is that interest is tax deductible.

6. A journal entry is not recorded on what date?
   a. Date of declaration.
   b. Date of record.
   c. Date of payment.
   d. None of the above. (A journal entry is recorded on all of the above dates.)

7. Which of the following transactions will increase the return on equity?
   a. Declare and issue a stock dividend.
   b. Split the stock 2-for-1.
   c. Repurchase the company's stock.
   d. None of the above.

8. Which statement regarding dividends is false?
   a. Dividends represent a sharing of corporate profits with owners.
   b. Both stock and cash dividends reduce retained earnings.
   c. Cash dividends paid to stockholders reduce net income.
   d. None of the above.
9. When treasury stock is purchased with cash, what is the impact on the balance sheet equation?
   a. No change—the reduction of the asset Cash is offset with the addition of the asset Treasury Stock.
   b. Assets decrease and Stockholders' Equity increases.
   c. Assets increase and Stockholders' Equity decreases.
   d. Assets decrease and Stockholders' Equity decreases.
10. In what situation does an investor's personal wealth increase immediately?
   a. When receiving a cash dividend.
   b. When receiving a stock dividend.
   c. When a stock split is announced.
   d. In all of the above situations.

---

**Solutions to Multiple-Choice Questions**

1. a   2. d   3. d   4. a   5. c   6. b   7. c   8. c   9. d   10. a

---

## Mini Exercises 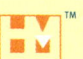 Available with McGraw-Hill's Homework Manager

**LO1**

### M13-1 Favoring Equity versus Debt Financing
Indicate whether each of the following favors the use of equity (E) or debt (D) financing.

____ 1. Interest is tax deductible.

____ 2. Dividends are optional.

____ 3. Debt must be repaid.

____ 4. Additional stock issuances dilute existing stockholders' control.

**LO1**

### M13-2 Evaluating Stockholders' Rights
Name four rights of common stockholders. Which of these seems most important? Why?

**LO2**

### M13-3 Computing the Number of Unissued Shares
The balance sheet for Crutcher Corporation reported 147,000 shares outstanding, 300,000 shares authorized, and 10,000 shares in treasury stock. Compute the maximum number of new shares that Crutcher could issue.

**LO2**

### M13-4 Recording the Sale of Common Stock
To expand operations, Aragon Consulting issued 100,000 shares of previously unissued common stock with a par value of $1. The selling price for the stock was $75 per share. Record the journal entry for this sale of stock. Would your answer be different if the par value were $2 per share? If so, record the sale of stock with a par value of $2.

**LO2**

### M13-5 Recording the Sale of Common Stock
Refer to M13-4. Assume the issued stock has no par value. Record the journal entry for the sale of no-par value stock at $75. Do the effects on total assets, total liabilities, and total stockholders' equity differ from those in M13-4?

**LO2**

Sonic Corporation

### M13-6 Comparing Common Stock and Preferred Stock
Your parents have just retired and have asked you for some financial advice. They have decided to invest $100,000 in a company very similar to Sonic Corp. The company has issued both common and preferred stock. Which type of stock would you recommend? What factors would you consider in giving them advice?

**LO2**

### M13-7 Determining the Effects of Treasury Stock Transactions
Trans Union Corporation sold 5,000 shares for $50 per share in 2007, and it sold 10,000 shares for $37 per share in 2008. In 2009, the company purchased 2,000 shares of its own stock for $45 per share. Determine the impact (increase, decrease, or no change) of each of these transactions on the following classifications:

1. Total assets.
2. Total liabilities.
3. Total stockholders' equity.
4. Net income.

**M13-8 Comparing Stockholder's Equity to Owner's Equity**

LO2

On January 1, Daniel Harrison contributed $20,000 to start his business. At the end of that year, the business had generated $30,000 in sales revenues, incurred $18,000 in operating expenses, and distributed $5,000 for Daniel to use to pay some personal expenses. Prepare the section of the balance sheet showing (a) his stockholder's equity, assuming this is a corporation with no-par value stock or (b) his owner's equity, assuming this is a sole proprietorship.

**M13-9 Determining the Amount of a Dividend**

LO3

Netpass Company has 300,000 shares of common stock authorized, 270,000 shares issued, and 50,000 shares of treasury stock. The company's board of directors declares a dividend of 50 cents per share on common stock. What is the total amount of the dividend that will be paid?

**M13-10 Recording Dividends**

LO3

On April 15, 2009, the board of directors for Auction.com declared a cash dividend of 40 cents per share payable to stockholders of record on May 20. The dividends will be paid on June 14. The company has 500,000 shares of stock outstanding. Prepare any necessary journal entries for each date.

**M13-11 Determining the Impact of a Stock Dividend**

LO3

Sturdy Stone Tools, Inc., announced a 100 percent stock dividend. Determine the impact (increase, decrease, no change) of this dividend on the following:

1. Total assets.
2. Total liabilities.
3. Common stock.
4. Total stockholders' equity.
5. Market value per share of common stock.

**M13-12 Determining the Impact of a Stock Split**

LO3

Complete the requirements of M13-11 assuming that the company announced a 2-for-1 stock split.

**M13-13 Recording a Small Stock Dividend**

LO3

Shriver Food Systems, Inc., declared a 10 percent stock dividend on May 1. The company has 800,000 shares authorized and 200,000 shares outstanding. The par value of the stock is $1 per share and the market value is $100 per share. The dividend was issued on May 21. Prepare the journal entries to record the declaration and issuance of this stock dividend.

**M13-14 Recording a Large Stock Dividend**

LO3

Refer to M13-13. Assume the company declared and issued a 50 percent stock dividend on the dates indicated. Prepare the journal entries to record the declaration and issuance.

**M13-15 Determining the Amount of a Preferred Dividend**

LO3

Colliers, Inc., has 100,000 shares of cumulative preferred stock outstanding. The preferred stock pays dividends in the amount of $2 per share but because of cash flow problems, the company did not pay any dividends last year. The board of directors plans to pay dividends in the amount of $1 million this year. What amount will go to preferred stockholders? How much will be available for common stock dividends?

**M13-16 Calculating and Interpreting Earnings per Share (EPS)**

LO4

Academy Driving School reported the following amount in its financial statements:

|  | 2010 | 2009 |
|---|---|---|
| Number of common shares | 11,500 | 11,500 |
| Net income | $23,000 | $18,000 |
| Cash dividends paid on common stock | $ 3,000 | $ 3,000 |

Calculate 2010 EPS. Another driving school in the same city reported a higher net income ($45,000) in 2010, yet its EPS ratio was lower than that for the Academy Driving School. Explain how this apparent inconsistency could occur.

**LO4**

**M13-17 Determining the Impact of Transactions on Earnings per Share (EPS)**

Identify and explain the direction of effect (+ for increase, − for decrease, or NE for no effect) of each of the following transactions on EPS.

- *a.* Purchased 50 shares into treasury.
- *b.* Declared and paid a cash dividend.
- *c.* Declared and issued a stock dividend.
- *d.* Sold inventory at an amount more than cost.
- *e.* Sold and issued 6,000 shares of common stock for cash.

**LO4**

**M13-18 Inferring Financial Information Using the P/E Ratio**

In 2008, Rec Room Sports reported earnings per share of $8.50 when its stock was selling for $212.50. In 2009, its earnings increased by 20 percent. If all other relationships remain constant, what is the price of the stock in 2009? Explain.

# Exercises    Available with McGraw-Hill's Homework Manager

**LO2**

**Big Dog Holdings**

**E13-1 Computing Shares Outstanding**

Big Dog Holdings reported that, as of September 30, 2007, 30 million shares of common stock had been authorized. As of that date, 11,182,808 shares had been issued and 1,710,598 shares were held as treasury stock.

*Required:*

Determine the number of shares outstanding on September 30, 2007.

**LO2, 3**

**E13-2 Reporting Stockholders' Equity and Determining Dividend Policy**

Incentive Corporation was organized as a corporation in 2008 to operate a financial consulting business. The charter authorized the following capital stock: common stock, par value $4 per share, 12,000 shares. During the first year, the following selected transactions were completed:

- *a.* Sold and issued 6,000 shares of common stock for cash at $20 per share.
- *b.* Sold and issued 2,000 shares of common stock for cash at $23 per share.

*Required:*

1. Give the journal entry required for each of these transactions.
2. At year-end, the Income Summary account reflected a profit of $10,000. Give the journal entry to close this account to Retained Earnings.
3. Prepare the Stockholders' Equity section as it should be reported on the 2008 year-end balance sheet.
4. Incentive Corporation has $30,000 cash in the company's bank account. What is the maximum amount of cash dividends the company can declare at this time? Explain.

**LO2**

**E13-3 Reporting the Stockholders' Equity Section of the Balance Sheet**

North Wind Aviation received its corporate charter during January 2009. The charter authorized the following capital stock:

Common stock: par $7, authorized 50,000 shares.

Preferred stock: 8 percent, par $10, authorized 20,000 shares.

During 2009, the following transactions occurred in the order given:

- *a.* Issued a total of 40,000 shares of the common stock to the company's founders for $11 per share.
- *b.* Sold 5,000 shares of the preferred stock at $18 per share.
- *c.* Sold 3,000 shares of the common stock at $14 per share and 1,000 shares of the preferred stock at $28.
- *d.* Net income for the first year was $48,000, and no dividends were declared.

*Required:*

Prepare the Stockholders' Equity section of the balance sheet at December 31, 2009.

**LO2, 3**

**E13-4 Reporting the Stockholders' Equity Section of the Balance Sheet**

Shelby Corporation was organized in January 2010 by 10 stockholders to operate an air conditioning sales and service business. The charter issued by the state authorized the following capital stock:

Common stock, $1 par value, 200,000 shares.

Preferred stock, 6 percent, $8 par value, 50,000 shares.

During January and February 2010, the following stock transactions were completed:

a.  Collected $40,000 cash from each of the 10 organizers and issued 2,000 shares of common stock to each of them.

b.  Sold 15,000 shares of preferred stock at $25 per share; collected the cash and immediately issued the stock.

Net income for 2010 was $40,000; cash dividends declared and paid at year-end were $10,000.

*Required:*
Prepare the Stockholders' Equity section of the balance sheet at December 31, 2010.

**E13-5 Determining the Effects of the Issuance of Common and Preferred Stock**          LO2

Inside Incorporated was issued a charter on January 15, 2009, that authorized the following capital stock:

Common stock, $6 par, 100,000 shares, one vote per share.

Preferred stock, 7 percent, par value $10 per share, 5,000 shares, nonvoting.

During 2009, the following selected transactions were completed in the order given:

a.  Sold and issued 20,000 shares of the $6 par common stock at $18 cash per share.

b.  Sold and issued 3,000 shares of preferred stock at $22 cash per share.

c.  At the end of 2009, the Income Summary account included net income of $38,000.

*Required:*

1.  Prepare journal entries to record transactions a and b, and to close Income Summary to Retained Earnings in c.

2.  Prepare the Stockholders' Equity section of the balance sheet at December 31, 2009.

3.  Assume that you are a common stockholder. If Inside Incorporated needed additional capital, would you prefer to have it issue additional common stock or additional preferred stock? Explain.

**E13-6 Recording and Reporting Stockholders' Equity Transactions**          LO2

AvA School of Learning obtained a charter at the start of 2009 that authorized 50,000 shares of no-par common stock and 20,000 shares of preferred stock, par value $10, 5% noncumulative dividend. During 2009, the following selected transactions occurred:

a.  Collected $40 cash per share from four individuals and issued 5,000 shares of common stock to each.

b.  Sold and issued 6,000 shares of common stock to an outside investor at $40 cash per share.

c.  Sold and issued 8,000 shares of preferred stock at $15 cash per share.

*Required:*

1.  Give the journal entries indicated for each of these transactions.

2.  Prepare the Stockholders' Equity section of the balance sheet at December 31, 2009. At the end of 2009, the accounts reflected net income of $36,000.

**E13-7 Finding Amounts Missing from the Stockholders' Equity Section**          LO2

The Stockholders' Equity section on the December 31, 2009, balance sheet of Chemfast Corporation follows:

| Stockholders' Equity | |
| --- | --- |
| Contributed capital | |
| Preferred stock (par $20; authorized 10,000 shares, ? issued, of which 500 shares are held as treasury stock) | $104,000 |
| Additional paid-in capital, preferred | 14,300 |
| Common stock (no par; authorized 20,000 shares, issued and outstanding 8,000 shares) | 600,000 |
| Retained earnings | 30,000 |
| Cost of 500 shares of preferred treasury stock | 9,500 |

*Required:*

Complete the following statements and show your computations.

1. The number of shares of preferred stock issued was _____.
2. The number of shares of preferred stock outstanding was _____.
3. The average sales price of the preferred stock when issued was $_____ per share.
4. The average issue price of the common stock was $_____.
5. The treasury stock transaction increased (decreased) stockholders' equity by _____.
6. How much did the treasury stock cost per share? $_____.
7. Total stockholders' equity is $_____.

**LO2**

**E13-8 Recording Treasury Stock Transactions and Analyzing Their Impact**

During 2009, the following selected transactions affecting stockholders' equity occurred for Corner Corporation:

 a.  Feb.  1  Purchased 400 shares of the company's own common stock at $22 cash per share.
 b.  Jul.  15  Sold 100 of the shares purchased on February 1, 2009, for $24 cash per share.
 c.  Sept. 1  Sold 60 more of the shares purchased on February 1, 2009, for $20 cash per share.

*Required:*

1. Give journal entries for each of the transactions.
2. What impact does the purchase of treasury stock have on dividends paid?
3. What impact does the sale of treasury stock for an amount higher than the purchase price have on net income?

**LO2, 3**

**E13-9 Comparing Owners' Equity Sections for a Sole Proprietorship and Corporation**

Assume for each of the following independent cases that the annual accounting period ends on December 31, 2009, and that the Income Summary held a credit balance of $20,000.

**Case A:** Assume that the company is a *sole proprietorship* owned by Proprietor A. Prior to the closing entries, the capital account reflected a credit balance of $50,000 and the drawings account a balance of $8,000.

**Case B:** Assume that the company is a *corporation*. Prior to the closing entries, the stockholders' equity accounts showed the following: Common Stock, par $10, 30,000 shares authorized, 15,000 shares issued and outstanding; Additional Paid-In Capital, $5,000; Retained Earnings, $65,000. No dividends were declared.

*Required:*

1. Give all the closing entries required at December 31, 2009, for each case.
2. Show the body of (a) a statement of owner's equity and (b) a statement of retained earnings for the year ended December 31, 2009.
3. Show how the Equity section of the balance sheet would appear at December 31, 2009, for each case.

**LO2, 3**

**E13-10 Recording Stockholders' Equity Transactions**

The annual report for Malibu Beachwear reported the following transactions affecting stockholders' equity:

 a.  Purchased $35,000 in treasury stock.
 b.  Declared cash dividends in the amount of $25,420.
 c.  Paid cash dividends in the amount of $25,420.
 d.  Declared 10 percent common stock dividend, which would require issuing 20,000 additional $1 par value shares with a market price of $15 per share.
 e.  Issued the stock dividend in transaction d.

*Required:*

1. Prepare journal entries to record each of these transactions.
2. Indicate the effect (increase, decrease, or no effect) of each of these transactions on total assets, liabilities, and stockholders' equity.

**E13-11 Computing Dividends on Common and Preferred Stock and Analyzing Differences**    LO3

The records of Hoffman Company reflected the following balances in the stockholders' equity accounts at December 31, 2009:

> Common stock, par $12 per share, 40,000 shares outstanding.
>
> Preferred stock, 8 percent, par $10 per share, 6,000 shares outstanding.
>
> Retained earnings, $220,000.

On January 1, 2010, the board of directors was considering the distribution of a $62,000 cash dividend. No dividends were paid during 2008 and 2009.

*Required:*

1. Determine the total and per share amounts that would be paid to the common stockholders and to the preferred stockholders under two independent assumptions:

    a.  The preferred stock is noncumulative.

    b.  The preferred stock is cumulative.

2. Briefly explain why the dividends per share of common stock were less for the second assumption.
3. What factors would cause a more favorable dividend for the common stockholders?

**E13-12 Recording the Payment of Dividends and Preparing a Statement of Retained Earnings**    LO3

The 2009 annual report for Sneers Corporation disclosed that the company declared and paid preferred dividends in the amount of $119.9 million in 2009. It also declared and paid dividends on common stock in the amount of $2 per share. During 2009, Sneers had 1,000,000,000 shares of common authorized; 387,570,300 shares had been issued; and 41,670,300 shares were in treasury stock. The balance in Retained Earnings was $1,554 million on December 31, 2008 and net income was $858 million for 2009.

*Required:*

1. Prepare journal entries to record the declaration of dividends on (a) preferred stock and (b) common stock.
2. Prepare journal entries to record the payment of dividends on (a) preferred stock and (b) common stock.
3. Prepare a journal entry to close 2009 net income into Retained Earnings from Income Summary.
4. Using the information given above, prepare a statement of retained earnings for the year ended December 31, 2009.

**E13-13 Analyzing Stock Dividends**    LO3

On December 31, 2008, the Stockholders' Equity section of the balance sheet of R & B Corporation reflected the following:

| | |
|---|---:|
| Common stock (par $10; authorized 60,000 shares, outstanding 25,000 shares) | $250,000 |
| Additional paid-in capital | 12,000 |
| Retained earnings | 75,000 |

On February 1, 2009, the board of directors declared a 12 percent stock dividend to be issued April 30, 2009. The market value of the stock on February 1, 2009, was $18 per share.

*Required:*

1. For comparative purposes, prepare the Stockholders' Equity section of the balance sheet both (a) immediately before the stock dividend and (b) immediately after the stock dividend. Consider using side-by-side columns for the amounts in parts (a) and (b).
2. Explain the effects of this stock dividend on the assets, liabilities, and stockholders' equity.
3. How would your answers to requirements 1 and 2 change if the stock dividend were 100 percent?

**E13-14 Recording Dividends**    LO3

Black & Decker is a leading global manufacturer and marketer of power tools, hardware, and home improvement products. A press release on October 17, 2007, contained the following announcement:

**BLACK&DECKER**

> ... its Board of Directors declared a quarterly cash dividend of $0.42 per share on the Corporation's outstanding common stock payable December 28, 2007, to stockholders of record at the close of business on December 14, 2007.

At the time of the press release, Black & Decker had 150,000,000 shares authorized and 62,536,000 outstanding. The par value for the company's stock is $.50 per share.

*Required:*

Prepare journal entries as appropriate for each of the three dates mentioned above.

**LO3**    **E13-15 Comparing Stock Dividends and Splits**

On July 1, 2009, Jones Corporation had the following capital structure:

| | |
|---|---:|
| Common stock, $1 par, 200,000 authorized shares, 150,000 issued and outstanding | $150,000 |
| Additional paid-in capital | 88,000 |
| Retained earnings | 172,000 |
| Treasury stock | None |

*Required:*

Complete the following table based on three independent cases involving stock transactions:

**Case 1:** The board of directors declared and issued a 10 percent stock dividend when the stock was selling at $8 per share.

**Case 2:** The board of directors declared and issued a 100 percent stock dividend when the stock was selling at $8 per share.

**Case 3:** The board of directors voted a 2-for-1 stock split. The market price prior to the split was $8 per share.

| | | CASE 1 | CASE 2 | CASE 3 |
|---|---|---|---|---|
| Items | Before Stock Transactions | After 10% Stock Dividend | After 100% Stock Dividend | After Stock Split |
| Number of shares outstanding | | | | |
| Par per share | $    1 | $ | $ | $ |
| Common stock account | $ | $ | $ | $ |
| Additional paid-in capital | 88,000 | | | |
| Retained earnings | 172,000 | | | |
| Total stockholders' equity | $ | $ | $ | $ |

**LO2, 3**    **E13-16 Analyzing Dividends in Arrears**

Mission Critical Software, Inc., was a leading provider of systems management software for Windows NT network and Internet infrastructure. Like many start-up companies, Mission Critical struggled with cash flows as it developed new business opportunities. A student found a financial statement for Mission Critical that stated that the increase in dividends in arrears on preferred stock this year was $264,000.

The student who read the note suggested that the Mission Critical preferred stock would be a good investment because of the large amount of dividend income that would be earned when the company started paying dividends again: "As the owner of the stock, I'll get dividends for the period I hold the stock plus some previous periods when I didn't even own the stock." Do you agree? Explain.

**LO3**    **E13-17 Determining the Impact of Cash and Stock Dividends**

Superior Corporation has the following capital stock outstanding on January 1, 2009:

Common stock, par $8, outstanding shares, 30,000.

Preferred stock, 6 percent, par $15, outstanding shares, 8,000.

On October 1, 2009, the board of directors declared dividends that would be paid, or issued, to stockholders of record on December 1, 2009:

Common stock: 10 percent common stock dividend, to be issued on December 20, 2009.

Preferred stock: Cash dividend, 6 percent, payable December 20, 2009.

On October 1, 2009, the market prices were preferred stock, $40, and common stock, $32. On December 20, 2009, the dividends were paid, or issued.

*Required:*

At each date indicated above, present journal entries for the dividends on (a) preferred stock and (b) common stock.

**E13-18 Determining the Financial Statement Effects of Cash and Stock Dividends**  LO3

Lynn Company has outstanding 60,000 shares of $10 par value common stock and 25,000 shares of $20 par value preferred stock (8 percent). On December 1, 2009, the board of directors voted an 8 percent cash dividend on the preferred stock and a 10 percent stock dividend on the common stock. At the date of declaration, the common stock was selling at $35 and the preferred at $20 per share. The dividends are to be paid, or issued, on February 15, 2010. The annual accounting period ends December 31.

*Required:*

Explain the comparative effects of the two dividends on the assets, liabilities, and stockholders' equity (a) through December 31, 2009, (b) on February 15, 2010, and (c) overall from December 1, 2009, through February 15, 2010. A schedule using the following structure might be helpful:

|  | COMPARATIVE EFFECTS EXPLAINED | |
|---|---|---|
| Item | Cash Dividend on Preferred | Stock Dividend on Common |
| (a) Through December 31, 2009: | | |
| Effect on assets | | |
| Effect on liabilities | | |
| Effect on stockholders' equity | | |

**E13-19 Preparing a Statement of Retained Earnings and Partial Balance Sheet and Evaluating Dividend Policy**  LO2, 3, 4

The following account balances were selected from the records of Blake Corporation at December 31, 2009, after all adjusting entries were completed. The company had not issued or repurchased any additional shares this year.

| | |
|---|---|
| Common stock (par $15; authorized 100,000 shares, issued 35,000 shares, of which 1,000 shares are held as treasury stock) | $525,000 |
| Additional paid-in capital | 180,000 |
| Dividends on common stock declared and paid in 2009 | 28,000 |
| Retained earnings, January 1, 2009 | 76,000 |
| Treasury stock at cost (1,000 shares) | 20,000 |
| Net income for the year. | 48,000 |

*Required:*

1. Prepare the statement of retained earnings for the year ended December 31, 2009, and the Stockholders' Equity section of the balance sheet at December 31, 2009.
2. Determine the number of shares of stock that received dividends.
3. Compute the EPS ratio for the year ended December 31, 2009. Is it better or worse than the $1.32 earnings per share in 2008?

**E13-20 Analyzing Stock Repurchases and Stock Dividends**  LO3, 4

Winnebago is a familiar name on vehicles traveling U.S. highways. The company manufactures and sells large motor homes for vacation travel. These motor homes can be quickly recognized because of the company's "flying W" trademark. An April 12, 2006, press release contained the following information:

*Winnebago*

Winnebago Industries, Inc., (NYSE: WGO) announced that in a meeting held today, the Company's Board of Directors announced a new $60 million stock repurchase authorization. Winnebago Industries has repurchased approximately 24.4 million shares of common stock for approximately $356.8 million since December 31, 1997.

*Required:*

1.  Explain the impact of a $60 million stock repurchase on the financial statements.
2.  Why do you think the board decided to repurchase the stock?
3.  Assuming that Winnebago continues its current level of annual dividend payments, what impact will this purchase have on Winnebago's future dividends per share?
4.  On January 14, 2004, the company's board of directors declared a 100 percent stock dividend that was distributed on March 5, 2004. Why would Winnebago choose a stock dividend rather than a 2-for-1 stock split?
5.  What impact would this stock dividend have had on Winnebago's financial statements? What impact would it have had on the EPS ratio?

## Problems—Set A     Available with McGraw-Hill's Homework Manager

**LO2**

### PA13-1 Recording Journal Entries and Preparing a Partial Balance Sheet after Stock Issue, Purchase, and Reissue Transactions

Worldwide Company obtained a charter from the state in January 2009, which authorized 200,000 shares of common stock, $10 par value. During the first year, the company earned $38,200, and the following selected transactions occurred in the order given:

a.  Sold 60,000 shares of the common stock at $12 per share.
b.  Purchased 2,000 shares at $15 cash per share from one of the 30 stockholders who needed cash and wanted to sell the stock back to the company.
c.  Resold 1,000 of the shares of the treasury stock purchased in transaction *b* two months later to another individual at $18 cash per share.

*Required:*

1.  Prepare journal entries to record each transaction.
2.  Prepare the Stockholders' Equity section of the balance sheet at December 31, 2009. Because this is the first year of operations, Retained Earnings has a zero balance at the beginning of the year.

**LO3**

**Macy's**

### PA13-2 Recording Dividends

Prior to changing its corporate name to Macy's, Inc., on June 1, 2007, Federated Department Stores issued a press release with the following information:

CINCINNATI—May 19, 2006—The Board of Directors of Federated Department Stores, Inc. (NYSE:FD) today approved a split of the company's common stock on a two-for-one basis. Additional shares issued as a result of the stock dividend will be distributed after close of trading on June 9, 2006, to shareholders of record on May 26, 2006. At the company's Annual Meeting this morning, Federated shareholders approved an increase in the number of authorized shares of Federated common stock from 500 million to 1 billion. With the stock split, Federated's quarterly dividend will be 12.75 cents per outstanding common share, payable July 3, 2006, to Federated shareholders of record at the close of business on June 16, 2006.

*Required:*

1.  Although the press release refers to a stock split, the transaction actually involved a 100 percent stock dividend, to be recorded at par value. Prepare any journal entries that Federated Department Stores should have made as the result of the stock dividend and the cash dividend. Assume that, at the time of the stock dividend, the company had 175 million shares outstanding, the par value was $0.01 per share, and the market value was $73 per share.

2.  What two requirements would the board of directors have considered before making the dividend decision?

## PA13-3 Finding Missing Amounts

LO2, 3, 4

At December 31, 2009, the records of Nortech Corporation provided the following selected and incomplete data:

Authorized shares of common stock, 200,000.

Balance in common stock account $1,250,000 (par $10; no changes during 2009).

Common stock issued in prior year at a price of $17 per share.

Shares held as treasury stock, 3,000 shares, cost $20 per share (no changes during 2009).

Net income for 2009, $118,000.

Dividends declared and paid during 2009, $73,200.

Retained earnings balance, January 1, 2009, $155,000.

*Required:*

1.  Complete the following:

    Shares authorized _____.

    Shares issued _____.

    Shares outstanding _____.

2.  The balance in the Additional Paid-In Capital account would be $ _____.

3.  Earnings per share is $ _____.

4.  Dividends paid per share of common stock is $ _____.

5.  Treasury stock should be reported in the Stockholders' Equity section of the balance sheet in the amount of $ _____.

6.  Assume that the board of directors approved a 2-for-1 stock split. After the stock split, the par value per share will be $_____ and the number of outstanding shares will be _____. (The treasury stock was acquired after the split was issued.)

7.  Disregard the stock split (assumed above). Assume instead a 100 percent stock dividend was declared and issued after the treasury stock was acquired, when the market price of the common stock was $21. Give any journal entry that should be made.

## PA13-4 Recording Journal Entries and Preparing a Partial Balance Sheet after Common Stock Issue, Purchase, Reissue, and Cash Dividends

LO2, 3

www.mhhe.com/LLPW1e

American Laser, Inc. reported the following stockholders' equity account balances on January 1, 2009.

| | |
|---|---|
| Common stock, 10,000 shares of $1 par | $ 10,000 |
| Retained earnings | 120,000 |
| Additional paid-in capital—common | 90,000 |
| Treasury stock | 0 |

The company entered into the following transactions during 2009.

Jan.  15  Issued 5,000 shares of $1 par common stock for $50,000 cash.

Feb.  15  Purchased 3,000 shares of $1 par common stock into treasury for $33,000 cash.

Mar.  15  Reissued 2,000 shares of treasury stock for $24,000 cash.

Aug.  15  Reissued 600 shares of treasury stock for $4,600 cash.

Sept. 15  Declared (but did not pay) a $1 cash dividend on each outstanding share of common stock.

*Required:*

1.  Prepare journal entries to record each transaction.

2.  Prepare the Stockholders' Equity section of the balance sheet at December 31, 2009. At the end of 2009, the accounts reflected net income of $20,000. The company was authorized to issue 200,000 shares.

**LO2, 3**

www.mhhe.com/LLPW1e

### PA13-5 Comparing Stock and Cash Dividends

Water Tower Company had the following stock outstanding and retained earnings at December 31, 2009:

| | |
|---|---:|
| Common stock (par $8; outstanding, 30,000 shares) | $240,000 |
| Preferred stock, 7% (par $10; outstanding, 6,000 shares) | 60,000 |
| Retained earnings | 280,000 |

The board of directors is considering the distribution of a cash dividend to the common and preferred stockholders. No dividends were declared during 2007 or 2008. Three independent cases are assumed:

**Case A:** The preferred stock is noncumulative; the total amount of dividends is $30,000.

**Case B:** The preferred stock is cumulative; the total amount of dividends is $12,600.

**Case C:** Same as Case B, except the amount is $66,000.

*Required:*

1.  Compute the amount of dividends, in total and per share (rounded to the nearest penny), that would be payable to each class of stockholders for each case. Show computations.

2.  Assume that a 100 percent common stock dividend was issued when the market value per share was $24. Complete the following schedule.

| | AMOUNT OF DOLLAR INCREASE (DECREASE) | |
|---|---|---|
| Item | Cash Dividend, Case C | Stock Dividend |
| Assets | $ | $ |
| Liabilities | | |
| Stockholders' equity | | |

**LO4**

**Aaron Rents, Inc.**
**Rent-A-Center, Inc.**

www.mhhe.com/LLPW1e

### PA13-6 Computing and Interpreting Earnings per Share (EPS) and Price/Earnings (P/E) Ratios

Aaron Rents, Inc., and Rent-A-Center, Inc., are two publicly traded rental companies. They reported the following in their 2006 financial statements (in thousands, except per share amounts):

| | AARON RENTS, INC. | | RENT-A-CENTER, INC. | |
|---|---|---|---|---|
| | 2005 | 2006 | 2005 | 2006 |
| Average number of common shares | 49,994 | 52,423 | 72,977 | 69,657 |
| Average number of preferred shares | 0 | 0 | 0 | 0 |
| Net income | $ 57,993 | $ 78,635 | $ 135,738 | $ 103,092 |
| Stock price when annual results reported | 23.10 | 27.60 | 20.80 | 28.50 |

*Required:*

1.  Compute the 2006 EPS for each company (rounded to the nearest penny). In 2005, Aaron Rents reported EPS of $1.16, whereas Rent-A-Center reported EPS of $1.86. Which company appears to have improved its performance in 2006?

2.  Compute the 2006 P/E ratio for each company. Do investors appear to value one company more than the other? Explain.

# Problems—Set B  Available with McGraw-Hill's Homework Manager

**PB13-1 Recording Journal Entries and Preparing a Partial Balance Sheet after Stock Issue and Purchase Transactions**

Global Marine obtained a charter from the state in January 2009, which authorized 1,000,000 shares of common stock, $5 par value. During the first year of operations, the company earned $429,000, and the following selected transactions occurred in the order given:

LO2

  a.  Sold 700,000 shares of the common stock at $54 per share. Collected the cash and issued the stock.
  b.  Purchased 25,000 shares at $50 cash per share to use as stock incentives for senior management.

**Required:**

1.  Prepare journal entries to record each transaction.
2.  Prepare the Stockholders' Equity section of the balance sheet at December 31, 2009.

**PB13-2 Recording Dividends**

National Beverage Corp. produces soft drinks, bottled waters, and juices sold under the brand names Shasta, Faygo, and Everfresh. A press release contained the following information:

LO3
**National Beverage Corp.**

> March 5—National Beverage Corp. today announced that its Board of Directors has declared a special "one-time" cash dividend of $1.00 per share on approximately 36.6 million outstanding shares. The dividend will be paid on or before April 30 to shareholders of record at the close of business on March 26.

**Required:**

1.  Prepare any journal entries that National Beverage Corp. should make to record the cash dividend.
2.  On March 5, National Beverage Corp. also declared a 100 percent stock dividend, which was distributed on March 22. Prepare any journal entries that National Beverage Corp. should have made to record this stock dividend. Assume that the company had 18.3 million shares outstanding on March 5, the par value is $0.01 per share, and the market value is $10 per share.
3.  What two requirements would the board of directors have considered before making the dividend decisions?

**PB13-3 Finding Missing Amounts**

At December 31, 2009, the records of Kozmetsky Corporation provided the following selected and incomplete data:

LO2, 3, 4

Common stock (par $1; no changes during 2009).
Shares authorized, 5,000,000.
Shares issued, ___?___; issue price $80 per share.
Shares held as treasury stock, 100,000 shares, cost $60 per share (no changes during 2009).
Net income for 2009, $4,800,000.
Common Stock account, $1,500,000.
Dividends declared and paid during 2009, $2 per share.
Retained Earnings balance, January 1, 2009, $82,900,000.

**Required:**

1.  Complete the following:
    Shares issued _____.
    Shares outstanding_____.
2.  The balance in the Additional Paid-In Capital account would be $_____.
3.  Earnings per share is $_____.
4.  Total dividends paid on common stock during 2009 is $_____.
5.  Treasury stock should be reported in the Stockholders' Equity section of the balance sheet in the amount of $_____.

6.  Assume that the board of directors voted a 2-for-1 stock split. After the stock split, the par value per share will be $_____, and the number of outstanding shares will be_____. The treasury stock was acquired after the split was issued.

7.  Disregard the stock split (assumed above). Assume instead a 100 percent stock dividend was declared and issued after the treasury stock was acquired, when the market price of the common stock was $21. Explain how stockholders' equity will change.

LO2, 3    **PB13-4 Recording Journal Entries and Preparing a Partial Balance Sheet after Common Stock Issue, Purchase, Reissue, and Cash Dividends**
Waste Control, Inc. reported the following stockholders' equity account balances on January 1, 2009.

| | |
|---|---|
| Common stock, 20,000 shares of $1 par | $ 20,000 |
| Retained earnings | 110,000 |
| Additional paid-in capital—common | 180,000 |
| Treasury stock | 0 |

The company entered into the following transactions during 2009.

Jan.  12  Issued 5,000 shares of $1 par common stock for $50,000 cash.
Feb.   3  Purchased 3,000 shares of $1 par common stock into treasury for $27,000 cash.
Mar.   4  Reissued 2,000 shares of treasury stock for $20,000 cash.
Aug.   5  Reissued 600 shares of treasury stock for $5,400 cash.
Sept. 15  Declared (but did not pay) a $2 cash dividend on each outstanding share of common stock.

*Required:*
1.  Prepare journal entries to record each transaction.
2.  Prepare the Stockholders' Equity section of the balance sheet at December 31, 2009. At the end of 2009, the accounts reflected net income of $50,000. The company was authorized to issue 500,000 shares.

LO2, 3    **PB13-5 Comparing Stock and Cash Dividends**
Ritz Company had the following stock outstanding and Retained Earnings at December 31, 2009:

| | |
|---|---|
| Common stock (par $1; outstanding, 500,000 shares) | $500,000 |
| Preferred stock, 8% (par $10; outstanding, 21,000 shares) | 210,000 |
| Retained earnings | 900,000 |

The board of directors is considering the distribution of a cash dividend to the common and preferred stockholders. No dividends were declared during 2007 or 2008. Three independent cases are assumed:

**Case A:** The preferred stock is noncumulative; the total amount of dividends is $30,000.
**Case B:** The preferred stock is cumulative; the total amount of dividends is $30,000.
**Case C:** Same as Case B, except the amount is $75,000.

*Required:*
1.  Compute the amount of dividends, in total and per share (rounded to the nearest penny), payable to each class of stockholders for each case. Show computations.
2.  Assume that the company issued a 100 percent stock dividend on the outstanding common shares when the market value per share was $50. Complete the following schedule.

| Item | AMOUNT OF DOLLAR INCREASE (DECREASE) | |
|---|---|---|
| | Cash Dividend, Case C | Stock Dividend |
| Assets | $ | $ |
| Liabilities | | |
| Stockholders' equity | | |

**PB13-6 Computing and Interpreting Earnings per Share (EPS) and Price/Earnings (P/E) Ratios**      LO4

Two magazine companies reported the following in their 2008 financial statements:

|  | BUSINESSWORLD | | FUN AND GAMES | |
|---|---|---|---|---|
|  | 2007 | 2008 | 2007 | 2008 |
| Average number of common shares | 20,000 | 22,000 | 40,000 | 45,000 |
| Net income | $65,000 | $76,000 | $84,000 | $180,000 |
| Preferred dividends | 10,000 | 10,000 | 0 | 0 |
| Stock price when annual results reported | 54.60 | 51.00 | 32.55 | 59.60 |

*Required:*

1. Compute the 2008 EPS for each company. In 2007, BusinessWorld reported EPS of $2.75, whereas Fun and Games reported EPS of $2.10. Which company appears to have improved its performance in 2008?

2. Compute the 2008 P/E ratio for each company. Do investors appear to value one company more than the other? Explain.

# Cases and Projects

## CP13-1 Finding Financial Information      LO2, 3, 4

Refer to the financial statements of The Home Depot in Appendix A at the end of this book, or download the annual report from the Cases and Projects section of the text's Web site at www.mhhe.com/LLPW1e.

*Required:*

1. As of February 3, 2008, how many shares of common stock were authorized? How many shares were issued? How many shares were held in treasury? What does this suggest to you about the number of shares outstanding?

2. According to the Retained Earnings column in the Statement of Stockholders' Equity, how much did the company declare in dividends during the year ended February 3, 2008?

3. According to the income statement, how has The Home Depot's net earnings changed over the past three years? Has the company's basic earnings per share changed over the past three years? How do you explain these seemingly inconsistent patterns?

## CP13-2 Comparing Financial Information      LO2, 3, 4

Refer to the financial statements of The Home Depot in Appendix A and Lowe's in Appendix B at the end of this book, or download the annual reports from the Cases and Projects section of the text's Web site at www.mhhe.com/LLPW1e.

Lowe's

*Required:*

1. Did Lowe's have more or fewer authorized shares of common stock than The Home Depot at the beginning of February 2008?

2. From the Retained Earnings column in the statement of stockholders' equity, what total amount of cash dividends did Lowe's declare during the year ended February 1, 2008? Compared to The Home Depot, is Lowe's policy on dividends better, worse, or just different?

3. How have Lowe's net earnings changed over the past three years? How has the company's basic earnings per share changed over the past three years? According to financial statement note 11, were the changes in EPS caused only by changes in Lowe's net earnings?

## CP13-3 Examining an Annual Report: Internet-Based Team Research      LO3, 4

As a team, select an industry to analyze. Using your Web browser, each team member should acquire the annual report or 10-K for one publicly traded company in the industry, with each member selecting a different company. (See CP1-3 in Chapter 1 for a description of possible resources for these tasks.)

*Required:*

1. On an individual basis, each team member should write a short report that incorporates the following:

   *a.* Has the company declared cash or stock dividends during the past three years?

   *b.* What is the trend in the company's EPS over the past three years?

   *c.* Compute and analyze the P/E ratio over the past two years.

2. Then, as a team, write a short report comparing and contrasting your companies using these attributes. Discuss any patterns across the companies that you as a team observe. Provide potential explanations for any differences discovered.

LO2

Activision, Inc.

### CP13-4 Making Ethical Decisions: A Real-Life Example

Activision became a public company with an initial public offering of stock on June 9, 1983, at $12 per share. In June 2002, Activision issued 7.5 million additional shares to the public at approximately $33 per share. In October 2002, when its stock was trading at about $22 per share, Activision executives announced that the company would spend up to $150 million to buy back stock from investors. On January 8, 2003, *The Wall Street Journal* reported that several analysts were criticizing Activision's executives because the company had sold the shares to the public at a high price ($33) and then were offering to buy them back at the going market price, which was considerably lower than the issue price in 2002.

*Required:*

1. Do you think it was inappropriate for Activision to offer to buy back the stock at a lower price in October 2002?

2. Would your answer to requirement 1 be different if Activision had not issued additional stock in June 2002?

3. *The Wall Street Journal* article also reported that Activision executives had purchased over 530,000 shares of company stock in December 2002 at the then-current price of $13.32 per share. If you were an investor, how would you feel about executives buying stock in their own company?

4. Would your answer to requirement 3 be different if you also learned that the executives had sold nearly 2.5 million shares of Activision stock earlier that year, when the price was at least $26.08 per share?

LO3

### CP13-5 Making Ethical Decisions: A Mini Case

You are the president of a very successful Internet company that has had a remarkably profitable year. You have determined that the company has more than $10 million in cash generated by operating activities not needed in the business. You are thinking about paying it out to stockholders as a special dividend. You discuss the idea with your vice president, who reacts angrily to your suggestion:

> Our stock price has gone up by 200 percent in the last year alone. What more do we have to do for the owners? The people who really earned that money are the employees who have been working 12 hours a day, six or seven days a week to make the company successful. Most of them didn't even take vacations last year. I say we have to pay out bonuses and nothing extra for the stockholders.

As president, you know that you are hired by the board of directors, which is elected by the stockholders.

*Required:*

What is your responsibility to both groups? To which group would you give the $10 million? Why?

LO3

### CP13-6 Thinking Critically Making a Decision as an Investor

You have retired after a long and successful career as a business executive and now spend a good portion of your time managing your retirement portfolio. You are considering two basic investment alternatives. You can invest in (1) conservative stocks that pay substantial dividends (typically 5 percent of the stock price every year) or (2) growth-oriented technology stocks that pay no dividends.

*Required:*

Analyze each of these alternatives and select one. Justify your selection.

**CP13-7 Charting Stock Price Movement around Important Announcement Dates**    LO3

Using a Web search engine like Google, find either an earnings or dividend announcement for two different companies. Using a source such as bigcharts.com, determine the closing stock price for each company for each day during the five business days before and after the announcement. Using a separate worksheet for each company, prepare a line chart of its stock price movement.

*Required:*

Examine the charts for each company. Does the stock price appear to change as a consequence of their announcements? Explain why or why not.

# Long-Term Liabilities

## LEARNING OBJECTIVES

**After completing this chapter, you should be able to:**

**LO1** Explain how to measure long-term liabilities.

**LO2** Demonstrate how to account for discounted notes payable.

**LO3** Demonstrate how to account for bonds payable.

**LO4** Explain how to account for lease liabilities.

**LO5** Calculate and interpret the debt-to-assets and times interest earned ratios.

Lectured presentation–14-1
www.mhhe.com/LLPW1e

# GENERAL MILLS

## Focus Company: GENERAL MILLS, INC.

## Maker of Pillsbury, Green Giant, Cheerios, and More

www.generalmills.com

After turning in their report, they eagerly await their grade. They are expecting an A and would be devastated if they got a B. A group of high-achieving students waiting for their project grade? They could be, but these hopeful characters are actually the Jolly Green Giant, Lucky the Leprechaun, Poppin' Fresh, and their corporate bosses at General Mills.

That's right, this magically delicious company and all its brands receive a letter grade just as you do. The grading process is a bit different from yours because credit-rating agencies such as Standard & Poor's, Fitch, and Moody's assign their grades based on the company's ability to pay its liabilities on time. And instead of ranging from A to F, their grade can range from AAA to D. The AAA rating is given only to companies in rock-solid financial condition, and the D goes to those likely to pay less than half of what they owe. In general, any grade above a BB is considered a good to high-quality credit rating, which is what General Mills typically earns.

In this chapter, you will learn about the accounting procedures and financial ratios used to report and interpret long-term liabilities and how they influence a company's credit rating. Although we focus on business reporting and analysis, this chapter can also help you understand information that is used to assess your personal credit rating.

| LONG-TERM LIABILITIES | ACCOUNTING FOR LONG-TERM LIABILITIES | ANALYZING LONG-TERM LIABILITIES |
|---|---|---|
| • Making Financing Decisions<br>• Measuring Liabilities | • Discounted Notes<br>• Bonds Payable<br>• Lease Liabilities | • Debt-to-Assets Ratio<br>• Times Interest Earned Ratio |

# LONG-TERM LIABILITIES

## Making Financing Decisions

**Learning Objective 1**

Explain how to measure long-term liabilities.

Businesses of all forms, including sole proprietorships, partnerships, and corporations, usually require long-term financing at some time during their lives. This financing may be used to purchase new equipment, expand buildings, or acquire other businesses. Long-term financing generally involves borrowing money from lenders (debt) or obtaining money from owners (equity). Chapter 13 introduced the relative advantages of these two sources of financing when evaluated by corporations. See Exhibit 14.1 for similar ideas that apply to other organizational forms.

After a decision is made to rely on long-term debt financing, further decisions must be made about the type of debt to use. Long-term debt includes any liabilities that will require repayment over more than one year or if longer, the company's operating cycle. These long-term liabilities, which we explain in the following sections of this chapter, include notes payable, bonds payable, and lease liabilities. Although important differences for these types of debt exist, all liabilities are reported in the financial statements using the same principles, which we discuss next.

## Measuring Liabilities

In Chapter 11, we noted that all liabilities are first recorded at their cash-equivalent amount— that is, the amount of cash that would be accepted in full settlement of the liability at the moment it is created. This amount excludes interest. Interest arises and is recorded as an expense as time passes.

In many instances, the cash-equivalent amount is readily apparent. For example, bank loans or interest-bearing notes (discussed in Chapter 11) refer specifically to separate principal and interest components. In these situations, the principal clearly represents the cash-equivalent amount. To illustrate, consider a $100,000 interest-bearing note that requires principal and

---

**Exhibit 14.1**   Reasons to Use Debt or Equity Financing

| Reasons to Use Debt Financing | Reasons to Use Equity Financing |
|---|---|
| 1. Owners may not have sufficient resources to contribute to the business.<br>2. Interest paid on business loans is tax deductible, but withdrawals paid to owners are not tax deductible.<br>3. Debt does not usually change an owner's control, but admitting new owners does. | 1. A business must repay (or refinance) debt when it matures. Equity contributions by owners do not mature or require repayment.<br>2. Interest on debt must be repaid regardless of the financial condition of the business. Owners may forgo withdrawals to help the business survive its financial difficulties. |

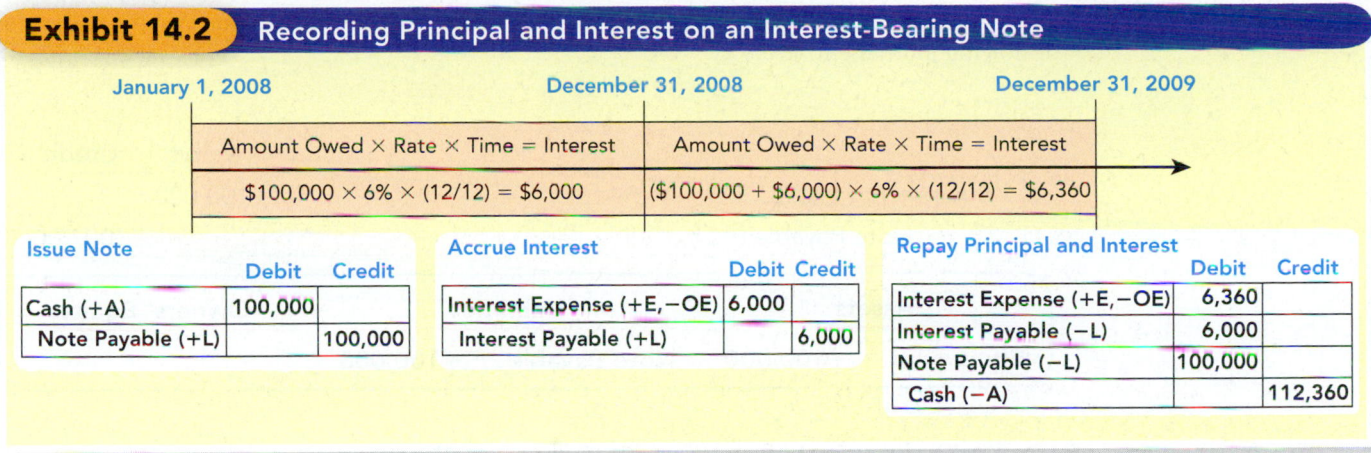

**Exhibit 14.2**   Recording Principal and Interest on an Interest-Bearing Note

January 1, 2008     December 31, 2008     December 31, 2009

| Amount Owed × Rate × Time = Interest | Amount Owed × Rate × Time = Interest |
|---|---|
| $100,000 × 6% × (12/12) = $6,000 | ($100,000 + $6,000) × 6% × (12/12) = $6,360 |

**Issue Note**

| | Debit | Credit |
|---|---|---|
| Cash (+A) | 100,000 | |
| Note Payable (+L) | | 100,000 |

**Accrue Interest**

| | Debit | Credit |
|---|---|---|
| Interest Expense (+E, −OE) | 6,000 | |
| Interest Payable (+L) | | 6,000 |

**Repay Principal and Interest**

| | Debit | Credit |
|---|---|---|
| Interest Expense (+E, −OE) | 6,360 | |
| Interest Payable (−L) | 6,000 | |
| Note Payable (−L) | 100,000 | |
| Cash (−A) | | 112,360 |

interest payments in two years with interest calculated at the rate of 6 percent of the unpaid balance each year. In this example, the principal is $100,000 and the total interest over the two years is $12,360. See Exhibit 14.2 for a review of how to calculate and record the principal and interest on the note. This long-term note is accounted for the same way as the short-term note payable you encountered in Chapter 11 except the long-term note is outstanding for two years rather than one.

The liabilities discussed in the remainder of this chapter apply these same principles, but they do not explicitly separate the principal and interest components. The separate components do exist, but they must be calculated before they can be recorded as principal or interest. A *discounted note payable*, for example, typically describes only the dollar amounts to be paid, such as requiring a payment of $112,360 in two years. Of this payment, part represents the principal and part is assumed to be built-in interest covering the two-year period. The accountant must determine what part is principal and what part is interest so that the cash-equivalent amount (the amount of the principal) can be initially recorded as a Note Payable. As time passes, interest is calculated and recorded, as you will see in the next section.

The procedures used for recording discounted notes are also used to record bonds and lease liabilities, as you will see in later sections. So take your time when learning about discounted notes, and you will find the other topics easier to learn.

The method that accountants use to determine the principal or cash-equivalent amount is called **discounting** or present value analysis. In effect, discounting allows accountants to remove the built-in interest component, leaving a **present value** that represents the note's principal (cash-equivalent) component on the date the liability was created. Supplement 14A explains the steps used in discounting various long-term liabilities.

# ACCOUNTING FOR LONG-TERM LIABILITIES

## Discounted Notes

Discounted notes are accounted for in the same way as interest-bearing notes with two exceptions. First, the accountant must discount the payments to be made on the note to determine the principal (cash-equivalent) amount to record in Notes Payable. Second, interest on a discounted note is accrued in the Notes Payable account. (Interest on interest-bearing notes is accrued in the Interest Payable account.)

Assume that on January 1, 2008, General Mills buys a new piece of equipment. Rather than pay cash, General Mills offers a note that promises to pay $112,360 on December 31, 2009. General Mills typically borrows at a 6 percent interest rate. Because this note does not explicitly state an interest rate, it must be discounted to remove the 6 percent interest that is presumed to be built into the $112,360 payment. By discounting the $112,360 payment using the steps explained in Supplement 14A (see page 616), we can determine that the note's present value on January 1, 2008, is $100,000. That amount is the principal, or

**Learning Objective 2**

Demonstrate how to account for discounted notes payable.

Video 14-1
www.mhhe.com/LLPW1e

cash-equivalent, amount of the note. The liability is recorded as a Note Payable using the following journal entry:

| | Debit | Credit |
|---|---|---|
| Equipment (+A) | 100,000 | |
|     Note Payable (+L) | | 100,000 |

| Assets | = | Liabilities | + | Owners' Equity |
|---|---|---|---|---|
| Equipment   +100,000 | | Note Payable   +100,000 | | |

**Under the matching principle, General Mills will need to adjust its records to account for the interest incurred each accounting period.** In reality, General Mills would make such an adjustment every month or quarter, but for the sake of simplicity, we assume that it occurs only once each year on December 31. Interest for the year ended December 31, 2008, is calculated by multiplying the amount of the liability by the interest rate for the full 12 months of the year ($100,000 × 6% × 12/12 = $6,000). This amount is an expense in 2008, and because it has not yet been paid, it also increases liabilities, as recorded in the following journal entry:

| | Debit | Credit |
|---|---|---|
| Interest Expense (+E, −OE) | 6,000 | |
|     Note Payable (+L) | | 6,000 |

| Assets | = | Liabilities | + | Owners' Equity |
|---|---|---|---|---|
| | | Note Payable   +6,000 | | Interest Expense (+E)   −6,000 |

**Coach's Tip**

Unpaid interest is recorded in Notes Payable because it will be paid with the principal when the note matures.

After this journal entry has been recorded, the balance in the Note Payable account increases from $100,000 to $106,000. We use this new balance in calculating the interest for the following year ($106,000 × 6% × 12/12 = $6,360). This amount is matched to the period in which it was incurred by recording the following journal entry on December 31, 2009, when General Mills makes the required payment of $112,360:

| | Debit | Credit |
|---|---|---|
| Interest Expense (+E, −OE) | 6,360 | |
| Note Payable (−L) | 106,000 | |
|     Cash (−A) | | 112,360 |

| Assets | = | Liabilities | + | Owners' Equity |
|---|---|---|---|---|
| Cash   −112,360 | | Note Payable   −106,000 | | Interest Expense (+E)   −6,360 |

Refer to Exhibit 14.3 for a summary of these calculations and journal entries. If you compare Exhibit 14.3 to Exhibit 14.2 (page 601), you will see that recording the liability and interest on discounted notes is similar to recording them on interest-bearing notes.

Before moving to bonds payable, try the following Self-Study Practice to make sure you understand how to account for discounted notes.

## Exhibit 14.3   Recording Principal and Interest on a Discounted Note

| January 1, 2008 | December 31, 2008 | December 31, 2009 |
|---|---|---|
| Amount Owed × Rate × Time = Interest | Amount Owed × Rate × Time = Interest | |
| $100,000 × 6% × (12/12) = $6,000 | ($100,000 + $6,000) × 6% × (12/12) = $6,360 | |

**Issue Note**

| | Debit | Credit |
|---|---|---|
| Equipment | 100,000 | |
| Note Payable | | 100,000 |

**Accrue Interest**

| | Debit | Credit |
|---|---|---|
| Interest Expense | 6,000 | |
| Note Payable | | 6,000 |

**Repay Principal and Interest**

| | Debit | Credit |
|---|---|---|
| Interest Expense | 6,360 | |
| Note Payable | 106,000 | |
| Cash | | 112,360 |

---

**SELF-STUDY PRACTICE**

Assume that Starbucks issued a discounted note on January 1, 2008, to acquire new equipment. The note requires a payment of $55,125 on December 31, 2009. Using an annual interest rate of 5 percent to discount the payment, you determine that the note's present value on January 1, 2008, was $50,000. Record the journal entries and accounting equation effects for (1) the equipment purchase, (2) the interest adjustment on December 31, 2008, and (3) the $55,125 payment on December 31, 2009.

Starbucks

1.

| | Debit | Credit |
|---|---|---|
| | | |
| | | |

Assets   =   Liabilities   +   Owners' Equity

2.

| | Debit | Credit |
|---|---|---|
| | | |
| | | |
| | | |

Assets   =   Liabilities   +   Owners' Equity

3.

| | Debit | Credit |
|---|---|---|
| | | |
| | | |
| | | |
| | | |

Assets   =   Liabilities   +   Owners' Equity

*After you have finished, check your answers with the solution at the bottom of the next page.*

Video 14-2
www.mhhe.com/LLPW1e

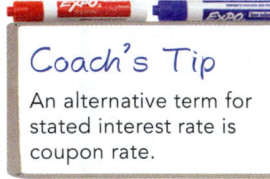

**Coach's Tip**

An alternative term for stated interest rate is coupon rate.

# Bonds Payable

Occasionally, governments and very large companies such as General Mills need to borrow more money than any single lender can provide. In 2007, for example, General Mills needed to borrow $700 million. Because issuing a promissory note for such a large amount of money was impractical, the company instead issued bonds. A sample bond certificate is shown here.

Bonds are financial instruments that outline the future payments a company promises to make in exchange for receiving a sum of money now. From the company's perspective, the bond is a long-term liability. From the bondholder's perspective, the bond is an investment. After a company issues the bonds, they can be traded on established exchanges such as the New York Bond Exchange. The ability to sell a bond on the bond exchange is attractive to bondholders because it provides them liquidity, or the ability to receive cash for the bond whenever they wish to sell it. In return for this liquidity, bondholders will accept a lower interest rate, which benefits the company by lowering the cost of long-term borrowing.

As you can see from the sample bond certificate shown here, three key elements of a bond are (1) the maturity date, (2) the amount payable on the maturity date (often called the face value), and (3) the stated interest rate. In most cases, the face value of each bond is $1,000.

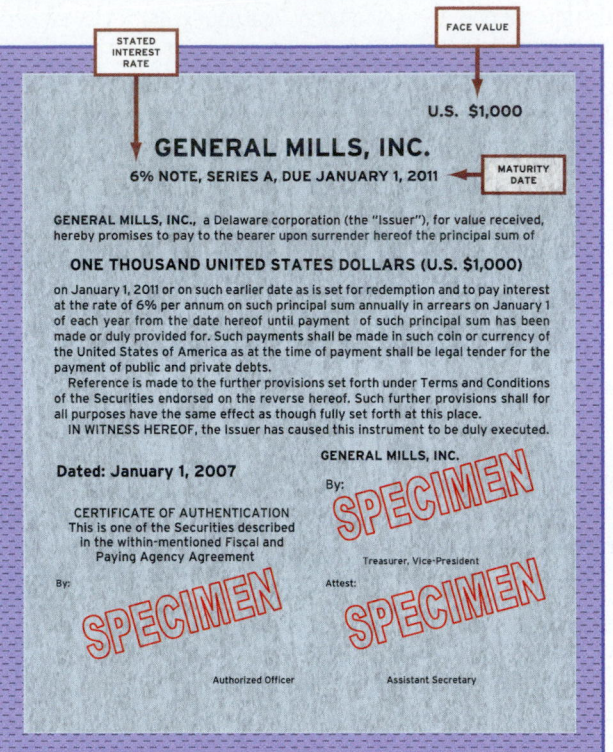

Solution to
Self-Study Practice

1.

| | Debit | Credit |
|---|---|---|
| Equipment (+A) | 50,000 | |
| Note Payable (+L) | | 50,000 |

| Assets | = | Liabilities | + | Owners' Equity |
|---|---|---|---|---|
| Equipment    +50,000 | | Note Payable    +50,000 | | |

2.

| | Debit | Credit |
|---|---|---|
| Interest Expense (+E, −OE) | 2,500 | |
| Note Payable (+L) | | 2,500 |
| [$50,000 × 5% × 12/12 = $2,500] | | |

| Assets | = | Liabilities | + | Owners' Equity |
|---|---|---|---|---|
| | | Note Payable    +2,500 | | Interest Expense (+E)    −2,500 |

3.

| | Debit | Debit |
|---|---|---|
| Interest Expense (+E, −OE) | 2,625 | |
| Note Payable (−L) | 52,500 | |
| Cash (−A) | | 55,125 |
| [($50,000 + $2,500) × 5% × 12/12 = $2,625] | | |

| Assets | = | Liabilities | + | Owners' Equity |
|---|---|---|---|---|
| Cash    −55,125 | | Note Payable    −52,500 | | Interest Expense (+E)    −2,625 |

The stated interest rate is always expressed as an annual rate although some bonds require interest payments every six months (that is, semiannually). Each interest payment is computed by multiplying the face value times the stated interest rate (times the fraction of the year if payments are made semiannually). As you will see later, for good economic reasons, bonds may be sold at amounts above or below their face value. A bond's selling price does not affect the amount of each interest payment, however. For example, a 6 percent bond with a face value of $1,000 will always pay interest of $60 cash each year (= $1,000 × 6% × 12/12).

## Spotlight On FINANCIAL REPORTING

The financial press reports bond prices each day based on transactions that occurred on the bond exchange. The following is typical of the information you will find:

| Company Bond | Close | Yield | Volume | Change |
|---|---|---|---|---|
| Safeway 5.5 2013 | 97.2 | 6.80 | 58 | −1/4 |
| General Mills 6.0 2011 | 101.4 | 5.77 | 250 | +3/8 |
| Harrah's 7.0 2020 | 104.1 | 6.90 | 580 | −7/8 |

**GENERAL MILLS**

This listing reports that the General Mills bond has a stated interest rate of 6.0 percent and will mature in the year 2011. The bond's price is quoted as a percentage of face value; in this case, 101.4 percent of face value, or $1,014 ($1,000 × 1.014). At this price, the bond payments represent a cash yield of 5.77 percent. On the date reported, 250 bonds were sold, and the price increased 3/8 of a point from the closing price on the day before (a point is 1 percent).

**Daily changes in bond prices arise from transactions among bondholders, which do not directly involve the company. Consequently, they do not affect the company's financial statements.** The company accounts for its bonds using the historical face value and historical interest rates that existed when the bonds were first sold to the public.

## Bond Pricing

Neither the company nor its financial advisers determine the price at which bonds sell. Instead, the market determines the price by discounting the cash payments that the company promises to make on the bond. Supplement 14A at the end of this chapter shows the calculations for the $1,000, 6 percent General Mills bond (see page 616). Although it is useful to know how to do these calculations, they are not a necessary step in accounting for a bond issue. Instead, what we really need to know is the amount of cash received from the market when the bonds were first sold. This cash-equivalent amount is the value at which the liability for the bonds is recorded.

Because the market determines the price at which bonds sell, the company may receive an amount of cash that is equal to the face value, above the face value, or below the face value. A bond issued for more than its face value is said to have been issued at a **premium**, which is the excess of the bond's issue price over its face value. A bond issued for less than its face value is said to have been issued at a **discount**, which is the amount by which the issue price falls short of the bond's face value. The following sections show how to account for bonds issued at face value, at a premium, and at a discount.

**Bonds Issued at Face Value.** If General Mills receives $100,000 cash in exchange for issuing 100 bonds at their $1,000 face value, the company's accountants will record the following journal entry:

> **Coach's Tip**
> Bond prices are typically quoted as a percentage of face value (although the percentage symbol is often omitted).

| | Debit | Credit |
|---|---|---|
| Cash (+A) | 100,000 | |
| Bonds Payable (+L) | | 100,000 |

| Assets | = | Liabilities | + | Owners' Equity |
|---|---|---|---|---|
| Cash +100,000 | | Bonds Payable +100,000 | | |

**Bonds Issued at a Premium.** If General Mills receives $107,260 for bonds with a total face value of $100,000, the cash-equivalent amount is $107,260, which represents the total liability on that date. The company's accountants will distinguish the $100,000 face value from the $7,260 premium by recording them in separate liability accounts as in the following journal entry:

|  | Debit | Credit |
|---|---|---|
| Cash (+A) | 107,260 | |
| Bonds Payable (+L) | | 100,000 |
| Premium on Bonds Payable (+L) | | 7,260 |

| Assets | = | Liabilities | + | Owners' Equity |
|---|---|---|---|---|
| Cash +107,260 | | Bonds Payable +100,000 | | |
| | | Premium on Bonds Payable +7,260 | | |

Why would bondholders be willing to pay a premium? For the same reason that you might pay a premium to acquire tickets to a great concert or a big game. If a bond offers something attractive, such as a high interest rate, bondholders may be willing to pay a premium to acquire it.

**Bonds Issued at a Discount.** If General Mills receives $93,376 for bonds with a total face value of $100,000, the cash-equivalent amount is $93,376, which represents the liability on that date. The discount of $6,624 (= $100,000 − $93,376) offsets the face value, so accountants will record it in a contra-account. A contra-account to a liability is recorded as a debit as in the following journal entry:

|  | Debit | Credit |
|---|---|---|
| Cash (+A) | 93,376 | |
| Discount on Bonds Payable (+xL, −L) | 6,624 | |
| Bonds Payable (+L) | | 100,000 |

| Assets | = | Liabilities | + | Owners' Equity |
|---|---|---|---|---|
| Cash +93,376 | | Bonds Payable +100,000 | | |
| | | Discount on Bonds Payable (+xL) −6,624 | | |

Why would companies such as General Mills be willing to discount a bond? The answer is that they must if they want to sell it. If a bond promises to pay interest at a stated rate of 6 percent when other financial instruments offer 8 percent, no one will be willing to buy the bond unless the company discounts it. The discount reduces the initial price of the bond without changing the interest payments and the face value to be paid at maturity. In effect, a discount increases the return that bondholders earn on their initial investment.

To illustrate, suppose you could buy a $1,000 bond that pays a stated interest rate of 6 percent and matures in one year. After one year, you would receive the stated interest of $60 ($1,000 × 6% × 12/12) plus the face value of $1,000. If you had paid $1,000 for the bond, you would receive 1.06 times as much as your initial investment [($60 + $1,000) ÷ $1,000]—a return of 6 percent. If instead the bond price were discounted $19, so that you paid only $981 for it, you would receive 1.08 times as much your initial investment [($60 + $1,000) ÷ $981 = 1.08]—a return of 8 percent. This percentage represents both the bondholder's rate of return and the company's cost of borrowing. It is commonly referred to as the **market interest rate**.

**Exhibit 14.4**    Balance Sheet Reporting of Bond Liabilities

| Bonds issued at a premium | |
|---|---|
| Bonds payable | $100,000 |
| Premium on bonds payable | 7,260 |
| Unpaid bond liability | 107,260 |

| Bonds issued at face value | |
|---|---|
| Bonds payable | $100,000 |

| Bonds issued at a discount | |
|---|---|
| Bonds payable | $100,000 |
| Discount on bonds payable | (6,624) |
| Unpaid bond liability | 93,376 |

**Reporting Bond Liabilities.**  The total face value of a bond plus any related premium or minus any related discount is reported in the liabilities section of the balance sheet as in Exhibit 14.4 for our three examples. The amount of the unpaid bond liability, after taking into account any premium or discount, is referred to as the bond's **carrying value**.

To determine whether a bond will be issued at a premium, at face value, or at a discount, you need consider only the relationship between the stated interest rate on the bond (what the bond pays in cash) and the market interest rate (the return that bondholders require). Exhibit 14.5 illustrates this relationship.

**Exhibit 14.5**    Relationships between Interest Rates and Bond Pricing

Before you continue, try the following Self-Study Practice to make sure you understand how bonds are priced.

---

For each of the following independent situations, indicate whether the bonds were issued at a premium, at a discount, or at face value.

1. Stated interest rate = 7% and market interest rate = 7%.    _____
2. Stated interest rate = 5% and market interest rate = 6%.    _____
3. Bond issue price = $10,100 and bond face value = $10,000.    _____

*After you have finished, check your answers with the solution at the bottom of the page.*

**SELF-STUDY PRACTICE**

---

## Interest Expense

As time passes, a bond liability creates interest expense, which is matched to each period in which the liability is outstanding. Because interest expense arises from a financing decision (not an operating decision), it is reported below the Income from Operations line on the company's income statement as in Exhibit 14.6.

---

1.  Face value.
2.  Discount—the market requires a better rate of return than the interest stated on the bond.
3.  Premium—the market is willing to pay more than face value to obtain the bond's higher interest rate.

Solution to
Self-Study Practice

| **Exhibit 14.6** | **Reporting Interest Expense on the Income Statement** |

**General Mills, Inc.**
**Income Statement**
**For the Quarter Ended August 26, 2007**
**(in millions)**

| | |
|---|---:|
| Net sales | $3,072.0 |
| Cost of sales | 1,915.8 |
| Selling, general, and administrative expenses | 631.6 |
| Other operating expenses | 14.5 |
| | 2,561.9 |
| Income from operations | 510.1 |
| **Interest expense** | **113.3** |
| Other expenses (revenues) | (22.4) |
| Income before income taxes | 419.2 |
| Income tax expense | 130.3 |
| Net income | $ 288.9 |

The process of calculating and recording interest on bonds is similar to that for notes payable, particularly when the bonds are issued at face value. Assume, for example, that General Mills issues bonds on July 1, 2009, at their total face value of $100,000. If the bonds carry an annual stated interest rate of 6 percent payable in cash on June 30 of each year, General Mills will need to accrue both an expense and a liability for interest at the end of each accounting period. On December 31, assuming no previous accrual of interest, General Mills would record interest of $3,000 (= $100,000 × 6% × 6/12) with the following entry:

| | Debit | Credit |
|---|---|---|
| Interest Expense (+E, −OE) | 3,000 | |
| Interest Payable (+L) | | 3,000 |

| Assets | = | Liabilities | + | Owners' Equity |
|---|---|---|---|---|
| | | Interest Payable  +3,000 | | Interest Expense (+E)    −3,000 |

General Mills reports Interest Payable as a current liability because the company will pay this amount within the coming year. When it is paid, Interest Payable will be debited and Cash will be credited.

In comparison to this procedure for reporting interest expense on bonds issued at face value, the procedures for reporting interest expense on bonds issued at a premium or a discount are slightly more complicated. The complication arises because the premium or discount represents an adjustment to the interest rate stated on the bond. A premium reduces the company's cost of borrowing, so it reduces Interest Expense over the life of the bond. A discount increases the company's cost of borrowing, so it increases Interest Expense over the life of the bond. The process of recording these adjustments to interest expense is called amortization. Two methods may be used to amortize premiums and discounts, the effective-interest method (explained in Supplement 14B) and the straight-line method (explained in Supplement 14C).

## Bond Retirement

Most bonds are retired (paid off) at maturity. If interest has been fully paid at the time of maturity, the only remaining account to settle will be Bonds Payable. Assuming the General

Mills bonds in our example were retired with a payment equal to their $100,000 face value, the following journal entry would be recorded:

|  | Debit | Credit |
|---|---|---|
| Bonds Payable (−L) | 100,000 | |
|     Cash (−A) | | 100,000 |

| Assets | = | Liabilities | + | Owners' Equity |
|---|---|---|---|---|
| Cash   −100,000 | | Bonds Payable   −100,000 | | |

Rather than wait until the maturity date to retire the bonds, however, the company may retire them early. Companies with a lot of cash often retire their bonds early to reduce future interest expense and increase net income. Even companies that do not have extra cash may decide to retire their bonds early if interest rates have fallen since issuing the original bonds. In this case, the companies would issue new bonds at the lower interest rate and use the money they receive from the new bonds to retire the old ones before maturity. Again, this decision reduces future interest expense, which increases future earnings.

The early retirement of bonds has three financial effects. The company (1) pays cash, (2) eliminates the bond liability, and (3) reports either a gain or a loss. A gain arises if the cash paid to retire the bonds is less than the carrying value of the bond liability. A loss is incurred if the company pays more than the carrying value at the time of retirement.

To illustrate these effects, assume that in 2000, General Mills issued $100,000 of bonds at face value. Nine years later, in 2009, the company retired the bonds early. At the time, the bond price was 103, so General Mills made a payment of $103,000 (= $100,000 × 103%) to retire the bonds. The following journal entry recorded the retirement:

|  | Debit | Credit |
|---|---|---|
| Bonds Payable (−L) | 100,000 | |
| Loss on Bond Retirement (+E, −OE) | 3,000 | |
|     Cash (−A) | | 103,000 |

| Assets | = | Liabilities | + | Owners' Equity |
|---|---|---|---|---|
| | | | | Loss on Bond |
| Cash  −103,000 | | Bonds Payable  −100,000 | | Retirement (+E)  −3,000 |

Notice two features of this example. First, because the bond retirement is a financing decision, the loss would be reported after the Income from Operations line on the income statement. In Exhibit 14.6, this loss would be included in Other Expenses; a gain would be included in Other Revenues. Second, this retirement does not involve the removal of a bond discount or bond premium account because the bonds were issued at face value. If the bonds had been issued below or above face value, any premium or discount balance that existed at the time of retirement would need to be removed as well.

## Types of Bonds

When you first start learning about bonds, it may seem the number of new terms that describe the bonds are limitless. These terms can generally be grouped into two categories: (1) those that describe the type of organization that issued the bonds and (2) those that describe specific features of the bond. In the first category are bonds issued by the U.S. Treasury Department ("treasuries"); municipal organizations such as states, cities, counties, and towns ("munis"); and corporations ("corporates"). In the second category are bonds that are backed by collateral ("secured") or not ("debentures"), that the issuing corporation can call in and exchange for cash ("callable") or convert into shares of its stock ("convertible"), and that mature in a series of installments ("serial bonds") or include no periodic interest payments ("zero-coupon bonds" and "strips"). The basic procedures shown in the previous sections for recording bond liabilities and interest expense apply equally to these various types of bonds.

Be sure you understand the basics of bond accounting by trying the following Self-Study Practice before you move to the next section.

In January 2008, Target Corporation issued bonds with a face value of $2,250,000, a stated interest rate of 7.0 percent, and a maturity date of January 15, 2038. The bonds issued at a price of 99.318. Based on this issue price, (1) indicate whether the market interest rate was higher or lower than the stated interest rate at the time of issue and (2) prepare the journal entry to record the bond issue.

*After you have finished, check your answers with the solution at the bottom of the page.*

**Learning Objective 4**

Explain how to account for lease liabilities.

# Lease Liabilities

A lease is a rental agreement between the owner of property (the lessor) and the renter of that property (the lessee). Depending on the terms of the rental agreement, a lease may be accounted for as an operating lease or a capital lease.

## Operating Leases

An operating lease allows a company to use property temporarily while the lessor continues to own it. An apartment lease and a daily or weekly car rental from Hertz or Avis are examples of operating leases.

When a company obtains the use of property through an operating lease, accountants record the payments made or owed to the lessor as an operating expense. For example, in 2007, General Mills rented warehouse space at a total cost of $46 million. Assuming that the company paid $40 million in cash and owed $6 million at the end of the year, accountants would record the following journal entry (in millions):

|  | Debit | Credit |
| --- | --- | --- |
| Rent Expense (+E, −OE) | 46 | |
| Rent Payable (+L) | | 6 |
| Cash (−A) | | 40 |

| Assets | = | Liabilities | + | Owners' Equity |
| --- | --- | --- | --- | --- |
| Cash    −40 | | Rent Payable    +6 | | Rent Expense (+E)    −46 |

## Capital Leases

A capital lease allows a lessee to use rented property in exchange for payments to the lessor, but unlike an operating lease, it transfers virtually all risks and rewards of owning the property to the lessee. In effect, the lessee purchases the property from the lessor through a series of payments made over the term of the lease. To account for this arrangement, the lessee records the property and the lease liability at the cash-equivalent amount. The cash-equivalent amount is calculated by discounting the payments the lessee will make over the term of the lease. Supplement 14A explains the procedure for discounting the payments (see page 616).

**Solution to Self-Study Practice**

1. The bonds are issued at a discount (99.318 percent of face value), which implies that the stated interest rate was not as attractive as other interest rates available in the market. That is, the market interest rate was higher than the stated interest rate.

2. Issue price = $2,250,000 × .99318 = $2,234,655.

|  | Debit | Credit |
| --- | --- | --- |
| Cash (+A) | 2,234,655 | |
| Discount on Bonds Payable (+xL, −L) | 15,345 | |
| Bonds Payable (+L) | | 2,250,000 |

General Mills obtains some of its equipment through capital leases. To illustrate the accounting, assume that the company has promised to make payments over a five-year period that equate to the cash-equivalent (discounted) amount of $42,124. When the equipment is obtained, General Mills would record the following journal entry:

| | Debit | Credit |
|---|---|---|
| Equipment (+A) | 42,124 | |
| Lease Liability (+L) | | 42,124 |

| Assets | = | Liabilities | + | Owners' Equity |
|---|---|---|---|---|
| Equipment +42,124 | | Lease Liability +42,124 | | |

In the periods that follow, General Mills would record Depreciation Expense on the equipment and Interest Expense on the lease liability.

## ANALYZING LONG-TERM LIABILITIES

In evaluating a company's ability to pay its liabilities, a good place to start is with the reports credit-rating agencies issue. These agencies do not report on all companies, however, particularly the smaller ones. Even if they did, their reports might not address your specific concerns. So, you need to know how to analyze a set of financial statements in the same way that a credit rater would.

Essentially, you want to assess what proportion of a company's assets are financed by liabilities and whether or not the company is likely to generate the resources needed to pay the interest on those liabilities. Two financial ratios are commonly used to make these assessments: the debt-to-assets ratio and the times interest earned ratio.

> **Learning Objective 5**
>
> Calculate and interpret the debt-to-assets and times interest earned ratios.

### Financial Analysis Tools

| Name of Measure | Formula | What It Tells You |
|---|---|---|
| Debt-to-assets ratio | $\dfrac{\text{Total Liabilities}}{\text{Total Assets}}$ | • The proportion of assets financed by liabilities <br> • The higher the number the greater the financing risk |
| Times interest earned ratio | $\dfrac{(\text{Net Income} + \text{Interest Expense} + \text{Income Tax Expense})}{\text{Interest Expense}}$ | • Whether sufficient resources are generated to cover interest costs <br> • The higher the number the better the coverage |

## Debt-to-Assets Ratio

The debt-to-assets ratio compares total liabilities to total assets. Usually calculated to three decimal places, it can be expressed as a percentage by multiplying it by 100. This ratio indicates the proportion of total assets that are financed by debt. It is important to know how much debt is used to finance assets because debt must be repaid whether or not a company is doing well. If a company finances its assets mainly by debt rather than equity, then the debt-to-assets ratio will be high, suggesting that the company's financing strategy is risky. Ultimately, a company can be forced into bankruptcy if it takes on more debt than it could ever repay.

Refer to Exhibit 14.7 for an illustration of how debt plays a major role in financing General Mills' assets: 64.5 percent of the company's assets were financed by debt at the end of 2007. That percentage is not nearly as large, however, as the one for rival Kellogg's, whose debt-to-assets ratio was more than 80 percent. Although these ratios are typical of the food processing industry, they are high compared to other industries. Companies in the video game industry, for example, have much lower debt-to-assets ratios (Activision's is 13.7 percent).

**Exhibit 14.7**    Debt-to-Assets Ratios in the Food Processing Industry

| Company | Relevant Information (in millions) | | 2007 Debt-to-Assets Ratio | |
|---|---|---|---|---|
| | | 2007 | 2006 | |
| GENERAL MILLS | Total liabilities | $11,726 | $11,167 | $\dfrac{\$11,726}{\$18,184}$ = 0.645 or 64.5% |
| | Total assets | 18,184 | 18,075 | |
| Kellogg's | | 2007 | 2006 | |
| | Total liabilities | $ 8,645 | $ 8,291 | $\dfrac{\$\,8,645}{\$10,714}$ = 0.807 or 80.7% |
| | Total assets | 10,714 | 10,575 | |

## Spotlight on ETHICS

### Doctoring the Debt-to-Assets Ratio

The debt-to-assets ratio can be a useful measure of the extent to which a company relies on debt to finance its assets. Analysts should be aware, however, that seemingly normal transactions that occur just before the end of an accounting period can influence this ratio. For example, the ratio can be reduced by repaying a loan just prior to the financial statement date. Although this transaction decreases total liabilities and total assets by the same amount, it has a greater impact on liabilities than on assets, thus reducing the ratio. If a company's debt-to-assets ratio is 10 to 15 (67 percent) before repayment of a $5 loan, it will be 5 to 10 (50 percent) after repayment.

## Times Interest Earned Ratio

One way to judge a company's ability to pay interest is to ask whether it has generated enough income to cover its interest expense. The measure that most analysts use for this purpose is the times interest earned ratio.

The financial analysis tools box (on page 611) showed the formula for the times interest earned ratio. It is reproduced after the following paragraph. Notice that in this ratio, interest and income tax expenses are added back into net income. The reason for this is simple: Analysts want to know whether a company generates enough income to cover its interest expense **before the costs of financing and taxes.** In general, a high times interest earned ratio is viewed more favorably than a low one. A high ratio indicates an extra margin of protection should the company's profitability decline in the future.

Using the information in the income statement in Exhibit 14.6 on page 608, we can compute the times interest earned ratio for General Mills as follows.

$$\frac{\text{Net Income} + \text{Interest Expense} + \text{Income Tax Expense}}{\text{Interest Expense}} = \frac{\$288.9 + \$113.3 + \$130.3}{\$113.3} = 4.70$$

This ratio means that General Mills generates $4.70 of income (before the costs of financing and taxes) for each dollar of interest expense. No doubt this ratio is part of the reason that General Mills has earned a favorable credit rating of BBB or higher.

Every now and then you will see a times interest earned ratio that is less than 1.0 or even negative. **When the times interest earned ratio is less than 1.0, a company is not generating enough income to cover its interest expense.** Most companies with a negative times interest earned ratio survive only a couple of years before declaring bankruptcy.

Before you conclude your reading of this chapter, try the following Self-Study Practice to make sure you understand how to analyze long-term liabilities.

1. Use the information in Exhibit 14.7 to calculate the 2006 debt-to-assets ratios for General Mills and Kellogg's. Show the ratios as whole numbers calculated to three decimal places and as percentages.
2. Compare the ratios calculated in part (1) to the ratios in Exhibit 14.7. Did the two companies' financing risk increase or decrease in 2007 relative to 2006?

*After you have finished, check your answers with the solutions at the bottom of the page.*

# Demonstration Case A
## Discounted Notes

On January 1, 2008, Central University (CU) bought new gymnastics equipment. Rather than pay cash, CU gave a note that promised payment of $20,000 on January 1, 2011. CU typically borrows at a 4 percent interest rate. Using a 4 percent interest rate to discount the $20,000 payment, CU determined that the present value of this liability on January 1, 2008, was $17,780.

*Required:*

1. Give the journal entry required to record the equipment purchase on January 1, 2008.
2. Calculate the interest expense on the note in 2008. If this amount is added to the note amount on December 31, 2008, what will be the new balance in Note Payable on December 31, 2008? Continue these calculations for 2009 and 2010. What will be the balance in Notes Payable immediately prior to payment of the note on January 1, 2011? Round all calculations to the nearest dollar.
3. Assuming CU adjusts its accounting records once each year on December 31, give the journal entries required to accrue interest on the note on December 31, 2008, 2009, and 2010.

## Suggested Solution

1.

|  | Debit | Credit |
|---|---|---|
| Equipment (+A) | 17,780 |  |
|     Note Payable (+L) |  | 17,780 |

| Assets | = | Liabilities | + | Owners' Equity |
|---|---|---|---|---|
| Equipment   +17,780 | | Note Payable   +17,780 | | |

2.

|  | Note Payable, January 1 | Interest Expense | Note Payable, December 31 |
|---|---|---|---|
| 2008 | $17,780 | $17,780 × 4% × 12/12 = $711 | $17,780 + $711 = $18,491 |
| 2009 | 18,491 | 18,491 × 4% × 12/12 = 740 | 18,491 + 740 = 19,231 |
| 2010 | 19,231 | 19,231 × 4% × 12/12 = 769 | 19,231 + 769 = 20,000 |

1. General Mills = $11,167 / $18,075 = 0.618 or 61.8%.
   Kellogg's = $8,291 / $10,575 = 0.784 or 78.4%.
2. Both companies increased their reliance on debt in 2007, suggesting an increase in the risk that they would be unable to repay their borrowings.

3.    December 31, 2008:

|  | Debit | Credit |
|---|---|---|
| Interest Expense (+E, −OE) | 711 | |
| Note Payable (+L) | | 711 |

| Assets | = | Liabilities | + | Owners' Equity |
|---|---|---|---|---|
| | | Note Payable    +711 | | Interest Expense (+E)    −711 |

December 31, 2009:

|  | Debit | Credit |
|---|---|---|
| Interest Expense (+E, −OE) | 740 | |
| Note Payable (+L) | | 740 |

| Assets | = | Liabilities | + | Owners' Equity |
|---|---|---|---|---|
| | | Note Payable    +740 | | Interest Expense (+E)    −740 |

December 31, 2010:

|  | Debit | Credit |
|---|---|---|
| Interest Expense (+E, −OE) | 769 | |
| Note Payable (+L) | | 769 |

| Assets | = | Liabilities | + | Owners' Equity |
|---|---|---|---|---|
| | | Note Payable    +769 | | Interest Expense (+E)    −769 |

# Demonstration Case B

## Bonds

On February 1, 2006, Black & Decker Corporation issued 300,000 bonds at 5.75 percent, each with a face value of $1,000 and a maturity date of January 31, 2016. The bonds were issued at 99.6. Of the cash received from the issue, $154.6 million was used to retire some 7 percent bonds. Assume the 7 percent bonds had been previously issued at a face value of $155 million.

*Required:*

1.    How much cash did Black & Decker Corporation receive from the sale of the bonds payable? Show your computations.

2.    What was the amount of the premium or discount on the bonds payable?

3.    Give the journal entry for recording the issue of the 5.75 percent bonds on February 1, 2006.

4.    Show how the bonds would be reported on the balance sheet on February 1, 2006.

5.    Give the journal entry to record the retirement of the 7 percent bonds.

## Suggested Solution

1.    Sale price of the bonds: 300,000 bonds × $1,000 face value × 99.6% = $298,800,000, or $298.8 million.

2.    Discount on the bonds payable: $300 million − $298.8 million = $1.2 million.

3.    February 1, 2006 (in millions):

|  | Debit | Credit |
|---|---|---|
| Cash (+A) | 298.8 | |
| Discount on Bonds Payable (+xL, −L) | 1.2 | |
|    Bonds Payable (+L) | | 300.0 |

| Assets | = | Liabilities | + | Owners' Equity |
|---|---|---|---|---|
| Cash   +298.8 | | Bonds Payable   +300.0 | | |
| | | Discount on Bonds Payable (+xL)   −1.2 | | |

4.    Balance sheet reporting (long-term liabilities) (in millions):

| | |
|---|---|
| Bonds Payable | $300.0 |
| Discount on Bond Payable | (1.2) |
| Unpaid Bond Liability | 298.8 |

5.    (in millions)

| | |
|---|---|
| Face value | $ 155.0 |
| Paid to retire | (154.6) |
| Gain | $  0.4 |

|  | Debit | Credit |
|---|---|---|
| Bonds Payable (−L) | 155.0 | |
|    Gain on Bond Retirement (+R, +OE) | | 0.4 |
|    Cash (−A) | | 154.6 |

| Assets | = | Liabilities | + | Owners' Equity |
|---|---|---|---|---|
| Cash   −154.6 | | Bonds Payable   −155.0 | | Gain on Bond Retirement (+R)   +0.4 |

# Demonstration Case C

## Leases

AMR Corporation provides air transportation to customers through its American Airlines and American Eagle business units. As of December 31, 2006, AMR operated 1,003 aircraft, 231 of which were obtained through operating leases and 90 through capital leases. For the year ended December 31, 2006, AMR incurred $606 million in aircraft rental expense. At the end of the year, the company owed $927 million for aircraft obtained via capital leases. The aircraft were capitalized as a noncurrent asset at a total cost of $1,744 million.

**AMR**

*Required:*

1.    Does the aircraft rental expense relate to operating leases or capital leases?
2.    Describe the two adjustments that would be made each year with respect to the aircraft and obligations related to capital leases.

## Suggested Solution

1.    The aircraft rental expense relates to operating leases. (When payments are made for capital leases, they are reported as interest expense and reductions in the principal owed on the lease liability.)
2.    An adjustment would be recorded each accounting period for (a) depreciation on the aircraft obtained through capital leases and (b) interest on the lease liability. (Rent on the operating leases would be accrued as well.)

## Supplement 14A
### Discounting Future Payments

This supplement is based on the simple notion that you can invest cash today to earn interest over time, resulting in a larger amount in the future. The future value of your investment is larger than its present value because interest is added to the original investment, in a process called compounding. The following timeline shows how $1,000 invested today at a 10 percent interest rate becomes $1,100 one year from now ($1,000 × 1.10 = $1,100):

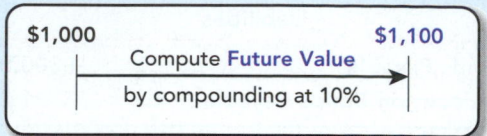

In finance, many problems involve determining the future value that can be generated from some present value. In accounting, however, our focus is just the opposite: We want to know the present (cash-equivalent) value today of amounts that will be paid in the future. This process of starting with the future value and working back to the present value is **discounting**. The following timeline shows the same situation as in the first timeline except that it works backward from the future value of $1,100 to a present value of $1,000, assuming a 10 percent discount rate:

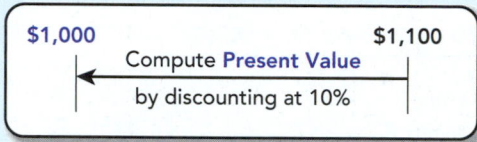

Two different discounting situations arise in business. The first involves discounting a **single amount** paid only once. This situation is illustrated in our timeline. To calculate the present value of a single amount, you divide the future payment by the rate at which interest accumulates in each period. Because our example involves only one period, the calculation is straightforward: $1,100 ÷ 1.10 = $1,000.

As the number of periods increases, this method becomes tiresome. An alternative approach is to use present value tables. Table 14A-1 shows the present value of $1 at various combinations of interest rates

**Table 14A-1    Present Value of $1**

| Periods | 2% | 3% | 3.75% | 4% | 4.25% | 5% | 6% | 7% | 8% |
|---|---|---|---|---|---|---|---|---|---|
| 1 | 0.9804 | 0.9709 | 0.9639 | 0.9615 | 0.9592 | 0.9524 | 0.9434 | 0.9346 | 0.9259 |
| 2 | 0.9612 | 0.9426 | 0.9290 | 0.9246 | 0.9201 | 0.9070 | 0.8900 | 0.8734 | 0.8573 |
| 3 | 0.9423 | 0.9151 | 0.8954 | 0.8890 | 0.8826 | 0.8638 | 0.8396 | 0.8163 | 0.7938 |
| 4 | 0.9238 | 0.8885 | 0.8631 | 0.8548 | 0.8466 | 0.8227 | 0.7921 | 0.7629 | 0.7350 |
| 5 | 0.9057 | 0.8626 | 0.8319 | 0.8219 | 0.8121 | 0.7835 | 0.7473 | 0.7130 | 0.6806 |
| 6 | 0.8880 | 0.8375 | 0.8018 | 0.7903 | 0.7790 | 0.7462 | 0.7050 | 0.6663 | 0.6302 |
| 7 | 0.8706 | 0.8131 | 0.7728 | 0.7599 | 0.7473 | 0.7107 | 0.6651 | 0.6227 | 0.5835 |
| 8 | 0.8535 | 0.7894 | 0.7449 | 0.7307 | 0.7168 | 0.6768 | 0.6274 | 0.5820 | 0.5403 |
| 9 | 0.8368 | 0.7664 | 0.7180 | 0.7026 | 0.6876 | 0.6446 | 0.5919 | 0.5439 | 0.5002 |
| 10 | 0.8203 | 0.7441 | 0.6920 | 0.6756 | 0.6595 | 0.6139 | 0.5584 | 0.5083 | 0.4632 |
| 20 | 0.6730 | 0.5537 | 0.4789 | 0.4564 | 0.4350 | 0.3769 | 0.3118 | 0.2584 | 0.2145 |

| Periods | 9% | 10% | 11% | 12% | 13% | 14% | 15% | 20% | 25% |
|---|---|---|---|---|---|---|---|---|---|
| 1 | 0.9174 | 0.9091 | 0.9009 | 0.8929 | 0.8850 | 0.8772 | 0.8696 | 0.8333 | 0.8000 |
| 2 | 0.8417 | 0.8264 | 0.8116 | 0.7972 | 0.7831 | 0.7695 | 0.7561 | 0.6944 | 0.6400 |
| 3 | 0.7722 | 0.7513 | 0.7312 | 0.7118 | 0.6931 | 0.6750 | 0.6575 | 0.5787 | 0.5120 |
| 4 | 0.7084 | 0.6830 | 0.6587 | 0.6355 | 0.6133 | 0.5921 | 0.5718 | 0.4823 | 0.4096 |
| 5 | 0.6499 | 0.6209 | 0.5935 | 0.5674 | 0.5428 | 0.5194 | 0.4972 | 0.4019 | 0.3277 |
| 6 | 0.5963 | 0.5645 | 0.5346 | 0.5066 | 0.4803 | 0.4556 | 0.4323 | 0.3349 | 0.2621 |
| 7 | 0.5470 | 0.5132 | 0.4817 | 0.4523 | 0.4251 | 0.3996 | 0.3759 | 0.2791 | 0.2097 |
| 8 | 0.5019 | 0.4665 | 0.4339 | 0.4039 | 0.3762 | 0.3506 | 0.3269 | 0.2326 | 0.1678 |
| 9 | 0.4604 | 0.4241 | 0.3909 | 0.3606 | 0.3329 | 0.3075 | 0.2843 | 0.1938 | 0.1342 |
| 10 | 0.4224 | 0.3855 | 0.3522 | 0.3220 | 0.2946 | 0.2697 | 0.2472 | 0.1615 | 0.1074 |
| 20 | 0.1784 | 0.1486 | 0.1240 | 0.1037 | 0.0868 | 0.0728 | 0.0611 | 0.0261 | 0.0115 |

and time periods. To solve the problem in our example, we would look for the value at the intersection of 10 percent and one period, which is 0.9091. This value implies that $1 paid one year from now equals $0.9091 today. To apply it to a $1,100 payment in one year, we would simply multiply it by $1,100 to obtain a present value of $1,000 (rounded).

The second type of discounting situation that arises in business involves a series of equal amounts, called an **annuity**. The following timeline illustrates an annuity:

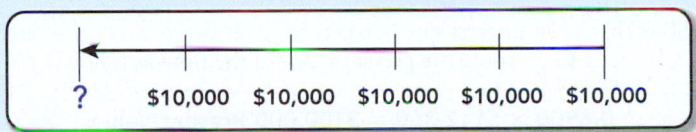

Although we could treat each payment in this annuity as a single amount to be discounted separately (and then totaled), such an approach would be cumbersome. To save time, we can use Table 14A-2, which shows the present value of a $1 annuity received at the end of several periods given various combinations of interest rates and periods. Assuming an interest rate of 6 percent for five years, we simply multiply the discounting factor in the table, 4.2124, by the annuity amount of $10,000 to obtain a present value of $42,124.

The following sections show how to apply these discounting techniques to discounted notes, bonds payable, and capital leases.

## Discounted Notes

Assume that General Mills has just signed a note that requires a $112,360 payment in two years. The note does not state an interest rate, but General Mills typically incurs a 6 percent annual rate.

### Table 14A-2  Present Value of Annuity of $1

| Periods* | 2% | 3% | 3.75% | 4% | 4.25% | 5% | 6% | 7% | 8% |
|---|---|---|---|---|---|---|---|---|---|
| 1 | 0.9804 | 0.9709 | 0.9639 | 0.9615 | 0.9592 | 0.9524 | 0.9434 | 0.9346 | 0.9259 |
| 2 | 1.9416 | 1.9135 | 1.8929 | 1.8861 | 1.8794 | 1.8594 | 1.8334 | 1.8080 | 1.7833 |
| 3 | 2.8839 | 2.8286 | 2.7883 | 2.7751 | 2.7620 | 2.7232 | 2.6730 | 2.6243 | 2.5771 |
| 4 | 3.8077 | 3.7171 | 3.6514 | 3.6299 | 3.6086 | 3.5460 | 3.4651 | 3.3872 | 3.3121 |
| 5 | 4.7135 | 4.5797 | 4.4833 | 4.4518 | 4.4207 | 4.3295 | 4.2124 | 4.1002 | 3.9927 |
| 6 | 5.6014 | 5.4172 | 5.2851 | 5.2421 | 5.1997 | 5.0757 | 4.9173 | 4.7665 | 4.6229 |
| 7 | 6.4720 | 6.2303 | 6.0579 | 6.0021 | 5.9470 | 5.7864 | 5.5824 | 5.3893 | 5.2064 |
| 8 | 7.3255 | 7.0197 | 6.8028 | 6.7327 | 6.6638 | 6.4632 | 6.2098 | 5.9713 | 5.7466 |
| 9 | 8.1622 | 7.7861 | 7.5208 | 7.4353 | 7.3513 | 7.1078 | 6.8017 | 6.5152 | 6.2469 |
| 10 | 8.9826 | 8.5302 | 8.2128 | 8.1109 | 8.0109 | 7.7217 | 7.3601 | 7.0236 | 6.7101 |
| 20 | 16.3514 | 14.8775 | 13.8962 | 13.5903 | 13.2944 | 12.4622 | 11.4699 | 10.5940 | 9.8181 |

| Periods* | 9% | 10% | 11% | 12% | 13% | 14% | 15% | 20% | 25% |
|---|---|---|---|---|---|---|---|---|---|
| 1 | 0.9174 | 0.9091 | 0.9009 | 0.8929 | 0.8550 | 0.8772 | 0.8696 | 0.8333 | 0.8000 |
| 2 | 1.7591 | 1.7355 | 1.7125 | 1.6901 | 1.6681 | 1.6467 | 1.6257 | 1.5278 | 1.4400 |
| 3 | 2.5313 | 2.4869 | 2.4437 | 2.4018 | 2.3612 | 2.3216 | 2.2832 | 2.1065 | 1.9520 |
| 4 | 3.2397 | 3.1699 | 3.1024 | 3.0373 | 2.9745 | 2.9137 | 2.8550 | 2.5887 | 2.3616 |
| 5 | 3.8897 | 3.7908 | 3.6959 | 3.6048 | 3.5172 | 3.4331 | 3.3522 | 2.9906 | 2.6893 |
| 6 | 4.4859 | 4.3553 | 4.2305 | 4.1114 | 3.9975 | 3.8887 | 3.7845 | 3.3255 | 2.9514 |
| 7 | 5.0330 | 4.8684 | 4.7122 | 4.5638 | 4.4226 | 4.2883 | 4.1604 | 3.6046 | 3.1611 |
| 8 | 5.5348 | 5.3349 | 5.1461 | 4.9676 | 4.7988 | 4.6389 | 4.4873 | 3.8372 | 3.3289 |
| 9 | 5.9952 | 5.7590 | 5.5370 | 5.3282 | 4.1317 | 4.9464 | 4.7716 | 4.0310 | 3.4631 |
| 10 | 6.4177 | 6.1446 | 5.8892 | 5.6502 | 5.4262 | 5.2161 | 5.0188 | 4.1925 | 3.5705 |
| 20 | 9.1285 | 8.5136 | 7.9633 | 7.4694 | 7.0248 | 6.6231 | 6.2593 | 4.8696 | 3.9539 |

* There is one payment each period.

We use that rate to discount the future payment of $112,360 to today's present value as in the following timeline:

Table 14A-1 shows that at an interest rate of 6 percent over two periods, the discounting factor we should use is 0.8900. So, we can compute the present value of the note as follows:

$$0.8900 \times \$112,360 = \$100,000 \text{ Present Value}$$

## Bonds Payable

A bond represents a promise to pay a specified **face value** at maturity plus a **stated interest rate** each period until maturity. The following timeline illustrates these payments using the example in which General Mills issued 100 bonds, each with a face value of $1,000, to be repaid at maturity in four years. The stated interest rate of 6 percent is to be paid annually, which means a total annual interest payment of $6,000 (100 bonds × $1,000 × 6%). The two question marks on the timeline indicate that the $100,000 face value (a single amount) should be discounted separately from the $6,000 interest payments (an annuity). The total of the two present values will equal the value that the bond market places on these bonds.

Coach's Tip

A bond certificate describes the future payments to be made on the bond. The amount that a bond investor would pay to receive those future payments depends on the market interest rate when the bond is issued.

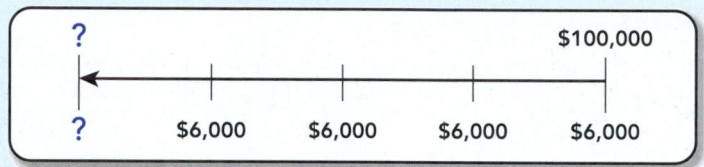

The value the market places on bond payments depends on three factors: (1) the amount of the payments for face value and interest, (2) the period covered by each payment, and (3) the market interest rate when the bond is issued. The following examples show how differences in the market interest rate affect the computations.

### Bonds Issued at Face Value.
Exhibit 14.5 (on page 607) shows that bonds will be issued at their face value if their stated interest rate (what the bond pays) equals the market interest rate (what the market demands). To illustrate, assume that the market interest rate is 6 percent, which equals the 6 percent stated interest rate used to compute the interest payments shown in the timeline. Table 14A-1 shows that the discounting factor for a single amount at 6 percent for four periods is 0.7921; Table 14A-2 shows that the discounting factor for an annuity at 6 percent for four periods 3.4651. We can multiply these factors by the future payments to get the present values:

| | |
|---|---:|
| Present value of $100,000 face value ($100,000 × 0.7921) | $ 79,210 |
| Present value of $6,000 annuity ($6,000 × 3.4651) | 20,790 |
| Total present value of bond | $100,000 |

We should mention that, because the discounting factors are rounded to four decimal places, small rounding errors can arise. For example, if you calculate $6,000 × 3.4651 in the previous example, you will find it equals $20,790.60. We have rounded this down so that the total present value equals $100,000.

### Bonds Issued above Face Value (at a Premium).
Bonds will be issued at a premium if their stated interest rate is higher than the market interest rate. Assume, for example, that the stated interest rate is 6 percent, but the market interest rate is only 4 percent. The discounting factor for a single amount at 4 percent for four periods is 0.8548 (see Table 14A-1); the discounting factor for an annuity at the same 4 percent interest rate for the same number of periods is 3.6299 (see Table 14A-2). If we multiply these factors by the future payments, we get the present values:

| | |
|---|---:|
| Present value of $100,000 face value ($100,000 × 0.8548) | $ 85,480 |
| Present value of $6,000 annuity ($6,000 × 3.6299) | 21,780 |
| Total present value of bond | $107,260 |

## Bonds Issued below Face Value (at a Discount).

Bonds will be issued at a discount if their stated interest rate is lower than the market interest rate. Assume, for example, that the stated interest rate is 6 percent, but the market interest rate is 8 percent. The discounting factor for a single amount at 8 percent for four periods is 0.7350 (see Table 14A-1); the discounting factor for an annuity at the same 8 percent rate for the same number of periods is 3.3121 (see Table 14A-2). If we multiply these factors by the future payments, we get the present values:

| | |
|---|---:|
| Present value of $100,000 face value ($100,000 × 0.7350) | $73,503 |
| Present value of $6,000 annuity ($6,000 × 3.3121) | 19,873 |
| Total present value of bond | $93,376 |

Again, we need to mention that because the present value factors are rounded to four decimal places, small rounding differences may arise. In the preceding calculation, for example, we have shown $73,503, which is the actual present value unaffected by rounding, rather than the amount obtained by multiplying $100,000 by the rounded factor of 0.7350.

## Capital Leases

A capital lease is a rental agreement that typically requires the lessee to make a series of equal payments over the term of the lease. Those payments represent an annuity. To compute the present (cash-equivalent) value of the annuity when a company enters into the lease, we can simply multiply the payment by the appropriate annuity factor in Table 14A-2.

To illustrate, assume General Mills has agreed to rent a piece of equipment for five years in return for five annual payments of $10,000 at an implied interest rate of 6 percent. The discounting factor for an annuity at 6 percent over five periods is 4.2124 (see Table 14A-2). We can use this factor to calculate the present (cash-equivalent) value of the five payments when a company enters into the agreement as follows:

$$\$10,000 \times 4.2124 = \$42,124 \text{ present value}$$

## Interest Rates and Interest Periods

The preceding illustrations assumed annual interest periods. Although interest *rates* are always quoted on an annual basis, interest *periods* may cover less than a year. For example, semiannual interest implies two interest periods each year; quarterly interest implies four periods per year. When interest periods are less than a year, both the number of periods and the interest rate must be restated to be consistent with the length of the interest period.

To illustrate, 12 percent interest compounded annually for five years implies an interest rate of 12 percent and five periods. If interest is compounded quarterly, however, the interest period is one-quarter of a year (four periods per year), and the quarterly interest rate is one-quarter of the annual rate (3 percent per quarter). Therefore, 12 percent interest compounded quarterly for five years implies an interest rate of 3 percent per period over 20 interest periods (5 years × 4 periods per year).

# Supplement 14B
## Effective-Interest Method of Amortization

When a bond is issued at a premium or a discount, the amount of the bond premium or discount must be matched to the periods in which the bond is outstanding. This process, called bond amortization, may be accomplished using the effective-interest method, which ensures that interest expense represents the company's actual cost of borrowing. To calculate the interest expense for each interest period, accountants multiply the unpaid bond liability by the market interest rate that existed when the bonds were issued. Then they record the difference between the interest expense and the amount of interest paid (or accrued) that period as a reduction in the bond premium or discount as in the following examples.

**Coach's Tip**

The effective-interest method computes interest expense by multiplying a **constant** interest rate (the market interest rate) by the unpaid bond liability.

## Bond Premiums

A premium arises when the bond issuer receives more cash than the issuer repays at maturity. In effect, the premium reduces the company's cost of borrowing, so that in each accounting period, interest expense is lower than the actual interest payment. The excess of the interest payment over the interest expense is recorded as a reduction in the Premium on Bonds Payable liability account.

In our earlier example, General Mills received $107,260 for bonds with a total face value of $100,000. The company received a premium because the stated interest rate on the bonds (6 percent) was higher than the market interest rate at the time the bonds were issued (4 percent). The stated interest rate determines the interest payment that is made each period ($100,000 × 6% × 12/12 = $6,000). Interest expense, however, is based on the market interest rate, as follows:

> **Interest Expense = Unpaid Bond Liability × Market Interest Rate × n/12**
>
> Unpaid Bond Liability = Bonds Payable + Premium on Bonds Payable
>
> n = Number of Months in Each Interest Period

For the first year ended December 31, 2007, interest expense for these bonds would be $4,290 ($107,260 × 4% × 12/12). The interest payment is $6,000 ($100,000 × 6% × 12/12). You can think of the difference between the $6,000 payment and the $4,290 interest expense ($6,000 − $4,290 = $1,710) as a partial repayment of the Premium on Bonds Payable. These effects would be recorded on December 31, 2007, in the following journal entry:

| | Debit | Credit |
|---|---|---|
| Interest Expense (+E, −OE) | 4,290 | |
| Premium on Bonds Payable (−L) | 1,710 | |
| Cash (−A) | | 6,000 |

| Assets | = | Liabilities | + | Owners' Equity |
|---|---|---|---|---|
| Cash −6,000 | | Premium on Bonds Payable −1,710 | | Interest Expense (+E) −4,290 |

**Coach's Tip**

The beginning balance on January 1, 2008, is the same as the ending balance on December 31, 2007.

Now that the journal entry has reduced the Premium on Bonds Payable, the unpaid bond liability in 2008 is smaller than it was in 2007 ($107,260 − $1,710 = $105,550). Thus, the calculation of Interest Expense in 2008 reflects this change, by multiplying the unpaid bond liability on January 1, 2008, by the market rate of interest for the full year ($105,550 × 4% × 12/12 = $4,222). Again, think of the difference between the $6,000 payment in 2008 and the $4,222 interest expense as another partial repayment of the Premium on Bonds Payable ($6,000 − $4,222 = $1,778). These effects would be recorded with the following journal entry:

| | Debit | Credit |
|---|---|---|
| Interest Expense (+E, −OE) | 4,222 | |
| Premium on Bonds Payable (−L) | 1,778 | |
| Cash (−A) | | 6,000 |

| Assets | = | Liabilities | + | Owners' Equity |
|---|---|---|---|---|
| Cash −6,000 | | Premium on Bonds Payable −1,778 | | Interest Expense (+E) −4,222 |

In each remaining year, General Mills will pay $6,000 as promised on the bond certificate. As you have just seen, a portion of that payment will represent Interest Expense and a portion reduces the original Premium on Bonds Payable. The following bond amortization schedule summarizes these effects:

### BOND PREMIUM AMORTIZATION SCHEDULE: EFFECTIVE-INTEREST METHOD

| | CHANGES DURING THE PERIOD | | | ENDING BOND LIABILITY BALANCES | | |
|---|---|---|---|---|---|---|
| Period Ended | (A) Interest Expense | (B) Interest Payable | (C) (= B − A) Amortization of Premium | (D) Bonds Payable | (E) Premium on Bonds Payable | (F) (= D + E) Unpaid Bond Liability |
| 01/01/07 | — | — | — | $100,000 | $7,260 | $107,260 |
| 12/31/07 | $4,290 | $6,000 | $1,710 | 100,000 | 5,550 | 105,550 |
| 12/31/08 | 4,222 | 6,000 | 1,778 | 100,000 | 3,772 | 103,772 |
| 12/31/09 | 4,151 | 6,000 | 1,849 | 100,000 | 1,923 | 101,923 |
| 12/31/10 | 4,077 | 6,000 | 1,923 | 100,000 | 0 | 100,000 |

## Bond Discounts

A discount arises when the bond issuer receives less cash than the issuer must repay at maturity. In effect, the discount increases the company's cost of borrowing so that in each accounting period, interest expense is higher than the company's interest payment. The excess amount represents an increase in the unpaid bond liability, which will be paid at maturity. To report this effect, accountants record a decrease in the contra-liability account Discount on Bonds Payable. Decreasing this contra-liability increases the carrying value of the bond liability.

In our earlier example, General Mills received $93,376 for bonds with a total face value of $100,000. The company gave buyers a discount because the stated interest rate on the bonds (6 percent) was less than the market interest rate at the time the bonds were issued (8 percent). The stated interest rate determines the interest payment that must be made each period ($100,000 × 6% × 12/12 = $6,000). The interest expense is based on the market interest rate, as follows:

> **Interest Expense = Unpaid Bond Liability × Market Interest Rate × n/12**
>
> Unpaid Bond Liability = Bonds Payable − Discount on Bonds Payable
>
> n = Number of Months in Each Interest Period

For the first year ended December 31, 2007, interest expense on these bonds would be $7,470 ($93,376 × 8% × 12/12). The interest payment is $6,000 ($100,000 × 6% × 12/12). The difference between the interest expense and the payment ($7,470 − $6,000 = $1,470) represents the amortization of the bond discount in 2007. These effects would be recorded on December 31, 2007, in the following journal entry:

|  | Debit | Credit |
|---|---|---|
| Interest Expense (+E, −OE) | 7,470 |  |
| Discount on Bonds Payable  (−xL, +L) |  | 1,470 |
| Cash (−A) |  | 6,000 |

| Assets | = | Liabilities | + | Owners' Equity |
|---|---|---|---|---|
| Cash −6,000 |  | Discount on Bonds Payable (−xL) +1,470 |  | Interest Expense (+E) −7,470 |

Because the 2007 interest expense was not paid in full, the unpaid bond liability at the beginning of 2008 will be more than it was in the last year ($93,376 + $1,470 = $94,846). Interest expense for the following year will reflect this change in the unpaid bond liability. Interest expense in 2008 would be calculated by multiplying the unpaid bond liability on January 1, 2008, by the market rate of interest for the full year ($94,846 × 8% × 12/12 = $7,588). Again, the difference between the $7,588 interest expense and the $6,000 interest paid in 2008 represents amortization of the bond discount in 2008 ($7,588 − $6,000 = $1,588). These effects would be recorded with the following journal entry:

**Coach's Tip**

The unpaid bond liability at the beginning of 2008 can also be computed by subtracting the balance in the Discount on Bonds Payable account from Bonds Payable.

|  | Debit | Credit |
|---|---|---|
| Interest Expense (+E, −OE) | 7,588 |  |
| Discount on Bonds Payable  (−xL, +L) |  | 1,588 |
| Cash (−A) |  | 6,000 |

| Assets | = | Liabilities | + | Owners' Equity |
|---|---|---|---|---|
| Cash −6,000 |  | Discount on Bonds Payable (−xL) +1,588 |  | Interest Expense (+E) −7,588 |

In each remaining year, General Mills will pay $6,000 interest, as promised on the bond certificate. As we have seen, however, this payment will be less than the interest expense, so the unpaid bond liability will continue to increase (through decreases in the contra-liability account Discount on Bonds Payable). These effects are summarized in the following bond amortization schedule:

### BOND DISCOUNT AMORTIZATION SCHEDULE: EFFECTIVE-INTEREST METHOD

| | CHANGES DURING THE PERIOD | | | ENDING BOND LIABILITY BALANCES | | |
| | (A) Interest Expense | (B) Interest Payable | (C) (= A − B) Amortization of Discount | (D) Bonds Payable | (E) Discount on Bonds Payable | (F) (= D − E) Unpaid Bond Liability |
| Period Ended | | | | | | |
| --- | --- | --- | --- | --- | --- | --- |
| 01/01/07 | — | — | — | $100,000 | $6,624 | $ 93,376 |
| 12/31/07 | $7,470 | $6,000 | $1,470 | 100,000 | 5,154 | 94,846 |
| 12/31/08 | 7,588 | 6,000 | 1,588 | 100,000 | 3,566 | 96,434 |
| 12/31/09 | 7,715 | 6,000 | 1,715 | 100,000 | 1,851 | 98,149 |
| 12/31/10 | 7,851 | 6,000 | 1,851 | 100,000 | 0 | 100,000 |

**Coach's Tip**

The straight-line method amortizes a bond premium or discount by adjusting Interest Expense each period by a **constant** dollar amount.

# Supplement 14C
## Straight-Line Method of Amortization

The aim of the straight-line method of amortization is to **match** any bond premium or discount to the periods in which the bond liability remains unpaid. Rather than adjust the rate used to calculate the interest expense, the straight-line method allocates the total premium or discount evenly over each year. Because this method results in an equal amount of interest expense each period, it is easy to apply. However, constant interest expense does not reflect reality because the bond liability changes each period. Consequently, the straight-line method may be used only when it does not materially differ from the effective-interest method of amortization (presented in Supplement 14B).

### Bond Premiums

A premium arises when the bond issuer receives more cash than the issuer repays at maturity. In effect, a premium reduces the company's cost of borrowing, so amortization of the premium causes interest expense to be lower than the interest payment each period. The difference is recorded as a reduction in the Premium on Bonds Payable liability account.

In our earlier example, General Mills received $107,260 for four-year bonds with a total face value of $100,000, implying a premium of $7,260. Using the straight-line method, amortization of the premium in each of the four years that the bonds remain unpaid would be $1,815 (= $7,260 ÷ 4). This amount would be subtracted from the interest to be paid ($6,000) to arrive at the amount of interest expense ($4,185). The effects would be recorded in the following journal entry:

| | Debit | Credit |
| --- | --- | --- |
| Interest Expense (+E, −OE) | 4,185 | |
| Premium on Bonds Payable (−L) | 1,185 | |
| Cash (−A) | | 6,000 |

| Assets | = | Liabilities | + | Owners' Equity |
| --- | --- | --- | --- | --- |
| Cash    −6,000 | | Premium on Bonds Payable    −1,815 | | Interest Expense (+E)   −4,185 |

This journal entry would be recorded each year on December 31 until the bonds mature. The following bond amortization schedule summarizes the effects:

## BOND PREMIUM AMORTIZATION SCHEDULE: STRAIGHT-LINE METHOD

| | CHANGES DURING THE PERIOD | | | ENDING BOND LIABILITY BALANCES | | |
|---|---|---|---|---|---|---|
| Period Ended | (A) Interest Payable | (B) Amortization of Premium | (C) (= A − B) Interest Expense | (D) Bonds Payable | (E) Premium on Bonds Payable | (F) (= D + E) Unpaid Bond Liability |
| 01/01/07 | — | — | — | $100,000 | $7,260 | $107,260 |
| 12/31/07 | $6,000 | $1,815 | $4,185 | 100,000 | 5,445 | 105,445 |
| 12/31/08 | 6,000 | 1,815 | 4,185 | 100,000 | 3,630 | 103,630 |
| 12/31/09 | 6,000 | 1,815 | 4,185 | 100,000 | 1,815 | 101,815 |
| 12/31/10 | 6,000 | 1,815 | 4,185 | 100,000 | 0 | 100,000 |

## Bond Discounts

A discount arises when the bond issuer receives less cash than the issuer repays at maturity. In effect, a discount increases the company's cost of borrowing, so amortization of the discount causes interest expense to be higher than the interest payment each period. To report this effect, accountants record a decrease in Discount on Bonds Payable and an increase in Interest Expense.

In our earlier example, General Mills received $93,376 for four-year bonds with a total face value of $100,000, implying a discount of $6,624. Using the straight-line method, amortization of the discount in each of the four years that the bonds remain unpaid would be $1,656 (= $6,624 ÷ 4). This amount would be added to the interest to be paid ($6,000) to calculate the amount of Interest Expense ($7,656). The effects would be recorded in the following journal entry:

| | Debit | Credit |
|---|---|---|
| Interest Expense (+E, −OE) | 7,656 | |
| Discount on Bonds Payable (−xL, +L) | | 1,656 |
| Cash (−A) | | 6,000 |

| Assets | = | Liabilities | + | Owners' Equity |
|---|---|---|---|---|
| Cash −6,000 | | Discount on Bonds Payable (−xL) +1,656 | | Interest Expense (+E) −7,656 |

This journal entry would be recorded each year on December 31 until the bonds mature. The effects are summarized in the following bond amortization schedule:

## BOND DISCOUNT AMORTIZATION SCHEDULE: STRAIGHT-LINE METHOD

| | CHANGES DURING THE PERIOD | | | ENDING BOND LIABILITY BALANCES | | |
|---|---|---|---|---|---|---|
| Period Ended | (A) Interest Payable | (B) Amortization of Discount | (C) (= A + B) Interest Expense | (D) Bonds Payable | (E) Discount on Bonds Payable | (F) (= D − E) Unpaid Bond Liability |
| 01/01/07 | — | — | — | $100,000 | $6,624 | $ 93,376 |
| 12/31/07 | $6,000 | $1,656 | $7,656 | 100,000 | 4,968 | 95,032 |
| 12/31/08 | 6,000 | 1,656 | 7,656 | 100,000 | 3,312 | 96,688 |
| 12/31/09 | 6,000 | 1,656 | 7,656 | 100,000 | 1,656 | 98,344 |
| 12/31/10 | 6,000 | 1,656 | 7,656 | 100,000 | 0 | 100,000 |

## Chapter Summary

### LO1 Explain how to measure long-term liabilities. p. 600

- Long-term liabilities are first recorded at their cash-equivalent amount, which is the amount of cash that would be accepted as full settlement of the liability at the moment it is created.

- The cash-equivalent amount is calculated using the discounting techniques explained in Supplement 14A. It excludes interest that arises (and is later recorded) with the passage of time.

### LO2  Demonstrate how to account for discounted notes payable. p. 601

- Discounted notes are recorded at their cash-equivalent amount, which is computed using the discounting techniques explained in Supplement 14A.
- As time passes, interest on a discounted note is accrued in the Note Payable account.

### LO3  Demonstrate how to account for bonds payable. p. 604

- The account Bonds Payable reports the face value of the bonds, which must be paid at maturity.
- If a company receives more cash when a bond is issued than the amount it promises to repay at maturity (perhaps because the bond pays an attractive rate of interest), the excess is recorded as a liability Premium on Bonds Payable.
- If the company receives less cash when a bond is issued than the amount it promises to repay at maturity (perhaps because the bond pays an unattractive rate of interest), the difference is recorded as a Discount on Bonds Payable, a contra-liability account that is deducted from Bonds Payable.
- Interest expense is the cost of borrowing; it equals the periodic interest payments plus (or minus) the amount of the bond discount (or premium) amortized in the current interest period.
- When a bond is retired, three financial effects are recorded: (1) a reduction in Cash for the amount paid, (2) the elimination of any balances in the bond liability account(s), and (3) a gain (or loss) if the amount paid is less (or more) than the carrying value of the bond liability accounts.

### LO4  Explain how to account for lease liabilities. p. 610

- An operating lease allows a company (the lessee) to temporarily use property belonging to another company (the lessor) in exchange for payments that the lessee records as Rent Expense.
- A capital lease allows a lessee to use rented property in exchange for paying the lessor, but unlike an operating lease, it transfers virtually all risks and rewards of owning the property to the lessee. To account for a capital lease, the lessee records the property as an asset and a long-term lease liability equal to the cash-equivalent amount of the future lease payments.

### LO5  Calculate and interpret the debt-to-assets and times interest earned ratios. p. 611

- The debt-to-assets ratio measures the extent to which a company's total assets have been financed by liabilities.
- The times interest earned ratio measures a company's ability to meet its interest obligations using resources generated by profit-making activities.

#### Financial Analysis Tools

| Name of Measure | Formula | What It Tells You |
|---|---|---|
| Debt-to-assets ratio | $\dfrac{\text{Total Liabilities}}{\text{Total Assets}}$ | • The proportion of assets financed by liabilities<br>• The higher the number the greater the financing risk |
| Times interest earned ratio | $\dfrac{(\text{Net Income} + \text{Interest Expense} + \text{Income Tax Expense})}{\text{Interest Expense}}$ | • Whether sufficient resources are generated to cover interest costs<br>• The higher the number the greater the coverage |

## Key Terms

Bonds (p. 604)
Cash-Equivalent Amount (p. 600)
Capital Lease (p. 610)
Carrying Value (p. 607)
Debt-to-Assets Ratio (p. 611)

Discount (p. 605)
Discounting (p. 601)
Face Value (p. 604)
Long-term Debt (p. 600)
Market Interest Rate (p. 606)

Maturity Date (p. 604)
Operating Lease (p. 610)
Premium (p. 605)
Stated Interest Rate (p. 604)
Times Interest Earned Ratio (p. 612)

See complete glossary in back of text.

# Questions

1. Why might a business finance using debt rather than equity? Why might a different business rely on equity rather than debt?

2. What term describes the amount at which liabilities are first recorded? Does this include interest? Why or why not?

3. How does a discounted note payable differ from an interest-bearing note payable, a topic introduced in Chapter 11? In what two ways does the accounting for these notes differ?

4. What accounting principle requires that interest expense be recorded each period even when interest has not been paid?

5. What are the three key elements of a bond, and which is/are indicated on the face of a bond certificate?

6. How are bond prices typically quoted? If an issuer sells 900 bonds, each with a face value of $1,000, at an issue price of 99.8, how much cash is received by the issuer? Describe how this would be reported by the issuer in the financial statements on the date of issue.

7. What are the reasons that some bonds are issued at a discount and others are issued at a premium?

8. Assuming simple annual compounding, how much should you pay for a one-year bond with a stated interest rate of 5 percent and a face value of $1,000 if you want to earn a return of 5 percent? What is the maximum you would be willing to pay if you want to earn a return of 8 percent? What is the maximum you would be willing to pay if you require a return of 4 percent?

9. What is the difference between the stated interest rate and the market interest rate on a bond?

10. Will the stated interest rate be higher than the market interest rate or will the market interest rate be higher than the stated interest rate when a bond is issued at (a) face value, (b) a discount, and (c) a premium?

11. In the context of bonds payable, to what does the term "carrying value" refer? In this same context, to what does the term "amortization" refer?

12. What three financial effects arise when a bond is retired early?

13. What two categories can be used to characterize seemingly limitless types of bonds?

14. What aspect of a lease agreement distinguishes a capital lease from an operating lease? In what ways does the accounting for capital leases differ from the accounting for operating leases?

15. If a company's debt-to-assets ratio increases, is it more or less likely to be able to pay the amounts it owes? If a company's times interest earned ratio decreases, has it become a better or worse credit risk?

16. (Supplement 14A) How does the purpose of compounding differ from the purpose of discounting? Which procedure (compounding or discounting) is more likely to be used in accounting?

17. (Supplement 14A) If you are asked to compute the present value of an amount compounded quarterly using an annual rate of 8 percent for five years, what combination of interest rates and interest periods should you use?

18. (Supplement 14B) How is interest expense calculated using the effective-interest method of amortization for a bond issued at (a) a discount and (b) a premium?

19. (Supplement 14C) How is interest expense calculated using the straight-line method of amortization for a bond issued at (a) a discount and (b) a premium?

# Multiple Choice

1. Which of the following best describes a reason for using debt rather than equity financing?

   Quiz 14-1
   www.mhhe.com/LLPW1e

   a. Owners may not have sufficient resources available to contribute to the business.
   b. Debt must be repaid (or refinanced) when it matures.
   c. Owners may forgo withdrawals to help the business survive its financial difficulties.
   d. None of the above.

2. A company purchases a piece of equipment and pays for it by signing a discounted note payable that requires a single payment of $134,776 in three years. How does the company account for this transaction?

   a. The payment of $134,776 is reported as a noncurrent liability on the date of purchase.
   b. Nothing is reported until the payment of $134,776 is made.
   c. The accountant computes the present value of $134,776 and records that amount as a noncurrent liability on the date of purchase.

   d. The accountant computes the future value of $134,776 and records that amount as a noncurrent liability on the date of purchase.

3. A three-year discounted note payable, which requires a payment of $595,508 at maturity on December 31, 2010, had an adjusted balance of $530,000 at December 31, 2008. Assuming 6 percent annual interest, which of the following adjusting journal entries should be recorded on December 31, 2009?

| | | | |
|---|---|---|---|
| a. | Interest Expense | 31,800 | |
| | Interest Payable | | 31,800 |
| b. | Interest Expense | 31,800 | |
| | Cash | | 31,800 |
| c. | Interest Expense | 31,800 | |
| | Note Payable | | 31,800 |
| d. | Interest Expense | 65,508 | |
| | Note Payable | 530,000 | |
| | Cash | | 595,508 |

4.  A corporate bond issued at 102 is currently trading at 97. Which of the following is true?
    a.  The corporation reports a bond discount on the balance sheet.
    b.  The corporation reports a bond premium on the income statement.
    c.  The stated interest rate was less than the market interest rate on the date of issue.
    d.  None of the above.

5.  Which of the following does not impact the calculation of the cash interest payments to be made to bondholders?
    a.  Face value of the bond.
    b.  Stated interest rate.
    c.  Market interest rate.
    d.  Length of time between payments.

6.  Which of the following is false when a bond is issued at a premium?
    a.  The bond is issued at an amount above its face value.
    b.  Interest expense will exceed the cash interest payments.
    c.  The market interest rate is lower than the stated interest rate.
    d.  The issue price will be quoted at a number more than 100.

7.  Which of the following terms describes bonds that are issued without security?
    a.  Zero coupon.       c.  Serial.
    b.  Debentures.        d.  Callable.

8.  To determine whether a bond will be issued at a premium, discount, or at face value, one must know which of the following pairs of information?
    a.  The face value and the stated interest rate on the date the bonds were issued.
    b.  The face value and the market interest rate on the date the bonds were issued.
    c.  The stated interest rate and the market interest rate on the date the bonds were issued.
    d.  You cannot tell without having more information.

9.  For the year ended December 31, 2006, Land O' Lakes, Inc., reported income from operations of $124,195, net income of $88,666, interest expense of $58,360, and income tax expense of $7,806. What was this dairy company's times interest earned ratio for the year?
    a.  0.65              c.  2.13
    b.  1.51              d.  2.65

10. Which of the following expenses is recorded on an operating lease?
    a.  Depreciation Expense.
    b.  Interest Expense.
    c.  Rent Expense.
    d.  All of the above.

---

**Solutions to Multiple-Choice Questions**

1. a    2. c    3. c    4. d    5. c    6. b    7. b
8. c    9. d    10. c

---

## Mini Exercises    Available with McGraw-Hill's Homework Manager

**LO2**

### M14-1 Recording Discounted Note Issue and Interest Accruals
On January 1, 2008, Steelmet Furniture purchased new welding equipment by issuing a note that promises to pay $27,783 on December 31, 2010. Assuming a 5 percent annual interest rate, the cash-equivalent amount on January 1, 2008, is $24,000. Prepare journal entries needed on (a) January 1, 2008, (b) December 31, 2008, and (c) December 31, 2009.

**LO2**

### M14-2 Recording Discounted Note Issue and Interest Accruals
On January 1, 2009, Shaw Cable purchased new computer switching equipment by issuing a note that promises to pay $115,762.50 on December 31, 2011. Assuming a 5 percent annual interest rate, the cash-equivalent amount on January 1, 2009, is $100,000. Prepare journal entries needed on (a) January 1, 2009, (b) December 31, 2009, and (c) December 31, 2010.

**LO2**

### M14-3 Recording Discounted Note Issue, Interest, and Maturity Repayment
On January 1, 2008, Touchstone Developments purchased a new excavator by issuing a note that promises to pay $22,898 on December 31, 2009. Assuming a 7 percent annual interest rate, the cash-equivalent amount on January 1, 2008, is $20,000. Prepare journal entries needed on (a) January 1, 2008, (b) December 31, 2008, and (c) December 31, 2009.

**LO2**

### M14-4 Recording Discounted Note Issue, Interest, and Maturity Repayment
On January 1, 2009, ACME Corporation purchased new aviation equipment by issuing a note that promises to pay $110,250 on December 31, 2010. Assuming a 5 percent annual interest rate, the cash-equivalent amount on January 1, 2009, is $100,000. Prepare journal entries needed on (a) January 1, 2009, (b) December 31, 2009, and (c) December 31, 2010.

**LO3**

Ford Motor Company

### M14-5 Determining Bond Discount or Premium from Quoted Price
On October 1, 2006, biz.yahoo.com quoted a bond price of 101.5 for Ford Motor Company's 9.875 percent bonds maturing on August 10, 2011. Were the bonds selling at a discount or premium? Does this mean the market interest rate for comparable bonds was higher or lower than 9.875 percent?

**M14-6 Computing and Reporting a Bond Liability at an Issuance Price of 98**
E-Tech Initiatives Limited plans to issue $500,000, 10-year, 4 percent bonds. Interest is payable annually on December 31. All of the bonds will be issued on January 1, 2009. Show how the bonds would be reported on the January 2, 2009, balance sheet if they are issued at 98.

LO3

**M14-7 Computing and Reporting a Bond Liability at an Issuance Price of 103**
Repeat M14-6 assuming the bonds are issued at 103.

LO3

**M14-8 Recording Bonds Issued at Face Value**
Schlitterbahn Waterslide Company issued 25,000, 10-year, 6 percent, $100 bonds on January 1, 2009, at face value. Interest is payable each December 31. Show the journal entries and accounting equation effects for (a) the bond issue on January 1, 2009, and (b) the interest payment on December 31, 2009.

LO3

**M14-9 Recording Bonds Issued at Face Value**
Shark's Pool Company issued 2,000, 10-year, 6 percent, $1,000 bonds on July 1, 2009, at face value. Interest is payable each June 30. Show the journal entries and accounting equation effects for (a) the issuance of these bonds on July 1, 2009, and (b) accrual of interest on December 31, 2009.

LO3

**M14-10 Determining Financial Statement Effects of an Early Retirement of Debt**
If the market price of a bond increased after it was issued and the company decided to retire its debt early, would you expect the company to report a gain or loss on debt retirement? Describe the financial statement effects of a debt retirement under these circumstances.

LO3

**M14-11 Recording Early Retirement of Bonds**
Refer to M14-9. Prepare journal entries that would be recorded if the bonds were retired early by repurchasing them at a price of (a) 99 or (b) 100.5. Explain why an early bond retirement is likely to result in a gain or loss.

LO3

**M14-12 Recording Operating and Capital Leases**
Prepare the journal entries that Hamilton Property should make on June 30, 2008, to record the following transactions, in which Hamilton is the lessee.

LO4

   a.   Made a lease payment of $8,000 on June 30, 2008, for equipment rented in June under an operating lease agreement.
   b.   Leased a new building, which requires 10 annual payments of $50,000. Assuming an annual interest rate of 6 percent, the cash-equivalent amount on June 30, 2008, is $368,005.

**M14-13 Computing the Debt-to-Assets Ratio and the Times Interest Earned Ratio**
The balance sheet for Food Maker Corporation (FMC) reported the following: total assets, $250,000; noncurrent assets, $150,000; current liabilities, $40,000; total stockholders' equity, $90,000; net income, $3,320; interest expense, $4,400; and income before income taxes, $5,280. Compute FMC's debt-to-assets ratio and times interest earned ratio. Based on these calculations and the ratios reported in Exhibit 14.7, does it appear FMC will be able to meet its obligations to pay liabilities and interest obligations as they become payable?

LO5

**M14-14 Analyzing the Impact of Transactions on the Debt-to-Assets Ratio**
BSO, Inc., has total liabilities of $500,000 and total assets of $1,000,000, resulting in a debt-to-assets ratio of 0.50 (or 50 percent). For each of the following independent events, determine whether the debt-to-assets ratio will increase, decrease, or remain the same.

LO5

   a.   Purchased $20,000 of new inventory on credit.
   b.   Paid accounts payable in the amount of $50,000.
   c.   Recorded accrued salaries in the amount of $10,000.
   d.   Borrowed $250,000 from a local bank on an interest-bearing note to be repaid in 90 days.

**M14-15 (Supplement 14A) Calculating Present Values**
Refer to M14-1. Show how Steelmet's accountants determined that the cash-equivalent amount on January 1, 2008, was $24,000.

**M14-16 (Supplement 14A) Calculating Present Values**
Refer to M14-2. Show how Shaw's accountants determined that the cash-equivalent amount on January 1, 2009, was $100,000.

**M14-17 (Supplement 14A) Calculating Present Values**
Refer to M14-3. Show how Touchstone's accountants determined that the cash-equivalent amount on January 1, 2008, was $20,000.

**M14-18 (Supplement 14A) Calculating Present Values**

Refer to M14-4. Show how ACME's accountants determined that the cash-equivalent amount on January 1, 2009, was $100,000.

**M14-19 (Supplement 14A) Calculating Present Values**

Refer to M14-12. Show how Hamilton's accountants determined that the cash-equivalent amount on June 30, 2008, was $368,005.

**M14-20 (Supplement 14B) Recording Bond Issuance and Interest Payment (Effective-Interest Amortization)**

Clem Company issued $800,000, 10-year, 5 percent bonds on January 1, 2009. The bonds sold for $741,000. Interest is payable annually on January 1. Using effective-interest amortization, prepare journal entries to record (*a*) the bond issuance on January 1, 2009, and (*b*) the payment of interest on January 1, 2010. The market interest rate on the bonds is 6 percent.

**M14-21 (Supplement 14C) Recording Bond Issuance and Interest Payment (Straight-Line Amortization)**

Simko Company issued $600,000, 10-year, 5 percent bonds on January 1, 2009. The bonds were issued for $580,000. Interest is payable annually on January 1. Using straight-line amortization, prepare journal entries to record (*a*) the bond issuance on January 1, 2009, and (*b*) the payment of interest on January 1, 2010.

# Exercises  Available with McGraw-Hill's Homework Manager

**LO1**

**E14-1 Choosing between Debt and Equity Financing**

Novelty Productions is operated as a sole proprietorship by its founder, Tina Wilkins. Tina is an inventor who recently created a new product that is growing in popularity. Tina needs to expand the business but has already contributed all personal resources to the business. Tina estimates that $100,000 is needed to purchase new equipment, and is confident that this investment will return about $25,000 cash each year for the next five years. Given the secret nature of the business, Tina is reluctant to admit partners. She rarely withdraws funds from the sole proprietorship.

*Required:*

How should Tina finance the expansion of her business? Provide reasons supporting your recommendation.

**LO1**

**E14-2 Accounting for an Interest-Bearing Note Issue, Interest, and Maturity**

Right Foot Shoes issued a two-year, $50,000 interest-bearing note on January 1, 2008, in exchange for new equipment. Interest accrues at 6 percent annually but is not paid until maturity.

*Required:*

Record the journal entries and accounting equation effects for each of the following.

1. The equipment purchase on January 1, 2008.
2. The interest adjustment on December 31, 2008.
3. The payment on December 31, 2009.

**LO2**

**E14-3 Accounting for a Discounted Note Issue, Interest, and Maturity**

Left Foot Shoes issued a discounted note on January 1, 2008, in exchange for new equipment. The note requires a payment of $56,180 on December 31, 2009. Using an annual interest rate of 6 percent to discount the payment, you determine that the note's present value on January 1, 2008, was $50,000.

*Required:*

Record the journal entries and accounting equation effects for each of the following.

1. The equipment purchase on January 1, 2008.
2. The interest adjustment on December 31, 2008.
3. The $56,180 payment on December 31, 2009.

**LO2**

**E14-4 Accounting for a Discounted Note Issue, Interest, and Maturity**

Deep Powder Corporation issued a discounted note on January 1, 2008, in exchange for new snow-making equipment. The note requires a $121,551 payment on December 31, 2011. Using an annual interest rate of 5 percent to discount the payment, you determine that the note's present value on January 1, 2008, was $100,000.

*Required:*

Record the journal entries for each of the following. (Round interest calculations to the nearest dollar.)

1. The equipment purchase on January 1, 2008.
2. The interest adjustments on December 31, 2008, 2009, and 2010.
3. The $121,551 payment on December 31, 2011.

### E14-5 Accounting for Bonds Issued at Face Value with Interest Accrual and Early Retirement    LO3

On October 1, 2009, Garden Equipment Corporation issued 2,000 bonds at face value. The bond certificates indicate a face value of $1,000, a stated interest rate of 7 percent paid annually on September 30, and a September 30, 2020 maturity date.

*Required:*

1. Give the journal entry to record the bond issue on October 1, 2009.
2. Give the adjusting entry required on December 31, 2009.
3. Assume Garden Equipment retires the bond early on October 1, 2012, at a price of 103. Give the journal entry to record this early retirement.

### E14-6 Accounting for Bonds Issued at Face Value with Interest Accrual and Maturity Repayment    LO3

On January 1, 2009, Arena Enterprises issued 300 bonds at face value. The bond certificates indicate a face value of $1,000, a stated interest rate of 6 percent paid annually on December 31, and a December 31, 2010, maturity date.

*Required:*

1. Give the journal entry to record the bond issue on January 1, 2009.
2. Give the journal entry required on December 31, 2009.
3. Give the journal entry to record the payment on December 31, 2010.

### E14-7 Determining Bond Price and Preparing Journal Entries to Record Bond Issue and Interest Payment    LO3

On January 1, 2008, Applied Technologies Corporation (ATC) issued 600 bonds, each with a face value of $1,000 and a maturity date of December 31, 2017. The bonds have a stated interest rate of 10 percent. When the bonds were issued, the market interest rate was 10 percent. The bonds pay interest once per year on December 31.

*Required:*

1. Determine the price at which the bonds were issued and the amount of cash that ATC received.
2. Prepare the journal entry to record the bond issue.
3. Prepare the journal entry to record the interest payment on December 31, 2008.

### E14-8 Preparing Journal Entries to Record Issuance of a Bond at Face Value, Payment of Interest, and Early Retirement    LO3

On January 1, 2009, Innovative Solutions, Inc., issued 200 bonds at face value ($1,000 each). The bonds have a stated interest rate of 6 percent, mature in 10 years, and pay interest annually on December 31.

*Required:*

1. Prepare the journal entry to record the bond issue.
2. Prepare the journal entry to record the interest payment on December 31, 2009.
3. Assume the bond was retired immediately after the first interest payment on January 1, 2010, at a quoted price of 102. Prepare the journal entry to record the early retirement of the bond.

### E14-9 Describing the Effects of a Premium Bond Issue and Interest Payment on the Financial Statements, Debt-to-Assets Ratio, and Times Interest Earned Ratio    LO3, 5

Grocery Corporation received $300,328 for $250,000, 11 percent bonds issued on January 1, 2008, at a market interest rate of 8 percent. The bonds stated that interest would be paid each December 31 and that they mature on December 31, 2017.

*Required:*

1. Describe how the bond issue affects the balance sheet and income statement, specifically identifying the account names and direction of effects (ignore amounts). Also, describe its impact on the debt-to-assets ratio and times interest earned ratio.
2. Without doing calculations, describe which balance sheet and income statement accounts are affected by the recording of interest on December 31, 2008.

**LO3**

### E14-10 Computing Price for One-Year Bond

Speedy Housing issued 200 bonds, each with a face value of $1,000 and stated interest rate of 5 percent to be paid out exactly one year after the issue date.

*Required:*

Determine your return on the 200 bonds if you purchased them all on the issue date for

1. $200,000.
2. $201,924.
3. $198,114.

**LO4**

### E14-11 Recording Lease Transactions

On June 1, 2009, National Equipment Rental leased equipment to the Glendale Community Club and Craig Legal Services. Glendale signed a lease indicating the club would rent portable tables for the month of June 2009 at a cost of $1,000 to be paid in July 2009. Craig Legal Services signed a lease indicating that the business would rent computer equipment for the three-year period ended May 31, 2012. Craig is required to pay $10,000 at the end of each year; these payments equate to a present value of $26,730 on June 1, 2009.

*Required:*

1. Prepare the journal entry that Glendale Community Club should record on June 30, 2009.
2. Prepare the journal entry that Craig Legal Services should record on June 1, 2009.

**LO5**

**Kraft**

### E14-12 Calculating and Interpreting the Debt-to-Assets Ratio and Times Interest Earned Ratio

According to its Web site, Kraft Foods Inc. sells enough Kool-Aid mix to make 1,000 gallons of the drink every minute during the summer and more than 560 million gallons each year. At December 31, 2007, the company reported the following amounts (in millions) in its financial statements:

|  | 2007 | 2006 |
|---|---|---|
| Total assets | $ 67,993 | $ 55,574 |
| Total liabilities | 40,698 | 27,019 |
| Interest expense | 698 | 579 |
| Income tax expense | 1,137 | 951 |
| Net income | 2,590 | 3,060 |

*Required:*

1. Compute the debt-to-assets ratio (to three decimal places) and times interest earned ratio (to two decimal places) for 2007 and 2006.
2. Does the trend in these ratios suggest Kraft has relied more or less on debt financing? Is Kraft's financial position more or less risky than that for the companies in Exhibit 14.7?

**LO5**

**TJX Companies Inc.**

### E14-13 Reporting Long-term Liabilities on a Classified Balance Sheet

TJX Companies, Inc., owns discount clothing stores operating in the United States under the store names Marshall's and TJ Maxx. For its year ended January 27, 2007, TJX Companies reported the following liabilities (all amounts in thousands). Prepare the Liabilities section of its classified balance sheet.

| | | | |
|---|---|---|---|
| Accounts payable | $1,372,352 | Bond debentures payable | $200,000 |
| Accrued liabilities | 1,008,774 | Discount on bond debentures payable | 183 |
| Other long-term liabilities | 604,572 | Zero-coupon bonds payable | 517,497 |
| Lease liability, long-term | 22,382 | Discount on zero-coupon bonds payable | 126,485 |
| Lease liability, short-term | 1,854 | Other long-term borrowings | 194,816 |

### E14-14 (Supplement 14A) Calculating Present Values

Refer to E14-3. Show how, Left Foot Shoes determined that the cash-equivalent amount on January 1, 2008, was $50,000.

### E14-15 (Supplement 14A) Calculating Present Values

Refer to E14-4. Show how Deep Powder's accountants determined that the cash-equivalent amount on January 1, 2008, was $100,000.

## E14-16 (Supplement 14A) Calculating Present Values

Refer to E14-9. Show how investors determined the price of Grocery Corporation's bonds on January 1, 2008 to be $300,328.

## E14-17 (Supplement 14A) Calculating Present Values

Refer to E14-11. Show how Craig Legal Services determined the cash-equivalent amount of $26,730 on June 1, 2009. What interest rate does this imply?

## E14-18 (Supplement 14B) Recording the Effects of a Premium Bond Issue and First Interest Payment (Effective-Interest Amortization)

Refer to the information in E14-9 and assume Grocery Corporation uses the effective-interest method to amortize the bond premium.

*Required:*

1. Prepare the journal entry to record the bond issue.
2. Prepare the journal entries to record the December 31 interest payments in 2008 and 2009.

## E14-19 (Supplement 14C) Recording the Effects of a Premium Bond Issue and First Interest Payment (Straight-Line Amortization)

Refer to the information in E14-9 and assume Grocery Corporation uses the straight-line method to amortize the bond premium.

*Required:*

1. Prepare the journal entry to record the bond issue.
2. Prepare the journal entries to record the December 31 interest payments in 2008 and 2009.

## E14-20 (Supplement 14B) Recording the Effects of a Discount Bond Issue and First Interest Payment and Preparing a Discount Amortization Schedule (Effective-Interest Amortization)

On January 1, 2009, when the market interest rate was 9 percent, Seton Corporation sold a $200,000, 8 percent bond issue for $187,163. The bonds were dated January 1, 2009, pay interest each December 31, and mature December 31, 2018. Seton amortizes the bond discount using the effective-interest method.

*Required:*

1. Prepare the journal entry to record the bond issue.
2. Prepare the journal entry to record the interest payment on December 31, 2009.
3. Prepare a bond discount amortization schedule for these bonds using the format shown in Supplement 14B.

## E14-21 (Supplement 14C) Recording the Effects of a Discount Bond Issue and First Interest Payment and Preparing a Discount Amortization Schedule (Straight-Line Amortization)

Refer to the information in E14-20 but assume Seton Corporation uses the straight-line method to amortize the bond discount.

*Required:*

1. Prepare the journal entry to record the bond issuance.
2. Prepare the journal entry to record the interest payment on December 31, 2009.
3. Prepare a bond discount amortization schedule for these bonds, using the format shown in Supplement 14C.

# Problems—Set A  Available with McGraw-Hill's Homework Manager

## PA14-1 Comparing and Recording a Discounted Note Payable and Capital Lease Liability

LO2, 4 ,5

Rockwell Industries is evaluating whether to purchase a piece of equipment or rent it. The company is a little short on cash, so a purchase would require Rockwell to finance the equipment's cost by signing a promissory note that requires a single payment of $100,000 three years after the purchase date. The present value of this payment is $83,960. If Rockwell were to rent the equipment, the company would pay $31,410.40 at the end of each of the following three years. This rental agreement would transfer to Rockwell virtually all risks and rewards of owning the equipment. The present value of these payments is $83,960. Rockwell's bank requires that the company's debt-to-assets ratio not exceed 0.50. Prior to acquiring the equipment, Rockwell has liabilities totaling $490,000 and assets totaling $1,000,000.

*Required:*

1. Prepare the journal entry to record the purchase of the equipment by issuing a promissory note.
2. Prepare the journal entry to record acquisition of the equipment through a capital lease.
3. Describe any significant differences in your answers to requirements 1 and 2.
4. Calculate the debt-to-assets ratio before and after the equipment acquisition. What are the possible consequences of acquiring the equipment through purchase or capital lease? How would you advise Rockwell to proceed?

**LO3**

### PA14-2 Comparing Bonds Issued at Face Value, Discount, and Premium

Sikes Corporation, whose annual accounting period ends on December 31, issued the following bonds:

Date of bonds: January 1, 2008.

Maturity amount and date: $200,000 due in 10 years (December 31, 2017).

Interest: 10 percent per year payable each December 31.

Date issued: January 1, 2008.

*Required:*

1. Provide the following amounts to be reported on the January 1, 2008, financial statements immediately after the bonds are issued:

|  | Case A (issued at 100) | Case B (issued at 96) | Case C (issued at 102) |
|---|---|---|---|
| *a.* Bonds payable | $ | $ | $ |
| *b.* Unamortized premium or discount | | | |
| *c.* Unpaid bond liability | | | |

2. Assume that a retired person has written to you (an investment adviser) asking, "Why should I buy a bond at a premium when I can find one at a discount? Is it not the case that paying a premium is like paying list price for a car instead of negotiating a discount?" Write a brief message in response to the question.

### PA14-3 (Supplement 14A) Comparing and Recording a Discounted Note Payable and Capital Lease Liability with Present Value Computations

Refer to PA14-1. Assume Rockwell Industries can acquire a comparable piece of equipment by signing a promissory note that requires a single payment of $80,000 three years after the purchase date or rent it by paying $25,128.32 at the end of each of the following three years. Rockwell typically borrows at a 6 percent annual interest rate.

*Required:*

1. Calculate the present value of the promissory note, and prepare the journal entry to record the purchase of the equipment.
2. Calculate the present value of the lease payments, and prepare the journal entry to record acquisition of the equipment through a capital lease.
3. Describe any significant differences in your answers to requirements 1 and 2.
4. Calculate the debt-to-assets ratio before and after the equipment acquisition. What are the possible consequences of acquiring the equipment through purchase or capital lease? How would you advise Rockwell to proceed?

**eXcel**

www.mhhe.com/LLPW1e

### PA14-4 (Supplement 14B) Recording Bond Issue, Interest Payments (Effective-Interest Amortization), and Early Retirement

Southwest Corporation issued bonds with the following details:

Face value: $600,000.

Interest: 9 percent per year paid each December 31.

Terms: Bonds issued January 1, 2009, maturing on December 31, 2013.

The annual accounting period ends December 31. The bonds were issued at 104 on January 1, 2009, implying an 8 percent market interest rate. Assume the company uses effective-interest amortization.

*Required:*

1. Compute the bond issue price (show computations).
2. Give the journal entry to record the bond issue.
3. Give the journal entries to record the interest payments on December 31, 2009 and 2010.

4.  How much interest expense would be reported on the income statements for 2009 and 2010? Show how the liability related to the bonds should be reported on the balance sheets at December 31, 2009 and 2010.

5.  Assume the bonds are retired on January 1, 2011, at a price of 101. Give the journal entry to record the bond retirement.

**PA14-5 (Supplement 14C) Recording Bond Issue, Interest Payments (Straight-Line Amortization), and Early Retirement**

Complete the requirements of PA14-4, assuming Southwest Corporation uses straight-line amortization.

**PA14-6 (Supplement 14B) Interpreting and Completing an Amortization Schedule (Effective-Interest Amortization)**

Hondor Corporation issued bonds and received cash for the issue price. The bonds were dated and issued on January 1, 2008. The stated interest rate was payable at the end of each year. The bonds mature at the end of four years. The following schedule has been completed (amounts in thousands):

| Date | Cash Paid | Interest Expense | Amortization | Unpaid Bond Liability |
|---|---|---|---|---|
| January 1, 2008 | — | — | — | $6,101 |
| End of year 2008 | $450 | $427 | $23 | 6,078 |
| End of year 2009 | 450 | 426 | 24 | 6,054 |
| End of year 2010 | 450 | ? | ? | ? |
| End of year 2011 | 450 | ? | 28 | 6,000 |

*Required:*

1.  What was the total face value to be paid at maturity?
2.  How much cash was received at date of issuance (sale) of the bonds?
3.  Was there a premium or a discount? If so, which was it and how much was it?
4.  How much cash will be paid for interest each period and in total for the full life of the bond issue?
5.  What is the stated interest rate?
6.  What is the market interest rate?
7.  Complete the amortization schedule by replacing the four ?s with appropriate amounts.
8.  What amount should be reported on the income statement each year?
9.  Show how the bonds should be reported on the balance sheet at the end of 2008 and 2009.

**PA14-7 (Supplement 14C) Interpreting and Completing an Amortization Schedule (Straight-Line Amortization)**

The Peg Corporation (TPC) issued bonds and received cash in full for the issue price. The bonds were dated and issued on January 1, 2009. The stated interest rate was payable at the end of each year. The bonds mature at the end of four years. The following schedule has been prepared (amounts in thousands):

| Date | Cash Paid | Interest Expense | Amortization | Unpaid Bond Liability |
|---|---|---|---|---|
| January 1, 2009 | — | — | — | $6,101 |
| End of year 2009 | $450 | $425 | $25 | ? |
| End of year 2010 | 450 | ? | 25 | 6,051 |
| End of year 2011 | 450 | ? | 25 | 6,026 |
| End of year 2012 | 450 | 424 | 26 | 6,000 |

*Required:*

1.  What was the total face value to be paid at maturity?
2.  How much cash was received at date of issuance (sale) of the bonds?
3.  Was there a premium or a discount? If so, which was it and how much was it?
4.  How much cash will be paid for interest each period and in total for the full life of the bond issue?
5.  What is the stated interest rate?
6.  Complete the amortization schedule by replacing the three ?s with appropriate amounts.
7.  What amount should be reported on the income statement each year?
8.  Show how the bonds should be reported on the balance sheet at the end of 2009 and 2010.

eXcel

www.mhhe.com/LLPW1e

www.mhhe.com/LLPW1e

**PA14-8 (Supplements 14A and 14B) Computing Bond Issue Price with Present Values, and Recording Bond Issue, Interest Payments (Effective-Interest Amortization), and Early Bond Retirement**

On January 1, 2008, Surreal Manufacturing issued 600 bonds, each with a face value of $1,000, a stated interest rate of 3 percent paid annually on December 31, and a maturity date of December 31, 2010. On the issue date, the market interest rate was 4 percent. Surreal uses the effective-interest method of amortization.

*Required:*

1. Compute the bond issue price (show computations).
2. Prepare a bond amortization schedule similar to that shown in Supplement 14B.
3. Give the journal entry to record the bond issue.
4. Give the journal entries to record the interest payments on December 31, 2008 and 2009.
5. Give the journal entry to record the interest and face value payment on December 31, 2010.
6. Assume, instead, that the bonds are retired on January 1, 2010, at a price of 101. Give the journal entry to record the bond retirement.

**PA14-9 (Supplements 14A and 14C) Computing Bonds Issue Price with Present Values, and Recording Bond Issue, Interest Payments (Straight-Line Amortization), and Early Bond Retirement**

On January 1, 2008, Loop Raceway issued 600 bonds, each with a face value of $1,000, a stated interest rate of 5 percent paid annually on December 31, and a maturity date of December 31, 2010. On the issue date, the market interest rate was 6 percent. Loop uses the straight-line method of amortization.

*Required:*

1. Compute the bond issue price (show computations).
2. Prepare a bond amortization schedule similar to that shown in Supplement 14C.
3. Give the journal entry to record the bond issue.
4. Give the journal entries to record the interest payments on December 31, 2008 and 2009.
5. Give the journal entry to record the interest and face value payment on December 31, 2010.
6. Assume, instead, that the bonds are retired on January 1, 2010, at a price of 98. Give the journal entry to record the bond retirement.

# Problems—Set B  Available with McGraw-Hill's Homework Manager

**LO2, 4, 5**

**PB14-1 Comparing and Recording a Discounted Note Payable and Capital Lease Liability**

Bridge Construction Company is evaluating whether to purchase a piece of equipment or rent it. The company is short on cash, so a purchase would require Bridge to finance the equipment's cost by signing a promissory note that requires a single payment of $200,000 three years after the purchase date. The present value of this payment is $167,920. If Bridge were to rent the equipment, the company would pay $62,820.80 at the end of each of the following three years. This rental agreement would transfer to Bridge virtually all risks and rewards of owning the equipment. The present value of these payments is $167,920. Bridge's bank requires that the company's debt-to-assets ratio not exceed 0.50. Prior to acquiring the equipment, Bridge has liabilities totaling $980,000 and assets totaling $2,000,000.

*Required:*

1. Prepare the journal entry to record the purchase of the equipment by issuing a promissory note.
2. Prepare the journal entry to record acquisition of the equipment through a capital lease.
3. Describe any significant differences in your answers to requirements 1 and 2.
4. Calculate the debt-to-assets ratio before and after the equipment acquisition. What are the possible consequences of acquiring the equipment through purchase or capital lease? How would you advise Bridge to proceed?

**LO3**

**PB14-2 Comparing Bonds Issued at Par, Discount, and Premium**

Net Work Corporation, whose annual accounting period ends on December 31, issued the following bonds:

Date of bonds: January 1, 2009.

Maturity amount and date: $200,000 due in 10 years (December 31, 2018).

Interest: 10 percent per year payable each December 31.

Date issued: January 1, 2009.

*Required:*

1.  Provide the following amounts to be reported on the January 1, 2009, financial statements immediately after the bonds were issued:

| | Case A (issued at 100) | Case B (issued at 97) | Case C (issued at 101) |
|---|---|---|---|
| *a.* Bonds payable | $ | $ | $ |
| *b.* Unamortized premium or discount | | | |
| *c.* Unpaid bond liability | | | |

2.  Assume that a retired person has written to you (an investment adviser) asking, "Why did you encourage me to buy a bond at a premium when my friend bought a different one at a discount? Have I paid too much for the bond I bought?" Write a brief message in response to the question.

## PB14-3 (Supplement 14A) Comparing and Recording a Discounted Note Payable and Capital Lease Liability with Present Value Computations

Refer to PB14-1. Assume that Bridge Construction Company can acquire a comparable piece of equipment by signing a promissory note that requires a single payment of $160,000 three years after the purchase date, or rent it by paying $50,256.64 at the end of each of the following three years. Bridge typically borrows at a 6% annual interest rate.

*Required:*

1.  Calculate the present value of the promissory note, and prepare the journal entry to record the purchase of the equipment.
2.  Calculate the present value of the lease payments, and prepare the journal entry to record acquisition of the equipment through a capital lease.
3.  Describe any significant differences in your answers to requirements 1 and 2.
4.  Calculate the debt-to-assets ratio before and after the equipment acquisition. What are the possible consequences of acquiring the equipment through purchase or capital lease? How would you advise Bridge to proceed?

## PB14-4 (Supplement 14B) Recording Bond Issue, Interest Payments (Effective-Interest Amortization), and Early Retirement

WestCoast Airlines Corporation issued bonds with the following details:

Face value: $500,000.

Interest: 7 percent per year paid each December 31.

Terms: Bonds issued January 1, 2009, maturing on December 31, 2014.

The annual accounting period ends December 31. The bonds were issued at 95.38 on January 1, 2009, implying an 8 percent market interest rate. Assume the company uses effective-interest amortization.

*Required:*

1.  Compute the bond issue price (show computations).
2.  Give the journal entry to record the bond issue.
3.  Give the journal entries to record the interest payments on December 31, 2009 and 2010.
4.  How much interest expense would be reported on the income statements for 2009 and 2010? Show how the liability related to the bonds should be reported on the balance sheets at December 31, 2009 and 2010.
5.  Assume the bonds are retired on January 1, 2011, at a price of 101. Give the journal entry to record the bond retirement.

## PB14-5 (Supplement 14C) Recording Bond Issue, Interest Payments (Straight-Line Amortization), and Early Retirement

Complete the requirements of PA14-4, assuming WestCoast Airlines Corporation uses straight-line amortization.

## PB14-6 (Supplement 14B) Interpreting and Completing an Amortization Schedule (Effective-Interest Amortization)

Amhert Corporation issued bonds and received cash for the issue price. The bonds were dated and issued on January 1, 2008. The stated interest rate was payable at the end of each year. The bonds mature at the end of four years. The following schedule has been completed (amounts in thousands):

| Date | Cash Paid | Interest Expense | Amortization | Unpaid Bond Liability |
|---|---|---|---|---|
| January 1, 2008 | — | — | — | $11,800 |
| End of year 2008 | $900 | $944 | $44 | 11,844 |
| End of year 2009 | 900 | ? | 48 | 11,892 |
| End of year 2010 | 900 | ? | ? | ? |
| End of year 2011 | 900 | 957 | 57 | 12,000 |

*Required:*

1. What was the total face value to be paid at maturity?
2. How much cash was received at date of issuance (sale) of the bonds?
3. Was there a premium or a discount? If so, which was it and how much was it?
4. How much cash will be paid for interest each period and in total for the full life of the bond issue?
5. What is the stated interest rate?
6. What is the market interest rate?
7. Complete the amortization schedule by replacing the four ?s with appropriate amounts.
8. What amount should be reported on the income statement each year?
9. Show how the bonds should be reported on the balance sheet at the end of 2008 and 2009.

## PB14-7 (Supplement 14C) Interpreting and Completing an Amortization Schedule (Straight-Line Amortization)

Toon Corporation (TC) issued bonds and received cash in full for the issue price. The bonds were dated and issued on January 1, 2009. The stated interest rate was payable at the end of each year. The bonds mature at the end of four years. The following schedule has been prepared (amounts in thousands):

| Date | Cash Paid | Interest Expense | Amortization | Unpaid Bond Liability |
|---|---|---|---|---|
| January 1, 2009 | — | — | — | $11,800 |
| End of year 2009 | $900 | $950 | $50 | ? |
| End of year 2010 | 900 | ? | 50 | 11,900 |
| End of year 2011 | 900 | ? | 50 | 11,950 |
| End of year 2012 | 900 | 950 | 50 | 12,000 |

*Required:*

1. What was the total face value to be paid at maturity?
2. How much cash was received at date of issuance (sale) of the bonds?
3. Was there a premium or a discount? If so, which was it and how much was it?
4. How much cash will be paid for interest each period and in total for the full life of the bond issue?
5. What is the stated interest rate?
6. Complete the amortization schedule by replacing the three ?s with appropriate amounts.
7. What amount should be reported on the income statement each year?
8. Show how the bonds should be reported on the balance sheet at the end of 2009 and 2010.

## PB14-8 (Supplements 14A and 14B) Computing Bond Issue Price with Present Values, and Recording Bond Issue, Interest Payments (Effective-Interest Amortization), and Early Bond Retirement

On January 1, 2008, Methodical Manufacturing issued 100 bonds, each with a face value of $1,000, a stated interest rate of 5 percent paid annually on December 31, and a maturity date of December 31, 2010. On the issue date, the market interest rate was 4.25 percent. Methodical uses the effective-interest method of amortization.

*Required:*

1. Compute the bond issue price (show computations).
2. Prepare a bond amortization schedule similar to that shown in Supplement 14B.
3. Give the journal entry to record the bond issue.
4. Give the journal entries to record the interest payments on December 31, 2008 and 2009.
5. Give the journal entry to record the interest and face value payment on December 31, 2010.
6. Assume the bonds are retired on January 1, 2010, at a price of 101. Give the journal entries to record the bond retirement.

**PB14-9 (Supplements 14A and 14C) Computing Bond Issue Price with Present Values, and Recording Bond Issue, Interest Payments (Straight-Line Amortization), and Early Bond Retirement**
Refer to PB14-8. Assume Methodical uses the straight-line method of amortization.

*Required:*

1. Compute the bond issue price (show computations).
2. Prepare a bond amortization schedule similar to that shown in Supplement 14C.
3. Give the journal entry to record the bond issue.
4. Give the journal entries to record the interest payments on December 31, 2008 and 2009.
5. Give the journal entry to record the interest and face value payment on December 31, 2010.
6. Assume the bonds are retired on January 1, 2010, at a price of 102. Give the journal entry to record the bond retirement.

# Cases and Projects

### CP14-1 Finding Financial Information
Refer to the financial statements of The Home Depot in Appendix A at the end of this book, or download the annual report from the Cases and Projects section of the text's Web site at www.mhhe.com/LLPW1e.

LO5

*Required:*

1. Calculate, to two decimal places, the company's debt-to-assets ratio using amounts reported in its financial statements for the years ended February 3, 2008, and January 28, 2007. What do the changes in this ratio suggest about the company's ability to pay its liabilities?
2. Calculate, to two decimal places, the company's times interest earned ratio for the year ended February 3, 2008. Does this ratio cause you any concern about the company's ability to meet future interest obligations as they become due?

### CP14-2 Comparing Financial Information
Refer to the financial statements of The Home Depot in Appendix A and Lowe's in Appendix B at the end of this book, or download the annual reports from the Cases and Projects section of the text's Web site at www.mhhe.com/LLPW1e.

LO5

Lowe's

*Required:*

1. Calculate, to two decimal places, the companies' debt-to-assets ratios using amounts reported in the financial statements for the years ending in early 2008 and 2007. What do the changes in this ratio suggest about the companies' ability to pay their liabilities? Does it appear that Lowe's or The Home Depot has a greater financing risk?
2. Calculate, to two decimal places, the companies' times interest earned ratios for the year ended in February 2008. Does it appear that Lowe's or The Home Depot will be better able to meet future interest obligations as they become payable?

### CP14-3 Examining an Annual Report: Internet-Based Team Research
As a team, select an industry to analyze. Using your Web browser, each team member should acquire the annual report or 10-K for one publicly traded company in the industry, with each member selecting a different company. (See CP1-3 in Chapter 1 for a description of possible resources for these tasks.)

LO1, 5

*Required:*

1. On an individual basis, each team member should read the company's financial statement note regarding long-term debt and then write a short report that incorporates the following:

   *a.* What are the types of long-term debt owed by the company?
   *b.* Does the company have any significant amounts coming due in the next five years?
   *c.* Compute and analyze the debt-to-assets ratios and times interest earned ratios for the two most recent years.

2. Then, as a team, write a short report comparing and contrasting your companies using these attributes. Discuss any patterns across the companies that you as a team observe. Provide potential explanations for any differences discovered.

**LO3    CP14-4 Making Ethical Decisions: A Real-Life Example**

Many retired people invest a significant portion of their money in bonds of corporations because of their relatively low level of risk. During the 1980s, significant inflation caused some interest rates to rise to as high as 15 percent. Retired people who bought bonds that paid only 6 percent continued to earn at the lower rate. During the 1990s, inflation subsided and interest rates declined. Many corporations took advantage of the callability feature of these bonds and retired the bonds early. Many of these early retirements of high interest rate bonds were replaced with low interest rate bonds.

*Required:*

In your judgment, is it ethical for corporations to continue paying low interest rates when rates increase but to call bonds when rates decrease? Why or why not?

**LO3    CP14-5 Making Ethical Decisions: A Mini Case**

Assume you are a portfolio manager for a large insurance company. The majority of the money you manage is from retired school teachers who depend on the income you earn on their investments. You have invested a significant amount of money in the bonds of a large corporation and have just read a news release from the company's president explaining that it is unable to meet its current interest obligations because of deteriorating business operations related to increased international competition. The president has a recovery plan that will take at least two years. During that time, the company will not be able to pay interest on the bonds and, she admits, if the plan does not work, bondholders will probably lose more than half of their money. As a creditor, you can force the company into immediate bankruptcy and probably get back at least 90 percent of the bondholders' money. You also know that your decision will cause at least 10,000 people to lose their jobs if the company ceases operations.

*Required:*

Given only these two options, what should you do? Consider who would be helped or harmed by the two options.

**LO1, 5    CP14-6 Thinking Critically: Evaluating Effects on Debt-to-Assets Ratio**

Assume you work as an assistant to the chief financial officer (CFO) of Little Chip Company. The CFO reminds you that the fiscal year end is only one month away and that he is looking to you to ensure the company adheres to its loan covenant to maintain a debt-to-assets ratio of 0.50 or lower. A review of the general ledger indicates that assets total $1,690,000 and total liabilities are $820,000. Your company will soon need additional warehouse space that could be obtained by issuing a long-term, interest-bearing promissory note for $200,000 and using that money to purchase a nearby building. Alternatively, the building owner is willing to rent the space on either a long-term or month-to-month basis.

*Required:*

1. Determine whether the company is currently in compliance with its loan covenant. Show calculations (to three decimal places) in support of your answer.

2. Evaluate whether Little Chip should purchase the building before year-end. Show calculations in support of your answer.

3. Evaluate whether Little Chip should enter into a lease agreement before year-end. Explain your answer.

**CP14-7 (Supplement 14B) Preparing a Bond Amortization Schedule (Effective-Interest Amortization)**

Assume the authors of a popular accounting principles text have hired you to create spreadsheets that will calculate bond discount amortization schedules like those shown in Supplements 14B and 14C.

You e-mail your friend Sally for some guidance. Much to your disappointment, you receive an auto-reply message from Sally indicating that she's gone skiing in New Zealand. After a bit of panicking, you realize you can refer to Sally's previous e-mail messages for spreadsheet advice that will help you complete this task. From her advice for Chapter 10, you decide to create a data input section for the stated interest rate, market interest rate, face value, issue price, and years to maturity. The spreadsheet file also will have a separate amortization schedule worksheet that contains only formulas, references to the cells in the data input section, and references to other cells in the amortization schedule. All amounts will be rounded to the nearest dollar (using the Round function in Excel), which means the discount amortization in the final year might be off a few dollars (unless you use the If function in Excel to eliminate any remaining discount in the final year of the bond's life, in the same way that Sally showed in Chapter 10 for declining-balance depreciation).

*Required:*

Prepare a worksheet that reproduces the effective-interest bond discount amortization schedule shown in Supplement 14B (page 622). Provide a printout showing both the amortization schedule and the formulas underlying it. (Formulas can be revealed in Excel by entering Ctrl ~).

### CP14-8 (Supplement 14C) Preparing a Bond Amortization Schedule (Straight-Line Amortization)

Refer to the information in CP14-7 and prepare a worksheet that reproduces the straight-line bond discount amortization schedule shown in Supplement 14C (page 623). Provide a printout showing both the amortization schedule and the formulas underlying it. (Formulas can be revealed in Excel by entering Ctrl ~).

# 15 Accounting for Investments

## LEARNING OBJECTIVES

**After studying this chapter, you should be able to:**

**LO1** Explain why companies invest in debt and stock securities.

Lectured presentations–15-1
www.mhhe.com/LLPW1e

**LO2** Identify investment types and the related accounting methods.

**LO3** Analyze and report bond investments held to maturity.

**LO4** Analyze and report passive investments in securities using the market value method.

**LO5** Analyze and report investments involving significant influence using the equity method.

**LO6** Explain the reporting of investments in controlling interests.

**LO7** Analyze and interpret the return on assets ratio.

# Focus Company: THE WASHINGTON POST COMPANY

## Investment Strategies

www.washpostco.com

Have you ever wondered how big companies become big? The answer, for many companies, is by investing in other companies. One such business is The Washington Post Company, best known for publishing the most important newspaper in our nation's capital. However, The Washington Post Company does much more than that. It owns television stations, *Newsweek* magazine, Cable One (a TV cable company), and a variety of community newspapers.

Many users of this text have already been Washington Post customers without knowing it. The company also owns Kaplan, Inc., the king of admissions test preparation services that will even help you prepare for the certified public accountant or chartered financial analyst exams. The Washington Post Company also recognizes that new technologies bring increased efficiency to its operations while expanding business opportunities. For example, it publishes electronic versions of *The Washington Post* and *Newsweek* and shares news resources with NBC News and MSNBC.

The company has achieved its diversity in part by investing in the stock of other companies. For example, it spent $350 million over the last three years to purchase other companies including the online magazine *Slate* and a variety of private education companies around the world. It jointly owns (with another publisher) the company that produces the European, Middle Eastern, and African editions of *Newsweek*. It also jointly owns one of the major providers of the paper on which *The Washington Post* is printed. In addition, the company's investment portfolio consists of more than $350 million worth of stock of other companies.

In this chapter, you will see how to account for four different types of investments. To understand these investments and the reasons why they are accounted for in certain ways, you first need to answer the following question: Why do companies invest in other companies?

| **AN OVERVIEW** | **ACCOUNTING FOR PASSIVE INVESTMENTS** | **ACCOUNTING FOR INFLUENTIAL INVESTMENTS** | **EVALUATING TOTAL INVESTED CAPITAL** |
|---|---|---|---|
| • Reasons Companies Invest<br>• Identifying Investment Types and Accounting Methods<br> • Passive Investments in Debt and Equity Securities<br> • Investments in Stock for Significant Influence<br> • Investments in Stock for Control | • Debt Investments Held to Maturity: Amortized Cost Method<br>• Securities Available for Sale: Market Value Method<br>• Comparison of Available-for-Sale and Trading Securities | • Investments for Significant Influence: Equity Method<br>• Investments with Controlling Interests: Consolidated Statements | • Return on Assets (ROA)<br>• Comparison to Benchmarks |

## AN OVERVIEW

### Reasons Companies Invest

**Learning Objective 1**

Explain why companies invest in debt and stock securities.

Many factors motivate managers to invest in securities. Some do so **because the very nature of their business requires it.** For example, pension funds, insurance companies, and mutual funds receive large sums of cash from their clients. To generate earnings—an important source of revenue in these companies—they invest the cash in the securities of other companies. Investments are significant assets to these companies. State Farm Mutual Automobile Insurance Company, for example, holds more than $90 billion in securities that generate more than $3 billion in income each year.

Other managers invest in securities **to even out seasonal fluctuations in cash.** A manager whose company has extra cash at the end of a busy season may want to earn a return on the idle funds until they are needed for other purposes, such as repaying loans, purchasing property and equipment, or paying dividends. Excess cash can be invested in the stocks and bonds of other companies, either long or short term. Managers may also invest excess cash to provide a cushion against future downturns in the economy or unanticipated emergencies. Such investments in securities are referred to as **passive investments** because the investors are not interested in influencing or controlling the companies that issued the securities. The Washington Post Company's 2006 balance sheet in Exhibit 15.1 reflects both short-term and long-term Investments in Marketable Securities accounts—passive investments.

Sometimes managers want to expand their company's presence in a related industry or market. They do so by investing in another company **with the purpose of influencing, but not controlling, the company's policies and activities.** Washington Post's balance sheet reports these types of investments as Investments in Affiliates in Exhibit 15.1—investments for significant influence.

Finally, managers may want **to control another company,** either by purchasing it directly or by becoming the majority shareholder. In this case, the two companies combine their financial reports into **consolidated** financial statements, as Washington Post has done (see the title to its "consolidated" balance sheet). In the notes to the annual report, we find that Washington Post's recent acquisitions include PMBR, a bar exam test preparation company, and *Slate* magazine. As you saw in Chapter 10, when one company purchases another for more than the fair value of its assets and liabilities, the company records the difference as Goodwill (see Exhibit 15.1).

## Exhibit 15.1   The Washington Post Company's Balance Sheet

THE WASHINGTON POST COMPANY
CONSOLIDATED BALANCE SHEET
December 31, 2006
(Dollars in millions)

| ASSETS: | | LIABILITIES & STOCKHOLDERS' EQUITY | |
|---|---|---|---|
| Current assets: | | Current liabilities: | |
| Cash and cash equivalents | $   348 | Accounts payable | $   514 |
| Investments in marketable securities | 29 | Current portion of long-term debt | 6 |
| Other current assets (*summarized*) | 558 | Other current liabilities (*summarized*) | 283 |
| Total current assets | 935 | Total current liabilities | 803 |
| Investments in marketable securities | 326 | Long-term debt | 402 |
| Investments in affiliates | 54 | Other liabilities | 1,005 |
| Plant, property, and equipment (net) | 1,218 | Stockholders' equity: | |
| Goodwill | 1,790 | Common stock | 32 |
| Other assets (*summarized*) | 1,059 | Additional paid-in capital | 206 |
| | | Retained earnings | 4,120 |
| | | Accumulated other comprehensive income: | |
| | | Unrealized gain on investments | 85 |
| | | Other (*summarized*) | 293 |
| | | Less: Treasury stock | (1,564) |
| Total assets | $5,382 | Total liabilities and stockholders' equity | $5,382 |

Control →

Passive →

Passive →

Significant Influence →

Related to passive investments ←

# Identifying Investment Types and Accounting Methods

The accounting methods used to record investments are directly related to the purpose of the investment.

## Passive Investments in Debt and Equity Securities

Investors make **passive investments** to earn a high rate of return on funds that may be needed in the future for either short- or long-term purposes. This category includes investments in both debt securities (bonds and notes) and equity securities (stock):

- **Investments in equity securities** are presumed to be passive if the investing company owns less than 20 percent of the other company's outstanding voting shares or any amount of nonvoting shares. The market value method is used to measure and report these investments.
- **Investments in debt securities** are always considered to be passive. If they are meant to be sold before maturity, they are treated as equity securities and reported using the market value method (also called fair market value method). If the company intends and has the ability to hold them until the maturity date, however, the company measures and reports them at amortized cost.

## Investments in Stock for Significant Influence

**Active investments** are those in which a company owns enough stock in another business to influence or control that business. An investor or company that owns enough shares of voting stock of another company to have an important impact on its operating and financing policies is said to have **significant influence.** Significant influence is presumed to exist if the investing company owns from 20 to 50 percent of the outstanding voting shares. However, other factors may also indicate significant influence, including membership on the board of directors of the other company, participation in its policy-making processes, evidence of material transactions between the two companies, an interchange of managerial personnel, and technological dependency. The equity method is used to measure and report this type of investment.

## Investments in Stock for Control

**Control** is the ability to determine the operating and financial policies of another company through ownership of its voting stock. For all practical purposes, control is presumed when

Investments in the Securities of Other Companies . . . . . . . .

Passive
Debt securities, nonvoting equity securities, and <20% of outstanding voting equity securities

Significant Influence
20–50% of outstanding voting stock

Control
>50% of outstanding voting stock

the investing company owns more than 50 percent of the outstanding voting stock. These investments are accounted for by combining the two companies using the consolidated statement method.

The three investment types and the appropriate measuring and reporting methods for each may be summarized as follows:

| Investment Category | Investment in Debt Securities of Another Entity | | Investment in the Voting Common Stock of Another Entity | | |
|---|---|---|---|---|---|
| | Passive | | Passive | Significant Influence | Control |
| Level of ownership | Held to maturity | Not held to maturity | <20% of outstanding shares | 20–50% of outstanding shares | >50% of outstanding shares |
| Measuring and reporting method | Amortized cost method | Market value method | | Equity method | Consolidation method |

Let's look more closely at the accounting and reporting rules for each of these investment types.

# ACCOUNTING FOR PASSIVE INVESTMENTS

## Debt Investments Held to Maturity: Amortized Cost Method

When management plans to hold a bond investment until the maturity date (when the principal is due), it is reported in the account appropriately named **Investments Held to Maturity.** Bonds should be classified as investments held to maturity if management has both the intent and the ability to hold them until the maturity date. These bonds are reported at **amortized cost**—that is, at cost adjusted for the amortization of any bond discount or premium. We illustrate how to account for these investments from their purchase date through the maturity date.

### Bond Purchases

On the date of purchase, a bond may be acquired at the maturity amount (at par), for less than the maturity amount (at a discount), or for more than the maturity amount (at a premium).[1] Following the cost principle, the bond's total cost, including all acquisition costs such as transfer fees and brokers' commissions, is debited to the Investments Held to Maturity account.

To illustrate, assume that on October 1, 2010, The Washington Post Company paid the par value of $100 million[2] for 8 percent bonds due to mature on October 1, 2015. The 8 percent interest is paid each September 30. Management plans and has the ability to hold the bonds for five years until their maturity date. The journal entry to record the purchase of the bonds on October 1, 2010, is:

| (In millions) | Debit | Credit |
|---|---|---|
| Investments Held to Maturity (+A) | 100 | |
|     Cash (−A) | | 100 |

| Assets | | = | Liabilities | + Owners' Equity |
|---|---|---|---|---|
| Investments Held to Maturity | +100 | | | |
| Cash | −100 | | | |

---

[1] The price of the bond is determined based on the present value techniques discussed in Chapter 14. Many analysts refer to a bond price as a percentage of par. For example, *The Wall Street Journal* might report that an ExxonMobil bond with a par value of $1,000 is selling at 82.97. This statement means that the bond costs $829.70 (82.97 percent of $1,000).

[2] When bond investors accept an interest rate that is the same as the rate stated on the bonds, the bonds will sell at par (that is, at 100 percent of face value).

## Interest Earned

In this illustration, the company purchased the bonds at par, or face value. Because there is no premium or discount to amortize, the book value remains constant over the life of the investment. In such situations, the revenue earned on the investment each period is measured as the amount of interest collected in cash or accrued at year-end. The following journal entry records the accrual of $2 million in interest on December 31 [$100 million face value × 0.08 (or 8%) × 3/12 of a year (since the October 1 purchase)]:

| (In millions) | Debit | Credit |
|---|---|---|
| Interest Receivable (+A) | 2 | |
|    Interest Revenue (+R, +OE) | | 2 |

| Assets | | = | Liabilities | + | Owners' Equity | |
|---|---|---|---|---|---|---|
| Interest Receivable | +2 | | | | Interest Revenue (+R) | +2 |

On September 30, 2011, when the investor receives a full year of interest ($2 million each quarter × 4 quarters = $8 million), the following journal entry is made:

| (In millions) | Debit | Credit |
|---|---|---|
| Cash (+A) | 8 | |
|    Interest Receivable (−A) | | 2 |
|    Interest Revenue (+R, +OE) | | 6 |

| Assets | | = | Liabilities | + | Owners' Equity | |
|---|---|---|---|---|---|---|
| Cash | +8 | | | | Interest Revenue (+R) | +6 |
| Interest Receivable | −2 | | | | | |

The same entry is made for succeeding interest payments. On the income statement, Interest Revenue is reported in the Other Items section.

## Principal at Maturity

When the bonds mature on October 1, 2015, the journal entry to record receipt of the $100 million principal payment is:

| (In millions) | Debit | Credit |
|---|---|---|
| Cash (+A) | 100 | |
|    Investments Held to Maturity (−A) | | 100 |

| Assets | | = | Liabilities | + | Owners' Equity |
|---|---|---|---|---|---|
| Cash | +100 | | | | |
| Investments Held to Maturity | −100 | | | | |

Note the following:

- If the bond investment is sold before maturity, any difference between the market value (the proceeds from the sale) and the net book value (the unamortized cost) is reported in the income statement as a gain or loss on the sale.
- If management intends to sell the bonds before (or is unable to hold them until) the maturity date, they should be treated in the same way as stock investments classified as securities available for sale, which we discuss in the next section.

**SELF-STUDY PRACTICE**

On February 1, 2011, Rodriguez Company had $200,000 in excess cash. The company invested it in a three-year bond, purchased at par, which pays 12 percent interest each year on January 31. Rodriguez expects and is able to hold the bond to maturity. Answer the following questions.

1. What type of investment is this, and how should Rodriguez account for it?
2. Record the journal entry on the purchase date, February 1, 2011.

| | Debit | Credit |
| --- | --- | --- |
| | | |
| | | |

3. Record the journal entry on December 31, 2011, the company's year-end.

| | Debit | Credit |
| --- | --- | --- |
| | | |
| | | |

4. Record the journal entry on the first interest payment date, January 31, 2012.

| | Debit | Credit |
| --- | --- | --- |
| | | |
| | | |
| | | |

5. Record the journal entry on the maturity date, February 1, 2014.

| | Debit | Credit |
| --- | --- | --- |
| | | |
| | | |

*After you have finished, check your answers with the solution at the bottom of the next page.*

# Securities Available for Sale: Market Value Method

**Learning Objective 4**

Analyze and report passive investments in securities using the market value method.

When the investing company owns less than 20 percent of the outstanding voting stock in another company or any level of nonvoting stock, its investment in equity securities is considered passive. Among the assets and liabilities shown on the balance sheet, only passive investments in marketable securities (that is, stock and debt that is not held to maturity) are reported using the market value method.

## Classifying Passive Investments

Depending on management's intent, passive investments may be classified as either trading securities or securities available for sale:

**Trading Securities.** Trading securities are traded actively with the objective of generating short-term profits on changes in the securities' price. This approach is similar to the one taken by many mutual funds whose portfolio managers actively buy and sell securities. On the balance sheet, Trading Securities are classified as current assets.

**Securities Available for Sale.** Most companies do not actively trade the securities of other companies. Instead they invest in them to earn a return on funds they may need in the near future for operating purposes. These investments are called Securities Available for Sale.

On the balance sheet, they are classified as either current or noncurrent assets, depending on whether management intends to sell them within the next year.

Because securities available for sale are the most common type of passive investment, we focus on this category in the next section by analyzing Washington Post's investing activities.

## Recording and Reporting Securities Available for Sale

Washington Post's Investments in Marketable Securities accounts are reported for the year 2006 at $29 million for the current asset and $326 million for the noncurrent asset (see Exhibit 15.1). The notes to Washington Post's annual report contain the following information concerning this investment portfolio:

---

### NOTES TO CONSOLIDATED FINANCIAL STATEMENTS

#### A. SUMMARY OF SIGNIFICANT ACCOUNTING POLICIES

**Investments in Marketable Equity Securities.** The Company's investments in marketable equity securities are classified as **available-for-sale** and therefore are recorded at fair market value in the Consolidated Balance Sheets, with the change in fair market value during the period excluded from earnings and recorded net of tax as a separate component of comprehensive income. Marketable equity securities the Company expects to hold long term are classified as non-current assets. If the fair market value of a marketable equity security declines below its cost basis, and the decline is considered other than temporary, the Company will record a write-down, which is included in earnings [*emphasis added*].

---

WASHINGTON POST

2006 Annual Report

Here is how the market value method is applied:

- Washington Post invests in equity securities, acquiring a passive interest in the stock of other companies. These assets are reported on the balance sheet (Exhibit 15.1) as both current and noncurrent assets. The note to the annual report indicates both groups are accounted for as securities available for sale. Like most companies, Washington Post does not invest in trading securities.
- When the company purchases securities available for sale, accountants record them at cost in the account Securities Available for Sale (part of Investments in Marketable Securities on Washington Post's balance sheet).

Solution to
Self-Study Practice

1. Because Rodriguez intends to hold the bond until maturity, it is a passive investment called Investments Held to Maturity. It should be accounted for using the amortized cost method.

2.

|  | Debit | Credit |
|---|---|---|
| Investments Held to Maturity (+A) | 200,000 |  |
| Cash (−A) |  | 200,000 |

3.

|  | Debit | Credit |
|---|---|---|
| Interest Receivable (+A) | 22,000 |  |
| Interest Revenue (+R, +OE) |  | 22,000 |
| [$200,000 \times 0.12 \times 11/12$] |  |  |

4.

|  | Debit | Credit |
|---|---|---|
| Cash (+A) | 24,000 |  |
| Interest Receivable (−A) |  | 22,000 |
| Interest Revenue (+R, +OE) |  | 2,000 |

5.

|  | Debit | Credit |
|---|---|---|
| Cash (+A) | 200,000 |  |
| Investments Held to Maturity (−A) |  | 200,000 |

**Coach's Tip**

A realized gain or loss occurs when a company actually **sells** its investments. Gains or losses from simply **holding** the available-for-sale investments are not realized because no sale has occurred.

- In reporting the market value of the investments on the balance sheet at year-end, accountants record an adjusting entry for any temporary change up or down in the stock's market value since it was acquired. These changes are called **unrealized holding gains or losses.** Accountants use a special account, a valuation allowance, to show the change in the market value above or below acquisition cost. If the investments' market value has increased since they were purchased, the valuation allowance is added to the cost of the securities in the Securities Available for Sale account. If their market value has decreased, the valuation allowance is subtracted from the cost of the investments.

- Because a journal entry must affect at least two accounts, the other half of the adjusting entry is made to another account, reported in the Stockholders' Equity section of the balance sheet under Accumulated Other Comprehensive Income. Note in Exhibit 15.1 that Washington Post reported unrealized gains of $85 million in Stockholders' Equity. Because the amount reported for the long-term asset Investments in Marketable Securities was $326 million, the **cost** of the securities available for sale must have been $241 million with a valuation allowance of $85 million for unrealized gains ($326 million reported − $85 million unrealized gain = $241 million cost).

This process may sound complicated. To illustrate the market value method, let's assume that Washington Post had no passive investments at the end of 2009. In the following example, we apply the market value method, the accounting policy used by Washington Post, to a sample securities purchase.

**Purchase of Stock.** Assume that on January 2, 2010, Washington Post purchased 1,000,000 shares of Internet Financial News[3] (IFN) common stock for $60 per share, paying $60,000,000. On that date, 10,000,000 shares were outstanding, so Washington Post owned 10 percent of IFN (1,000,000 ÷ 10,000,000). This investment would be treated as a passive investment that is recorded initially (on January 2, 2010) at cost:

| (In millions) | Debit | Credit |
|---|---|---|
| Securities Available for Sale (+A) | 60 | |
| Cash (−A) | | 60 |

| | Assets | = | Liabilities | + | Owners' Equity |
|---|---|---|---|---|---|
| Securities Available for Sale | +60 | | | | |
| Cash | −60 | | | | |

See Exhibit 15.2 on page 651 for this entry and those that follow posted to T-accounts.

**Dividends Earned.** Investments in equity securities earn a return from two sources: (1) price increases and (2) dividend income. Price increases (or decreases) are analyzed both at year-end and when a security is sold. On the income statement, dividends earned are reported as Investment Income (or Dividend Revenue) and included in the computation of net income for the period. Let's assume that on December 15, 2010, Washington Post received a $1 per share cash dividend from IFN totaling $1,000,000 ($1 × 1,000,000 shares). The entry to record the receipt is:

| (In millions) | Debit | Credit |
|---|---|---|
| Cash (+A) | 1 | |
| Investment Income (+R, +OE) | | 1 |

| | Assets | = | Liabilities | + | Owners' Equity | |
|---|---|---|---|---|---|---|
| Cash | +1 | | | | Investment Income (+R) | +1 |

This entry is the same for both trading securities and available-for-sale securities.

---

[3] Internet Financial News is a fictitious company.

**Year-End Valuation.** At the end of the accounting period, Washington Post reports passive investments on the balance sheet **at their market value.** Assume that IFN had a $58 per share market value at the end of the year. That is, the investment lost value ($60 − $58 = $2 per share). Because the shares were not sold, however, the loss is a holding loss, not a realized loss.

Reporting securities available for sale at market value requires adjusting the account to market value at the end of each period using the valuation account **Market Value Allowance.** The offset to the Market Value Allowance is the **Unrealized Gain (or Loss) on Investments** account. If the Market Value Allowance account has a **debit balance,** it is **added** to the Securities Available for Sale account. If it has a **credit balance,** it is **subtracted.** The Unrealized Gain (or Loss) on Investments account is then reported in the Stockholders' Equity section of the balance sheet under Accumulated Other Comprehensive Income. Thus, the balance sheet remains in balance.

The following chart shows the computation of any unrealized gain or loss in the securities available for sale portfolio. The amounts are given in millions of dollars:

> **Coach's Tip**
> Because there were no passive investments at the end of the prior year, the beginning balance in the Market Value Allowance account is $0.

| Year: 2010 | In millions | |
|---|---|---|
| Market value | $58 | ($58 per share × 1 million shares) |
| − Cost | − 60 | ($60 per share × 1 million shares) |
| Balance needed in Market Value Allowance | (2) | A credit balance is needed. |
| − Unadjusted balance in Market Value Allowance | − 0 | |
| Amount for adjusting entry | ($ 2) | Credit |

**Market Value Allowance**

| | |
|---|---|
| | 0   12/31/09 |
| | 2    AJE |
| | 2   12/31/10 |

The adjusting entry on December 31, 2010, would be recorded as follows:

| (In millions) | Debit | Credit |
|---|---|---|
| Unrealized Gain (Loss) on Investments (−OE) | 2 | |
| Market Value Allowance (−A) | | 2 |

| Assets | = | Liabilities | + | Owners' Equity |
|---|---|---|---|---|
| Market Value Allowance  −2 | | | | Unrealized Gain (Loss) on Investments  −2 |

On the 2010 balance sheet under Investments in Marketable Securities, Washington Post reports securities available for sale of $58,000,000 ($60,000,000 cost − the $2,000,000 credit balance in the valuation allowance). The company also reports, under Accumulated Other Comprehensive Income (Stockholders' Equity), Unrealized Loss on Investments of $2,000,000 for securities available for sale. Because these investments are expected to be held into the future, the company does not report the unrealized holding loss as part of net income. (Recall that only when a security is sold are any realized gains or losses included in net income.) The only item that would be reported on the income statement for 2010 is investment income of $1,000,000 (from dividends earned), classified under Other Items.

**On the Balance Sheet:** *(in millions)*

*Assets*
| | |
|---|---|
| Investments in Marketable Securities | $ 60 |
| Market Value Allowance | (2) |
| Net investment | $ 58 |

*Stockholders' Equity*
Other Comprehensive Income:
| | |
|---|---|
| Unrealized Loss on Investments | $(2) |

Now let's assume that Washington Post held the IFN securities through the year 2011. At the end of 2011, the stock had a market value of $61 per share. The adjustment for 2011 is computed as follows:

| Year: 2011 | In millions | |
|---|---|---|
| Market value | $ 61 | ($61 per share × 1 million shares) |
| − Cost | − 60 | ($60 per share × 1 million shares) |
| Balance needed in Market Value Allowance | 1 | |
| − Unadjusted balance in Market Value Allowance | − (2) | |
| Amount for adjusting entry | $ 3 | Debit |

**Market Value Allowance**

| | | | |
|---|---|---|---|
| | | 0 | 12/31/09 |
| | | 2 | AJE |
| | | 2 | 12/31/10 |
| AJE | 3 | | |
| 12/31/11 | 1 | | |

The adjusting entry on December 31, 2011, is:

| (in millions) | Debit | Credit |
|---|---|---|
| Market Value Allowance (+A) | 3 | |
| Unrealized Gain (Loss) on Investments (+OE) | | 3 |

| Assets | = | Liabilities | + | Owners' Equity |
|---|---|---|---|---|
| Market Value Allowance   +3 | | | | Unrealized Gain (Loss) on Investments   +3 |

**On the Balance Sheet:**    (*in millions*)

*Assets*

Investments in Marketable Securities    $60

Market Value Allowance    1

Net investment    $61

*Stockholders' Equity*

Other Comprehensive Income:

Unrealized Gain on Investments    $ 1

**Sale of Stock.** Let's assume that on March 17, 2012, Washington Post sold all of its investment in IFN for $64 per share. The company receives $64,000,000 in cash ($64 × 1,000,000 shares) for stock purchased at $60,000,000 in 2010 ($60 × 1,000,000 shares). On that date, accountants record a $4,000,000 **realized gain** on the sale ($64 million − $60 million) and then eliminate the Securities Available for Sale account.

| (in millions) | Debit | Credit |
|---|---|---|
| Cash (+A) | 64 | |
| Securities Available for Sale (−A) | | 60 |
| Gain on Sale of Investments (+R, +OE) | | 4 |

| Assets | = | Liabilities | + | Owners' Equity |
|---|---|---|---|---|
| Cash   +64 | | | | Gain on Sale |
| Securities Available for Sale   −60 | | | | of Investments (+R)   +4 |

You may be wondering what a company does with the Market Value Allowance and the Unrealized Gain (Loss) on Investments accounts when investments are sold. The answer is that they adjust the account balances to $0 at the end of the year, similar to the process in the preceding example. Because Washington Post has no investment in IFN at December 31, 2012, it would eliminate the $1 balance in each account.

| (in millions) | Debit | Credit |
|---|---|---|
| Unrealized Gain (Loss) on Investments  (−OE) | 1 | |
| Market Value Allowance  (−A) | | 1 |

| Assets | = | Liabilities | + | Owners' Equity |
|---|---|---|---|---|
| Market Value Allowance   −1 | | | | Unrealized Gain (Loss) on Investments   −1 |

You now can review the T-accounts for all of the transactions from 2010 to 2012 in Exhibit 15.2.

# Comparison of Available-for-Sale and Trading Securities

The impact of unrealized holding gains or losses on the financial statements depends on whether an investment is a trading security or a security available for sale.

## Available-for-Sale Securities

As you learned in the last section, the balance in the Unrealized Gain (Loss) on Investments account is reported as a separate component of stockholders' equity under **Accumulated Other**

## Exhibit 15.2   T-Accounts for the Illustrated Transactions

**Balance Sheet Accounts** (in millions)

| Securities Available for Sale (at cost) (A) | | Market Value Allowance (A) | | Unrealized Gain (Loss) on Investments (OE) | |
|---|---|---|---|---|---|
| 12/31/09           0 | | | 0            12/31/09 | 12/31/09           0 | |
| 1/2/10 Purchase  60 | | | 2   AJE 12/31/10 | 12/31/10 AJE      2 | |
| 12/31/10          60 | | | 2            12/31/10 | 12/31/10          2 | |
| | | 12/31/11 AJE   3 | | | 3   AJE 12/31/11 |
| 12/31/11          60 | | 12/31/11          1 | | | 1            12/31/11 |
| | 60   Sale 3/17/12 | | 1   AJE 12/31/12 | 12/31/12 AJE      1 | |
| 12/31/12           0 | | | 0            12/31/12 | 12/31/12          0 | |

**Income Statement Accounts** (in millions)

| Investment Income (R) | | Gain on Sale of Investments (R) | |
|---|---|---|---|
| | 1   Earned 12/15/10 | | 4   Sale 3/17/12 |
| | 1            12/31/10 | | 4            12/31/12 |

**Comprehensive Income.** It is not reported on the income statement because it does not affect net income.

However, at the time of sale, the difference between the proceeds from the sale and the original cost of the investment is recorded as a gain or loss on the sale of investments. It is reported on the income statement because the gain has been realized. At the end of the year, the Unrealized Gain (Loss) on Investments account and the Market Value Allowance account are adjusted.

## Trading Securities

For trading securities, the amount of the adjustment to record a holding gain or loss is included **in each period's income statement** (that is, it is treated as realized). Holding gains increase net income, and holding losses decrease net income. The amount that is recorded as Unrealized Gain (Loss) on Trading Securities is also closed to Retained Earnings at the end of the period as are other temporary accounts on the income statement. When a trading security is sold, the affected accounts are Cash, Trading Securities, and Market Value Allowance plus any additional Gain (Loss) on Sale of Investments.

See Exhibit 15.3 for a comparison of the treatment of trading securities and securities available for sale using Washington Post's transactions from 2010 to 2012. **Note that the total investment income reported for the three years is the same for both trading securities and securities available for sale ($5 million). Only the allocation across periods differs.**

| | EFFECT ON INCOME STATEMENT (in millions) | |
|---|---|---|
| | Trading Securities | Securities Available for Sale |
| 2010  Investment income | $1 | $1 |
| 2010  Unrealized loss | (2) | — |
| 2011  Unrealized gain | 3 | — |
| 2012  Gain on sale | 3 | 4 |
| Total income | $5 | $5 |

**Exhibit 15.3** Comparison of Accounting for Trading and Available-for-Sale Securities

| Part A: Journal Entries | Trading Securities (in millions) | | Securities Available for Sale (in millions) | |
|---|---|---|---|---|
| **2010** | | | | |
| • Purchase (for $60 million cash) | Trading Securities (+A) | 60 | Securities Available for Sale (+A) | 60 |
| | Cash (−A) | 60 | Cash (−A) | 60 |
| • Receipt of dividends ($1 million cash) | Cash (+A) | 1 | Cash (+A) | 1 |
| | Investment Income (+R, +OE) | 1 | Investment Income (+R, +OE) | 1 |
| • Year-end adjustment to market (market = $58 million) | Unrealized Loss on Trading Securities (+E, −OE) | 2 | Unrealized Gain (Loss) on Investments (−OE) | 2 |
| | Market Value Allowance (−A) | 2 | Market Value Allowance (−A) | 2 |
| **2011** | | | | |
| • Year-end adjustment to market (market = $61 million) | Market Value Allowance (+A) | 3 | Market Value Allowance (+A) | 3 |
| | Unrealized Gain on Trading Securities (+R, + OE) | 3 | Unrealized Gain (Loss) on Investments (+OE) | 3 |
| **2012** | | | | |
| • Sale (for $64 million) | Cash (+A) | 64 | Cash (+A) | 64 |
| | Trading Securities (−A) | 60 | Securities Available for Sale (−A) | 60 |
| | Market Value Allowance (−A) | 1 | Gain on Sale of Investments (+R, + OE) | 4 |
| | Gain on Sale of Investments (+R, +OE) | 3 | | |
| • Year-end adjustment to market (market = $0 because investments have been sold) | None | | Unrealized Gain (Loss) on Investments (−OE) | 1 |
| | | | Market Value Allowance (−A) | 1 |

| Part B: Financial Statements | Trading Securities | | | Securities Available for Sale | | | |
|---|---|---|---|---|---|---|---|
| **Balance Sheet** | *Assets* | 2012 | 2011 | 2010 | *Assets* | 2012 | 2011 | 2010 |

| | | 2012 | 2011 | 2010 | | 2012 | 2011 | 2010 |
|---|---|---|---|---|---|---|---|---|
| *Assets* | | | | | *Assets* | | | |
| Investment in marketable securities | | — | $60 | $60 | Investment in marketable securities | — | $60 | $60 |
| Market value allowance | | = | 1 | (2) | Market value allowance | — | 1 | (2) |
| Net investment in trading securities | | = | $61 | $58 | Net investments available for sale | = | $61 | $58 |
| | | | | | *Stockholders' Equity* | | | |
| | | | | | Unrealized gain (loss) on investments | — | $1 | $(2) |
| **Income Statement** | | 2012 | 2011 | 2010 | | 2012 | 2011 | 2010 |
| Investment income | | — | — | $1 | Investment income | — | — | $1 |
| Unrealized gain (loss) on trading securities. | | — | $3 | $(2) | Gain on sale of investments | $4 | — | — |
| Gain on sale of investments | | $3 | — | — | | | | |

Let's reconstruct the investment activities Washington Post undertook in a recent year, with a few transactions assumed. Use the following T-accounts to infer the amounts. Then prepare journal entries and answer questions. The dollars are stated in millions.

**Balance Sheet Accounts**

(In Accumulated Other Comprehensive Income)

| Securities Available for Sale | | | | Market Value Allowance | | | Unrealized Gain (Loss) on Investments | |
|---|---|---|---|---|---|---|---|---|
| 1/1 | 361 | | | 1/1 | 58 | | 58 | 1/1 |
| Purchase | 43 | ? | Sale | AJE | ? | | ? | AJE |
| 12/31 | 355 | | | 12/31 | 85 | | 85 | 12/31 |

**Income Statement Accounts**

| Investment Income | | | Gain on Sale of Investments | | |
|---|---|---|---|---|---|
| | ? | Earned | | 34 | Sale |
| | 73 | 12/31 | | 34 | 12/31 |

1. Purchased securities available for sale for cash as a noncurrent asset. Prepare the journal entry.
2. Received cash dividends on the investments. Prepare the journal entry.
3. Sold securities available for sale at a gain. Prepare the journal entry.
4. At year-end, the securities available for sale portfolio had a market value of $440. Prepare the adjusting entry.
5. What would be reported for investments on the balance sheet on December 31? On the income statement for the year? Indicate classifications, account titles, and amounts.
6. How would year-end reporting change if the investments were categorized as trading securities instead of securities available for sale? Assume the market value allowance for the trading securities sold was $20.

*After you have finished, check your answers with the solution at the bottom of the page.*

---

Solution to Self-Study Practice

| 1. | Securities Available for Sale (+A) | 43 | |
|---|---|---|---|
| | Cash (−A) | | 43 |
| 2. | Cash (+A) | 73 | |
| | Investment Income (+R, +OE) | | 73 |
| 3. | Cash (+A) | 83 | |
| | Gain on Sale of Investments (+R +OE) | | 34 |
| | Securities Available for Sale (−A) | | 49 |
| | (Beg. bal. $361 + purchase $43 − end. bal. $355 = $49 cost of securities sold) | | |
| 4. | Market Value Allowance (+A) | 27 | |
| | Unrealized Gain (Loss) on Investments (+OE) | | 27 |

| | *In Millions* |
|---|---|
| Market value | $440 |
| − Cost | − 355 |
| Balance needed in Market Value Allowance | 85 |
| − Unadjusted balance in Market Value Allowance | − 58 |
| Amount for adjusting entry | $ 27 |

5.

| Balance Sheet | Income Statement |
|---|---|
| *Assets (noncurrent)* | *Other Items* |
| Investments in Marketable Securities  $440 | Gain on Sale of Investments   $ 34 |
| *Stockholders' Equity* | Investment Income        73 |
| Accumulated Other Comprehensive | |
| Income: | |
| Unrealized Gain (Loss) on | |
| Investments            85 | |

6.

| Balance Sheet | Income Statement |
|---|---|
| *Assets (Current)* | *Other Items* |
| Investments in Marketable Securities  $440 | Gain on Sale of Investments  $ 14 |
| | Investment Income        73 |

When trading securities were sold, the journal entry was:

| Cash (+A) | 83 | |
|---|---|---|
| Investments in Marketable Securities (−A) | | 49 |
| Market Value Allowance (−A) | | 20   Assumed |
| Gain on Sale of Investments (+R, +OE) | | 14 |

## Spotlight On FINANCIAL REPORTING

### Passive Investments and the Fair Value Option

Both U.S. GAAP and international financial reporting standards (IFRS) allow the option to account for bonds held to maturity and securities available for sale at **fair value.** Fair value is the price the seller would receive if the assets were sold. The election is made when each security is purchased. If a company decides to account for a held-to-maturity or available-for-sale security at fair value, it is transferred to the trading securities portfolio and is accounted for in the same manner as other trading securities.

# ACCOUNTING FOR INFLUENTIAL INVESTMENTS

## Investments for Significant Influence: Equity Method

For a variety of reasons, an investor may want to exert significant influence (by owning 20 to 50 percent of a company's outstanding voting stock) without becoming the controlling shareholder (by acquiring over 50 percent of the voting stock). For example:

- A retailer may want to influence a manufacturer to ensure obtaining certain products designed to its specifications.
- A manufacturer may want to influence a computer consulting firm to incorporate the firm's cutting-edge technology in its manufacturing processes.
- A manufacturer may recognize that a parts supplier lacks experienced management and could prosper with additional managerial support.

When an investor can exert **significant influence** over an **investee** (the company it partially owns), accountants must use the **equity method** to value the investment. As you have seen, when Washington Post invests in securities as a passive investor, the company reports those investments on the balance sheet as Investments in Marketable Securities. However, when Washington Post owns 20 to 50 percent of the outstanding voting stock, the company is presumed to be taking a more active role as an investor. On the balance sheet, Washington Post reports these long-term **investments for significant influence** as Investments in Affiliates (see Exhibit 15.1). Washington Post reported one primary investment in an affiliated company in its 2006 annual report. It sold another affiliated company during 2006:

**WASHINGTON POST**
2006 Annual Report

### NOTES TO FINANCIAL STATEMENTS

#### A. SUMMARY OF SIGNIFICANT ACCOUNTING POLICIES

**Investments in Affiliates.** The Company uses the equity method of accounting for its investments in and earnings or losses of associated companies that it does not control, but over which it does exert significant influence. . . .

#### C. INVESTMENTS

. . .

**Investments in Affiliates.** The Company's investments in affiliates at December 31, 2006 and January 1, 2006 include the following (in millions):

|  | 2006 | 2005 |
|---|---|---|
| Bowater Mersey Paper Company | $49 | $55 |
| BrassRing | — | 11 |
| Other | 5 | 1 |
|  | $54 | $67 |

At the end of 2006, the Company's investments in affiliates consisted of a 49% interest in the common stock of Bowater Mersey Paper Company Limited, which owns and operates a newsprint mill in Nova Scotia, and other investments.

. . . On November 13, 2006, the Company sold its 49% interest in BrassRing and recorded a $43.2 million pre-tax gain that is included in "Other income (expense), net" in the Consolidated Statements of Income.

## Recording Investments under the Equity Method

With a passive investment (less than 20 percent stock ownership), an investor usually cannot influence the investee's operating and financing activities—for example, by compelling the investee to pay dividends. So, the investor reports any dividends received from the investee as dividend revenue.

Under the equity method, however, the investor's 20 to 50 percent ownership in a company presumes significant influence over the investee's operating and financing policies. Often the investee's board of directors may include a representative of the investor who influences the investee's board to declare dividends among other decisions. Because of this influence, the investment is accounted for as if the two companies were one. That is, the net income the investee earned increases the investee's net assets (assets − liabilities). Likewise, the investor should report a portion of the investee's net income as its income and an increase in the investment account. Dividends paid by the investee decrease the investee's net assets. Similarly, the receipt of dividends by the investor is treated as a reduction of the investment account, not revenue. A summary follows:

**Net Income of Investee.** If the investee reports positive results from operations for the year, the investor records investment income equal to its **percentage share of the investee's net income** and increases the asset account Investments in Affiliates. If the investee reports a net loss, the investor records the opposite effect.

**Dividends paid by Investee.** If the investee declares and pays dividends to the investor during the year (a financing decision), the investor reduces the investment account and increases cash.

| + | Investments in Affiliates (A) | − |
|---|---|---|
| Beginning balance Purchases of affiliated companies | Sales of affiliated companies | |
| Investor's percentage share of investee's net income (credit Equity in Investee Earnings) | Investor's percentage share of investee's net loss (debit Equity in Investee Losses) | |
| | Company's percentage share of investee's dividends declared for the period (debit Cash) | |
| Ending balance | | |

**Purchase of Stock.** For simplicity, let's assume that at the end of 2009, Washington Post had no long-term investments in companies over which it exerted significant influence. On January 2, 2010, Washington Post purchased 4 million shares of the outstanding voting stock of IFN for $240,000,000 cash. Because IFN had 10 million shares of common stock outstanding, Washington Post acquired a 40 percent interest (4 million ÷ 10 million shares) and was presumed to have significant influence over the investee. Therefore, Washington Post must use the equity method to account for the investment. The purchase of the asset would be recorded on January 2, 2010, at cost in Investments in Affiliates.

| (in millions) | Debit | Credit |
|---|---|---|
| Investments in Affiliates (+A) | 240 | |
| Cash (−A) | | 240 |

| Assets | | = | Liabilities | + | Owners' Equity |
|---|---|---|---|---|---|
| Investments in Affiliates | +240 | | | | |
| Cash | −240 | | | | |

**Investee Earnings.** Because the investor can influence the investee's income-earning process, the investor bases its investment income on the investee's earnings rather than on the dividends paid. In 2010, IFN reported net income of $50,000,000. Washington Post's percentage share of that income, $20,000,000 (40% × $50,000,000), would be recorded on December 31, 2010, as follows:

| (in millions) | Debit | Credit |
|---|---|---|
| Investments in Affiliates (+A) | 20 | |
|     Equity in Investee Earnings (+R, +OE) | | 20 |

| Assets | = | Liabilities | + | Owners' Equity | |
|---|---|---|---|---|---|
| | | | | Equity in Investee | |
| Investments in Affiliates   +20 | | | | Earnings (+R) | +20 |

If reporting a net loss, the investor records its share of the loss by decreasing the investment account and recording the loss under Equity in Investee Losses. Equity in Investee Earnings (or Losses) is reported in the Other Items section of the income statement along with interest revenue, interest expense, and gains and losses on sales of assets.

### Dividends Received.

Because Washington Post can influence the dividend policies of its investees, the company should **not** record any dividends it receives as investment income. Instead, dividends reduce its investment account. On December 1, 2010, IFN declared and paid a cash dividend of $2 per share to stockholders. Washington Post received $8,000,000 in cash ($2 per share × 4,000,000 shares) from IFN, and recorded this on December 1, 2010, as follows:

| (in millions) | Debit | Credit |
|---|---|---|
| Cash (+A) | 8 | |
|     Investments in Affiliates (−A) | | 8 |

| Assets | | = | Liabilities | + | Owners' Equity |
|---|---|---|---|---|---|
| Investments in Affiliates | −8 | | | | |
| Cash | +8 | | | | |

The cumulative effects of the IFN purchase, earnings, and dividends for 2010 are reflected in the following T-accounts (in millions of dollars):

| Investments in Affiliates | | | | Equity in Investee Earnings | | | |
|---|---|---|---|---|---|---|---|
| 1/1/10 | 0 | | | | | 0 | 1/1/10 |
| Purchases | 240 | | | | | | |
| Share of investee | | | Share of | | | | Share of investee |
|   net earnings | 20 | 8 | investee dividends | | | 20 | net earnings |
| 12/31/10 | 252 | | | | | 20 | 12/31/10 |

### Sale of Stock.

Companies record any sale of stock in affiliated companies in the same way as sales of other assets. Investment in Affiliates is reduced by the percentage of stock sold, Cash is debited, and the difference is recorded as either a Gain (or Loss) on Sale of Investments.

Let's assume that on January 2, 2011, Washington Post decided to sell 1,000,000 of the 4,000,000 shares of stock it owned in IFN for $70 million. That represents 25 percent of Washington Post's Investment in Affiliates. One-fourth of the balance in the account is equal to $63 million ($252 million × ¼), so the entry in January 2011 is:

| (in millions) | Debit | Credit |
|---|---|---|
| Cash (+A) | 70 | |
|     Investments in Affiliates (−A) | | 63 |
|     Gain on Sale of Investments (+R, +OE) | | 7 |

| Assets | | = | Liabilities | + | Owners' Equity | |
|---|---|---|---|---|---|---|
| Cash | +70 | | | | Gain on Sale of | |
| Investments in Affiliates | −63 | | | | Investments (+R) | +7 |

**Coach's Tip**

Because Washington Post owned 40 percent of IFN prior to the sale (4 million of the 10 million shares outstanding), it will then own 30 percent (3 million of 10 million shares) after the sale. Thus, **it must still apply the equity method.**

## Reporting Investments under the Equity Method

On the balance sheet, Investments in Affiliates is reported as a long-term asset. However, as the year-end entries show, the investment account does not reflect either cost or market value. Instead, the following occurs:

- The investment account increases with the cost of the purchased shares and the proportional share of the investee's income.
- The investment account decreases with the dividends received from the investee, the proportional share of any investee losses, and any sale of shares in the investee.

At the end of the accounting period, accountants **do not adjust the investment account to reflect changes in the market value** of the securities. When the securities are sold, accountants record the difference between the cash received and the book value of the investment as a Gain (Loss) on Sale of Investments and report the amount on the income statement in the Other Items section.

## Spotlight On **ETHICS**

### Improper Influence

A key assumption in accounting is that all transactions occur at "arm's length." That is, each party to the transaction is acting in his or her own self-interest. But when one company exerts significant influence over another (that is, when it owns 20 to 50 percent of the voting common stock), it is unreasonable to assume that transactions between the two companies are made at arm's length.

Consider what might happen if an investor company could affect the investee's dividend policy. If the investor reported dividends paid by the investee as dividend income, the investor could manipulate its own income by influencing the other company's dividend policy. In a bad year, the investor might request large dividend payments to bolster its income. In a good year, it might try to cut dividend payments to build up the investee's retained earnings, which would support large dividends in the future.

The equity method prevents this type of manipulation. Instead of recognizing dividends as income, this method bases income from the investment on a percentage of the affiliated company's reported net income.

**SELF-STUDY PRACTICE**

Let's reconstruct some actions Washington Post undertook recently regarding its investments in affiliated companies with a few transactions assumed. Prepare the following journal entries and answer the following questions. Use the T-accounts that follow to infer the amounts. The dollars are given in millions.

| Investments in Affiliates | | | | Equity in Investee Earnings | | |
|---|---|---|---|---|---|---|
| 1/1 | 67 | | | | 0 | 1/1 |
| Purchases | 3 | 15 | Sales of investments | | | |
| Share of investee earnings | ? | 2 | Share of investee dividends | | 1 | Share of investee earnings |
| 12/31 | 54 | | | | 1 | 12/31 |

1. Purchased additional investments in affiliated companies for cash. Prepare the journal entry.
2. Sold a portion of investments in affiliated companies for $58 cash. Prepare the journal entry.
3. Received cash dividends on the investments. Prepare the journal entry.
4. At year-end, the affiliated companies reported a total of $5 in net income, and investments in affiliates had a market value of $42. Prepare the adjusting entry. What percentage of the investee's stock is owned by the Washington Post?
5. What would be reported on the year-end balance sheet regarding the investments in affiliates? What would be reported on the income statement for the year?

*After you have finished, check your answers with the solution at the bottom of the next page.*

## Spotlight On FINANCIAL REPORTING

### Selecting Accounting Methods

Managers can choose freely between LIFO and FIFO for measuring inventory or between accelerated depreciation and straight-line depreciation for measuring the use of long-lived assets. In the case of minority investments (50 percent or less), however, they may **not** choose between the market value and equity methods. Investments in less than 20 percent of a company's outstanding stock are usually accounted for using the market value method. Investments of 20 to 50 percent are accounted for using the equity method.

However, managers may be able to structure acquisitions in a way that permits them to use the accounting methods they prefer. For example, a company that wants to use the market value method could purchase only 19.9 percent of the outstanding stock of another company and achieve essentially the same investment goals as it would with a 20 percent investment. Why might managers want to avoid using the equity method? Most managers prefer to minimize variations in reported earnings. If a company were planning to buy stock in a firm that reported large earnings in some years and large losses in others, it might want to use the market value method to avoid reporting its share of the investee's earnings and losses.

In short, analysts who compare companies must understand management's reporting choices and the way in which differences between the market value and equity methods can affect a company's earnings.

## Investments with Controlling Interests: Consolidated Statements

### Why Control Other Companies?

**Learning Objective 6**

Explain the reporting of investments in controlling interests.

Before we discuss financial reporting of investments that involve ownership of more than 50 percent of another company's outstanding voting stock, we should consider the reasons for acquiring this level of ownership. Following are some of these reasons:

1. **Vertical integration.** In this type of acquisition, one company acquires another company that operates on a different level in the distribution channel. For example, Washington Post owns a newsprint company that provides raw materials.

2. **Horizontal growth.** Horizontal acquisitions involve companies that operate on the same level of the distribution channel. For example, Washington Post has expanded internationally by creating or acquiring newspaper companies in major international markets.

**Solution to Self-Study Practice**

| 1. | Investments in Affiliates (+A) | 3 | |
| | Cash (−A) | | 3 |
| 2. | Cash (+A) | 58 | |
| | Investments in Affiliates (−A) | | 15 |
| | Gain on Sale of Investments (+R, +OE) | | 43 |
| 3. | Cash (+A) | 2 | |
| | Investments in Affiliates (−A) | | 2 |
| 4. | Investments in Affiliates (+A) | 1 | |
| | Equity in Investee Earnings (+R, +OE) | | 1 |
| | Washington Post owns 20 percent of affiliates' stock (20% × $5 net income = $1 equity in investee earnings). | | |

Under the equity method, there is no entry at year-end to adjust the Investments in Affiliates account to market value.

5.

| Balance Sheet | | Income Statement | |
|---|---|---|---|
| *Assets* (under noncurrent assets) | | *Other Items* | |
| Investments in Affiliates | $54 | Equity in Investee Earnings | $ 1 |
| | | Gain on Sale of Investments | 43 |

3. **Synergy.** Two companies operating together may be more profitable than two companies operating separately. Washington Post has created or purchased a number of broadcast and Internet services. Merging these companies and sharing news content may create more profits than operating separate entities could.

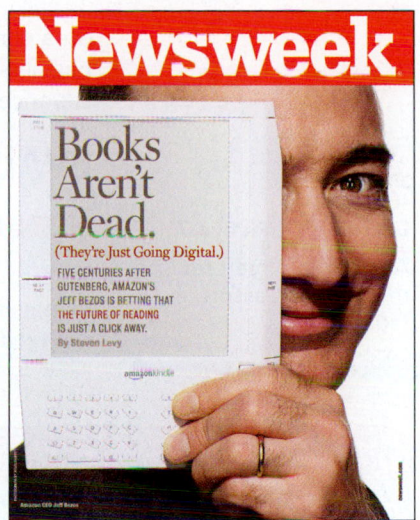

Understanding why one company has acquired control over other companies is a key factor in understanding that company's business strategy.

## What Are Consolidated Statements?

Any corporate acquisition involves two companies. A merger occurs when one company purchases all assets and liabilities of another company and the **acquired company goes out of existence.** When the acquired company remains in business, the company that gains control over it by acquiring all or a majority of the voting stock is the **parent company.** The **subsidiary company** is the company that the parent acquired.[4] Following is a list of three corporations and some of the well-known companies they own:

| The Gap, Inc. | YUM! Brands, Inc. | The Walt Disney Company |
|---|---|---|
| Gap | Pizza Hut | ABC Television Network |
| Old Navy | KFC | ESPN |
| Banana Republic | Taco Bell | Disneyland |
| Forth & Towne | Long John Silver's | Pixar Animation Studios |
| | A&W All-American Restaurants | Touchstone Pictures |

When one company acquires another, the results of their operations must be reported together in consolidated statements. Consolidated financial statements **combine the operations of two or more companies into a single set of statements,** usually identified by the word consolidated in the statement titles. For example, the title of the statement in Exhibit 15.1 is *Consolidated* Balance Sheet. Consolidated statements may be thought of as adding together the financial statements for two or more companies so that they appear to be a single company. Thus, the cash accounts for the companies are summed, along with the inventory accounts, the land accounts, and all other accounts. Combining all financial information into one set of consolidated statements gives users better information on the size and scope of operations in companies controlled by the parent corporation.

The notes to Washington Post's 2006 annual report provide the following information:

### NOTES TO FINANCIAL STATEMENTS

#### A. SUMMARY OF SIGNIFICANT ACCOUNTING POLICIES

**Principles of Consolidation.** The accompanying financial statements include the accounts of the Company and its subsidiaries; significant intercompany transactions have been eliminated.

**WASHINGTON POST**

2006 Annual Report

As the note indicates, when consolidated statements are prepared, intercompany items such as loans from the parent company to the subsidiaries must be eliminated. Remember that consolidated statements imply that a single company exists when in fact there are two or more separate legal entities. Intercompany items do not exist in a single corporation. For example, a debt Washington Post (the parent) owes to its newsprint subsidiary is not reported

---

[4] The discussion assumes acquisition of 100 percent of another company. Any acquisition of 51 to 99 percent of another company creates a minority interest that is discussed in advanced accounting courses.

on a consolidated statement because a company cannot owe money to itself. Accounting for business acquisitions and preparing consolidated financial statements are discussed in detail in advanced accounting courses.

# EVALUATING TOTAL INVESTED CAPITAL

## Return on Assets (ROA)

**Learning Objective 7**
Analyze and interpret the return on assets ratio.

Investments are assets that are used to generate profits for their owners. To assess how well management has used the company's assets to earn income, analysts and managers compute the **return on assets (ROA)** ratio.

| Accounting Decision Tools | | |
|---|---|---|
| **Name of Measure** | **Formula** | **What It Tells You** |
| Return on assets (ROA) | $\dfrac{\text{Net Income*}}{\text{Average Total Assets}^\dagger} \times 100$ | • The percentage of income earned on each dollar invested in assets<br>• The higher the ratio, the more effectively managers are using total assets |

*In more complicated analyses, interest expense (net of tax) and minority interest are added back to net income because the measure assesses return on assets independent of their source.

†Average Total Assets = (Beginning Total Assets + Ending Total Assets) ÷ 2

The ROA ratio measures how much the firm earned for each dollar invested in assets. It is the broadest measure of profitability and managerial effectiveness independent of financial strategy. Using the information from Washington Post's 2006 10-K report (with dollars given in thousands), the company's ROA is computed as follows:

$$\frac{\text{Return on}}{\text{Assets}} = \frac{\text{Net Income}}{\text{Average Total Assets}} \times 100 = \frac{\$324,469}{(\$5,381,372 + \$4,584,773) \div 2} \times 100 = 6.5\%$$

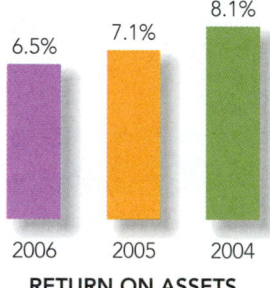

**RETURN ON ASSETS**

The Washington Post

The return on assets ratio is helpful both in analyzing management's effectiveness in using assets to generate profits and in comparing one company or division to another. Companies often compute this measure on a division-by-division basis and then use it to evaluate divisional managers' performance. A higher ROA means that the managers are doing a better job at selecting new investments in assets, all other things held equal.

As you can see from the graph in the margin, Washington Post's ROA for 2006 was below its ROA for the preceding two years. In 2006, Washington Post generated 6.5 cents of income for every dollar of assets; in 2005 and 2004, the company generated 7.1 cents and 8.1 cents of income, respectively, for every dollar of assets. ROA allows investors to compare management's investment performance against alternative investment options. Firms with higher ROAs are doing a better job of selecting new investments, all other things equal.

## Comparison to Benchmarks

Comparing a company's ROA ratio to those of competing companies provides additional information on management's effectiveness. As noted in Exhibit 15.4, in 2006, the Gannett Co., Inc., and the Tribune Company reported ROAs of 7.3 percent and 4.7 percent, respectively. By comparison, Washington Post's 2006 ROA of 6.5 percent was in the middle.

Be aware that ROAs can vary greatly from one industry to the next. As noted in Exhibit 15.4, footwear companies recently reported an average return on assets ratio of 16.4 percent compared to 1.0 percent for banks and 13.6 percent for nonalcoholic beverage companies.

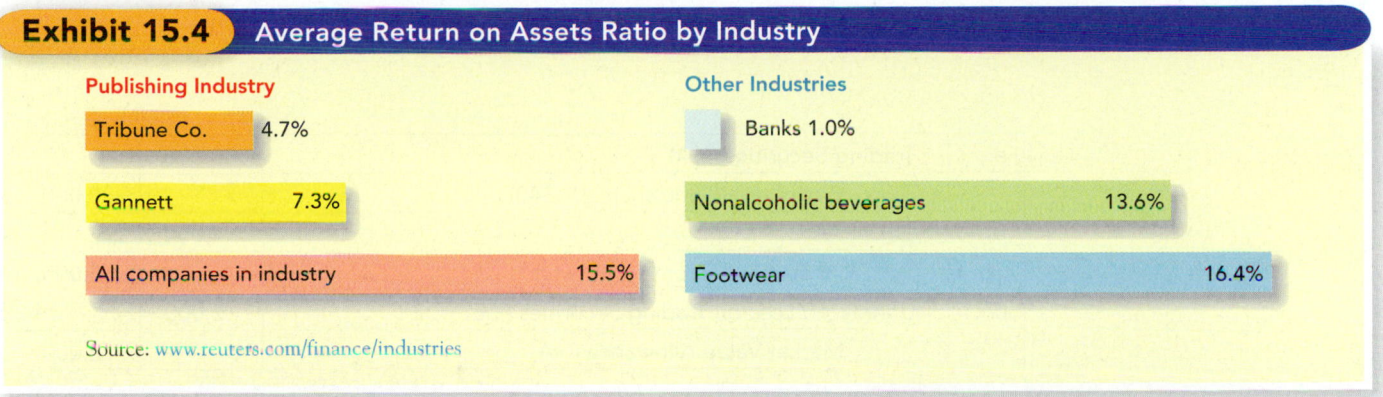

**Exhibit 15.4**   Average Return on Assets Ratio by Industry

| Publishing Industry | | Other Industries | |
|---|---|---|---|
| Tribune Co. | 4.7% | Banks | 1.0% |
| Gannett | 7.3% | Nonalcoholic beverages | 13.6% |
| All companies in industry | 15.5% | Footwear | 16.4% |

Source: www.reuters.com/finance/industries

## Spotlight On BUSINESS DECISIONS

### The Big Get Bigger

We began this chapter by asking how big companies become big and suggesting that acquisitions of stock in other companies is a common strategy. As this chapter was being written, Dow Jones, another major player in the publishing industry, was acquired by News Corporation, a diversified entertainment company headquartered in Australia with worldwide operations in film (e.g., 20th Century Fox), television and cable network programming (e.g., Fox network), magazines (e.g., TV Guide), newspapers (e.g., New York Post), and other segments. News Corporation has more than $62 billion in total assets, and its annual revenues exceed $28 billion. With the $5 billion Dow Jones acquisition, News Corporation will grow by 8 percent. On December 13, 2007, Dow Jones issued the following press release:

> **NEW YORK** — Dow Jones & Company, Inc. (NYSE: DJ) announced today that its stockholders voted at a special meeting to approve the previously announced merger agreement with News Corporation. The stockholder vote satisfies the final condition for the completion of the transaction. The merger is expected to close and become effective at approximately the close of business on Dec. 13, 2007.

**DOWJONES**

2007 Press Release

## Demonstration Case A

(Try to resolve the following requirements before proceeding to the suggested solution that follows.) Howell Equipment Corporation sells and services a major line of farm equipment. Both sales and service operations have been profitable. The following transactions affected the company during 2009:

*a.* Jan.  1  Purchased 2,000 shares of common stock in Dear Company at $40 per share. Purchase represented 1 percent of the shares outstanding. Management intends to trade these shares actively.

*b.* Dec. 28  Received $4,000 cash dividend on Dear Company stock.

*c.* Dec. 31  Determined that the current market price of Dear stock was $39.

*Required:*

1. Prepare the journal entry for each of these transactions.
2. What accounts and amounts will be reported on the balance sheet at the end of 2009 and on the income statement for 2009?

## Suggested Solution for Case A

1.

| | | | |
|---|---|---|---|
| a. | Trading Securities (+A) | 80,000 | |
| | Cash (−A) (2,000 shares × $40) | | 80,000 |
| b. | Cash (+A) | 4,000 | |
| | Investment Income (+R, +OE) | | 4,000 |
| c. | Unrealized Loss on Trading Securities (+E −OE) | 2,000 | |
| | Market Value Allowance (−A) | | 2,000 |

**Year: 2009**

| | | |
|---|---|---|
| Market value | $78,000 | ($39 per share × 2,000 shares) |
| − Cost | −80,000 | ($40 per share × 2,000 shares) |
| Balance needed in Market Value Allowance | (2,000) | A credit balance |
| − Unadjusted balance in Market Value Allowance | − 0 | |
| Amount for adjusting entry | $ (2,000) | An unrealized loss **to income** |

2.  On the balance sheet                                    On the income statement

| *Current Assets* | | *Other Items* | |
|---|---|---|---|
| Investment in Marketable Securities | $78,000 | Investment Income | $4,000 |
| ($80,000 cost − $2,000 allowance) | | Unrealized Loss on | |
| | | Trading Securities | (2,000) |

# Demonstration Case B

Assume the same facts as in Case A except that the shares were purchased as securities available for sale rather than as trading securities.

**Required:**

1.  Prepare the journal entry for each of these transactions.
2.  What accounts and amounts will be reported on the balance sheet at the end of 2009 and on the income statement for 2009?

## Suggested Solution for Case B

1.

| | | | |
|---|---|---|---|
| a. | Securities Available for Sale (+A) | 80,000 | |
| | Cash (−A) (2,000 shares × $40) | | 80,000 |
| b. | Cash (+A) | 4,000 | |
| | Investment Income (+R, +OE) | | 4,000 |
| c. | Unrealized Gain (Loss) on Investments (−OE) | 2,000 | |
| | Market Value Allowance (−A) | | 2,000 |

**Year: 2009**

| | | |
|---|---|---|
| Market value | $78,000 | ($39 per share × 2,000 shares) |
| − Cost | − 80,000 | ($40 per share × 2,000 shares) |
| Balance needed in Market Value Allowance | (2,000) | A credit balance |
| − Unadjusted balance in Market Value Allowance − | 0 | |
| Amount for adjusting entry | $ (2,000) | An unrealized loss **to owners' equity** |

2.  On the balance sheet                                              On the income statement

| **Current or noncurrent assets** | | **Other items** | |
|---|---|---|---|
| Investments in marketable securities | $78,000 | Investment income | $4,000 |
| ($80,000 cost − $2,000 allowance) | | | |
| **Owners' equity** | | | |
| Accumulated other comprehensive income: | | | |
| Unrealized loss on investments | (2,000) | | |

# Demonstration Case C

On January 1, 2010, Connaught Company purchased 40 percent of the outstanding voting shares of London Company on the open market for $85,000 cash. London declared $10,000 in cash dividends on December 1, 2010, and reported net income of $60,000 for the year on December 31, 2010.

**Required:**

1.  Prepare the journal entries for 2010.
2.  What accounts and amounts were reported on Connaught's balance sheet at the end of 2010 and on Connaught's income statement for 2010?

## Suggested Solution for Case C

1.

| Jan.  1 | Investments in Affiliates (+A) | 85,000 | |
|---|---|---|---|
| | Cash (−A) | | 85,000 |
| Dec.  1 | Cash (+A)   (40% × $10,000) | 4,000 | |
| | Investments in Affiliates (−A) | | 4,000 |
| Dec. 31 | Investments in Affiliates (+A)   (40% × $60,000) | 24,000 | |
| | Equity in Investee Earnings (+R, +OE) | | 24,000 |

2.  On the balance sheet                                              On the income statement

| **Noncurrent assets** | | **Other items** | |
|---|---|---|---|
| Investments in affiliates | $105,000 | Equity in investee earnings | $24,000 |
| $ 85,000 cost | | | |
| −    4,000 dividends | | | |
| +  24,000 percentage of investee's net income | | | |
| $105,000 balance in Investments account | | | |

# Chapter Summary

**LO1  Explain why companies invest in debt and stock securities. p. 642**

- Businesses that receive large amounts of cash invest in the debt and stock securities of other companies to generate earnings.
- Companies with seasonal businesses that have extra cash on hand at the end of the busy season may invest in the stocks and bonds of other companies to earn a return on idle funds.
- Companies with a growth strategy may acquire the stock of other companies to significantly influence their financial and operating policies or to actually control their activities

**LO2  Identify investment types and the related accounting methods. p. 643**

- Passive investments in debt and equity securities
  - Debt securities that are accounted for and reported as
    - Held-to-maturity investments, accounted for under the cost method or
    - Investments not intended to be held to maturity, accounted for under the market value method.
  - Equity securities (stock) amounting to less than 20 percent of the outstanding voting stock of another company, accounted for and reported under the market value method.
- Investments in stock for significant influence
  - Investments that amount to 20 to 50 percent of the outstanding voting stock of another company are presumed to result in significant influence over the other company. These investments are accounted for and reported under the equity method.
- Investments in stock for control
  - Investments that amount to more than 50 percent of the outstanding voting stock of another company result in control over that company. These investments are combined with the parent company in consolidated financial statements.

**LO3  Analyze and report bond investments held to maturity. p. 644**

- Debt investments held to maturity: Amortized cost
  - When management intends to hold a bond investment until it matures, the bond is recorded at **cost** when acquired and at amortized cost on the balance sheet. Any interest earned during the period is reported on the income statement.

**LO4  Analyze and report passive investments in securities using the market value method. p. 646**

- Securities available for sale: Market value method
  - Depending on management's intent, passive investments may be classified as either
    - Trading securities (those that are actively traded to maximize their return) or
    - Securities available for sale (those that earn a return but are not as actively traded). Most companies classify investments as available for sale.
  - Debt securities that are not intended to be held to maturity and passive stock investments are recorded at cost and adjusted to market value at year-end. A valuation allowance is increased or decreased to arrive at the market value. The resulting unrealized holding gain or loss is recorded
    - For trading securities, in net income.
    - For securities available for sale, as a component of stockholders' equity in Accumulated Other Comprehensive Income.
  - Any dividends or interest earned are reported in the Other Items section of the income statement along with any gains or losses on sales of passive investments.
- Comparing available-for-sale and trading securities
  - Trading securities are always classified as current assets.
  - Accounting for trading securities is almost identical to accounting for securities available for sale. The primary difference is that any unrealized holding gains or losses are reported directly on the income statement.

**LO5  Analyze and report investments involving significant influence using the equity method. p. 654**

- Investments for significant influence: Equity method
  - Under the equity method, the investor records an investment at cost on the acquisition date. Each period after that, the investment's value is increased (or decreased) by the investor's percentage share of the investee's reported net income (or loss) and decreased by the investor's percentage share of the dividends declared by the investee. Each period, the investor recognizes as revenue its share of the net income (or loss) reported by the investee.
  - Equity in the investee's earnings or losses (that is, the investor's percentage share of the investee's net income or loss for the period) is reported in the Other Items section of the income statement along with any gains or losses on the sale of investments.

## LO6 Explain the reporting of investments in controlling interests. p. 658

- **Investments with controlling interest: Consolidated statements**
  - A company acquires control of another company by purchasing more than 50 percent of the acquired company's outstanding voting shares. Often acquisitions are made to achieve vertical integration (with a different level in the distribution channel), horizontal growth (on the same level of the distribution channel), or synergy (more efficient operations, which increase profitability).
  - Mergers occur when one company purchases all net assets of another and the acquired company ceases to exist as a separate legal entity. When the acquired company remains in business, the purchaser is the parent company and the acquired company is the subsidiary.
  - The concept of consolidation is based on the view that a parent company and its subsidiaries constitute a single economic entity. Therefore, their separate income statements, balance sheets, and statements of cash flows should be combined each period on an item-by-item basis to form a single set of consolidated financial statements.

## LO7 Analyze and interpret the return on assets ratio. p. 660

- **Return on assets (ROA)**
  - The return on assets ratio is computed by dividing net income by average total assets. This ratio measures how much income a company earned with each dollar of assets. It provides information on both a company's profitability and management's effectiveness in using assets. An increasing ratio suggests increased managerial efficiency.

### Accounting Decision Tools

| Name of Measure | Formula | What It Tells You |
|---|---|---|
| Return on assets (ROA) | $\dfrac{\text{Net Income*}}{\text{Average Total Assets}^\dagger} \times 100$ | • The percentage of income earned on each dollar invested in assets<br>• The higher the ratio, the more effectively managers are using total assets |

* In more complicated analyses, interest expense (net of tax) and minority interest are added back to net income because the measure assesses return on assets independent of their source.

† Average Total Assets = (Beginning Total Assets + Ending Total Assets) ÷ 2

## Key Terms

Active Investments (p. 643)
Amortized Cost (p. 644)
Consolidated Financial Statements (p. 659)
Equity Method (p. 654)
Investments Held to Maturity (p. 644)

Investments for Significant Influence (p. 654)
Market Value Method (p. 646)
Merger (p. 659)
Parent Company (p. 659)
Passive Investments (p. 643)

Return on Assets (ROA) (p. 660)
Securities Available for Sale (p. 646)
Subsidiary Company (p. 659)
Trading Securities (p. 646)
Unrealized Holding Gains or Losses (p. 648)

See complete glossary in the back of text.

## Questions

1. Explain the difference between a short-term investment and a long-term investment.
2. Why do companies invest in debt and stock securities?
3. What are
   a. Passive investments?
   b. Investments for significant influence?
   c. Investments for control?
4. What are the accounting methods used for passive investments, investments in which the investor can exert significant influence, and investments in which the investor has control over another entity?
5. Explain how to report bonds held to maturity on the balance sheet.
6. What are trading securities? How are they reported on the balance sheet, and how is income determined and reported on the income statement?
7. What are securities available for sale? How are they reported on the balance sheet, and how is income determined and reported on the income statement?
8. Under the market value method, when and how does the investor company measure investment revenue?

9. Under the equity method, why does the investor company measure revenue on a proportionate basis when the investee company reports income rather than when dividends are declared?

10. Under the equity method, dividends received from the investee company are not recorded as revenue. To record dividends as revenue involves double counting. Explain.

11. What is a parent–subsidiary relationship?

12. Explain the basic concept underlying consolidated statements.

## Multiple Choice

1. Company A owns 40 percent of Company B and exercises significant influence over Company B management. Therefore, Company A uses what method of accounting for and reporting its ownership of stock in Company B?

    Quiz 15-1
    www.mhhe.com/LLPW1e

    a. Amortized cost method.
    b. Market-value method.
    c. Equity method.
    d. Consolidation of the financial statements of companies A and B.

2. Company A purchases 10 percent of Company X and intends to hold the stock for at least five years. At the end of the current year, how would Company A report on its December 31 (year-end) balance sheet its investment in Company X?

    a. At original cost in the Current Assets section.
    b. At the December 31 market value in the Current Assets section.
    c. At original cost in the Long-Term Assets section.
    d. At the December 31 market value in the Long-Term Assets section.

3. Dividends received from a stock that is reported as a security available for sale in the Long-Term Assets section of the balance sheet are reported as which of the following?

    a. Increase to cash and a decrease to the Investment in Marketable Securities account.
    b. Increase to cash and an unrealized gain on the balance sheet.
    c. Increase to cash and an increase to revenue.
    d. Increase to cash and an unrealized gain on the income statement.

4. Realized gains and losses are recorded on the income statement for which of the following transactions in Trading Securities and Securities Available for Sale?

    a. When adjusting a trading security to its market value.
    b. When adjusting a security available for sale to its market value.
    c. Only when recording the sale of a trading security.
    d. When recording the sale of either a trading security or an available-for-sale security.

5. When recording dividends received from a stock investment accounted for using the equity method, which of the following statements is true?

    a. Total assets are increased and net income is increased.
    b. Total assets are increased and total owners' equity is increased.

    c. Total assets are decreased and total owners' equity is decreased.
    d. Total assets and total owners' equity do not change.

6. When using the equity method, when is revenue recorded on the books of the investor company?

    a. When the market value of the investee stock increases.
    b. When a dividend is received from the investee.
    c. When the investee company reports net income.
    d. Both (b) and (c).

7. Kelly Company acquired 500 shares of stock of Drucker Company at $60 per share as a long-term investment. This represents 10 percent of the outstanding voting shares of Drucker. During the year, Drucker paid stockholders $2 per share in dividends. At year-end, Drucker reported net income of $40,000. Drucker's stock price at year-end was $63 per share. The amount of investments reported on the balance sheet at year-end and the amount reported on the income statement for the year would be:

    | | Balance Sheet | Income Statement |
    |---|---|---|
    | a. | $31,500 | $1,000 |
    | b. | $30,000 | $1,000 |
    | c. | $33,000 | $4,000 |
    | d. | $31,500 | $4,000 |

8. Kelly Company acquired 500 shares of stock of Drucker Company at $60 per share as a long-term investment. This represents 40 percent of the outstanding voting shares of Drucker. During the year, Drucker paid stockholders $2 per share in dividends. At year-end, Drucker reported net income of $40,000. Drucker's stock price at year-end was $63 per share. The amount of investments reported on the balance sheet at year-end and the amount reported on the income statement for the year would be:

    | | Balance Sheet | Income Statement |
    |---|---|---|
    | a. | $31,500 | $ 1,000 |
    | b. | $45,000 | $16,000 |
    | c. | $31,000 | $ 0 |
    | d. | $31,500 | $16,000 |

9. Consolidated financial statements are required in which of the following situations?

    a. Only when a company can exert significant influence over another company.
    b. Only when a company acquires another company for more than it is valued.

c. Only when a parent company can exercise control over its subsidiary.

d. Only when a company acquires another company for passive investment.

10. Which of the following is true regarding the use of the return on assets ratio?

a. Evaluates the efficiency of a company given the capital contributed by owners.

b. Evaluates the financing strategy of a company.

c. Evaluates the profit generated for every dollar of sales.

d. Evaluates how efficiently a company uses its total assets to earn income.

---

**Solutions to Multiple-Choice Questions**

1. c    2. d    3. c    4. d    5. d    6. c    7. a    8. b    9. c    10. d

---

# Mini Exercises

**Available with McGraw-Hill's Homework Manager**

## M15-1 Matching Measurement and Reporting Methods                    LO2
Match the following. Answers may be used more than once.

**Measurement Method**

A. Market value method
B. Equity method
C. Consolidation
D. Amortized cost

1. _____ More than 50 percent ownership
2. _____ Bonds held to maturity
3. _____ Less than 20 percent ownership
4. _____ At least 20 but not more than 50 percent ownership
5. _____ Current market value
6. _____ Original cost less any amortization of premium or discount associated with the purchase
7. _____ Original cost plus proportionate part of the income of the investee less proportionate part of the dividends declared by investee

## M15-2 Recording a Bond Investment                                   LO3
Wall Company purchased $1,000,000, 8 percent bonds issued by Janice Company on January 1, 2010. The purchase price of the bonds was $1,070,000. Management plans and has the ability to hold bonds until their maturity date. Interest is payable semiannually each June 30 and December 31. Record the purchase of the bonds on January 1, 2010.

## M15-3 Recording Trading Securities Transactions                     LO4
During 2009, Princeton Company acquired some of the 50,000 outstanding shares of the common stock, par $10, of Cox Corporation as trading securities. The accounting period for both companies ends December 31. Give the journal entries for each of the following transactions that occurred during 2009:

July   2   Purchased 8,000 shares of Cox common stock at $28 per share.
Dec. 15   Recorded receipt of Cox Corporation's cash dividends of $2 per share.
     31   Determined the current market price of Cox stock to be $25 per share.

## M15-4 Recording Available-for-Sale Securities Transactions          LO4
Using the data in M15-3, assume Princeton Company purchased the voting stock of Cox Corporation for the available-for-sale portfolio instead of the trading securities portfolio. Give the journal entries for each of the transactions listed.

## M15-5 Determining Financial Statement Effects of Trading Securities Transactions   LO4
Using the information in M15-3, indicate in the following table the effects and amounts of each transaction listed. Use + for increase, − for decrease, and NE for no effect.

| | BALANCE SHEET | | | INCOME STATEMENT | | |
|---|---|---|---|---|---|---|
| Transaction | Assets | Liabilities | Owners' Equity | Revenues/ Gains | Expenses/ Losses | Net Income |
| July  2 | | | | | | |
| Dec. 15 | | | | | | |
| Dec. 31 | | | | | | |

**LO4**

**M15-6 Determining Financial Statement Effects of Available-for-Sale Securities Transactions**

Using the information in M15-4, indicate in the following table the effects and amounts of each transaction listed. Use + for increase, − for decrease, and NE for no effect.

| | BALANCE SHEET | | | INCOME STATEMENT | | |
|---|---|---|---|---|---|---|
| Transaction | Assets | Liabilities | Owners' Equity | Revenues/ Gains | Expenses/ Losses | Net Income |
| July  2 | | | | | | |
| Dec. 15 | | | | | | |
| Dec. 31 | | | | | | |

**LO5**

**M15-7 Recording Equity Method Securities Transactions**

On January 1, 2011, Ubuy.com acquired 25 percent (10,000 shares) of the common stock of E-Net Corporation. The accounting period for both companies ends December 31. Give the journal entries for each of the following transactions that occurred during 2011:

July   2   E-Net declared and paid a cash dividend of $3 per share.

Dec. 31   E-Net reported net income of $200,000.

**LO5**

**M15-8 Determining Financial Statement Effects of Equity Method Securities**

Using the information in M15-7, indicate in the following table the effects and amounts of each transaction listed. Use + for increase, − for decrease, and NE for no effect.

| | BALANCE SHEET | | | INCOME STATEMENT | | |
|---|---|---|---|---|---|---|
| Transaction | Assets | Liabilities | Owners' Equity | Revenues/ Gains | Expenses/ Losses | Net Income |
| July  2 | | | | | | |
| Dec. 31 | | | | | | |

**LO7**

**M15-9 Computing and Interpreting Return on Assets Ratio**

M.A.D. Company reported the following information at the end of each year:

| Year | Net Income | Total Assets |
|---|---|---|
| 2008 | $152,000 | $ 52,000 |
| 2009 | 195,000 | 68,000 |
| 2010 | 201,000 | 134,000 |
| 2011 | 212,000 | 145,000 |

Compute return on assets for 2009, 2010, and 2011. What do the results suggest about M.A.D. Company?

## Exercises  Available with McGraw-Hill's Homework Manager

**LO3**

Macy's, Inc.

**E15-1 Explaining Investing Decisions and Recording Bonds Held to Maturity**

Macy's, Inc. (formerly Federated Department Stores, Inc.) operates more than 880 department and furniture stores under the names of Macy's and Bloomingdales. The company does more than $20 billion in sales each year.

Assume that as part of its cash management strategy, Macy's purchased $10 million in bonds at par for cash on July 1, 2009. The bonds pay 10 percent annual interest each June 30 and December 31 and mature in 10 years. Macy's plans to hold the bonds until maturity.

*Required:*

1. Record the purchase of the bonds on July 1, 2009.
2. Record the receipt of interest on December 31, 2009.

## E15-2 Comparing Market Value and Equity Methods

LO4, 5

Company A purchased a certain number of Company B's outstanding voting shares at $19 per share as a long-term investment. Company B had outstanding 20,000 shares of $10 par value stock.

*Required:*

Complete the following matrix relating to the measurement and reporting by Company A after the acquisition of the shares of Company B stock.

| | Market Value Method | Equity Method |
|---|---|---|
| 1. What is the applicable level of ownership by Company A of Company B to apply the method? | _____ % | _____ % |
| For 2, 3, 6, 7, and 8, assume the following: | | |
| Number of shares acquired of Company B stock | 1,000 | 5,000 |
| Net income reported by Company B in the first year | $50,000 | $50,000 |
| Dividends declared by Company B in the first year | $10,000 | $10,000 |
| Market price at end of the first year, Company B stock | $ 15 | $ 15 |
| 2. What is the percentage ownership of Company B by Company A? | _____ | _____ |
| 3. At acquisition, the investment account on the books of Company A should be debited at what amount? | _____ | _____ |
| 4. When should Company A recognize revenue earned on the stock of Company B? Explanation required. | _____ | _____ |
| 5. After the acquisition date, how should Company A change the balance of the investment account net of the allowance with respect to the stock owned in Company B (other than for disposal of the investment)? Explanation required. | _____ | _____ |
| 6. What is the net amount of investment reported on the balance sheet of Company A at the end of the first year? | _____ | _____ |
| 7. What amount of revenue from the investment in Company B should Company A report at the end of the first year? | _____ | _____ |
| 8. What amount of unrealized loss should Company A report at the end of the first year? | _____ | _____ |

## E15-3 Recording Transactions in the Trading Securities Portfolio

LO4

On June 30, 2009, MetroMedia, Inc., purchased 10,000 shares of Mitek stock for $20 per share. Management purchased the stock for speculative purposes and recorded the stock in the trading securities portfolio. The following information pertains to the price per share of Mitek stock:

|  | Price |
|---|---|
| 12/31/2009 | $24 |
| 12/31/2010 | 31 |
| 12/31/2011 | 25 |

MetroMedia sold all of the Mitek stock on February 14, 2012, at a price of $22 per share. Prepare any journal entries that are required by the facts presented in this case.

## E15-4 Recording Transactions in the Available-for-Sale Portfolio

LO4

Using the data in E15-3, assume MetroMedia's management purchased the Mitek stock for the available-for-sale portfolio instead of the trading securities portfolio. Prepare any journal entries required by the facts presented in the case.

## E15-5 Recording Transactions in the Trading Securities Portfolio

LO4

On March 10, 2009, General Solutions, Inc., purchased 5,000 shares of MicroTech stock for $50 per share. Management purchased the stock for speculative purposes and recorded it in the trading securities portfolio. The following information pertains to the price per share of MicroTech stock:

| | Price |
|---|---|
| 12/31/2009 | $55 |
| 12/31/2010 | 40 |
| 12/31/2011 | 42 |

General Solutions sold all of the MicroTech stock on September 12, 2012, at a price of $39 per share. Prepare any journal entries required by the facts presented in this case.

**LO4**

**E15-6 Recording Transactions in the Available-for-Sale Portfolio**
Using the data in E15-5, assume General Solutions' management purchased the MicroTech stock for the available-for-sale portfolio instead of the trading securities portfolio. Prepare any journal entries required by the facts presented in the case.

**LO5**

**E15-7 Recording and Reporting an Equity Method Investment**
Felicia Company acquired some of the 60,000 shares of outstanding common stock (no par) of Nueces Corporation during 2010 as a long-term investment. The annual accounting period for both companies ends December 31. The following transactions occurred during 2010:

Jan. 10    Purchased 21,000 shares of Nueces common stock at $12 per share.
Dec. 31    a.    Received the 2010 financial statements of Nueces Corporation that reported net income of $90,000.
            b.    Nueces Corporation declared and paid a cash dividend of $0.60 per share.
            c.    Determined the market price of Nueces stock to be $11 per share.

*Required:*

1.    What accounting method should the company use? Why?
2.    Give the journal entries for each of these transactions. If no entry is required, explain why.
3.    Show how the long-term investment and the related revenue should be reported in the 2010 financial statements of the company.

**LO6**

The Colgate-Palmolive
Company

**E15-8 Determining the Appropriate Accounting Treatment for an Acquisition**
The notes of Colgate-Palmolive's recent financial statements contained the following information:

**Note 3**

*Acquisitions*
On May 1, 2006, the Company completed the purchase of 84% of the outstanding shares of Tom's of Maine, Inc., for approximately $100 plus transaction costs. Tom's of Maine gives Colgate the opportunity to enter the fast-growing health and specialty trade channel where Tom's of Maine toothpaste and deodorant are market leaders.

How would Colgate-Palmolive report the acquisition? Explain why.

**LO7**

Timberland

**E15-9 Analyzing and Interpreting the Return on Assets Ratio**
The Timberland Company is a leading designer of shoes and clothing. In a recent year, it reported the following (in thousands of dollars):

| | Current Year | Prior Year |
|---|---|---|
| Revenue | $1,567,619 | $1,565,681 |
| Net income | 106,432 | 164,624 |
| Total assets | 843,105 | 788,654 |
| Total stockholders' equity | 560,817 | 528,187 |

*Required:*

1.    Determine the return on assets ratio for the current year.
2.    Explain the meaning of the ratio.
3.    The footwear industry ratio is 16.4 percent. What do your results for Timberland suggest about the company?

# Problems—Set A    Available with McGraw-Hill's Homework Manager

## PA15-1 Determining Financial Statement Effects for Bonds Held to Maturity

Starbucks is a rapidly expanding company that provides high-quality coffee products. Assume as part of its expansion strategy, Starbucks plans to open numerous new stores in Mexico in five years. The company has $5 million to support the expansion and has decided to invest the funds in corporate bonds until the money is needed. Assume Starbucks purchased bonds with $5 million face value at par for cash on July 1, 2010. The bonds pay 8 percent interest each June 30 and December 31 and mature in five years. Starbucks plans to hold the bonds until maturity.

**LO3**

**Starbucks Corporation**

### Required:

1. What accounts are affected when the bonds are purchased on July 1, 2010?
2. What accounts are affected when interest is received on December 31, 2010?
3. Should Starbucks prepare a journal entry if the market value of the bonds decreased to $4,000,000 on December 31, 2010? Explain.

## PA15-2 Recording Passive Investments

On March 1, 2009, HiTech Industries purchased 10,000 shares of Integrated Services Company for $20 per share. The following information applies to the stock price of Integrated Services:

**LO4**

| | Price |
|---|---|
| 12/31/2009 | $17 |
| 12/31/2010 | 24 |
| 12/31/2011 | 31 |

www.mhhe.com/LLPW1e

### Required:

1. Prepare journal entries to record the facts in the case assuming HiTech purchased the shares for the trading portfolio.
2. Prepare journal entries to record the facts in the case assuming HiTech purchased the shares for the available-for-sale portfolio.

## PA15-3 Reporting Passive Investments

During January 2010, Nash Glass Company purchased the following shares as a long-term investment:

**LO4**

| Stock | Number of Shares Outstanding | Purchase | Cost per Share |
|---|---|---|---|
| Q Corporation Common (no par) | 90,000 | 12,600 | $ 5 |
| R Corporation Preferred, nonvoting (par $10) | 20,000 | 12,000 | 30 |

Subsequent to acquisition, the following data were available:

| | 2010 | 2011 |
|---|---|---|
| Net income reported at December 31 | | |
| Q Corporation | $30,000 | $36,000 |
| R Corporation | 40,000 | 48,000 |
| Dividends declared and paid per share during the year | | |
| Q Corporation common stock | $ 0.85 | $ 0.90 |
| R Corporation preferred stock | 1.00 | 1.10 |
| Market value per share at December 31 | | |
| Q Corporation common stock | $ 4.00 | $ 4.00 |
| R Corporation preferred stock | 29.00 | 31.00 |

### Required:

1. What accounting method should the company use for the investment in Q Corporation common stock? In R Corporation preferred stock? Why?
2. Give the journal entries for the company for each year in parallel columns (if none, explain why) for each of the following:
   a. Purchase of the investments.
   b. Income reported by Q and R corporations.

    *c.*  Dividends received from Q and R corporations.

    *d.*  Market value effects at year-end.

3.  For each year, show how the following items and their balances should be reported on the financial statements:

    *a.*  Long-term investments.

    *b.*  Owners' equity—unrealized gains and losses.

    *c.*  Revenues.

**LO4, 5**

www.mhhe.com/LLPW1e

**PA15-4 Recording Passive Investments and Investments for Significant Influence**

On August 4, 2009, Coffman Corporation purchased 1,000 shares of Dittman Company for $45,000. The following information applies to the stock price of Dittman Company:

|  | Price |
| --- | --- |
| 12/31/2009 | $52 |
| 12/31/2010 | 47 |
| 12/31/2011 | 38 |

Dittman Company declares and pays cash dividends of $2 per share on June 1 of each year.

*Required:*

1.  Prepare journal entries to record the facts in the case assuming Coffman purchased the shares for the trading portfolio.

2.  Prepare journal entries to record the facts in the case assuming Coffman purchased the shares for the available-for-sale portfolio.

3.  Prepare journal entries to record the facts in the case assuming Coffman used the equity method to account for the investment. Coffman owns 30 percent of Dittman and Dittman reported $50,000 in income each year.

**LO4, 5**

**PA15-5 Comparing Methods to Account for Various Levels of Ownership of Voting Stock**

Company Chi had outstanding 30,000 shares of common stock, par value $10 per share. On January 1, 2009, Company Delta purchased some of these shares as a long-term investment at $25 per share. At the end of 2009, Company Chi reported the following: income, $50,000, and cash dividends declared and paid during the year, $25,500. The market value of Company Chi stock at the end of 2009 was $22 per share.

*Required:*

1.  For each of the following cases (in the tabulation), identify the method of accounting that Company Delta should use. Explain why.

2.  Give the journal entries for Company Delta at the dates indicated for each of the two independent cases, assuming that the investments will be held long term. If no entry is required, explain why. Use the following format:

| Tabulation of Items | Case A: 3,600 Shares Purchased | Case B: 10,500 Shares Purchased |
| --- | --- | --- |
| 1. Accounting method? |  |  |
| 2. Journal entries: |  |  |
|    *a.* To record the acquisition at January 1, 2009. |  |  |
|    *b.* To recognize the income reported by Company Chi for 2009. |  |  |
|    *c.* To recognize the dividends declared and paid by Company Chi. |  |  |
|    *d.* To recognize the market value effect at the end of 2009. |  |  |

3.  Complete the following schedule to show the separate amounts that should be reported on the 2009 financial statements of Company Delta:

DOLLAR AMOUNTS

| | Case A | Case B |
|---|---|---|

**Balance sheet**
  Investments
  Owners' equity
**Income statement**
  Investment income
  Equity in investee earnings

4.  Explain why assets, owners' equity, and revenues for the two cases are different.

## PA15-6 Comparing the Market Value and Equity Methods

LO4, 5, 6

www.mhhe.com/LLPW1e

Ship Corporation had outstanding 100,000 shares of no-par common stock. On January 10, 2011, Shore Company purchased a block of these shares in the open market at $20 per share for long-term investment purposes. At the end of 2011, Ship reported net income of $300,000 and cash dividends of $.60 per share. At December 31, 2011, Ship's stock was selling at $18 per share. This problem involves two separate cases:

Case A:  Purchase of 10,000 shares of Ship common stock.
Case B:  Purchase of 40,000 shares of Ship common stock.

*Required:*

1.  For each case, identify the accounting method that Shore Company should use. Explain why.
2.  For each case, in parallel columns, give the journal entries for each of the following (if no entry is required, explain why):
    *a.*  Acquisition.
    *b.*  Revenue recognition.
    *c.*  Dividends received.
    *d.*  Market value effects.
3.  For each case, show how the following should be reported on the 2011 financial statements:
    *a.*  Long-term investments.
    *b.*  Owners' equity.
    *c.*  Revenues.
4.  Explain why the amounts reported for the two cases in requirement 3 differ.
5.  Explain whether either of the two cases requires preparing consolidated financial statements? Why?

## PA15-7 Comparing Methods for Sales of Securities

LO4, 5

Using the data in PA15-6, assume that Shore Company management sold 10,000 shares of its investment in Ship Corporation stock on January 10, 2012, at $19 per share. This problem involves two separate cases.

*Required:*

1.  For each case, what level of ownership did Shore Company have in Ship Corporation after the sale?
2.  For each case, what method should Shore Company use for its investment in Ship Corporation after the sale?
3.  For each case, give the journal entry for the sale of the investment and any entry needed on December 31, 2012.

## PA15-8 Interpreting the Return on Assets Ratio

LO7

The Cheesecake Factory Incorporated operates more than 120 upscale casual dining restaurants. The following information was reported in the company's 10-K annual report dated January 2, 2007:

| (in thousands) | 2006 | 2005 | 2004 | 2003 |
|---|---|---|---|---|
| Net income | $ 81,282 | $ 87,948 | $ 65,366 | $ 55,585 |
| Total assets | 1,039,731 | 926,250 | 758,994 | 610,116 |

*Required:*

1.  Compute the return on assets ratio for 2006, 2005, and 2004.
2.  What do the results in requirement 1 suggest about The Cheesecake Factory?

## Problems—Set B  Available with McGraw-Hill's Homework Manager

**LO3**

Sonic Corporation

### PB15-1 Determining Financial Statement Effects for Bonds Held to Maturity

Sonic Corporation operates and franchises a chain of quick-service drive-in restaurants in most of the United States and in Mexico. Customers drive up to a canopied parking space and order food through an intercom speaker system. A carhop then delivers the food to the customer. Assume Sonic has $10 million in cash to support future expansion and has decided to invest the funds in corporate bonds until the money is needed. Sonic purchases bonds with a face value of $10 million for $10.3 million cash on January 1, 2011. The bonds pay 8 percent interest each June 30 and December 31 and mature in four years. Sonic plans to hold the bonds until maturity.

*Required:*

1. What accounts were affected when the bonds were purchased on January 1, 2011?
2. What accounts were affected when interest was received on June 30, 2011?
3. Should Sonic prepare a journal entry if the market value of the bonds decreased to $9,700,000 on December 31, 2011? Explain.

**LO4**

### PB15-2 Recording Passive Investments

On September 15, 2010, James Media Corporation purchased 5,000 shares of Community Broadcasting Company for $32 per share. The following information applies to the stock price of Community Broadcasting:

|  | Price |
|---|---|
| 12/31/2010 | $34 |
| 12/31/2011 | 25 |
| 12/31/2012 | 21 |

*Required:*

1. Prepare journal entries to record the facts in the case assuming James Media purchased the shares for the trading portfolio.
2. Prepare journal entries to record the facts in the case assuming James Media purchased the shares for the available-for-sale portfolio.

**LO4**

### PB15-3 Reporting Passive Investments

During January 2009, Stevie's Bike Shop purchased the following shares as a long-term investment:

| Stock | Number of Shares Outstanding | Purchase | Cost per Share |
|---|---|---|---|
| Chrome Corporation Common (no par) | 100,000 | 15,000 | $ 25 |
| Leather Company Preferred, nonvoting (par $10) | 30,000 | 20,000 | 10 |

Subsequent to acquisition, the following data were available:

|  | 2009 | 2010 |
|---|---|---|
| Net income reported at December 31 |  |  |
| Chrome Corporation | $60,000 | $72,000 |
| Leather Company | 80,000 | 96,000 |
| Dividends declared and paid per share during the year |  |  |
| Chrome Corporation common stock | $ 1.20 | $ 1.00 |
| Leather Company preferred stock | 2.00 | 1.20 |
| Market value per share at December 31 |  |  |
| Chrome Corporation common stock | $ 24.00 | $ 24.00 |
| Leather Company preferred stock | 9.00 | 11.00 |

*Required:*

1. What accounting method should Stevie's Bike Shop use for the investment in Chrome Corporation common stock? In Leather Company preferred stock? Why?

2. Give the journal entries for Stevie's Bike Shop for each year in parallel columns (if none, explain why) for each of the following:
   a. Purchase of the investments.
   b. Income reported by Chrome Corporation and Leather Company.
   c. Dividends received from Chrome Corporation and Leather Company.
   d. Market value effects at year-end.

3. For each year, show how the following amounts should be reported on the financial statements:
   a. Long-term investments.
   b. Owners' equity—unrealized gain/loss.
   c. Revenues.

**PB15-4 Recording Passive Investments and Investments for Significant Influence**    LO4, 5
On March 1, 2010, St. Denis Corporation purchased 10,000 shares of Carey Company for $520,000. The following information applies to the stock price of Carey Company:

| | Price |
|---|---|
| 12/31/2010 | $54 |
| 12/31/2011 | 49 |
| 12/31/2012 | 40 |

Carey Company declares and pays cash dividends of $1.50 per share on June 1 of each year.

*Required:*

1. Prepare journal entries to record the facts in the case assuming St. Denis purchased the shares for the trading portfolio.

2. Prepare journal entries to record the facts in the case assuming St. Denis purchased the shares for the available-for-sale portfolio.

3. Prepare journal entries to record the facts in the case assuming St. Denis used the equity method to account for the investment. St. Denis owns 30 percent of Carey and Carey reported $150,000 in income each year.

**PB15-5 Comparing Methods to Account for Various Levels of Ownership of Voting Stock**    LO4, 5
Zeta Company had outstanding 100,000 shares of common stock, par-value $5 per share. On January 1, 2010, Beta Company purchased some of these shares as a long-term investment at $15 per share. At the end of 2010, Zeta Company reported the following: income, $100,000, and cash dividends declared and paid during the year, $2,500. The market value of Zeta Company stock at the end of 2010 was $12 per share.

*Required:*

1. For each of the following cases (in the tabulation), identify the method of accounting that Beta Company should use. Explain why.

2. Give the journal entries for Beta Company at the dates indicated for each of the two independent cases assuming the investments will be held long term. If no entry is required, explain why. Use the following format:

| Tabulation of Items | Case A: 4,000 Shares Purchased | Case B: 40,000 Shares Purchased |
|---|---|---|

1. Accounting method?
2. Journal entries:
   a. To record the acquisition at January 1, 2010.
   b. To recognize the income reported by Zeta Company for 2010.
   c. To recognize the dividends declared and paid by Zeta Company.
   d. To recognize the market value effect at the end of 2010.

3. Complete the following schedule to show the separate amounts that should be reported on the 2010 financial statements of Beta Company:

DOLLAR AMOUNTS

|  | Case A | Case B |
|---|---|---|
| **Balance sheet** | | |
| Investments | | |
| Owners' equity | | |
| **Income statement** | | |
| Investment income | | |
| Equity in investee earnings | | |

4. Explain why assets, owners' equity, and revenues for the two cases are different.

**LO4, 5, 6**

### PB15-6 Comparing the Market Value and Equity Methods

Boston Corporation had outstanding 200,000 shares of common stock. On October 1, 2009, Packer Company purchased a block of these shares in the open market at $15 per share for long-term investment purposes. At the end of 2009, Boston reported net income of $560,000 and cash dividends of $1.20 per share. At December 31, 2009, Boston's stock was selling at $17 per share. This problem involves two separate cases:

**Case A:** Purchase of 30,000 shares of Boston common stock.
**Case B:** Purchase of 80,000 shares of Boston common stock.

*Required:*

1. For each case, identify the accounting method that Packer Company should use. Explain why.
2. For each case, in parallel columns, give the journal entries for each of the following (if no entry is required, explain why).
   a. Acquisition.
   b. Revenue recognition.
   c. Dividends received.
   d. Market value effects.
3. For each case, show how the following should be reported on the 2009 financial statements:
   a. Long-term investments.
   b. Owners' equity.
   c. Revenues.
4. Explain why the amounts reported for the two cases in requirement 3 are different.
5. Explain whether either of the two cases requires preparing consolidated financial statements? Why?

**LO4, 5**

### PB15-7 Comparing Methods for Sales of Securities

Using the data in PB15–6, assume that Packer Company's management sold 20,000 shares of its investment in Boston Corporation stock on January 10, 2010, at $16 per share. This problem involves two separate cases.

*Required:*

1. For each case, what level of ownership did Packer Company have in Boston Corporation after the sale?
2. For each case, what method should Packer Company use for its investment in Boston Corporation after the sale?
3. For each case, give the journal entry for the sale of the investment and any entry needed on December 31, 2010.

**LO7**

**Marriott
International, Inc.**

### PB15-8 Interpreting the Return on Assets Ratio

Marriott International, Inc., is a global leader in the hospitality industry operating or franchising more than 2,800 lodging units and 2,000 furnished corporate housing units around the world. The following information was reported in the company's 2006 annual report (in millions of dollars):

| (in millions) | 2006 | 2005 | 2004 | 2003 |
|---|---|---|---|---|
| Net income | $ 608 | $ 669 | $ 596 | $ 502 |
| Total assets | 8,588 | 8,530 | 8,668 | 8,117 |

**Required:**

1. Compute the return on assets ratio for 2006, 2005, and 2004.
2. What do the results in requirement 1 suggest about Marriott?

# Cases and Projects

### CP15-1 Finding Financial Information

LO4, 5, 6

Refer to the financial statements of The Home Depot in Appendix A at the end of this book, or download the annual report from the *Cases* section of the text's Web site at www.mhhe.com/LLPW1e.

**Required:**

1. What was the balance in short-term investments reported by the company on February 3, 2008?
2. How much cash did the company realize from investments that matured or were sold during the year ended February 3, 2008?
3. What companies did The Home Depot acquire in 2007? What was the total purchase price of these acquisitions for the year?

### CP15-2 Comparing Financial Information

LO4, 5, 6, 7

Refer to the financial statements of The Home Depot in Appendix A and Lowe's in Appendix B at the end of this book, or download the annual reports from the *Cases* section of the text's Web site at www.mhhe.com/LLPW1e.

Lowe's

**Required:**

1. What was the balance in short-term investments reported by Lowe's on February 1, 2008? By The Home Depot on February 3, 2008? What types of securities were included in short-term investments for each company?
2. Compute the net profit margin, total asset turnover, and return on assets ratios for both The Home Depot and Lowe's for the current year. Which company provided the higher return on its total investments during the current year?
3. Was the difference in ROA due primarily to profitability or efficiency differences? How did you know?

### CP15-3 Examining an Annual Report: Internet-Based Team Research Project

LO2, 3, 4, 5, 6, 7

As a team, select an industry to analyze. Using your Web browser, each team member should acquire the annual report or 10-K for one publicly traded company in the industry with each member selecting a different company.

**Required:**

1. On an individual basis, each team member should write a short report that answers the following questions:
   a. Determine whether the company prepared consolidated financial statements. How do you know?
   b. Does the company use the equity method for any of its investments?
   c. Does the company hold any investments in securities? If so, what is their market value? Does the company have any unrealized gains or losses?
   d. Identify the company's lines of business. Why does management want to engage in these business activities?
   e. Compute the return on assets ratio for the two most recent years reported. What do the results suggest about your company?
2. Discuss any patterns that you as a team observe. Then, as a team, write a short report comparing and contrasting your companies according to the preceding attributes. Provide potential explanations for any differences discovered.

**LO1**

**CP15-4 Evaluating an Ethical Dilemma: Using Inside Information**

Assume you are on the board of directors of a company that has decided to buy 80 percent of the outstanding stock of another company within the next three or four months. The discussions have convinced you that this company is an excellent investment opportunity, so you decide to buy $10,000 worth of the company's stock.

*Required:*

1. Is there an ethical problem with your decision?
2. Would your answer be different if you planned to invest $500,000?
3. Are there different ethical considerations if you do not buy the stock but recommend that your brother do so?

**LO6**

**CP15-5 Evaluating an Acquisition from the Standpoint of a Financial Analyst**

Assume you are a financial analyst for a large investment banking firm. You are responsible for analyzing companies in the retail sales industry. You have just learned that a large West Coast retailer has acquired a large East Coast retail chain for a price more than the net book value of the acquired company. You have reviewed the separate financial statements for the two companies before the announcement of the acquisition.

*Required:*

Write a brief report explaining what will happen when the financial results of the companies are consolidated as well as the impact on the return on assets ratio.

# 16 Reporting and Interpreting the Statement of Cash Flows

## LEARNING OBJECTIVES

**After completing this chapter, you should be able to:**

**LO1** Identify cash flows from operating, investing, and financing activities.

Lectured presentation–16-1
www.mhhe.com/LLPW1e

**LO2** Report cash flows from operating activities using the indirect method.

**LO3** Report cash flows from investing activities.

**LO4** Report cash flows from financing activities.

**LO5** Prepare and evaluate the statement of cash flows.

## Focus Company: NAUTILUS INC.

## "Helping People Achieve a Fit and Healthy Lifestyle Through Proper Exercise, Rest and Nutrition."

www.nautilusinc.com

Have you ever studied your bank statements to see how much money you bring in and pay out during a typical month? You do not have to be a financial genius to know that if you are spending more than you earn, your savings will quickly disappear, and you will need to get a loan or some other source of financing to see you through.

Most businesses face the same issues you do. In 2005, for example, Nautilus Inc.— maker of Stairmaster and Bowflex fitness equipment—reported a net cash outflow from day-to-day operating activities. To ensure the company's long-term survival, managers had to stay on top of this change in the cash situation. Fortunately, the company had saved a great deal of cash in prior years. Managers were also able to negotiate some new loans to keep the business from running out of cash. By 2006, the company was again experiencing a positive net cash inflow from operating activities.

Investors and creditors also monitor a company's cash inflows and outflows to predict whether they are likely to receive dividends and other amounts they are owed. They can find the information they need to make such predictions reported in the statement of cash flows, which is similar to your bank statement in that it reports changes in the company's cash situation. In this chapter, we will investigate how cash flows from operating, investing, and financing activities are classified and reported on the statement of cash flows. We also examine some of the tools investors and creditors use to evaluate the statement of cash flows.

| CLASSIFICATIONS OF THE STATEMENT OF CASH FLOWS | REPORTING CASH FLOWS FROM OPERATING ACTIVITIES— INDIRECT METHOD | REPORTING CASH FLOWS FROM INVESTING ACTIVITIES | REPORTING CASH FLOWS FROM FINANCING ACTIVITIES | PREPARING AND EVALUATING THE STATEMENT OF CASH FLOWS |
|---|---|---|---|---|
| • The Relationship between Business Activities and Cash Flows<br>• Cash Flows from Operating Activities<br>• Cash Flows from Investing Activities<br>• Cash Flows from Financing Activities<br>• Net Increase (Decrease) in Cash<br>• Relationships to the Balance Sheet and Income Statement | • Depreciation and Gains and Losses on Sale of Long-Term Assets<br>• Changes in Current Assets and Current Liabilities | • Plant and Equipment<br>• Land and Investments | • Long-Term Debt<br>• Contributed Capital<br>• Retained Earnings | • Format for the Statement of Cash Flows<br>• Noncash Investing and Financing Activities<br>• Supplemental Cash Flow Information<br>• Free Cash Flow<br>• Quality of Income Ratio |

# CLASSIFICATIONS OF THE STATEMENT OF CASH FLOWS

**Learning Objective 1**

Identify cash flows from operating, investing, and financing activities.

Video 16-1
www.mhhe.com/LLPW1e

To this point, we have analyzed business activities to identify their financial effects on assets, liabilities, owners' equity, revenues, and expenses. We have emphasized that business activities have financial effects even when they do not involve cash. That is why accrual accounting exists. When accurately reported, accrual-based net income is the best measure of whether a company has been profitable during the period.

Despite the importance of net income as a measure of profit, however, companies cannot use net income to pay wages, dividends, or loans. Because those activities require cash, financial statement users need information about the company's cash situation.

## The Relationship between Business Activities and Cash Flows

Neither the balance sheet nor the income statement provides all of the needed information about the company's cash situation. Although the balance sheet shows a company's cash balance at a point in time, it does not indicate where the cash came from. Cash might have been generated by the company's day-to-day operations, by the sale of the company's buildings, or by the negotiation of new loans. What financial statement users really need is a report that identifies the activities that produced the amount of cash reported on the balance sheet.

Furthermore, the timing of cash receipts and payments may differ from the items shown on the income statement, which reports revenues when they are earned and expenses when they are incurred. Nautilus, for example, reported a hefty amount of net income in each quarter of 2006, yet its cash flows were negative in two of those four quarters. Such differences between net income and cash flows are the reason that GAAP requires every company to report a statement of cash flows. **The statement of cash flows shows each major type of business activity that caused a company's cash to increase or decrease during the accounting period.** For the purposes of this statement, cash is defined to include cash and cash equivalents. As you have seen before, cash equivalents are short-term, highly liquid investments that are both (1) readily convertible to known amounts of cash and (2) so near to maturity that there is little risk their value will change. All of a company's cash inflows and outflows must be classified under operating, investing, or financing activities. Exhibit 16.1 shows the general form of the statement. Note that each category of activities can result in net cash inflows (represented by a positive number)

| Exhibit 16.1 | Categories in the Statement of Cash Flows |
|---|---|

Net cash provided by (used for) operating activities
± Net cash provided by (used for) investing activities
± Net cash provided by (used for) financing activities

Net increase (decrease) in cash and cash equivalents
+ Cash and cash equivalents at beginning of period
Cash and cash equivalents at end of period

or net cash outflows (represented by a negative number in brackets). The sum of the three categories of cash flows explains the change in cash on the balance sheet for the period.

# Cash Flows from Operating Activities

**Cash flows from operating activities** (or **cash flows from operations**) are the cash inflows and outflows related directly to the revenues and expenses reported on the income statement. Operating activities involve day-to-day business activities with customers, suppliers, employees, landlords, and others. Typical cash flows from operating activities include:

| Inflows | Outflows |
|---|---|
| **Cash provided by** | **Cash used for** |
| Customers | Purchase of goods for resale and services (electricity, etc.) |
| Dividends and interest on investments | Salaries and wages |
| | Income taxes |
| | Interest on liabilities |

The difference between these cash inflows and outflows is reported on the statement of cash flows as a subtotal, Net Cash Provided by (Used for) Operating Activities.

The two different methods for presenting the operating activities in the cash flow statement are:

1. The **direct method** reports the total cash inflow or outflow from each major type of transaction (that is, transactions with customers, suppliers, etc.). The difference between those cash inflows and outflows equals the Net Cash Provided by (Used for) Operating Activities.

2. The **indirect method** starts with net income from the income statement and adjusts it by removing items that do not involve cash and adding items that do involve cash. Adjusting net income for these items yields the amount of Net Cash Provided by (Used for) Operating Activities.

Net income
± Adjustments
Net cash provided by (used for) operating activities

The point to remember about these two methods is that they are simply different ways to arrive at the same number. **Net cash flows provided by (used for) operating activities is the same under both methods.** Also, the choice between the two methods affects only the operating activities section of the statement of cash flows, not the investing and financing sections.

Each company's management is allowed to choose which method to use. Nearly 99 percent of large U.S. companies, including Nautilus, choose the indirect method.[1] For this reason, we

---

[1] American Institute of Certified Public Accountants, *Accounting Trends & Techniques* (New York: AICPA, 2006). Some people have speculated that the indirect method is preferred so overwhelmingly because the FASB requires that companies using the direct method also report a reconciliation of net income to cash flow. That reconciliation is identical to the indirect method.

**Coach's Tip**

Remember that each category of activities can show a positive or negative net cash flow. Use parentheses ($XXX) to denote a negative cash flow.

examine the indirect method in detail within this chapter. We present the less commonly used direct method in Supplement 16A at the end of the chapter.

## Cash Flows from Investing Activities

Cash flows from investing activities are the cash inflows and outflows related to the purchase and disposal of investments and long-lived assets. Typical cash flows from investing activities include:

| Inflows | Outflows |
|---|---|
| *Cash provided by* | *Cash used for* |
| Sale or disposal of property, plant, and equipment | Purchase of property, plant, and equipment |
| Sale or maturity of investments in securities | Purchase of investments in securities |

The difference between these cash inflows and outflows is reported on the statement of cash flows as a subtotal, Net Cash Provided by (Used for) Investing Activities.

## Cash Flows from Financing Activities

Cash flows from financing activities include exchanges of cash with stockholders and cash exchanges with lenders (for principal on loans). Common cash flows from financing activities include:

| Inflows | Outflows |
|---|---|
| *Cash provided by* | *Cash used for* |
| Borrowing from lenders through formal debt contracts | Repaying principal to lenders |
| Issuing stock to owners | Repurchasing stock from owners |
| | Paying dividends to owners |

The difference between these cash inflows and outflows is reported on the statement of cash flows as a subtotal, Net Cash Provided by (Used for) Financing Activities.

## Net Increase (Decrease) in Cash

Together, **the net cash flows from operating activities, investing activities, and financing activities must equal the net increase (decrease) in cash** for the period. For 2006, Nautilus reported a net decrease in cash of $1,000. That explains the change in cash on the company's balance sheet from the beginning balance of $8,000 to the ending balance of $7,000 (all amounts in $thousands):

| | |
|---|---:|
| Net cash provided by operating activities | $29,000 |
| − Net cash used for investing activities | (11,000) |
| − Net cash used for financing activities | (19,000) |
| Net decrease in cash and cash equivalents | (1,000) |
| + Cash and cash equivalents at beginning of period | 8,000 |
| Cash and cash equivalents at end of period | $ 7,000 |

In the next section, we examine Nautilus's statement of cash flows in more detail, including the way in which it relates to the balance sheet and income statement. Then we see how each section of the statement describes a set of important decisions made by Nautilus's management, and how financial analysts use those sections to evaluate the company's performance. But first, to make sure you understand how to classify cash flows, complete the following Self-Study Practice.

**Brunswick Corporation** produces the Life Fitness line of gym equipment, which competes head to head with Nautilus. A list of some of the company's cash flows follows. Indicate whether each item should be disclosed in the operating activities (O), investing activities (I), or financing activities (F) section of the statement of cash flows.

____ 1. Stock issued to owners for cash
____ 2. Collections from customers
____ 3. Interest paid on debt
____ 4. Purchase of equipment
____ 5. Purchase of investment securities
____ 6. Dividends paid to owners

Brunswick Corporation

*After you have finished, check your answers with the solution at the bottom of the page.*

## Spotlight On ETHICS

### Cash Is Not Estimated

Critics of accrual-based net income claim that it can be manipulated because it includes many estimated amounts (for bad debts, the market values of inventory, and assets' useful lives, for example). Because cash flows are not estimated, these critics claim the cash flows are not so easily manipulated. Indeed, a cash balance changes only when cash has been received or paid.

One particularly dramatic illustration of the subjectivity of net income compared to cash is the bankruptcy of a department store chain operated by W. T. Grant Company. Through biased estimates, the company reported net income for nine consecutive years and then shocked everyone by declaring bankruptcy and closing. At the time, GAAP did not require a statement of cash flows. Had this been required, it would have shown that the company's operations led to net cash outflows in 7 of the company's last 10 years.

## Relationships to the Balance Sheet and Income Statement

One way to classify cash flows into operating, investing, and financing categories is to think about the balance sheet accounts to which the cash flows relate. Although exceptions exist, the general rule is that operating cash flows cause changes in current assets and current liabilities; investing cash flows affect long-lived assets; and financing cash flows affect noncurrent liabilities or owners' equity accounts.[2] See Exhibit 16.2 for the way this general rule relates the three sections of the statement of cash flows to the main sections of the classified balance sheet.

The statement of cash flows is intended to provide a cash-based view of a company's business activities during the accounting period. So, a company cannot prepare this statement directly from the ledger accounts because those amounts are based on accrual accounting. Instead, the company must analyze the numbers recorded under the accrual method and convert them to a cash basis. To prepare a statement of cash flows, you need the following:

1. **Comparative balance sheets**, showing beginning and ending balances for use in calculating the cash flows from all activities (operating, investing, and financing).
2. **A complete income statement** for use primarily in calculating cash flows from operating activities.
3. **Additional details** concerning selected accounts that increase and decrease as a result of investing and/or financing activities.

[2] Intermediate accounting discusses exceptions to this general rule in detail. They include investing activities that affect current assets (for example, short-term investments) and financing activities that affect current liabilities (for example, dividends payable and short-term notes payable).

Solution to Self-Study Practice
1. F    4. I
2. O    5. I
3. O    6. F

| Exhibit 16.2 | Relationships between Balance Sheet and Cash Flow Categories |
|---|---|

| Operating Activities Affect | |
|---|---|
| Current assets | Current liabilities |

| Investing Activities Affect | Financing Activities Affect |
|---|---|
| Noncurrent assets | Noncurrent liabilities |
| | Owners' equity |

This approach to preparing the cash flow statement focuses on changes in the balance sheet accounts. It relies on a simple rearrangement of the balance sheet equation:

$$\text{Assets} = \text{Liabilities} + \text{Owners' Equity}$$

First, assets can be separated into cash and all other assets, which we call noncash assets:

$$\text{Cash} + \text{Noncash Assets} = \text{Liabilities} + \text{Owners' Equity}$$

If we move the noncash assets to the right side of the equation, we get

$$\text{Cash} = \text{Liabilities} + \text{Owners' Equity} - \text{Noncash Assets}$$

Given this relationship, the changes ($\Delta$) in cash from the beginning to the end of the period must equal the changes ($\Delta$) in the amounts on the right side of the equation from the beginning to the end of the period:

$$\Delta \text{ Cash} = \Delta \text{ Liabilities} + \Delta \text{ Owners' Equity} - \Delta \text{ Noncash Assets}$$

This equation says that **changes in cash must be accompanied by, and can be explained by, changes in liabilities, owners' equity, and noncash assets.** See Exhibit 16.3 for examples of this basic idea using selected cash transactions.

Before beginning to prepare the statement of cash flows, it is helpful to compute the change in each balance sheet account (that is, the ending balance minus the beginning

| Exhibit 16.3 | Effects of Cash Transactions on Other Balance Sheet Accounts |
|---|---|

| Category | Transaction | Cash Effect | Other Account Affected |
|---|---|---|---|
| Operating | Collect accounts receivable | + Cash | − Accounts Receivable (A) |
| | Pay accounts payable | − Cash | − Accounts Payable (L) |
| | Prepay rent | − Cash | + Prepaid Rent (A) |
| | Pay interest | − Cash | − Retained Earnings (OE) |
| | Sell goods/services for cash | + Cash | + Retained Earnings (OE) |
| Investing | Purchase equipment for cash | − Cash | + Equipment (A) |
| | Sell investment securities for cash | + Cash | − Investments (A) |
| Financing | Pay back debt to bank | − Cash | − Bank Loan Payable (L) |
| | Issue stock for cash | + Cash | + Contributed Capital (OE) |

balance). The next step is to relate each account to operating (O), investing (I), or financing (F) activities by marking it with the appropriate letter. **Operating activities** typically affect the following accounts:

- *Current assets* are used up or converted into cash through the company's regular operating activities. For example, the sale of inventories creates accounts receivable, which are turned into cash when they are collected. When marking an O beside the current assets related to operating activities, you should exclude cash (because the change in cash is what you are trying to explain).
- *Current liabilities* such as accounts payable and accrued liabilities arise from the purchase of goods or services that are used in the company's operations. Mark these items with an O.
- *Accumulated Depreciation* is a contra-asset account that increases each period by the amount of depreciation expense and decreases when the asset is sold. Because depreciation expense affects net income, this account is related to operating activities.
- *Retained Earnings* increases each period by the amount of net income, which is the starting point for the operating activities section. It decreases when dividends are declared and paid (a financing activity). To show that this account relates to both operating and financing activities, mark it with an O and an F.

After classifying all accounts related to operating activities, you should relate other balance sheet accounts to investing (I) or financing (F) activities. **All remaining asset accounts will be related to investing (I) and all remaining liability and owners' equity accounts will be related to financing (F).**

In Exhibit 16.4, the left-hand column shows how to classify the balance sheet accounts for Nautilus. The right-hand column shows the changes in the account balances, which we use in the following sections.

# REPORTING CASH FLOWS FROM OPERATING ACTIVITIES—INDIRECT METHOD

**Learning Objective 2**

Report cash flows from operating activities using the indirect method.

As we defined them earlier, operating cash flows are cash inflows and outflows that are directly related to the revenues and expenses reported on the income statement. These cash flows arise from transactions with customers, suppliers, employees, landlords, and others.

The indirect method begins with the creation of a schedule of operating activities in the following format:

| Operating Activities |
|---|
| Net income |
|     Add/Subtract to convert to cash basis |
| + Depreciation expense |
| − Gain on sale of long-term assets |
| + Loss on sale of long-term assets |
| + Decreases in current assets |
| + Increases in current liabilities |
| − Increases in current assets |
| − Decreases in current liabilities |
| **Net cash flow from operating activities** |

As the format suggests, the conversion process begins with net income, which is taken from the bottom line of the company's income statement. The schedule for Nautilus is in Exhibit 16.5. Notice that the schedule begins with the $31,000 net income reported on the income statement in Exhibit 16.4.

**Exhibit 16.4**     Nautilus, Inc.: Comparative Balance Sheet and Current Income Statement     `Nautilus`

## Nautilus, Inc.
### Balance Sheet*
### (in thousands)

| Related Cash Flow Section | Assets | December 31, 2006 | December 31, 2005 | Change |
|---|---|---|---|---|
| **Change in Cash** | Current assets | | | *Change* |
| | Cash and cash equivalents | $ 7,000 | $ 8,000 | −1,000 |
| O | Accounts receivable | 138,000 | 117,000 | +21,000 |
| O | Inventories | 76,000 | 96,000 | −20,000 |
| O | Prepaid expenses | 33,000 | 24,000 | +9,000 |
| | Total current assets | 254,000 | 245,000 | |
| I | Plant and equipment | 219,000 | 203,000 | +16,000 |
| O | Less: Accumulated depreciation | (54,000) | (47,000) | −7,000 |
| I | Land | 10,000 | 12,000 | −2,000 |
| | Total assets | $429,000 | $413,000 | |
| | | | | |
| | Liabilities and Stockholders' Equity | | | |
| | Current liabilities | | | |
| O | Accounts payable | $ 64,000 | $ 61,000 | +3,000 |
| O | Accrued liabilities | 38,000 | 37,000 | +1,000 |
| | Total current liabilities | 102,000 | 98,000 | |
| F | Long-term debt | 67,000 | 63,000 | +4,000 |
| | Total liabilities | 169,000 | 161,000 | |
| | Stockholders' equity | | | |
| F | Contributed capital | 5,000 | 4,000 | +1,000 |
| O, F | Retained earnings† | 255,000 | 248,000 | +7,000 |
| | Total stockholders' equity | 260,000 | 252,000 | |
| | Total liabilities and stockholders' equity | $429,000 | $413,000 | |

## Nautilus, Inc.
### Income Statement *
### For the Year Ended December 31, 2006
### (in thousands)

| | |
|---|---|
| Net sales | $680,000 |
| Cost of goods sold | 382,000 |
| Gross profit | 298,000 |
| Operating expenses | |
| Selling, general, and administrative expenses | 250,000 |
| Depreciation | 7,000 |
| Total operating expenses | 257,000 |
| Operating income | 41,000 |
| Gain on sale of land | 3,000 |
| Interest revenue (expense) | (1,000) |
| Net income before taxes | 43,000 |
| Income tax expense | 12,000 |
| Net income | $ 31,000 |

\* Certain balances have been adjusted to simplify the presentation.
† This line item includes transactions related to both operating and financing activities.

| **Exhibit 16.5** | **Schedule for Conversion of Net Income to Net Cash Flow from Operating Activities** |

| Items | Amount (in thousands) | Explanation |
|---|---|---|
| Net income | $31,000 | From income statement. |
| Add (subtract) to convert to cash basis | | |
| Depreciation | +7,000 | Add because depreciation expense does not affect cash but was subtracted in computing net income. |
| Gain on sale of land | −3,000 | Subtract because all cash collected from sale of long-lived assets are investing cash flows. |
| Accounts receivable increase | −21,000 | Subtract because cash collected from customers was less than accrual-based revenues. |
| Inventory decrease | +20,000 | Add because purchases were less than cost of goods sold expense. |
| Prepaid expense increase | −9,000 | Subtract because cash prepayments for expenses were more than accrual-based expenses. |
| Accounts payable increase | +3,000 | Add because amounts purchased on account (that is, borrowed from suppliers) were more than cash payments made to suppliers. |
| Accrued liabilities increase | +1,000 | Add because accrual-based expenses were more than cash payments for expenses. |
| Net cash inflow (outflow) | $29,000 | Subtotal for the operating cash flows section. |

By starting with net income, it appears we are assuming all revenues resulted in cash inflows and all expenses resulted in cash outflows. Because we know that is not true, however, we must adjust net income for the effects of the items we marked with an O on the balance sheet (see Exhibit 16.4). Those items reflect differences in the timing of accrual-basis net income and cash flows. The process of adjusting net income has two steps.

# Depreciation and Gains and Losses on Sale of Long-Term Assets

**Step 1  Adjust net income for depreciation expense and gains and losses on sale of long-term assets.** On the income statement, depreciation is subtracted to determine net income. But depreciation does not affect cash, so we must eliminate its effect by adding it back to net income. In the case of Nautilus, we remove its effect by adding back the $7,000 of depreciation expense that had been subtracted to determine net income: See Exhibit 16.5.[3]

If Nautilus sells plant and equipment or land or investments at a gain or loss, the amount of cash received would be classified as an investing cash inflow. Because all of the cash received is an investing cash flow, an adjustment must also be made in the operating activities section to avoid double counting the gain or loss. **Gains on sales of property, plant, and equipment or investments are subtracted, and losses on such sales are added** to convert net income to cash flow from operating activities. Nautilus sold land at a gain of $3,000 ($5,000 cash received less cost of $2,000) that must be subtracted in Exhibit 16.5.

# Changes in Current Assets and Current Liabilities

**Step 2  Adjust net income for changes in current assets and current liabilities.** Each change in current assets (other than cash) and current liabilities causes a difference between

**Coach's Tip**

Adding back depreciation is not intended to suggest that depreciation creates an increase in cash. Rather, it shows that depreciation does not cause a decrease in cash. This is a subtle but very important point.

---

[3] Amortization expense for intangible assets and depletion expense for natural resources (discussed in Chapter 10) is handled in exactly the same way as depreciation expense.

net income and cash flow from operating activities. In converting net income to cash flow from operating activities, apply the following general rules:

- **Add the change when a current asset decreases or a current liability increases.**
- **Subtract the change when a current asset increases or a current liability decreases.**

Understanding what causes current assets and current liabilities to increase and decrease is the key to understanding the logic behind these additions and subtractions. Take your time reading the following explanations and make sure you understand the reasons for the changes.

### Change in Accounts Receivable

The first operating item (O) listed on the Nautilus balance sheet in Exhibit 16.4 is Accounts Receivable. Remember that the income statement reflects sales revenue, but the cash flow statement must reflect cash collections from customers. As the following T-account for accounts receivable shows, when sales revenues are recorded, Accounts Receivable increases; when cash is collected from customers, the amount in the Accounts Receivable account decreases.

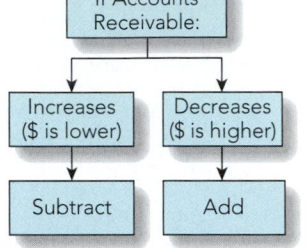

| Accounts Receivable (A) | | |
|---|---|---|
| Beginning balance | 117,000 | |
| Sales revenue (on account) | 680,000 | Cash collected from customers 659,000 |
| Ending balance | 138,000 | |

*Change +$21,000*

In the case of Nautilus, Accounts Receivable increased, which means that sales revenue was greater than cash collected from customers. To convert from the higher sales amount included in net income to the lower amount of cash collected from customers, we must subtract the difference ($680,000 − $659,000 = $21,000), which is the same as the change in Accounts Receivable.

| | |
|---|---|
| Ending balance | $138,000 |
| − Beginning balance | 117,000 |
| Change | $ 21,000 |

This procedure suggests a shortcut for determining adjustments to net income: Simply adjust for the **changes** in the current asset and current liability accounts that are related to operating activities. The sign of the adjustment fits the general rule just given. In the case of Nautilus, the net increase in Accounts Receivable is subtracted from net income. If Accounts Receivable had decreased, the net decrease would be added to net income.

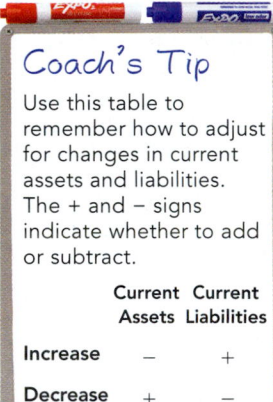

**Coach's Tip**

Use this table to remember how to adjust for changes in current assets and liabilities. The + and − signs indicate whether to add or subtract.

| | Current Assets | Current Liabilities |
|---|---|---|
| **Increase** | − | + |
| **Decrease** | + | − |

| Accounts Receivable (A) | | |
|---|---|---|
| Beg. bal. | 117,000 | |
| Increase | 21,000 | |
| End. bal. | 138,000 | |

| Cash Flows from Operating Activities | |
|---|---|
| Net income | 31,000 |
| Accts rec. increase | (21,000) |
| . . . | . . . |
| Net cash inflow | |

### Change in Inventory

The income statement reports the cost of merchandise sold during the period, but cash flow from operating activities must report cash purchases of inventory. As the following T-accounts show, recording purchases of goods (left) increases the balance in the Inventories account; recording cost of goods sold (right) decreases the balance in the Inventories account:

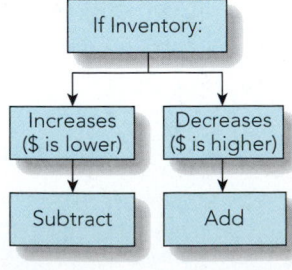

| Inventories (A) | | |
|---|---|---|
| Beg. bal. | | |
| Purchases | | Cost of goods sold |
| End. bal. | | |

| Inventories (A) | | |
|---|---|---|
| Beg. bal. | 96,000 | |
| | | Decrease   20,000 |
| End. bal. | 76,000 | |

The balance sheet in Exhibit 16.4 indicates that Nautilus's inventory decreased by $20,000, which means that purchases were less than the amount of merchandise sold. This decrease (that is, the use of existing inventories) must be added to net income to convert to cash flow from operating activities: See Exhibit 16.5. (An increase in inventories would be subtracted.)

## Change in Prepaid Expenses

The income statement reports expenses for the period, but cash flow from operating activities must report cash payments. As the following T-accounts show, cash prepayments increase the balance in Prepaid Expenses; the recording of expenses decreases the balance:

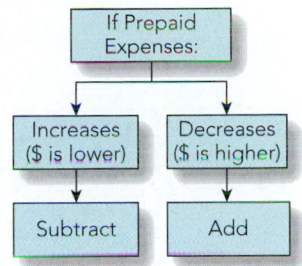

| Prepaid Expenses (A) | |
|---|---|
| Beg. bal. | |
| Cash prepayments | Used up/expensed |
| End. bal. | |

| Prepaid Expenses (A) | | |
|---|---|---|
| Beg. bal. | 24,000 | |
| Increase | 9,000 | |
| End. bal. | 33,000 | |

The balance sheet for Nautilus (see Exhibit 16.4) shows a $9,000 increase in Prepaid Expenses, which means that new cash prepayments were more than recorded expenses. This increase (the extra cash prepayments) must be subtracted from net income in Exhibit 16.5. (A decrease in Prepaid Expenses would be added.)

## Change in Accounts Payable

Cash flow from operations must reflect cash purchases, but not all purchases are paid for in cash. Purchases made on account increase Accounts Payable; cash paid to suppliers decreases Accounts Payable:

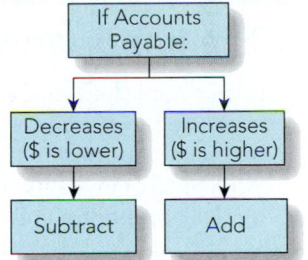

| Accounts Payable (L) | |
|---|---|
| | Beg. bal. |
| Cash payments | Purchases on account |
| | End. bal. |

| Accounts Payable (L) | | |
|---|---|---|
| | Beg. bal. | 61,000 |
| | Increase | 3,000 |
| | End. bal. | 64,000 |

For Nautilus, Accounts Payable increased by $3,000 during the period (see Exhibit 16.4). That means cash payments to suppliers were less than purchases made on account. This increase in Accounts Payable must be added to net income in Exhibit 16.5. (A decrease in Accounts Payable would be subtracted.)

## Change in Accrued Liabilities

The income statement reports all accrued expenses, but the cash flow statement must report actual payments for those expenses. Recording accrued expenses increases the balance in the Accrued Liabilities account; cash payments for these expenses decrease Accrued Liabilities:

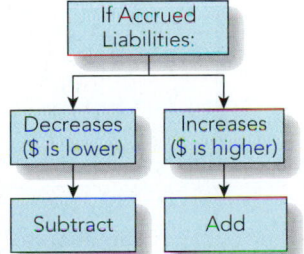

| Accounts Liabilities (L) | |
|---|---|
| | Beg. bal. |
| Cash payments | Accrued expenses |
| | End. bal. |

| Accrued Liabilities (L) | | |
|---|---|---|
| | Beg. bal. | 37,000 |
| | Increase | 1,000 |
| | End. bal. | 38,000 |

According to Exhibit 16.4, Nautilus's Accrued Liabilities increased by $1,000, which means that cash payments were less than accrued expenses. This increase in Accrued Liabilities must be added to net income in Exhibit 16.5. (A decrease in Accrued Liabilities would be subtracted.)

## Summary

We can summarize the typical additions and subtractions required to reconcile net income with cash flow from operating activities as follows:

| ADDITIONS AND SUBTRACTIONS TO RECONCILE NET INCOME TO CASH FLOW FROM OPERATING ACTIVITIES | | |
|---|:---:|:---:|
| Item | When Item Increases | When Item Decreases |
| Depreciation and amortization | + | NA |
| Gain on sale of long-term asset | − | NA |
| Loss on sale of long-term asset | + | NA |
| Accounts receivable | − | + |
| Inventory | − | + |
| Prepaid expenses | − | + |
| Accounts payable | + | − |
| Accrued liabilities | + | − |

Notice that to reconcile net income to cash flow from operations, you must:

- **Add the change when a current asset decreases or a current liability increases.**
- **Subtract the change when a current asset increases or a current liability decreases.**

## Spotlight On BUSINESS DECISIONS

### The Importance of Cash Flow from Operations

In an established business, operating activities are important to investors and creditors. Financial statement users are interested in a company's ability to generate enough cash flows from operations to continue investing in assets and repay its debt on time. Creditors and investors will tolerate poor operating cash flows only so long before they stop lending to or investing in a company. For a company to survive over the long run, then, the amount of cash generated by daily operating activities must exceed the amount of cash spent on them.

**SELF-STUDY PRACTICE**

Compute cash flow from operating activities assuming the following list includes all amounts related to operating activities.

| | | | |
|---|---:|---|---:|
| Net income | $10,000 | Inventory decrease | $ 300 |
| Accounts receivable increase | 600 | Loss on sale of investments | 100 |
| Accounts payable decrease | 700 | Depreciation expense | 3,000 |

*After you have finished, check your answers with the solution at the bottom of the page.*

**Solution to Self-Study Practice**

| | |
|---|---:|
| Net income | $10,000 |
| + Depreciation expense | 3,000 |
| + Loss on sale of investments | 100 |
| − Accounts receivable increase | (600) |
| + Inventory decrease | 300 |
| − Accounts payable decrease | (700) |
| Cash Flow from Operating Activities | $12,100 |

# REPORTING CASH FLOWS FROM INVESTING ACTIVITIES

To prepare the second section of the statement of cash flows, we must analyze the accounts related to investments and to property, plant, and equipment.[4] In the operating activities section, we were concerned with only the **net** change in selected accounts. In the investing activities section, however (as well as in the financing activities section), we must identify the causes of **both** increases and decreases in selected accounts. The following activities and their related accounts are the ones you will encounter most often:

| Related Balance Sheet Accounts | Investing Activity | Cash Flow Effect |
|---|---|---|
| Investments | Purchase of investment securities for cash | Outflow |
| | Sale (maturity) of investment securities for cash | Inflow |
| Property, Plant, and Equipment | Purchase of property, plant, and equipment for cash | Outflow |
| | Sale of property, plant, and equipment for cash | Inflow |

In the case of Nautilus, the balance sheet in Exhibit 16.4 shows two investment-related accounts (noted with an I) that changed during the year: Plant and Equipment, and Land. To determine the cause(s) for the changes in these accounts, we need to examine the records for these accounts. Purchases of plant and equipment or land increase the account; sales decrease it.

## Plant and Equipment

Assume Nautilus purchased equipment for $16,000 cash. This purchase caused a cash outflow, which we must subtract on the schedule of investing activities in Exhibit 16.6. This purchase explains the change in the Plant and Equipment account.

| Plant and Equipment (A) | | | |
|---|---|---|---|
| Beg. bal. | 203,000 | | |
| Purchases | 16,000 | Sales | 0 |
| End. bal. | 219,000 | | |

**Exhibit 16.6**    **Nautilus, Inc.: Schedule for Net Cash Flow from Investing Activities**

| Items | Amount (in thousands) | Explanations |
|---|---|---|
| Purchases of plant and equipment | $(16,000) | Payment of cash for equipment |
| Sales of land | 5,000 | Sale of land for cash |
| Net cash inflow (outflow) | $(11,000) | Subtotal for the statement of cash flows |

---

[4] Although they are not shown here, cash flows for intangible assets are similar to those for property, plant, and equipment.

If Nautilus had sold any plant and equipment during the period, regardless of the amount of any gain or loss on the sale, the total amount of cash received would have been an investing cash inflow.

## Land and Investments

Nautilus sold land for $5,000 in cash. The land's book value on the balance sheet at the time of sale was $2,000. Consequently, a gain of $3,000 ($5,000 − $2,000) occurred on the sale. Regardless of the amount of any gain or loss on the sale, the total amount of cash received from the sale, $5,000, is an investing cash inflow.

| Land (A) | | | |
|---|---|---|---|
| Beg. bal. | 12,000 | | |
| Purchases | 0 | Sales | 2,000 |
| End. bal. | 10,000 | | |

If Nautilus had purchased or sold any investments during the period, they would be treated in the same manner as the land in this example.

**SELF-STUDY PRACTICE**

Compute cash flow from investing activities assuming the following list includes all amounts related to purchases and sales of plant and equipment, land, and investments.

a. Purchased investments for cash, $10,000.
b. Sold land with a book value of $17,000 for $18,000 cash.
c. Purchased plant and equipment for $25,000 cash.
d. Sold investments with a book value of $15,000 for $12,000 cash.

*After you have finished, check your answers with the solution at the bottom of the page.*

## REPORTING CASH FLOWS FROM FINANCING ACTIVITIES

**Learning Objective 4**
Report cash flows from financing activities.

The third section of the statement of cash flows includes changes in the liabilities owed to owners (such as dividends payable) and financial institutions (such as bank loans payable, notes payable, and long-term debt) as well as changes in owners' equity. (Because earning interest is considered an operating activity, it is excluded from cash flows from financing.) The following activities and their related accounts are the ones you will encounter most often:

**Coach's Tip**
Remember that the dividends received from investing in other companies, as well as interest received and interest paid, affect net income. Thus, they are reported as **operating** (not investing or financing) cash flows.

| Related Balance Sheet Accounts | Financing Activity | Cash Flow Effect |
|---|---|---|
| Notes Payable | Borrowing cash from banks or other financial institutions | Inflow |
| | Repayment of loan principal | Outflow |
| Long-Term Debt | Issuance of bonds for cash | Inflow |
| | Repayment of bond principal | Outflow |
| Contributed Capital | Issuance of stock for cash | Inflow |
| | Repurchase of stock with cash | Outflow |
| Retained Earnings | Payment of cash dividends | Outflow |

Solution to
Self-Study Practice

| | |
|---|---|
| Purchased plant and equipment | ($25,000) |
| Purchased investments | (10,000) |
| Sold land | 18,000 |
| Sold investments | 12,000 |
| Cash flow from investing activities | ($ 5,000) |

To compute the cash flows from financing activities, we must review the changes in all debt and owners' equity accounts. Looking at changes in Nautilus's balance sheet (Exhibit 16.4), we find that the Long-Term Debt, Contributed Capital, and Retained Earnings accounts (noted with an F) all changed during the period. In the financing activities section (as in the investing activities section), we must **separately** identify the causes of both increases and decreases in selected accounts. This means that, in addition to the change in the balance sheet account, the accounting records related to the account must be examined.

## Long-Term Debt

Suppose the accounting records indicate that the $4,000 increase in Long-Term Debt on the balance sheet resulted from a combination of new borrowing of $6,000 and repayment of $2,000 in **principal** on existing debt. We will include both the inflow and outflow in the schedule of financing activities in Exhibit 16.7.

| Long-Term Debt (L) | | | |
|---|---|---|---|
| | | Beg. bal. | 63,000 |
| Repayments | 2,000 | Borrowings | 6,000 |
| | | End. bal. | 67,000 |

## Contributed Capital

The change in the Contributed Capital account resulted from an issue of company stock for $1,000 in cash, which produced a cash inflow. This $1,000 increase in contributed capital should be listed on the schedule of financing activities in Exhibit 16.7.

| Contributed Capital (OE) | |
|---|---|
| Beg. bal. | 4,000 |
| Issuance of stock | 1,000 |
| End. bal. | 5,000 |

## Retained Earnings

Net income increases the amount in the Retained Earnings account; dividends decrease Retained Earnings. We have already included the cash effects related to net income in the operating activities section of the statement of cash flows. The only change in retained earnings that remains to be accounted for is the cash outflow for any dividends paid.

From the income statement in Exhibit 16.4, we know that Nautilus reported net income of $31,000. From the statement of retained earnings (or statement of owners' equity), we know that Nautilus declared dividends of $24,000. The balance sheet does not report any dividends payable, so the full amount of dividends must have been paid in cash. This outflow is included in the schedule of financing activities in Exhibit 16.7. Together, net income

**Exhibit 16.7** Nautilus, Inc.: Schedule for Net Cash Flow from Financing Activities

| Items | Amount (in thousands) | Explanation |
|---|---|---|
| Additional borrowings of long-term debt | $ 6,000 | Cash received when new loan obtained |
| Repayment of principal on existing debt | (2,000) | Cash paid to repay principal on existing debt |
| Issuance of company stock | 1,000 | Cash received from issuing stock |
| Cash dividends paid | (24,000) | Cash paid to stockholders as dividend |
| Net cash inflow (outflow) | $(19,000) | Subtotal for the statement of cash flows |

and dividends account for the $7,000 increase in Retained Earnings as in the following T-account.

| Retained Earnings (OE) | | | |
|---|---|---|---|
| | | Beg. bal. | 248,000 |
| Dividends | 24,000 | Net Income | 31,000 |
| | | End. bal. | 255,000 |

**SELF-STUDY PRACTICE**

Compute cash flow from financing activities assuming the following list includes all financing activities of the period and some nonfinancing activities

| | | | |
|---|---|---|---|
| Purchased investments for cash | $10,000 | Additional short-term borrowing from bank | $19,000 |
| Dividends paid | 25,000 | Interest paid | 8,000 |

*After you have finished, check your answers with the solution at the bottom of the page.*

# PREPARING AND EVALUATING THE STATEMENT OF CASH FLOWS

## Format for the Statement of Cash Flows

**Learning Objective 5**

Prepare and evaluate the statement of cash flows.

Now that we have determined the cash flows for the three main types of business activity, we can prepare the statement of cash flows. In Exhibit 16.8, we show the format for the statement of cash flows using the indirect method. The statement of cash flows combines cash flows from operating, investing, and financing activities to produce an overall net increase (or decrease) in cash. This net change is added to the beginning cash balance to arrive at the ending cash balance, which is the same as the cash balance reported on the balance sheet.

## Noncash Investing and Financing Activities

Certain transactions are important investing and financing activities but have no cash flow effects. These are called **noncash investing and financing activities.** For example, the purchase of a $100,000 building with a $100,000 mortgage given by the former owner does not cause either an inflow or an outflow of cash. As a result, these noncash activities are not listed in the three main sections of the cash flow statement. However, supplemental disclosure of these transactions is required, in either narrative or schedule form. Nautilus statement of cash flows does not list any noncash investing and financing activities. However, when Northwest Airlines purchases airplanes from AIRBUS or Boeing, the manufacturer provides some of the

Solution to Self-Study Practice

| | |
|---|---|
| Dividends paid | ($25,000) |
| Additional short-term borrowing from bank | 19,000 |
| Cash flow from financing activities | ($6,000) |

## Exhibit 16.8    Format for the Statement of Cash Flows—Indirect Method

### Nautilus, Inc.
### Statement of Cash Flows*
### For the Year Ended December 31, 2006
### (in thousands)

| | |
|---|---:|
| **Cash Flows from Operating Activities** | |
| Net income | $31,000 |
| Adjustments to reconcile net income to net cash provided by operating activities: | |
| Depreciation | 7,000 |
| Gain on sale of land | (3,000) |
| Changes in assets and liabilities: | |
| Accounts receivable | (21,000) |
| Inventories | 20,000 |
| Prepaid expenses | (9,000) |
| Accounts payable | 3,000 |
| Accrued liabilities | 1,000 |
| **Net cash provided by operating activities** | 29,000 |
| **Cash Flows from Investing Activities** | |
| Purchases of plant and equipment | (16,000) |
| Sales of land | 5,000 |
| **Net cash used by investing activities** | (11,000) |
| **Cash Flows from Financing Activities** | |
| Additional borrowings of long-term debt | 6,000 |
| Repayment of principal on existing debt | (2,000) |
| Issuance of common stock | 1,000 |
| Cash dividends paid | (24,000) |
| **Net cash used by financing activities** | (19,000) |
| **Net decrease in cash and cash equivalents** | (1,000) |
| **Cash and cash equivalents at beginning of period** | 8,000 |
| **Cash and cash equivalents at end of period** | $ 7,000 |

*Certain amounts have been adjusted to simplify the presentation.

**Nautilus**

financing for those purchases. These amounts are disclosed as follows at the bottom of its cash flow statement:

### NORTHWEST AIRLINES CORPORATION

| (in millions) | Year ended December 31, | | |
|---|---:|---:|---:|
| **Investing and Financing Activities Not Affecting Cash:** | 2007 | 2006 | 2005 |
| Manufacturer financing of aircraft and other non-cash transactions | $ 502 | $ 280 | $ 344 |

**Northwest**

## Supplemental Cash Flow Information

Companies that use the indirect method of presenting cash flows from operations also must provide two other figures: cash paid for interest and cash paid for income taxes. These are normally listed at the bottom of the statement or in the notes.

## Free Cash Flow

In evaluating the statement of cash flows, a good place to start is with the subtotals in each of the three main sections. Cash flow patterns differ from one company to the next, depending on how well established a company is. A healthy, well-established company will show positive cash flows from operations that are large enough to pay for the replacement of current property, plant, and equipment and pay dividends to stockholders.

Any additional cash beyond that required to meet a company's basic needs is called **free cash flow.** Free cash flow can be used (a) to expand the business through additional investing activities, (b) for financing (for example, to pay down debt or pay future dividends), or (c) simply to build the company's cash balance.

### Financial Analysis Tools

| Name of Measure | Formula | What It Tells You |
|---|---|---|
| Free Cash Flow | Net Cash Flow from Operating Activities<br>– Purchases of Property and Equipment<br>– Dividends Paid | • Ability to make additional capital investments without external financing.<br>• Ability to pay down debt or repurchase stock.<br>• Ability to pay future dividends. |

Nautilus's free cash flow would be computed as follows:

> **Free Cash Flow = Net Cash Flow from Operating Activities − Purchases of Property and Equipment − Dividends Paid**
> **= $29,000 − $16,000 − $24,000 = ($11,000)**

## Quality of Income Ratio

The operating activities section of the statement of cash flows indicates how well a company can generate cash internally through its operations and its management of current assets and current liabilities. Most analysts believe this section is the most important one because in the long run, operations are the only continuing source of cash. Investors will not invest in a company if they do not believe that cash generated from operations will be available to pay dividends or expand the company. Similarly, creditors will not lend money if they believe that cash generated from operations will not be sufficient to repay them.

In evaluating the operating activities section of the statement of cash flows, consider the absolute amount of the cash flow; is it positive or negative? Keep in mind that for a company to be successful, operating cash flows must be positive over the long run. You can also look at the relationship between operating cash flows and net income by using the quality of income ratio. This ratio measures the portion of net income that was generated in cash. All other things held equal, a quality of income ratio near 1.0 indicates a high likelihood that revenues are realized in cash and that expenses are associated with cash outflows.

| Financial Analysis Tools | | |
|---|---|---|
| Name of Measure | Formula | What It Tells You |
| Quality of income ratio | Net Cash Flow from Operating Activities / Net Income | • Portion of net income generated in cash<br>• Ratio near 1.0 means that operating cash flows and net income are in sync. |

Nautilus's quality of income ratio would be computed as follows:

$$\text{Quality of Income Ratio} = \frac{\text{Net Cash Flow from Operating Activities}}{\text{Net Income}} = \frac{\$29,000}{\$31,000} = 0.94 \text{ times}$$

The quality of income ratio is most useful when it is compared to those of competitors in the same industry or to that of the same company in prior periods. Any major deviations—say, below 0.5 or above 1.5—should be investigated. In some cases, a deviation may be nothing to worry about, but in others it could be the first sign of serious problems.

There are three potential causes of deviations in this ratio. The first is **the corporate life cycle, or growth in sales.** New companies often experience rapid sales growth. When sales are increasing, accounts receivable and inventory normally increase faster than cash flows from sales. This lag in collections often reduces operating cash flows below net income, which in turn reduces the ratio. The problem is not serious provided that the company can get sufficient cash from financing activities to meet its needs until operating activities begin to generate positive cash flows.

A second potential cause of a deviation in the quality of income ratio is a **change in management of operating activities.** If a company's operating assets (such as Accounts Receivable and Inventories) are allowed to grow out of control, its operating cash flows and quality of income ratio will decrease. More efficient management will have the opposite effect. To investigate this potential cause more closely, use the inventory and accounts receivable turnover ratios covered in prior chapters

A third cause of deviation in this ratio is a **change in revenue and expense recognition.** Most cases of fraudulent financial reporting involve aggressive revenue recognition (that is, recording revenues before they are earned) or delayed expense recognition (that is, failing to report expenses). Both tactics cause net income to increase in the current period, suggesting that the company has improved its performance. However, neither of these tactics affects cash flows from operating activities. As a result, if revenue and expense recognition policies are used to artificially boost net income, the quality of income ratio will drop, providing one of the first warning signs that the financial statements might contain errors or fraud.

# Demonstration Case A: Indirect Method

For a recent quarter ended March 31, Brunswick Corporation reported net income of $3,800 (all numbers in thousands). On December 31 of the year before, the balance in cash and cash equivalents had been $351,400; by March 31, it was $280,000. The company reported the following additional activities:

a. Received $2,200 from debt borrowings.
b. Accounts receivable increased by $40,300.
c. Paid $31,800 in cash for purchase of property, plant, and equipment.
d. Recorded depreciation of $35,600.
e. Salaries payable increased by $10,210.
f. Other accrued liabilities decreased by $35,000.
g. Prepaid expenses decreased by $14,500.

h.   Inventories increased by $20,810.

i.   Accounts payable decreased by $10,200.

j.   Issued stock to employees for $400 in cash.

**Required:**

Based on this information, prepare the statement of cash flows using the indirect method. Evaluate the cash flows reported in the statement.

## Suggested Solution

**Brunswick Corporation**
**Statement of Cash Flows**
**For the Quarter Ended March 31**
**(in thousands)**

| | |
|---|---:|
| **Cash flows from operating activities** | |
| Net income | $    3,800 |
| Adjustments | |
| Depreciation | 35,600 |
| Increase in accounts receivable | (40,300) |
| Increase in inventories | (20,810) |
| Decrease in prepaid expenses | 14,500 |
| Decrease in accounts payable | (10,200) |
| Increase in salaries payable | 10,210 |
| Decrease in other accrued liabilities | (35,000) |
| Net cash provided by (used for) operating activities | (42,200) |
| **Cash flows from investing activities** | |
| Additions to property, plant, and equipment | (31,800) |
| Net cash provided by (used for) investing activities | (31,800) |
| **Cash flows from financing activities** | |
| Proceeds from debt borrowings | 2,200 |
| Proceeds from issuance of stock to employees | 400 |
| Net cash provided by (used for) financing activities | 2,600 |
| Increase (decrease) in cash and cash equivalents | (71,400) |
| Cash and cash equivalents, December 31 | 351,400 |
| Cash and cash equivalents, March 31 | $280,000 |

Despite reporting a profit this quarter, the company has experienced negative cash flow from operations. The drop was caused primarily by a buildup of accounts receivable and inventories with no corresponding reduction in spending on accounts payable and other accrued liabilities. This negative cash flow from operations could be troublesome because it suggests that the company may be encountering difficulties in selling its products and collecting on past sales. In addition to the drain on cash for operating activities, the company spent more than $30 million for additional property, plant, and equipment. Financing activities had relatively little effect on cash flows during the period, however. The company entered the quarter with a lot of cash (more than $350 million). Despite the shortfall in cash flow, it still has a lot of cash remaining to finance future activities.

## Supplement 16A

### Reporting Cash Flows from Operating Activities—Direct Method

The direct method summarizes all operating transactions that result in either a debit or a credit to Cash. It is prepared by adjusting each revenue and expense on the income statement from an accrual basis to a cash basis. We demonstrate this process using the revenues and expenses reported in Nautilus's income statement (Exhibit 16.4). See Exhibit 16A.1 for the schedule for converting from an accrual to a cash basis using the direct method. Notice that in this method, we work directly with each revenue and expense listed on the income statement, ignoring any totals or subtotals (such as net income).

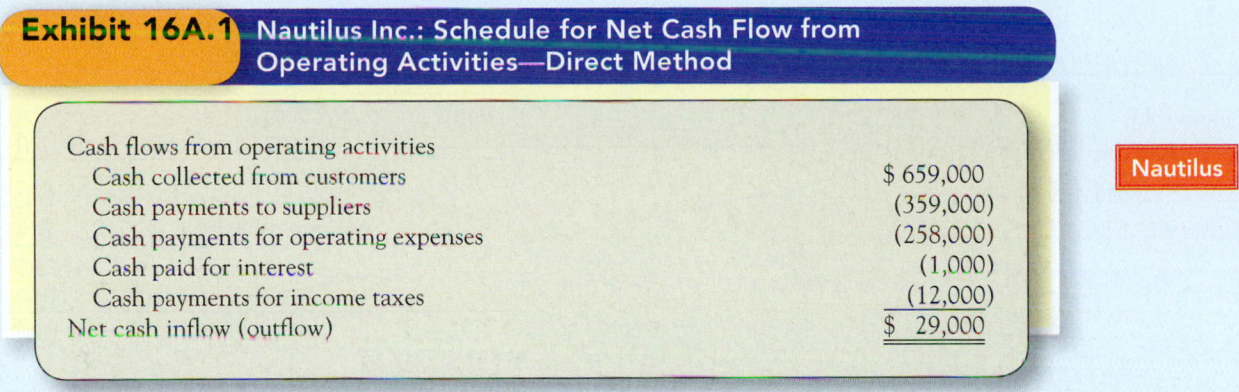

**Exhibit 16A.1**    Nautilus Inc.: Schedule for Net Cash Flow from Operating Activities—Direct Method

| | |
|---|---|
| Cash flows from operating activities | |
| Cash collected from customers | $ 659,000 |
| Cash payments to suppliers | (359,000) |
| Cash payments for operating expenses | (258,000) |
| Cash paid for interest | (1,000) |
| Cash payments for income taxes | (12,000) |
| Net cash inflow (outflow) | $  29,000 |

Nautilus

## Converting Sales Revenues to a Cash Inflow

When a company records sales, its Accounts Receivable increases; when the company collects cash, Accounts Receivable decreases. Thus, if Accounts Receivable increases by $21,000, sales on account must have been $21,000 more than cash collections. To convert sales revenue to cash collected, then, we need to subtract $21,000 from sales revenue. The following diagram shows this process:

Using information from Nautilus's income statement and balance sheet in Exhibit 16.4, we can compute cash collected from customers as follows:

| | |
|---|---|
| Net sales | $680,000 |
| − Increase in accounts receivable | 21,000 |
| Cash collected from customers | $659,000 |

| Accounts Receivable (A) | | |
|---|---|---|
| Beg. | 117,000 | |
| Increase | 21,000 | |
| End. | 138,000 | |

## Converting Cost of Goods Sold to Cash Paid to Suppliers

Cost of goods sold represents the cost of merchandise sold during the accounting period. It may be more or less than the amount of cash paid to suppliers during the period. In the case of Nautilus, inventory decreased during the year because the company sold more merchandise than it purchased. If the company paid cash to inventory suppliers, it would have paid less cash than the amount of cost of goods sold. So, the decrease in inventory must be subtracted from the cost of goods sold to compute the cash paid to suppliers.

Typically, companies buy their inventory on account from suppliers (as indicated by an accounts payable balance on the balance sheet). Consequently, we need to consider more than just the change in Inventory to convert the cost of goods sold to cash paid to suppliers. We must also consider the credit purchases and payments recorded in Accounts Payable. Credit purchases increase Accounts Payable; cash payments decrease it. The overall increase in Accounts Payable reported by Nautilus in Exhibit 16.4 indicates that cash payments were less than credit purchases, so we must subtract the difference to compute the total cash payments to suppliers. In other words, to fully convert the cost of goods sold to a cash basis, we must consider the changes in both Inventory and Accounts Payable, in the following manner:

Using information from Exhibit 16.4, we can compute cash paid to suppliers as follows:

| Cost of goods sold | $382,000 |
|---|---|
| − Decrease in inventory | 20,000 |
| − Increase in accounts payable | 3,000 |
| Cash payments to suppliers | $359,000 |

**Inventories (A)**

| Beg. | 96,000 | | |
|---|---|---|---|
| | | Decrease | 20,000 |
| End. | 76,000 | | |

**Accounts Payable (L)**

| | | Beg. | 61,000 |
|---|---|---|---|
| | | Increase | 3,000 |
| | | End. | 64,000 |

## Converting Operating Expenses to a Cash Outflow

The total amount of expense on the income statement may differ from the cash outflow associated with that activity. Some amounts, such as that for prepaid rent, are paid **before** they are recognized as expenses. When prepayments are made, the balance in the asset Prepaid Expenses increases. When expenses are recorded, Prepaid Expenses decreases. When Nautilus's Prepaid Expenses increase by $9,000, we know that the company paid more cash than it recorded in operating expenses. This increase in Prepaid Expenses must be added to net income to determine cash paid for operating expenses.

Some operating expenses, such as accrued wages, are paid **after** they are recorded. In that case, when the expenses are recorded, the balance in the Accrued Liabilities account increases. When the payments are made, Accrued Liabilities decreases. When Nautilus's Accrued Liabilities increase by $1,000, then we know the company paid that much less cash than it recorded as operating expenses. This amount must be subtracted in computing cash paid for expenses.

Generally, other operating expenses can be converted from an accrual basis to a cash basis in the following manner:

Using income statement information from Exhibit 16.4, we can compute cash paid for expenses as follows:

| Selling, general, and administrative expenses | $250,000 |
|---|---|
| + Increase in prepaid expenses | 9,000 |
| − Increase in accrued liabilities | 1,000 |
| Cash payments for expenses | $258,000 |

**Prepaid Expenses (A)**

| Beg. | 24,000 | | |
|---|---|---|---|
| Increase | 9,000 | | |
| End. | 33,000 | | |

**Accrued Liabilities (L)**

| | | Beg. | 37,000 |
|---|---|---|---|
| | | Increase | 1,000 |
| | | End. | 38,000 |

It is easy to convert depreciation expense to a cash basis because depreciation does not involve cash. Thus, the direct method of preparing the statement of cash flows omits noncash expenses such as depreciation (as well as revenues, gains, and losses that do not affect cash).

The next line on the income statement in Exhibit 16.4 is interest expense of $1,000. Because the Interest Payable account has no balance, all interest expense must have been paid in cash. Thus, the interest expense equals the interest paid:

| Interest expense | $1,000 |
|---|---|
| No change in interest payable | 0 |
| Cash payments for interest | $1,000 |

The same logic can be applied to income taxes. Nautilus reported income tax expense of $12,000. Because Income Taxes Payable (or any other tax account) on the balance sheet in Exhibit 16.4 has no balance, the income tax paid must equal the income tax expense:

| | |
|---|---|
| Income tax expense | $12,000 |
| No change in taxes payable | 0 |
| Cash payments for income taxes | $12,000 |

**Coach's Tip**

The amount Cash Flows from Operating Activities ($29,000 in this example) will **always** be the same regardless of whether it is computed with the direct or indirect method. (Compare the bottom lines of Exhibits 16A.1 and 16.5.)

Now that we have considered all of the line items shown on the income statement in Exhibit 16.4, it is time to gather all operating cash inflows and outflows that we have calculated (See Exhibit 16A.1). If Nautilus were to report its statement of cash flows using the direct method, Exhibit 16A.1 would replace the Cash Flows from Operating Activities section in Exhibit 16.8.

The following chart summarizes the adjustments that must be made to convert income statement items to operating cash flows. Before you move to the next section, review it carefully and then complete the self-study practice that follows to make sure you understand how to compute cash flow from operations (direct method).

| Income Statement Account | ±Change in Balance Sheet Account(s) | = Operating Cash Flow |
|---|---|---|
| Sales Revenue | +Decrease in Accounts Receivable (A) | |
| | −Increase in Accounts Receivable (A) | = Collections from customers |
| Cost of Goods Sold | +Increase in Inventory (A) | |
| | −Decrease in Inventory (A) | |
| | −Increase in Accounts Payable (L) | |
| | +Decrease in Accounts Payable (L) | = Payments to suppliers of inventory |
| Other Expenses | +Increase in Prepaid Expenses (A) | |
| | −Decrease in Prepaid Expenses (A) | |
| | −Increase in Accrued Expenses (L) | = Payments to suppliers of services |
| | +Decrease in Accrued Expenses (L) | (e.g., rent, utilities, wages, interest) |
| Interest Expense | −Increase in Interest Payable (L) | |
| | +Decrease in Interest Payable (L) | = Payments of interest |
| Income Tax Expense | +Increase in Prepaid Income Taxes (Deferred Taxes) (A) | |
| | −Decrease in Prepaid Income Taxes (Deferred Taxes) (A) | |
| | −Increase in Income Taxes Payable (Deferred Taxes) (L) | |
| | +Decrease in Income Taxes Payable (Deferred Taxes) (L) | = Payments of income taxes |

**SELF-STUDY PRACTICE**

Indicate which of the following items taken from a cash flow statement would be added (+), subtracted (−), or not included (0) when calculating cash flow from operations using the direct method.

___1. Payments to suppliers of inventories.        ___4. Purchase of plant and equipment for cash.

___2. Payment of dividends to stockholders.        ___5. Payments of interest to lenders.

___3. Cash collections from customers.             ___6. Payment of taxes to the government.

*After you have finished, check your answers with the solution at the bottom of the page.*

1. −    2. 0    3. +    4. 0    5. −    6. −

Solution to Self-Study Practice

# Demonstration Case B: Direct Method (Supplement A)

During a recent quarter ended March 29, Cybex International reported that cash and cash equivalents had increased from $216 on December 31 to $469 on March 29 (all amounts in thousands). The company also reported the following:

  a. Paid $13,229 to suppliers for inventory purchases.
  b. Borrowed $2,400 from one of the company's main stockholders.
  c. Paid $554 in cash for purchase of property, plant, and equipment.
  d. Reported sales on account of $20,608 (accounts receivable were $13,628 at the beginning of the quarter and $12,386 at the end of the quarter).
  e. Paid operating expenses totaling $6,188.
  f. Made cash payments for interest totaling $1,060.
  g. Made payments of $2,625 for principal owed on long-term debt.
  h. Paid $284 cash for other financing activities.
  i. Paid $57 cash for income taxes.

**Required:**
Based on this information, prepare the statement of cash flows using the direct method. Evaluate the cash flows reported in the statement.

## Suggested Solution

**Cybex International**
**Statement of Cash Flows**
**For the Quarter Ended March 29**
**(in thousands)**

| | |
|---|---|
| Operating activities | |
| Cash collected from customers ($20,608 + $13,628 − $12,386) | $ 21,850 |
| Cash paid to suppliers | (13,229) |
| Cash paid for operating expenses | (6,188) |
| Cash paid for interest | (1,060) |
| Cash paid for income taxes | (57) |
| Net cash provided by operating activities | 1,316 |
| Investing activities | |
| Additions to property, plant, and equipment | (554) |
| Net cash used for investing activities | (554) |
| Financing activities | |
| Borrowed cash from related party (stockholder) | 2,400 |
| Repaid principal owed on long-term debt | (2,625) |
| Cash paid for other financing activities | (284) |
| Net cash used for financing activities | (509) |
| Increase in cash and cash equivalents | 253 |
| Cash and cash equivalents, December 31 | 216 |
| Cash and cash equivalents, March 29 | $   469 |

Cybex reported a net cash inflow of $1,316 from operating activities during the quarter. This cash inflow was more than enough to pay for the property, plant, and equipment purchased during the quarter. Some of the extra cash from operations (that is, free cash flow) that was not needed to purchase property, plant, and equipment could have been used to pay down debt or increase the company's cash balance. The Financing Activities section suggests that the company did pay down a significant amount of long-term debt ($2,625) in part by borrowing funds from a related party ($2,400). Borrowing from a related party—particularly a major stockholder—is unusual, and would prompt analysts to investigate further. The company's quarterly report explains that lenders had demanded immediate repayment of their loans after the company violated its debt covenants. A major stockholder lent money to the company to make the repayment.

## Supplement 16B
### Spreadsheet Approach: Indirect Method

As a company's situation becomes more complex, the analytical approach that we used to prepare the statement of cash flows for Nautilus becomes cumbersome and inefficient. In practice, many companies use a spreadsheet to prepare the statement of cash flows. This approach is based on the same logic as our earlier approach. Its primary advantage is its systematic way of keeping track of detailed information. You may find it useful even in simple situations.

Exhibit 16B.1 is a spreadsheet for Nautilus, which we created using the following procedure:

1. Starting from the right side of the spreadsheet, set up four columns to record dollar amounts. The first column should hold the beginning balances for the items reported on the balance sheet. The next two columns should show debit and credit changes in those balances. The final column should show the ending balances in these balance sheet accounts.

2. On the top half of the spreadsheet, on the left side, enter each account name from the balance sheet.

3. On the bottom half of the spreadsheet, on the left side, enter the name of each item to be reported on the statement of cash flows. Do this as you analyze the change in each balance sheet account.

**Coach's Tip**
Think of the bottom half of the spreadsheet as a big Cash T-account.

Note that in the top half of the spreadsheet, you analyze changes in the balance sheet accounts in terms of debits and credits. In the bottom half of the spreadsheet, you record the offsetting debits and credits in terms of their impact on cash flows. Each change in the noncash balance sheet accounts explains part of the change in the Cash account.

Let's go through each of the entries in the spreadsheet in Exhibit 16B.1, starting with the first one in the bottom half:

a. Net income of $31,000 is shown as an inflow in the operating activities section. The corresponding credit in the top half of the spreadsheet goes to Retained Earnings (to show that net income increased Retained Earnings).

b. Depreciation expense of $7,000 is added back to net income because this expense does not cause a cash outflow. The corresponding credit explains the increase in the Accumulated Depreciation account during the period.

c. The $21,000 increase in Accounts Receivable means that cash collections from customers were less than sales made on account. Because net income includes the sales made on account, we must subtract that amount to adjust to the actual cash collected. This adjustment appears on the spreadsheet as a credit to Cash and a corresponding debit to Accounts Receivable.

d. This $20,000 entry reconciles purchases of inventory with the cost of goods sold. The amount is added to net income because more inventory was sold than was purchased.

e. This $9,000 entry reconciles the prepayment of expenses with their expiration. The amount is subtracted from net income because cash prepayments were more than the amounts reported as expired expenses.

f. This $3,000 entry reconciles cash paid to suppliers with purchases made on account. The amount is added because more was borrowed (by purchasing on account) than was paid in cash.

g. This $1,000 entry reconciles the accrual of liabilities for operating expenses with payments for those expenses. The amount is added because the cash paid for accrued liabilities was less than the expenses recorded for accrued liabilities. Note that the debit to Cash corresponds to the net credit to Accrued Liabilities.

h. This $16,000 entry records purchases of new equipment for cash.

i. This $5,000 entry records the sale of land for cash.

j. This $2,000 entry records cash repaid for principal on existing debt.

k. This $6,000 entry records cash obtained through additional long-term debt.

l. This $1,000 entry records cash received from an issue of company stock.

m. This $24,000 entry records the payment of dividends in cash.

n. This $1,000 entry shows that the change in cash (on the top part of the spreadsheet) is accounted for by the net cash flows listed on the bottom part of the spreadsheet.

Finally, check to make sure that the debits equal the credits on your spreadsheet. If they do not, you have missed something. If they do, you can then use the bottom part of the spreadsheet to prepare the statement of cash flows in Exhibit 16.8.

**Exhibit 16B.1**    Spreadsheet to Prepare Statement of Cash Flows, Indirect Method    Nautilus

## Nautilus, Inc.
### For the Year Ended December 31, 2006
### (in thousands)

|  | Beginning Balances, December 31, 2005 | ANALYSIS OF CHANGES Debit | | ANALYSIS OF CHANGES Credit | | Ending Balances, December 31, 2006 |
|---|---|---|---|---|---|---|
| **Items from Balance Sheet** | | | | | | |
| Cash and cash equivalents (A) | 8,000 | | | (n) | 1,000 | 7,000 |
| Accounts receivable (A) | 117,000 | (c) | 21,000 | | | 138,000 |
| Inventories (A) | 96,000 | | | (d) | 20,000 | 76,000 |
| Prepaid expenses (A) | 24,000 | (e) | 9,000 | | | 33,000 |
| Plant and Equipment (A) | 203,000 | (h) | 16,000 | | | 219,000 |
| Accumulated depreciation (xA) | (47,000) | | | (b) | 7,000 | (54,000) |
| Land (A) | 12,000 | | | (i) | 2,000 | 10,000 |
| Accounts payable (L) | (61,000) | | | (f) | 3,000 | (64,000) |
| Accrued liabilities (L) | (37,000) | | | (g) | 1,000 | (38,000) |
| Long-term debt (L) | (63,000) | (j) | 2,000 | (k) | 6,000 | (67,000) |
| Contributed capital (OE) | (4,000) | | | (l) | 1,000 | (5,000) |
| Retained earnings (OE) | (248,000) | (m) | 24,000 | (a) | 31,000 | (255,000) |

|  |  | CASH Inflows | | Outflows | | Subtotals |
|---|---|---|---|---|---|---|
| **Statement of Cash Flows** | | | | | | |
| **Cash flows from operating activities** | | | | | | |
| Net income | (a) | 31,000 | | | | |
| Adjustments to reconcile net income to cash provided by operating activities | | | | | | |
| Depreciation | (b) | 7,000 | | | | |
| Gain on sale of land | (i) | | | 3,000 | | |
| Changes in assets and liabilities | | | | | | |
| Accounts receivable | (c) | | | 21,000 | | |
| Inventories | (d) | 20,000 | | | | |
| Prepaid expenses | (e) | | | 9,000 | | |
| Accounts payable | (f) | 3,000 | | | | |
| Accrued liabilities | (g) | 1,000 | | | | |
|  | | | | | | 29,000 |
| **Cash flows from investing activities** | | | | | | |
| Purchases of equipment | (h) | | | 16,000 | | |
| Sale of land | (i) | 5,000 | | | | |
|  | | | | | | (11,000) |
| **Cash flows from financing activities** | | | | | | |
| Repayment of principal on existing debt | (j) | | | 2,000 | | |
| Additional long-term debt borrowed | (k) | 6,000 | | | | |
| Stock issuance | (l) | 1,000 | | | | |
| Cash dividends paid | (m) | | | 24,000 | | |
|  | | | | | | (19,000) |
| Net decrease in cash and cash equivalents | (n) | 1,000 | | | | |
|  | | 147,000 | | 147,000 | | (1,000) |

# Chapter Summary

**LO1  Identify cash flows from operating, investing, and financing activities. p. 682**

- The statement of cash flows has three main sections: cash flows from operating activities, which are related to income earned from normal operations; cash flows from investing activities, which are related to the acquisition and sale of productive assets; and cash flows from financing activities, which are related to external financing of the enterprise.
- The net cash inflow or outflow for the period equals the increase or decrease in cash and cash equivalents on the balance sheet for the period. Cash equivalents are highly liquid investments with original maturities of less than three months.

**LO2  Report cash flows from operating activities using the indirect method. p. 687**

- The indirect method for reporting cash flows from operating activities converts net income to net cash flow from operating activities.
- The conversion involves additions and subtractions for (1) expenses (such as depreciation expense) and revenues that do not affect cash and gains and losses from sale of long-lived assets and (2) changes in each of the individual current assets (other than cash) and current liabilities that reflect differences in the timing of accrual-based net income and cash flows.

**LO3  Report cash flows from investing activities. p. 693**

- Investing activities reported on the statement of cash flows include cash payments to acquire property, plant, and equipment, investments, and cash proceeds from their sale.

**LO4  Report cash flows from financing activities. p. 694**

- Cash inflows from financing activities include cash proceeds from the issue of debt and common stock. Cash outflows include cash repayments of principal on debt, cash paid for the repurchase of the company's stock, and cash dividend payments. (Cash payments associated with interest are a cash flow from operating activities.)

**LO5  Prepare and evaluate the statement of cash flows. p. 696**

- A healthy company will generate positive cash flows from operations, some of which will be used to pay for purchases of property, plant, and equipment. Any additional cash, called free cash flow, can be used to further expand the business or pay down some of the company's debt, or it can be returned to owners. A company is in trouble if it cannot generate positive cash flows from operations over the long run because creditors will eventually stop lending to the company, and stockholders will stop investing in it.
- Two common measures for assessing operating, investing, and financing cash flows are free cash flow and the quality of income ratio.

| Financial Analysis Tools | | |
| --- | --- | --- |
| Name of Measure | Formula | What It Tells You |
| Free Cash Flow | Net Cash Flow from Operating Activities – Purchases of Property and Equipment – Dividends Paid | • Ability to make additional capital investments without external financing. • Ability to pay down debt or repurchase stock. • Ability to pay future dividends. |
| Quality of income ratio | $\dfrac{\text{Net Cash Flow from Operating Activities}}{\text{Net Incomes}}$ | • Portion of net income generated in cash • Ratio near 1.0 means that operating cash flows and net income are in sync. |

# Key Terms

Cash Equivalents (p. 682)

Cash Flows from Financing Activities (p. 684)

Cash Flows from Investing Activities (p. 684)

Cash Flows from Operating Activities (Cash Flows from Operations) (p. 683)

Direct Method (p. 683)

Indirect Method (p. 683)

See complete glossary in back of text.

# Questions

1. Compare the purposes of the income statement, the balance sheet, and the statement of cash flows.

2. What information does the statement of cash flows report that is not reported on the other required financial statements?

3. What are cash equivalents? How are they reported on the statement of cash flows?

4. What are the major categories of business activities reported on the statement of cash flows? Define each of these activities.

5. What are the typical cash inflows from operating activities? What are the typical cash outflows from operating activities?

6. Describe the types of items used to compute cash flows from operating activities under the two alternative methods of reporting.

7. Under the indirect method, depreciation expense is added to net income to report cash flows from operating activities. Does depreciation cause an inflow of cash?

8. Explain why cash outflows during the period for purchases and salaries are not specifically reported on a statement of cash flows prepared using the indirect method.

9. Explain why a $50,000 increase in inventory during the year must be included in computing cash flows from operating activities under the indirect method.

10. What are the typical cash inflows from investing activities? What are the typical cash outflows from investing activities?

11. What are the typical cash inflows from financing activities? What are the typical cash outflows from financing activities?

12. What are noncash investing and financing activities? Give one example. How are noncash investing and financing activities reported on the statement of cash flows?

# Multiple Choice

1. Where is the change in cash shown in the statement of cash flows?
   a. In the top part, before the operating activities section.
   b. In one of the operating, investing, or financing activities sections.
   c. In the bottom part, following the financing activities section.
   d. None of the above.

Quiz 16-1
www.mhhe.com/LLPW1e

2. In what order do the three sections of the statement of cash flows appear when reading from top to bottom?
   a. Financing, investing, operating.
   b. Investing, operating, financing.
   c. Operating, financing, investing.
   d. Operating, investing, financing.

3. Total cash inflow in the operating section of the statement of cash flows should include which of the following?
   a. Cash received from customers at the point of sale.
   b. Cash collections from customer accounts receivable.
   c. Cash received in advance of revenue recognition (unearned revenue).
   d. All of the above.

4. If the balance in Prepaid Expenses increased during the year, what action should be taken on the statement of cash flows when following the indirect method, and why?
   a. The change in the account balance should be subtracted from net income because the net increase in Prepaid Expenses did not impact net income but did reduce the Cash balance.
   b. The change in the account balance should be added to net income because the net increase in Prepaid Expenses did not impact net income but did increase the Cash balance.

   c. The net change in Prepaid Expenses should be subtracted from net income to reverse the income statement effect that had no impact on Cash.
   d. The net change in Prepaid Expenses should be added to net income to reverse the income statement effect that had no impact on Cash.

**Coach's Tip**
To practice more multiple choice questions, go to www.mhhe.com/LLPW1e.

5. Which of the following would not appear in the investing section of the statement of cash flows?
   a. Purchase of inventory.
   b. Sale of investments.
   c. Purchase of land.
   d. All of the above would appear in the investing section of the statement of cash flows.

6. Which of the following items would not appear in the financing section of the statement of cash flows?
   a. The issuance of the company's own stock.
   b. The repayment of debt.
   c. The payment of dividends.
   d. All of the above would appear in the financing section of the statement of cash flows.

7. Which of the following is not added when computing cash flows from operations using the indirect method?
   a. The net increase in Accounts Payable.
   b. The net decrease in Accounts Receivable.
   c. The net decrease in Inventory.
   d. None of the above.

8. If a company engages in a material transaction that is noncash, which of the following is required?
   a. The company must include an explanatory narrative or schedule accompanying the statement of cash flows.
   b. No disclosure is necessary.
   c. The company must include an explanatory narrative or schedule accompanying the balance sheet.
   d. It must be reported in the investing and financing sections of the statement of cash flows.

9. The **total** change in cash as shown near the bottom of the statement of cash flows for the year should agree with which of the following?
   a. The difference in retained earnings when reviewing the comparative balance sheet.
   b. Net income or net loss as found on the income statement.
   c. The difference in cash when reviewing the comparative balance sheet.
   d. None of the above.

10. Which of the following is a ratio or amount used to assess whether cash flows from operations are sufficiently large to pay for replacing current property, plant, and equipment and to pay dividends to stockholders?
   a. Free cash flow.
   b. Fixed asset turnover ratio.
   c. Cash coverage ratio.
   d. Quality of income ratio.

| Solutions to Multiple-Choice Questions | | | | | | |
| --- | --- | --- | --- | --- | --- | --- |
| 1. c | 2. d | 3. d | 4. a | 5. a | 6. d | 7. d |
| 8. a | 9. c | 10. a | | | | |

# Mini-Exercises  Available with McGraw-Hill's Homework Manager

## M16-1 Identifying Companies from Cash Flow Patterns
LO1, 5

Based on the cash flows shown, classify each of the following cases as a growing start-up company (S), a healthy established company (E), or an established company facing financial difficulties (F).

| | Case 1 | Case 2 | Case 3 |
| --- | --- | --- | --- |
| Cash provided by (used for) operating activities | $(120,000) | $ 3,000 | $ 80,000 |
| Cash provided by (used for) investing activities | 10,000 | (70,000) | (40,000) |
| Cash provided by (used for) financing activities | 75,000 | 75,000 | (30,000) |
| Net change in cash | (35,000) | 8,000 | 10,000 |
| Cash position at beginning of year | 40,000 | 2,000 | 30,000 |
| Cash position at end of year | $ 5,000 | $10,000 | $ 40,000 |

## M16-2 Matching Items Reported to Cash Flow Statement Categories (Indirect Method)
LO1

Buckle

The Buckle, Inc., operates more than 330 stores in 38 states, selling brand name apparel such as Lucky Jeans and Fossil belts and watches. Some of the items included in its recent statement of cash flows presented using the indirect method are listed here. Indicate whether each item is disclosed in the operating activities (O), investing activities (I), or financing activities (F) section of the statement or (NA) if the item does not appear on the statement.

_____ 1. Purchase of investments.
_____ 2. Proceeds from issuance of stock.
_____ 3. Purchase of property and equipment.
_____ 4. Depreciation.
_____ 5. Accouts payable (decrease).
_____ 6. Inventories (increase).

## M16-3 Determining the Effects of Account Changes on Cash Flows from Operating Activities (Indirect Method)
LO2

Indicate whether each item would be added (+) or subtracted (−) in the computation of cash flow from operating activities using the indirect method.

_____ 1. Depreciation.
_____ 2. Inventories (decrease).
_____ 3. Accounts payable (decrease).
_____ 4. Accounts receivable (increase).
_____ 5. Accrued liabilities (increase).

**LO2**

**M16-4 Computing Cash Flows from Operating Activities (Indirect Method)**

For each of the following independent cases, compute cash flows from operating activities. Assume the following list includes all balance sheet accounts related to operating activities.

|  | Case A | Case B |
|---|---|---|
| Net income | $ 200,000 | $ 360,000 |
| Depreciation expense | 40,000 | 80,000 |
| Accounts receivable increase (decrease) | 100,000 | (20,000) |
| Inventory increase (decrease) | (50,000) | 50,000 |
| Accounts payable increase (decrease) | (110,000) | 70,000 |
| Accrued liabilities increase (decrease) | 60,000 | (80,000) |

**LO2**

**M16-5 Computing Cash Flows from Operating Activities (Indirect Method)**

For the following two independent cases, show the Cash Flows from Operating Activities section of the 2011 statement of cash flows using the indirect method.

|  | CASE A | | CASE B | |
|---|---|---|---|---|
|  | 2011 | 2010 | 2011 | 2010 |
| Sales revenue | $ 10,000 | $ 9,000 | $ 21,000 | $ 18,000 |
| Cost of goods sold | 6,000 | 5,500 | 12,000 | 11,000 |
| Gross profit | 4,000 | 3,500 | 9,000 | 7,000 |
| Depreciation expense | 1,000 | 1,000 | 2,000 | 1,500 |
| Salaries expense | 2,500 | 2,000 | 5,000 | 5,000 |
| Net income | 500 | 500 | 2,000 | 500 |
| Accounts receivable | 300 | 400 | 750 | 600 |
| Inventories | 600 | 500 | 790 | 800 |
| Accounts payable | 800 | 700 | 800 | 850 |
| Salaries payable | 1,000 | 1,200 | 200 | 250 |

**LO3**

**M16-6 Computing Cash Flows from Investing Activities**

Based on the following information, compute cash flows from investing activities.

| Cash collections from customers | $800 |
|---|---|
| Purchase of used equipment | 850 |
| Depreciation expense | 200 |
| Proceeds from sale of investments | 300 |

**LO4**

**M16-7 Computing Cash Flows from Financing Activities**

Based on the following information, compute cash flows from financing activities.

| Purchase of investments | $ 250 |
|---|---|
| Dividends paid | 800 |
| Interest paid | 400 |
| Additional short-term borrowing from bank | 2,000 |

**LO3, 4, 5**

**M16-8 Reporting Noncash Investing and Financing Activities**

Which of the following transactions would be considered noncash investing and financing activities?

_____1. Additional borrowing from bank.

_____2. Purchase of equipment with investments.

_____3. Dividends paid in cash.

_____4. Purchase of building with promissory note.

**LO5**

**M16-9 Interpreting Cash Flows from Operating, Investing, and Financing Activities**

Quantum Dots, Inc., is a nanotechnology company that manufactures "quantum dots," which are tiny pieces of silicon consisting of 100 or more molecules. Quantum dots can be used to illuminate very small objects, enabling scientists to see the blood vessels beneath a mouse's skin ripple with each heartbeat, at the rate of 100 times per second. Evaluate this research intensive company's cash flows assuming the following was reported in its statement of cash flows.

| | Current Year | Previous Year |
|---|---|---|
| **Cash flows from operating activities** | | |
| Net cash provided by (used for) operating activities | $ (50,790) | $ (46,730) |
| **Cash flows from investing activities** | | |
| Purchases of research equipment | (250,770) | (480,145) |
| Proceeds from selling all short-term investments | 35,000 | — |
| Net cash provided by (used for) investing activities | (215,770) | (480,145) |
| **Cash flows from financing activities** | | |
| Additional long-term debt borrowed | 100,000 | 200,000 |
| Proceeds from stock issuance | 140,000 | 200,000 |
| Cash dividends paid | — | (10,000) |
| Net cash provided by (used for) financing activities | 240,000 | 390,000 |
| **Net increase (decrease) in cash** | (26,560) | (136,875) |
| Cash at beginning of period | 29,025 | 165,900 |
| Cash at end of period | $  2,465 | $ 29,025 |

**M16-10 Calculating and Interpreting Free Cash Flow**                                        LO5

Capital Corporation reported the following information in its statement of cash flows:

| | 2010 | 2011 | 2012 |
|---|---|---|---|
| Net cash flow from operating activities | $35,000 | $32,000 | $23,000 |
| Dividends paid | 2,000 | 3,000 | 2,500 |
| Income taxes paid | 9,000 | 8,500 | 6,500 |
| Purchases of property, plant, and equipment | 31,818 | 22,857 | 20,325 |

Calculate the total free cash flow for the period covering 2010–2012 and the free cash flow for each year during the period. What does this analysis tell you about the company's need for using external financing to replace property, plant, and equipment and pay dividends?

**M16-11 Calculating and Interpreting the Quality of Income Ratio**                           LO5

Dan's Products, Inc., reported net income of $80,000, depreciation expense of $2,000, and cash flow from operations of $60,000. Compute the quality of income ratio. What does the ratio tell you about the company's accrual of revenues and/or deferral of expenses?

**M16-12 (Supplement A) Matching Items Reported to Cash Flow Statement Categories (Direct Method)**

Prestige Manufacturing Corporation reports the following items in its 2011 statement of cash flows presented using the direct method. Indicate whether each item is disclosed in the operating activities (O), investing activities (I), or financing activities (F) section of the statement or (NA) if the item does not appear on the statement.

_____1. Payment for equipment purchase.        _____4. Proceeds from issuance of stock.

_____2. Repayments of bank loan.               _____5. Interest paid.

_____3. Dividends paid.                         _____6. Receipts from customers.

**M16-13 (Supplement A) Computing Cash Flows from Operating Activities (Direct Method)**

For each of the following independent cases, compute cash flows from operating activities using the direct method. Assume the following list includes all items relevant to operating activities.

| | Case A | Case B |
|---|---|---|
| Sales revenue | $ 70,000 | $ 55,000 |
| Cost of goods sold | 35,000 | 32,000 |
| Depreciation expense | 10,000 | 2,000 |
| Other operating expenses | 5,000 | 13,000 |
| Net income | 20,000 | 8,000 |
| Accounts receivable increase (decrease) | (1,000) | 4,000 |
| Inventory increase (decrease) | 2,000 | 0 |
| Accounts payable increase (decrease) | 0 | 3,000 |
| Accrued liabilities increase (decrease) | 1,000 | (2,000) |

**M16-14 (Supplement A) Computing Cash Flows from Operating Activities (Direct Method)**
Refer to the two cases presented in M16-5, and show the Cash Flow from Operating Activities section of the 2011 statement of cash flows using the direct method.

## Exercises 🟧 ™   Available with McGraw-Hill's Homework Manager

**LO1, 2**
**Nike**

**E16-1 Matching Items Reported to Cash Flow Statement Categories (Indirect Method)**
Nike, Inc., is the best-known sports shoe, apparel, and equipment company in the world because of its association with sports stars such as LeBron James. Some of the items included in its recent statement of cash flows presented using the indirect method are listed here.

Indicate whether each item is disclosed in the operating activities (O), investing activities (I), or financing activities (F) section of the statement or (NA) if the item does not appear on the statement.

_____ 1. Additions to long-term debt (new borrowing).

_____ 2. Depreciation.

_____ 3. Additions to property, plant, and equipment (paid in cash).

_____ 4. Increase (decrease) in notes payable. (The amount is owed to financial institutions.)

_____ 5. (Increase) decrease in other current assets.

_____ 6. Cash received from disposal of property, plant, and equipment.

_____ 7. Reductions in long-term debt (repayment).

_____ 8. Issuance of stock (for cash).

_____ 9. (Increase) decrease in inventory.

_____10. Net income.

**LO1, 2**

**E16-2 Comparing the Direct and Indirect Methods**
To compare statement of cash flows reporting under the direct and indirect methods, enter check marks to indicate which line items are reported on the statement of cash flows with each method.

| Cash Flows (and Related Changes) | Statement of Cash Flows Method | |
|---|---|---|
| | Direct | Indirect |
| 1. Net income. | _____ | _____ |
| 2. Receipts from customers. | _____ | _____ |
| 3. Accounts receivable increase or decrease. | _____ | _____ |
| 4. Payments to suppliers. | _____ | _____ |
| 5. Inventory increase or decrease. | _____ | _____ |
| 6. Accounts payable increase or decrease. | _____ | _____ |
| 7. Payments to employees. | _____ | _____ |
| 8. Wages payable, increase or decrease. | _____ | _____ |
| 9. Depreciation expense. | _____ | _____ |
| 10. Cash flows from operating activities. | _____ | _____ |
| 11. Cash flows from investing activities. | _____ | _____ |
| 12. Cash flows from financing activities. | _____ | _____ |
| 13. Net increase or decrease in cash during the period. | _____ | _____ |

**LO2**

**E16-3 Reporting Cash Flows from Operating Activities (Indirect Method)**
The following information pertains to Guy's Gear Company for 2010:

| | | |
|---|---|---|
| Sales | | $80,000 |
| Expenses | | |
| Cost of goods sold | $50,000 | |
| Depreciation expense | 6,000 | |
| Salaries expense | 12,000 | 68,000 |
| Net income | | $12,000 |

| Partial Balance Sheet | 2010 | 2009 |
|---|---|---|
| Accounts receivable | $ 15,000 | $ 20,000 |
| Merchandise inventory | 18,000 | 10,000 |
| Salaries payable | 2,500 | 2,000 |

*Required:*
Present the operating activities section of the statement of cash flows for Guy's Gear Company using the indirect method.

**E16-4 Reporting and Interpreting Cash Flows from Operating Activities from an Analyst's Perspective (Indirect Method)**                               LO2, 5

New Vision Company completed its income statement and balance sheet for 2010 and provided the following information:

| | | |
|---|---|---|
| Service revenue | | $66,000 |
| Expenses | | |
| Salaries | $42,000 | |
| Depreciation | 7,300 | |
| Utilities | 7,000 | |
| Loss on sale of machine | 1,700 | 58,000 |
| Net income | | $ 8,000 |

| Partial Balance Sheet | 2010 | 2009 |
|---|---|---|
| Accounts receivable | $12,000 | $24,000 |
| Salaries payable | 19,000 | 10,000 |
| Other accrued liabilities | 5,000 | 9,000 |
| Land | 52,000 | 57,000 |

*Required:*
1.  Present the operating activities section of the statement of cash flows for New Vision Company using the indirect method.

2.  Of the potential causes of differences between cash flow from operations and net income, which are the most important to financial analysts?

**E16-5 Reporting and Interpreting Cash Flows from Operating Activities from an Analyst's Perspective (Indirect Method)**                               LO2, 5

Sizzler, Inc., operates 700 family restaurants around the world. The company's annual report contained the following information (in thousands):

| Operating Activities | |
|---|---|
| Net loss | $(9,482) |
| Depreciation | 33,305 |
| Increase in receivables | 170 |
| Decrease in inventories | 643 |
| Increase in prepaid expenses | 664 |
| Decrease in accounts payable | 2,282 |
| Decrease in accrued liabilities | 719 |
| Increase in income taxes payable | 1,861 |
| Reduction of long-term debt | 12,691 |
| Additions to equipment | 29,073 |

*Required:*
1.  Based on this information, compute cash flow from operating activities using the indirect method.

2.  What were the major reasons that Sizzler was able to report a net loss but positive cash flow from operations?

3.  Of the potential causes of differences between cash flow from operations and net income, which are the most important to financial analysts?

**LO2, 3**

**AMC Theatres**

**E16-6 Determining Cash Flows from the Sale of Property (Indirect Method)**

The first in the theatre industry to introduce a customer loyalty program (like frequent flyer miles for movie watchers) was AMC Theatres. During the prior year, the company sold property for $5,494,000 cash and recorded a gain on sale of $1,385,000. During the current year, the company sold property for $9,289,000 cash and recorded a gain on sale of $2,590,000.

*Required:*

For the property sold by AMC each year, show how the disposals would be reported on the comparative statements of cash flows using the following format (which assumes the indirect method). Indicate the sign and amount of the effects.

|  | Prior Year | Current Year |
|---|---|---|
| **Cash flows from operating activities** | | |
| Gain on sale of property | _____ | _____ |
| **Cash flows from investing activities** | | |
| Proceeds from disposition of property | _____ | _____ |

**LO2, 3**

**Gymboree**

**E16-7 Determining Cash Flows from the Sale of Property (Indirect Method)**

The Gymboree Corporation, a specialty retailer, offers apparel, accessories, and play programs for children in the United States and Canada. During the prior year, the company sold property for $18,823,000 cash and recorded a loss on sale of $4,419,000. During the current year, the company sold property for $12,648,000 cash and recorded a loss on sale of $2,964,000.

*Required:*

For the property sold by Gymboree each year, show how the disposals would be reported on the comparative statements of cash flows, using the following format (which assumes the indirect method). Indicate the sign and amount of the effects.

|  | Prior Year | Current Year |
|---|---|---|
| **Cash flows from operating activities** | | |
| Loss on sale of property | _____ | _____ |
| **Cash flows from investing activities** | | |
| Proceeds from disposition of property | _____ | _____ |

**LO2**

**Colgate-Palmolive**

**E16-8 Inferring Balance Sheet Changes from the Cash Flow Statement (Indirect Method)**

Colgate-Palmolive was founded in 1806. Its statement of cash flows for the first quarter of a recent year reported the following information (in millions):

| Operating Activities | |
|---|---|
| Net income | $  952.2 |
| Depreciation | 243.5 |
| Cash effect of changes in | |
| Accounts receivable | (122.9) |
| Inventories | (128.9) |
| Accounts payable | 122.8 |
| Other | 303.2 |
| Net cash provided by operations | $1,369.9 |

*Required:*

Based on the information reported in the operating activities section of the statement of cash flows for Colgate-Palmolive, determine whether the following accounts increased or decreased during the period: Accounts Receivable, Inventories, and Accounts Payable.

**LO2**

**Apple**

**E16-9 Inferring Balance Sheet Changes from the Cash Flow Statement (Indirect Method)**

The statement of cash flows for Apple for the six-month period ended April 1 of a recent year contained the following information (in millions):

| Operating Activities | |
|---|---|
| Net income | $975 |
| Depreciation | 102 |
| Changes in assets and liabilities | |
| Accounts receivable | 34 |
| Inventories | (39) |
| Other current assets | (892) |
| Accounts payable | 329 |
| Other adjustments | (351) |
| Net cash provided by operations | $158 |

**Required:**

For each of the asset and liability accounts listed in the operating activities section of the statement of cash flows, determine whether the account balances increased or decreased during the period.

**E16-10 Analyzing Cash Flows from Operating Activities (Indirect Method) and Calculating and Interpreting the Quality of Income Ratio**

LO2, 5

PepsiCo

A recent annual report for PepsiCo contained the following information for the period (in millions):

| | |
|---|---|
| Net income | $4,078 |
| Cash dividends paid | 1,642 |
| Depreciation | 1,308 |
| Increase in accounts receivable | 272 |
| Increase in inventory | 132 |
| Increase in prepaid expense | 56 |
| Increase in accounts payable | 188 |
| Increase in taxes payable | 609 |
| Decrease in other liabilities related to operations | 791 |

**Required:**

1. Compute cash flows from operating activities for PepsiCo using the indirect method.
2. Compute the quality of income ratio to one decimal place.
3. What was the main reason that PepsiCo's quality of income ratio did not equal 1.0?

**E16-11 Calculating and Understanding Operating Cash Flows Relating to Inventory Purchases (Indirect Method)**

LO2

The following information was reported by three companies. When completing the requirements, assume that any and all purchases on account are for inventory.

| | Aztec Corporation | Bikes Unlimited | Campus Cycles |
|---|---|---|---|
| Cost of goods sold | $175 | $175 | $350 |
| Inventory purchases from suppliers made using cash | 200 | 0 | 200 |
| Inventory purchases from suppliers made on account | 0 | 200 | 200 |
| Cash payments to suppliers on account | 0 | 160 | 160 |
| Beginning inventory | 100 | 100 | 200 |
| Ending inventory | 125 | 125 | 250 |
| Beginning accounts payable | 0 | 80 | 80 |
| Ending accounts payable | 0 | 120 | 120 |

**Required:**

1. What amount did each company deduct on the income statement related to inventory?
2. What total amount did each company pay in cash during the period related to inventory?
3. By what amount do your answers in 1 and 2 differ for each company?

4.  By what amount did each company's inventory increase (decrease)? By what amount did each company's accounts payable increase (decrease)?

5.  Using the indirect method of presentation, what amount(s) must each company add (deduct) from net income to convert from accrual to cash basis?

6.  Describe any similarities in your answers to requirements 3 and 5. Are these answers the same? Why or why not?

**LO3, 4**

### E16-12 Reporting Cash Flows from Investing and Financing Activities

Randell Furniture Corporation is a North Carolina–based manufacturer of furniture. In a recent quarter, it reported the following activities:

| | |
|---|---|
| Net income | $ 4,135 |
| Purchase of property, plant, and equipment | 871 |
| Borrowings under line of credit (bank) | 1,417 |
| Proceeds from issuance of stock | 11 |
| Cash received from customers | 29,164 |
| Payments to reduce long-term debt | 46 |
| Sale of investments | 134 |
| Proceeds from sale of property and equipment | 6,594 |
| Dividends paid | 277 |
| Interest paid | 90 |

*Required:*

Based on this information, present the cash flows from investing and financing activities sections of the cash flow statement.

**LO3, 4, 5**

GIBRALTAR
INDUSTRIES

### E16-13 Reporting and Interpreting Cash Flows from Investing and Financing Activities with Discussion of Management Strategy

Gibraltar Steel Corporation is a Buffalo, New York–based manufacturer of steel products. In a recent year, it reported the following activities:

| | |
|---|---|
| Net income | $ 5,213 |
| Purchase of property, plant, and equipment | 10,468 |
| Payments of notes payable (bank) | 8,598 |
| Net proceeds of stock issuance | 26,061 |
| Depreciation | 3,399 |
| Long-term debt reduction | 17,832 |
| Proceeds from sale of investments | 131 |
| Proceeds from sale of property, plant, and equipment | 1,817 |
| Proceeds from long-term debt borrowed | 10,242 |
| Decrease in accounts receivable | 1,137 |
| Proceeds from notes payable (bank) | 3,848 |

*Required:*

1.  Based on this information, present the cash flows from investing and financing activities sections of the cash flow statement.

2.  Referring to your response to requirement 1, comment on what you think Gibraltar's management plan was for the use of the cash generated by the stock issuance.

**LO5**

**Disney**

### E16-14 Calculating and Interpreting Free Cash Flow

The Disney Company reported the following in its 2007 annual report.

| | 2007 | 2006 | 2005 |
|---|---|---|---|
| Net income | $4,687 | $3,374 | $2,533 |
| Net cash provided by operating activities | 5,421 | 6,058 | 4,269 |
| Purchase of parks, resorts, and other property | (1,566) | (1,299) | (1,823) |
| Cash paid for interest | 551 | 617 | 641 |
| Cash paid for income taxes | 2,796 | 1,857 | 1,572 |
| Cash paid for dividends | 637 | 519 | 490 |

*Required:*

1.  Calculate the total free cash flow for the period covering 2005–2007 and the free cash flow for each year.

2.  Interpret the results of your calculation in requirement 1. What do they suggest about the company's need for external financing to acquire property and equipment and pay dividends?

### E16-15 Calculating and Interpreting the Quality of Income Ratio

Refer to the information about the Disney Company in E16-14.

LO5
Disney

*Required:*

1.  Calculate to one decimal place the quality of income ratio for each year.

2.  Interpret the results of your calculations in requirement 1. Given what you know about the Walt Disney Company from your own personal observations, provide one reason that could explain the sizable difference between net income and net cash provided by operating activities.

### E16-16 (Supplement A) Reporting and Interpreting Cash Flows from Operating Activities from an Analyst's Perspective (Direct Method)

Refer to the information for New Vision Company in E16-4.

*Required:*

1.  Present the operating activities section of the statement of cash flows for New Vision Company using the direct method. Assume other accrued liabilities relate to other expenses on the income statement.

2.  Of the potential causes of differences between cash flow from operations and net income, which are the most important to financial analysts?

### E16-17 (Supplement A) Reporting and Interpreting Cash Flows from Operating Activities from an Analyst's Perspective (Direct Method)

Refer to the information given for E16-5 plus the following summarized income statement for Sizzler, Inc.:

| | |
|---|---:|
| Revenues | $136,500 |
| Cost of sales | 45,500 |
| Gross margin | 91,000 |
| Salary expense | 56,835 |
| Depreciation | 33,305 |
| Other expenses | 7,781 |
| Net loss before income taxes | (6,921) |
| Income tax expense | 2,561 |
| Net loss | $ (9,482) |

*Required:*

1.  Based on this information, compute the cash flow from operating activities using the direct method. Assume prepaid expenses and accrued liabilities relate to other expenses.

2.  What were the major reasons that Sizzler was able to report a net loss but positive cash flow from operations?

3.  Of the potential causes of differences between cash flow from operations and net income, which are the most important to financial analysts?

### E16-18 (Supplement B) Preparing a Statement of Cash Flows, Indirect Method: Complete Spreadsheet

To prepare a statement of cash flows for Golf Champion Store, you examined the company's accounts, noting the following transactions:

a.  Purchased equipment, $20,000, and issued a promissory note in full payment.
b.  Purchased a long-term investment for cash, $15,000.

c.  Paid cash dividend, $12,000.
d.  Sold land for $24,000 cash (the land was purchased for $21,000).
e.  Issued shares of stock, 500 shares at $12 per share cash.

You also created the following spreadsheet to use when preparing the statement of cash flows.

## ANALYSIS OF CHANGES

| | Beginning Balances, December 31, 2010 | Debit | Credit | Ending Balances, December 31, 2011 |
|---|---|---|---|---|
| **Income statement items** | | | | |
| Sales | | | $140,000 | |
| Cost of goods sold | | $59,000 | | |
| Depreciation | | 3,000 | | |
| Wage expense | | 28,000 | | |
| Income tax expense | | 9,000 | | |
| Interest expense | | 5,000 | | |
| Other expenses | | 15,800 | | |
| Gain on the sale of land | | | 3,000 | |
| Net income | | 23,200 | | |
| **Balance sheet items** | | | | |
| Cash | $ 20,500 | | | $ 37,200 |
| Accounts receivable | 22,000 | | | 22,000 |
| Merchandise inventory | 68,000 | | | 75,000 |
| Investments | 0 | | | 15,000 |
| Land | 21,000 | | | 0 |
| Equipment | 114,500 | | | 134,500 |
| Total debits | $246,000 | | | $283,700 |
| | | | | |
| Accumulated depreciation | $ 32,000 | | | $ 35,000 |
| Accounts payable | 17,000 | | | 14,000 |
| Wages payable | 2,500 | | | 1,500 |
| Income taxes payable | 3,000 | | | 4,500 |
| Notes payable | 75,000 | | | 95,000 |
| Contributed capital | 100,000 | | | 106,000 |
| Retained earnings | 16,500 | | | 27,700 |
| Total credits | $246,000 | | | $283,700 |
| | | Inflows | Outflows | |

**Statement of Cash Flows**
Cash flows from operating activities
Cash flows from investing activities
Cash flows from financing activities
Net increase (decrease) in cash
Totals

*Required:*
Prepare a spreadsheet to prepare the statement of cash flows using the indirect method. Follow the format in Exhibit 16B.1.

# Problems—Set A     Available with McGraw-Hill's Homework Manager

### PA16-1 Determining Cash Flow Statement Effects of Transactions    LO1

Motif Furniture is an Austin-based furniture company. For each of the following first-quarter transactions, indicate whether operating (O), investing (I), or financing activities (F) are affected and whether the effect is a cash inflow (+) or outflow (−), or (NE) if the transaction has no effect on cash.

_____1. Bought used equipment for cash.

_____2. Paid cash to purchase new equipment.

_____3. Declared and paid cash dividends to stockholders.

_____4. Collected payments on account from customers.

_____5. Recorded an adjusting entry to record accrued salaries expense.

_____6. Recorded and paid interest on debt to creditors.

_____7. Repaid principal on loan from bank.

_____8. Prepaid rent for the following period.

_____9. Made payment to suppliers on account.

### PA16-2 Computing Cash Flows from Operating Activities (Indirect Method)    LO2

The income statement and selected balance sheet information for Direct Products Company for the year ended December 31, 2011, follow.

www.mhhe.com/LLPW1e

### Income Statement

| | |
|---|---|
| Sales revenue | $49,600 |
| Expenses | |
| Cost of goods sold | 21,000 |
| Depreciation expense | 2,000 |
| Salaries expense | 9,000 |
| Rent expense | 4,500 |
| Insurance expense | 1,900 |
| Interest expense | 1,800 |
| Utilities expense | 1,400 |
| Loss on sale of land | 1,000 |
| Net income | $ 7,000 |

### Selected Balance Sheet Accounts

| | 2011 | 2010 |
|---|---|---|
| Accounts receivable | $560 | $580 |
| Merchandise inventory | 990 | 770 |
| Accounts payable | 440 | 460 |
| Salaries payable | 100 | 70 |
| Utilities payable | 20 | 15 |
| Prepaid rent | 25 | 20 |
| Prepaid insurance | 25 | 28 |

**Required:**
Prepare the Cash Flows from Operating Activities section of the 2011 statement of cash flows using the indirect method.

### PA16-3 Preparing a Statement of Cash Flows (Indirect Method)    LO2, 3, 4, 5

XS Supply Company is developing its annual financial statements at December 31, 2011. The statements are complete except for the statement of cash flows. The completed comparative balance sheets and income statement are summarized:

|                                      | 2011      | 2010      |
|--------------------------------------|-----------|-----------|
| **Balance sheet at December 31**     |           |           |
| Cash                                 | $ 34,000  | $ 29,000  |
| Accounts receivable                  | 35,000    | 28,000    |
| Merchandise inventory                | 41,000    | 38,000    |
| Property and equipment               | 121,000   | 100,000   |
| Less: Accumulated depreciation       | (30,000)  | (25,000)  |
|                                      | $201,000  | $170,000  |
|                                      |           |           |
| Accounts payable                     | $ 36,000  | $ 27,000  |
| Wages payable                        | 1,200     | 1,400     |
| Note payable, long term              | 38,000    | 44,000    |
| Contributed capital                  | 88,600    | 72,600    |
| Retained earnings                    | 37,200    | 25,000    |
|                                      | $201,000  | $170,000  |
|                                      |           |           |
| **Income statement for 2011**        |           |           |
| Sales                                | $120,000  |           |
| Cost of goods sold                   | 70,000    |           |
| Other expenses                       | 37,800    |           |
| Net income                           | $ 12,200  |           |

**Additional Data:**

a. Bought equipment for cash, $21,000.
b. Paid $6,000 on the long-term note payable.
c. Issued new shares of stock for $16,000 cash.
d. No dividends were declared or paid.
e. Other expenses included depreciation, $5,000; wages, $20,000; taxes, $6,000; other, $6,800.
f. Accounts Payable includes only inventory purchases made on credit. Because there are no liability accounts relating to taxes or other expenses, assume that these expenses were fully paid in cash.

**Required:**

1. Prepare the statement of cash flows for the year ended December 31, 2011, using the indirect method.
2. Evaluate the statement of cash flows.

LO2, 3, 4, 5

www.mhhe.com/LLPW1e

**PA16-4 Preparing and Interpreting a Statement of Cash Flows (Indirect Method)**
Heads Up Company was started several years ago by two hockey instructors. The company's comparative balance sheets and income statement with additional information follow.

|                                      | 2012      | 2011      |
|--------------------------------------|-----------|-----------|
| **Balance sheet at December 31**     |           |           |
| Cash                                 | $ 6,000   | $ 4,000   |
| Accounts receivable                  | 1,000     | 1,750     |
| Equipment                            | 5,500     | 5,000     |
| Less: Accumulated depreciation       | (1,500)   | (1,250)   |
|                                      | $11,000   | $ 9,500   |
|                                      |           |           |
| Accounts payable                     | $    500  | $ 1,000   |
| Wages payable                        | 500       | 750       |
| Bank loan payable                    | 1,500     | 500       |
| Contributed capital                  | 5,000     | 5,000     |
| Retained earnings                    | 3,500     | 2,250     |
|                                      | $11,000   | $ 9,500   |
|                                      |           |           |
| **Income statement for 2012**        |           |           |
| Lessons revenue                      | $37,500   |           |
| Wages expense                        | 35,000    |           |
| Other expenses                       | 1,250     |           |
| Net income                           | $ 1,250   |           |

**Additional Data:**

a. Bought new hockey equipment for cash, $500.
b. Borrowed $1,000 cash from the bank during the year.

c.  Other expenses included depreciation, $250; rent, $500; taxes, $500.

d.  Accounts Payable includes only purchases of services made on credit for operating purposes. Because there are no liability accounts relating to utilities or taxes, assume that these expenses were fully paid in cash.

**Required:**

1.  Prepare the statement of cash flows for the year ended December 31, 2012, using the indirect method.

2.  Use the statement of cash flows to evaluate the company's cash flows.

**TIP:** The demonstration cases provide good examples of information to consider when evaluating cash flows.

### PA16-5 (Supplement A) Computing Cash Flows from Operating Activities (Direct Method)
Refer to the information in PA16-2.

www.mhhe.com/LLPW1e

**Required:**
Prepare the cash flows from the operating activities section of the 2011 statement of cash flows using the direct method.

### PA16-6 (Supplement A) Preparing and Interpreting a Statement of Cash Flows (Direct Method)
Refer to PA16-4.

**Required:**
Complete requirements 1 and 2 using the direct method.

## Problems—Set B   Available with McGraw-Hill's Homework Manager

### PB16-1 Determining Cash Flow Statement Effects of Transactions
LO1

Fantatech Inc. designs, develops, and produces high-tech entertainment products, including VirtuaSports, that allow novice players to experience hazardous and difficult real-life sports in virtual reality. The company also produces a 4D theater system that combines 3D visual effects with special effects such as vibrating chairs, simulated drops, and scented air blasts. For each of the following transactions listed in Fantatech's annual report, indicate whether operating (O), investing (I), or financing activities (F) are affected and whether the effect is a cash inflow (+) or outflow (−), or (NE) if the transaction has no effect on cash.

_____1.  Received deposits from customers for products to be delivered the following period.

_____2.  Principal repayments on loan.

_____3.  Paid cash to purchase new equipment.

_____4.  Received proceeds from loan.

_____5.  Collected payments on account from customers.

_____6.  Recorded and paid salaries to employees.

_____7.  Paid cash for building construction.

_____8.  Recorded and paid interest to debt holders.

### PB16-2 Computing Cash Flows from Operating Activities (Indirect Method)
LO2

The income statement and selected balance sheet information for Calendars Incorporated for the year ended December 31, 2011, follow.

| Income Statement | |
|---|---|
| Sales revenue | $78,000 |
| Expenses | |
| Cost of goods sold | 36,000 |
| Depreciation expense | 16,000 |
| Salaries expense | 10,000 |
| Rent expense | 2,500 |
| Insurance expense | 1,300 |
| Interest expense | 1,200 |
| Utilities expense | 1,000 |
| Net income | $10,000 |

| Selected Balance Sheet Accounts | 2011 | 2010 |
|---|---|---|
| Merchandise inventory | $ 430 | $ 490 |
| Accounts receivable | 1,800 | 1,500 |
| Accounts payable | 1,200 | 1,300 |
| Salaries payable | 450 | 300 |
| Utilities payable | 100 | 0 |
| Prepaid rent | 50 | 100 |
| Prepaid insurance | 70 | 90 |

**Required:**
Prepare the Cash Flows from Operating Activities section of the 2011 statement of cash flows using the indirect method.

**LO2, 3, 4, 5**

### PB16-3 Preparing a Statement of Cash Flows (Indirect Method)

Audio City, Inc., is developing its annual financial statements at December 31, 2011. The statements are complete except for the statement of cash flows. The completed comparative balance sheets and income statement are summarized:

| | 2011 | 2010 |
|---|---|---|
| **Balance sheet at December 31** | | |
| Cash | $ 63,000 | $ 65,000 |
| Accounts receivable | 15,000 | 20,000 |
| Merchandise inventory | 22,000 | 20,000 |
| Property and equipment | 210,000 | 150,000 |
| Less: Accumulated depreciation | (60,000) | (45,000) |
| | $250,000 | $210,000 |
| | | |
| Accounts payable | $ 8,000 | $ 19,000 |
| Wages payable | 2,000 | 1,000 |
| Note payable, long term | 60,000 | 75,000 |
| Contributed capital | 100,000 | 70,000 |
| Retained earnings | 80,000 | 45,000 |
| | $250,000 | $210,000 |
| **Income statement for 2011** | | |
| Sales | $190,000 | |
| Cost of goods sold | 90,000 | |
| Other expenses | 60,000 | |
| Net income | $ 40,000 | |

**Additional Data:**
a. Bought equipment for cash, $60,000.
b. Paid $15,000 on the long-term note payable.
c. Issued new shares of stock for $30,000 cash.
d. Paid dividends of $5,000 in cash.
e. Other expenses included depreciation, $15,000; wages, $20,000; taxes, $25,000.
f. Accounts Payable includes only inventory purchases made on credit. Because a liability relating to taxes does not exist, assume they were fully paid in cash.

**Required:**
1. Prepare the statement of cash flows for the year ended December 31, 2011, using the indirect method.
2. Evaluate the statement of cash flows.

**PB16-4 Preparing and Interpreting a Statement of Cash Flows (Indirect Method)**    LO2, 3, 4, 5

Dive In Company was started several years ago by two diving instructors. The company's comparative balance sheets and income statement with additional information follow.

|  | 2012 | 2011 |
|---|---|---|
| **Balance sheet at December 31** | | |
| Cash | $ 3,200 | $ 4,000 |
| Accounts receivable | 1,000 | 500 |
| Prepaid expenses | 100 | 50 |
|  | $ 4,300 | $ 4,550 |
| | | |
| Wages payable | $ 350 | $ 1,100 |
| Contributed capital | 1,200 | 1,000 |
| Retained earnings | 2,750 | 2,450 |
|  | $ 4,300 | $ 4,550 |
| | | |
| **Income statement for 2012** | | |
| Lessons revenue | $33,950 | |
| Wages expense | 30,000 | |
| Other expenses | 3,650 | |
| Net income | $ 300 | |

*Additional Data:*

a.  Prepaid expenses relate to rent paid in advance.
b.  Other operating expenses were paid in cash.
c.  An owner contributed capital by paying $200 cash in exchange for the company's stock.

*Required:*

1.  Prepare the statement of cash flows for the year ended December 31, 2012, using the indirect method.
2.  Use the statement of cash flows to evaluate the company's cash flows.

**PB16-5 (Supplement A) Computing Cash Flows from Operating Activities (Direct Method)**

Refer to the information in PB16-2.

*Required:*

Prepare the Cash Flows from Operating Activities section of the 2011 statement of cash flows using the direct method.

**PB16-6 (Supplement A) Preparing and Interpreting a Statement of Cash Flows (Direct Method)**

Refer to PB16-4.

*Required:*

Complete requirements 1 and 2 using the direct method.

# Cases and Projects

**CP16-1 Finding Financial Information**    LO1, 5

Refer to the financial statements of The Home Depot in Appendix A at the end of this book, or download the annual report from the *Cases* section of the text's Web site at www.mhhe.com/LLPW1e.

*Required:*

1.  Which of the two basic reporting approaches for the cash flows from operating activities did The Home Depot use?
2.  What amount of tax payments did The Home Depot make during the current year? Where did you find this information?
3.  In the most recent year reported, The Home Depot generated $5,727 million from operating activities. Where did The Home Depot spend this money? List the two largest cash outflows.

**LO1, 5**

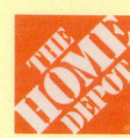

Lowe's

### CP16-2 Comparing Financial Information

Refer to the financial statements of The Home Depot in Appendix A and Lowe's in Appendix B at the end of this book, or download the annual reports from the *Cases* section of the text's Web site at www.mhhe.com/LLPW1e.

*Required:*

1. Which of the two basic reporting approaches for the cash flows from operating activities did Lowe's use? Is this the same as what The Home Depot used?
2. What amount of cash did Lowe's receive during fiscal 2007 from issuing long-term debt?
3. In fiscal 2007, Lowe's generated $4,347 million from operating activities. Where did Lowe's spend this money? List the two largest cash outflows reported in the investing or financing activities sections. Do Lowe's uses differ significantly from The Home Depot's?

**LO5**

### CP16-3 Examining an Annual Report: Internet-Based Team Research

As a team, select an industry to analyze. Using your Web browser, each team member should acquire the annual report or 10-K for one publicly traded company in the industry, with each member selecting a different company. (See CP1-3 in Chapter 1 for a description of possible resources for these tasks.)

*Required:*

1. On an individual basis, each team member should write a short report that incorporates the following:
   a. Has the company generated positive or negative operating cash flows during the past three years?
   b. Has the company been expanding over the period? If so, what appears to have been the source of financing for this expansion (operating cash flow, additional borrowing, issuance of stock)?
   c. Compute and analyze the quality of income ratio in each of the past three years.
2. Then, as a team, write a short report comparing and contrasting your companies using these attributes. Discuss any patterns across the companies that you as a team observe. Provide potential explanations for any differences discovered.

**LO1, 2, 5**

### CP16-4 Making Ethical Decisions: A Mini Case

Assume you serve on the board of a local golf and country club. In preparation for renegotiating the club's bank loans, the president indicates that the club needs to increase its operating cash flows before the end of the current year. With a wink and sly smile, the club's treasurer reassures the president and other board members that he knows a couple of ways to boost the club's operating cash flows. First, he says, the club can sell some of its accounts receivable to a collections company that is willing to pay the club $97,000 up front for the right to collect $100,000 of the overdue accounts. That will immediately boost operating cash flows. Second, he indicates that the club paid about $200,000 last month to relocate the 18th fairway and green closer to the clubhouse. The treasurer indicates that although these costs have been reported as expenses in the club's own monthly financial statements, he feels an argument can be made for reporting them as part of land and land improvements (a long-lived asset) in the year-end financial statements that would be provided to the bank. He explains that, by recording these payments as an addition to a long-lived asset, they will not be shown as a reduction in operating cash flows.

*Required:*

1. Does the sale of accounts receivable to generate immediate cash harm or mislead anyone? Would you consider it an ethical business activity?
2. If cash is spent on long-lived assets, such as land improvements, how is it typically classified in the statement of cash flows? If cash is spent on expenses, such as costs for regular upkeep of the grounds, how is it typically classified in the statement of cash flows?
3. What facts are relevant to deciding whether the costs of the 18th hole relocation should be reported as an asset or as an expense? Is it appropriate to make this decision based on the impact it could have on operating cash flows?
4. As a member of the board, how would you ensure that an ethical decision is made?

**LO2**

### CP16-5 Thinking Critically: Interpreting Adjustments Reported on the Statement of Cash Flows from a Management Perspective (Indirect Method)

QuickServe, a chain of convenience stores, was experiencing some serious cash flow difficulties because of rapid growth. The company did not generate sufficient cash from operating activities to finance its new stores, and creditors were not willing to lend money because the company had not produced any income for the previous three years. The new controller for QuickServe proposed a reduction in the estimated life of store equipment to increase depreciation expense; thus, "we can improve cash flows from operating activities because depreciation expense is added back on the statement of cash flows." Other executives were not sure that this was a good idea because the increase in depreciation would make it more difficult to have positive earnings: "Without income, the bank will never lend us money."

*Required:*

What action would you recommend for QuickServe? Why?

**CP16-6 Using a Spreadsheet that Calculates Cash Flows from Operating Activities (Indirect Method)**                      LO2

You've recently been hired by B2B Consultants to provide financial advisory services to small business managers. B2B's clients often need advice on how to improve their operating cash flows and, given your accounting background, you are frequently called upon to show them how operating cash flows would change if they were to speed up their sales of inventory and their collections of accounts receivable or delay their payment of accounts payable. Each time you are asked to show the effects of these business decisions on the cash flows from operating activities, you get the uneasy feeling that you might inadvertently miscalculate their effects. To deal with this once and for all, you e-mail your friend Owen and ask him to prepare a template that automatically calculates the net operating cash flows from a simple comparative balance sheet. You received his reply today.

| | |
|---|---|
| From: | Owentheaccountant@yahoo.com |
| To: | Helpme@hotmail.com |
| Cc: | |
| Subject: | Excel Help |

Hey, pal. I like your idea of working smarter, not harder. Too bad it involved me doing the thinking. Anyhow, I've created a spreadsheet file that contains four worksheets. The first two tabs (labeled BS and IS) are the input sheets where you would enter the numbers from each client's comparative balance sheet and income statement. Your clients are small, so this template allows for only the usual accounts. Also, I've assumed that depreciation is the only reason for a change in accumulated depreciation. If your clients' business activities differ from these, you'll need to contact me for more complex templates. The third worksheet calculates the operating cash flows using the indirect method, and the fourth does this calculation using the direct method. I'll attach the screenshots of each of the worksheets so you can create your own. To answer "what if" questions, all you'll need to do is change selected amounts in the balance sheet and income statement.

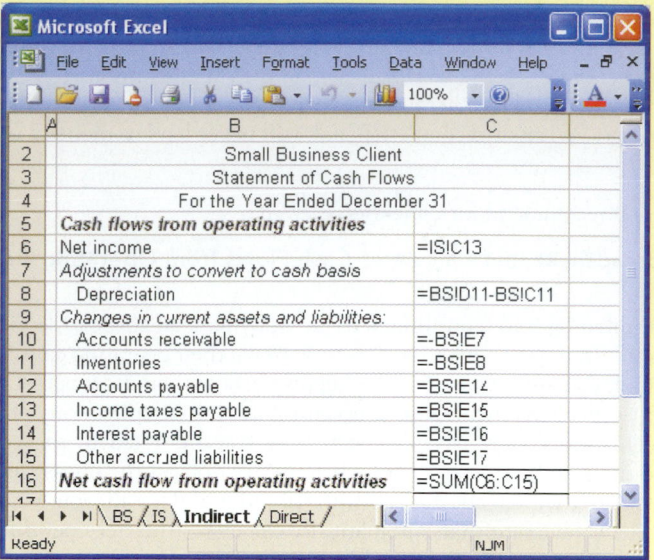

*Required:*

Copy the information from the worksheets for the balance sheet, income statement, and statement of cash flows (indirect method only) into a spreadsheet file. What was the net cash flow from operating activities?

# 17 Financial Statement Analysis

## LEARNING OBJECTIVES

**After completing this chapter, you should be able to:**

**LO1** Describe how financial statement information is communicated to external users.

**LO2** Use horizontal (trend) analysis to recognize financial changes that unfold over time.

**LO3** Use vertical (common size) analysis to understand important relationships within financial statements.

**LO4** Calculate and use financial ratios to assess profitability, liquidity, and solvency.

# Focus Company: LOWE'S

## "Let's Build Something Together"

www.lowes.com

Measuring and evaluating financial performance is like judging gymnastics or figure skating at the Olympics. You have to know three things: (1) the general categories to evaluate for each event, (2) the particular elements to consider within each category, and (3) how to measure performance for each element. On the financial side, analysts follow the same process. They evaluate general categories such as profitability, liquidity, and solvency, which are separated into particular elements such as gross profit margin and net profit margin. For each of these elements, analysts measure performance by computing various percentages and ratios, which themselves are based on information reported in the financial statements.

In this chapter, we focus on Lowe's, the second largest home improvement retailer in the world. Lowe's is a giant with nearly 1,400 stores and 210,000 employees. Yet the company's continued success still requires innovations to increase sales in existing markets and to successfully enter new markets. At the same time, Lowe's must control costs while maintaining a high level of customer service in their stores. Finally, Lowe's management must anticipate the actions of its larger rival, The Home Depot, and deal with changes in overall demand for building products over which it has no control.

How do analysts, investors, and creditors assess Lowe's success in meeting these challenges? This is the purpose of financial statement analysis. Our discussion begins with an explanation of how companies release their financial statement information and where that information can be found. We then explain how to use trend and ratio analysis to understand the financial results of a company's business activities. We conclude the chapter with a review of the key accounting decisions analysts consider when evaluating financial statements.

729

**RELEASE OF FINANCIAL INFORMATION**

- Preliminary Press Release
- Quarterly and Annual Reports
- Securities and Exchange Commission (SEC) Filings
- Investor Information Web Sites

**HORIZONTAL (TREND) ANALYSIS**

- Preparing Comparative Balance Sheets and Comparative Income Statements
- Revealing Changes through Trend Analyses

**VERTICAL (COMMON SIZE) ANALYSIS**

- Preparing a Common Size Balance Sheet and Income Statement
- Interpreting Common Size Statements

**FINANCIAL RATIOS**

- Profitability Ratios
- Liquidity Ratios
- Solvency Ratios
- Accounting Decisions and Ratio Analysis

# RELEASE OF FINANCIAL INFORMATION

## Preliminary Press Release

**Learning Objective 1**

Describe how financial statement information is communicated to external users.

Video 17-1
www.mhhe.com/LLPW1e

To provide timely information to external users, public companies such as Lowe's announce their annual and quarterly financial results in a press release sent to news agencies three to five weeks after the accounting period ends. The press release typically includes key figures, a discussion of the results of the company's business activities, and a condensed income statement and balance sheet. During the time between the end of the company's year and the date of the press release, accountants are busy making adjusting journal entries and preparing the financial statements, and managers are preparing their analysis and discussion of the results.

Today, many companies, including Lowe's, follow up the press release with a conference call that is broadcast over the Internet. This call allows analysts to grill senior executives about the company's financial results. By listening to these calls, investors can learn much about a company's business strategy, its expectations for the future, and the key factors analysts consider when they evaluate a company. (To access this useful source of information, visit a company's Web site or check the archive of conference calls at biz.yahoo.com/cc.)

## Quarterly and Annual Reports

Several weeks after the preliminary press release, public companies release their complete financial statements as part of the annual or quarterly report. The annual report has two main sections. The first half usually begins with a friendly letter to investors from the company's CEO followed by glossy photographs of the company's products and glowing commentaries on the company's brilliant future. After developing the right mood with these jazzy marketing tactics, the company then presents the financial section, the meat and potatoes of the report. See Exhibit 17.1 for a list of the typical elements of the financial section and the information they contain. The third column of the exhibit gives the pages in Appendix A (at the end of this book) where you will find an example of each element.

A company's quarterly report looks like a condensed version of its annual report. Following a short letter to stockholders and abbreviated discussion of the financial results, a quarterly report presents a condensed income statement for the quarter, a condensed balance sheet dated at the end of the quarter, and a condensed statement of cash flows. These condensed financial statements typically show less detail than the annual statements, often omitting the statement of retained earnings or stockholders' equity and many notes to the financial statements. Items 4, 7, 8, and 9 in Exhibit 17.1 are typically omitted. Because the quarterly financial statements are not audited, they are labeled unaudited. With these limitations, the quarterly reports are not as informative as the annual reports, but they are released on a timelier basis (every three months rather than every year). So, they also have a major impact on investor and creditor judgments about the company.

## Exhibit 17.1    Typical Elements of the Financial Section of an Annual Report

| Name of Financial Section | Information Presented |
|---|---|
| 1. Summarized financial data | • Key figures covering a period of 5 or 10 years |
| 2. Management's discussion and analysis (MD&A) | • Honest and detailed analysis of the company's financial condition and operating results—a must-read for any serious financial statement user |
| 3. Management's report on internal control | • Statements that describe management's responsibility for ensuring adequate internal control over financial reporting and report on the effectiveness of those controls during the year |
| 4. Auditor's report | • Auditor's conclusion about whether GAAP was followed (and for public companies, whether internal controls were effective) |
| 5. Comparative financial statements | • Multiyear presentation of the four basic statements |
| 6. Financial statement notes | • Further information about the financial statements, crucial to understanding the financial statement data |
| 7. Recent stock price data | • Brief summary of highs and lows during the year |
| 8. Unaudited quarterly data | • Condensed summary of each quarter's results |
| 9. Directors and officers | • List of the individuals who are overseeing and running the company |

## Securities and Exchange Commission (SEC) Filings

To ensure that timely information is available to investors, the SEC requires public companies to file certain reports with the SEC electronically. These reports include an annual report on Form 10-K, quarterly reports on Form 10-Q, and current event reports on Form 8-K. Several of these reports include information beyond that reported in the quarterly or annual reports. For example, Lowe's 2006 10-K describes the significant business risks the company faces and outlines the strategies for addressing those risks. The 8-K reports significant business events that occurred between financial statement dates, such as the acquisition of another company or a change in auditor.

These filings are available to the public as soon as the SEC's Electronic Data Gathering and Retrieval Service (EDGAR) receives them. As a result, most users can get all the details of a company's financial results from the SEC filings several weeks before the company's glossy reports reach them in the mail. (To find a company's SEC filings, click on "Search for Company Filings" at www.sec.gov.)

## Investor Information Web Sites

Investor information Web sites such as Hoovers.com, TheStreet.com, Fool.com, and Yahoo!Finance offer information about public companies. Some sections of these Web sites provide useful information for evaluating and predicting a company's financial performance. For example, at Yahoo!Finance, you can obtain valuable financial information about Lowe's and its industry sector including financial ratios similar to those you will read about later in this chapter. It is important to note that many Web sites do not show the formulas used to calculate the ratios. That can be a serious drawback because ratios and amounts with similar-sounding names may be calculated differently.

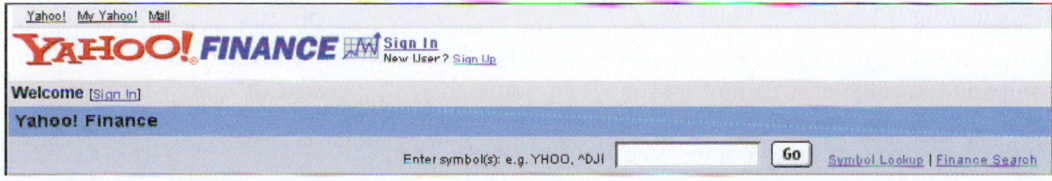

Most good stories have a plot, one the reader comes to understand as it unfolds over time. In the same way, the story of a business and its activities unfolds gradually. To understand and evaluate the results of business activities, then, you need to look at a company over time from many different angles. Only after you have combined the results of all your evaluations into a complete story will you understand whether or not a business is truly successful and why. The first financial analysis tool that we discuss is horizontal or trend analysis.

# HORIZONTAL (TREND) ANALYSIS

**Learning Objective 2**

Use horizontal (trend) analysis to recognize financial changes that unfold over time.

Horizontal (trend) analysis helps financial statement users to recognize financial changes that unfold over time. This approach compares individual financial statement items from year to year with the general goal of identifying significant sustained changes or trends. For example, trend analysis can be used to determine the dollar and percentage changes in the cost of goods sold this year relative to prior years. Because this type of analysis compares the results on each line of the financial statements across several years, trend analysis is also known as horizontal analysis. Because it compares results over a series of periods, it is sometimes called **time-series analysis.**

## Preparing Comparative Balance Sheets and Comparative Income Statements

Regardless of the name, trend analyses are usually calculated in terms of year-to-year dollar and percentage changes. A year-to-year percentage change expresses the current year's dollar change as a percentage of the prior year's total by using the following calculation:

$$\text{Year-to-Year Change (\%)} = \frac{\text{Change This Year}}{\text{Prior Year's Total}} \times 100 = \frac{(\text{Current Year's Total} - \text{Prior Year's Total})}{\text{Prior Year's Total}} \times 100$$

To demonstrate how to calculate a trend, we analyze Lowe's financial statements. Summaries of Lowe's balance sheets and income statements from three recent years appear in Exhibits 17.2 and 17.3. Dollar and percentage changes from fiscal year 2005 to 2006[1] are shown to the right of the balance sheet and income statement. The dollar changes were calculated by subtracting the 2005 balances from the 2006 balances. The percentage changes were calculated by dividing those differences by the 2005 balances. For example, according to Exhibit 17.2, Cash decreased by $59 = ($364 − $423) in 2006 relative to 2005 (all numbers in millions). That dollar amount represented a decrease of 13.9% [= ($59 ÷ $423) × 100]. To avoid focusing on unimportant changes, use the percentage changes to identify potentially significant changes and then check the dollar change to make sure that it too is significant.

## Revealing Changes through Trend Analyses

Data in Exhibits 17.2 and 17.3 indicate that Lowe's grew significantly in 2006 despite a slowdown in the housing market. Exhibit 17.2, for example, shows that total assets increased approximately 12.7 percent in 2006. Similarly, Exhibit 17.3 shows that net sales revenues, gross profit, and net income also rose in 2006 by 8.5, 9.5, and 12.3 percent, respectively.

The major drivers of these changes are explained in the Management's Discussion and Analysis (MD&A) section of the company's 2006 annual report. Lowe's opened 155 new stores in 2006 and was planning to open more than 400 additional stores in the future. Installed sales, which reflect a trend away from do-it-yourself projects and toward do-it-for-me projects, increased by 9 percent in 2006, outpacing the company's overall sales growth. Even more impressive was growth in sales to commercial businesses, which grew at nearly double the company's average growth rate and made up more than 25 percent of Lowe's total sales in 2006. To expand online sales, the company also continued to refine the functionality and product offerings on its corporate Web site.

---

[1] Like many retail companies, Lowe's fiscal year ends at the end of January.

**Exhibit 17.2** | Trend (Horizontal) Analysis of Lowe's Summarized Balance Sheets | Lowe's

Lowe's
Balance Sheets
(in millions)

| Year Ended: | Fiscal 2006 | Fiscal 2005 | INCREASE (DECREASE) Amount | Percent |
|---|---|---|---|---|
| **ASSETS** | | | | |
| Current assets | | | | |
| Cash | $ 364 | $ 423 | $ (59) | (13.9)% |
| Short-term investments | 432 | 453 | (21) | (4.6) |
| Accounts receivable | | | — | 0.0 |
| Inventories | 7,144 | 6,635 | 509 | 7.7 |
| Other current assets | 374 | 277 | 97 | 35.0 |
| Total current assets | 8,314 | 7,788 | 526 | 6.8 |
| Property and equipment, net | 18,971 | 16,354 | 2,617 | 16.0 |
| Long-term Investments and other assets | 482 | 497 | (15) | (3.0) |
| Total assets | $27,767 | $24,639 | $3,128 | 12.7 |
| | | | | |
| **LIABILITIES and STOCKHOLDERS' EQUITY** | | | | |
| Current liabilities | $ 6,539 | $ 5,832 | $ 707 | 12.1 |
| Long-term liabilities | 5,503 | 4,511 | 992 | 22.0 |
| Total liabilities | 12,042 | 10,343 | 1,699 | 16.4 |
| Stockholders' equity | 15,725 | 14,296 | 1,429 | 10.0 |
| Total liabilities and stockholders' equity | $27,767 | $24,639 | $3,128 | 12.7 |

**Exhibit 17.3** | Trend (Horizontal) Analysis of Lowe's Summarized Income Statements | Lowe's

Lowe's
Income Statements
(in millions)

| Year Ended: | Fiscal 2006 | Fiscal 2005 | INCREASE (DECREASE) Amount | Percent |
|---|---|---|---|---|
| Net sales revenue | $46,927 | $43,243 | $3,684 | 8.5% |
| Cost of revenues | 30,729 | 28,453 | 2,276 | 8.0 |
| Gross profit | 16,198 | 14,790 | 1,408 | 9.5 |
| Operating and other expenses | 11,046 | 10,136 | 910 | 9.0 |
| Interest expense | 154 | 158 | (4) | (2.5) |
| Income tax expense | 1,893 | 1,731 | 162 | 9.4 |
| Net income | $ 3,105 | $ 2,765 | $ 340 | 12.3 |
| Earnings per share | $ 2.02 | $ 1.78 | $ 0.24 | 13.5 |

In sum, the story told by our trend analysis is that Lowe's grew significantly from 2005 to 2006. While that growth increased sales and gross profit, it also increased operating expenses. Fortunately, the growth in sales more than offset the growth in expenses.

## VERTICAL (COMMON SIZE) ANALYSIS

A second type of analysis, **vertical (common size) analysis,** focuses on important relationships within financial statements. When a company is growing or shrinking overall, it is difficult to tell from the dollar amounts whether the proportions within each statement category are changing. Common size financial statements provide this information by expressing each financial statement amount as a percentage of another amount on that statement. The usefulness of common size statements is illustrated by the fact that Lowe's presents its balance sheet and income statements in the common size format illustrated in Exhibits 17.4 and 17.5.

**Exhibit 17.4**  Vertical (Common Size) Analysis of Lowe's Summarized Balance Sheets  Lowe's

**Lowe's**
**Balance Sheets**
**(in millions)**

| Year Ended | FISCAL 2006 | | FISCAL 2005 | |
|---|---|---|---|---|
| | Amount | Percent | Amount | Percent |
| **ASSETS** | | | | |
| Current assets | | | | |
| Cash | $ 364 | 1.3% | $ 423 | 1.7% |
| Short-term investments | 432 | 1.6 | 453 | 1.8 |
| Inventories | 7,144 | 25.7 | 6,635 | 26.9 |
| Other current assets | 374 | 1.3 | 277 | 1.1 |
| Property and equipment, net | 18,971 | 68.3 | 16,354 | 66.4 |
| Long-term investments and other assets | 482 | 1.7 | 497 | 2.0 |
| Total assets | $27,767 | 100.0% | $24,639 | 100.0% |
| **LIABILITIES and STOCKHOLDERS' EQUITY** | | | | |
| Current liabilities | $ 6,539 | 23.5% | $ 5,832 | 23.7% |
| Long-term liabilities | 5,503 | 19.8 | 4,511 | 18.3 |
| Stockholders' equity | 15,725 | 56.6 | 14,296 | 58.0 |
| Total liabilities and stockholders' equity | $27,767 | 100.0% | $24,639 | 100.0% |

**Exhibit 17.5**  Vertical (Common Size) Analysis of Lowe's Summarized Income Statements  Lowe's

**Lowe's**
**Income Statements**
**(in millions)**

| Year Ended | FISCAL 2006 | | FISCAL 2005 | |
|---|---|---|---|---|
| | Amount | Percent | Amount | Percent |
| Net sales revenue | $46,927 | 100.0% | $43,243 | 100.0% |
| Cost of revenues | 30,729 | 65.5 | 28,453 | 65.8 |
| Gross profit | 16,198 | 34.5 | 14,790 | 34.2 |
| Operating and other expenses | 11,046 | 23.5 | 10,136 | 23.4 |
| Interest expense | 154 | 0.3 | 158 | 0.4 |
| Income tax expense | 1,893 | 4.0 | 1,731 | 4.0 |
| Net income | $ 3,105 | 6.6% | $ 2,765 | 6.4% |

# Preparing a Common Size Balance Sheet and Income Statement

In a common size balance sheet, each asset appears as a percent of total assets, and each liability or stockholders' equity item appears as a percent of total liabilities and stockholders' equity. For example, in Exhibit 17.4, which presents Lowe's common size balance sheets, cash was 1.3% of total assets [= ($364 ÷ $27,767) × 100] at the end of fiscal 2006.

The common size income statement reports each income statement item as a percentage of sales. For example, cost of revenues was equal to 65.5 percent of net sales revenue in 2006 [= ($30,729 ÷ $46,927) × 100]. Exhibit 17.5 presents common size income statements for Lowe's for 2005 and 2006.

# Interpreting Common Size Statements

Although Lowe's balance sheet indicates growth during 2006, the common size balance sheet suggests that the increase on the assets side reflected relative increases in property and equipment resulting from the opening of new stores combined with relative declines in most other assets as a percentage of total assets. The decline in inventory reflects both lower costs of certain materials sold by Lowe's and the expected slowdown in the housing market in 2007. These increases in assets were financed more by increases in long-term liabilities than by current liabilities or stockholders' equity as evidenced by the increase in the long-term liabilities percentage.

The common size income statements tell us how Lowe's was able to increase its net income as a percent of sales from 6.4 percent to 6.6 percent. Lowe's accomplished this feat by reducing cost of goods sold as a percent of sales by 0.3 percent, which was partially offset by small increases in operating and other expenses. In its MD&A, Lowe's explains the improvement as resulting from a shift in sales mix to more profitable products and a switch to lower cost foreign-made products. A 0.3 percent decrease in cost of goods sold as a percent of sales may seem to be a small effect at first. But this improvement accounted for $141 million of Lowe's net income for 2006.

These findings from the vertical (common size) analysis are consistent with the results of the horizontal (trend) analysis discussed earlier. Opening 155 new stores involves a significant additional investment in property and equipment and start-up efforts at the new stores tend to add to other operating expenses.

**SELF-STUDY PRACTICE**

For the year ended January 28, 2007, The Home Depot reported net income of $5.76 billion on sales of $90.8 billion. If the company's cost of sales in fiscal 2006 was $61.1 billion, what percentages would be shown on a common size income statement for gross profit and net income? If sales were $81.5 billion in 2005, what was the year-to-year percentage increase in 2006? Round your answers to one decimal place.

$$\text{Gross Profit Percentage} = \frac{(\$\underline{\quad} - \underline{\quad}) \text{ billion}}{\$90.8 \text{ billion}} \times 100$$

$$\text{Net Profit Margin} = \frac{\$5.76 \text{ billion}}{\$\underline{\quad}} \times 100$$

$$\text{Sales Increase (Percentage)} = \frac{(\$\underline{\quad} - \underline{\quad}) \text{ billion}}{\$\underline{\quad} \text{ billion}} \times 100$$

*After you have finished, check your answers with the solution at the bottom of the page.*

Solution to Self-Study Practice

Gross profit percentage = [($90.8 − $61.1) ÷ 90.8] × 100
= 32.7%
Net profit margin = [$(5.76) ÷ 90.8] × 100 = 6.3%
Sales increase (percentage) = [($90.8 − $81.5) ÷ 81.5] ÷ 100
= 11.4%

# FINANCIAL RATIOS

**Ratio analyses** help financial statement users to understand relationships among various items reported in the financial statements. This type of analysis compares the amounts for one or more line items to the amounts for other line items in the same year. Like common size statements, ratio analyses are useful because they consider differences in the size of the amounts being compared, which allows users to evaluate how well a company has performed given the level of its other resources. In fact, some of the most popular ratios, such as net profit margin and debt to assets ratios, are taken directly from the common size statements.

Most analysts classify ratios into three categories:

1. **Profitability** ratios, which relate to the company's performance in the current period—in particular, the company's ability to generate income.
2. **Liquidity** ratios, which relate to the company's short-term survival—in particular, the company's ability to use current assets to repay liabilities as they become due.
3. **Solvency** ratios, which relate to the company's long-run survival—in particular, the company's ability to repay lenders when debt matures and to make the required interest payments prior to the date of maturity.

These three categories emphasize different aspects of a company's performance, which may or may not be important depending on the purpose of the analysis.

In the next section, we demonstrate how to calculate financial trends and ratios. We must emphasize at the start, however, that **no analysis is complete unless it leads to an interpretation that helps financial statement users to understand and evaluate a company's financial results.** Without interpretation, trends and ratios are nothing more than a list of apparently unrelated numbers. See Exhibit 17.6 for a summary of the most commonly used ratios, many of which were introduced in Chapters 4–16, categorized as profitability, liquidity, or solvency ratios.

As you have seen in other chapters, benchmarks help to interpret a company's ratios. Benchmarks can include the company's prior year results and those of close competitors, as well as industry averages. In a competitive economy, companies strive to outperform one another, so comparisons with other companies can suggest which are likely to survive and thrive in the long run.

For Lowe's, the industry average encompasses home improvement stores of all sizes and types. The Home Depot, the largest home improvement retailer in the world, is Lowe's closest competitor, with 2,147 stores located in the United States, Canada, China, and Mexico. (Both Lowe's and The Home Depot's annual reports for fiscal 2007 are reproduced in Appendix A and B at the end of this book.) Lowe's is the second largest company in the industry. Its customer-oriented marketing strategy focuses on attracting women. The Home Depot's marketing strategy focuses on contractors and other experienced builders as well as homeowners with a do-it-yourself attitude. In the following sections, we compare Lowe's financial ratios to the prior year and in some cases to those for The Home Depot and the industry as a whole.

## Profitability Ratios

The financial analyses in this section focus on the level of profits Lowe's generated during the period. We will compute and interpret ratios (1) through (8) in Exhibit 17.6. The computation shown for each ratio is for 2006 and is based on the statements in Exhibits 17.4 and 17.5. Our first two profitability ratios come right from the common size income statement in Exhibit 17.5.

### Net Profit Margin

Net profit margin indicates the percentage of sales revenues that remain in net income after expenses have been deducted. Using the equation in Exhibit 17.6, Lowe's net profit margin in each of the last two years was:

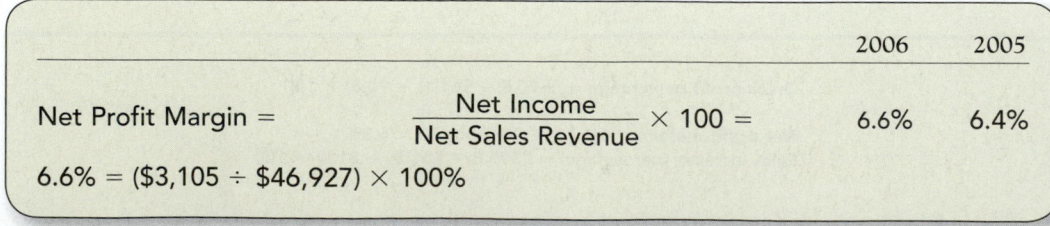

|  | | 2006 | 2005 |
|---|---|---|---|
| Net Profit Margin = | $\dfrac{\text{Net Income}}{\text{Net Sales Revenue}} \times 100 =$ | 6.6% | 6.4% |

$6.6\% = (\$3,105 \div \$46,927) \times 100\%$

## Exhibit 17.6  Common Ratios Used in Financial Statement Analysis

### Profitability Ratios

(1)  Net Profit Margin  $= \dfrac{\text{Net Income}}{\text{Net Sales Revenue}} \times 100$

(2)  Gross Profit Percentage  $= \dfrac{\text{Net Sales Revenue} - \text{Cost of Goods Sold}}{\text{Net Sales Revenue}} \times 100$

(3)  Asset Turnover  $= \dfrac{\text{Net Sales Revenue}}{\text{Average Total Assets}}$

(4)  Fixed Asset Turnover  $= \dfrac{\text{Net Sales Revenue}}{\text{Average Net Fixed Assets}}$

(5)  Return on Assets (ROA)  $= \dfrac{\text{Net Income*}}{\text{Average Total Assets}} \times 100$

(6)  Return on Equity (ROE)  $= \dfrac{\text{Net Income}}{\text{Average Stockholders' Equity}} \times 100$

(7)  Earnings per Share (EPS)  $= \dfrac{\text{Net Income} - \text{Preferred Dividends}}{\text{Average Number of Common Shares Outstanding}}$

(8)  Price/Earnings  $= \dfrac{\text{Stock Price}}{\text{EPS}}$

### Liquidity Ratios

(9)  Receivables Turnover  $= \dfrac{\text{Net Sales Revenue}}{\text{Average Net Receivables}}$

    Days to Collect  $= \dfrac{365}{\text{Receivables Turnover Ratio}}$

(10)  Inventory Turnover  $= \dfrac{\text{Cost of Goods Sold}}{\text{Average Inventory}}$

    Days to Sell  $= \dfrac{365}{\text{Inventory Turnover Ratio}}$

(11)  Current Ratio  $= \dfrac{\text{Current Assets}}{\text{Current Liabilities}}$

(12)  Quick Ratio  $= \dfrac{\text{Quick Assets}}{\text{Current Liabilities}}$

### Solvency Ratios

(13)  Debt to Assets  $= \dfrac{\text{Total Liabilities}}{\text{Total Assets}}$

(14)  Times Interest Earned  $= \dfrac{\text{Net Income} + \text{Interest Expense} + \text{Income Tax Expense}}{\text{Interest Expense}}$

(15)  Free Cash Flow  $=$ Net Cash Flow from Operating Activities $-$ Purchases of Property and Equipment $-$ Dividends Paid

\* In more complex ROA analyses, interest expense (net of tax) and minority interest are added back to net income in the numerator because the ratio assesses return on capital independent of source.

The net profit margin of 6.6 percent for 2006 indicates that for each dollar of sales, Lowe's generated 6.6 cents of net income. That is quite good compared to the average home improvement retailer, which according to Yahoo!Finance enjoyed a net profit margin of 5.9 percent that year. The seemingly small increase from 6.4 percent in 2005 to 6.6 percent in 2006 was significant, yielding an additional $94 million in profit on the company's $47 billion in sales.

## Gross Profit Percentage

Our earlier analysis indicated that Lowe's gross profits from 2005 to 2006 increased in terms of total dollars, but it did not indicate whether those increases were caused by more total sales or more profit per sale. The gross profit percentage is particularly helpful in this kind of analysis because it indicates how much profit was made, on average, on each dollar of sales after deducting the cost of goods sold. Lowe's gross profit percentage for the last two years was:

$$\text{Gross Profit Percentage} = \frac{\text{Net Sales} - \text{Cost of Goods Sold}}{\text{Net Sales}} \times 100 = \begin{array}{cc} 2006 & 2005 \\ 34.5\% & 34.2\% \end{array}$$

$$34.5\% = [(\$46,927 - \$30,729) \div \$46,927] \times 100$$

This analysis shows that in 2006, after payment of the cost of merchandise sold, 34.5 cents of each sales dollar were left to cover other costs, such as employee wages, advertising, and utilities and to provide profits to the stockholders. The increase in the gross profit percentage from 2005 to 2006 (34.5% − 34.2%) means that Lowe's made 0.3¢ more gross profit on each dollar of sales in 2006 than in 2005. There are two potential explanations for this increase: (1) Lowe's charged higher selling prices without paying a corresponding increase in the cost of merchandise and (2) Lowe's obtained merchandise at a lower unit cost. The MD&A section of Lowe's annual report explains that the increase in gross profit percentage came from a reduction in the cost of merchandise, primarily because of an increase in the proportion of imported goods.

## Asset Turnover

The asset turnover ratio indicates the amount of sales revenue generated for each dollar invested in assets. Lowe's ratios for the two years were:

$$\text{Asset Turnover} = \frac{\text{Net Sales Revenue}}{\text{Average Total Assets}} = \begin{array}{cc} 2006 & 2005 \\ 1.8 & 1.9 \end{array}$$

$$1.79 = \$46,927 \div [(\$27,767 + \$24,639) \div 2]$$

The asset turnover ratio suggests that Lowe's assets did not generate sales as efficiently in 2006 as in the prior year. To understand why, it is helpful to focus on the key assets used to generate sales. For a retailer such as Lowe's, the key asset is store properties, which we can compare to sales using the fixed asset turnover ratio, discussed next.

## Fixed Asset Turnover

The fixed asset turnover ratio indicates how much revenue the company generates in sales for each dollar invested in fixed assets, such as store buildings and the property they sit on. Lowe's fixed asset turnover ratios for the two years were:

$$\text{Fixed Asset Turnover} = \frac{\text{Net Sales Revenue}}{\text{Average Net Fixed Assets}} = \begin{array}{cc} 2006 & 2005 \\ 2.7 & 2.9 \end{array}$$

$$2.7 = \$46,927 \div [(\$18,971 + \$16,354) \div 2]$$

This analysis shows that Lowe's had $2.66 of sales in 2006 for each dollar invested in fixed assets. Although the decline from 2005 was not good, it is understandable because Lowe's added 155 stores during these two years. Those stores will likely need some time to establish a strong customer base and begin generating sales at full capacity. Moreover, as additional stores are opened, they are likely to be located in areas of greater competition. Still, Lowe's fixed asset turnover ratio is low compared to that of its main competitor, The Home Depot, whose fixed asset turnover ratio was 3.53 in 2006. In terms of using fixed assets to generate sales revenue, The Home Depot has a competitive advantage over Lowe's. In other words, Lowe's is operating less efficiently than its major competitor.

## Return on Assets (ROA)

The return on assets ratio compares the amount of net income to average total assets. ROA measures how much the firm earned for each dollar of investment. It is the broadest measure of profitability and management effectiveness, independent of financing strategy. ROA allows investors to compare management's investment performance against alternative investment options. Firms with higher ROA are doing a better job of selecting new investments, all other things equal. Company managers often compute the measure on a division-by-division basis and use it to evaluate division managers' relative performance.[2]

|  |  | 2006 | 2005 |
|---|---|---|---|
| Return on Assets (ROA) = $\frac{\text{Net Income}}{\text{Average Total Assets}} \times 100 =$ | | 11.8% | 12.1% |

$$11.8\% = (\$3,105 \div [(\$27,767 + \$24,639) \div 2]) \times 100$$

Even though Lowe's net income increased in 2006, its ROA fell slightly because of the increase in assets during the period. Net profit margin and total asset turnover affect return on assets in the following fashion:

$$\text{ROA} = \text{Net Profit Margin} \times \text{Asset Turnover}$$
$$11.8\% = 6.6\% \times 1.79$$

The decline resulted from the decline in total asset turnover discussed earlier, which was partially offset by the increase in net profit margin.

## Return on Equity (ROE)

The return on equity ratio compares the amount of net income to average stockholders' equity. ROE reports the net amount earned during the period as a percentage of each dollar contributed by stockholders and retained in the business. Lowe's ROE ratios for the past two years were:

|  |  | 2006 | 2005 |
|---|---|---|---|
| Return on Equity (ROE) = $\frac{\text{Net Income}}{\text{Average Stockholders' Equity}} \times 100 =$ | | 20.7% | 21.4% |

$$20.7\% = (\$3,105 \div [(\$15,725 + \$14,296) \div 2]) \times 100$$

Lowe's ROE fell to 20.7 percent because average stockholders' equity increased. Lowe's ROE was close to the industry average of 20.0 percent in 2006, but it lagged behind The Home Depot's, which was 22.2 percent. Lowe's ROE is higher than its ROA because it is earning a higher return on its borrowed funds than it is paying to creditors for interest.

[2] In more complex ROA analyses, interest expense (net of tax) and minority interest are added back to net income in the numerator because the ratio assesses return on capital independent of source.

## Earnings Per Share (EPS)

Earnings per share (EPS) indicates the amount of earnings generated for each share of outstanding common stock. It is reported on the income statement. Lowe's reported average shares outstanding of 1,535 and 1,555 in 2006 and 2005, respectively. It has no preferred dividends. Despite the decline in Lowe's ROE, its EPS ratio increased in 2006 because the company repurchased some of its shares (which reduced the number of common shares outstanding). Lowe's EPS for the past two years was:

|  |  | 2006 | 2005 |
|---|---|---|---|
| Earnings per Share (EPS) = | $\dfrac{\text{Net Income} - \text{Preferred Dividends}}{\text{Average Number of Common Shares}}$ = | $2.02 | $1.78 |

$2.02 = $3,105 ÷ 1,535

## Price/Earnings (P/E) Ratio

The P/E ratio relates the company's stock price to its EPS, as follows:

|  |  | 2006 | 2005 |
|---|---|---|---|
| Price/earnings = | $\dfrac{\text{Stock Price}}{\text{EPS}}$ = | 15.3 | 16.3 |

15.3 = $31 ÷ $2.02

Using the going price for Lowe's stock when its 2006 earnings were announced, its P/E ratio was 15.3, meaning that investors were willing to pay 15.3 times its earnings per share to buy a share of stock. According to Yahoo! Finance, the average P/E ratio for home improvement stores at that time was about 14.8, suggesting that investors were more willing to buy stock in Lowe's than in other home improvement retailers.

Let's pause to summarize what we have learned so far. Despite a slowdown in the housing market, Lowe's increased its profit margin in 2006. Management did so primarily by (1) reducing merchandise costs by importing more merchandise and (2) growing sales by opening new stores, increasing sales to commercial builders, and placing more emphasis on online sales. These increases in gross profit were partly eaten up by operating expenses, which grew at a rate of 9 percent. Despite a decline in ROE during 2006, the company's EPS ratio increased as a result of share repurchases. Asset turnover and fixed asset turnover both declined, meaning that the company was not using its assets to generate sales as efficiently as in the past. Lowe's P/E ratio, which was slightly higher than the industry average, suggests that investors were willing to overlook those declines and were more willing to buy stock in Lowe's than in other home improvement retailers. The bottom line is that Lowe's has fared reasonably well during the housing slump, although the company currently trails its main competitor, The Home Depot, on a number of key ratios.

# Liquidity Ratios

The analyses in this section focus on Lowe's ability to survive in the short term by converting its assets to cash to pay current liabilities as they come due. We interpret ratios (9) through (12) from Exhibit 17.6.

## Receivables Turnover

Most home improvement retailers have low levels of accounts receivable relative to sales revenue because they collect the majority of their sales immediately in cash. Lowe's sells its small amounts of accounts receivable to a bank. Although the formula for this ratio calls for net **credit** sales in the numerator, companies rarely report their credit sales and cash sales separately. Consequently, financial statement users must use total sales revenue in the numerator, which results in a receivables turnover ratio that is not terribly meaningful for businesses that make few sales on account. This ratio is presented in Exhibit 17.6 simply to remind you of how it is calculated.

## Inventory Turnover

The inventory turnover ratio indicates how many times inventory is bought and sold during the year. The ratio "days to sell" converts inventory turnover into the number of days needed to sell each purchase of inventory.

|  |  |  | 2006 | 2005 |
|---|---|---|---|---|
| Inventory Turnover = | $\dfrac{\text{Cost of Goods Sold}}{\text{Average Inventory}}$ = | | 4.5 | 4.5 |

$4.5 = \$30,729 \div [(\$7,144 + \$6,635) \div 2]$

|  |  |  | 2006 | 2005 |
|---|---|---|---|---|
| Days to sell = | $\dfrac{365}{\text{Inventory Turnover Ratio}}$ = | | 81.1 | 81.1 |

$81.1 \text{ days} = 365 \div 4.5$

The inventory turnover ratio is critical to Lowe's because the company wants to offer customers the right product when they need it at a price that beats the competition. Historically, The Home Depot has enjoyed a significant advantage over Lowe's in terms of inventory management. However, in recent years, Lowe's has been able to close the gap. In 2006, The Home Depot had an inventory turnover ratio of 5.04—only slightly better than Lowe's ratio of 4.5.

Turnover ratios vary significantly from one industry to the next. Companies in the food industry (restaurants and grocery stores) have high inventory turnover ratios because their inventory is subject to spoilage. Companies that sell expensive merchandise (automobiles and high-fashion clothes) have much lower ratios because sales of those items are infrequent, but customers want to have a wide selection to choose from when they do buy.

## Current Ratio

The current ratio compares current assets to current liabilities, as follows:

|  |  |  | 2006 | 2005 |
|---|---|---|---|---|
| Current Ratio = | $\dfrac{\text{Current Assets}}{\text{Current Liabilities}}$ = | | 1.27 | 1.34 |

$1.27 = \$8,314 \div \$6,539$

This ratio measures the company's ability to pay its current liabilities. The slight drop in Lowe's current ratio from 2005 to 2006 probably is not something to be concerned about so long as the decline does not continue. The 2006 current ratio of 1.27 indicates that the company's current assets were 127 percent of its current liabilities. Most analysts would judge that ratio to be very strong, especially considering Lowe's ability to generate cash. In this industry, a current ratio of more than 1.0 is considered to be acceptable.

## Quick Ratio

The quick ratio compares the sum of cash, accounts receivable, and short-term investments to current liabilities as follows:

|  | | 2006 | 2005 |
|---|---|---|---|
| Quick Ratio = $\dfrac{\text{Quick Assets}}{\text{Current Liabilities}}$ = | | 0.12 | 0.15 |
| 0.12 = ($364 + $432) ÷ $6,539 | | | |

The quick ratio is a more stringent test of short-term liquidity than is the current ratio. The quick ratio compares quick assets, defined as cash and near-cash assets, to current liabilities. Quick assets include cash, short-term investments, and accounts receivable (net of the allowance for doubtful accounts). Inventory is omitted from quick assets because of the uncertainty of the timing of cash flows from its sale. Prepaid expenses are also excluded from quick assets.

# Solvency Ratios

The analyses in this section focus on Lowe's ability to survive over the long term—that is, its ability to repay debt when it matures, pay interest until that time, and finance the replacement and/or expansion of long-term assets. We interpret ratios (13) through (15) from Exhibit 17.6.

## Debt to Assets

The debt-to-assets ratio indicates the proportion of total assets that creditors finance. Remember that creditors must be paid regardless of how difficult a year the company may have had. The higher this ratio, the riskier is the company's financing strategy. Lowe's ratio for the two years was:

|  | | 2006 | 2005 |
|---|---|---|---|
| Debt to Assets = $\dfrac{\text{Total Liabilities}}{\text{Total Assets}}$ = | | 0.43 | 0.42 |
| 0.43 = $12,042 ÷ $27,767 | | | |

> **Coach's Tip**
>
> Instead of the debt-to-assets ratio, analysts might use the **debt-to-equity ratio,** which gives the same basic information as debt to assets. The debt-to-equity ratio is typically calculated as Total Liabilities ÷ Total Stockholders' Equity. As with debt to assets, the higher the debt-to-equity ratio, the more the company relies on debt (rather than equity) financing.

Lowe's ratio of 0.43 in 2006 indicates that creditors contributed 43 percent of the company's financing, implying that stockholders' equity was the company's main source of financing at 57 percent. This ratio did not change significantly from 2005 to 2006. Lowe's currently relies less on debt financing than The Home Depot, which had a debt-to-assets ratio of 52 percent in 2006.

## Times Interest Earned

The times interest earned ratio indicates how many times the company's interest expense was covered by its operating results. This ratio is calculated using accrual-based interest expense and net income before interest and income taxes, as follows:

> **Coach's Tip**
>
> If a company reports a net loss instead of net income, you should include the loss in the formula as a negative number. A negative ratio indicates that the company's operating results (before the costs of financing and taxes) do not cover its interest costs.

|  | | 2006 | 2005 |
|---|---|---|---|
| Times Interest Earned = $\dfrac{\text{Net Income + Interest Expense + Income Tax Expense}}{\text{Interest Expense}}$ = | | 33.5 | 29.5 |
| 33.5 = ($3,105 + $154 + $1,893) ÷ $154 | | | |

A times interest earned ratio higher than 1.0 indicates that net income (before the costs of financing and taxes have been deducted) is sufficient to cover the company's interest expense. Lowe's ratio of 33.5 indicates that the company is generating more than enough profit to cover its interest expense.

## Free Cash Flow

Free cash flow measures a company's ability to make capital investments and pay dividends from its operating cash flows. Lowe's free cash flow for the two years was:

|  |  | 2006 | 2005 |
|---|---|---|---|
| Free Cash Flow = | Net Cash Flow from Operating Activities <br> −Purchases of Property and Equipment = <br> −Dividends Paid | $366 | $323 |

$366 = $4,502 − $3,860 − $276

The amounts in the computation come from the cash flow statement, which is not shown in this chapter. The positive free cash flow in the two years (in millions) indicates that Lowe's is a healthy company with enough cash flow from operations to purchase property, plant, and equipment and pay dividends to stockholders.

In sum, these solvency ratios suggest that Lowe's has grown significantly and has financed its growth through both operating cash flows and debt financing. Lowe's reliance on debt financing has remained relatively steady, and the company is in an excellent position to cover the interest expense associated with its debt. Overall, analysts would consider Lowe's to have a low-risk profile, one that bodes well for the company's long-term survival.

**SELF-STUDY PRACTICE**

**Lowe's**

1. Show the computations for the following two ratios for Lowe's for 2005. Use the information in Exhibits 17.2 and 17.3 (all numbers are in millions).

   a. Gross profit percentage ratio.
   b. Current ratio.

2. Assume that in 2006, Lowe's recorded a $25 (in millions) expiration of prepaid expenses. Complete the following table by showing its impact (+, −, or no change) on selected measures of profitability, and liquidity.

   **Impact of Prepaid Expense Expiration**

   a. Net profit margin ratio.
   b. Current ratio.

*After you have finished, check your answers with the solution at the bottom of the page.*

Solution to
Self-Study Practice

1.

$$\frac{\text{Net Sales Revenue} - \text{Cost of Goods Sold}}{\text{Net Sales Revenue}} = \frac{\$43,243 - \$28,453}{\$43,243} \times 100 = 34.2\%$$

$$\frac{\text{Current Assets}}{\text{Current Liabilities}} = \frac{\$7,788}{\$5,832} = 1.34$$

2. The expiration of prepaid expenses would decrease prepaid expenses on the balance sheet and increase expenses on the income statement. The effects on the ratios are:

   a. "−" net income, the numerator of the ratio, decreases when expenses increase, so the ratio decreases
   b. "−" current assets, the numerator of the ratio, decreases when prepaid expenses decreases, so the ratio decreases

| Exhibit 17.7 | Comparison of Accounting Methods Used by Three Home Improvement Retailers |
|---|---|

| | Lowe's | The Home Depot | Builder's FirstSource |
|---|---|---|---|
| **Inventory** | FIFO | FIFO | Weighted Average Cost |
| **Depreciation** | **Straight line**<br>Buildings: 10–40 yrs<br>Equipment: 3–15 yrs | **Straight line**<br>Buildings: 10–45 yrs<br>Equipment: 3–20 yrs | **Straight line**<br>Buildings: 20–40 yrs<br>Equipment: 3–10 yrs |

## Accounting Decisions and Ratio Analysis

In the analyses just presented, we compared Lowe's results with those of The Home Depot. When appropriate, we discussed how differences in the two companies' strategies (for example, relying on debt versus equity financing) and business operations (for example, targeting do-it-yourselfers versus professionals) affected their financial ratios. We should also consider whether differences between the two companies' financial ratios might be caused by differences in their accounting decisions.

Information about a company's accounting decisions is presented in a note to the financial statements. Data in Exhibit 17.7 compare the policies that three home improvement retailers follow in accounting for inventory and depreciation—two line items that can have a noticeable impact on a retailer's results. Take a moment to study the exhibit.

As you can see, the three companies follow similar but not identical policies. Lowe's and The Home Depot use the FIFO method of accounting for ending inventory and the cost of goods sold; Builder's FirstSource uses the weighted average method. Although these two methods result in different numbers, the overall impact on the companies' financial ratios should be minor.

All three companies calculate depreciation using the straight-line method with a similar range of estimated useful lives for buildings and equipment. Because buildings and equipment make up such a large portion of each company's assets, these similarities go a long way toward making their financial results comparable. In conclusion, although the companies' accounting policies have some differences, they are unlikely to have a major impact on our comparisons.

## Spotlight On FINANCIAL REPORTING

### International Differences in Accounting Standards

Cross-national differences in accounting standards also create differences in the accounting methods different companies use. Many countries, including the members of the European Union, are committed to adopting the international financial reporting standards (IFRS) issued by the International Accounting Standards Board (IASB). Although IFRS are similar to GAAP, several important differences exist. Two of the differences relate to inventory accounting.

| Difference | U.S. GAAP | IFRS |
|---|---|---|
| Last-in, first-out method for inventory | Permitted | Prohibited |
| Reversal of inventory write-downs | Prohibited | Required |

These differences would make it difficult to compare a U.S. automaker such as Ford that follows U.S. GAAP with a European competitor such as BMW that follows IFRS.

Source: *Deloitte IAS Plus*, February 2007.

# Demonstration Case

The following information was taken from The Home Depot's recent annual report.

| (in millions of dollars) | Year ended January 28, 2007 | |
|---|---|---|
| Net sales revenue | $90,837 | |
| Cost of goods sold | 61,054 | |
| Net income | 5,761 | |
| | **January 28, 2007** | **January 29, 2006** |
| Inventory | $12,822 | $11,401 |
| Current assets | 18,000 | 15,269 |
| Net property and equipment | 26,605 | 24,901 |
| Total assets | 52,263 | 44,405 |
| Current liabilities | 12,931 | 12,706 |
| Total liabilities | 27,233 | 17,496 |

*Required:*

1. Compute the following ratios for The Home Depot for the year ended January 28, 2007.

   Fixed Asset Turnover
   Return on Equity
   Days to Sell
   Current Ratio
   Debt to Assets

2. Interpret the meaning of the ratios you calculated in requirement 1.

## Suggested Solution

1. Calculating ratios:

**Fixed Asset Turnover**
= Net Sales Revenue/Average Net Fixed Assets
= $90,837 ÷ [(26,605 + 24,901) ÷ 2]
= 3.53

**Return on Equity**
= Net Income/Average Stockholders' Equity
= $5,761 ÷ [(25,030 + 26,909) ÷ 2]
= 0.2218, or 22.2%

**Days to Sell**
= 365 ÷ Inventory Turnover Ratio
= 365 ÷ (Cost of Goods Sold/Average Inventory)
= 365 ÷ [61,054 ÷ [(12,822 + 11,401) ÷ 2]]
= 72

**Current Ratio**
= Current Assets/Current Liabilities
= $18,000 ÷ 12,931
= 1.39

**Debt to Assets**
= Total Liabilities/Total Assets
= $27,233 ÷ 52,263
= 0.52

2. Interpreting ratios

- The fixed asset turnover ratio of 3.53 means that on average, The Home Depot generated $3.53 of sales for each dollar of fixed assets.
- The return on equity of 22.2 percent means that The Home Depot's net income for the year was 22.2 percent of the amount investors contributed to and left in the company.
- The days to sell ratio of 72 means that on average, 72 days elapsed between the time The Home Depot acquired the inventory and the time the company sold it.

- The current ratio of 1.39 means that at year-end, The Home Depot had $1.39 of current assets for each dollar of current liabilities.
- The debt-to-assets ratio of 0.52 means that The Home Depot relied on short-term and long-term debt to finance 52 percent of its assets, implying that stockholders' equity financed 48 percent (=100 − 52) of its total assets.

# Supplement 17A
## Nonrecurring and Other Special Items

Until 2005, three different types of nonrecurring item were reported in income statements: discontinued operations, extraordinary items, and the cumulative effects of changes in accounting methods. Recently, however, **new accounting standards have nearly eliminated reporting of extraordinary items and the cumulative effects of changes in accounting methods.** In fact, the definition of the term **extraordinary** has become so restricted that few events—not even losses that arose from the terrorist attacks of September 11, 2001—now qualify as extraordinary. The cumulative effects of changes in accounting methods are reported as adjustments to retained earnings rather than as part of the income statement in the period when the change is made. That leaves only one remaining nonrecurring item, discontinued operations.

Discontinued operations result from the abandonment or sale of a major business component. The discontinued operations line on the income statement includes any gain or loss on the disposal of the discontinued operation as well as any operating income generated before its disposal. Because gains or losses from discontinued operations appear below the income tax expense line on the income statement, any additional tax effects related to those gains or losses are included in the reported amounts. Obviously, the sale of a particular business unit can happen only once, so these results are reported separately to inform users that they will not affect the company's future results. Exhibit 17A.1 shows how Newell Rubbermaid reported discontinued operations in 2005 and 2006 when the company divested its Little Tikes division and its Home Décor Europe and European Cookware operations.

In some cases, additional items may appear after the net income (loss) line on the income statement. Those items may be added to or subtracted from net income to arrive at the amount of **comprehensive income.** As you can learn in detail in intermediate financial accounting courses, those items represent gains or losses related to changes in the value of certain balance sheet accounts. While most gains and losses are included in the computation of net income, some (those related to changes in foreign currency exchange rates and the value of certain investments, for example) are excluded from net income and included only in comprehensive income. The main reason for excluding these gains and losses from net income is that the changes in value that created them may well disappear before the gains or losses are

**Exhibit 17A.1**    **Reporting of Nonrecurring Items on the Income Statement**    Newell Rubbermaid

### Newell Rubbermaid
### Condensed Income Statements
### December 31,
### (in millions)

|  | 2006 | 2005 |
|---|---|---|
| **Net sales** | $6,201.0 | $5,717.2 |
| Cost of products sold | 4,131.0 | 3,959.1 |
| Selling, general, and administrative expenses | 1,347.0 | 1,117.7 |
| Impairment charges and restructuring costs | 66.4 | 73.0 |
| **Operating income (loss)** | 656.6 | 567.4 |
| Interest and other expenses, net | 141.7 | 104.0 |
| **Income (loss) before income taxes** | 514.9 | 463.4 |
| Income tax expense (benefit) | 44.2 | 57.1 |
| **Net income (loss) from continuing operations** | 470.7 | 406.3 |
| Gain (loss) on sale of discontinued operations, net of income taxes | (85.7) | (155.0) |
| **Net income (loss)** | $ 385.0 | $ 251.3 |

ever realized (when the company sells the related assets or liabilities). For this reason, most analysts will take a moment to consider the size of these special items in relation to net income. If the amount is not large, they will exclude the items in calculating profitability ratios.[3]

## Chapter Summary

**LO1  Describe how financial statement information is communicated to external users. p. 730**

- The issuance of quarterly and annual reports is preceded by press releases containing preliminary results.
- Publicly owned companies file with the Securities and Exchange Commission more detailed information on Forms 10-Q, 10K, and 8-K, which are available first on the Web.

**LO2  Use horizontal (trend) analysis to recognize financial changes that unfold over time. p. 732**

- Horizontal analysis (also called trend analysis) compares financial statement items to comparable amounts in prior periods with the goal of identifying sustained changes, or trends.
- Trend analysis involves computing the dollar amount by which each account changes from one period to the next and expressing that change as a percentage of the balance for the prior period.

**LO3  Use vertical (common size) analysis to understand important relationships within financial statements. p. 734**

- Common size financial statements express each line of the income statement (or balance sheet) as a percentage of total sales (or total assets).
- The statements tell the reader whether the proportions within each statement category are changing.

**LO4  Calculate and use financial ratios to assess profitability, liquidity, and solvency. p. 736**

- Financial ratios are commonly classified with relation to profitability, liquidity, or solvency. Exhibit 17.6 lists common ratios in these three categories and shows how to compute them.
- Profitability ratios focus on measuring the adequacy of a company's income by comparing it to other items reported on the financial statements.
- Liquidity ratios measure a company's ability to meet its current debt obligations.
- Solvency ratios measure a company's ability to meet its long-term debt obligations.
- In comparing trends and ratios over time and across companies, watch for possible differences in accounting policies and nonrecurring events that could affect reported financial results.

## Key Terms

Horizontal (Trend) Analysis (p. 732)     Profitability (p. 736)     Vertical (Common Size)
Liquidity (p. 736)                       Solvency (p. 736)          Analysis (p. 734)

**See complete glossary in back of text.**

## Questions

1. What are the major categories of information in the annual report financial section?
2. What is the general goal of trend analysis?
3. How is a year-to-year percentage change calculated?
4. What is ratio analysis? Why is it useful?
5. What benchmarks are commonly used for interpreting ratios?
6. Into what three categories of performance are most financial ratios classified? To what in particular does each of these categories relate?
7. (Supplement 17A) Name the most commonly reported nonrecurring item, and explain where and how it is reported on the income statement.

## Multiple Choice

1. Which of the following ratios is not used to analyze profitability?
   a. Fixed asset turnover ratio.
   b. Gross profit percentage.
   c. Current ratio.
   d. Return on equity.

   Quiz 17-1
   www.mhhe.com/LLPW1e

2. Which of the following would not directly change the receivables turnover ratio for your company?
   a. Increases in the selling prices of your inventory.
   b. A change in your credit policy.
   c. Increases in the cost you incur to purchase inventory.
   d. None of the above.

---

[3] Instead of showing the computation of comprehensive income on the face of the income statement, companies are allowed to show it in either a statement of stockholders' equity or a separate statement of comprehensive income. One survey indicates that about 70 percent of companies show the computation in a statement of stockholders' equity. See American Institute of Public Accountants (New York: AICPA, 2006). *Accounting Trends & Techniques*.

3. Which of the following ratios is used to analyze liquidity?
   a. Earnings per share.
   b. Debt to assets.
   c. Current ratio.
   d. Both debt to assets and current ratio.

4. Analysts use ratios to
   a. Compare different companies in the same industry.
   b. Track a company's performance over time.
   c. Compare a company's performance to industry averages.
   d. All of the above.

5. Which of the following incorporates cash flows from operations?
   a. Inventory turnover.          c. Free cash flow.
   b. Earnings per share.          d. All of the above.

6. Given the following ratios for four companies, which company is least likely to experience problems paying its current liabilities promptly?

|     | Current Ratio | Receivables Turnover Ratio |
|-----|---------------|----------------------------|
| a.  | 1.2           | 7.0                        |
| b.  | 1.2           | 6.0                        |
| c.  | 1.0           | 6.0                        |
| d.  | 0.5           | 7.0                        |

7. A decrease in selling and administrative expenses would directly impact what ratio?
   a. Fixed asset turnover ratio.   c. Current ratio.
   b. Times interest earned.        d. Gross profit percentage.

8. A bank is least likely to use which of the following ratios when analyzing the likelihood that a borrower will pay interest and principal on its loans?
   a. Free cash flow.               c. Times interest earned ratio.
   b. Debt-to-assets ratio.         d. Return on equity ratio.

9. Which of the following accounting concepts do accountants and auditors assess by using financial analyses?
   a. Cost benefit.                 c. Industry practices.
   b. Materiality.                  d. Going-concern assumption.

10. (Supplement 17A) Which of the following items is reported net of related income taxes?
    a. Gain or loss from discontinued operations.
    b. Gain or loss from disposal of property, plant, and equipment.
    c. Interest on long-term debt.
    d. Gain or loss from early extinguishment of debt.

---

Solutions to Multiple-Choice Questions

1. c     2. c     3. c     4. d     5. c     6. a     7. b
8. d     9. d     10. a

---

## Mini Exercises  Available with McGraw-Hill's Homework Manager

**LO2**     **M17-1 Calculations and Interpretations of Horizontal (Trend) Analyses**

**Lockey Fencing Corporation**
**Income Statements**
**For the Years Ended December 31**

|                                                    | 2009      | 2008      |
|----------------------------------------------------|-----------|-----------|
| Net sales                                          | $100,000  | $75,000   |
| Cost of goods sold                                 | 58,000    | 45,000    |
| Gross profit                                       | 42,000    | 30,000    |
| Selling, general, and administrative expenses      | 9,000     | 4,500     |
| Interest expense                                   | 3,000     | 3,750     |
| Income before income taxes                         | 30,000    | 21,750    |
| Income tax expense                                 | 9,000     | 6,525     |
| Net income                                         | $ 21,000  | $15,225   |

What are the two most significant year-to-year changes in terms of dollars and in terms of percentages?

**LO3**     **M17-2 Calculations and Interpretations of Vertical (Common Size) Analyses**
Using the information in M17-1, prepare common size income statements to determine how the company increased its net income as a percent of revenues in 2009.

**M17-3 Computing the Return on Equity Ratio**                                 LO4

Given the following data, compute the 2008 return on equity ratio (expressed as a percentage to one decimal place).

|                       | 2008        | 2007        |
|-----------------------|-------------|-------------|
| Net income            | $ 1,850,000 | $ 1,600,000 |
| Stockholders' equity  | 10,000,000  | 13,125,000  |
| Total assets          | 24,000,000  | 26,000,000  |
| Interest expense      | 400,000     | 300,000     |

**M17-4 Analyzing the Inventory Turnover Ratio**                               LO4

A manufacturer reported an inventory turnover ratio of 8.6 during 2009. During 2010, management introduced a new inventory control system that was expected to reduce average inventory levels by 25 percent without affecting sales volume or cost of goods sold. Given these circumstances, would you expect the inventory turnover ratio to increase or decrease during 2010? Explain.

**M17-5 Analyzing the Impact of Accounting Alternatives**                      LO4

Nevis Corporation operates in an industry in which costs are falling. The company is considering changing its inventory method from FIFO to LIFO and wants to determine the impact that the change would have on selected accounting ratios in future years. In general, what impact would you expect on the following ratios: net profit margin, fixed asset turnover, and current ratio?

**M17-6 Inferring Financial Information Using the P/E Ratio**                   LO4

In 2009, Big W Company reported earnings per share of $2.50 when its stock was selling for $50.00. In 2010, its earnings increased by 10 percent. If all other relationships remain constant, what is the price of the stock? Explain.

**M17-7 Identifying Relevant Ratios**                                          LO4

Identify the ratio that is relevant to answering each of the following questions.

1. How much net income does the company earn from each dollar of sales?
2. Is the company financed primarily by debt or equity?
3. How many dollars of sales were generated for each dollar invested in fixed assets?
4. How many days, on average, does it take the company to collect on credit sales made to customers?
5. How much net income does the company earn for each dollar owners have invested in it?
6. Does the company have sufficient assets to convert into cash for paying liabilities as they come due in the upcoming year?

**M17-8 Interpreting Ratios**                                                  LO4

Generally speaking, do the following indicate good or bad news?

1. Increase in times interest earned ratio.
2. Decrease in days to sell.
3. Increase in gross profit percentage.
4. Decrease in EPS.
5. Increase in asset turnover ratio.

# Exercises 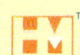   Available with McGraw-Hill's Homework Manager

**E17-1 Preparing and Interpreting a Horizontal (Trend) Analysis**             LO2

The average price of a gallon of gas in 2005 jumped $0.43 (24 percent) from $1.81 in 2004 to $2.24 in 2005. Let's see whether these changes are reflected in the income statement of Chevron Corp. for the year ended December 31, 2005 (amounts in millions).

Chevron

| | 2005 | 2004 |
|---|---|---|
| Total revenues | $198,200 | $155,300 |
| Costs of crude oil and products | 140,902 | 104,948 |
| Other operating costs | 32,101 | 29,801 |
| Income before income tax expense | 25,197 | 20,551 |
| Income tax expense | 11,098 | 7,223 |
| Net income | $ 14,099 | $ 13,328 |

**Required:**

Conduct a horizontal analysis by calculating the year-to-year changes in each line item expressed in dollars and in percentages (rounded to one decimal place). How did the change in gas prices compare to the changes in Chevron Corp.'s total revenues and costs of crude oil and products?

**LO3**

**Chevron**

### E17-2 Preparing and Interpreting a Vertical (Common Size) Analysis

Use the information for Chevron Corp. in E17-1 to conduct a vertical (common size) analysis of the income statements and then answer the following questions.

**Required:**

1. Was Chevron able to raise gas prices to offset the increase in its costs of crude oil and products?
2. How did you know?
3. Did other operating costs rise as fast as gas prices? How did you know? Why do you think this is so?

**LO4**

**Chevron**

### E17-3 Computing and Interpreting Profitability Ratios

Use the information for Chevron Corp. in E17-1 to complete the following requirements.

**Required:**

1. Compute the gross profit percentage for each year (one decimal place). Assuming the change for 2004 to 2005 is the beginning of a sustained trend, is Chevron likely to earn more or less gross profit from each dollar of sales in 2006?
2. Compute the net profit margin for each year (expressed as a percentage with one decimal place). Given your calculations here and in requirement 1, explain whether Chevron did a better or worse job of controlling expenses other than the costs of crude oil and products in 2005 relative to 2004.
3. Chevron reported average net fixed assets of $54.2 billion in 2005 and $45.1 billion in 2004. Compute the fixed asset turnover ratios for both years (round to two decimal places). Did the company better utilize its investment in fixed assets to generate revenues in 2005 or 2004?
4. Chevron reported average stockholders' equity of $54.0 billion in 2005 and $40.8 billion in 2004. Compute the return on equity ratios for both years (expressed as a percentage with one decimal place). Did the company generate higher returns for stockholders in 2005 or 2004?

**LO4**

**Chevron**

### E17-4 Computing a Commonly Used Solvency Ratio

Use the information for Chevron Corp. in E17-1 to complete the following requirement.

**Required:**

Interest expense in the amount of $482 million was included with Other Operating Costs in 2005 ($406 million in 2004). Compute the times interest earned ratios for each year (round to one decimal place). In your opinion, does Chevron generate sufficient net income (before taxes and interest) to cover the cost of debt financing?

**LO2**

### E17-5 Preparing and Interpreting a Horizontal (Trend) Analysis

The average selling price of low-end laptops fell about $200 (25 percent) from $800 in 2008 to $600 in 2009. Let's see whether these changes are reflected in the income statement of Computer Tycoon Inc. for the year ended December 31, 2009.

|                                   | 2008      | 2009     |
|-----------------------------------|-----------|----------|
| Sales revenues                    | $121,761  | $98,913  |
| Cost of goods sold                | 71,583    | 59,249   |
| Operating expenses                | 36,934    | 36,943   |
| Interest expense                  | 474       | 565      |
| Income before income tax expense  | 12,770    | 2,156    |
| Income tax expense                | 5,540     | 1,024    |
| Net income                        | $ 7,230   | $ 1,132  |

*Required:*

Conduct a horizontal analysis by calculating the year-to-year changes in each line item expressed in dollars and in percentages (rounded to one decimal place). How did the change in computer prices compare to the changes in Computer Tycoon's sales revenues?

## E17-6 Preparing and Interpreting a Vertical (Common Size) Analysis                                    LO3

Use the information in E17-5 to conduct a vertical (common size) analysis of Computer Tycoon's income statements and then answer the following questions.

*Required:*

1.  Was Computer Tycoon able to lower its costs of goods to offset the decrease in selling price? How did you know?
2.  What was the main reason Computer Tycoon's net income as a percent of revenues decreased?

## E17-7 Computing Profitability Ratios                                                                   LO4

Use the information in E17-5 for Computer Tycoon to complete the following requirements.

*Required:*

1.  Compute the gross profit percentage for each year (one decimal place). Assuming that the change for 2008 to 2009 is the beginning of a sustained trend, is Computer Tycoon likely to earn higher or lower gross profit from each dollar of sales in 2010?
2.  Compute the net profit margin for each year (expressed as a percentage with one decimal place). Given your calculations here and in requirement 1, explain whether Computer Tycoon did a better or worse job of controlling operating expenses in 2009 relative to 2008.
3.  Computer Tycoon reported average net fixed assets of $54,200 in 2009 and $45,100 in 2008. Compute the fixed asset turnover ratio for each year (round to two decimal places). Did the company better utilize its investment in fixed assets to generate revenues in 2009 or 2008?
4.  Computer Tycoon reported average stockholders' equity of $54,000 in 2009 and $40,800 in 2008. Compute the return on equity ratio for each year (expressed as a percentage with one decimal place). Did the company generate greater returns for stockholders in 2009 or 2008?

## E17-8 Computing a Commonly Used Solvency Ratio                                                         LO4

Use the information in E17-5 for Computer Tycoon to complete the following requirement.

*Required:*

Compute the times interest earned ratios for 2009 and 2008. In your opinion, does Computer Tycoon generate sufficient net income (before taxes and interest) to cover the cost of debt financing?

## E17-9 Matching Each Ratio with Its Computational Formula                                               LO4

Match each ratio or percentage with its formula by entering the appropriate letter for each numbered item.

| Ratios or Percentages | Formula |
|---|---|
| ___ 1. Current ratio | A. Net income ÷ Net sales revenue. |
| ___ 2. Net profit margin | B. (Net sales revenue − Cost of goods sold) ÷ Net sales revenue. |
| ___ 3. Inventory turnover | C. Current assets ÷ Current liabilities. |
| ___ 4. Asset turnover | D. Cost of goods sold ÷ Average inventory. |
| ___ 5. Fixed asset turnover | E. Net credit sales revenue ÷ Average net receivables. |
| ___ 6. Free cash flow | F. Net income ÷ Average number of common shares outstanding. |
| ___ 7. Return on equity | G. Total liabilities ÷ Total assets. |
| ___ 8. Times interest earned | H. (Net income + Interest expense + Income tax expense) ÷ Interest expense. |
| ___ 9. Debt to assets | I. Net cash flows from operating activities − Purchases of property and equipment − Dividends paid |
| ___ 10. Price/earnings | J. Current stock price per share ÷ Earnings per share. |
| ___ 11. Receivables turnover | K. Net income ÷ Average total stockholders' equity. |
| ___ 12. Earnings per share | L. Net sales revenue ÷ Average total assets. |
| ___ 13. Gross profit percentage | M. Net sales revenue ÷ Average net fixed assets. |

**LO4**

### E17-10 Computing and Interpreting Selected Liquidity Ratios

DuckWing Stores (DWS) reported sales of $600,000 for the year; one-half of sales were on credit. The average gross profit percentage was 40 percent on sales. Account balances follow:

| | Beginning | Ending |
|---|---|---|
| Accounts receivable (net) | $45,000 | $55,000 |
| Inventory | 60,000 | 40,000 |

*Required:*

1. Compute the turnover ratios for accounts receivable and inventory (round to one decimal place).
2. Calculate the average days to collect receivables and the average days to sell inventory (round to one decimal place).
3. Explain what each of these ratios and measures means.

**LO4**

### E17-11 Computing and Interpreting Liquidity Ratios

Cintas Corporation is the largest uniform supplier in North America. More than 5 million people wear Cintas clothing each day. Selected information from a recent balance sheet follows. For Year 2, the company reported sales revenue of $2,686,585 and cost of goods sold of $1,567,377 (in thousands).

| Cintas | Year 2 | Year 1 |
|---|---|---|
| **Balance Sheet (amounts in thousands)** | | |
| Cash | $ 32,239 | $ 52,182 |
| Accounts receivable, less allowance of $7,737 and $9,229 | 278,147 | 225,735 |
| Inventories | 228,410 | 164,906 |
| Prepaid expenses | 7,607 | 7,237 |
| Other current assets | 25,420 | 57,640 |
| Accounts payable | 53,909 | 60,393 |
| Wages payable | 25,252 | 29,004 |
| Income taxes payable | 69,545 | 73,163 |
| Accrued liabilities | 127,882 | 131,705 |
| Long-term debt due within one year | 28,251 | 18,369 |

*Required:*

Assuming that 60 percent of sales are on credit, compute the current ratio (two decimal places), inventory turnover ratio (one decimal place), and accounts receivable turnover ratio (one decimal place) for Year 2. Explain what each ratio means.

### E17-12 Analyzing the Impact of Selected Transactions on the Current Ratio      LO4

In its most recent annual report, Appalachian Beverages reported current assets of $54,000 and a current ratio of 1.80. Assume that the following transactions were completed: (1) purchased merchandise for $6,000 on account and (2) purchased a delivery truck for $10,000, paying $1,000 cash and signing a two-year promissory note for the balance.

*Required:*

Compute the updated current ratio, rounded to two decimal places, after each transaction.

### E17-13 Analyzing the Impact of Selected Transactions on the Current Ratio      LO4

In its most recent annual report, Sunrise Enterprises reported current assets of $1,090,000 and current liabilities of $602,000.

*Required:*

Determine the impact of the following transactions on the current ratio for Sunrise:

1. Sold long-term assets for cash.
2. Accrued severance pay for terminated employees.
3. Wrote down the carrying value of certain inventory items that were deemed to be obsolete.
4. Acquired new inventory by signing an 18-month promissory note (the supplier was not willing to provide normal credit terms).

### E17-14 Analyzing the Impact of Selected Transactions on the Current Ratio      LO4

Sports Authority, Inc., is the country's largest private full-line sporting goods retailer. Stores are operated under four brand names: Sports Authority, Gart Sports, Oshman's, and Sportmart. Assume one of the Sports Authority stores reported current assets of $88,000 and its current ratio was 1.75. Assume also the following transactions were completed: (1) paid $6,000 on accounts payable, (2) purchased a delivery truck for $10,000 cash, (3) wrote off a bad account receivable for $2,000 under the allowance method, and (4) paid previously declared dividends in the amount of $25,000 (the dividends were declared in the prior period and paid in the current period).

**Sports Authority**

*Required:*

Compute the updated current ratio, rounded to two decimal places, after each transaction.

### E17-15 Analyzing the Impact of Selected Transactions on the Current Ratio      LO4

Current assets totaled $500,000, the current ratio was 2.00, and the company uses the perpetual inventory method. Assume that the following transactions were completed: (1) sold $12,000 in merchandise on short-term credit for $15,000, (2) declared but did not pay dividends of $50,000, (3) paid prepaid rent in the amount of $12,000, (4) paid previously declared dividends in the amount of $50,000, (5) collected an account receivable in the amount of $12,000, and (6) reclassified $40,000 of long-term debt as a current liability.

*Required:*

Compute the updated current ratio, rounded to two decimal places, after each transaction.

### E17-16 Computing the Accounts Receivable and Inventory Turnover Ratios      LO4

Procter & Gamble is a multinational corporation that manufactures and markets many products that are probably in your home or dorm room. In 2006, sales for the company were $68,222 (all amounts in millions). The annual report did not report the amount of credit sales, so we assume all sales were on credit. The average gross profit percentage was 51 percent. Account balances follow:

**P&G**

|                             | Beginning | Ending |
|-----------------------------|-----------|--------|
| Accounts receivable (net)   | $5,266    | $7,336 |
| Inventory                   | 5,006     | 6,291  |

*Required:*

1. Compute the turnover ratios (rounded to one decimal place) for accounts receivable and inventory.
2. Calculate the average days to collect receivables and the average days to sell inventory.
3. Interpret what these ratios and measures mean.

**LO4**

**Dollar General**

**E17-17 Inferring Financial Information from Profitability and Liquidity Ratios**

Dollar General Corporation operates approximately 8,250 general merchandise stores that feature quality merchandise at low prices to meet the needs of middle-, low-, and fixed-income families in southern, eastern, and midwestern states. For the year ended February 3, 2006, the company reported average inventories of $1,425 (in millions) and an inventory turnover of 4.3. Average total fixed assets were $1,137 (million), and the fixed asset turnover ratio was 7.5.

*Required:*

1.  Calculate Dollar General's gross profit percentage (expressed as a percentage with one decimal place). What does this imply about the amount of gross profit made from each dollar of sales?
2.  Is this an improvement from the gross profit percentage of 29.5 percent earned during the year ended January 28, 2005?

**TIP:** Work backward from the fixed asset turnover and inventory turnover ratios to compute the amounts needed for the gross profit percentage.

**LO4**

**E17-18 Using Financial Information to Identify Mystery Companies**

The following selected financial data pertain to four unidentified companies (balance sheet amounts reported in millions):

|  | COMPANY | | | |
|---|---|---|---|---|
|  | 1 | 2 | 3 | 4 |
| **Balance Sheet Data** | | | | |
| Cash | $ 5.1 | $ 8.8 | $ 6.3 | $ 10.4 |
| Accounts receivable | 13.1 | 41.5 | 13.8 | 4.9 |
| Inventory | 4.6 | 3.6 | 65.1 | 35.8 |
| Property and equipment | 53.1 | 23.0 | 8.8 | 35.7 |
| **Selected Ratios** | | | | |
| Gross profit percentage | N/A* | N/A | 45.2 | 22.5 |
| Net profit margin ratio (%) | 0.3 | 16.0 | 3.9 | 1.5 |
| Current ratio | 0.7 | 2.2 | 1.9 | 1.4 |
| Inventory turnover | N/A | N/A | 1.4 | 15.5 |
| Debt to assets | 0.7 | 0.5 | 0.6 | 0.7 |

* N/A = Not applicable.

This financial information pertains to the following companies:

a.  Cable TV company.
b.  Grocery store.
c.  Accounting firm.
d.  Retail jewelry store.

*Required:*

Match each company with its financial information, and explain the basis for your answers.

**LO4**

**E17-19 Analyzing the Impact of Alternative Inventory Methods on Selected Ratios**

Company A uses the FIFO method to cost inventory, and Company B uses the LIFO method. The two companies are exactly alike except for the difference in inventory costing methods. Costs of inventory items for both companies have been falling steadily in recent years, and each company has increased its inventory each year. Ignore income tax effects.

*Required:*

Identify which company will report the higher amount for each of the following ratios. If it is not possible to identify which will report the higher amount, explain why.

1.  Current ratio.
2.  Debt-to-assets ratio.
3.  Earnings per share.

# Problems—Set A

 **Available with McGraw-Hill's Homework Manager**

**PA17-1 Analyzing Financial Statements Using Horizontal (Trend) and Vertical (Common Size) Analysis**

**LO2, 3**

The comparative financial statements prepared at December 31, 2009, for Pinnacle Plus showed the following summarized data:

www.mhhe.com/LLPW1e

| | 2009 | 2008 | INCREASE (DECREASE) 2009 OVER 2008 Amount | Percentage |
|---|---|---|---|---|
| **Income Statement** | | | | |
| Sales revenue* | $110,000 | $ 99,000 | | |
| Cost of goods sold | 52,000 | 48,000 | | |
| Gross profit | 58,000 | 51,000 | | |
| Operating expenses | 36,000 | 33,000 | | |
| Interest expense | 4,000 | 4,000 | | |
| Income before income taxes | 18,000 | 14,000 | | |
| Income tax expense (30%) | 5,400 | 4,200 | | |
| Net income | $ 12,600 | $ 9,800 | | |
| **Balance Sheet** | | | | |
| Cash | $ 49,500 | $ 18,000 | | |
| Accounts receivable (net) | 37,000 | 32,000 | | |
| Inventory | 25,000 | 38,000 | | |
| Property and equipment (net) | 95,000 | 105,000 | | |
| Total assets | $206,500 | $193,000 | | |
| Accounts payable | $ 42,000 | $ 35,000 | | |
| Income taxes payable | 1,000 | 500 | | |
| Note payable, long term | 40,000 | 40,000 | | |
| Total liabilities | 83,000 | 75,500 | | |
| Common stock (par $10) | 90,000 | 90,000 | | |
| Retained earnings† | 33,500 | 27,500 | | |
| Total liabilities and stockholders' equity | $206,500 | $193,000 | | |

\* One-half of all sales are on credit.
† During 2009, cash dividends amounting to $6,600 were declared and paid.

*Required:*

1. Complete the Amount and Percentage columns in Pinnacle Plus's comparative financial statements to prepare a horizontal (trend) analysis. Round the percentages to one decimal place. Does anything significant jump out at you from the year-to-year analyses?

2. Prepare common size income statements and balance sheets for the two years. Round the percentages to one decimal place. What significant changes have taken place in the relationship among items in the balance sheet and income statement?

**PA17-2 Analyzing Comparative Financial Statements Using Selected Ratios**

**LO4**

Use the data given in PA17-1 for Pinnacle Plus.

*Required:*

1. Compute the gross profit percentages in 2009 and 2008. Round the percentages to one decimal place. Is the trend going in the right direction?
2. Compute the net profit margin ratios in 2009 and 2008. Round the percentages to one decimal place. Is the trend going in the right direction?
3. Compute the earnings per share for 2009 and 2008. Does the trend look good or bad? Explain.
4. Stockholders' equity totaled $100,000 at the end of 2007. Compute the return on equity (ROE) ratios for 2008 and 2009. Express the ROE as percentages rounded to one decimal place. Is the trend going in the right direction?
5. Net property and equipment totaled $110,000 at the end of 2007. Compute the fixed asset turnover ratios for 2009 and 2008. Round the ratios to two decimal places. Is the trend going in the right direction?
6. Compute the debt-to-assets ratios for 2009 and 2008. Round the ratios to two decimal places. Is debt providing financing for a larger or smaller proportion of the company's asset growth? Explain.
7. Compute the times interest earned ratios for 2009 and 2008. Round the ratios to one decimal place. Do they look good or bad? Explain.
8. After Pinnacle Plus released its 2009 financial statements, the company's stock was trading at $18. After the release of its 2008 financial statements, the company's stock price was $15 per share. Compute the P/E ratios for both years rounded to one decimal place. Does it appear that investors have become more (or less) optimistic about Pinnacle's future success?

**LO4**
Coca-Cola & Pepsico

**PA17-3 Interpreting Profitability, Liquidity, Solvency, and P/E Ratios**

Coke and Pepsi are well-known international brands. Coca-Cola sells more than $23 billion worth of beverages each year while annual sales of Pepsi products exceed $32 billion. Compare the two companies as a potential investment based on the following ratios:

| Ratio | Coca-Cola | PepsiCo |
|---|---|---|
| Gross profit percentage | 48.5 % | 49.0 % |
| Net profit margin | 2.6 % | 4.1 % |
| Return on equity | 66.2 % | 23.3 % |
| EPS | $ 3.40 | $ 1.54 |
| Receivables turnover | 11.5 | 9.8 |
| Inventory turnover | 15.1 | 12.8 |
| Current ratio | 1.47 | 1.40 |
| Debt to assets | 0.94 | 0.72 |
| Price/Earnings | 16.4 | 18.7 |

*Required:*

1. Which company appears more profitable? Describe the ratio(s) that you used to reach this decision.
2. Which company appears more liquid? Describe the ratio(s) that you used to reach this decision.
3. Which company appears more solvent? Describe the ratio(s) that you used to reach this decision.
4. Are the conclusions from your analyses in requirements 1–3 consistent with the value of the two companies suggested by the P/E ratio of each company? If not, offer one explanation for any apparent inconsistency.

**LO4**

**PA17-4 Using Ratios to Compare Loan Requests from Two Companies**

The 2008 financial statements for Royale and Cavalier companies are summarized here:

| | Royale Company | Cavalier Company |
|---|---|---|
| **Balance Sheet** | | |
| Cash | $ 25,000 | $ 45,000 |
| Accounts receivable (net) | 55,000 | 5,000 |
| Inventory | 110,000 | 25,000 |
| Property and equipment (net) | 550,000 | 160,000 |
| Other assets | 140,000 | 57,000 |
| Total assets | $880,000 | $292,000 |
| Current liabilities | $120,000 | $ 15,000 |
| Long-term debt | 190,000 | 55,000 |
| Capital stock (par $20) | 480,000 | 210,000 |
| Additional paid-in capital | 50,000 | 4,000 |
| Retained earnings | 40,000 | 8,000 |
| Total liabilities and stockholders' equity | $880,000 | $292,000 |
| **Income Statement** | | |
| Sales revenue | $800,000 | $280,000 |
| Cost of goods sold | (480,000) | (150,000) |
| Expenses (including interest and income tax) | (240,000) | (95,000) |
| Net income | $ 80,000 | $ 35,000 |
| **Selected Data from 2007 Statements** | | |
| Accounts receivable, net | $ 47,000 | $ 11,000 |
| Long-term debt | 190,000 | 55,000 |
| Property and equipment, net | 550,000 | 160,000 |
| Inventory | 95,000 | 38,000 |
| Total stockholders' equity | 570,000 | 202,000 |
| **Other Data** | | |
| Per share price at end of 2008 | $   14.00 | $   11.00 |
| Average income tax rate | 30% | 30% |

These two companies are in the same line of business and in the same state but in different cities. One-half of Royale's sales are on credit whereas one-quarter of Cavalier's sales are on credit. Each company has been in operation for about 10 years. Both companies received an unqualified audit opinion on the financial statements, which means the independent auditors found nothing wrong. Royale Company wants to borrow $75,000 cash, and Cavalier Company is asking for $30,000. The loans will be for a two-year period. Both companies estimate bad debts based on an aging analysis, but Cavalier has estimated slightly higher uncollectible rates than Royale.

**Required:**

1.  Complete a schedule that reflects the following ratios for each company: return on equity, gross profit percentage, net profit margin, earnings per share, fixed asset turnover, price earnings, current, receivables turnover, inventory turnover, debt to assets.
2.  Assume you work in the loan department of a local bank. You have been asked to analyze the situation and recommend which loan is preferable. Based on the data given, your analysis prepared in requirement 1, and any other information, give your choice and the supporting explanation.

### PA17-5 Analyzing an Investment by Comparing Selected Ratios          LO4

You have the opportunity to invest $10,000 in one of two companies from a single industry. The only information you have is shown here. The word *high* refers to the top third of the industry; *average* is the middle third; *low* is the bottom third.

| Ratio | Company A | Company B |
|---|---|---|
| Current | Low | High |
| Inventory turnover | High | Low |
| Debt to assets | Low | Average |
| Times interest earned | High | Average |
| Price/earnings | High | Average |

**Required:**

Which company would you select? Write a brief explanation for your recommendation.

## Problems—Set B     Available with McGraw-Hill's Homework Manager

**LO2, 3**    **PB17-1 Analyzing Financial Statements Using Ratios and Percentage Changes**

The comparative financial statements prepared at December 31, 2010, for Tiger Audio showed the following summarized data:

| | 2010 | 2009 | INCREASE (DECREASE) 2010 OVER 2009 Amount | Percentage |
|---|---|---|---|---|
| **Income Statement** | | | | |
| Sales revenue* | $222,000 | $185,000 | | |
| Cost of goods sold | 127,650 | 111,000 | | |
| Gross profit | 94,350 | 74,000 | | |
| Operating expenses | 39,600 | 33,730 | | |
| Interest expense | 4,000 | 3,270 | | |
| Income before income taxes | 50,750 | 37,000 | | |
| Income tax expense (30%) | 15,225 | 11,100 | | |
| Net income | $ 35,525 | $ 25,900 | | |
| **Balance Sheet** | | | | |
| Cash | $ 40,000 | $ 38,000 | | |
| Accounts receivable (net) | 18,500 | 16,000 | | |
| Inventory | 25,000 | 22,000 | | |
| Property and equipment (net) | 127,000 | 119,000 | | |
| Total assets | $210,500 | $195,000 | | |
| Accounts payable | $ 27,000 | $ 25,000 | | |
| Income taxes payable | 3,000 | 2,800 | | |
| Note payable, long term | 75,500 | 92,200 | | |
| Total liabilities | 105,500 | 120,000 | | |
| Capital stock (par $1) | 25,000 | 25,000 | | |
| Retained earnings† | 80,000 | 50,000 | | |
| Total liabilities and stockholders' equity | $210,500 | $195,000 | | |

\* One-half of all sales are on credit.
† During 2010, cash dividends amounting to $5,525 were declared and paid.

*Required:*

1.  Complete the Amount and Percentage columns in Tiger Audio's comparative financial statements to prepare a horizontal (trend) analysis. Round the percentages to one decimal place. Does anything significant jump out at you from the year-to-year analyses?
2.  Prepare common size income statements and balance sheets for the two years. Round the percentages to one decimal place. What significant changes have taken place in the relationship among items in the balance sheet and income statement?

**PB17-2 Analyzing Comparative Financial Statements Using Selected Ratios**          LO4

Use the data given in PB17-1 for Tiger Audio.

*Required:*

1.  Compute the gross profit percentages in 2010 and 2009. Is the trend going in the right direction?
2.  Compute the net profit margin ratios in 2010 and 2009. Is the trend going in the right direction?
3.  Compute the earnings per share for 2010 and 2009. Does the trend look good or bad? Explain.
4.  Stockholders' equity totaled $65,000 at the end of 2008. Compute the return on equity ratios for 2010 and 2009. Is the trend going in the right direction?
5.  Net property and equipment totaled $115,000 at the end of 2008. Compute the fixed asset turnover ratios for 2010 and 2009. Is the trend going in the right direction?
6.  Compute the debt-to-assets ratios for 2010 and 2009. Is debt providing financing for a larger or smaller proportion of the company's asset growth? Explain.
7.  Compute the times interest earned ratios for 2010 and 2009. Do they look good or bad? Explain.
8.  After Tiger released its 2010 financial statements, the company's stock was trading at $17. After the release of its 2009 financial statements, the company's stock price was $12 per share. Compute the P/E ratios for both years rounded to one decimal place. Does it appear that investors have become more (or less) optimistic about Tiger Audio's future success?

**PB17-3 Interpreting Profitability, Liquidity, Solvency, and P/E Ratios**          LO4

Mattel and Hasbro are the two largest makers of games and toys in the world. Mattel sells more than $5 billion of products each year while annual sales of Hasbro products exceed $3 billion. Compare the two companies as a potential investment based on the following ratios:

Hasbro

| Ratio | Mattel | Hasbro |
|---|---|---|
| Gross profit percentage | 48.3 % | 58.7 % |
| Net profit margin | 10.3 % | 5.7 % |
| Return on equity | 23.6 % | 13.6 % |
| EPS | $ 1.23 | $ 0.91 |
| Receivables turnover | 7.2 | 6.4 |
| Inventory turnover | 5.5 | 5.7 |
| Current ratio | 1.86 | 1.89 |
| Debt to assets | 0.24 | 0.33 |
| Price/Earnings | 15.2 | 18.9 |

*Required:*

1.  Which company appears more profitable? Describe the ratio(s) that you used to reach this decision.
2.  Which company appears more liquid? Describe the ratio(s) that you used to reach this decision.
3.  Which company appears more solvent? Describe the ratio(s) that you used to reach this decision.
4.  Are the conclusions from your analyses in requirements 1–3 consistent with the value of the two companies suggested by the P/E ratio of each company? If not, offer one explanation for any apparent inconsistency.

**LO4**

**PB17-4 Using Ratios to Compare Loan Requests from Two Companies**

The 2010 financial statements for Thor and Gunnar Companies are summarized here:

|  | Thor Company | Gunnar Company |
| --- | --- | --- |
| **Balance Sheet** | | |
| Cash | $     35,000 | $   54,000 |
| Accounts receivable (net) | 77,000 | 6,000 |
| Inventory | 154,000 | 30,000 |
| Property and equipment (net) | 770,000 | 192,000 |
| Other assets | 196,000 | 68,400 |
| Total assets | $1,232,000 | $ 350,400 |
| | | |
| Current liabilities | $  168,000 | $  18,000 |
| Long-term debt (12% interest rate) | 266,000 | 66,000 |
| Capital stock (par $20) | 672,000 | 252,000 |
| Additional paid-in capital | 70,000 | 4,800 |
| Retained earnings | 56,000 | 9,600 |
| Total liabilities and stockholders' equity | $1,232,000 | $ 350,400 |
| | | |
| **Income Statement** | | |
| Sales revenue | $1,120,000 | $ 336,000 |
| Cost of goods sold | (672,000) | (180,000) |
| Expenses (including interest and income tax) | (336,000) | (114,000) |
| Net income | $  112,000 | $  42,000 |
| | | |
| **Selected Data from 2009 Statements** | | |
| Accounts receivable, net | $    65,800 | $  13,200 |
| Inventory | 133,000 | 45,600 |
| Property and equipment, net | 770,000 | 192,000 |
| Long-term debt (12% interest rate) | 266,000 | 66,000 |
| Total stockholders' equity | 798,000 | 266,400 |
| | | |
| **Other Data** | | |
| Per share price at end of 2010 | $      13.20 | $     19.60 |
| Average income tax rate | 30% | 30% |

These two companies are in the same line of business and in the same state but in different cities. One-half of Thor's sales are on credit, whereas one-quarter of Gunnar's sales are on credit. Each company has been in operation for about 10 years. Both companies received an unqualified audit opinion on the financial statements, which means the independent auditors found nothing wrong. Thor Company wants to borrow $105,000 cash, and Gunnar Company is asking for $36,000. The loans will be for a two-year period.

*Required:*

1. Complete a schedule that reflects the following ratios for each company: return on equity, gross profit percentage, net profit margin, earnings per share, fixed asset turnover, price earnings, current, receivables turnover, inventory turnover, debt to assets.

2. Assume you work in the loan department of a local bank. You have been asked to analyze the situation and recommend which loan is preferable. Based on the data given, your analysis prepared in requirement 1, and any other information, give your choice and the supporting explanation.

**LO4**

**PB17-5 Analyzing an Investment by Comparing Selected Ratios**

You have the opportunity to invest $10,000 in one of two companies from a single industry. The only information you have is shown here. The word *high* refers to the top third of the industry; *average* is the middle third; *low* is the bottom third.

| Ratio | Company A | Company B |
|---|---|---|
| EPS | High | High |
| Return on equity | High | Average |
| Debt to assets | High | Low |
| Current | Low | Average |
| Price/Earnings | Low | High |

*Required:*

Which company would you select? Write a brief explanation for your recommendation.

# Cases and Projects

### CP17-1 Finding Financial Information

Refer to the financial statements of The Home Depot in Appendix A at the end of this book, or download the annual report from the *Cases* section of the text's Web site at www.mhhe.com/LLPW1e. Compute and interpret the ratios discussed in the chapter for the most recent year presented. Assume that the stock price was $30.44.

LO4

### CP17-2 Comparing Financial Information

Refer to the financial statements of Lowe's in Appendix B at the end of this book, or download the annual report from the *Cases* section of the text's Web site at www.mhhe.com/LLPW1e. From the list of ratios that were discussed in this chapter, compute and interpret the ratios that help you compare Lowe's to the results for The Home Depot for the most recent year presented. Assume that Lowe's stock price was $25.55 and The Home Depot's stock price was $30.44.

LO4

Lowe's

### CP17-3 Examining an Annual Report: Internet-Based Team Research

As a team, select an industry to analyze. Using your Web browser, each team member should acquire the annual report or 10-K for one publicly traded company in the industry with each member selecting a different company. (See CP1-3 in Chapter 1 for a description of possible resources for these tasks.)

LO1, 2, 3, 4

*Required:*

1. On an individual basis, each team member should write a short report that incorporates trend analysis and as many of the ratios from the chapter as are applicable given the nature of the selected company.

2. Then, as a team, write a short report comparing and contrasting your companies using these attributes. Discuss any patterns across the companies that you as a team observe. Provide potential explanations for any differences discovered.

### CP17-4 Making Ethical Decisions: A Real-Life Example

During its deliberations on the Sarbanes-Oxley Act, the U.S. Senate considered numerous reports evaluating the quality of work done by external auditors. One study by Weiss Ratings, Inc., focused on auditors' ability to predict bankruptcy. The study criticized auditors for failing to identify and report going-concern problems for audit clients that later went bankrupt. Based on a sample of 45 bankrupt companies, the Weiss study concluded that had auditors noted unusual levels for just two of seven typical financial ratios, they would have identified 89 percent of the sample companies that later went bankrupt. A follow-up to the Weiss study found that had the criteria in the Weiss study been applied to a larger sample of nonbankrupt companies, 46.9 percent of nonbankrupt companies would have been predicted to go bankrupt.* In other words, the Weiss criteria would have incorrectly predicted bankruptcy for nearly half of the companies in the follow-up study and would have led the auditors to report that these clients had substantial going-concern problems when, in fact, they did not.

LO4

---

* Michael D. Akers, Meredith A. Maher, and Don E. Giacomino, "Going-Concern Opinions: Broadening the Expectations Gap," *CPA Journal*, October 2003 (n. d.), www.nysscpa.org/cpajournal/2003/1003/features/f103803.htm (November 20, 2006).

*Required:*

Discuss the negative consequences that arise when auditors fail to predict companies that go bankrupt. Who is harmed by these failures? Discuss the negative consequences that arise when auditors incorrectly predict bankruptcy. Who is harmed by these errors? In your opinion, which of the potential consequences is worse?

**LO4**

### CP17-5 Making Ethical Decisions: A Mini Case

Capital Investments Corporation (CIC) requested a sizable loan from First Federal Bank to acquire a large piece of land for future expansion. CIC reported current assets of $1,900,000 (including $430,000 in cash) and current liabilities of $1,075,000. First Federal denied the loan request for a number of reasons, including the fact that the current ratio was below 2:1. When CIC was informed of the loan denial, the controller of the company immediately paid $420,000 that was owed to several trade creditors. The controller then asked First Federal to reconsider the loan application.

*Required:*

Based on these abbreviated facts, would you recommend that First Federal approve the loan request? Why? Are the controller's actions ethical?

**LO4**

### CP17-6 Thinking Critically: Analyzing the Impact of Alternative Depreciation Methods on Ratio Analysis

Speedy Company uses the double-declining-balance method to depreciate its property, plant, and equipment. Turtle Company uses the straight-line method. The two companies are exactly alike except for the difference in depreciation methods.

*Required:*

1. Identify the financial ratios discussed in this chapter that are likely to be affected by the difference in depreciation methods.
2. Which company will report the higher amount for each ratio that you have identified? If you cannot be certain, explain why.

**LO4**

### CP17-7 Using a Spreadsheet to Calculate Financial Statement Ratios

Use the financial statement information from Exhibits 17.2, and 17.3.

*Required:*

Enter the financial information for each exhibit into two separate worksheets in one spreadsheet file. Create a third worksheet that uses the formulas in Exhibit 17.6 to recalculate ratios (1) through (14) for Lowe's for 2006. (For the EPS ratio, simply import the amount reported on the face of the income statement stock price is $31 per share.)

# 18 Managerial Accounting

## LEARNING OBJECTIVES

**After completing this chapter, you should be able to:**

**LO1** Describe the key differences between financial accounting and managerial accounting.

**LO2** Explain the functions of management.

**LO3** Define and give examples of different types of cost:
   a. Out-of-pocket and opportunity costs
   b. Direct and indirect costs
   c. Variable and fixed costs
   d. Relevant and irrelevant costs
   e. Manufacturing and nonmanufacturing costs
   f. Product and period costs

**LO4** Compare the financial statements of merchandising and manufacturing firms.

**LO5** Prepare a cost of goods manufactured report.

Lectured presentations 18-1
www.mhhe.com/LLPW1e

The past 17 chapters (and 700 plus pages) were devoted to preparing and interpreting financial accounting reports. The information provided in those reports is critical to small business owners such as Mauricio Rosa, owner of Pizza Aroma, as well as huge corporations such as Wal-Mart, which must report their financial and operating results to investors, creditors, and government regulators. In this chapter, we shift our focus to managerial accounting, the branch of accounting that specializes in meeting the information needs of internal business managers.

To illustrate the role of managerial accounting in organizations, we use the story of two brothers from Wisconsin who started out much like Mauricio Rosa, as owners of a small pizza business. In 1960, the Simek brothers began selling pizza at a small tavern across the street from the local cemetery, aptly named the Tombstone Tap. As the buzz about the Simeks' delicious pizza spread, other local businesses began to buy and serve it to their own customers. By 1966, the two brothers had bought the first in what would eventually become a fleet of refrigerated trucks that deliver Tombstone Pizza to small businesses and grocery stores across the country. In 1986, Kraft Foods made the brothers an offer they couldn't refuse, and Tombstone Pizza became a subsidiary—that is, a freestanding operating unit—of Kraft Foods.

As you read the chapter, try putting yourself in the shoes of one of the following managers at Tombstone Pizza:

- Regional sales manager responsible for sales and distribution to grocery stores in California, Nevada, Utah, and Arizona.
- Marketing manager responsible for pricing and promotion of existing products.
- New product development manager responsible for the development and introduction of a new whole wheat pizza.

- Production manager responsible for the rising-crust production line.
- Human resource manager responsible for hiring, training, and evaluating Tombstone employees.

Think about the activities you would engage in and the decisions you would make in your chosen role and, most of all, the information you would need as a manager. Chances are that much of that information would come from the company's managerial accounting system.

## ORGANIZATION OF THE CHAPTER

**ROLE OF MANAGERIAL ACCOUNTING IN ORGANIZATIONS**
- Decision-Making Orientation
- Comparison of Financial and Managerial Accounting
- Functions of Management

**COST CLASSIFICATIONS AND DEFINITIONS**
- Definition of Cost
- Out-of-Pocket versus Opportunity Costs
- Direct versus Indirect Costs
- Variable versus Fixed Costs
- Relevant versus Irrelevant Costs
- Manufacturing versus Nonmanufacturing Costs
- Product versus Period Costs

**COSTS IN MANUFACTURING VERSUS NONMANUFACTURING FIRMS**
- Balance Sheets of Merchandising versus Manufacturing Firms
- Cost of Goods Manufactured Report
- Income Statements of Merchandising versus Manufacturing Firms

# ROLE OF MANAGERIAL ACCOUNTING IN ORGANIZATIONS

## Decision-Making Orientation

Video 18-1
www.mhhe.com/LLPW1e

The purpose of managerial accounting is to provide useful information to internal managers to help them make decisions that arise as they manage people, projects, products, or segments of the business. For example, managers at Tombstone Pizza might need to answer the following questions:

- How much should we charge for our pizza? Should we base the price on how much each pizza costs us to make or how much our competitors charge for their pizza?
- Should we make the pizza sauce ourselves or buy it in large quantities from a supplier?
- What kind of advertisements and promotions should we use to make consumers aware of our products?
- Should we invest in automated equipment or continue to make our pizza dough by hand?

Throughout this chapter, we focus on the role of managerial accounting in helping managers to answer questions such as these.

## Comparison of Financial and Managerial Accounting

**Learning Objective 1**

Describe the key differences between financial accounting and managerial accounting.

The major difference between financial accounting and managerial accounting is the intended user of the information. **Financial accounting** information is used by external parties, such as investors, creditors, and regulators; **managerial accounting** information is used by internal managers. Of course, different users have different needs. Financial statements prepared

## Exhibit 18.1   Differences between Financial and Managerial Accounting

| | Financial Accounting | Managerial Accounting |
|---|---|---|
| |  | |
| **User prespective** | Used by external parties, such as investors, creditors, and regulators | Used by internal parties, such as managers and employees |
| **Types of reports** | Classified financial statements prepared according to GAAP | Various non-GAAP reports, such as budgets, performance evaluations, and cost reports |
| **Nature of information** | Objective, reliable, historical | Subjective, relevant, future oriented |
| **Frequency of reporting** | Prepared periodically (monthly, quarterly, annually) | Prepared as needed, perhaps day-to-day or even in real time |
| **Level of detail** | Information reported for the company as a whole | Information reported at the decision-making level (by product, region, customer, or other business segment) |

according to generally accepted accounting principles (GAAP) provide external users certain advantages in terms of their comparability and objectivity. However, internal managers often need more detailed information that is not restricted by GAAP—information that is not captured in the financial reports prepared for external parties. More often than not, the information managers seek is relevant, future oriented, or subjective. See Exhibit 18.1 for a summary of these key differences between financial accounting and managerial accounting.

To illustrate these differences, let's return to Tombstone Pizza. For purposes of external financial reporting, Kraft Foods combines the Tombstone Pizza subsidiary with other well-known brands, such as DiGiorno pizza, Kraft macaroni and cheese, and Oscar Mayer hot dogs. At the end of the fiscal year, accountants at Kraft Foods prepare the company's annual report, including a consolidated income statement, balance sheet, and statement of cash flows, along with other relevant information and disclosures. These financial statements are audited by an independent public accounting firm, such as PricewaterhouseCoopers LLC. They are publicly available to anyone with an interest in Kraft Foods, including government regulators, financial analysts, and investors who are considering buying or selling stock in the company.

Although financial statements are an extremely important source of information to external decision makers, they probably are not that useful to individual managers responsible for making decisions in Kraft's Tombstone Pizza division. In particular, financial reports tend to be too focused on the past and too general for managerial decision making. Managers often need more detailed information related to their specific responsibilities—information that focuses on what will happen in the future rather than on what happened in the past. For example, a manager who is responsible for new product development must be able to predict, identify, and interpret consumers' ever-changing tastes to develop products that will appeal to consumer preferences.

To better understand the role of managerial accounting, let's consider the various functions that managers at Tombstone Pizza perform and the information they need to perform them.

# Functions of Management

Regardless of the type of organization or size of the business unit they manage, all managers perform the same basic functions, which revolve around planning, organizing, leading/directing, and control. In the course of performing each of these functions, managers make a

## Coach's Tip

Financial accounting is sometimes referred to as **external** reporting while managerial accounting is referred to as **internal** reporting. The difference is whether the intended users are inside or outside the company.

## Learning Objective 2

Explain the functions of management.

**Exhibit 18.2**    Functions of Management

variety of decisions, many of which are based on managerial accounting information. Refer to Exhibit 18.2 for an illustration of the managerial process.

**Planning** is the future-oriented aspect of the managerial process. It involves setting long-term goals and objectives, along with the short-term tactics necessary to achieve them. Assume, for example, that Tombstone Pizza plans to introduce a new low-calorie pizza with a whole wheat crust to appeal to health-conscious consumers. The planning process would include setting long-term objectives for sales volume and market share over the first few years of the product's life cycle. Once the objectives have been set, managers would then identify and define the short-term tactics with which to achieve those objectives. Tactics would include the details of how to develop, test, produce, market, distribute, and sell the new product. Once the planning stage is complete, managers must begin **organizing**, or arranging for the necessary resources needed to achieve the plan. As part of the organization process, managers would need to develop a **budget** that details how much time and money should be spent on each of these critical tasks.

The next managerial function, **directing/leading**, relates to putting the plan into action and making all of the managerial decisions needed to implement the plan. In addition to leading, managers must motivate their employees to work toward the plan's success. For example, managers might offer bonuses for meeting project deadlines and staying within budget in each phase of the new product's development and introduction. They might also use incentives to motivate the sales force to sell the new whole wheat pizza as well as negotiate with retailers for shelf space for the product.

The final managerial function, **control**, involves comparing actual results to planned results, to see whether the company's objectives are being met. If not, managers must take corrective action to adjust the objectives and/or their implementation of the plan. For example, if managers determined that sales of Tombstone's whole wheat pizza were falling short of expectations, they might decide to spend more money on marketing to advertise the new product's health benefits.

As you can see, the managerial functions of planning, organizing, directing/leading, and control are interconnected: one function feeds into another, and feedback from the process is used to improve future decision making. Throughout, managers must make a variety of decisions based on relevant, up-to-date information including cost estimates, competitor pricing, market demand, and consumer preferences. Much of the information managers need to make these decisions comes from the managerial accounting system.

In the next section, we discuss the role of cost information in helping managers to make some of their decisions. But first take a moment to complete the following Self-Study Practice to make sure you understand the functions of management and the differences between financial and managerial accounting.

## SELF-STUDY PRACTICE

1. Which of the following statements best describes the difference between financial accounting and managerial accounting?

    a. Managerial accounting is targeted at external stakeholders, while financial accounting is targeted at individuals within the company.

    b. Financial accounting relies more on subjective, future-oriented information than managerial accounting does.

    c. The major focus of managerial accounting is the preparation of the income statement, balance sheet, and statement of cash flows.

    d. Managerial accounting tends to focus on relevant, subjective, and future-oriented information while financial accounting relies primarily on objective, reliable, and historical information.

    e. All the above statements are false.

2. Which of the following statements regarding the key management functions is false? (You may select more than one answer.)

    a. Planning involves setting both long-term objectives and the short-term tactics necessary to achieve those objectives.

    b. Directing/leading involves comparing actual results to planned objectives and making any adjustments as necessary.

    c. Each of the management functions (planning, organizing, leading/directing, and controlling) is completely independent of the others.

    d. All of the above.

*When you are have finished, check your answers with the solutions at the bottom of the page.*

# COST CLASSIFICATIONS AND DEFINITIONS

One of the key roles of managerial accounting is to measure the cost of various products, services, and customers. For example, a marketing manager at Tombstone Pizza would probably want to know how much each pizza costs to determine what price to charge. Similarly, a production manager might want to know how much it costs to make the pizza sauce in-house as opposed to buying it from a supplier. You may not realize it, but these two examples use the word **cost** in subtly different ways. Let's look more closely at the meaning of the word **cost.**

## Definition of Cost

When you incur a cost, you give up one thing, such as money or time, in exchange for something else. Cost is the value of what is given up during this exchange. Determining what something costs is fairly straightforward if you are paying cash or credit for an item. It is a

Video 18-2
www.mhhe.com/LLPW1e

**Learning Objective 3**

Define and give examples of different types of cost.

Solution to
Self-Study Practice

1. D
2. B and C. (Item B describes control, not leading/directing. Item C is false because the management functions are interdependent).

lot trickier when you are giving up something of less obvious value, such as your time, your services, or your expertise. In this section, we classify and define various types of cost including those that are stated routinely in dollars and cents and those that are not.

## Out-of-Pocket versus Opportunity Costs

Out-of-pocket costs involve an actual outlay of cash. In your personal life, these are the costs you pay "out of your pocket" for things such as food, clothing, and entertainment. For Tombstone Pizza, these costs would include payments for items such as rent, wages, utilities, advertising, and insurance.

Unlike an out-of-pocket cost which involves an outlay of cash, an opportunity cost is the cost of **not** doing something. In other words, it is the forgone benefit (or lost opportunity) of the path not taken. Anytime you choose to do one thing instead of another because of a limit on your time or money, you incur an opportunity cost. For example, if you are going to school full-time, you are giving up the opportunity to earn money by working full-time. The potential earnings you give up to go to school are an opportunity cost of pursuing your education.

Similarly, business managers incur an opportunity cost any time they are forced to choose between one alternative or another because of limited resources, such as cash, equipment, or space. If Tombstone Pizza has a limited number of ovens in which to bake its various pizza products, for example, managers may need to reduce production of an existing pizza product in order to produce the new whole wheat pizza. If so, the value of the lost sales from the existing product should be treated as an opportunity cost of introducing the new whole wheat pizza.

## Spotlight On BUSINESS DECISIONS

### Should You Continue Your Education?

You have obviously made the decision to further your education by taking this class. At some point in the future, you may even think of getting an advanced degree, such as an MBA, law degree, or medical degree.

The decision to pursue a degree is a very important one that should consider both the costs and benefits. As you know, the costs of education, including tuition, fees, and books, are very high. You also incur opportunity costs when you forgo working to go to school. These costs must be offset by the future career opportunities (and higher salary) the degree will bring.

If you ever consider getting an MBA, Forbes has an online decision tool that can help you weigh the costs and benefits of the advanced degree.* This tool estimates the five-year gain from getting an MBA as the difference between the salary and bonuses you would expect to earn in the five years after graduation minus the tuition and potential earnings you would give up while getting your MBA. Because these costs and benefits occur across a number of years, the online tool factors in the time value of money, or the opportunity cost of giving up cash today to earn cash at some point in the future.

This same approach can be applied to almost any decision so long as you can estimate the future costs and benefits of the particular decision you are trying to make.

---
* http://www.forbes.com/2005/08/16/cz_05mba_business_schools_gain_calulator.html

**Coach's Tip**

Whether a cost is treated as direct or indirect depends on whether tracing it is both **possible** and **feasible**. Some minor costs, such as the cost of glue or other supplies, may not be worth the effort needed to trace to individual products. These costs are classified as **indirect costs**.

## Direct versus Indirect Costs

When managers request cost information, they typically want to know the cost of something specific, whether it is a specific unit of product (such as a 16-inch pizza), a particular component of the product (such as the pizza dough), or an area or division in the company (such as the baking department). The item for which they are trying to determine cost is the cost object.

Costs that can be traced directly to a specific cost object are direct costs. Costs that cannot be traced to a specific cost object, or that are not worth the effort of tracing, are indirect costs. Assume, for example, you want to know the cost of taking a specific course, such as this accounting course. Some costs, such as those for tuition and books, can be traced directly to the course, so they would be considered direct costs. If you are taking multiple courses, some costs may not be directly traceable to a single course. Examples would be the cost of traveling to and from campus, the cost of your personal computer, and the supplies you use in class. These costs would be considered indirect costs.

For Tombstone Pizza, direct costs would include the costs of materials and labor that can be traced directly to each pizza produced. Indirect costs would include items such as depreciation on the ovens used to bake the pizzas as well as the costs of utilities, advertising, and plant supervision. See Exhibit 18.3 for some examples of direct and indirect costs at other real-world companies.

| Exhibit 18.3 | Real-World Examples of Direct versus Indirect Costs | | |
|---|---|---|---|
| **Company** | **Cost Object** | **Direct Costs** | **Indirect Costs** |
| **Toni and Guy Hair Salons** | Individual haircut and style | Stylist's time | Styling products, receptionist's service, depreciation on equipment |
| **Federal Express** | Package delivered | Packaging of materials (envelopes, etc.) | Planes, delivery personnel |
| **GAP** | Pair of blue jeans | Cost of the jeans, commissions paid to salesperson | Store supervision, rent, and inventory control |
| **Dell Computer** | Personal computer | Cost of the components, wages of workers who assembled the computer, and delivery costs | Production supervision, factory space, and quality control |

## Variable versus Fixed Costs

For internal decision making, managers are often interested in how costs will change with a change in activity level, such as the number of units produced or sold. Variable costs are those that change, in total, in direct proportion to changes in activity levels. For example, if Tombstone Pizza were to increase its production of pizzas by 20 percent, certain costs, such as those for direct materials, direct labor, and the power required to run the ovens, would increase proportionally.

Fixed costs are those that stay the same, in total, regardless of activity level, at least within some range of activity. For example, the costs of factory space, depreciation on equipment, insurance, and supervision probably would not increase as a result of a 20 percent increase in production. Because the distinction between fixed and variable costs is so important to many managerial decisions, we will analyze it in detail in Chapter 21.

### Coach's Tip

In deciding whether a cost is variable or fixed, be sure to think about whether the **total cost** will change. Looking at average or unit cost will reveal an entirely different pattern, which we will examine more closely in Chapter 21.

## Spotlight On BUSINESS DECISIONS

### The Need to Understand Fixed and Variable Costs

Assume you are the treasurer of a university club and you are on the planning committee for the end-of-year social event. The committee is in charge of finding a location, renting tables and chairs, and hiring a DJ, photographer, and caterer for the event. Your responsibility as treasurer is to set the budget for the event and make sure the committee stays within that budget. One of the first questions you would need to know is how many people are likely to attend the event.

Which costs would you expect to vary with the number of people attending? Which costs will be the same regardless of how many people attend the event? Why is it important for you to know the answers to these questions to prepare a budget? Check the Coach's Tip on the next page for answers to these questions.

Managers must answer these same questions when making business decisions. They need to understand which costs will vary with the number of units produced or the number of customers served, and which will be incurred regardless of these factors.

# Relevant versus Irrelevant Costs

Often managers are interested only in those costs that are relevant to a particular decision. A **relevant cost** is one that has the potential to influence a decision; an **irrelevant cost** is one that will not influence a decision. For a cost to be relevant, it must meet both of the following criteria:

- It must differ between the decision alternatives.
- It must be incurred in the future rather than in the past.

The first criterion means that the cost must change depending on the choice the manager makes. Costs that differ across decision alternatives are also called **differential costs**. The second criterion, that the cost must be incurred in the future, eliminates costs that have already been incurred or **sunk costs**. Because those costs have already been paid for (that is, they are sunk), they will not change with the manager's decision. Therefore, they are not relevant to future decisions.

Assume, for example, you are thinking of selling your old car and buying a new one. Is the amount you paid for your old car a relevant cost? The answer is no; it is a sunk cost that will not change regardless of what you do in the future. However, the amount of money you can get for your old car now (its current value) and the cost of the new car are relevant to your decision. Any difference in fuel costs and insurance for the old and the new cars would also be relevant. What about the parking fee you pay each semester—is that a relevant cost? The answer is no because you will have to pay for parking no matter which car you drive.

Now assume that you are thinking of getting rid of your car altogether and either riding a bike or relying on public transportation. Would the cost of on-campus parking be relevant to that decision? In this case, it would be relevant because it will change depending on whether or not you own a car. In Chapter 22, we rely heavily on this concept of relevant versus irrelevant costs to analyze a variety of managerial decisions.

# Manufacturing versus Nonmanufacturing Costs

Another important distinction between costs is whether they are related to manufacturing or nonmanufacturing activities. This distinction is important only in companies that make a physical product, such as Apple (iPods), Toyota (cars and trucks), Harley Davidson (motorcycles), or Maytag (appliances). Businesses that sell services or purchased goods do not need to make this distinction.

**Manufacturing costs** include all costs incurred to produce the final product. They are generally classified into one of three categories:

**Prime Cost =**

**Direct Materials
+
Direct Labor**

**Conversion Cost =**

**Direct Labor
+
Manufacturing
Overhead**

- **Direct materials** are the major material inputs that can be physically and conveniently traced to the final product. For Tombstone Pizza, direct materials would include the major ingredients (dough, sauce, cheese, and meat), as well as packaging materials (plastic and cardboard). This category would not include minor materials that cannot be conveniently traced to individual units (such as seasoning and glue).
- **Direct labor** is the cost of labor that can be physically and conveniently traced to the product. This category includes all hands-on labor associated with making the physical product. It would not include the labor of those who do not touch the physical product, such as supervisors, maintenance workers, and engineers.
- **Manufacturing overhead** includes all manufacturing costs **other than direct materials and direct labor** that must be incurred to manufacture a physical product. For Tombstone Pizza, examples would include rent, insurance, utilities, and supervision at the manufacturing facility. Costs that are not related to manufacturing (such as distribution or marketing costs) should not be included in manufacturing overhead.

Taken together, direct materials and direct labor are referred to as **prime cost** because they represent the primary costs that can be traced to the end product. Similarly, direct labor and manufacturing overhead are referred to as **conversion cost**—that is, the total cost required to convert direct materials into the finished product.

**Nonmanufacturing costs** are the costs associated with running the business and selling the product, as opposed to manufacturing the product. They are generally classified into two groups:

- **Marketing or selling costs** are incurred to get the final product to the customer. For Tombstone Pizza, examples would include the cost of the trucks that deliver the pizzas to supermarkets, the sales managers' salaries, and advertising costs.

- **Administrative costs** are associated with running the overall organization. They include general management's salaries, rent and utilities for corporate headquarters, and corporate service functions, such as the accounting, payroll, and legal departments.

## Product versus Period Costs

The distinction between product and period costs is closely tied to the distinction between manufacturing and nonmanufacturing costs. This terminology has to do with the way in which different costs are treated from a financial accounting perspective. Specifically, the distinction depends on **when** the cost is matched against revenue on the income statement.

For financial reporting purposes, GAAP requires that all manufacturing costs be treated as product costs, or costs that are attached to the product during production. Product costs are sometimes called inventoriable costs because they are initially counted as part of the cost of inventory. In contrast, period costs are never counted as inventory. Rather, they are expensed during the period they are incurred. For financial reporting purposes, GAAP requires that all nonmanufacturing costs be expensed in the period incurred. Note, however, that **these rules pertain only to external reporting.** For internal purposes, companies may use other accounting methods that are more useful in managerial decision making. Refer to Exhibit 18.4 for an illustration of the different treatment of product and period costs under GAAP.

### Exhibit 18.4    Accounting Treatment of Product versus Period Costs

In the next section, we see how various costs are reported in the financial statements. Chapter 19 will present costs in even more detail. For now, it is important that you understand the basic cost terminology and definitions. Before continuing take the Self-Study Practice on the next page to see how well you understand this terminology.

## COSTS IN MANUFACTURING VERSUS NONMANUFACTURING FIRMS

Most businesses can be classified into one of three categories. Service companies provide services to other businesses or consumers. Examples of service companies include United Parcel Service (UPS), Regis hair salons, LA Fitness clubs, and Verizon Wireless. Merchandising companies purchase goods from others and sell them to other businesses or consumers. Examples of merchandising companies include Safeway, Sam's Club, Abercrombie and Fitch, and Amazon.com. Manufacturing firms purchase raw materials from suppliers and use them

## SELF-STUDY PRACTICE

Match the appropriate description on the right to the terms on the left.

____ 1. Cost

____ 2. Product costs

____ 3. Period costs

____ 4. Manufacturing costs

____ 5. Nonmanufacturing costs

____ 6. Variable costs

____ 7. Fixed costs

____ 8. Direct costs

____ 9. Indirect costs

____10. Out-of-pocket costs

____11. Opportunity cost

____12. Sunk costs

A. Costs that remain the same in total regardless of the activity level

B. Costs that involve an outlay of cash for items such as rent, utilities, and salaries

C. The benefit that you forgo when you select one alternative over another

D. Costs that can be traced conveniently and physically to a specific cost object

E. Costs that have already been incurred and thus are not relevant to future decisions

F. Costs that are expensed in the period when they are incurred

G. Costs that are incurred while making a physical product, such as direct materials, direct labor, and manufacturing overhead

H. Costs that cannot be traced conveniently or physically to a specific cost object

I. Costs that change in total in direct proportion to a change in the activity level

J. Costs that are attached to the product being produced and are included in inventory until the product is sold

K. The value that is given up in an exchange of goods or services

L. Costs that are not related to producing a product, such as selling and administrative costs

*When you have finished, check your answers with the solutions at the bottom of the page.*

to make a finished product, which they sell to other businesses or consumers. Examples of manufacturing firms include Tombstone Pizza, Harley Davidson, Levis, and Ford Motor Company.

As you might expect, the financial statements of manufacturing firms are more complicated than those of service or merchandising companies because they must account for all costs of transforming raw materials into finished products. Because manufacturing firms play such an important (although diminishing) role in the U.S. economy, the remainder of this chapter will be devoted to issues that arise in manufacturing firms. To start, let's consider how a manufacturing firm's balance sheet differs from that of a merchandising firm.

**Solution to Self-Study Practice**

1. K
2. J
3. F
4. G
5. L
6. I
7. A
8. D
9. H
10. B
11. C
12. E

# Balance Sheets of Merchandising versus Manufacturing Firms

The major difference between the balance sheets of merchandising and manufacturing firms is the treatment of inventory. Merchandisers report only one form of inventory (merchandise inventory) on their balance sheets; manufacturing firms report three types: raw materials, work in process, and finished goods (see Exhibit 18.5).

| **Exhibit 18.5** | **Balance Sheets for Merchandising and Manufacturing Firms** |
| --- | --- |

| Merchandising Firm's Balance Sheet | | Manufacturing Firm's Balance Sheet | |
| --- | --- | --- | --- |
| **Assets** | | **Assets** | |
| Cash | $ 15,000 | Cash | $ 20,000 |
| Accounts receivable | 35,000 | Accounts receivable | 30,000 |
| Merchandise inventory | 50,000 | Raw materials inventory | 15,000 |
| Property, plant, and equipment | 100,000 | Work in process inventory | 27,000 |
| Total assets | $200,000 | Finished goods inventory | 40,000 |
| | | Property, plant, and equipment | 78,000 |
| | | Total assets | $210,000 |

**Raw Materials Inventory** represents the cost of all materials purchased from suppliers but not yet used. For Tombstone Pizza, this amount would include the cost of all ingredients for making the pizza (cheese, dough, sauce, and spices) as well as the cost of all packaging materials (cardboard and plastic). As raw materials are used in production, these costs are transferred to the Work in Process Inventory account.

**Work in Process Inventory** represents the cost of units that have been started but are not yet complete. In addition to the cost of the direct materials transferred out of the raw materials account, this inventory account accumulates direct labor costs and manufacturing overhead costs, such as factory rent, depreciation, insurance, and utilities. Once the product is complete, these costs are transferred to the finished goods inventory account.

**Finished Goods Inventory** represents the cost of all units that have been completed but not yet sold. The cost of each unit manufactured remains in the Finished Goods Inventory account until the product is sold. After the product's sale, the cost is transferred to the Cost of Goods Sold account on the income statement.

Recall from our discussion of product costs (page 773) that GAAP requires all manufacturing costs initially be treated as part of the cost of inventory. As units make their way through the manufacturing process, the manufacturing costs flow into and out of the three inventory accounts (see Exhibit 18.6). At first, raw materials are recorded in the Raw Materials Inventory account. As materials are issued into production, their costs are transferred to the Work in Process Inventory account, which also accumulates direct labor and manufacturing overhead costs. When the product is complete, the total manufacturing cost is transferred out of the Work in Process Inventory account and into the Finished Goods Inventory account. Finally, when the product is sold, the manufacturing cost is transferred out of Finished Goods Inventory and into the Cost of Goods Sold account.

# Cost of Goods Manufactured Report

The total cost that is transferred out of Work in Process and into Finished Goods is called the **cost of goods manufactured**. It represents the total cost of all units completed during a given period regardless of whether or not they have been sold. To calculate the cost of goods manufactured, accountants sum the direct materials, direct labor, and manufacturing overhead costs recorded during the period and then adjust them using the beginning and ending values in the Raw Materials Inventory and Work in Process Inventory accounts.

## Exhibit 18.6    Manufacturing Cost Flows

**Raw Materials Inventory**

| Beginning Raw Materials + Raw Material Purchases | − Raw Materials Used in Production |
|---|---|
| Ending Raw Materials | |

Note: This assumes that only direct materials are included in Raw Materials Inventory. Indirect materials are ignored for now.

**Work in Process Inventory**

| Beginning Work in Process + Direct Material Used + Direct Labor + Manufacturing Overhead | − Cost of Goods Manufactured |
|---|---|
| Ending Work in Process | |

**Cost of goods manufactured**

**Finished Goods Inventory**

| Beginning Finished Goods + Cost of Goods Manufactured | − Cost of Goods Sold |
|---|---|
| Ending Finished Goods | |

**Cost of goods sold**

> **Coach's Tip**
> Cost of goods manufactured is sometimes called cost of goods completed. It is the cost of the units completed during the period, regardless of whether or not they have been sold.

The total cost of goods manufactured or completed is reported in the cost of goods manufactured report. See Exhibit 18.7 for such a report.

## Income Statements of Merchandising versus Manufacturing Firms

The main difference between the income statements of merchandising and manufacturing firms is the calculation of the cost of goods sold. These differences may be summarized as follows:

### Merchandiser Cost of Goods Sold

Beginning Merchandise Inventory + Merchandise Purchases − Ending Merchandise Inventory = Cost of Goods Sold

## Manufacturer Cost of Goods Sold

| Beginning Finished Goods Inventory | | Cost of Goods Manufactured | | Ending Finished Goods Inventory | | Cost of Goods Sold |
|:---:|:---:|:---:|:---:|:---:|:---:|:---:|
| | + | | − | | = | |

**Exhibit 18.7**  Cost of Goods Manufactured Report

### Schedule of Cost of Goods Manufactured

| | | | |
|---|---:|---:|---:|
| Beginning raw materials inventory | $ 10,000 | | |
| Plus: Raw material purchases | 95,000 | | |
| Total raw material available for use | 105,000 | | |
| Less: Ending raw materials inventory | 15,000 | | |
| Raw material used in production | | $90,000 | |
| Direct labor | | 50,000 | |
| Manufacturing overhead costs | | | |
| Factory rent | 25,000 | | |
| Supervisors' salaries | 18,000 | | |
| Factory insurance | 9,000 | | |
| Factory utilities | 8,000 | | |
| Other manufacturing overhead cost | 12,000 | 72,000 | |
| Total current manufacturing costs | | | $212,000 |
| Plus: Beginning work in process inventory | | | 15,000 |
| Total work in process | | | 227,000 |
| Less: Ending work in process inventory | | | 27,000 |
| Cost of goods manufactured | | | $200,000 |

Because merchandising firms purchase finished goods from someone else (rather than making the products themselves), they calculate cost of goods sold by adding the value of the merchandise on hand at the beginning of the period to the value of goods purchased during the period and then subtracting the value of any merchandise remaining at the end of the period. Manufacturing firms make a similar calculation that considers the values of the beginning and ending finished goods inventory. However, because manufacturing firms make their products instead of purchasing them, they use the term **cost of goods manufactured** instead of **merchandise purchases.**

See Exhibit 18.8 for these differences in calculation, which are ultimately summarized in the Cost of Goods Sold section of the income statement. Notice that the only difference is

**Exhibit 18.8**  Income Statements for Merchandising and Manufacturing Firms

| Merchandising Company Income Statement | | Manufacturing Company Income Statement | |
|---|---:|---|---:|
| Sales | $200,000 | Sales | $300,000 |
| Less: Cost of goods sold | | Less: Cost of goods sold | |
| Beginning merchandise inventory | 40,000 | Beginning finished goods inventory | 50,000 |
| Plus: Purchases | 150,000 | Plus: Cost of goods manufactured | 200,000 |
| Cost of goods available for sale | 190,000 | Cost of goods available for sale | 250,000 |
| Less: Ending merchandise inventory | 50,000 | Less: Ending finished goods inventory | 40,000 |
| Cost of goods sold | 140,000 | Cost of goods sold | 210,000 |
| Gross profit | 60,000 | Gross profit | 90,000 |
| Less: Operating expenses | 20,000 | Less: Operating expenses | 40,000 |
| Income from operations | $ 40,000 | Income from operations | $ 50,000 |

that the merchandising firm bases cost of goods sold on purchases of merchandise, while the manufacturing firm bases cost of goods sold on the cost of goods manufactured.

To make sure you understand how to calculate a manufacturing firm's cost of goods manufactured and cost of goods sold, complete the following self-study practice.

**SELF-STUDY PRACTICE**

**DiGiorno Pizza** reported the following inventory balances at the beginning and end of January 2009.

|  | Beginning Inventory (1/1/2009) | Ending Inventory (1/31/2009) |
| --- | --- | --- |
| Raw materials inventory | $15,000 | $25,000 |
| Work in process inventory | 30,000 | 15,000 |
| Finished goods inventory | 50,000 | 40,000 |

Additional information for the month of January follows:

| Raw material purchases | $ 80,000 |
| --- | --- |
| Direct labor | 50,000 |
| Manufacturing overhead costs | 100,000 |

Based on this information, compute the following:

1. Cost of raw material used in production.
2. Total current manufacturing costs.
3. Cost of goods manufactured.
4. Cost of goods sold.

*When you have finished, check your answers with the solutions at the bottom of the page.*

# Demonstration Case

Barnaby's Bicycle Company manufactures high-quality mountain bikes. The company's managerial accountant has come to you for help. She needs to classify and identify each of the following costs before she can calculate the cost to produce each mountain bike.

**Part 1:** Classify each of the costs listed on the following chart into three categories based on the following questions.

1.  Can this cost be directly and conveniently traced to each bicycle that is manufactured, or is doing so either not possible or not worth the effort?
2.  Is this cost related to manufacturing the bicycles or to some other activity, such as selling them or managing the overall business?

**Solution to Self-Study Practice**

1. $ 15,000 + $80,000 − $ 25,000 = $ 70,000
2. $ 70,000 + $50,000 + $100,000 = $220,000
3. $220,000 + $30,000 − $ 15,000 = $235,000
4. $235,000 + $50,000 − $ 40,000 = $245,000

3.  Will the total cost vary with the number of bicycles manufactured or sold, or will it remain the same regardless of how many bikes are produced and sold?

The first item in the chart is completed as an example.

| | QUESTION 1 | | QUESTION 2 | | | | QUESTION 3 | |
| --- | --- | --- | --- | --- | --- | --- | --- | --- |
| | | | MANUFACTURING (PRODUCT) COSTS: | | | | COST BEHAVIOR | |
| | Direct Cost | Indirect Cost | Direct Materials | Direct Labor | Mfg. Overhead | Nonmfg. (period) Expenses | Variable Cost | Fixed Cost |
| Alloy tubing used to make the bicycle frames | X | | X | | | | X | |
| Wages paid to employees who cut and weld the alloy tubing | | | | | | | | |
| Factory rent | | | | | | | | |
| Bicycle wheels and tires | | | | | | | | |
| Miscellaneous bicycle components | | | | | | | | |
| Insurance on the factory | | | | | | | | |
| Insurance on the president's company car | | | | | | | | |

**Part 2:** On July 1, Barnaby's Bicycle Company had the following inventory on hand:

| | |
| --- | --- |
| Raw materials inventory | $15,000 |
| Work in process inventory | 25,000 |
| Finished goods inventory (500 bikes @ $90 each) | 45,000 |

Additional information recorded during July follows.

| | |
| --- | --- |
| Raw material purchases | $100,000 |
| Raw materials used in production | 105,000 |
| Direct labor | 30,000 |
| Manufacturing overhead costs | 40,000 |
| Selling and administrative expenses | 49,000 |

During July, workers completed 2,000 bikes and transferred $180,000 worth of goods from Work in Process to Finished Goods, leaving $20,000 worth of goods still in process. A monthly cost summary revealed that the average cost of each bike produced that month was $90. At the end of the month, 400 bikes, valued at a total cost of $36,000, were in finished goods inventory. The company sold 2,100 bikes in July at a retail price of $200 each.

*Required:*

1. Prepare a cost of goods manufactured report for the month of July.
2. Prepare the income statement for Barnaby's Bicycle Company for the month of July; include a detailed calculation of the cost of goods sold.

## Suggested Solution
Part 1:

| Example: | QUESTION 1 | | QUESTION 2 MANUFACTURING (PRODUCT) COSTS: | | | | QUESTION 3 COST BEHAVIOR | |
|---|---|---|---|---|---|---|---|---|
| | Direct Cost | Indirect Cost | Direct Materials | Direct Labor | Mfg. Overhead | Nonmfg. (period) Expenses | Variable Cost | Fixed Cost |
| Alloy tubing used to make the bicycle frames | X | | X | | | | X | |
| Wages paid to employees who cut and weld the alloy tubing | X | | | X | | | X | |
| Factory rent | | X | | | X | | | X |
| Bicycle wheels and tires | X | | X | | | | X | |
| Miscellaneous bicycle components | | X | | | X | | X | |
| Insurance on the factory | | X | | | X | | | X |
| Insurance on the president's company car | | X | | | | X | | X |

Part 2:
1.

**Barnaby's Bicycle Company**
**Cost of Goods Manufactured**
**for the Month of July**

| | | |
|---|---|---|
| Beginning raw materials inventory | $ 15,000 | |
| Plus: Raw material purchases | 100,000 | |
| Total raw materials available for use | 115,000 | |
| Less: Ending raw materials inventory | 10,000 | |
| Raw materials used in production | | $105,000 |
| Direct labor | | 30,000 |
| Manufacturing overhead | | 40,000 |
| Total current manufacturing costs | | $175,000 |
| Plus: Beginning work in process inventory | | 25,000 |
| Total work in process | | 200,000 |
| Less: Ending work in process inventory | | 20,000 |
| Cost of goods manufactured | | $180,000 |

2.

| Barnaby's Bicycle Company<br>Income Statement<br>for the Month of July | | |
|---|---:|---:|
| Sales revenue (2,100 bikes × $200) | | $420,000 |
| Less: Cost of goods sold | | |
| Beginning finished goods inventory | $ 45,000 | |
| Plus: Cost of goods manufactured | 180,000 | |
| Cost of goods available for sale | 225,000 | |
| Less: Ending finished goods inventory | 36,000 | |
| Cost of goods sold | | 189,000 |
| Gross profit | | 231,000 |
| Less: Selling and administrative expenses | | 49,000 |
| Income from operations | | $182,000 |

# Chapter Summary

### LO1  Describe the key differences between financial accounting and managerial accounting. p. 766

- Financial accounting is used by external stakeholders, such as investors, creditors, and bankers.
- Managerial accounting is used by managers inside the organization.
- Other differences:
  - Financial accounting information tends to be reliable, objective, and historical in nature.
  - Managerial accounting information tends to be relevant, timely, and future oriented.
  - Financial accounting is reported through the income statement, balance sheet, and cash flow statement.
  - Managerial accounting relies on a variety of reports targeted at specific decisions, including budgets, cost reports, and performance evaluations.
  - Financial accounting reports are prepared on a monthly, quarterly, or annual basis.
  - Managerial accounting reports are prepared as needed.
  - Financial accounting reports are prepared at the company level.
  - Managerial accounting reports are prepared at the divisional or departmental level appropriate to the decision being made.

### LO2  Explain the functions of management. p. 767

- The managerial decision making process can be described as including four interrelated functions:
- Planning, or the process of setting long-term objectives along with the short-term tactics needed to achieve those objectives.
- Organizing, or gathering the necessary resources to carry out the plan.
- Directing/Leading, or performing the steps involved in putting the plan into action.
- Control, or monitoring actual results against the plan and making any necessary adjustments.

### LO3  Define and give examples of different types of costs. p. 769

- When you incur a cost, you give up something of value in exchange for something else.
- Costs can be classified in a variety of ways:
  - Out-of-pocket costs require a cash outlay.
  - Opportunity costs are the benefits you give up when you choose one alternative over another.
  - Direct costs can be traced directly to a specific cost object.
  - Indirect costs either cannot be traced to a specific cost object or are not worth the effort to do so.
  - Variable costs change in direct proportion to changes in the level of activity.
  - Fixed costs remain the same, in total, regardless of the level of activity.
  - Relevant costs are those that differ between alternatives.
  - Irrelevant costs are those that remain the same regardless of the alternatives and thus will not affect the decision.
  - Manufacturing costs are associated with making a physical product.
  - Nonmanufacturing costs are associated with selling a product or service or running the overall business.

- GAAP requires manufacturing costs to be treated as product costs and nonmanufacturing costs to be expensed as period costs.
- Product costs are assigned to a product as it is being produced; they accumulate in inventory accounts until the product is sold.
- Period costs are reported as expenses as they are incurred.

### LO4  Compare the financial statements of merchandising and manufacturing firms. p. 775

- The major difference between the balance sheets of merchandising and manufacturing firms is the reporting of inventory: Merchandising firms report the total value of merchandise inventory; manufacturing firms break it down into three different categories.
- Manufacturing firms report three types of inventory on their balance sheets: Raw materials, Work in process, and Finished goods.
- The primary difference between the income statements of merchandising and manufacturing firms is the calculation of the cost of goods sold.
- Merchandising firms calculate cost of goods sold based on the cost of merchandise purchased adjusted for the beginning and ending values of merchandise inventory.
- Manufacturing firms calculate cost of goods sold based on the cost of goods manufactured adjusted for the beginning and ending values of finished goods inventory.

### LO5  Prepare a cost of goods manufactured report. p. 775

- The cost of goods manufactured is the total cost to manufacture all units completed during the period; this amount is transferred out of the Work in Process Inventory account and into the Finished Goods Inventory account when the products are complete.
- To calculate the cost of goods manufactured, first account for the total manufacturing costs (direct materials, direct labor, and manufacturing overhead) and then make adjustments for the beginning and ending values of the raw materials and work in process inventories.
- The cost of goods completed remains on the balance sheet as part of Finished Goods Inventory until the products are sold, at which point it is reported as part of cost of goods sold on the income statement.

## Key Terms

Administrative Costs (p. 773)
Budget (p. 768)
Control (p. 768)
Conversion Cost (p. 772)
Cost (p. 769)
Cost Object (p. 770)
Cost of Goods Manufactured (p. 775)
Differential Cost (p. 772)
Direct Costs (p. 770)
Directing/Leading (p. 768)
Direct Labor (p. 772)
Direct Materials (p. 772)
Financial Accounting (p. 776)

Finished Goods Inventory (p. 775)
Fixed Costs (p. 771)
Indirect Costs (p. 770)
Inventoriable Cost (p. 773)
Irrelevant Cost (p. 772)
Managerial Accounting (p. 766)
Manufacturing Costs (p. 772)
Manufacturing Overhead (p. 772)
Marketing or Selling Costs (p. 772)
Merchandising Company (p. 774)
Manufacturing Firm (p. 774)
Nonmanufacturing Costs (p. 772)
Opportunity Cost (p. 770)

Organizing (p. 768)
Out-of-Pocket Costs (p. 770)
Period Cost (p. 773)
Planning (p. 768)
Prime Cost (p. 772)
Product Costs (p. 773)
Raw Materials Inventory (p. 775)
Relevant Cost (p. 772)
Service Company (p. 783)
Sunk Cost (p. 772)
Variable Costs (p. 771)
Work in Process Inventory (p. 775)

See complete glossary in the back of text.

## Questions

1. What is the primary difference between financial accounting and managerial accounting?

2. Explain how the primary difference between financial and managerial accounting results in other differences between the two.

3. Why are traditional, GAAP-based financial statements not necessarily useful to managers and other internal parties?

4. What are the four basic functions that all managers perform? How are these functions interrelated?

5. Think about all of the choices you make on a day-to-day basis: everything from driving versus riding a bike to school or deciding where to have lunch. Pick three decisions you have made today. Identify the out-of-pocket and opportunity costs of each decision.

6. Why is it important for managers to be able to cost a particular item? Name one decision that a company might make using cost information.

7. Explain the difference between a direct cost and an indirect cost. Look at the pen or pencil you are using to do your homework. Give an example of a direct cost that went into making that pen or pencil and an indirect cost of making the pen or pencil.

8. What types of costs are included in manufacturing overhead? Other than direct materials and direct labor, what costs would not be included in manufacturing overhead?

9. Why can't prime cost and conversion cost be added together to arrive at a total manufacturing cost?

10. Explain why product costs are also called inventoriable costs and how those costs move through a company's financial statements.

11. Explain the difference in fixed and variable costs. Give an example of a cost that varies with the number of miles you drive your car each week and an example of a cost that is fixed regardless of how many miles you drive your car each week.

12. Suppose you and your friends are planning a trip for spring break. You have narrowed the destination choices to Panama City, Florida, and Galveston Bay, Texas. List three relevant costs for this decision. List two costs that are irrelevant to this decision.

13. Explain the difference between service companies, merchandising companies, and manufacturing companies.

14. Consider the area in a 3-mile radius of your campus. What service companies, merchandising companies, and manufacturing firms are located within that area?

15. Suppose you have been given a balance sheet for Garcia Company. Without knowing any information about the company, how would the balance sheet help you determine what type of company Garcia is?

16. What are the three types of inventory accounts that you would expect to see on a manufacturing firm's balance sheet? Explain what each one represents and how a particular cost would move through these accounts.

17. What triggers the movement of product costs from an asset on the balance sheet to an expense on the income statement?

18. What is the cost of goods manufactured? What type of costs should be included in cost of goods manufactured?

19. Explain why ending work in process inventory is subtracted from total manufacturing costs to arrive at cost of goods manufactured.

20. Explain the relationship between cost of goods manufactured and cost of goods sold.

## Multiple Choice

1. The **primary** difference between financial accounting and managerial accounting is that

    Quiz 18-1
    www.mhhe.com/LLPW1e

    a. Financial accounting is used by internal parties, while managerial accounting is used by external parties.
    b. Managerial accounting is future oriented, while financial accounting is historical in nature.
    c. Financial accounting is used by external parties, while managerial accounting is used by internal parties.
    d. Financial accounting is prepared as needed (perhaps even daily), but managerial accounting is prepared periodically (monthly, quarterly, annually).

2. Which of the following is not one of the four basic functions of management?
    a. Directing.           c. Planning.
    b. Control.             d. Customer service.

3. Which of the four basic functions of management involves monitoring actual results to see whether the objectives set in the planning stage are being met and, if necessary, taking corrective action to adjust the objectives or implementation of the plan?
    a. Directing.           c. Planning.
    b. Control.             d. Organizing.

4. Suppose you have decided that you would like to purchase a new home in five years. To do this, you will need a down payment of approximately $20,000, which means that you need to save $350 each month for the next five years. This is an example of
    a. Directing.           c. Planning.
    b. Control.             d. Organizing.

Use the following information regarding Garcia Company for questions 5–7.

| | |
|---|---|
| Factory rent | $5,000 |
| Direct labor | 8,000 |
| Indirect materials | 1,000 |
| Direct materials used | 3,500 |
| Sales commissions | 2,500 |
| Factory manager's salary | 4,000 |
| Advertising | 1,500 |

5. What is Garcia's total current manufacturing cost?
    a. $25,500.
    b. $24,000.
    c. $21,500.
    d. $10,000.

6.  What is Garcia's prime cost?
    a.  $11,500.
    b.  $12,500.
    c.  $15,500.
    d.  $21,500.

7.  What is Garcia's manufacturing overhead?
    a.  $24,000.
    b.  $12,500.
    c.  $14,000.
    d.  $10,000.

8.  Suppose you are trying to decide whether to sell your
    accounting book at the end of the semester or keep it for a
    reference book in future courses. If you decide to keep the book,
    the money you would have received from selling it is a(n)
    a.  Sunk cost.
    b.  Opportunity cost.
    c.  Out-of-pocket cost.
    d.  Indirect cost.

9.  Work in Process Inventory would appear as an asset on the
    balance sheet for which type of company?
    a.  Manufacturing.
    b.  Merchandising.
    c.  Service.
    d.  All of the above.

10. Nguyen, Inc., has the following information available for
    January:

    | | |
    |---|---|
    | Cost of goods manufactured | $15,000 |
    | Finished goods inventory (1-31) | 4,000 |
    | Finished goods inventory (1-1) | 2,000 |

    What amount will appear on Nguyen's income statement as
    cost of goods sold?
    a.  $21,000.
    b.  $17,000.
    c.  $13,000.
    d.  $11,000.

---

Solutions to Multiple-Choice Questions

1. c    2. d    3. b    4. c    5. c    6. a    7. d    8. b    9. a    10. c

---

## Mini Exercises  Available with McGraw-Hill's Homework Manager

LO1     **M18-1 Comparing Financial and Managerial Accounting**
Match each of the following characteristics that describe **financial** accounting, **managerial** accounting,
**both** financial and managerial accounting, or **neither** financial and managerial accounting.

_____ 1.  Is future oriented.

_____ 2.  Is used primarily by external parties.

_____ 3.  Is relied on for making decisions.

_____ 4.  Is historical in nature.

_____ 5.  Can be obtained through the company
          Web site or requested from the company
          CFO.

_____ 6.  Is reported in aggregate for the company
          as a whole.

_____ 7.  May be reported daily or even in real time.

_____ 8.  Is used mostly by managers within the
          company.

_____ 9.  Must be accurate to help decision makers.

_____ 10. Is always available on the Internet to any
          interested party.

A.  Financial accounting

B.  Managerial accounting

C.  Both financial and managerial accounting

D.  Neither financial nor managerial accounting

LO2     **M18-2 Identifying Management Functions**
You were recently hired as a production manager for Medallion Company. You just received a memo
regarding a company meeting being held this week. The memo stated that one topic of discussion will

be the basic management functions as they relate to the Production Department. You are expected to lead this discussion. To prepare for the discussion, briefly list the four basic functions of any management and how those functions might relate to your position as production manager.

## M18-3 Classifying Costs

LO3

Top Shelf Company builds oak bookcases. Determine whether each of the following is a direct material (DM), direct labor (DL), manufacturing overhead (MOH), or a period cost (P) for Top Shelf.

_____ 1.   Depreciation on factory equipment.

_____ 2.   Depreciation on delivery trucks.

_____ 3.   Wood used to build a bookcase.

_____ 4.   Production supervisor's salary.

_____ 5.   Glue and screws used in the bookcases.

_____ 6.   Wages of persons who assemble the bookcases.

_____ 7.   Cost to run an ad on local radio stations.

_____ 8.   Rent for the factory.

_____ 9.   Accounts payable manager's salary.

_____10.   Wages of person who sands the wood after it is cut.

## M18-4 Classifying and Calculating Cost

LO3, 5

Refer to M18-3. Assume that you have following about Top Shelf's costs for the most recent month.

| | |
|---|---:|
| Depreciation on factory equipment | $2,000 |
| Depreciation on delivery trucks | 900 |
| Wood used to build bookcases | 1,300 |
| Production supervisor's salary | 3,000 |
| Glue and screws used in the bookcases | 250 |
| Wages of persons who assemble the bookcases | 2,800 |
| Cost to run an ad on local radio stations | 1,200 |
| Rent for the factory | 4,000 |
| Accounts payable manager's salary | 1,500 |
| Wages of person who sands the wood after it is cut | 1,600 |

Determine each of the following costs for Top Shelf.

1.   Direct materials used.
2.   Direct labor.
3.   Manufacturing overhead.
4.   Prime.
5.   Conversion.
6.   Total current manufacturing.
7.   Total nonmanufacturing (period).

## M18-5 Classifying Costs

LO3

You are considering the possibility of pursuing a master's degree after completing your undergraduate degree.

1.   List three costs (or benefits) that would be relevant to this decision including at least one opportunity cost.
2.   List two costs that would be irrelevant to this decision.

## M18-6 Classifying Costs

LO3

Lighten Up Lamps, Inc., manufactures table lamps and other lighting products. For each of the following costs, use an X to indicate the category of product cost and whether it is a prime cost, conversion cost, or both.

PRODUCT COSTS

| | Direct Materials | Direct Labor | Mfg. Overhead | Prime Cost | Conversion Cost |
|---|---|---|---|---|---|
| Production supervisor salary | | | | | |
| Cost of lamp shades | | | | | |
| Wages of person who assembles lamps | | | | | |
| Factory rent | | | | | |
| Wages of person who paints lamps | | | | | |
| Factory utilities | | | | | |
| Screws used to assemble lamps | | | | | |

**LO3**

**M18-7 Calculating Missing Amounts**

For each of the following independent cases A–D, compute the missing values in the table below

| Case | Direct Materials | Direct Labor | Manufacturing Overhead | Prime Cost | Conversion Cost |
|---|---|---|---|---|---|
| A | $800 | $1,400 | $2,100 | $ ? | $ ? |
| B | 400 | ? | 1,325 | 2,550 | ? |
| C | ? | 675 | 1,500 | 2,880 | ? |
| D | ? | 750 | ? | 1,500 | 2,000 |

**LO4**

**M18-8 Classifying Type of Company**

Indicate whether each of the following businesses would most likely be classified as a service company (S), merchandising company (Mer), or manufacturing company (Man).

_____ 1.  Merry Maids.

_____ 2.  Dell Computer.

_____ 3.  Brinks Security.

_____ 4.  Kmart.

_____ 5.  PetSmart.

_____ 6.  Ford Motor Company.

_____ 7.  Bank One.

_____ 8.  Ralph Lauren.

_____ 9.  Dillard's.

_____10.  Sam's Club.

**LO4, 5**

**M18-9 Calculating Missing Amounts and Cost of Goods Manufactured**

For each of the following independent cases A–D, compute the missing values in the table below.

| Case | Total Current Manufacturing Costs | Beginning Work in Process Inventory | Ending Work in Process Inventory | Cost of Goods Manufactured |
|---|---|---|---|---|
| A | $4,800 | $1,400 | $1,100 | $ ? |
| B | 2,200 | ? | 1,325 | 2,550 |
| C | ? | 675 | 1,500 | 6,880 |
| D | 7,900 | 750 | ? | 6.875 |

**LO5**

**M18-10 Calculating Missing Amounts and Cost of Goods Sold**

For each of the following independent cases A–D, compute the missing values in the table below.

| Case | Cost of Goods Manufactured | Beginning Finished Goods Inventory | Ending Finished Goods Inventory | Cost of Goods Sold |
|---|---|---|---|---|
| A | $ 3,100 | $ 400 | $ 100 | $ ? |
| B | 4,250 | ? | 1,325 | 4,550 |
| C | ? | 950 | 500 | 4,375 |
| D | 10,900 | 2,200 | ? | 9,750 |

# Exercises ▪▪ᵀᴹ    Available with McGraw-Hill's Homework Manager

## E18-1 Making Decisions Using Managerial Accounting                    LO1

Suppose you are a sales manager for Books on Wheels, Inc., which makes rolling book carts often used by libraries. The company is considering adding a new product aimed at university students. The new product will be a small, collapsible, wheeled tote designed specifically to aid students in transporting textbooks across campus.

*Required:*

1.  List five questions you and the company would need to answer before proceeding with the development and marketing of this new product.

2.  For each question identified in requirement 1, identify the information you would need to answer the question as well as the expected source of that information.

3.  Identify three serious consequences of either not obtaining the information you need or obtaining inaccurate information.

## E18-2 Identifying Management Functions                    LO2

Refer to E18-1. Suppose that after a thorough investigation, Books on Wheels decided to go forward with the new product aimed at university students. The product, The Campus Cart, has gone into production and the first units have already been delivered to campuses across the country.

*Required:*

Match each of the following steps that took place as Books on Wheels moved through the decision making, production, marketing, and sale of The Campus Cart with the correct phase of the management process: planning (setting long- and short-term objectives), organizing (organizing the necessary resources to implement the plan), directing/leading (taking action to implement the plan), and control (making adjustments to the plan based on actual results).

_____1.  Identifying five college campuses to serve as test markets.                    A.  Planning

_____2.  Setting the goal of 1 million in annual sales by the year 2015.                    B.  Organizing

_____3.  Hiring workers for the manufacturing facility.                    C.  Directing/Leading

_____4.  Overseeing the production and shipment of The Campus Cart.                    D.  Control

_____5.  Preparing one-, three-, and five-year budgets that detail the necessary resources and costs that will be incurred to meet the projected sales forecasts.

_____6.  Deciding which new markets to expand into based on the first year's sales results.

_____7.  Implementing a bonus system to reward employees for meeting sales and production goals.

_____8.  Deciding to spend more advertising dollars in regions where sales were slower than expected.

## E18-3 Classifying Costs                    LO3

Suppose you have just finished your third year of college and expect to graduate with a bachelor's degree in accounting after completing two more semesters of coursework. The salary for entry-level positions with an accounting degree is approximately $48,000 in your area. Shelton Industries has just offered you a position in its northwest regional office. The position has an annual salary of $40,000 and would not require you to complete your undergraduate degree. If you accept the position, you would have to move to Seattle.

*Required:*

Identify with an X whether each of the following costs-benefits would be relevant to the decision to accept the offer from Shelton or stay in school. You may have more than one X for each item.

| | Relevant Cost or Benefit | Irrelevant Cost or Benefit | Sunk Cost | Opportunity Cost |
|---|---|---|---|---|
| $40,000 salary from Shelton | | | | |
| Anticipated $48,000 salary with an accounting degree | | | | |
| Tuition and books for years 1–3 of college | | | | |
| Cost to relocate to Seattle | | | | |
| Tuition and books for remaining two semesters | | | | |
| $19,000 from your part-time job, which you plan to keep until you graduate | | | | |
| Cost to rent an apartment in Seattle (assume you are currently living at home with your parents) | | | | |
| Food and entertainment expenses, which are expected to be the same in Seattle as where you currently live | | | | |
| Increased promotional opportunities that will come from having a college degree | | | | |

**LO3**    **E18-4 Classifying Costs**

Seth's Skateboard Company has provided the following information about its company.

*Required:*

For each of the following costs, use an X to indicate the category of product cost and whether it is a prime cost, conversion cost, both or neither.

### PRODUCT COSTS

| | Direct Materials | Direct Labor | Mfg. Overhead | Period Cost | Prime Cost | Conversion Cost |
|---|---|---|---|---|---|---|
| Production supervisor salary | | | | | | |
| Cost of fiberglass | | | | | | |
| Wages of assembly person | | | | | | |
| Sales commission | | | | | | |
| Cost of high-grade wheels | | | | | | |
| Screws | | | | | | |
| Factory rent | | | | | | |
| Wages of skateboard painter | | | | | | |
| Factory utilities | | | | | | |
| Utilities for corporate office | | | | | | |

**LO3**    **E18-5 Calculating Costs**

Cotton White, Inc. makes specialty clothing for chefs. The company reported the following costs for 2009:

| | |
|---|---:|
| Factory rent | $36,000 |
| Company advertising | 24,000 |
| Wages paid to seamstresses | 75,000 |
| Depreciation on salespersons' vehicles | 30,000 |
| Thread | 1,000 |
| Utilities for factory | 23,000 |
| Cutting room supervisor's salary | 30,000 |
| President's salary | 75,000 |
| Premium quality cotton material | 40,000 |
| Buttons | 750 |
| Factory insurance | 18,000 |
| Depreciation on sewing machines | 6,000 |
| Wages paid to cutters | 50,000 |

*Required:*
Compute the following for Cotton White:

1. Direct materials cost.
2. Direct labor cost.
3. Manufacturing overhead.
4. Total current manufacturing cost.
5. Prime cost.
6. Conversion cost.
7. Total period cost.

## E18-6 Preparing an Income Statement    LO4
Refer to the information in E18-5 regarding Cotton White, Inc.

*Required:*
Prepare the company's income statement for 2009 assuming that all inventory accounts (Raw Materials, Work in Process, and Finished Goods) had a zero balance at both the beginning and end of the year. Cotton White's sales revenue for the year was $735,000.

## E18-7 Calculating Missing Amounts    LO3, 5

*Required:*
For each of the following independent cases (A–E), compute the missing values in the table below.

| Case | Prime Cost | Conversion Cost | Direct Materials | Direct Labor | Manufacturing Overhead | Total Manufacturing Cost |
|---|---|---|---|---|---|---|
| A | $ ? | $ ? | $2,000 | $1,000 | $3,500 | $ ? |
| B | 6,800 | 11,500 | 2,300 | ? | 7,000 | ? |
| C | ? | 7,850 | 1,400 | 3,250 | ? | 9,250 |
| D | ? | ? | ? | 2,100 | 3,100 | 5,800 |
| E | 11,500 | 20,500 | 3,500 | ? | ? | ? |

## E18-8 Calculating Missing Amounts and Cost of Goods Manufactured and Sold    LO4, 5

*Required:*
For each of the following independent cases (A–D), compute the missing values in the table below.

|  | Case A | Case B | Case C | Case D |
|---|---|---|---|---|
| Beginning raw materials inventory | $ 5,000 | ? | $ 20,000 | $110,000 |
| Raw material purchases | 45,000 | 12,250 | 41,640 | ? |
| Ending raw materials inventory | 3,000 | 3,250 | ? | 95,500 |
| Raw materials used | ? | 13,500 | 33,720 | ? |
| Direct labor | 29,000 | ? | ? | 123,250 |
| Manufacturing overhead | 52,000 | 40,350 | 31,080 | 541,730 |
| Total current manufacturing costs | ? | 75,600 | 92,900 | ? |
| Beginning work in process inventory | 41,000 | 32,600 | ? | 102,520 |
| Ending work in process inventory | ? | ? | 41,250 | 236,100 |
| Cost of goods manufactured | 139,000 | 79,800 | 89,225 | 825,900 |
| Beginning finished goods inventory | 72,000 | ? | 51,900 | ? |
| Ending finished goods inventory | 80,000 | 30,100 | ? | 397,200 |
| Cost of goods sold | ? | 71,000 | 113,375 | 839,400 |

LO4, 5  **E18-9 Classifying Costs and Calculating Cost of Goods Manufactured and Sold**

The following information is available for Wonderway, Inc., for 2010.

| | |
|---|---|
| Factory rent | $28,000 |
| Company advertising | 19,000 |
| Wages paid to laborers | 83,500 |
| Depreciation for president's vehicle | 8,000 |
| Indirect production labor | 1,800 |
| Utilities for factory | 30,000 |
| Production supervisor salary | 30,000 |
| President's salary | 60,000 |
| Direct material purchases | 32,500 |
| Sales commissions | 7,500 |
| Factory insurance | 12,000 |
| Depreciation on factory equipment | 26,000 |

Additionally, Wonderway provided the following:

| | |
|---|---|
| Beginning raw materials inventory | $ 5,000 |
| Ending raw materials inventory | 3,000 |
| Beginning work in process inventory | 20,000 |
| Ending work in process inventory | 25,000 |
| Beginning finished goods inventory | 37,500 |
| Ending finished goods inventory | 45,000 |

*Required:*

Calculate the amount for each of the following for Wonderway:

1.  Direct materials used (assume all material is direct).
2.  Direct labor.
3.  Manufacturing overhead.
4.  Total current manufacturing costs.
5.  Cost of goods manufactured.
6.  Cost of goods sold.
7.  Period expenses.

LO4  **E18-10 Preparing an Income Statement**

Refer to the information in E18-9 for Wonderway.

*Required:*

Prepare the company's income statement assuming sales revenue for the year was $500,000.

**E18-11 Calculating Cost of Goods Manufactured and Sold and Preparing an Income Statement**    LO4, 5

StorSmart Company makes plastic organizing bins. The company has the following inventory balances at the beginning and end of March.

|  | Beginning Inventory | Ending Inventory |
|---|---|---|
| Raw materials | $30,000 | $25,000 |
| Work in process | 23,000 | 45,000 |
| Finished goods | 80,000 | 68,000 |

Additional information for the month of March follows.

| | |
|---|---|
| Raw material purchases | $ 42,000 |
| Direct labor | 64,000 |
| Manufacturing overhead | 37,000 |
| Selling and administrative expenses | 25,000 |
| Sales revenue | 236,000 |

**Required:**

Based on this information, prepare the following for StorSmart:

1.  Cost of goods manufactured report.
2.  Income statement for the month of March.

# Problems—Set A  Available with McGraw-Hill's Homework Manager

**PA18-1 Comparing Financial and Managerial Accounting**    LO1

You have been asked to take part in an upcoming Young Professionals meeting in your area. The program planned for the evening will cover many aspects of today's business world. Specifically, you have been asked to explain why there are two types of accounting—financial and managerial—and why they are both relevant to a company's employees. The program director would like for you to cover differences between the two types of accounting as well as how each type plays a role within today's competitive environment.

You will have 15 minutes for your presentation plus a 15-minute question-and-answer period at the end. Your audience is comprised primarily of entry-level managers from all fields (marketing, human resources, production, etc.). Assume that they all have some familiarity with accounting, but few are practicing accountants.

**Required:**

1.  Prepare a detailed outline for your discussion identifying your topic of discussion.
2.  List at least five questions you may be asked during the question-and-answer period. Briefly discuss your answers to these questions.

**PA18-2 Identifying Management Functions**    LO2

Your friend, Suzie Whitson, has designed a new type of outdoor children's toy that helps youngsters learn basic concepts such as colors, numbers, and shapes. Suzie's product will be targeted for two groups: day care centers in warm climates and home school programs for which few activity-intensive programs aim at toddlers' developmental processes. Suzie has come to you for help in getting her idea off the ground. She has never managed a business before and is not sure what functions she will need to perform to make her venture successful.

**Required:**

Briefly explain to Suzie the four major functions of management. For each function, give three examples of questions that Suzie will need to answer to make her business venture a success.

**PA18-3 Classifying Costs; Calculating Total Costs; Identifying Impact of Misclassification**    LO3

Assume that Suzie Whitson (PA18-2) has decided to begin production of her outdoor children's game. Her company is Jiffy Jet where costs for last month follow.

www.mhhe.com/LLPW1e

| | |
|---|---:|
| Factory rent | $3,000 |
| Company advertising | 1,000 |
| Wages paid to assembly workers | 30,000 |
| Depreciation for salespersons' vehicles | 2,000 |
| Screws | 500 |
| Utilities for factory | 800 |
| Assembly supervisor's salary | 3,500 |
| Sandpaper | 150 |
| President's salary | 5,000 |
| Plastic tubing | 4,000 |
| Paint | 250 |
| Sales commissions | 1,200 |
| Factory insurance | 1,000 |
| Depreciation on cutting machines | 2,000 |
| Wages paid to painters | 7,500 |

**Required:**

1. Identify each of the preceding costs as either a product or a period cost. If the cost is a product cost, decide whether it is direct materials (DM), direct labor (DL), or manufacturing overhead (MOH).

2. Determine the total amount for each of the following.

   a. Direct material.

   b. Direct labor.

   c. Manufacturing overhead.

   d. Prime cost.

   e. Conversion cost.

   f. Total product cost.

3. Suppose all period costs were incorrectly identified as product costs. What impact could that have on Jiffy Jet's financial statements? Be specific.

LO3, 4, 5

www.mhhe.com/LLPW1e

**PA18-4 Identifying Types of Companies and Preparing Financial Statements**
Following are the Assets section of comparative balance sheets for Dixie Industries for 2008 and 2009.

| Dixie Industries Comparative Balance Sheet | | |
|---|---:|---:|
| | 12/31/2008 | 12/31/2009 |
| **Assets** | | |
| Cash | $130,400 | $ 97,800 |
| Accounts receivable | 35,600 | 45,300 |
| Merchandise inventory | 59,200 | 51,700 |
| Property, plant, & equipment | 354,700 | 301,600 |
| Total assets | $579,900 | $496,400 |

Information available for Dixie's operations in 2009 includes the following.

| | |
|---|---:|
| President's salary | $ 78,000 |
| Depreciation on office equipment | 12,000 |
| Merchandise purchases | 205,800 |
| Sales commissions | 25,000 |
| Utilities for corporate office | 15,500 |
| Sales revenue | 763,900 |
| Salaries for office personnel | 225,000 |

*Required:*

1. Is Dixie a service, merchandising, or manufacturing firm? How can you tell?
2. Would Dixie have a cost of goods manufactured report?
3. Compute Dixie's cost of goods sold.
4. Prepare Dixie's income statement.

## PA18-5 Identifying Types of Companies, and Preparing Financial Statements

Following are the Assets section of comparative balance sheets for Bettie Company for 2008 and 2009.

LO3, 4, 5

www.mhhe.com/LLPW1e

|  | 12/31/2008 | 12/31/2009 |
|---|---|---|
| Assets |  |  |
| Cash | $ 30,300 | $ 37,800 |
| Accounts receivable | 17,900 | 15,600 |
| Direct materials inventory | 12,900 | 13,850 |
| Work in process inventory | 21,450 | 25,190 |
| Finished goods inventory | 35,670 | 31,700 |
| Property, plant, & equipment | 138,200 | 143,600 |
| Total assets | $256,420 | $267,740 |

Information available for Bettie's operations in 2009 includes the following.

| | |
|---|---|
| President's salary | $ 68,000 |
| Direct material purchases | 36,780 |
| Depreciation on office equipment | 12,000 |
| Depreciation on factory equipment | 62,400 |
| Indirect materials | 1,200 |
| Direct labor | 140,400 |
| Sales commissions | 17,200 |
| Utilities on factory | 17,230 |
| Production supervisor's salary | 38,500 |
| Utilities for corporate office | 9,300 |
| Sales revenue | 653,100 |
| Salaries for office personnel | 95,000 |

*Required:*

1. Is Bettie a service, merchandising, or manufacturing firm? How can you tell?
2. Prepare Bettie's cost of goods manufactured report.
3. Compute Bettie's cost of goods sold. Include any necessary supporting schedules.
4. Prepare Bettie's income statement.

## Problems—Set B  Available with McGraw-Hill's Homework Manager

### PB18-1 Comparing Product and Period Costs

LO3

You have been asked to take part in an upcoming Young Professionals meeting in your area. The program planned for the evening focuses on today's manufacturing environment. Specifically, you have been asked to explain how manufacturing firms determine how much it costs to make their product and why some costs are initially recorded as inventory while other costs are expensed immediately. The program director would like for you to discuss (1) the rules for determining whether a cost should be treated as a product cost or period cost and (2) explain the types of costs that would be included in each category, how each flows through the accounting system, and the implications of the distinction between product costs and period costs for financial reporting (income statement versus balance sheet).

You will have 15 minutes for your presentation plus a 15-minute question-and-answer period at the end. Your audience is comprised primarily of entry-level production personnel although people from other fields (marketing, human resources, production, etc.) will be attending. Assume that they all have some familiarity with accounting but few are practicing accountants.

*Required:*

1. Prepare a detailed outline for your discussion identifying your topic of discussion.
2. List at least five questions you may be asked during the question-and-answer period. Briefly discuss your answers to these questions

**LO2**

### PB18-2 Identifying Management Functions

Your friend, Maria Cottonwood, has designed a new type of fire extinguisher that is very small and easy to use. It will be targeted for two groups of people: elderly or people with disabilities who often have trouble operating the heavy traditional extinguishers and for people who need to store it in small spaces such as a vehicle or storage room where the size of traditional extinguishers makes them cumbersome. Maria has come to you for help in getting her idea off the ground. She has never managed a business before and she is not sure what functions she will need to perform to make her venture successful.

*Required:*

Briefly explain to Maria the four major functions of management. For each function, give three examples of questions that Maria will need to answer to make her business venture a success.

**LO3**

### PB18-3 Classifying Costs, Calculating Total Costs, and Identifying Impact of Classifications

Assume that Maria Cottonwood (PB18-2) has decided to begin production of her fire extinguisher. Her company is Blaze Be Gone whose costs for last month follow.

| | |
|---|---:|
| Factory rent | $2,000 |
| Company advertising | 500 |
| Wages paid to assembly workers | 25,000 |
| Depreciation for salespersons' vehicles | 1,000 |
| Screws | 250 |
| Utilities for factory | 1,200 |
| Production supervisor's salary | 4,500 |
| Sandpaper | 150 |
| President's salary | 6,000 |
| Sheet metal | 8,000 |
| Paint | 750 |
| Sales commissions | 1,700 |
| Factory insurance | 3,000 |
| Depreciation on factory machinery | 5,000 |
| Wages paid to painters | 5,500 |

*Required:*

1. Identify each of the preceding costs as either a product or a period cost. If the cost is a product cost, decide whether it is direct materials (DM), direct labor (DL) or manufacturing overhead (MOH).
2. Determine the total amount for each of the following.
   a. Direct material.
   b. Direct labor.
   c. Manufacturing overhead.
   d. Prime cost.
   e. Conversion cost.
   f. Total product cost.
3. Assume that Maria wants you to explain why the depreciation on the salespersons' vehicles is treated differently than the depreciation on the factory machines. Explain why these costs are treated differently and what the implications are for Maria's financial statements in terms of the balance sheet and income statement.

**LO3, 4, 5**

### PB18-4 Identifying Types of Companies Classifying Costs, and Preparing Financial Statements

Following are the Assets sections of comparative balance sheets for Wynflow Company for 2008 and 2009.

|                               | 2008      | 2009      |
|-------------------------------|-----------|-----------|
| Assets                        |           |           |
| Cash                          | $ 90,300  | $ 87,200  |
| Accounts receivable           | 37,300    | 25,800    |
| Direct materials inventory    | 22,500    | 19,530    |
| Work in process inventory     | 40,150    | 55,000    |
| Finished goods inventory      | 105,290   | 91,200    |
| Property, plant, & equipment  | 278,100   | 288,600   |
| Total assets                  | $573,640  | $567,330  |

Information available for Wynflow's operations in 2009 includes the following.

| | |
|---|---|
| President's salary | $ 72,000 |
| Direct material purchases | 56,870 |
| Depreciation on office equipment | 19,200 |
| Depreciation on factory equipment | 122,700 |
| Indirect materials | 2,150 |
| Direct labor | 187,900 |
| Sales commissions | 34,200 |
| Utilities on factory | 28,540 |
| Production supervisor's salary | 49,500 |
| Utilities for corporate office | 12,900 |
| Sales revenue | 788,100 |
| Salaries for office personnel | 106,500 |

**Required:**

1. Is Wynflow a service, merchandising, or manufacturing firm? How can you tell?
2. If possible, prepare Wynflow's cost of goods manufactured report.
3. Compute Wynflow's cost of goods sold. Include any necessary supporting schedules.
4. Prepare Wynflow's income statement.

**PB18-5 Identifying Costs, Classifying Types of Companies, and Preparing Financial Statements**     LO3, 4, 5

Following are the Assets sections of comparative balance sheets for Ratliff Industries the 2008 and 2009.

Ratliff Industries Comparative Balance Sheet

|                               | 12/31/2008 | 12/31/2009 |
|-------------------------------|------------|------------|
| Assets                        |            |            |
| Cash                          | $ 69,600   | $ 57,290   |
| Accounts receivable           | 30,550     | 25,700     |
| Merchandise inventory         | 24,500     | 31,100     |
| Property, plant, & equipment  | 164,700    | 121,900    |
| Total assets                  | $289,350   | $235,990   |

Information available for Ratliff's operations in 2009 includes the following.

| | |
|---|---|
| President's salary | $ 59,300 |
| Depreciation on office equipment | 4,000 |
| Merchandise purchases | 128,300 |
| Sales commissions | 6,300 |
| Utilities for corporate office | 7,500 |
| Sales revenue | 389,900 |
| Salaries for office personnel | 65,000 |

*Required:*

1. Is Ratliff a service, merchandising, or manufacturing firm? How can you tell?
2. If possible, prepare Ratliff's cost of goods manufactured report.
3. Compute Ratliff's cost of goods sold.
4. Prepare Ratliff's income statement.

## Cases and Projects

**LO1, 3**   **CP18-1 Researching Cost Components of Everyday Item**

Choose one item that you use each day—anything from a toothbrush to your favorite soda to an automobile.

*Required:*

Research online the company that produces this item to find out as much information as you can about the manufacturing process used to create the product. Prepare a report on the product and its manufacturer including the following.

1. A summary of the company including information about its manufacturing facilities.
2. How the company's managerial accounting information would differ from its financial accounting information and specific users of each information type.
3. For the specific product you chose, provide three examples of each of the following.
   a. Direct costs.
   b. Indirect costs.
   c. Variable costs.
   d. Fixed costs.
   e. Product costs.
   f. Period costs.
4. At least two potential suppliers of raw materials used to manufacture the item.
5. The typical price that you pay for this item.

**LO1, 3**   **CP18-2 Identifying Changes in Manufacturing Process and Costs Due to Automation**

In recent years, many companies have converted from a labor-intensive manufacturing process to an automated one. As an example, think of a car wash company that used to wash cars by hand but has now invested in an automatic washing and drying system.

*Required:*

Think of another company that might upgrade to an automated system and answer the following questions.

1. What physical changes would the conversion to automation cause in the manufacturing process?
2. What impact, both positive and negative, might automation have on company morale?
3. What impact might automation have on the skill level of the company's workforce?
4. How might automation affect the quality of the product manufactured and the efficiency of the manufacturing process?
5. How would you expect automation to affect direct material, direct labor, and manufacturing overhead costs? Would you expect any of these costs to increase or decrease?
6. How would you expect automation to affect variable costs and fixed costs? Would you expect either of these costs to increase or decrease?
7. How might this change in manufacturing process affect the price consumers pay for the product?
8. How might this change in manufacturing process affect the company's bottom line both immediately and several years in the future?

**LO1**   **CP18-3 Finding Future-Oriented Information in Financial Statements**

Consider the following statement about the use of forward-looking information on Kraft's Web site.

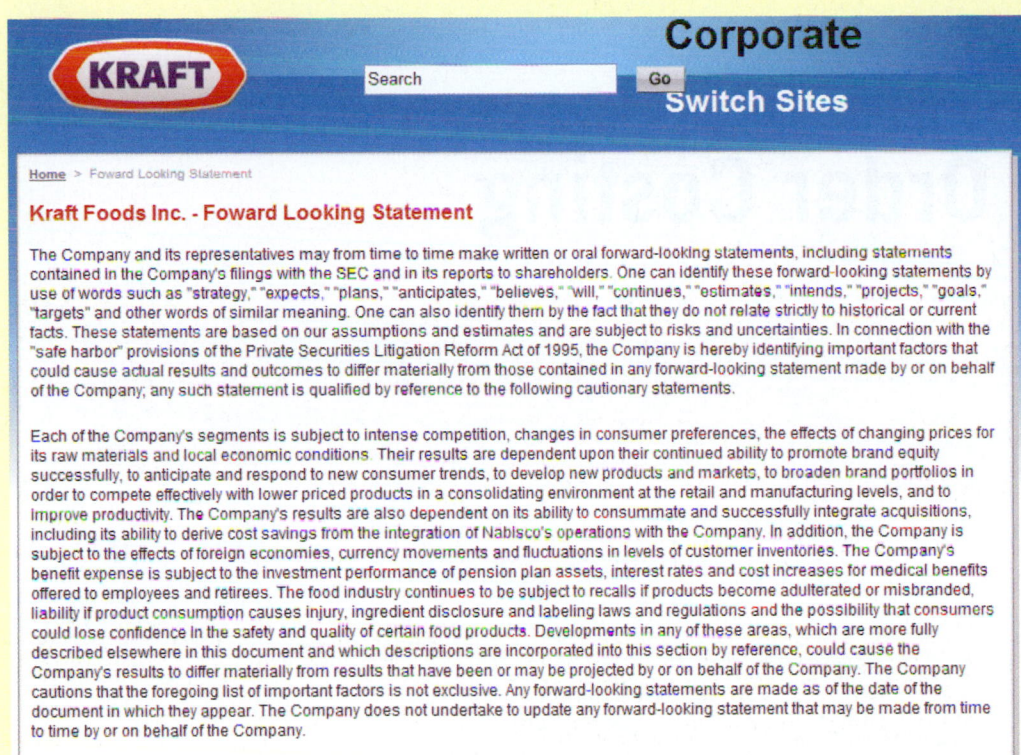

**Kraft Foods Inc. - Foward Looking Statement**

The Company and its representatives may from time to time make written or oral forward-looking statements, including statements contained in the Company's filings with the SEC and in its reports to shareholders. One can identify these forward-looking statements by use of words such as "strategy," "expects," "plans," "anticipates," "believes," "will," "continues," "estimates," "intends," "projects," "goals," "targets" and other words of similar meaning. One can also identify them by the fact that they do not relate strictly to historical or current facts. These statements are based on our assumptions and estimates and are subject to risks and uncertainties. In connection with the "safe harbor" provisions of the Private Securities Litigation Reform Act of 1995, the Company is hereby identifying important factors that could cause actual results and outcomes to differ materially from those contained in any forward-looking statement made by or on behalf of the Company; any such statement is qualified by reference to the following cautionary statements.

Each of the Company's segments is subject to intense competition, changes in consumer preferences, the effects of changing prices for its raw materials and local economic conditions. Their results are dependent upon their continued ability to promote brand equity successfully, to anticipate and respond to new consumer trends, to develop new products and markets, to broaden brand portfolios in order to compete effectively with lower priced products in a consolidating environment at the retail and manufacturing levels, and to improve productivity. The Company's results are also dependent on its ability to consummate and successfully integrate acquisitions, including its ability to derive cost savings from the integration of Nabisco's operations with the Company. In addition, the Company is subject to the effects of foreign economies, currency movements and fluctuations in levels of customer inventories. The Company's benefit expense is subject to the investment performance of pension plan assets, interest rates and cost increases for medical benefits offered to employees and retirees. The food industry continues to be subject to recalls if products become adulterated or misbranded, liability if product consumption causes injury, ingredient disclosure and labeling laws and regulations and the possibility that consumers could lose confidence in the safety and quality of certain food products. Developments in any of these areas, which are more fully described elsewhere in this document and which descriptions are incorporated into this section by reference, could cause the Company's results to differ materially from results that have been or may be projected by or on behalf of the Company. The Company cautions that the foregoing list of important factors is not exclusive. Any forward-looking statements are made as of the date of the document in which they appear. The Company does not undertake to update any forward-looking statement that may be made from time to time by or on behalf of the Company.

*Required:*

1. What was the safe harbor provision of the Private Securities Litigation Reform Act of 1995? What was its intended purpose?

2. Does Kraft have to make similar statements about reports prepared for internal (managerial) use? Would you expect to see more or less forward-looking information in internal reports than external reports?

3. Can you think of other words that accountants might use to describe what they expect to happen in the future other than "strategy," "expects," "plans," "anticipates," "believes," "will," "continues," "estimates," "intends," "projects," "goals," or "targets"? (*Hint:* See the title to Chapter 23).

4. Go to the Web site of another public company and find a similar statement about the use of forward-looking information. Alternatively, you can search for "forward-looking information" and "safe harbor" using a search engine such as Google. What factors does the company list as potential reasons that actual results may differ from the "forward-looking" information. Why does the company list these factors?

## CP18-4 Identifing Service, Merchandising, and Manufacturing Firms: Internet Research    LO4

As discussed in the chapter, companies can be classified into one of three categories: service, merchandising, and manufacturing.

*Required:*

1. Choose one publicly traded company from each category and explore that company's Web site. On the Web site, find a brief company description as well as the most recent published financial statements. Based on the company description, support your categorization of the company as service, merchandising, or manufacturing. If the company falls into more than one of these categories, describe how.

2. Look at the income statement and balance sheet for the company and list any factors that would support your categorization of the company as a service, merchandising, or manufacturing organization.

# 19 Job Order Costing

## LEARNING OBJECTIVES

**After completing this chapter, you should be able to:**

**LO1** Describe the key differences between job order costing and process costing.

Lectured presentation–LP19-1
www.mhhe.com/LLPW1e

**LO2** Describe the source documents used to track direct materials and direct labor costs to the job cost sheet.

**LO3** Calculate a predetermined overhead rate and use it to apply manufacturing overhead cost to jobs.

**LO4** Prepare journal entries to record the flow of manufacturing and nonmanufacturing costs.

**LO5** Calculate and dispose of overapplied or underapplied manufacturing overhead.

**LO6** Calculate the cost of goods manufactured and cost of goods sold.

# Focus Company: TOLL BROTHERS INC.

## "America's Luxury Home Builder"

**Toll Brothers**
America's Luxury Home Builder®

www.tollbrothers.com

Consider the following situation. You go out to a trendy new restaurant with a group of friends. You are on a limited budget, so you order the cheapest dish on the menu and a glass of ice water. Meanwhile, your friends indulge in a full-course meal with drinks, appetizers, entrees, and dessert. When it is time to pay the bill, would you prefer to split the check or get a separate tab for each person at the table?

This common scenario illustrates the basic difference between the two costing systems discussed in the next two chapters. Process costing is similar to splitting the check, spreading the total cost over the number of units produced (or in the case of the restaurant meal, the number of customers at the table). This simple method works well as long as each unit (or customer) consumes about the same amount of cost (or food). Process costing will be covered in Chapter 20.

With job order costing, a separate cost record is kept for each individual product or customer, similar to getting separate checks at a restaurant. This method makes sense when products or customers consume vastly different resources and thus have different costs. Job order costing systems are used for companies that provide customized products or services, such as a custom home builder.

Imagine that you have just landed a great new job and are building your dream home with a luxury home builder such as Toll Brothers Inc. Founded by Bruce and Robert Toll in 1967, Toll Brothers has grown from a small family-owned business to become the nation's leading luxury home builder, with operations in all of the major regions throughout the United States. Toll Brothers prides itself on "building communities in picturesque settings where luxury meets convenience, and where neighbors become lifelong friends."

In this chapter, we track the cost of building a custom home using a job order costing system. Of course, we simplify many of the details, and the numbers we use are fictional. Nevertheless, this extended example should give you a good idea of how an actual job order costing system works—and how your dream home will be accounted for should you be fortunate enough to build one someday.

| JOB ORDER VERSUS PROCESS COSTING | ASSIGNMENT OF MANUFACTURING COSTS TO JOBS | JOURNAL ENTRIES FOR JOB ORDER COSTING | OVERAPPLIED OR UNDERAPPLIED MANUFACTURING OVERHEAD |
|---|---|---|---|
| • Process Costing<br>• Job Order Costing | • Manufacturing Cost Categories<br>• Materials Requisition Form<br>• Direct Labor Time Tickets<br>• Job Cost Sheet<br>• Predetermined Overhead Rates | • Recording the Purchase and Issue of Materials<br>• Recording Labor Costs<br>• Recording Actual Manufacturing Overhead<br>• Recording Applied Manufacturing Overhead<br>• Transferring Costs to Finished Goods Inventory and Cost of Goods Sold<br>• Recording Nonmanufacturing Costs | • Calculating Overapplied and Underapplied Manufacturing Overhead<br>• Disposing of Overapplied or Underapplied Manufacturing Overhead<br>• Calculating Cost of Goods Manufactured and Cost of Goods Sold |

# JOB ORDER VERSUS PROCESS COSTING

Throughout the remainder of this book, you will learn about several different types of cost systems including job order cost systems, process cost systems, activity-based cost systems, full absorption cost systems, variable cost systems, and standard cost systems. Although this may sound a little overwhelming at this point, the most important thing to keep in mind is that these cost systems are not mutually exclusive. In other words, a company could use job order costing, activity-based costing, full absorption costing, and standard costing at the same time.

For now, we focus on the difference between job order and process costing. This distinction has to do with the type of product or service that the company provides and whether the product or service is highly standardized or unique.

## Process Costing

Video 19-1
www.mhhe.com/LLPW1e

Process costing is used by companies that make **homogeneous (standardized)** products or services, such as:

- Coca-Cola beverages.
- Kraft macaroni and cheese.
- Charmin toilet tissue.
- Exxon petroleum products.

These and many other common products are produced in a continuous manufacturing process in which raw materials are put through a standardized production process so that each unit of the final product comes out identical to the next. Process costing breaks the production process down into its basic steps, or processes, and then averages the total cost of the process over the number of units produced. The basic process costing formula is:

$$\text{Average Unit Cost} = \frac{\text{Total Manufacturing Cost}}{\text{Total Units Produced}}$$

Although this formula makes process costing sound simple, a few questions complicate its use in the real world. For example, how much cost should Coca-Cola assign to soft drinks that are still in process at the end of the month—that is, when all the ingredients have been added but the bottling process is not yet complete? These issues will be discussed in more detail in the next chapter, which focuses specifically on process costing.

## Job Order Costing

Video 19-2
www.mhhe.com/LLPW1e

Job order costing is used in companies that offer **customized** or **unique** products or services. Unlike process costing, in which each unit is identical to the next, job order costing is used for situations in which each unit or customer tends to be very different from the next. Examples include:

- A custom home built by Toll Brothers.
- A skyscraper built by Trump Industries.
- A nuclear submarine built for the U.S. Department of Defense.
- A one-of-a-kind wedding gown designed by Vera Wang.

Job order costing is also common in service industries that serve clients or customers with unique needs. For example, the accounting firm Ernst and Young, LLP tracks the billable hours spent on each individual client's account. Law firms, architectural firms, and consulting firms also track the costs of serving individual clients.

In the next section, we illustrate the basics of job order costing using the example of a custom home built by Toll Brothers. First, to make sure you understand the difference between job order costing and process costing, take a moment to complete the following Self-Study Practice.

> **Coach's Tip**
>
> In job order costing, each unique product or customer order is called a **job**. The cost of each unique job is recorded on a document called a **job cost sheet**.

**SELF-STUDY PRACTICE**

Indicate which of the following statements are true (T) and which are false (F).

\_\_\_\_\_ 1. Job order costing systems are more appropriate for companies that produce many units of an identical product.

\_\_\_\_\_ 2. Job order costing is often used in service industries in which each client or customer has unique requirements.

\_\_\_\_\_ 3. A builder of custom pools is more likely to use process costing than job order costing.

\_\_\_\_\_ 4. A company such as Coca-Cola is more likely to use a process costing system than a job order costing system.

\_\_\_\_\_ 5. In process costing, costs are averaged to determine the unit cost of homogeneous goods and services.

*After you have finished, check your answers with the solutions at the bottom of the page.*

## ASSIGNMENT OF MANUFACTURING COSTS TO JOBS

### Manufacturing Cost Categories

As you learned in Chapter 18, the three categories of manufacturing cost are direct materials, direct labor, and manufacturing overhead. Recall that **direct materials** are the primary material inputs that can be directly and conveniently traced to each job. Examples of direct materials used in building a home include concrete, piping, lumber, drywall, fixtures, and appliances. **Direct labor** is the hands-on work that goes into producing a product or service. Examples of direct labor used in building a home include the work of pouring the foundation, framing the home, and installing the plumbing. **Manufacturing overhead** includes all other costs of producing a product that cannot be directly or

> **Coach's Tip**
>
> If you have ever done your own home improvement project, think of the direct materials as the materials you purchased at The Home Depot and the direct labor as the number of hours you put into the job. Unlike do-it-yourself enthusiasts, large construction companies also have many **indirect costs** including equipment, supervision, and insurance. These costs are called **manufacturing overhead**.

Solution to
Self-Study Practice

1. F   2. T   3. F   4. T   5. T

conveniently traced to an individual unit. Examples of the manufacturing overhead required to build (not sell) a home include the costs of site supervision, construction insurance, depreciation on construction equipment, and indirect materials (nails, screws, and so on).

All of these manufacturing costs are recorded on a document called the job cost sheet, which provides a detailed record of the cost incurred to complete a specific job. Refer to Exhibit 19.1 for an illustration of how the three types of manufacturing costs are assigned in a job order cost system.

The most important thing to notice in Exhibit 19.1 is that direct materials and direct labor costs are assigned to jobs differently than manufacturing overhead costs. For the direct costs, all that is needed to keep track of the costs of specific jobs is a set of records called source documents. These documents provide the detailed information needed to record direct materials and direct labor costs. In contrast, manufacturing overhead is made up of all the costs that cannot be directly or conveniently traced to specific jobs. To assign these indirect costs to jobs, accountants must use a predetermined overhead rate that is based on some secondary allocation measure, or cost driver.

Let's start by assigning the direct cost to specific jobs using materials requisition forms and direct labor time tickets.

**Exhibit 19.1    Assignment of Manufacturing Costs to Jobs**

# Materials Requisition Form

Before materials can be used on a job, a materials requisition form—a form that lists the quantity and cost of the direct materials used on a specific job—must be filled out. This form is used to control the physical flow of materials out of inventory and into production. It is also the basis for the journal entries that record the costs of raw materials used in production.

Assume that Toll Brothers is getting ready to frame the interior and exterior walls of the Simpson family's new 2,500 square-foot custom home. The Simpson home has been assigned Job 2719. Before the lumber can be delivered to the job site, a materials requisition form like the one that follows must be completed.

| Materials Requisition Number: | MR 5236 | Date: | 8/11/2008 | |
|---|---|---|---|---|

Job Number    2719
Description:    Simpson Home, Lot 79, Cambridge Subdivision

| Material Description | Quantity | Unit Cost | Total Cost |
|---|---|---|---|
| 2 X 6 Exterior studs | 6,362 board ft. | $0.50 | $3,181 |
| 2 X 6 Double plate | 2,600 board ft. | 0.49 | 1,274 |
| 2 X 6 Pressure treated | 450 board ft. | 0.68 | 306 |
| 2 X 4 Interior studs | 5,400 board ft. | 0.21 | 1,134 |
| 2 X 4 Pressure treated | 300 board ft. | 0.35 | 105 |
| Total cost | | | $6,000 |

Authorized Signature _____

**Coach's Tip**

Source documents always include identification numbers that can be used to cross reference the documents in the accounting records. Here, the total cost on this materials requisition form ($6,000) will be posted to Job 2719.

# Direct Labor Time Tickets

To determine how much direct labor cost is incurred on specific jobs, many companies use computers, bar codes, and handheld devices to track the time employees spend on various tasks. Others rely on the old-fashioned method, having employees record their time manually on labor time tickets. A **direct labor time ticket** is a source document that shows how much time a worker has spent on various jobs each week, as in the following illustration.

Direct Labor Time Ticket        Dates:    Monday 8/11 – Friday 8/15, 2008
Ticket Number:        TT 335
Employee        Bill Robertson

| Date | Time Started | Time Ended | Total Hours | Hourly Rate | Total Amount | Job Number |
|---|---|---|---|---|---|---|
| 8/11/2008 | 7:00 AM | 3:00 PM | 8 hours | $25 | $ 200 | 2719 |
| 8/12/2008 | 7:00 AM | 3:00 PM | 8 hours | 25 | 200 | 2719 |
| 8/13/2008 | 7:00 AM | 3:00 PM | 8 hours | 25 | 200 | 2719 |
| 8/14/2008 | 7:00 AM | 11:00 AM | 4 hours | 25 | 100 | 2719 |
| 8/14/2008 | 12:00 PM | 4:00 PM | 4 hours | 25 | 100 | 3335 |
| 8/15/2008 | 7:00 AM | 3:00 PM | 8 hours | 25 | 200 | 3335 |
| | | Weekly totals | 40 hours | | 1,000 | |

Authorized Signature _____

**Coach's Tip**

This time ticket shows that Bill Robertson spent 28 hours on Job 2719. Because Bill makes $25 per hour, accountants would charge a total of $700 (28 × $25) to Job 2719. The rest of Bill's time would be charged to Job 3335.

# Job Cost Sheet

All costs assigned to an individual job are summarized on a source document called the **job cost sheet.** For example, the costs from the preceding materials requisition form and labor time ticket would be posted to the job cost sheet for the Simpson home (Job 2719).

Job Cost Sheet
Job Number    2719
Date Started:    7/12/2008
Date Completed:
Description:    Simpson Home, Lot 79, Cambridge Subdivision

| Direct Materials | | Direct Labor | | | Applied Manufacturing Overhead |
|---|---|---|---|---|---|
| Req. No | Amount | Ticket | Hours | Amount | |
| MR 5236 | $6,000 | TT 335 | 28 | $700 | ? |

# Predetermined Overhead Rates

The third type of cost that must be recorded is **manufacturing overhead.** Unlike direct materials and direct labor costs, which can be traced to individual jobs using source documents, manufacturing overhead cannot be directly traced to specific jobs. The production supervisor's salary, for example, and depreciation on construction equipment are common costs that relate to multiple jobs. Theoretically, some indirect costs such as indirect materials (screws, nails, and so on) could be traced to individual jobs, but doing so is probably not worth the effort.

Instead, indirect manufacturing overhead costs are **assigned** to specific jobs using an allocation base, or a secondary measure that allocates, or assigns, indirect costs to jobs. Ideally, the allocation base should explain why the cost is incurred. An allocation base that is causally related to cost incurrence is sometimes called a **cost driver.** For example, some manufacturing overhead costs, such as employee taxes and site supervision, are probably driven by the number of direct labor hours worked. Other manufacturing overhead costs, such as machine maintenance and fuel, are driven by the length of time that construction equipment is used. The cost of indirect materials such as glue, sandpaper, and insulation might be driven by the square footage of the home under construction.

For the sake of simplicity, in this chapter, we use a single allocation base for assigning manufacturing overhead costs to jobs. Because home building is a labor-intensive business, let's assume that Toll Brothers uses direct labor hours as the single allocation base for assigning manufacturing overhead. (For a more accurate way to assign overhead cost using multiple cost drivers, see Chapter 20.)

Once an allocation base has been selected, the predetermined overhead rate is calculated as follows:

$$\text{Predetermined Overhead Rate} = \frac{\text{Estimated Total Manufacturing Overhead Cost}}{\text{Estimated Units in the Allocation Base}}$$

This overhead rate is calculated for an entire accounting period (month, quarter, or year) and is based on **estimated** rather than actual values. We often do not know the actual manufacturing overhead cost until after the month, quarter, or year has ended. Thus, accountants must use their best estimate of manufacturing overhead based on past experience and any expectations they have about how the costs might change in the future.

Assume Toll Brothers estimates the total manufacturing overhead cost for the year to be $750,000 and direct labor hours to be 10,000. Based on these estimates, the predetermined overhead rate would be calculated as follows:

$$\frac{\text{Estimated Total Manufacturing Overhead Cost}}{\text{Estimated Direct Labor Hours}} = \frac{\$750,000}{10,000} = \text{Predetermined Overhead Rate (\$75 per direct labor hour)}$$

This rate suggests that the company needs to assign $75 in manufacturing overhead cost for each direct labor hour worked. This is not the cost of the direct labor, but all of the **indirect costs** of building a home such as indirect materials, depreciation on construction equipment, supervisors' salaries, and insurance.

Once the predetermined overhead rate has been established, accountants use it to determine the amount of overhead to apply to each job. They calculate the **applied manufacturing overhead** by multiplying the predetermined overhead rate by the actual value of the allocation base used on the job, as follows:

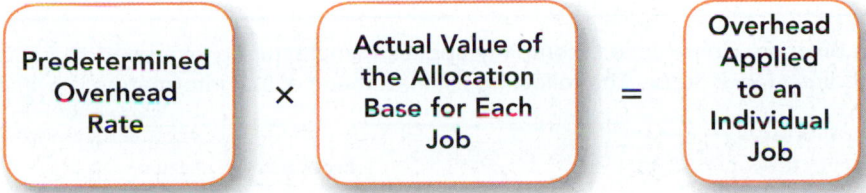

Assume that during the first week of construction, the Simpson home (Job 2719) required a total of 300 direct labor hours. Because the predetermined overhead rate is $75 per direct labor hour, the total applied manufacturing overhead for the week would be $22,500, calculated as follows:

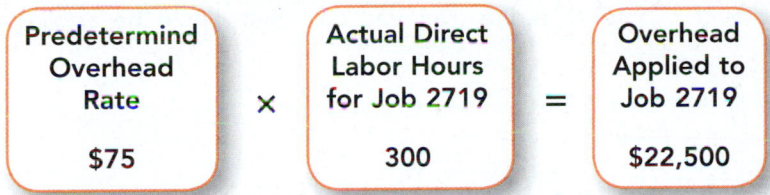

Accountants can apply manufacturing overhead costs when they record direct labor hours, or they can wait until the job is completed and apply all of it at once. If some jobs are still in process at the end of an accounting period, however, accountants must make sure that all cost records are up to date by applying overhead to all jobs in process at the end of the period. The job cost sheet for the Simpson home at the end of the first week follows.

Job Cost Sheet
Job Number   2719
Date Started: 7/12/2008
Date Completed:
Description:    Simpson Home, Lot 79, Cambridge Subdivision

| Direct Materials | | Direct Labor | | | Applied Manufacturing Overhead | | |
|---|---|---|---|---|---|---|---|
| Req. No | Amount | Ticket | Hours | Amount | Hours | Rate | Amount |
| MR 3345 | $ 8,000 | TT 335 | 28 | $ 700 | 28 | $75 | $ 2,100 |
| MR 3372 | 6,000 | TT 340 | 90 | 2,250 | 90 | 75 | 6,750 |
| MR 4251 | 4,500 | TT 385 | 90 | 2,250 | 90 | 75 | 6,750 |
| MR 4827 | 5,500 | TT 425 | 52 | 1,300 | 52 | 75 | 3,900 |
| MR 5236 | 6,000 | TT 445 | 40 | 1,000 | 40 | 75 | 3,000 |
| | $30,000 | | 300 | $7,500 | 300 | $75 | $22,500 |

| Cost Summary | |
|---|---|
| Direct Materials Cost | $30,000 |
| Direct Labor Cost | 7,500 |
| Applied Manufacturing Overhead | 22,500 |
| Total Cost | $60,000 |

Coach's Tip
Notice that the overhead cost applied on the job cost sheet is based on the predetermined (estimated) overhead rate multiplied by the actual number of direct labor hours worked on that job.

Notice that manufacturing overhead was applied to the job cost sheet based on the predetermined overhead rate of $75 per direct labor hour. Because this rate was based on estimated data, applied manufacturing overhead is unlikely to be exactly the same as the actual manufacturing overhead cost incurred. You will see how to record actual manufacturing overhead cost and how to account for any difference between actual and applied manufacturing overhead later in this chapter. First, complete the following Self-Study Practice to make sure you know how to calculate the predetermined overhead rate and apply manufacturing overhead cost to jobs.

**SELF-STUDY PRACTICE**

Carlton Brothers Construction Company applies manufacturing overhead to jobs on the basis of direct labor hours. The following estimated and actual information is available.

|  | Estimated | Actual |
|---|---|---|
| Total manufacturing overhead | $96,000 | $90,000 |
| Total direct labor hours | 12,000 | 11,000 |

Based on these data, calculate the following:

1. Predetermined overhead rate.
2. Total amount of manufacturing overhead cost that would be applied during the period.

*After you have finished, check your answers with the solutions at the bottom of the page.*

## JOURNAL ENTRIES FOR JOB ORDER COSTING

As you learned in Chapter 18, GAAP requires that all manufacturing costs be counted as inventory costs until a product is sold. The three inventory accounts that are used to record manufacturing costs are as follows:

- Raw Materials Inventory represents the cost of materials purchased but not yet issued to production. This account includes costs for both direct materials (lumber, piping) and indirect materials (screws, nails, and so on).
- Work in Process Inventory represents the cost of jobs still in process. Any cost that is added to work in process must also be added to the job cost sheet. Thus, the total cost of all jobs in process should equal the balance in the Work in Process Inventory account.
- Finished Goods Inventory represents the cost of jobs completed but not yet sold. Once a job has been sold, its total cost is transferred to Cost of Goods Sold, which is matched against sales revenue on the income statement.

See Exhibit 19.2 for an illustration of the flow of manufacturing costs through these inventory accounts before being recognized as part of the Cost of Goods Sold.

As the top row in Exhibit 19.2 shows, direct materials and direct labor are recorded directly into the Raw Materials Inventory and Work in Process Inventory accounts. Eventually, when the job is completed, they are transferred to the Finished Goods Inventory account. When the job is sold, the costs are moved to the Cost of Goods Sold account.

Manufacturing overhead costs, in contrast, are not added directly to the Work in Process Inventory account. The Manufacturing Overhead account is a temporary holding account that is used to accumulate actual and applied manufacturing overhead costs. Actual manufacturing overhead, or the actual **indirect** manufacturing costs incurred during the period, appears on the debit side of the Manufacturing Overhead account. **Applied manufacturing overhead,** or the amount that is applied to jobs based on the predetermined overhead rate and the allocation base, appears on the credit side of the Manufacturing Overhead account. The balance in the manufacturing Overhead account represents the difference between actual and applied manufacturing overhead, which is adjusted at the end of the accounting period.

**Solution to Self-Study Practice**

1.

$96,000 / 12,000 = $8.00 per Direct Labor Hour

2.

$8.00 × 11,000 Actual Direct Labor Hours = $88,000

**Exhibit 19.2** Flow of Manufacturing Costs through the Inventory Accounts

The journal entries to record manufacturing costs are described in the following sections. For the sake of simplicity, we assume that none of the accounts had a beginning balance, and that the company worked on only two jobs during the period.

## Recording the Purchase and Issue of Materials

When materials are purchased, the total cost is debited to the Raw Materials Inventory account. The credit should be to Cash or Accounts Payable, depending on the form of payment.

Assume that Toll Brothers purchased $150,000 in raw materials on account. The journal entry to record the purchase of raw materials follows:

| | Debit | Credit |
|---|---|---|
| Raw Materials Inventory | 150,000 | |
| Accounts Payable | | 150,000 |

When materials are placed into production, the cost is debited to either Work in Process Inventory or Manufacturing Overhead, depending on whether the materials can be traced directly to a specific job. Only materials that can be traced directly to a specific job are debited to the Work in Process Inventory account, with a corresponding entry on the job cost sheet. Indirect materials—those that cannot be traced easily or conveniently to a specific job—are debited to the Manufacturing Overhead account. The credit entry should be to Raw Materials Inventory (if the materials come from inventory) or to Accounts Payable (if they are delivered directly from a supplier).

Assume that $150,000 worth of materials is withdrawn from inventory for the following uses:

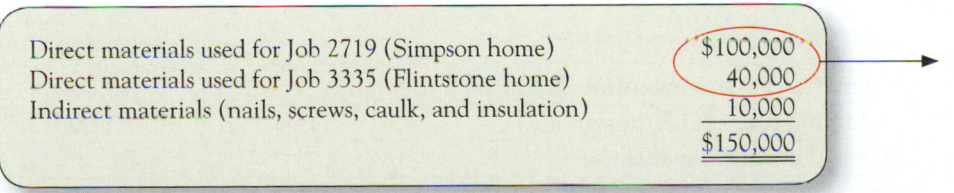

| | |
|---|---|
| Direct materials used for Job 2719 (Simpson home) | $100,000 |
| Direct materials used for Job 3335 (Flintstone home) | 40,000 |
| Indirect materials (nails, screws, caulk, and insulation) | 10,000 |
| | $150,000 |

**Learning Objective 4**

Prepare journal entries to record the flow of manufacturing and nonmanufacturing costs.

*Coach's Tip*

Only **direct** materials are debited to Work in Process. **Indirect** materials are debited to Manufacturing Overhead because they cannot be traced to specific jobs.

The entry to record the issuance of direct and indirect materials follows:

|  | Debit | Credit |
|---|---|---|
| Work in Process Inventory ($100,000 + $40,000) | 140,000 | |
| Manufacturing Overhead | 10,000 | |
| Raw Materials Inventory | | 150,000 |

See Exhibit 19.3 for a summary of the flow of direct and indirect materials costs through the Raw Materials Inventory, Work in Process, and Manufacturing Overhead accounts.

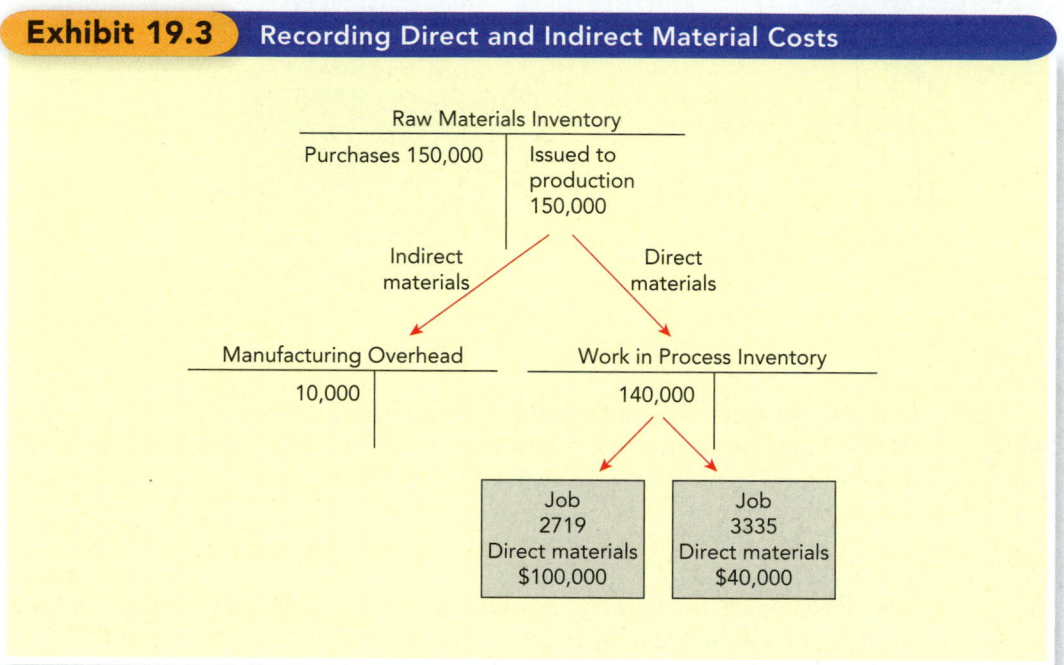

**Exhibit 19.3**     Recording Direct and Indirect Material Costs

## Recording Labor Costs

Labor costs are recorded in much the same way as direct materials: based on the direct labor time tickets that are filled out each week to show how much time was spent on each job. If the time can be traced directly to a specific job, the cost is added to the job cost sheet and debited to the Work in Process Inventory account. If it is not traceable directly to a specific job, the cost is considered indirect labor and is debited to the Manufacturing Overhead account. The corresponding credit should be to Wages Payable.

Assume Toll Brothers recorded the following information:

| | |
|---|---|
| Direct labor on Job 2719 (Simpson home) | $30,000 |
| Direct labor on Job 3335 (Flintstone home) | 20,000 |
| Indirect labor (such as maintenance and inspection work) | 5,000 |
| | $55,000 |

The journal entry to record the direct and indirect labor follows:

|  | Debit | Credit |
|---|---|---|
| Work in Process Inventory ($30,000 + $20,000) | 50,000 | |
| Manufacturing Overhead | 5,000 | |
| Wages Payable | | 55,000 |

See Exhibit 19.4 for a summary of the posting of this entry to the Manufacturing Overhead and Work in Process Inventory accounts.

**Exhibit 19.4    Recording Direct and Indirect Labor Costs**

## Recording Actual Manufacturing Overhead

Remember that actual manufacturing overhead costs are not recorded directly in the Work in Process Inventory account. Instead, these indirect costs are accumulated in the Manufacturing Overhead account.

We have already recorded the indirect materials and indirect labor costs in the Manufacturing Overhead account. Assume Toll Brothers recorded the following additional manufacturing overhead costs during the month:

| | |
|---|---|
| Salary paid to construction site supervisor | $12,000 |
| Salary owed to a construction engineer | 8,000 |
| Property taxes owed but not yet paid | 6,000 |
| Expired insurance premium for construction site | 4,000 |
| Depreciation on construction equipment | 18,000 |
| | $48,000 |

These actual manufacturing overhead costs would be debited to the Manufacturing Overhead account. The credit would be to Cash, Accounts Payable, Prepaid Assets, and/or Accumulated Depreciation, depending on the nature of the transaction. The journal entry to record these actual manufacturing overhead costs is:

| | Debit | Credit |
|---|---|---|
| Manufacturing Overhead | 48,000 | |
| Cash | | 12,000 |
| Salaries Payable | | 8,000 |
| Taxes Payable | | 6,000 |
| Prepaid Insurance | | 4,000 |
| Accumulated Depreciation | | 18,000 |

## Recording Applied Manufacturing Overhead

Manufacturing overhead costs are **applied** to jobs based on the predetermined overhead rate that was estimated at the beginning of the accounting period. As jobs are actually worked on during the period, accountants multiply that predetermined overhead rate by the actual number of direct labor hours worked to determine the amount of manufacturing overhead cost to apply to specific jobs.

In our home-building example, we estimated the manufacturing overhead rate to be $75 per direct labor hour. This rate is not the cost of the direct labor itself, but rather the amount of manufacturing overhead cost that needs to be added for each direct labor hour worked to cover the indirect costs of building the home (equipment depreciation, insurance, supervision, etc.). Assume Toll Brothers' labor time tickets for the month revealed the following:

|  | Job Number | Direct Labor Hours Spent |
| --- | --- | --- |
| Simpson home | 2719 | 600 |
| Flintstone home | 3335 | 200 |
| Total direct labor hours |  | 800 |

Because the overhead rate is $75 per direct labor hour, we need to apply a total of $60,000 (800 hours × $75 per direct labor hour) in manufacturing overhead costs to the Work in Process Inventory account. A corresponding credit should be made to the Manufacturing Overhead account. The journal entry to apply manufacturing overhead to work in process is:

|  | Debit | Credit |
| --- | --- | --- |
| Work in Process Inventory | 60,000 |  |
| Manufacturing Overhead |  | 60,000 |

Again, anytime that we debit Work in Process Inventory, we must also update the individual job cost sheets. For the Simpson home, we would apply $45,000 (600 hours × $75 per hour) to Job 2719. For the Flintstone home, we would apply $15,000 (200 hours × $75) to Job 3335. See Exhibit 19.5 for a summary of the recording of actual and applied manufacturing overhead costs.

**Exhibit 19.5**    **Recording Actual and Applied Manufacturing Overhead Costs**

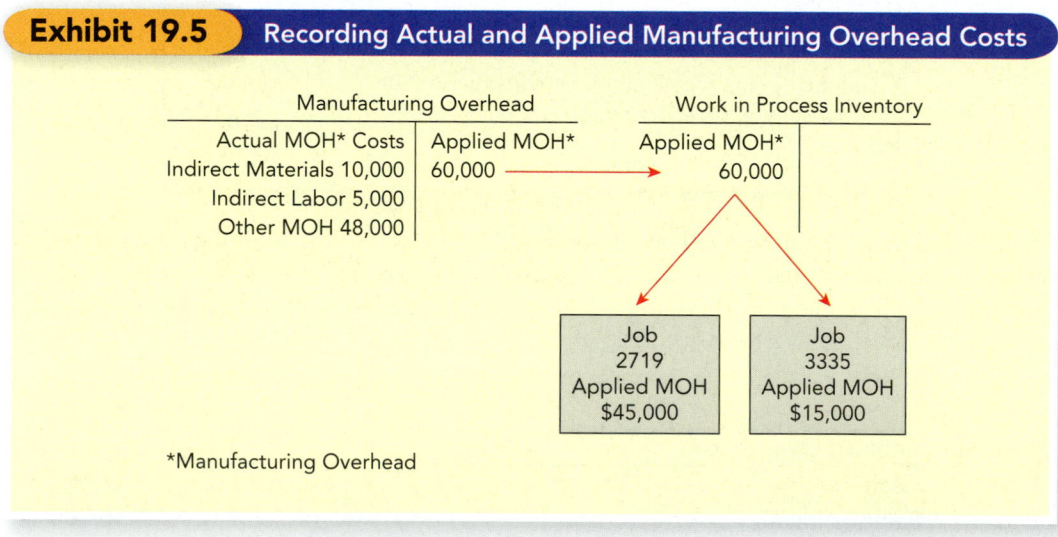

Notice that the amount of overhead that is applied to Work in Process Inventory of $60,000 is not equal to the actual manufacturing overhead cost incurred of $63,000 ($10,000 + $5,000 + $48,000). There are several reasons why the applied amount may be more or less than the actual amount; we discuss those reasons in detail in Chapter 24. For now, just remember that the applied amount is based on estimates made at the beginning of the period. We discuss how to handle the difference between actual and applied overhead costs later in this chapter.

# Transferring Costs to Finished Goods Inventory and Cost of Goods Sold

When a job is finally completed, the job cost sheet must be updated to reflect all direct materials, direct labor, and applied overhead costs that should be charged to the job. Once all manufacturing costs for the Simpson home have been updated, the summary section of the final job cost sheet appears as follows:

| Job Cost Sheet | |
|---|---|
| Job Number    2719 | |
| Date Started:    7/12/2008 | |
| Date Completed: | |
| Description:    Simpson Home, Lot 79, Cambridge Subdivision | |
| Cost Summary | |
| Direct materials cost | $100,000 |
| Direct labor cost | 30,000 |
| Applied manufacturing overhead | 45,000 |
| Total cost | $175,000 |

The total cost to complete the job is referred to as the **cost of goods manufactured** or cost of goods completed. This is the total cost that must be transferred from the Work in Process Inventory account to the Finished Goods Inventory account. When Toll Brothers completes the Simpsons' home at a total cost of $175,000, the company's accountant should make the following journal entry to transfer the completed job from Work in Process Inventory to Finished Goods Inventory.

| | Debit | Credit |
|---|---|---|
| Finished Goods Inventory | 175,000 | |
| Work in Process Inventory | | 175,000 |

The effect of this entry on the T-accounts follows.

| Work in Process Inventory | | | | | | | | | |
|---|---|---|---|---|---|---|---|---|---|

| Work in Process Inventory | | Finished Goods Inventory | | Cost of Goods Sold | |
|---|---|---|---|---|---|
| Direct material 140,000 | When job is | Cost of goods | When job | | |
| Direct labor 50,000 | completed | completed | is sold | | |
| Applied MOH* 60,000 | 175,000 → *Job 2719* → | 175,000 | 175,000 → *Job 2719* → | 175,000 | |
| | | | | | |
| Balance 75,000 | | | | | |
| * Manufacturing overhead. | | | | | |

Because this home was built for a specific customer, the new owners should take ownership shortly after construction is complete (and it passes the owners' inspection). Once the sale is final, accountants will move the total cost of the job from the Finished Goods Inventory account to Cost of Goods Sold. They will also make an entry to recognize the revenue that Toll Brothers earned on the sale. If the Simpsons agreed to pay $275,000 for their home, accountants would make the following journal entries to record the sales revenue and cost of the home.

| | Debit | Credit |
|---|---|---|
| Cash or Accounts Receivable | 275,000 | |
| Sales Revenue | | 275,000 |
| Cost of Goods Sold | 175,000 | |
| Finished Goods Inventory | | 175,000 |

**Coach's Tip**

Remember that the difference between sales revenue and cost of goods sold is **gross profit,** or the profit before nonmanufacturing expenses have been deducted. In this case, the gross profit on the Simpson home is $100,000 ($275,000 − $175,000).

The $175,000 in the Cost of Goods Sold account includes all manufacturing costs of building the Simpson home. But we still need to account for the nonmanufacturing costs.

## Recording Nonmanufacturing Costs

In addition to the manufacturing costs just described, companies incur many other **nonmanufacturing costs** to market their products and run their businesses. Nonmanufacturing costs are treated differently than manufacturing costs. Instead of being treated as part of the product cost (included in inventory and eventually the cost of goods sold), nonmanufacturing costs are expensed during the period in which they are incurred.

Assume Toll Brothers incurred the following nonmanufacturing expenses last month:

| | |
|---|---|
| Commissions to sales agents | $20,000 |
| Advertising expense | 5,000 |
| Depreciation on office equipment | 6,000 |
| Other selling and administrative expenses | 4,000 |
| Total | $35,000 |

The journal entries to record these nonmanufacturing costs are:

| | Debit | Credit |
|---|---|---|
| Commissions Expense | 20,000 | |
|    Cash or Commissions Payable | | 20,000 |
| Advertising Expense | 5,000 | |
|    Cash or Prepaid Advertising | | 5,000 |
| Depreciation Expense | 6,000 | |
|    Accumulated Depreciation | | 6,000 |
| Selling and Administrative Expenses | 4,000 | |
|    Cash, Prepaids, or Payables | | 4,000 |

**Coach's Tip**

Notice that depreciation on office equipment is treated as a period expense while depreciation on construction equipment was treated as manufacturing overhead (a product cost). The difference has to do with whether the asset being depreciated is used for manufacturing or nonmanufacturing activities.

# OVERAPPLIED OR UNDERAPPLIED MANUFACTURING OVERHEAD

## Calculating Overapplied and Underapplied Manufacturing Overhead

Because the amount of **applied** manufacturing overhead is based on a predetermined overhead rate that is estimated before the accounting period begins, it will probably differ from the **actual** manufacturing overhead cost incurred during the period. The difference between actual and applied overhead is called overapplied or underapplied overhead. Overhead cost is overapplied if the amount applied is more than the actual overhead cost. It is underapplied if the amount applied is less than the actual cost.

After recording the actual and applied manufacturing overhead in our home-building example, the Manufacturing Overhead account would appear as follows:

| Manufacturing Overhead | | | |
|---|---|---|---|
| Actual Mfg. Overhead | | Applied Mfg. Overhead | |
| Indirect Materials | 10,000 | | |
| Indirect Labor | 5,000 | | |
| Supervisor Salaries | 12,000 | | |
| Engineering Salaries | 8,000 | | |
| Property Taxes | 6,000 | $60,000 | Applied Overhead |
| Plant Insurance | 4,000 | | |
| Factory Depreciation | 18,000 | | |
| Balance | 3,000 | | |

**Coach's Tip**

The debit balance in Manufacturing Overhead means that actual overhead cost was $3,000 more than the applied overhead cost. That is, overhead was **underapplied.** A credit balance will appear when actual overhead is less than applied overhead—that is, when overhead is **overapplied.**

Notice that actual overhead cost was $63,000, but applied overhead was only $60,000, resulting in $3,000 of **underapplied overhead.** We will see how to dispose of this overhead balance next.

# Disposing of Overapplied or Underapplied Manufacturing Overhead

**The most common method for disposing of the balance in Manufacturing Overhead is to make a direct adjustment to Cost of Goods Sold.** Doing so makes sense as long as most of the jobs that were worked on during the period were completed and sold. However, if a significant amount of cost remains in the Work in Process Inventory or Finished Goods Inventory accounts, then part of the over- or underapplied manufacturing overhead technically should be adjusted to those accounts.

In the example we just examined, the company worked on only two jobs. One was completed and sold, but the other was still in process. In reality, most companies complete and sell many more jobs during the accounting period. Thus, we demonstrate the simplest and most common method of transferring the balance in the Manufacturing Overhead account directly to Cost of Goods Sold. (The more complicated approach of adjusting multiple accounts is covered in advanced accounting textbooks.)

To eliminate the $3,000 debit balance in the Manufacturing Overhead account, we need to credit the Manufacturing Overhead account and debit the Cost of Goods Sold account. The journal entry to dispose of the underapplied overhead is:

| | Debit | Credit |
|---|---|---|
| Cost of Goods Sold | 3,000 | |
| Manufacturing Overhead | | 3,000 |

**Learning Objective 5**

Calculate and dispose of overapplied or underapplied manufacturing overhead.

The effect of this entry is to increase the Cost of Goods Sold account by $3,000. Increasing Cost of Goods Sold makes sense in this case because manufacturing overhead was underapplied. In other words, we did not apply enough cost to the jobs that were completed and eventually sold.

If Manufacturing Overhead had been overapplied (with a credit balance), we would have debited the Manufacturing Overhead account to eliminate the balance and credited the Cost of Goods Sold account. Crediting the Cost of Goods Sold account decreases the cost to reflect the fact that actual manufacturing overhead was less than applied overhead—that is, overhead was overapplied. The effect of disposing of the Manufacturing Overhead balance to the Cost of Goods Sold account is as follows:

Take a moment to make sure you understand how to calculate over- and underapplied manufacturing overhead by completing this Self-Study Practice.

## SELF-STUDY PRACTICE

Carlton Brothers Construction Company applies manufacturing overhead to jobs on the basis of direct labor hours. The following estimated and actual information is available.

|  | Estimated | Actual |
|---|---|---|
| Total manufacturing overhead | $96,000 | $90,000 |
| Total direct labor hours | 12,000 | 11,000 |

1. Calculate the over- or underapplied overhead.
2. Show the journal entry needed to close that amount to the Cost of Goods Sold account.

*After you have finished, check your answers with the solutions at the bottom of the page.*

### Solution to Self-Study Practice

1.

Predetermined Overhead Rate = $96,000 / 12,000 = $8.00 per Direct Labor (DL) Hour
Applied Overhead = $8.00 × 11,000 actual DL hours = $88,000

| Applied overhead | = | $88,000 (credit) |
|---|---|---|
| Actual overhead | = | $90,000 (debit) |
| Underapplied overhead | = | $ 2,000 (debit balance) |

2.

|  | Debit | Credit |
|---|---|---|
| Cost of Goods Sold | 2,000 | |
| Manufacturing Overhead | | 2,000 |

### Coach's Tip

It is easy to become confused about whether to use actual or estimated data in calculating applied manufacturing overhead. Remember that applied overhead is calculated by multiplying the predetermined **(estimated)** overhead rate by the **actual** value of the allocation base.

# Calculating the Cost of Goods Manufactured and Cost of Goods Sold

**Learning Objective 6**

Calculate the cost of goods manufactured and cost of goods sold.

The preceding example illustrated how to record manufacturing and nonmanufacturing costs. See Exhibit 19.6 for the final balance in each of the major accounts after all of the previous transactions have been posted.

Recall that the company only worked on two jobs during the period. Because only one job (#3335) is still in process at the end of the accounting period, the balance in the Work in Process Inventory account will be equal to the total cost recorded on that job ($75,000). The ending balance in Finished Goods Inventory is zero because the only job completed during the period was also sold. The ending balance in Cost of Goods Sold represents the cost of Job #2719 ($175,000), plus the adjustment for underapplied manufacturing overhead ($3,000).

**Exhibit 19.6    Summary of Recorded Manufacturing and Nonmanufacturing Costs**

Using the T-accounts shown in Exhibit 19.6, we can prepare a cost of goods manufactured and sold report. The first part of this report is very similar to the one you learned to prepare in Chapter 18, with a few important differences:

- Because the Raw Materials Inventory account includes both direct and indirect materials, we need to subtract the indirect materials from the total materials purchased to determine how much direct materials were used in production. Remember that only direct materials will flow into the Work in Process Inventory account, while indirect materials will flow through the Manufacturing Overhead account.
- The total current manufacturing costs debited to Work in Process Inventory includes direct material, direct labor, and applied (not actual) manufacturing overhead. Any difference between actual and applied manufacturing overhead is made as a direct adjustment to Cost of Goods Sold.

The cost of goods manufactured and sold report for our home-building example follows, along with the resulting income statement.

## Toll Brothers Inc.
### Cost of Goods Manufactured and Sold

| | |
|---|---:|
| Beginning raw materials inventory | 0 |
| Plus: Raw material purchases | $150,000 |
| Less: Indirect materials used | – 10,000 |
| Less: Ending raw materials inventory | 0 |
| Direct materials used in production | 140,000 |
| Direct labor | 50,000 |
| Manufacturing overhead applied | 60,000 |
| Total current manufacturing costs | 250,000 |
| Plus: Beginning work in process inventory | 0 |
| Less: Ending work in process inventory | – 75,000 |
| Cost of goods manufactured | 175,000 |
| Plus: Beginning finished goods inventory | 0 |
| Less: Ending finished goods inventory | 0 |
| Unadjusted Cost of goods sold | 175,000 |
| Adjustment for underapplied manufacturing overhead | + 3,000 |
| Cost of Goods Sold | $178,000 |

## Toll Brothers Inc.
### Income Statement

| | |
|---|---:|
| Sales revenue | $275,000 |
| Less: Cost of goods sold | 178,000 |
| Gross profit | 97,000 |
| Less: Selling and administrative expenses | 35,000 |
| Income from Operations | $ 62,000 |

**Coach's Tip**

Notice that cost of goods manufactured and cost of goods sold are initially based on the amount of overhead **applied** to Work in Process Inventory, Finished Goods Inventory, and Cost of Goods Sold. Any difference between the actual and applied overhead is adjusted directly to Cost of Goods Sold at the end of the year.

**Coach's Tip**

Earlier in the chapter, we reported that the gross profit earned on the sale of the Simpson home was $100,000. The adjusted gross profit is less because we did not apply enough manufacturing overhead to the job.

# Demonstration Case

Pacific Pool Company (PPC) builds custom swimming pools for homeowners in California, Arizona, and Nevada. PPC uses material requisition forms and direct labor time tickets to trace direct materials and direct labor costs to specific jobs. Manufacturing overhead is applied to jobs at a rate of $100 per direct labor hour. During the most recent month, the company recorded the following transactions:

a. Purchased $200,000 in raw materials on account.
b. Issued $150,000 in raw materials to production.
- $130,000 of this cost was directly traceable to specific jobs;
- $20,000 was not directly traceable to specific jobs.
c. Recorded the following labor costs (paid in cash):
- Direct labor                  $50,000
- Construction supervision       30,000
d. Recorded the following actual manufacturing overhead costs:
- Construction insurance (prepaid)        $ 5,000
- Construction equipment depreciation      25,000
- Pool permits and inspections              5,000

e.  Recorded the following nonmanufacturing costs:
- Office equipment depreciation                    $ 3,000
- Rent and insurance on owner's company car      2,000
- Advertising costs                                 10,000

f.  Applied manufacturing overhead to jobs in process based on 900 actual direct labor hours.

g.  Completed 15 pools at a total cost of $195,000.

h.  Finalized the sale of 13 pools that cost $176,000. The other 2 pools are completed and awaiting inspection by the customer before the sale is finalized.

i.  Recorded sales revenue of $325,000 on the 13 pools that were sold.

j.  Closed the Manufacturing Overhead account balance to Cost of Goods Sold.

**Required:**

1.  Prepare journal entries to record these transactions. Unless otherwise indicated, assume all expenses are paid in cash.

2.  Assuming there were no beginning balances in any of the accounts, calculate the following:
    a.  Ending Work in Process Inventory.
    b.  Ending Finished Goods Inventory.
    c.  Cost of Goods Sold (after the overhead adjustment).
    d.  Gross profit (after the overhead adjustment).

## Suggested Solution

1.

|     |                                          | Debit   | Credit  |
|-----|------------------------------------------|---------|---------|
| a.  | Raw Materials Inventory                  | 200,000 |         |
|     | Accounts Payable                         |         | 200,000 |
| b.  | Work in Process Inventory                | 130,000 |         |
|     | Manufacturing Overhead                   | 20,000  |         |
|     | Raw Materials Inventory                  |         | 150,000 |
| c.  | Work in Process Inventory                | 50,000  |         |
|     | Manufacturing Overhead                   | 30,000  |         |
|     | Cash                                     |         | 80,000  |
| d.  | Manufacturing Overhead                   | 35,000  |         |
|     | Prepaid Construction Insurance           |         | 5,000   |
|     | Accumulated Depreciation                 |         | 25,000  |
|     | Cash                                     |         | 5,000   |
| e.  | Depreciation Expense                     | 3,000   |         |
|     | Rent and Insurance Expense               | 2,000   |         |
|     | Advertising Expense                      | 10,000  |         |
|     | Accumulated Depreciation                 |         | 3,000   |
|     | Cash                                     |         | 12,000  |
| f.  | Work in Process Inventory (900 × $100)   | 90,000  |         |
|     | Manufacturing Overhead                   |         | 90,000  |
| g.  | Finished Goods Inventory                 | 195,000 |         |
|     | Work in Process Inventory                |         | 195,000 |
| h.  | Cost of Goods Sold                       | 176,000 |         |
|     | Finished Goods Inventory                 |         | 176,000 |
| i.  | Cash                                     | 325,000 |         |
|     | Sales Revenue                            |         | 325,000 |
| j.  | Manufacturing Overhead                   | 5,000   |         |
|     | Cost of Goods Sold                       |         | 5,000   |

| Manufacturing Overhead | |
|---|---|
| b. 20,000 | f. 90,000 |
| c. 30,000 | |
| d. 35,000 | |
| | Balance 5,000 |
| j. 5,000 to remove | overapplied |

2.

| Work in Process Inventory | |
|---|---|
| b. 130,000 | g. 195,000 |
| c.  50,000 | |
| f.  90,000 | |
| Balance   75,000 | |

| Finished Goods Inventory | |
|---|---|
| g. 195,000 | h. 176,000 |
| Balance 19,000 | |

| Cost of Goods Sold | |
|---|---|
| h. 176,000 | j. 5,000 |
| Balance 171,000 | |

| | |
|---|---|
| Sales revenue | 325,000 |
| Cost of goods sold | (171,000) |
| Gross profit | 154,000 |

## Chapter Summary

### LO1  Describe the key differences between job order costing and process costing. p. 800

- Process costing is used in companies that make very homogeneous products using a continuous production process.
- Job order costing is used in companies that make unique products or provide specialized services.

### LO2  Describe the source documents used to track direct materials and direct labor costs to the job cost sheet. p. 802

- Direct materials are issued to production by using a materials requisition form showing the costs and quantities of all materials requested and the job on which the materials were used.
- Direct labor costs are recorded using labor time tickets on which each worker records the amount of time spent on each specific job.
- The costs incurred for each job are recorded on a separate job cost sheet.

### LO3  Calculate a predetermined overhead rate and use it to apply manufacturing overhead cost to jobs. p. 804

- Because manufacturing overhead costs cannot be traced directly to individual jobs, we must use an allocation base or cost driver to apply manufacturing overhead cost to specific jobs.
- The predetermined overhead rate is calculated by dividing the estimated total manufacturing overhead cost by the estimated value of the allocation base.
- Manufacturing overhead is applied to specific jobs by multiplying the predetermined overhead rate by the actual amount of the allocation base used on the job.

### LO4  Prepare journal entries to record the flow of manufacturing and nonmanufacturing costs. p. 807

- Initially, raw material purchases are recorded in the Raw Materials Inventory account.
- When materials are placed into production, direct materials are recorded in the Work in Process Inventory account; indirect materials are recorded in the Manufacturing Overhead account.
- When labor costs are incurred, direct labor is recorded in the Work in Process Inventory account; indirect labor is recorded in the Manufacturing Overhead account.

- Actual manufacturing overhead costs are recorded with a debit to Manufacturing Overhead and a credit to the appropriate asset or liability account.
- When manufacturing overhead is applied to specific jobs, the Work in Process Inventory account is debited and the Manufacturing Overhead account is credited.
- When a job is completed, the total cost of goods completed is transferred from the Work in Process Inventory account to the Finished Goods Inventory account.
- When the job is delivered to the customer, the total cost is transferred from Finished Goods Inventory to Cost of Goods Sold.
- Nonmanufacturing costs are recorded as period expenses rather than as part of the manufacturing cost flow.

### LO5 Calculate and dispose of overapplied or underapplied manufacturing overhead. p. 813

- Actual overhead costs are recorded on the debit side of the Manufacturing Overhead account; applied manufacturing overhead costs are recorded on the credit side. Thus, the balance in the Manufacturing Overhead account represents the amount of overapplied or underapplied overhead.
- If the overhead account has a debit balance, actual overhead costs were higher than applied overhead costs; that is, overhead was underapplied.
- If the overhead account has a credit balance, applied overhead costs were higher than actual overhead costs; that is, overhead was overapplied.
- At the end of the year, the remaining overhead balance is typically transferred to the Cost of Goods Sold account. Overapplied overhead decreases (credits) the Cost of Goods Sold account; underapplied overhead increases (debits) the Cost of Goods Sold account.

### LO6 Calculate the cost of goods manufactured and cost of goods sold. p. 815

- The flow of manufacturing costs out of the Work in Process account and into the Finished Goods Inventory account is the cost of good manufactured. When the product is sold, this amount is transferred to the Cost of Goods Sold account.
- Initially, the cost of goods manufactured and the cost of goods sold are based on direct materials, direct labor, and **applied manufacturing overhead** costs.
- The cost of goods sold account is updated to reflect actual manufacturing overhead costs through an adjustment for overapplied or underapplied manufacturing overhead.

| Key Formulas | |
|---|---|
| **To Calculate** | **Formula** |
| Predetermined overhead rate | $\dfrac{\text{Estimated Total Manufacturing Overhead Cost}}{\text{Estimated Units of the Allocation Base}}$ |
| Applied overhead | Predetermined Overhead Rate $\times$ Actual Units of the Allocation Base |
| Overapplied or underapplied overhead | Applied Overhead $-$ Actual Overhead<br>A positive value indicates that overhead cost was overapplied.<br>A negative value indicates that overhead cost was underapplied. |

## Key Terms

Actual Manufacturing Overhead (p. 806)

Allocation Base (p. 804)

Cost of Goods Completed (p. 811)

Cost of Goods Sold (p. 806)

Direct Labor Time Ticket (p. 803)

Indirect Materials (p. 807)

Job Cost Sheet (p. 802)

Job Order Costing (p. 801)

Materials Requisition Form (p. 802)

Overapplied Overhead (p. 812)

Predetermined Overhead Rate (p. 804)

Process Costing (p. 800)

Underapplied Overhead (p. 812)

See complete glossary in the back of text.

## Questions

1. What is the difference between job order and process costing?
2. What types of companies are likely to use job order costing? Give three examples.
3. What types of companies are likely to use process costing? Give three examples.
4. Many service industries use job order costing to keep track of the cost of serving clients. Can you think of a service industry that provides fairly homogeneous services? Describe the industry and explain why it might use process costing rather than job order costing.

5. Many companies use a modified costing system that blends certain elements of process costing and job order costing. Can you think of a company that makes products that have certain similarities from unit to unit (similar to process costing) but also allows a certain degree of customization (similar to job order costing)? Give an example.

6. Describe the three major types of manufacturing costs that are accounted for in a job order cost system. Give an example of each type of cost for an auto repair shop that uses job order costing.

7. What is the purpose of a job order cost sheet? What information should it contain?

8. The job order cost sheet serves as a subsidiary ledger to the Work in Process Inventory account. Explain what this means and how you would verify this.

9. What is the purpose of a materials requisition form? What information should it contain?

10. Explain why the cost of direct materials is debited to Work in Process Inventory while the cost of indirect materials is debited to Manufacturing Overhead.

11. What is the primary source document used to trace the cost of direct labor to specific jobs? What information should it contain?

12. Some would argue that costs would be more accurate if overhead costs were assigned to jobs using an overhead rate based on actual direct labor and actual value of the allocation base. Do you agree or disagree with this view? Explain.

13. Why is manufacturing overhead assigned to Work in Process Inventory in a different manner than direct materials and direct labor? Explain how it is different.

14. Explain how and why depreciation on office equipment is treated differently than depreciation on manufacturing equipment.

15. How is a predetermined overhead rate calculated? How does a company decide on an allocation base to use to calculate the rate?

16. How do you apply manufacturing overhead to the Work in Process Inventory account? Is it based on estimated or actual data?

17. Will the amount of manufacturing overhead that is applied to Work in Process Inventory be equal to the actual amount of manufacturing overhead costs incurred? Why or why not?

18. How do you know when manufacturing overhead is overapplied? What type of balance would you expect to see in the Manufacturing Overhead account?

19. How do you know when manufacturing overhead is underapplied? What type of balance would you expect to see in the Manufacturing Overhead account?

20. Explain the most common method of eliminating any balance in the Manufacturing Overhead account at year-end. What account(s) is (are) adjusted? What happens to the account(s) when manufacturing overhead is overapplied? Underapplied?

## Multiple Choice

1. Why would a company choose to use process costing rather than job order costing to compute product cost?
   a. The company produces units to customer specifications.
   b. The company manufactures a product using a series of continuous processes that results in units that are virtually identical from one to the next.
   c. The company wants to track the cost of material, labor, and overhead to specific customers.
   d. The company wants to allocate manufacturing overhead using an overhead application rate based on direct labor hours.
   e. All of the above.

Quiz 19-1
www.mhhe.com/LLPW1e

2. The source document used to specify the quantity and unit costs of raw materials issued into production is called a:
   a. Production order form.
   b. Materials requisition form.
   c. Direct labor time ticket.
   d. Predetermined overhead rate.
   e. Job order cost sheet.

3. Which of the following source documents serves as a subsidiary ledger for the Work in Process Inventory account?
   a. Production order form.
   b. Materials requisition form.

   c. Direct labor time ticket.
   d. Predetermined overhead rate.
   e. Job order cost sheet.

4. Comstock Company uses a predetermined overhead rate based on machine hours to apply manufacturing overhead to jobs. Estimated and actual total manufacturing overhead costs and machine hours follow.

|  | Estimated | Actual |
|---|---|---|
| Total overhead cost | $100,000 | $110,250 |
| Machine hours | 20,000 | 21,000 |

   What is the predetermined overhead rate per machine hour?
   a. $4.75.       c. $5.25.
   b. $5.00.       d. $5.51.

5. Refer to the information in question 4 above. How much is over- or underapplied overhead?
   a. $10,250 overapplied.      d. $ 5,250 underapplied.
   b. $10,250 underapplied.      e. None of the above.
   c. $ 5,250 overapplied.

6. When raw materials are purchased on account, the journal entry would:
   a. Include a Debit to Work in Process Inventory.
   b. Include a Debit to Raw Materials Inventory.
   c. Include a Credit to Accounts Payable.
   d. Both A and C.
   e. Both B and C.

7. The journal entry to record actual overhead costs incurred would:
   a. Include a debit to Work in Process Inventory.
   b. Include a debit to Manufacturing Overhead.
   c. Include a credit to Manufacturing Overhead.
   d. Include both A and C.
   e. Not be recorded.

8. The journal entry to record applied manufacturing overhead costs would:
   a. Include a debit to Work in Process Inventory.
   b. Include a debit to Manufacturing Overhead.
   c. Include a credit to Manufacturing Overhead.
   d. Include both A and C.
   e. Not be recorded.

9. Carlton Construction Company sold a home that it built for a total cost of $150,000 for a sales price of $250,000. The journal entries to record the sales revenue and cost of the sale would include:
   a. A debit to Cost of Goods Sold for $150,000.
   b. A credit to Finished Goods for $150,000.
   c. A debit to Sales Revenue for $250,000.
   d. A credit to Accounts Receivable for $250,000.
   e. A and B.

10. Before disposing of its year-end manufacturing overhead balance, Delphi Corporation had the following amounts in Manufacturing Overhead and Cost of Goods Sold.

| | |
|---|---|
| Applied manufacturing overhead | $100,000 |
| Actual manufacturing overhead | 90,000 |
| Unadjusted cost of goods sold | 800,000 |

If Delphi closes the balance of its Manufacturing Overhead account directly to Cost of Goods Sold, how much is adjusted cost of goods sold?
   a. $790,000.
   b. $810,000.
   c. $890,000.
   d. $900,000.
   e. None of the above.

| Solutions to Multiple-Choice Questions |
|---|
| 1. b   2. b   3. e   4. b   5. d   6. e   7. b |
| 8. d   9. e   10. a |

## Mini Exercises  Available with McGraw-Hill's Homework Manager

### M19-1 Identifying Companies that Use Job Order versus Process Costing
LO1

Indicate whether each of the following companies is likely to use job order (j) or process costing (p).

___ 1. Golf ball manufacturer.
___ 2. Landscaping business.
___ 3. Tile manufacturer.
___ 4. Auto repair shop.
___ 5. Pet food manufacturer.
___ 6. Light bulb manufacturer.
___ 7. Water bottling company.
___ 8. Appliance repair business.
___ 9. DVD manufacturer.
___ 10. Music video production company.

### M19-2 Calculating Total Current Manufacturing Cost
LO6

The following information is available for Carefree Industries.

| | |
|---|---|
| Beginning work in process inventory | $ 75,000 |
| Ending work in process inventory | 90,000 |
| Cost of goods manufactured | 300,000 |

Compute total current manufacturing costs.

### M19-3 Calculating Cost of Goods Sold
LO6

The following information is available for Carefree Industries.

| | |
|---|---|
| Cost of goods manufactured | $300,000 |
| Beginning finished goods inventory | 140,000 |
| Ending finished goods inventory | 120,000 |

Compute cost of goods sold.

**LO6**

### M19-4 Calculating Direct Material Used in Production

The following information is available for Carefree Industries.

| | |
|---|---|
| Direct labor | $100,000 |
| Total current manufacturing costs | 370,000 |

Manufacturing overhead is applied to production at 150 percent of direct labor cost. Determine how much direct material was used in production.

**LO3**

### M19-5 Calculating Predetermined Overhead Rates

Willard Company applies manufacturing overhead costs to products as a percentage of direct labor dollars. Estimated and actual values of manufacturing overhead and direct labor costs are summarized here:

| | Estimated | Actual |
|---|---|---|
| Direct labor cost | $400,000 | $350,000 |
| Manufacturing overhead | 800,000 | 725,000 |

1. Compute the predetermined overhead rate.
2. Interpret this rate and explain how it will be used to apply manufacturing overhead to jobs.
3. Explain whether you used estimated or actual values to compute the rate, and why.

**LO3**

### M19-6 Calculating Applied Manufacturing Overhead

Refer to M19-5 for Willard Company.

1. Determine how much overhead to apply to production.
2. Explain whether applied overhead was based on actual values, estimated values, or both.

**LO4**

### M19-7 Calculating Over- or Underapplied Manufacturing Overhead

Refer to M19-5 for Willard Company.

1. Compute over- or underapplied overhead.
2. Explain how you would handle the over- or underapplied overhead at the end of the accounting period. Which accounts will be affected? Will the accounts be increased or decreased?

**LO2, 4**

### M19-8 Recording the Purchase and Issue of Raw Materials

Kelly Company's raw materials inventory transactions for the most recent month are summarized here.

| | | |
|---|---|---|
| Beginning raw materials | $ 10,000 | |
| Purchases of raw materials | 100,000 | |
| Raw materials issued | | |
| Material Requisition #1445 | 50,000 | For Job 101 |
| Material Requisition #1446 | 40,000 | For Job 102 |
| Material Requisition #1447 | 15,000 | Used on multiple jobs |

1. Prepare the journal entries to record the purchase and issuance of raw materials.
2. In addition to the Work in Process Inventory account, on what subsidiary record would the $50,000 and $40,000 direct material costs be recorded?
3. Compute the ending balance in the Raw Materials Inventory account.

**LO4**

### M19-9 Recording Direct and Indirect Labor Costs

Kelly Company's payroll costs for the most recent month are summarized here:

| Item | Description | | Total Cost |
|---|---|---|---|
| Hourly labor wages | 750 hours @ $25 per hour | | |
| | 200 hours for Job 101 = | $5,000 | |
| | 300 hours for Job 102 = | 7,500 | |
| | 250 hours for Job 103 = | 6,250 | $18,750 |
| Factory supervision | | | 4,250 |
| Production engineer | | | 6,000 |
| Factory janitorial work | | | 2,000 |
| General and administrative salaries | | | 8,000 |
| Total payroll costs | | | $39,000 |

1. Prepare the journal entry to record the month's payroll costs.
2. Explain why some labor costs are recorded as work in process, some as manufacturing overhead, and some as period costs.

**M19-10 Recording Applied Manufacturing Overhead Costs**                                      LO3, 4
Refer to M19-9 for Kelly Company. The company applies manufacturing overhead to products at a predetermined rate of $50 per direct labor hour.
   Prepare the journal entry to apply manufacturing overhead to production.

**M19-11 Calculating Over- or Underapplied Overhead Costs**                                     LO3, 4, 5
Refer to M19-10 for Kelly Company. Its actual manufacturing costs for the most recent period are summarized here:

| Item | Description | | Total Cost |
|---|---|---|---|
| Direct material | Used on Jobs 101 and 102 | | $90,000 |
| Indirect material | Used on multiple jobs | | 15,000 |
| Hourly labor wages | 750 hours @ $25 per hour | | |
| | 200 hours for Job 101 = | $5,000 | |
| | 300 hours for Job 102 = | 7,500 | |
| | 250 hours for Job 103 = | 6,250 | 18,750 |
| Factory supervision | | | 4,250 |
| Production engineer | | | 6,000 |
| Factory janitorial work | | | 2,000 |
| General and administrative salaries | | | 8,000 |
| Other manufacturing overhead costs (factory rent, insurance, depreciation, etc.) | | | 7,000 |
| Other general and administrative costs (office rent, insurance, depreciation, etc.) | | | 5,000 |

1. Compute over- or underapplied manufacturing overhead.
2. Prepare the journal entry to close the Manufacturing Overhead account balance to Cost of Goods Sold.
3. Explain whether the entry in requirement 2 will increase or decrease Cost of Goods Sold and why.

# Exercises  Available with McGraw-Hill's Homework Manager

**E19-1 Recording Materials Based on Materials Requisitions**                                   LO2, 4
A recent materials requisition form for Christopher Creek Furniture Manufacturers follows.

| Requisition Number | Job Number | Item Description | Total Cost |
|---|---|---|---|
| MR 234 | 25 | ¼" maple planks | $400 |
| MR 235 | 26 | ¼" cherry planks | 500 |
| MR 236 | 27 | ½" birch planks | 450 |
| MR 237 | Indirect | Wood screws, etc | 100 |

*Required:*
Prepare the journal entry to record the issuance of materials.

**E19-2 Recording Direct Materials, Direct Labor, and Applied Overhead**                         LO2, 3, 4
Stone Creek Furniture Factory (SCFF), a custom furniture manufacturer, uses job order costing to keep track of the cost of each customer order. On March 1, SCFF had two jobs in process with the following costs:

| Work in Process | Balance on 3/1 |
|---|---|
| Job 33 | $5,000 |
| Job 34 | 4,000 |
| | $9,000 |

Source documents revealed the following during March.

|  | Amount on Materials Requisitions Forms | Amount on Labor Time Tickets | Status of Job at Month-End |
|---|---|---|---|
| Job 33 | $ 3,000 | $ 5,000 | Completed and sold |
| Job 34 | 3,000 | 4,000 | Completed, but not sold |
| Job 35 | 4,000 | 3,000 | In process |
| Indirect | 1,000 | 2,000 | |
| | $11,000 | $14,000 | |

The company applies overhead to products at a rate of 75 percent of direct labor cost.

*Required:*

1. Prepare journal entries to record the material requisitions, labor costs, and applied overhead.
2. Calculate the balance in the Work in Process Inventory, Finished Goods Inventory, and Cost of Goods Sold accounts at month-end.

**LO2,4**    **E19-3 Analyzing Labor Time Tickets and Recording Labor Costs**
A weekly time ticket for Jim Bolton follows.

| Direct Labor Time Ticket | | Dates: | Monday 8/12 – Friday 8/16, 2008 | |
|---|---|---|---|---|
| Ticket Number: | TT338 | | | |
| Employee: | Jim Bolton | | | |
| Date | Time Started | Time Ended | Total Hours | Job Number |
| 8/12/2008 | 7:00 AM | 3:00 PM | 8 hours | Job 271 |
| 8/13/2008 | 7:00 AM | 3:00 PM | 8 hours | Job 271 |
| 8/14/2008 | 7:00 AM | 3:00 PM | 8 hours | Job 272 |
| 8/15/2008 | 7:00 AM | 11:00 AM | 4 hours | Job 272 |
| 8/15/2008 | 12:00 PM | 4:00 PM | 4 hours | Maintenance |
| 8/16/2008 | 7:00 AM | 3:00 PM | 8 hours | Job 273 |
| | | Weekly Total | 40 hours | |
| | | Hourly Labor Rate | $25 | |
| | | Total Wages Earned | $1,000 | |

*Required:*

1. Determine how much of the $1,000 that Jim earned during this week would be charged to Job 271, Job 272, and Job 273.
2. Explain how would the time spent doing maintenance work would be treated.
3. Prepare a journal entry to record the wages for Jim assuming they have not yet been paid.

**LO3, 6**    **E19-4 Finding Unknown Values in the Cost of Goods Manufactured and Sold Report**
Mulligan Manufacturing Company uses a job order cost system with overhead applied to products at a rate of 200 percent of direct labor cost. Selected manufacturing data follow.

|  | Case 1 | Case 2 | Case 3* |
|---|---|---|---|
| Direct material used | $ 10,000 | f. | $15,000 |
| Direct labor | 15,000 | e. | i. |
| Manufacturing overhead applied | a. | 16,000 | j. |
| Total current manufacturing costs | b. | 35,000 | 27,000 |
| Beginning work in process inventory | 8,000 | g. | 7,000 |
| Ending work in process inventory | 6,000 | 8,000 | k. |
| Cost of goods manufactured | c. | 40,000 | 30,000 |
| Beginning finished goods inventory | 5,000 | 10,000 | l. |
| Ending finished goods inventory | 7,000 | h. | 5,000 |
| Cost of goods sold | d. | 42,000 | 33,000 |

* **Hint:** For Case 3 (parts i. and j.), first solve for conversion costs and then determine how much of that is direct labor and how much is manufacturing overhead.

*Required:*

Treat each case independently. Find the missing amounts for letters a–l. You should do them in the order listed.

**E19-5 Calculating Overhead Rates, Recording Actual and Applied Manufacturing Overhead, and Analyzing Over- or Underapplied Manufacturing Overhead**    LO3, 4, 5

Cayman Custom Manufacturing Company applies manufacturing overhead on the basis of machine hours. At the beginning of the year, the company estimated its total overhead cost to be $300,000 and machine hours to be 15,000. Actual manufacturing overhead and machine hours were $340,000 and 16,000, respectively.

*Required:*

1. Compute the predetermined overhead rate.
2. Compute applied manufacturing overhead.
3. Prepare the journal entries to record actual and applied manufacturing overhead.
4. Compute over- or underapplied manufacturing overhead.
5. Prepare the journal entry to transfer the overhead balance to Cost of Goods Sold.

**E19-6 Calculating and Recording the Total Cost to Complete a Job and Sales Revenue**    LO3, 4, 6

Aquazona Pool Company is a custom pool builder. It recently completed a pool for the Drayna family (Job 1324), as summarized on the following incomplete job cost sheet.

Job Cost Sheet
Job Number    1324
Date Started:  7/12/2008
Date Completed:
Description:    Drayna Pool

| Direct Materials | | Direct Labor | | | Applied Manufacturing Overhead | | |
|---|---|---|---|---|---|---|---|
| Req. No | Amount | Ticket | Hours | Amount | Hours | Rate | Amount |
| MR 3345 | $1,500 | TT 335 | 28 | $ 600 | | | |
| MR 3372 | 1,000 | TT 340 | 40 | 800 | | | |
| MR 4251 | 1,250 | TT 385 | 30 | 600 | | | |
| MR 4263 | 1,750 | TT 425 | 35 | 700 | | | |
| MR 5236 | 2,000 | TT 445 | 25 | 500 | | | |
| | $7,500 | | 158 | $3,200 | ? | ? | ? |

Cost Summary

| | |
|---|---|
| Direct Material Cost | $7,500 |
| Direct Labor Cost | 3,200 |
| Applied Manufacturing Overhead | |
| Total Cost | |

The company applies overhead to jobs at a rate of $10 per direct labor hour.

*Required:*

1. Calculate how much overhead would be applied to Job 1324.
2. Compute the total cost of Job 1324.
3. Assume the company bids its pools at total manufacturing cost plus 30 percent. If actual costs were the same as estimated, determine how much revenue the company would report on the sale of Job 1324.
4. Prepare journal entries to show the completion of Job 1324 and to recognize the sales revenue. Assume the total cost of Job 1324 is currently in the Finished Goods Inventory Account and that the Draynas paid for the pool with cash.
5. Calculate how much gross profit Aquazona made on the sale of the Drayna pool.

**E19-7 Recording Manufacturing Costs**    LO4

The flow of costs through a company's cost accounting system is summarized in the following T-accounts.

| Raw Materials Inventory | | Manufacturing Overhead | |
|---|---|---|---|
| a. | b. | b. | d. |
| | | c. | |
| | | e. | |

| Work in Process Inventory | | Finished Goods Inventory | |
|---|---|---|---|
| b. | g. | g. | h. |
| c. | | | |
| d. | | | |

| Sales Revenue | | Cost of Goods Sold | |
|---|---|---|---|
| | i. | h. | |

| Selling and Administrative Expenses | | Other Assets or Liabilities | |
|---|---|---|---|
| c. | | i. | a. |
| f. | | | c. |
| | | | e. |
| | | | f. |

**Required:**

Describe the transactions represented by letters a–i. When more than one debit appears in a single transaction, explain why the costs are debited to different accounts.

**LO3, 4**

**E19-8 Preparing Entries for Manufacturing Costs**

Roy's Appliance Repair Shop uses a job order costing system to keep track of the cost of each repair. Roy applies its "garage or shop" overhead at a rate of $25 per direct labor hour spent on each repair. Roy's uses the following accounts to keep track of the cost of all repairs.

| Raw Materials (parts and supplies) | | Repair Jobs in Process | | Cost of Repairs Completed and Sold | | Garage/Shop* Overhead Costs | |
|---|---|---|---|---|---|---|---|
| | | | | | | | |

\* Because an auto shop does not manufacture a product, the overhead cost would include all of the indirect costs that are incurred in the "garage or shop" that cannot be traced to a specific repair job.

The following transactions occurred during the most recent month:

a. Purchased raw materials (parts and supplies) on account $21,000.

b. Used $16,000 in raw materials (parts and supplies). Of this, $14,000 was for major parts that were traceable to individual repair jobs, and the remainder was for incidental supplies such as lubricants, rags, fuel, and so on.

c. Recorded a total of $8,000 in direct labor cost (for 400 hours) that are owed but not yet paid.

d. Applied overhead to repair jobs at a rate of $25 per direct labor hour.

e. Recorded the following actual overhead costs:

| | |
|---|---|
| Repair shop rent (prepaid) | $ 14,000 |
| Depreciation on diagnostic equipment | 2,000 |
| Repair shop supervision (owed but not paid) | 3,000 |

f. Completed repair jobs costing $45,000 and charged customers at cost plus 30 percent. (**Note:** You can bypass the Finished Goods Inventory account, which is not appropriate in this context).

**Required:**

Prepare journal entries for transactions a–f using the account names shown and other appropriate accounts such as Cash, Payables, Accumulated Depreciation, Prepaids, and Sales Revenue.

**LO4, 5**

**E19-9 Recording Actual and Applied Manufacturing Overhead Costs, and Calculating Over- or Underapplied Overhead Costs**

Verizox Company uses a job order costing system with manufacturing overhead applied to products based on direct labor hours. At the beginning of the most recent year, the company estimated its manufacturing overhead cost at $200,000. Estimated direct labor cost was $500,000 for 20,000 hours (average of $25 per hour). Actual costs for the most recent month are summarized here:

| Item Description | Total Cost |
|---|---|
| Direct labor (2,000 hours @ $26 per hour) | $52,000 |
| Indirect costs | |
|     Indirect labor | 2,400 |
|     Indirect material | 3,300 |
|     Factory rent | 3,200 |
|     Factory supervision | 4,700 |
|     Factory depreciation | 5,600 |
|     Factory janitorial work | 1,100 |
|     Factory insurance | 1,700 |
|     General and administrative salaries | 4,100 |
|     Selling expenses | 5,300 |

**Required:**

1. Calculate the predetermined overhead rate.
2. Prepare the journal entry to apply manufacturing overhead to Work in Process Inventory.
3. Calculate actual manufacturing overhead costs. Explain which costs you excluded and why.
4. Prepare the journal entry to record actual manufacturing overhead costs. The credit can be to a generic account titled Cash, Payables, etc.
5. Compute over- or underapplied overhead.
6. Prepare the journal entry to transfer the Manufacturing Overhead account balance to Cost of Goods Sold. Does this increase or decrease Cost of Goods Sold? Why?

**E19-10 Recording Manufacturing and Nonmanufacturing Costs**                          LO4
Reyes Manufacturing Company uses a job order costing system. At the beginning of January, the company had one job in process (Job 201) and one job that was completed but not yet sold (Job 200). Other select account balances follow (ignore any accounts that are not listed).

| Raw Materials Inventory | | Work in Process Inventory | | Finished Goods Inventory | |
|---|---|---|---|---|---|
| 1/1 32,000 | | 1/1 15,500 | | 1/1 20,000 | |

| Cost of Goods Sold | | Manufacturing Overhead | | Sales Revenue | |
|---|---|---|---|---|---|
| | | | | | |

During January, the company had the following transactions.
    a.  Purchased $60,000 worth of material on account.
    b.  Recorded materials issued to production as follows:

| Job Number | Total Cost |
|---|---|
| 201 | $ 10,000 |
| 202 | 20,000 |
| Indirect materials | 5,000 |
| | $ 35,000 |

    c.  Recorded factory payroll costs from direct labor time tickets that revealed the following:

| Job Number | Hours | Total Cost |
|---|---|---|
| 201 | 120 | $ 3,000 |
| 202 | 400 | 10,000 |
| Factory supervision | | 4,000 |
| | | $ 17,000 |

d.  Applied overhead to production at a rate of $30 per direct labor hour for 520 actual direct labor hours.

e.  Recorded the following actual manufacturing overhead costs.

| Item | Total Cost | Description |
|---|---|---|
| Factory rent | $ 2,000 | Paid in cash |
| Depreciation | 3,000 | Factory equipment |
| Factory utilities | 2,500 | Incurred but not paid |
| Factory insurance | 1,500 | Prepaid policy |
| | $ 9,000 | |

f.  Job 201 was completed and transferred to Finished Goods Inventory.

g.  Sold Job 200 for $50,000.

Job 202 was still in process at the end of January.

*Required:*

1.  Complete the following job cost summary to calculate the total cost of the jobs that were worked on during the period.

| Job number | Beg. Balance (given) | Direct Material Cost | Direct Labor Cost | MOH* Applied @ $30 per DL† hour | Total Cost of Job |
|---|---|---|---|---|---|
| 200 | $20,000 | $ 0 | $ 0 | $ 0 | $20,000 |
| 201 | 15,500 | | | | |
| 202 | 0 | | | | |

\* Manufacturing Overhead
† Direct labor

2.  Post the preceding transactions to the T-accounts. Create an additional account called Miscellaneous to capture the offsetting debits and credits to other accounts such as Cash, Payables, Accumulated Depreciation, and so on.

3.  Compute the ending balance in the following accounts:

Raw Materials Inventory
Work in Process Inventory
Finished Goods Inventory
Cost of Goods Sold
Manufacturing Overhead

4.  Explain which jobs would appear in Work in Process Inventory, Finished Goods Inventory, and Cost of Goods Sold. Confirm that the total cost of each job is equal to the ending balance in its respective control accounts.

## Problems—Set A       Available with McGraw-Hill's Homework Manager

**LO3, 4, 5**

### PA19-1 Calculating Predetermined Overhead Rates, Recording Manufacturing Cost Flows, and Analyzing Overhead

Tyler Tooling Company uses a job order costing system with overhead applied to products on the basis of machine hours. For the upcoming year, the company estimated its total manufacturing overhead cost at $250,000 and total machine hours at 62,500. During the first month of operations, the company worked on three jobs and recorded the following actual direct materials cost, direct labor cost, and machine hours for each job.

| | Job 101 | Job 102 | Job 103 | Total |
|---|---|---|---|---|
| Direct materials cost | $12,000 | $9,000 | $6,000 | $27,000 |
| Direct labor cost | $18,000 | $7,000 | $6,000 | $31,000 |
| Machine hours | 2,000 hours | 3,000 hours | 1,000 hours | 6,000 hours |

Job 101 was completed and sold for $50,000.

Job 102 was completed but not sold.

Job 103 is still in process.

Actual overhead costs recorded during the first month of operations were $25,000.

**Required:**

1. Calculate the predetermined overhead rate.
2. Compute the total manufacturing overhead applied to the Work in Process Inventory account during the first month of operations.
3. Compute the balance in the Work in Process Inventory account at the end of the first month.
4. Prepare a journal entry showing the transfer of Job 102 into Finished Goods Inventory upon its completion.
5. Prepare the journal entries to recognize the sales revenue and cost of goods sold for Job 101. How much gross profit would the company report during the first month of operations before making an adjustment for over- or underapplied manufacturing overhead?
6. Determine the balance in the Manufacturing Overhead account at the end of the first month. Is it over or underapplied?
7. Prepare the journal entry to transfer the balance of the Manufacturing Overhead account to Cost of Goods Sold. How much is adjusted Cost of Goods Sold and adjusted gross profit?

**PA19-2 Recording Manufacturing Costs and Analyzing Manufacturing Overhead**

LO4, 5

www.mhhe.com/LLPW1e

Christopher's Custom Cabinet Company uses a job order costing system with overhead applied as a percentage of direct labor costs. Inventory balances at the beginning of 2009 follow:

| | |
|---|---|
| Raw materials inventory | $15,000 |
| Work in process inventory | 5,000 |
| Finished goods inventory | 20,000 |

The following transactions occurred during January.

    *a.* Purchased materials on account for $26,000.

    *b.* Issued materials to production totaling $22,000, 90 percent of which was traced to specific jobs and the remainder treated as indirect materials.

    *c.* Payroll costs totaling $15,500 were recorded as follows:

        $10,000 for assembly workers

          3,000 for factory supervision

          1,000 for administrative personnel

          1,500 for sales commissions

    *d.* Recorded depreciation: $6,000 for machines, $1,000 for office copier.

    *e.* Had $2,000 in insurance expire, allocated equally between manufacturing and administrative expenses.

    *f.* Paid $6,500 in other factory costs in cash.

    *g.* Applied manufacturing overhead at a rate of 200 percent of direct labor cost.

    *h.* Completed all jobs but one; the job cost sheet for this job shows $2,100 for direct materials, $2,000 for direct labor, and $4,000 for applied overhead.

    *i.* Sold jobs costing $50,000; the company uses cost-plus pricing with a markup of 30 percent.

**Required:**

1. Set up T-accounts, record the beginning balances, post the January transactions, and compute the final balance for the following accounts:

Raw Materials Inventory

Work in Process Inventory

Finished Goods Inventory

Cost of Goods Sold

Manufacturing Overhead

Selling and Administrative Expenses

Sales Revenue

Other accounts (Cash, Payables, etc.)

2.    Determine how much gross profit the company would report during the month of January **before** any adjustment is made for the overhead balance.

3.    Determine the amount of over- or underapplied overhead.

4.    Compute adjusted gross profit assuming that any over- or underapplied overhead balance is adjusted directly to Cost of Goods Sold.

**LO4, 5**

**PA19-3 Finding Unknowns in the Cost of Goods Manufacturing and Sold Report and Analyzing Manufacturing Overhead**

The following information was obtained from the records of Appleton Corporation during 2009.

1.    Manufacturing Overhead was applied at a rate of 80 percent of direct labor dollars.

2.    Beginning value of inventory follows:

    a.    Beginning Work in Process, Inventory $10,000.

    b.    Beginning Finished Goods, Inventory $20,000.

3.    Work in Process Inventory increased by 20 percent during the period; Finished Goods Inventory decreased by 25 percent during the period.

4.    Actual manufacturing overhead costs were $85,000.

5.    Sales were $400,000.

6.    Adjusted Cost of Goods Sold was $300,000.

*Required:*
Use the above information to find the missing values in the table below.

| Item | Amount |
|---|---|
| Direct materials used in production | $    ? |
| Direct labor | ? |
| Manufacturing overhead applied | 80,000 |
| Total current manufacturing costs | ? |
| Plus: Beginning work in process inventory | 10,000 |
| Less: Ending work in process inventory | ? |
| Cost of goods manufactured | ? |
| Plus: Beginning finished goods inventory | 20,000 |
| Less: Ending finished goods inventory | ? |
| Unadjusted cost of goods sold | ? |
| Overhead adjustment | ? |
| Adjusted cost of goods sold | $300,000 |

**LO3, 5**

www.mhhe.com/LLPW1e

**PA19-4 Selecting Allocation Base and Analyzing Manufacturing Overhead**

Amberjack Company is trying to decide on an allocation base to use to assign manufacturing overhead to jobs. In the past, the company has always used direct labor hours to assign manufacturing overhead to products, but it is trying to decide whether it should use a different allocation base such as direct labor dollars or machine hours.

Actual and estimated data for manufacturing overhead, direct labor cost, direct labor hours, and machine hours for the most recent fiscal year are summarized here:

|  | Estimated Value | Actual Value |
|---|---|---|
| Manufacturing overhead cost | $700,000 | $655,000 |
| Direct labor cost | $350,000 | $360,000 |
| Direct labor hours | 17,500 hours | 16,000 hours |
| Machine hours | 14,000 hours | 13,000 hours |

*Required:*

1.    Based on the company's current allocation base (direct labor hours), compute the following:

    a.    Predetermined overhead rate.

    b.    Applied manufacturing overhead.

    c.    Over- or underapplied manufacturing overhead.

2.  If the company had used direct labor dollars (instead of direct labor hours) as its allocation base, compute the following:

    a.  Predetermined overhead rate.
    b.  Applied manufacturing overhead.
    c.  Over- or underapplied manufacturing overhead.

3.  If the company had used machine hours (instead of direct labor hours) as its allocation base, compute the following:

    a.  Predetermined overhead rate.
    b.  Applied manufacturing overhead.
    c.  Over- or underapplied manufacturing overhead.

4.  Based on last year's data alone, which allocation base would have provided the most accurate measure for applying manufacturing overhead costs to production?

5.  How does a company decide on an allocation base to use in applying manufacturing overhead? What factors should be considered?

## PA19-5 Recording Manufacturing Costs, Preparing a Cost of Goods Manufactured and Sold Report, and Calculating Income from Operations    LO3, 4, 5, 6

Dobson Manufacturing Company uses a job order costing system with manufacturing overhead applied to products on the basis of direct labor dollars. At the beginning of the most recent period, the company estimated its total direct labor cost to be $50,000 and its total manufacturing overhead cost to be $75,000. Several incomplete general ledger accounts showing the transactions that occurred during the most recent accounting period follow.

| Raw Materials Inventory | | |
|---|---|---|
| Beginning Balance | 15,000 | ? |
| Purchases | 95,000 | |
| Ending Balance | 30,000 | |

| Work in Process Inventory | | |
|---|---|---|
| Beginning Balance | 30,000 | ? |
| Direct Materials | 70,000 | |
| Direct Labor | 40,000 | |
| Applied Overhead | ? | |
| Ending Balance | 20,000 | |

| Finished Goods Inventory | | |
|---|---|---|
| Beginning Balance | 40,000 | ? |
| Cost of Goods Completed | ? | |
| Ending Balance | 50,000 | |

| Cost of Goods Sold | |
|---|---|
| Unadjusted Cost of Goods Sold | ? |
| Adjusted Cost of Goods Sold | ? |

| Manufacturing Overhead | | | |
|---|---|---|---|
| Indirect Materials | 10,000 | ? | Applied Overhead |
| Indirect Labor | 15,000 | | |
| Factory Depreciation | 13,000 | | |
| Factory Rent | 7,000 | | |
| Factory Utilities | 3,000 | | |
| Other Factory Costs | 10,000 | | |
| Actual Overhead | 58,000 | | |

| Sales Revenue | | |
|---|---|---|
| | 300,000 | Sales Revenue |

| Selling and Administrative Expenses | |
|---|---|
| Adm. Salaries | 28,000 |
| Office Depreciation | 20,000 |
| Advertising | 15,000 |
| Ending balance | 63,000 |

*Required:*

1.  Calculate the predetermined overhead rate.
2.  Fill in the missing values in the T-accounts.
3.  Compute over- or underapplied overhead.
4.  Prepare a statement of cost of goods manufactured and sold including the adjustment for over- or underapplied overhead.
5.  Prepare a brief income statement for the company.

## Problems—Set B  Available with McGraw-Hill's Homework Manager

LO3, 4, 5

**PB19-1 Calculating Predetermined Overhead Rates, Recording Manufacturing and Cost Flows, and Analyzing Overhead**

Babson Company uses a job order costing system with overhead applied to products on the basis of machine hours. For the upcoming year, Babson estimated its total manufacturing overhead cost at $360,000 and its total machine hours at 125,000. During the first month of operation, the company worked on three jobs and recorded the following actual direct materials cost, direct labor cost, and machine hours for each job.

|  | Job 101 | Job 102 | Job 103 | Total |
|---|---|---|---|---|
| Direct materials cost | $15,000 | $10,000 | $5,000 | $30,000 |
| Direct labor cost | $ 7,000 | $ 5,000 | $8,000 | $20,000 |
| Machine hours | 5,000 hours | 4,000 hours | 1,000 hours | 10,000 hours |

Job 101 was completed and sold for $50,000.

Job 102 was completed but not sold.

Job 103 is still in process.

Actual overhead costs recorded during the first month of operations were $28,000.

**Required:**

1. Calculate the predetermined overhead rate.
2. Compute the total overhead applied to the Work in Process Inventory account during the first month of operations.
3. Compute the balance in the Work in Process Inventory account at the end of the first month.
4. Prepare a journal entry showing the transfer of Job 102 into Finished Goods Inventory upon its completion.
5. Prepare the journal entries to recognize the sales revenue and cost of goods sold for Job 101. How much gross profit would the company report during the first month of operations before making an adjustment for over- or underapplied manufacturing overhead?
6. Determine the balance in the Manufacturing Overhead account at the end of the first month. Is it over- or underapplied?
7. Prepare the journal entry to close Manufacturing Overhead to the Cost of Goods Sold account. How much is adjusted Cost of Goods Sold and adjusted gross profit?

LO4, 5

**PB19-2 Recording Manufacturing Costs and Analyzing Manufacturing Overhead**

Carrington Custom Cabinet Company uses a job order costing system with overhead applied based on direct labor cost. Inventory balances at the beginning of 2009 follow.

| | |
|---|---|
| Raw materials inventory | $25,000 |
| Work in process inventory | 30,000 |
| Finished goods inventory | 40,000 |

The following transactions occurred during January.

a. Purchased materials on account for $40,000.

b. Issued materials to production totaling $30,000, 80 percent of which was traced to specific jobs and the remainder treated as indirect materials.

c. Payroll costs totaling $25,500 were recorded as follows:

$15,000 for assembly workers

6,000 for factory supervision

2,000 for administrative personnel

2,500 for sales commissions

d. Recorded depreciation: $5,000 for machines, $2,000 for office copier.

e. Had $4,000 in insurance expire; allocated equally between manufacturing and administrative expenses.

f. Paid $8,500 in other factory costs in cash.

g. Applied manufacturing overhead at a rate of 150 percent of direct labor cost.

h.   Completed all jobs but one; the job cost sheet for this job shows $7,000 for direct materials, $6,000 for direct labor, and $9,000 for applied overhead.

i.   Sold jobs costing $60,000 during the period; the company uses cost-plus pricing with a markup of 35 percent.

**Required:**

1.   Set up T-accounts, record the beginning balances, post the January transactions, and compute the final balance for the following accounts:

Raw Materials Inventory

Work in Process Inventory

Finished Goods Inventory

Cost of Goods Sold

Manufacturing Overhead

Selling and Administrative Expenses

Sales Revenue

Other accounts (Cash, payables, etc.)

2.   Determine how much gross profit the company would report during the month of January **before** any adjustment is made for the overhead balance.

3.   Determine the amount of over- or underapplied overhead.

4.   Compute adjusted gross profit assuming that any over- or underapplied overhead is adjusted directly to Cost of Goods Sold.

## PB19-3 Finding Unknowns in the Cost of Goods Manufacturing and Sold Report, and Analyzing Manufacturing Overhead

LO5, 6

The following information was obtained from the records of Carrington Corporation during 2009.

1.   Manufacturing overhead was applied at a rate of 150 percent of direct labor dollars.

2.   Beginning value of inventory follows:

a.   Beginning Work in Process Inventory $20,000.

b.   Beginning Finished Goods Inventory $10,000.

3.   Work in Process Inventory decreased by 20 percent during the period; Finished Goods Inventory increased by 25 percent during the period.

4.   Actual manufacturing overhead costs were $85,000.

5.   Sales were $500,000.

6.   Adjusted Cost of Goods Sold was $350,000.

**Required:**

Use the above information to find the missing values in the table below.

| Item | Amount |
|---|---|
| Direct materials used in production | $   ? |
| Direct labor | ? |
| Manufacturing overhead applied | 90,000 |
| Current manufacturing costs | ? |
| Plus: Beginning work in process inventory | 20,000 |
| Less: Ending work in process inventory | ? |
| Cost of goods manufactured | ? |
| Plus: Beginning finished goods inventory | 10,000 |
| Less: Ending finished goods inventory | ? |
| Unadjusted cost of goods sold | ? |
| Overhead adjustment | ? |
| Adjusted cost of goods sold | $350,000 |

## PB19-4 Selecting Allocation Base and Analyzing Manufacturing Overhead

LO3, 5

Timberland Company is trying to decide on an allocation base to use to assign manufacturing overhead to jobs. In the past, the company has always used direct labor hours to assign manufacturing overhead to products, but it is trying to decide whether it should use a different allocation base such as direct labor dollars or machine hours.

Actual and estimated results for manufacturing overhead, direct labor cost, direct labor hours, and machine hours for the most recent fiscal year are summarized here:

|  | Estimated Value | Actual Value |
|---|---|---|
| Manufacturing overhead cost | $900,000 | $890,000 |
| Direct labor cost | $450,000 | $464,000 |
| Direct labor hours | 30,000 hours | 29,000 hours |
| Machine hours | 15,000 hours | 15,000 hours |

*Required:*

1. Based on the company's current allocation base (direct labor hours), compute the following:
   a. Predetermined overhead rate.
   b. Applied manufacturing overhead.
   c. Over- or underapplied manufacturing overhead.

2. If the company had used direct labor dollars (instead of direct labor hours) as its allocation base, compute the following:
   a. Predetermined overhead rate.
   b. Applied manufacturing overhead.
   c. Over- or underapplied manufacturing overhead.

3. If the company had used machine hours (instead of direct labor hours) as its allocation base, compute the following:
   a. Predetermined overhead rate.
   b. Applied manufacturing overhead.
   c. Over- or underapplied manufacturing overhead

4. Based on last year's data alone, which allocation base would have provided the most accurate measure for applying manufacturing overhead costs to production?

5. How does a company decide on an allocation base to use in applying manufacturing overhead? What factors should be considered?

**LO3, 4, 5, 6**    **PB19-5 Recording Manufacturing Costs, Preparing a Cost of Goods Manufactured, and Sold Report, and Calculating from Operations Income**

Carlton Manufacturing Company uses a job order costing system with manufacturing overhead applied to products on the basis of direct labor dollars. At the beginning of the most recent period, the company estimated its total direct labor cost to be $30,000 and its total manufacturing overhead cost to be $60,000. Several incomplete general ledger accounts showing the transactions that occurred during the most recent accounting period follow.

### Raw Materials Inventory

| | | |
|---|---|---|
| Beginning Balance | 10,000 | ? |
| Purchases | 85,000 | |
| Ending Balance | 20,000 | |

### Work in Process Inventory

| | | |
|---|---|---|
| Beginning Balance | 30,000 | ? |
| Direct Materials | ? | |
| Direct Labor | 35,000 | |
| Applied Overhead | ? | |
| Ending Balance | 20,000 | |

### Finished Goods Inventory

| | | |
|---|---|---|
| Beginning Balance | 60,000 | ? |
| Cost of Goods Completed | ? | |
| Ending Balance | 40,000 | |

### Cost of Goods Sold

| | |
|---|---|
| Unadjusted Cost of Goods Sold | ? |
| Adjusted Cost of Goods Sold | ? |

### Manufacturing Overhead

| | | | |
|---|---|---|---|
| Indirect Materials | 10,000 | ? | Applied Overhead |
| Indirect Labor | 20,000 | | |
| Factory Depreciation | 13,000 | | |
| Factory Rent | 12,000 | | |
| Factory Utilities | 5,000 | | |
| Other Factory Costs | 14,000 | | |
| Actual Overhead | 74,000 | | |

### Sales Revenue

| | |
|---|---|
| | 280,000 Sales Revenue |

### Selling and Administrative Expenses

| | |
|---|---|
| Adm. Salaries | 30,000 |
| Office Depreciation | 20,000 |
| Advertising | 19,000 |
| Ending Balance | 69,000 |

*Required:*

1. Calculate the predetermined overhead rate.
2. Fill in the missing values in the T-accounts.
3. Compute over- or underapplied overhead.
4. Prepare a statement of cost of goods manufactured and sold including the adjustment for over- or underapplied overhead
5. Prepare a brief income statement for the company.

# Cases and Projects

## CP19-1 Multiple Allocation Bases and Ethical Dilemmas                          LO3

Assume you recently accepted a job with a company that designs and builds helicopters for commercial and military use. The company has numerous contracts with the U.S. military that require the use of cost-plus pricing. In other words, the contracted price for each helicopter is calculated at a certain percentage (about 130 percent) of the total cost to produce it. Unlike the cost-plus pricing approach used for military contracts, the prices for civilian helicopters are based on the amount that individuals and corporations are willing to pay for a state-of-the-art helicopter.

As your first assignment, the company controller has asked you to reevaluate the costing system currently used to determine the cost of producing helicopters. Currently, the company assigns manufacturing overhead based on the number of units produced. The result is that every helicopter is assigned the same amount of overhead regardless of whether it is for military or civilian use.

As part of your assignment, you collected the following information about two other potential allocation bases (direct labor hours and machine hours) and how they differ for the two types of customers the company serves:

|  | MILITARY CONTRACTS | | CIVILIAN CONTRACTS | | |
|  | Units in Allocation Base | Percent of Total | Units in Allocation Base | Percent of Total | Total |
| --- | --- | --- | --- | --- | --- |
| Units produced | 1,000 | 50% | 1,000 | 50% | 2,000 |
| Labor hours | 800,000 | 40 | 1,200,000 | 60 | 2,000,000 |
| Machine hours | 700,000 | 70 | 300,000 | 30 | 1,000,000 |

These data show that while the company produces an equal number of military and civilian helicopters (1,000 of each), they require a different amount of direct labor and machine hours. In particular, civilian helicopters require relatively more direct labor hours (60 percent of the total) perhaps because of the labor required to install all of the "bells and whistles" that wealthy consumers expect on a luxury helicopter. However, military helicopters require more machine time (70 percent of the total) due to the precise machining and intensive instrument testing required to comply with the military contracts. Further analysis revealed that some of the manufacturing overhead items are logically related to labor hours (such as supervision and use of indirect materials) while other overhead items (such as machine depreciation and power) are more highly related to machine hours.

When you presented these data to the controller, you recommended that the company move to an allocation system whereby part of the overhead would be allocated based on direct labor hours and part of it based on machine hours. He responded that he wanted you to choose the system that would assign the highest percentage of the total overhead cost to the military contracts. His reasoning was that the cost-plus agreement with the U.S. government would result in a higher contract price for military helicopters without affecting the price of civilian helicopters, which are set by the market.

*Required:*

1. Explain how changing the allocation base can impact the profitability of the two types of products.
2. Which allocation base(s) do you think the company should use to apply manufacturing overhead to the two types of products?
3. Identify the ethical issues involved in this scenario. What are your potential courses of action for responding to the controller's request? What are the potential personal, professional, and legal implications of the alternative courses of action you considered? How would you ultimately respond to this situation?

**LO1, 2, 3**    **CP19-2 Applying Job Order Costing to an Entrepreneurial Business**

Assume you are going to become an entrepreneur and start your own business. Think about your talents and interests and come up with an idea for a small business venture that provides a unique product or service to local customers. You can select any business venture you want, but if you are struggling to come up with an idea, here are some examples:

> Catering
> Wedding-planning consulting
> Video production company
> Pool building company
> Personal shopping service
> Interior design business
> Flower shop
> Rock-climbing guide service
> River-rafting company
> Web design company

*Required:*

For whatever business venture you select, answer the following questions:

1. What would the major costs of your business be? Try to classify the costs into the areas of direct materials, direct labor, manufacturing overhead, general and administrative costs, and selling costs. (**Hint:** Not all businesses will have all of these cost classifications.)
2. Why would you need to determine the cost of providing your product or service to individual customers? In other words, what types of decisions would you expect to make based on job order cost information?
3. In general, would you expect your company's indirect (overhead) costs to be less or more than the direct costs (direct labor and materials)? What allocation base do you think you would use to charge overhead costs to individual customers? How much do you think the overhead rate would need to be?
4. Think about a hypothetical "average" customer and create a job cost sheet for this customer that includes estimates of the major costs of serving that customer. How much do you think you would need to charge the customer to cover all of the costs plus provide a reasonable profit for yourself?

**LO3, 4, 5, 6**    **CP19-3 Comprehensive Job Order Costing Case**

Sampson Company uses a job order cost system with overhead applied to products based on direct labor hours. Based on previous history, the company estimated its total overhead for the coming year (2009) to be $240,000 and its total direct labor hours to be 6,000.

On January 1, 2009, the general ledger of Sampson Company revealed that it had one job in process (Job 102) for which it had incurred a total cost of $15,000. Job 101 had been finished the previous month for a total cost of $30,000 but was not yet sold. The company had a contract for Job 103 but had not started working on it yet. Other balances in Raw Materials Inventory and other assets, liabilities and owner's equity accounts are summarized here:

## Sampson Company
## General Ledger Accounts

### Raw Materials Inventory

| | | | |
|---|---|---|---|
| 1/1 Balance | 10,000 | | |

### Manufacturing Overhead

| | | | |
|---|---|---|---|
| | | | |

### Work in Process Inventory

| | | | |
|---|---|---|---|
| 1/1 Balance | 15,000 | | |

### Individual Job Cost Sheets (subsidiary ledgers to WIP)

| | Job 102 | Job 103 |
|---|---|---|
| Beg. Balance | 15,000 | — |
| + Direct Material | | |
| + Direct Labor | | |
| + Applied OH | | |
| Total Mfg. Cost | | |

### Finished Goods Inventory

| | | | |
|---|---|---|---|
| 1/1 Balance | 30,000 | | |

### Cost of Goods Sold

| | | | |
|---|---|---|---|
| | | | |

### Sales Revenue

| | | | |
|---|---|---|---|
| | | | |

### Selling and Administrative Expenses

| | | | |
|---|---|---|---|
| | | | |

### Cash and Other Assets

| | | | |
|---|---|---|---|
| 1/1 Balance | 100,000 | | |

### Payables and Other Liabilities

| | | |
|---|---|---|
| | 85,000 | 1/1 Balance |

### Stockholder's Equity

| | | |
|---|---|---|
| | 70,000 | 1/1 Balance |

During January, the company had the following transactions:

a. Purchased $10,000 worth of raw materials on account.

b. Issued the following materials into production:

| Item | Cost | Explanation |
|---|---|---|
| Direct materials | $7,000 | Job 102, $2,000; Job 103, $5,000 |
| Indirect materials | 2,000 | Used on both jobs |
| Total materials issued | $9,000 | |

c. Recorded salaries and wages payable as follows:

| Item | Cost | Explanation |
|---|---|---|
| Direct labor | $10,000 | Job 102, $6,000; Job 103, $4,000 |
| Indirect labor | 4,000 | For factory supervision |
| Salaries | 5,000 | For administrative staff |
| Total payroll cost | $19,000 | |

d. Applied overhead to jobs based on the direct labor hours required:

| Job Number | Direct Labor Hours |
|---|---|
| Job 102 | 300 hours |
| Job 103 | 200 hours |
| Total | 500 hours |

e. Recorded the following actual manufacturing costs:

| Item | Cost | Explanation |
|---|---|---|
| Rent | $ 6,000 | Paid factory rent in cash |
| Depreciation | 5,000 | Factory equipment |
| Insurance | 3,000 | Had one month of factory insurance policy expire |
| Utilities | 2,000 | Received factory utility bill but did not pay it |
| Total Cost | $16,000 | |

f. Recorded the following general and administrative costs:

| Item | Cost | Explanation |
|---|---|---|
| Advertising | $ 2,000 | Advertising paid in cash |
| Depreciation | 3,000 | Office equipment |
| Other expenses | 1,000 | Miscellaneous expenses owed but not paid |
| Total Cost | $ 6,000 | |

g. Sold Job 101, which is recorded in Finished Goods Inventory at a cost of $30,000, for $55,000.
h. Completed Job 102 but did not sell it; Job 103 is still in process at year-end.

**Required:**

1. Compute and interpret the predetermined overhead rate.
2. How much overhead would be applied to jobs during the period?
3. Compute the total cost of Jobs 102 and 103 at the end of the period. Where would the cost of each of these jobs appear on the year-end balance sheet?
4. Prepare journal entries to record the January transactions and post the entries to the general ledger T-accounts given earlier in the problem.
5. Calculate the amount of over- or underapplied overhead.
6. Prepare the journal entry to dispose of the overhead balance assuming that it had been a year-end balance instead of a month-end balance. Post the effect to the general ledger T-accounts.
7. Prepare a statement of cost of goods manufactured and sold report including the adjustment for over- or underapplied overhead.
8. Prepare a brief income statement for Sampson Company.

# Process Costing and Activity Based Costing

## LEARNING OBJECTIVES

**After completing this chapter, you should be able to:**

**LO1**   Describe the key features of a process costing system.

**LO2**   Prepare journal entries to record product costs using process costing.

**LO3**   Reconcile the number of physical units that were worked on during the period.

**LO4**   Calculate equivalent units of production using the FIFO method.

**LO5**   Prepare a process costing production report.

**LO6**   Calculate the cost of products using activity based costing.

Lectured presentation–LP20-1
www.mhhe.com/LLPW1e

## Focus Company: CK MONDAVI FAMILY VINEYARDS

## "Trust in a Family Name"

www.ckmondavi.com

**W**hy does a hamburger sell for $10 or more at an upscale restaurant when you can buy one at McDonald's for only a dollar or two? The same question can be asked about bottles of wine, which range in price from $5 to more than $50. While higher quality ingredients are used in the finer versions of these products, much of the difference in cost has to do with how the products are made. In other words, different resources, activities, and processes are used to create a dish in an upscale restaurant than to mass-produce standard variety fare at a fast-food franchise. Similarly, it takes different activities and processes to produce a truly outstanding bottle of wine than a more standard variety.

In this chapter, we study two methods that can be used to determine the cost of a product or service. **Process costing** is used to calculate the cost of highly similar (homogeneous) goods and services that are produced using standardized processes. McDonald's hamburgers and high-volume wine production would both fall into this category. Activity based costing (ABC) is appropriate for companies that offer a diverse range of products or services, some of which require more costly resources or activities than others. An example is a winery that produces its most popular wine in large batches using stainless steel containers, but also produces a small batch of "vintage reserve" that is aged in French oak barrels.

To illustrate these topics, we visit the CK Mondavi winery in Napa Valley, California. The Mondavi family history reads like a great American novel or soap opera.[1] In 1943, Italian immigrants Cesare and Rosa Mondavi purchased the Charles Krug (CK) winery, which had fallen on hard times during the depression. Sons Robert and Peter worked with their parents to turn the troubled winery into a successful business. Then in 1966, brotherly rivalry turned bitter when Peter took command of the family vineyards and Robert left, determined to build

[1] www.ckmondavi.com/family; www.charleskrug.com/familyhistory.

his own wine dynasty. Robert was extremely successful in that regard, turning the Mondavi name into a household brand. But he eventually lost control of his huge corporation and was forced to sell to Constallation Brands Inc.[2] Meanwhile, Peter Mondavi and his heirs continue to run the private family business (CK Mondavi) with an emphasis on quality and innovation.

Throughout this chapter, we use the CK Mondavi winery to demonstrate how to determine the cost of a bottle of wine. Although we will simplify things and the numbers we will use in our example are fictional, the accounting methods we show are actually used by wineries to determine the cost of their wines.

## ORGANIZATION OF THE CHAPTER

**BASIC CONCEPTS IN PROCESS COSTING**
- Job Order versus Process Costing
- Flow of Costs in Process Costing
- Journal Entries for Process Costing

**PROCESS COSTING PRODUCTION REPORT**
- Step 1: Reconcile the Number of Physical Units
- Step 2: Translate Physical Units into Equivalent Units
- Step 3: Calculate Cost per Equivalent Unit
- Step 4: Reconcile the Total Cost of Work in Process
- Step 5: Prepare a Production Report
- Additional Factors in Process Costing

**ACTIVITY BASED COSTING (ABC)**
- Step 1: Identify and Classify Activities
- Step 2: Form Activity Cost Pools and Assign Indirect Costs to Each Pool
- Step 3: Select an Activity Cost Driver and Calculate an Activity Rate for Each Cost Pool
- Step 4: Assign Indirect Costs to Products or Services Based on Their Activity Demands

# BASIC CONCEPTS IN PROCESS COSTING

In the last chapter, you learned about job order costing systems. This chapter introduces another type of costing system, process costing. Later in the chapter, you will also learn about a costing approach called activity based costing (ABC). ABC can be used with with either job order or process costing. For now, let's focus on the differences between job order and process costing.

## Job Order versus Process Costing

Job order costing is used by companies that offer **customized** products or services, such as a custom-built home, highway construction project, or legal defense. Because each individual product or customer is unique, a job cost sheet is used to keep track of the costs of each individual unit, or job, in a job order costing system.

Process costing is used by companies that produce **homogeneous** products or services using a series of standardized processes. Canned and bottled goods, frozen foods, paper products, and petroleum products are all examples of homogeneous products that result from a standardized process. Although process costing is most often identified with manufacturing companies, it can also be used in businesses that provide high-volume, standardized services, such as oil and filter changes at Jiffy Lube, standardized medical tests (X-rays, blood work at hospitals and clinics), and haircuts at Supercuts.

Because the products or services that result from standardized processes are the same, keeping a separate cost record for each individual unit is not necessary. Instead, process costing tracks the total cost of each production process and spreads that cost over the total number of units that flow through the process. See Exhibit 20.1 for a summary of the differences between job order and process costing.

Video 20-1
www.mhhe.com/LLPW1e

---

[2] Julia Flynn Siler, *The House of Mondavi: The Rise and Fall of an American Wine Dynasty.* New York: Gotham Books, 2007.

## Exhibit 20.1 — Job Order Costing versus Process Costing

| | Job Order Costing | Process Costing |
|---|---|---|
| Type of product | Unique products and services, such as a custom-built ship | Homogeneous products and services, such as cans of soda |
| Manufacturing approach | Customized to the needs of the customer or client | Mass-production of products in series of standardized processes |
| Cost accumulation | Costs accumulated by job or customer | Costs accumulated by process |
| Major cost report | Job cost sheet for each unique unit, customer, or job | Production report for each major production process |

# Flow of Costs in Process Costing

Like job order costing, process costing relies on three inventory accounts to keep track of manufacturing costs:

- **Raw Materials Inventory** represents the cost of materials purchased from suppliers but not yet put into production.
- **Work in Process Inventory** represents the cost of units started in the manufacturing operation but not yet finished.
- **Finished Goods Inventory** represents the cost of units finished but not yet sold.

When the company sells the final product, it transfers the total manufacturing cost from Finished Goods Inventory to the **Cost of Goods Sold** account, where it will be reported as an expense and matched against sales revenue on the income statement. In terms of cost flows, the main difference between job order costing and process costing is that **process costing, has a different Work in Process Inventory account for each of the major processes the product must go through as it is being manufactured.**

See Exhibit 20.2 for an illustration of the process costing flow for a winery. As indicated, several production processes are required to convert raw materials (grapes) into the finished product (wine), including crushing, fermenting, aging, and bottling.

Wine making is an example of a **sequential** process. In other words, the grapes must be crushed before they can be fermented and then aged, which must occur before the wine can be bottled. Other companies may use a **parallel** processing approach in which more than one production process occurs at the same time. For example, Toyota Motor Company could have two different assembly processes running in parallel, one that produces engines and another that produces transmissions.

A process costing system will have a separate Work in Process Inventory account for each of the major processes the product must go through during production. To simplify our examples, we combine the crushing, fermenting, and aging processes into a single process, which we will refer to as the CFA process.

Recall from Chapter 19 that three categories of manufacturing cost must be traced to the product and recorded as inventory until the product is sold:

- **Direct materials** are the material inputs that can be traced directly to the product. For a winery, this category includes the cost of grapes and any other major material inputs, such as the bottles, labels, and boxes used in the packaging process.

**Exhibit 20.2**   Process Costing Flow for a Winery

**Conversion Cost =**

**Direct Labor**
**+**
**Manufacturing Overhead**

- **Direct labor** is the cost of labor that can be traced directly to the product. This category includes the cost of manual labor involved in the process, such as the work of pouring the grapes into crushing bins, testing the fermenting mix, and bottling the wine.
- **Manufacturing overhead** includes all manufacturing costs **other than direct materials and direct labor** that must be incurred to make the final product. For a winery, this category includes rent or mortgage payments, insurance, utilities, equipment depreciation, and supervision.

Because today's wineries tend to be highly automated, direct labor is typically a very small portion of the total manufacturing cost. Thus, wineries and other process-oriented industries may combine direct labor and manufacturing overhead costs together in a single category called **conversion cost.** This category represents the total cost of converting raw materials (grapes) into the finished product (wine).

Remember that **nonmanufacturing costs,** including marketing, distribution, and general and administrative costs, are expensed during the period incurred rather than inventoried as part of the cost of the final product.

# Journal Entries for Process Costing

**Learning Objective 2**

Prepare journal entries to record product costs using process costing.

In this section, we focus on the journal entries that record the flow of manufacturing costs in a process costing system. For the sake of simplicity, we begin our example on the first day of operations. Thus, there are no beginning balances in any of the accounts.

## Purchase of Raw Materials

When materials are purchased, they are recorded in the Raw Materials Inventory account. Assume, for example, that CK Mondavi purchased $35,000 of direct materials (grapes, bottles, and corks) on account from various suppliers. The journal entry to record the purchase of raw materials is:

|  | Debit | Credit |
|---|---|---|
| Raw Materials Inventory | 35,000 |  |
| Accounts Payable |  | 35,000 |

## Issue of Raw Materials into Production

When raw materials are taken out of storage and placed into production, the cost is debited to the Work in Process Inventory account for the first production process. Assume, for example, that $20,000 worth of grapes is added to the CFA process. The journal entry to record the issue of direct materials into production is:

|  | Debit | Credit |
| --- | --- | --- |
| Work in Process Inventory (CFA) | 20,000 |  |
| Raw Materials Inventory |  | 20,000 |

## Recording Actual and Applied Conversion Costs

Remember that conversion costs include direct labor and manufacturing overhead. Most accounting systems will maintain a separate general ledger account for each of these components. However, direct labor is likely to be a very small percentage of the total conversion cost in a winery and many other process-oriented industries. For this reason, we will combine direct labor and manufacturing overhead in a single account called Conversion Cost. This account is almost identical to the Manufacturing Overhead account we used in Chapter 19, except that it now includes a small amount of direct labor cost. We will use this account to record actual and applied conversion cost, just as we recorded actual and applied manufacturing overhead in Chapter 19. Actual costs will be debited to the Conversion Cost account and applied costs will be credited to the Conversion Cost account. Any difference between actual and applied conversion cost will be transferred to Cost of Goods Sold at the end of the accounting period.

To illustrate this process, assume that CK Mondavi incurred the following actual conversion costs:

| | |
| --- | --- |
| Direct labor and supervision paid | $16,000 |
| Winery utilities owed but not yet paid | 5,000 |
| Depreciation on winery equipment | 15,250 |
| Total conversion cost | $36,250 |

These actual conversion costs would be debited to the Conversion Cost account. Depending on the nature of the transaction, the credit would be to Cash, Payables, Prepaid Assets, or Accumulated Depreciation. The journal entry to record the actual conversion costs follows.

|  | Debit | Credit |
| --- | --- | --- |
| Conversion Cost | 36,250 |  |
| Cash |  | 16,000 |
| Utilities Payable |  | 5,000 |
| Accumulated Depreciation |  | 15,250 |

**Coach's Tip**

The process of accounting for conversion cost is the same as the process we used for manufacturing overhead in the last chapter. The only difference is that conversion cost also includes a small amount of direct labor. These costs were directly traced to jobs in the last chapter but are treated as indirect costs in this chapter.

Conversion costs are then applied to Work in Process Inventory using a predetermined allocation base. For example, a winery might apply conversion cost based on the number of barrels, the number of fermentation tanks, or the cost of the grapes that are processed. Direct labor hours and machine hours are also common allocation bases. Assume that CK Mondavi applies conversion cost in the CFA process at a rate equal to 125 percent of direct materials cost. In other words, for every $1.00 of direct materials cost, an additional $1.25 must be applied to cover the direct labor and manufacturing overhead costs. In a preceding transaction, we recorded the issue of $20,000 worth of direct materials into the CFA Work in Process account. Now we need to apply $25,000 ($20,000 × 125%) of conversion cost to Work in Process. The journal entry to apply the conversion cost to the Work in Process Inventory account follows.

|  | Debit | Credit |
| --- | --- | --- |
| Work in Process Inventory (CFA) | 25,000 |  |
| Conversion Cost |  | 25,000 |

At the end of the accounting period, we will need to account for any difference in actual and applied conversion cost. We will do this after we have recorded all transactions for this example.

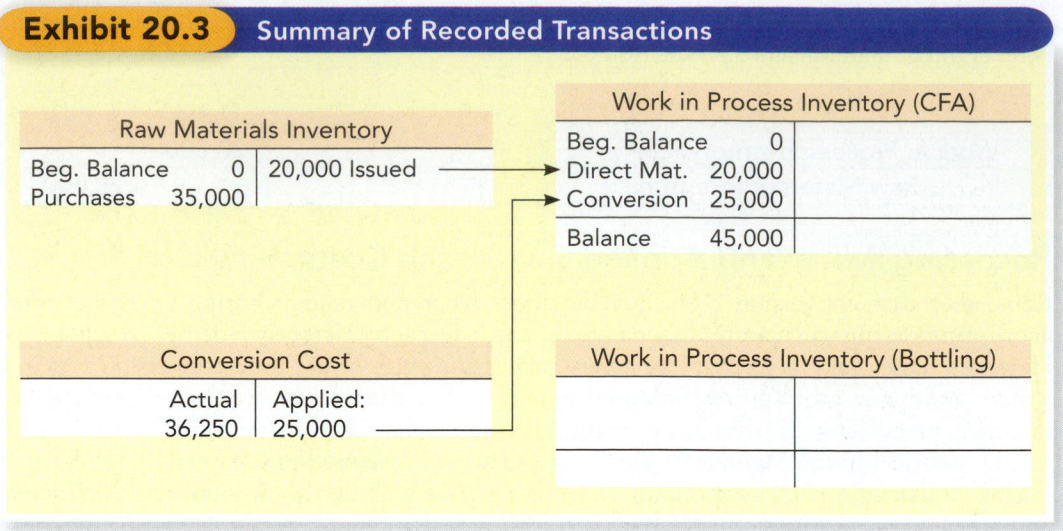

**Exhibit 20.3**    Summary of Recorded Transactions

## Transfer of Cost from One Work in Process Inventory Account to the Next

Once the wine has completed the CFA process, its total manufacturing cost must be transferred to the bottling process. See Exhibit 20.3 for a summary of the costs that have been recorded to this point.

Note that a total of $45,000 has been recorded in the CFA Work in Process Inventory account. This cost needs to be transferred out of Work in Process Inventory (CFA) and into the next process (Bottling), which will have its own Work in Process Inventory account. The journal entry to transfer the total manufacturing costs from one process to the other follows:

|  | Debit | Credit |
|---|---|---|
| Work in Process Inventory (Bottling) | 45,000 | |
| Work in Process Inventory (CFA) | | 45,000 |

Once the wine is in the bottling process, the company will incur more direct material costs for items such as bottles, corks, and boxes. Assume that CK Mondavi issues $10,000 worth of direct materials into the bottling process. The journal entry to record the issue of these direct materials into production is:

|  | Debit | Credit |
|---|---|---|
| Work in Process Inventory (Bottling) | 10,000 | |
| Raw Materials Inventory | | 10,000 |

Next we need to apply conversion cost to the bottling department's Work in Process Inventory account. Let's assume that the rate for applying conversion cost to the bottling process is 87.5 percent of direct materials cost. Because we just recorded $10,000 in direct materials cost, we need to apply an additional $8,750 ($10,000 × 87.5%) in conversion cost. The journal entry to apply conversion cost to the Work in Process Inventory account is:

|  | Debit | Credit |
|---|---|---|
| Work in Process Inventory (Bottling) | 8,750 | |
| Conversion Cost | | 8,750 |

Exhibit 20.4 shows the updated T-accounts.

**Exhibit 20.4    Updated Summary of Recorded Transactions**

So far, we have recorded a total of $63,750 in the Work in Process Inventory (Bottling) account. Once the wine is through the bottling process, this amount will be transferred to Finished Goods Inventory. The journal entry to transfer cost from the last Work in Process account to Finished Goods Inventory is:

|  | Debit | Credit |
|---|---|---|
| Finished Goods Inventory | 63,750 | |
|     Work in Process Inventory (Bottling) | | 63,750 |

Assuming that the $63,750 transferred to the Finished Goods Inventory account represents the cost of processing 15,000 bottles (or 1,250 cases) of wine, the costs per case and per bottle would be calculated as follows:

| | |
|---|---|
| Total manufacturing cost | $63,750 |
| Total number of cases | 1,250 |
| Total number of bottles | 15,000 |
| Cost per case ($63,750/1,250) | $ 51.00 |
| Cost per bottle ($63,750/15,000) | $  4.25 |

If CK Mondavi sold 12,000 bottles (1,000 cases) of this wine in the winery gift shop at a retail price of $8 per bottle, we would make additional journal entries to record cost of goods sold and sales revenue. The journal entry to record the cost of goods sold for 12,000 bottles at a cost of $4.25 per bottle is:

|  | Debit | Credit |
|---|---|---|
| Cost of Goods Sold (12,000 × $4.25) | 51,000 | |
|     Finished Goods Inventory | | 51,000 |

The journal entry to record the sale of 12,000 bottles at a price of $8 per bottle is:

|  | Debit | Credit |
|---|---|---|
| Cash (12,000 × $8.00) | 96,000 | |
|     Sales Revenue | | 96,000 |

Notice that the $4.25 cost per bottle was based on the amount of conversion cost **applied** to the Work in Process Inventory accounts, then transferred to Finished Goods Inventory and Cost of Goods Sold. But what if **actual** conversion costs was more or less than **applied** conversion cost? The Conversion Cost account for our example may be summarized as follows:

| Conversion Cost | |
|---|---|
| Actual<br>36,250 | Applied<br>25,000<br>8,750  > 33,750 |
| 2,500<br>Underapplied | |

**Coach's Tip**

A debit balance indicates that actual conversion cost was more than applied conversion cost; that is, conversion cost was underapplied. Overapplied conversion cost would be reflected by a credit balance (because the applied cost was more than the actual cost).

This account shows that actual conversion cost was $36,250, but only $33,750 was applied. In short, conversion cost was **underapplied** by $2,500.

Because most of the applied conversion cost is now in the Cost of Goods Sold account, the easiest way to handle the $2,500 in underapplied conversion cost is to increase Cost of Goods Sold. The journal entry to adjust for $2,500 in underapplied conversion cost is:

| | Debit | Credit |
|---|---|---|
| Cost of Goods Sold | 2,500 | |
| Conversion Cost | | 2,500 |

If the conversion cost had been **overapplied,** we would have **decreased** Cost of Goods Sold. Thus, the journal entry just given would be reversed (that is, Conversion Cost would be debited and Cost of Goods Sold would be credited). See Exhibit 20.5 for the Cost of Goods Sold and Finished Goods Inventory accounts after these entries have been made.

**Coach's Tip**

For simplicity, we will close the entire amount of underapplied conversion cost to the Cost of Goods Sold account. A more precise approach would have been to adjust the Work in Process Inventory, Finished Goods Inventory, and Cost of Goods Sold accounts based on the amount of conversion cost in each (if any). This more complicated method is covered in intermediate-level accounting books.

**Exhibit 20.5    Final Summary of Recorded Transactions**

| Conversion Cost | |
|---|---|
| Actual<br>36,250 | Applied:<br>25,000<br>8,750 |
| 2,500<br>Underapplied | 2,500<br>Closed to CGS |

| Finished Goods Inventory | | Cost of Goods Sold | |
|---|---|---|---|
| Beginning Balance 0 | CGS 51,000 | Unadjusted 51,000 | |
| Transferred from Bottling 63,750 | | Underapplied Conversion Cost 2,500 | |
| End. Balance 12,750 | | Adjusted 53,500 | |

The example we have just illustrated shows how process costing works in a simplified production environment. Unfortunately, in the real world, production processes are not usually so simple. Specifically, the company may have units that are only partially complete at the end of an accounting period. For example, wine needs to age for months, or even years, before it is ready for bottling. How do we account for wine that is still in barrels at the end of an accounting period? According to Generally Accepted Accounting Principles (GAAP), the manufacturing cost of units that are not yet sold must be counted as inventory. But how do we value a partially complete unit? This question is the focus of the next section. First, make sure you understand the basic concepts of process costing by completing the following Self-Study Practice.

1. Which of the following statements about process costing is false?

   a. Process costing is used in companies that produce very homogeneous products or services.

   b. Process costing uses the same type of inventory accounts as job order costing to record the flow of manufacturing costs.

   c. Process costing will typically have more Work in Process Inventory accounts than job order costing will.

   d. Process costing keeps a separate record, or cost sheet, for each unit produced.

   e. All of these statements are true.

2. The journal entry to apply conversion cost to Work in Process Inventory would include a:

   a. Debit to Work in Process Inventory.

   b. Debit to Conversion Cost.

   c. Credit to Conversion Cost.

   d. Credit to Cash, Accounts Payables, and other accounts.

   e. A and C.

   f. B and D.

3. The journal entry to record actual conversion costs would include a:

   a. Debit to Work in Process Inventory.

   b. Debit to Conversion Cost.

   c. Credit to Conversion Cost.

   d. Credit to Cash, Accounts Payables, and other accounts.

   e. A and C.

   f. B and D.

*After you have finished, check your answers with the solutions at the bottom of the page.*

# PROCESS COSTING PRODUCTION REPORT

The production report is the main report in a process costing system. It provides information about manufacturing costs and the number of units that flowed into and out of the production process during a given period. A separate report is prepared for each production process on either a monthly or a quarterly basis.

In this section we discuss how to prepare a production report for the crushing, fermenting, and aging (CFA) process at CK Mondavi. For this process, we define a unit as one barrel of wine. About 740 pounds of crushed grapes are required to fill a standard barrel of wine. After the crushed grapes have been fermented and the wine aged for an appropriate period, the barrels are transferred to the next process (Bottling). Each barrel yields about 300 bottles, or 25 cases, of wine.

To prepare the production report we use four steps:

1. Reconcile the number of physical units worked on during the period.

2. Translate physical units into equivalent units.

3. Calculate the cost per equivalent unit.

4. Reconcile the total cost of Work in Process Inventory.

First, however, we must make an assumption about how the units flow through the production process. In this chapter, we assume that they follow a first-in, first-out (FIFO) pattern in which the units that were started first are also completed first. For most process-oriented industries, this assumption is a reasonable one.

An alternative approach, the weighted average method, averages the cost of units in beginning inventory with the cost of units started during the current period. This method works well for companies that do not maintain large amounts of inventory or have very stable inventory levels. We present the weighted average method in Supplement 20.

# Step 1: Reconcile the Number of Physical Units

**Learning Objective 3**

Reconcile the number of physical units that were worked on during the period.

The first step in preparing a production report is to reconcile the number of physical units. To do so, we first calculate the total number of units worked on during the period by adding the number of units in beginning inventory to the number of units started during the current period. Then we determine whether those units were completed during the period or were still being worked on at the end of the period. The formula to reconcile the number of physical units is as follows:

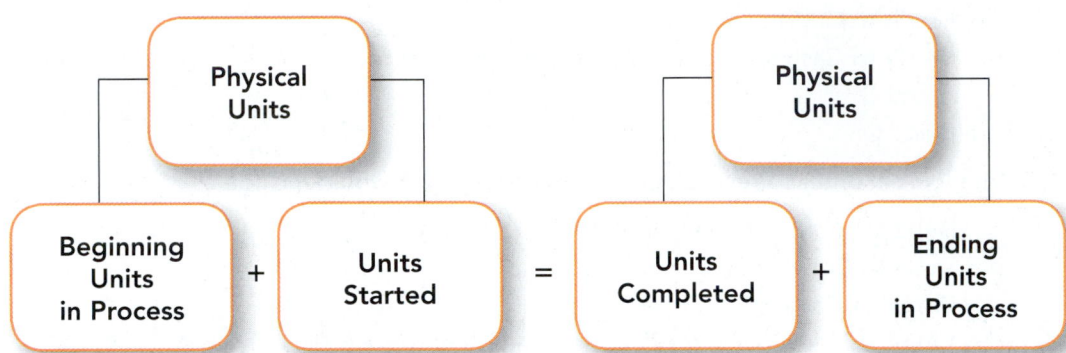

**Coach's Tip**

This formula ignores any units that may have been lost due to spoilage or waste. Accounting for lost or spoiled units is covered in more advanced accounting texts.

As an example, assume CK Mondavi had 200 barrels of wine in process at the start of a new accounting period. Last period's production report valued these partially complete units at $165,600. During the period, workers started another 1,800 barrels into the CFA process. At the end of the period, 400 barrels of wine were still in the CFA process. Based on this information, can you answer this question: How many barrels of wine were transferred out of the CFA process and into bottling during the current period?

To answer this question, we can prepare a reconciliation of physical units as follows:

**Coach's Tip**

The number of units completed is 1,600. A total of 2,000 units were worked on during the period, and 400 of them were still being worked on at the end of the period, so 1,600 of them must have been completed.

| | **Physical Units** | | **Physical Units** |
|---|---|---|---|
| Beginning units | 200 | Units completed | ? |
| Units started | 1,800 | Ending units | 400 |
| Total units | 2,000 | Total units | 2,000 |

We must account for a total of 2,000 units, 200 that were on hand at the beginning of the period plus 1,800 that were started this period. If we only have 400 on hand at the end of the period, we must have completed 1,600 units.

The next step is to determine how many units were both started **and** completed during the current period. Those units would have made it all the way through the CFA process during the current period, so they would not be part of either beginning or ending inventory, as the following formula shows:

Remember that FIFO assumes that the units in beginning inventory were completed first. Thus, not all units that were completed during the current period were started during the current period; the units that were in the beginning inventory were started during the last period. Likewise, some of the units that were started during the period were not completed; they remain in the ending inventory.

In our example, we had a total of 2,000 physical units to account for: 200 from the beginning inventory plus 1,800 that were started during the period. During the period, 1,600 units were completed; 400 were still in process at the end of the period. How many units were both started **and** completed during the current period? The answer is 1,400 units, as shown in the following formulas:

To summarize step 1, the number of physical units worked on during the period can be reconciled as follows:

|  | Physical Units |
| --- | --- |
| Beginning inventory | 200 |
| Started **and** completed | 1,400 |
| Ending inventory | 400 |
| Total units | 2,000 |

**Coach's Tip**

The 1,400 units started **and** completed can be calculated as 1,600 units completed less 200 units in beginning inventory or as 1,800 units started less 400 units in ending inventory.

# Step 2: Translate Physical Units into Equivalent Units

The next step in preparing the production report is to calculate the number of equivalent units. An **equivalent unit** is a measure of the amount of work or effort expended during the current period to produce both fully and partially completed units. Why must we calculate equivalent units? Companies often have units in process at the beginning and end of an accounting period. Even though those units are incomplete, their cost must be recorded on the balance sheet as Work in Process Inventory. Remember that GAAP requires all manufacturing costs to be counted as part of the cost of the product and reported as inventory (an asset) until the product is sold. By converting partially completed units into equivalent units, we can assign an appropriate value to those units for financial statement reporting.

**Learning Objective 4**

Calculate equivalent units of production using the FIFO method.

To illustrate the calculation of equivalent units in our winery example, we assume the following additional details about the CFA process at CK Mondavi.

- Direct materials (grapes) are added at the beginning of the process. Thus, once a unit has started the CFA process, it will have 100 percent of the required direct materials.
- Conversion costs (direct labor and manufacturing overhead) are incurred uniformly throughout the process.
- The 200 units in beginning inventory were 70 percent through the CFA process. For these units, all direct materials and 70 percent of the conversion cost were incurred **in the last period.**
- Only 1,400 of the units that were started during the current period were completed during the current period. Thus, those units made it all the way through the CFA process without getting "stuck" in beginning or ending inventory.
- The 400 units in ending inventory were 60 percent through the CFA conversion process. Thus, these units have all required direct materials (crushed grapes) but only 60 percent of the conversion effort (fermenting and aging).

These details are presented in the form of a diagram of the production process in Exhibit 20.6.

**Exhibit 20.6**    Diagram of the Crushing, Fermenting, and Aging (CFA) Process, FIFO Method

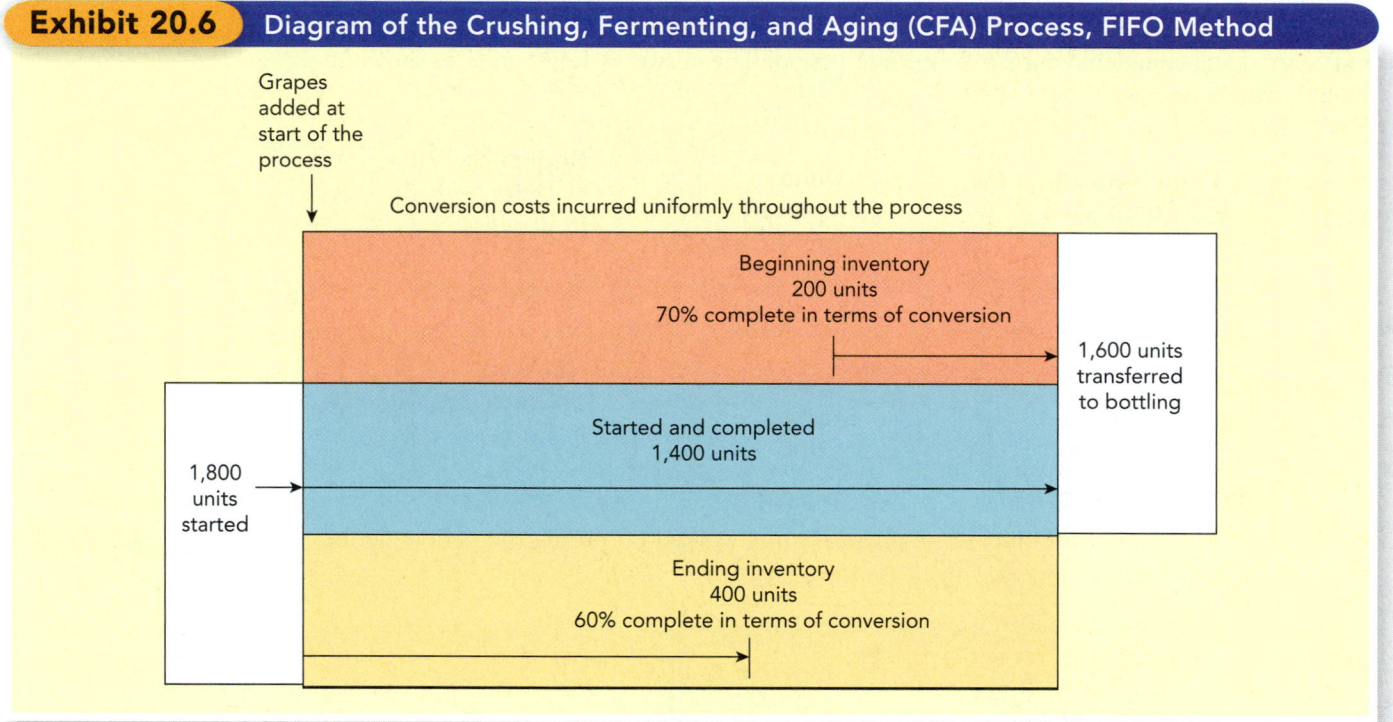

To calculate the number of equivalent units, we need to consider how much work was done during the **current** period to complete the 200 units in beginning inventory, to produce 1,400 units from start to finish, and to get the 400 units in ending inventory 60 percent complete with respect to conversion cost. This calculation must be made separately for direct materials and conversion costs because each of those costs are added at different points in the production process. See Exhibit 20.7 for a summary of the calculation of equivalent units.

Because direct materials are added at the beginning of the process, we did not need to add any direct materials to the beginning inventory during the current period. Thus, for the beginning inventory, we calculate zero equivalent units of direct materials. Because those units were already 70 percent of the way through the conversion process, they required only 30 percent conversion effort during the current period. So, we multiply the 200 physical units by 30 percent to arrive at 60 equivalent units of conversion cost for the beginning inventory units.

The 1,400 units that were started **and** completed went all the way through the CFA process during the current period. Because all work on those units happened during the current period, the number of equivalent units is the same as the number of physical units.

## Exhibit 20.7 — Calculation of Equivalent Units, FIFO Method

| | Physical Units | EQUIVALENT UNITS | |
| | | Direct Materials | Conversion Cost |
| --- | --- | --- | --- |
| Beginning inventory | 200 | 0 (200 × (100% − 100%)) | 60 (200 × (100% − 70%)) |
| Started and completed | 1,400 | 1,400 (1,400 × 100%) | 1,400 (1,400 × 100%) |
| Ending inventory | 400 | 400 (400 × 100%) | 240 (400 × 60%) |
| Total | 2,000 | 1,800 | 1,700 |

The 400 units in ending inventory were started during the current period and received the entire amount of direct materials at the beginning of the process. Thus, the number of equivalent units for direct materials is the same as the 400 physical units in ending inventory. Those units went only 60 percent of the way through the conversion process during the current period, however. Therefore, the number of equivalent units for conversion would be 60 percent of the 400 units in ending inventory, or 240.

Finally, we calculate the number of total equivalent units by adding the number of equivalent units for beginning inventory, units started and completed, and ending inventory. This calculation gives us 1,800 equivalent units of direct materials and 1,700 equivalent units of conversion cost. In the next step of preparing the production report, we use these numbers to calculate the cost per equivalent unit.

## Step 3: Calculate Cost per Equivalent Unit

To calculate the cost per equivalent unit under FIFO, we divide the current period's costs by the total number of equivalent units calculated in Step 2, as follows:

$$\text{Cost per Equivalent Unit} = \frac{\text{Current Period Costs}}{\text{Equivalent Units}}$$

Only current period costs are included in this calculation because **equivalent units relate only to work that was performed during the current period.** We do not include the cost of beginning inventory because those costs were incurred in a prior period. Because the number of equivalent units differs for direct materials and conversion cost, we must calculate each category separately.

Exhibit 20.8 shows the cost per equivalent unit calculations for our winery example. The cost per equivalent unit is $450 for direct materials and $540 for conversion. In the next step, we use these costs per equivalent unit to determine the cost of the units completed and transferred to bottling as well as the cost of the units that are still in process.

> **Coach's Tip**
>
> To calculate the number of equivalent units, ask yourself the following questions: What did we do during the **current** period to get the beginning inventory units from 70 percent complete to fully complete? What did we do during the **current** period to start the ending inventory units and get them 60 percent complete?

## Exhibit 20.8 — Calculation of the Cost per Equivalent Unit, FIFO Method

| | Direct Materials | Conversion Cost |
| --- | --- | --- |
| Current Period Cost (given) | $810,000 | $918,000 |
| Equivalent Units (from Exhibit 20.7) | ÷ 1,800 | ÷ 1,700 |
| Cost per Equivalent Unit | $ 450 | $ 540 |

## Step 4: Reconcile the Total Cost of Work in Process

The final step in preparing the production report is to reconcile the total cost recorded in the Work in Process account. Its total cost includes the cost that was already in the account at the beginning of the period plus the direct materials and conversion costs that were added to the process during the period. See the following T-account for the costs for our winery example.

| Work in Process Inventory (CFA) | | | |
|---|---:|---|---|
| Beginning Balance | 165,600 | Cost of Goods Completed | |
| Direct Materials | 810,000 | and Transferred to Bottling | ? |
| Conversion Cost Applied | 918,000 | | |
| | 1,893,600 | | |
| Ending Balance | ? | | |

In all, we need to account for a total cost of $1,893,600 for the CFA process. A portion of this cost will be transferred out of the CFA process and into the next department (Bottling), and part of it will remain in the CFA department as the ending balance in Work in Process Inventory.

Notice that $165,600 of this cost relates to the units that were already in process at the beginning of the period. Because FIFO assumes that these units are completed first, the cost of the beginning inventory is transferred out of the Work in Process Inventory account with the units that are completed and transferred. The $810,000 and $918,000 represent the current period's costs, which were included in the calculation of the cost per equivalent unit in Step 3. To determine how much of this cost should be transferred out and how much should remain in ending inventory, we must multiply the cost per equivalent unit (from Exhibit 20.8) by the number of equivalent units (calculated in Exhibit 20.7). See Exhibit 20.9 for the calculations.

- The 200 units in beginning inventory carried a cost of $165,600 from the prior period. During the current period, the company incurred an additional 60 equivalent units of conversion at a cost of $540 per equivalent unit, for a total cost of $32,400 (60 × $540). Under the FIFO cost assumption, the total cost of the beginning inventory $198,000 ($165,600 + $32,400) is transferred out of the department with the units completed.

- The 1,400 units that were started **and** completed during the current period would be transferred out at the full cost per equivalent unit of $450 for direct materials and $540 for conversion, for a total cost of $1,386,000 [1,400 × ($450 + $540)].

**Exhibit 20.9**    Calculation of the Cost of Goods Completed and Ending Inventory Costs, FIFO Method

| | Prior Period Costs | CURRENT PERIOD COSTS | | Total Cost Accounted for | |
|---|---|---|---|---|---|
| | | EQUIVALENT UNITS × COST PER EQUIVALENT UNIT | | | |
| | | Direct Materials | Conversion Cost | | |
| Beginning inventory | $165,600 | — | 60 × $540 = $ 32,400 | $ 198,000 | $1,584,000 cost of goods completed and transferred |
| Started and completed | — | 1,400 × $450 = $630,000 | 1,400 × $540 = 756,000 | 1,386,000 | |
| Ending inventory | — | 400 × $450 = 180,000 | 240 × $540 = 129,600 | 309,600 | |
| Total cost to account for | $165,600 | | $810,000 | $918,000  $1,893,600 | |

- The total cost transferred out of CFA work in process (for the units in beginning inventory plus the units started and completed) is $1,584,000 ($198,000 + $1,386,000). This cost would be debited to the next Work in Process Inventory account (bottling).
- The 400 units that remain in ending inventory are valued at the full $450 per equivalent unit for direct materials or $180,000 (400 × $450). The conversion cost attached to these units would be $129,600 (240 equivalent units × $540 per equivalent unit), for a total ending inventory cost of $309,600 ($180,000 + $129,600).

After we transfer $1,584,000 out of the Work in Process Inventory (CFA) account, the $309,600 cost of the ending inventory units remain in the Work in Process Inventory (CFA) account as in the following T-account.

| Work in Process Inventory (CFA) | | | |
|---|---|---|---|
| Beginning Balance | 165,600 | Cost of Goods Completed | 1,584,000 |
| Direct Materials | 810,000 | and Transferred to Bottling | |
| Conversion Cost Applied | 918,000 | | |
| Ending Balance | 309,600 | | |

# Step 5: Prepare a Production Report

The final step in process costing is to summarize the results of Steps 1–4 into a single document called the **production report**. The production report is essentially a summary of what occurred in the production process during the accounting period. It includes information about the number of physical units (Step 1) and equivalent units (Step 2) as well as cost per equivalent unit (Step 3), and a reconciliation of the cost of work in process (Step 4).

Refer to Exhibit 20.10 for the production report based on Steps 1–4 for our winery example. This single document summarizes the four steps we followed to determine the cost of the CFA process.

> **Learning Objective 5**
>
> Prepare a process costing production report.

**Exhibit 20.10    FIFO Process Costing Production Report**

|  | CK Mondavi Winery | | | | |
|---|---|---|---|---|---|
|  | Process Costing Production Report (FIFO Method) | | | | |
|  | Crushing, Fermenting and Aging (CFA) Department | | | | |
|  | For the Quarter Ended March 31, 2009 | | | | |
| **UNITS** | **Step 1 Reconcile Physical Units** | | | | |
| 1 Units to be accounted for: | | | | | |
| 2   Beginning work in process | 200 | | | | |
| 3   Started into production | 1,800 | | | | |
| 4   Total units | 2,000 | | | | |
| 5 | | **Step 2 Calculate Equivalent Units** | | | |
| 6 Units accounted for as follows: | | Direct Materials | Conversion | | |
| 7   Beginning work in process | 200 | 0 | 60 | | |
| 8   Started and completed | 1,400 | 1,400 | 1,400 | | |
| 9   Ending work in process | 400 | 400 | 240 | | |
| 10  Total units | 2,000 | 1,800 | 1,700 | | |
| 11 **COSTS** | | **Step 3:  Calculate cost per equivalent unit** | | | |
| 12 | | | | | |
| 13 | | Direct Materials | Conversion | | |
| 14   Current period costs: | | $      810,000 | $   918,000 | | |
| 15   Equivalent units (Row 10) | | 1,800 | 1,700 | | |
| 16   Cost per equivalent unit | | $          450 | $      540 | | |
| 17 | | **Step 4:  Reconcile the total cost of work in process** | | | |
|  Cost to be accounted for: | | Direct Materials | Conversion | | Total |
| 18   Beginning work in process | | | | $ | 165,600 |
| 19   Current period costs | | $      810,000 | $   918,000 | | 1,728,000 |
| 20   Total cost | | | | $ | 1,893,600 |
| 21 | | | | | |
| 22 Cost accounted for as follows: | | | | | |
| 23   Beginning inventory balance (transferred out) | | | | $ | 165,600 |
| 24   Cost to complete beginning inventory (Row 7 x Row 16) | | $          - | $    32,400 | | 32,400 |
| 25   Started and completed (Row 8 x Row 16) | | 630,000 | 756,000 | | 1,386,000 |
| 26   Ending inventory (Row 9 x Row 16) | | 180,000 | 129,600 | | 309,600 |
| 27   Total cost | | | | $ | 1,893,600 |

## Additional Factors in Process Costing

The example you have just studied illustrates most aspects of process costing. However, you should be aware of two issues that were not included in the example. First, as was mentioned earlier, many process-oriented companies use an alternative method called weighted average process costing. The weighted average method does not separately account for the units in beginning inventory. Instead, it assumes that all units completed were started during the current period. As long as a company has minimal or very stable inventory levels, this method will approximate the results of FIFO.

Supplement 20 illustrates the weighted average method using the same data we used for our winery example. Your instructor may want you to learn the FIFO method, the weighted average method, or both. The steps for preparing the production report are the same. The only difference is how you treat the units and costs of the beginning inventory.

The second issue we did not consider is how to account for subsequent departments in process costing. We showed the first process in the production chain (CFA), but we did not extend the example to show how costs flow through the next process (Bottling). The cost of the wine transferred out of the CFA process ($1,584,000) would enter the Work in Process Inventory (Bottling) account in the same way that the cost of direct materials (grapes) were added to the Work in Process Inventory (CFA) account. Each subsequent department must then keep track of the costs that were transferred in from the prior departments in addition to the costs that are added during the process.

Before we move to activity based costing, make sure you understand the steps necessary to prepare a production report by completing the following Self-Study Practice.

**SELF-STUDY PRACTICE**

Aqua-Fit manufactures and sells fitness drinks (with added vitamins and minerals) to fitness clubs across the country. The company uses a FIFO process costing system to determine the cost of the fitness drinks. All materials (water, juice, vitamins, and bottles) are added at the beginning of the process, and conversion costs are added uniformly.

At the start of the most recent period, the company had 1,000 bottles that were about 40 percent through the conversion process. During the period, an additional 9,000 bottles were started in the process. The period ended with 3,000 bottles that were 20 percent of the way through the process.

1. How many units were **completed** during the period?
2. How many units were **started and completed** during the period?
3. How many equivalent units of conversion would be required to **complete** the beginning inventory?
4. Calculate the equivalent units of direct materials and conversion for the units in ending inventory.

*After you have finished, check your answers with the solutions at the bottom of the page.*

Video 20-2
www.mhhe.com/LLPW1e

## ACTIVITY BASED COSTING (ABC)

We started this chapter by asking what makes a $5 bottle of wine different from a $50 bottle of wine. To answer this question, we expand our example to assume that CK Mondavi produces two types of wine. The first is a standard-variety chardonnay produced in large batches and aged for a relatively short period (about four months) in large metal containers called vats. The vats are very easy to clean and maintain and can be reused hundreds of times before they wear out. This wine is the company's highest volume product. Over the years, Mondavi has learned to produce it with a minimum of quality testing on each batch.

Solution to
Self-Study Practice

1. 7,000 (1,000 + 9,000 − 3,000)
2. 6,000 (7,000 − 1,000) or (9,000 − 3,000)
3. 600 [1,000 × (100% − 40%)]
4. 3,000 equivalent units of direct materials, 600 equivalent units of conversion (3,000 × 20%)

The second wine is a limited-edition cabernet that is made in very small batches from premium grapes and then aged for more than three years in special French oak barrels to provide a particular taste. The barrels require significant maintenance between batches and can be used only a few times before they lose some of the oak flavor that they transfer to the wine. The company maintains extremely tight quality control over this wine to ensure that it is produced to the most exacting standards.

In this scenario, averaging the manufacturing costs of the two products does not make sense. The chardonnay, which is produced in high volume, accumulates more of certain kinds of costs, but the limited-edition cabernet requires more care and attention. This situation is precisely what activity based costing was designed for.

**Activity Based Costing (ABC)** is a method of assigning indirect costs to products and services based on the underlying activities performed in the manufacturing process. Costs related to direct materials and direct labor can be traced directly to individual products or services so they are assigned directly to those products or services as they are incurred. Indirect costs, which cannot be directly traced to a specific product or service, are assigned using an **allocation base** or **cost driver**:

**Learning Objective 6**
Calculate the cost of products using activity based costing.

Most traditional (non-ABC) cost systems use measures such as number of direct labor hours, machine hours, or direct materials cost to apply indirect costs to products or services. We call these measures **volume-based allocation measures** because they are directly related to the number of units produced or the number of customers served. Volume-based allocation measures generally assign the highest cost to the products with the highest volume. In our example, a volume-based measure would assign higher cost to the standard chardonnay than to the limited-edition cabernet simply because the chardonnay is produced in higher volume and therefore requires more total labor hours, machine hours, and direct materials cost.

Unlike traditional cost systems which rely strictly on volume-based allocation measures, ABC systems include measures that capture something other than the volume of units produced or sold. These measures are called **nonvolume-based cost drivers**. Some common examples of volume-based and nonvolume-based measures are:

| Volume-Based Allocation Measures (used in traditional cost systems) | Nonvolume-Based Cost Drivers (used in activity based costing) |
|---|---|
| Number of units produced | Number of batches or setup time |
| Number of direct labor hours | Processing time per unit |
| Number of machine hours | Number of quality inspections |
| Direct materials cost | Number of design changes |

**Coach's Tip**
A traditional (non-ABC) costing system includes only volume-based measures such as those in the left column. An ABC system may include some volume measures, but it also includes nonvolume-based measures, such as those in the right column.

By incorporating allocation measures that capture other aspects of the production process besides volume, ABC can assign more cost to products that require more setup time, longer processing, more quality control, or more engineering. In our winery example, an ABC system would assign more cost to the limited edition cabernet than to the standard chardonnay because the cabernet is produced in small batches and requires more setups, longer aging, and more quality control.

Activity based costing involves four basic steps:

1. Identify and classify activities.
2. Form activity cost pools and assign indirect costs to each pool.
3. Select an activity cost driver and calculate an activity rate for each cost pool.
4. Assign indirect costs to products or services based on their activity demands.

Video 20-3
www.mhhe.com/LLPW1e

In the following sections, we use the example of CK Mondavi to complete these steps.

## Step 1: Identify and Classify Activities

The first step in activity based costing is to identify all activities that must occur to make a product or provide a service and then classify them into one of the following categories:

- **Unit level activities** are performed for each unit or customer (one at a time).
- **Batch-level activities** are performed all at once for a group of units or customers.
- **Product-level activities** are performed to support a specific product line.
- **Customer-level activities** are performed for a specific customer.
- **Facility-level activities** are performed for the overall company to benefit multiple customers or product lines.

For a sample of activities as CK Mondavi would categorize them, see Exhibit 20.11.

**Exhibit 20.11    Categorization of Activities at CK Mondavi**

**Activity Categories**

**Facility-Level Activities**
Performed to support all of the company's products or services

**Customer-Level Activities**
Performed for specific customers

**Product-Level Activities**
Performed to support individual product lines

**Batch-Level Activities**
Performed for a group of units or customers all at once

**Unit-Level Activities**
Performed for each unit or customer (one at a time)

**Sample Activities**

Installing and maintaining equipment
Paying for insurance, utilities, taxes

Designing a special customer label
Negotiating a contract for a large customer

Performing research and development for new wine
Obtaining special equipment (e.g., oak barrels) used only for certain wines

Aging wine in barrels or vats
Testing each barrel or vat for quality

Pouring wine into bottles
Labeling bottles, inserting corks

## Step 2: Form Activity Cost Pools and Assign Indirect Costs to Each Pool

The next ABC step is to combine related activities into activity cost pools. The goal is to create as few activity cost pools as possible (to keep the approach manageable) while capturing the major activities identified in Step 1 (to provide useful information). Assume that CK Mondavi has determined that the following five categories capture its major production activities:

- Purchasing, receiving, and crushing grapes.
- Setting up and maintaining equipment.
- Fermenting and aging the wine in barrels.
- Performing quality control.
- Bottling and labeling the wine.

Next we must determine how much indirect cost CK Mondavi incurred to support each of these activities. Doing so means taking a detailed look at the Manufacturing Overhead Cost account to determine how much each activity costs. For example, managers at the winery might determine that the salary of a materials purchasing agent is related primarily to purchasing, receiving, and crushing the grapes. Similarly, the cost of setting up and maintaining the equipment would belong in the setup activity cost pool. The quality control supervisor's salary would be assigned to the quality control pool. Depreciation on the barrels used in the fermenting and aging process would be assigned to fermenting and aging, and the cost of the equipment used in bottling and packaging would be assigned to the bottling and packaging pool.

Some indirect costs may need to be spread over or allocated to more than one activity. For example, a production supervisor might be responsible for overseeing all five activities; thus, the supervisor's salary would be allocated to all five activities based on the amount of supervisory time spent on each. In this example, we assume CK Mondavi has divided a total of $880,000 in manufacturing overhead cost among the five activity cost pools as in the following diagram.

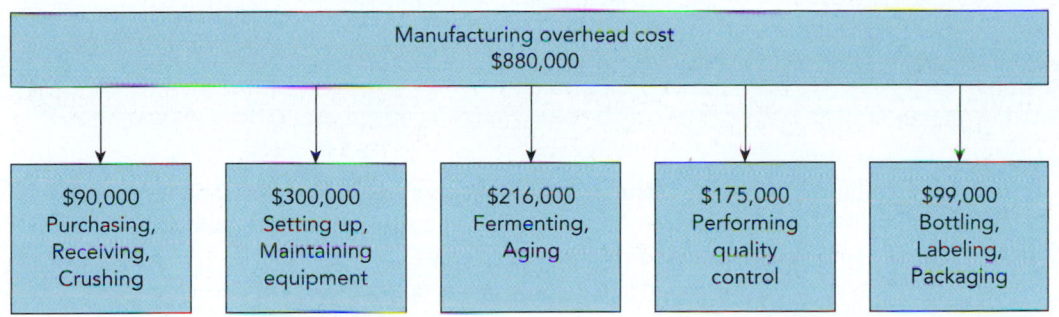

# Step 3: Select an Activity Cost Driver and Calculate an Activity Rate for Each Cost Pool

The next step is to select an activity cost driver for each of the cost pools created in Step 2. An **activity cost driver** is an underlying measure that is used to assign the activity that occurs in an activity cost pool to individual products and services. Assume that CK Mondavi has identified the following cost drivers for its five activity cost pools:

- Purchasing, receiving, and crushing is driven by the weight (pounds) of grapes purchased, received, and then crushed.
- Setting up and maintaining equipment is driven by the number of setups.
- Fermenting and aging is driven by the number of days the wine remains in the vat or barrel.
- Quality control is driven by the number of quality inspections.
- Bottling, labeling and packaging is driven by the number of bottles processed.

We can incorporate these cost drivers in our diagram of the activity cost pools:

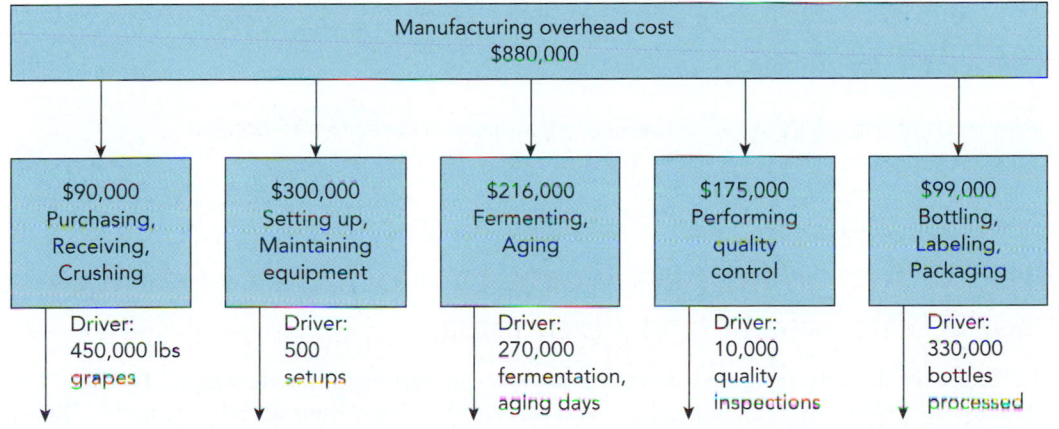

Once we have selected an appropriate activity cost driver for each cost pool, we can calculate the activity rate by dividing the total cost of each pool by the total activity cost driver, as follows:

$$\text{Activity Rate} = \frac{\text{Total Activity Cost}}{\text{Total Activity Driver}}$$

---

**Coach's Tip**

The process of assigning indirect costs to the activity cost pools is sometimes referred to as the first stage of allocation under activity based costing. In this chapter, our primary focus is on the second stage that assigns costs to products and services based on their activity cost drivers.

**Coach's Tip**

Remember that these rates are intended to cover only the **indirect** costs of making the wine. The cost of the grapes, bottles, and direct labor can be traced directly to each unit produced and thus are not subject to activity based costing.

## Exhibit 20.12    Calculation of CK Mondavi's Activity Rates

| Activity Cost Pool | Total Indirect Cost | / Activity Cost Driver | = | Activity Rate |
|---|---|---|---|---|
| Purchasing, receiving, and crushing | $ 90,000 | / 450,000 pounds of grapes | = | $ 0.20 per pound |
| Setting up a production run | 300,000 | / 500 setups | = | 600.00 per setup |
| Fermenting, aging in barrels | 216,000 | / 270,000 fermentating and aging days | = | 0.80 per day |
| Performing quality control | 175,000 | / 10,000 quality inspections | = | 17.50 per inspection |
| Bottling, labeling, packaging | 99,000 | / 330,000 bottles | = | 0.30 per bottle |

Refer to Exhibit 20.12 for the calculation of the activity rates for CK Mondavi's cost pools. Before we move to the final step in activity based costing, take the following Self-Study Practice to make sure you understand the first three steps.

### SELF-STUDY PRACTICE

1. Which of the following would be classified as a unit-level activity by an ice cream manufacturer such as Ben & Jerry's?

   a.   Purchasing the ingredients to make a batch of cookie dough ice cream.
   b.   Performing quality checks on each batch produced to make sure the flavor is right.
   c.   Conducting research and development on a new flavor of ice cream.
   d.   Maintaining the equipment used to produce various flavors of ice cream.
   e.   Pouring the ice cream into containers before freezing it.

2. Which of the activities in question 1 (a–e) would be classified as a product-level activity by an ice cream manufacturer such as Ben & Jerry's?

3. One of Ben & Jerry's major activities is changing over the equipment to produce a new flavor of ice cream. The total annual cost and the activity driver for this cost pool are:

   | | |
   |---|---|
   | Total annual cost of activity | $100,000 |
   | Activity driver | 500 change-overs |

What is the activity rate for this activity?

*After you have finished, check your answers with the solutions at the bottom of the page.*

## Step 4: Assign Indirect Costs to Products or Services Based on Their Activity Demands

The final step in activity based costing is to use the activity rates developed in Step 3 to calculate the cost of individual products and services based on their activity demands. To see how this works, let's compare the activities needed for CK Mondavi to produce one batch of

**Solution to Self-Study Practice**

1.  e
2.  c
3.  $200 per setup ($100,000/500)

standard chardonnay to the activities needed to produce one batch of vintage cabernet. We assume these two hypothetical products have the following activity requirements:

| Activity Requirements | Standard Chardonnay | Vintage Cabernet |
|---|---|---|
| Pounds of grapes | 1,250 pounds per batch | 375 pounds per batch |
| Number of setups | 1 setup per batch | 1 setup per batch |
| Fermentation, aging days | 150 days per batch | 900 days per batch |
| Number of quality inspections | 1 every 15 days (10 per batch) | 1 every 10 days (90 per batch) |
| Number of bottles | 1,000 bottles per batch | 150 bottles per batch |

To calculate the manufacturing overhead cost of each product, we simply multiply these activity requirements by the activity rates developed in Step 3 (see Exhibit 20.13).

**Exhibit 20.13  Calculation of CK Mondavi's Activity-Based Costs**

| Activity Cost Pool | (From Exhibit 20.12) Activity Rate | STANDARD CHARDONNAY Activity Cost Driver | ABC Cost | VINTAGE CABERNET Activity Cost Driver | ABC Cost |
|---|---|---|---|---|---|
| Purchasing, receiving, crushing | $ 0.20 per pound | 1,250 pounds | $250.00 | 375 pounds | $75.00 |
| Setting up a production run | 600.00 per set-up | 1 setup | 600.00 | 1 setup | 600.00 |
| Fermenting, aging in barrels | 0.80 per day | 150 days | 120.00 | 900 days | 720.00 |
| Performing quality control | 17.50 per inspection | 10 inspections | 175.00 | 90 inspections | 1,575.00 |
| Bottling, labeling, packaging | 0.30 per bottle | 1,000 bottles | 300.00 | 150 bottles | 45.00 |
| Manufacturing overhead cost per batch | | | $1,445.00 | | $3,015.00 |
| Number of bottles per batch | | | 1,000 | | 150 |
| Manufacturing overhead cost per bottle | | | $1.45 | | $20.10 |

The $1.45 and $20.10 in manufacturing overhead cost per bottle for the standard chardonnay and vintage cabernet represent only the indirect portion of the manufacturing costs. Direct materials costs and direct labor costs, which can be traced directly to each product, must still be added to the manufacturing overhead costs to determine the full manufacturing cost per unit under ABC. Assume the direct materials and direct labor costs per bottle follow:

| Manufacturing Cost per Bottle | Standard Chardonnay | Vintage Cabernet |
|---|---|---|
| Direct materials cost | $2.00 | $ 4.00 |
| Direct labor cost | 1.00 | 2.00 |
| Manufacturing overhead (ABC) cost | 1.45 | 20.10 |
| Total manufacturing cost | $4.45 | $26.10 |

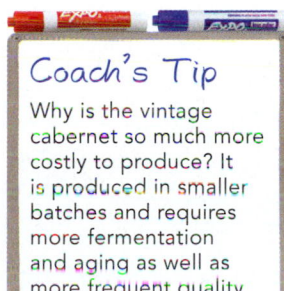

**Coach's Tip**

Why is the vintage cabernet so much more costly to produce? It is produced in smaller batches and requires more fermentation and aging as well as more frequent quality inspections.

This ABC analysis shows that it costs about $26.10 to produce a bottle of vintage cabernet compared to about $4.45 for a bottle of standard chardonnay. Although the cost of direct materials and direct labor for the two products differ, most of the difference in total cost is due to the manufacturing overhead cost per unit.

To summarize, activity based costing is a method of assigning indirect costs to products or services based on the activities required to produce them. ABC uses both volume-based cost drivers (such as the number of bottles produced or the number of pounds of materials used) and nonvolume-based cost drivers (such as the number of setups required, the number of days spent in fermentation and aging, and the number of quality inspections performed). The goal of ABC is to provide more valuable information about the cost of products and services so that managers can make better decisions about what prices to charge, whether to offer certain products or services, and how to reduce costs.

# Demonstration Case A (Process Costing)

Bellagio Olive Oil Company manufactures extra virgin olive oil using a series of processes to convert olives into olive oil. These steps include cleaning the olives, grinding them into a paste, mixing to increase olive oil yield, separating the olive oil from the fruit, extracting the olive oil, storing, and bottling.

In the mixing department, direct materials (olives) are added at the beginning of the process, and conversion costs are incurred uniformly throughout the process. At the beginning of the most recent accounting period, Bellagio had 20,000 units in the mixing process, 30 percent complete. It started an additional 150,000 units into the process, and ended the period with 40,000 units in process, 40 percent complete. The mixing department's partially completed production report is shown below:

| | A | B | C | D | E | F |
|---|---|---|---|---|---|---|
| 1 | | | Bellagio Olive Oil | | | |
| 2 | | | Process Costing Production Report (FIFO Method) | | | |
| 3 | | | Mixing Department | | | |
| 4 | | | For the Quarter Ended December 31, 2009 | | | |
| 5 | | | Step 1 | | | |
| 6 | | UNITS | Reconcile | | | |
| 7 | 1 | Units to be accounted for: | Physical Units | | | |
| 8 | 2 | Beginning work in process | 20,000 | | | |
| 9 | 3 | Started into production | 150,000 | | | |
| 10 | 4 | Total units | 170,000 | Step 2 | | |
| 11 | 5 | | | Calculate Equivalent Units | | |
| 12 | 6 | Units accounted for as follows: | | Direct Materials | Conversion | |
| 13 | 7 | Beginning work in process | ? | ? | ? | |
| 14 | 8 | Started and completed | ? | ? | ? | |
| 15 | 9 | Ending work in process | 40,000 | ? | ? | |
| 16 | 10 | Total units | ? | ? | ? | |
| 17 | 11 | COSTS | | Step 3:  Calculate cost per | | |
| 18 | 12 | | | equivalent unit | | |
| 19 | 13 | | | Direct Materials | Conversion | |
| 20 | 14 | Current period costs | | $    450,000 | $    679,000 | |
| 21 | 15 | Equivalent units (from step 2 above) | | ? | ? | |
| 22 | 16 | Cost per equivalent unit | | ? | ? | |
| 23 | 17 | | | Step 4:  Reconcile the total cost of work in process | | |
| 24 | 18 | Costs to be accounted for: | | Direct Materials | Conversion | Total |
| 25 | 19 | Beginning work in process | | | | $    301,000 |
| 26 | 20 | Current period costs | | $    450,000 | $    679,000 | 1,129,000 |
| 27 | 21 | Total cost | | | | $   1,430,000 |
| 28 | 22 | | | | | |
| 29 | 23 | Costs accounted for as follows: | | | | |
| 30 | 24 | Beginning inventory balance (transferred out) | | | | ? |
| 31 | 25 | Cost to complete beginning inentory (Row 7 x Row 16) | | ? | ? | ? |
| 32 | 26 | Started and completed (Row 8 x Row 16) | | ? | ? | ? |
| 33 | 27 | Ending inventory (Row 9 x Row 16) | | ? | ? | ? |
| 34 | 28 | Total cost | | | | ? |

## Required:

1. Complete steps 1–4 by filling in Bellagio's production report.
2. What is the balance in Work in Process Inventory (Mixing) at the end of the quarter?
3. Prepare the journal entry to show the transfer of cost from Work in Process Inventory (Mixing) to Work in Process Inventory (Separating) for all of the units completed during the quarter.

## Suggested Solution

1.

| | A | B | C | D | E | F |
|---|---|---|---|---|---|---|
| 1 | | | Bellagio Olive Oil | | | |
| 2 | | | Process Costing Production Report (FIFO Method) | | | |
| 3 | | | Mixing Department | | | |
| 4 | | | For the Quarter Ended December 31, 2009 | | | |
| 5 | | | Step 1 | | | |
| 6 | | **UNITS** | **Reconcile** | | | |
| 7 | 1 | Units to be acccunted for: | **Physical Units** | | | |
| 8 | 2 | Beginning work in process | 20,000 | | | |
| 9 | 3 | Started into production | 150,000 | | | |
| 10 | 4 | Total units | 170,000 | **Step 2** | | |
| 11 | 5 | | | Calculate Equivalent Units | | |
| 12 | 6 | Units accounted for as follows: | | Direct Materials | Conversion | |
| 13 | 7 | Beginning work in process | 20,000 | 0 | 4,000 | |
| 14 | 8 | Started and completed | 110,000 | 110,000 | 110,000 | |
| 15 | 9 | Ending work in process | 40,000 | 40,000 | 16,000 | |
| 16 | 10 | Total units | 170,000 | 150,000 | 140,000 | |
| 17 | 11 | | | Step 3:  Calculate cost per | | |
| 18 | 12 | **COSTS** | | equivalent unit | | |
| 19 | 13 | | | Direct Materials | Conversion | |
| 20 | 14 | Current period costs | | $    450,000 | $    679,000 | |
| 21 | 15 | Equivalent units (from step 2 above) | | 150,000 | 140,000 | |
| 22 | 16 | Cost per equivalent unit | | $    3.00 | $    4.85 | |
| 23 | 17 | | | Step 4:  Reconcile the total cost of work in process | | |
| 24 | 18 | Costs to be accounted for: | | Direct Materials | Conversion | Total |
| 25 | 19 | Beginning work in process | | | | $    301,000 |
| 26 | 20 | Current period costs | | $    450,000 | $    679,000 | 1,129,000 |
| 27 | 21 | Total costs | | | | $    1,430,000 |
| 28 | 22 | | | | | |
| 29 | 23 | Costs accounted for as follows: | | | | |
| 30 | 24 | Beginning inventory balance (transferred out) | | | | $    301,000 |
| 31 | 25 | Cost to complete beginning inentory (Row 7 x Row 16) | | $    - | $    67,900 | 67,900 |
| 32 | 26 | Started and completed (Row 8 x Row 16) | | 330,000 | 533,500 | 863,500 |
| 33 | 27 | Ending inventory (Row 9 x Row 16) | | 120,000 | 77,600 | 197,600 |
| 34 | 28 | | | | | $    1,430,000 |

2.    Ending balance in Work in Process Inventory (Mixing) is $197,600

3.    Journal entry to transfer completed units from Mixing to Separating:

| | Debit | Credit |
|---|---|---|
| Work in Process Inventory (Separating) | 1,232,400 | |
| Work in Process Inventory (Mixing) | | 1,232,400 |
| $301,000 + $67,900 + $863,500 = $1,232,400 | | |

# Demonstration Case B (Activity Based Costing)

Tom and Terry's Ice Cream Company uses activity based costing to assign manufacturing overhead cost to various ice cream products. The company has completed the first few steps in the ABC process by identifying and pooling major activities, assigning manufacturing overhead cost to each pool, and developing an appropriate activity driver for each pool, as follows:

| Activity Cost Pool | Total Cost | Total Activity Cost Driver |
|---|---|---|
| Purchasing ingredients | $200,000 | 400,000 pounds |
| Setting up equipment | 150,000 | 500 setups |
| Performing quality testing | 200,000 | 2,000 quality inspections |
| Packaging | 40,000 | 200,000 pints |

Using this information, the company is trying to determine how much it costs to manufacture chocolate chunk ice cream. The activity requirements for the chocolate chunk product follow.

| Direct Costs | Chocolate Chunk per Pint |
|---|---|
| Direct materials cost | $0.75 |
| Direct labor cost | 0.25 |

| Activity Requirements | Activity Drivers |
|---|---|
| Total pints produced | 100,000 |
| Pounds of materials required | 15,000 |
| Number of setups | 1 per batch |
| Batch size | 5,000 pints (20 batches) |
| Quality testing | 6 times per batch (120 total) |

**Required:**

1. Calculate an activity rate for each of the four activity cost pools.
2. Use the activity rates calculated in question 1 to assign manufacturing overhead cost to the chocolate chunk product.
3. Calculate the total manufacturing cost per pint of chocolate chunk ice cream.

## Suggested Solution

1.

| Activity | Total Cost | Total Activity Cost Driver | Activity Rate |
|---|---|---|---|
| Purchasing ingredients | $200,000 | 400,000 pounds | $ 0.50 per pound |
| Setting up equipment | 150,000 | 500 setups | 300.00 per setup |
| Performing quality testing | 200,000 | 2,000 quality inspections | 100.00 per quality inspection |
| Packaging | 40,000 | 200,000 pints | 0.20 per pint |

2.

| Activity Rate | Chocolate Chunk Requirements | ABC Cost Allocation |
|---|---|---|
| $ 0.50 per pound | 15,000 pounds | $ 7,500 |
| 300.00 per setup | 20 setups | 6,000 |
| 100.00 per quality inspection | 120 quality inspections | 12,000 |
| 0.20 per pint | 100,000 pints | 20,000 |
| Total manufacturing overhead cost (using ABC) | | $45,500 |
| | | 100,000 pints |
| Manufacturing overhead cost per pint (from ABC) | | $0.455 |

3.

| | Chocolate Chunk |
|---|---|
| Direct materials cost | $0.75 per pint |
| Direct labor cost | 0.25 per pint |
| Manufacturing overhead per pint | 0.46 (rounded from ABC in preceding table) |
| Total manufacturing cost per pint | $1.46 |

# Supplement 20A
## Weighted Average Method

This supplement demonstrates how to prepare a process costing production report using the weighted average method. The example used to demonstrate the weighted average method is the same as the one we used to prepare a production report using the FIFO method (see page 855):

The main difference between the FIFO and weighted average methods is that the FIFO method assumes that the units in beginning inventory are completed before any new units enter the process. The weighted average method assumes that all units completed during the current period were started in the current period. Thus, the weighted average method ignores the fact that the units in beginning inventory were partially complete at the start of the period. That is, the weighted average method ignores the percentage of completion of units in beginning inventory and instead treats them as if they were started in the current period.

Because the FIFO method pays more attention to how much work went into fully and partially completed units during the period, it is generally more accurate than the weighted average method. However, the weighted average method is simpler than the FIFO method and provides similar results for companies with minimal inventory or very stable production and inventory patterns. The weighted average method is used more often than the FIFO method and is expected to become even more common as companies move toward just-in-time inventory systems, which minimize inventory levels.

Regardless of whether a company uses the FIFO or weighted average method, the same four steps are followed in preparing the production report:

1. Reconcile the number of physical units.
2. Translate physical units into equivalent units.
3. Calculate the cost per equivalent unit.
4. Reconcile the total cost of Work in Process Inventory.

## Step 1: Reconcile the Number of Physical Units

The first step in preparing the production report is to reconcile the number of physical units. First you calculate the total number of units that were worked on during the period by adding the number of units in beginning inventory to the number of units that were started in the current period. Then you determine whether those units were completed during the period or were still being worked on at the end of the period. The formula for reconciling the number of physical units is:

> **Coach's Tip**
>
> This formula ignores any units that may have been lost due to spoilage or waste. Accounting for lost or spoiled units is covered in more advanced texts.

To apply this formula, let's return to the CFA process at CK Mondavi. For this example, assume the company had 200 barrels of wine in process at the start of a new accounting period. Last period's production report valued these partially complete units at $165,600 ($84,500 for direct materials + $81,100 for conversion cost). During the period, workers started another 1,800 barrels into the CFA process. At the end of the period, 400 barrels of wine were still in the CFA process. Based on this information, you can answer the following question: How many barrels of wine were transferred out of the CFA process and into bottling during the current period?

To answer this question, you can prepare a reconciliation of physical units, as follows:

> **Coach's Tip**
>
> The number of units completed and transferred to bottling is 1,600. During the period, 2,000 units were worked on and 400 units were still being worked on at the end of the period, so 1,600 units must have been completed.

| Physical Units | | Physical Units | |
|---|---|---|---|
| Beginning units | 200 | Units completed | ? |
| Units started | 1,800 | Ending units | 400 |
| Total units | 2,000 | Total Units | 2,000 |

## Step 2: Translate Physical Units into Equivalent Units

The next step in preparing the production report is to calculate **equivalent units,** a measure of the amount of work or effort that occurred during the current period to produce full and partially completed units. Under the weighted average method, the only partially completed units we need to deal with are the units in inventory at the end of the period. The weighted average method ignores the beginning inventory, assuming that those units were started in the current period.

To determine the number of equivalent units in our winery example, we use the following additional details about CK Mondavi's production process.

- Direct materials (grapes) are added at the beginning of the process. Thus, once a unit has been started in the process, it has 100 percent of direct materials.
- Conversion costs (direct labor and manufacturing overhead) are incurred uniformly throughout the process.
- Although some units may have been in process at the beginning of the period, the weighted average method ignores that fact and assumes that the 1,600 units completed this period were all started in the current period.
- The 400 units in ending inventory were 60 percent of the way through the CFA process. Those units have all of the direct materials added but only 60 percent of the conversion cost.

See Exhibit 20A.1 for a summary of these details.

**Exhibit 20A.1**    Diagram of the Crushing, Fermenting, and Aging (CFA) Process, Weighted Average Method

To determine the number of equivalent units, we must consider how much work went into the units that were completed in the current period and those that remain in ending inventory. We need to make separate calculations for direct materials and conversion cost because these costs are incurred at different points in the process. See Exhibit 20A.2 for a demonstration of the calculation of equivalent units. Notice that for the completed units, the equivalent units equal the physical units. That is because the weighted average method assumes that all units completed during the current period were started during the period. Thus, we ignore any units in beginning inventory.

The only adjustment we need to make is for the units in ending inventory. Remember that direct materials are added at the beginning of the process, so the 400 units in ending inventory are 100 percent complete with respect to direct materials. For direct materials, then, the number of equivalent units is the same as the number of physical units. For conversion cost, the units in ending inventory have gone only 60 percent of the way through the production process. Therefore,

## Exhibit 20A.2    Calculation of Equivalent Units, Weighted Average Method

|  | Number of Physical Units | EQUIVALENT UNITS | | | |
|---|---|---|---|---|---|
|  |  | Direct Materials | | Conversion Cost | |
| Completed | 1,600 | 1,600 | (1,600 × 100%) | 1,600 | (1,600 × 100%) |
| Ending Inventory | 400 | 400 | (400 × 100%) | 240 | (400 × 60%) |
| Total | 2,000 | 2,000 | | 1,840 | |

the number of equivalent units for conversion cost would be 60 percent of the 400 units in ending inventory, or 240.

We can calculate the total number of equivalent units by summing the equivalent units for the units completed during the period and the units in ending inventory. The total equivalent units is 2,000 for direct materials and 1,840 for conversion cost. In the next step, we use these numbers to calculate the cost per equivalent unit.

## Step 3: Calculate the Cost per Equivalent Unit

To calculate the cost per equivalent unit, we divide the total cost of work in process by the total number of equivalent units (calculated in Step 2):

$$\text{Cost per Equivalent Unit} = \frac{\text{Beginning Inventory + Current Costs}}{\text{Equivalent Units}}$$

As this formula shows, the weighted average method combines the cost of the beginning inventory with the costs that were added to the process during the current period. This calculation should be done separately for direct materials and conversion costs.

In our winery example, the cost per equivalent unit is calculated as follows:

|  | Direct Materials | Conversion Cost |
|---|---|---|
| Beginning inventory costs | $ 84,500 | $ 81,100 |
| Current period cost | 810,000 | 918,000 |
| Total costs | $894,500 | $999,100 |
| Equivalent units (from Step 2) | 2,000 | 1,840 |
| Cost per equivalent unit | $ 447.25 | $ 542.99 |

In the next section, we use the cost per equivalent unit of $447.25 for direct materials and $542.99 (rounded) for conversion to calculate the cost of units completed and transferred out of the process as well as the cost of units still in process at the end of the period.

## Step 4: Reconcile the Total Cost of Work in Process

The final step in the preparation of the production report is to reconcile the total cost recorded in the Work in Process Inventory account. The total cost of Work in Process Inventory includes the cost that was already in the account at the beginning of the period plus the direct materials and conversion costs added to the process during the period. The following T-account shows the costs for our winery example:

| Work In Process Inventory (CFA) | | | |
|---|---:|---|---:|
| Beginning balance | | Cost of goods completed | ? |
|    Direct materials | 84,500 | (transferred to bottling) | |
|    Conversion cost applied | 81,100 | | |
| Current period costs | | | |
|    Direct materials | 810,000 | | |
|    Conversion cost applied | 918,000 | | |
| Total cost to account for | 1,893,600 | | |
|   Ending balance | ? | | |

This T-account shows that we must account for a total cost of $1,893,600 for the CFA process. Some of that total cost will be transferred out of the Work in Process Inventory account with the units completed and transferred to the next department, and some will remain as Work in Process Inventory. To determine how much of the cost should be transferred out and how much should be kept with the ending inventory, we simply multiply the costs per equivalent unit of $447.25 for direct materials and $542.99 (rounded) for conversion by the number of equivalent units calculated in Step 2. See Exhibit 20A.3 for the calculations for our winery example.

## Exhibit 20A.3  Reconciliation of the Total Cost of Work in Process, Weighted Average Method

CURRENT PERIOD COSTS

(EQUIVALENT UNITS × COST PER EQUIVALENT UNITS)

| | Direct Materials | Conversion Cost | Total Cost Accounted for as Follows: |
|---|---|---|---|
| Units completed | 1,600 × $447.25 = $715,600 | 1,600 × $542.99* = $868,783 | $1,584,383 |
| Ending inventory | 400 × $447.25 = $178,900 | 240 × $542.99* = $130,317 | $ 309,217 |
| Total cost to account for: | | | $1,893,600* |

* $542.9891 is used to eliminate the rounding error.

After we transfer $1,584,383 out of the Work in Process account to reflect the cost of units completed and transferred to the next process, the T-account for the CFA process should appear as follows:

| Work In Process Inventory (CFA) | | | |
|---|---:|---|---:|
| Beginning balance | 165,600 | Cost of goods completed | |
|    Direct materials | 810,000 | (transferred to bottling) | $1,584,383 |
|    Conversion cost applied | 918,000 | | |
| Total cost to account for | 1,893,600 | | |
|   Ending balance | 309,217 | | |

## Step 5: Prepare a Production Report

The final step in process costing is to summarize the results of Steps 1–4 into a single document, the production report. The production report is essentially a summary of what occurred in the production process during the accounting period. It includes information about the number of physical units (Step 1) and equivalent units (Step 2) as well as the cost per equivalent unit (Step 3), and a reconciliation of the cost of work in process (Step 4).

Exhibit 20A.4 is a production report for the winery example. This single document summarizes the four steps used to determine the cost of the CFA process.

**Exhibit 20A.4**    Weighted Average Process Costing Production Report

| | A | B | C | D | E | F |
|---|---|---|---|---|---|---|
| 1 | | | CK Mondavi Winery | | | |
| 2 | | | Process Costing Production Report (Weighted Average Method) | | | |
| 3 | | | Crushing, Fermenting and Aging (CFA) Department | | | |
| 4 | | | For the Quarter Ended March 31, 2009 | | | |
| 5 | | | Step 1 | | | |
| 6 | | UNITS | Reconcile | | | |
| 7 | 1 | Units to be accounted for: | Physical Units | | | |
| 8 | 2 | Beginning work in process | 200 | | | |
| 9 | 3 | Started into production | 1,800 | | | |
| 10 | 4 | Total units | 2,000 | Step 2 | | |
| 11 | 5 | | | Calculate Equivalent Units | | |
| 12 | 6 | Units accounted for as follows: | | Direct Materials | Conversion | |
| 13 | 7 | Completed and transferred | 1,600 | 1,600 | 1,600 | |
| 14 | 8 | Ending work in process | 400 | 400 | 240 | |
| 15 | 9 | Total units | 2,000 | 2,000 | 1,840 | |
| 16 | 10 | COSTS | | Step 3: Calculate cost per | | |
| 17 | 11 | | | equivalent unit | | |
| 18 | 12 | | | Direct Materials | Conversion | |
| 19 | 13 | Cost of beginning inventory | | $   84,500 | $   81,100 | |
| 20 | 14 | Current period costs | | 810,000 | 918,000 | |
| 21 | 15 | Total cost of units in process | | $ 894,500 | $ 999,100 | |
| 22 | 16 | Equivalent units (from step 2 above) | | 2,000 | 1,840 | |
| 23 | 17 | Cost per equivalent unit | | $    447.25 | $ 542.9891 | * |
| 24 | 18 | | | Step 4: Reconcile the total cost of work in process | | |
| 25 | 19 | Costs to be accounted for: | | Direct Materials | Conversion | Total |
| 26 | 20 | Beginning work in process | | $   84,500 | $   81,100 | $   165,600 |
| 27 | 21 | Current period costs | | $ 810,000 | $ 918,000 | 1,728,000 |
| 28 | 22 | Total costs | | | | $ 1,893,600 |
| 29 | 23 | | | | | |
| 30 | 24 | Costs accounted for as follows: | | | | |
| 31 | 25 | Units completed and transferred (Row 7 x Row 17) | | 715,600 | 868,783 | 1,584,383 |
| 32 | 26 | Ending inventory (Row 8 x Row 17) | | 178,900 | 130,317 | 309,217 |
| 33 | 27 | | | | | $ 1,893,600 |
| 34 | | | | | | |
| 35 | | *This number must be kept to 4 decimal places for the the reconciliation in step 4 to balance. | | | | |

# Chapter Summary

## LO1  Describe the key features of a process costing system. (p. 842)

- Process costing is used by companies that produce homogeneous (similar) goods or services in a series of standardized processes.
- The flow of costs in process costing is very similar to that in job order costing. Manufacturing costs are recorded in the Raw Materials, Work in Process, and Finished Goods Inventory accounts until the product is sold, at which point they become part of the Cost of Goods Sold.
- Process costing systems maintain a separate Work in Process Inventory account for each major production process. As the product flows through the various production processes, the total cost is transferred from one Work in Process Inventory account to the next.

## LO2  Prepare journal entries to record product costs using process costing. (p. 844)

- The three major categories of product costs are direct materials, direct labor, and manufacturing overhead. This chapter combined direct labor and manufacturing overhead into the single account Conversion Cost.
- Product costs are recorded in one of three inventory accounts: Raw Materials Inventory, Work in Process Inventory, or Finished Goods Inventory. Each major process has a separate Work in Process Inventory account, and the costs are transferred to the appropriate account as the product is manufactured.
- Actual and applied conversion costs can be recorded in a control account, much the same way that actual and applied manufacturing overhead costs were dealt with in Chapter 19. Any under- or overapplied balance is closed directly to Cost of Goods Sold at the end of the accounting period.

**LO3 Reconcile the number of physical units that were worked on during the period. (p. 850)**

- The first step in process costing is to reconcile the number of physical units.
- The number of units in beginning inventory plus the number of units started must equal the number of units completed plus the number of units in ending inventory.
- The number of units started and completed equals the number of units completed minus the number of units in beginning inventory or the number of units started minus the number of units in ending inventory.

**LO4 Calculate equivalent units of production using the FIFO method. (p. 851)**

- The second step is to translate physical units into equivalent units.
- An equivalent unit is an adjustment that is made to the number of physical units to reflect the amount of work or effort that went into full and partially completed units during the period.

**LO5 Prepare a process costing production report. (p. 855)**

- The production report summarizes the costs and units that flow into and out of the production process during a given period. It will summarize the following steps:
- Step 1: Reconcile the number of physical units.
- Step 2: Translate physical units into equivalent units.
- Step 3: Calculate cost per equivalent units.
- Step 4: Reconcile the total cost of work in process by multiplying the number of equivalent units by the cost per equivalent unit.
- Step 5: Prepare a production report by summarizing Steps 1–4.

**LO6 Calculate the cost of products using activity based costing. (p. 857)**

- Activity based costing is a method of assigning indirect costs to products or services based on their underlying activity requirements.
- Unlike traditional costing systems, which rely exclusively on volume-based cost drivers, ABC also incorporates nonvolume-based cost drivers, such as the number of setups, inspections, or design changes.
  ABC uses four steps
- Step 1: Identify the firm's key activities and classify them as either unit-level, batch-level, product-level, customer-level, or facility-level activities.
- Step 2: Form activity cost pools and assign the company's indirect costs to those cost pools.
- Step 3: Select an activity driver and calculate an activity rate for each pool by dividing the total cost by the total value of the activity driver.
- Step 4: Assign indirect costs to individual products or services by multiplying the activity rates by their activity requirements.

## Key Terms

Activity Cost Driver (p. 859)
Activity Based Costing (p. 857)
Batch-Level Activities (p. 858)
Cost Driver (p. 857)

Customer-Level Activities (p. 858)
Equivalent Unit (p. 851)
Facility-Level Activities (p. 858)
Nonvolume Allocation Measures (p. 857)

Product-Level Activities (p. 858)
Production Report (p. 855)
Unit-Level Activities (p. 858)
Volume-Based Allocation Measures (p. 857)

See complete glossary in back of text.

## Questions

1. Briefly describe the differences between job order, process, and activity based costing. Give an example of a type of company that would use each one.
2. Explain the differences between Raw Materials, Work in Process and Finished Goods inventories.
3. Explain the flow of costs in a manufacturing company including the type of account and the respective financial statement on which the cost appears.
4. What are the four steps to prepare a production report?
5. Why is a production report important to a company?
6. What is the difference between conversion cost and manufacturing overhead? Why would a company use a conversion cost account instead of a manufacturing overhead account?
7. How is the number of physical units reconciled in a production report?

8. Why must a company calculate equivalent units when using process costing?

9. How can a unit be 100% complete with respect to materials, but only partially complete in terms of conversion effort?

10. What does a credit to the Work in Process Inventory account represent?

11. What types of business might use activity based costing?

12. How does activity based costing differ from process costing in its assignment of overhead?

13. What is an allocation base? What is the difference between a volume-based allocation measure and a nonvolume-based allocation measure?

14. What are the advantages and disadvantages of an activity based costing system?

15. What are the four basic steps in ABC?

16. With ABC, why must costs be classified into different categories? What is the basis for these categories?

17. How do the weighted average and the FIFO methods treat beginning inventory.

18. Is the weighted average method or FIFO method usually more accurate? Why?

19. What are the four steps of preparing a weighted average production report? Is this different than the steps used for a FIFO production report?

# Multiple Choice

1. The journal entry to record the issuance of direct materials into production includes
    a. A credit to cash.
    b. A debit to Work in Process Inventory.
    c. A credit to Finished Goods Inventory.
    d. A debit to Cost of Goods Sold.

Quiz 20-1
www.mhhe.com/LLPW1e

2. Which of the following is most likely to use a process costing system?
    a. A company that builds and installs custom cabinetry.
    b. A company that makes one style of office chair.
    c. A janitorial service.
    d. A paving company.

3. Suppose Shadow Company has 250 units in beginning inventory, 400 units started in production, and 175 units in ending inventory. How many units did Shadow complete?
    a. 25.        c. 475.
    b. 325.       d. Number cannot be determined.

4. If Wilson Corp. has 450 units that are estimated to be 60 percent complete, how many equivalent units are there?
    a. 270.       c. 100.
    b. 210.       d. 450.

5. Masterson Company has calculated a cost per unit of $4 for materials and $8.50 for conversion to manufacture a specific product. Ending work in process has 1,000 units that are fully complete for materials and 70 percent complete for conversion. What amount will Masterson have as ending Work in Process Inventory?
    a. $12,500.   c. $5,950.
    b. $8,750.    d. $9,950.

6. Which of the following is a nonvolume-based allocation measure?
    a. Machine hours.
    b. Direct labor hours.

    c. Number of batches.
    d. Direct labor cost.

7. Taylor Company has an overhead rate for machine setups of $200 per setup. Last month, Product A had 40 setups and Product B had 70 setups. How much overhead did Taylor assign to each product?
    a. $11,000 to Product A, $11,000 to Product B.
    b. $8,000 to Product A, $14,000 to Product B.
    c. $4,000 to Product A, $7,000 to Product B.
    d. Amount cannot be determined.

8. Which of the following is not a facility level activity?
    a. Maintenance on the factory building.
    b. Factory utilities.
    c. Research and development for a new product.
    d. Salaries for plant administration.

9. The primary difference between FIFO and weighted average methods of process costing has to do with the treatment of
    a. Beginning inventory.
    b. Ending inventory.
    c. Number of units started.
    d. Direct materials.

10. When calculating product cost using the weighted average method, which of the following amounts are combined?
    a. Ending finished goods and cost of goods sold.
    b. Beginning finished goods and cost of goods sold.
    c. Beginning work in process and beginning finished goods.
    d. Beginning work in process and current period costs.

Solutions to Multiple-Choice Questions

1. b    2. b    3. c    4. a    5. d    6. c    7. b
8. c    9. a    10. d

# Mini Exercises  Available with McGraw-Hill's Homework Manager

**LO3**

## M20-1 Calculating Physical Units

Roundtree company had 575 units in work in process on January 1. During the month, Roundtree completed 2,400 units and had 1,000 units in process on January 31. Determine how many units Roundtree started during January.

**LO3**

## M20-2 Calculating Physical Units

For each of the following independent cases (A–D), compute the missing value in the table.

| Case | Beginning Units | Units Started | Units Completed | Ending Units |
|------|----------------|---------------|-----------------|--------------|
| A | 400 | 2,300 | 1,650 | ? |
| B | 1,200 | 800 | ? | 1,600 |
| C | ? | 750 | 1,230 | 2,560 |
| D | 345 | ? | 900 | 680 |

**LO3, 4**

## M20-3 Calculating Physical Units and Equivalent Units (FIFO)

Bedford Company produces carrying cases for CDs. It has compiled the following information for the month of June.

| | Physical Units | Percent Complete for Conversion |
|---|---|---|
| Beginning work in process | 35,000 | 55% |
| Ending work in process | 46,000 | 70 |

Bedford adds all materials at the beginning of its manufacturing process. During the month, it started 90,000 units.

Using the FIFO method, reconcile the number of physical units and calculate the number of equivalent units.

**LO3, 4**

## M20-4 Calculating Cost per Equivalent Unit (FIFO)

Incontro Company manufactures file cabinets. The following cost information is available for the month of December.

| | |
|---|---|
| Beginning work in process | |
| Direct materials | $ 34,000 |
| Conversion cost | 62,000 |
| December costs | |
| Direct materials | 68,000 |
| Conversion cost | 105,000 |

Incontro had 8,500 equivalent units of direct materials and 6,000 equivalent units of conversion activity during the month. Using the FIFO method, calculate Incontro's cost per equivalent unit for materials and conversion during December.

**LO6**

## M20-5 Classifying Activities in ABC

For each of the following activities, indicate the appropriate category (unit, batch, product, customer, or facility level) and suggest a possible cost driver for each pool.

1. Factory utilities.
2. Machine setups.
3. Research and development for a new product.
4. Sanding rough edges of the product.
5. Packaging the product for shipment.
6. Developing new packaging for a special order of 200 units.
7. Maintaining equipment.
8. Assembling the product's component parts.
9. Materials-handling costs.
10. Quality control testing.

**M20-6 Calculating Activity Rates and Assigning Costs to Products in ABC**                    LO6

Newkirk Co. has identified one of its cost pools to be quality control and assigned $50,000 to that pool. The number of inspections has been chosen as the cost driver for this pool. Newkirk performs 25,000 quality control inspections. Suppose Newkirk manufactures two products that consume 10,000 and 15,000 inspections each. Determine how much quality control cost will be assigned to each of Newkirk's product lines.

**M20-7 Calculating Physical Units and Equivalent Units (Weighted Average) (Supplement)**

Refer to M20-3 for information regarding Bedford Company. Using the weighted average method, reconcile the number of physical units and calculate the number of equivalent units.

**M20-8 Calculating Cost per Equivalent Unit (Weighted average) (Supplement)**

Refer to M20-4 for information regarding Incontro Company. Using the weighted average method, calculate Incontro's cost per equivalent unit for materials and conversion during December.

# Exercises  Available with McGraw-Hill's Homework Manager

**E20-1 Recording Manufacturing Costs in Process Costing**                    LO2

Forrest Co. makes wooden tables.

*Required:*

Prepare the journal entries to record each of the following transactions.

 a.  Purchased $20,000 of raw materials on credit.
 b.  Issued $18,000 of direct materials into production.
 c.  Applied $47,500 of conversion cost.
 d.  Paid in full the raw materials purchased on credit.
 e.  Completed $52,750 in tables.
 f.  Recorded actual conversion costs of $42,000.
 g.  Sold tables for $93,000 that cost $50,000 to produce.
 h.  Disposed of any over- or underapplied conversion cost.

**E20-2 Recording Manufacturing Costs in Process Costing**                    LO2

Rock-On Company produces wooden rocking chairs. The company has two sequential production departments, Cutting and Assembly. The wood is cut and sanded in Cutting, and then transferred to Assembly to be assembled and painted. From Assembly, the chairs are transferred to Finished Goods Inventory and then sold.

Rock-On has compiled the following information for the month of February.

|  | Cutting Department | Assembly Department |
|---|---|---|
| Direct materials | $ 75,000 | $ 12,000 |
| Direct labor | 65,000 | 99,000 |
| Applied manufacturing overhead | 150,000 | 167,000 |
| Cost of goods completed and transferred out | 234,000 | 253,000 |

*Required:*

Prepare the following journal entries for Rock-On.

1.  Amount of direct materials, direct labor, and manufacturing overhead incurred for the Cutting Department.
2.  Transfer of products from Cutting to Assembly.
3.  Amount of direct materials, direct labor, and manufacturing overhead incurred by the Assembly Department.
4.  Transfer of chairs from Assembly to Finished Goods.

**LO3, 4**     **E20-3 Calculating Equivalent Units, Cost per Equivalent Unit and Reconciling the Cost of Work in Process (FIFO)**

GoFly Company manufactures kites and has the following information available for the month of April.

| | |
|---|---|
| Work in process, April 1 | |
| (100% complete for materials, 40% for conversion) | 26,000 units |
| Direct materials | $ 40,000 |
| Conversion cost | $ 55,000 |
| | |
| Number of units started | 79,000 |
| April costs | |
| Direct materials | $113,000 |
| Conversion cost | $168,000 |
| | |
| Work in process, April 30 | |
| (100% complete for materials, 20% for conversion) | 40,000 units |

*Required:*

Using the FIFO method of process costing, complete each of the following steps:

1.   Reconcile the number of physical units worked on during the period.
2.   Calculate the number of equivalent units.
3.   Calculate the cost per equivalent unit, rounded to five decimal places.
4.   Reconcile the total cost of work in process.

**E20-4 Calculating Equivalent Units, Cost per Equivalent Unit and Reconciling the Cost of Work in Process (Weighted Average) (Supplement)**

GoFly Company manufactures kites and has the following information available for the month of April.

| | |
|---|---|
| Work in process, April 1 | |
| (100% complete for materials, 40% for conversion) | 26,000 units |
| Direct materials | $ 40,000 |
| Conversion cost | $ 55,000 |
| | |
| Number of units started | 79,000 |
| | |
| April costs | |
| Direct materials | $113,000 |
| Conversion cost | $168,000 |
| | |
| Work in process, April 30 | |
| (100% complete for materials, 20% for conversion) | 40,000 units |

*Required:*

Using the weighted average method, complete each of the following steps:

1.   Reconcile the number of physical units worked on during the period.
2.   Calculate the number of equivalent units.
3.   Calculate the cost per equivalent unit, rounded to five decimal places.
4.   Reconcile the total cost of work in process.

**LO3, 4**     **E20-5 Calculating Equivalent Units, Cost per Equivalent Unit, and Reconciling the Cost of Work in Process (FIFO)**

Raindrop Company manufactures umbrellas and has the following information available for the month of May.

| | |
|---|---|
| Work in process, May 1 | |
| (100% complete for materials, 90% for conversion) | 72,000 units |
|    Direct materials | $129,000 |
|    Conversion cost | $175,000 |
| | |
| Number of units started | 181,000 |
| | |
| May costs | |
|    Direct materials | $206,000 |
|    Conversion cost | $379,000 |
| | |
| Work in process, May 31 | |
| (100% complete for materials, 20% for conversion) | 67,000 units |

**Required:**
Using the FIFO method of process costing, complete each of the following steps:

1. Reconcile the number of physical units worked on during the period.
2. Calculate the number of equivalent units.
3. Calculate the cost per equivalent unit, rounded to five decimal places.
4. Reconcile the total cost of work in process.

**E20-6 Calculating Equivalent Units, Cost per Equivalent Unit, and Reconciling the Cost of Work in Process (Weighted Average) (Supplement)**
Refer to E20-5 for information regarding Raindrop Company.

**Required:**
Using the weighted average method, complete each of the following steps:

1. Reconcile the number of physical units worked on during the period.
2. Calculate the number of equivalent units.
3. Calculate the cost per equivalent unit, rounded to five decimal places.
4. Reconcile the total cost of work in process.

**E20-7 Calculating Activity Rates and Assigning Costs to Products in ABC**                 LO6
Titan Corp. has identified the following information about its cost pools and cost drivers.

| | |
|---|---|
| Cost pools | |
|    Materials handling | $40,000 |
|    Machine maintenance | 25,500 |
| | |
| Cost drivers | |
|    Number of material moves | 800 |
|    Number of machine hours | 75,000 |

**Required:**

1. Calculate Titan's activity rate for each cost pool.
2. Determine the amount of overhead assigned to Titan's Product A and Product B if each has the following requirements:

| | Product A | Product B |
|---|---|---|
| Number of material moves | 500 | 300 |
| Number of machine hours | 42,000 | 33,000 |

**E20-8 Calculating Activity Rates and Assigning Cost to Products in ABC**                 LO6
Matson Corp. manufactures automobile floor mats. It currently has two product lines, standard and deluxe. Matson has identified the following information about its overhead activity pools and the standard product line.

| Activity Pools | Cost Driver | Activity Rate | Activity Cost Driver for Standard Floor Mat Line |
|---|---|---|---|
| Materials handling | Number of moves | $25 per move | 40 moves |
| Quality control | Number of inspections | 7 per inspection | 600 inspections |
| Machine maintenance | Number of machine hours | 2 per machine hour | 3,000 machine hours |

*Required:*

Calculate the amount of overhead that Matson will assign to the standard floor mat product line.

**LO6**    **E20-9 Calculating Activity Rates and Assigning Costs to Products in ABC**

Refer to the activity pool, cost driver, and activity rate information given in E20-8. Suppose Matson has compiled the following information for its deluxe floor mat line.

**Activity Cost Driver for Deluxe Floor Mat Line**

60 moves
720 inspections
4,150 machine hours

*Required:*

Calculate the amount of overhead that Matson will assign to the deluxe product line.

## Problems—Set A     Available with McGraw-Hill's Homework Manager

**LO3, 4, 5**    **PA20-1 Preparing a Process Costing Production Report (FIFO)**

Boxer Corporation manufactures metal toolboxes. It adds all materials at the beginning of the manufacturing process. The company has provided the following information.

| | |
|---|---:|
| Beginning work in process | 40,000 units |
|    Direct materials (30% complete) | $ 40,000 |
|    Conversion cost | 95,000 |
| Total cost of beginning work in process | $ 135,000 |
| | |
| Number of units started | 76,000 |
| Number of units completed and transferred to finished goods | 82,000 |
| | |
| Ending work in process: Conversion | 50% complete |
| | |
| Direct materials cost incurred | $ 90,000 |
| Conversion cost applied | 157,000 |
|    Total cost added | $ 247,000 |

*Required:*

1.  Using the FIFO method of process costing, complete each of the following steps:

    a.  Reconcile the number of physical units worked on during the period.
    b.  Calculate the number of equivalent units.
    c.  Calculate the cost per equivalent unit, rounded to five decimal points.
    d.  Reconcile the total cost of work in process.

2.  Summarize the preceding steps in a production report for Boxer Corporation.

**PA20-2 Preparing a Process Costing Production Report (Weighted Average) (Supplement)**

Refer to the information for Boxer Corporation in PA20-1.

*Required:*

Complete all requirements for PA20-1 using the weighted average method.

**PA20-3 Recording Manufacturing Costs and Preparing a Process Costing Production Report (FIFO)**

LO2, 3, 4, 5

www.mhhe.com/LLPW1e

Seemore Company makes camping lanterns using a single production process. All direct materials are added at the beginning of the manufacturing process. Information for the month of March follows.

| | |
|---|---:|
| Beginning work in process (30% complete) | 58,900 units |
|    Direct materials | $ 96,000 |
|    Conversion cost | 172,000 |
| Total cost of beginning work in process | $ 268,000 |
| | |
| Number of units started | 121,500 |
| Number of units completed and transferred to finished goods | 167,400 |
| | |
| Ending work in process (65% complete) | |
| | |
| Direct materials cost incurred | $ 253,700 |
| Conversion cost applied | 324,000 |
|    Total cost added | $ 577,700 |

*Required:*

1. Using the FIFO method of process costing, complete each of the following steps:

   a. Reconcile the number of physical units worked on during the period.
   b. Calculate the number of equivalent units.
   c. Calculate the cost per equivalent unit, rounded to five decimal places.
   d. Reconcile the total cost of work in process.

2. Summarize the preceding steps in a March production report for Seemore Company.
3. Prepare Seemore's journal entries to record each of the following transactions.

   *a.* Added direct materials to production during March.
   *b.* Applied conversion cost during March.
   *c.* Transferred completed units to Finished Goods Inventory.
   *d.* Sold units costing $650,000 for $1,000,000.
   *e.* Recorded $329,000 of actual conversion cost.
   *f.* Disposed of the ending balance in the Conversion Cost account.

**PA20-4 Recording Manufacturing Costs and Preparing a Process Costing Production Report (Weighted Average) (Supplement)**

eXcel

www.mhhe.com/LLPW1e

Refer to the information in PA20-3 for Seemore Company.

*Required:*

Complete all requirements for PA20-3 using the weighted average method.

**PA20-5 Calculating Activity Rates and Assigning Costs to Products in ABC**

LO6

Gutierrez Company makes two models of children's playhouses, the Castle and the Mansion.

Information for Gutierrez follows.

| | Castle | Mansion |
|---|:---:|:---:|
| Direct materials cost per unit | $45 | $72 |
| Direct labor cost per unit | $23 | $35 |
| Sales price per unit | $1,350 | $1,565 |
| Expected production per month | 350 units | 200 units |

Gutierrez has monthly overhead of $219,000 that is divided into the following cost pools.

| | |
|---|---|
| Setup costs | $ 85,000 |
| Quality control | 73,000 |
| Maintenance | 61,000 |
| Total | $ 219,000 |

The company has also compiled the following information about its chosen cost drivers:

| Number of | Castle | Mansion | Total |
|---|---|---|---|
| Setups required | 42 | 58 | 100 |
| Inspections | 340 | 390 | 730 |
| Machine hours | 1,750 | 1,300 | 3,050 |

**Required:**

Complete the following for Gutierrez.

1. Select the appropriate cost driver for each cost pool and calculate the activity rates.
2. Assign overhead costs to each product based on activity demands.
3. Calculate the production cost per unit for each of Gutierrez's products.

## Problems—Set B  Available with McGraw-Hill's Homework Manager

**LO3, 4, 5**

### PB20-1 Preparing a Process Costing Production Report (FIFO)

Zoinks Inc. produces a popular brand of energy drink. It adds all materials at the beginning of the manufacturing process. The company has provided the following information.

| | |
|---|---|
| Beginning work in process (30% complete) | 20,000 units |
| Direct materials | $ 10,000 |
| Conversion cost | 46,000 |
| Total cost of beginning work in process | $ 56,000 |
| | |
| Number of units started | 52,000 |
| Number of units completed and transferred to finished goods | 49,000 |
| | |
| Ending work in process (70% complete) | |
| | |
| Direct materials cost incurred | $ 31,000 |
| Conversion cost applied | 82,000 |
| Total cost added | $ 113,000 |

**Required:**

1. Using the FIFO method of process costing, complete each of the following steps:

    a. Reconcile the number of physical units worked on during the period.
    b. Calculate the number of equivalent units.
    c. Calculate the cost per equivalent unit, rounded to five decimal places.
    d. Reconcile the total cost of work in process.
2. Summarize the preceding steps in a production report for Zoinks Inc.

### PB20-2 Preparing a Process Costing Production Report (Weighted Average) (Supplement)

Refer to the information about Zoinks Inc. in PB20-1.

**Required:**

Complete all requirements for PB20-1 using the weighted average method.

**PB20-3 Recording Manufacturing Costs and Preparing a Process Costing Production Report (FIFO)**                                    LO2, 3, 4, 5

Firelight Company makes camping tents in a single production department. All direct materials are added at the beginning of the manufacturing process. Information for the month of July follows.

| | |
|---|---:|
| Beginning work in process (30% complete) | 23,100 units |
| Direct materials | $ 121,000 |
| Conversion cost | 184,000 |
| Total cost of beginning work in process | $ 305,000 |
| | |
| Number of units started | 62,500 |
| Number of units completed and transferred to finished goods | 77,400 |
| | |
| Ending work-in-process (35% complete) | |
| | |
| Direct materials cost incurred | $ 281,700 |
| Conversion cost applied | 386,200 |
| Total cost added | $ 667,900 |

*Required:*

1.  Using the FIFO method of process costing, complete each of the following steps:

    a.  Reconcile the number of physical units worked on during the period.
    b.  Calculate the number of equivalent units.
    c.  Calculate the cost per equivalent unit, rounded to five decimal places.
    d.  Reconcile the total cost of work in process.
2.  Summarize the preceding steps in a July production report for Firelight Company.
3.  Prepare Firelight's journal entries to record each of the following transactions.

    a.  Added direct materials to production during July.
    b.  Applied conversion cost during July.
    c.  Transferred completed units to Finished Goods Inventory.
    d.  Sold units costing $450,000 for $800,000.
    e.  Recorded $367,000 of actual conversion cost.
    f.  Disposed of ending the balance in the Conversion Cost account.

**PB20-4 Recording Manufacturing Costs and Preparing a Process Costing Production Report (Weighted Average) (Supplement)**

Refer to the information in PB20-3 for Firelight Company.

*Required:*

Complete all requirements for PB20-3 using the weighted average method.

**PB20-5 Calculating Activity Rates and Assigning Costs to Products in ABC**                                    LO5

Wayward Company makes two models of automobile navigation systems, the SeldomLost and the NeverLost.

Information for Wayward follows.

| | SeldomLost | NeverLost |
|---|---|---|
| Direct materials cost per unit | $ 92 | $ 115 |
| Direct labor cost per unit | $ 51 | $ 75 |
| Sales price per unit | $850 | $1,065 |
| Expected production per month | 400 units | 900 units |

Wayward has monthly overhead of $521,870 that is divided into the following cost pools.

| | |
|---|---:|
| Setup costs | $ 170,455 |
| Quality control | 203,775 |
| Maintenance | 65,700 |
| Engineering | 81,940 |
| Total | $ 521,870 |

The company has also compiled the following information about its chosen cost drivers.

| | ACTIVITY REQUIREMENTS | | |
|---|---|---|---|
| | SeldomLost | NeverLost | Total |
| Number of setups required | 60 | 86 | 146 |
| Number of inspections | 975 | 675 | 1,650 |
| Number of machine hours | 1,540 | 2,840 | 4,380 |
| Number of engineering hours | 352 | 612 | 964 |

**Required:**
Complete the following for Wayward.

1. Select the appropriate cost driver for each cost pool and calculate the activity rate.
2. Assign overhead costs to each product based on activity demands.
3. Calculate the production cost per unit for each of Wayward's products.

# Cases and Projects

LO1    **CP20-1 Researching Companies That Use Process Costing**

Consider the many different manufactured products a person might use or consume in a typical day, everything from toothpaste to a custom-made Harley Davidson motorcycle.

**Required:**

Choose three items that you use regularly and whose manufacturer you believe is likely to use process costing. Investigate the manufacturing company of each item and its Web site for information to support or contradict your belief.

LO1    **CP20-2 Evaluating the Implications of Process Costing in a Service Industry**

Overnight package delivery is a multimillion dollar industry that has grown steadily since it began. The four largest carriers are the US Postal Service (USPS), Federal Express (FedEx), United Parcel Service (UPS), and Airborne Express. Suppose you have a document that must be delivered to each of the following cities by the close of business tomorrow. Using each company's Web site, determine the price to ship your letter and and record the information in the following table.

| | Carefree, AZ | Happy Valley, TN | Experiment, PA | Opportunity, MT |
|---|---|---|---|---|
| USPS | | | | |
| FedEx | | | | |
| UPS | | | | |
| Airborne | | | | |

To answer the following questions, assume that the prices charged by the companies are directly related to the cost of delivery.

**Required:**

1. Based on their pricing, which of the delivery companies appear(s) to use process costing?
2. For the companies that do(es) not appear to use process costing, what factors are likely to impact the cost (and thus pricing) of the overnight delivery service?
3. In this industry, what are the potential advantages and disadvantages of process costing?

**CP20-3 Researching Companies That Have Implemented Activity Based Costing**    LO6

*Required:*

Review recent issues of business publications (e.g., *BusinessWeek*, *The Wall Street Journal*) for information about companies that have implemented activity based costing. Choose one company to research in detail and then answer the following questions.

1.   Give a brief description of the company, its products, and its history.
2.   If the company has multiple divisions or segments, has one or more of them implemented ABC?
3.   If one or more divisions or segments do use ABC, what factor(s) prompted the decision to do so?
4.   What type of costing system was utilized prior to the conversion to ABC?
5.   Were any specific difficulties experienced during the switch?
6.   What benefits has the company or one or more of its divisions or segments identified as a result of implementing ABC?
7.   Did the move to an ABC system impact other areas of the company and/or result in changes to other aspects of its operation?
8.   Does the company view the ABC implementation as successful?

# 21 Cost Behavior and Cost-Volume-Profit Analysis

## LEARNING OBJECTIVES

**After completing this chapter, you should be able to:**

Lectured slideshow—LP21-1
www.mhhe.com/LLPW1e

**LO1** Identify costs as either variable, fixed, step, or mixed.

**LO2** Prepare a scattergraph to illustrate the relationship between total cost and activity.

**LO3** Use the high-low method to analyze mixed costs.

**LO4** Prepare and interpret a contribution margin income statement.

**LO5** Use cost-volume-profit analysis to find the break-even point.

**LO6** Use cost-volume-profit analysis to determine the sales needed to achieve a target profit.

## Focus Company: STARBUCKS COFFEE

## "Beyond a Cup of Coffee"

www.starbucks.com

These days you don't have to go far to buy a cup of Starbucks coffee. Started as a small coffee shop in Seattle's Pike Place Market over three decades ago, Starbucks Coffee can now be found on street corners, college campuses, and airports across the country and abroad. Consider the following facts about Starbucks:

- From 2002–2007, Starbucks opened approximately five new locations every day. By 2008, the company realized it could not sustain that rate of growth and announced that it was closing 600 stores.
- The average customer spends $4.05 per visit at Starbucks.
- Starbucks spends more on employee health insurance than on coffee beans.
- When Starbucks eliminated the 8-ounce cup from its menu (making the "tall" the new "small"), it increased revenue by 25 cents per cup with only 2 cents of added product cost.[1]

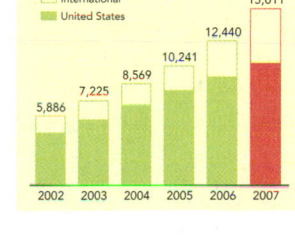

stores open at fiscal year-end
(number of company operated and licensed stores)

STARBUCKS COFFEE

☐ International
▩ United States

5,886  7,225  8,569  10,241  12,440  15,011
2002  2003  2004  2005  2006  2007

How does Starbucks decide how much to charge for a cup of coffee? How does the relationship between revenue, cost, and volume affect the bottom line, or profit?

This chapter illustrates two managerial accounting topics that can help managers answer these questions. The first topic, cost behavior, helps managers understand how total costs will change as the company's volume of activity changes. The second topic, cost-volume-profit analysis, focuses on the relationship among product prices, volume, costs, and profits. This approach allows managers to determine the number of units or customers needed to make a certain profit and to analyze how changing prices or costs will impact profit.

Throughout this chapter, we use a hypothetical Starbucks coffeeshop as our focus company, but we limit our analysis to the sale of coffee. So, forget about all of the other goodies that Starbucks sells, such as pastries, CDs, T-shirts, and appliances. To keep things simple, we have also made up some numbers for our examples—but that is only appropriate for the company that invented the words "venti" and "doppio."

---

[1] Taylor Clark, *Starbucked: A Double Tall Tale of Caffeine, Commerce, and Culture* (New York: Little, Brown and Company, 2007).

# COST BEHAVIOR PATTERNS

**Cost behavior** is defined as the way in which total costs change when some measure of activity changes. Activities that cause total cost to change are referred to as **cost drivers.** Some of the most common measures of activity include the number of direct labor hours, machine hours, units produced, and customers served.

## Relevant Range

When we classify cost according to behavior, we must limit the range of activity, called the relevant range. The **relevant range** is the range of activity over which we expect our assumptions about cost behavior to hold true. For example, fixed costs will remain constant only over a limited range of activity. At some point, fixed costs must increase to accommodate more activity. In this chapter, we use a straight line to define the relationship between total cost and activity. In reality, the relationship between total cost and activity probably is not perfectly linear. However, so long as we limit our analysis to a fairly narrow range of activity—that is, the relevant range—we can **assume** that the relationship is linear and come close to estimating true cost behavior.

## Variable Costs

Recall from Chapter 18 that variable costs are those that change, in total, in direct proportion to changes in activity levels. If the activity level increases by 50 percent, total variable cost also increases by 50 percent. If the activity level decreases by 20 percent, total variable cost should decrease by 20 percent. Examples of variable costs for Starbucks Coffee include the cost of coffee beans, milk, sugar, cups, and other paper products. All of these costs will increase, in total, as Starbucks sells more coffee drinks.

Although **total** variable costs change with activity, variable cost **per unit** remains constant. For example, the cost of coffee used in each cup should be the same regardless of how many cups are served. This ignores any type of discount that a company may get by purchasing ingredients in large quantities.

See Exhibit 21.1 for charts of how the total and per unit cost of ingredients such as coffee beans change with the number of coffee drinks served.

As the graph on the left shows, the total cost of ingredients increases in direct proportion to increases in the number of coffee drinks served. As the graph on the right shows, however, the **per unit** cost of ingredients remains constant at about $0.50 per drink, regardless of how many drinks are served.

## Fixed Costs

Fixed costs remain the same **in total** regardless of activity level. For a Starbucks Coffee shop, fixed costs include rent, the manager's salary, depreciation on equipment, and insurance. These costs

---

**Coach's Tip**

The terms cost and expense are used interchangeably in this chapter, although they have different meanings in financial accounting.

---

**Learning Objective 1**

Identify costs as either variable, fixed, step, or mixed.

## Exhibit 21.1 | Variable Cost Behavior

remain the same in total regardless of how many coffee drinks the shop serves each month. On a **per unit** basis, however, fixed costs decrease with increases in activity levels (see Exhibit 21.2).

The fact that per unit fixed cost decreases with increases in activity level does not mean that a manager can drive down costs simply by increasing the number of units produced. Imagine what would happen if a Starbucks manager decided to make as many cups of coffee as possible each day regardless of whether there were enough customers to buy them. Although doing so would drive down the per unit cost of each cup, it would also result in a lot of coffee being thrown away, with no revenue from customers to cover the cost.

Although this example may seem far fetched, it is not uncommon for managers to believe that they can drive down costs by producing as many units as possible. The difference is that in most companies, the unsold units are not thrown away at the end of the day like a cold cup of coffee. Instead, unsold units are stored in a warehouse as inventory—a solution that adds unnecessary costs for insurance, shipping and handling, and so on. The bottom line is that while increasing production lowers the average cost of each unit produced (because the fixed costs are spread over more units), it does not translate into increased profit without increased sales.

## Exhibit 21.2 | Fixed Cost Behavior

## Step Costs

**Step costs** are fixed over some range of activity and then increase in a steplike fashion when a capacity limit is reached. Depending on the width of the steps, step costs may be treated as either step-variable or step-fixed costs as in Exhibit 21.3.

As the graph on the left shows, **step-variable costs** tend to be fixed over a fairly narrow range and rise in multiple steps across the relevant range. At Starbucks Coffee, a step-variable cost includes the wages paid to servers. Starbucks relies heavily on part-time labor, and managers try to schedule more workers when more customers are expected to arrive. Once employees are

## Exhibit 21.3 | Step Cost Behavior

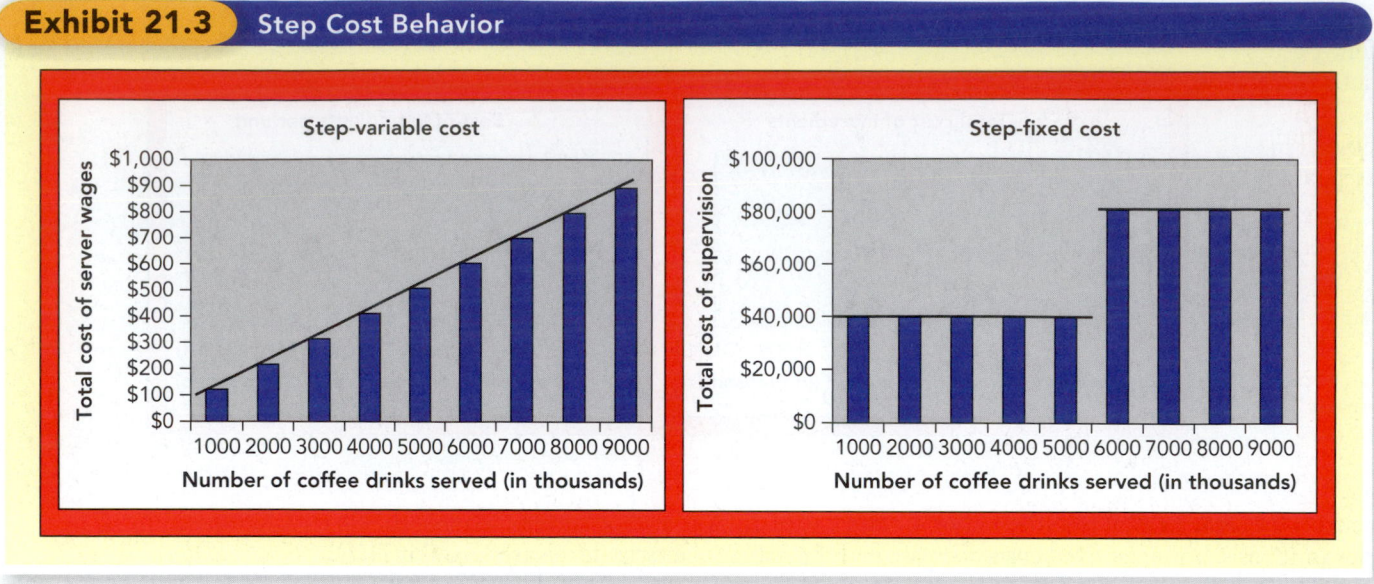

on the job, however, they must be paid regardless of how many customers they serve. Because the steps between servers' wages are so narrow and the total cost increases with the number of coffee drinks served, Starbucks can treat the cost of server wages as a variable cost.

As the graph on the right side of Exhibit 21.3 shows, **step-fixed costs** are fixed over a much wider range of activity than step-variable costs. To allow more customers to be served, for example, Starbucks might decide to hire an additional supervisor or rent additional space or equipment. Because these costs are fixed over a fairly wide range of activity, they are treated as fixed costs, at least within a limited range of activity.

## Mixed Costs

**Coach's Tip**

When you see total cost increasing and per unit cost decreasing with activity level, you can conclude that the cost has both a fixed and a variable component. That is, it is a mixed cost.

**Mixed costs**, also known as semivariable costs, have both a fixed and a variable component. The fixed portion represents the base amount that is incurred regardless of activity. The variable cost is the amount that is based on activity or usage. An example of a mixed cost is a long-distance calling plan that has a fixed charge each month plus an additional charge for each minute of usage. Many utility expenses behave the same way. Most companies incur a minimum utility charge each month regardless of activity, but the total utility expense increases with increased activity. The activity driver for utility costs could be the number of hours a company is open or the number of hours that employees use electrical equipment.

Because mixed costs have both a fixed and a variable component, both the total cost and the per unit cost change with the level of activity (see Exhibit 21.4). Because part of the

## Exhibit 21.4 | Mixed Cost Behavior

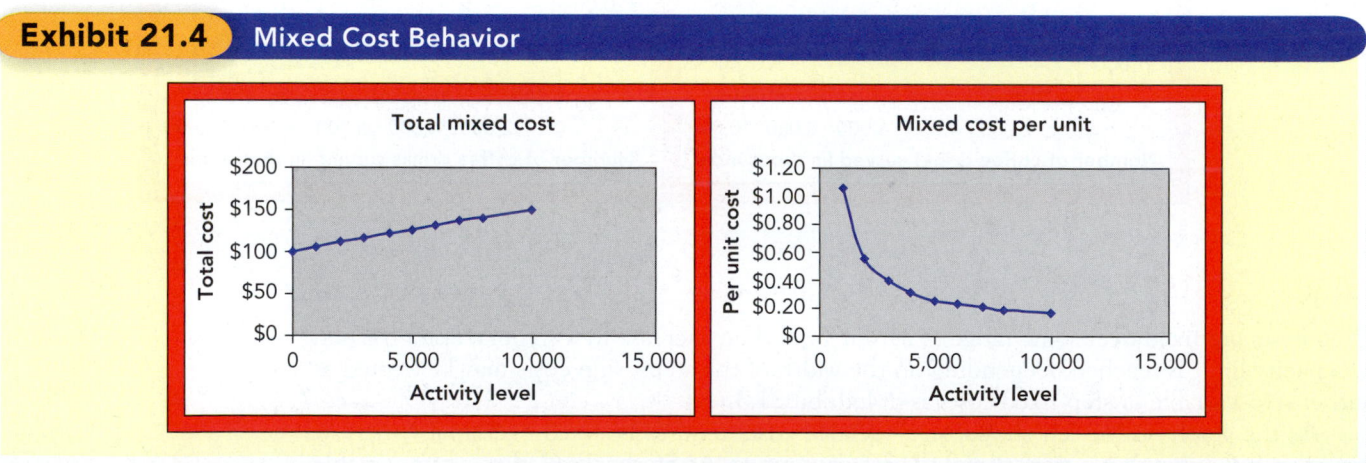

cost is variable, the total mixed cost rises with increases in activity as in the graph on the left. Because part of the cost is fixed, however, the mixed cost per unit falls with increases in activity as in the graph on the right.

The next section discusses how to separate the fixed and variable components of mixed costs. First take a moment to make sure you understand the difference between fixed, variable, step, and mixed costs by completing the following Self-Study Practice.

---

**SELF-STUDY PRACTICE**

1. Which of the following statements is true?

   a.  If activity increases by 10 percent, total fixed cost will increase by 10 percent.
   b.  If activity increases by 10 percent, per unit variable cost will increase by 10 percent.
   c.  If activity increases by 10 percent, per unit fixed cost will decrease by 10 percent.
   d.  If activity increases by 10 percent, total variable cost will increase by 10 percent.

2. For each row in the following table, indicate whether the cost is variable, fixed, step, or mixed.

| | UNITS OF ACTIVITY | | | | |
| --- | --- | --- | --- | --- | --- |
| | 0 Units | 100 Units | 200 Units | 300 Units | 400 Units |
| Total cost of A | $ 0 | $200 | $400 | $600 | $800 |
| Total cost of B | 500 | 500 | 500 | 750 | 750 |
| Total cost of C | 350 | 400 | 450 | 500 | 550 |
| Total cost of D | 750 | 750 | 750 | 750 | 750 |

After you have finished, check your answers with the solutions at the bottom of the page.

---

# ESTIMATING COST BEHAVIOR

## Preparing a Scattergraph

One of the easiest ways to identify cost behavior is by using a visual representation or graph. A scattergraph is a graph with total cost plotted on the vertical (Y) axis and some measure of activity on the horizontal (X) axis. It is useful for getting a "feel" for the data and helps answer preliminary questions about the nature of the relationship between total cost and activity and whether the data have any unusual patterns or blips.

A scattergraph can be created by manually plotting data points on graph paper, or by using the following steps in Excel:

1. Enter the data in Excel and highlight the data that you want to plot.
2. Select the Chart Wizard from the toolbar.
3. Select XY (Scatter) as the chart type. Be sure total cost is on the Y axis with the activity driver on the X axis.
4. Add a chart title and labels for the X and Y axes.

To apply these steps, consider the following data showing the total overhead cost (Y) and the number of customers served (X) for our hypothetical Starbucks location.

---

1. D.

2. A, variable cost; B, step cost; C, mixed cost; and D, fixed cost.

Solution to
Self-Study Practice

**Learning Objective 2**

Prepare a scattergraph to illustrate the relationship between total cost and activity.

| Month | Number of Customers Served (X) | Total Overhead Cost (Y) |
|---|---|---|
| January | 9,000 | $15,000 |
| February | 15,000 | 15,750 |
| March | 12,500 | 16,000 |
| April | 6,000 | 12,500 |
| May | 5,000 | 13,250 |
| June | 10,000 | 13,000 |

See Exhibit 21.5 for an illustration of how to create a scattergraph of these data using Excel.

**Exhibit 21.5**    Creating a Scattergraph in Excel

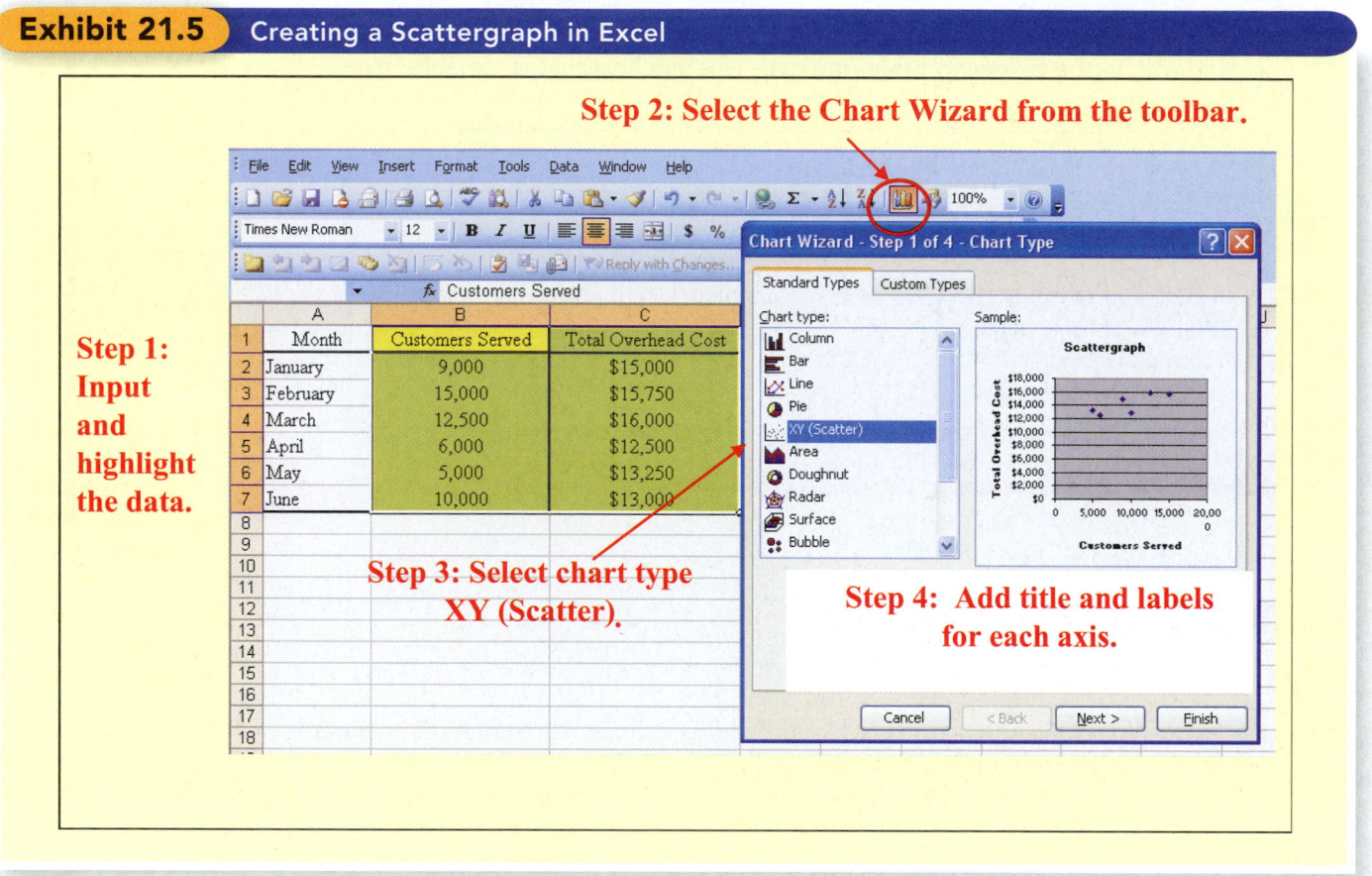

Refer to Exhibit 21.6 for the scattergraph that results from these steps. We have added a red line to the graph to show the general trend in the data. Although the data points do not fall in a perfect line, they are close enough so that we can use the line to approximate the relationship between total overhead cost (Y) and activity (X). In a later section, we discuss several ways to determine the line, but for now, let's focus on what the line reveals about the relationship between total overhead cost (Y) and the number of customers served (X).

This scattergraph reveals a slightly positive relationship between total overhead cost (Y) and the number of customers served (X). At least a portion of the overhead cost is variable. But we can also see that a large part of the overhead cost is fixed.

**The slope of the red line represents the variable cost per unit of X.** It indicates the amount by which total overhead will increase with each additional customer served. For Starbucks, the variable overhead cost would be for items such as paper supplies, sugar, cream, and power to run the coffee machines.

**Exhibit 21.6** | Scattergraph of Total Overhead Cost (Y) and Customers Served (X)

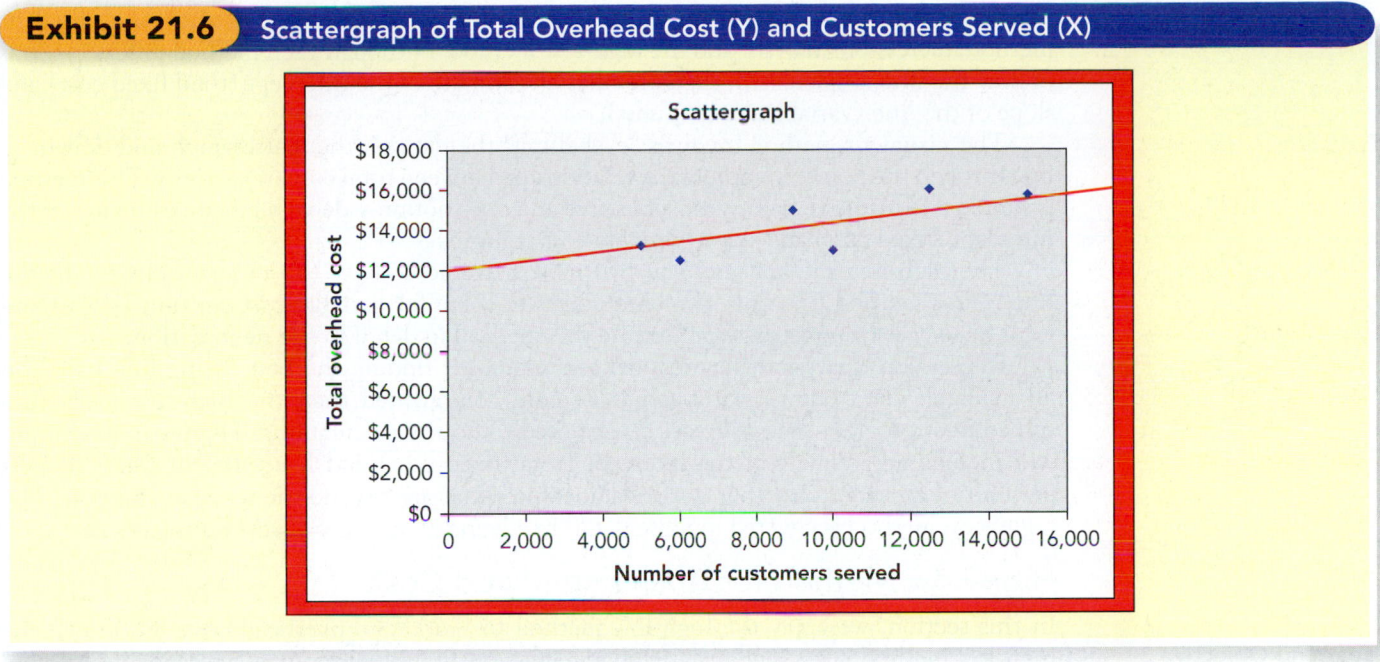

The intercept, or the point at which the red line connects with the Y axis, represents the fixed cost. This is also sometimes called the **constant,** because it reflects the amount of cost expected at zero activity. In this example, the fixed cost appears to be about $12,000. For Starbucks, the fixed overhead costs would be for items such as rent, insurance, the manager's salary, and other costs that will be incurred each month regardless of how many customers are served.

The next section discusses several methods for finding the variable cost per unit (slope of the line) and the total fixed cost (intercept).

## Linear Approaches to Analyzing Mixed Costs

The linear approach to cost estimation is based on the following formulas:

These terms are interpreted as follows.

- **Y** is total cost, which is shown on the vertical axis. It is called the **dependent variable** because we assume that Y is dependent on X.
- **X** is the activity that causes Y (total cost) to change. This variable is also called the **cost driver** or the **independent variable.**
- **A** is the amount of cost that will be incurred regardless of the activity level (X), or the **total fixed cost.** This term is also called the **intercept term** or the **constant.**
- **B** indicates how much Y (total cost) will increase with each additional unit of X (activity). In other words, it is the **variable cost per unit of X** and is represented by the **slope** of the line.

### Coach's Tip

We often use a straight line to represent the relationship between total cost (Y) and activity (X). Although the data do not fall perfectly on the line, we can use a straight line to approximate or estimate the relationship. Of course, our estimates will be good only if our assumption of linearity is reasonable.

There are three linear approaches that can be used to analyze mixed costs: the visual fit method, regression analysis, and the high-low method. Although each method differs in terms of how the line is calculated, each provides an estimate of the intercept (total fixed cost) and slope of the line (variable cost per unit).

The **visual fit method** involves "eyeballing" the data on the scattergraph and drawing a line through the points to capture the relationship between total cost and activity. This method is simple and intuitive but is very subjective and does not provide very precise estimates of the intercept (fixed cost) and slope (variable cost per unit).

The **high-low method** uses the two most extreme activity (X) observations to "fit the line." This method uses only two data points to solve for variable cost per unit (slope) and total fixed cost (intercept). We illustrate this method in detail in the next section.

**Regression analysis** is a statistical technique for finding the best fitting line based on all available data points. Although it is more complicated than the high-low method, a spreadsheet program such as Excel can be used to do the calculations. The program's output will include an estimate of the intercept (total fixed cost) and X coefficient (variable cost per unit of X) as well as other statistical measures that are beyond the scope of this text. The regression method is covered in more detail in advanced managerial accounting books.

## High-Low Method for Analyzing Mixed Costs

**Learning Objective 3**

Use the high-low method to analyze mixed costs.

In this section, we apply the high-low method to Starbucks' overhead costs. Although the high-low method is less sophisticated than regression analysis, it provides a reasonable estimate of the fixed and variable costs as long as the high and low data points represent the trend in the overall data, which appears to be the case in this example.

The first step in the high-low method is to find the two most extreme activity (X) observations. The data we have been using for our Starbucks example follow:

**Coach's Tip**

Be sure to pick the highest and lowest X (customers served).

Notice that this is not necessarily the same as the highest and lowest Y (total cost).

| Month | Number of Customers Served (X) | Total Overhead Cost (Y) | |
|---|---|---|---|
| January | 9,000 | $15,000 | |
| February | 15,000 | 15,750 | High X |
| March | 12,500 | 16,000 | |
| April | 6,000 | 12,500 | |
| May | 5,000 | 13,250 | Low X |
| June | 10,000 | 13,000 | |

The high-low method uses only the high (February) and low (May) data points to estimate the variable cost per unit and the total fixed cost.

The second step is to calculate the slope of the line based on the high and low data points. You may recall from your high school algebra class that the slope of the line is calculated as "rise over run," or the change in Y over the change in X. We use the same logic here to calculate how much total cost (Y) changes with a corresponding change in activity level (X).

**Coach's Tip**

Students sometimes wonder if it matters whether they subtract the high values from the low, or the low values from the high. As long as you use the same order for both the numerator and the denominator, you will get the same results.

$$\boxed{\text{Variable Cost per Unit}} = \boxed{\frac{\text{Difference in Total Cost (Y)}}{\text{Difference in Activity (X)}}}$$

Applying this formula to the data from February and May results in the following:

$$\boxed{\begin{array}{c}\text{Variable Cost} = \$0.25 \\ \text{per Unit}\end{array}} = \boxed{\frac{(\$15,750 - \$13,250) = \$2,500}{(15,000 - 5,000) = 10,000}}$$

The high-low method shows that total overhead cost increased by $2,500 when the number of customers served increased by 10,000. This results in a variable overhead cost of $0.25 per customer served.

The third step is to solve for total fixed cost using the following equation:

| Total Fixed Cost | = | Total Cost | − | Total Variable Cost (Variable Cost per Unit × X) |
|---|---|---|---|---|

Because we now know that the variable cost is $0.25 per customer served and we know the total cost, we can solve for the fixed cost. To do this, we can use **EITHER** the high or the low data point to determine the fixed cost. The high and low data points for our Starbucks example follow.

| Month | Number of Customers Served (X) | Total Overhead Cost (Y) | |
|---|---|---|---|
| February | 15,000 | $15,750 | High X |
| May | 5,000 | 13,250 | Low X |

First let's use the data from February to solve for the total fixed cost:

| Total Fixed Cost $12,000 | = | Total Cost (February) $15,750 | − | Total Variable Cost (February) $0.25 × 15,000 Customers Served $3,750 |
|---|---|---|---|---|

We get exactly the same result if we use May instead:

| Total Fixed Cost $12,000 | = | Total Cost (May) $13,250 | − | Total Variable Cost (May) $0.25 × 5,000 Customers Served $1,250 |
|---|---|---|---|---|

Regardless of whether we use the high (February) or low (May) data points, we arrive at a total fixed cost of $12,000. You should recall that this is the same estimate of fixed costs shown in Exhibit 21.6 where the red line intercepted the Y axis. If you look back to this exhibit, you will see that the red line was drawn so that it went through both the high and the low data points. Based on the high-low method, we now know that the red line can be more specifically defined as follows:

| Total Overhead Cost | = | Total Fixed Cost $12,000 | + | Total Variable Cost $.25 × Customers Served |
|---|---|---|---|---|

We can use this formula to predict total overhead cost in the future, so long as we have an estimate of the number of customers to be served. For example, if Starbucks expects to serve 8,000 customers in July, it would budget for $12,000 in fixed overhead cost plus $2,000 ($0.25 × 8,000 customers) in variable costs for a total of $14,000.

Before you continue, complete the following self-study practice to make sure you understand how to estimate fixed and variable cost using the high-low method.

**SELF-STUDY PRACTICE**

A travel agent has collected the following information regarding the number of reservations made and the total cost of running the agency for the past four months:

| Month | Number of Reservations Booked | Total Cost |
|---|---|---|
| January | 600 | $41,000 |
| February | 400 | 32,000 |
| March | 860 | 55,000 |
| April | 740 | 56,000 |

Using the high-low method, determine the variable cost per reservation and the total fixed cost.

*After you have finished, check your answers with the solutions at the bottom of the page.*

# CONTRIBUTION MARGIN

## Contribution Margin Income Statement

**Learning Objective 4**

Prepare and interpret a contribution margin income statement.

Now that you have learned how to separate mixed costs into their fixed and variable components, you can prepare a type of income statement called the **contribution margin income statement.** A contribution margin income statement categorizes costs as variable or fixed. Unlike financial statements meant for external users, which are prepared according to GAAP, a contribution margin income statement is used only for internal purposes. It is extremely useful for addressing a variety of managerial questions because cost behavior is the key to many managerial decisions.

To illustrate, let's construct a contribution margin income statement for our hypothetical Starbucks coffee shop for the month of February when it served 15,000 cups of coffee. For this analysis, we assume that the total variable cost per unit is $1.00. This includes not only the variable overhead calculated using the high-low method, but also the direct material cost (ingredients) and direct labor (server wages). We assume an average sales price of $2.50 per unit and total fixed overhead cost of $12,000. Based on this information, the contribution margin income statement would appear as follows:

**Coach's Tip**

Notice that fixed costs are stated on a total basis rather than per unit or as a percentage of sales because those measures will change as the sales volume changes. When you see fixed cost stated on a per unit basis, you should immediately calculate the total fixed cost because that is the number that is truly fixed.

**Starbucks Coffee**
**Contribution Margin Income Statement**
**For the Month of February 2009**

**15,000 Units sold**

| | Total | Per Unit | Percent of Sales |
|---|---|---|---|
| Sales revenue | $37,500 | $2.50 | 100% |
| Less: Variable costs | 15,000 | 1.00 | 40 |
| Contribution margin | 22,500 | $1.50 | 60% |
| Less: Fixed costs | 12,000 | | |
| Profit (loss) | $10,500 | | |

**Solution to Self-Study Practice**

High, March; Low, February

Variable Cost = ($55,000 − $32,000) / (860 − 400) = $23,000 / 460 = $50 per reservation
Total Fixed Cost = $55,000 − ($50 × 860) = $12,000, or $32,000 − ($50 × 400) = $12,000

# Contribution Margin Formula

The key to the contribution margin income statement is the contribution margin, which is the difference between sales revenue and variable costs:

$$\boxed{\text{Contribution Margin}} \;=\; \boxed{\text{Sales Revenue}} \;-\; \boxed{\text{Variable Costs}}$$

The contribution margin represents the amount left over from sales revenue after variable costs have been covered to contribute to fixed costs and then provide a profit. In the preceding example, the total contribution margin was $22,500. Once the monthly fixed costs of $12,000 were deducted, $10,500 remained as profit.

What happens if the contribution margin is not enough to cover fixed costs? The company will incur a loss. If the contribution margin exactly equals fixed costs, the company earns zero profit. This concept lies at the heart of break-even analysis, which is covered later in this chapter.

As the next section discusses, the contribution margin formula can be used to find not only the total contribution margin but also the contribution margin per unit and as a percentage of sales.

# Unit Contribution Margin

The contribution margin is often stated on a per unit basis. The unit contribution margin tells us how much each additional unit contributes to fixed costs and profit. It is very useful in solving cost-volume-profit questions involving the way changes in the number of units sold will affect the bottom line.

In our Starbucks example, each coffee drink provides $1.50 in contribution margin. Because fixed costs do not change with each additional unit sold, the contribution margin earned on each unit will have a direct effect on the bottom-line profit. What would happen if Starbucks sold 1,000 more coffee drinks in March than in February? Recall that the coffeehouse sold 15,000 units in February and made a profit of $10,500. Because the contribution margin per unit is $1.50, the profit would be $1,500 higher (1,000 × $1.50) than it was in February, or $12,000 ($10,500 + $1,500).

We can verify this answer by creating a new contribution margin income statement based on 16,000 units as follows:

## Starbucks Coffee
### Contribution Margin Income Statement
### For the Month of March 2009

#### 16,000 Units sold

|  | Total | Per Unit | Percent of Sales |
|---|---|---|---|
| Sales revenue | $40,000 | $2.50 | 100% |
| Less: Variable costs | 16,000 | 1.00 | 40 |
| Contribution margin | 24,000 | $1.50 | 60% |
| Less: Fixed costs | 12,000 |  |  |
| Net profit | $12,000 |  |  |

# Contribution Margin Ratio

The contribution margin can also be stated as percentage of sales, called the contribution margin ratio, that is calculated as follows:

$$\boxed{\text{Contribution Margin Ratio}} \;=\; \frac{\text{Contribution Margin}}{\text{Sales Revenue}}$$

The contribution margin ratio indicates how much additional contribution margin is generated by each dollar of sales. In our Starbucks example, the 60 percent contribution margin means that every

**Coach's Tip**

The contribution margin ratio can be calculated based on total contribution margin or per unit contribution margin. For example, a 60 percent contribution margin ratio can be calculated in one of two ways:

$24,000 / $40,000 = 60%

or

$1.50 / $2.50 = 60%

**Coach's Tip**

The contribution margin ratio provides a shortcut for determining the effect of an increase in sales on profit. Another way to find the effect is to prepare two contribution margin income statements and note whether profit increases or decreases. Although this approach takes longer, it is a good way to verify that your calculations are correct.

$1.00 in sales will generate $0.60 in contribution margin. Because fixed costs do not increase with increases in sales, this increased contribution margin will have a direct effect on the bottom line.

The contribution margin ratio is useful for answering cost-volume-profit questions involving how changes in total sales revenue will affect profitability. Assume, for example, Starbucks' manager is thinking of investing $2,000 per month in local advertising in hope of boosting monthly sales by $5,000. What effect would this decision have on profit? Because we know that the contribution margin ratio is 60 percent, we can quickly determine that a $5,000 increase in sales would increase the contribution margin by $3,000. Of course, fixed costs would go up by $2,000, so the net effect on profit would be a $1,000 increase, as follows:

| | | |
|---|---|---|
| Increased sales | | $5,000 |
| Increased contribution margin | ($5,000 × 60%) | 3,000 |
| Increased fixed expenses | | 2,000 |
| Increased profit | | 1,000 |

Before we continue on, take a moment to complete the following Self-Study Practice.

**SELF-STUDY PRACTICE**

In the same month that a company sold 750 units for $80 each, it reported total variable costs of $45,000 and total fixed expenses of $10,000.
Prepare a contribution margin income statement to calculate the following:

1. Total contribution margin.
2. Contribution margin per unit.
3. Contribution margin ratio.
4. Net profit.

*After you have finished, check your answers with the solutions at the bottom of the page.*

## COST-VOLUME-PROFIT ANALYSIS

This section extends the analysis of cost behavior to a specific application called cost-volume-profit analysis (CVP). Cost-volume-profit analysis is a managerial decision-making tool that focuses on the relationships among sales price, volume of units sold, fixed and variable costs, and profit. The basic approach allows managers to see how a change in any one of these variables will impact profitability while holding everything else constant.

Video 21-1
www.mhhe.com/LLPW1e

## Assumption of Cost-Volume-Profit

While CVP is very useful in answering certain questions, it requires managers to make several important assumptions. Like all business modeling approaches, the results are only as good as the underlying assumptions. The key assumptions of CVP analysis are:

1. A straight line can be used to model how total cost and total revenue change across the relevant range of activity.
2. All costs can be accurately described as either fixed or variable.
3. Changes in total cost are due strictly to changes in activity level rather than other factors, such as gains in efficiency.
4. Production and sales are equal so that inventory levels remain constant.
5. Companies that sell more than one product maintain a constant sales mix, or proportion of products sold.

If any of these assumptions are violated, the results of CVP analysis may not be accurate.

Solution to
Self-Study Practice

1. (750 × $80) − $45,000 = $15,000
2. $15,000/750 = $20
3. $20/$80 = 25%
4. $15,000 − $10,000 = $5,000

# Break-Even Analysis

Break-even analysis is one of the most common applications of cost-volume-profit analysis. The goal of **break-even analysis** is to determine the level of sales (in either units or sales dollars) required for a company to break even, or earn zero profit.

**Learning Objective 5**
Use cost-volume-profit analysis to find the break-even point.

Recall that contribution margin is the amount of sales revenue that remains after variable costs have been covered, and is available to cover fixed costs and provide a profit. The **break-even point** is the point at which the company would make zero profit. In terms of the contribution margin, the break-even point means that contribution margin must equal fixed costs so that nothing is left over as profit.

Recall too that we can express the contribution margin either on a per unit basis or as a percentage of sales. Let's state our formula for the contribution margin in terms of the number of units sold:

## Unit Contribution Margin Approach

**Coach's Tip**

This general framework can be used to solve many CVP problems. In break-even analysis, we set the profit equal to zero. If we want the profit to be something other than zero, we modify the equation to include the target profit.

To express the break-even point in terms of the number of units sold, we simply set the profit in this equation equal to zero. Then we rearrange the terms so that only the number of units sold appears to the left of the equal sign, which yields the following formula for the break-even point:

$$\text{Break-Even Units} = \frac{\text{Total Fixed Costs}}{\text{Unit Contribution Margin}}$$

Recall from our Starbucks example that monthly fixed costs were $12,000 and that each coffee drink provided a contribution margin of $1.50 ($2.50 price − $1.00 variable cost per unit). Thus, the number of coffee drinks that Starbucks needs to sell to break even would be calculated as follows:

Break-Even Units = $12,000 / $1.50 per drink
Break-Even Units = 8,000 Coffee Drinks

The break-even formula shows that Starbucks needs to sell 8,000 coffee drinks per month just to cover its fixed costs. Because we know that the average price of a coffee drink is $2.50, this result translates into $20,000 in total sales revenue (8,000 units × $2.50 price).

A more direct way to calculate the break-even point in total sales dollars is to use the contribution margin (CM) ratio. Recall that the CM ratio indicates how much total CM every dollar of sales generates. Thus, we can convert the total contribution margin to sales dollars using the CM ratio, as follows:

**Contribution Margin Ratio Approach**

If we rearrange the terms of this equation so that only total sales dollars appears to the left of the equal sign, we arrive at the following formula:

$$\text{Break-Even Sales} = \frac{\text{Total Fixed Costs}}{\text{Contribution Margin Ratio (\%)}}$$

Because Starbucks' CM ratio is 60 percent, the total sales needed to break even can be calculated as follows:

$$\text{Break-Even Units} = \$12,000 / 60\%$$
$$\text{Break-Even Sales} = \$20,000$$

## Margin of Safety

The margin of safety is the difference between actual or budgeted sales and the break-even point. Think of the margin of safety as a buffer zone that identifies how much sales can drop before the business will begin operating at a loss. This application of CVP analysis is most relevant to companies that face a significant risk of **not** making a profit, such as start-up businesses or companies that face extreme competition or abrupt changes in demand. The formula for calculating the margin of safety is:

$$\text{Margin of Safety} = \text{Actual or Budgeted Sales} - \text{Break-Even Sales}$$

Existing companies base the margin of safety on actual sales; new businesses or those in a new location base it on budgeted sales. For example, if you were thinking of opening a new Starbucks location and had developed a business plan based on an anticipated sales level, it would be wise to compare that level to the break-even point. Doing so would show you how much of a cushion you have between making a profit and suffering a loss.

To see how to apply the margin of safety to actual sales, let's return to the month of February when our Starbucks coffee location sold 15,000 coffee drinks:

**Starbucks Coffee House**
**Contribution Margin Income Statement**
**For the Month of February 2009**

15,000 units sold

|  | Total | Per Unit |
|---|---|---|
| Sales revenue | $37,500 | $2.50 |
| Less: Variable costs | 15,000 | 1.00 |
| Contribution margin | 22,500 | $1.50 |
| Less: Fixed costs | 12,000 | |
| Profit (Loss) | $10,500 | |

Notice that the company operated above the break-even point during February with sales of $37,500 and a profit of $10,500. Recall that the break-even point was 8,000 units, or $20,000 in total sales. Thus, the margin of safety is calculated as follows:

| Margin of Safety | = | Actual or Budgeted Sales | − | Break-Even Sales |
|---|---|---|---|---|
| $17,500 | | $37,500 | | $20,000 |

Expressing the margin of safety as a percentage of actual sales provides a better idea of how large this buffer zone is. In this case, the margin of safety as a percentage of actual sales would be 46.7 percent ($17,500 / $37,500). That means that Starbucks' monthly sales could fall 46.7 percent below the February sales level before the company would begin to incur a loss.

## Target Profit Analysis

Most managers want to do more than just break even; they want to earn a profit for the owners or shareholders. **Target profit analysis** is an extension of break-even analysis that allows managers to determine the number of units or total sales revenue needed to earn a target profit. To do so, the total contribution margin must be enough to cover the fixed costs plus the target profit as follows:

$$\text{Total Contribution Margin} = \text{Total Fixed Costs} + \text{Target Profit}$$

We can easily modify the break-even formulas presented in the last section to incorporate a target profit as follows:

$$\text{Target Units} = \frac{\text{Total Fixed Costs} + \text{Target Profit}}{\text{Unit Contribution Margin}}$$

$$\text{Target Sales} = \frac{\text{Total Fixed Costs} + \text{Target Profit}}{\text{Contribution Margin Ratio (\%)}}$$

**Learning Objective 6**
Use cost-volume-profit analysis to determine the sales needed to achieve a target profit.

**Coach's Tip**
The only difference between the target profit formula and the break-even formula is that the target profit formula adds the target profit to fixed costs. The amount in the denominater depends on whether the purpose is to find the target in terms of units or total sales dollars.

For example, if the Starbucks' manager wants to earn $18,000 in profit each month, the target units and target sales would be calculated as follows:

$$\text{Target Units} = \frac{\$12,000 + \$18,000}{\$1.50 \text{ per Drink}} = 20,000 \text{ Coffee Drinks}$$

$$\text{Target Sales} = \frac{\$12,000 + \$18,000}{60\%} = \$50,000$$

## Cost-Volume-Profit Relationships in Graphic Form

Cost-volume-profit relationships can be shown graphically. Sometimes called a break-even chart, a **CVP graph** is useful for visualizing the relationships among unit sales volume, total revenue, and total costs. It also shows how activity levels above or below the break-even point will produce a profit or loss. Refer to Exhibit 21.7 for a **CVP** graph based on the cost and revenue data we have been using for Starbucks Coffee.

You can quickly see that the company needs to sell 8,000 coffee drinks or earn $20,000 in total sales revenue to break even. The difference between the total revenue and total cost lines is the profit (or loss). For example, if Starbucks sells 20,000 coffee drinks, or $50,000 in sales, it will earn the target profit of $18,000.

CVP graphs are also useful for determining what will happen if different elements of the CVP relationship change—for example, the unit sales price, the variable cost, or the fixed costs. What would happen to the break-even point, for example, if fixed costs increased but the unit price and variable cost remained the same? The total cost line would shift upward by the amount of the added fixed cost, but its slope would remain the same because the variable cost per unit did not change. This change would shift the break-even point upward and to the right, raising the break-even point in terms of both units and total sales dollars, as shown in Exhibit 21.8.

Try visualizing how other changes to the CVP graph would affect the break-even point. For example, increasing the unit sales price would make the slope of the total revenue line steeper, which would lower the break-even point. Lowering the variable cost per unit would flatten the total cost line, which would also lower the break-even point.

**Coach's Tip**
The point where the total cost and total revenue lines cross is the break-even point. Activity levels below the break-even point will produce a loss; activity levels above the break-even point will generate a profit.

**Exhibit 21.7    Cost-Volume-Profit Graph**

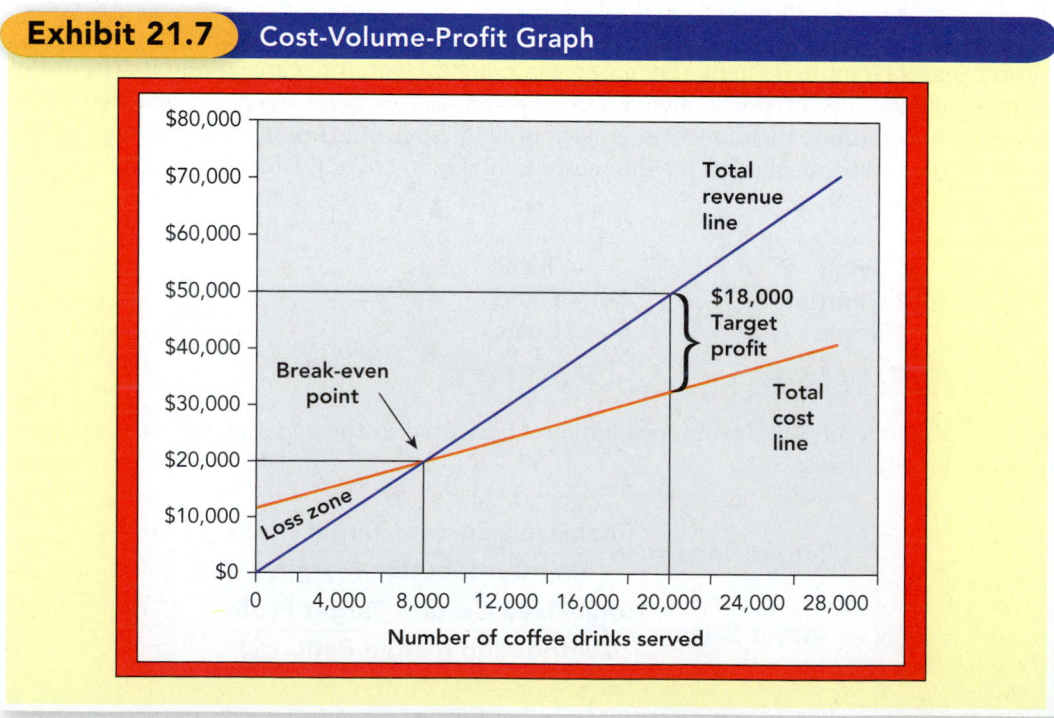

**Exhibit 21.8**    Effect of an Increase in Fixed Costs on the Break-Even Point

## Multiproduct Cost-Volume-Profit Analysis

Throughout this chapter, we simplified the CVP analysis by assuming that Starbucks sells only a single product: coffee. But in reality Starbucks and most other businesses offer more than one product or service. For example, Starbucks sells various types of coffee and tea, as well as pastries, sandwiches, mugs, T-shirts, and other novelty items. The fact that each of these products has a different price (and different cost) makes the CVP analysis more complex.

To extend the single product CVP analysis to a multiproduct setting requires calculating an **average** contribution margin based on all of the products or services that the company offers. This average contribution margin should be weighted according to the volume of sales generated by the various products and services. For example, if 80 percent of a company's sales come from a particular product, that product's contribution margin should be weighted at 80 percent, with the other products receiving 20 percent of the weight. Once the average contribution margin is calculated, we can apply the same formulas we used to perform CVP analysis earlier in the chapter. Of course, the analysis will be valid only if the sales mix used to calculate the weighted average contribution margin remains constant.

The specific details for how to use the weighted average contribution margin to perform multiproduct cost-volume-profit analysis are covered in more advanced management accounting books.

To make sure you understand how to analyze cost-volume-profit for a single product company, complete the following Self-Study Practice.

A company sells a product for $60 per unit. Variable costs per unit are $36, and monthly fixed costs are $120,000. Answer the following questions.

1. What is the break-even point in units and in total sales dollars?
2. What is the contribution margin ratio?
3. What level of total sales would be required to earn a target profit of $60,000?
4. Assuming the company achieves the level of sales required in part 3, what is the margin of safety as a percentage of sales?

*After you have finished, check your answers with the solutions at the bottom of the next page.*

## Demonstration Case

In 2004, two young entrepreneurs realized that almost everyone loves cereal but no one ever eats it outside of their own home. So they opened Cereality, a cereal bar and café in the student union at Arizona State University. This innovative concept in fast food appealed to students and others who loved the idea of mixing Cocoa Puffs and Lucky Charms at almost any time of the day. Since then, Cereality franchises have opened at other college campuses around the country.

Based on market research, the young entrepreneurs decided to charge $3.75 for customers to create their own cereal combinations. But the entrepreneurs still needed to understand how much it would cost to run the business. They knew that costs such as cereal, milk, and paper products would vary with the number of customers but that other costs such as rent and insurance would be incurred each month even if the store were closed.

Assume the total operating costs and number of customers served during Cereality's first four months of operation were as follows:

| Month | Total Operating Costs | Total Number of Customers |
|---|---|---|
| August | $7,500 | 2,000 |
| September | 8,000 | 2,600 |
| October | 8,700 | 3,600 |
| November | 8,800 | 3,400 |

*Required:*

1. Use the high-low method to determine the variable cost per customer and the total fixed operating costs.
2. Calculate and interpret the unit contribution margin and contribution margin ratio.
3. How many customers must Cereality serve each month to break even?
4. How much total sales revenue must Cereality earn each month to break even?
5. If the owners want to earn an operating profit of $7,500 per month, how many customers must they serve?

## Suggested Solution

1. The high-low method should be based on the high and low × (total number of customers):

| | Total Operating Cost (Y) | Total Number of Customers (X) | |
|---|---|---|---|
| August | $7,500 | 2,000 | Low activity |
| October | 8,700 | 3,600 | High activity |

Variable Cost = ($8,700 − $7,500)/(3,600 − 2,000) = $1,200/1,600 = $0.75 per Customer
Fixed Cost (based on August) = $7,500 − (2,000 × $0.75 per Customer) = $6,000
Fixed Cost (based on October) = $8,700 − (3,600 × $0.75 per Customer) = $6,000

2. Unit Contribution Margin = $3.75 Selling Price − $0.75 Variable Cost = $3.00 per Customer
Contribution Margin Ratio = $3.00 / $3.75 = 80%

The unit contribution margin of $3 means that each additional customer served generates $3 in contribution margin, which goes to cover fixed costs and then operating profit.
The contribution margin ratio of 80 percent means that each $1.00 of sales generates $0.80 in contribution margin, which goes to cover fixed costs and then operating profit.

**Solution to Self-Study Practice**

1. Break-Even Units = Fixed Costs / CM per unit = $120,000 / ($60 − $36) = 5,000 units
   Break-Even Sales Dollars = 5,000 units × $60 price = $300,000

2. CM Ratio = $24 / $60 = 40%

3. Target Sales $ = (Fixed Costs + Target Profit) / CM Ratio = ($120,000 + 60,000) / 40% = $450,000

4. Margin of Safety = Actual Sales − Break-Even Sales = $450,000 − $300,000 = $150,000
   Margin of Safety Percentage = $150,000 / $450,000 = 33%

3.  Break-Even Units = Fixed Cost / Unit Contribution Margin = $6,000 / $3.00 = 2,000 Customers

4.  Break-Even Sales Dollar = Fixed Cost / Contribution Margin Ratio = $6,000 / 80% = $7,500

5.  Target Units = (Fixed Costs + Target Profit) / Unit Contribution Margin
    = ($6,000 + $7,500) / $3.00 = 4,500 Units

# Supplement 21A
## Variable Costing

This chapter discussed how to prepare a contribution margin income statement. The statement categorizes costs according to their behavior based on how total costs respond to changes in the activity level. Because this approach classifies costs as either variable or fixed, it is called **variable costing.**

In the early chapters of this book, you learned to prepare financial statements for external users. Those statements were prepared to comply with the rules of GAAP, which does not distinguish between variable or fixed costs. Instead, GAAP requires that all manufacturing costs be treated as part of the cost of the product and inventoried until the product is sold. This approach is called **full absorption costing** because the product must "fully absorb" all costs incurred to produce it regardless of whether they are variable or fixed or whether units of the product have or have not been sold.

See Exhibit 21A.1 for a summary of the differences between variable costing and full absorption costing.

| Exhibit 21A.1 | Calculation and Uses of Full Absorption Costing and Variable Costing |
| --- | --- |

|  | Full Absorption Costing | Variable Costing |
| --- | --- | --- |
| Purpose | External financial reporting | Internal decision making |
| Cost classification | Manufacturing versus Nonmanufacturing costs | Variable versus fixed costs |
| Income statement formulas | Sales <br> − Cost of goods sold <br> Gross margin <br> − Nonmanufacturing expenses <br> Net income from operations | Sales <br> − Variable costs <br> Contribution margin <br> − Fixed expenses <br> Net income from operations |
| Treatment of fixed overhead | Divided between cost of goods sold and ending inventory | Expensed during the period incurred |

**Coach's Tip**

Notice that gross margin and contribution margin are not the same. Contribution margin is the difference between sales revenue and variable costs; it is used only for internal reporting. Gross margin is the difference between sales revenue and the cost of goods sold; it appears on external financial statements.

## Differences between Variable Costing and Full Absorption Costing

In terms of the effect on the bottom line, variable costing and full absorption costing have one critical difference: the treatment of fixed manufacturing overhead. Full absorption costing (GAAP) requires that fixed manufacturing overhead costs be treated as product cost, which means that the cost will be included as either cost of goods sold or inventory, depending on whether the product has been sold. Variable costing deducts all fixed costs, including fixed manufacturing overhead, during the period they are incurred.

To see how this difference can impact the bottom line, consider a company that produces and sells only one product. Assume this is the company's first month of operation, so no inventory was on hand at the beginning of the month. Costs and unit production follow.

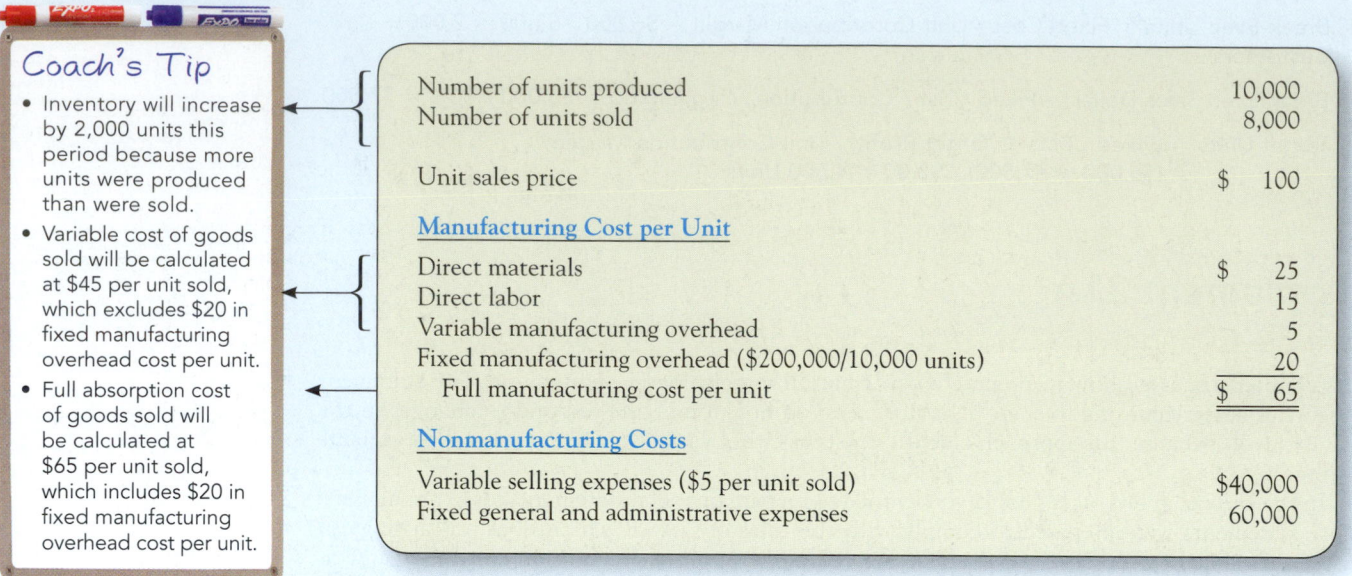

**Coach's Tip**

- Inventory will increase by 2,000 units this period because more units were produced than were sold.
- Variable cost of goods sold will be calculated at $45 per unit sold, which excludes $20 in fixed manufacturing overhead cost per unit.
- Full absorption cost of goods sold will be calculated at $65 per unit sold, which includes $20 in fixed manufacturing overhead cost per unit.

| | |
|---|---:|
| Number of units produced | 10,000 |
| Number of units sold | 8,000 |
| | |
| Unit sales price | $ 100 |
| **Manufacturing Cost per Unit** | |
| Direct materials | $ 25 |
| Direct labor | 15 |
| Variable manufacturing overhead | 5 |
| Fixed manufacturing overhead ($200,000/10,000 units) | 20 |
|    Full manufacturing cost per unit | $ 65 |
| **Nonmanufacturing Costs** | |
| Variable selling expenses ($5 per unit sold) | $40,000 |
| Fixed general and administrative expenses | 60,000 |

Refer to Exhibit 21A.2 for a comparision of the company's income statement under the two methods.

## Reconciling Income under Full Absorption Costing and Variable Costing

The $40,000 difference in income between the two income statements in Exhibit 21A.2 is due to the different treatment of fixed manufacturing overhead under the two costing methods. Full absorption costing requires that this cost be spread over the number of units produced and then assigned either to the cost of goods sold or to ending inventory. As the cost and unit production data above indicate, the fixed manufacturing overhead cost of $200,000 is spread over the 10,000 units produced, for a fixed overhead rate of $20 per unit. This cost is then split between the 8,000 units sold and the 2,000 units remaining in ending inventory. Because the 2,000 units are not yet sold, full absorption costing reports

---

### Exhibit 21A.2    Income Statement under Two Costing Approaches

#### Full Absorption Costing Income Statement

| | | |
|---|---:|---:|
| **Sales ($100 × 8,000 units)** | | $800,000 |
| **Less: Cost of Goods Sold** | | |
|    Inventory, January 1 | $ — | |
|    Cost of Goods Manufactured | | |
|       (10,000 × $65) | 650,000 | |
|    Cost of Goods Available for Sale | 650,000 | |
|    Less: Ending Inventory | | |
|       (2,000 × $65) | 130,000 | |
|    Cost of Goods Sold | | |
|       (8,000 × $65) | | 520,000 |
| **Gross Margin** | | 280,000 |
| Less: Nonmanufacturing Expenses | | |
|    Variable Selling Expenses | | |
|       ($5 × 8,000) | | 40,000 |
|    Fixed General and Administrative | | |
|       Expenses | | 60,000 |
| **Income from Operations** | | **$180,000** |

#### Variable Costing Income Statement

| | | |
|---|---:|---:|
| **Sales ($100 × 8,000 units)** | | $ 800,000 |
| **Less: Variable Cost of Goods Sold** | | |
|    Inventory, January 1 | $ — | |
|    Variable Manufacturing Costs | | |
|       (10,000 × $45) | 450,000 | |
|    Cost of Goods Available for Sale | 450,000 | |
|    Less: Ending Inventory | | |
|       (2,000 × $45) | 90,000 | |
|    Variable Cost of Goods Sold | | |
|       (8,000 × $45) | | 360,000 |
|    Variable Selling Expenses | | |
|       (8,000 × $5) | | 40,000 |
| **Contribution Margin** | | **400,000** |
| Less: Fixed Expenses | | |
|    Fixed Manufacturing Overhead | | 200,000 |
|    Fixed General and Administrative | | |
|       Expenses | | 60,000 |
| **Income from Operations** | | **$140,000** |

**$40,000 Difference in income**

$40,000 of the $200,000 in fixed overhead as an asset on the balance sheet rather than as an expense on the income statement. This cost will eventually be expensed but not until the units are sold.

In contrast, variable costing deducts the entire $200,000 in fixed manufacturing overhead as an expense during the current period. The rationale is that this cost is incurred regardless of how many units are produced and sold. Thus, variable costing assigns $20 less to each of the 2,000 units in ending inventory, or a total of $40,000. This difference in the treatment of fixed manufacturing overhead explains the $40,000 difference in income between the two methods.

In sum, the difference in income between full absorption costing and variable costing is directly related to the fixed manufacturing overhead cost per unit and the change in ending inventory, as in the following formula:

| Difference between Full Absorption and Variable Costing Income | = | Change in Units in Ending Inventory (Production − Sales) | × | Fixed Manufacturing Overhead Cost per Unit |

The difference in income equals 2,000 units × $20 per unit, or $40,000. Income is higher under full absorption costing than under variable costing because full absorption costing counts a portion of the fixed manufacturing overhead as ending inventory instead of a period expense.

If the company had sold exactly the same number of units that it produced, the number of units in inventory would not change, and the two methods would give identical results. If production had been **lower** than sales, or the inventory level had **decreased,** variable costing would have produced a higher income than full absorption costing for exactly the opposite reason. Inventory units have a higher value under full absorption costing than under variable costing. Thus, when those units are finally sold, they must be deducted from income as part of the cost of goods sold at a higher value than under variable costing.

The illustration in Exhibit 21A.3 summarizes the effect of changes in inventory on income under full absorption versus variable costing.

**Exhibit 21A.3    Effect of Changes in Inventory under Full Absorption Costing and Variable Costing**

# Chapter Summary

**LO1  Identify costs as either variable, fixed, step, or mixed. p. 884**

- Costs can be classified as either variable, fixed, step, or mixed.
- Variable costs increase in total in direct proportion to increases in the activity level.
- Fixed costs remain constant in total regardless of changes in the activity level.
- Step costs increase in a steplike fashion when a capacity constraint is reached.
- Mixed costs contain a fixed component plus a variable component that changes with the level of activity.

**LO2  Prepare a scattergraph to illustrate the relationship between total cost and activity. p. 888**

- A scattergraph provides a visual representation of the relationship between total cost and activity.
- A scattergraph is created by plotting the activity level on the horizontal (X) axis and the total cost on the vertical (Y) axis.
- If the scattergraph suggests that the relationship between cost and activity is roughly linear, a straight line can be used to approximate that relationship.
- The slope of the line represents the variable cost per unit of activity.
- The intercept of the line represents the total fixed cost.

**LO3  Use the high-low method to analyze mixed costs. p. 890**

- The high-low method is one of three linear methods that can be used to estimate the relationship between total cost and activity. The steps of the high-low method are:
- Identify the points that represent the highest and lowest activity (X) levels.
- Calculate the variable cost per unit by dividing the change in total cost across the high and low points by the change in activity level across the high and low points.
- Calculate the total fixed cost by subtracting the total variable cost from the total cost at either the high or low point.

**LO4  Prepare and interpret a contribution margin income statement. p. 892**

- Contribution margin is the difference between sales revenue and variable costs. The contribution margin can be expressed on a total, per unit, or percentage basis.
- The unit contribution margin, which is the difference between a unit's selling price and its variable cost, indicates how profit will change as a result of selling one more or one less unit.
- The contribution margin ratio is computed by dividing the unit contribution margin by the unit selling price or by dividing the total contribution margin by total sales. The contribution margin ratio shows how much a $1 increase in sales will affect the contribution margin and net operating income.

**LO5  Use cost-volume-profit analysis to find the break-even point. p. 895**

- The break-even point is that point at which contribution margin exactly equals fixed costs, indicating that the company is making zero profit.
- To find the break-even point in units, divide total fixed costs by the unit contribution margin. This is the number of units needed to break even.
- To find the break-even point in sales dollars, divide total fixed costs by the contribution margin ratio. This identifies the total sales that are needed to break even.
- The margin of safety is the difference between actual or budgeted sales and break-even sales. It indicates how much cushion there is between the current (or expected) level of sales and the break-even point.

**LO6  Use cost-volume-profit analysis to determine the sales needed to achieve a target profit. p. 897**

- For a business to earn a profit, the total contribution margin must be enough to cover fixed costs plus the desired target profit.
- To determine the number of units needed to earn a target profit, divide the target contribution margin (fixed cost plus target profit) by the unit contribution margin.
- To determine the total sales needed to earn a target profit, divide the target contribution margin (fixed cost plus target profit) by the contribution margin ratio.

## Managerial Analysis Tools

| Name of Measure | Formula |
|---|---|
| Variable cost (VC) per unit | $\dfrac{\text{Difference in Total Cost (Y)}}{\text{Difference in Activity Level (X)}}$ |
| Total fixed costs | Fixed Costs = Total Cost − (Variable Cost per Unit × Activity) |
| Contribution margin per unit | Unit Sales Price − Variable Cost per Unit <br><br> or <br><br> $\dfrac{\text{Total Contribution Margin}}{\text{Number of Units Sold}}$ |
| Contribution margin ratio | $\dfrac{\text{Unit Contribution Margin}}{\text{Unit Sales Price}}$ <br><br> or <br><br> $\dfrac{\text{Total Contribution Margin}}{\text{Total Sales Revenue}}$ |
| Break-even units | $\dfrac{\text{Total Fixed Costs}}{\text{Unit Contribution Margin}}$ |
| Break-even sales | Break-even Units × Unit Sales Price <br><br> or <br><br> $\dfrac{\text{Total Fixed Costs}}{\text{Contribution Margin Ratio}}$ |
| Target units | $\dfrac{\text{Total Fixed Costs} + \text{Target Profit}}{\text{Unit Contribution Margin}}$ |
| Target sales revenue | Target Units × Unit Sales Price <br><br> or <br><br> $\dfrac{\text{Total Fixed Costs} + \text{Target Profit}}{\text{Contribution Margin Ratio}}$ |
| Margin of safety | Actual or Budgeted Sales − Break-Even Sales |
| Margin of safety percentage | $\dfrac{\text{Actual or Budgeted Sales} - \text{Break-Even Sales}}{\text{Actual or Budgeted Sales}}$ |

# Key Terms

Break-Even Analysis (p. 895)

Break-Even Point (p. 895)

Contribution Margin (p. 893)

Contribution Margin Income Statement (p. 892)

Contribution Margin Ratio (p. 893)

Cost Behavior (p. 884)

Cost-Volume-Profit Analysis (p. 894)

CVP Graph (p. 898)

Dependent Variable (p. 889)

High-Low Method (p. 890)

Independent Variable (p. 889)

Margin of Safety (p. 896)

Mixed Costs (p. 886)

Regression Analysis (p. 890)

Relevant Range (p. 884)

Scattergraph (p. 887)

Step Costs (p. 885)

Step-Fixed Cost (p. 886)

Step-Variable Cost (p. 885)

Target Profit Analysis (p. 897)

Unit Contribution Margin (p. 893)

Visual Fit Method (p. 890)

**See complete glossary in back of text.**

## Questions

1. Explain the difference between variable cost, fixed cost, step cost, and mixed cost, and give an example of each.
2. When activity level decreases, explain what happens to:
   a. Total fixed cost.
   b. Total variable cost.
   c. Total mixed cost.
   d. Fixed cost per unit.
   e. Variable cost per unit.
   f. Mixed cost per unit.
3. What are the key assumptions of cost-volume-profit analysis? Why are they important?
4. Why is the relevant range important in cost-volume-profit analysis?
5. Why is separating the fixed and variable components of a mixed cost important? What might happen if that is not done?
6. The formula for analyzing mixed costs is Y = A + B(X). Explain what each component represents.
7. Why is a scattergraph useful?
8. Describe the three methods of analyzing mixed costs. What are the strengths and weaknesses of each method? Will these methods always yield the same results?
9. Why is a contribution margin income statement more useful to managerial decision makers than an income statement intended for external users?
10. Explain how to calculate total contribution margin, contribution margin per unit, and the contribution margin ratio. What is the meaning of each?
11. When activity level increases, explain what happens to:
    a. Contribution margin per unit.
    b. Contribution margin ratio.
    c. Total contribution margin.
    d. Total fixed cost.
    e. Profit.
12. Why is it important for a company to know its break-even point? What happens to the break-even point

if variable cost per unit decreases? If total fixed cost increases?
13. A company's cost structure can have a high proportion of fixed costs or a high proportion of variable costs. Which cost structure is more vulnerable to decreases in demand? Why?
14. Explain the difference in calculating the break-even point in units and in dollars. How can one be used to double-check the other?
15. Apple Company and Baker Company are competitors in the same industry. They produce the same product and have similar variable costs per unit and selling prices, but Baker has more fixed costs. Explain the impact of this on the break-even point of each company.
16. Bert Company and Ernie Company are competitors in the same industry. The companies produce the same product and have the same amount of fixed costs and the same selling price per unit. However, Bert has higher variable cost per unit. Compare the break-even point of each company.
17. Explain the difference between break-even analysis and target profit analysis.
18. Why is it important for managers to create a CVP graph?
19. Your supervisor has requested that you prepare a CVP graph for your company's product but does not understand its meaning or how changes would affect the graph. Explain to your supervisor how your graph would be affected by:
    a. an increase in the selling price.
    b. a decrease in variable cost per unit.
    c. an increase in fixed costs.
20. Explain margin of safety. Why is it important for managers to know their margin of safety? Give an example of a company to which margin of safety is particularly important.
21. Explain the difference between absorption costing and variable costing. Why do internal users need variable costing?
22. When will variable costing show the same income as absorption costing? When will they be different and why?

## Multiple Choice

1. Which of the following would increase when the activity level increases?
   a. Total variable cost.
   b. Total fixed cost.
   c. Total mixed cost.
   d. Both a and c.

   Quiz 21-1
   www.mhhe.com/LLPW1e

2. Which of the following is **not** a method used to separate mixed costs?
   a. Regression analysis.      c. High-low method.
   b. Break-even analysis.      d. Visual fit method.

3. Consider the following information for a local concession stand's first four weeks of operation:

| Week | Drinks Served | Total Cost |
|---|---|---|
| 1 | 1,000 | $2,500 |
| 2 | 2,000 | 3,250 |
| 3 | 1,750 | 3,000 |
| 4 | 2,250 | 3,200 |

Using the high-low method, what is the equation for total operating cost for this concession stand?
a. Operating Cost = $1,750 + $0.75 × (Number of drinks served).
b. Operating Cost = $1,000 + $1.75 × (Number of drinks served).
c. Operating Cost = $1,940 + $0.56 × (Number of drinks served).
d. Operating Cost = $1,750 + $0.56 × (Number of drinks served).

4. Bombay Co. sells handmade rugs. Bombay's variable cost per rug is $30 and each rug sells for $50. What are Bombay's contribution margin per unit and contribution margin ratio?
   a. $20 and 40 percent.
   c. $20 and 60 percent.
   b. $30 and 60 percent.
   d. $30 and 40 percent.

5. Whistler Co. sells one model of radio. Suppose its cost per radio is $125 and its total fixed costs are $4,130. Each radio sells for $195. How many radios must Whistler sell to break even?
   a. 33.
   c. 45.
   b. 21.
   d. 59.

6. Recent information for Shady Co., which makes automobile sunscreens, follows.

   | | |
   |---|---|
   | Selling price per screen | $   18 |
   | Total fixed cost per month | 1,225 |
   | Variable cost per screen | 7 |

   If Shady wants to earn $1,250 profit next month, how many screens must it sell?
   a. 109.
   c. 186.
   b. 136.
   d. 225.

7. Various information for Happy Camper Co., which makes sleeping bags, follows.

   | | |
   |---|---|
   | Selling price per bag | $   30 |
   | Total fixed cost per month | 2,250 |
   | Variable cost per bag | 21 |
   | Last month's profit | 1,260 |

   How many sleeping bags did the company sell last month?
   a. 159.
   c. 140.
   b. 250.
   d. 390.

8. Refer to the information in question 7 above. Suppose Happy Camper decides to lower its selling price to $27. How many sleeping bags must it sell to match last month's profit?
   a. 585.
   c. 780.
   b. 375.
   d. 130.

9. Which of the following statements about a CVP graph is true?
   a. Total revenue is a downward-sloping line.
   b. Break even is the point at which the total revenue and total cost lines intersect.
   c. The dollar value of sales revenue and total cost are plotted on the horizontal (X) axis.
   d. The total cost line includes only fixed costs.

10. Hathaway Corp. manufactures garden hoses. Last month its ending inventory level increased. In comparing absorption costing to variable costing,
    a. Both would show the same amount of profit.
    b. Variable costing would show more profit.
    c. Absorption costing would show more profit.
    d. Effect on income cannot be determined.

---

Solutions to Multiple-Choice Questions

1. d   2. b   3. c   4. a   5. d   6. d   7. d   8. a   9. b   10. c

---

# Mini Exercises  Available with McGraw-Hill's Homework Manager

### M21-1 Identifying Cost Behavior                                                         LO1
Martha Trent is trying to prepare a budget and has come up with the following list of monthly costs. Identify each cost as fixed, variable, or mixed. Indicate a possible cost driver for any variable or mixed cost.

1. Rent.
2. Utilities.
3. Car payment.
4. Telephone.
5. Gasoline.
6. Cable bill.
7. Groceries.
8. Dining out.

### M21-2 Identifying Cost Behavior                                                         LO1
Steve's Snow Cones is a small refreshment stand located near a football stadium. Steve's fixed expenses total $300 per week, and the variable cost per snow cone is $0.35. Complete the following table for the various levels.

| Number of snow cones | 500 | 1,000 | 1,500 |
|---|---|---|---|
| Total fixed cost | | | |
| Fixed cost per snow cone | | | |
| Total variable cost | | | |
| Variable cost per snow cone | | | |
| Total cost | | | |
| Cost per snow cone | | | |

**LO2**

### M21-3 Preparing a Scattergraph

Taylor's Tan-O-Rama is a local tanning salon. The information below reflects Taylor's number of appointments and total costs for the first half of the year:

| Month | Number of Appointments | Total Cost |
|---|---|---|
| January | 500 | $5,400 |
| February | 600 | 5,900 |
| March | 1,000 | 6,700 |
| April | 450 | 5,675 |
| May | 300 | 5,328 |
| June | 350 | 5,325 |

Prepare a scattergraph by plotting Taylor's data on a graph. Then draw a line that you believe best fits the data points. Using the graph and line you have drawn, estimate Taylor's total fixed cost per month.

**LO3**

### M21-4 Analyzing Mixed Costs Using High-Low Method

Refer to the Tan-O-Rama data in M21-3. Using the high-low method, calculate the fixed cost per month and the variable cost per tanning appointment. How does the estimate of fixed cost compare to what you estimated in M21-3?

**LO3**

### M21-5 Analyzing Mixed Costs Using High-Low Method

Wendy's Widgits builds the world's best widgits. The information for the last eight months of Wendy's operations follows.

| Month | Number of Widgits Produced | Total Cost |
|---|---|---|
| January | 4,000 | $7,000 |
| February | 2,250 | 5,000 |
| March | 3,500 | 6,250 |
| April | 4,300 | 7,750 |
| May | 1,875 | 5,000 |
| June | 3,000 | 6,250 |
| July | 1,500 | 4,250 |
| August | 2,500 | 5,750 |

Using the high-low method, calculate the fixed cost per month and the variable cost per widgit produced.

**LO4**

### M21-6 Preparing a Contribution Margin Income Statement

Following is relevant information for Sunsplash Smoothie Shop, a small business that serves fruit drinks.

| | |
|---|---|
| Total fixed cost per month | $1,200.00 |
| Variable cost per drink | 1.25 |
| Sales price per drink | 4.75 |

During the month of June, Sunsplash sold 500 smoothies. Using the preceding information, prepare Sunsplash's contribution margin income statement for the month of June.

**LO4**

### M21-7 Calculating Contribution Margin and Contribution Margin Ratio

Lezoli Enterprises sells handmade clocks. Its variable cost per clock is $6, and each clock sells for $15. Calculate Lezoli's contribution margin per unit and contribution margin ratio. Suppose Lezoli sells 2,000 clocks this year. Calculate the total contribution margin.

**M21-8 Calculating Break-Even Point**                                                     LO5
Refer to the information for Lezoli Enterprises in M21-7. If the company's fixed costs total $6,660 this
year, determine how many clocks Lezoli must sell to break even.

**M21-9 Calculating Target Profit**                                                        LO6
Theodora Patel makes stuffed teddy bears. Recent information for her business follows.

| | |
|---|---:|
| Selling price per bear | $    25.00 |
| Total fixed cost per month | 1,500.00 |
| Variable cost per bear | 15.00 |

If Theodora wants to earn $1,250 profit next month, how many bears will she have to sell?

**M21-10 Identifying Margin of Safety**                                                    LO5
Refer to the information in M21-9 for Theodora Patel. If Theodora sells 275 bears next month, what is the
margin of safety in number of units? What is the margin of safety in sales dollars and as a percentage of sales?

# Exercises  Available with McGraw-Hill's Homework Manager

**E21-1 Analyzing Mixed Costs Using High-Low Method**                                      LO3
Valley Dental Services is a specialized dental practice whose only service is filling cavities. Valley has
identified the following monthly costs.

| Month | Number of Cavities Filled | Total Cost |
|---|---|---|
| January | 625 | $2,800 |
| February | 700 | 2,900 |
| March | 500 | 2,100 |
| April | 425 | 2,000 |
| May | 450 | 2,200 |
| June | 300 | 1,700 |
| July | 375 | 1,800 |
| August | 550 | 2,400 |
| September | 575 | 2,600 |

*Required:*

1.  Use the high-low method to estimate the cost formula. Using this formula, calculate Valley's total
    cost for filling 500 cavities.
2.  How closely does your estimate match the actual cost for March? Why would these be different?

**E21-2 Analyzing Mixed Costs Using Scattergraph Method**                                  LO2
Refer to the information in E21-1 regarding Valley Dental.

1.  Create a scattergraph using Valley's activity and cost information and draw a line on the graph
    that you believe has the best fit.
2.  Using this graph and best fitting line, estimate Valley Dental's total fixed cost.
3.  Does your visual fit line differ from the one calculated using the high-low method? If so, why?

**E21-3 Analyzing Mixed Costs Using High-Low Method and Scattergraph**                     LO2, 3
Aspen, Inc., manufactures one model of computer desk. The following data are available regarding units
shipped and total shipping costs.

| Month | Number of Units Shipped | Total Shipping Cost |
|---|---|---|
| January | 30 | $3,600 |
| February | 60 | 2,300 |
| March | 40 | 1,700 |
| April | 20 | 1,200 |
| May | 70 | 2,300 |
| June | 80 | 2,700 |
| July | 50 | 2,000 |

*Required:*

1. Prepare a scattergraph of Aspen's shipping cost and draw the line you believe best fits the data.
2. Based on this graph, estimate Aspen's total fixed shipping costs per month.
3. Using the high-low method, calculate Aspen's total fixed shipping costs and variable shipping cost per unit.

**LO1, 4**    **E21-4 Determining Cost Behavior and Preparing Contribution Margin Income Statement**

Paddle Away, Inc., makes one model of wooden canoe. Partial information for it follows.

| | 450 | 600 | 750 |
|---|---|---|---|
| Number of canoes produced and sold | 450 | 600 | 750 |
| Total costs | | | |
| Variable costs | $ 67,500 | ? | ? |
| Fixed costs | 150,000 | ? | ? |
| Total costs | $217,500 | ? | ? |
| Cost per unit | | | |
| Variable cost per unit | ? | ? | ? |
| Fixed cost per unit | ? | ? | ? |
| Total cost per unit | ? | ? | ? |

*Required:*

1. Complete the preceding table.
2. Identify three costs that would be classified as fixed costs and three variable costs for Paddle Away.
3. Suppose Paddle Away sells its canoes for $500 each. Calculate the contribution margin per canoe and the contribution margin ratio.
4. This year Paddle Away expects to sell 800 canoes. Prepare a contribution margin income statement for the company.

**LO5**    **E21- 5 Identifying Break-Even Point and Margin of Safety**

Refer to the information in E21-4 regarding Paddle Away.

*Required:*

1. Calculate Paddle Away's break-even point in units and in sales dollars.
2. If Paddle Away sells 650 canoes, compute its margin of safety in units and as a percentage of sales.

**LO3, 4, 5**    **E21-6 Analyzing Break Even and Preparing Contribution Margin Income Statement**

Cory Bryant runs a courier service in downtown Phoenix. He charges clients $0.50 per mile driven. Cory has determined that if he drives 3,000 miles in a month, his total operating cost is $875. If he drives 4,000 miles in a month, his total operating cost is $1,025.

*Required:*

1. Using the high-low method, determine Cory's variable and fixed operating cost components. Show this as a cost formula.
2. Determine how many miles Cory will need to drive to break even.
3. Prepare a contribution margin income statement for Cory assuming he drove 2,400 miles last month.

**LO5, 6**    **E21-7 Analyzing Break-Even Point and Preparing CVP Graph**

Peggy's Ribbon World makes award rosettes. Following is information about the company.

| | |
|---|---|
| Variable cost per rosette | $ 1.10 |
| Sales price per rosette | 2.50 |
| Total fixed costs per month | 889.00 |

*Required:*

1. Determine how many rosettes Peggy must sell to break even.
2. Calculate the break-even point in sales dollars.
3. Prepare a CVP graph for Peggy assuming the relevant range is zero to 1,500 rosettes.

### E21-8 Identifying Target Profit and Margin of Safety                LO6

Refer to the information regarding Peggy's Ribbon World in E21-7.

*Required:*

1. Suppose Peggy would like to generate a profit of $800. Determine how many rosettes she must sell to achieve this target profit.
2. If Peggy sells 1,100 rosettes, compute her margin of safety in units, in sales dollers, and as a percentage of sales.

### E21-9 (Supplement) Comparing Full Absorption Costing and Variable Costing

The following information pertains to Sonic Boom Radios, Inc. for its first year of operation:

| | |
|---|---:|
| Number of units produced | 3,000 |
| Number of units sold | 2,500 |
| Unit sales price | $ 350 |
| Direct materials per unit | 70 |
| Direct labor per unit | 60 |
| Variable manufacturing overhead | 10 |
| Fixed manufacturing overhead ($225,000/3,000 units) | 75 |
| Variable selling expenses ($15/unit sold) | 37,500 |
| Fixed general and administrative expenses | 65,000 |

*Required:*

Prepare Sonic Boom's full absorption costing income statement and variable costing income statement for the year.

## Problems—Set A  Available with McGraw-Hill's Homework Manager

### PA21-1 Analyzing Mixed Costs, Using High-Low Method, Preparing a Contribution Margin     LO3, 4, 5, 6
Income Statement, Analyzing Break-Even Point, and Setting Target Profit

Fred Carson delivers parts for several local auto parts stores. He charges clients $0.75 per mile driven. Fred has determined that if he drives 2,000 miles in a month, his average operating cost is $0.55 per mile. If he drives 4,000 miles in a month, his average operating cost is $0.40 per mile.

*Required:*

1. Using the high-low method, determine Fred's variable and fixed operating cost components. Show this as a cost formula.
2. Determine how many miles Fred will need to drive to break even.
3. Assume Fred drove 1,500 miles last month. Without making any additional calculations, determine whether he earned a profit or a loss last month.
4. Prepare a contribution margin income statement for Fred's business last month.
5. If Fred wants to earn $1,000 a month, determine how many miles he must drive.

### PA21-2 Preparing a Contribution Margin Income Statement and Analyzing Break-Even Point     LO1, 4, 5

Simpson Company produces one model of golf cart. A partially complete table of company costs follows.

| | 600 | 800 | 1,000 |
|---|---:|---:|---:|
| Number of golf carts produced and sold | 600 | 800 | 1,000 |
| Total costs | | | |
|   Variable costs | $  ? | $400,000 | $  ? |
|   Fixed costs per year | ? | 500,000 | ? |
|   Total costs | ? | $900,000 | ? |
| Cost per unit | | | |
|   Variable cost per unit | ? | ? | ? |
|   Fixed cost per unit | ? | ? | ? |
|   Total cost per unit | ? | ? | ? |

*Required:*

1. Complete the table.
2. Simpson sells its carts for $1,200 each. Prepare a contribution margin income statement for each of the three production levels given in the table.
3. Based on these three statements (and without any additional calculations), estimate Simpson's break-even point in units.
4. Calculate Simpson's break-even point in number of units and in sales dollars.
5. Assume Simpson sold 700 carts last year. Without performing any calculations: determine whether Simpson earned a profit last year.

**LO4, 5, 6**

**PA21-3 Preparing a CVP Graph and Calculating Contribution Margin, Contribution Margin Ratio, and Break-Even Point**

Cardinal Castles, Inc. makes one type of birdhouse that it sells for $30 each. Its variable cost is $14 per house, and its fixed costs total $13,840 per year. Cardinal currently has the capacity to produce up to 2,000 birdhouses per year, so its relevant range is zero to 2,000 houses.

*Required:*

1. Prepare a contribution margin income statement for Cardinal assuming it sells 1,100 birdhouses this year.
2. Without any calculations, determine Cardinal's total contribution margin if the company breaks even.
3. Calculate Cardinal's contribution margin per unit and its contribution margin ratio.
4. Calculate Cardinal's break-even point in number of units and in sales dollars.
5. Suppose Cardinal wants to earn $20,000 this year. Determine how many birdhouses it must sell to generate this amount of profit. Is this possible?
6. Prepare a cost-volume-profit graph for Cardinal including lines for both total cost and sales revenue. Clearly identify fixed cost and the break-even point on your graph.

**LO1, 5**

www.mhhe.com/LLPW1e

**PA21-4 Calculating Contribution Margin, Contribution Margin Ratio, and Break-Even Point**

Overhill, Inc. produces one model of mountain bike. Partial information for the company follows.

| | 500 | 800 | 1,000 |
|---|---|---|---|
| Number of bikes produced and sold | 500 | 800 | 1,000 |
| Total costs | | | |
| Variable costs | $125,000 | $ ? | $ ? |
| Fixed costs per year | ? | ? | ? |
| Total costs | ? | ? | ? |
| Cost per unit | | | |
| Variable cost per unit | ? | ? | ? |
| Fixed cost per unit | ? | ? | ? |
| Total cost per unit | ? | $543.75 | ? |

*Required:*

1. Complete the table.
2. Calculate Overhill's contribution margin ratio and its total contribution margin at each sales level indicated in the table assuming the company sells each bike for $650.
3. Consider the contribution margins just calculated and total fixed costs. Determine whether Overhill's break-even point will be more or less than 500 units and 800 units.
4. Calculate Overhill's break-even point in units and sales dollars.

www.mhhe.com/LLPW1e

**PA21-5 (Supplement) Determining Income Using Variable Costing**

Refer to the information for Overhill, Inc., in PA21-4. Additional information available for Overhill's first year of operations follows.

| | |
|---|---:|
| Number of units produced | 2,000 |
| Number of units sold | 1,300 |
| Sales price per unit | $  650.00 |
| Direct materials per unit | 110.00 |
| Direct labor per unit | 90.00 |
| Variable manufacturing overhead | 40.00 |
| Fixed manufacturing overhead ($235,000/2,000 units) | 117.50 |
| Variable selling expenses ($10 per unit sold) | 13,000.00 |
| Fixed general and administrative expenses | 70,000.00 |

*Required:*

1.  Consider the computations performed in PA21-4 (and without further calculation). Explain whether Overhill earned a profit during its first year of operations.

2.  Did Overhill's inventory increase or decrease last year? Without any calculation, explain whether Overhill's income will be higher with full absorption costing or variable costing.

3.  Prepare a full absorption costing income statement and a variable costing income statement for Overhill.

4.  Compute the difference in profit between full absorption costing and variable costing. Explain what is causing the difference.

# Problems—Set B  Available with McGraw-Hill's Homework Manager

## PB21-1 Analyzing Mixed Costs Using High-Low Method, Preparing a Contribution Margin Income Statement, Analyzing Break-Even Point, and Setting Target Profit

LO3, 4, 5

Tina Sutton delivers flowers for several local flower stores. She charges clients $0.85 per mile driven. Tina has determined that if she drives 1,200 miles in a month, her average operating cost is $0.70 per mile. If she drives 2,000 miles in a month, her average operating cost is $0.60 per mile.

*Required:*

1.  Using the high-low method, determine Tina's variable and fixed operating cost components. Show this as a cost formula.

2.  Determine how many miles Tina will need to drive to break even.

3.  Assume Tina drove 900 miles last month. Without making any additional calculations, determine whether she earned a profit or a loss last month.

4.  Prepare a contribution margin income statement for Tina's business last month.

5.  If Tina wants to earn $800 a month, determine how many miles she must drive.

## PB21-2 Preparing a Contribution Margin Income Statement and Analyzing Break-Even Point

LO1, 4, 5

StaySafe Company produces one model of security door. A partially complete table of company costs follows.

| | 400 | 500 | 700 |
|---|---:|---:|---:|
| Number of doors produced and sold | 400 | 500 | 700 |
| Total costs | | | |
| Variable costs | $30,000 | $  ? | $  ? |
| Fixed costs per year | 65,000 | ? | ? |
| Total costs | 95,000 | ? | ? |
| Cost per unit | | | |
| Variable cost per unit | ? | ? | ? |
| Fixed cost per unit | ? | ? | ? |
| Total cost per unit | ? | ? | ? |

*Required:*

1. Complete the table.
2. StaySafe sells its doors for $200 each. Prepare a contribution margin income statement for each of the three production levels in the table.
3. Based on these three statements (and without any additional calculations), estimate StaySafe's break-even point in units.
4. Calculate Staysafe's break-even point in number of units and in sales dollars.
5. Assume StaySafe sold 600 doors last year. Without performing any calculations, determine whether StaySafe earned a profit last year.

**LO4, 5, 6**

**PB21-3 Preparing a CVP Graph and Calculating Contribution Margin, Contribution Margin Ratio and Break-Even Point**

Hot Dog, Inc. makes one type of doggie sweater that it sells for $25 each. Its variable cost is $11 per sweater and its fixed costs total $8,600 per year. Hot Dog currently has the capacity to produce up to 1,000 sweaters per year, so its relevant range is zero to 1,000 sweaters.

*Required:*

1. Prepare a contribution margin income statement for Hot Dog assuming it sells 600 sweaters this year.
2. Without any calculations, determine Hot Dog's total contribution margin if the company breaks even.
3. Calculate Hot Dog's contribution margin per unit and its contribution margin ratio.
4. Calculate Hot Dog's break-even point in number of units and in sales dollars.
5. Suppose Hot Dog wants to earn $3,000 this year. Determine how many sweaters it must sell to generate this amount of profit. Is this possible?
6. Prepare a cost-volume-profit graph for Hot Dog including lines for both total cost and sales revenue. Clearly identify fixed cost and the break-even point on your graph.

**LO1, 5**

**PB21-4 Calculating Contribution Margin, Contribution Margin Ratio and Break-Even Point**

CoverUp, Inc. produces one model of seatcover. Partial information for the company follows:

| | | | |
|---|---|---|---|
| Number of seatcovers produced and sold | 1,500 | 1,700 | 2,100 |
| Total costs | | | |
| Variable costs | $? | $? | $15,750 |
| Fixed costs per year | ? | ? | ? |
| Total costs | ? | ? | ? |
| Cost per unit | | | |
| Variable cost per unit | ? | ? | ? |
| Fixed cost per unit | ? | ? | ? |
| Total cost per unit | $31.00 | ? | ? |

*Required:*

1. Complete the table.
2. Calculate CoverUp's contribution margin ratio and its total contribution margin at each sales level indicated in the table assuming the company sells each seatcover for $30.
3. Consider the contribution margins just calculated and total fixed costs for the company. Determine whether CoverUp's break-even point will be more or less than 1,500 units and 1,700 units.
4. Calculate CoverUp's break-even point in units and sales dollar.

**PB21-5 (Supplement) Determining Variable Costing**

Refer to the information for CoverUp in PB21-4. Additional information available for CoverUp's most recent year of operation follows.

| Number of units produced | | 3,000 |
|---|---|---|
| Number of units sold | | 2,800 |
| Sales price per unit | $ | 30.00 |
| Direct materials per unit | | 3.00 |
| Direct labor per unit | | 2.00 |
| Variable manufacturing overhead | | 1.50 |
| Fixed manufacturing overhead ($15,000/3,000 units) | | 5.00 |
| Variable selling expenses ($1 per unit sold) | | 2,800.00 |
| Fixed general and administrative expenses | | 20,250.00 |

*Required:*

1. Consider the computations performed in PB21-4 and without further calculation, explain whether CoverUp earned a profit during its first year of operations.

2. Did CoverUp's inventory increase or decrease last year? Without any calculation, explain whether CoverUp's income will be higher with full absorption costing or variable costing.

3. Prepare a full absorption costing income statement and a variable costing income statement for CoverUp.

4. Compute the difference in profit between full absorption costing and variable costing. Explain what is causing the difference.

# Cases & Projects

### CP21-1 Analyzing Cost Behavior and the Impact on Break-Even    LO1, 6

Ink Spot, Inc., is a new business located in upstate New York. It offers local businesses the service of printing and distributing promotional flyers at public places or events in the area. The flyers are either placed on the windshield of cars in parking lots or distributed by hand to people.

Ink Spot's owner, Dana Everhart, is facing a difficult decision. She could purchase a commercial printer and produce the flyers in-house. However, the machinery, costing approximately $20,000, is quite expensive. The printer has an estimated useful life of four years and would be depreciated using the straight-line method with no salvage value. If Dana purchases the printer, she would also have to buy paper and toner for the machine and pay for maintenance or repairs as needed. She estimates that it would cost $0.02 per page to print the flyers herself.

Alternatively, Dana could pay a local printing company $0.05 per copy to print the flyers. She would not incur any printing costs in addition to the $0.05 per page if she chooses this alternative. However, $0.05 per page is considerably more than Dana would have to pay for paper and toner if she owned a commercial printer.

Dana plans to charge customers $0.08 per page for each flyer Ink Spot distributes.

*Required:*

1. Name at least three other costs (other than the cost of producing the flyers) that a business such as Ink Spot would incur and identify the cost behavior of each one.

2. Considering the decision Dana must make, determine the cost behavior of each alternative. For any mixed cost, determine the amount of each component as much as possible.

3. Discuss whether Dana's choice will impact the break-even point for Ink Spot. Why might this be important?

4. Discuss other factors about Ink Spot's operating environment that Dana should consider.

5. Discuss factors other than cost that Dana should consider.

### CP21-2 Evaluating the Effect of Decisions on Contribution Margin, Break-Even, and Margin of Safety    LO1, 5

Companies must make many decisions regarding day-to-day business activities. For each of the following decision-making situations, discuss the impact on a company's contribution margin (both total and per unit), break-even point, margin of safety, and ability to withstand fluctuation in product demand.

*Required:*

1. Whether to pay employees a fixed salary or an hourly wage.
2. Whether to pay commissions to salespeople.
3. Whether to purchase a building or rent space.
4. Whether to purchase component parts or manufacture them.
5. Whether to create its own delivery department (including the purchase and maintenance of delivery vehicles) or contract with a delivery company.

**LO1, 5**      **CP21-3 Researching the Cost of Operating a Vending Machine and Performing Cost-Volume-Profit Analysis**

Suppose that you have decided to start a small business selling snacks from vending machines. You have secured a location for one candy vending machine in a local bookstore. Rental for the space will cost $200 per month.

Vending machines can be purchased at wholesale clubs such as Sam's Club or Costco. You can also purchase the snacks to stock the machines in bulk at warehouse clubs.

*Required:*

1. Either visit a local warehouse club or review the club's Web site to determine the initial cost to purchase a snack vending machine.
2. Assume you are going to have only one type of snack bar in your machine initially. What type of snack bar will you choose? If you purchase the bars in bulk, what is your cost per bar?
3. How much will you charge for each bar sold?
4. What is your contribution margin per bar? How many bars must you sell to cover the cost of the vending machine?
5. Once you have covered the initial investment, what is the monthly break-even point in number of bars? In sales dollars?
6. Repeat requirements 2–5 assuming you decided to have a drink vending machine instead of a snack machine. Remember to look up the price for a beverage vending machine. You may assume rental for the vending machine space is $200 per month regardless of its type.

**LO1, 5, 6**      **CP21-4 Researching a Company Web Site and Performing Cost-Volume-Profit Analysis**

Pink Jeep Tours offers off-road tours to individuals and groups visiting the Southwestern U.S. hotspots of Sedona, Arizona, and Las Vegas, Nevada. Take a tour of the company's Web site at www.pinkjeep.com. Suppose you are a manager for the Pink Jeep office in Sedona. From the company Web site, choose two tours offered in Sedona. One tour should last all day and the other should be a shorter tour of 2–4 hours.

For the following requirements, assume that each Jeep tour has four adult passengers plus a tour guide.

*Required:*

1. Make a list of the various costs Pink Jeep would incur to offer each tour. Indicate whether each cost identified is variable, fixed, or mixed based on the number of tours offered.
2. Briefly research each cost listed in requirement 1 and estimate its amount. Estimate variable costs on a per Jeep tour basis and fixed costs on a monthly basis. Break any mixed cost into variable and fixed components. State any assumptions that you must make when estimating these costs (and be aware that many assumptions must be made).
3. What is Pink Jeep's total variable cost for each tour? Does this cost differ for each type of tour? Explain.
4. Using the current tour prices listed on Pink Jeep's Web site, determine the contribution margin per Jeep tour for each tour type.
5. Assume Pink Jeep ran **only** the all-day excursion tour in the month of August. In this case, how many tours must the company complete to break even?
6. Assume Pink Jeep ran **only** the shorter tour during August. In this case, how many tours must the company complete to earn $30,000 in profit for the month?

# 22 Incremental Analysis and Capital Budgeting

## LEARNING OBJECTIVES

**After completing this chapter, you should be able to:**

**LO1** Describe the five steps in the decision-making process.

**LO2** Define and identify relevant costs and benefits.

**LO3** Use incremental analysis to analyze the following managerial decisions:
   a. Special-order decisions.
   b. Make-or-buy decisions.
   c. Keep-or-drop decisions.
   d. Sell-or-process further decisions.

**LO4** Analyze investment decisions using the following capital budgeting techniques:
   a. Accounting rate of return.
   b. Payback period.
   c. Net present value.
   d. Internal rate of return.

Lectured presentation–LP22-1
www.mhhe.com/LLPW1e

# Focus Company: MATTEL TOYS

## "The World's Premier Toy Brands"

I n 1945, two friends named Matt and Elliot combined their names, money, and artistic skills to form a company called Mattel. They started out producing picture frames but quickly expanded into dollhouse furniture. Matt soon left the business and Elliot's wife, Ruth, joined the management team. Based on their early success with the dollhouse furniture, Elliot and Ruth decided to focus Mattel's efforts on the production and sale of toys.

After more than a decade of satisfactory but not stellar performance, Mattel struck it big in 1959 with the introduction of Barbie, a doll named after Ruth and Elliot's own daughter Barbara. Since then, Barbie and her fabulous friends, clothes, and accessories have entertained generations of young girls and, no doubt a few boys.

Today, Mattel's success hinges on much more than Barbie dolls. The company has a huge portfolio of products for children of all ages, including Fisher Price toys, Matchbox cars and trucks, Hot Wheels, Mattel classic games, and American Girl dolls. Mattel has also had its share of controversy over the years, including critics who question whether Barbie is an appropriate role model for young girls. More recently, Mattel experienced a wave of bad press when it recalled millions of toys that were manufactured in China and contained toxic levels of lead-based paint.

This chapter discusses how managers at Mattel use managerial accounting information to make both short- and long-term business decisions such as:

- Whether to accept an order from a large university to produce a special Barbie doll who wears the school logo and colors.
- Whether to make or buy the packaging materials for the American Girl doll collection.
- Whether to discontinue one of the Power Wheels products.
- Whether to add more features to a remote control toy.
- Whether to invest in a children's MP3 product that would allow parents to download children's books, music, and educational materials from Mattel's Web site.

To make these decisions, we use two different decision-making approaches. The first, incremental analysis, is a short-term analysis that compares the costs and benefits of different decision alternatives. The second technique, capital budgeting, is a long-term decision-making framework to help managers make decisions about the investment of assets. Although we will use fictitious scenarios and numbers to illustrate these techniques, we make them as realistic as possible to illustrate how Mattel's managers might approach these and other decisions.

Before we dive into these two topics, let's first discuss the decision-making process and some basic principles that apply to making any decision.

## ORGANIZATION OF THE CHAPTER

| MANAGERIAL DECISION-MAKING PROCESS | RELEVANT VERSUS IRRELEVANT COSTS AND BENEFITS | INCREMENTAL ANALYSIS OF SHORT-TERM DECISIONS | CAPITAL BUDGETING FOR LONG-TERM INVESTMENT DECISIONS |
|---|---|---|---|
| • Step 1: Identify the Decision Problem<br>• Step 2: Determine the Decision Alternatives<br>• Step 3: Evaluate the Costs and Benefits of the Alternatives<br>• Step 4: Make the Decision<br>• Step 5: Review the Results of the Decision-Making Process | • Relevant Costs<br>• Irrelevant Costs | • Special-Order Decisions<br>• Make-or-Buy Decisions<br>• Keep-or-Drop Decisions<br>• Sell-or-Process Further Decisions | • Nondiscounting Methods<br>• Discounted Cash Flow Methods |

# MANAGERIAL DECISION-MAKING PROCESS

The managerial decision-making process has five basic steps (see Exhibit 22.1).

## Step 1: Identify the Decision Problem

The first step in the decision-making process is to identify the decision problem. See Exhibit 22.2 for a description of a decision problem that you may have encountered yourself: deciding where to live. You can apply the same type of decision analysis to many other personal decisions, such as deciding where to go to college or what kind of vehicle to buy. Later in this chapter, we apply a similar process to a variety of problems that managers face in the business world.

## Step 2: Determine the Decision Alternatives

Once managers have identified the problem, the next step is to determine the possible solutions to the problem, called decision alternatives. This is a critical step because the remainder of the decision process hinges on the decision alternatives identified here. If a potential alternative

**Exhibit 22.1    Managerial Decision-Making Process**

| Step 1:<br>Identify the decision problem | → | Step 2:<br>Determine the decision alternatives | → | Step 3:<br>Evaluate the costs and benefits of the alternatives | → | Step 4:<br>Make the decision | → | Step 5:<br>Review the results of the decision-making process |

Improve future decisions

is not included in this initial stage, it will not be included in the later phases of the analysis. The housing decision described in Exhibit 22.2 identified two potential decision alternatives: lease a house with two roommates or rent a one-bedroom apartment on your own. We have eliminated other potential alternatives such as living with parents or buying your own home; thus, these alternatives will not be considered in the analysis.

## Step 3: Evaluate the Costs and Benefits of the Alternatives

Our primary focus in this chapter is the third step of the decision process, which involves comparing the costs and benefits of the decision alternatives identified in Step 2. For decision making, we consider only those costs and benefits that differ between alternatives, an approach called incremental analysis or **differential analysis**. This approach is sometimes called relevant costing because it focuses only on those costs (and benefits) that are relevant to the decision to be made. The identification of relevant costs and benefits are discussed in more detail shortly.

## Step 4: Make the Decision

Once managers have evaluated the costs and benefits of the decision alternatives, they are ready to make the decision. However, they will probably not base it strictly on the numerical analysis performed in Step 3. Managers should incorporate a variety of other factors, such

| Exhibit 22.2 | Application of the Five-Step Managerial Decision-Making Process to a Personal Decision |
|---|---|
| **Step 1: Identify the decision problem.** | Your freshman year living in the dorm is almost up and you must decide where you are going to live next year. |
| **Step 2: Determine the decision alternatives.** | You narrowed it down to two options:<br>• Lease a 3-bedroom house with two roommates.<br>• Lease a 1-bedroom apartment. |
| **Step 3: Evaluate the costs and benefits of the alternatives.** | After doing some research, you have gathered the following information.<br>• The rent on the house is $1,800 per month ($600 per person). The rent on the apartment is $800 per month. Thus, sharing the house is $200 per month less expensive assuming you can find two roommates.<br>• The monthly utility bills at the house are $450 ($150 per person). The monthly utilities at the apartment are $150. Because the cost to you is the same, it is not relevant to your decision, and you can ignore it.<br>• Advertising in the student paper for two new roommates would cost you about $50.<br>• The apartment is near the campus so you could bike to school. You estimate your monthly savings on fuel and parking to be about $75 per month.<br>• The house is large and has a great backyard, but you are tired of sharing space with loud, messy roommates. You think you would enjoy the one-bedroom apartment, especially for studying and quiet entertaining.<br><br>In summary,<br>• The house is the less expensive alternative by about $125 per month ($200 in rent savings less $75 in additional vehicle expenses per month). However, you would need to spend some money ($50) to find new roommates.<br>• The one-bedroom apartment has certain advantages that are more difficult to quantify (it is close to campus and very quiet). |
| **Step 4: Make the decision.** | You will have to make a trade-off between the cost advantages of the house and the qualitative advantages of the one-bedroom apartment. Let's assume you are on a very tight budget and have decided to sign the lease on the house and begin the search for new roommates. |
| **Step 5: Review the results of the decision-making process.** | Looking back on the outcome, you will later determine whether your decision was a good one. If you were unable to find two good roommates, the decision may prove to be a bad one. If you find that your roommates are great and will become lifelong friends, your decision was a good one. Either way, you are likely to learn something that will affect the way you make similar decisions in the future. |

as strategic issues, quality considerations, legal and ethical issues, and the like. For all of the decisions that we analyze throughout this chapter, we first perform a numerical or quantitative analysis to determine which alternative is "best" based strictly on the numbers. We then discuss what qualitative factors might come into play to influence managers' decisions. For example, in the housing scenario illustrated in Exhibit 22.2, the numeric analysis showed that sharing a house with two roommates was the least costly alternative (by about $125 per month). However, the apartment may have other advantages (such as privacy and quiet) that might influence your decision about which housing alternative to choose.

## Step 5: Review the Results of the Decision-Making Process

Once managers make the decision based on the relevant costs and benefits identified in Step 3 as well as any additional qualitative factors in Step 4, the managers will eventually need to review the results of the decision-making process to determine whether they made the correct decision, or did not make the correct decision and should use a different decision-making approach in the future. The role of managerial accounting in helping managers evaluate performance to improve future decisions is discussed in detail in Chapters 24 and 25.

# RELEVANT VERSUS IRRELEVANT COSTS AND BENEFITS

Most of our attention throughout the remainder of this chapter focuses on the third step of the decision-making process, which involves comparing the costs and benefits of the decision alternatives. In particular, we want to compare only those costs and benefits that are **relevant** to the decision being made. Although the decision-making process should include consideration of both costs and benefits, our examples focus primarily on the **cost** side of the process. As you will see shortly, not all costs are relevant to a particular decision. Benefits are also incorporated only when they are relevant to the particular decision.

## Relevant Costs

> **Learning Objective 2**
>
> Define and identify relevant costs and benefits.

A relevant cost is one that will change depending on which alternative a manager selects. Costs that differ between alternatives are also called differential costs or incremental costs. In Exhibit 22.2, the difference in monthly rent between the house and the apartment was $200. This cost was relevant to the decision of whether to rent the house or the apartment.

Another term for relevant cost is avoidable cost—that is, a cost the manager can avoid by choosing one alternative instead of another. In Exhibit 22.2, the costs of fuel and on-campus parking could be avoided if you lived in an apartment near campus and could ride your bike to class. This cost was relevant to the decision because it differed between the two alternatives.

Managers must also identify any opportunity costs that are relevant to the decision. Recall from Chapter 18 that an opportunity cost is a benefit that you give up when you choose one alternative over another. Although opportunity costs are relevant for decision making, they are often difficult to estimate and measure because they are associated with the "path not taken." Whenever possible, however, managers should include opportunity costs in their analyses.

## Irrelevant Costs

Irrelevant costs are those that do not differ between alternatives. Two types of cost do not change depending on the alternative selected, and should therefore be ignored:

- **Costs that have already been incurred, called** sunk costs. Because these costs have already been spent (that is, they are sunk), they will not change depending on which alternative the manager selects.

- **Costs that are the same regardless of the alternative the manager chooses.** In Exhibit 22.2, the monthly utility costs were the same regardless of whether you share the rental house or rent the apartment. You ignored that cost because it did not differ between the alternatives. In other words, it was an irrelevant cost.

Next we apply the concept of relevant costs, or incremental analysis, to Mattel, the world's leading toy company. First make sure that you understand the decision-making process and can correctly identify relevant costs by completing the following Self-Study Practice.

**SELF-STUDY PRACTICE**

1. Which of the following steps in the decision-making process are out of sequence?
   a. Identify the decision problem.
   b. Evaluate the costs and benefits of the alternatives.
   c. Determine the decision alternatives.
   d. Make the decision.
   e. Review the results of the decision-making process.

2. Which of the following costs would **not** be relevant to the decision of whether to take the bus or drive your vehicle to school for a semester? Assume that you will continue to own your vehicle under either alternative.
   a. The cost of the fuel you use driving to and from campus.
   b. The cost of on-campus parking.
   c. The wear and tear on your vehicle due to the extra mileage.
   d. The time you could spend studying while traveling on the bus instead of driving to school.
   e. The monthly cost of liability insurance on your vehicle.

*After you have finished, check your answers with the solutions at the bottom of the page.*

# INCREMENTAL ANALYSIS OF SHORT-TERM DECISIONS

In this section, we illustrate how to use incremental analysis to make four common business decisions: special-order, make-or-buy, keep-or-drop, and sell or process further decisions. In the real world, the specific decisions managers need to make depend on a variety of factors, such as the type of business they are running, their level of responsibility, and the particular problems they are trying to solve. Nevertheless, the approach we use to address these problems can be applied to many other short-term managerial decisions.

## Special-Order Decisions

Managers must often decide whether to accept or reject an order that is outside the scope of normal sales. These so-called one-time or special orders often carry a lower sales price than the normal sales price of the product or service. The decision that managers must make is whether to accept or reject the offer. We can analyze this decision by comparing the incremental costs to the incremental benefits (revenue) of the special order.

As an example, assume that a major university has asked Mattel to produce a special **University Barbie** dressed in a sporty outfit and carrying a backpack with the school's logo and colors. The university bookstore has offered to buy 25,000 of these dolls at a price of $7 each,

Video 22-1
www.mhhe.com/LLPW1e

**Learning Objective 3a**

Use incremental analysis to analyze special-order decisions.

Solution to
Self-Study Practice

1. b and c are reversed.
2. e.

which it would then sell in the bookstore and in alumni catalogues for a retail price of $15 each. Mattel has the capacity to fill the order without affecting production of other Barbie products, which are normally sold to toy stores and discount chains for about $9 each. Assume the estimated cost to produce the University Barbie is as follows:

|  | Unit Cost |
|---|---|
| Direct materials (silicone rubber, clothing, accessories) | $3.50 |
| Direct labor | 1.00 |
| Variable manufacturing overhead (indirect materials, power, etc.) | 0.50 |
| Fixed manufacturing overhead (factory rent, insurance, etc.) | 2.50 |
| Total manufacturing cost | $7.50 |

At first glance, it appears that Mattel should reject the offer because the $7.00 price is less than the $7.50 it will cost to make the University Barbie. But is that analysis correct?

Recall the relevant cost concept. Will **all** of the company's costs change if Mattel accepts the special order? To answer this question, we need to perform an incremental analysis below:

## Quantitative Analysis

The incremental analysis of Mattel's special order decision is shown below:

### Incremental Analysis of the Special Order for 25,000 University Barbie Dolls

|  | Per Unit | Total |
|---|---|---|
| Incremental revenue | $7.00 | $175,000 |
| Less: Incremental costs |  |  |
| Direct materials | 3.50 | 87,500 |
| Direct labor | 1.00 | 25,000 |
| Variable overhead | 0.50 | 12,500 |
| Fixed overhead | — | — |
| Total incremental cost | 5.00 | 125,000 |
| Incremental profit | $2.00 | $ 50,000 |

Notice that this incremental analysis does not include fixed manufacturing overhead costs. The reason these costs have been excluded is that fixed costs such as rent, insurance, and supervision will be incurred regardless of whether Mattel accepts the special order. Because the special order does not cause total fixed costs to increase, only the variable costs of producing the University Barbie are relevant. Compared to the special order price of $7, the $5 in variable cost per unit means that each Barbie sold would generate $2 in incremental profit, or a total of $50,000 in added profit.

## Qualitative Analysis

Two important cautions should be kept in mind in doing this type of short-term analysis. First, this analysis is valid only for one-time or special orders. Managers would not want to use this type of analysis to make long-term pricing decisions because in the long run, prices must cover

**Coach's Tip**

A key assumption in analyzing special orders is that it will not affect the production and sale of units that are sold through regular channels. That means the company must have the extra capacity (in terms of machines, people, etc.) to fill the special order without disrupting normal operations.

**Coach's Tip**

Fixed costs are excluded from the incremental analysis because they will be incurred regardless of whether the company accepts the special order. In the short term, fixed costs will not change, so any price that exceeds the variable costs of production will yield an incremental profit.

all costs, including fixed costs, if the company is to be profitable. They would also want to consider whether accepting the special order would have any effect on the price that regular customers are willing to pay for sales made through regular channels.

Second, this analysis is valid only if the company has excess, or idle, production capacity. If the company does not have the capacity to fill the order, it must either incur additional fixed costs (by renting more factory space, machines, etc.) or reduce the production and sale of other products, which would create an opportunity cost. Either way, the company would incur additional incremental costs that may make the special order unprofitable.

Before we discuss make-or-buy decisions, complete the following Self-Study Practice to make sure you understand how to analyze special-order decisions.

**SELF-STUDY PRACTICE**

Big Top Tent Company has received a special order for 10,000 units of its product at a discounted price of $100. The product, which normally sells for $150, has the following manufacturing costs.

|  | Cost per Unit |
|---|---|
| Direct materials | $ 40 |
| Direct labor | 20 |
| Variable manufacturing overhead | 20 |
| Fixed manufacturing overhead | 30 |
| Unit cost | $110 |

Assume Big Top has enough extra capacity to fill the order without affecting the production or sale of its product to regular customers. If Big Top accepts the offer, what effect will the order have on the company's short-term profit?

a. $100,000 increase
b. $100,000 decrease
c. $200,000 increase
d. $400,000 decrease

*After you have finished, check your answers with the solutions at the bottom of the page.*

# Make-or-Buy Decisions

The next managerial decision we analyze is whether to make certain parts of the product or provide a service in-house or to buy it from an outside supplier. Traditionally, these decisions have been called make-or-buy decisions, but more recently they have been referred to as insourcing versus outsourcing decisions.

In making this type of decision, we must compare the relevant costs of making a component or providing a service internally to the cost of buying it from an external supplier. To determine which costs to include in the analysis, we must again keep in mind the definition of a relevant cost. In other words, we want to include only those costs that will change depending on

**Learning Objective 3b**

Use incremental analysis to analyze make-or-buy decisions.

---

c.   ($100 price − $80 variable cost) = $20 incremental profit × 10,000 units = $200,000

Solution to
Self-Study Practice

whether we make the item internally or buy it from an outside supplier. In addition, we should consider whether we give up any opportunity or benefits by choosing to make something internally instead of buying it externally (or vice versa).

Assume, for example, Mattel's managers are trying to decide whether to package the company's toys in-house or to outsource the packaging process to an external supplier. The design, marketing, and production of appealing toys are Mattel's competitive strengths, so outsourcing less critical activities may make sense. To see how Mattel might approach this decision, consider the following scenario in which Mattel currently performs all packaging of the American Girl dolls internally. Assume Mattel produces a total of 200,000 American Girl dolls annually; cost data for the product line follow:

**Coach's Tip**

When you see fixed costs stated on a per unit basis, be careful. What really counts is the **total** fixed cost and whether that total cost will change depending on the decision.

### Internal Cost of Packaging
### 200,000 American Girl Dolls per Year

|  | Annual Cost | Cost per Unit |
| --- | --- | --- |
| Packaging materials (cardboard, plastic, etc.) | $300,000 | $1.50 |
| Packaging direct labor | 90,000 | 0.45 |
| Indirect materials (e.g., glue) | 60,000 | 0.30 |
| Packaging supervision | 50,000 | 0.25 |
| Other fixed manufacturing overhead | 200,000 | 1.00 |
| Total packaging cost | $700,000 | $3.50 |

Mattel has been negotiating with a reputable supplier to provide the packaging for the American Girl collection. After several discussions, the supplier has finally agreed to a price of $3 per unit for all packaging-related activities. The agreement includes a three-year contract for a minimum of 200,000 units per year. Should Mattel package the product internally or outsource this process to the supplier?

As you have seen, we cannot simply compare the internal cost of packaging of $3.50 per unit to the $3.00 price that the supplier will charge. Some of the costs included in the $3.50 per unit may not be relevant to the decision. We should also consider whether any opportunity costs are associated with continuing to package the product internally. After investigating the proposed agreement further, Mattel's managers learn the following:

| Information Gathered | Manager's Analysis |
| --- | --- |
| • All costs directly related to the packaging activities including all direct and indirect materials, labor, and supervision could be avoided. | • Because these costs can be avoided, they should be considered a relevant cost of internal packaging. |
| • Other total fixed manufacturing overhead costs would remain unchanged. | • Because these costs will be incurred under either alternative, they should be excluded from the analysis. |
| • The factory space now used for packaging the American Girl collection could be used to expand production of a popular product line. The expansion would generate an additional $150,000 in profit per year. | • Mattel will receive this benefit by outsourcing the packaging but not if they keep the packaging in-house. This amount can be considered a benefit of outsourcing or an opportunity cost of insourcing, but not both. |

## Quantitative Analysis

Based on this information and analysis, the incremental cost of making the packaging versus buying it would be as follows:

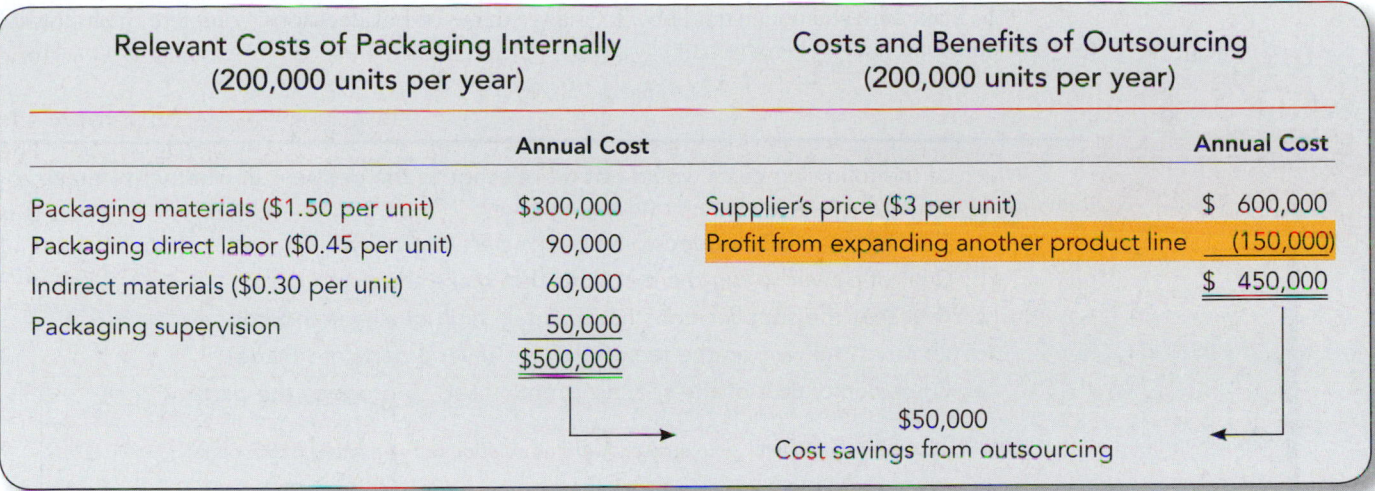

| Relevant Costs of Packaging Internally (200,000 units per year) | | Costs and Benefits of Outsourcing (200,000 units per year) | |
|---|---|---|---|
| | **Annual Cost** | | **Annual Cost** |
| Packaging materials ($1.50 per unit) | $300,000 | Supplier's price ($3 per unit) | $ 600,000 |
| Packaging direct labor ($0.45 per unit) | 90,000 | Profit from expanding another product line | (150,000) |
| Indirect materials ($0.30 per unit) | 60,000 | | $ 450,000 |
| Packaging supervision | 50,000 | | |
| | $500,000 | | |

$50,000
Cost savings from outsourcing

The quantitative analysis suggests that Mattel will save $50,000 per year by outsourcing the packaging to the external supplier.

## Qualitative Analysis

Of course, quantitative analysis has its limitations. Before making a final decision, Mattel's managers would want to consider other qualitative factors, such as the following:

- Will the quality of the packaging be as good as Mattel and its customers expect?
- Will the supplier be reliable in delivering the packaging?
- What will happen if demand for the product drops below 200,000 units or rises significantly higher than 200,000? Does the supplier have the capacity to meet the increased demand? Will the supplier charge a higher or lower price for the additional units?
- What will happen in three years? Will the price of packaging increase significantly? Going back to internal packaging would be difficult after the space has been converted for another purpose.
- What if the predicted profit from expanding the other product line has been substantially over- or underestimated?
- Does outsourcing the packaging create any additional risks, such as those described in the accompanying spotlight on business decisions?

## Spotlight On BUSINESS DECISIONS

### Mattel Becomes the Poster Child for the Dangers of Outsourcing to China

**Outsourcing** occurs when a company hires a third party to do part of its work. Often the third party is located in a foreign country, such as India or China, where labor is much less expensive.

Although many companies have recently started outsourcing to control costs, Mattel has been producing its toys overseas for almost 50 years. Most of its toys are produced in "company-owned" plants in China where Mattel can maintain strict quality standards. But the company also outsources production of some toys to other Chinese manufacturers that may not maintain the same quality standards.

This decision came back to haunt Mattel in the fall of 2007 when the company was forced to recall millions of "toxic toys" that contained unsafe levels of lead-based paint. The costs to Mattel were high including consumer lawsuits, a drop in the company's stock price, sanctions by Congress, and a general loss in consumer and investor confidence.

The lesson is that outsourcing decisions must be made carefully and include an analysis of both the benefits and risks. Mattel's experience also highlights the need to build strict quality control standards into outsourcing agreements regardless of whether the outsourcing contract is with a company overseas or in the United States.

The New York Times, September 29, 2007
**Recalls Make Toy Shopping a Source of Anxiety**

**Mattel issues a third toy recall**
Los Angeles Times, September 5, 2007

St. Petersburg Times, August 15, 2007
**Lead scare crosses all lines**

Fisher-Price recalls 1M toys
CNN.com, August 1, 2007

To make sure you understand how to analyze make-or-buy decisions, complete the following self-study practice.

Which of the following costs would **not** be relevant to the decision of whether to make a part internally or buy it from an outside supplier?

   a. Cost of materials needed to make the part internally.

   b. Cost of power to run the machines that make the part.

   c. Fact that the supplier does not maintain high quality standards.

   d. Share of the rent on the factory (where several parts are made).

   e. Opportunity cost of the space currently used to produce the part.

*After you have finished, check your answers with the solution at the bottom of the page.*

## Keep-or-Drop Decisions

**Learning Objective 3c**

Use incremental analysis to analyze keep-or-drop decisions.

The next decision we consider is whether to continue or discontinue making a particular product or offering a specific service. Managers face this decision frequently, particularly when products and services are not generating as much profit as expected. Again, our approach determines which costs and benefits will change as a result of the decision. Because some of the costs of making a product or providing a service will be incurred regardless, we need to do an incremental analysis to determine the net effect on the bottom line.

Assume, for example, that Mattel has three versions of its Power-Wheels battery-powered vehicles sold under the Fisher Price brand. The hypothetical income statement in Exhibit 22.3 shows the revenues and costs for those product lines.

The company is considering eliminating the Barbie Ford Mustang product because it has shown a loss for the past few years.

**Exhibit 22.3    Segmented Income Statement for the Power Wheels Product Lines**

|  | Jeep Wrangler 4 × 4 | Barbie Ford Mustang | Dora the Explorer Jeep | Total |
|---|---|---|---|---|
| Sales revenue | $500,000 | $ 150,000 | $350,000 | $1,000,000 |
| Variable costs | 200,000 | 100,000 | 140,000 | 440,000 |
| Contribution margin | 300,000 | 50,000 | 210,000 | 560,000 |
| Fixed costs* | 200,000 | 60,000 | 140,000 | 400,000 |
| Profit margin | $100,000 | $ (10,000) | $ 70,000 | $ 160,000 |

*Fixed costs are allocated based on total sales dollars.

### Quantitative Analysis

What effect would the elimination of the Barbie Ford Mustang product have on the company's overall profitability? To answer this question, assume that managers have gathered the following additional information:

d    (The rent on the factory will remain unchanged and is therefore irrelevant.)

| Information Gathered | Manager's Analysis | Differential Profit |
|---|---|---|
| Elimination of the Barbie Ford Mustang will reduce the revenue and variable costs that are directly attributable to this individual product line. | Lost sales = $(150,000) <br> Reduced costs = $100,000 <br> Lost contribution margin = ($50,000) | $(50,000) |
| Elimination of the Barbie Ford Mustang will increase sales of the Dora the Explorer Jeep by 20% with no effect on the Jeep 4 × 4. | Increased sales from the Dora line: <br> $350,000 × 20% = $70,000 | 70,000 |
| Total variable costs of the Dora the Explorer Jeep will increase as a result of the increased sales. Variable costs of the Dora Jeep are 40% of sales. | Increased variable costs of the Dora line: $70,000 × 40% = $28,000 | (28,000) |
| Total fixed costs will not be affected by the elimination of the Barbie Ford Mustang. They will be reallocated to the remaining products based on total sales dollars. | Because the total cost will not change, it is not relevant to the decision. | — |
| Overall effect on profit of dropping the Barbie Ford Mustang: | | $(8,000) |

This differential analysis suggests that dropping the Barbie Ford Mustang will reduce Mattel's profit by $8,000. To confirm that the analysis is correct, we can recreate the income statement in Exhibit 22.3 without the Barbie Ford Mustang (see Exhibit 22.4). Notice that this new statement shows a profit of $152,000, which is $8,000 less than the company earned with the Barbie Ford Mustang line. The reason for the reduction in profit is that the elimination of the Barbie Ford Mustang reduced the overall contribution margin. However, the total fixed costs did not change with the elimination of the Barbie Ford Mustang. Instead, these costs were simply reallocated to the two remaining product lines:

**Exhibit 22.4    Segmented Income Statement for the Power Wheel Product Lines after Elimination of the Barbie Ford Mustang**

| | Jeep Wrangler 4 × 4 | Dora the Explorer Jeep | Total after Elimination of Barbie Ford Mustang | Total before Elimination of Barbie Ford Mustang |
|---|---|---|---|---|
| Sales revenue | $500,000 | $ 420,000  (350,000 × 120%) | $920,000 | $1,000,000 |
| Variable costs | 200,000 | 168,000  (420,000 × 40%) | 368,000 | 440,000 |
| Contribution margin | 300,000 | 252,000 | 552,000 | 560,000 |
| Fixed costs* | 216,000 | 184,000 | 400,000 | 400,000 |
| Profit margin | $ 84,000 | $ 68,000 | $152,000 | $160,000 |

*Fixed costs were reallocated based on the new sales revenue of the remaining products

$8,000 Reduction in Profit from Elimination of the Barbie Ford Mustang

## Qualitative Analysis

As always, short-term quantitative analysis has its limitations, including these:

- What if the expected increase in sales of the Dora the Explorer product line has been underestimated?
- Will the elimination of the Barbie Ford Mustang free up resources (people, space, or machines) that could be used in another way?
- Can the company introduce another product that will yield more than $8,000 in incremental profit?
- Are there any other opportunity costs associated with keeping the Barbie Ford Mustang?

Before we continue, complete the following Self-Study Practice to make sure you can analyze keep-or-drop decisions correctly.

**SELF-STUDY PRACTICE**

Big Top Tent Company is trying to decide whether to keep or drop one of its outdoor wedding tents. The company's segmented income statement shows that this product is generating a net loss, as follows:

|  | Total |
| --- | --- |
| Sales | $100,000 |
| Variable cost (canvas, ropes, and direct labor) | 70,000 |
| Contribution margin | 30,000 |
| Fixed costs (allocated based on sales dollars) | 40,000 |
| Net loss | $(10,000) |

The company estimates that eliminating this product line will increase the contribution margin on a related product line by $20,000 and save $15,000 in allocated fixed costs. Based on this information, what impact would dropping the line have on the company's overall profitability?

a. $10,000 increase.

b. $25,000 increase.

c. $5,000 increase.

d. $5,000 decrease.

*After you have finished, check your answers with the solutions at the bottom of the page.*

# Sell-or-Process Further Decisions

**Learning Objective 3d**

Use incremental analysis to analyze sell-or-process further decisions.

The next managerial decision we consider is whether to sell a product "as is," or spend additional money to process the product so that it can be sold for a higher price. Once again, we can analyze this decision by comparing the incremental costs and benefits of this decision. If the increased revenue is enough to offset the incremental cost, the company should process further; otherwise the company is better off selling the product "as is."

As an example, assume that Mattel has developed a remote control Hummer toy. So far, the company has spent a total of $250,000 on research and development. Based on the features that are currently included in the product, managers estimate that they could sell 100,000 units at a price of $15 each.

One of the product designers has proposed that additional features to be added to the Hummer, such as moveable parts, music, and lights. If the company spends an additional $100,000 on development, it could sell the enhanced product for $18 per unit. However, the enhanced product would have a slightly higher manufacturing cost because it would require additional components and more labor in the assembly and machining departments. The following table summarizes the expected costs and revenues from selling the product based on the current design versus selling it with the enhanced features.

**Solution to Self-Study Practice**

c

| | |
| --- | --- |
| Lost Contribution Margin | ($30,000) |
| Gained Contribution Margin | 20,000 |
| Fixed Costs Avoided | 15,000 |
| Net Increase in Profit | $ 5,000 |

|  | Current Design | Enhanced Design |
|---|---|---|
| Estimated demand | 100,000 units | 100,000 units |
| Estimated sales price | $15 per unit | $18 per unit |
| Estimated manufacturing costs (per unit) | | |
|    Direct materials | $3.00 | $4.25 |
|    Direct labor | 1.50 | 1.75 |
|    Variable manufacturing overhead | 0.50 | 0.75 |
|    Fixed manufacturing overhead | 2.00 | 2.00 |
| Unit manufacturing costs | $7.00 | $8.75 |
| Research and development costs | $250,000 | $350,000 |

Should the company sell the product as it is currently designed or spend more money to create the enhanced design? To answer this question, we can compare the incremental revenue and incremental costs of the two alternatives as shown in the following table:

| | |
|---|---|
| Increased sales revenue 100,000 units × $3 ($18 − $15) | $300,000 |
| Increased manufacturing costs 100,000 units × $1.75 ($8.75 − $7.00) | (175,000) |
| Increased research and development costs | (100,000) |
|    Increased profit | $ 25,000 |

This analysis suggests that the company would make an additional $25,000 in profit by incorporating additional features in the toy. The increase in development and manufacturing costs would be more than offset by the increased sales revenue generated by the higher sales price.

Notice, however, that no opportunity costs were incorporated in the analysis. By spending time on creating the enhanced design for the Hummer toy, Mattel's product designers may be sacrificing time that could be better spent designing new products that could be sold at an even higher profit. Whenever possible, managers need to incorporate these opportunity costs into the decision-making process.

## CAPITAL BUDGETING FOR LONG-TERM INVESTMENT DECISIONS

Long-term capital investment decisions, called capital budgeting decisions, are decisions concerning major capital assets, including projects, production facilities, machines, land, and other assets. Examples include:

- Whether Mattel should replace old equipment with more modern and efficient equipment.
- Whether Mattel should invest in a new information system that will provide the company with more accurate and up-to-date information.
- Whether Mattel should automate part of the production process to save on long-term labor costs.
- How Mattel should invest its limited research and development budget when faced with multiple options for future products.

All of these decisions involve a significant up-front cash investment with the expectation of receiving future benefits in the form of either revenues or cost savings. Managers make two different types of capital investment decisions:

- Screening decisions require managers to evaluate a proposed capital investment to determine whether it meets some minimum criteria. In other words, they must decide whether a project is acceptable or not.

Video 22-2
www.mhhe.com/LLPW1e

- **Preference decisions** require managers to choose from among a set of alternative capital investment opportunities. Because companies typically have limited funds to invest in capital projects, managers must prioritize and select from the available options.

Several different capital budgeting techniques are available to help managers make these decisions. Some of those techniques are **nondiscounting methods**—that is, methods that do not consider the time value of money. We examine two nondiscounting methods, the annual rate of return and the payback period. Techniques that do incorporate the time value of money are called **discounted cash flow methods**. We consider two such methods, net present value and the internal rate of return. Because capital investment decisions affect a company's cash flow for many years, approaches that incorporate the time value of money are considered superior to the nondiscounting methods. To see how the various capital budgeting methods work, let's consider a possible scenario at Mattel.

Assume that Mattel's managers are evaluating a proposal to create a children's MP3 product that would allow parents to download children's music, books, and educational products from Mattel's Web site. This new product, the Learning Pod or L Pod, would require an up-front investment of $1,100,000. The product's estimated life cycle is five years, at which point the residual assets (equipment and so on) would have an estimated salvage value of about $100,000.

Based on preliminary market research and production cost estimates, Mattel has estimated the new product's net income over the next five years as follows:

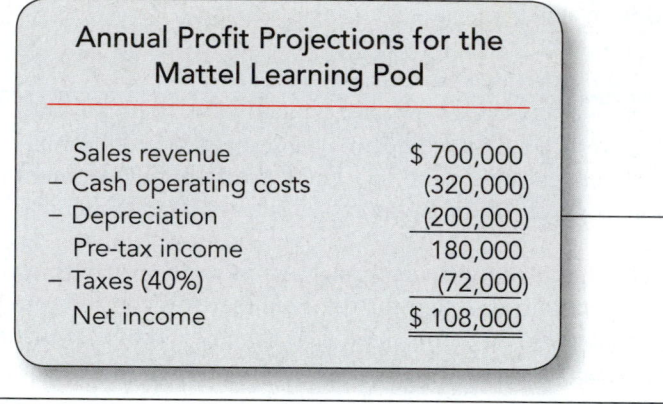

**Annual Profit Projections for the Mattel Learning Pod**

| | |
|---|---|
| Sales revenue | $ 700,000 |
| − Cash operating costs | (320,000) |
| − Depreciation | (200,000) |
| Pre-tax income | 180,000 |
| − Taxes (40%) | (72,000) |
| Net income | $ 108,000 |

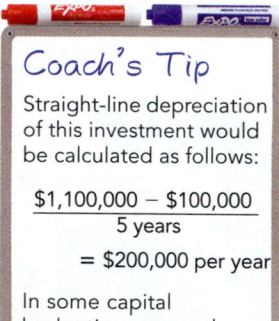

**Coach's Tip**

Straight-line depreciation of this investment would be calculated as follows:

$$\frac{\$1,100,000 - \$100,000}{5 \text{ years}}$$

= $200,000 per year

In some capital budgeting approaches, we need to add this amount back to net income to calculate cash flow.

Should Mattel invest in this project? Answering this question fully requires much more information and analysis than we can cover in this chapter. To illustrate how managers might begin to address this question, however, let's apply the four capital budgeting techniques.

# Nondiscounting Methods

The two nondiscounting methods we will discuss are the accounting rate of return and the payback period. These methods are fairly simple to use but suffer from the limitation that they do not take into account the time value of money.

## Accounting Rate of Return

**Learning Objective 4a**

Analyze investment decisions using the accounting rate of return.

The **accounting rate of return**, also called the **annual rate of return**, is an estimate of the average annual return on investment that a project is expected to generate over its life. It is calculated as follows:

$$\text{Accounting Rate of Return} = \text{Annual Net Income} \div \text{Average Investment Level}$$

To find the average investment level, we start with the original cost of $1,100,000, which will eventually be depreciated down to a salvage value of $100,000. Thus, the average investment is the average of these two numbers, or $600,000 (see Exhibit 22.5).

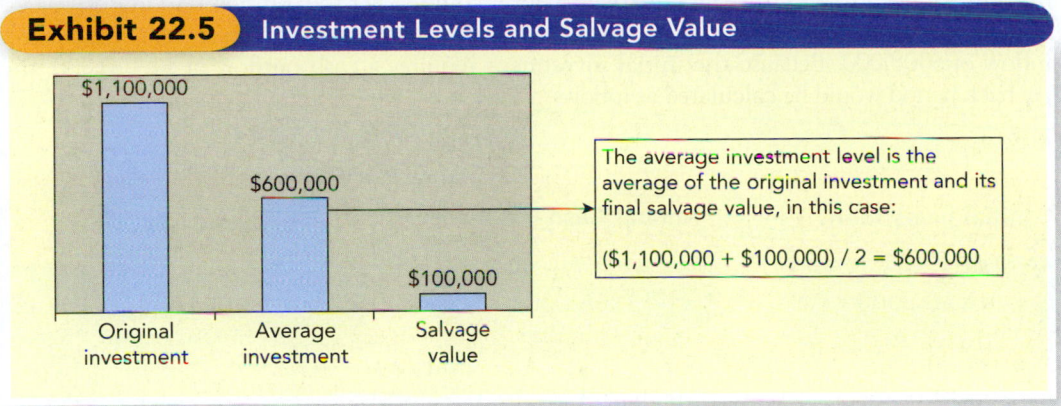

**Exhibit 22.5**  Investment Levels and Salvage Value

$1,100,000

$600,000

$100,000

The average investment level is the average of the original investment and its final salvage value, in this case:

($1,100,000 + $100,000) / 2 = $600,000

Original investment

Average investment

Salvage value

In our example, the proposed project is expected to generate an annual net income of $108,000. So, the accounting rate of return is calculated as follows:

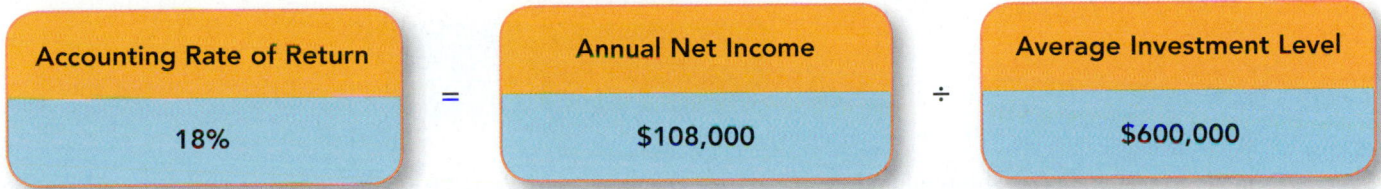

| Accounting Rate of Return | | Annual Net Income | | Average Investment Level |
| --- | --- | --- | --- | --- |
| 18% | = | $108,000 | ÷ | $600,000 |

To make a screening decision on this project, Mattel's managers would compare its 18 percent accounting rate of return to the company's minimum required rate of return, sometimes called the **hurdle rate**. The hurdle rate should reflect the company's cost of capital, which is a function of the interest rate the company pays on its debt as well as the cost of equity financing. If the accounting rate of return is higher than the hurdle rate, the project is acceptable; if not, it is unacceptable.

To make a preference decision on the project, managers would compare the project's accounting rate of return to the rate that could be earned on other potential projects. They would also need to consider other factors, such as the level of risk associated with each project.

The accounting rate of return is the only method we present that is based on the accounting measures of net income and investment. The other three methods focus on cash flows rather than net income.

## Payback Period

The **payback period** is the amount of time needed for a capital investment to "pay for itself." The payback period is calculated as follows:

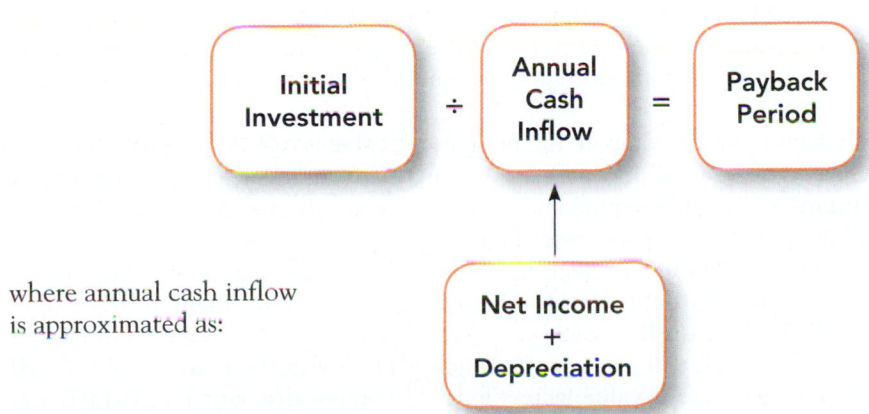

| Initial Investment | ÷ | Annual Cash Inflow | = | Payback Period |
| --- | --- | --- | --- | --- |

where annual cash inflow is approximated as:

Net Income + Depreciation

**Learning Objective 4b**

Analyze investment decisions using the payback period.

**Coach's Tip**

Recall from Chapter 16 that depreciation is only one factor that causes net income to differ from cash flow. For the sake of simplicity, we ignore the other differences, which arise from accrual accounting, and the indirect cash savings that result from the tax benefits of depreciation.

To apply these formulas, we must first calculate the annual cash flow from the investment. We estimated Mattel's annual net income to be $108,000 after a $200,000 deduction for depreciation expense. Because depreciation is a noncash expense that was deducted in the calculation of net income, we need to add this amount back to net income to get to cash flow. Adding $200,000 in depreciation to the $108,000 in net income provides an estimate of the project's annual cash inflow of $308,000. Because the initial investment requires a cash outflow of $1,100,000, the payback period would be calculated as follows.

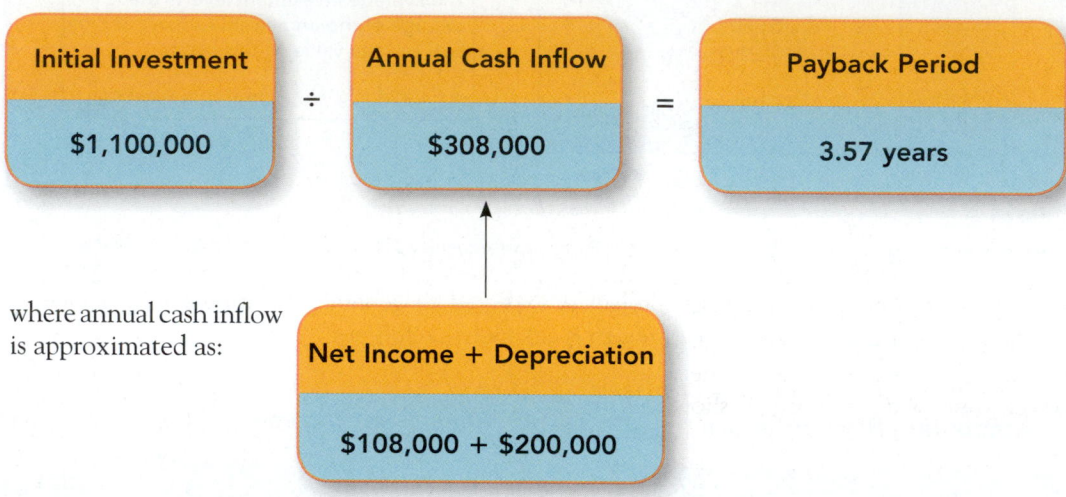

where annual cash inflow is approximated as:

This result tells managers that the project is expected to pay back the original cash investment in a little more than three and one-half years. In general, projects with short cash payback periods are considered safer investments than those with long payback periods. However, this approach is a very simplistic one that does not consider the timing of the cash flows or anything that happens after the payback period. For example, we completely ignored the salvage value of the equipment because that cash inflow does not occur until the end of the project, long after the cash inflows from the first three and one-half years are expected to pay back the original investment.

## Discounted Cash Flow Methods

The next two methods we focus on consider the timing of all cash flows, recognizing that cash received today is more valuable than cash received in the future. Present value concepts lie at the heart of the discounted cash flow methods, so you may want to review the present value concepts discussed in Appendix C.

### Net Present Value

**Learning Objective 4c**

Analyze investment decisions using the net present value method.

The **net present value (NPV) method** compares the present value of a project's future cash flows to the original investment made at the start of the project. The difference between the present value of the cash inflows and outflows over the life of the project is the net present value.

The discounting factor used to compute the net present value is called the required rate of return, hurdle rate, or cost of capital. In general terms, a positive NPV means that the project will generate a return in excess of the required rate of return; a negative net present value means that the project will not cover the required rate of return.

To compute the NPV for Mattel's project, let's assume that the required rate of return, or hurdle rate, is 12 percent. Recall that the project requires an initial investment of $1,100,000 and will generate $308,000 in cash flow each year. In addition, the assets have an estimated salvage value of $100,000, which will create a one-time cash inflow at the end of year 5. Based on this information and the present value factors for a 12 percent discount rate (which you will find in Appendix C), the NPV of this project would be calculated as follows:

| Year | Cash Flow | | Present Value Factor (12%) | | Present Value |
|------|-----------|---|----------------------------|---|---------------|
| 0 | $(1,100,000) | | — | | $(1,100,000) |
| 1 | 308,000 | × | 0.8929 | = | 275,013 |
| 2 | 308,000 | × | 0.7972 | = | 245,538 |
| 3 | 308,000 | × | 0.7118 | = | 219,234 |
| 4 | 308,000 | × | 0.6355 | = | 195,734 |
| 5 | 408,000 | × | 0.5674 | = | 231,499 |
| | | | Net present value | = | $    67,018 |

The resulting net present value of $67,018 indicates that the present value of the project's cash inflows is $67,018 more than the cost of the original investment. In general, a positive NPV indicates that a project is acceptable; a negative NPV indicates that it is not acceptable.

Since the $308,000 annual cash inflow happens in each of the five years of the project, we could have used the present value of an annuity (or stream of cash flows) to calculate the NPV of the project. But we would still need to do a separate calculation for the $100,000 salvage value, because this happens at only one point in the future (at the end of year five). This analysis, which yields the same NPV, is shown below.

| Year | Cash Flow | | Present Value Factor (12%) | | Present Value |
|------|-----------|---|----------------------------|---|---------------|
| 0 | $(1,100,000) | | — | | $(1,100,000) |
| 1–5 | 308,000 | × | 3.6048* | = | 1,110,278 |
| 5 | 100,000 | × | 0.5674** | = | 56,740 |
| | | | Net present value | = | $    67,018 |

\* 3.6048 is the PV of an annuity for 5 years at 12%.
\*\* 0.5674 is the PV of $1 in 5 years at 12%.

## Internal Rate of Return

We know from the positive NPV we just calculated that the expected cash flows from the proposed project will generate a return that is higher than the 12 percent required rate of return. It would be nice to have an exact number for the estimated return. We cannot rely on the 18 percent accounting rate of return we calculated earlier, however, because that approach was based on net income rather than cash flow and did not consider the time value of money. Instead, we need to find the discount rate that will equate the NPV of the future cash flows with the initial cash outflow. The rate at which the present value of the cash inflows exactly equals the present value of the cash outflows is called the **internal rate of return (IRR)**. It is also the discount rate at which the project's NPV would be zero.

Consider what would happen if we increased the discount rate used to evaluate the Mattel project from 12% to 13%, 14% and 15%:

**Learning Objective 4d**

Analyze investment decisions using the internal rate of return.

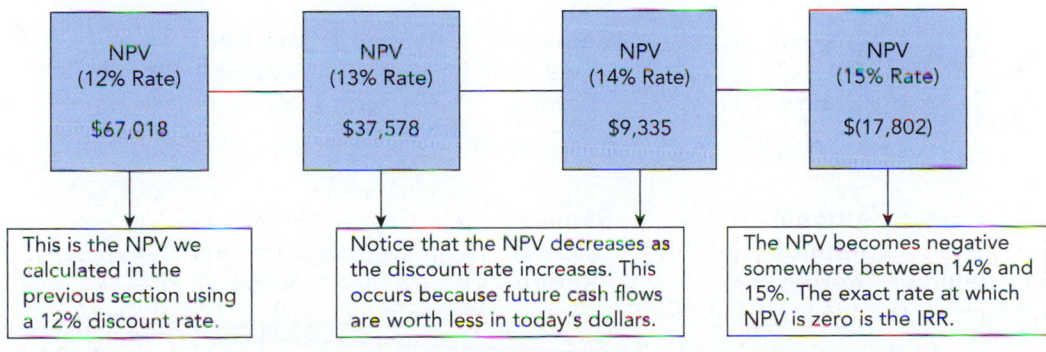

The previous diagram shows that the NPV is positive at a 14% discount rate, but becomes negative at a 15% discount rate. The point at which the NPV is zero is the internal rate of return (IRR).

To calculate the exact IRR, we would need to use a computer program such as Excel. These steps are illustrated in Exhibit 22.6

**Exhibit 22.6    Calculating IRR Using Excel**

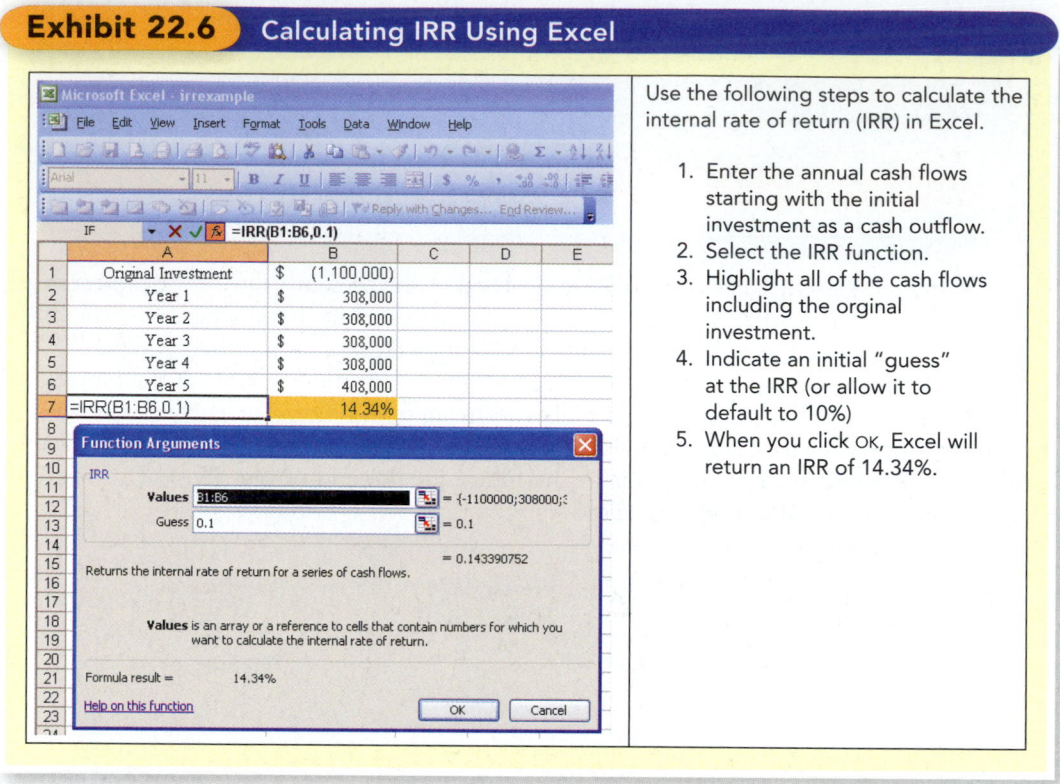

Use the following steps to calculate the internal rate of return (IRR) in Excel.

1. Enter the annual cash flows starting with the initial investment as a cash outflow.
2. Select the IRR function.
3. Highlight all of the cash flows including the orginal investment.
4. Indicate an initial "guess" at the IRR (or allow it to default to 10%)
5. When you click OK, Excel will return an IRR of 14.34%.

Following these steps results in an IRR of 14.34 percent. As we predicted based on the NPV analysis, the IRR was between 14 percent and 15 percent.

As you can see, the IRR is closely related to the NPV method. The NPV uses the company's required rate of return as the discount rate to determine whether the present value of the project's expected cash flows is sufficient to cover the original investment. The IRR is the return that will yield a zero net present value. The following diagram summarizes the relationship between the IRR, the required rate of return, and the NPV.

To make sure you understand the four capital budgeting techniques, complete the following Self-Study Practice.

1. Which of the following statements regarding the four capital budgeting techniques is **true?** You may select more than one answer.
   a. Both the accounting rate of return and the payback period consider the time value of money.
   b. Both the accounting rate of return and the payback period are based on net income rather than on cash flow.
   c. Both the NPV method and the IRR ignore the time value of money.
   d. The accounting rate of return is based on net income, the other three methods are based on cash flow.
   e. All of these statements are true.

2. Jackson Company's required rate of return is 10 percent. The NPV of a project using the 10 percent discount rate is $(15,333). Which of the following statements regarding the NPV and IRR is **true?** You may select more than one answer.
   a. The present value of the project's future cash flows is more than the original cost of the investment.
   b. The present value of the project's future cash flows is less than the original cost of the investment.
   c. The IRR on this project is less than 10 percent.
   d. The IRR on this project is more than 10 percent.

*After you have finished, check your answers with the solutions at the bottom of the page.*

# Demonstration Case A

Assume you need to buy a new vehicle. The junker that you paid $5,000 for two years ago has a current value of $1,500. You have narrowed the choice down to a used 2002 Jeep Cherokee with a blue book value of $8,000 and a new Hyundai Elantra with a sticker price of $12,995. You plan to drive either vehicle for at least five more years.

*Required:*

1. List the five steps in the decision-making process and briefly describe the key factors you would consider at each step.
2. Indicate whether each of the following factors would be relevant or irrelevant to your decision:

   a. The $5,000 you paid for your junker two years ago.
   b. The $1,500 your vehicle is worth today.
   c. The blue book value of the Jeep Cherokee.
   d. The sticker price of the Hyundai Elantra.
   e. The difference in fuel economy for the Jeep and the Hyundai.
   f. The cost of on-campus parking.
   g. The difference in insurance cost for the Jeep and the Hyundai.
   h. The difference in resale value five years from now for the Jeep and the Hyundai.
   i. The fact that the Hyundai comes with a warranty but the Jeep does not.

1.  d is the only true statement.
2.  b and c are true statements.

Solution to Self-Study Practice

3. Consider only the costs you just classified as irrelevant.

    a. Would any of these costs be relevant if you were deciding whether to keep your present vehicle or buy a new one?

    b. Would any of these costs be relevant if you were deciding whether to get rid of your vehicle and ride your bike to work and school?

## Suggested Solution

1.

| Factors to Consider: | |
|---|---|
| **Step 1: Identify the decision problem.** | You need (or want) to buy a new vehicle, presumable because your old one is no longer fulfilling its purpose. |
| **Step 2: Determine the decision alternatives.** | What kind of vehicle should you buy (a car, a truck, an SUV)? Should you buy a new or a used vehicle? What is your price range? What kind of fuel economy should the vehicle you buy offer? What other features are important to you? |
| **Step 3: Evaluate the costs and benefits of the alternatives.** | What is the difference in price for each alternatives: fuel economy, the cost of insurance, the cost of maintenance, reliability ratings, future resale value, and other benefits or costs? |
| **Step 4: Make the decision.** | Which cost and qualitative considerations, such as style and function, outweigh the others? |
| **Step 5: Review the results of the decision-making process.** | Does the vehicle you selected meet your needs? Is it reliable? Are you comfortable in it? Can you make the payments? |

2.
    a. Sunk cost.
    b. Same under both options.
    c. Relevant.
    d. Relevant.
    e. Relevant.
    f. Same under both options.
    g. Relevant.
    h. Relevant.
    i. Relevant.

3.

    a. Yes, the $1,500 value of your current vehicle would be relevant because you could sell it under one option but not the other.

    b. Yes, the cost of on-campus parking would be relevant because you could avoid it if you did not own a vehicle.

## Demonstration Case B

Maddox Company is considering investing $800,000 in a new project. Projected annual revenues, expenses, and profit for the next four years follow:

| | |
|---|---:|
| Sales revenue | $ 600,000 |
| −Cash operating costs | (300,000) |
| −Depreciation ($800,000 / 4) | (200,000) |
| Pre-Tax income | 100,000 |
| −Taxes (40%) | (40,000) |
| Net income | $  60,000 |

The project's assets are expected to have no salvage value at the end of four years. The company's required rate of return is 12 percent.

**Required:**

1. Compute the accounting rate of return.
2. Compute the payback period.
3. Compute the four-year NPV using a 12 percent discount rate.
4. Without computing the exact IRR, explain whether it would be higher or lower than the 12 percent required rate of return.
5. Compute the exact IRR using Excel's IRR function.

## Suggested Solution

1. Accounting rate of return = $60,000 / [($800,000 + 0) / 2] = 15\%$
2. Payback period = $800,000 / ($60,000 + $200,000) = 3.08$ years
3.

| Year | Cash Flow | PV Factor (12%) | Present Value |
|------|-----------|-----------------|---------------|
| 0 | ($ 800,000) | – | $(800,000) |
| 1-4 | $ 60,000 + $ 200,000 = $260,000 $\times$ | 3.0373* | 789,689 |
| | | Net Present Value = | $ (10,302) |

*3.0373 is the PV of an annuity for 4 years at 12%.

4. Because the NPV is negative at a discount rate of 12 percent, the IRR must be less than 12 percent.
5. The exact IRR is 11.3879 percent.

## Chapter Summary

### LO1 Describe the five steps in the decision-making process. p. 920

- The managerial decision-making process has five steps:
  - Identify the decision problem.
  - Determine the decision alternatives.
  - Evaluate the costs and benefits of the alternatives.
  - Make the decision.
  - Review the results of the decision-making process.

### LO2 Define and identify relevant costs and benefits. p. 922

- When making decisions, managers should focus only on costs and benefits that are relevant to the decision. To be relevant, a cost or benefit must meet the following criteria:
  - It must occur in the future, not the past. Sunk costs are never relevant.
  - The total amount of the cost or benefit must change depending on which alternative is selected.
  - Relevant costs are sometimes called **differential costs, incremental costs,** or **avoidable costs.** Costs that will not change regardless of the alternative that is selected are irrelevant and should be ignored.

### LO3 Use incremental analysis to make short-term decisions. p. 923

- Incremental analysis is a short-term decision-making approach that compares the incremental costs and benefits of various alternatives. This approach can be used to address several common managerial decisions, including:
  - **Special-order decisions.** As long as the price of a special order is more than the incremental costs of filling it, a special order will contribute to short-term profit.
  - **Make-or-buy decisions.** Managers should compare the relevant (that is, differential) costs of making the product or providing the service internally to the cost of buying it from an outside supplier.

- **Keep-or-drop decisions.** In deciding whether to eliminate a product or service, managers should compare the lost revenue with the resulting reduction in cost to determine the overall impact on profit and should consider the effect of the decision on other product lines.
    - **Sell-or-process further decisions.** To decide whether to sell a product "as is" or continue spending money to enhance it, managers should compare the incremental revenue with the incremental costs that will result from the additional processing.
- In making all of these decisions, it is important for managers to consider opportunity costs as well as factors that cannot be quantified, such as quality concerns.

**LO4  Analyze investment decisions using four capital budgeting techniques. p. 932**

- Managers use several approaches to make long-term capital budgeting decisions including the four considered here.
    - The accounting rate of return is a nondiscounting approach that estimates the average accounting rate of return on a project. This approach is the only one that focuses on net income rather than cash flow.
    - The payback period is the total amount of time needed for a capital investment project to pay back the company's original investment. This simple approach does not take into account the time value of money.
    - Net present value is a discounted cash flow technique that compares the present value of a project's future cash flows to the original investment.
    - The internal rate of return is related to the net present value. It is calculated by finding the discount rate that would generate a zero NPV. In other words, the IRR is the rate at which the present value of a project's future cash flows equals the original cash outflow. An IRR that is higher than the required rate of return will generate a positive net present value. An IRR that is lower than the required rate of return will generate a negative net present value.

## Key Terms

Accounting Rate of Return (p. 932)

Annual Rate of Return (p. 932)

Avoidable Cost (p. 922)

Capital Budgeting (p. 920)

Capital Budgeting Decisions (p. 931)

Differential Analysis (p. 921)

Differential Cost (p. 922)

Discounted Cash Flow Method (p. 932)

Hurdle Rate (p. 933)

Incremental Analysis (p. 920)

Incremental Cost (p. 922)

Internal Rate of Return (IRR) (p. 935)

Irrelevant Cost (p. 922)

Net Present Value (NPV) Method (p. 934)

Nondiscounting Methods (p. 932)

Payback Period (p. 933)

Preference Decisions (p. 932)

Relevant Cost (p. 922)

Screening Decisions (p. 931)

Sunk Costs (p. 922)

**See complete glossary in the back of text.**

## Questions

1. How do incremental analysis and capital budgeting differ? How are they similar?

2. Briefly describe the five steps of the management decision-making process.

3. Suppose you are considering a part-time job to earn some extra spending money. List four factors that could affect that decision and would be included in Step 3 of your decision-making process.

4. Tom Ellis recently bought a plasma television and has since stated that he would not recommend that brand to others. This indicates that Tom has completed which step of the decision-making process?

5. What are the criteria for a cost to be considered relevant to any decision?

6. How is an avoidable cost related to a relevant cost?

7. Explain opportunity cost and give two opportunity costs of your decision to enroll in classes this semester.

8. Why should opportunity costs be factored into the decision-making process and why is it often difficult to do?

9. What is a special-order decision? Why can managers ignore fixed overhead costs when making special-order decisions?

10. How might the acceptance of a special order have negative consequences for a company?

11. Briefly explain what excess capacity means. How does it impact a special-order decision?

12. Suppose that you are a manager of a local deli and sandwich shop. Give an example of each of the following decisions that

you might have to make and identify three factors that would be relevant to each decision.

   a.   Special order.

   b.   Make or buy.

   c.   Keep or drop.

13. Briefly describe three problems that might result from a decision to buy a component part from an external supplier. For each problem, identify one way to avoid or correct it.

14. How do opportunity costs affect make-or-buy decisions? How are opportunity costs shown in a make-or-buy analysis?

15. When a product line is eliminated, why are the fixed costs allocated to that line not automatically eliminated as well?

16. How might the decision to drop a product line affect a company's remaining products?

17. Briefly explain what happens to total variable costs when a product line is dropped.

18. Identify three opportunity costs that might be involved in a keep-or-drop decision.

19. Explain the difference between screening decisions and preference decisions.

20. How do nondiscounting methods and discounting methods of capital budgeting differ? Which is considered superior, and why?

21. Briefly explain what the time value of money means.

22. What is a company's hurdle rate? How is it relevant to capital budgeting?

23. In everyday terms, explain what information the payback period provides about an investment.

24. What do a positive net present value (NPV) and a negative NPV indicate about an investment?

25. When would you use an annuity factor in a net present value calculation instead of a present value factor for a single cash flow?

26. Explain how the internal rate of return and net present value are related. If a project has a net present value of $50,000 using a 10 percent discount factor, what does this imply about that project's IRR?

## Multiple Choice

1. The decision-making approach in which a manager considers only costs and benefits that differ for alternatives is called:

Quiz 22-1
www.mhhe.com/LLPW1e

   a.   Incremental analysis.

   b.   Outsourcing.

   c.   Differential analysis.

   d.   Either a or c.

2. Which of the following is not a step of the management decision-making process?

   a.  Review results of the decision-making process.

   b.  Contact competitors who have made similar decisions.

   c.  Evaluate the costs and benefits of the alternatives.

   d.  Determine the decision alternatives.

3. Sunk costs are always

   a.   Opportunity costs.     c.   Relevant.

   b.   Avoidable.         d.   Irrelevant.

4. When making a one-time special-order decision, a company can ignore fixed overhead because

   a.   The cost is not avoidable.

   b.   The cost is avoidable.

   c.   The cost cannot be determined.

   d.   None of the above.

5. When making make-or-buy decisions, managers should consider

   a.   Alternate uses for any facility currently being used to make the item.

   b.   The costs of direct materials included in making the item.

   c.   Qualitative factors such as whether the supplier can deliver the item on time and to the company's quality standards.

   d.   All of the above.

6. Which of the following costs is not likely to be completely eliminated by a decision to drop a product line?

   a.   The variable overhead traced to that product line.

   b.   The cost of direct materials used to produce the product.

   c.   The portion of fixed overhead allocated to that product line.

   d.   All of the above will be completely eliminated.

7. Which of the following requires managers to determine whether a proposed capital investment meets some minimum criteria?

   a.   Preference decision.     c.   Cash payback period.

   b.   Screening decision.      d.   None of the above.

8. ABC Company is considering a $500,000 investment to automate its production process. The new equipment will allow ABC to save $75,000 each year in labor costs. What is this project's payback period?

   a.   4.00 years.         c.   6.67 years.

   b.   5.67 years.        d.   8.00 years.

9. Discounting methods of capital budgeting are considered superior to nondiscounting methods because

   a.   Discounting methods recognize the time value of money.

   b.   Discounting methods are simpler to calculate.

   c.   Discounting methods are always based on accounting measurements of net income and investment.

   d.   Both a and c are correct.

10. Jennings Company has evaluated a project and found that its internal rate of return is approximately 13.5 percent.

Suppose Jennings' cost of capital is 12 percent. What, if anything, can you infer about the net present value (NPV) of this project?

a.   The NPV is less than zero.

b.   The NPV is more than zero.

c.   The NPV is exactly zero.

d.   Nothing can be determined about the project's NPV.

| Solutions to Multiple-Choice Questions |
|---|
| 1. d    2. b    3. d    4. a    5. d    6. c    7. b |
| 8. c    9. a    10. b |

## Mini Exercises  Available with McGraw-Hill's Homework Manager

**LO1, 2, 3, 4**     **M22-1 Matching Key Terms and Concepts to Definitions**
A number of terms and concepts from this chapter and a list of descriptions, definitions, and explanations follow. For each term listed on the left, choose at least one corresponding item from the right. Note that a single term may have more than one description and a single description may be used more than once or not at all.

_____  1.   Time value of money
_____  2.   Identify the decision problem
_____  3.   Payback period
_____  4.   Special order decision
_____  5.   Net present value method
_____  6.   Differential costs
_____  7.   Evaluate the costs and benefits of alternatives
_____  8.   Make-or-buy decision
_____  9.   Preference decision
_____ 10.   Sunk costs
_____ 11.   Opportunity costs
_____ 12.   Keep-or-drop decision
_____ 13.   Internal rate of return method
_____ 14.   Screening decision
_____ 15.   Accounting rate of return
_____ 16.   Avoidable costs

A.   Short-term management decision made using differential analysis.
B.   Discounting method of capital budgeting.
C.   Estimate of the average annual return on investment a project will generate.
D.   Management decision based on comparing lost revenue with the reduction of costs to determine the overall effect on profit.
E.   Capital budgeting method that finds the discount rate that generates a zero net present value.
F.   Decision made when managers evaluate potential capital investments to determine whether they meet a minimum criteria.
G.   The only capital budgeting method based on accounting measures of net income and investment.
H.   Costs that have already been incurred.
I.   Management decision based on ignoring fixed manufacturing overhead so long as there is enough excess capacity to meet the order.
J.   Costs that can be avoided by choosing one option over another.
K.   Concept recognizing that cash received today is more valuable than cash received in the future.
L.   Step 5 of the management decision-making process.
M.   Management decision based on the relevant costs of making a product internally compared with the cost of purchasing that product.
N.   Cost that is relevant to short-term decision making.
O.   Decision that requires a manager to choose from a set of alternatives.
P.   Step 1 of the management decision-making process.
Q.   Costs that are always irrelevant to management decisions.
R.   Method that calculates how long it will take for a particular capital investment to pay for itself.
S.   Benefits given up when one alternative is chosen over another.
T.   Capital budgeting technique that compares the present value of the future cash flows for a project to its original investment.
U.   Costs that change across decision alternatives.
V.   Nondiscounting method of capital budgeting.
W.   Step 3 of the management decision-making process.

### M22-2 Identifying Relevant and Irrelevant Costs

LO2

Sarah Ramirez is considering taking a part-time job at a local clothing store. Sarah loves the store and shops there often, but unfortunately, employee discounts are given only to full-time employees. If Sarah takes this job, she will have to withdraw from her Tuesday night basket-weaving class to work. Accepting the job would also mean that Sarah must give up her volunteer work at the local animal sanctuary, an activity that she enjoys a great deal. The new job would pay approximately $125 per week but would cost Sarah $15 per week in gas. Sarah would be able to keep her Saturday afternoon job at the library that pays $40 per week.

A list of factors that Sarah has identified follows. For each one, indicate whether it is relevant or irrelevant to Sarah's decision.

1. The $125 income from the new job.
2. The $40 income from the library.
3. The $50 nonrefundable registration fee Sarah paid for the basket-weaving class.
4. The $15 cost for gas.
5. The $75 per month that Sarah spends for clothing.
6. The time Sarah spends volunteering at the animal sanctuary.

### M22-3 Identifying Relevant and Irrelevant Costs

LO2

The local summer baseball league wants to buy new uniforms for its teams. The current uniforms are quite old and will require $400 in repairs before they can be handed out to players next week for the upcoming season. The old uniforms will be replaced as soon as new ones can be purchased. League leaders have investigated several possible fund-raisers and have narrowed the choice down to two options: candy sales or car washes. Each option can generate the $2,500 that the new uniforms would cost.

*Option 1:*
The candy sales option would require the league to purchase 2,000 candy bars at a cost of $0.75 each. The players and coaches would then sell the bars for $2.00 each. The league estimates that it would take about four weeks to sell the candy and collect all of the money.

*Option 2:*
The car wash option would require about $200 for buckets, sponges, soap, and towels. A local business has offered to donate the water (estimated at $300 total) and a location. The car washes would be held on Saturdays, and each team would be required to provide workers. Each car wash day is expected to generate $450 in proceeds, so the league expects that it would take six weeks to raise $2,500.

*Required:*

1. Several factors related to the league's choice follow. Indicate whether each factor is relevant or irrelevant to deciding which project to engage in and briefly explain your reason.

    a. Repair costs for the old uniforms, $400.
    b. Initial outlay to purchase the candy bars, $1,500.
    c. Initial outlay to purchase car wash supplies, $200.
    d. Cost of water for the car wash option, $300.
    e. Cost of the new uniforms, $2,500.
    f. Additional two weeks that the car wash option would require to raise the money.

2. List three qualitative factors that the league should consider in making its choice.

**Questions M22-4–M22-6 refer to Flyaway Company, which produces window fans. Consider each question independently.**

### M22-4 Analyzing a Special-Order Decision

LO2, 3

Flyaway Company has just received a one-time offer to purchase 10,000 units of its Breezy model for a price of $20 each. The Breezy model costs $25 to produce ($17 in variable costs and $8 of fixed overhead). Because the offer came during a slow production month, Flyaway has enough excess capacity to accept the order.

*Required:*

1. Should Flyaway accept the special order offer?
2. Determine the impact the special order would have on Flyaway's net income.

### M22-5 Analyzing a Keep-or-Drop Decision

LO2, 3

Suppose that Flyaway Company also produces the Windy model fan, which currently has a net loss of $40,000 as follows:

| Sales | $ 160,000 |
| Variable costs | (130,000) |
| Contribution margin | 30,000 |
| Allocated fixed costs | (70,000) |
| Profit (Loss) | $ (40,000) |

Dropping the Windy product line will eliminate $20,000 of fixed costs. The remaining $50,000 will be redistributed to Flyaway's remaining product lines.

Determine whether Flyaway should drop the Windy fan line. Why or why not?

**LO2, 3**  **M22-6 Analyzing a Make-or-Buy decision**

Flyaway Company also has the Cyclone fan model. It is the company's top-selling model, with sales of 30,000 units per year. This model has a dual fan as well as a thermostat component that causes the fan to cycle on and off depending on the room temperature. Flyaway has always manufactured the thermostat component but is considering buying the part from a supplier.

It costs Flyaway $5 to make each thermostat ($3 variable and $2 fixed). Mostat Co. has offered to sell the component to Flyaway for $4. Flyaway's decision to purchase the part from Mostat will eliminate all variable costs but none of the fixed costs. Flyaway has no other possible uses for the area currently dedicated to the thermostat production.

Determine whether Flyaway should continue to make the thermostat or purchase the part from Mostat Co. Justify your answer.

**LO4**  **M22-7 Calculating the Accounting Rate of Return and Payback Period**

Milo Company is considering purchasing new equipment for its factory. The equipment will cost $250,000 and have a $50,000 salvage value in five years. The annual net income from the equipment is expected to be $30,000, and depreciation is $40,000 per year.

Calculate and evaluate Milo's:

*Required:*

1. Annual rate of return on the equipment.
2. Payback period for the equipment.

**LO4**  **M22-8 Calculating Net Present Value and Predicting the Internal Rate of Return**

Otis Company has the following information about a potential capital investment:

| Initial investment | $400,000 |
| Annual cash inflow | $ 70,000 |
| Expected life | 10 years |
| Cost of capital | 11% |

1. Calculate and evaluate the net present value of this project.
2. Without any calculations, explain whether the internal rate of return on this project is more or less than 11 percent.

# Exercises  <sup>TM</sup>

**Available with McGraw-Hill's Homework Manager**

**LO1, 2**  **E22-1 Identifying Relevant Costs and Calculating Differential Costs**

Maria Turner has just graduated from college with a degree in accounting. She had planned to enroll immediately in the master's program at her university but has been offered a lucrative job at a well-known company. The job is exactly what Maria had hoped to find after obtaining her graduate degree.

In anticipation of master's program classes, Maria has already spent $450 to apply for the program. Tuition for the master's program is $8,000 per year, and it will take two years to complete. Maria's expected salary after completing the master's program is approximately $60,000. If she pursues the master's degree, Maria would stay in her current home that is near the campus and costs $600 per month in rent. She would also remain at her current job that pays $25,000 per year. Additionally, Maria's immediate family is nearby.

She spends considerable time with family and friends, especially during the holidays. This would not be possible if she accepts the job offer because of the distance from her new location.

The job Maria has been offered includes a salary of $50,000. She would have to relocate to another state, but her employer would pay the $5,000 of moving expenses. Maria's rent in the new location would be approximately $800 per month. The new location is a fast-growing, active city that offers a number of cultural activities that Maria would enjoy. The city is also home to Maria's favorite Major League Baseball team, and she would expect to buy season tickets.

**Required:**

1. Help Maria make her decision by categorizing the factors involved in making her choice. Complete the following chart regarding the factors in Maria's decision. A single factor may have multiple columns checked.

|  | Relevant | Irrelevant | Sunk Cost | Qualitative |
|---|---|---|---|---|
| $450 spent on application fee |  |  |  |  |
| $8,000 per year tuition |  |  |  |  |
| $60,000 salary with master's degree |  |  |  |  |
| $600 per month current rent |  |  |  |  |
| $25,000 current salary |  |  |  |  |
| Time spent with family and friends |  |  |  |  |
| $50,000 new salary |  |  |  |  |
| $5,000 moving expenses |  |  |  |  |
| $800 rent per month in new location |  |  |  |  |
| Cultural activities in the new location |  |  |  |  |
| Ability to have MLB season tickets |  |  |  |  |

2. For each item following, determine the differential amount in Maria's alternatives. For example, the incremental cost of tuition is $16,000 if Maria chooses to pursue the master's degree.

   a. Rent.
   b. Salary for the next two years.
   c. Salary after two years.
   d. Moving expenses.

**The following information pertains to E22-2 through E22-5.**
Electronic Playground, Inc. (EPI) manufactures and sells computer games for children. The company has several product lines based on the age range of the target market and whether the games are marketed as educational or entertainment. EPI sells both individual games as well as packaged sets. All games are in CD format, and some utilize accessories such as steering wheels, electronic tablets, and hand controls. To date, EPI has developed and manufactured all CDs itself as well as the accessories and packaging for all of its products.

The gaming market has traditionally been targeted at teenagers and young adults. However, the increasing affordability of computers and the incorporation of computer activities into junior high and elementary school curriculums has led to a significant increase in sales to younger children. EPI has always included games for younger children but now wants to expand its business to capitalize on changes in the industry. The company currently has excess capacity and is investigating several possible ways to improve profitability.

**E22-2 Analyzing a Special-Order Decision**                                                LO2, 3
EPI has been approached by a fourth-grade teacher from Phoenix about the possibility of creating a specially designed game that would be customized for her classroom and environment. The teacher would like an educational game to correspond to her classroom coverage of the history of the desert Southwest and the state of Arizona in particular. EPI has not sold its products directly to teachers or school systems in the past, but that possibility was identified during a recent meeting of EPI's Marketing Department.

The teacher has offered to buy 1,000 copies of the CD at a price of $5 each. EPI could easily modify one of its existing educational programs about U.S. history to accommodate the request. The modifications would cost approximately $500. A summary of the information related to production of EPI's current history program follows.

| | |
|---|---|
| Direct materials | $ 1.25 |
| Direct labor | 0.50 |
| Variable manufacturing overhead | 2.25 |
| Fixed manufacturing overhead | 2.00 |
| Total cost per unit | $ 6.00 |
| Sales price per unit | $12.00 |

*Required:*

1. Determine the impact this special order would have on EPI's total profit.

2. Should EPI accept the special order?

3. Suppose that the special offer had been to purchase 1,000 copies of the program for $4.50 each. What effect would that offer have on EPI's total profit?

4. Explain why a company might accept a special order that did not increase profits.

**LO2, 3**

### E22-3 Analyzing a Make-or-Buy Decision

EPI is considering outsourcing the production of the handheld control module used with some of its products. The company has received a bid from Control Freak Co. (CFC) to produce 10,000 units of the module per year for $15 each. The following information pertains to EPI's production of the control modules.

| | |
|---|---|
| Direct materials | $ 8 |
| Direct labor | 3 |
| Variable manufacturing overhead | 2 |
| Fixed manufacturing overhead | 3 |
| Total cost per unit | $16 |

EPI has determined that it could eliminate all variable costs if the control modules were produced externally, but none of the fixed overhead is avoidable. At this time, EPI has no specific use in mind for the space that is currently dedicated to the control module production.

*Required:*

1. Determine the impact this decision will have on EPI's annual income.

2. Should EPI buy the modules from CFC or continue to make them?

3. Suppose that the EPI space currently used for the modules could be utilized by a new product line that would generate $35,000 in annual profit. Does this change your recommendation to EPI? If so, how?

**LO2, 3**

### E22-4 Analyzing a Keep-or-Drop Decision

EPI is considering eliminating a product from its ToddleTown Tours collection. This collection is aimed at children one to three years of age and includes "tours" of a hypothetical town. Two products, The Pet Store Parade and The Grocery Getaway, have impressive sales. However, sales for the third CD in the collection, The Post Office Polka, have lagged the others. Several other CDs are planned for this collection, but none is ready for production.

EPI's information related to the ToddleTown Tours collection follows.

SEGMENTED INCOME STATEMENT FOR EPI'S
TODDLETOWN TOURS PRODUCT LINES

|  | Pet Store Parade | Grocery Getaway | Post Office Polka | Total |
|---|---|---|---|---|
| Sales revenue | $50,000 | $45,000 | $15,000 | $110,000 |
| Variable costs | 23,000 | 19,000 | 10,000 | 52,000 |
| Contribution margin | 27,000 | 26,000 | 5,000 | 58,000 |
| Allocated fixed costs | 19,200 | 15,600 | 5,200 | 40,000 |
| Profit (loss) | $ 7,800 | $10,400 | $ (200) | $ 18,000 |

EPI has determined that elimination of the Post Office Polka (POP) program will not impact sales of the other two items. Additionally, total fixed cost will be reduced by only $1,500. The remaining fixed overhead currently allocated to the POP program will be redistributed to the remaining two products.

*Required:*

1. Determine what will happen to the company's total profit, if EPI drops the POP product. What is your recommendation about the elimination?
2. Suppose that the full amount of fixed overhead ($5,200) allocated to POP is avoidable. Would your recommendation to EPI change? Why or why not?

**E22-5 Identifying Qualitative Factors in Short-Term Decision Making**                     LO2, 3
Refer to E22-2 through E22-4.

*Required:*
Identify at least three qualitative factors that EPI should consider when making each decision.

**E22-6 Calculating the Accounting Rate of Return and Payback Period**                     LO4
Midway Printing Co. is considering the purchase of new electronic printing equipment. The new equipment would allow Midway to increase its annual before-tax profit by $100,000. Midway has a 40 percent tax rate. Other information about this proposed project follows:

| | |
|---|---|
| Initial investment | $300,000 |
| Useful life | 5 years |
| Salvage value | $100,000 |

*Required:*
Calculate and evaluate Midway's

1. Annual rate of return.
2. Payback period.

**E22-7 Calculating Net Present Value and Internal Rate of Return**                     LO4
Lancer Corp. has the following information available about a potential capital investment:

| | |
|---|---|
| Initial investment | $1,300,000 |
| Annual net income | $ 200,000 |
| Expected life | 8 years |
| Salvage value | $ 350,000 |
| Lancer's cost of capital | 10% |

*Required:*

1. Calculate and evaluate the net present value of this project.
2. Without making any calculations, determine whether the internal rate of return on this project is more or less than 10 percent.

3.  Calculate the net present value using a 20% discount rate.
4.  Estimate the project's internal rate of return (IRR).

LO4    **E22-8 Calculating the Accounting Rate of Return, Payback Period, and Net Present Value**
Lenny's Limousine Service (LLS) is considering the purchase of two Hummer limousines. Various information about the proposed investment follows.

| | |
|---|---|
| Initial investment (2 limos) | $600,000 |
| Useful life | 8 years |
| Salvage value | $100,000 |
| Annual net income generated | $ 48,000 |
| LLS's cost of capital | 12% |

*Required:*
Help LLS evaluate this project by calculating each of the following:

1.  Annual rate of return.
2.  Payback period.
3.  Net present value.
4.  Based on your calculation of net present value, what would you estimate the project's internal rate of return to be?

LO4    **E22-9 Analyzing the Relationship between Net Present Value and Internal Rate of Return**
Consider the relationship between a project's net present value (NPV), its internal rate of return (IRR), and a company's cost of capital. For each scenario that follows, indicate the relative value of the unknown. If cost of capital is unknown, indicate whether it would be higher or lower than the stated IRR. If NPV is unknown, indicate whether it would be higher or lower than zero. Project 1 is shown as an example.

| | Net Present Value | Cost of Capital | Internal Rate of Return |
|---|---|---|---|
| Project 1 | < 0 | 13% | <13% |
| Project 2 | > 0 | ? | 10 |
| Project 3 | ? | 14 | 12 |
| Project 4 | > 0 | 10 | ? |
| Project 5 | < 0 | ? | 9 |
| Project 6 | ? | 9 | 10 |

# Problems—Set A     **Available with McGraw-Hill's Homework Manager**

LO2, 3    **PA22-1 Analyzing a Special-Order Decision**
Sunblocker Corp. makes several varieties of beach umbrellas and accessories. It has been approached about producing a special order for custom umbrellas. The special-order umbrellas with logo of Randolph Industries would be distributed to participants at an upcoming convention sponsored by Randolph.

Randolph has offered to buy 1,500 of the No-More-Squint (NMS) model umbrellas at a price of $8 each. Sunblocker currently has the excess capacity necessary to accept the offer. The following information is related to production of Sunblocker's NMS umbrella.

| | |
|---|---|
| Direct materials | $ 2.25 |
| Direct labor | 0.75 |
| Variable manufacturing overhead | 3.50 |
| Fixed manufacturing overhead | 2.50 |
| Total cost | $ 9.00 |
| Regular sales price | $19.00 |

*Required:*

1. Determine the impact this special order would have on Sunblocker's total profit.
2. Should Sunblocker accept the special order?
3. Suppose that the special offer had been to purchase 2,000 umbrellas for $7.50 each. What effect would that offer have on Sunblocker's total profit?

## PA22-2 Analyzing a Make-or-Buy Decision

LO2, 3

Sunblocker Corp. (see PA22-1) is considering the possibility of outsourcing production of the umbrella tote bag included with some of its products. The company has received a bid from CarryAll Co. to produce 8,000 units per year for $6 each. Sunblocker has the following information about its own production of the tote bags:

| | |
|---|---|
| Direct materials | $3 |
| Direct labor | 1 |
| Variable manufacturing overhead | 1 |
| Fixed manufacturing overhead | 2 |
| Total cost per unit | $7 |

Sunblocker has determined that all variable costs could be eliminated by dropping production of the tote bags, but none of the fixed overhead is avoidable. At this time, Sunblocker has no specific use in mind for the space currently dedicated to producing the tote bags.

*Required:*

1. Determine the impact this decision will have on Sunblocker's annual income.
2. Should Sunblocker buy the tote bags from CarryAll or continue to make them?
3. Suppose that the space Sunblocker currently uses to make the bags could be utilized by a new product line that would generate $10,000 in annual profits. Does this change your recommendation to Sunblocker? If so, how?

## PA22-3 Analyzing a Keep-or-Drop Decision

LO2, 3

Sunblocker Corp. (see PA22-1 and PA22-2) is considering eliminating a product from its Happy Sand line of beach umbrellas. This collection is aimed at people who spend time on the beach or have an outdoor patio near the beach. Two products, the Happy Day and Morning Sun umbrellas, have impressive sales. However, sales for another umbrella, the Rolling Surf model, have been dismal.

Sunblocker's information related to the Happy Sand line follows.

| Segmented Income Statement for Sunblocker's Happy Sand Beach Umbrella Products | | | | |
|---|---|---|---|---|
| | Happy Day | Morning Sun | Rolling Surf | Total |
| Sales Revenue | $60,000 | $60,000 | $ 30,000 | $150,000 |
| Variable Costs | 34,000 | 31,000 | 23,000 | 88,000 |
| Contribution Margin | 26,000 | 29,000 | 7,000 | 62,000 |
| Allocated Fixed Costs* | 20,000 | 20,000 | 10,000 | 50,000 |
| Profit | $ 6,000 | $ 9,000 | $ (3,000) | $ 12,000 |

* Allocated based on total sales dollars.

Sunblocker has determined that eliminating the Rolling Surf model will cause sales of the Happy Day and the Morning Sun models to increase by 10 percent and 15 percent, respectively. Variable costs for these two models will increase proportionately. Additionally, none of the fixed cost allocated to the Rolling Surf model is avoidable. The fixed overhead currently allocated to the Rolling Surf model will be redistributed to the remaining two products.

*Required:*

1.  Determine what will happen to the company's total profit, if Sunblocker drops the Rolling Surf product. What is your recommendation to Sunblocker?
2.  Suppose that the full amount of fixed overhead allocated to Rolling Surf is avoidable. Would your recommendation to Sunblocker change? Why or why not?

**LO4**

www.mhhe.com/LLPW1e

### PA22-4 Calculating the Accounting Rate of Return, Payback Period, and Net Present Value

Hot Air Highlights (HAH) is considering the purchase of two new hot air balloons so that it can expand its desert sunset tours. Various information about the proposed investment follows.

| | |
|---|---|
| Initial investment (for two hot air balloons) | $500,000 |
| Useful life | 10 years |
| Salvage value | $ 50,000 |
| Annual net income generated | $ 42,000 |
| HAH's cost of capital | 11% |

*Required:*

Help HAH evaluate this project by calculating each of the following:

1.  Annual rate of return.
2.  Payback period.
3.  Net present value (NPV).
4.  Recalculate the NPV assuming HAH's cost of capital is 15 percent.
5.  Based on your calculation of NPV, what would you estimate the project's internal rate of return to be?

**LO4**

www.mhhe.com/LLPW1e

### PA22-5 Calculating the Accounting Rate of Return, Payback Period, and Net Present Value

Wing Walker Aces (WWA), Inc., is considering the purchase of a small plane to be used in its wing-walking demonstrations and aerial tour business. Various information about the proposed investment follows.

| | |
|---|---|
| Initial investment | $110,000 |
| Useful life | 12 years |
| Salvage value | $ 10,000 |
| Annual net income generated | $ 5,400 |
| WWA's cost of capital | 10% |

*Required:*

Help WWA evaluate this project by calculating each of the following:

1.  Annual rate of return.
2.  Payback period.
3.  Net present value (NPV).
4.  Recalculate WWA's NPV assuming the cost of capital is 6 percent.
5.  Based on your calculations of NPV, what would you estimate the project's internal rate of return to be?

## Problems—Set B     Available with McGraw-Hill's Homework Manager

**LO2, 3**

### PB22-1 Analyzing a Special-Order Decision

Woodchuck Corp. makes several varieties of wooden furniture. It has been approached about producing a special order for rocking chairs. A local senior citizens group would use the special-order chairs in a newly remodeled activity center.

The senior citizens have offered to buy 80 of the Rock-On model chairs at a price of $70 each. Woodchuck currently has the excess capacity necessary to accept the offer. A summary of the information related to production of Woodchuck's Rock-On model follows.

| | |
|---|---|
| Direct materials | $30 |
| Direct labor | 20 |
| Variable manufacturing overhead | 12 |
| Fixed manufacturing overhead | 11 |
| Total cost | $73 |
| Regular sales price | $99 |

*Required:*

1. What impact would this special order have on Woodchuck's total profit?
2. Should Woodchuck accept the special order?
3. Suppose that the special offer had been to purchase 100 rocking chairs for $65 each. What effect would that offer have on Woodchuck's total profit?

**PB22-2 Analyzing a Make-or-Buy Decision**    LO2, 3

Woodchuck Corp. (see PB22-1) is considering the possibility of outsourcing the production of upholstered chair pads that are included with some of its wooden chairs. The company has received a bid from Padalong Co. to produce 1,000 units per year for $9 each. Woodchuck has the following information about its own production of the chair pads:

| | |
|---|---|
| Direct materials | $ 4 |
| Direct labor | 2 |
| Variable manufacturing overhead | 2 |
| Fixed manufacturing overhead | 3 |
| Total cost per unit | $11 |

Woodchuck has determined that all variable costs could be eliminated by dropping production of the chair pads, but none of the fixed overhead is avoidable. At this time, Woodchuck has no specific use in mind for the space currently dedicated to producing the chair pads.

*Required:*

1. Determine the impact this decision will have on Woodchuck's annual income.
2. Should Woodchuck buy the chair pads from Padalong or continue to make them?
3. Suppose that a new product line that Woodchuck wants to develop could utilize the Woodchuck space currently used for the chair pads. What amount of income must be generated by the new product line for Woodchuck to outsource the chair pads?

**PB22-3 Analyzing a Keep-or-Drop Decision**    LO2, 3

Woodchuck Corp. (see PB22-1 and PB22-2) is considering eliminating a product from its line of outdoor tables. Two products, the Oak-A and Fiesta tables, have impressive sales. However, sales for the Studio model have been dismal.

Information related to Woodchuck's outdoor table line follows.

### Segmented Income Statement for Woodchuck's Outdoor Table Products

| | Oak-A | Fiesta | Studio | Total |
|---|---|---|---|---|
| Sales revenue | $110,000 | $77,000 | $33,000 | $220,000 |
| Variable costs | 77,000 | 52,000 | 24,000 | 153,000 |
| Contribution margin | 33,000 | 25,000 | 9,000 | 67,000 |
| Allocated fixed costs* | 20,000 | 14,000 | 6,000 | 40,000 |
| Profit | $ 13,000 | $11,000 | $ 3,000 | $ 27,000 |

*Allocated based on total sales dollars

Woodchuck has determined that eliminating the Studio model will cause sales of the Oak-A and the Fiesta tables to increase by 20 percent and 5 percent, respectively. Variable costs for these two models will increase proportionately. Additionally, $1,000 of the fixed cost allocated to the Studio model is avoidable. The remaining fixed overhead currently allocated to the Studio model will be redistributed to the remaining two products.

*Required:*

1. Determine what will happen to the company's total profit, if Woodchuck drops the Studio product. What is your recommendation to Woodchuck?
2. Suppose that $4,000 of fixed overhead allocated to the Studio model is avoidable. Would your recommendation to Woodchuck change? Why or why not?

**LO4**

**PB22-4 Calculating the Accounting Rate of Return, Payback Period, and Net Present Value**
Ted's Taxi Company (TTC) is considering the purchase of four new taxi cabs. Various information about the proposed investment follows.

| | |
|---|---|
| Initial investment (for 4 vehicles) | $220,000 |
| Useful life | 5 years |
| Salvage value | $ 20,000 |
| Annual net income generated | $ 27,000 |
| TTC's cost of capital | 9% |

*Required:*
Help TTC evaluate this project by calculating each of the following:

1. Annual rate of return.
2. Payback period.
3. Net present value (NPV).
4. Recalculate the NPV assuming the cost of capital is 15 percent.
5. Based on your calculations of NPV, what would you estimate the project's internal rate of return to be?

**LO4**

**PB22-5 Calculating the Accounting Rate of Return, Payback Period, and Net Present Value**
Titan Production Co. is considering an investment in new machinery for its factory. Various information about the proposed investment follows.

| | |
|---|---|
| Initial investment | $750,000 |
| Useful life | 6 years |
| Salvage value | $120,000 |
| Annual net income generated | $ 66,000 |
| Titan's cost of capital | 11% |

*Required:*
Help Titan evaluate this project by calculating each of the following:

1. Annual rate of return.
2. Payback period.
3. Net present value (NPV).
4. Recalculate Titan's NPV assuming its cost of capital is 12 percent.
5. Based on your calculations of NPV, what would you estimate the project's internal rate of return to be?

# Cases and Projects

**CP22-1 Evaluating a University's Decision to Eliminate Collegiate Sports Programs:**      **LO3**
**Quantitative and Qualitative Considerations**

Due to budget cutbacks, colleges and universities across the country are struggling to cut expenses. Frequent casualties of these money-saving decisions are organized sport teams. Suppose that a fictional college, West Tennessee State (WTS), has identified three teams to be eliminated in its effort to cut costs: men's lacrosse, women's softball, and men's diving. A summary of each sport's annual revenue and costs follow:

|  | Men's Lacrosse | Women's Softball | Men's Diving |
|---|---|---|---|
| Revenue | $  25,600 | $  37,800 | $  14,900 |
| Less: Expenses |  |  |  |
| Scholarships | 150,000 | 130,000 | 40,000 |
| Coaches' salaries | 53,000 | 49,700 | 62,800 |
| Team travel | 21,100 | 28,500 | 13,200 |
| Venue maintenance | 15,000 | 20,000 | 35,000 |
| Equipment | 4,300 | 2,800 | 800 |
| Team support | 16,600 | 11,200 | 6,300 |
| Net income (loss) | $(234,400) | $(204,400) | $(143,200) |

The combined net loss from these three programs is $(582,000).

*Required:*

1. Do you think WTS will see an immediate improvement in the college's bottom line (loss) of $582,000? Why or why not?

2. Determine whether the decision for each individual line item will be completely eliminated, partially eliminated, or not eliminated. Label the items as avoidable, partially avoidable, or unavoidable and explain any assumptions you made in determining the classification.

3. Research actual examples of the colleges or universities that have eliminated sports programs. List five colleges or universities that have eliminated sports teams in the past three years and identify which teams were eliminated.

4. Major sports such as men's football and basketball are seldom, if ever, eliminated even though they generally have the highest dollar amount of expenses. Why are these sports retained? What other factors may affect which teams are eliminated?

5. Choose one of the institutions identified in requirement 3 to investigate in more detail. For that university, discuss the factors that led to its choice(s), the anticipated impact on direct participants (coaches, athletes, etc.), and the total amount of savings expected. Also include reactions from the student body and the local and college communities.

**C22-2 Evaluating Wal-Mart's Decision to Eliminate Product Offerings: Quantitative**      **LO3**
**and Qualitative Considerations**

During 2006 and 2007, Wal-Mart decided to eliminate two long-standing components of its business: merchandise layaway and by-the-bolt sales of fabric. Each of these decisions was met with considerable controversy among Wal-Mart customers.

*Required:*

1. Research these two decisions by Wal-Mart and write a brief paragraph explaining the company's point of view in making each decision. Include any information you can find about the profitability of the segment and possible plans for an alternative in the fabric decision.

2. Describe the "typical" Wal-Mart customer who will be most impacted by these decisions.

3. Write a brief paragraph from this typical customer's point of view explaining how Wal-Mart's decision would impact the customer.

4. Identify three possible effects of each decision on other segments of Wal-Mart's business. Be specific in terms of both the segment and the possible impact.

5. Consider a small, rural community in an economically depressed area of the United States. How might each of these decisions impact the people in that community? Contrast this to the impact felt in larger, urban areas of the country.

LO3 **CP22-3 Researching Outsourcing Issues in the National and Local Press**

Outsourcing, particularly to overseas companies, is a hot-button topic that has garnered much attention in the academic, national, and local business media.

*Required:*

1. Do a quick search at www.wikipedia.org for a high-level overview of outsourcing. What are some of the major reasons that companies decide to follow this practice? What are the advantages and disadvantages to outsourcing from the perspective of the company and its stockholders, managers, employees, and local community?

2. Search for a recent article on outsourcing in a national business publication such as *Fortune*, *BusinessWeek*, or *The Wall Street Journal*. Briefly summarize the article's main points, including any outsourcing trends, companies making outsourcing decisions, or issues related to politics or the U.S. economy.

3. Search the archives of your local or regional newspaper for articles about outsourcing. Try to identify a specific company in your area that has outsourced part of its operations. Describe the part of the business that was outsourced. For example, did the company outsource part of its manufacturing operation or a support function such as information technology or customer support? What likely factors came into play in the decision? What impact, if any, will this decision have on customers, employees, and the local community?

4. Discuss whether you or someone you know has been personally affected by a company's decision to outsource.

LO4 **CP22-4 Analyzing a Personal Decision to Pursue a Graduate Degree**

Assume that your friend Greg Ellis is thinking of getting an MBA. He is a resident of Arizona and is currently earning $45,000 per year. One of the schools Greg is considering is Brigham Young University (BYU) in Provo, Utah. He went to the Forbes Web site and used the "Should You Get an M.B.A." decision tool to calculate the "five-year gain" from getting an MBA at BYU. The results of that analysis follow.

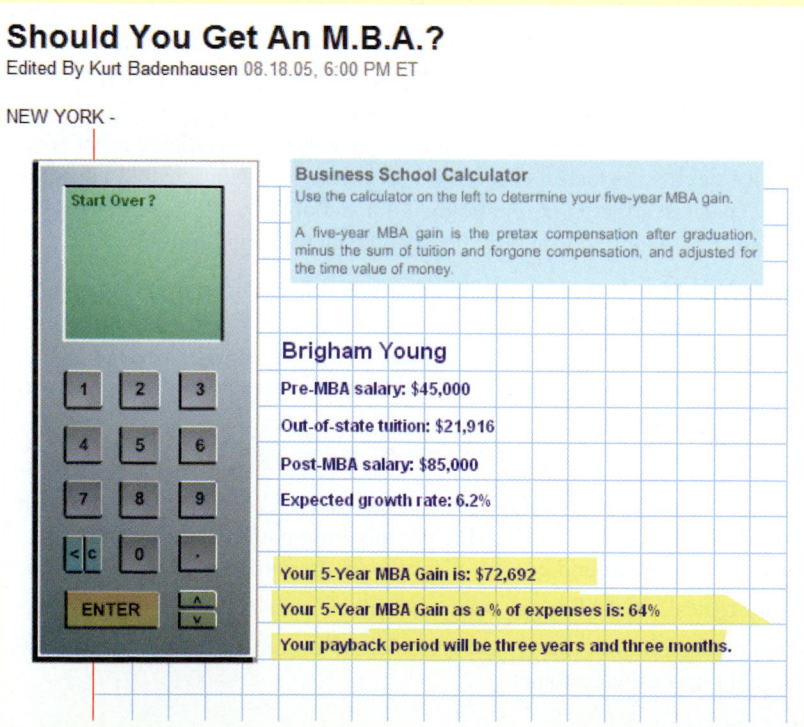

From: http://www.forbes.com/2005/08/16/cz_05mba_business_schools_gain_calulator.html

Greg was pleased to see that his five-year gain from getting an MBA was $72,692 and that the payback time on his investment would be just a little over three years. He is also considering a few other options:

- Getting a degree at Arizona State University (ASU) where he would qualify for in-state tuition. Greg believes his post-MBA salary would be the same with a degree from ASU as with one from BYU.
- Getting a degree at Harvard University. Greg believes he would be able to earn a higher starting salary coming out of Harvard (estimated at $100,000).

*Required:*

1. Go to the Forbes Web site and calculate the five-year gain from getting an MBA at ASU. State any assumption you are asked to make. Explain what factors caused the five-year gain to be higher or lower at ASU than at BYU.

2. Go to the Forbes Web site and calculate the five-year gain from getting an MBA at Harvard. State any assumption you are asked to make. Explain what factors caused the five-year gain to be higher or lower at Harvard than at BYU.

3. The Forbes decision tool takes into account both out-of-pocket costs and opportunity costs. Give examples of each.

4. The Forbes decision tool also takes into account the time value of money. Without making specific calculations, explain how the time value of money is likely to differ for the Harvard and ASU alternatives. Keep in mind that the up-front tuition is likely to be much lower at ASU than at Harvard, but the future benefits in terms of salary are likely to be higher at Harvard than ASU. How would these differences affect the time value of money?

5. Is the $45,000 pre-MBA salary relevant to Greg's decision about whether to go to Harvard, ASU, or BYU? Why or why not?

6. Suppose instead that Greg was trying to decide whether to continue with his current career path or get an MBA. Is his current salary relevant to this decision? Why or why not?

# Budgetary Planning

## LEARNING OBJECTIVES

**After completing this chapter, you should be able to:**

**LO1** Describe the phases of the planning and control process.

**LO2** List the key benefits of budgeting.

**LO3** Explain the behavioral effects of budgets and provide guidelines for implementing a budget.

**LO4** Describe the major components of the master budget and their interrelationships.

**LO5** Prepare the following components of the operating budget:

   a. Sales budget.
   b. Production budget.
   c. Raw materials purchases budget.
   d. Direct labor budget.
   e. Manufacturing overhead budget.
   f. Selling and administrative expense budget.

**LO6** Prepare the cash budget and describe the other financial budgets required to produce a budgeted balance sheet.

Lectured presentation–LP23-1
www.mhhe.com/LLPW1e

## Focus Company: COLD STONE CREAMERY

## "Because the world deserves better ice cream."

www.coldstonecreamery.com

Have you ever spent time planning a major event, such as a graduation party, bar or bat mitzvah, or wedding? If so, you probably realize the importance of having a **budget** to guide your decisions about where to hold the event, how many people to invite, and what food to serve. These and many other decisions affect the cost and success of any event.

Businesses use budgets in a similar way. Rather than budgeting for a one-time event, however, organizations use budgets to plan their ongoing operations so they will be able to meet their short-term and long-term objectives. Both profit-oriented and nonprofit organizations use budgets. The only difference is whether their short- and long-term objectives are oriented to earning a profit or reaching some nonprofit objective, such as providing education, feeding the poor, or improving health care.

In this chapter, we describe the budgeting process in a company that many of you may be familiar with, Cold Stone Creamery. Founded in 1988 by two ice cream lovers in Tempe, Arizona, Cold Stone Creamery now has more than 1,500 locations in countries around the world including Korea and Japan. The company's employees prepare delicious, custom-made ice cream creations on a piece of cold granite by mixing freshly made ice cream with a wide variety of high-quality ingredients. Consumers may choose one of Cold Stone's best-selling flavors, such as Peanut Butter Cup Perfection or Cheesecake Fantasy, or create their own unique flavor choosing from dozens of mix-ins, such as nuts, candy, cookies, and fruit. A Harvard business student has estimated that the average person would need more than 421 lifetimes to try all of the more than 11.5 million possible Cold Stone Creamery creations—but only by starting on the day he or she was born!

In this chapter, we prepare an entire master budget for a hypothetical Cold Stone Creamery location. In the next chapter, we determine whether Cold Stone Creamery achieved its budget by comparing actual to budgeted results. First, let's cover some basic concepts in budgeting.

**ROLE OF BUDGETS IN THE PLANNING AND CONTROL CYCLE**

- Planning Process
- Benefits of Budgeting
- Behavioral Effects of Budgets

**COMPONENTS OF THE MASTER BUDGET**

**PREPARATION OF THE OPERATING BUDGETS**

- Sales Budget
- Production Budget
- Raw Materials Purchases Budget
- Direct Labor Budget
- Manufacturing Overhead Budget
- Budgeted Cost of Goods Sold
- Selling and Administrative Expense Budget
- Budgeted Income Statement

**PREPARATION OF FINANCIAL BUDGETS**

- Cash Budget
- Budgeted Balance Sheet
- Budgeting in a Merchandising Company

## ROLE OF BUDGETS IN THE PLANNING AND CONTROL CYCLE

**Learning Objective 1**

Describe the phases of the planning and control process.

Chapter 18 introduced the four functions of management: planning, organizing, directing/ leading, and control. This process, which is illustrated in Exhibit 23.1, is sometimes referred to as the planning and control cycles.

**Planning** is the forward-looking phase of the planning and control process that involves setting long-term objectives and defining short-term tactics that will help to achieve them. Once the plan is in place, managers must beginning **organizing** or arranging for the necessary resources needed to achieve the plan. An important part of the organizing process is the

**Exhibit 23.1** Planning and Control Cycles

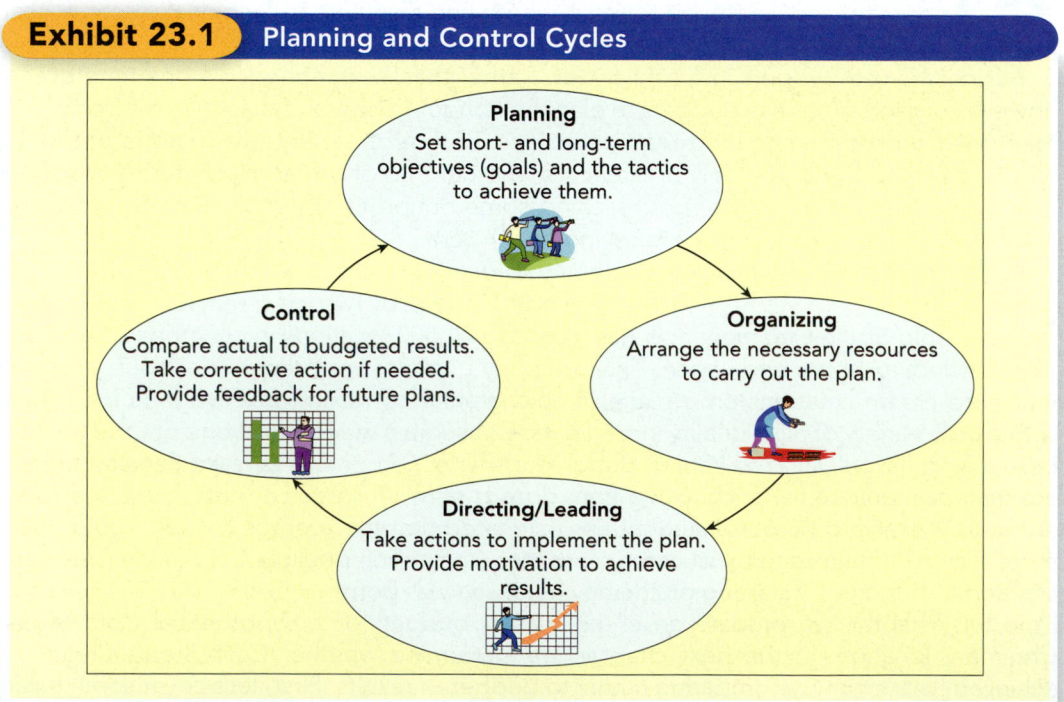

Planning
Set short- and long-term objectives (goals) and the tactics to achieve them.

Organizing
Arrange the necessary resources to carry out the plan.

Directing/Leading
Take actions to implement the plan. Provide motivation to achieve results.

Control
Compare actual to budgeted results. Take corrective action if needed. Provide feedback for future plans.

creation of a **budget,** a detailed plan that translates the company's objectives into financial terms, identifying the resources and expenditures that will be required over a limited planning horizon (typically a year) which can be broken into shorter periods (for example, months or quarters). The next step, **directing/leading,** involves all actions managers must take to implement the plan including motivating employees to achieve results. As you will see shortly, a budget can have either motivating or demotivating effects on behavior, depending on how it is implemented. As the plan is implemented, the managerial accounting system keeps track of the results, which are used later in the control process. The **control** function is the backward-looking part of the planning and control cycle. In this phase, managers compare actual to budgeted results to determine whether employees have met the objectives set during the planning stage. If not, managers should take corrective action where necessary. We focus more closely on the control process in Chapter 24, when we calculate variances that compare to budgeted results.

## Planning Process

The starting point of the planning process is managers' **strategic plan**—their vision of what they want the organization to achieve over the long term. The strategic plan is then translated into long-term and short-term objectives (that is, goals) and the tactics necessary to achieve those objectives. A **long-term objective** is a specific goal that managers want to achieve over the long term, typically 5 to 10 years. A **short-term objective** is a specific goal that managers need to achieve in no more than a year to reach their long-term goals. **Tactics** are the specific actions or mechanisms managers plan to use to achieve their objectives.

For example, consider a company's long-term objective that is to gain a 50 percent share of the market over the next five years. A short-term objective might be to increase sales revenue by 10 percent during the next year. One possible tactic for achieving that goal would be to increase the amount spent on advertising and promotion to generate additional sales.

Consider Cold Stone Creamery's strategic vision, the "Pyramid of Success 2010" in Exhibit 23.2. It is a strategic plan that identifies what the company wants to achieve by the year 2010. The top of the pyramid shows the company's strategic vision, which is to become "the #1 best-selling ice cream brand in America by December 31, 2009." This goal, which was set in 2005, represents a specific long-term objective. To achieve this long-term goal, managers then set their short-term objectives and tactics. Although Cold Stone Creamery's objectives and tactics are not available to the general public (or to competitors), we can get a sense of their nature by examining the other levels of the pyramid.

The pyramid indicates that Cold Stone Creamery's daily purpose is to sell more ice cream to more people more often in more locations. Thus, we can assume that many of the company's short-term objectives are based on growth rates for sales revenue, the number of new stores opened, and the company's overall market share. In addition to these financial objectives, Cold Stone's success depends on its ability to introduce appealing new ice cream products and to hire and retain employees who can keep customers happy by providing the "ultimate ice cream experience." Thus, the company is likely to have objectives for new product development, employee training and retention, and customer satisfaction. In the last chapter of this book, we discuss the importance of developing nonfinancial measures to track performance in these areas.

## Benefits of Budgeting

Budgeting has several benefits (see Exhibit 23.3). **One of the major advantages of budgeting is that it forces managers to look to the future.** In your own life, you or your parents may have prepared a budget to help save for college, a future vacation, or retirement. In business, budgets force managers to look ahead and address potential problems. For example, a budget can help managers plan to ensure they always have enough cash on hand to pay the company's bills or to avoid running out of inventory during periods of peak demand.

**Budgets also play an important communication role within organizations.** They provide a mechanism for managers to share expectations and priorities for the future. Because budgets span the entire organization, they also require managers from different functional areas to communicate and coordinate their activities.

### Coach's Tip

The terms **budgeted, predicted, estimated, forecasted, anticipated, expected,** and **planned** are used interchangeably to reflect the future-oriented aspects of the budgeting process.

Video 23-1
www.mhhe.com/LLPW1e

### Learning Objective 2

List the key benefits of budgeting.

**Exhibit 23.2** Cold Stone Creamery's Strategic Vision: Pyramid of Success 2010

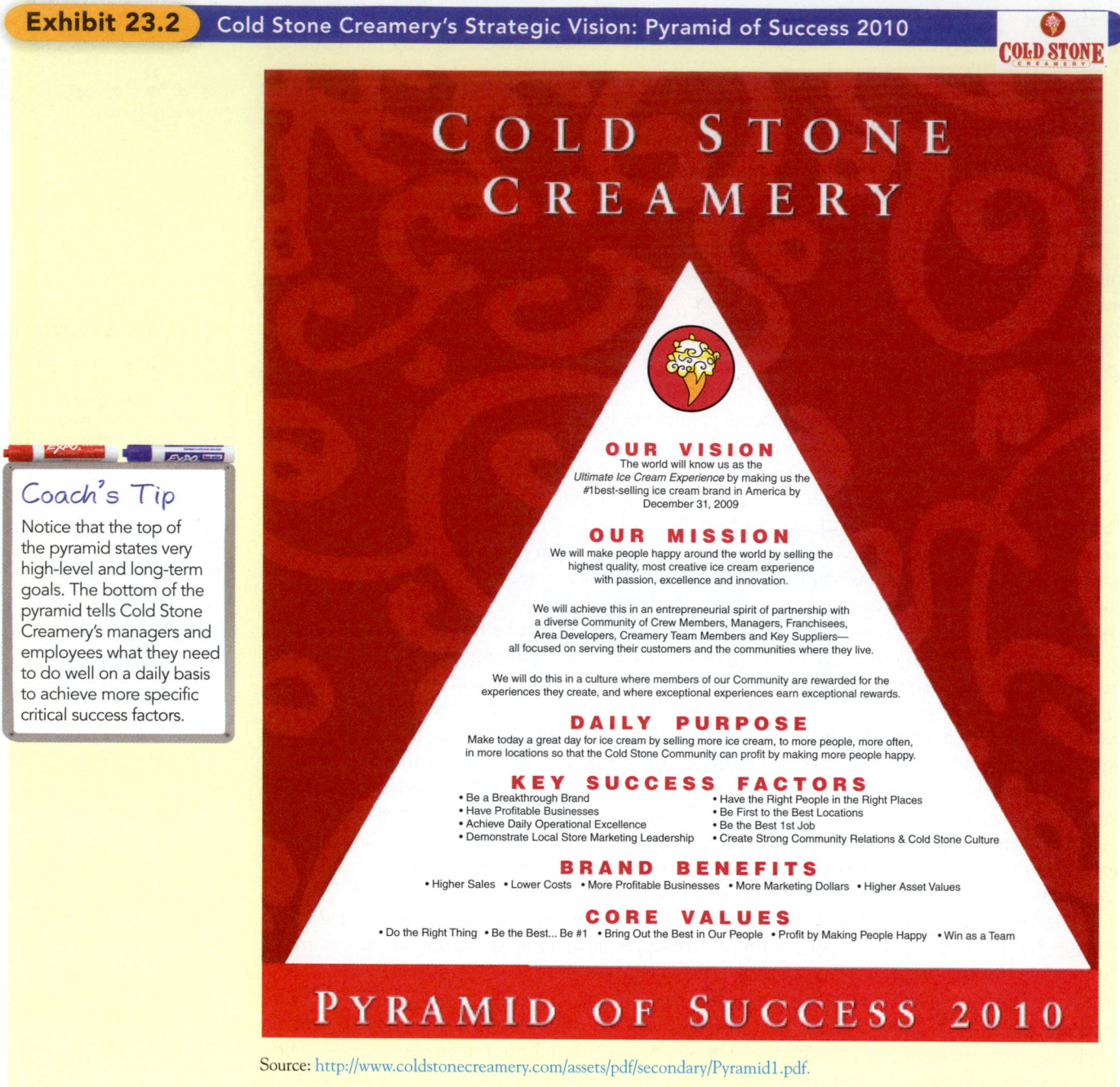

**Coach's Tip**

Notice that the top of the pyramid states very high-level and long-term goals. The bottom of the pyramid tells Cold Stone Creamery's managers and employees what they need to do well on a daily basis to achieve more specific critical success factors.

Source: http://www.coldstonecreamery.com/assets/pdf/secondary/Pyramid1.pdf.

Finally, **budgets serve an important role in motivating and rewarding employees.** If a budget is implemented correctly, it should motivate employees to work to meet the organization's objectives. **Budgets also provide a useful benchmark for evaluating and rewarding employee performance.** We discuss the motivational effects of budgets in the next section; their role in performance evaluation is addressed in the next two chapters.

## Behavioral Effects of Budgets

Although budgets are intended to motivate employees to work to achieve the organization's goals, they can sometimes create unintended effects. The way in which managers and employees behave in response to budgets depends, in large part, on how goals and budgets are set. Two considerations are especially critical: the relative difficulty of meeting goals and the degree of employee participation in establishing goals.

In setting budgetary goals, finding the right level of difficulty is important. Research suggests that **budgets that are tight but attainable are more likely to motivate people** than

| **Exhibit 23.3** | **Benefits of Budgeting** |

| Thinking ahead | Communication | Motivation |
|---|---|---|
| • Forcing managers to look ahead and state their goals for the future<br>• Providing lead time to solve potential problems | • Communicating management's expectations and priorities<br>• Promoting cooperation and coordination between functional areas of the organization | • Providing motivation for employees to work toward organizational objectives<br>• Providing a benchmark for evaluating performance |

budgets that are either too easy or too difficult to achieve. Think about your own personal goals. If your goal is too easy, you will not have to work very hard to achieve it. If you set your goal too high, however, you will quickly become frustrated and give up. Similarly, managers must try to find the just-right level of difficulty in setting an organization's budgetary goals to have a motivating rather than a demotivating effect on employee behavior.

Involving employees at all levels of the organization in the budgeting process is also important. **Participative budgeting** allows employees throughout the organization to have input into the budget-setting process. This bottom-up approach to budgeting can be contrasted with a **top-down approach** in which top management sets the budget and imposes it on lower levels of the organization. In general, **a participative approach is more likely to motivate people to work toward an organization's goals than a top-down approach.**

One downside to participative budgeting is that managers may try to build a little extra cushion, or **budget slack**, into their budgets. They can do so by understating expected sales or overstating budgeted expenses, making it more likely that they will come in under budget for expenses or over budget for revenues. Budgets can also create a "use-it-or-lose-it" mentality that encourages managers to spend their entire budgets to avoid a reduction in the next budget period. Some of these dysfunctional behaviors can be minimized by implementing the following budget-setting guidelines:

- **Use different budgets for planning and for performance evaluation.** Although budget slack causes problems in planning, it provides a way for managers to hedge against uncertainty. In organizations that face major fluctuations in demand or costs that are beyond the manager's control, some slack can be beneficial.

- **Use a continuous, or rolling budget, approach.** Under continuous budgeting, the company maintains a rolling budget that always extends a certain period into the future. When one budget period passes, another is automatically added at the end. This approach keeps managers in a continuous planning mode, always looking into the future rather than at the end of a specific budget period.

- **Use a zero-based budgeting approach.** Under zero-based budgeting, the entire budget must be constructed from zero each period rather than starting with the last period's actual results.

As this discussion indicates, managers must take a variety of behavioral factors into account in designing and implementing a budget system. There is not a "one-size-fits-all" solution to

**Learning Objective 3**

Explain the behavioral effects of budgets and provide guidelines for implementing a budget.

## Spotlight On **ETHICS**

### Playing Budget Games

Managers who are evaluated and rewarded for meeting budgetary goals may engage in game playing. For example, a sales manager who has reached his or her sales quota for the week may try to defer sales to a future period by telling customers to come back later to make their purchases. Managers may even be tempted to post-date purchase orders so that purchases **appear** to have been made in a later period. Alternatively, a salesperson who has not met his or her quota may cut prices at the end of the period to increase sales volume and meet the sales goal.

By engaging in these tactics, managers are putting their own self-interest ahead of the organization's objectives. Although the complete elimination of such budget games is difficult to achieve, organizations must try to design their budgets and control systems to minimize these dysfunctional behaviors.

budgeting. The best approach depends on the nature of the business environment, type of organization, and tasks managers must perform within the organization.

Before continuing, take a moment to make sure you understand the basic principles of budgeting by completing the following Self-Study Practice.

**SELF-STUDY PRACTICE**

Which of the following statements is false? (You may select more than one answer.)

1. Planning is the forward-looking phase of the planning and control cycle; control is the backward-looking phase of the cycle.

2. Short-term objectives are the specific goals that managers would like to achieve; tactics are the specific mechanisms they will use to achieve those goals.

3. Employees are more likely to be motivated by a top-down approach to budgeting than by a participative approach.

4. The creation of budget slack is not a problem for planning purposes, but it does cause problems in evaluating employees' performance.

*After you have finished, check your answers with the solutions at the bottom of the page.*

## COMPONENTS OF THE MASTER BUDGET

A **master budget** is a comprehensive set of budgets that covers all phases of an organization's planned activities for a specific period. Within the master budget, individual budgets can be classified as either operating budgets or financial budgets. See Exhibit 23.4 for an illustration of the components of the master budget. Note that each component is either based on or provides input for another component.

**Operating budgets** cover the organization's planned operating activities for a particular period including expected sales, production, raw materials purchases, direct labor, manufacturing overhead, and selling and administrative expenses. When all of these individual budgets are combined, they form a **budgeted income statement**.

**Financial budgets** focus on the financial resources needed to support operations including cash receipts and disbursements, inventory, capital expenditures, and financing. Note that each of these budgets relates in some way either to an asset (for example, cash, inventory, and capital investments) or to liabilities and equity (for example, the way operating activities are financed). Thus, the financial budgets can be combined to form a **budgeted balance sheet**.

**Learning Objective 4**

Describe the major components of the master budget and their interrelationships.

**Solution to Self-Study Practice**    Statements 3 and 4 are false.

| Exhibit 23.4 | Components of the Master Budget |
| --- | --- |

The starting point for preparing the master budget is the **sales budget**, or sales forecast, an estimate of the number of units to be sold and the total sales revenue to be generated each period. Various sources are used to determine the sales forecast including:

- Actual sales for the preceding period.
- Research on overall industry trends.
- Input from top management about overall sales objectives (for example, market share goals).
- Input from research and development about new product introductions, new features of existing products, and so on.
- Planned marketing activities (for example, advertising and sales promotions).

By considering all of these factors, sales managers determine their best estimate of future sales, which is reflected in the sales budget.

When the sales budget has been set, managers prepare the **production budget**, which shows how many units must be produced each period. The number of units to be produced may differ from the number of units to be sold depending on the company's **inventory budget**, which shows planned levels of the finished goods, work in process, and raw materials inventories at the beginning and end of each period.

When managers know how many units to produce, they can prepare budgets estimating the materials, labor, and manufacturing overhead costs they will need to produce those units.

- The **raw materials purchases budget** indicates the amount of raw materials needed to meet production goals and allow for planned levels of raw materials inventory.
- The **direct labor budget** identifies the amount of direct labor needed to meet production needs.
- The **manufacturing overhead budget** indicates the manufacturing overhead cost needed to support budgeted production.

All of these manufacturing budgets are combined to calculate the **budgeted manufacturing cost per unit**, which is used to determine the **budgeted cost of goods sold**. This cost is calculated by multiplying the budgeted cost per unit by the number of units of expected sales. Based on the sales forecast, managers can also prepare a **selling and administrative expense budget**, which identifies how much they need to spend on selling and administrative costs to support planned sales levels.

The operating budgets in turn are used to prepare the budgeted income statement. Essentially, each of the operating budgets, starting with the sales budget, becomes a line item in the budgeted income statement. Managers then subtract the budgeted cost of goods sold, which incorporates all budgeted manufacturing costs, to arrive at the budgeted gross margin. Finally, managers subtract budgeted selling and administrative expenses to arrive at the budgeted operating profit (before taxes).

Note in Exhibit 23.4 that all operating budgets are connected in some way to one or more financial budgets. The primary financial budget that we prepare in this chapter is the cash budget, which provides information about budgeted cash receipts and disbursements. Based on the cash budget and the other financial budgets, we can then prepare a budgeted balance sheet to show the balances of all of the company's assets, liabilities, and owners' equity accounts at the end of the period.

# PREPARATION OF THE OPERATING BUDGETS

In this section, we prepare the operating budgets for a hypothetical Cold Stone Creamery location. Although we make a number of simplifying assumptions and the numbers do not necessarily represent Cold Stone's actual cost of operations, the objective of this example is to show the key components of the various operating budgets and how they relate to one another.

## Sales Budget

**Learning Objective 5a**

Prepare the sales budget.

As mentioned, the starting point for the master budget is the sales forecast or sales budget. The sales department typically provides this information based on a variety of sources, including prior sales, industry trends, and marketing activities.

Preparation of the sales budget requires multiplying the number of units expected to be sold each period by the budgeted sales price. See Exhibit 23.5 for Cold Stone Creamery's quarter-by-quarter estimate of unit sales for the year 2010.

Notice that budgeted unit sales are high during the summer months and low during the winter months. The budgeted sales price is expected to remain constant at an average of $5 per unit, for a total budgeted sales revenue of $425,000.

**Exhibit 23.5    Sales Budget**

|  | Quarter 1 Jan.–Mar. | Quarter 2 Apr.–June | Quarter 3 July–Sept. | Quarter 4 Oct.–Dec. | Yearly Total |
|---|---|---|---|---|---|
| Budgeted unit sales | 15,000 | 20,000 | 27,000 | 23,000 | 85,000 |
| Budgeted sales price | × $ 5.00 | × $ 5.00 | × $ 5.00 | × $ 5.00 | × $ 5.00 |
| Budgeted sales revenue | $75,000 | $100,000 | $135,000 | $115,000 | $425,000 |

## Production Budget

The production budget is directly related to the sales budget and to the amount of inventory the company wants to have on hand at the beginning and end of each period. If the company is planning to build inventory, production needs to exceed sales. If the company is planning to reduce its inventory, sales should be more than production. The relationship between budgeted production, sales, and inventory is summarized in the following formula:

**Coach's Tip**

Today, many service businesses and manufacturing companies produce their products and services to order. These companies have no finished goods inventory, so the sales budget and the production budget are identical.

**Budgeted Production Units** = **Budgeted Unit Sales** + **Budgeted Ending Finished Goods Inventory** − **Budgeted Beginning Finished Goods Inventory**

In the past, manufacturing companies held substantial inventories of finished goods, which created a marked difference between the sales budget and the production budget. Today, however, companies such as Dell and Nike are moving toward a make-to-order approach in which the final product is manufactured to fill a specific customer order.

Cold Stone Creamery is a make-to-order company that produces its ice cream creations at the customer's request. Thus, the company holds virtually no finished goods inventory. The only exception is the "grab and go" containers that Cold Stone stocks for customers who want to enjoy a frozen creation at home. Traditional manufacturing companies maintain a much larger finished goods inventory as a buffer between expected sales and production. To make our example more consistent with that of a traditional manufacturing company, we assume that **Cold Stone Creamery maintains a small stock of finished goods inventory equal to 5 percent of the current period's budgeted sales.** See Exhibit 23.6 for the resulting production budget for Cold Stone Creamery based on this assumption and on the sales budget in Exhibit 23.5.

As expected, production is budgeted to be highest during the summer months when budgeted sales are at their highest. Notice that the ending finished goods inventory is calculated as 5 percent of the current period sales. In quarter 1, ending inventory is budgeted at 750 units (15,000 units × 5 percent). This ending inventory value becomes the beginning inventory value for the next quarter.

> **Learning Objective 5b**
> Prepare the production budget.

**Exhibit 23.6** | **Production Budget**

| | Quarter 1 Jan.–Mar. | Quarter 2 Apr.–June | Quarter 3 July–Sept. | Quarter 4 Oct.–Dec. | Yearly Total |
|---|---|---|---|---|---|
| Budgeted unit sales (from Exhibit 23.5) | 15,000 | 20,000 | 27,000 | 23,000 | 85,000 |
| +Budgeted ending inventory 5% of current period budgeted sales | + 750* | + 1,000 | + 1,350 | + 1,150 | + 1,150 |
| – Budgeted beginning inventory | – 900† | – 750 | – 1,000 | – 1,350 | – 900 |
| Budgeted production | 14,850 | 20,250 | 27,350 | 22,800 | 85,250 |

\* Ending inventory for quarter 1 = 15,000 × 5% = 750
† Beginning inventory for quarter 1 is assumed to be 900 units.

# Raw Materials Purchases Budget

Next managers must determine what amount of raw materials to purchase. Budgeted purchases depend on budgeted production needs and on the planned levels for beginning and ending raw materials inventory. The formula follows:

> **Learning Objective 5c**
> Prepare the raw materials purchases budget.

$$\boxed{\text{Budgeted Raw Material Purchases}} = \boxed{\text{Budgeted Production Needs}} + \boxed{\text{Budgeted Ending Raw Materials Inventory}} - \boxed{\text{Budgeted Beginning Raw Materials Inventory}}$$

Let's apply this formula to the primary ingredients used to make ice cream: milk, cream, and sugar. The super-premium ice cream made at Cold Stone Creamery contains a relatively high proportion of cream (as opposed to milk) compared to most commercially manufactured ice cream. The specific mix of ingredients is what creates the rich and creamy taste of the ice cream, as well as the relatively high price (since cream is much more expensive than milk). In reality, Cold Stone Creamery would prepare a separate budget for each of these major ingredients. However, for simplicity we will combine the purchase of milk, cream, and sugar into a single budget. We assume that each Cold Stone creation requires a total of 10 ounces of milk, cream, and sugar, and that the average price of this ingredient mix is $.05 per ounce. Because of the company's emphasis on freshness and quality, managers will want to keep the inventory of raw materials to a minimum. For this example, we assume that Cold Stone Creamery plans its purchase of raw materials so that the ending inventory is equal to 3 percent of **next period's** production needs. Exhibit 23.7 shows Cold Stone Creamery's raw materials purchases budget based on these assumptions.

Notice that raw materials purchases are based on budgeted **production** levels (not sales levels). We multiply budgeted production by the materials requirement per unit (10 ounces)

> **Coach's Tip**
> Notice that the formula for budgeted raw material purchases is very similar to the one for the budgeted production. The only difference is that it starts with production (not sales) and adjusts for beginning and ending raw materials inventory.
>
> In these formulas, always add the ending inventory and subtract the beginning inventory.

**Exhibit 23.7**    Raw Materials Purchases Budget (Milk, Sugar, and Cream)

|  | Quarter 1 Jan.–Mar. | Quarter 2 Apr.–June | Quarter 3 July–Sept. | Quarter 4 Oct.–Dec. | Yearly Total |
|---|---|---|---|---|---|
| Budgeted production (from Exhibit 23.6) | 14,850 | 20,250 | 27,350 | 22,800 | 85,250 |
| Materials requirement (10 oz. per unit) | × 10 oz. | × 10 oz. | × 10 oz. | × 10 oz. | × 10 oz. |
| Total material needed for production | 148,500 | 202,500 | 273,500 | 228,000 | 852,500 |
| + Planned ending inventory (3% of next month's production needs) | + 6,075* | + 8,205 | + 6,840 | + 3,510‡ | + 3,510 |
| − Planned beginning inventory (3% of current month's production needs) | − 4,455† | − 6,075 | − 8,205 | − 6,840 | − 4,455 |
| Total purchases of raw materials | 150,120 | 204,630 | 272,135 | 224,670 | 851,555 |
| Average cost per ounce | × $ 0.05 | × $ 0.05 | × $ 0.05 | × $ 0.05 | × $ 0.05 |
| Budgeted cost of raw materials purchases | $ 7,506 | $ 10,232 | $ 13,607 | $ 11,233 | $ 42,578 |

\* Ending inventory for quarter 1 = 202,500 × 3% = 6,075
† Beginning inventory for quarter 1 = 148,500 × 3% = 4,455
‡ Ending inventory for quarter 4 is assumed to be 3,510 ounces. Cannot determine based on information given.

to find the total amount of materials needed for production. Then we add the budgeted ending raw materials inventory and subtract the beginning raw materials inventory to determine how much ice cream to purchase. In this case, the ending inventory is based on 3 percent of the **next period's** production needs, so the first quarter ending inventory equals 3 percent of 202,500, or 6,075 ounces. This value becomes the beginning inventory for the next period.

Cold Stone Creamery would construct similar budgets for all other raw materials including the various candies and nuts used to make its ice cream creations. For this example, we assume the purchase cost of these additional ingredients is about 40 percent of the cost of the milk, sugar, and cream (see Exhibit 23.8).

**Exhibit 23.8**    Total Raw Materials Purchases

|  | Quarter 1 Jan.–Mar. | Quarter 2 Apr.–June | Quarter 3 July–Sept. | Quarter 4 Oct.–Dec. | Yearly Total |
|---|---|---|---|---|---|
| Total purchases of milk, sugar, and cream | $ 7,506 | $10,232 | $13,607 | $11,233 | $42,578 |
| Total purchases of mix-in ingredients* | 3,002 | 4,093 | 5,443 | 4,493 | 17,031 |
| Total cost of raw materials purchased | $10,508 | $14,325 | $19,050 | $15,726 | $59,609 |

\* Assumed to be 40 percent of the cost of milk, sugar, and cream.

## Direct Labor Budget

**Learning Objective 5d**

Prepare the direct labor budget.

Next we can determine how much direct labor will be needed to support budgeted production levels. We assume each Cold Stone Creamery creation requires .10 hour (6 minutes) of labor time including the time needed to take customers' orders, mix and serve the ice cream, take customers' payments, as well as cleanup time and employee breaks. See Exhibit 23.9 for the resulting direct labor budget based on budgeted production levels and an average labor rate of $8 per hour.

| **Exhibit 23.9** | **Direct Labor Budget** | | | | |
|---|---|---|---|---|---|
| | Quarter 1<br>Jan.–Mar. | Quarter 2<br>Apr.–June | Quarter 3<br>July–Sept. | Quarter 4<br>Oct.–Dec. | Yearly<br>Total |
| Budgeted production<br>  (from Exhibit 23.6) | 14,850 | 20,250 | 27,350 | 22,800 | 85,250 |
| Direct labor requirements<br>  (.10 hour per unit) | × .10 hr. | × .10 hr. | × .10 hr. | × .10 hr. | × .10 hr. |
| Total direct labor hours required | 1,485 | 2,025 | 2,735 | 2,280 | 8,525 |
| Direct labor cost per hour | × $ 8 | × $ 8 | × $ 8 | × $ 8 | × $ 8 |
| Total direct labor cost | $11,880 | $16,200 | $21,880 | $18,240 | $68,200 |

# Manufacturing Overhead Budget

Next we can prepare the manufacturing overhead budget. Although Cold Stone Creamery is not a traditional manufacturing company, it does create and serve a physical product. Thus, we define manufacturing overhead as all costs other than direct materials and direct labor that the company must incur to make the ice cream and serve it to customers. This amount includes the costs of rent, depreciation on equipment, and other indirect costs such as utilities, paper supplies, and the like. It does not include selling costs, such as advertising and promotion, or administrative costs for legal counsel, accounting services, insurance, franchise fees, and so on.

> **Learning Objective 5e**
>
> Prepare the manufacturing overhead budget.

Some manufacturing overhead costs, such as those for indirect materials and paper supplies, vary with the number of units produced. Other costs, such as those for rent and depreciation, are incurred regardless of the number of units produced. We assume Cold Stone Creamery's variable manufacturing overhead cost is $0.10 per unit produced and the fixed manufacturing overhead cost is $8,525 per quarter. Refer to Exhibit 23.10 for the resulting manufacturing overhead cost budget.

Notice that the variable manufacturing overhead cost is highest during the summer, when production is highest but fixed manufacturing overhead cost is constant each period.

| **Exhibit 23.10** | **Manufacturing Overhead Budget** | | | | |
|---|---|---|---|---|---|
| | Quarter 1<br>Jan.–Mar. | Quarter 2<br>Apr.–June | Quarter 3<br>July–Sept. | Quarter 4<br>Oct.–Dec. | Yearly<br>Total |
| Budgeted production | 14,850 | 20,250 | 27,350 | 22,800 | 85,250 |
| Variable overhead rate | × $ 0.10 | × $ 0.10 | × $ 0.10 | × $ 0.10 | × $ 0.10 |
| Total variable manufacturing overhead cost | $ 1,485 | $ 2,025 | $ 2,735 | $ 2,280 | $ 8,525 |
| Fixed manufacturing overhead | 8,525 | 8,525 | 8,525 | 8,525 | 34,100 |
| Total budgeted manufacturing overhead cost | $10,010 | $ 10,550 | $ 11,260 | $10,805 | $42,625 |

# Budgeted Cost of Goods Sold

The budgeted cost of goods sold should reflect all costs required to manufacture the product including raw materials, direct labor, and manufacturing overhead. See Exhibit 23.11 for the calculation of the budgeted cost of each ice cream creation using information from the manufacturing cost budgets in Exhibits 23.8 through 23.10.

Notice that all variable manufacturing costs were calculated based on the variable manufacturing overhead cost per unit, but fixed manufacturing overhead cost was calculated

**Exhibit 23.11**   Budgeted Manufacturing Cost Per Unit

| | |
|---|---:|
| Budgeted cost of milk, sugar and cream (10 ounces × $0.05 per ounce) | $0.50 |
| Budgeted cost of mix-in ingredients (40% of the cost of milk, sugar and cream) | 0.20 |
| Budgeted direct labor (.10 hours × $8.00 per hour) | 0.80 |
| Budgeted variable manufacturing overhead ($.10 per unit) | 0.10 |
| Budgeted fixed manufacturing overhead ($34,100 per year / 85,250 units) | 0.40 |
| Budgeted manufacturing cost per unit | $2.00 |

based on the total annual cost and yearly production. Fixed manufacturing overhead costs do not change with production levels. Calculating the fixed manufacturing overhead cost in this way avoids the changes in unit cost that occur from quarter to quarter due to seasonal fluctuations in production levels.

Using the budgeted manufacturing cost of $2 per unit calculated in Exhibit 23.11, we can calculate the budgeted cost of goods sold for each period (Exhibit 23.12).

Notice that budgeted cost of goods sold is calculated based on the sales budget (Exhibit 23.5), not the production budgeted (Exhibit 23.6). The cost of the units produced but not sold appears on the budgeted balance sheet as inventory.

**Exhibit 23.12**   Budget Cost of Goods Sold

| | Quarter 1 Jan.–Mar. | Quarter 2 Apr.–June | Quarter 3 July–Sept. | Quarter 4 Oct.–Dec. | Yearly Total |
|---|---:|---:|---:|---:|---:|
| Budgeted unit sales (from Exhibit 23.5) | 15,000 | 20,000 | 27,000 | 23,000 | 85,000 |
| Budgeted manufacturing cost per unit | × $ 2.00 | × $ 2.00 | × $ 2.00 | × $ 2.00 | × $ 2.00 |
| Budgeted cost of goods sold | $30,000 | $40,000 | $54,000 | $46,000 | $170,000 |

## Selling and Administrative Expense Budget

**Learning Objective 5f**

Prepare the selling and administrative expense budget.

The last operating budget we need to prepare is the selling and administrative expense budget, which includes all the costs related to selling the product (such as advertising and promotion) and managing the business (such as franchise fees, legal counsel, accounting services, and insurance). We assume that Cold Stone Creamery's selling costs are budgeted at 5 percent of sales revenue. Fixed administrative expenses are estimated to be $10,000 per quarter. The resulting selling and administrative expense budget is in Exhibit 23.13.

## Budgeted Income Statement

Finally, we can combine all of the operating budgets we just prepared to form a budgeted income statement for Cold Stone Creamery (Exhibit 23.14).

**Exhibit 23.13**   Selling and Administrative Expense Budget

| | Quarter 1 Jan.–Mar. | Quarter 2 Apr.–June | Quarter 3 July–Sept. | Quarter 4 Oct.–Dec. | Yearly Total |
|---|---:|---:|---:|---:|---:|
| Budgeted sales revenue (from Exhibit 23.5) | $75,000 | $100,000 | $135,000 | $115,000 | $425,000 |
| 5% of sales revenue | × $ .05 | × .05 | × .05 | × .05 | × .05 |
| Variable selling expenses | 3,750 | 5,000 | 6,750 | 5,750 | 21,250 |
| Fixed administrative expenses | 10,000 | 10,000 | 10,000 | 10,000 | 40,000 |
| Budgeted selling and administrative expense | $13,750 | $ 15,000 | $ 16,750 | $ 15,750 | $ 61,250 |

**Exhibit 23.14**   Budgeted Income Statement

**Cold Stone Creamery**
**Budgeted Income Statement**
**For the Year Ended December 31, 2010**

|  | Quarter 1 Jan.–Mar. | Quarter 2 Apr.–June | Quarter 3 July–Sept. | Quarter 4 Oct.–Dec. | Yearly Total |
|---|---|---|---|---|---|
| Budgeted sales revenue (from Exhibit 23.5) | $75,000 | $100,000 | $135,000 | $115,000 | $425,000 |
| Less: Budgeted cost of goods sold (from Exhibit 23.12) | 30,000 | 40,000 | 54,000 | 46,000 | 170,000 |
| Budgeted gross margin | 45,000 | 60,000 | 81,000 | 69,000 | 255,000 |
| Less: Budgeted selling and administrative expenses (from Exhibit 23.13) | 13,750 | 15,000 | 16,750 | 15,750 | 61,250 |
| Budgeted operating income | $31,250 | $ 45,000 | $ 64,250 | $ 53,250 | $193,750 |

Before you move to the financial budgets, take a moment to make sure you understand the key relationships among the operating budgets by completing the following Self-Study Practice.

**SELF-STUDY PRACTICE**

1. Taylor Made's sales forecast for the next four quarters follows:

|  | Quarter 1 | Quarter 2 | Quarter 3 | Quarter 4 |
|---|---|---|---|---|
| Sales forecast (units) | 12,000 | 14,000 | 15,000 | 18,000 |

   If the company wants to maintain a finished goods inventory equal to 20 percent of sales for the next quarter, how many units should it produce during the second quarter?

2. Calico Coat Company's production budget follows:

|  | Quater 1 | Quarter 2 | Quarter 3 | Quarter 4 |
|---|---|---|---|---|
| Production budget (units) | 15,000 | 13,000 | 14,000 | 12,000 |

   Each unit requires 5 yards of raw materials at a cost of $3 per yard. The company plans its raw materials purchases so that ending raw materials inventory equals 10 percent of the production needs for the current quarter. At the beginning of the first quarter, 5,000 yards of materials were on hand.
   What is the budgeted cost of raw materials purchases during the first quarter?

*After you have finished, check your answers with the solutions at the bottom of the page.*

Solution to
Self-Study Practice

1.  14,200 = 14,000 + (.20 × 15,000) − (.20 × 14,000)
2.  Current production needs = 15,000 × 5 = 75,000 yards
    Ending raw materials inventory = 75,000 × .10 = 7,500
    Beginning raw materials inventory = 5,000
    75,000 + 7,500 − 5,000 = 77,500 × $3.00 per yard = $232,500

# PREPARATION OF THE FINANCIAL BUDGETS

As mentioned earlier, the financial budgets focus on the financial resources needed to support the company's operations including cash receipts and disbursements, inventory, capital purchases, and financing. To review the relationship between the financial budgets and the operating budgets, take a moment to review Exhibit 23.4 on page 963. In this section, we concentrate on two financial budgets, the cash budget and the budgeted balance sheet.

## Cash Budget

> **Learning Objective 6**
>
> Prepare the cash budget and describe the other financial budgets required to produce a budgeted balance sheet.

The **cash budget** is a future-oriented version of the statement of cash flows, which you learned about in Chapter 16. Recall that cash inflows (receipts) can come from operating activities or from financing and investing activities. Similarly, cash outflows (disbursements) can be made for operating activities or for investing and financing activities. In this chapter, we focus strictly on cash flows that arise from operating activities, which are directly related to the operating budgets described previously. We do not consider cash flows that arise from investing or financing activities, which would appear in the capital purchases budget (for investing activities) and the financing budget (for financing).

The basic formula for the cash budget follows:

$$\boxed{\text{Ending Cash Balance}} = \boxed{\text{Beginning Cash Balance}} + \boxed{\text{Budgeted Cash Receipts}} - \boxed{\text{Budgeted Cash Disbursements}}$$

Because we are focusing strictly on operating activities, all budgeted cash receipts come from sales revenue. Remember, however, that sales revenue is not the same as cash. Sales are recognized when revenue is earned, not when cash is received. Thus, to calculate the budgeted cash receipts, we need to know what type of sales are made (cash or credit) and how credit sales are collected.

We assume 60 percent of Cold Stone Creamery's sales are paid for in cash and 40 percent are paid with credit cards. Credit card sales are collected immediately subject to a 5 percent transaction fee. Cold Stone's cash receipts budget is in Exhibit 23.15.

**Exhibit 23.15  Cash Receipts Budget**

|  | Quarter 1 Jan.–Mar. | Quarter 2 Apr.–June | Quarter 3 July–Sept. | Quarter 4 Oct.–Dec. | Yearly Total |
|---|---|---|---|---|---|
| Budgeted sales revenue (from Exhibit 23.5) | $ 75,000 | $100,000 | $135,000 | $115,000 | $425,000 |
| Cash collections (60% of sales) | 45,000* | 60,000 | 81,000 | 69,000 | 255,000 |
| Credit card collections (40% of sales less a 5% service fee) | 28,500† | 38,000 | 51,300 | 43,700 | 161,500 |
| Budgeted cash (receipts) | $ 73,500 | $ 98,000 | $132,300 | $112,700 | $416,500 |

*Quarter 1 cash collections = $75,000 × 60% = $45,000
†Quarter 1 credit collections = $75,000 × 40% × (100% − 5%) = $28,500

As you can see, budgeted cash receipts are not the same thing as budgeted sales. Similarly, cash disbursements do not necessarily equal budgeted expenses. To calculate budgeted cash disbursements it is necessary to know when the company pays for raw materials purchases, direct labor costs, manufacturing overhead costs, and selling and administrative costs. To continue our Cold Stone Creamery example, assume the following:

- Of raw materials purchases, 70 percent is paid for during the quarter purchased; 30 percent is paid for in the following quarter. Assume last year's quarter 4 raw materials purchases totaled $10,000.
- Direct labor, manufacturing overhead costs, and selling and administrative costs are paid for during the quarter in which they are incurred.
- The fixed manufacturing overhead cost budget includes $3,000 in depreciation (a noncash expense).

See Exhibit 23.16 for the Cold Stone Creamery's budgeted cash disbursements using this information.

## Exhibit 23.16  Cash Disbursements Budget

| | Quarter 1 Jan.–March | Quarter 2 April–June | Quarter 3 July–Sept. | Quarter 4 Oct.–Dec. | Yearly Total |
|---|---|---|---|---|---|
| Budgeted direct materials purchased (from Exhibit 23.8) | $10,508 | $14,325 | $19,050 | $15,726 | $ 59,609 |
| **Budgeted Cash Payments:** | | | | | |
| 70% of raw materials purchases paid for in current quarter | 7,356* | 10,028 | 13,335 | 11,008 | 41,727 |
| 30% of raw materials purchases paid for in the next quarter | 3,000 | 3,152† | 4,298 | 5,715 | 16,165 |
| Budgeted payments for raw materials purchases | 10,356 | 13,180 | 17,633 | 16,723 | 57,892 |
| Budgeted direct labor costs (from Exhibit 23.9) | 11,880 | 16,200 | 21,880 | 18,240 | 68,200 |
| Budgeted manufacturing overhead costs (from Exhibit 23.10) | 10,010 | 10,550 | 11,260 | 10,805 | 42,625 |
| Less depreciation (noncash expense) | (3,000) | (3,000) | (3,000) | (3,000) | (12,000) |
| Budgeted selling and administrative expenses (from Exhibit 23.13) | 13,750 | 15,000 | 16,750 | 15,750 | 61,250 |
| Budgeted cash disbursements | $42,996 | $51,930 | $64,523 | $58,518 | $217,967 |

* Quarter 1 cash paid for current quarter's materials purchases = $10,508 × 70% = $7,356
† Quarter 2 cash paid for previous quarter raw materials purchases = $10,508 × 30% = $3,152

The cash receipts and cash disbursements can then be combined into a summary cash budget. Cold Stone Creamery's cash budget for the year, assuming it had $100,000 cash on hand at the beginning of the year is in Exhibit 23.17.

## Exhibit 23.17  Cash Budget

| | Quarter 1 Jan.–Mar. | Quarter 2 Apr.–June | Quarter 3 July–Sept. | Quarter 4 Oct.–Dec. | Yearly Total |
|---|---|---|---|---|---|
| Beginning balance of cash | $ 100,000 | $130,504 | $176,574 | $244,351 | $100,000 |
| Plus: Budgeted cash receipts (from Exhibit 23.15) | 73,500 | 98,000 | 132,300 | 112,700 | 416,500 |
| Less: Budgeted cash disbursements (from Exhibit 23.16) | (42,996) | (51,930) | (64,523) | (58,518) | (217,967) |
| Ending Balance of Cash | $ 130,504 | $176,574 | $244,351 | $298,533 | $ 298,533 |

Believe it or not, Cold Stone Creamery's cash budget is relatively straightforward because most customers pay in cash at the time of sale. Sales made on credit card are collected almost instantaneously minus the fee the credit card company charges. But some businesses sell goods or services on credit terms that allow the customer to take weeks or even months to pay. In these situations, the cash receipts component of the cash budget is slightly more complicated because part of the cash receipts are based on the previous period sales number rather than the current period sales. To see whether you can complete a cash budget when credit sales are collected in a later period, complete the Self-Study Practice on the next page.

# Budgeted Balance Sheet

The final financial budget that we discuss is the budgeted balance sheet. Just as the operating budgets were combined into a pro forma (forward-looking) income statement, all of the financial budgets can be combined into a pro forma (forward-looking) balance sheet. A number of financial budgets including the inventory budget, the capital expenditures budget, and the financing budget must be created before we can prepare a complete balance sheet. For the sake of simplicity, we do not show how to prepare those budgets. Just make sure you understand the structure of the **budgeted balance sheet** (Exhibit 23.18).

**Exhibit 23.18**  Budgeted Balance Sheet

COLD STONE

### Cold Stone Creamery
### Budgeted Balance Sheet
### December 31, 2010

| Assets | | Liabilities | |
|---|---|---|---|
| Cash (from Exhibit 23.17) | $298,533 | Accounts payable | $ 4,718 |
| Accounts receivable | 13,274 | Long-term liability | 250,000 |
| Inventory | 2,300 | Total liabilities | 254,718 |
| Long-term assets | 170,000 | **Owners' Equity** | 229,389 |
| Total assets | $484,107 | Total liabilities and owners' equity | $484,107 |

## Budgeting in a Merchandising Company

Throughout this chapter, we have used Cold Stone Creamery to illustrate how to prepare the operating and financial budgets for a manufacturing company that purchases raw materials and converts them into a final product.

The budgets for a merchandising company differ slightly from those of a manufacturing firm. Recall that a merchandising company purchases finished goods for resale. As such, one of the primary operating budgets a merchandiser needs to prepare is the merchandise purchases budget. This budget is very similar to the raw materials purchases budget in Exhibit 23.7. However, instead of considering production needs and raw materials inventory, this budget is based on budgeted sales and the need to maintain adequate levels of finished goods inventory as in the following formula:

| Budgeted Merchandise Purchases | = | Budgeted Sales | + | Budgeted Ending Finished Goods Inventory | − | Budgeted Beginning Finished Goods Inventory |

The other major difference between merchandising and manufacturing firms' budgets is that merchandising firms do not have a raw materials, direct labor, or manufacturing overhead expense budget. Remember that these are all categories of manufacturing costs and apply only to manufacturing companies.

**SELF-STUDY PRACTICE**

Big Ben Clock Company's total sales for the first two quarters of the year are budgeted as follows:

| | Quarter 1 | Quarter 2 |
|---|---|---|
| Total sales budget | $120,000 | $140,000 |

Of total sales, 60 percent is expected to be cash with the remaining 40 percent on credit. Of the credit sales, 30 percent will be collected in the quarter in which the sales are made, 65 percent the following quarter, and 5 percent will never be collected.

Based on this information, calculate Big Ben's budgeted cash receipts for Quarter 2 only.

*After you have finished, check your answers with the solutions at the bottom of the page.*

**Solution to Self-Study Practice**

Cash Sales (Quarter 2) = $140,000 × .60 = $84,000
Credit Sales (Quarter 2) = $140,000 × .40 × .30 = $16,800
Credit Sales (Quarter 1) = $120,000 × .40 × .65 = $31,200
Budgeted Cash Receipts (Quarter 2) = $132,000

# Demonstration Case A
## Operating Budgets

Sky High Parachute Company manufactures and sells parachutes to adventure companies. The company's sales forecast for the coming year is as follows:

|  | Quarter 1 | Quarter 2 | Quarter 3 | Quarter 4 |
|---|---|---|---|---|
| Sales (units) | 40,000 | 35,000 | 45,000 | 50,000 |

Other budgeted information follows:

- The budgeted sales price for each parachute is $1,000 per unit.
- The company budgets production so that ending finished goods inventory equals 10 percent of the next quarter's budgeted sales.
- Each parachute requires 20 square yards of specialty material at a price of $15 per square yard.
- The company purchases raw materials so that about 10 percent of each quarter's production needs are left over at the end of the quarter to be used as beginning inventory in the next quarter. At the beginning of the first quarter, 70,000 square yards of material were on hand.
- Each parachute requires 15 hours of direct labor at a rate of $12 per hour.
- Manufacturing overhead costs are budgeted at $1,000,000 per quarter plus $50 per unit produced.
- Selling and administrative expenses are budgeted at $500,000 per quarter plus 10 percent of total sales revenue.

*Required:*
Prepare the following operating budgets for quarters 1–3. (You do not have enough information to prepare all of the budgets, for quarter 4.)

1. Sales budget.
2. Production budget.
3. Raw materials purchases budget.
4. Direct labor budget.
5. Manufacturing overhead budget.
6. Selling and administrative expense budget.

## Suggested Solution

1.

|  | Quarter 1 | Quarter 2 | Quarter 3 | Quarter 4 |
|---|---|---|---|---|
| Sales forecast (units) | 40,000 | 35,000 | 45,000 | 50,000 |
| Price per unit | × $ 1,000 | × $ 1,000 | × $ 1,000 | × $ 1,000 |
| Sales budget (dollars) | $40,000,000 | $35,000,000 | $45,000,000 | $50,000,000 |

2.

|  | Quarter 1 | Quarter 2 | Quarter 3 | Quarter 4 |
|---|---|---|---|---|
| Unit sales forecast (from requirement 1) | 40,000 | 35,000 | 45,000 | 50,000 |
| Plus: Desired ending inventory | 3,500 | 4,500 | 5,000 |  |
| Less: Planned beginning inventory | 4,000 | 3,500 | 4,500 |  |
| Production budget (units) | 39,500 | 36,000 | 45,500 |  |

3.

|  | Quarter 1 | Quarter 2 | Quarter 3 |
|---|---|---|---|
| Production budget (from requirement 2 in units) | 39,500 | 36,000 | 45,500 |
| Raw materials requirements (per unit in sq. yards) | × 20 | × 20 | × 20 |
| Total raw materials needed for production (sq. yards) | 790,000 | 720,000 | 910,000 |
| Plus: Desired ending inventory | 79,000 | 72,000 | 91,000 |
| Less: Planned beginning inventory | 70,000 | 79,000 | 72,000 |
| Budgeted raw materials purchases (sq. yards) | 799,000 | 713,000 | 929,000 |
| Budgeted cost per square yard | × $ 15 | × $ 15 | × $ 15 |
| Total raw materials purchases | $11,985,000 | $10,695,000 | $13,935,000 |

4.

|  | Quarter 1 | Quarter 2 | Quarter 3 |
|---|---|---|---|
| Production budget (from requirement 2 in units) | 39,500 | 36,000 | 45,500 |
| Direct labor requirements (hours per unit) | × 15 | × 15 | × 15 |
| Total labor hours required | 592,500 | 540,000 | 682,500 |
| Direct labor rate (per hour) | × $ 12 | × $ 12 | × $ 12 |
| Total direct labor cost | $7,110,000 | $6,480,000 | $8,190,000 |

5.

|  | Quarter 1 | Quarter 2 | Quarter 3 |
|---|---|---|---|
| Production budget (from requirement 2 in units) | 39,500 | 36,000 | 45,500 |
| Variable overhead rate ($50 per unit) | × $ 50 | × $ 50 | × $ 50 |
| Variable overhead budget | $1,975,000 | $1,800,000 | $2,275,000 |
| Fixed overhead budget | 1,000,000 | 1,000,000 | 1,000,000 |
| Total manufacturing overhead budget | $2,975,000 | $2,800,000 | $3,275,000 |

6.

|  | Quarter 1 | Quarter 2 | Quarter 3 |
|---|---|---|---|
| Sales budget (from requirement 1) | $40,000,000 | $35,000,000 | $45,000,000 |
|  | × .10 | × .10 | × .10 |
| Variable selling expenses (10% of sales dollars) | 4,000,000 | 3,500,000 | 4,500,000 |
| Fixed selling expenses | 500,000 | 500,000 | 500,000 |
| Budgeted selling and administrative expenses | $ 4,500,000 | $ 4,000,000 | $ 5,000,000 |

# Demonstration Case B
## Cash Budget

Assume that Sky High Parachute Company's budgeted income statement is as follows:

|  | Quarter 1 | Quarter 2 | Quarter 3 | Quarter 4 |
|---|---|---|---|---|
| Budgeted sales revenue | $40,000,000 | $35,000,000 | $45,000,000 | $50,000,000 |
| Budgeted cost of goods sold | 15,600,000 | 13,650,000 | 17,550,000 | 19,500,000 |
| Budgeted gross margin | 24,400,000 | 21,350,000 | 27,450,000 | 30,500,000 |
| Budgeted selling and administrative expenses | 4,500,000 | 4,000,000 | 5,000,000 | 5,500,000 |
| Budgeted income from operations | $19,900,000 | $17,350,000 | $22,450,000 | $25,000,000 |

Budgeted sales revenue is collected as follows:

- 60 percent of sales revenue is collected in cash.
- The remainder of sales is on credit and is collected as follows:
  - During the quarter of sale, 35 percent.
  - During the quarter following the sale 60 percent.
  - Uncollected, 5 percent.

Cost of goods sold (manufacturing costs) consists of the following:

- Materials purchases represent 70 percent of cost of goods sold. The company pays for 40 percent of materials during the quarter of purchase and the remainder the next quarter.
- The remaining 30 percent of cost of goods sold is made up of direct labor and manufacturing overhead including $400,000 in depreciation (a noncash expense). All of the cash disbursements for direct labor and overhead are paid during the quarter incurred.
- Selling and administrative expenses are paid in the next quarter.

*Required:*
Prepare the following schedules for quarters 2, 3, and 4.

1. Cash receipts budget.
2. Cash disbursements budget.
3. Cash budget.

**Note:** You do not have enough information to prepare the cash budget for quarter 1, so assume its ending cash balance is $500,000.

## Suggested Solution

1.

|  | Quarter 1 | Quarter 2 | Quarter 3 | Quarter 4 |
|---|---|---|---|---|
| Budgetes sales revenue (given) | $40,000,000 | $35,000,000 | $45,000,000 | $50,000,000 |
| Budgeted cash receipts |  |  |  |  |
| Cash sales (60% of current quarter sales) |  | $21,000,000 | $27,000,000 | $30,000,000 |
| Credit sales collected in current quarter (40% of current quarter sales × 35%) |  | 4,900,000 | 6,300,000 | 7,000,000 |
| Credit sales collected in following quarter (40% of previous quarter sales × 60%) |  | 9,600,000 | 8,400,000 | 10,800,000 |
| Budgeted cash receipts |  | $35,500,000 | $41,700,000 | $47,800,000 |

2.

| | Quarter 1 | Quarter 2 | Quarter 3 | Quarter 4 |
|---|---|---|---|---|
| Budgeted cost of goods sold (given) | $15,600,000 | $13,650,000 | $17,550,000 | $19,500,000 |
| Raw materials purchases (70% of cost of goods sold) | 10,920,000 | 9,555,000 | 12,285,000 | 13,650,000 |
| Direct labor and manufacturing overhead (30% of cost of goods sold) | 4,680,000 | 4,095,000 | 5,265,000 | 5,850,000 |
| Budgeted selling and administrative expenses (given) | 4,500,000 | 4,000,000 | 5,000,000 | 5,500,000 |
| Raw materials paid for in current quarter (40% of current quarter purchases) | | 3,822,000 | 4,914,000 | 5,460,000 |
| Raw materials paid for in next quarter (60% of previous quarter purchases) | | 6,552,000 | 5,733,000 | 7,371,000 |
| Cash paid for direct labor and overhead (Less: $400,000 in depreciation) | | 3,695,000 | 4,865,000 | 5,450,000 |
| Cash paid for selling and administrative expenses | | 4,500,000 | 4,000,000 | 5,000,000 |
| Budgeted cash disbursements | | $18,569,000 | $19,512,000 | $23,281,000 |

3.

| | Quarter 1 | Quarter 2 | Quarter 3 | Quarter 4 |
|---|---|---|---|---|
| Beginning balance of cash | | $   500,000 | $ 17,431,000 | $ 39,619,000 |
| Plus: Budgeted cash receipts | | 35,500,000 | 41,700,000 | 47,800,000 |
| Less: Budgeted cash disbursements | | (18,569,000) | (19,512,000) | (23,281,000) |
| Ending balance of cash | $500,000 | $17,431,000 | $39,619,000 | $64,138,000 |

## Chapter Summary

### LO1  Describe the phases of the planning and control process. p. 958

- Planning is the forward-looking phase of the managerial process. It involves setting both long- and short-term objectives and identifying the tactics used to achieve them.
- Organizing involves arranging for the necessary resources needed to achieve the plan, including the preparation of a budget.
- Directing/leading is the action phase of the managerial process. It involves implementing the objectives developed in the planning phase including motivating employees to achieve the objectives.
- Control is the backward-looking phase of the managerial process. It involves comparing actual results to budgeted figures and taking corrective action if necessary.

### LO2  List the key benefits of budgeting. p. 959

Budgeting has several benefits:
- Forces managers to plan ahead.
- Serves as a basis for communication throughout the organization.
- Motivates employees to work toward the organization's goals.

### LO3  Explain the behavioral effects of budgets and provide guidelines for implementing a budget. p. 961

- Budgets can create a number of behavioral effects that should be considered in designing and implementing a budgetary control system.
- Budgets that are "tight but attainable" are more likely to motivate people to work harder than budgets that are either too easy or impossible to achieve.

- Participative budgeting allows individuals to provide input into the budget-setting process. However, it may lead to the creation of budget slack.
- Using different budgets for planning than for performance evaluations, rolling budgets, or zero-based budgets can mitigate some of the game playing that occurs in the budgeting process.

## LO4  Describe the major components of the master budget and their interrelationships. p. 962

- The master budget is a comprehensive set of budgets that covers all phases of an organization's planned activities for a specific period.
- The master budget contains two types of budgets: operatings budgets and financial budgets.
- Operating budgets include all budgets needed to prepare a budgeted income statement including the sales budget, production budget, raw materials purchases budget, direct labor budget, manufacturing overhead cost budget, and selling and administrative expense budget.
- Financial budgets provide the information on financial resources and obligations needed to prepare a budgeted balance sheet. These budgets include the cash budget, inventory budget, capital expenditures budget, and financing budget.

## LO5  Prepare the following components of the operating budget. p. 964

- **Sales budget.** The starting point for the operating budget is the sales budget. It is based on a variety of inputs and affects all other components of the master budget.
- **Production budget.** This budget is based on the sales budget and the planned levels of beginning and ending finished goods inventory.
- **Raw materials purchases budget.** This budget is based on the production budget and the planned levels of the beginning and ending raw materials inventory.
- **Direct labor budget.** It is based on the production budget and shows how much labor is required to produce (or serve) each unit.
- **Manufacturing overhead cost budget.** This budget provides information about expected variable and fixed manufacturing overhead costs.
- **Selling and administrative expense budget.** Information about expected selling and administrative expenses is in this budget.
- Information from all operating budgets can be combined to prepare a budgeted income statement.

## LO6  Prepare the cash budget and describe the other financial budgets required to produce a budgeted balance sheet. p. 976

- The cash budget is a future-oriented version of the statement of cash flows; it includes budgeted cash receipts and budgeted cash disbursements.
- The ending balance of the cash budget appears on the budgeted balance sheet along with the budgeted balances for all other asset, liability, and equity accounts.
- Other financial budgets needed to prepare a comprehensive budgeted balance sheet include the inventory budget, capital purchases budget, and financing budget.

# Key Terms

Budgeted Balance Sheet (p.962)
Budgeted Cost of Goods Sold (p. 963)
Budgeted Gross Margin (p. 964)
Budgeted Manufacturing Cost per Unit (p. 963)
Budgeted Income Statement (p. 962)
Budget Slack (p. 961)
Cash Budget (p. 964)
Direct Labor Budget (p. 963)

Financial Budget (p. 962)
Inventory Budget (p. 963)
Long-Term Objective (p. 959)
Manufacturing Overhead Budget (p. 963)
Master Budget (p. 962)
Operating Budgets (p. 962)
Participative Budgeting (p. 961)
Production Budget (p. 963)
Raw Materials Purchases Budget (p. 963)

Sales Forecast Budget (p. 963)
Selling and Administrative Expense Budget (p. 963)
Short-Term Objective (p. 959)
Strategic Plan (p. 959)
Tactics (p. 959)
Top-Down Approach (p. 961)

See complete glossary in back of text.

## Questions

1. Briefly describe why budgetary planning is crucial to companies.
2. What role do budgets play in the planning and control cycle?
3. What is a strategic plan? How does a strategic plan involve both short- and long-term goals?
4. Suppose that your strategic plan is to retire comfortably at the age of 55. List several long-term objectives, short-term objectives, and tactics that will enable you to accomplish this goal.
5. Identify and briefly discuss the benefits of budgeting.
6. Suppose a company chooses not to develop budgets. Describe three potential negative consequences of this decision.
7. What are the advantages and disadvantages of participative budgeting over top-down budgeting?
8. Explain the concept of budgetary slack. How might budgetary slack be detrimental to a company?
9. Briefly explain how each of the following helps to minimize dysfunctional behaviors caused by budgeting:
   a. Different budgets for different purposes.
   b. Continuous budgeting.
   c. Zero-based budgeting.
10. What is the master budget? What are its components?
11. Explain why the sales budget is the starting point for a company's budgeting process. Which budgets does the sales budget affect? Which budgets does the sales budget not affect?
12. What sources does a company utilize to determine its sales forecast? What could happen if one of the sources used is inaccurate?
13. What are the components of the operating budget?
14. What are the components of the financial budget?

## Multiple Choice

1. Budgets help companies
   a. Meet short-term objectives.
   b. Meet long-term objectives.
   c. Both a and b.
   d. None of the above.

2. Which phases of the management process does budgeting impact?
   a. Planning.        c. Control.
   b. Directing/leading.   d. All of the above.
3. Which of the following statements is true?
   a. GAAP requires all companies to prepare budgets.
   b. Only newly formed companies need budgets.
   c. Budgets are used by all companies.
   d. Most companies would benefit from budgeting.
4. Shasta Company plans to double profits in five years. This is an example of a
   a. Long-term objective.   c. Tactic.
   b. Short-term objective.   d. Sales forecast.
5. Which of the following is not considered a direct benefit of budgeting?
   a. Better communication.
   b. Motivating employees.
   c. Developing new product lines.
   d. Forcing managers to think ahead.
6. Which of the following budgets would be prepared earliest in a company's budgeting process?
   a. Budgeted income statement.
   b. Budgeted balance sheet.
   c. Raw materials purchases budget.
   d. Production budget.
7. Which of the following budgets does the sales budget impact?
   a. Direct labor budget.
   b. Cash receipts and disbursements budget.
   c. Selling and administrative budget.
   d. All of the above.
8. ABC Company expects to sell 100,000 units of its primary product in January. Expected beginning and ending finished goods inventory for January are 20,000 and 45,000 units, respectively. How many units should ABC produce?
   a. 100,000.        c. 75,000.
   b. 125,000.        d. 35,000.
9. Which of the following is not considered an operating budget?
   a. Cash budget.
   b. Budgeted income statement.
   c. Selling and administrative expense budget.
   d. Raw materials purchases budget.
10. Raya Company is calculating its expected cash receipts for the month of June. This should not include
   a. Cash sales made during June.
   b. Credit sales made during May.
   c. Credit sales made during June.
   d. Credit sales made during July.

| Solutions to Multiple-Choice Questions | | | | | | |
|---|---|---|---|---|---|---|
| 1. c | 2. d | 3. d | 4. a | 5. c | 6. d | 7. d |
| 8. b | 9. a | 10. d | | | | |

# Mini Exercises 

**Available with McGraw-Hill's Homework Manager**

**M23-1 Explaining the Role of Managerial Accounting in the Planning and Control Cycle**
Your boss believes that the three management functions of planning, directing/leading, and control are unrelated. He also thinks that managerial accounting has no role in any of the functions. Is your boss correct? Explain why or why not.

LO1

**M23-2 Describing the Advantages of Budgetary Planning**
Calypso Cal (CC) has a "Live today, worry about tomorrow later" motto. In keeping with this philosophy, CC has not set any long-term or short-term objectives or budgets for the company, which manufactures surfboards. Describe three potential consequences of CC's philosophy.

LO2

**M23-3 Classifying and Ordering the Components of the Master Budget**
Indicate whether each of the following budgets is an operating (O) or financing (F) budget and the order in which they would be prepared.

LO4

| | O or F | Order of Preparation |
|---|---|---|
| Cash receipts and disbursements budget | | |
| Sales budget | | |
| Raw materials purchases budget | | |
| Selling and administrative expense budget | | |
| Budgeted balance sheet | | |
| Manufacturing overhead budget | | |
| Direct labor budget | | |
| Budgeted income statement | | |
| Production budget | | |

**M23-4 Preparing a Sales Budget**
Ranger Company estimates that unit sales of its weather radios will be 8,000 in October; 8,200 in November; and 9,350 in December. Prepare Ranger's sales budget for the fourth quarter assuming each unit sells for $27.50.

LO5

**M23-5 Preparing a Purchases Budget**
Pascall Corp. expects to sell 1,300 units of its camera bags in March and 900 units in April. Each unit sells for $110. Pascall's ending inventory policy is 40 percent of the following month's sales. Pascall pays its supplier $50 per unit. Prepare Pascall's purchases budget for March.

LO5

**M23-6 Preparing a Raw Materials Purchases Budget**
CubbyHole, Inc., manufactures wooden shelving units for collecting and sorting mail. The company expects to produce 310 units in July and 400 units in August. Each unit requires 10 feet of wood at a cost of $1.20 per foot. CubbyHole wants to always have 300 feet of wood on hand in materials inventory. Prepare CubbyHole's raw materials purchases budget for July and August.

LO5

**M23-7 Preparing a Direct Labor Budget**
Refer to the information in M23-6 for CubbyHole, Inc. Each unit requires 1.5 hours of direct labor, and labor wages average $9 per hour. Prepare CubbyHole's direct labor budget for July and August.

LO5

**M23-8 Preparing a Manufacturing Overhead Cost Budget**
Damon Company expects sales of its headphones to be $200,000 in the first quarter and $236,000 in the second quarter. Its variable overhead is approximately 17 percent of sales, and fixed overhead costs are $52,000 per quarter. Prepare Damon's manufacturing overhead cost budgets for the first two quarters.

LO5

**M23-9 Preparing a Selling and Administrative Expense Budget**
Affleck, Inc., expects sales of its housing for electric motors to be $83,000, $79,000 and $88,000 for January, February, and March, respectively. Its variable selling and administrative expenses are 9 percent of sales, and fixed selling and administrative expenses are $11,000 per month. Prepare Affleck's selling and administrative expense budget for January, February, and March.

LO5

## Exercises 🔶™    Available with McGraw-Hill's Homework Manager

**LO4**    **E23-1 Classifying and Ordering the Components of the Master Budget**
Organize the following budgets in order of preparation by placing the number before it and indicate how each would be affected by a sales forecast that is understated.

_____ Cash receipts and disbursements budget.

_____ Selling and administrative expense budget.

_____ Manufacturing overhead budget.

_____ Raw materials purchases budget.

_____ Budgeted balance sheet.

_____ Sales budget.

_____ Direct labor budget.

_____ Budgeted income statement.

_____ Budgeted cost of goods sold.

_____ Production budget.

**LO5**    **E23-2 Calculating Unknowns Based on Production, Sales, and Beginning and Ending Inventory Values**
Complete the following table.

### NUMBER OF UNITS

| Production | Sales | Ending Inventory | Beginning Inventory |
|-----------|-------|------------------|---------------------|
| ? | 500 | 100 | 75 |
| 800 | ? | 90 | 125 |
| 750 | 675 | ? | 80 |
| 900 | 1,200 | 100 | ? |
| 665 | ? | 225 | 160 |
| 845 | 795 | 305 | ? |

**LO5**    **E23-3 Calculating the Sales and Production Budgets**
Rainwater Corp. expects to sell 600 umbrellas in January and 400 umbrellas in February. Each umbrella sells for $15. Rainwater's beginning and ending finished goods inventories for January are 75 and 50 units, respectively. Ending finished goods inventory for February will be 60 units.

_Required:_

1.  Prepare Rainwater's sales budget for January and February.
2.  Prepare Rainwater's production budget for January and February.

**LO5**    **E23-4 Preparing the Raw Materials Purchases and Manufacturing Overhead Cost Budgets**
Refer to the information in E23-3 for Rainwater Corp. Assume its production budget calls for production of 605 umbrellas in May and 530 umbrellas in June. Each umbrella requires an opening mechanism that the company purchases from a supplier at a cost of $2 each. Rainwater wants to have 30 mechanisms on hand at May 1, 20 mechanisms at May 31, and 25 mechanisms at June 30. Additionally, Rainwater's fixed manufacturing overhead is $1,000 per month, and variable manufacturing overhead is $1.25 per unit produced.

_Required:_

1.  Prepare Rainwater's May and June raw materials purchases budget for these mechanisms.
2.  Prepare Rainwater's manufacturing overhead budget for May and June.

## E23-5 Calculating Cash Receipts    LO6
Refer to information in E23-3 and E23-4 for Rainwater Corp. It expects the following unit sales for the third quarter.

| | |
|---|---|
| July | 525 |
| August | 490 |
| September | 450 |

Sixty percent of Rainwater's sales are cash. Of the credit sales, one-half is collected in the month of the sale, 45 percent is collected during the following month, and 5 percent is never collected.

**Required:**
Calculate Rainwater's total cash receipts for sales for August and September.

## E23-6 Preparing a Selling and Administrative Expense Budget    LO5
The following information is available for Revelle Company.

- Sales price per unit is $80.
- In November and December, sales were 3,100 and 3,550 units, respectively.
- Variable costs are 11 percent of sales (6 percent commission, 2 percent advertising, 3 percent shipping).
- Fixed costs per month are sales salaries, $5,000; office salaries, $2,500; depreciation, $2,500; building rent, $3,500; insurance, $1,500; and utilities, $800.

**Required:**
Prepare Revelle's selling and administrative expense budgets for November and December.

## E23-7 Preparing a Cash Budget    LO6
Garcia Company has the following information for the month of March.

| | |
|---|---|
| Cash balance, March 1 | $15,575 |
| Collections from customers | 34,650 |
| Paid to suppliers | 22,300 |
| Manufacturing overhead | 6,100 |
| Direct labor | 8,250 |
| Selling and administrative expenses | 4,200 |

Wages are paid in the month incurred. Manufacturing overhead includes $1,200 for machinery depreciation, but the amount for selling and administrative expenses is exclusive of depreciation. Additionally, Garcia also expects to sell a piece of property for $15,000 during March.

**Required:**
Prepare Garcia's cash budget for the month of March.

## E23-8 Calculating Cash Receipts    LO6
For Wright Company, 75 percent of sales are cash. Credit sales are collected as follows: 65 percent in the month of the sale and 35 percent in the month following the sale.
Wright's budgeted sales for upcoming months are:

| | |
|---|---|
| June | $22,500 |
| July | 25,000 |
| August | 23,000 |
| September | 21,000 |

**Required:**
Compute Wright's expected cash receipts for August.

## Problems—Set A  Available with McGraw-Hill's Homework Manager

For problems PA23-1 through PA23-3, refer to the following information about Bamboo You, Inc., which manufactures bamboo picture frames that sell for $20 each. Each frame requires 4 linear feet of bamboo, which costs $1.50 per foot. Each frame takes approximately 30 minutes to build, and the labor rate averages $10.00 per hour.

Bamboo You has the following inventory policies:

Ending finished goods inventory should be 40 percent of the next month's sales.

Ending raw materials inventory should be 30 percent of the next month's production.

Expected sales in number of frames for the upcoming months are:

| | |
|---|---|
| March | 275 |
| April | 250 |
| May | 300 |
| June | 400 |
| July | 375 |
| August | 425 |

Variable manufacturing overhead is incurred at a rate of $0.25 per unit produced. Annual fixed manufacturing overhead is estimated to be $7,200 ($600 per month) for an expected production of 4,000 units for the year. Selling and administrative expenses are estimated at $650 per month plus $0.60 per unit sold.

**LO5**

www.mhhe.com/LLPW1e

### PA23-1 Preparing the Components of the Operating Budget

*Required:*

Prepare the following for Bamboo You, Inc., for the second quarter. Include each month (April–June) as well as the quarter 2 total in your budgets.

1.  Sales budget.
2.  Production budget.
3.  Raw materials purchases budget.
4.  Direct labor budget.
5.  Manufacturing overhead cost budget.
6.  Budgeted cost of goods sold.
7.  Selling and administrative expense budget.

**LO5**

www.mhhe.com/LLPW1e

### PA23-2 Preparing a Budgeted Income Statement

Refer to the information in PA23-1.

*Required:*

Prepare Bamboo You's budgeted income statement for Quarter 2.

**LO6**

www.mhhe.com/LLPW1e

### PA23-3 Preparing a Cash Budget

Refer to the information in PA23-1. Bamboo You, Inc., had $9,800 cash on hand at April 1. Seventy percent of sales are cash. Of the credit sales, 40 percent is collected during the month of the sale and 60 percent is collected during the month following the sale.

Eighty percent of direct material purchases is paid for during the month purchased. Twenty percent is paid in the following month. Raw materials purchases for March 1 totaled $2,000. All other operating costs are paid during the month incurred. Monthly fixed manufacturing overhead includes $150 in depreciation.

*Required:*

Prepare the following for Bamboo You.

1.  Budgeted cash receipts for Quarter 2. Include each month (April–June) as well as quarter 2 totals.
2.  Budgeted cash disbursements for Quarter 2.
3.  Cash budget for Quarter 2.

**LO5**

BLACK&DECKER.

### PA23-4 Preparing the Components of the Operating Budget

Black & Decker (B&D) manufactures a wide variety of tools and accessories. One of its more popular items is a cordless power Handisaw. Use the following fictitious information about this product line to complete the problem requirements. Each Handisaw sells for $40. B&D expects the following sales in number of units.

|          |       |
|----------|-------|
| January  | 2,000 |
| February | 2,200 |
| March    | 2,700 |
| April    | 2,500 |
| May      | 1,900 |

B&D's ending finished goods inventory policy is 25 percent of the following month's sales.

Suppose each Handisaw takes approximately 0.75 hours to manufacture, and B&D pays an average labor wage of $16.50 per hour.

Each Handisaw requires a plastic housing. B&D purchases these housings from a supplier at a cost of $7 each. The company has a raw materials inventory policy of 20 percent of the following month's production requirements. Materials other than the housing unit total $4.50 per Handisaw.

Manufacturing overhead for this product includes $72,000 annual fixed overhead (based on production of 27,000 units) and $1.10 per unit variable manufacturing overhead. B&D's selling expenses are 7 percent of sales dollars, and administrative expenses are fixed at $18,000 per month.

**Required:**
Prepare the following for B&D.
1. Sales budget for the first quarter.
2. First quarter production budget.
3. B&D's First quarter raw materials purchases budget for the plastic housings.
4. First quarter direct labor budget.
5. Cost of goods sold budget for the first quarter.
6. First quarter selling and administrative expense budget.

# Problems—Set B   Available with McGraw-Hill's Homework Manager

For problems PB23-1 through PB23-3, refer to the following information about Flying High Company, which manufactures kites that sell for $15 each. Each kite requires 2 yards of lightweight canvas, which costs $0.50 per yard. Each kite takes approximately 45 minutes to build, and the labor rate averages $8.00 per hour.

Flying High has the following inventory policies:

Ending finished goods inventory should be 30 percent of next month's sales.

Ending raw materials inventory should be 20 percent of next month's production.

Expected sales in number of kites for the upcoming months are:

|        |     |
|--------|-----|
| March  | 850 |
| April  | 700 |
| May    | 650 |
| June   | 720 |
| July   | 830 |
| August | 760 |

Variable manufacturing overhead is incurred at a rate of $0.30 per unit produced. Annual fixed manufacturing overhead is estimated to be $9,000 ($750 per month) for an expected production of 9,000 units for the year. Selling and administrative expenses are estimated at $820 per month plus $0.75 per unit sold.

## PB23-1 Preparing the Components of the Operating Budget                    LO5
**Required:**
Prepare the following for Flying High for the second quarter. Include each month (April–June) as well as the quarter 2 total in your budgets.

1. Sales budget.
2. Production budget.
3. Raw materials purchases budget.

4. Direct labor budget.
5. Manufacturing overhead cost budget.
6. Budgeted cost of goods sold.
7. Selling and administrative expenses budget.

**LO5**

**PB23-2 Preparing a Budgeted Income Statement**
Refer to the information in PB23-1.

*Required:*
Prepare Flying High's budgeted income statement for Quarter 2.

**LO6**

**PB23-3 Preparing a Cash Budget**
Refer to the information in PB23-1. Flying High Company had $12,200 cash on hand at April 1. Eighty percent of sales are cash. Of the credit sales, 60 percent is collected during the month of the sale and 40 percent is collected during the month following the sale.

Seventy percent of raw material purchases is paid for during the month purchased. Thirty percent is paid in the following month. Raw materials purchases for March totaled $800. All other operating costs are paid during the month incurred. Monthly fixed manufacturing overhead includes $280 in depreciation.

*Required:*
Prepare the following for Flying High.
1. Budgeted cash receipts for Quarter 2. Include each month (April–June) as well as quarter 2 totals.
2. Budgeted cash disbursements for Quarter 2.
3. Cash budget for Quarter 2.

**LO5**

**PB23-4 Preparing the Components of the Operating Budget**
Black & Decker (B&D) manufactures a wide variety of tools and accessories. One of its more popular craft-related items is the Cord Free Glue Gun. Use the following fictitious information about this product to complete the problem requirements. Each glue gun sells for $25. B&D expects the following sales in number of glue guns.

| | |
|---|---|
| January | 8,000 |
| February | 7,400 |
| March | 8,700 |
| April | 9,500 |
| May | 9,150 |

B&D's ending finished goods inventory policy is 30 percent of the following month's sales.

Suppose each glue gun takes approximately 0.5 hours to manufacture, and B&D pays an average labor wage of $16.50 per hour.

Each glue gun requires a heating element. B&D purchases these heating elements from a supplier at a cost of $1.25 each. The company has a raw materials inventory policy of 40 percent of the following month's production requirements. Materials other than the heating elements total $3.25 per glue gun.

Manufacturing overhead for this product includes $96,900 annual fixed overhead (based on production of 102,000 units) and variable manufacturing overhead of 0.80 per unit. B&D's selling expenses are 5 percent of sales dollars, and administrative expenses for this product are fixed at $17,500 per month.

*Required:*
Prepare the following for B&D.
1. Sales budget for the first quarter.
2. First quarter production budget.
3. First quarter raw materials purchases budget for the heating element.
4. First quarter direct labor budget.
5. Cost of goods sold budget for the first quarter.
6. First quarter selling and administrative expense budget.

# Cases and Projects

**CP23-1 Evaluating the Impact of Corporate Culture and Pressure to Meet the Numbers in the Accounting Reporting Environment**          LO3

In 1995, *BusinessWeek* ran a cover story entitled "Blind Ambition: How the Pursuit of Results Got Out of Hand at Bausch and Lomb." The two-part article details a number of games Bausch and Lomb (B&L) managers played to artificially achieve short-term results at the expense of long-term value.

The "numbers-oriented" culture at B&L was far from unique, as evidenced by the high-profile accounting scandals that occurred over the past decade. Since then, numerous reforms, including the Sarbanes-Oxley Act of 2002, have been implemented to improve the corporate reporting environment.

*Required:*

1.  Find *BusinessWeek's* "Blind Ambition" article on the Internet. Read it and list five specific examples of actions that B&L managers took to artificially boost short-term results.
2.  Were the actions taken at B&L unethical, illegal, or both? What was the likely impact on long-term results and stockholder value?
3.  Explain how the corporate culture at B&L may have contributed to managers' pressure to achieve budgetary results.
4.  How did the bonus and compensation systems affect the behavior of individual B&L managers?
5.  Conduct an Internet search on the Sarbanes-Oxley Act. What was its intent? Did it include any requirements aimed at improving corporate culture as a means to reduce fraudulent reporting?

**CP23-2 Interviewing and Writing a Report on a Real-World Budget Process.**          LO2, 3

Budgets can be used in almost any type of organization including large corporations, small businesses, government organizations, universities, churches, and student clubs.

*Required:*

Choose any organization and interview two people who are involved in its budget process. Try to choose one person who actually worked on preparing the budget (e.g., an accountant or treasurer of the organization) and another person who is affected by the budget (e.g., a person in charge of spending the budget, or an employee who is evaluated based on his or her ability to meet budgetary goals).

1.  Based on your interviews, write a brief description of the budgeting process within this organization. The description should be a factual account of the steps taken to develop and distribute the budget without any qualitative evaluations of the process. You should identify the type of budgeting (top down or participative) and the personnel involved in the budgeting procedure as well as any recent and/or anticipated adjustments to the process and the overall importance management place on budgets.
2.  Separately consider each of the people you interviewed. How satisfied does each seem with the organization's budgeting process? With what step(s) of the process were they the most and least satisfied? Did either of your interviewees identify a particular step of the process that has been troublesome?
3.  Suppose the organization you investigated has retained you as a consultant. Based on the information compiled from the organization and your knowledge from this course, what recommendations would you make to this organization regarding its budgeting process?

**CP23-3 Researching Online Budget Tools.**          LO2, 3

Numerous personal financial planning or budgeting tools are available on the Internet, many of them free. Choose at least two different online budgeting calculators and input information for a typical person of your age. (**Note:** You may either create a fictitious profile or use your own personal information. If you choose to use your personal data, be sure to read the sites' privacy policies.)

*Required:*

1.  Develop weekly, monthly, and annual budgets.
2.  Compare and contrast the two online budgeting tools. Do you prefer aspects of one over the other? Are there things that you dislike?
3.  What tools other than budgeting calculators are available online?
4.  How helpful do you think such tools are in personal financial management?

# 24 Budgetary Control

## LEARNING OBJECTIVES

**After completing this chapter, you should be able to:**

**LO1** Describe the standard-setting process and explain how standard costs relate to budgets and variances.

Lectured slideshow–LP24-1
www.mhhe.com/LLPW1e

**LO2** Prepare a flexible budget and show how total costs change with sales volume.

**LO3** Calculate and interpret the direct materials price and quantity variances.

**LO4** Calculate and interpret the direct labor rate and efficiency variances.

**LO5** Calculate and interpret the variable overhead rate and efficiency variances.

**LO6** Calculate and interpret the fixed overhead spending and volume variances.

**Focus Company:** COLD STONE CREAMERY

**"Because the World Deserves Better Ice Cream."**

www.coldstonecreamery.com

The last chapter focused on the role of budgets in the planning and control process. This chapter discusses the use of variances in the control phase of that process. A **variance** is simply the difference between actual costs and budgeted or standard costs. Variances act as signals to managers that their planned results are (or are not) being achieved.

Think of the planning and control process in terms of flying an airplane. Before takeoff, the pilot must file a flight plan that states where the plane is going and how it will get there. The flight plan is similar to the role of a budget in business. The budget states where the business is going and how managers plan to get it there.

Likewise, the system of signals that guides pilots and air traffic controllers during the flight serves as an aviation control process. Just as the pilot monitors the plane's instrument panel to follow these signals, managers keep a close eye on key indicators, including variances, to determine whether they are on track to achieve their plan. If they go too far off course, managers need a signal that they should take corrective action.

In the last chapter, you began the study of the planning and control process by preparing a master budget for a hypothetical Cold Stone Creamery location. In this chapter, we continue this example to calculate Cold Stone's cost variances for direct materials, direct labor, and manufacturing overhead. We also discuss how to prepare a different kind of budget, the **flexible budget.** First, we need to become familiar with **standard cost systems,** the basis for these budgets and variances.

**STANDARD COST SYSTEMS**

- Ideal versus Attainable Standards
- Types of Standard
- Standard Cost Card
- Favorable versus Unfavorable Variances

**USE OF FLEXIBLE BUDGETS TO CALCULATE COST VARIANCES**

- Master Budgets versus Flexible Budgets
- Flexible Budget as a Benchmark
- Volume Variance versus Spending Variance

**DIRECT MATERIALS AND DIRECT LABOR VARIANCES**

- Variance Framework
- Direct Materials Variances
- Direct Labor Variances

**MANUFACTURING OVERHEAD COST VARIANCES**

- Variable Manufacturing Overhead Variances
- Fixed Manufacturing Overhead Variances
- Summary of Variances

# STANDARD COST SYSTEMS

A standard cost system is the foundation of a managerial control system. The key difference between a standard cost system and the cost systems covered in earlier chapters is that a standard cost system records cost at standard rather than actual amounts. The standards are set in advance to reflect what managers think a particular cost **should** be. Managers can then use these standards to create budgets, set prices for products and services, and make a variety of other decisions.

## Ideal versus Attainable Standards

Standards can be set at varying levels of difficulty or achievability. The most extreme case is an ideal standard, or one that can be achieved only under perfect or ideal conditions. An example is the performance standard of a world-class athlete, such as a 4-minute mile. Standards that are almost impossible to achieve are unlikely to motivate people to work hard to try to achieve the standards. At the other end of the spectrum is an easily attainable standard, or one that can be met without much effort. Research suggests that **tight but attainable standards**—the happy medium between these two extremes—are best for motivating individuals to work hard.

What these general guidelines mean to a particular business depends on the type of task and the person performing it. Imagine, for example, that you just started training for a 10-K charity run. You can run a 10-minute mile with relative ease but would like to improve your running time. It probably would not be realistic to set a 4-minute mile as your performance standard because most people are not physically capable of achieving that ideal standard. What standard would motivate you to train harder without being so difficult that it would cause you to give up? This type of standard is sometimes called a "stretch goal"—one you must stretch yourself to achieve. Similarly, organizations should set standard costs so that they are difficult but not impossible to achieve. To foster continuous improvement, the standards should increase in difficulty over time, just as you would decrease your target running time as your strength and training improve.

## Types of Standard

Standard cost systems rely on two types of standard, quantity standards and price standards:

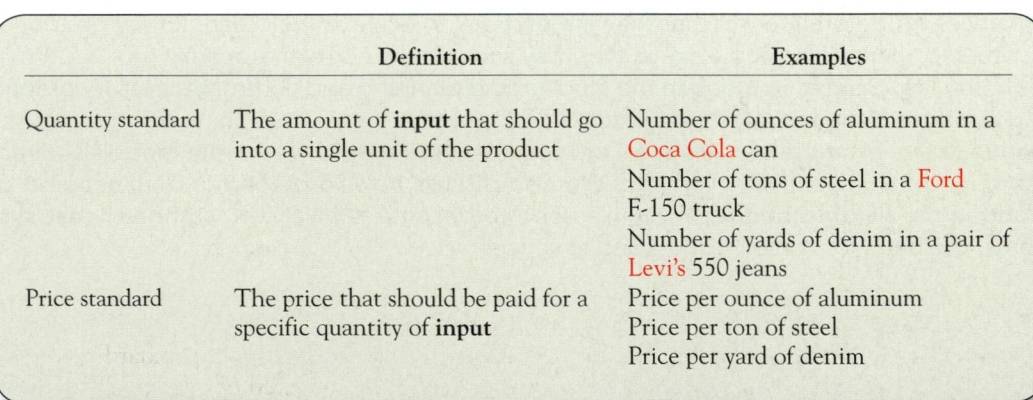

|  | Definition | Examples |
|---|---|---|
| Quantity standard | The amount of **input** that should go into a single unit of the product | Number of ounces of aluminum in a Coca Cola can<br>Number of tons of steel in a Ford F-150 truck<br>Number of yards of denim in a pair of Levi's 550 jeans |
| Price standard | The price that should be paid for a specific quantity of **input** | Price per ounce of aluminum<br>Price per ton of steel<br>Price per yard of denim |

**Coach's Tip**

Managers should set standards at realistic levels that allow a certain amount of downtime for preventive maintenance, employee breaks and training, and the like. Failure to build these factors into the standards can reduce performance over the long run because of machine breakdowns, low employee morale, and high turnover rates.

Video 24-1
www.mhhe.com/LLPW1e

**Coach's Tip**

You may wonder how companies set their price and quantity standards. Managers use many types of information including historical data, industry averages, and the results of process studies to determine how much time and money they **should** spend to make a product.

Notice that these standards are stated in terms of the quantity and price of the **input** (ounces, tons, or yards) that **should** be used to create a single unit of output. Similar quantity and price standards are developed for direct labor cost. The quantity standard for direct labor is the amount of time (in hours, minutes, or seconds) that workers **should** take to produce a single unit of product. The price standard for labor, called the **standard labor rate,** is the expected hourly cost of labor including employee taxes and benefits.

## Standard Cost Card

The price standard is multiplied by the quantity standard for each input to get the standard unit cost. Then all standard costs are summarized on a standard cost card, a form that shows what the company **should** spend to make a single unit of product based on expected production and sales for the coming period. Exhibit 24.1 shows a hypothetical standard cost card for Cold Stone Creamery.

**Exhibit 24.1  Standard Cost Card for Cold Stone Creamery**  COLD STONE

| | Standard Quantity | Standard Price (Rate) | Standard Unit Cost |
|---|---|---|---|
| **Direct costs** | | | |
| Ice cream* | 10 oz. | $0.05 per oz. | $ 0.50 |
| Mix-in ingredients | 2 oz. | 0.10 per oz. | 0.20 |
| Direct labor | .10 hrs. | 8.00 per hr. | 0.80 |
| **Manufacturing overhead costs** | | | |
| Variable manufacturing overhead (based on number of direct labor hours) | .10 hrs. | 1.00 per hr. | 0.10 |
| Fixed manufacturing overhead $6,000 / 15,000 units = $0.40 per unit | | | .40 |
| **Standard manufacturing cost per unit** | | | $2.00 |

*In reality, Cold Stone Creamery purchases milk, cream, and sugar and uses these raw ingredients to make fresh ice cream at each individual store. For simplicity, we assume that the ice cream is purchased from a regional distribution center. The standard cost card focuses only on mixing the ice cream with ingredients to create and serve a Cold Stone Creation to customers.

According to the standard cost card, Cold Stone should use 10 ounces of ice cream and 2 ounces of mix-in ingredients (fruits, candy, nuts) to make each unit of product. The standard price is $0.05 per ounce for ice cream and $0.10 per ounce for mix-ins, which results in a standard unit cost for materials of $0.70 ($0.50 + $0.20).

The direct labor standard assumes that employees can produce and serve an average of 10 units per hour—including the time needed to prepare, serve, and clean up after each unit, as well as an allowance for training time, breaks, and the like. Converting this direct labor standard to a per unit basis produces a standard amount of time to produce each unit of .10 hours (6 minutes). Because the standard labor rate (including taxes and benefits) is $8.00 per hour, the standard direct labor cost per unit is $0.80.

Variable manufacturing costs are applied to the product at a rate of $1.00 per direct labor hour. When this standard variable overhead rate is multiplied by the standard quantity of .10 labor hours per unit, we get a standard unit cost of $0.10 for variable overhead. Fixed overhead costs are budgeted at $6,000 per month. If that amount is spread over the 15,000 units we expect to produce and sell, we get a fixed manufacturing overhead cost of $0.40 per unit. Adding all of these standard cost components, we arrive at a standard manufacturing cost of $2.00 per unit.

**Learning Objective 1**

Describe the standard-setting process and explain how standard costs relate to budgets and variances.

## Favorable versus Unfavorable Variances

Cost variances are calculated by comparing actual costs to budgeted or standard costs. A favorable variance (F) occurs when actual costs are less than budgeted or standard costs. An

**unfavorable variance** (U) occurs when actual costs are more than budgeted or standard costs. Common causes of favorable and unfavorable variances include the following:

| Causes of Favorable Variances | Causes of Unfavorable Variances |
|---|---|
| • Paying a **lower price** than expected for direct materials | • Paying a **higher price** than expected for direct materials |
| • Using **less** direct materials than expected | • Using **more** direct materials than expected |
| • Paying a **lower** rate than expected for direct labor | • Paying a **higher** rate than expected for direct labor |
| • Producing a unit in **less** time than expected | • Producing a unit in **more** time than expected |
| • Paying **less** than expected for manufacturing overhead costs | • Paying **more** than expected for manufacturing overhead costs |
| • Using **less** of a variable overhead resource than expected | • Using **more** of a variable overhead resource than expected |
| • Using **more** of a fixed overhead resource than expected | • Using **less** of a fixed overhead resource than expected |

**Coach's Tip**

The words **favorable** and **unfavorable** do not necessarily indicate good and bad performance. Rather, they reflect a difference between actual and standard costs. Sometimes a favorable variance can signal bad performance and an unfavorable variance can indicate good performance.

In the remainder of this chapter, we calculate cost variances that illustrate each of these potential causes. First, we need to discuss and develop a flexible budget.

## USE OF FLEXIBLE BUDGETS TO CALCULATE COST VARIANCES

Video 24-2
www.mhhe.com/LLPW1e

As mentioned in the previous section, we calculate variances by comparing actual costs to budgeted or standard costs. Although we often use the terms **standard** and **budget** interchangeably, they have slightly different meanings. Standards are expressed at a very detailed level to reflect the cost and quantity of the **inputs** that go into a product or service. A simple example of an input is the amount of flour that is needed to make a cake. A budget, on the other hand, is the total dollar amount that we expect to spend to achieve a certain level of **output.** In other words, a budget depends not only on the standards that are stated in terms of the input but also on the level of output, such as the number of cakes that will be made. As you will see shortly, we can develop different budgets for different levels of output, but the standards we use to develop those budgets remain the same.

### Master Budgets versus Flexible Budgets

**Learning Objective 2**

Prepare a flexible budget and show how total costs change with sales volume.

In the last chapter, you prepared an entire master budget for Cold Stone Creamery. Recall that the master budget is an integrated set of operating and financial budgets that reflects what managers expect to achieve in a future accounting period. The starting point for preparing the master budget is the sales forecast, or the company's best estimate of future sales. All other components of the master budget are based on the sales forecast, including the production budget, the raw materials purchases budget, the direct labor budget, the manufacturing overhead budget, and the selling and administrative expense budget.

The master budget is an example of a static budget—that is, a budget that is based on a single (fixed) estimate of sales volume. Because predicting sales volume with 100 percent certainty is impossible, managers often find it useful to prepare a flexible budget that shows how budgeted costs and revenues will change across different levels of sales volume. As you should recall from Chapter 21, variable costs are those that change (in total) in response to a change in production or sales volume. Fixed costs are those that remain the same (in total) regardless of production or sales volume. For the sake of simplicity, we assume that production and sales are equal throughout this chapter. See Exhibit 24.2 for a flexible budget for Cold Stone Creamery's manufacturing costs.

Two points are important to keep in mind when preparing a flexible budget. **First, total variable costs change in direct proportion to changes in volume.** For example, if Cold Stone's sales volume increases from 15,000 units to 18,000 units (see Exhibit 24.2), the total cost of ice cream should increase from $7,500 to $9,000. The 20 percent increase in sales

## Exhibit 24.2    Preparation of the Master and Flexible Budgets

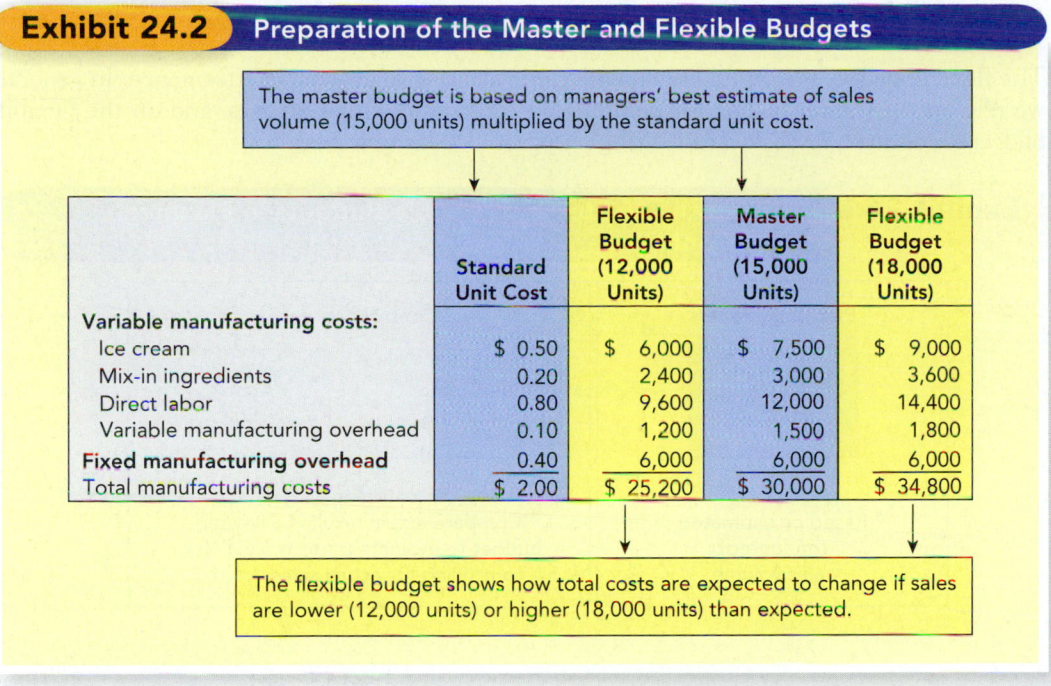

The master budget is based on managers' best estimate of sales volume (15,000 units) multiplied by the standard unit cost.

| | Standard Unit Cost | Flexible Budget (12,000 Units) | Master Budget (15,000 Units) | Flexible Budget (18,000 Units) |
|---|---|---|---|---|
| **Variable manufacturing costs:** | | | | |
| Ice cream | $ 0.50 | $  6,000 | $  7,500 | $  9,000 |
| Mix-in ingredients | 0.20 | 2,400 | 3,000 | 3,600 |
| Direct labor | 0.80 | 9,600 | 12,000 | 14,400 |
| Variable manufacturing overhead | 0.10 | 1,200 | 1,500 | 1,800 |
| **Fixed manufacturing overhead** | 0.40 | 6,000 | 6,000 | 6,000 |
| Total manufacturing costs | $ 2.00 | $ 25,200 | $ 30,000 | $ 34,800 |

The flexible budget shows how total costs are expected to change if sales are lower (12,000 units) or higher (18,000 units) than expected.

volume (3,000 / 15,000 = 20%) produces a 20 percent increase in the total cost of ice cream ($1,500 / $7,500 = 20%). The same effect will occur for all other variable costs.

**Second, total fixed costs should remain the same, regardless of volume.** Cold Stone's budgeted fixed cost is $6,000 regardless of the number of units produced or sold. Thus, the fixed cost of $0.40 per unit shown in the standard unit cost column is valid only for the master budget of 15,000 units ($6,000 / 15,000 = $0.40).

Before we continue, complete the following Self-Study Practice to make sure you understand how to prepare a flexible budget.

---

### SELF-STUDY PRACTICE

Assume that Papa John's standard unit cost and master budget for 20,000 units are as follows.

| | Standard Unit Cost | Master Budget (20,000 units) | Flexible Budget (25,000 units) |
|---|---|---|---|
| 1. Pizza dough | $0.80 | $16,000 | |
| 2. Pizza sauce | 0.20 | 4,000 | |
| 3. Direct labor | 1.00 | 20,000 | |
| 4. Variable manufacturing overhead | 0.25 | 5,000 | |
| 5. Fixed manufacturing overhead | 0.50 | 10,000 | |
| | $2.75 | $55,000 | |

PIZZA
PAPA JOHNS
Better Ingredients.
Better Pizza.

Calculate a flexible budget for 25,000 units and enter the amounts in the Flexible Budget column.

*After you have finished, check your answers with the solutions at the bottom of the page.*

Solution to
Self-Study Practice

1. $20,000 (25,000 × $0.80)
2. $ 5,000 (25,000 × $0.20)
3. $25,000 (25,000 × $1.00)
4. $ 6,250 (25,000 × $0.25)
5. $10,000 (remains the same)
   $66,250

## Flexible Budget as a Benchmark

The flexible budget is a useful benchmark for evaluating managerial performance. In general, we rely on the master budget for planning, or forward-looking purposes, and on the flexible budget for control, or backward-looking purposes. See Exhibit 24.3.

**Exhibit 24.3    Use of the Master and Flexible Budgets in Planning and Control**

| Planning process | Control process |
|---|---|
| Master budget | Flexible budget — Actual results |
| ↓ | ↓ |
| Based on estimated (budgeted) sales volume | Compare actual results to flexible budget to evaluate performance after controlling for actual sales volume |

To illustrate the use of a flexible budget for performance evaluation, assume you are a store manager at Cold Stone Creamery and part of your responsibility is to control the cost of the ice cream used to make Cold Stone Creations. Based on the master budget sales forecast of 15,000 units, your ice cream budget was set at $7,500 ($0.50 per unit × 15,000 units). After the budget period, you learned that the actual cost of ice cream was $8,000, or $500 higher than budgeted. Based on this information, how should the company evaluate your performance at controlling ice cream costs?

To answer this question, we need to think about the two possible reasons that the cost might have been higher than budgeted:

- You may have spent more than $0.50 per unit for ice cream.
- You may have produced more than 15,000 units.

Now we learn that the company actually produced and sold 18,000 units for the period. Would that knowledge change how we should evaluate your performance at controlling direct materials costs? In this case, we can blame the increased cost on the increase in volume. In fact, when we compare the budgeted cost for 18,000 units in Exhibit 24.2 to the actual cost, we can see that you spent **less** than $0.50 per unit on ice cream.

The lesson here is that to evaluate cost control, we cannot just compare actual results to the master budget. Although the master budget is very useful in planning, a flexible budget is more useful in evaluating past managerial performance because it helps separate the effects that are due to spending from those that are due to volume.

## Volume Variance versus Spending Variance

**Coach's Tip**

Some volume variances are driven by the difference in actual and budgeted **sales** volume, while others are driven by the difference in actual and budgeted **production** volume. To keep things simple, we assume that sales and production are equal.

Using the flexible budget for performance evaluation allows us to separate the effect of volume from the effect of spending. The only difference between the master budget and the flexible budget, in fact, is the volume used to create each budget. Thus, any comparison of the master budget to the flexible budget creates a volume variance that represents the difference between actual and budgeted volume. Spending variances are calculated by comparing actual costs to the flexible budget (not the master budget). Because both numbers are based on the same volume, this provides an "apples to apples" comparison of spending.

See Exhibit 24.4 for a comparison of the master and flexible budgets based on the ice cream example presented in the previous section. Remember that your budget for ice cream was $0.50 for each unit produced and sold. The master budget cost of $7,500 is based on the 15,000 units you expected to produce ($0.50 × 15,000 = $7,500). The flexible budget cost

**Exhibit 24.4**    Calculation of Spending and Volume Variances

of $9,000 is based on the 18,000 units you actually produced and sold ($0.50 × 18,000 = $9,000). The volume variance is the difference between these two amounts ($9,000 − $7,500 = $1,500). In this example, the volume variance is unfavorable because producing more units than expected **should** result in higher ice cream cost. However, this volume variance only considers the cost of the ice cream and ignores other production costs, as well as the additional revenue you would get from increased sales. From an overall company perspective, selling more units than expected is favorable so long as the sales price is high enough to cover the increased variable costs. We do not consider revenue variances in this chapter as they are covered in more advanced managerial accounting texts.

Exhibit 24.4 also includes a comparison of actual ice cream costs to the flexible budget. Recall that you actually spent $8,000 on ice cream to produce 18,000 units. The flexible budget shows that it **should** have cost $9,000 to produce 18,000 units (18,000 × $0.50). The difference is a favorable spending variance of $1,000 ($9,000 − $8,000). It is favorable because you spent less on ice cream than the flexible budget allowed. Notice that volume is held constant between these two numbers at 18,000 units. So the entire variance can be attributed to your **spending** on ice cream, as opposed to the number of units produced. There are several possible explanations for this favorable spending variance. Perhaps you were able to negotiate a reduced price for the ice cream. Or perhaps employees skimped on the amount of ice cream they put into each Cold Stone Creation. In the next section we will calculate price and quantity variances that break the overall spending variance into more detailed components, so that we can hold a specific manager responsible for it.

# DIRECT MATERIALS AND DIRECT LABOR VARIANCES

Direct material and direct labor costs are those that can be directly attributed to each unit produced. We can use the same basic framework to analyze these direct costs. This framework allows us to divide the overall spending variance into two unique components: a price variance and a quantity variance.

## Variance Framework

The price variance relates to the amount **paid** for a particular **input** that goes into the final product. For Cold Stone Creamery, the direct inputs to the final product are ice cream, mix-in ingredients, and employee time. The price variance compares the price we actually paid for each of these inputs to the price we **should have** paid. Notice that when we talk about price in this context, we are talking about the amount paid for something (cost), not the price we charged the final customer (revenue). Thus, the price variance is actually a cost variance.

The quantity variance relates to the quantity of **input** used to make the final product. For Cold Stone, the quantity of input can be measured in terms of **ounces** of ice cream and mix-in ingredients, or **hours** of employee time. For simplicity, we assume that the quantity of input purchased equals the quantity used. That way we won't need to worry about changes in inventory, which complicates the calculations.

Exhibit 24.5 illustrates the framework we will use to analyze the direct cost variances.

**Coach's Tip**

In calculating variances, we always isolate the effect of a single factor while holding all other factors constant. Doing so makes it easier to assign responsibility to the manager who has control over that factor.

**Exhibit 24.5** | Calculation of Direct Cost Variances

AP: Actual price per unit of input
AQ: Actual quantity of input
SP: Standard price per unit of input
SQ: Standard quantity of input allowed to achieve the actual units of output

**Coach's Tip**

Spending variances are calculated by comparing actual costs to the flexible budget. The master budget is used to calculate volume variances, so it is shown outside the box in this diagram.

Exhibit 24.5 shows that direct cost variances can be calculated in two ways. The first approach is to calculate the total cost in each of the orange boxes shown in Exhibit 24.5. Then calculate the difference (variance) between each box by subtracting one value from the other. The second approach is to use the formulas that are shown in the blue boxes. Either of these approaches will provide the same answer, because the variance formulas were derived by subtracting the equations in the orange boxes from one another, as follows:

**Price variance = [(SP × AQ) − (AP × AQ)] = AQ × (SP − AP)**
**Quantity variance = [(SP × SQ) − (SP × AQ)] = SP × (SQ − AQ)**

Notice that each variance formula allows only one factor (either price or quantity) to vary, while holding the other factor constant. Isolating the variance this way allows managers to identify the specific cause of the variance so that a specific manager can be held responsible for it.

**Learning Objective 3**

Calculate and interpret the direct materials price and quantity variances.

## Direct Materials Variances

In an earlier example, we learned that Cold Stone Creamery had a $1,000 unfavorable spending variance for ice cream. Let's see if we can find the specific cause of that variance. The standard cost information for Cold Stone's ice cream is as follows:

| Direct Costs | Standard Quantity | Standard Price | Standard Unit Cost |
|---|---|---|---|
| Ice cream | 10 oz. | $0.05 per oz. | $0.50 |

Cold Stone's actual results were as follows:

- Produced and sold 18,000 units.
- Purchased and used 200,000 ounces of ice cream at a total cost of $8,000.

Let's start by identifying the following terms:

Actual price: $8,000 / 200,000 = $0.04 per ounce.

Actual quantity: 200,000 ounces.

Standard price: $0.05 per ounce.

Standard quantity: 10 ounces per unit × 18,000 actual units = 180,000 ounces.

**Coach's Tip**

Try entering these numbers into Exhibit 24.5 to see whether you can calculate the variances yourself. Then look at the answers in Exhibit 24.6.

The **direct materials price variance** is the difference between the actual price and the standard price for direct materials multiplied by the actual quantity of direct materials purchased. In this case, the actual price of the ice cream was $0.04 per ounce; the standard price was $0.05 per ounce. To get the variance, we need to multiply the difference by the 200,000 ounces that were actually purchased.

The **direct materials quantity variance** is the difference between the actual quantity and the standard quantity of direct materials used, multiplied by the standard price. This variance is sometimes called the **direct materials usage variance.** Because the standard quantity for ice cream is 10 ounces for each unit produced, the standard quantity allowed for 18,000 units is 180,000 ounces. However, the company actually used 200,000 ounces. To get the variance, we need to multiply the difference by the $0.05 standard price.

Entering these numbers into Exhibit 24.5 provides the variances in Exhibit 24.6.

**Exhibit 24.6   Cold Stone Creamery's Direct Materials Variances**

DM: Direct materials
AP: Actual price per unit of input
AQ: Actual quantity of input
SP: Standard price per unit of input
SQ: Standard quantity of input allowed to achieve the actual units of output

**Coach's Tip**

It may seem odd that we are using the actual number of units to calculate SQ. But remember that SQ is the standard quantity of **input** needed to achieve the actual units of output.

We can draw two conclusions from this diagram. First, the direct materials price variance is $2,000 favorable because the company paid $0.01 less than the standard cost for the 200,000 ounces of materials purchased. **The direct materials purchasing manager is responsible for this favorable direct materials price variance.** A favorable price variance is not always good, however. Although it has a positive effect on short-term spending, it could have a negative effect over the long term if customers can detect a difference in product quality.

What are some potential explanations for this favorable price variance? Perhaps the purchasing manager purchased lower quality ingredients or negotiated a reduced price. Or perhaps the company received a quantity discount that was not factored into the standard price. Maybe the price difference reflects a market fluctuation in the price of ice cream in the same way that dairy prices fluctuate at the grocery store.

Second, the direct materials quantity variance is $1,000 unfavorable because the company used 200,000 ounces of ice cream to make 18,000 units, when only 180,000 ounces were allowed by the standard. **The production manager is typically responsible for the direct materials quantity variance**—in this case, the manager who oversees the employees who make and serve the ice cream creations. What are some potential explanations for this unfavorable usage variance? Perhaps employees put too much ice cream into each unit. Or perhaps the standard quantity does not account for ice cream given away to customers in taste tests or thrown away at the end of the day. Managers would need to investigate further to determine the exact cause, but the variance gives them a starting point for their investigation.

The total **direct materials spending variance** combines the direct materials price and quantity variances. Because the price variance is $2,000 F and the quantity variance is $1,000 U, we add them together to get a $1,000 favorable spending variance. Notice that this is the same number we calculated in Exhibit 24.4 (page 993) by comparing actual costs to the flexible budget costs. Now, however, we have a better idea of **why** the company spent less money than planned on ice cream. These variances can provide feedback to managers who may need to change their behavior. Alternatively, they may signal that the company's standards need to be updated to reflect new pricing or production methods.

Before you continue, complete the following Self-Study Practice to see whether you can calculate the direct materials variances for Cold Stone Creamery's mix-in ingredients.

---

**SELF-STUDY PRACTICE**

Cold Stone Creamery's standard cost card for mix-in ingredients follows:

| Direct costs | Standard Quantity | Standard Price | Standard Unit Cost |
|---|---|---|---|
| Mix-in ingredients | 2 oz. | $0.10 per oz. | $0.20 |

Actual results were as follows:

- Produced and sold 18,000 units.
- Purchased and used 35,000 ounces of mix-in ingredients at a total cost of $4,200 ($0.12 per ounce).

Calculate the following variances and label them as favorable (F) or unfavorable (U):

1. Direct materials price variance.
2. Direct materials quantity variance.
3. Total direct materials spending variance.

*After you have finished, check your answers with the solutions at the bottom of the page.*

---

## Direct Labor Variances

The method for calculating direct labor variances is similar to the one for direct materials variances with a few modifications:

- Because the price of direct labor is called the direct labor rate, **the price variance for labor is called the direct labor rate (not price) variance.**
- Because direct labor quantity is measured in hours, **the quantity variance for labor is called the direct labor efficiency variance.**

Let's use Exhibit 24.7 to analyze Cold Stone Creamery's actual and standard direct labor costs. The labor portion of Cold Stone's standard cost card may be summarized as follows:

| Input | Standard Quantity | Standard Price | Standard Unit Cost |
|---|---|---|---|
| Direct labor | .10 hrs. | $8.00 per hr. | $0.80 |

Cold Stone's actual results were as follows:

- Actual number of units produced was 18,000.
- Actual direct labor costs were $16,500 for 2,000 hours.

---

**Solution to Self-Study Practice**

1. DM Price Variance = AQ × (SP − AP) = 35,000 × ($0.10 − $0.12) = $700 U
2. DM Quantity Variance = SP × (SQ − AQ) = $0.10 (36,000 − 35,000) = $100 F
3. Total DM Spending Variance = $700 Unfavorable + $100 Favorable = $600 U

**Exhibit 24.7**    **Calculation of Direct Labor Variances**

AR: Actual hourly labor rate
AH: Actual labor hours
SR: Standard hourly labor rate
SH: Standard labor hours allowed to achieve the actual units of output
DL: Direct labor

**Coach's Tip**

SH is the number of direct labor hours we **should have used** to produce 18,000 actual units of output.

Let's start by filling in the following terms:

Actual labor rate: $16,500 / 2,000 hours = $8.25 per hour.

Actual labor hours: 2,000 hours.

Standard labor rate: $8.00 per hour.

Standard labor hours: 0.10 hours × 18,000 units = 1,800 hours.

**Coach's Tip**

Try using these numbers in Exhibit 24.7 to see whether you can calculate the variances yourself. Then look at the answers in Exhibit 24.8.

The **direct labor rate variance** is the difference between the actual labor rate and the standard labor rate multiplied by the actual labor hours used. The **direct labor efficiency variance** is the difference between the actual number of labor hours used and the standard number of labor hours multiplied by the standard labor rate. Cold Stone's direct labor standard indicates that an employee should take .10 hours (6 minutes) to produce a single unit of output. Because Cold Stone's employees produced 18,000 units, they should have used only 1,800 direct labor hours. Actually, employees worked 2,000 direct labor hours to produce 18,000 units.

Using these numbers in Exhibit 24.7 gives the results in Exhibit 24.8.

The direct labor rate variance is $500 unfavorable because the company paid $0.25 more per hour than the standard labor rate (on average) for the 2,000 labor hours worked. **Holding an individual manager responsible for the direct labor rate variance is difficult** because many factors can influence the variance including labor market conditions, how and when workers were hired and promoted, and turnover rates in the organization. In this case, the variance is unfavorable because the actual labor rate was slightly higher (on average) than the standard rate. The market wage rate may have increased, or the standard wage rate may not have been adjusted to reflect that market reality.

The direct labor efficiency variance is unfavorable because workers took 200 more hours than they **should** have (based on the standard) to produce 18,000 units. When we multiply the 200 extra hours by the standard labor rate of $8.00 per hour, we get an unfavorable efficiency variance of $1,600. **In general, the production manager is responsible for the direct labor efficiency variance.** A variety of factors can affect this variance, including how quickly workers can make the product and how closely production can be matched with customer demand. Unlike a traditional manufacturing firm, which can use inventory to keep production levels stable, Cold Stone Creamery cannot produce its product until a customer walks through the door. If employees are standing around with no customers to serve, it will negatively affect the direct labor efficiency variance. This variance can signal to managers that the staffing schedule should be modified.

The total **direct labor spending variance** is the sum of the direct labor rate and direct labor efficiency variances. In this case, because both variances are unfavorable, we add them together to arrive at an unfavorable spending variance of $2,100 ($500U + $1,600U = $2,100U).

**Exhibit 24.8**  Calculation of Cold Stone Creamery's Direct Labor Variances

DL: Direct labor
AR: Actual hourly labor rate
AH: Actual labor hours
SR: Standard hourly labor rate
SH: Standard labor hours allowed to achieve the actual units of output

# MANUFACTURING OVERHEAD COST VARIANCES

Because manufacturing overhead costs cannot be traced directly to specific units, they must be **applied** to products using a predetermined overhead rate and a secondary allocation measure such as direct labor hours. The standard overhead rates are estimated before the accounting period begins based on budgeted costs and budgeted levels of the overhead cost drivers. Overhead is then applied to specific units during the period by multiplying the budgeted (standard) rate by the standard quantity of the cost driver.

This is a key difference between a standard cost system and the "normal" cost system described in Chapter 19. In Chapter 19, we established a budgeted manufacturing overhead rate based on budgeted costs and budgeted levels of the activity drivers. Then we applied overhead cost to products by multiplying the budgeted rate by the **actual** number of units produced. In this chapter, we multiply the budgeted (standard) overhead rate by the **standard** value of the cost driver.

The overall difference (variance) between actual and applied manufacturing overhead is still called over- or underapplied overhead. Now, however, we can break the overall variance down into more detailed variances to gain some insight into **why** manufacturing overhead costs were over- or underapplied. As you will see shortly, our interpretation of these overhead variances changes greatly depending on whether the overhead cost is variable or fixed.

## Variable Manufacturing Overhead Variances

Variable manufacturing overhead costs include the costs of indirect materials, such as cleaning supplies and paper products, as well as the power to run machines and other incidental costs that vary with some activity measure. In this chapter, we assume these costs vary in direct proportion to direct labor hours—a realistic assumption for a labor-oriented business such as Cold Stone Creamery. As you learned in earlier chapters, however, overhead costs can vary with many other factors including number of machine hours and nonvolume activity drivers such as the number of setups, materials-handling transactions, and the like. Companies that have activity-based cost systems would do a separate analysis for each major overhead cost driver (a task that is beyond the scope of this book).

Video 24-3
www.mhhe.com/LLPW1e

**Learning Objective 5**

Calculate and interpret the variable overhead rate and efficiency variances.

**Exhibit 24.9**   Calculation of Variable Overhead Variances

VOH: Variable manufacturing overhead
AR:   Actual variable overhead rate
AH:   Actual direct labor hours (or other allocation base)
SR:   Standard variable overhead rate
SH:   Standard direct labor hours (or other allocation base) allowed to
       achieve the actual units of output

Because we are assuming that variable overhead (VOH) costs are driven by direct labor hours (DLH), we can simply substitute the variable overhead rate for the direct labor rate in the direct labor variance framework (see Exhibit 24.9 for the modified diagram).

Let's apply this framework to our Cold Stone Creamery example. The variable manufacturing overhead standards are as follows:

|  | Standard Quantity | Standard Price | Standard Unit Cost |
|---|---|---|---|
| Variable manufacturing overhead applied at $1.00 per direct labor hour | 0.10 hrs. | $1.00 per hr. | $0.10 |

The company's actual results were as follows:

- Actual units produced were 18,000.
- Actual direct labor hours were 2,000.
- Actual VOH costs were $1,800.

Let's start by identifying the following terms:

Actual variable overhead rate: $1,800 / 2,000 hours = $0.90 per hour.
Actual DLH: 2,000 hours.
Standard VOH rate: $1.00 per hour.
Standard DLH: .10 hours × 18,000 units = 1,800 hours.

**Coach's Tip**

Enter these numbers into Exhibit 24.9 to see whether you can calculate the variances yourself. Then look at the answers in Exhibit 24.10.

The **variable overhead (VOH) rate variance** is the difference between the actual variable overhead rate and the standard variable overhead rate multiplied by the actual value of the cost driver (DLH). In this case, the actual cost of VOH is $0.90 per direct labor hour, and the standard variable overhead rate is $1.00 per direct labor hour. The **variable overhead**

**Exhibit 24.10** Calculation of Cold Stone Creamery's Variable Overhead Variances

VOH: Variable manufacturing overhead
AR:    Actual variable overhead rate
AH:    Actual direct labor hours (or other allocation base)
SR:    Standard variable overhead rate
SH:    Standard direct labor hours (or other allocation base)
        allowed to achieve the actual units of output

**Coach's Tip**

The VOH spending variance is also the amount of over- or underapplied variable overhead. In this case, actual VOH cost is exactly equal to the amount applied based on 18,000 units.

efficiency variance is the difference between the number of actual DLH used and the number of standard DLH, multiplied by the standard variable overhead rate. In this case, the actual number of DLH was 2,000, but according to the standard, only 1,800 hours should have been required to produce 18,000 units.

See Exhibit 24.10 for the results of substituting these numbers into the formulas in Exhibit 24.9.

The variable overhead rate variance is favorable because the actual variable overhead cost per direct labor hour was less than the standard variable overhead rate. When we multiply the $0.10 difference by the 2,000 actual direct labor hours, we get a favorable variable overhead rate variance of $200. What caused this variance? Managers may have paid less for variable overhead items (cleaning supplies, napkins, or power) than the standard allows, or the relationship between the variable overhead cost and the number of direct labor hours may not be perfectly proportional. Even if the variable overhead costs are partially driven by direct labor hours, other factors are likely to influence spending on variable overhead costs.

The variable overhead efficiency variance is unfavorable because the company used 200 more direct labor hours than **should** have been needed to produce 18,000 units. Multiplying the 200 extra hours by the $1.00 standard variable overhead rate gives a $200 unfavorable variable overhead efficiency variance. Although this variance is called the variable overhead efficiency variance, it is really driven by the efficiency (or inefficiency) of the underlying allocation driver (that is, direct labor hours). This variance is a mirror reflection of the direct labor efficiency variance. The assumption is that as managers use more direct labor hours, they also incur additional variable overhead costs.

The total variable overhead spending variance is the sum of the variable overhead rate variance and the variable overhead efficiency variance. In this case, it is zero because the $200 favorable variable overhead rate variance exactly offsets the $200 unfavorable variable overhead efficiency variance.

Before you continue, complete the following Self-Study Practice to make sure you can calculate the direct labor and variable overhead variances.

**SELF-STUDY PRACTICE**

Papa John's standard cost card for direct labor and variable overhead includes the following costs.

| Direct costs | Standard Quantity | Standard Price |
|---|---|---|
| Direct labor | .3 hrs. | $10.00 per hr. |
| Variable overhead | .3 hrs. | 2.50 per hr. |

PIZZA
PAPA JOHNS®
Better Ingredients.
Better Pizza.

Actual results were as follows:

- The number of units sold and produced was 15,000.
- The direct labor cost was $38,000 for 4,000 hours ($9.50 per hour).
- The variable overhead cost was $12,000 for 4,000 hours ($3.00 per hour).

Calculate the following variances and label them as favorable or unfavorable:

1. Direct labor rate variance
2. Direct labor efficiency variance
3. Total direct labor spending variance
4. Variable overhead rate variance
5. Variable overhead efficiency variance
6. Total variable overhead spending variance
7. Briefly explain the relationship between the direct labor efficiency variance and the variable overhead efficiency variance.

*After you have finished, check your answers with the solutions at the bottom of the page.*

# Fixed Manufacturing Overhead Variances

The calculation and interpretation of fixed manufacturing overhead variances is completely different from that of the variable manufacturing cost variances. Fixed manufacturing overhead includes costs that are independent of volume, such as supervisors' salaries, rent, equipment depreciation, and insurance.

Although fixed manufacturing overhead costs are unrelated to volume, we must still establish a budgeted (standard) fixed overhead rate based on the budgeted cost and budgeted production volume. For Cold Stone Creamery, we calculated that rate as follows:

> **Budgeted Fixed Overhead Rate = $6,000 / 15,000 Units = $0.40 per Unit**

**Learning Objective 6**

Calculate and interpret the fixed overhead spending and volume variances.

Solution to
Self-Study Practice

1.  DL Rate Variance: AH × (SR − AR) = 4,000 × ($10.00 − $9.50) = $2,000 F
2.  DL Efficiency Variance: SR × (SH − AH) = $10.00 × (4,500 − 4,000) = $5,000 F
3.  Total DL Spending Variance = $2,000 F + $5,000 F = $7,000 F
4.  VOH Rate Variance: AH × (SR − AR) = 4,000 × ($2.50 − $3.00) = $2,000 U
5.  VOH Efficiency Variance: SR × (SH − AH) = $2.50 × (4,500 − 4,000) = $1,250 F
6.  Total VOH Spending Variance = $2,000 U + $1,250 F = $750 U
7.  The direct labor efficiency variance and the variable overhead efficiency variance are both driven by the difference between actual labor hours and standard labor hours. The variable overhead efficiency variance is 25% of the direct labor efficiency variance, because the variable overhead rate is based on the direct labor rate.

Of course, this rate will be accurate only if we correctly estimate the fixed manufacturing overhead cost (in the numerator) and the budgeted number of units (in the denominator).

Refer to Exhibit 24.11 for the calculation of the fixed manufacturing overhead variances. The two variances we calculate for fixed manufacturing overhead relate directly to the numerator and the denominator in the fixed overhead rate. The **fixed overhead spending variance,** which relates to the numerator, is the difference between the actual fixed manufacturing overhead cost and budgeted fixed manufacturing overhead cost. The **fixed overhead volume variance,** which relates to the denominator, is the difference between the actual production volume and budgeted production volume. Essentially, if managers produce more units than allowed for in the budget, they will apply too much fixed overhead cost to the product. On the other hand, if they do not produce as many units as allowed for in the budget, they will apply too little fixed overhead cost to the product.

**Coach's Tip**

Although the model for analyzing fixed manufacturing overhead variances looks similar to the model we used to analyze the variable costs, it is actually quite different. As such, the interpretation of the variances is very different.

**Exhibit 24.11    Calculation of Fixed Overhead Variances**

FOH: Fixed manufacturing overhead
FOH Rate: Budgeted FOH cost / Budgeted units

To apply the framework in Exhibit 24.11, assume that Cold Stone Creamery's fixed manufacturing costs were as follows:

Budgeted results
    Fixed manufacturing overhead costs      $6,000
    Budgeted production/sales      15,000 units
Actual results
    Fixed manufacturing overhead costs      $6,300
    Actual production/sales      18,000 units

Substituting these numbers into Exhibit 24.11 produces the results in Exhibit 24.12.

The fixed overhead spending variance is the difference between actual ($6,300) and budgeted ($6,000) fixed overhead cost. It is unfavorable because actual costs were $300 more than budgeted. Perhaps managers failed to anticipate an increase in fixed costs. Even though fixed costs are considered to be independent of volume, they can still change over time as the cost of items such as rent, insurance, and supervision increases.

The fixed overhead volume is driven by the difference in actual production (18,000 units) and budgeted production (15,000 units). Multiplying the 3,000 unit difference by the $0.40 fixed overhead rate results in a $1,200 favorable volume variance. It is favorable because producing more units than expected drives down the cost per unit (getting more volume out of the same cost). But remember that the fixed overhead rate was set in advance based on 15,000 units. The volume variance simply tells managers that they should have been basing the fixed overhead rate on 18,000 units instead of 15,000 units.

**Exhibit 24.12** Calculation of Cold Stone Creamery's Fixed Overhead Variances

FOH: Fixed manufacturing overhead
FOH Rate: Budgeted FOH cost / Budgeted units

**Coach's Tip**
Note that the fixed overhead volume variance is the difference between the master budget volume and the flexible budget volume. This is the only time the master budget is used to calculate a cost variance.

**Over- or underapplied fixed overhead** is the sum of the fixed overhead spending and volume variances. Here, the total fixed overhead variance is $900 favorable because the fixed overhead spending variance was $300 unfavorable and the fixed overhead volume variance was $1,200 favorable ($300 U + $1,200 F = $900 F). This total variance also shows that fixed manufacturing overhead was $900 overapplied, because actual fixed overhead was less than applied. This means that the overhead rate used to apply fixed overhead was too high. Instead of applying fixed overhead cost at the rate of $.40 per unit ($6,000 / 15,000 units), the company **should** have applied it at the rate of $.35 per unit ($6,300 / 18,000 units). In many ways, the fixed overhead variance reflects managers' ability to accurately predict fixed costs and volume, and has very little to do with how well the manager is controlling costs.

## Summary of Variances

In this chapter we calculated many different variances. You are probably beginning to suffer from calculation overload. How in the world are you going to remember all those variances and how to calculate them? Exhibit 24.13 provides a summary of all of the variances calculated in this chapter, along with a definition of the terms used in the formulas.

Of course calculating the variance is only part of it. Here are some other tips for understanding and interpreting the variances.

- Variances are always calculated by comparing actual results to budgeted, or standard, results. Variances signal managers that they are (or are not) achieving their plans so they can take corrective action if necessary.
- Companies try to hold specific managers responsible for specific variances, while removing the effects of factors that are beyond managers' control.
- The formulas for variances allow only one factor such as price, quantity, or volume to change, while holding everything else constant at either actual or standard values (depending on the type of variance).

- The driving factor for a variance always appears in parentheses in the formula, as well as in the name of the variance. If you forget the name of a particular variance, just look at the terms in parentheses to figure out the cause of the variance.
- Try not to memorize rules or rely on the formulas to determine whether a variance is favorable or unfavorable; just think about it. Spending or using more of a variable resource is unfavorable. Using more of a fixed resource is favorable because it drives down the fixed cost per unit.

**Exhibit 24.13    Summary of Variance Formulas and Terminology**

| Variance | Formula |
|---|---|
| DM Price Variance | $AQ \times (SP - AP)$ |
| DM Quantity Variance | $SP \times (SQ - AQ)$ |
| DM Spending Variance | Sum of DM Price and DM Quantity Variances |
| DL Rate Variance | $AH \times (SR - AR)$ |
| DL Efficiency Variance | $SR \times (SH - AH)$ |
| DL Spending Variance | Sum of DL Rate and DL Efficiency Variances |
| VOH Rate Variance | $AH \times (SR - AR)$ |
| VOH Efficiency Variance | $SR \times (SH - AH)$ |
| VOH Spending Variance | Sum of VOH Rate and VOH Efficiency Variances |
| Over or Underapplied VOH | Applied − Actual VOH |
| FOH Spending Variance | Budgeted − Actual FOH Costs |
| FOH Budget Variance | Same as FOH Spending Variance |
| FOH Volume Variance | FOH Rate × (Actual − Budgeted Units) |
| Over or Under applied FOH | Applied − Actual FOH |

Where:

DM:   Direct materials
DL:   Direct labor
VOH:  Variable manufacturing overhead
FOH:  Fixed manufacturing overhead
AP:   Actual price of input
AQ:   Actual quantity of input
SP:   Standard price of input
SQ:   Standard quantity of input allowed for actual units produced
AR:   Actual labor rate (or VOH rate for VOH variances)
AH:   Actual labor hours
SR:   Standard labor rate (or standard VOH rate for VOH variances)
SH:   Standard labor hours allowed for actual units produced

Finally, you need to understand how all of the variances fit together. See Exhibit 24.14 for a summary of all of the manufacturing cost variances calculated in this chapter, and how they can be used to explain the difference in Cold Stone Creamery's actual and budgeted results.

In a standard cost system, all manufacturing costs are initially recorded at the standard amount, in either an inventory or the Cost of Goods Sold account. Recall that Cold Stone's standard unit cost was $2.00. Thus, cost of goods sold for 18,000 units would be $36,000 (18,000 × $2.00). The company's actual manufacturing cost was $36,800. Thus, the overall variance in manufacturing cost was $800 unfavorable.

Throughout the accounting period, the individual variances are accumulated in variance accounts before being closed to the Cost of Goods Sold account at the end of the period. The $800 adjustment to Cost of Goods Sold will increase it from the standard cost of $36,000 to the actual cost of $36,800. The specific journal entries needed to record manufacturing costs and variances in a standard cost system are illustrated in Supplement 24A.

**Exhibit 24.14    Summary of Variances for Cold Stone Creamery**

### Variance Report for Cold Stone Creamery

| | Actual cost | Spending variances | | Flexible budget | | Applied cost |
|---|---|---|---|---|---|---|
| **Direct materials:** | | DM price variance | DM quantity variance | | For variable costs, flexible budget and applied cost are the same. It is only different for fixed costs because of the volume variance. | |
| Ice cream | $ 8,000 | 2,000 F | 1,000 U | $ 9,000 | | $ 9,000 |
| **Mix-in ingredients** (from Self-Study Practice) | 4,200 | 700 U | 100 F | 3,600 | | 3,600 |
| | | DL rate variance | DL efficiency variance | | | |
| **Direct labor** | 16,500 | 500 U | 1,600 U | 14,400 | | 14,400 |
| **Variable manufacturing overhead** | 1,800 | VOH rate variance 200 F | VOH efficiency variance 200 U | 1,800 | | 1,800 |
| **Fixed manufacturing overhead** | 6,300 | FOH spending variance 300 U | | 6,000 | FOH volume variance 1,200 F | 7,200 |
| **Total manufacturing cost** | $ 36,800 | Total spending variances 2,000 U | | $ 34,800 | | $ 36,000 |

**Coach's Tip**
Actual cost ($36,800) is higher than the flexible budget ($34,800). Spending variances are used to explain the $2,000 difference in actual and flexible budget costs.

**Coach's Tip**
The flexible budget is the budget we would have prepared had we known (in advance) that we were going to produce and sell 18,000 units.

**Coach's Tip**
Recall that the standard unit cost was $2.00 per unit. So when we produce and sell 18,000 units, we record (apply) $36,000 ($2.00 × 18,000 units) in total standard cost.

## Demonstration Case

Bunko Beds produces bunk beds for children. It sells the beds through Pottery Barn Kids and other retail outlets. The standard cost of producing one of Bunko's most popular beds follows:

### STANDARD COST CARD FOR BUNKO BEDS

| | Standard Quantity | Standard Price | Standard Unit Cost |
|---|---|---|---|
| Direct materials (1 × 12" treated pine) | 50 ft. | $ 2.50 per ft. | $125.00 |
| Direct labor | 5 hrs. | 10.00 per hr. | 50.00 |
| Manufacturing overhead costs | | | |
|   Variable manufacturing overhead (based on direct labor hours) | 5 hrs. | 5.00 per hr. | 25.00 |
|   Fixed manufacturing overhead $120,000 / 3,000 units = $40 per unit | | | 40.00 |
| Standard manufacturing cost per unit | | | $240.00 |

Bunko's master budget was based on the planned production and sale of 3,000 units. Actual results were as follows:

- Produced 2,500 units.
- Purchased and used 130,000 feet of direct materials at a total cost of $312,000.
- Total direct labor cost was $123,750 for 11,250 hours.
- Variable overhead cost was $54,000.
- Fixed overhead cost was $115,000.

*Required:*
Calculate the following variances and label them as favorable (F) or unfavorable (U).

1.  Direct materials variances:

    a.  Direct materials price variance.
    b.  Direct materials quantity variance.
    c.  Total direct materials spending variance.

2.  Direct labor variances:

    a.  Direct labor rate variance.
    b.  Direct labor efficiency variance.
    c.  Total direct labor spending variance.

3.  Variable manufacturing overhead variances:

    a.  Variable overhead rate variance.
    b.  Variable overhead efficiency variance.
    c.  Total variable overhead spending variance.

4.  Fixed manufacturing overhead variances:

    a.  Fixed overhead spending variance.
    b.  Fixed overhead volume variance.
    c.  Over- or underapplied fixed overhead.

## Suggested Solution

1.  Direct materials variances:

    $AQ = 130,000$ ft.
    $AP = \$312,000 \,/\, 130,000 = \$2.40$ per ft.
    $SQ = 50$ ft. $\times$ 2,500 actual units $= 125,000$ ft.
    $SP = \$2.50$ per ft.

2.  Direct labor variances:

    $AH = 11,250$ hrs.
    $AR = \$123,750 \,/\, 11,250 = \$11$ per hr.

SH = 5 hrs. × 2,500 actual units = 12,500 hrs.
SR = $10 per hr.

3.   Variable manufacturing overhead variances:

AH = 11,250
AR = $54,000 / 11,250 = $4.80 per hour
SH = 5 hrs. × 2,500 units = 12,500
SR = $5.00 per hour

4.   Fixed manufacturing overhead variances:

Actual FOH = $115,000
Actual units = 2,500
Budgeted FOH = $120,000
Budgeted Units = 3,000
FOH Rate = $120,000 / 3,000 = $40

# Supplement 24A
## Recording Standard Costs and Variances in a Standard Cost System

This supplement focuses on the journal entries used to record the variances generated by a standard cost system. In preparing journal entries for a standard cost system, keep in mind these common rules:

- The initial debit to an inventory account (Raw Materials, Work in Process, or Finished Goods) and the eventual debit to Cost of Goods Sold should be based on the standard, not actual, cost.
- Cash, payables, and other accounts, such as accumulated depreciation or prepaid assets, should be credited for the actual cost incurred.
- The difference between the standard cost (debit) and the actual cost (credit) should be recorded as the cost variance.
- Unfavorable variances should appear as debit entries; favorable variances should appear as credit entries.
- At the end of the accounting period, all variances should be closed to the Cost of Goods Sold account to adjust the standard cost up or down to the actual cost.

Recall from earlier chapters that manufacturing costs are initially recorded in inventory and are later recognized as Cost of Goods Sold as in Exhibit 24A.1.

A standard cost system initially records manufacturing costs at the standard rather than the actual amounts. Thus, the journal entries used to record manufacturing costs always involve a debit to an inventory account or to Cost of Goods Sold for the standard amount.

We illustrate this process using the variances we calculated for Cold Stone Creamery. Because the company does not make the product until a customer orders it, there is no need to keep Work in Process or Finished Goods Inventory accounts. Instead, we can bypass those accounts and transfer raw materials costs directly from the Raw Materials Inventory account to the Cost of Goods Sold account. Similarly, we can record direct labor and manufacturing overhead costs directly in the Cost of Goods Sold account (see Exhibit 24A.2).

**Exhibit 24A.1   Recording Manufacturing Costs in a Standard Cost System**

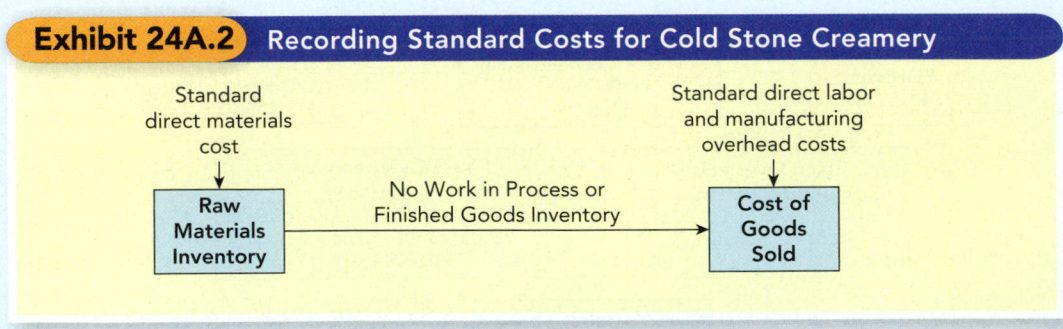

**Exhibit 24A.2   Recording Standard Costs for Cold Stone Creamery**

## Direct Materials Costs

Let's start with the entry to record the purchase of raw materials. Assume Cold Stone's price and quantity standards for ice cream follow:

| Direct costs | Standard Quantity | Standard Price | Standard Unit Cost |
|---|---|---|---|
| Ice cream | 10 oz. | $0.05 per oz. | $0.50 |

During the period, the purchasing manager bought 200,000 ounces of ice cream on account for a total of $8,000, at an average actual price of $.04 per ounce. The journal entry to record the purchase of raw materials would be:

| | Debit | Credit |
|---|---|---|
| Raw Materials Inventory (200,000 × $0.05) | 10,000 | |
| Direct Materials Price Variance (200,000 × $0.01) | | 2,000 |
| Accounts Payable (200,000 × $0.04) | | 8,000 |

**Coach's Tip**

Notice that the variance is the "plug figure" that makes the debits and credits balance. Here the actual cost (credit) is less than the standard cost (debit), resulting in a favorable (credit) variance.

Notice that the debit to Raw Materials Inventory is based on the standard price per unit of $0.05, but the credit to Accounts Payable is based on the actual price of $0.04 per unit. The difference between the actual price and the standard price is the direct materials price variance calculated earlier by multiplying the $0.01 difference in price by 200,000 ounces of ice cream. This variance is favorable because the actual price was less than the standard price.

Next let's record the journal entry to transfer the cost of the ice cream out of Raw Materials Inventory and into Cost of Goods Sold. During the period, Cold Stone's employees used 200,000 ounces of ice cream to produce 18,000 units. The entry to transfer the cost of the ice cream from Raw Materials Inventory to Cost of Goods Sold is:

| | Debit | Credit |
|---|---|---|
| Cost of Goods Sold (180,000 ounces × $0.05) | 9,000 | |
| Direct Materials Quantity Variance (20,000 × $0.05) | 1,000 | |
| Raw Materials Inventory (200,000 × $0.05) | | 10,000 |

**Coach's Tip**

A debit entry reflects an unfavorable variance. The quantity of materials actually taken from Raw Materials Inventory (a credit) was more than the standard quantity that should have been used to make 18,000 units (a debit).

Notice that the amount debited to Cost of Goods Sold is based on the flexible budget, or what it **should have cost** the company to produce 18,000 units. Because each unit requires 10 ounces of ice cream, we multiply the standard quantity of 180,000 ounces by the standard price of $0.05 per ounce. The amount that is transferred out of Raw Materials Inventory, however, is based on the 200,000 ounces that were actually used multiplied by the standard price of $0.05. When we multiply the 20,000 ounce difference by the standard price of $0.05, we get an unfavorable direct materials quantity variance of $1,000. Notice that this unfavorable variance appears as a debit entry; a favorable variance would appear as a credit entry.

Before you continue, complete the Self-Study Practice to see whether you can record the purchase and use of Cold Stone Creamery's mix-in ingredients.

**SELF-STUDY PRACTICE**

Cold Stone Creamery's standard cost card for mix-in ingredients follows.

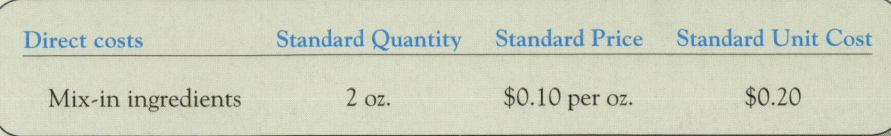

| Direct costs | Standard Quantity | Standard Price | Standard Unit Cost |
|---|---|---|---|
| Mix-in ingredients | 2 oz. | $0.10 per oz. | $0.20 |

Actual results were as follows:

- Purchased 35,000 ounces of mix-in ingredients at a total cost of $4,200, for an average cost of $0.12 per ounce.
- Used 35,000 ounces of mix-in ingredients to produce the 18,000 units sold.

Prepare the journal entries to record the purchase of raw materials and the transfer of their cost to the Cost of Goods Sold account.

*After you have finished, check your answers with the solutions at the bottom of the page.*

## Direct Labor and Manufacturing Overhead Costs

The entries to record direct labor and manufacturing overhead costs are simpler than those to record direct materials costs because the cost can be recorded directly into Cost of Goods Sold. The following journal entries record direct labor, variable manufacturing overhead, and fixed manufacturing overhead costs. The entry to record direct labor costs would be:

| | Debit | Credit |
|---|---|---|
| Cost of Goods Sold (1,800 hrs. × $8.00 per hr.) | 14,400 | |
| Direct Labor Rate Variance [2,000 × ($8.00 − 8.25)] | 500 | |
| Direct Labor Efficiency Variance [$8.00 × (1,800 − 2,000)] | 1,600 | |
| Wages Payable or Cash (2,000 hrs. × $8.25 per hr.) | | 16,500 |

The entry to record variable manufacturing overhead costs would be:

| | Debit | Credit |
|---|---|---|
| Cost of Goods Sold (1,800 hrs. × $1.00 per hr.) | 1,800 | |
| Variable Overhead Efficiency Variance [$1.00 × (1,800 − 2,000)] | 200 | |
| Variable Overhead Rate Variance [2,000 × ($1.00 − $0.90)] | | 200 |
| Wages Payable, Cash, etc. (2,000 hrs. × $0.90 per hr.) | | 1,800 |

**Solution to Self-Study Practice**

**Purchase of Raw Materials**

| | | |
|---|---|---|
| Raw Materials Inventory (35,000 × $0.10) | 3,500 | |
| Direct Materials Price Variance | 700 | |
| Accounts Payable (35,000 × $0.12) | | 4,200 |

**Transfer to Cost of Goods Sold When Used**

| | | |
|---|---|---|
| Cost of Goods Sold (36,000 × $0.10) | 3,600 | |
| Direct Materials Quantity Variance | | 100 |
| Raw Materials Inventory (35,000 × $0.10) | | 3,500 |

The entry to record fixed manufacturing overhead costs would be:

|  | Debit | Credit |
|---|---|---|
| Cost of Goods Sold (18,000 units × $0.40  per unit) | 7,200 |  |
| Fixed Overhead Spending Variance ($6,000 − $6,300) | 300 |  |
|    Fixed Overhead Volume Variance (18,000 − 15,000 units) × $0.40 |  | 1,200 |
| Salaries Payable or Cash |  | 6,300 |

## Cost of Goods Sold and Cost Variance Summary

After all variances have been recorded, the Cost of Goods Sold and variance summary account[1] will appear as follows:

| Cost of Goods Sold | | | | Cost Variance Summary | | | |
|---|---|---|---|---|---|---|---|
| Ice Cream | 9,000 | | | Ice Cream Quantity Variance | 1,000 | 2,000 | Ice Cream Price Variance |
| Mix-ins | 3,600 | | | Mix-in Price Variance | 700 | 100 | Mix-in Quantity Variance |
| Direct Labor | 14,400 | | | DL Rate Variance | 500 | 200 | VOH Rate Variance |
| Var. Mfg. Overhead | 1,800 | | | DL Efficiency Variance | 1,600 | 1,200 | FOH Volume Variance |
| Fixed Mfg. Overhead | 7,200 | | | VOH Efficiency Variance | 200 | | |
| | | | | FOH Spending Variance | 300 | | |
| Applied/Standard Cost | 36,000 | | | | | | |
| Variance Adjustment | 800 | ← | | Balance | 800 | | |
| Actual Cost of Goods Sold | 36,800 | | | | | | |

Notice that Cost of Goods Sold in the previous T-account is based initially on the standard cost of $36,000. The standard cost card shown at the beginning of this chapter (see Exhibit 24.1 on page 989) indicated that each unit produced should cost $2.00. Because Cold Stone Creamery sold 18,000 units, the cost of goods sold in the T-account is stated initially at $36,000.

The Cost Variance Summary account indicates how much higher or lower the actual costs were compared to the standard costs. Overall, Cold Stone had more unfavorable variances than favorable variances, resulting in a debit (unfavorable) balance of $800. At the end of the accounting period, each individual variance is closed to Cost of Goods Sold, which has the net effect of increasing its amount by $800.

The combined entry to close the variance accounts to Cost of Goods Sold would be:

|  | Debit | Credit |
|---|---|---|
| Ice Cream Price Variance | 2,000 |  |
| Mix-In Quantity Variance | 100 |  |
| Variable Overhead Rate Variance | 200 |  |
| Fixed Overhead Volume Variance | 1,200 |  |
| Cost of Goods Sold | 800 |  |
|    Ice Cream Quantity Variance |  | 1,000 |
|    Mix-In Price Variance |  | 700 |
|    Direct Labor Rate Variance |  | 500 |
|    Direct Labor Efficiency Variance |  | 1,600 |
|    Variable Overhead Efficiency Variance |  | 200 |
|    Fixed Overhead Spending Variance |  | 300 |

Notice that the closing entry debits the favorable variances to eliminate their credit balance and credits the unfavorable variances to eliminate their debit balance. The "plug figure" that makes the debits and credits equal is used to increase or decrease the Cost of Goods Sold account. In this case, we debited (increased) Cost of Goods Sold by $800, which raises it from the standard cost of $36,000 to the actual cost of $36,800.

Adjusting the Cost of Goods Sold account is the easiest and most common method of dealing with variances. However, if Cold Stone had had significant Work in Process or Finished Goods inventory, adjusting those accounts may also have been necessary. That treatment of the variance accounts, which is rare in practice, is beyond the scope of this textbook.

---

[1] For the sake of simplicity, we have shown all variances in a single summary account. In reality, each variance would be accumulated in a separate account so that the manager who is responsible for the variance can monitor it.

# Chapter Summary

**LO1 Describe the standard-setting process and explain how standard costs relate to budgets and variances. p. 989**

- Standard costs, which are set at the beginning of the accounting period to reflect what management believes costs should be, should be set so that they are difficult but not impossible to achieve.
- The two types of standard are price standard and quantity standard.
- The standard price is the amount that **should** be paid for a particular quantity of input.
- The standard quantity is the amount of input that **should** be used to produce a single unit of output.
- Budgeted costs are based on the standard costs for inputs multiplied by a specific level of output.
- Variances are the difference between actual and budgeted or standard costs.

**LO2 Prepare a flexible budget and show how total costs change with sales volume. p. 990**

- A master budget is a static budget based on the estimated sales volume.
- A flexible budget shows how total costs are expected to change if actual sales are more or less than expected.
- A flexible budget is used to evaluate managerial performance after the fact by separating the effect of spending (that is, cost control) from the effects of volume.
- Spending variances are calculated by comparing actual costs to the flexible budget.
- Volume variances are calculated by comparing the flexible budget to the master budget.

**LO3 Calculate and interpret the direct materials price and quantity variances. p. 994**

- The direct materials price variance is driven by the difference between the actual and the standard price paid for direct materials.
- The direct materials quantity variance is driven by the difference between the actual quantity and the standard quantity of materials used in production. The standard quantity should be based on the actual volume of output.
- The direct materials purchasing manager is responsible for the direct materials price variance. The production manager is responsible for the direct materials quantity (usage) variance.
- The total direct materials spending variance is the sum of the direct materials price and direct materials quantity variances.

**LO4 Calculate and interpret the direct labor rate and efficiency variances. p. 996**

- The direct labor rate variance is driven by the difference in the actual direct labor rate and the standard direct labor rate.
- The direct labor efficiency variance is driven by the difference between the actual number of labor hours and the standard number of labor hours allowed for the actual volume of output.
- Assigning direct responsibility for the direct labor rate variance is difficult. The production manager is responsible for the direct labor efficiency variance.
- The total direct labor spending variance is the sum of the direct labor rate and direct labor efficiency variances.

**LO5 Calculate and interpret the variable overhead rate and efficiency variances. p. 998**

- The variable overhead rate variance is driven by the difference between the actual variable overhead cost and the standard variable overhead cost per unit of the allocation base (such as direct labor hours).
- The variable overhead efficiency variance is driven by the difference between the actual number of labor hours and the standard number of labor hours allowed for production. It is a mirror reflection of the direct labor efficiency variance.
- The total variable overhead spending variance is the sum of the variable overhead rate and the variable overhead efficiency variances.

**LO6 Calculate and interpret the fixed overhead spending and volume variances. p. 1001**

- The fixed overhead spending variance is the difference between actual fixed overhead cost and budgeted fixed overhead cost.
- The fixed overhead volume variance is driven by the difference between actual production volume and budgeted production volume.
- The fixed overhead volume variance is favorable when a company produces more units than expected because the fixed cost is spread over more units.
- The fixed overhead volume variance is unfavorable when a company produces fewer units than expected because the fixed cost is spread over fewer units.

## Key Terms

Direct Labor Efficiency Variance (p. 997)
Direct Labor Rate Variance (p. 997)
Direct Labor Spending Variance (p. 997)
Direct Materials Price Variance (p. 995)
Direct Materials Quantity Variance (p. 995)
Direct Materials Spending Variance (p. 996)
Easily Attainable Standard (p. 988)
Favorable Variance (p. 989)

Fixed Overhead Spending Variance (p. 1002)
Fixed Overhead Volume Variance (p. 1002)
Flexible Budget (p. 990)
Ideal Standard (p. 988)
Over- or Underapplied Fixed Overhead (p. 1003)
Spending Variances (p. 992)
Standard Cost Card (p. 989)

Standard Cost System (p. 988)
Standard Unit Cost (p. 989)
Static Budget (p. 990)
Unfavorable Variance (p. 990)
Variance (p. 987)
Variable Overhead Efficiency Variance (p. 987)
Variable Overhead Rate Variance (p. 999)
Volume Variance (p. 992)

**See complete glossary in back of text.**

## Questions

1. Briefly describe the difference between the budgetary planning and control processes.

2. What are standard costs? When are they set?

3. Explain a standard cost system and how a company uses it.

4. What is the difference between ideal and easily attainable standards?

5. What type of standard is best for motivating individuals to work hard?

6. Briefly describe the two types of standards on which a standard cost system relies.

7. What is a standard cost card and why is it important?

8. How do the terms standard and budget relate to one another and how do they differ?

9. Explain what the terms favorable variance and unfavorable variance mean.

10. How do the master budget, flexible budget, and static budget differ from one another?

11. What type of variance is created by comparing the master budget to the flexible budget?

12. What type of variance is calculated by comparing actual costs to the costs in the flexible budget?

13. The spending variance can be separated into two components. Name and briefly describe them.

14. What are the two direct materials variances? Who is most likely responsible for each of these?

15. What are the two direct labor variances? Who is most likely responsible for each of these?

16. What are the two variable overhead variances? Who is most likely responsible for each of these?

17. What are the two fixed overhead variances? Who is most likely responsible for each of these?

## Multiple Choice

Quiz 24-1
www.mhhe.com/LLPW1e

1. In general, variances tell managers
   a. Nothing.
   b. Whom to promote and whom to fire.
   c. Whether budgeted goals are being achieved.
   d. Which departments are running at full capacity.

2. In distinguishing between budgets and standards, which of the following is true?
   a. The terms mean exactly the same thing.
   b. Standards are used to develop budgets.
   c. Budgets are used to develop standards.
   d. Budgets and standards are unrelated.

3. Variances are always noted as favorable or unfavorable. What do these terms indicate?
   a. Whether actual costs are more or less than expected costs.
   b. Whether the manager in a particular department is doing a good job.

   c. Whether a company is performing as well as its competitors.
   d. All of the above.

4. What type of budget is an integrated set of operating and financial budgets that reflects managements' expectations for a given sales level, and what type shows how budgeted costs and revenues will change across different levels of sales?
   a. Flexible budget, master budget.
   b. Standard budget, flexible budget.
   c. Master budget, static budget.
   d. Master budget, flexible budget.

5. When evaluating performance in a standard cost system, actual results are compared to
   a. The flexible budget.
   b. The master budget.
   c. The variances.
   d. Last year's actual results.

6.  Spending variances may be broken down into
    a.  Price and quantity variances.
    b.  Price and volume variances.
    c.  Volume and quantity variances.
    d.  Quantity and quality variances.

7.  Temecula Company has calculated its direct materials price variance to be $1,000 favorable and its direct materials quantity variance to be $3,000 unfavorable. Which of the following could explain both of these variances?
    a.  The production manager has recently hired more skilled laborers.
    b.  The purchases manager found less expensive raw materials but they were also of lesser quality.
    c.  A machine in the factory malfunctioned resulting in considerable wasted raw materials.
    d.  The purchases manager bought higher quality materials.

8.  In producing its product, Ranger Company used 1,500 hours of direct labor at an actual cost of $15 per hour. The standard for Ranger's production level is 1,400 hours at $14 per hour. What is Ranger's direct labor rate variance?
    a.  $1,500 favorable.
    b.  $1,400 favorable.
    c.  $1,500 unfavorable.
    d.  $1,400 unfavorable.

9.  In producing its product, Ranger Company used 1,500 pounds of direct materials at an actual cost of $1.50 per pound. The standard for Ranger's production level was 1,400 pounds at $1.40 per pound. What is Ranger's direct materials quantity variance?
    a.  $150 favorable.
    b.  $140 favorable.
    c.  $150 unfavorable.
    d.  $140 unfavorable.

10. An unfavorable fixed overhead volume variance indicates that a company
    a.  manufactured fewer units than it expected.
    b.  manufactured more units than it expected.
    c.  underestimated its total fixed overhead cost.
    d.  overestimated its total fixed overhead cost.

| Solutions to Multiple-Choice Questions |
|---|
| 1. c    2. b    3. a    4. d    5. a    6. a    7. b |
| 8. c    9. d    10. a |

# Mini Exercises  Available with McGraw-Hill's Homework Manager

**LO1**  **M24-1 Creating a Grading Scale Based on Ideal, Tight but Attainable and Easily Attainable Standards**

Consider the grading scale for a university class that has 500 possible points. The possible course grades are A, B, C, D, and F. Create a grading scale for the class that would fall into each of the following categories: an ideal standard, an easily attainable standard, and a tight but attainable standard.

**LO2**  **M24-2 Explaining the Costs That Will Change with Flexible Budget Activity**

When preparing a company's flexible budget, which manufacturing cost(s) will change as the volume increases or decreases? Which manufacturing cost(s) will not change as the volume changes?

**LO1**  **M24-3 Describing How Standards Are Set in a Standard Cost System**

Dabney Company manufactures widgets and would like to use a standard cost system. Explain how Dabney will determine the standards for direct materials and direct labor to use in its costing system.

**LO4**  **M24-4 Calculating Unknown Values for Direct Labor Variances**

For each of the following independent cases, fill in the missing amounts in the following table.

| Case | Direct Labor Rate Variance | Direct Labor Efficiency Variance | Direct Labor Spending Variance |
|---|---|---|---|
| A | $  750 F | $1,200 F | $    ? |
| B | 2,000 U | ? | 3,500 U |
| C | 1,000 F | ? | 1,800 U |
| D | ? | 500 F | 2,500 U |
| E | ? | 1,100 U | 1,950 U |
| F | 650 F | 1,150 U | ? |

**LO3**  **M24-5 Interpreting Direct Materials Cost Variances**

Phantom Corp. has calculated its direct materials price and quantity variances to be $500 favorable and $800 unfavorable, respectively. Phantom's production manager believes that these variances indicate that the purchasing department is doing a good job but production is doing a poor job. Explain whether the production manager's conclusions are correct.

**M24-6 Calculating Direct Materials Cost Variances**    LO3
Randolph, Inc., has determined a standard direct materials cost per unit of $6 (2 feet × $3 per foot). Last month, Randolph purchased and used 4,200 feet of direct materials for which it paid $12,180. The company produced and sold 2,000 units during the month. Calculate the direct materials price, quantity, and spending variances.

**M24-7 Calculating Direct Labor Cost Variances**    LO4
Clayton Corp. has determined a standard labor cost per unit of $12 (1 hour × $12 per hour). Last month, Clayton incurred 1,900 direct labor hours for which it paid $23,940. The company also produced and sold 2,000 units during the month. Calculate the direct labor rate, efficiency, and spending variances.

**M24-8 Calculating Variable Manufacturing Overhead Variances**    LO5
Montour Company has determined a standard variable overhead rate of $1.10 per direct labor hour and expects 1 labor hour per unit produced. Last month, Montour incurred 1,900 actual direct labor hours in the production of 2,000 units. The company has also determined that its actual variable overhead rate is $1.20 per direct labor hour. Calculate the variable overhead rate and efficiency variances as well as the total amount of over- or underapplied variable overhead.

**M24-9 Calculating Fixed Manufacturing Overhead Variances**    LO6
LaPaz Company has determined a standard fixed overhead rate of $0.30 per unit based on an expectation of 30,000 units and $9,000 fixed manufacturing overhead. Actual results for the month of October reveal that LaPaz produced 28,000 units and had $9,200 in fixed manufacturing overhead costs. Calculate LaPaz's fixed overhead spending variance, fixed overhead volume variance, and the total amount of over- or underapplied fixed overhead.

**M24-10 Preparing Journal Entries to Record Direct Material Costs and Variances (Supplement)**
During May, Willett Corp. purchased direct materials for 4,250 units at a cost of $61,625. Willett's standard materials cost per unit is $14. Prepare the journal entry to record this transaction.

**M24-11 Preparing Journal Entries to Record Direct Labor Costs and Variances (Supplement)**
Bowman Company reported the following information for the month of November. The standard cost of labor for the month was $38,000, but actual wages paid were $40,000. Bowman has calculated its direct labor rate and efficiency variances to be $2,500 unfavorable and $500 favorable, respectively. Prepare the necessary journal entry to record Bowman's direct labor cost for the month, assuming that standard labor costs are recorded directly to Cost of Goods Sold.

# Exercises        Available with McGraw-Hill's Homework Manager

**E24-1 Calculating Unknown Values for Direct Materials and Direct Labor Variances**    LO3, 4
Three Pigs Company manufactures cast-iron barbeque cookware. During a recent windstorm, it lost some of its cost accounting records. Three Pigs has managed to reconstruct portions of its standard cost system database but is still missing a few pieces of information.

|  | Direct Materials | Direct Labor |
| --- | --- | --- |
| Standard amount per pan produced | 2.5 lb. | 1.25 hr. |
| Standard cost | $4.00 per lb. | $16.00 per hr. |
| Actual amount used per pan produced | 2.4 lb. | 1.20 hr. |
| Actual cost | $4.10 per lb. | $15.50 per hr. |
| Actual number of pans produced and sold | 2,500 pans | 2,500 pans |
| Direct materials price variance | ? |  |
| Direct materials quantity variance | ? |  |
| Direct materials spending variance | ? |  |
| Direct labor rate variance |  | ? |
| Direct labor efficiency variance |  | ? |
| Direct labor spending variance |  | ? |

*Required:*

Use the information in the table to determine the unknown amounts. You may assume that Three Pigs does not keep any raw materials on hand.

**LO2**

### E24-2 Preparing a Flexible Budget for Manufacturing Costs

Follett Company makes handwoven blankets. The company's master budget appears in the first column of the table.

| | Master Budget (5,000 units) | Flexible Budget (4,000 units) | Flexible Budget (6,000 units) | Flexible Budget (7,000 units) |
|---|---|---|---|---|
| Direct materials | $ 7,500 | | | |
| Direct labor | 20,000 | | | |
| Variable manufacturing overhead | 8,000 | | | |
| Fixed manufacturing overhead | 18,000 | | | |
| Total manufacturing cost | $53,500 | | | |

*Required:*

Complete the table by preparing Follett's flexible budget for 4,000, 6,000 and 7,000 units.

**LO3**

### E24-3 Interpreting the Direct Materials Price and Quantity Variances

Cody's Collar Company makes custom leather pet collars. The company expects each collar to require 1.5 feet of leather and predicts leather will cost $2.25 per foot. Suppose Cody's made 60 collars during February. For these 60 collars, the company actually averaged 1.6 feet of leather per collar and paid $2.00 per foot for it.

*Required:*

1.   Compute the standard direct materials cost per unit.

2.   Without performing any calculations, determine whether the direct materials price variance will be favorable or unfavorable.

3.   Without performing any calculations, determine whether the direct materials quantity variance will be favorable or unfavorable.

4.   Give a potential explanation for this pattern of variances.

5.   Where would you begin to investigate the variances?

6.   Calculate the direct materials price and quantity variances.

**LO3, 4**

### E24-4 Calculating Direct Materials and Direct Labor Variances

Rub-a-Dub Dogs is a local pet grooming shop owned by Max Aslett. Max has prepared the following standard cost card for each dog bath given.

| | Standard Quantity | Standard Rate | Standard Unit Cost |
|---|---|---|---|
| Direct costs | | | |
| Shampoo | 2 oz. | $ 0.10 per oz. | $0.20 |
| Water | 20 gal. | $ 0.05 per gal. | 1.00 |
| Direct labor | .75 hr. | $ 9.00 per hr. | 6.75 |

During the month of July, Max's employees gave 345 baths. The actual results were 725 ounces of shampoo used (total cost $87), 6,500 gallons of water used (cost of $390), and labor costs for 250 hours (cost of $2,300).

*Required:*

1.   Calculate Rub-a-Dub Dogs' direct materials variances for both shampoo and water for the month of July.

2.   Calculate Rub-a-Dub Dogs' direct labor variances for the month of July.

3.   Identify a possible cause of each variance.

## E24-5 Preparing Journal Entries to Record Direct Materials and Direct Labor Costs and Variances (Supplement)

Refer to the information presented in E24-4 regarding Rub-a-Dub Dogs.

*Required:*

Prepare journal entries to record Rub-a-Dub's July direct materials and labor transactions. (**Hint:** Record all costs directly to Cost of Goods Sold.)

## E24-6 Calculating Direct Materials and Direct Labor Variances

LO3, 4

Lucky Charm Company makes handcrafted silver charms that attach to jewelry such as a necklace or bracelet. Each charm is adorned with two crystals of various colors. Standard costs follow.

|  | Standard Quantity | Standard Price (Rate) | Standard Unit Cost |
|---|---|---|---|
| Direct costs |  |  |  |
| Silver | 0.25 oz. | $20.00 per oz. | $ 5.00 |
| Crystals | 2 | $ 0.25 per each | $ 0.50 |
| Direct labor | 1.5 hrs. | $15.00 per hr. | $22.50 |

During the month of January, Lucky Charm made 1,500 charms. The company used 350 ounces of silver (total cost of $7,350), 3,050 crystals (total cost of $701.50), and paid for 2,400 actual direct labor hours (cost of $34,800).

*Required:*

1. Calculate Lucky Charm's direct materials variances for silver and crystals for the month of January.

2. Calculate Lucky Charm's direct labor variances for the month of January.

3. Identify a possible cause of each variance.

## E24-7 Preparing Journal Entries to Record Direct Material and Direct Labor Costs and Variances (Supplement)

Refer to the information in E24-6 regarding Lucky Charm Company.

*Required:*

Prepare journal entries to record Lucky Charm's January direct materials and labor transactions. (**Hint:** Record all costs directly to Cost of Goods Sold.)

## E24-8 Calculating Variable and Fixed Manufacturing Overhead Variances

LO5, 6

Slim Shady Company (SSC) manufactures lamp shades. It applies variable overhead on the basis of the number of direct labor hours used. Information regarding SSC's overhead for the month of August follows.

|  | Standard Quantity | Standard Rate | Standard Unit Cost |
|---|---|---|---|
| Variable manufacturing overhead | 0.5 direct labor hour per shade | $0.80 per direct labor hour | $0.40 |
| Fixed manufacturing overhead ($30,000 / 24,000 units) |  |  | 1.25 |

During August, SSC had the following actual results

| | |
|---|---|
| Units produced and sold | 25,000 |
| Actual variable overhead | $ 9,490 |
| Actual direct labor hours | 13,000 |
| Actual fixed overhead | $29,000 |

*Required:*

1. Compute SSC's variable overhead rate and efficiency variances as well as the over- or underapplied variable overhead.
2. Compute SSC's fixed overhead spending and volume variances as well as its over- or underapplied fixed overhead.

### E24-9 Preparing Journal Entries to Record Manufacturing Overhead Cost and Variances (Supplement)

Refer to the information in E24-8 regarding Slim Shady Company.

*Required:*

Prepare journal entries to record SSC's overhead transactions for August.

**LO5, 6**

### E24-10 Calculating Variable and Fixed Manufacturing Overhead Variances

ClearView Company manufactures clear plastic CD cases. It applies variable overhead based on the number of machine hours used. Information regarding ClearView's overhead for the month of December follows.

|  | Standard Quantity | Standard Rate | Standard Unit Cost |
|---|---|---|---|
| Variable manufacturing overhead | 0.1 machine hours per case | $.50 per machine hour | $0.05 |
| Fixed manufacturing overhead ($180,000 / 600,000 units) |  |  | 0.30 |

During December, ClearView had the following actual results.

| | |
|---|---|
| Number of units produced and sold | 625,000 |
| Actual variable overhead cost | $  30,240 |
| Actual machine hours | 63,000 |
| Actual fixed overhead | $  195,000 |

*Required:*

1. Compute ClearView's variable overhead rate and efficiency variances as well as its over- or underapplied variable overhead.
2. Compute ClearView's fixed overhead spending and volume variances as well as its over- or underapplied FOH Fixed overhead.

### E24-11 Preparing Journal Entries to Record Manufacturing Overhead Cost and Variances (Supplement)

Refer to the information presented in E24-10 regarding ClearView Company.

*Required:*

Prepare journal entries to record ClearView's overhead transactions for December.

## Problems—Set A    Available with McGraw-Hill's Homework Manager

**LO3, 4, 5, 6**

### PA24-1 Calculating Direct Material, Direct Labor, Variable Manufacturing Overhead, and Fixed Manufacturing Overhead Variances

Drink Well, Inc., manufactures custom-ordered commemorative beer steins. Its standard cost information follows.

| | Standard Quantity | Standard Price (Rate) | Standard Unit Cost |
|---|---|---|---|
| Direct costs | | | |
| Clay | 1.5 lbs. | $ 1.60 per lb. | $ 2.40 |
| Direct labor | 1.5 hrs. | $12.00 per hr. | 18.00 |
| Variable MOH | | $ 1.20 per direct labor hour | 1.80 |
| Fixed MOH ($250,000 / 100,000 units) | | | 2.50 |

Drink Well had the following actual results last year.

| | |
|---|---|
| Number of units produced and sold | 110,000 |
| Number of pounds of clay used | 180,000 |
| Cost of clay | $ 279,000 |
| Number of labor hours worked | 150,000 |
| Direct labor cost | $1,950,000 |
| Variable overhead cost | $ 195,000 |
| Fixed overhead cost | $ 295,000 |

**Required:**
1. Calculate Drink Well's direct materials variances.
2. Calculate Drink Well's direct labor variances.
3. Compute Drink Well's variable overhead rate and efficiency variances and its over- or underapplied variable overhead.
4. Compute Drink Well's fixed overhead spending and volume variances and its over- or underapplied fixed overhead.

**PA24-2 Preparing Journal Entries to Record Direct Material, Direct Labor, Variable Manufacturing Overhead, and Fixed Manufacturing Overhead Costs and Variances (Supplement)**
Refer to the information in PA24-1 for Drink Well. Prepare journal entries to record all its manufacturing costs for last year. Assume the company purchases raw materials as needed and does not maintain any ending inventories.

**PA24-3 Calculating Direct Materials, Direct Labor, Variable Manufacturing Overhead, and Fixed Manufacturing Overhead Variances**
Darting Around Company manufactures dart boards. Its standard cost information follows.

LO3, 4, 5, 6

| | Standard Quantity | Standard Price (Rate) | Standard Unit Cost |
|---|---|---|---|
| Direct costs | | | |
| Corkboard | 2.5 sq. ft. | $ 2.00 per sq. ft. | $ 5.00 |
| Direct labor | 1 hr. | $14.00 per hr. | 14.00 |
| Variable manufacturing overhead | | $ .50 per direct labor hour | 0.50 |
| Fixed manufacturing overhead ($20,000 / 80,000 units) | | | 0.25 |

Darting Around had the following actual results for the month of September.

| | |
|---|---|
| Number of units produced and sold | 70,000 |
| Number of square feet of corkboard used | 180,000 |
| Cost of corkboard used | $378,000 |
| Number of labor hours worked | 75,000 |
| Direct labor cost | $975,000 |
| Variable overhead cost | $ 36,000 |
| Fixed overhead cost | $ 25,000 |

*Required:*

1. Calculate Darting Around's direct materials variances.
2. Calculate Darting Around's direct labor variances.
3. Compute Darting Around's variable overhead rate and efficiency variances and its over- or underapplied variable overhead.
4. Compute Darting Around's fixed overhead spending and volume variances and its over- or underapplied fixed overhead.

**PA24-4 Preparing Journal Entries to Record Direct Material, Direct Labor, Variable Manufacturing Overhead, and Fixed Manufacturing Overhead Costs and Variances (Supplement)**
Refer to the information in PA24-3 for Darting Around Company. Prepare journal entries to record its manufacturing costs for September. Assume the company purchases raw materials as needed and does not maintain any ending inventories.

LO3, 4, 5, 6

www.mhhe.com/LLPW1e

**PA24-5 Calculating Direct Materials, Direct Labor, Variable Manufacturing Overhead, and Fixed Manufacturing Overhead Variances**
Catch a Wave Company manufactures surf boards. Its standard cost information follows.

| | Standard Quantity | Standard Price (Rate) | Standard Unit Cost |
|---|---|---|---|
| **Direct costs** | | | |
| Fiberglass | 15 sq. ft. | $ 5 per sq. ft. | $ 75.00 |
| Direct labor | 10 hrs. | $15 per hr. | 150.00 |
| Variable manufacturing overhead | | $ 6 per direct labor hour | 60.00 |
| Fixed manufacturing overhead ($20,000 / 250 units) | | | 80.00 |

Catch a Wave had the following actual results for the month of June.

| | |
|---|---|
| Number of units produced and sold | 260 |
| Number of square feet of fiberglass used | 4,100 |
| Cost of fiberglass used | $22,550 |
| Number of labor hours worked | 2,550 |
| Direct labor cost | $39,525 |
| Variable overhead cost | $14,790 |
| Fixed overhead cost | $20,500 |

*Required:*

1. Calculate Catch a Wave's direct materials variances.
2. Calculate Catch a Wave's direct labor variances.

3.  Compute Catch a Wave's variable overhead rate and efficiency variances and its over- or underapplied variable overhead.

4.  Compute Catch a Wave's fixed overhead spending and volume variances and its over- or underapplied fixed overhead.

**PA24-6 Preparing Journal Entries to Record Direct Materials, Direct Labor, Variable Manufacturing Overhead, and Fixed Manufacturing Overhead Costs and Variances (Supplement)**
Refer to the information in PA24-5 for Catch a Wave. Prepare journal entries to record all of its transactions for June. Assume the company purchases raw materials as needed and does not maintain any ending inventories.

## Problems—Set B  Available with McGraw-Hill's Homework Manager

**PB24-1 Calculating Direct Material, Direct Labor, Variable Manufacturing Overhead, and Fixed Manufacturing Overhead Variances**

LO3, 4, 5, 6

CandleGlow, Inc., manufactures scented pillar candles. Its standard cost information for the month of February follows.

|  | Standard Quantity | Standard Price (Rate) | Standard Unit Cost |
|---|---|---|---|
| Direct costs |  |  |  |
| Wax | 15 oz. | $ 0.05 per oz. | $0.75 |
| Direct labor | .25 hr. | $14.00 per hr. | 3.50 |
| Variable manufacturing overhead |  | $ 0.40 per direct labor hour | 0.10 |
| Fixed manufacturing overhead ($10,000 / 40,000 units) |  |  | 0.25 |

CandleGlow had the following actual results for the month of February.

| | |
|---|---|
| Number of units produced and sold | 35,000 |
| Number of ounces of wax purchased and used | 530,000 |
| Cost of wax used | $ 31,800 |
| Number of labor hours worked | 9,000 |
| Direct labor cost | $123,750 |
| Variable overhead cost | $  3,300 |
| Fixed overhead cost | $  9,700 |

*Required:*

1.  Calculate CandleGlow's direct materials variances.
2.  Calculate CandleGlow's direct labor variances.
3.  Compute CandleGlow's variable overhead rate and efficiency variances and its over- or underapplied variable overhead.
4.  Compute CandleGlow's fixed overhead spending and volume variances and its over- or underapplied fixed overhead.

**PB24-2 Preparing Journal Entries to Record Direct Material, Direct Labor, Variable Manufacturing Overhead, and Fixed Manufacturing Overhead Costs and Variances (Supplement)**
Refer to the information in PB24-1 for CandleGlow. Prepare journal entries to record its manufacturing costs for February. Assume the company purchases raw materials as needed and does not maintain any ending inventories.

**LO3, 4, 5, 6**    **PB24-3 Calculating Direct Materials, Direct Labor, Variable Manufacturing Overhead, and Fixed Manufacturing Overhead Variances**

Gotta Cotta, Inc., manufactures basic terra cotta planters. Its standard cost information for the past year follows.

|  | Standard Quantity | Standard Price (Rate) | Standard Unit Cost |
|---|---|---|---|
| **Direct costs** | | | |
| Clay | 2 lbs. | $ 0.80 per lb. | $1.60 |
| Direct labor | .5 hr. | $12.00 per hr. | 6.00 |
| Variable manufacturing overhead | | $ 0.40 per direct labor hour | 0.20 |
| Fixed manufacturing overhead ($480,000 / 800,000 units) | | | 0.60 |

Gotta Cotta had the following actual results for the past year.

| | |
|---|---|
| Number of units produced and sold | 750,000 |
| Number of pounds of clay used | 1,450,000 |
| Cost of clay purchased and used | $1,087,500 |
| Number of labor hours worked | 375,000 |
| Direct labor cost | $3,937,500 |
| Variable overhead cost | $ 157,500 |
| Fixed overhead cost | $ 505,000 |

*Required:*

1. Calculate Gotta Cotta's direct materials variances.
2. Calculate Gotta Cotta's direct labor variances.
3. Compute Gotta Cotta's variable overhead rate and efficiency variances and its over- or underapplied variable overhead.
4. Compute Gotta Cotta's fixed overhead spending and volume variances and its over- or underapplied fixed overhead.

**PB24-4 Preparing Journal Entries to Record Direct Materials, Direct Labor, Variable Manufacturing Overhead, and Fixed Manufacturing Overhead Costs and Variances (Supplement)**

Refer to the information in PB24-3 for Gotta Cotta. Prepare journal entries to record its manufacturing costs for the past year. Assume the company purchases raw materials as needed and does not maintain any ending inventories.

**LO3, 4, 5, 6**    **PB24-5 Calculating Direct Material, Direct Labor, Variable Manufacturing Overhead, and Fixed Manufacturing Overhead Variances**

Easy Roller, Inc., manufactures plastic mats for use with rolling office chairs. Its standard cost information for last year follows.

|  | Standard Quantity | Standard Price (Rate) | Standard Unit Cost |
|---|---|---|---|
| **Direct costs** | | | |
| Plastic | 12 sq ft. | $ 0.75 per sq. ft. | $9.00 |
| Direct labor | .25 hr. | $12.00 per hr. | 3.00 |
| Variable manufacturing overhead | | $ 1.20 per direct labor hour | 0.30 |
| Fixed manufacturing overhead ($360,000 / 900,000 units) | | | 0.40 |

Easy Roller had the following actual results for the past year.

| | |
|---|---|
| Number of units produced and sold | 1,000,000 |
| Number of square feet of plastic used | 11,800,000 |
| Cost of plastic purchased and used | $ 8,260,000 |
| Number of labor hours worked | 245,000 |
| Direct labor cost | $ 2,891,000 |
| Variable overhead cost | $ 318,500 |
| Fixed overhead cost | $ 355,000 |

**Required:**

1. Calculate Easy Roller's direct materials variances.
2. Calculate Easy Roller's direct labor variances.
3. Compute Easy Roller's variable overhead rate and efficiency variances and its over- or underapplied variable overhead.
4. Compute Easy Roller's fixed overhead spending and volume variances and its over- or underapplied fixed overhead.

**PB24-6 Preparing Journal Entries to Record Direct Materials, Direct Labor, Variable Manufacturing Overhead, and Fixed Manufacturing Overhead Costs and Variances (Supplement)**
Refer to the information in PB24-5 for Easy Roller. Prepare journal entries to record its manufacturing costs for the past year. Assume the company purchases raw materials as needed and does not maintain any ending inventories.

# Cases and Projects

**CP24-1: Evaluating Managerial Performance by Comparing Actual to Budgeted Results**    LO1
Suppose Acore Pharmaceuticals has four sales representatives assigned to the State of Arizona. These sales reps are responsible for visiting physicians in their assigned area, introducing the company's current or upcoming products, providing samples, getting feedback about the products, and generating sales. Each sales rep is given an expense budget that includes samples of Acore's products, travel expenses related to the company vehicle that Acore provides, and entertainment expenses such as buying meals or hosting small "meet and greet" receptions.

The following table includes both budgeted and actual amounts for each sales rep for the first half of the current year. As you can see, each sales rep was allotted the same amount of resources and expected to generate the same amount of sales for the six-month period.

| | Samples | | Travel | | Entertainment | | Sales | |
|---|---|---|---|---|---|---|---|---|
| Sales Rep | Budget | Actual | Budget | Actual | Budget | Actual | Budget | Actual |
| Terry | $7,200 | $ 4,200 | $18,000 | $28,000 | $4,800 | $1,900 | $90,000 | $ 78,000 |
| Maria | 7,200 | 15,500 | 18,000 | 12,000 | 4,800 | 9,900 | 90,000 | 130,000 |
| Samantha | 7,200 | 2,900 | 18,000 | 18,000 | 4,800 | 4,600 | 90,000 | 43,000 |
| Abraham | 7,200 | 5,300 | 18,000 | 16,200 | 4,800 | 4,500 | 90,000 | 92,000 |

**Required:**

1. Calculate the expense and sales variances for each rep. Evaluate each of them and rank them in order of performance. Explain your rationale for these rankings. Suppose $100,000 in bonuses is available to be split among these sales reps. How would you allocate the money to them?

2. Now suppose that you find additional information about the territories to which Acore's Arizona reps are assigned. (If you're not familiar with Arizona, you can find a map at this Web site: www.mapofarizona.net)

- Terry has the northern Arizona territory that includes everything north of Phoenix between the California and New Mexico borders. This territory encompasses a large amount of Native American reservation land as well as the Grand Canyon National Park. Flagstaff is the largest city in the territory.

- Maria has the Phoenix area that includes only the Phoenix metropolitan area including all suburbs of Phoenix such as Glendale, Scottsdale, Mesa, and Sun City.

- Samantha's Southwestern Arizona territory includes all areas south and west of Phoenix. Yuma is the largest city in this region.

- Abraham's southeastern Arizona area includes everything south and east of Phoenix. Tucson is included in this territory.

Does this new information change your evaluation of Acore's Arizona sales reps? If so, how? Does your allocation of the bonus money change as a result of the additional information? If so, explain how.

3. Do you need any other information to evaluate these employees' performances for the first half of the year?

4. What, if any, adjustments would you make to the budgets for the remainder of the year?

5. Do you think that Acore's policy of allocating the four sales reps the same amount of expenses and expected sales is adequate? What factors would you use in setting budgets for next year?

**LO1**    **CP24-2 Developing Standard Costs Using Time Studies and Incentives to Distort the Standard**

For a company to use a standard costing system, it must be able to develop the standards that will serve as the guide for the amount of a resource (e.g., direct materials, direct labor) that should be consumed in the production of a unit. One way to accomplish this is to conduct a time or process study that examines the work of one individual whose results are then used as the standard. This standard serves as a base against which actual results can be compared and ultimately affects performance evaluations.

Suppose you work for an ice packaging service company and your job is to fill each plastic bag with 7 pounds of crushed ice and close the bag with a metal fastener. These bags are then delivered to local grocery and convenience stores for sale. Assume also you were chosen as the subject for a time or process study. Because some amount of spillage is normal, the study will measure the amount of ice each bag has. Your time to fill and fasten each bag will also be measured. These numbers will then serve as company standards for everyone within the company doing your job.

*Required:*

1. Is there any motivation for you to intentionally spill some ice or to purposefully take longer than normal to fill and/or fasten the bag?

2. How might these standards affect employees (including you) later?

3. How might the company mitigate this problem?

**LO1**    **CP24-3 Investigating the Use of Variance Analysis in Business by Reading a Case Study Article on the Use of Variances in the Construction Industry**

Not all companies are manufacturing companies. For that reason, the variances calculated in this chapter are not appropriate for every organization. Industries and/or individual companies must often develop and use variances that make the most sense for evaluating performance within their specific circumstances. The construction industry is one example.

*Required:*

1. Go to http://www.constructionequipment.com/article/CA6568297.html and read the article that explains how budget variances can be used with respect to construction equipment.

2. Explain how construction equipment costs are separated into owning costs and operating costs.

3. If you were a manager for this company, how would you interpret and evaluate the company's performance for each class of equipment?

4. Does this manner of evaluation make sense for a construction company? Why or why not?

5. Give examples of two other companies or industries that would not necessarily use the variances calculated in this chapter.

# 25 Decentralized Performance Evaluation

## LEARNING OBJECTIVES

**After completing this chapter, you should be able to:**

**LO1** List and explain the advantages and disadvantages of decentralization.

**LO2** Describe the different types of responsibility centers and explain how managers in each type are evaluated.

**LO3** Compute and interpret an investment center's return on investment.

**LO4** Compute and interpret an investment center's residual income.

**LO5** Describe the four dimensions of the balanced scorecard and explain how they are used to evaluate managerial performance.

**LO6** Explain how transfer prices are set in decentralized organizations.

Lectured slideshow–LP25-1
www.mhhe.com/LLPW1e

Think about the last time you rented a movie. Did you go to your neighborhood rental store such as Blockbuster or get it from an online rental service such as Netflix? The battle between Blockbuster and Netflix has been raging for more than a decade. Founded in 1986, Blockbuster Inc. became the world's largest provider of in-home movie entertainment, but now it is struggling to survive in this rapidly changing industry. Many industry experts have predicted the demise of Blockbuster and other "bricks and mortar" rental stores due to competition from online rental services such as Netflix, the increasingly affordable cost of DVDs, and rapid advances in technology for downloadable movies. Although Blockbuster still faces significant challenges in this battle, the company has made major strides and remains a prominent player in the entertainment industry.

As you read this chapter, put yourself in the shoes of a stakeholder at Blockbuster and ask yourself the following questions:

- As a customer of Blockbuster, how would you measure the company's performance?
- If you were a manager at a local Blockbuster store (responsible for all aspects of store management), how would your boss evaluate your performance?
- If you were a manager in Blockbuster's distribution warehouse (responsible for shipping DVDs to individual stores), how would your boss evaluate your performance?
- If you were a senior executive at Blockbuster (responsible for developing and delivering entertainment using new delivery channels), how would your boss evaluate your performance?
- If you owned stock in Blockbuster, how would you measure the company's performance?

Each of these questions involves measuring or evaluating the performance of a manager, a segment of the business, or the entire company. As the questions indicate, performance can be measured in different ways depending on what and who is being evaluated.

In this chapter, we present a variety of methods for measuring the performance of business units and managers. To do so, we apply the techniques to Blockbuster and its various divisions. Although some details and the numbers we use in our examples are hypothetical, they are intended to illustrate the techniques that Blockbuster and other companies use to evaluate the performance of their managers and business units.

## ORGANIZATION OF THE CHAPTER

| DECENTRALIZATION OF RESPONSIBILITY | RESPONSIBILITY CENTERS | EVALUATION OF INVESTMENT CENTER PERFORMANCE | TRANSFER PRICING |
|---|---|---|---|
| | • Cost Centers <br> • Revenue Centers <br> • Profit Centers <br> • Investment Centers | • Return on Investment (ROI) <br> • Residual Income <br> • Return on Investment versus Residual Income <br> • Limitations of Financial Performance Measures <br> • Balanced Scorecard | • Market-Price Method <br> • Cost-Based Method <br> • Negotiation |

# DECENTRALIZATION OF RESPONSIBILITY

As children, most of us couldn't wait to grow up and do everything our parents told us we were too young to do—drive a car, stay out late, date, or get a job. It didn't take long, though, to realize that all that freedom comes with a great deal of responsibility. Wikipedia defines responsibility as the "state of being responsible, accountable or answerable." With responsibility comes the authority to make decisions for ourselves, to take action on behalf of others, and ultimately, to be held accountable for both our decisions and our actions.

In business, employees are given the responsibility and authority to make decisions on behalf of their employer. How do organizations make sure that employees act responsibly or make decisions that are in the organization's best interest? The methods they use are not that different from the ones parents use to monitor and control their children, including setting clear rules and guidelines for conduct, directly observing behavior, indirectly measuring the decisions being made, and evaluating the outcome of those decisions.

Think, for example, about how parents teach their children to drive. They establish clear rules of conduct, such as how fast, and when and where to drive, and how many passengers can be in the car. At first, they may insist on being in the car with the new driver (direct observation). Many parents also enroll their children in a driver's education course and receive report cards that assess their children's driving skills (indirect observation). At some point, parents must trust that their children have learned the rules of the road and will drive responsibly. Even so, parents may still check the odometer from time to time, install a GPS unit, or use some other means of indirect monitoring.

Organizations need similar mechanisms to ensure that managers are making responsible decisions—those that are in the best interests of the organization. The approach organizations use depends on how centralized or decentralized the decision-making authority is spread throughout the organization.

In a decentralized organization, decision-making authority is spread throughout the organization, and managers are given a great deal of autonomy to decide how to manage their individual units. In a centralized organization, decision-making authority is kept at the very top of the organization. High-level executives make all strategic and operational decisions and charge lower-level managers with implementing those decisions.

In deciding how much decision-making authority to delegate, organizations must weigh the advantages and disadvantages of decentralization. See Exhibit 25.1 for a summary of the pros and cons of decentralization.

In most organizations, the distinction between centralized and decentralized operations is not an either-or matter but a question of **how much** decision-making authority to delegate.

## Exhibit 25.1  Advantages and Disadvantages of Decentralization

**Centralized decisions**

**Decentralized decisions (organization wide)**

| Advantages of Decentralization | Disadvantages of Decentralization |
|---|---|
| • Recognizes that managers have specialized knowledge and can react quickly to local information | • Has the potential to duplicate resources |
| • Allows the development of managerial expertise | • Allows managers the opportunity to make decisions that are good for themselves or their division, but which are not in the best interests of the organization overall |
| • Fosters competition among divisions | |
| • Allows top managers to focus on strategic issues | |

As companies grow, become geographically dispersed, or begin to offer more diversified products and services, keeping all decision-making authority at the top of the organization may not be possible or even desirable.

When decision-making authority has been decentralized, the organization must find a way to monitor and evaluate managerial performance in much the same way that parents monitor and evaluate their children's driving behavior. Ideally, the company's performance measurement system should be designed so that the manager's goals and incentives are aligned with the organization's goals and objectives. Unfortunately, that is much easier said than done and is not always achieved in practice.

In the next section, we use Blockbuster Inc. to illustrate a variety of methods for measuring and evaluating managerial responsibility. Consider the simplified organizational chart for Blockbuster Inc. in Exhibit 25.2 as background. To manage this large, geographically dispersed company, Blockbuster must delegate decision-making responsibility throughout the organization.

Video 25-1
www.mhhe.com/LLPW1e

## Exhibit 25.2  Organization Chart for Blockbuster Inc.

**Blockbuster**

**Corporate support functions**
Advertising
Human resources
Purchasing
Distribution/Logistics
Information technology
Legal services
Accounting

**Domestic operations**
Blockbuster-owned stores
Franchised locations
Online rentals

**International operations**
Blockbuster International
Xtra-Vision (Ireland)
Gamestation (United Kingdom)
Game Rush (Canada)

Western region | Southwest region | Midwest region | Northeast region | Southeast region

The next section discusses the various methods Blockbuster might use to measure and evaluate managerial performance in these various business segments.

# RESPONSIBILITY CENTERS

Responsibility accounting gives managers authority and responsibility for a particular part of the organization and then evaluates them based on the results of that area of responsibility. The part of the organization for which managers are responsible is called a responsibility center. It can be established based on business function, product or service offerings, or geographic area.

As described in Exhibit 25.2, Blockbuster is divided into segments (divisions) based on all three characteristics: business support functions such as human resources, legal services, and accounting; service offerings including Blockbuster-owned stores, franchised stores, and online rentals; and geographic areas such as international, domestic, and regional. Many of these areas could be broken down further. For example, each of the geographic regions could be divided into districts, cities, towns, and individual stores.

One of the most important concepts in responsibility accounting is the controllability principle, which states that managers should be held responsible only for what they can control. The four different types of responsibility centers vary according to what the business managers can control and, thus, what they should be held responsible for:

- The manager of a cost center is responsible for controlling **cost.**
- The manager of a revenue center is responsible for generating **revenue.**
- The manager of a profit center is responsible for **profit** (revenue − cost).
- The manager of an investment center is responsible for **profit** (revenue − cost) and the **investment of assets.**

**Learning Objective 2**

Describe the different types of responsibility center and explain how managers in each type are evaluated.

We next discuss each responsibility center and some common measures used to evaluate managerial performance in each.

## Cost Centers

**Cost center managers** have the authority to incur costs to support their areas of responsibility. All of Blockbuster's corporate support functions listed in Exhibit 25.2 would be treated as cost centers: advertising, human resources, purchasing, distribution and logistics, information technology, legal services, and accounting. Note that these centers do not generate revenue directly from customers, although they can have an indirect impact on revenue. For example, dollars spent on advertising should have an impact on the generation of revenue.

To understand the responsibilities of cost center managers, consider the following actual job descriptions posted recently on Blockbuster.com:

| Cost Center Managers | Job Description/Responsibilities | Blockbuster |
|---|---|---|
| **Distribution Center Manager** | • Responsible for the operation and management of the Distribution Center. | |
| | • Supervise warehouse employees and provide training to ensure that productivity standards are met or exceeded. | |
| | • Responsible for planning and management of the daily work activities of one or more departments within the warehouse (i.e., processing, returning, and packing) to performance metrics in the areas of throughput, cost, and customer service. | |
| **Human Resource Manager** | • Manage the field Human Resources function within a specified area of responsibility. | |
| | • Provide strategic direction and coaching to District Managers on the succession planning and development of employees. | |
| | • Partner with region, district, and store management on HR related issues and with corporate HR on training and recruiting issues. | |

One of the primary tools that cost center managers use to manage costs is the budgetary control system described in Chapters 23 and 24. However, cost center managers are responsible for more than just controlling costs. Usually they are also responsible for providing a high level of service to the rest of the organization whether in distribution, human resources, accounting, legal services, or some other internal function. Later in this chapter we discuss the use of the **balanced scorecard** to assess how well managers perform on dimensions other than cost, including internal processes, customer service, and employee satisfaction and turnover.

# Revenue Centers

**Revenue center managers** are responsible for generating revenue within their areas of the organization. The following revenue center positions were posted recently on Blockbuster.com:

| Revenue Center Managers | Job Description/ Responsibilities | Blockbuster |
|---|---|---|
| **Sales Manager** | • Overall responsibility for meeting sales goals set by the strategic sales plan.<br>• Responsible for implementing sales processes for training, communicating and tracking progress.<br>• Interact with customers in person and on the phone and utilize the computerized point of sale system to complete both credit and cash transactions and maintain member accounts. | |
| **Customer Care Associate** | • Manage service interactions by exhibiting a superior level of customer service and quality. Win back profitable customers through effective negotiations.<br>• Take personal ownership of meeting average handle time, response time, and contract resolution rates to ensure service level agreements are met while effectively communicating value and service offerings to build and retain current membership base. | |

Revenue center managers generally receive sales targets or quotas for a particular period and are evaluated based on whether they meet those targets. Later in this chapter, we discuss some other measures for evaluating revenue center managers including customer satisfaction, customer retention, and customer turnover.

# Profit Centers

**Profit center managers** are responsible for generating a profit (revenue − cost) within their area of the business: a store, district, region, division, or other business segment. Because they are responsible for both costs and revenues, profit center managers often supervise revenue and cost center managers. Consider the following profit center positions posted recently on Blockbuster.com:

| Profit Center Positions | Job Description/Responsibilities |
|---|---|
| **Store Manager (Tempe, AZ)** | • Hire, train and develop store employees. Schedule, organize and direct assignments<br>• Resolve customer problems or complaints by determining optimal solutions<br>• Ensure interior and exterior of store is maintained to company standards<br>• Utilize labor management tools including effective scheduling to maximize productivity, profitability and margins<br>• Analyze store's financial data and take action to grow revenues, control costs, and ensure appropriate inventory management (maintain product and sell-through merchandise inventories) to achieve sales and profit goals. |

| Regional Director of Operations (Seattle) | • General Manager responsible for the results of the overall regional business unit. |
|---|---|
|  | • Responsible for maximizing earnings through the growth of rental and retail sales revenues, effective control of expenses and the use of leadership and mentoring skills to maximize team performance. |
| | • Provide coaching, vision and direction to the Region management team, monitor and manage performance, and develop strategies and people to achieve Region growth, service and financial goals. |

The most common method of evaluating a profit center manager is by using the **segmented income statement**, which measures the profitability of a business segment during a particular period. One of the key features of a segmented income statement is that it distinguishes between costs that the segment manager can and cannot control. **Remember that managers should be held accountable only for those costs that are within their control.** The following hypothetical segmented income statement reports on Blockbuster's Seattle District, which includes several retail stores throughout the area:

**Blockbuster**

### Blockbuster
### Segmented Income Statement for Seattle District
### For the Quarter Ended March 31, 2010

| | Amount | Percentage |
|---|---|---|
| Revenues | | |
| Movie and game rental, merchandise sales, etc. | $1,200,000 | 100% |
| Less: Variable cost of rentals and merchandise sold | 240,000 | 20 |
| Contribution margin | 960,000 | 80 |
| Less: Direct operating expenses | | |
| Occupancy costs, labor, and supervision costs | 300,000 | 25 |
| **Segment margin** | **660,000** | **55** |
| Less: Indirect operating expense (advertising, general and administrative expenses, etc.) | 564,000 | 47 |
| Income from operations | $    96,000 | 8% |

**Coach's Tip**

Only these items are controllable by the division's manager, who is evaluated based on the segment margin.

These costs are controlled at the corporate level, so they should be excluded from the segment manager's performance evaluation.

The most important line on the segmented income statement is the **segment margin**, which is calculated as revenue minus all costs that are directly traceable to the segment, division, or region. In Blockbuster's segmented income statement for the Seattle district, the variable costs of rentals and merchandise sold plus the direct operating expenses of occupancy costs (rent), labor, and supervision are all directly attributable to the Seattle District. Thus, those costs are deducted from sales revenue to find the segment margin. Notice that indirect costs, such as advertising and general and administrative expenses, are deducted **after** segment margin. Those costs are incurred at corporate headquarters and allocated to the individual divisions, so they should not be included in the segment margin. In short, a profit center manager should be evaluated based on the segment margin, not the profit margin (that is, operating income), because the segment margin includes only those costs that are within the manager's control.

# Investment Centers

**Investment center managers** are responsible for generating a profit (revenue − cost) **and** investing assets. To understand the difference between a profit center manager and an investment center manager, consider the two types of Blockbuster store, company-owned stores and franchised locations. Blockbuster Inc. owns and operates about 80 percent of the individual stores in the United States. For these company-owned stores, senior executives at corporate headquarters make all major investment decisions, including new store openings, store closings, adopting new technologies, and other decisions requiring major investments of capital. Because the lower-level managers at Blockbuster-owned stores do not make decisions concerning the investment of assets, they are profit center managers, not investment center managers.

The other 20 percent of Blockbuster stores are franchised locations owned by other companies or individuals. The owners of these stores pay a franchise fee in exchange for the use of Blockbuster's name, national advertising and promotion, and other benefits, such as access to the company's proprietary software. The owners/managers of these stores are free to make their own decisions about where to locate, how much money to invest in physical assets and local advertising, and how to price their products. The following excerpt is from a recent annual report from Blockbuster.

> **Excerpted from:**
> **BLOCKBUSTER INC.**
> **FORM 10-K**
> **For the Fiscal Year Ended December 31, 2006**
>
> Our franchisees have control over all operating and pricing decisions at their respective locations. For example, our franchisees have control over whether or not to eliminate extended viewing fees . . . and over whether or not to participate in the BLOCKBUSTER Total Access program. . . . A franchisee has sole responsibility for all financial commitments relating to the development, opening and operation of its stores, including rent, utilities, payroll and other capital and incidental expenses. We cannot offer assurances that our franchisees will be able to achieve profitability levels in their businesses sufficient to pay our franchise fees.

**Blockbuster**

As the report notes, the owner/manager of a franchised Blockbuster store has significantly more responsibility than the manager of a company-owned Blockbuster store. Because the owner/managers of franchised stores have control over the investment of assets, they are investment center managers.

The next section focuses on the evaluation of an investment center manager's performance. First, complete the following Self-Study Practice to make sure that you understand the differences between the four types of responsibility centers.

**SELF-STUDY PRACTICE**

Which of the following statements about responsibility centers is true? You may select more than one answer.

1. Cost center managers are responsible for generating sales in their area of the business.
2. Revenue center managers are responsible for controlling costs and generating revenue in their area of the business.
3. Profit center managers are responsible for controlling costs and generating revenue but not for investing assets.
4. Investment center managers are responsible for investing assets but not for controlling costs or generating revenue.
5. None of these statements is true.

*After you have finished, check your answers with the solutions at the bottom of the page.*

3 is the only true statement

Solution to
Self-Study Practice

# EVALUATION OF INVESTMENT CENTER PERFORMANCE

As described in the previous section, investment center managers are responsible for generating profit and investing assets. As such, they will be evaluated based on their ability to generate enough profit to compensate for the investment in assets. Next we discuss two common measures for evaluating investment center performance: return on investment and residual income.

## Return on Investment (ROI)

The most common method of evaluating investment center performance is by using the rate of return on invested assets. Also called return on invested assets, the **return on investment (ROI)** is calculated as follows:

$$\text{Return on Investment (ROI)} = \frac{\text{Operating Income}}{\text{Invested Assets}}$$

ROI is calculated as the return on the segment's assets (measured by its operating profit) divided by the value of those assets. Thus, the higher a segment's operating profit relative to its investment base, the higher its ROI.

Consider the following sample data for two different segments of Blockbuster.

### COMPARISON OF RETURN ON INVESTMENT FOR TWO BLOCKBUSTER BUSINESS SEGMENTS

|  | Blockbuster Western Region | Blockbuster Online Rentals Division |
|---|---|---|
| $\dfrac{\text{Operating Income}}{\text{Average invested assets}} =$ | $\dfrac{\$\ 120{,}000}{\$2{,}000{,}000}$ | $\dfrac{\$\ 600{,}000}{\$2{,}000{,}000}$ |
| Return on Investment | 6% | 30% |

Notice that the two divisions have the same level of investment, with average assets of $2,000,000. Yet Online Rentals generates a much higher operating profit ($600,000) and, thus, has a higher ROI (30 percent) than the Western Region (6 percent). This comparison of the two ROIs is a good starting point for evaluating the two investment centers, but it does not provide much information about **why** the Online Rentals Division managed to generate a higher ROI.

To really understand ROI, we need to break it into two separate components, **investment turnover** and **profit margin**:

$$\text{Return on Investment (ROI)} = \text{Investment Turnover} \times \text{Profit Margin}$$

$$\frac{\text{Operating Income}}{\text{Invested Assets}} = \frac{\text{Sales Revenue}}{\text{Invested Assets}} \times \frac{\text{Operating Income}}{\text{Sales Revenue}}$$

In the preceding formula, **investment turnover** is the ratio of sales revenue to the invested assets; **profit margin** is the ratio of operating income to sales revenue. Essentially, this formula states that to increase ROI, managers must either generate more sales revenue from their assets (investment turnover) or keep a larger percentage of sales revenue as profit (profit margin). Developed by executives at DuPont in the early 1900s, the formula is often referred to as the **DuPont method**.

Applying the DuPont method to Blockbuster's two segments provides the following results:

## COMPARISON OF RETURN ON INVESTMENT, PROFIT MARGIN, AND INVESTMENT TURNOVER FOR TWO BLOCKBUSTER BUSINESS SEGMENTS

| | Blockbuster Western Region | Blockbuster Online Rentals Division |
|---|---|---|
| Sales revenue | $3,000,000 | $6,000,000 |
| Less: Operating expenses | (2,880,000) | (5,400,000) |
| Operating income | 120,000 | 600,000 |
| Average invested assets | 2,000,000 | 2,000,000 |
| Investment Turnover = $\frac{\text{Sales Revenue}}{\text{Invested Assets}}$ | $\frac{3,000,000}{2,000,000} = 1.5$ | $\frac{6,000,000}{2,000,000} = 3$ |
| Profit Margin = $\frac{\text{Operating Income}}{\text{Sales Revenue}}$ | $\frac{120,000}{3,000,000} = 4\%$ | $\frac{600,000}{6,000,000} = 10\%$ |
| ROI = $\frac{\text{Operating Income}}{\text{Invested Assets}}$ | $\frac{120,000}{2,000,000} = 6\%$ | $\frac{600,000}{2,000,000} = 30\%$ |
| ROI = $\frac{\text{Investment}}{\text{Turnover}} \times \frac{\text{Profit}}{\text{Margin}}$ | $1.5 \times 4\% = 6\%$ | $10\% \times 3 = 30\%$ |

**Coach's Tip**

Online Rentals generates more revenue than the Western Region from the same amount of invested assets.

Online Rentals earns more profit (or incurs less cost) than the Western Region for each dollar of sales.

The combined effect is a much higher return on investment for Online Rentals than for the Western Region.

This analysis shows that two factors are driving the difference in ROI for Blockbuster's two segments. The first factor is the amount of sales revenue generated for every dollar of investment. The investment turnover ratio shows how efficiently assets are used to generate sales revenue. The Western Region generates sales equal to 1.5 times its investment base; Online Rental Division generates twice that amount—3 times its investment base—from the same level of investment.

The second factor that drives the difference in ROI is the profit margins of the two business segments. The profit margin shows how much of a segment's sales revenue remains as operating profit after the operating costs have been covered. The Online Rental Division generates $0.10 in operating profit for every dollar of sales; the Western Region generates only $0.04 for every dollar of sales. This difference in profit margin is rooted in the different cost structures of the two segments. Blockbuster's bricks and mortar stores tend to have relatively high fixed costs (for rental space, utilities, and other overhead costs); Online Rentals Division has higher variable costs (for mailing movies back and forth to customers).

Multiplying these two effects gives the ROI, which can be reinvested in the company or paid to the owners. In sum, the Online Rentals Division generates more sales revenue from the same level of investment **and** keeps a higher percentage of the sales revenue as operating profit. The end result is that Online's ROI (30 percent) is much higher than that for the Western Region (6 percent). See these relationships shown in Exhibit 25.3.

To make sure you understand how to calculate ROI, profit margin, and investment turnover, complete the following Self-Study Practice.

**SELF-STUDY PRACTICE**

Consider the following sample data for Blockbuster's Midwestern Region:

| | |
|---|---|
| Sales | $1,000,000 |
| Operating expenses | 900,000 |
| Operating income | 100,000 |
| Invested assets | 400,000 |

1. Compute the region's ROI, profit margin, and investment turnover.
2. Show how the ROI is related to profit margin and investment turnover.

*After you have finished, check your answers with the solutions at the bottom of the next page.*

Coach's Tip

The investment turnover tells you how a given investment in assets is translated into sales revenue. This is represented by the megaphone effect in the diagram. The Online Division is able to generate twice as much sales revenue from the same investment base.

The profit margin tells you how much of that sales revenue trickles down to the bottom line as operating income. This is represented by the width of the funnel in the diagram. The Online Division keeps a greater percentage of its sales as income (as opposed to cost).

When you multiply these two effects together, you get return on investment.

**Exhibit 25.3**    Relationship between Investment Turnover, Profit Margin, and ROI

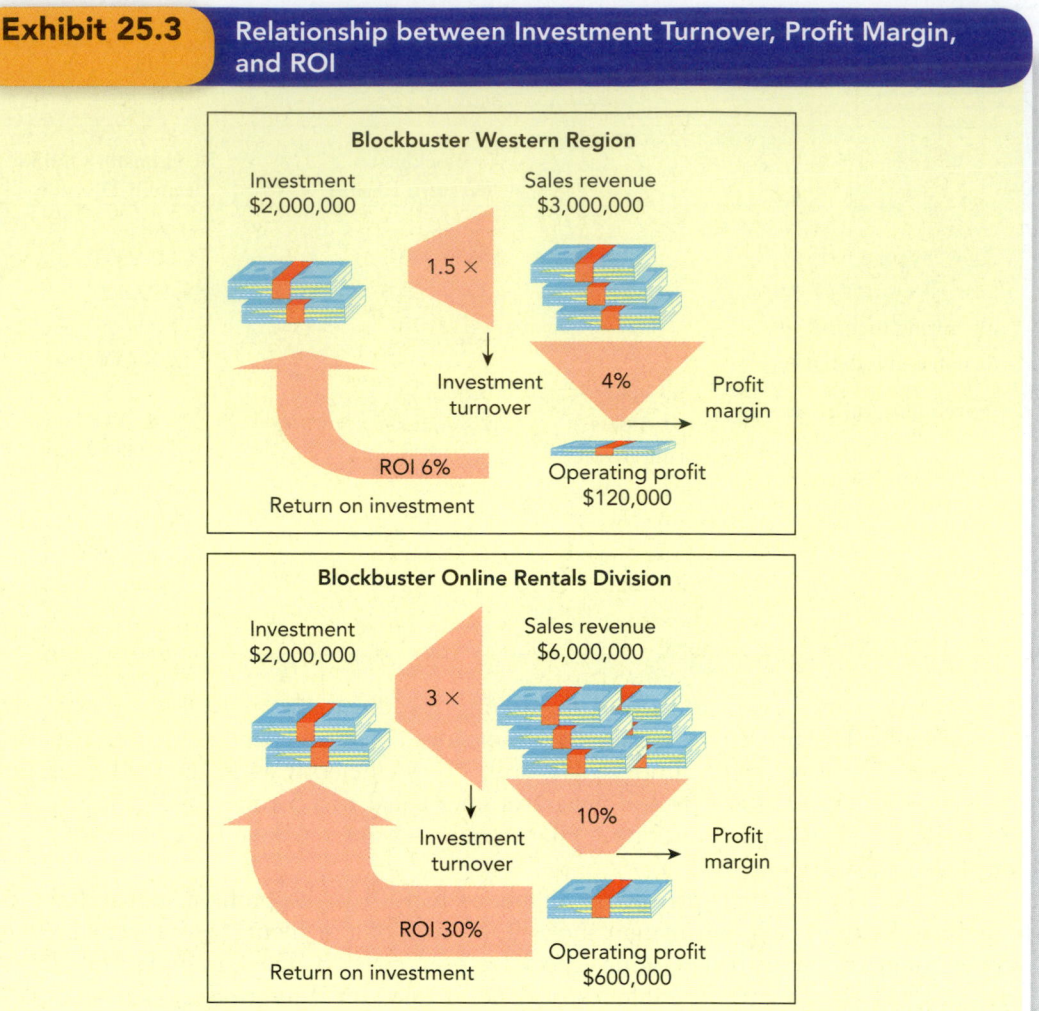

Learning Objective 4

Compute and interpret an investment center's residual income.

Coach's Tip

The **hurdle rate** is the minimum return that the organization will accept on invested assets. It is sometimes called the **cost of capital.**

**Residual income** is the organization's extra profit over and above that needed to cover the cost of capital.

# Residual Income

An alternative measure for evaluating an investment center's performance, called residual income, involves making a comparison between operating profit and the minimum required rate of return. Recall from Chapter 22 that organizations set the minimum required rate of return on an investment, sometimes called the **hurdle rate.** Residual income is the difference between the operating profit and the minimum profit the organization must earn to cover the hurdle rate as in the following formula:[1]

$$\boxed{\text{Residual Income}} = \boxed{\text{Operating Income}} - \boxed{\text{Invested Assets} \times \text{Hurdle Rate}}$$

Solution to
Self-Study Practice

1. ROI = $100,000 / $400,000 = 25%
   Profit margin = $100,000 / $1,000,000 = 10%
   Investment turnover = $1,000,000 / 400,000 = 2.5
2. ROI = Profit Margin × Investment Turnover = 10% × 2.5 = 25%

[1] A closely related technique for evaluating an investment center's performance is known as **economic value added,** or EVA™. This approach, which was devised by Stern, Stewart and Co., measures the economic wealth that is created when a company's operating income exceeds its cost of capital. Conceptually, EVA is very similar to residual income, but it requires a number of complex adjustments that are beyond the scope of this textbook.

Let's compute the residual incomes for two of Blockbuster's segments using a hurdle rate of 10 percent:

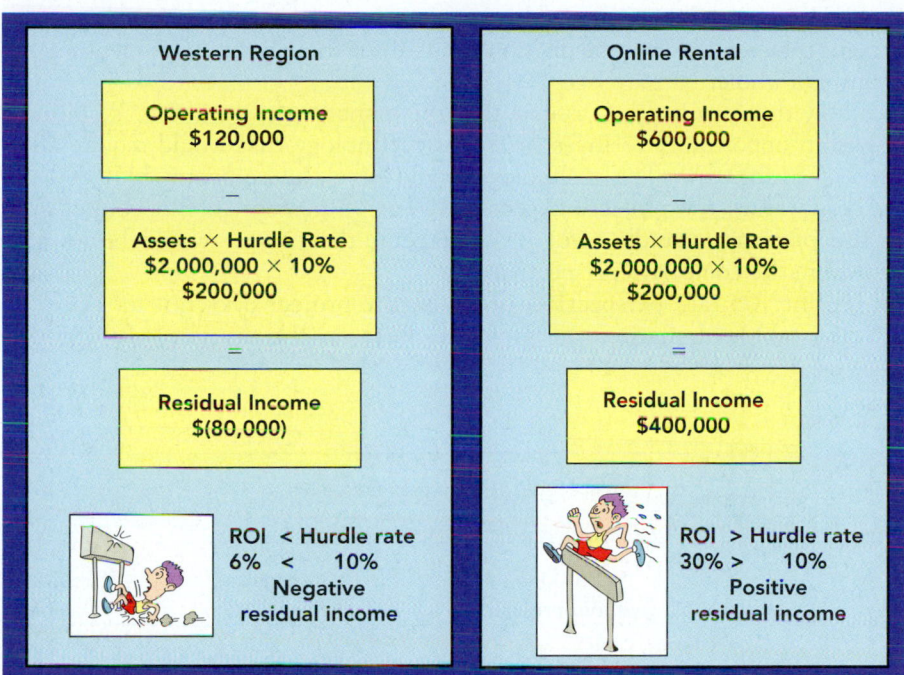

Notice that the Western Region has a negative residual income of $(80,000). That is, the region's operating profit is not high enough to cover its 10 percent hurdle rate. The ROI analysis on the previous page showed that the Western Region's ROI was only 6 percent—4 percent less than the hurdle rate. If you multiply the region's $2,000,000 investment by the 4 percent shortfall in its ROI (compared to the hurdle rate), you get the same result: a negative residual income of $(80,000).

The Online Division's residual income is $400,000, which is more than enough to cover the 10 percent required return on investment. The ROI analysis on the previous page showed that the Online Rentals Division was earning a 30 percent ROI. Multiplying the extra 20 percent return (over and above the 10 percent hurdle rate) by the division's $2,000,000 investment gives the same result: a residual income of $400,000. This amount is the additional profit Online Rentals earned over and above the required ROI.

Before you continue, complete the following Self-Study Practice to make sure you understand how to calculate residual income.

---

**SELF-STUDY PRACTICE**

Consider the following hypothetical data for Blockbuster's Midwest Region:

| | |
|---|---|
| Operating income | $100,000 |
| Invested assets | $400,000 |
| ROI | 25% |

1. Using a hurdle rate of 10 percent, compute the division's residual income.
2. Explain how the residual income is related to the 25 percent ROI.

*After you have finished, check your answers with the solutions at the bottom of the page.*

---

**Solution to Self-Study Practice**

1. Residual Income = Operating Income − (Invested Assets × Hurdle Rate) = $100,000 − ($400,000 × 10%) = $60,000
2. The 25 percent ROI is higher than the 10 percent hurdle rate.
   Excess of 15% × $400,000 Investment = $60,000 Residual Income.

# Return on Investment versus Residual Income

Return on investment is the most widely used method for evaluating investment center performance. However, it has one major disadvantage: It can sometimes cause managers to reject an investment that would lower the division's ROI, even though the investment might benefit the company as a whole.

To see how that can happen, assume that the manager of Blockbuster's Online Rentals Division has an opportunity to invest in a new technology that would require an up-front investment of $1,000,000. The technology would save the company $150,000 a year in operating costs. Thus, the project's expected ROI is 15 percent. If Blockbuster's minimum required rate of return (hurdle rate) is 10 percent, the project would be an acceptable investment from the company's perspective.

From Online Rentals' perspective, however, the project does not look as promising. The following table summarizes the project's effect on the division's ROI and residual income.

---

### EFFECT OF THE PROPOSED PROJECT ON ONLINE RENTALS' RETURN ON INVESTMENT AND RESIDUAL INCOME

| Return on investment analysis | Status Quo (without project) | Effect of Proposed Project | If Project Is Accepted |
|---|---|---|---|
| $\dfrac{\text{Operating Income}}{\text{Average Invested Assets}}$ = Return on Investment | $\dfrac{\$600{,}000}{\$2{,}000{,}000}=$ | $\dfrac{\$150{,}000}{\$1{,}000{,}000}=$ | $\dfrac{\$750{,}000}{\$3{,}000{,}000}=$ |
| | 30% | 15% | 25% |
| **Residual income analysis** | | | |
| Operating Income | $600,000 | $150,000 | $750,000 |
| Required Profit (10% of average invested assets) | (200,000) | (100,000) | (300,000) |
| Residual Income | $400,000 | $ 50,000 | $450,000 |

---

**Coach's Tip**

Notice that the project would have a negative effect on Online Rentals' ROI because its rate of return would be less than the current ROI of 30%. The project would generate a positive residual income, however, because its return is higher than the company's required rate of return, 10 percent.

Given these numbers, will the manager of Online Rentals want to invest in the project? The answer to this question depends on whether the manager is evaluated based on the division's ROI or its residual income. The proposed project would generate a positive residual income because it would earn more than the required 10 percent hurdle rate. However, it would have a negative impact on the division's ROI because the 15 percent return is less than the division's current ROI of 30 percent. If the manager invests in this project, the division's ROI will drop from 30 percent to 25 percent.

This example shows how a responsibility accounting system can create goal incongruence, or conflict between a manager and the organization as a whole. A manager who is evaluated based on ROI may not be willing to invest in a project that is in the best interest of the company as a whole simply because doing so would have a negative impact on the manager's own performance evaluation. The residual income method helps to align the manager's goals with the organization's objective of earning a minimum ROI of 10 percent. Regardless of the division's current ROI, its residual income will increase as long as the manager invests in projects that exceed the company's minimum required return.

# Limitations of Financial Performance Measures

Both ROI and residual income are lagging indicators of financial performance. In other words, they are based on historical information taken from a company's financial statements including past sales revenue, operating income, and assets. These measures tell how a company or a division has done in the past but not necessarily how it will do in the future.

Unfortunately, many of the actions that managers take to improve a company's financial performance in the short run can prove harmful to the organization over the long run. Examples include cutting back on research and development, reducing employee training, and using less expensive materials to make a product. While all of these decisions will improve short-run financial results, they will likely hurt the company in the long term through reduced sales, quality problems, customer complaints, and increased warranty expenses. To avoid these problems, organizations should evaluate and reward managers based on more than just short-term financial results. The next section discusses the balanced scorecard, a performance measurement system designed to focus managers' attention on more than just financial results.

# Balanced Scorecard

The balanced scorecard is a comprehensive performance measurement system that translates an organization's vision and strategy into a set of operational performance metrics. The balanced scorecard measures organizational performance on four key dimensions:

- **Customer perspective.**   How do we want our customers to see us?
- **Learning and growth perspective.**   How will we sustain our ability to change and improve?
- **Internal business processes.**   What internal processes will we require to meet the needs of our customers, employees, and shareholders?
- **Financial perspective.**   How do we satisfy our shareholders, regulators, and other stakeholders?

**Learning Objective 5**

Describe the four dimensions of the balanced scorecard and explain how they are used to evaluate managerial performance.

For each of these dimensions, managers must devise specific objectives, measures, and targets that can be used to gauge how well the company is performing and identify what needs to be done to improve performance. Those objectives, measures, and targets should be communicated to managers throughout the organization so that everyone knows what needs to be done to achieve long-term success, not just short-term financial results.

See the sample balanced scorecard for Blockbuster in Exhibit 25.4. Notice that the center of the scorecard is the company's strategic vision. In this example, Blockbuster's strategic vision is to remain the leading provider of in-home movies and gaming. Because of the dynamic nature of this industry, Blockbuster's managers cannot continue to operate as they have in the past, relying primarily on Blockbuster's neighborhood stores. Instead, they must gain market share in the market for online rentals and invest in new technologies that will allow the company to deliver downloadable movies and games.

The four boxes surrounding the center of Exhibit 25.4 represent the four key dimensions of Blockbuster's performance. Notice that each dimension lists specific objectives and measures that managers can use to evaluate the company's performance. For example, one of Blockbuster's internal business processes objectives is to reduce delivery time to customers. A specific measure that managers can use to assess the company's performance on this objective is the percentage of orders that reach customers within one business day. Blockbuster tracks this measure carefully. In a recent annual report, the company noted that its distribution system is set up to reach more than 90 percent of online subscribers within a single business day.

Similar measures must be developed and captured for the other dimensions of the balanced scorecard. For example, customer measures might include the percentage of revenue from online rentals, number of new contracts, and retention of existing customers. Measures for learning and growth might focus on employee education and internal level promotions as well as the amount of money spent on new technology. Measures of financial performance include reductions in operating costs, increase in investment turnover rates, and increases in the company's stock price.

Video 25-2
www.mhhe.com/LLPW1e

**Exhibit 25.4**    Balanced Scorecard for Blockbuster Inc.                    **Blockbuster**

**Customer Perspective**
**Objectives**
- Increase market share by providing the very best entertainment products
- Increase online customer base

**Measures**
- Percentage of revenue from online rentals
- Percentage of new contracts signed
- Percentage of existing customers retained

**Learning and Growth Perspective**
**Objectives**
- Hire and retain well-educated employees
- Provide on-the-job training and promotional opportunities
- Invest in new product–delivery technologies

**Measures**
- Average educational level of store managers
- Percentage of promotions from within
- Amount spent on new technology initiatives

**Vision:**
Remain the leading provider of in-home movie and game entertainment

**Internal Business Processes**
**Objectives**
- Reduce delivery time to customers
- Reduce inventory in the warehouse
- Increase automation in the warehouse

**Measures**
- Percentage of orders delivered within one business day
- Inventory turnover rate
- Number of data entry errors

**Financial Perspective**
**Objectives**
- Reduce the cost of operations
- Increase shareholders' return on investment

**Measures**
- Percentage decrease in operating costs
- Percentage increase in investment turnover
- Percentage change in stock price

# TRANSFER PRICING

Video 25-3
www.mhhe.com/LLPW1e

The final issue we consider in this chapter is how decentralized organizations deal with the transfer or sale of goods and services between divisions. A **transfer price** is the amount that one division charges when it sells goods or services to another division in the same company. Transfers happen quite often in today's business environment because many large corporations are composed of several relatively independent business units all owned by the same parent company. Business transactions between units or divisions in the same company are called **related-party transactions.**

Perhaps the easiest way to think about transfer prices is in terms of the deal you would get if you buy something from a relative. Maybe you want to buy a car from your brother-in-law's dealership, a meal at your cousin's restaurant, or a cut and style at your sister's hair salon. How much would you expect to pay for a product or service when buying from a relative? At a minimum, you should be willing to pay for any variable costs that your relative incurs (floor). For example, if your brother, an auto-mechanic, agrees to repair your car, you should at least be willing to pay for the parts. The maximum amount you should be willing to pay is the going market rate (ceiling) for the product or service. In other words, you should not be willing to pay more for the product or service than you would if you bought it elsewhere. See Exhibit 25.5 for this range of potential transfer prices.

The same rules apply to transfer prices in decentralized organizations. The only difference is that the managers of decentralized business units are not necessarily friendly relatives. In fact, if managers are evaluated based on their ability to control costs and/or generate revenue, their goals may be diametrically opposed even if they do work in the same company. The manager of the selling division is motivated to achieve the highest possible price; the manager of the buying division is motivated to pay the lowest possible price. Although the transfer price

## Exhibit 25.5 | Range of Potential Transfer Prices

does not really matter from the company's overall perspective,[2] it can make a big difference to individual managers. As in the famous line from the film *The Godfather*, "It's not personal, it's just business."

As a simple example, assume Blockbuster has a controlling interest in the hypothetical company Popcorn Ltd., which manufactures bags of microwave popcorn for sale in large buckets at Blockbuster and other movie rental stores. Because Popcorn Ltd. operates as a free-standing business unit of Blockbucker Inc., its managers are considered profit center managers.

Assume that Popcorn Ltd.'s costs to produce a single case (24 packs) of microwave popcorn are as follows.

### Popcorn Ltd.
### Cost to Produce 1 Case (24 packs)
### of Microwave Popcorn

| | | |
|---|---|---|
| Direct materials | $1.00 | |
| Direct labor | 0.25 | $1.50 |
| Variable overhead | 0.25 | |
| Fixed overhead ($350,000 / 100,000 unit capacity) | 3.50 | |
| Full manufacturing cost | $5.00 | |

The external market price (for non-Blockbuster buyers) is $10.00.

The manager of Blockbuster's Midwest Region has approached Popcorn Ltd. to buy popcorn for that region. What price should Popcorn Ltd. charge the manager for a case of popcorn?

There are three different ways to determine transfer prices such as this one: the market-price method, the cost-based method, and negotiation.

## Market-Price Method

The market price is the price that a company would charge to external customers. It is the maximum price that a buyer should be willing to pay. In this example, the market price is $10 per case of popcorn. The problem with using the market price as a transfer price is that the buyer has no incentive to purchase from within the company and so may consider buying from an outside supplier. Think of buying a car from someone other than your car-dealing brother-in-law because he is unwilling to give you a discount.

**Learning Objective 6**

Explain how transfer prices are set in decentralized organizations.

[2] Transfer prices **can** have a major impact on multinational companies due to variations in tax rates from one country to the next. This issue, which is extremely complex, is beyond the scope of this textbook.

**Exhibit 25.6**    Range of Transfer Prices for Blockbuster Popcorn

What is the appropriate transfer price?

Market price ← $10.00 ─ Ceiling

Seller's profit ($5.00)

Negotiated prices

$5.00

Cost-based prices ← 

Fixed costs ($3.50)

$1.50 ─ Floor

Variable costs ($1.50)

In our example, if the buying division (the Midwest Region) decides to buy from an outside supplier, the selling division (Popcorn Ltd.) loses the opportunity to profit from the sale just as your brother-in-law would lose the opportunity to earn a commission on your new car. As a result, the company as a whole may suffer. The only time that using a market price as a transfer price makes sense is when the selling division is operating at full capacity and cannot fill the order without giving up sales to external customers. If Popcorn Ltd. is already selling all the popcorn it can produce for $10 per case, for example, selling to the Midwest Region at a lower price would not make sense. The company would be losing more profitable business.

If the selling division has **excess capacity,** however, it can make a profit by selling at any price above the variable cost. (Remember that the total fixed cost is constant and does not change depending on the number of units produced and sold, at least within a limited range.) In this example, we assume Popcorn Ltd. has sufficient capacity to fill the Midwest Region's order without incurring additional fixed costs or losing sales to other customers. In that case, Popcorn Ltd. should be willing to sell the popcorn for less than the market price (see Exhibit 25.6). In the next section, we use the cost-based method to determine a transfer price for the popcorn.

## Cost-Based Method

The cost-based method uses either the variable cost or the full cost as the basis for setting the transfer price. At a minimum, the selling division should recover the incremental (that is, variable) costs of producing and selling the product. In this example, the transfer price should be set at no less than the variable cost of $1.50 per case of popcorn. Another option is to base the transfer price on the full manufacturing cost of $5.00 per case, which covers both variable and fixed costs.

Many companies have a predetermined "cost-plus" transfer price. For example, Blockbuster might have a policy of making all internal transfers at the full manufacturing cost plus 10 percent. If so, the transfer price per case of popcorn would be $5.00 + (10% of $5.00) = $5.50. If the transfer price were set at $5.50, both buyer and seller would benefit from the transfer. The buying division (Blockbuster's Midwest Region) would pay $5.50 per case, a $4.50 savings compared to the market price of $10.00. The selling division (Popcorn Ltd.) would make $5.50 minus $1.50 in variable costs for an increased profit of $4.00 per case.

## Negotiation

A final option is to let divisional managers negotiate transfer prices. In this method, the negotiated price can range anywhere from the variable cost ($1.50) to the full market price ($10.00). As in any negotiation, the final price will depend on the relative power of the buyer and seller, their negotiation skills, and how much inside information each has about the other division's cost, capacity, and demand.

Think of buying a car from a car dealer. You should not be willing to pay more than the market price, which we will assume is the sticker price. The dealer should not be willing to accept less than the variable cost; otherwise, the dealership will lose money on the sale. Knowing the variable cost of the car would certainly help you in your bargaining. On the other hand, if the dealer knows you really want the car and has another customer who is ready to buy it (and no more cars like it on the lot), you will not be in a good bargaining position.

Negotiating transfer prices can be time consuming and can force managers of the same parent company to act as adversaries. To avoid such situations, companies may dictate that the buying and selling divisions split the difference so that each receives an equal benefit from the internal transfer. In our example, the transfer price would be midway between the $10.00 market price and the $1.50 in variable costs, or $5.75. This approach creates a win–win situation for the managers: The buying division saves $4.25 per case ($10.00 − $5.75) by buying from inside, and the selling division makes an extra $4.25 per case ($5.75 − $1.50) in incremental profit.

To make sure you understand how to set transfer prices, complete the following Self-Study Practice.

---

**SELF-STUDY PRACTICE**

Kraft Foods owns both Tombstone Pizza and Kraft Cheese. Assume that Tombstone Pizza (the buyer) has approached Kraft Cheese (the seller) to ask for a special deal on the cheese used to produce Tombstone's frozen pizza.

Which of the following statements is true? You may select more than one answer.

1. If Kraft Cheese is operating at full capacity, the company should be willing to accept less than the market price for the cheese.
2. If Kraft Cheese has excess capacity, the company may be willing to accept less than the variable cost for the cheese.
3. Both statements above are true.
4. None of the statements above are true.

*After you have finished, check your answers with the solutions at the bottom of the page.*

---

# Demonstration Case

Consider the following data for two divisions of Peter Piper Pizza:

|  | Northwest Region | Southwest Region |
|---|---|---|
| Average invested assets | $ 6,000,000 | $6,000,000 |
| Sales revenue | $18,000,000 | $9,000,000 |
| Less: Operating expenses | (17,460,000) | (8,100,000) |
| Operating income | $    540,000 | $   900,000 |

**Required:**

1.   Compute the investment turnover, profit margin, return on investment, and residual income for each division. Assume a 10 percent hurdle rate.
2.   Explain the relationship between each division's residual income and its return on investment.
3.   The manager of the Southwest Region has the opportunity to invest an additional $2,000,000 in a project expected to generate additional operating income of $220,000 per year. Calculate Southwest's new return on investment and residual income if the manager accepts the project.
4.   Would Southwest's manager, who is evaluated based on the region's return on investment, want to invest in the project? If the evaluation were based on the region's residual income? Why or why not?

---

4 is the only true statement.

Solution to
Self-Study Practice

## Suggested Solution

1.

|  | | Northwest Region | Southwest Region |
|---|---|---|---|
| Investment Turnover | $= \dfrac{\text{Sales Revenue}}{\text{Invested Assets}}$ | $\dfrac{18,000,000}{6,000,000} = 3$ | $\dfrac{9,000,000}{6,000,000} = 1.50$ |
| Profit Margin | $= \dfrac{\text{Operating Income}}{\text{Sales Revenue}}$ | $\dfrac{540,000}{18,000,000} = 3\%$ | $\dfrac{900,000}{9,000,000} = 10\%$ |
| Return on Investment | $= \dfrac{\text{Operating Income}}{\text{Invested Assets}}$ | $\dfrac{540,000}{6,000,000} = 9\%$ | $\dfrac{900,000}{6,000,000} = 15\%$ |
| Operating Income | | 540,000 | 900,000 |
| Required Profit (10% of assets) | | (600,000) | (600,000) |
| Residual Income | | (60,000) | 300,000 |

2. The Northwest Region has a negative residual income because its return on investment, which is 9 percent, is less than the 10 percent hurdle rate, 1 percent of $6,000,000 = $(60,000).

The Southwest Region has a positive residual income because its return on investment, which is 15 percent, is higher than the 10 percent hurdle rate; 5 percent of $6,000,000 = $300,000.

3.

| | Southwest Region (before project) | Proposed Project | If Project Is Accepted |
|---|---|---|---|
| **Return on Investment Analysis** | | | |
| $\dfrac{\text{Operating income}}{\text{Average invested assets}}$ = Return on investment | $\dfrac{\$900,000}{\$6,000,000} = 15\%$ | $\dfrac{\$220,000}{\$2,000,000} = 11\%$ | $\dfrac{\$1,120,000}{\$8,000,000} = 14\%$ |
| **Residual Income Analysis** | | | |
| Operating income | $900,000 | $220,000 | $1,120,000 |
| Required profit (10% of assets) | (600,000) | (200,000) | (800,000) |
| Residual income | $300,000 | $ 20,000 | $ 320,000 |

4. If the evaluation is based on the region's return on investment (ROI), Southwest's regional manager probably would **not** want to invest in the project because it would lower the division's ROI. The project's expected ROI of 11 percent is less than the division's current ROI of 15 percent. Thus, investing the extra $2,000,000 would lower the region's ROI to 14 percent.

However, if the evaluation is based on the region's residual income, the manager **would** want to invest in the project because it would increase the region's residual income. Residual income will increase as long as the project's return (11 percent) is higher than the minimum required rate of return (10 percent).

# Chapter Summary

## LO1 List and explain the advantages and disadvantages of decentralization. p. 1028

- Decentralization is the delegation of decision-making authority to managers at all levels of the organization.
- The advantages of decentralization include the ability to make decisions more quickly based on local information; the development of managerial expertise; increased competition among managers; and increased opportunity for upper management to focus on strategic issues.
- The disadvantages of decentralization include the potential for duplicating resources and for making suboptimal decisions (those that are not made in the best interests of the organization as a whole).

## LO2 Describe the different types of responsibility centers and explain how managers in each type are evaluated. p. 1030

- **Cost center:** Managers are responsible for controlling costs within their area of responsibility, such as distribution, advertising, accounting, or human resources. Cost center managers are evaluated based on their ability to stay within budget and provide the necessary support to the organization.

- **Revenue center:** Managers are responsible for generating sales revenue within their area of responsibility, such as a store, a district, or a region. They are evaluated based on their ability to meet sales quotas and other measures of success, such as customer retention.
- **Profit center:** Managers are responsible for earning a profit within their area of responsibility through both revenue generation and cost control. They are typically evaluated based on a measure such as segment margin, which includes only those costs that are within the segment manager's direct control.
- **Investment center:** Managers are responsible for both profit (revenue − cost) and the investment of assets. They are evaluated based on measures that include both profit and investment, such as return on investment and residual income.

### LO3  Compute and interpret an investment center's return on investment. p. 1034

- Return on investment (ROI) is the most common measure for evaluating an investment center's performance.
- ROI equals the investment center's operating profit divided by its average investment in assets.
- The DuPont formula shows that ROI equals the profit margin multiplied by the investment turnover ratio.
- Profit margin is the amount of profit generated for every dollar of sales revenue.
- Investment turnover is the amount of sales revenue generated for every dollar of invested assets.
- Companies can increase ROI by either increasing profit margin (by reducing costs without reducing sales) or increasing asset turnover (by increasing sales without increasing assets).

### LO4  Compute and interpret an investment center's residual income. p. 1036

- Residual income is an alternative measure for evaluating an investment center's performance.
- Residual income equals the difference between an investment center's operating profit and the minimum profit it must make to cover its hurdle rate (that is, the minimum rate of return on its assets).
- Managers earn residual income by investing in projects that earn more than the minimum required rate of return (or hurdle rate).

### LO5  Describe the four dimensions of the balanced scorecard and explain how they are used to evaluate managerial performance. p. 1039

- The balanced scorecard is a comprehensive performance measurement system that translates the organization's vision and strategy into a set of operational performance measures.
- The balanced scorecard measures operational performances on four key dimensions: consumer perspective, learning and growth perspective, internal business processes, and financial perspective.
- The customer perspective focuses on the customer through measures such as customer retention, customer satisfaction, and market share.
- The learning and growth perspective focuses on the organization's ability to change and improve through measures such as the amount of money spent on research and development and employee education and training.
- The internal business processes focus on the internal processes required to meet customer needs through measures of on-time delivery, quality, and internal process efficiency.
- The financial perspective focuses on traditional financial measures of performance, such as return on investment, residual income, sales revenue, and profit.

### LO6  Explain how transfer prices are set in decentralized organizations. p. 1041

- A transfer price is the price charged when one unit or division of a company sells goods or services to another unit or division of the same company.
- The maximum transfer price is the external market price, or the amount that would be charged to an unrelated party. The minimum transfer price is the variable cost (to the seller) of selling to the other division.
- Cost-based transfer prices can be set based on variable cost, full cost, or cost plus some percentage markup.
- Transfer prices can also be set through negotiation between the buying and selling divisions.

## Key Terms

Balanced Scorecard (p. 1039)

Centralized Organization (p. 1028)

Controllability Principle (p. 1030)

Cost Center (p. 1030)

Decentralized Organization (p. 1028)

DuPont Method (p. 1034)

Goal Incongruence (p. 1038)

Investment Center (p. 1030)

Investment Turnover (p. 1034)

Profit Center (p. 1030)

Profit Margin (p. 1034)

Related-Party Transactions (p. 1040)

Residual Income (p. 1036)

Responsibility Accounting (p. 1030)

Responsibility Center (p. 1030)

Return on Investment (ROI) (p. 1034)

Revenue Center (p. 1030)

Segmented Income Statement (p. 1032)

Segment Margin (p. 1032)

Transfer Price (p. 1040)

See complete glossary in back of text.

# Questions

1. Explain how centralized and decentralized companies differ. What are the advantages and disadvantages of each?

2. How does decentralization create the need for responsibility accounting in an organization?

3. What is the controllability principle and why is it crucial to responsibility accounting?

4. Name the four types of responsibility centers and describe the managers' responsibilities and authority in each.

5. Why are profit center managers evaluated on segment margin instead of overall company income?

6. What role do return on investment and residual income play in responsibility accounting?

7. Return on investment may be separated into two components. Name them and describe what each of these components can tell you.

8. Explain how reliance on return on investment for performance evaluation of investment center managers could lead to goal incongruence.

9. How is residual income calculated?

10. What benefit does residual income offer in comparison to return on investment when evaluating performance?

11. What are the primary limitations of financial measures of performance?

12. Explain the balanced scorecard approach to performance evaluation. What advantages does this approach have over using only financial measurements?

13. What are the four perspective areas of a balanced scorecard? What does each perspective represent?

14. What is a transfer price?

15. Explain the minimum and maximum transfer prices and identify whether each would be determined by the buyer or the seller.

16. What is the market-price method of transfer pricing?

17. What does the term excess capacity mean? How does excess capacity affect a transfer price?

18. Describe the cost-based method of transfer pricing.

19. What are negotiated transfer prices? Explain two possible disadvantages of allowing managers to negotiate a transfer price.

# Multiple Choice

1. Sally Thorne is a profit center manager for ABC Company's Phoenix district. Last year, her performance evaluation was based on the operating performance of ABC's entire Southwest region. This is a violation of

    Quiz 25-1
    www.mhhe.com/LLPW1e

    a. The hurdle rate principle.
    b. The controllability principle.
    c. The balanced scorecard approach.
    d. Negotiated transfer pricing rules.

2. Responsibility centers include

    a. Cost centers.          d. Investment centers.
    b. Revenue centers.       e. All of these.
    c. Profit centers.

3. Which of the following statements is true?

    a. A profit center manager is responsible for investment of company assets.
    b. A cost center manager should be evaluated based on sales revenue.
    c. A profit center manager should be evaluated based on return on investment.
    d. An investment center manager is responsible for costs, revenue, and the investment of assets.

4. Which of the following is most likely to be classified as a cost center manager?

    a. Accounting manager.
    b. Sales manager.
    c. Regional manager.
    d. All of these are cost center managers.

5. Return on investment and residual income are useful in evaluating

    a. Cost center managers.
    b. Revenue center managers.
    c. Profit center managers.
    d. Investment center managers.

6. Return on investment can be separated into

    a. Investment turnover and profit margin.
    b. Profit margin and residual income.
    c. Investment turnover and residual income.
    d. Profit margin and operating income.

7. Raymond Calvin is an investment center manager for XYZ Corp. and is evaluated solely on the return on investment for his division. Which of the following will improve Raymond's evaluation?

    a. Increasing the amount invested in assets while keeping operating income the same.

b.   Increasing the amount of operating income while keeping invested assets the same.

c.   Decreasing the amount invested in assets while keeping operating income the same.

d.   Either b or c.

8.   Which of the following statements is true?

a.   Return on investment considers a company's hurdle rate for investments.

b.   Residual income considers a company's hurdle rate for investments.

c.   Projects may be declined based on return on investment even though they produce positive residual income.

d.   Both b and c.

9.   Which of the following is not a component of the balanced scorecard method of measuring performance?

a.   Customer perspective.

b.   Management perspective.

c.   Learning and growth perspective.

d.   Internal business processes.

e.   Financial perspective.

10.  Transfer price could be based on:

a.   Variable costs.

b.   Full cost.

c.   Market price.

d.   Any of the above.

---

**Solutions to Multiple-Choice Questions**

1. b    2. e    3. d    4. a    5. d    6. a    7. d    8. d    9. b    10. d

---

# Mini Exercises  Available with McGraw-Hill's Homework Manager

**M25-1 Describing the Difference in Centralized and Decentralized Organizations**    LO1

Lupe Bornes recently graduated from college and received job offers in management from two different companies. The positions are similar in terms of title, salary, and benefits, but the companies vary in organizational structure. Alpha Company is centralized while Beta Company is decentralized. Explain to Lupe what he can infer about each company and how it is likely to affect his position within each one.

**M25-2 Describing How Real-World Organizations' Responsibility Centers Are Structured**    LO2

Responsibility centers can be created in a variety of ways. Give a real-world example of a company whose responsibility centers would likely be created on the basis of each of the following: functional area, product line, and geographic area.

**M25-3 Applying the Balanced Scorecard to a Real-World Company**    LO5

Consider the manager of your local Applebee's restaurant. Using a balanced scorecard approach, identify five measures on which upper management could evaluate the manager's performance. At least three of the items listed should be nonfinancial measures.

**M25-4 Calculating Return on Investment and Residual Income**    LO3, 4

Kettle Company has sales of $450,000, operating income of $250,000, average invested assets of $800,000, and a hurdle rate of 10 percent. What are Kettle's return on investment and its residual income?

**M25-5 Calculating Return on Investment and Residual Income**    LO3, 4

Lowry Company has sales of $125,000, cost of goods sold of $70,000, operating expenses of $20,000, average invested assets of $400,000, and a hurdle rate of 8 percent. What are Lowry's return on investment and its residual income?

**M25-6 Calculating Return on Investment and Residual Income**    LO3, 4

Rally Corp's Eastern Division has sales of $190,000, cost of goods sold of $110,000, operating expenses of $35,000, average invested assets of $900,000, and a hurdle rate of 12 percent. What are the Eastern Division's return on investment and its residual income?

**M25-7 Describing the Implications of Transfer Pricing**    LO2, 6

Assume that your cousin Matilda Flores, manages a local glass shop that was recently bought by a company that produces custom picture frames. As a result, Matilda will soon be providing glass to the Frame Division. She has heard upper management mention a transfer price but does not understand what this term means or how it might affect her division. Briefly explain transfer pricing to Matilda and how it will impact her division's performance in the future.

**LO6**

**M25-8 Identifying Minimum and Maximum Transfer Prices**

Lancaster Company has two divisions, A and B. Division A manufactures a component that Division B uses. The variable cost to produce this component is $1.50 per unit; full cost is $2.00. The component sells on the open market for $5.00. Assuming Division A has excess capacity, what is the lowest price for which Division A will sell the component? What is the most that Division B will pay for it?

**LO6**

**M25-9 Calculating a Cost-Plus Transfer Price**

Bellows Company has two divisions, X and Y. Division X manufactures a wheel assembly that Division Y uses. The variable cost to produce this assembly is $4.00 per unit; full cost is $5.00. The component sells on the open market for $9.00. What will the transfer price be if Bellows uses a pricing rule of variable cost plus 40 percent?

# Exercises  Available with McGraw-Hill's Homework Manager

**LO1, 2, 5**

**E25-1 Explaining the Relationships among Decentralization, Responsibility Accounting, Controllability, and the Balanced Scorecard**

Assume you are the vice president of operations for a local company. Your company is in the process of converting from a small, centralized company in which its president makes all decisions to a larger, geographically dispersed organization with decentralized decision-making authority.

*Required:*

Write a brief memo to other company managers explaining how decentralization, responsibility accounting, controllability, and the balanced scorecard method of performance evaluation are all related. Include the most obvious changes the managers are likely to see as this transition takes place and how it will impact their performance evaluations in the future.

**LO2**

**E25-2 Identifying Types of Responsibility Centers**

*Required:*

Match the most likely type of responsibility center classification to each of the following positions. You may use a classification once, more than once, or not at all.

| Employment Positions | Possible Responsibility Center Classification |
|---|---|
| _____ Sales manager | a. Cost center |
| _____ Regional manager | b. Revenue center |
| _____ Company president | c. Profit center |
| _____ Purchasing manager | d. Investment center |
| _____ Human resources manager | |
| _____ Chief financial officer | |
| _____ Production facility manager | |

**LO3**

**E25-3 Finding Unknowns Using Return on Investment, Profit Margin, and Investment Turnover**

Tuttle Company recently had a computer malfunction and lost a portion of its accounting records. The company has reconstructed some of its financial performance measurements including components of the return on investment calculations.

*Required:*

Help Tuttle rebuild its information database by completing the following table.

| Return on Investment (percent) | Profit Margin (percent) | Investment Turnover |
|---|---|---|
| ? | 5% | 1.1 |
| 14 | ? | 2.0 |
| 3 | 4 | ? |
| 23 | ? | 0.4 |

**E25-4 Finding Unknowns Using Return on Investment, Profit Margin, and Investment Turnover**    LO3

Norshon Company recently had a computer malfunction and lost a portion of its accounting records. The company has reconstructed some of its financial performance measurements including components of the return on investment calculations.

**Required:**

Help Norshon rebuild its information database by completing the following table.

| Return on Investment (percent) | Profit Margin (percent) | Investment Turnover | Operating Income | Sales Revenue | Average Invested Assets |
|---|---|---|---|---|---|
| ? | ? | ? | $ 35,000 | $ 700,000 | $1,400,000 |
| ? | 10 | 0.40 | 100,000 | ? | 2,500,000 |
| ? | 15 | 1.25 | ? | 2,000,000 | ? |
| 12 | ? | 2.00 | ? | 500,000 | ? |

**E25-5 Calculating Return on Investment and Residual Income and Determining the Effect of Changes in Sales, Expenses, Invested Assets, and the Hurdle Rate on Each**    LO3, 4

Mancell Company has sales of $500,000, cost of goods sold of $370,000, other operating expenses of $50,000, invested assets of $1,400,000, and a hurdle rate of 8 percent.

**Required:**

1. Determine Mancell's return on investment (ROI), investment turnover, profit margin, and residual income.
2. Several possible changes that Mancell could face in the upcoming year follow. Determine each scenario's impact on Mancell's ROI and residual income. (Note: Treat each scenario independently.)

    a. Company sales and cost of goods sold increase by 30 percent.
    b. Operating expenses decrease by $10,000.
    c. Operating expenses increase by 20 percent.
    d. Average invested assets increase by $300,000.
    e. Mancell changes its hurdle rate to 12 percent.

**E25-6 Evaluating Managerial Performance Using Return on Investment and Residual Income**    LO3, 4

Francis Corp. has two divisions, Eastern and Western. The following information for the past year is for each division.

| | Eastern Division | Western Division |
|---|---|---|
| Sales | $ 600,000 | $ 900,000 |
| Cost of goods sold and operating expenses | 450,000 | 600,000 |
| Operating Income | $ 150,000 | $ 300,000 |
| Average invested assets | $1,000,000 | $1,500,000 |

Francis has established a hurdle rate of 9 percent.

**Required:**

1. Compute each division's return on investment (ROI) and residual income for last year. Determine which manager seems to be performing better.
2. Suppose Francis is investing in new technology that will increase each division's operating income by $144,000. The total investment required is $1,600,000, which will be split evenly between the two divisions. Calculate the ROI and return on investment for each division after the investment is made.
3. Determine whether both managers will support the investment. Explain how their support will differ depending on which performance measure (ROI or residual investment) is used.

**LO5**

**E25-7 Describing the Objectives and Perspectives of a Balanced Scorecard**

Your brother-in-law, Fred Miles, has just taken a new position as the plant manager of a local production facility. He has been told that the company uses a balanced scorecard approach to evaluate its managers. Fred is not familiar with this approach because his previous experience as a production manager focused on only whether the plant met the company's budgeted production.

*Required:*

1. Briefly explain to Fred how performance evaluations at his new company will differ from those at his previous company.
2. Give Fred five possible objectives that the new company will use in addition to production level in evaluating Fred's performance. For each objective that you identify, be sure to indicate a plausible metric for measuring that item.

**LO6**

**E25-8 Determining Minimum, Maximum, and Negotiated Transfer Prices**

Coleman Company is a lumber company that also manufactures custom cabinetry. It is made up of two divisions, Lumber and Cabinetry. Division L is responsible for harvesting and preparing lumber for use; Division C produces custom-ordered cabinetry. The lumber produced by Division L has a variable cost of $1.00 per linear foot and full cost of $1.50. Comparable quality wood sells on the open market for $3.00 per linear foot.

*Required:*

1. Assume you are the manager of Division C. Determine the maximum amount you would pay for lumber from Division L.
2. Assume you are the manager of Division L. Determine the minimum amount you would charge for the lumber sold to Division C if you have excess capacity. Repeat assuming you have no excess capacity.
3. Assume you were the president of Coleman and wanted to set a mutually beneficial transfer price. Determine the mutually beneficial transfer price.
4. Explain the possible consequences of simply letting the two division managers negotiate a price.

**LO6**

**E25-9 Identifying Minimum and Maximum Transfer Prices and Determining the Effect on Each Division's Profit**

Womack Company is made up of two divisions, A and B. Division A produces a widget that Division B uses in the production of its product. Variable cost per widget is $0.50; full cost is $0.70. Comparable widgets sell on the open market for $1.10 each. Division A can produce up to 2,000,000 widgets per year but is currently operating at only 50 percent capacity. Division B expects to use 100,000 widgets in the current year.

*Required:*

1. Determine the minimum and maximum transfers prices.
2. Calculate Womack Company's total benefit of having the widgets transferred between these divisions.
3. If the transfer price is set at $0.50 per unit, determine how much profit Division A will receive from the transfer. Determine how much Division B will save by not purchasing the widgets on the open market.
4. If the transfer price is set at $1.10 per unit, determine how much profit Division A will receive from the transfer. Determine how much Division B will save by not purchasing the widgets on the open market.
5. What transfer price would you recommend to split the difference?

## Problems—Set A  Available with McGraw-Hill's Homework Manager

**LO3, 4**

www.mhhe.com/LLPW1e

**PA25-1 Calculating Return on Investment and Residual Income and Determining the Effect of Changes in Sales, Expenses, Invested Assets, and the Hurdle Rate on Each**

Longview Company has the following information available for past year.

|  | Northern Division | Southern Division |
| --- | --- | --- |
| Sales | $1,200,000 | $1,800,000 |
| Cost of goods sold and operating expenses | 900,000 | 1,300,000 |
| Operating Income | $ 300,000 | $ 500,000 |
| Average invested assets | $1,000,000 | $1,500,000 |

The company's hurdle rate is 8 percent.

*Required:*

1. Calculate return on investment (ROI) and residual income for each division for last year.
2. Recalculate ROI and residual income for each division for each independent situation that follows.

   a. Operating income increase by 10 percent.
   b. Operating income decrease by 10 percent.
   c. The company invests $250,000 in each division, an amount that generates $100,000 additional income per division.
   d. Longview changes its hurdle rate to 6 percent.

**PA25-2 Calculating Unknowns and Predicting the Relationship among Return on Investment, Residual Income, and Hurdle Rates**   LO3, 4

The following is partial information for Dupre Company's most recent year of operation. Dupre manufactures pet toys and categorizes its operations into two divisions, Cat and Dog.

|  | Cat Division | Dog Division |
| --- | --- | --- |
| Sales revenue | ? | $600,000 |
| Average invested assets | $2,000,000 | ? |
| Operating income | $ 160,000 | $150,000 |
| Profit margin | 20% | ? |
| Investment turnover | ? | 0.2 |
| Return on investment | ? | ? |
| Residual income | $ 40,000 | $ (30,000) |

*Required:*

1. Without making any calculations, determine whether each division's return on investment is above or below Dupre's hurdle rate. How can you tell?
2. Determine the missing amounts in the preceding table.
3. What is Dupre's hurdle rate?
4. Suppose Dupre has the opportunity to purchase additional assets to help expand the company's market share. The expansion would require an average investment of $2,000,000 and would generate $140,000 in additional income. From Dupre's perspective, is this a viable investment? Why or why not?
5. Suppose the two divisions would equally share the investment and profits from the expansion project. If return on investment is used to evaluate performance, what will each division think about the proposed project?
6. In requirement 5, will either manager's preference change if residual income is used to measure division performance? Explain your answer.

**PA25-3 Identifying Minimum, Maximum, and Mutually Beneficial Transfer Prices**   LO6

Rideaway Corp. is a high-end bicycle manufacturing company that produces mountain bikes. SoftSaddle, Inc. is a division of Rideaway that manufactures bicycle seats. SoftSaddle's seats are used in Rideaway's bikes and are sold to other bike manufacturers. Cost information per seat follows.

| | |
| --- | --- |
| Variable cost | $22.00 |
| Full cost | 27.00 |
| Market price | 40.00 |

In addition, its capacity data follow.

| | |
|---|---|
| Capacity per year | 40,000 seats |
| Current production level | 30,000 seats |

*Required:*

1. Assuming Rideaway produces 3,000 bikes per year, determine the overall benefit of using seats from SoftSaddle instead of purchasing them externally.
2. Determine the maximum price that the bike production facility would be willing to pay to purchase the seats from SoftSaddle. How is the overall benefit split between the two divisions if this transfer price is used?
3. Determine the minimum that SoftSaddle will accept as a transfer price. How is the overall benefit split between the two divisions if this transfer price is used?
4. Determine the mutually beneficial transfer price for the bicycle seats.
5. How would your answer change if SoftSaddle were currently operating at capacity?

**LO6**

**PA25-4 Identifying Minimum, Maximum, and Mutually Beneficial Transfer Prices**

Travel Well, Inc., manufactures a variety of luggage for use by airline passengers. The company has several luggage production divisions as well as a wholly owned subsidiary, SecureLock, that manufactures small padlocks used on luggage. Each piece of luggage that Duffle Bag Division produces has two padlocks for which it previously paid the going market price of $3 each. Financial information for Travel Well's Duffle Bag Division and for SecureLock follow.

| | Duffle Bag Division | SecureLock |
|---|---|---|
| Sales | | |
| 4,500 bags × $150 each | $675,000 | |
| 200,000 locks × $3.00 each | | $600,000 |
| Variable expenses | | |
| 4,500 units × $85.00 each | 382,500 | |
| 200,000 × $0.60 each | | 120,000 |

SecureLock has a production capacity of 250,000 units.

*Required:*

1. Determine how much Travel Well will save on each padlock if Duffle Bag Division obtains them from SecureLock instead of an external supplier.
2. Determine the maximum and minimum transfer prices for the padlocks. Who sets these?
3. Suppose Travel Well has set a transfer price policy of variable cost plus 50 percent for all related-party transactions. Determine how much each party will benefit from the internal transfer.
4. Determine the mutually beneficial transfer price.

## Problems—Set B 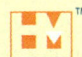  Available with McGraw-Hill's Homework Manager

**LO3, 4**

**PB25-1 Calculating Return on Investment and Residual Income and Determining the Effect of Changes in Sales, Expenses, Invested Assets, and the Hurdle Rate on Each**

Pascall Company has the following information available for the past year.

|  | Eastern Division | Western Division |
|---|---|---|
| Segment sales | $2,200,000 | $1,300,000 |
| Segment cost of goods sold and operating expenses | 1,700,000 | 1,000,000 |
| Segment income | $ 500,000 | $ 300,000 |
| Average invested assets | $3,800,000 | $2,500,000 |

The company's hurdle rate is 10 percent.

1. Determine Pascall's return on investment (ROI) and residual income for each division for last year.
2. Recalculate Pascall's ROI and residual income for each division for each independent situation that follows.

   a. Operating income increases by 10 percent.
   b. Operating income decreases by 10 percent.
   c. The company invests $400,000 in each division, an amount that generates $80,000 additional income per division.
   d. Pascall changes its hurdle rate to 15 percent.

3. For each scenario in requirement 2, indicate which division is performing better.

## PB25-2 Calculating Unknowns and Predicting the Relationship among Return on Investment, Residual Income, and Hurdle Rates

LO3, 4

The following is partial information for Xavier Company's most recent year of operation. Xavier manufactures children's shoes and categorizes its operations into two divisions, Girls and Boys.

|  | Girls Division | Boys Division |
|---|---|---|
| Sales revenue | $2,000,000 | ? |
| Average invested assets | ? | $1,000,000 |
| Operating income | $ 500,000 | $ 300,000 |
| Profit margin | ? | 15% |
| Investment turnover | 1.0 | ? |
| Return on investment | ? | ? |
| Residual income | $ 260,000 | $ 180,000 |

*Required:*

1. Without making any calculations, determine whether each division's return on investment is above or below Xavier's hurdle rate. How can you tell?
2. Determine the missing amounts in the preceding table.
3. What is Xavier's hurdle rate?
4. Suppose Xavier has the opportunity to purchase additional assets to help expand the company's market share. The expansion would require an investment of $4,000,000 and would generate $800,000 in additional income. From Xavier's perspective, is this a viable investment? Why or why not?
5. Suppose the two divisions would equally share the investment and profits from the expansion project. If return on investment is used to evaluate performance, what will each division think about the proposed project?
6. In requirement 5, will either manager's preference change if residual income is used to measure division performance? Explain your answer.

**LO6**

**PB25-3 Identifying Minimum, Maximum, and Mutually Beneficial Transfer Prices**

Snuggle Up Company produces outdoor gear. ZipIt is a division of Snuggle that manufactures unbreakable zippers used in Snuggle's gear and sold to other manufacturers. Cost information per zipper follows.

| | |
|---|---|
| Variable cost | $0.80 |
| Full cost | 1.10 |
| Market price | 3.00 |

In addition, ZipIt's capacity data follow.

| | |
|---|---|
| Capacity per year | 2,000,000 zippers |
| Current production level | 1,500,000 zippers |

*Required:*

1. Assuming Snuggle produces 300,000 sleeping bags per year, what is the overall benefit of using zippers from ZipIt instead of purchasing them externally?
2. Determine the maximum price that the sleeping bag production facility would be willing to pay to purchase the zippers from ZipIt. How is the overall benefit split between the two divisions if this transfer price is used?
3. Determine the minimum that ZipIt will accept as a transfer price. How is the overall benefit split between the two divisions if this transfer price is used?
4. Determine the mutually beneficial transfer price for the zippers.
5. How would your answer change if ZipIt were currently operating at capacity?

**LO6**

**PB25-4 Identifying Minimum, Maximum, and Mutually Beneficial Transfer Prices**

H2-Oh! produces bottled water. The company recently purchased PlastiCo., a manufacturer of plastic bottles. In the past, H2-Oh! has purchased plastic bottles on the open market at $0.25 each. Financial information for the past year for H2-Oh! and PlastiCo. follows.

| | H2-Oh! | PlastiCo. |
|---|---|---|
| Sales | | |
| 500,000 units × $2.00 each | $1,000,000 | |
| 1,200,000 units × $0.25 each | | $300,000 |
| Variable expenses | | |
| 500,000 units × $0.25 each | 125,000 | |
| 1,200,000 × $0.05 each | | 60,000 |

PlastiCo has a production capacity of 2,000,000 units.

*Required:*

1. Determine how much H2-Oh! will save on each bottle if it obtains them from PlastiCo. instead of an external supplier.
2. Determine the maximum and minimum transfer prices for the plastic bottles. Who sets these?
3. Suppose H2-Oh! has determined a transfer price rule of variable cost plus 40 percent for all related-party transactions. Determine how much each party will benefit from the internal transfer.
4. Determine the mutually beneficial transfer price.

# Cases and Projects

**LO6**

**CP25-1 Researching the Effect of Transfer Prices on Taxes**

The problems surrounding transfer pricing are not limited to internal decisions. Companies' transfer prices can have huge implications well beyond departmental profits including significant tax implications.

In September 2006, the U.K.-based pharmaceutical giant, Glaxo SmithKline (GSK), settled an ongoing dispute with the U.S. Internal Revenue Service. In doing so, GSK agreed to pay $3.4 billion dollars in back taxes and interest. This was the largest single tax dispute in U.S. history.

*Required:*

Research the GSK dispute and write a two-page memo summarizing the central issues of the dispute. Include in your summary the position of each side (IRS and GSK) as well as GSK's explanation for the settlement and any impact on company shareholders.

### CP25-2 Researching the Use of the Balanced Scorecard in Business                    LO5

This chapter discussed the use of the balanced scorecard for evaluating managerial and organizational performance. Many companies have adopted this performance measurement in recent years.

*Required:*

Do an Internet search to find an example of a company that has implemented the balanced scorecard and write a brief report of the company's experience. You should include information such as when the company implemented the balanced scorecard, what performance measurement approach it had used previously, any difficulties it experienced with the implementation, and the benefits received from the new method.

### CP25-3 Explaining the Impact of Organizational Structure and Budgetary Processes on      LO1
### Employee Morale

In the last several chapters, you have learned about many aspects of organizational structure, budgeting, and performance evaluation. None of these characteristics of a company operates in isolation: They all interrelate to form an organization's culture and influence employee morale. The following table has several combinations of organizational structure and budgeting preparation style.

| Organizational Structure | Budget Creation Process |
| --- | --- |
| Centralized | Administered |
| Decentralized | Participative |
| Centralized | Participative |
| Decentralized | Administered |

*Required:*

For each combination in the table, write a brief paragraph summarizing both the potential advantages and disadvantages for a company using the combination. Consider the impact on managers and other employees as well as the potential impact on outside parties such as customers or other organizational stakeholders.

# THE HOME DEPOT, INC. 2007 ANNUAL REPORT*

OUR APRONS, YOUR STORE
2007 Annual Report

\* This appendix contains excerpts. Go to the text Web site at www.mhhe.com/LLPW1e for the complete report.

# |DEAR SHAREHOLDERS, ASSOCIATES, CUSTOMERS, SUPPLIERS AND COMMUNITIES:

This past year was one of the most difficult our company has faced. Year-over-year retail sales declined by 2.1 percent, with comp sales down 6.7 percent. Our operating margin declined 186 basis points and our earnings per share from continuing operations were down 11 percent.

We began the year with the objectives of focusing on our retail business, investing in our associates and stores, and improving our customer service. We stayed true to those objectives despite the economic headwinds and invested over $2 billion in five key priorities: **associate engagement, product excitement, product availability, shopping environment and own the pro.** These investments put additional pressure on earnings in a difficult environment, but we are convinced the right long-term strategy starts with the customer experience in our stores. In each priority area, we made significant progress.

## ASSOCIATE ENGAGEMENT:

Our founders emphasized the importance of taking care of our associates who take care of our customers. This is as important today as it was twenty years ago. It is an investment we know will strengthen our market leadership position. This past year, we took significant steps to improve the compensation and recognition of our associates and to build on the expertise in our stores. We implemented a new restricted stock bonus program for our assistant store managers. We are the only retailer of our size to award equity grants at that level of management. For us, it is important that our assistant store managers feel and act like owners. We significantly increased participation and payout of our Success Sharing bonuses for hourly associates and rolled out a new Homer Badge merit program to recognize great customer service. I hope as you shop our stores you will notice the associates who are proudly wearing these badges. We hired more than 2,500 Master Trade Specialists in our plumbing and electrical departments. These associates are licensed plumbers and electricians and provide both knowledgeable service to our customers and great training for associates. As a result of these and other efforts, full time voluntary attrition was down almost 20 percent in 2007.

## PRODUCT EXCITEMENT:

Our customers expect great value and exciting products in our stores. In 2007, as in the past, we focused on meeting those expectations. We invested significantly in merchandising resets, drove product innovation through our successful launch of the Ryobi Lithium One+ line of power tools and our Eco Options program, and revamped product lines to drive greater value for our customers. We are particularly proud of the leadership we maintained in a number of categories including appliances, outdoor living, live goods, and paint.

## PRODUCT AVAILABILITY:

In 2007, we took an important first step in transforming our supply chain. We piloted a new distribution network and technology - Rapid Deployment Centers (RDCs). The pilot was successful, and we will be rolling out RDCs throughout 2008 and 2009. We are confident that our future supply chain will dramatically improve our supply chain efficiency, improve our in stock levels, improve our asset efficiency, and improve our ability to meet increasingly differentiated customer needs.

## SHOPPING ENVIRONMENT:

Our store base is getting older, and we have to protect one of our most important assets. We increased store maintenance in 2007, spending 38 percent more than our 2006 maintenance levels and two times our 2005 maintenance levels. We developed a sustainable programmatic approach to maintenance, with specific schedules for polishing floors, remodeling restrooms, and replacing major equipment such as air conditioners and service desks. As shown through our "Voice of the Customer" surveys, our customers appreciate these investments.

## OWN THE PRO:

We know that the professional customer is a critically important customer for us. This year we rolled out several programs aimed at better serving our pros. One of these is our pro bid room, which allows us to better manage large customer orders. Our professional customers look to us for the right products in the right quantities to make their jobs easier. We reinforced our job lot quantity program in our stores and revised our delivery service for better utilization. We are also leveraging our customer data to build stronger relationships with this key customer segment.

## INTERNATIONAL:

While discussing progress in 2007, I'd like to give special recognition to our international businesses in Mexico, Canada and China. Our stores in Mexico had double digit positive comps for the year. Our stores in Canada posted positive comps. In China, once we launched our Home Depot brand in August 2007, our stores posted positive comps. Our international stores contributed almost 10 percent of sales and 12 percent of operating profit in 2007. These results demonstrate how well our format translates and the sizable opportunity to

## VALUES WHEEL

expand to new areas such as Guam, where we opened our first store this year.

As I complete my first year in this role, I want to thank the Board of Directors for their support and dedication. I would especially like to recognize our directors that are retiring this year: John Clendenin, Claudio González, Mitch Hart, and Ken Langone – one of our founders. Their guidance and counsel has been instrumental in the success of our company.

### OUR STRATEGY IS SIMPLE:

We have clearly defined The Home Depot as a retail business. The sale of HD Supply in August of 2007 was the critical step in achieving that clarity and focus. We also defined our capital allocation strategy: We will be focused on improving our return on invested capital and will benchmark all uses of excess cash against the value created for shareholders through share repurchases. With that in mind, we used the proceeds from the sale of HD Supply and cash on hand to buy back $10.7 billion of stock. This puts us approximately halfway through our announced $22.5 billion recapitalization plan. Our cash flow will help determine the timing of the remaining steps in the recapitalization plan, as we look to maintain an adjusted debt/EBITDAR ratio of 2.5 times. We are targeting a payout ratio of 30 percent, amongst the highest ratios in retail.

Our strategy: focus on our retail business, invest in our people, improve our stores, bring great products at great value to our customers, drive a high return on invested capital, and return excess cash to our shareholders.

For 2008, we are expecting a year every bit as challenging as 2007. We plan on opening fewer stores than has been our historical practice as we continue to invest and sharpen our focus on existing stores. We will continue to invest in our business along the five priorities set

out in 2007. As part of our investment plan, we have aggressive plans to build out our U.S. supply chain, to put more associates on the selling floor through a major "aprons on the floor" initiative, and to take the first step in transforming our information technology infrastructure by converting our Canadian business to an Enterprise Resource Planning platform focused on enhancing our merchandising and customer facing activities. As our market improves and as the benefits of these investments in our business take hold, we look forward over the next four years to returning to a double digit operating margin.

We will also continue to build relationships and strengthen ties with our communities. This has been a hallmark of The Home Depot. One of the best parts of my job is hearing about the extraordinary things our associates do to help each other, help our customers and help our communities every day. We are a values based business, and we do our best to live and celebrate the values represented on the wheel depicted on this page. We recognize the self-reinforcing strength of these values builds great customer service. I hope, as you shop in our stores, you will notice our continuing improvement and the value of the investments we are making.

*Frank*

Francis S. Blake
Chairman & Chief Executive Officer
April 3, 2008

**Item 8.    Financial Statements and Supplementary Data.**

**Management's Responsibility for Financial Statements**

The financial statements presented in this Annual Report have been prepared with integrity and objectivity and are the responsibility of the management of The Home Depot, Inc. These financial statements have been prepared in conformity with U.S. generally accepted accounting principles and properly reflect certain estimates and judgments based upon the best available information.

The financial statements of the Company have been audited by KPMG LLP, an independent registered public accounting firm. Their accompanying report is based upon an audit conducted in accordance with the standards of the Public Company Accounting Oversight Board (United States).

The Audit Committee of the Board of Directors, consisting solely of outside directors, meets five times a year with the independent registered public accounting firm, the internal auditors and representatives of management to discuss auditing and financial reporting matters. In addition, a telephonic meeting is held prior to each quarterly earnings release. The Audit Committee retains the independent registered public accounting firm and regularly reviews the internal accounting controls, the activities of the independent registered public accounting firm and internal auditors and the financial condition of the Company. Both the Company's independent registered public accounting firm and the internal auditors have free access to the Audit Committee.

**Management's Report on Internal Control over Financial Reporting**

Our management is responsible for establishing and maintaining adequate internal control over financial reporting, as such term is defined in Rules 13a-15(f) promulgated under the Securities Exchange Act of 1934, as amended. Under the supervision and with the participation of our management, including our chief executive officer and chief financial officer, we conducted an evaluation of the effectiveness of our internal control over financial reporting as of February 3, 2008 based on the framework in *Internal Control – Integrated Framework* issued by the Committee of Sponsoring Organizations of the Treadway Commission (COSO). Based on our evaluation, our management concluded that our internal control over financial reporting was effective as of February 3, 2008 in providing reasonable assurance regarding the reliability of financial reporting and the preparation of financial statements for external purposes in accordance with generally accepted accounting principles. The effectiveness of our internal control over financial reporting as of February 3, 2008 has been audited by KPMG LLP, an independent registered public accounting firm, as stated in their report which is included on page 32 in this Form 10-K.

**/s/ FRANCIS S. BLAKE**

**/s/ CAROL B. TOMÉ**

**Francis S. Blake**
**Chairman &**
**Chief Executive Officer**

**Carol B. Tomé**
**Chief Financial Officer &**
**Executive Vice President – Corporate**
**Services**

## Report of Independent Registered Public Accounting Firm

The Board of Directors and Stockholders
The Home Depot, Inc.:

We have audited The Home Depot Inc.'s internal control over financial reporting as of February 3, 2008, based on criteria established in *Internal Control – Integrated Framework* issued by the Committee of Sponsoring Organizations of the Treadway Commission (COSO). The Home Depot Inc.'s management is responsible for maintaining effective internal control over financial reporting and for its assessment of the effectiveness of internal control over financial reporting, included in the accompanying Management's Report on Internal Control Over Financial Reporting. Our responsibility is to express an opinion on the Company's internal control over financial reporting based on our audit.

We conducted our audit in accordance with the standards of the Public Company Accounting Oversight Board (United States). Those standards require that we plan and perform the audit to obtain reasonable assurance about whether effective internal control over financial reporting was maintained in all material respects. Our audit included obtaining an understanding of internal control over financial reporting, assessing the risk that a material weakness exists, and testing and evaluating the design and operating effectiveness of internal control based on the assessed risk. Our audit also included performing such other procedures as we considered necessary in the circumstances. We believe that our audit provides a reasonable basis for our opinion.

A company's internal control over financial reporting is a process designed to provide reasonable assurance regarding the reliability of financial reporting and the preparation of financial statements for external purposes in accordance with generally accepted accounting principles. A company's internal control over financial reporting includes those policies and procedures that (1) pertain to the maintenance of records that, in reasonable detail, accurately and fairly reflect the transactions and dispositions of the assets of the company; (2) provide reasonable assurance that transactions are recorded as necessary to permit preparation of financial statements in accordance with generally accepted accounting principles, and that receipts and expenditures of the company are being made only in accordance with authorizations of management and directors of the company; and (3) provide reasonable assurance regarding prevention or timely detection of unauthorized acquisition, use, or disposition of the company's assets that could have a material effect on the financial statements.

Because of its inherent limitations, internal control over financial reporting may not prevent or detect misstatements. Also, projections of any evaluation of effectiveness to future periods are subject to the risk that controls may become inadequate because of changes in conditions, or that the degree of compliance with the policies or procedures may deteriorate.

In our opinion, The Home Depot, Inc. maintained, in all material respects, effective internal control over financial reporting as of February 3, 2008, based on criteria established in *Internal Control – Integrated Framework* issued by the Committee of Sponsoring Organizations of the Treadway Commission.

We also have audited, in accordance with the standards of the Public Company Accounting Oversight Board (United States), the Consolidated Balance Sheets of The Home Depot, Inc. and subsidiaries as of February 3, 2008 and January 28, 2007, and the related Consolidated Statements of Earnings, Stockholders' Equity and Comprehensive Income, and Cash Flows for each of the fiscal years in the three-year period ended February 3, 2008, and our report dated March 28, 2008 expressed an unqualified opinion on those consolidated financial statements.

/s/ KPMG LLP

Atlanta, Georgia
March 28, 2008

**Report of Independent Registered Public Accounting Firm**

The Board of Directors and Stockholders
The Home Depot, Inc.:

We have audited the accompanying Consolidated Balance Sheets of The Home Depot, Inc. and subsidiaries as of February 3, 2008 and January 28, 2007, and the related Consolidated Statements of Earnings, Stockholders' Equity and Comprehensive Income, and Cash Flows for each of the fiscal years in the three-year period ended February 3, 2008. These Consolidated Financial Statements are the responsibility of the Company's management. Our responsibility is to express an opinion on these Consolidated Financial Statements based on our audits.

We conducted our audits in accordance with the standards of the Public Company Accounting Oversight Board (United States). Those standards require that we plan and perform the audit to obtain reasonable assurance about whether the financial statements are free of material misstatement. An audit includes examining, on a test basis, evidence supporting the amounts and disclosures in the financial statements. An audit also includes assessing the accounting principles used and significant estimates made by management, as well as evaluating the overall financial statement presentation. We believe that our audits provide a reasonable basis for our opinion.

In our opinion, the Consolidated Financial Statements referred to above present fairly, in all material respects, the financial position of The Home Depot, Inc. and subsidiaries as of February 3, 2008 and January 28, 2007, and the results of their operations and their cash flows for each of the fiscal years in the three-year period ended February 3, 2008, in conformity with U.S. generally accepted accounting principles.

As discussed in Note 6 to the consolidated financial statements, effective January 29, 2007, the beginning of the fiscal year ended February 3, 2008, the Company adopted Financial Accounting Standards Board Interpretation No. 48, *Accounting for Uncertainty in Income Taxes* . Also, as discussed in Note 3 to the consolidated financial statements, effective January 30, 2006, the beginning of the fiscal year ended January 28, 2007, the Company adopted Securities and Exchange Commission Staff Accounting Bulletin No. 108, *Considering the Effects of Prior Year Misstatements when Quantifying Misstatements in the Current Year Financial Statements* .

We also have audited, in accordance with the standards of the Public Company Accounting Oversight Board (United States), The Home Depot, Inc.'s internal control over financial reporting as of February 3, 2008, based on criteria established in *Internal Control – Integrated Framework* issued by the Committee of Sponsoring Organizations of the Treadway Commission (COSO), and our report dated March 28, 2008 expressed an unqualified opinion on the effectiveness of the Company's internal control over financial reporting.

/s/ KPMG LLP

Atlanta, Georgia
March 28, 2008

**THE HOME DEPOT, INC. AND SUBSIDIARIES**

**CONSOLIDATED STATEMENTS OF EARNINGS**

|  | Fiscal Year Ended [1] | | |
|---|---|---|---|
| *amounts in millions, except per share data* | February 3, 2008 | January 28, 2007 | January 29, 2006 |
| **NET SALES** | $ 77,349 | $ 79,022 | $ 77,019 |
| Cost of Sales | 51,352 | 52,476 | 51,081 |
| **GROSS PROFIT** | 25,997 | 26,546 | 25,938 |
| Operating Expenses: | | | |
| Selling, General and Administrative | 17,053 | 16,106 | 15,480 |
| Depreciation and Amortization | 1,702 | 1,574 | 1,411 |
| Total Operating Expenses | 18,755 | 17,680 | 16,891 |
| **OPERATING INCOME** | 7,242 | 8,866 | 9,047 |
| Interest (Income) Expense: | | | |
| Interest and Investment Income | (74) | (27) | (62) |
| Interest Expense | 696 | 391 | 142 |
| Interest, net | 622 | 364 | 80 |
| **EARNINGS FROM CONTINUING OPERATIONS BEFORE PROVISION FOR INCOME TAXES** | 6,620 | 8,502 | 8,967 |
| Provision for Income Taxes | 2,410 | 3,236 | 3,326 |
| **EARNINGS FROM CONTINUING OPERATIONS** | 4,210 | 5,266 | 5,641 |
| **EARNINGS FROM DISCONTINUED OPERATIONS, NET OF TAX** | 185 | 495 | 197 |
| **NET EARNINGS** | $ 4,395 | $ 5,761 | $ 5,838 |
| Weighted Average Common Shares | 1,849 | 2,054 | 2,138 |
| **BASIC EARNINGS PER SHARE FROM CONTINUING OPERATIONS** | $ 2.28 | $ 2.56 | $ 2.64 |
| **BASIC EARNINGS PER SHARE FROM DISCONTINUED OPERATIONS** | $ 0.10 | $ 0.24 | $ 0.09 |
| **BASIC EARNINGS PER SHARE** | $ 2.38 | $ 2.80 | $ 2.73 |
| Diluted Weighted Average Common Shares | 1,856 | 2,062 | 2,147 |
| **DILUTED EARNINGS PER SHARE FROM CONTINUING OPERATIONS** | $ 2.27 | $ 2.55 | $ 2.63 |
| **DILUTED EARNINGS PER SHARE FROM DISCONTINUED OPERATIONS** | $ 0.10 | $ 0.24 | $ 0.09 |
| **DILUTED EARNINGS PER SHARE** | $ 2.37 | $ 2.79 | $ 2.72 |

*(1)    Fiscal year ended February 3, 2008 includes 53 weeks. Fiscal years ended January 28, 2007 and January 29, 2006 include 52 weeks.*

*See accompanying Notes to Consolidated Financial Statements.*

**THE HOME DEPOT, INC. AND SUBSIDIARIES**

**CONSOLIDATED BALANCE SHEETS**

| *amounts in millions, except share and per share data* | February 3, 2008 | January 28, 2007 |
|---|---:|---:|
| **ASSETS** | | |
| Current Assets: | | |
| Cash and Cash Equivalents | $ 445 | $ 600 |
| Short-Term Investments | 12 | 14 |
| Receivables, net | 1,259 | 3,223 |
| Merchandise Inventories | 11,731 | 12,822 |
| Other Current Assets | 1,227 | 1,341 |
| Total Current Assets | 14,674 | 18,000 |
| Property and Equipment, at cost: | | |
| Land | 8,398 | 8,355 |
| Buildings | 16,642 | 15,215 |
| Furniture, Fixtures and Equipment | 8,050 | 7,799 |
| Leasehold Improvements | 1,390 | 1,391 |
| Construction in Progress | 1,435 | 1,123 |
| Capital Leases | 497 | 475 |
| | 36,412 | 34,358 |
| Less Accumulated Depreciation and Amortization | 8,936 | 7,753 |
| Net Property and Equipment | 27,476 | 26,605 |
| Notes Receivable | 342 | 343 |
| Goodwill | 1,209 | 6,314 |
| Other Assets | 623 | 1,001 |
| Total Assets | $ 44,324 | $ 52,263 |
| **LIABILITIES AND STOCKHOLDERS' EQUITY** | | |
| Current Liabilities: | | |
| Short-Term Debt | $ 1,747 | $ — |
| Accounts Payable | 5,732 | 7,356 |
| Accrued Salaries and Related Expenses | 1,094 | 1,307 |
| Sales Taxes Payable | 445 | 475 |
| Deferred Revenue | 1,474 | 1,634 |
| Income Taxes Payable | 60 | 217 |
| Current Installments of Long-Term Debt | 300 | 18 |
| Other Accrued Expenses | 1,854 | 1,924 |
| Total Current Liabilities | 12,706 | 12,931 |
| Long-Term Debt, excluding current installments | 11,383 | 11,643 |
| Other Long-Term Liabilities | 1,833 | 1,243 |
| Deferred Income Taxes | 688 | 1,416 |
| Total Liabilities | 26,610 | 27,233 |
| **STOCKHOLDERS' EQUITY** | | |
| Common Stock, par value $0.05; authorized: 10 billion shares; issued 1.698 billion shares at February 3, 2008 and 2.421 billion shares at January 28, 2007; outstanding 1.690 billion shares at February 3, 2008 and 1.970 billion shares at January 28, 2007 | 85 | 121 |
| Paid-In Capital | 5,800 | 7,930 |
| Retained Earnings | 11,388 | 33,052 |
| Accumulated Other Comprehensive Income | 755 | 310 |
| Treasury Stock, at cost, 8 million shares at February 3, 2008 and 451 million shares at January 28, 2007 | (314) | (16,383) |
| Total Stockholders' Equity | 17,714 | 25,030 |
| Total Liabilities and Stockholders' Equity | $ 44,324 | $ 52,263 |

*See accompanying Notes to Consolidated Financial Statements.*

## THE HOME DEPOT, INC. AND SUBSIDIARIES

## CONSOLIDATED STATEMENTS OF STOCKHOLDERS' EQUITY AND COMPREHENSIVE INCOME

| amounts in millions, except per share data | Common Stock | | Paid-In Capital | Retained Earnings | Accumulated Other Comprehensive Income (Loss) | Treasury Stock | | Stockholders' Equity | Total Comprehensive Income |
|---|---|---|---|---|---|---|---|---|---|
| | Shares | Amount | | | | Shares | Amount | | |
| BALANCE, JANUARY 30, 2005 | 2,385 $ | 119 $ | 6,542 $ | 23,962 $ | 227 | (200) $ | (6,692) $ | 24,158 | |
| Net Earnings | — | — | — | 5,838 | — | — | — | 5,838 | $ 5,838 |
| Shares Issued Under Employee Stock Plans | 16 | 1 | 409 | — | — | — | — | 410 | |
| Tax Effect of Sale of Option Shares by Employees | — | — | 24 | — | — | — | — | 24 | |
| Translation Adjustments | — | — | — | — | 182 | — | — | 182 | 182 |
| Stock Options, Awards and Amortization of Restricted Stock | — | — | 174 | — | — | — | — | 174 | |
| Repurchase of Common Stock | — | — | — | — | — | (77) | (3,020) | (3,020) | |
| Cash Dividends ($0.40 per share) | — | — | — | (857) | — | — | — | (857) | |
| Comprehensive Income | | | | | | | | | $ 6,020 |
| BALANCE, JANUARY 29, 2006 | 2,401 $ | 120 $ | 7,149 $ | 28,943 $ | 409 | (277) $ | (9,712) $ | 26,909 | |
| Cumulative Effect of Adjustment Resulting from the Adoption of SAB 108, net of tax | — | — | 201 | (257) | — | — | — | (56) | |
| ADJUSTED BALANCE, JANUARY 29, 2006 | 2,401 $ | 120 $ | 7,350 $ | 28,686 $ | 409 | (277) $ | (9,712) $ | 26,853 | |
| Net Earnings | — | — | — | 5,761 | — | — | — | 5,761 | $ 5,761 |
| Shares Issued Under Employee Stock Plans | 20 | 1 | 351 | — | — | — | — | 352 | |
| Tax Effect of Sale of Option Shares by Employees | — | — | 18 | — | — | — | — | 18 | |
| Translation Adjustments | — | — | — | — | (77) | — | — | (77) | (77) |
| Cash Flow Hedges | — | — | — | — | (22) | — | — | (22) | (22) |
| Stock Options, Awards and Amortization of Restricted Stock | — | — | 296 | — | — | — | — | 296 | |
| Repurchase of Common Stock | — | — | — | — | — | (174) | (6,671) | (6,671) | |
| Cash Dividends ($0.675 per share) | — | — | — | (1,395) | — | — | — | (1,395) | |
| Other | — | — | (85) | — | — | — | — | (85) | |
| Comprehensive Income | | | | | | | | | $ 5,662 |
| BALANCE, JANUARY 28, 2007 | 2,421 $ | 121 $ | 7,930 $ | 33,052 $ | 310 | (451) $ | (16,383) $ | 25,030 | |
| Cumulative Effect of the Adoption of FIN 48 | — | — | — | (111) | — | — | — | (111) | |
| Net Earnings | — | — | — | 4,395 | — | — | — | 4,395 | $ 4,395 |
| Shares Issued Under Employee Stock Plans | 12 | 1 | 239 | — | — | — | — | 240 | |
| Tax Effect of Sale of Option Shares by Employees | — | — | 4 | — | — | — | — | 4 | |
| Translation Adjustments | — | — | — | — | 455 | — | — | 455 | 455 |
| Cash Flow Hedges | — | — | — | — | (10) | — | — | (10) | (10) |
| Stock Options, Awards and Amortization of Restricted Stock | — | — | 206 | — | — | — | — | 206 | |
| Repurchase of Common Stock | — | — | — | — | — | (292) | (10,815) | (10,815) | |
| Retirement of Treasury Stock | (735) | (37) | (2,608) | (24,239) | — | 735 | 26,884 | — | |
| Cash Dividends ($0.90 per share) | — | — | — | (1,709) | — | — | — | (1,709) | |
| Other | — | — | 29 | — | — | — | — | 29 | |
| Comprehensive Income | | | | | | | | | $ 4,840 |
| BALANCE, FEBRUARY 3, 2008 | 1,698 $ | 85 $ | 5,800 $ | 11,388 $ | 755 | (8) $ | (314) $ | 17,714 | |

*See accompanying Notes to Consolidated Financial Statements.*

**THE HOME DEPOT, INC. AND SUBSIDIARIES**

**CONSOLIDATED STATEMENTS OF CASH FLOWS**

| | Fiscal Year Ended [1] | | |
| --- | --- | --- | --- |
| amounts in millions | February 3, 2008 | January 28, 2007 | January 29, 2006 |
| **CASH FLOWS FROM OPERATING ACTIVITIES:** | | | |
| Net Earnings | $ 4,395 | $ 5,761 | $ 5,838 |
| Reconciliation of Net Earnings to Net Cash Provided by Operating Activities: | | | |
| Depreciation and Amortization | 1,906 | 1,886 | 1,579 |
| Stock-Based Compensation Expense | 207 | 297 | 175 |
| Changes in Assets and Liabilities, net of the effects of acquisitions and disposition: | | | |
| Decrease (Increase) in Receivables, net | 116 | 96 | (358) |
| Increase in Merchandise Inventories | (491) | (563) | (971) |
| Decrease (Increase) in Other Current Assets | 109 | (225) | 16 |
| (Decrease) Increase in Accounts Payable and Accrued Liabilities | (465) | 531 | 148 |
| (Decrease) Increase in Deferred Revenue | (159) | (123) | 209 |
| (Decrease) Increase in Income Taxes Payable | — | (172) | 175 |
| (Decrease) Increase in Deferred Income Taxes | (348) | 46 | (609) |
| Increase (Decrease) in Other Long-Term Liabilities | 186 | (51) | 151 |
| Other | 271 | 178 | 267 |
| Net Cash Provided by Operating Activities | 5,727 | 7,661 | 6,620 |
| **CASH FLOWS FROM INVESTING ACTIVITIES:** | | | |
| Capital Expenditures, net of $19, $49 and $51 of non-cash capital expenditures in fiscal 2007, 2006 and 2005, respectively | (3,558) | (3,542) | (3,881) |
| Proceeds from Sale of Business, net | 8,337 | — | — |
| Payments for Businesses Acquired, net | (13) | (4,268) | (2,546) |
| Proceeds from Sales of Property and Equipment | 318 | 138 | 164 |
| Purchases of Investments | (11,225) | (5,409) | (18,230) |
| Proceeds from Sales and Maturities of Investments | 10,899 | 5,434 | 19,907 |
| Net Cash Provided by (Used in) Investing Activities | 4,758 | (7,647) | (4,586) |
| **CASH FLOWS FROM FINANCING ACTIVITIES:** | | | |
| Proceeds from (Repayments of) Short-Term Borrowings, net | 1,734 | (900) | 900 |
| Proceeds from Long-Term Borrowings, net of discount | — | 8,935 | 995 |
| Repayments of Long-Term Debt | (20) | (509) | (24) |
| Repurchases of Common Stock | (10,815) | (6,684) | (3,040) |
| Proceeds from Sale of Common Stock | 276 | 381 | 414 |
| Cash Dividends Paid to Stockholders | (1,709) | (1,395) | (857) |
| Other Financing Activities | (105) | (31) | (136) |
| Net Cash Used in Financing Activities | (10,639) | (203) | (1,748) |
| (Decrease) Increase in Cash and Cash Equivalents | (154) | (189) | 286 |
| Effect of Exchange Rate Changes on Cash and Cash Equivalents | (1) | (4) | 1 |
| Cash and Cash Equivalents at Beginning of Year | 600 | 793 | 506 |
| Cash and Cash Equivalents at End of Year | $ 445 | $ 600 | $ 793 |
| **SUPPLEMENTAL DISCLOSURE OF CASH PAYMENTS MADE FOR:** | | | |
| Interest, net of interest capitalized | $ 672 | $ 270 | $ 114 |
| Income Taxes | $ 2,524 | $ 3,963 | $ 3,860 |

(1)    Fiscal year ended February 3, 2008 includes 53 weeks. Fiscal years ended January 28, 2007 and January 29, 2006 include 52 weeks.

See accompanying Notes to Consolidated Financial Statements.

**NOTES TO CONSOLIDATED FINANCIAL STATEMENTS**

## 1.    SUMMARY OF SIGNIFICANT ACCOUNTING POLICIES

### Business, Consolidation and Presentation

The Home Depot, Inc. and its subsidiaries (the "Company") operate The Home Depot stores, which are full-service, warehouse-style stores averaging approximately 105,000 square feet in size. The stores stock approximately 35,000 to 45,000 different kinds of building materials, home improvement supplies and lawn and garden products that are sold to do-it-yourself customers, do-it-for-me customers, home improvement contractors, tradespeople and building maintenance professionals. In addition, the Company operates EXPO Design Center stores ("EXPO"), which offer products and services primarily related to design and renovation projects. At the end of fiscal 2007, the Company was operating 2,234 stores in total, which included 1,950 The Home Depot stores, 34 EXPO stores, five Yardbirds stores and two THD Design Center stores in the United States, including the territories of Puerto Rico, the Virgin Islands and Guam ("U.S."), 165 The Home Depot stores in Canada, 66 The Home Depot stores in Mexico and 12 The Home Depot stores in China.

Information related to the Company's discontinued HD Supply business is discussed in Note 2. The Consolidated Financial Statements include the accounts of the Company and its wholly-owned subsidiaries. All significant intercompany transactions have been eliminated in consolidation.

### Fiscal Year

The Company's fiscal year is a 52- or 53-week period ending on the Sunday nearest to January 31. Fiscal year ended February 3, 2008 ("fiscal 2007") includes 53 weeks and fiscal years ended January 28, 2007 ("fiscal 2006") and January 29, 2006 ("fiscal 2005") include 52 weeks.

### Use of Estimates

Management of the Company has made a number of estimates and assumptions relating to the reporting of assets and liabilities, the disclosure of contingent assets and liabilities, and reported amounts of revenues and expenses in preparing these financial statements in conformity with generally accepted accounting principles in the U.S. Actual results could differ from these estimates.

### Fair Value of Financial Instruments

The carrying amounts of Cash and Cash Equivalents, Receivables, Short-Term Debt and Accounts Payable approximate fair value due to the short-term maturities of these financial instruments. The fair value of the Company's investments is discussed under the caption "Short-Term Investments" in this Note 1. The fair value of the Company's Long-Term Debt is discussed in Note 5.

### Cash Equivalents

The Company considers all highly liquid investments purchased with original maturities of three months or less to be cash equivalents. The Company's Cash Equivalents are carried at fair market value and consist primarily of high-grade commercial paper, money market funds and U.S. government agency securities.

### Short-Term Investments

Short-Term Investments are recorded at fair value based on current market rates and are classified as available-for-sale.

### Accounts Receivable

The Company has an agreement with a third-party service provider who directly extends credit to customers, manages the Company's private label credit card program and owns the related receivables. We evaluated the third-party entities holding the receivables under the program and concluded that they should not be consolidated by the Company in accordance with the provisions of Financial Accounting Standards Board ("FASB") Interpretation No. 46(R), "Consolidation of Variable Interest Entities." The agreement with the third-party service provider expires in 2011, with the Company having the option, but no obligation, to purchase the receivables at the end of the agreement. The deferred interest charges incurred by the Company for its deferred financing programs offered to its customers are included in Cost of Sales. The interchange fees charged to the Company for the customers' use of the cards and the profit sharing with the third-party administrator are included in Selling, General and Administrative expenses ("SG&A").

In addition, certain subsidiaries of the Company extend credit directly to customers in the ordinary course of business. The receivables due from customers were $57 million and $1.8 billion as of February 3, 2008 and January 28, 2007, respectively, a decrease resulting from the sale of HD Supply. The Company's valuation reserve related to accounts receivable was not material to the Consolidated Financial Statements of the Company as of the end of fiscal 2007 or 2006.

### Merchandise Inventories

The majority of the Company's Merchandise Inventories are stated at the lower of cost (first-in, first-out) or market, as determined by the retail inventory method. As the inventory retail value is adjusted regularly to reflect market conditions, the inventory valued using the retail method approximates the lower of cost or market. Certain subsidiaries, including retail operations in Mexico and China, and distribution centers record Merchandise Inventories at the lower of cost (first-in, first-out) or market, as determined by the cost method. These Merchandise Inventories represent approximately 11% of the total Merchandise Inventories balance. The Company evaluates the inventory valued using the cost method at the end of each quarter to ensure that it is carried at the lower of cost or market. The valuation allowance for Merchandise Inventories valued under the cost method was not material to the Consolidated Financial Statements of the Company as of the end of fiscal 2007 or 2006.

Independent physical inventory counts or cycle counts are taken on a regular basis in each store and distribution center to ensure that amounts reflected in the accompanying Consolidated Financial Statements for Merchandise Inventories are properly stated. During the period between physical inventory counts in stores, the Company accrues for estimated losses related to shrink on a store-by-store basis based on historical shrink results and current trends in the business. Shrink (or in the case of excess inventory, "swell") is the difference between the recorded amount of inventory and the physical inventory. Shrink may occur due to theft, loss, inaccurate records for the receipt of inventory or deterioration of goods, among other things.

## Income Taxes

The Company provides for federal, state and foreign income taxes currently payable, as well as for those deferred due to timing differences between reporting income and expenses for financial statement purposes versus tax purposes. Federal, state and foreign tax benefits are recorded as a reduction of income taxes. Deferred tax assets and liabilities are recognized for the future tax consequences attributable to temporary differences between the financial statement carrying amounts of existing assets and liabilities and their respective tax bases. Deferred tax assets and liabilities are measured using enacted income tax rates expected to apply to taxable income in the years in which those temporary differences are expected to be recovered or settled. The effect of a change in income tax rates is recognized as income or expense in the period that includes the enactment date.

The Company and its eligible subsidiaries file a consolidated U.S. federal income tax return. Non-U.S. subsidiaries and certain U.S. subsidiaries, which are consolidated for financial reporting purposes, are not eligible to be included in the Company's consolidated U.S. federal income tax return. Separate provisions for income taxes have been determined for these entities. The Company intends to reinvest substantially all of the unremitted earnings of its non-U.S. subsidiaries and postpone their remittance indefinitely. Accordingly, no provision for U.S. income taxes for these non-U.S. subsidiaries was recorded in the accompanying Consolidated Statements of Earnings.

## Depreciation and Amortization

The Company's Buildings, Furniture, Fixtures and Equipment are recorded at cost and depreciated using the straight-line method over the estimated useful lives of the assets. Leasehold Improvements are amortized using the straight-line method over the original term of the lease or the useful life of the improvement, whichever is shorter. The Company's Property and Equipment is depreciated using the following estimated useful lives:

| | Life |
|---|---|
| Buildings | 10-45 years |
| Furniture, Fixtures and Equipment | 3-20 years |
| Leasehold Improvements | 5-45 years |

## Capitalized Software Costs

The Company capitalizes certain costs related to the acquisition and development of software and amortizes these costs using the straight-line method over the estimated useful life of the software, which is three to six years. These costs are included in Furniture, Fixtures and Equipment in the accompanying Consolidated Balance Sheets. Certain development costs not meeting the criteria for capitalization are expensed as incurred.

## Revenues

The Company recognizes revenue, net of estimated returns and sales tax, at the time the customer takes possession of merchandise or receives services. The liability for sales returns is estimated based on historical return levels. When the Company receives payment from customers before the customer has taken possession of the merchandise or the service has been performed, the amount received is recorded as Deferred Revenue in the accompanying Consolidated Balance Sheets until the sale or service is complete. The Company also records Deferred Revenue for the sale of gift cards and recognizes this revenue upon the redemption of gift cards in Net Sales. Gift card breakage income is recognized based upon historical redemption patterns and represents the balance of gift cards for which the Company believes the likelihood of redemption by the customer is remote. During fiscal 2007, 2006 and 2005, the Company recognized $36 million, $33 million and $52 million, respectively, of gift card breakage income. Fiscal 2005 was the first year in which the Company recognized gift card breakage income, and therefore, the amount recognized includes the gift card breakage income related to gift cards sold since the inception of the gift card program. This income is recorded as other income and is included in the accompanying Consolidated Statements of Earnings as a reduction in SG&A.

## Services Revenue

Net Sales include services revenue generated through a variety of installation, home maintenance and professional service programs. In these programs, the customer selects and purchases material for a project and the Company provides or arranges professional installation. These programs are offered through the Company's stores. Under certain programs, when the Company provides or arranges the installation of a project and the subcontractor provides material as part of the installation, both the material and labor are included in services revenue. The Company recognizes this revenue when the service for the customer is complete.

All payments received prior to the completion of services are recorded in Deferred Revenue in the accompanying Consolidated Balance Sheets. Services revenue was $3.5 billion, $3.8 billion and $3.5 billion for fiscal 2007, 2006 and 2005, respectively.

## Self-Insurance

The Company is self-insured for certain losses related to general liability, product liability, automobile, workers' compensation and medical claims. The expected ultimate cost for claims incurred as of the balance sheet date is not discounted and is recognized as a liability. The expected ultimate cost of claims is estimated based upon analysis of historical data and actuarial estimates.

## Prepaid Advertising

Television and radio advertising production costs, along with media placement costs, are expensed when the advertisement first appears. Included in Other Current Assets in the accompanying Consolidated Balance Sheets are $31 million and $44 million, respectively, at the end of fiscal 2007 and 2006 relating to prepayments of production costs for print and broadcast advertising as well as sponsorship promotions.

## Vendor Allowances

Vendor allowances primarily consist of volume rebates that are earned as a result of attaining certain purchase levels and advertising co-op allowances for the promotion of vendors' products that are typically based on guaranteed minimum amounts with additional amounts being earned for attaining certain purchase levels. These vendor allowances are accrued as earned, with those allowances received as a result of attaining certain purchase levels accrued over the incentive period based on estimates of purchases.

Volume rebates and certain advertising co-op allowances earned are initially recorded as a reduction in Merchandise Inventories and a subsequent reduction in Cost of Sales when the related product is sold. Certain advertising co-op allowances that are reimbursements of specific, incremental and identifiable costs incurred to promote vendors' products are recorded as an offset against advertising expense. In fiscal 2007, 2006 and 2005, gross advertising expense was $1.2 billion, $1.2 billion and $1.1 billion, respectively, which was recorded in SG&A. Advertising co-op allowances were $120 million, $83 million and $50 million for fiscal 2007, 2006 and 2005, respectively, and were recorded as an offset to advertising expense in SG&A.

## Cost of Sales

Cost of Sales includes the actual cost of merchandise sold and services performed, the cost of transportation of merchandise from vendors to the Company's stores, locations or customers, the operating cost of the Company's sourcing and distribution network and the cost of deferred interest programs offered through the Company's private label credit card program.

The cost of handling and shipping merchandise from the Company's stores, locations or distribution centers to the customer is classified as SG&A. The cost of shipping and handling, including internal costs and payments to third parties, classified as SG&A was $571 million, $545 million and $480 million in fiscal 2007, 2006 and 2005, respectively.

## Goodwill and Other Intangible Assets

Goodwill represents the excess of purchase price over the fair value of net assets acquired. The Company does not amortize goodwill, but does assess the recoverability of goodwill in the third quarter of each fiscal year by determining whether the fair value of each reporting unit supports its carrying value. The fair values of the Company's identified reporting units were estimated using the expected present value of discounted cash flows.

The Company amortizes the cost of other intangible assets over their estimated useful lives, which range from 1 to 20 years, unless such lives are deemed indefinite. Intangible assets with indefinite lives are tested in the third quarter of each fiscal year for impairment. The Company recorded no impairment charges for goodwill or other intangible assets for fiscal 2007, 2006 or 2005.

## Impairment of Long-Lived Assets

The Company evaluates the carrying value of long-lived assets when management makes the decision to relocate or close a store or other location, or when circumstances indicate the carrying amount of an asset may not be recoverable. A store's assets are evaluated for impairment by comparing its undiscounted cash flows with its carrying value. If the carrying value is greater than the undiscounted cash flows, a provision is made to write down the related assets to fair value if the carrying value is greater than the fair value. Impairment losses are recorded as a component of SG&A in the accompanying Consolidated Statements of Earnings. When a location closes, the Company also recognizes in SG&A the net present value of future lease obligations, less estimated sublease income.

In fiscal 2005 the Company recorded $91 million in SG&A related to asset impairment charges and on-going lease obligations associated with closing 20 of its EXPO stores. Additionally, the Company recorded $29 million of expense in Cost of Sales in fiscal 2005 related to inventory markdowns in these stores. The Company also recorded impairments on other closings and relocations in the ordinary course of business, which were not material to the Consolidated Financial Statements of the Company in fiscal 2007, 2006 and 2005.

**Stock-Based Compensation**

Effective February 3, 2003, the Company adopted the fair value method of recording stock-based compensation expense in accordance with Statement of Financial Accounting Standards ("SFAS") No. 123, "Accounting for Stock-Based Compensation" ("SFAS 123"). The Company selected the prospective method of adoption as described in SFAS No. 148, "Accounting for Stock-Based Compensation – Transition and Disclosure," and accordingly, stock-based compensation expense was recognized for stock options granted, modified or settled and expense related to the Employee Stock Purchase Plan ("ESPP") after the beginning of fiscal 2003. Effective January 30, 2006, the Company adopted the fair value recognition provisions of SFAS No. 123(R), "Share-Based Payment" ("SFAS 123(R)"), using the modified prospective transition method. Under the modified prospective transition method, the Company began expensing unvested options granted prior to fiscal 2003 in addition to continuing to recognize stock-based compensation expense for all share-based payments awarded since the adoption of SFAS 123 in fiscal 2003. During fiscal 2006, the Company recognized additional stock compensation expense of approximately $40 million as a result of the adoption of SFAS 123(R). Results of prior periods have not been restated.

The per share weighted average fair value of stock options granted during fiscal 2007, 2006 and 2005 was $9.45, $11.88 and $12.83, respectively. The fair value of these options was determined at the date of grant using the Black-Scholes option-pricing model with the following assumptions:

|  | Fiscal Year Ended | | |
| --- | --- | --- | --- |
|  | February 3, 2008 | January 28, 2007 | January 29, 2006 |
| Risk-free interest rate | 4.4% | 4.7% | 4.3% |
| Assumed volatility | 25.5% | 28.5% | 33.7% |
| Assumed dividend yield | 2.4% | 1.5% | 1.1% |
| Assumed lives of option | 6 years | 5 years | 5 years |

The following table illustrates the effect on Net Earnings and Earnings per Share as if the Company had applied the fair value recognition provisions of SFAS 123(R) to all stock-based compensation in each period (amounts in millions, except per share data):

|  | Fiscal Year Ended | | |
| --- | --- | --- | --- |
|  | February 3, 2008 | January 28, 2007 | January 29, 2006 |
| Net Earnings, as reported | $ 4,395 | $ 5,761 | $ 5,838 |
| Add: Stock-based compensation expense included in reported Net Earnings, net of related tax effects | 131 | 186 | 110 |
| Deduct: Total stock-based compensation expense determined under fair value based method for all awards, net of related tax effects | (131) | (186) | (197) |
| Pro forma net earnings | $ 4,395 | $ 5,761 | $ 5,751 |
| Earnings per Share: |  |  |  |
| Basic – as reported | $ 2.38 | $ 2.80 | $ 2.73 |
| Basic – pro forma | $ 2.38 | $ 2.80 | $ 2.69 |
| Diluted – as reported | $ 2.37 | $ 2.79 | $ 2.72 |
| Diluted – pro forma | $ 2.37 | $ 2.79 | $ 2.68 |

**Derivatives**

The Company uses derivative financial instruments from time to time in the management of its interest rate exposure on long-term debt and its exposure on foreign currency fluctuations. The Company accounts for its derivative financial instruments in accordance with SFAS No. 133, "Accounting for Derivative Instruments and Hedging Activities."

**Comprehensive Income**

Comprehensive Income includes Net Earnings adjusted for certain revenues, expenses, gains and losses that are excluded from Net Earnings under generally accepted accounting principles in the U.S. Adjustments to Net Earnings and Accumulated Other Comprehensive Income consist primarily of foreign currency translation adjustments.

**Foreign Currency Translation**

Assets and Liabilities denominated in a foreign currency are translated into U.S. dollars at the current rate of exchange on the last day of the reporting period. Revenues and Expenses are generally translated using average exchange rates for the period and equity transactions are translated using the actual rate on the day of the transaction.

**Segment Information**

The Company operates within a single operating segment primarily within North America. Net Sales for the Company outside of the U.S. were $7.4 billion, $6.3 billion and $5.2 billion for fiscal 2007, 2006 and 2005, respectively. Long-lived assets outside of the U.S. totaled $3.1 billion and $2.5 billion as of February 3, 2008 and January 28, 2007, respectively.

**Reclassifications**

Certain amounts in prior fiscal years have been reclassified to conform with the presentation adopted in the current fiscal year.

## 2.  DISPOSITION AND ACQUISITIONS

On August 30, 2007, the Company closed the sale of HD Supply. The Company received $8.3 billion of net proceeds for the sale of HD Supply and recognized a $4 million loss, net of tax, on the sale of the business, subject to the finalization of working capital adjustments. Also in connection with the sale, the Company purchased a 12.5% equity interest in the newly formed HD Supply for $325 million, which is included in Other Assets in the accompanying Consolidated Balance Sheets.

Also in connection with the sale, the Company guaranteed a $1.0 billion senior secured loan ("guaranteed loan") of HD Supply. The fair value of the guarantee, which was determined to be approximately $16 million, is recorded as a liability of the Company and included in Other Long-Term Liabilities. The guaranteed loan has a term of five years and the Company would be responsible for up to $1.0 billion and any unpaid interest in the event of non-payment by HD Supply. The guaranteed loan is collateralized by certain assets of HD Supply.

In accordance with Statement of Financial Accounting Standards No. 144, "Accounting for the Impairment or Disposal of Long-Lived Assets" ("SFAS 144"), the Company reclassified the results of HD Supply as discontinued operations in its Consolidated Statements of Earnings for all periods presented.

The following table presents Net Sales and Earnings of HD Supply through August 30, 2007 which have been reclassified to discontinued operations in the Consolidated Statements of Earnings for fiscal 2007, 2006 and 2005 (amounts in millions):

|  | Fiscal Year Ended | | |
|---|---|---|---|
|  | February 3, 2008 | January 28, 2007 | January 29, 2006 |
| Net Sales | $ 7,391 | $ 11,815 | $ 4,492 |
| Earnings Before Provision for Income Taxes | $ 291 | $ 806 | $ 315 |
| Provision for Income Taxes | (102) | (311) | (118) |
| Loss on Discontinued Operations, net | (4) | — | — |
| Earnings from Discontinued Operations, net of tax | $ 185 | $ 495 | $ 197 |

During fiscal 2007, the Company acquired Ohio Water & Waste Supply, Inc. and Geosynthetics, Inc. These acquisitions operated under HD Supply and were included in the disposition. The aggregate purchase price for acquisitions in fiscal 2007, 2006 and 2005 was $25 million, $4.5 billion and $2.6 billion, respectively, including $3.5 billion for Hughes Supply in fiscal 2006. The Company recorded Goodwill related to the HD Supply businesses of $20 million, $2.8 billion and $1.8 billion for fiscal 2007, 2006 and 2005, respectively, and recorded no Goodwill related to its retail businesses for fiscal 2007 compared to $229 million and $111 million for fiscal 2006 and 2005, respectively, in the accompanying Consolidated Balance Sheets.

## 3.  STAFF ACCOUNTING BULLETIN NO. 108

In fiscal 2006, the Company adopted Staff Accounting Bulletin No. 108, "Considering the Effects of Prior Year Misstatements when Quantifying Misstatements in Current Year Financial Statements" ("SAB 108"). SAB 108 addresses the process of quantifying prior year financial statement misstatements and their impact on current year financial statements. The provisions of SAB 108 allowed companies to report the cumulative effect of correcting immaterial prior year misstatements, based on the Company's historical method for evaluating misstatements, by adjusting the opening balance of retained earnings in the financial statements of the year of adoption rather than amending previously filed reports. In accordance with SAB 108, the Company adjusted beginning Retained Earnings for fiscal 2006 in the accompanying Consolidated Financial Statements for the items described below. The Company does not consider these adjustments to have a material impact on the Company's consolidated financial statements in any of the prior years affected.

*Historical Stock Option Practices*

During fiscal 2006, the Company requested that its Board of Directors review its historical stock option granting practices. A subcommittee of the Audit Committee undertook the review with the assistance of independent outside counsel, and it has completed its review. The principal findings of the 2006 review were as follows:

- All options granted in the period from 2002 through the present had an exercise price based on the market price of the Company's stock on the date the grant was approved by the Board of Directors or an officer acting pursuant to delegated authority. During this period, the stock administration department corrected administrative errors retroactively and without separate approvals. The administrative errors included inadvertent omissions of grantees from lists that were approved previously and miscalculations of the number of options granted to particular employees on approved lists.

- All options granted from December 1, 2000 through the end of 2001 had an exercise price based on the market price of the Company's stock on the date of a meeting of the Board of Directors or some other date selected without the benefit of hindsight. The February 2001 annual grant was not finally allocated to recipients until several weeks after the grant was approved. During this period, the stock administration department also corrected administrative errors retroactively and without separate approvals as in the period 2002 to the present.

- For annual option grants and certain quarterly option grants from 1981 through November 2000, the stated grant date was routinely earlier than the actual date on which the grants were approved by a committee of the Board of Directors. In almost every instance, the stock price on the apparent approval date was higher than the price on the stated grant date. The backdating occurred for grants at all levels of the Company. Management personnel, who have since left the Company, generally followed a practice of reviewing closing prices for a prior period and selecting a date with a low stock price to increase the value of the options to employees on lists of grantees subsequently approved by a committee of the Board of Directors.

- The annual option grants in 1994 through 2000, as well as many quarterly grants during this period, were not finally allocated among the recipients until several weeks after the stated grant date. Because of the absence of records prior to 1994, it is unclear whether allocations also postdated the selected grant dates from 1981 through 1993. Moreover, for many of these annual and quarterly grants from 1981 through December 2000, there is insufficient documentation to determine with certainty when the grants were actually authorized by a committee of the Board of Directors. Finally, the Company's stock administration department also retroactively added employees to lists of approved grantees, or changed the number of options granted to specific employees, without authorization of the Board of Directors or a board committee, to correct administrative errors.

- Numerous option grants to rank-and-file employees were made pursuant to delegations of authority that may not have been effective under Delaware law.

- In numerous instances, and primarily prior to 2003, beneficiaries of grants who were required to report them to the SEC failed to do so in a timely manner or at all.

- The subcommittee concluded that there was no intentional wrongdoing by any current member of the Company's management team or its Board of Directors.

The Company believes that because of these errors, it had unrecorded expense over the affected period (1981 through 2005) of $227 million in the aggregate, including related tax items. In accordance with the provisions of SAB 108, the Company decreased beginning Retained Earnings for fiscal 2006 by $227 million within the accompanying Consolidated Financial Statements.

As previously disclosed, the staff of the SEC began in June 2006 an informal inquiry into the Company's stock option practices, and the U.S. Attorney for the Southern District of New York has also requested information on the subject. The Company is continuing to cooperate with these agencies. While the Company cannot predict the outcome of these matters, it does not believe that they will have a material adverse impact on its consolidated financial condition or results of operations.

The Company does not believe that the effect of the stock option adjustment was material, either quantitatively or qualitatively, in any of the years covered by the review of these items. In reaching that determination, the following quantitative measures were considered (dollars in millions):

| Fiscal Year | Net After-tax Effect of Adjustment | Reported Net Earnings | Percent of Reported Net Earnings |
|---|---|---|---|
| 2005 | $ 11 | $ 5,838 | 0.19% |
| 2004 | 18 | 5,001 | 0.36 |
| 2003 | 18 | 4,304 | 0.42 |
| 2002 | 21 | 3,664 | 0.57 |
| 1981-2001 | 159 | 14,531 | 1.09 |
| Total | $ 227 | $ 33,338 | 0.68% |

*Vendor Credits*

The Company records credits against vendor invoices for various issues related to the receipt of goods. The Company previously identified that it was not recording an allowance for subsequent reversals of these credits based on historical experience. Beginning Retained Earnings for fiscal 2006 was decreased by $30 million in the accompanying Consolidated Financial Statements to reflect the appropriate adjustments to Merchandise Inventories and Accounts Payable, net of tax.

*Impact of Adjustments*

The impact of each of the items noted above, net of tax, on fiscal 2006 beginning balances are presented below (amounts in millions):

| | Cumulative Effect as of January 30, 2006 | | |
| --- | --- | --- | --- |
| | Stock Option Practices | Vendor Credits | Total |
| Merchandise Inventories | $ — | $ 9 | $ 9 |
| Accounts Payable | — | (59) | (59) |
| Deferred Income Taxes | 11 | 20 | 31 |
| Other Accrued Expenses | (37) | — | (37) |
| Paid-In Capital | (201) | — | (201) |
| Retained Earnings | 227 | 30 | 257 |
| Total | $ — | $ — | $ — |

## 4.   INTANGIBLE ASSETS

The Company's intangible assets at the end of fiscal 2007 and 2006, which are included in Other Assets in the accompanying Consolidated Balance Sheets, consisted of the following (amounts in millions):

| | February 3, 2008 | January 28, 2007 |
| --- | --- | --- |
| Customer relationships | $ 11 | $ 756 |
| Trademarks and franchises | 83 | 106 |
| Other | 29 | 67 |
| Less accumulated amortization | (23) | (151) |
| Total | $ 100 | $ 778 |

The decrease in intangible assets from January 28, 2007 to February 3, 2008 was a result of the sale of HD Supply. Amortization expense related to intangible assets in continuing operations was $9 million, $10 million and less than $1 million for fiscal 2007, 2006 and 2005, respectively. Estimated future amortization expense for intangible assets recorded as of February 3, 2008 is $8 million, $8 million, $8 million, $5 million and $4 million for fiscal 2008 through fiscal 2012, respectively.

## 5.   DEBT

The Company has commercial paper programs that allow for borrowings up to $3.25 billion. All of the Company's short-term borrowings in fiscal 2007 and 2006 were under these commercial paper programs. In connection with the commercial paper programs, the Company has a back-up credit facility with a consortium of banks for borrowings up to $3.0 billion. The credit facility, which expires in December 2010, contains various restrictions, none of which is expected to materially impact the Company's liquidity or capital resources.

Short-Term Debt under the commercial paper program was as follows (dollars in millions):

| | February 3, 2008 | January 28, 2007 |
| --- | --- | --- |
| Balance outstanding at fiscal year-end | $ 1,747 | $ — |
| Maximum amount outstanding at any month-end | $ 1,747 | $ 1,470 |
| Average daily short-term borrowings | $ 526 | $ 300 |
| Weighted average interest rate | 5.0% | 5.1% |

The Company's Long-Term Debt at the end of fiscal 2007 and 2006 consisted of the following (amounts in millions):

| | February 3, 2008 | January 28, 2007 |
|---|---|---|
| 3.75% Senior Notes; due September 15, 2009; interest payable semi-annually on March 15 and September 15 | $ 998 | $ 997 |
| Floating Rate Senior Notes; due December 16, 2009; interest payable on March 16, June 16, September 16 and December 16 | 750 | 750 |
| 4.625% Senior Notes; due August 15, 2010; interest payable semi-annually on February 15 and August 15 | 998 | 997 |
| 5.20% Senior Notes; due March 1, 2011; interest payable semi-annually on March 1 and September 1 | 1,000 | 1,000 |
| 5.25% Senior Notes; due December 16, 2013; interest payable semi-annually on June 16 and December 16 | 1,244 | 1,243 |
| 5.40% Senior Notes; due March 1, 2016; interest payable semi-annually on March 1 and September 1 | 3,017 | 2,986 |
| 5.875% Senior Notes; due December 16, 2036; interest payable semi-annually on June 16 and December 16 | 2,959 | 2,958 |
| Capital Lease Obligations; payable in varying installments through January 31, 2055 | 415 | 419 |
| Other | 302 | 311 |
| Total Long-Term Debt | 11,683 | 11,661 |
| Less current installments | 300 | 18 |
| Long-Term Debt, excluding current installments | $ 11,383 | $ 11,643 |

At February 3, 2008, the Company had outstanding interest rate swaps, accounted for as fair value hedges, with notional amounts of $2.0 billion that swap fixed rate interest on the Company's $3.0 billion 5.40% Senior Notes for variable rate interest equal to LIBOR plus 60 to 149 basis points that expire on March 1, 2016. At February 3, 2008, the approximate fair value of these agreements was an asset of $29 million, which is the estimated amount the Company would have received to settle similar interest rate swap agreements at current interest rates.

At February 3, 2008, the Company had outstanding an interest rate swap, accounted for as a cash flow hedge, with a notional amount of $750 million that swaps variable rate interest on the Company's $750 million floating rate Senior Notes for fixed rate interest at 4.36% that expires on December 16, 2009. At February 3, 2008, the approximate fair value of this agreement was a liability of $17 million, which is the estimated amount the Company would have paid to settle similar interest rate swap agreements at current interest rates.

In December 2006, the Company issued $750 million of floating rate Senior Notes due December 16, 2009 at par value, $1.25 billion of 5.25% Senior Notes due December 16, 2013 at a discount of $7 million and $3.0 billion of 5.875% Senior Notes due December 16, 2036 at a discount of $42 million, together the "December 2006 Issuance." The net proceeds of the December 2006 Issuance were used to fund, in part, the Company's common stock repurchases, to repay outstanding commercial paper and for general corporate purposes. The $49 million discount and $37 million of issuance costs associated with the December 2006 Issuance are being amortized to interest expense over the term of the related Senior Notes.

Additionally in October 2006, the Company entered into a forward starting interest rate swap agreement with a notional amount of $1.0 billion, accounted for as a cash flow hedge, to hedge interest rate fluctuations in anticipation of the issuance of the 5.875% Senior Notes due December 16, 2036. Upon issuance of the hedged debt in December 2006, the Company settled its forward starting interest rate swap agreements and recorded an $11 million decrease, net of income taxes, to Accumulated Other Comprehensive Income, which will be amortized to interest expense over the life of the related debt.

In March 2006, the Company issued $1.0 billion of 5.20% Senior Notes due March 1, 2011 at a discount of $1 million and $3.0 billion of 5.40% Senior Notes due March 1, 2016 at a discount of $15 million, together the "March 2006 Issuance." The net proceeds of the March 2006 Issuance were used to pay for the acquisition price of Hughes Supply, Inc. and for the repayment of the Company's 5.375% Senior Notes due April 2006 in the aggregate principal amount of $500 million. The $16 million discount and $19 million of issuance costs associated with the March 2006 Issuance are being amortized to interest expense over the term of the related Senior Notes.

Additionally in March 2006, the Company entered into a forward starting interest rate swap agreement with a notional amount of $2.0 billion, accounted for as a cash flow hedge, to hedge interest rate fluctuations in anticipation of the issuance of the 5.40% Senior Notes due March 1, 2016. Upon issuance of the hedged debt, the Company settled its forward starting interest rate swap agreements and recorded a $12 million decrease, net of income taxes, to Accumulated Other Comprehensive Income, which will be amortized to interest expense over the life of the related debt.

In August 2005, the Company issued $1.0 billion of 4.625% Notes due August 15, 2010 ("August 2005 Issuance") at a discount of $5 million. The net proceeds of $995 million were used to pay for a portion of the acquisition price of National Waterworks, Inc. The $5 million discount and $7 million of issuance costs associated with the August 2005 Issuance are being amortized to interest expense over the term of the related Senior Notes.

The Company also had $1.0 billion of 3.75% Senior Notes due September 15, 2009 outstanding as of February 3, 2008, collectively referred to with the December 2006 Issuance, March 2006 Issuance and August 2005 Issuance as "Senior Notes." The Senior Notes may be redeemed by the Company at any time, in whole or in part, at a redemption price plus accrued interest up to the redemption date. The redemption price is equal to the greater of (1) 100% of the principal amount of the Senior Notes to be redeemed, or (2) the sum of the present values of the remaining scheduled payments of principal and interest to maturity. Additionally, if a Change in Control Triggering Event occurs, as defined by the terms of the December 2006 Issuance, holders of the December 2006 Issuance have the right to require the Company to redeem those notes at 101% of the aggregate principal amount of the notes plus accrued interest up to the redemption date.

The Company is generally not limited under the indenture governing the Senior Notes in its ability to incur additional indebtedness or required to maintain financial ratios or specified levels of net worth or liquidity. However, the indenture governing the Senior Notes contains various restrictive covenants, none of which is expected to impact the Company's liquidity or capital resources.

Interest Expense in the accompanying Consolidated Statements of Earnings is net of interest capitalized of $46 million, $47 million and $51 million in fiscal 2007, 2006 and 2005, respectively. Maturities of Long-Term Debt are $300 million for fiscal 2008, $1.8 billion for fiscal 2009, $1.0 billion for fiscal 2010, $1.0 billion for fiscal 2011, $23 million for fiscal 2012 and $7.5 billion thereafter.

As of February 3, 2008, the market value of the Senior Notes was approximately $10.5 billion. The estimated fair value of all other long-term borrowings, excluding capital lease obligations, was approximately $307 million compared to the carrying value of $302 million. These fair values were estimated using a discounted cash flow analysis based on the Company's incremental borrowing rate for similar liabilities.

## 6. INCOME TAXES

The components of Earnings From Continuing Operations before Provision for Income Taxes for fiscal 2007, 2006 and 2005 were as follows (amounts in millions):

|  | Fiscal Year Ended | | |
|---|---|---|---|
|  | February 3, 2008 | January 28, 2007 | January 29, 2006 |
| United States | $ 5,905 | $ 7,915 | $ 8,427 |
| Foreign | 715 | 587 | 540 |
| Total | $ 6,620 | $ 8,502 | $ 8,967 |

The Provision for Income Taxes consisted of the following (amounts in millions):

|  | Fiscal Year Ended | | |
|---|---|---|---|
|  | February 3, 2008 | January 28, 2007 | January 29, 2006 |
| Current: |  |  |  |
| Federal | $ 2,055 | $ 2,557 | $ 3,316 |
| State | 285 | 361 | 493 |
| Foreign | 310 | 326 | 155 |
|  | 2,650 | 3,244 | 3,964 |
| Deferred: |  |  |  |
| Federal | (242) | (2) | (553) |
| State | 17 | (1) | (110) |
| Foreign | (15) | (5) | 25 |
|  | (240) | (8) | (638) |
| Total | $ 2,410 | $ 3,236 | $ 3,326 |

The Company's combined federal, state and foreign effective tax rates for fiscal 2007, 2006 and 2005, net of offsets generated by federal, state and foreign tax benefits, were approximately 36.4%, 38.1% and 37.1%, respectively.

The reconciliation of the Provision for Income Taxes at the federal statutory rate of 35% to the actual tax expense for the applicable fiscal years was as follows (amounts in millions):

|  | Fiscal Year Ended | | |
| --- | --- | --- | --- |
|  | February 3, 2008 | January 28, 2007 | January 29, 2006 |
| Income taxes at federal statutory rate | $ 2,317 | $ 2,976 | $ 3,138 |
| State income taxes, net of federal income tax benefit | 196 | 234 | 249 |
| Other, net | (103) | 26 | (61) |
| Total | $ 2,410 | $ 3,236 | $ 3,326 |

The tax effects of temporary differences that give rise to significant portions of the deferred tax assets and deferred tax liabilities as of February 3, 2008 and January 28, 2007, were as follows (amounts in millions):

|  | February 3, 2008 | January 28, 2007 |
| --- | --- | --- |
| **Current:** | | |
| Deferred Tax Assets: | | |
| Accrued self-insurance liabilities | $ 155 | $ 94 |
| Other accrued liabilities | 601 | 603 |
| Current Deferred Tax Assets | 756 | 697 |
| Deferred Tax Liabilities: | | |
| Accelerated inventory deduction | (118) | (137) |
| Other | (113) | (29) |
| Current Deferred Tax Liabilities | (231) | (166) |
| Current Deferred Tax Assets, net | 525 | 531 |
| **Noncurrent:** | | |
| Deferred Tax Assets: | | |
| Accrued self-insurance liabilities | 285 | 325 |
| State income taxes | 105 | — |
| Capital loss carryover | 56 | — |
| Net operating losses | 52 | 66 |
| Other | 54 | — |
| Valuation allowance | (7) | — |
| Noncurrent Deferred Tax Assets | 545 | 391 |
| Deferred Tax Liabilities: | | |
| Property and equipment | (1,133) | (1,365) |
| Goodwill and other intangibles | (69) | (361) |
| Other | (31) | (74) |
| Noncurrent Deferred Tax Liabilities | (1,233) | (1,800) |
| Noncurrent Deferred Tax Liabilities, net | (688) | (1,409) |
| Net Deferred Tax Liabilities | $ (163) | $ (878) |

Current deferred tax assets and current deferred tax liabilities are netted by tax jurisdiction and noncurrent deferred tax assets and noncurrent deferred tax liabilities are netted by tax jurisdiction, and are included in the accompanying Consolidated Balance Sheets as follows (amounts in millions):

|  | February 3, 2008 | January 28, 2007 |
| --- | --- | --- |
| Other Current Assets | $ 535 | $ 561 |
| Other Assets | — | 7 |
| Other Accrued Expenses | (10) | (30) |
| Deferred Income Taxes | (688) | (1,416) |
| Net Deferred Tax Liabilities | $ (163) | $ (878) |

The Company believes that the realization of the deferred tax assets is more likely than not, based upon the expectation that it will generate the necessary taxable income in future periods and, except for certain net operating losses discussed below, no valuation reserves have been provided. As a result of disposition of HD Supply, $139 million of net deferred tax liabilities were transferred to the purchaser.

At February 3, 2008, the Company had state and foreign net operating loss carryforwards available to reduce future taxable income, expiring at various dates from 2010 to 2027. Management has concluded that it is more likely than not that the tax benefits related to the net operating losses will be realized. However, certain foreign net operating losses are in jurisdictions where the expiration period is too short to be assured of utilization. Therefore, a $7 million valuation allowance has been provided to reduce the deferred tax asset related to net operating losses to an amount that is more likely than not to be realized. Total valuation allowances at February 3, 2008 were $7 million.

As a result of its sale of HD Supply, the Company incurred a tax loss, resulting in a net capital loss carryover of approximately $159 million. The tax loss on sale resulted primarily from the Company's tax basis in excess of its book investment in HD Supply. The net capital loss carryover will expire in 2012. However, the Company has concluded that it is more likely than not that the tax benefits related to the capital loss carryover will be realized based on its ability to generate adequate capital gain income during the carryover period. Therefore, no valuation allowance has been provided.

The Company has not provided for U.S. deferred income taxes on approximately $1.3 billion of undistributed earnings of international subsidiaries because of its intention to indefinitely reinvest these earnings outside the U.S. The determination of the amount of the unrecognized deferred U.S. income tax liability related to the undistributed earnings is not practicable; however, unrecognized foreign income tax credits would be available to reduce a portion of this liability.

The Company's income tax returns are routinely under audit by domestic and foreign tax authorities. These audits generally include questions regarding the timing and amount of depreciation deductions and the allocation of income among various tax jurisdictions. In 2005, the U.S. Internal Revenue Service ("IRS") completed its examination of the Company's U.S. federal income tax returns for fiscal years 2001 and 2002. During 2007, the IRS also completed its examination of the Company's fiscal 2003 and 2004 income tax returns. Certain issues relating to the examinations of fiscal years 2001 through 2004 are under appeal, but only years after fiscal 2004 remain subject to future examination. The Mexican government is currently auditing the Mexican operating subsidiaries' fiscal year 2005 returns, although years after 2001 remain subject to audit. The Canadian governments, including various provinces, are currently auditing income tax returns for the years 2001 through 2005. There are also U.S. state and local audits covering tax years 2001 to 2005. At this time, the Company does not expect the results from any income tax audit to have a material impact on the Company's financial statements.

On January 29, 2007, the Company adopted FASB Interpretation No. 48, "Accounting for Uncertainty in Income Taxes – an Interpretation of FASB Statement No. 109" ("FIN 48"). Among other things, FIN 48 requires application of a "more likely than not" threshold to the recognition and derecognition of tax positions. It further requires that a change in judgment related to prior years' tax positions be recognized in the quarter of such change. The adoption of FIN 48 reduced the Company's Retained Earnings by $111 million. As a result of the implementation, the gross amount of unrecognized tax benefits at January 29, 2007 for continuing operations totaled $667 million. A reconciliation of the beginning and ending amount of gross unrecognized tax benefits for continuing operations is as follows (amounts in millions):

|  | February 3, 2008 |
| --- | --- |
| Unrecognized tax benefits balance at January 29, 2007 | $ 667 |
| Additions based on tax positions related to the current year | 66 |
| Additions for tax positions of prior years | 25 |
| Reductions for tax positions of prior years | (115) |
| Reductions due to settlements | (31) |
| Reductions due to lapse of statute of limitations | (4) |
| Unrecognized tax benefits balance at February 3, 2008 | $ 608 |

The gross amount of unrecognized tax benefits as of February 3, 2008 includes $368 million of net unrecognized tax benefits that, if recognized, would affect the annual effective income tax rate.

During fiscal 2007, the Company increased its interest accrual associated with uncertain tax positions by approximately $32 million and paid interest of approximately $8 million. Total accrued interest as of February 3, 2008 is $140 million. There were no penalty accruals during fiscal 2007. Interest and penalties are included in net interest expense and operating expenses, respectively. Our classification of interest and penalties did not change as a result of the adoption of FIN 48.

The Company believes that some individual adjustments under appeal for the completed IRS and Canada audits, as well as other state audits, will be agreed upon within the next twelve months. The IRS issues generally concern the useful life of assets and relevant transfer pricing for intangible assets provided to foreign operations. The Canada issues generally concern the relevant transfer pricing for intangible assets provided from the U.S. State issues generally concern related party expense add-back provisions and forced combination filings. The Company has classified approximately $6 million of the reserve for unrecognized tax benefits as a short-term liability in the accompanying Consolidated Balance Sheets. In addition, there is a reasonable possibility that the Company may resolve the Quebec assessment from prior years, which totaled $65 million at February 3, 2008, within the next twelve months. Final settlement of these audit issues may result in payments that are more or less than these amounts, but the Company does not anticipate the resolution of these matters will result in a material change to its consolidated financial position or results of operations.

## 7.    EMPLOYEE STOCK PLANS

The Home Depot, Inc. 2005 Omnibus Stock Incentive Plan ("2005 Plan") and The Home Depot, Inc. 1997 Omnibus Stock Incentive Plan ("1997 Plan" and collectively with the 2005 Plan, the "Plans") provide that incentive and non-qualified stock options, stock appreciation rights, restricted shares, performance shares, performance units and deferred shares may be issued to selected associates, officers and directors of the Company. Under the 2005 Plan, the maximum number of shares of the Company's common stock authorized for issuance is 255 million shares, with any award other than a stock option reducing the number of shares available for issuance by 2.11 shares. As of February 3, 2008, there were 224 million shares available for future grants under the 2005 Plan. No additional equity awards may be issued from the 1997 Plan after the adoption of the 2005 Plan on May 26, 2005.

Under the Plans, as of February 3, 2008, the Company had granted incentive and non-qualified stock options for 177 million shares, net of cancellations (of which 127 million have been exercised). Under the terms of the Plans, incentive stock options and non-qualified stock options are to be priced at or above the fair market value of the Company's stock on the date of the grant. Typically, incentive stock options and non-qualified stock options vest at the rate of 25% per year commencing on the first anniversary date of the grant and expire on the tenth anniversary date of the grant. The non-qualified stock options also include performance options which vest on the later of the first anniversary date of the grant and the date the closing price of the Company's common stock has been 25% greater than the exercise price of the options for 30 consecutive trading days. The Company recognized $61 million, $148 million and $117 million of stock-based compensation expense in fiscal 2007, 2006 and 2005, respectively, related to stock options.

Under the Plans, as of February 3, 2008, the Company had issued 16 million shares of restricted stock, net of cancellations (the restrictions on 5 million shares have lapsed). Generally, the restrictions on the restricted stock lapse according to one of the following schedules: (1) the restrictions on 100% of the restricted stock lapse at 3, 4 or 5 years, (2) the restrictions on 25% of the restricted stock lapse upon the third and sixth year anniversaries of the date of issuance with the remaining 50% of the restricted stock lapsing upon the associate's attainment of age 62, or (3) the restrictions on 25% of the restricted stock lapse upon the third and sixth year anniversaries of the date of issuance with the remaining 50% of the restricted stock lapsing upon the earlier of the associate's attainment of age 60 or the tenth anniversary date. The restricted stock also includes the Company's performance shares, the payout of which is dependent on the Company's total shareholders return percentile ranking compared to the performance of individual companies included in the S&P 500 index at the end of the three-year performance cycle. Additionally, certain awards may become non-forfeitable upon the attainment of age 60, provided the associate has had five years of continuous service. The fair value of the restricted stock is expensed over the period during which the restrictions lapse. The Company recorded stock-based compensation expense related to restricted stock of $122 million, $95 million and $32 million in fiscal 2007, 2006 and 2005, respectively.

In fiscal 2007, 2006 and 2005, there were 593,000, 417,000 and 461,000 deferred shares, respectively, granted under the Plans. Each deferred share entitles the associate to one share of common stock to be received up to five years after the vesting date of the deferred shares, subject to certain deferral rights of the associate. The Company recorded stock-based compensation expense related to deferred shares of $10 million, $37 million and $10 million in fiscal 2007, 2006 and 2005, respectively.

As of February 3, 2008, there were 2.5 million non-qualified stock options outstanding under non-qualified stock option plans that are not part of the Plans.

The Company maintains two ESPPs (U.S. and non-U.S. plans). The plan for U.S. associates is a tax-qualified plan under Section 423 of the Internal Revenue Code. The non-U.S. plan is not a Section 423 plan. The ESPPs allow associates to purchase up to 152 million shares of common stock, of which 128 million shares have been purchased from inception of the plans. The purchase price of shares under the ESPPs is equal to 85% of the stock's fair market value on the last day of the purchase period. During fiscal 2007, there were 3 million shares purchased under the ESPPs at an average price of $28.25. Under the outstanding ESPPs as of February 3, 2008, employees have contributed $8 million to purchase shares at 85% of the stock's fair market value on the last day (June 30, 2008) of the purchase period. The Company had 24 million shares available for issuance under the ESPPs at February 3, 2008. The Company recognized $14 million, $17 million and $16 million of stock-based compensation in fiscal 2007, 2006 and 2005, respectively, related to the ESPPs.

In total, the Company recorded stock-based compensation expense, including the expense of stock options, ESPPs, restricted stock and deferred stock units, of $207 million, $297 million and $175 million, in fiscal 2007, 2006 and 2005, respectively.

The following table summarizes stock options outstanding at February 3, 2008, January 28, 2007 and January 29, 2006, and changes during the fiscal years ended on these dates (shares in thousands):

| | Number of Shares | Weighted Average Exercise Price |
|---|---|---|
| Outstanding at January 30, 2005 | 86,394 | $ 36.12 |
| Granted | 17,721 | 37.96 |
| Exercised | (11,457) | 28.83 |
| Canceled | (8,626) | 38.65 |
| Outstanding at January 29, 2006 | 84,032 | $ 37.24 |
| Granted | 257 | 39.53 |
| Exercised | (10,045) | 28.69 |
| Canceled | (8,103) | 40.12 |
| Outstanding at January 28, 2007 | 66,141 | $ 38.20 |
| Granted | 2,926 | 37.80 |
| Exercised | (6,859) | 28.50 |
| Canceled | (9,843) | 40.68 |
| Outstanding at February 3, 2008 | 52,365 | $ 38.98 |

The total intrinsic value of stock options exercised during fiscal 2007 was $63 million.

As of February 3, 2008, there were approximately 52 million stock options outstanding with a weighted average remaining life of five years and an intrinsic value of $30 million. As of February 3, 2008, there were approximately 42 million options exercisable with a weighted average exercise price of $39.43 and an intrinsic value of $28 million. As of February 3, 2008, there were approximately 51 million shares vested or expected to ultimately vest. As of February 3, 2008, there was $84 million of unamortized stock-based compensation expense related to stock options which is expected to be recognized over a weighted average period of two years.

The following table summarizes restricted stock outstanding at February 3, 2008 (shares in thousands):

| | Number of Shares | Weighted Average Grant Date Fair Value |
|---|---|---|
| Outstanding at January 29, 2006 | 5,308 | $ 35.76 |
| Granted | 7,575 | 41.37 |
| Restrictions lapsed | (1,202) | 38.03 |
| Canceled | (1,551) | 39.00 |
| Outstanding at January 28, 2007 | 10,130 | $ 39.20 |
| Granted | 7,091 | 39.10 |
| Restrictions lapsed | (2,662) | 39.01 |
| Canceled | (2,844) | 39.37 |
| Outstanding at February 3, 2008 | 11,715 | $ 39.14 |

As of February 3, 2008, there was $267 million of unamortized stock-based compensation expense related to restricted stock which is expected to be recognized over a weighted average period of three years.

## 8.   LEASES

The Company leases certain retail locations, office space, warehouse and distribution space, equipment and vehicles. While most of the leases are operating leases, certain locations and equipment are leased under capital leases. As leases expire, it can be expected that, in the normal course of business, certain leases will be renewed or replaced.

Certain lease agreements include escalating rents over the lease terms. The Company expenses rent on a straight-line basis over the life of the lease which commences on the date the Company has the right to control the property. The cumulative expense recognized on a straight-line basis in excess of the cumulative payments is included in Other Accrued Expenses and Other Long-Term Liabilities in the accompanying Consolidated Balance Sheets.

The Company has a lease agreement under which the Company leases certain assets totaling $282 million. This lease was originally created under a structured financing arrangement and involves two special purpose entities. The Company financed a portion of its new stores opened in fiscal years 1997 through 2003 under this lease agreement. Under this agreement, the lessor purchased the properties, paid for the construction costs and subsequently leased the facilities to the Company. The Company records the rental payments under the terms of the operating lease agreements as SG&A in the accompanying Consolidated Statements of Earnings.

The $282 million lease agreement expires in fiscal 2008 with no renewal option. The lease provides for a substantial residual value guarantee limited to 79% of the initial book value of the assets and includes a purchase option at the original cost of each property. During fiscal 2005, the Company committed to exercise its option to purchase the assets under this lease for $282 million at the end of the lease term in fiscal 2008.

In the first quarter of fiscal 2004, the Company adopted the revised version of FASB Interpretation No. 46(R), "Consolidation of Variable Interest Entities" ("FIN 46"). FIN 46 requires consolidation of a variable interest entity if a company's variable interest absorbs a majority of the entity's expected losses or receives a majority of the entity's expected residual returns, or both. In accordance with FIN 46, the Company was required to consolidate one of the two aforementioned special purpose entities that, before the effective date of FIN 46, met the requirements for non-consolidation. The second special purpose entity that owns the assets leased by the Company totaling $282 million is not owned by or affiliated with the Company, its management or its officers. Pursuant to FIN 46, the Company was not deemed to have a variable interest, and therefore was not required to consolidate this entity.

FIN 46 requires the Company to measure the assets and liabilities at their carrying amounts, which amounts would have been recorded if FIN 46 had been effective at the inception of the transaction. Accordingly, during the first quarter of fiscal 2004, the Company recorded Long-Term Debt of $282 million and Long-Term Notes Receivable of $282 million on the Consolidated Balance Sheets. During fiscal 2007, the liability was reclassified to Current Installments of Long-Term Debt as it is due in fiscal 2008. The Company continues to record the rental payments under the operating lease agreements as SG&A in the Consolidated Statements of Earnings. The adoption of FIN 46 had no economic impact on the Company.

Total rent expense, net of minor sublease income for fiscal 2007, 2006 and 2005 was $824 million, $768 million and $720 million, respectively. Certain store leases also provide for contingent rent payments based on percentages of sales in excess of specified minimums. Contingent rent expense for fiscal 2007, 2006 and 2005 was approximately $6 million, $9 million and $9 million, respectively. Real estate taxes, insurance, maintenance and operating expenses applicable to the leased property are obligations of the Company under the lease agreements.

The approximate future minimum lease payments under capital and all other leases at February 3, 2008 were as follows (in millions):

| Fiscal Year | Capital Leases | | Operating Leases | |
|---|---|---|---|---|
| 2008 | $ | 79 | $ | 802 |
| 2009 | | 80 | | 716 |
| 2010 | | 82 | | 644 |
| 2011 | | 82 | | 582 |
| 2012 | | 82 | | 523 |
| Thereafter through 2097 | | 882 | | 5,664 |
| | | 1,287 | $ | 8,931 |
| Less imputed interest | | 872 | | |
| Net present value of capital lease obligations | | 415 | | |
| Less current installments | | 15 | | |
| Long-term capital lease obligations, excluding current installments | $ | 400 | | |

Short-term and long-term obligations for capital leases are included in the accompanying Consolidated Balance Sheets in Current Installments of Long-Term Debt and Long-Term Debt, respectively. The assets under capital leases recorded in Property and Equipment, net of amortization, totaled $327 million and $340 million at February 3, 2008 and January 28, 2007, respectively.

## 9.    EMPLOYEE BENEFIT PLANS

The Company maintains active defined contribution retirement plans for its employees ("the Benefit Plans"). All associates satisfying certain service requirements are eligible to participate in the Benefit Plans. The Company makes cash contributions each payroll period up to specified percentages of associates' contributions as approved by the Board of Directors.

The Company also maintains a restoration plan to provide certain associates deferred compensation that they would have received under the Benefit Plans as a matching contribution if not for the maximum compensation limits under the Internal Revenue Code. The Company funds the restoration plan through contributions made to a grantor trust, which are then used to purchase shares of the Company's common stock in the open market.

The Company's contributions to the Benefit Plans and the restoration plan were $152 million, $135 million and $122 million for fiscal 2007, 2006 and 2005, respectively. At February 3, 2008, the Benefit Plans and the restoration plan held a total of 22 million shares of the Company's common stock in trust for plan participants.

## 10.    BASIC AND DILUTED WEIGHTED AVERAGE COMMON SHARES

The reconciliation of basic to diluted weighted average common shares for fiscal 2007, 2006 and 2005 is as follows (amounts in millions):

|  | Fiscal Year Ended | | |
|  | February 3, 2008 | January 28, 2007 | January 29, 2006 |
|---|---|---|---|
| Weighted average common shares | 1,849 | 2,054 | 2,138 |
| Effect of potentially dilutive securities: | | | |
|   Stock Plans | 7 | 8 | 9 |
| Diluted weighted average common shares | 1,856 | 2,062 | 2,147 |

Stock plans include shares granted under the Company's employee stock plans as described in Note 7 to the Consolidated Financial Statements. Options to purchase 43.4 million, 45.4 million and 55.1 million shares of common stock at February 3, 2008, January 28, 2007 and January 29, 2006, respectively, were excluded from the computation of Diluted Earnings per Share because their effect would have been anti-dilutive.

## 11.    COMMITMENTS AND CONTINGENCIES

At February 3, 2008, the Company was contingently liable for approximately $730 million under outstanding letters of credit and open accounts issued for certain business transactions, including insurance programs, trade contracts and construction contracts. The Company's letters of credit are primarily performance-based and are not based on changes in variable components, a liability or an equity security of the other party.

The Company is a defendant in numerous cases containing class-action allegations in which the plaintiffs are current and former hourly associates who allege that the Company forced them to work "off the clock" or failed to provide work breaks, or otherwise that they were not paid for work performed. The complaints generally seek unspecified monetary damages, injunctive relief or both. Class or collective-action certification has yet to be addressed in most of these cases. The Company cannot reasonably estimate the possible loss or range of loss which may arise from these lawsuits. These matters, if decided adversely to or settled by the Company, individually or in the aggregate, may result in a liability material to the Company's consolidated financial condition or results of operations. The Company is vigorously defending itself against these actions.

## 12.  QUARTERLY FINANCIAL DATA (UNAUDITED)

The following is a summary of the quarterly consolidated results of operations from continuing operations for the fiscal years ended February 3, 2008 and January 28, 2007 (dollars in millions, except per share data):

| | Net Sales | Gross Profit | Earnings from Continuing Operations | Basic Earnings per Share from Continuing Operations | Diluted Earnings per Share from Continuing Operations |
|---|---|---|---|---|---|
| **Fiscal Year Ended February 3, 2008:** | | | | | |
| First Quarter | $    18,545 | $    6,263 | $    947 | $    0.48 | $    0.48 |
| Second Quarter | 22,184 | 7,341 | 1,521 | 0.78 | 0.77 |
| Third Quarter | 18,961 | 6,339 | 1,071 | 0.59 | 0.59 |
| Fourth Quarter | 17,659 | 6,054 | 671 | 0.40 | 0.40 |
| Fiscal Year | $    77,349 | $    25,997 | $    4,210 | $    2.28 | $    2.27 |
| | | | | | |
| **Fiscal Year Ended January 28, 2007:** | | | | | |
| First Quarter | $    19,378 | $    6,636 | $    1,391 | $    0.66 | $    0.66 |
| Second Quarter | 22,592 | 7,456 | 1,701 | 0.82 | 0.82 |
| Third Quarter | 19,648 | 6,604 | 1,333 | 0.65 | 0.65 |
| | 17,404 | 5,850 | 841 | 0.42 | 0.42 |
| Fiscal Year | $    79,022 | $    26,546 | $    5,266 | $    2.56 | $    2.55 |

*Note: The quarterly data may not sum to fiscal year totals.*

**10-Year Summary of Financial and Operating Results**
**The Home Depot, Inc. and Subsidiaries**

| amounts in millions, except where noted | 10-Year Compound Annual Growth Rate | 2007 [1] | 2006 | 2005 |
|---|---|---|---|---|
| STATEMENT OF EARNINGS DATA [2] | | | | |
| Net sales | 12.3% | $ 77,349 | $ 79,022 | $ 77,019 |
| Net sales increase (%) | — | (2.1) | 2.6 | 8.3 |
| Earnings before provision for income taxes | 13.3 | 6,620 | 8,502 | 8,967 |
| Net earnings | 13.8 | 4,210 | 5,266 | 5,641 |
| Net earnings increase (%) | — | (20.1) | (6.6) | 14.6 |
| Diluted earnings per share ($) | 15.9 | 2.27 | 2.55 | 2.63 |
| Diluted earnings per share increase (%) | — | (11.0) | (3.0) | 18.5 |
| Diluted weighted average number of common shares | (2.1) | 1,856 | 2,062 | 2,147 |
| Gross margin – % of sales | — | 33.6 | 33.6 | 33.7 |
| Total operating expenses – % of sales | — | 24.3 | 22.4 | 21.9 |
| Net interest expense (income) – % of sales | — | 0.8 | 0.5 | 0.1 |
| Earnings before provision for income taxes – % of sales | — | 8.6 | 10.8 | 11.6 |
| Net earnings – % of sales | — | 5.4 | 6.7 | 7.3 |
| | | | | |
| BALANCE SHEET DATA AND FINANCIAL RATIOS [3] | | | | |
| Total assets | 14.7% | $ 44,324 | $ 52,263 | $ 44,405 |
| Working capital | (0.2) | 1,968 | 5,069 | 2,563 |
| Merchandise inventories | 12.5 | 11,731 | 12,822 | 11,401 |
| Net property and equipment | 15.5 | 27,476 | 26,605 | 24,901 |
| Long-term debt | 24.2 | 11,383 | 11,643 | 2,672 |
| Stockholders' equity | 9.6 | 17,714 | 25,030 | 26,909 |
| Book value per share ($) | 12.5 | 10.48 | 12.71 | 12.67 |
| Long-term debt-to-equity (%) | — | 64.3 | 46.5 | 9.9 |
| Total debt-to-equity (%) | — | 75.8 | 46.6 | 15.2 |
| Current ratio | — | 1.15:1 | 1.39:1 | 1.20:1 |
| Inventory turnover [2] | — | 4.2x | 4.5x | 4.7x |
| Return on invested capital (%) [2] | — | 13.9 | 16.8 | 20.4 |
| | | | | |
| STATEMENT OF CASH FLOWS DATA | | | | |
| Depreciation and amortization | 21.0% | $ 1,906 | $ 1,886 | $ 1,579 |
| Capital expenditures | 9.3 | 3,558 | 3,542 | 3,881 |
| Payments for businesses acquired, net | (14.3) | 13 | 4,268 | 2,546 |
| Cash dividends per share ($) | 30.5 | 0.900 | 0.675 | 0.400 |
| | | | | |
| STORE DATA | | | | |
| Number of stores | 13.6% | 2,234 | 2,147 | 2,042 |
| Square footage at fiscal year-end | 13.5 | 235 | 224 | 215 |
| Increase in square footage (%) | — | 4.9 | 4.2 | 7.0 |
| Average square footage per store (in thousands) | (0.1) | 105 | 105 | 105 |
| | | | | |
| STORE SALES AND OTHER DATA | | | | |
| Comparable store sales increase (decrease) (%) [4][5] | — | (6.7) | (2.8) | 3.1 |
| Weighted average weekly sales per operating store (in thousands) | (2.3)% | $ 658 | $ 723 | $ 763 |
| Weighted average sales per square foot ($) | (2.0) | 332 | 358 | 377 |
| Number of customer transactions | 9.3 | 1,336 | 1,330 | 1,330 |
| Average ticket ($) | 2.8 | 57.48 | 58.90 | 57.98 |
| Number of associates at fiscal year-end [3] | 10.3 | 331,000 | 364,400 | 344,800 |

(1) Fiscal years 2007 and 2001 include 53 weeks; all other fiscal years reported include 52 weeks.
(2) Fiscal years 2003 through 2007 include Continuing Operations only. The discontinued operations prior to 2003 were not material.
(3) Fiscal year 2007 amounts include Continuing Operations only. Fiscal years 1998-2006 amounts include discontinued operations, except as noted.

|  | | 2004 | 2003 | 2002 | 2001 [1] | 2000 | 1999 | 1998 |
|---|---|---|---|---|---|---|---|---|
| *STATEMENT OF EARNINGS DATA* [2] | | | | | | | | |
| Net sales | $ | 71,100 $ | 63,660 $ | 58,247 $ | 53,553 $ | 45,738 $ | 38,434 $ | 30,219 |
| Net sales increase (%) | | 11.7 | 9.3 | 8.8 | 17.1 | 19.0 | 27.2 | 25.1 |
| Earnings before provision for income taxes | | 7,790 | 6,762 | 5,872 | 4,957 | 4,217 | 3,804 | 2,654 |
| Net earnings | | 4,922 | 4,253 | 3,664 | 3,044 | 2,581 | 2,320 | 1,614 |
| Net earnings increase (%) | | 15.7 | 16.1 | 20.4 | 17.9 | 11.3 | 43.7 | 31.9 |
| Diluted earnings per share ($) | | 2.22 | 1.86 | 1.56 | 1.29 | 1.10 | 1.00 | 0.71 |
| Diluted earnings per share increase (%) | | 19.4 | 19.2 | 20.9 | 17.3 | 10.0 | 40.8 | 29.1 |
| Diluted weighted average number of common shares | | 2,216 | 2,289 | 2,344 | 2,353 | 2,352 | 2,342 | 2,320 |
| Gross margin – % of sales | | 33.4 | 31.7 | 31.1 | 30.2 | 29.9 | 29.7 | 28.5 |
| Total operating expenses – % of sales | | 22.4 | 21.1 | 21.1 | 20.9 | 20.7 | 19.8 | 19.7 |
| Net interest expense (income) – % of sales | | — | — | (0.1) | — | — | — | — |
| Earnings before provision for income taxes – % of sales | | 11.0 | 10.6 | 10.1 | 9.3 | 9.2 | 9.9 | 8.8 |
| Net earnings – % of sales | | 6.9 | 6.7 | 6.3 | 5.7 | 5.6 | 6.0 | 5.3 |
| | | | | | | | | |
| *BALANCE SHEET DATA AND FINANCIAL RATIOS* [3] | | | | | | | | |
| Total assets | $ | 39,020 $ | 34,437 $ | 30,011 $ | 26,394 $ | 21,385 $ | 17,081 $ | 13,465 |
| Working capital | | 3,818 | 3,774 | 3,882 | 3,860 | 3,392 | 2,734 | 2,076 |
| Merchandise inventories | | 10,076 | 9,076 | 8,338 | 6,725 | 6,556 | 5,489 | 4,293 |
| Net property and equipment | | 22,726 | 20,063 | 17,168 | 15,375 | 13,068 | 10,227 | 8,160 |
| Long-term debt | | 2,148 | 856 | 1,321 | 1,250 | 1,545 | 750 | 1,566 |
| Stockholders' equity | | 24,158 | 22,407 | 19,802 | 18,082 | 15,004 | 12,341 | 8,740 |
| Book value per share ($) | | 11.06 | 9.93 | 8.38 | 7.71 | 6.46 | 5.36 | 3.95 |
| Long-term debt-to-equity (%) | | 8.9 | 3.8 | 6.7 | 6.9 | 10.3 | 6.1 | 17.9 |
| Total debt-to-equity (%) | | 8.9 | 6.1 | 6.7 | 6.9 | 10.3 | 6.1 | 17.9 |
| Current ratio | | 1.37:1 | 1.40:1 | 1.48:1 | 1.59:1 | 1.77:1 | 1.75:1 | 1.73:1 |
| Inventory turnover [2] | | 4.9x | 5.0x | 5.3x | 5.4x | 5.1x | 5.4x | 5.4x |
| Return on invested capital (%) [2] | | 19.9 | 19.2 | 18.8 | 18.3 | 19.6 | 22.5 | 19.3 |
| | | | | | | | | |
| *STATEMENT OF CASH FLOWS DATA* | | | | | | | | |
| Depreciation and amortization | $ | 1,319 $ | 1,076 $ | 903 $ | 764 $ | 601 $ | 463 $ | 373 |
| Capital expenditures | | 3,948 | 3,508 | 2,749 | 3,393 | 3,574 | 2,618 | 2,094 |
| Payments for businesses acquired, net | | 727 | 215 | 235 | 190 | 26 | 101 | 6 |
| Cash dividends per share ($) | | 0.325 | 0.26 | 0.21 | 0.17 | 0.16 | 0.11 | 0.08 |
| | | | | | | | | |
| *STORE DATA* | | | | | | | | |
| Number of stores | | 1,890 | 1,707 | 1,532 | 1,333 | 1,134 | 930 | 761 |
| Square footage at fiscal year-end | | 201 | 183 | 166 | 146 | 123 | 100 | 81 |
| Increase in square footage (%) | | 9.8 | 10.2 | 14.1 | 18.5 | 22.6 | 23.5 | 22.8 |
| Average square footage per store (in thousands) | | 106 | 107 | 108 | 109 | 108 | 108 | 107 |
| | | | | | | | | |
| *STORE SALES AND OTHER DATA* | | | | | | | | |
| Comparable store sales increase (decrease) (%) [4][5] | | 5.1 | 3.7 | (0.5) | — | 4 | 10 | 7 |
| Weighted average weekly sales per operating store (in thousands) | $ | 766 $ | 763 $ | 772 $ | 812 $ | 864 $ | 876 $ | 844 |
| Weighted average sales per square foot ($) | | 375 | 371 | 370 | 394 | 415 | 423 | 410 |
| Number of customer transactions | | 1,295 | 1,246 | 1,161 | 1,091 | 937 | 797 | 665 |
| Average ticket ($) | | 54.89 | 51.15 | 49.43 | 48.64 | 48.65 | 47.87 | 45.05 |
| Number of associates at fiscal year-end [3] | | 323,100 | 298,800 | 280,900 | 256,300 | 227,300 | 201,400 | 156,700 |

(4)    Includes Net Sales at locations open greater than 12 months, including relocated and remodeled stores. Stores become comparable on the Monday following their 365 th day of operation. Comparable store sales is intended only as supplemental information and is not a substitute for Net Sales or Net Earnings presented in accordance with generally accepted accounting principles.

(5)    Comparable store sales in fiscal years prior to 2002 were reported to the nearest percent.

# Corporate and Shareholder Information

**STORE SUPPORT CENTER**
The Home Depot, Inc.
2455 Paces Ferry Road, NW
Atlanta, GA 30339-4024
Telephone: (770) 433-8211

**THE HOME DEPOT WEB SITE**
www.homedepot.com

**TRANSFER AGENT AND REGISTRAR**
Computershare Trust Company, N.A.
P.O. Box 43078
Providence, RI 02490-3078
Telephone: (800) 577-0177
Internet address: www.computershare.com/investor

**INDEPENDENT REGISTERED PUBLIC
ACCOUNTING FIRM**
KPMG LLP
Suite 2000
303 Peachtree Street, NE
Atlanta, GA 30308

**STOCK EXCHANGE LISTING**
New York Stock Exchange
Trading symbol – HD

**ANNUAL MEETING**
The Annual Meeting of Shareholders will be held at 9
a.m., Eastern Time, May 22, 2008, at Cobb Galleria Centre
in Atlanta, Georgia.

**NUMBER OF SHAREHOLDERS**
As of March 24, 2008, there were approximately 160,000
shareholders of record and approximately 1,400,000
individual shareholders holding stock under nominee
security posting listings.

**DIVIDENDS DECLARED PER COMMON SHARE**

|  | First Quarter | Second Quarter | Third Quarter | Fourth Quarter |
|---|---|---|---|---|
| **Fiscal 2007** | **$0.225** | **$0.225** | **$0.225** | **$0.225** |
| Fiscal 2006 | $0.150 | $0.150 | $0.225 | $0.225 |

New investors may make an initial investment, and
shareholders of record may acquire additional shares
of our common stock through our direct stock purchase
and dividend reinvestment plan. Subject to certain
requirements, initial cash investments, cash dividends
and/or additional optional cash purchases may be invested
through this plan. To obtain enrollment materials
including the prospectus, access The Home Depot
web site, or call (877) HD-SHARE or (877) 437-4273.
For all other communications regarding these services,
contact Computershare.

**FINANCIAL AND OTHER
COMPANY INFORMATION**
Our Annual Report on Form 10-K for the fiscal year ended February 3, 2008 is available on our web site at www.
homedepot.com under the Investor Relations section. In
addition, financial reports, filing with the Securities and
Exchange Commission, news releases and other information are available on The Home Depot web site.

The Home Depot, Inc. has included as exhibits to its Annual Report on Form 10-K for the fiscal year ended February 3, 2008 certifications of The Home Depot's Chief
Executive Officer and Chief Financial Officer. The Home
Depot's Chief Executive Officer has also submitted to the
New York Stock Exchange (NYSE) a certificate certifying
that he is not aware of any violations by The Home Depot
of the NYSE corporate governance listing standards.

**QUARTERLY STOCK PRICE RANGE**

|  | First Quarter | Second Quarter | Third Quarter | Fourth Quarter |
|---|---|---|---|---|
| **Fiscal 2007** | | | | |
| **High** | **$41.76** | **$40.94** | **$38.31** | **$31.51** |
| **Low** | **$36.74** | **$36.75** | **$30.70** | **$24.71** |
| Fiscal 2006 | | | | |
| High | $43.95 | $41.61 | $38.24 | $41.84 |
| Low | $38.50 | $32.85 | $33.07 | $35.77 |

**Concept and Design:** Sagepath (www.sagepath.com)
**Photography:** Doug Coulter, Craig Bromley, Kim Steele
**Printer:** Cenveo

# LOWE'S COMPANIES, INC. 2007 FORM 10-K ANNUAL REPORT*

---

* This appendix contains excerpts. Go to the text Web site at www.mhhe.com/LLPW1e for the complete report.

**Management's Report on Internal Control Over Financial Reporting**

Management of Lowe's Companies, Inc. and its subsidiaries is responsible for establishing and maintaining adequate internal control over financial reporting (Internal Control) as defined in Rule 13a-15(f) under the Securities Exchange Act of 1934, as amended. Our Internal Control was designed to provide reasonable assurance to our management and the board of directors regarding the reliability of financial reporting and the preparation and fair presentation of published financial statements.

All internal control systems, no matter how well designed, have inherent limitations, including the possibility of human error and the circumvention or overriding of controls. Therefore, even those systems determined to be effective can provide only reasonable assurance with respect to the reliability of financial reporting and financial statement preparation and presentation. Further, because of changes in conditions, the effectiveness may vary over time.

Our management, with the participation of the Chief Executive Officer and Chief Financial Officer, evaluated the effectiveness of our Internal Control as of February 1, 2008. In evaluating our Internal Control, we used the criteria set forth by the Committee of Sponsoring Organizations of the Treadway Commission (COSO) in *Internal Control—Integrated Framework* . Based on our management's assessment, we have concluded that, as of February 1, 2008, our Internal Control is effective.

Deloitte & Touche LLP, the independent registered public accounting firm that audited the financial statements contained in this report, was engaged to audit our Internal Control . Their report appears on page 27.

**Report of Independent Registered Public Accounting Firm**

To the Board of Directors and Shareholders of Lowe's Companies, Inc.
Mooresville, North Carolina

We have audited the accompanying consolidated balance sheets of Lowe's Companies, Inc. and subsidiaries (the "Company") as of February 1, 2008 and February 2, 2007, and the related consolidated statements of earnings, shareholders' equity, and cash flows for each of the three fiscal years in the period ended February 1, 2008. These financial statements are the responsibility of the Company's management. Our responsibility is to express an opinion on these financial statements based on our audits.

We conducted our audits in accordance with the standards of the Public Company Accounting Oversight Board (United States). Those standards require that we plan and perform the audit to obtain reasonable assurance about whether the financial statements are free of material misstatement. An audit includes examining, on a test basis, evidence supporting the amounts and disclosures in the financial statements. An audit also includes assessing the accounting principles used and significant estimates made by management, as well as evaluating the overall financial statement presentation. We believe that our audits provide a reasonable basis for our opinion.

In our opinion, such consolidated financial statements present fairly, in all material respects, the financial position of the Company at February 1, 2008 and February 2, 2007, and the results of its operations and its cash flows for each of the three fiscal years in the period ended February 1, 2008, in conformity with accounting principles generally accepted in the United States of America.

We have also audited, in accordance with the standards of the Public Company Accounting Oversight Board (United States), the Company's internal control over financial reporting as of February 1, 2008, based on the criteria established in *Internal Control—Integrated Framework* issued by the Committee of Sponsoring Organizations of the Treadway Commission and our report dated April 1, 2008 expressed an unqualified opinion on the Company's internal control over financial reporting.


/s/ Deloitte & Touche LLP

Charlotte, North Carolina
April 1, 2008


**Report of Independent Registered Public Accounting Firm**

To the Board of Directors and Shareholders of Lowe's Companies, Inc.
Mooresville, North Carolina

We have audited the internal control over financial reporting of Lowe's Companies, Inc. and subsidiaries (the "Company") as of February 1, 2008 based on criteria established in *Internal Control — Integrated Framework* issued by the Committee of Sponsoring Organizations of the Treadway Commission. The Company's management is responsible for maintaining effective internal control over financial reporting and for its assessment of the effectiveness of internal control over financial reporting, included in the accompanying Management's Report on Internal Control Over Financial Reporting. Our responsibility is to express an opinion on the Company's internal control over financial reporting based on our audit.

We conducted our audit in accordance with the standards of the Public Company Accounting Oversight Board (United States). Those standards require that we plan and perform the audit to obtain reasonable assurance about whether effective internal control over financial reporting was maintained in all material respects. Our audit included obtaining an understanding of internal control over financial reporting, assessing the risk that a material weakness exists, testing and evaluating the design and operating effectiveness of internal control based on the assessed risk, and performing such other procedures as we considered necessary in the circumstances. We believe that our audit provides a reasonable basis for our opinion.

A company's internal control over financial reporting is a process designed by, or under the supervision of, the company's principal executive and principal financial officers, or persons performing similar functions, and effected by the company's board of directors, management, and other personnel to provide reasonable assurance regarding the reliability of financial reporting and the preparation of financial statements for external purposes in accordance with generally accepted accounting principles. A company's internal control over financial reporting includes those policies and procedures that (1) pertain to the maintenance of records that, in reasonable detail, accurately and fairly reflect the transactions and dispositions of the assets of the company; (2) provide reasonable assurance that transactions are recorded as necessary to permit preparation of financial statements in accordance with generally accepted accounting principles, and that receipts and expenditures of the company are being made only in accordance with authorizations of management and directors of the company; and (3) provide reasonable assurance regarding prevention or timely detection of unauthorized acquisition, use, or disposition of the company's assets that could have a material effect on the financial statements.

Because of the inherent limitations of internal control over financial reporting, including the possibility of collusion or improper management override of controls, material misstatements due to error or fraud may not be prevented or detected on a timely basis. Also, projections of any evaluation of the effectiveness of the internal control over financial reporting to future periods are subject to the risk that the controls may become inadequate because of changes in conditions, or that the degree of compliance with the policies or procedures may deteriorate.

In our opinion, the Company maintained, in all material respects, effective internal control over financial reporting as of February 1, 2008, based on the criteria established in *Internal Control — Integrated Framework* issued by the Committee of Sponsoring Organizations of the Treadway Commission.

We have also audited, in accordance with the standards of the Public Company Accounting Oversight Board (United States), the consolidated financial statements as of and for the fiscal year ended February 1, 2008 of the Company and our report dated April 1, 2008 expressed an unqualified opinion on those financial statements.

/s/ Deloitte & Touche LLP

Charlotte, North Carolina
April 1, 2008

**Lowe's Companies, Inc.**
**Consolidated Statements of Earnings**

| (In millions, except per share and percentage data)<br>Fiscal years ended on | February 1, 2008 | % Sales | February 2, 2007 | % Sales | February 3, 2006 | % Sales |
|---|---|---|---|---|---|---|
| Net sales (Note 1) | $ 48,283 | 100.00% | $ 46,927 | 100.00% | $ 43,243 | 100.00% |
| Cost of sales (Notes 1 and 14) | 31,556 | 65.36 | 30,729 | 65.48 | 28,453 | 65.80 |
| **Gross margin** | **16,727** | **34.64** | **16,198** | **34.52** | **14,790** | **34.20** |
| Expenses: | | | | | | |
| Selling, general and administrative (Notes 1, 8, 9 and 12) | 10,515 | 21.78 | 9,738 | 20.75 | 9,014 | 20.84 |
| Store opening costs (Note 1) | 141 | 0.29 | 146 | 0.31 | 142 | 0.33 |
| Depreciation (Notes 1 and 3) | 1,366 | 2.83 | 1,162 | 2.48 | 980 | 2.27 |
| Interest - net (Note 15) | 194 | 0.40 | 154 | 0.33 | 158 | 0.37 |
| **Total expenses** | **12,216** | **25.30** | **11,200** | **23.87** | **10,294** | **23.81** |
| **Pre-tax earnings** | **4,511** | **9.34** | **4,998** | **10.65** | **4,496** | **10.39** |
| Income tax provision (Notes 1 and 10) | 1,702 | 3.52 | 1,893 | 4.03 | 1,731 | 4.00 |
| **Net earnings** | $ **2,809** | **5.82%** | $ **3,105** | **6.62%** | $ **2,765** | **6.39%** |
| **Basic earnings per share (Note 11)** | $ **1.90** | | $ **2.02** | | $ **1.78** | |
| **Diluted earnings per share (Note 11)** | $ **1.86** | | $ **1.99** | | $ **1.73** | |
| **Cash dividends per share** | $ **0.29** | | $ **0.18** | | $ **0.11** | |

*See accompanying notes to the consolidated financial statements.*

**Lowe's Companies, Inc.**
**Consolidated Balance Sheets**

| (In millions, except par value and percentage data) | | February 1, 2008 | % Total | February 2, 2007 | % Total |
|---|---|---|---|---|---|
| **Assets** | | | | | |
| **Current assets:** | | | | | |
| Cash and cash equivalents (Note 1) | | $    281 | 0.9% $ | 364 | 1.3% |
| Short-term investments (Notes 1 and 2) | | 249 | 0.8 | 432 | 1.6 |
| Merchandise inventory - net (Note 1) | | 7,611 | 24.6 | 7,144 | 25.7 |
| Deferred income taxes - net (Notes 1 and 10) | | 247 | 0.8 | 161 | 0.6 |
| Other current assets (Note 1) | | 298 | 1.0 | 213 | 0.8 |
| **Total current assets** | | **8,686** | **28.1** | **8,314** | **30.0** |
| Property, less accumulated depreciation (Notes 1 and 3) | | 21,361 | 69.2 | 18,971 | 68.3 |
| Long-term investments (Notes 1 and 2) | | 509 | 1.7 | 165 | 0.6 |
| Other assets (Note 1) | | 313 | 1.0 | 317 | 1.1 |
| **Total assets** | | $  **30,869** | **100.0%** $ | **27,767** | **100.0%** |
| | | | | | |
| **Liabilities and shareholders' equity** | | | | | |
| **Current liabilities:** | | | | | |
| Short-term borrowings (Note 4) | | $  1,064 | 3.5% $ | 23 | 0.1% |
| Current maturities of long-term debt (Note 5) | | 40 | 0.1 | 88 | 0.3 |
| Accounts payable (Note 1) | | 3,713 | 12.0 | 3,524 | 12.7 |
| Accrued salaries and wages | | 424 | 1.4 | 425 | 1.5 |
| Self-insurance liabilities (Note 1) | | 671 | 2.2 | 650 | 2.4 |
| Deferred revenue (Note 1) | | 717 | 2.3 | 731 | 2.6 |
| Other current liabilities (Note 1) | | 1,122 | 3.6 | 1,098 | 3.9 |
| **Total current liabilities** | | **7,751** | **25.1** | **6,539** | **23.5** |
| Long-term debt, excluding current maturities (Notes 5, 6 and 12) | | 5,576 | 18.1 | 4,325 | 15.6 |
| Deferred income taxes - net (Notes 1 and 10) | | 670 | 2.2 | 735 | 2.7 |
| Other liabilities (Note 1) | | 774 | 2.5 | 443 | 1.6 |
| **Total liabilities** | | **14,771** | **47.9** | **12,042** | **43.4** |
| | | | | | |
| Commitments and contingencies (Note 13) | | | | | |
| | | | | | |
| **Shareholders' equity** (Note 7) : | | | | | |
| Preferred stock - $5 par value, none issued | | - | - | - | - |
| Common stock - $.50 par value; | | | | | |
| Shares issued and outstanding | | | | | |
| February 1, 2008 | 1,458 | | | | |
| February 2, 2007 | 1,525 | 729 | 2.3 | 762 | 2.7 |
| Capital in excess of par value | | 16 | 0.1 | 102 | 0.4 |
| Retained earnings | | 15,345 | 49.7 | 14,860 | 53.5 |
| Accumulated other comprehensive income (Note 1) | | 8 | - | 1 | - |
| **Total shareholders' equity** | | **16,098** | **52.1** | **15,725** | **56.6** |
| **Total liabilities and shareholders' equity** | | $  **30,869** | **100.0%** $ | **27,767** | **100.0%** |

*See accompanying notes to the consolidated financial statements.*

**Lowe's Companies, Inc.**
**Consolidated Statements of**
**Shareholders' Equity**

| (In millions) | Common Stock Shares | Common Stock Amount | Capital in Excess of Par Value | Retained Earnings | Accumulated Other Comprehensive Income | Total Shareholders' Equity |
|---|---|---|---|---|---|---|
| **Balance January 28, 2005** | **1,548** $ | **774** $ | **1,127** $ | **9,597** $ | **-** $ | **11,498** |
| Comprehensive income (Note 1): | | | | | | |
| Net earnings | | | | 2,765 | | |
| Foreign currency translation | | | | | 1 | |
| Total comprehensive income | | | | | | 2,766 |
| Tax effect of non-qualified stock options exercised | | | 59 | | | 59 |
| Cash dividends | | | | (171) | | (171) |
| Share-based payment expense (Note 8) | | | 76 | | | 76 |
| Repurchase of common stock (Note 7) | (25) | (12) | (762) | | | (774) |
| Conversion of debt to common stock (Note 5) | 28 | 14 | 551 | | | 565 |
| Employee stock options exercised and other (Note 8) | 15 | 7 | 205 | | | 212 |
| Employee stock purchase plan (Note 8) | 2 | 1 | 64 | | | 65 |
| **Balance February 3, 2006** | **1,568** $ | **784** $ | **1,320** $ | **12,191** $ | **1** $ | **14,296** |
| Comprehensive income (Note 1): | | | | | | |
| Net earnings | | | | 3,105 | | |
| Foreign currency translation | | | | | (2) | |
| Net unrealized investment gains (Note 2) | | | | | 2 | |
| Total comprehensive income | | | | | | 3,105 |
| Tax effect of non-qualified stock options exercised | | | 21 | | | 21 |
| Cash dividends | | | | (276) | | (276) |
| Share-based payment expense (Note 8) | | | 59 | | | 59 |
| Repurchase of common stock (Note 7) | (57) | (28) | (1,549) | (160) | | (1,737) |
| Conversion of debt to common stock (Note 5) | 4 | 2 | 80 | | | 82 |
| Employee stock options exercised and other (Note 8) | 7 | 3 | 96 | | | 99 |
| Employee stock purchase plan (Note 8) | 3 | 1 | 75 | | | 76 |
| **Balance February 2, 2007** | **1,525** $ | **762** $ | **102** $ | **14,860** $ | **1** $ | **15,725** |
| Cumulative effect adjustment (Note 10): | | | | (8) | | (8) |
| Comprehensive income (Note 1): | | | | | | |
| Net earnings | | | | 2,809 | | |
| Foreign currency translation | | | | | 7 | |
| Total comprehensive income | | | | | | 2,816 |
| Tax effect of non-qualified stock options exercised | | | 12 | | | 12 |
| Cash dividends | | | | (428) | | (428) |
| Share-based payment expense (Note 8) | | | 99 | | | 99 |
| Repurchase of common stock (Note 7) | (76) | (38) | (349) | (1,888) | | (2,275) |
| Conversion of debt to common stock (Note 5) | 1 | - | 13 | | | 13 |
| Employee stock options exercised and other (Note 8) | 5 | 3 | 61 | | | 64 |
| Employee stock purchase plan (Note 8) | 3 | 2 | 78 | | | 80 |
| **Balance February 1, 2008** | **1,458** $ | **729** $ | **16** $ | **15,345** $ | **8** $ | **16,098** |

*See accompanying notes to the consolidated financial statements.*

**Lowe's Companies, Inc.**
**Consolidated Statements of Cash Flows**

| (In millions)<br>Fiscal years ended on | February 1,<br>2008 | February 2,<br>2007 | February 3,<br>2006 |
|---|---|---|---|
| **Cash flows from operating activities:** | | | |
| Net earnings | $      2,809 | $      3,105 | $      2,765 |
| Adjustments to reconcile earnings to net cash provided by operating activities: | | | |
| Depreciation and amortization | 1,464 | 1,237 | 1,051 |
| Deferred income taxes | 2 | (6) | (37) |
| Loss on disposition/writedown of fixed and other assets | 51 | 23 | 31 |
| Share-based payment expense | 99 | 62 | 76 |
| Changes in operating assets and liabilities: | | | |
| Merchandise inventory - net | (464) | (509) | (785) |
| Other operating assets | (64) | (135) | (38) |
| Accounts payable | 185 | 692 | 137 |
| Other operating liabilities | 265 | 33 | 642 |
| **Net cash provided by operating activities** | **4,347** | **4,502** | **3,842** |
| | | | |
| **Cash flows from investing activities:** | | | |
| Purchases of short-term investments | (920) | (284) | (1,829) |
| Proceeds from sale/maturity of short-term investments | 1,183 | 572 | 1,802 |
| Purchases of long-term investments | (1,588) | (558) | (354) |
| Proceeds from sale/maturity of long-term investments | 1,162 | 415 | 55 |
| Increase in other long-term assets | (7) | (16) | (30) |
| Fixed assets acquired | (4,010) | (3,916) | (3,379) |
| Proceeds from the sale of fixed and other long-term assets | 57 | 72 | 61 |
| **Net cash used in investing activities** | **(4,123)** | **(3,715)** | **(3,674)** |
| | | | |
| **Cash flows from financing activities:** | | | |
| Net increase in short-term borrowings | 1,041 | 23 | - |
| Proceeds from issuance of long-term debt | 1,296 | 989 | 1,013 |
| Repayment of long-term debt | (96) | (33) | (633) |
| Proceeds from issuance of common stock under employee stock purchase plan | 80 | 76 | 65 |
| Proceeds from issuance of common stock from stock options exercised | 69 | 100 | 225 |
| Cash dividend payments | (428) | (276) | (171) |
| Repurchase of common stock | (2,275) | (1,737) | (774) |
| Excess tax benefits of share-based payments | 6 | 12 | - |
| **Net cash used in financing activities** | **(307)** | **(846)** | **(275)** |
| | | | |
| Net decrease in cash and cash equivalents | (83) | (59) | (107) |
| Cash and cash equivalents, beginning of year | 364 | 423 | 530 |
| **Cash and cash equivalents, end of year** | $      **281** | $      **364** | $      **423** |

*See accompanying notes to the consolidated financial statements.*

**NOTES TO CONSOLIDATED FINANCIAL STATEMENTS**
**YEARS ENDED FEBRUARY 1, 2008, FEBRUARY 2, 2007 AND FEBRUARY 3, 2006**

**NOTE 1 - Summary of Significant Accounting Policies:**

Lowe's Companies, Inc. and subsidiaries (the Company) is the world's second-largest home improvement retailer and operated 1,534 stores in the United States and Canada at February 1, 2008. Below are those accounting policies considered by the Company to be significant.

**Fiscal Year -** The Company's fiscal year ends on the Friday nearest the end of January. The fiscal years ended February 1, 2008 and February 2, 2007 contained 52 weeks. The fiscal year ended February 3, 2006 contained 53 weeks. All references herein for the years 2007, 2006 and 2005 represent the fiscal years ended February 1, 2008, February 2, 2007 and February 3, 2006, respectively.

**Principles of Consolidation -** The consolidated financial statements include the accounts of the Company and its wholly-owned or controlled operating subsidiaries. All material intercompany accounts and transactions have been eliminated.

**Use of Estimates -** The preparation of the Company's financial statements in accordance with accounting principles generally accepted in the United States of America requires management to make estimates that affect the reported amounts of assets, liabilities, sales and expenses, and related disclosures of contingent assets and liabilities. The Company bases these estimates on historical results and various other assumptions believed to be reasonable, all of which form the basis for making estimates concerning the carrying values of assets and liabilities that are not readily available from other sources. Actual results may differ from these estimates.

**Cash and Cash Equivalents -** Cash and cash equivalents include cash on hand, demand deposits and short-term investments with original maturities of three months or less when purchased. The majority of payments due from financial institutions for the settlement of credit card and debit card transactions process within two business days and are, therefore, classified as cash and cash equivalents.

**Investments -** The Company has a cash management program which provides for the investment of cash balances not expected to be used in current operations in financial instruments that have maturities of up to 10 years. Variable-rate demand notes, which have stated maturity dates in excess of 10 years, meet this maturity requirement of the cash management program because the maturity date of these investments is determined based on the interest rate reset date or par value put date for the purpose of applying this criteria.

Investments, exclusive of cash equivalents, with a stated maturity date of one year or less from the balance sheet date or that are expected to be used in current operations, are classified as short-term investments. All other investments are classified as long-term. As of February 1, 2008, investments consisted primarily of money market funds, certificates of deposit, municipal obligations and mutual funds. Restricted balances pledged as collateral for letters of credit for the Company's extended warranty program and for a portion of the Company's casualty insurance and installed sales program liabilities are also classified as investments.

The Company has classified all investment securities as available-for-sale, and they are carried at fair market value. Unrealized gains and losses on such securities are included in accumulated other comprehensive income in shareholders' equity.

**Merchandise Inventory -** Inventory is stated at the lower of cost or market using the first-in, first-out method of inventory accounting. The cost of inventory also includes certain costs associated with the preparation of inventory for resale and distribution center costs, net of vendor funds.

The Company records an inventory reserve for the loss associated with selling inventories below cost. This reserve is based on management's current knowledge with respect to inventory levels, sales trends and historical experience. Management does not believe the Company's merchandise inventories are subject to significant risk of obsolescence in the near term, and management has the ability to adjust purchasing practices based on anticipated sales trends and general economic conditions. However, changes in consumer purchasing patterns could result in the need for additional reserves. The Company also records an inventory reserve for the estimated shrinkage between physical inventories. This reserve is based primarily on actual shrink results from previous physical inventories. Changes in the estimated shrink reserve may be necessary based on the results of physical inventories. Management believes it has sufficient current and historical knowledge to record reasonable estimates for both of these inventory reserves.

**Derivative Financial Instruments -** The Company occasionally utilizes derivative financial instruments to manage certain business risks. However, the amounts were not material to the Company's consolidated financial statements in any of the years presented. The Company does not use derivative financial instruments for trading purposes.

**Credit Programs -** The majority of the Company's accounts receivable arises from sales of goods and services to Commercial Business Customers. In May 2004, the Company entered into an agreement with General Electric Company and its subsidiaries (GE) to sell its then-existing portfolio of commercial business accounts receivable to GE. During the term of the agreement, which ends on December 31, 2016, unless terminated sooner by the parties, GE also purchases at face value new commercial business accounts receivable originated by the Company and services these accounts. The Company accounts for these transfers as sales of accounts receivable. When the Company sells its commercial business accounts receivable, it retains certain interests in those receivables, including the funding of a loss reserve and its obligation related to GE's ongoing servicing of the receivables sold. Any gain or loss on the sale is determined based on the previous carrying amounts of the transferred assets allocated at fair value between the receivables sold and the interests retained. Fair value is based on the present value of expected future cash flows, taking into account the key assumptions of anticipated credit losses, payment rates, late fee rates, GE's servicing costs and the discount rate commensurate with the uncertainty involved. Due to the short-term nature of the receivables sold, changes to the key assumptions would not materially impact the recorded gain or loss on the sales of receivables or the fair value of the retained interests in the receivables.

Total commercial business accounts receivable sold to GE were $1.8 billion in both 2007 and 2006, and $1.7 billion in 2005. During 2007, 2006 and 2005, the Company recognized losses of $34 million, $35 million and $41 million, respectively, on these sales as selling, general and administrative (SG&A) expense, which primarily relates to the fair value of the obligations incurred related to servicing costs that are remitted to GE monthly. At February 1, 2008 and February 2, 2007, the fair value of the retained interests was insignificant and was determined based on the present value of expected future cash flows.

Sales generated through the Company's proprietary credit cards are not reflected in receivables. Under an agreement with GE, credit is extended directly to customers by GE. All credit program-related services are performed and controlled directly by GE. The Company has the option, but no obligation, to purchase the receivables at the end of the agreement in December 2016. Tender costs, including amounts associated with accepting the Company's proprietary credit cards, are recorded in SG&A in the consolidated financial statements.

The total portfolio of receivables held by GE, including both receivables originated by GE from the Company's private label credit cards and commercial business accounts receivable originated by the Company and sold to GE, approximated $6.6 billion at February 1, 2008, and $6.0 billion at February 2, 2007.

**Property and Depreciation** - Property is recorded at cost. Costs associated with major additions are capitalized and depreciated. Capital assets are expected to yield future benefits and have useful lives which exceed one year. The total cost of a capital asset generally includes all applicable sales taxes, delivery costs, installation costs and other appropriate costs incurred by the Company in the case of self-constructed assets. Upon disposal, the cost of properties and related accumulated depreciation are removed from the accounts, with gains and losses reflected in SG&A expense in the consolidated statements of earnings.

Depreciation is provided over the estimated useful lives of the depreciable assets. Assets are depreciated using the straight-line method. Leasehold improvements are depreciated over the shorter of their estimated useful lives or the term of the related lease, which may include one or more option renewal periods where failure to exercise such options would result in an economic penalty in such amount that renewal appears, at the inception of the lease, to be reasonably assured. During the term of a lease, if a substantial additional investment is made in a leased location, the Company reevaluates its definition of lease term to determine whether the investment, together with any penalties related to non-renewal, would constitute an economic penalty in such amount that renewal appears, at the time of the reevaluation, to be reasonably assured.

**Long-Lived Asset Impairment/Exit Activities** - The carrying amounts of long-lived assets are reviewed whenever events or changes in circumstances indicate that the carrying amount may not be recoverable.

For long-lived assets held for use, a potential impairment has occurred if projected future undiscounted cash flows expected to result from the use and eventual disposition of the assets are less than the carrying value of the assets. An impairment loss is recognized when the carrying amount of the long-lived asset is not recoverable and exceeds its fair value. The Company estimates fair value based on projected future discounted cash flows.

For long-lived assets to be abandoned, the Company considers the asset to be disposed of when it ceases to be used. Until it ceases to be used, the Company continues to classify the assets as held for use and tests for potential impairment accordingly. If the Company commits to a plan to abandon a long-lived asset before the end of its previously estimated useful life, depreciation estimates are revised.

For long-lived assets held for sale, an impairment charge is recorded if the carrying amount of the asset exceeds its fair value less cost to sell. Fair value is based on a market appraisal or a valuation technique that considers various factors, including local market conditions. A long-lived asset is not depreciated while it is classified as held for sale.

The net carrying value for relocated stores, closed stores and other excess properties that are expected to be sold within the next 12 months are classified as held for sale and included in other current assets in the consolidated balance sheets. Assets held for sale totaled $28 million at February 1, 2008. Assets held for sale at February 2, 2007 were not significant. The net carrying value for relocated stores, closed stores and other excess properties that do not meet the held for sale criteria are included in other assets (non-current) in the consolidated balance sheets and totaled $91 million and $113 million at February 1, 2008 and February 2, 2007, respectively.

When operating leased locations are closed, a liability is recognized for the fair value of future contractual obligations, including property taxes, utilities and common area maintenance, net of estimated sublease income. The liability, which is included in other current liabilities in the consolidated balance sheets, was $11 million and $19 million at February 1, 2008 and February 2, 2007, respectively.

The charge for impairment is included in SG&A expense and totaled $28 million, $5 million and $16 million in 2007, 2006 and 2005, respectively.

**Leases** - For lease agreements that provide for escalating rent payments or free-rent occupancy periods, the Company recognizes rent expense on a straight-line basis over the non-cancelable lease term and option renewal periods where failure to exercise such options would result in an economic penalty in such amount that renewal appears, at the inception of the lease, to be reasonably assured. The lease term commences on the date that that Company takes possession of or controls the physical use of the property. Deferred rent is included in other long-term liabilities in the consolidated balance sheets.

Assets under capital lease are amortized in accordance with the Company's normal depreciation policy for owned assets or, if shorter, over the non-cancelable lease term and any option renewal period where failure to exercise such option would result in an economic penalty in such amount that renewal appears, at the inception of the lease, to be reasonably assured. The amortization of the assets is included in depreciation expense in the consolidated financial statements. During the term of a lease, if a substantial additional investment is made in a leased location, the Company reevaluates its definition of lease term.

**Accounts Payable -** In June 2007, the Company entered into a customer-managed services agreement with a third party to provide an accounts payable tracking system which facilitates participating suppliers' ability to finance payment obligations from the Company with designated third-party financial institutions. Participating suppliers may, at their sole discretion, make offers to finance one or more payment obligations of the Company prior to their scheduled due dates at a discounted price to participating financial institutions. The Company's goal in entering into this arrangement is to capture overall supply chain savings, in the form of pricing, payment terms or vendor funding, created by facilitating suppliers' ability to finance payment obligations at more favorable discount rates, while providing them with greater working capital flexibility.

The Company's obligations to its suppliers, including amounts due and scheduled payment dates, are not impacted by suppliers' decisions to finance amounts under this arrangement. However, the Company's right to offset balances due from suppliers against payment obligations is restricted by this arrangement for those payment obligations that have been financed by suppliers. As of February 1, 2008, the Company had placed $77 million of payment obligations on the accounts payable tracking system, and participating suppliers had financed $48 million of those payment obligations to participating financial institutions.

**Self-Insurance** - The Company is self-insured for certain losses relating to workers' compensation, automobile, property, and general and product liability claims. The Company has stop-loss coverage to limit the exposure arising from these claims. The Company is also self-insured for certain losses relating to extended warranty and medical and dental claims. Self-insurance claims filed and claims incurred but not reported are accrued based upon management's estimates of the discounted ultimate cost for uninsured claims incurred using actuarial assumptions followed in the insurance industry and historical experience. Although management believes it has the ability to reasonably estimate losses related to claims, it is possible that actual results could differ from recorded self-insurance liabilities.

**Income Taxes** - The Company establishes deferred income tax assets and liabilities for temporary differences between the tax and financial accounting bases of assets and liabilities. The tax effects of such differences are reflected in the balance sheet at the enacted tax rates expected to be in effect when the differences reverse. A valuation allowance is recorded to reduce the carrying amount of deferred tax assets if it is more likely than not that all or a portion of the asset will not be realized. The tax balances and income tax expense recognized by the Company are based on management's interpretation of the tax statutes of multiple jurisdictions.

The Company establishes a reserve for tax positions for which there is uncertainty as to whether or not the position will be ultimately sustained. The Company includes interest related to tax issues as part of net interest in the consolidated financial statements. The Company records any applicable penalties related to tax issues within the income tax provision.

**Revenue Recognition -** The Company recognizes revenues, net of sales tax, when sales transactions occur and customers take possession of the merchandise. A provision for anticipated merchandise returns is provided through a reduction of sales and cost of sales in the period that the related sales are recorded. Revenues from product installation services are recognized when the installation is completed. Deferred revenues associated with amounts received for which customers have not yet taken possession of merchandise or for which installation has not yet been completed were $332 million and $364 million at February 1, 2008, and February 2, 2007, respectively.

Revenues from stored value cards, which include gift cards and returned merchandise credits, are deferred and recognized when the cards are redeemed. The liability associated with outstanding stored value cards was $385 million and $367 million at February 1, 2008, and February 2, 2007, respectively, and these amounts are included in deferred revenue in the accompanying consolidated balance sheets. The Company recognizes income from unredeemed stored value cards at the point at which redemption becomes remote. The Company's stored value cards have no expiration date or dormancy fees. Therefore, to determine when redemption is remote, the Company analyzes an aging of the unredeemed cards based on the date of last stored value card use.

**Extended Warranties -** Lowe's sells separately-priced extended warranty contracts under a Lowe's-branded program for which the Company is ultimately self-insured. The Company recognizes revenue from extended warranty sales on a straight-line basis over the respective contract term. Extended warranty contract terms primarily range from one to four years from the date of purchase or the end of the manufacturer's warranty, as applicable. The Company's extended warranty deferred revenue is included in other liabilities (non-current) in the accompanying consolidated balance sheets. Changes deferred revenue for extended warranty contracts are summarized as follows:

| (In millions) | | 2007 | | 2006 |
|---|---|---|---|---|
| Extended warranty deferred revenue, beginning of period | $ | 315 | $ | 206 |
| Additions to deferred revenue | | 175 | | 148 |
| Deferred revenue recognized | | (83) | | (39) |
| Extended warranty deferred revenue, end of period | $ | 407 | $ | 315 |

Incremental direct acquisition costs associated with the sale of extended warranties are also deferred and recognized as expense on a straight-line basis over the respective contract term. Deferred costs associated with extended warranty contracts were $91 million and $81 million at February 1, 2008 and February 2, 2007, respectively. The Company's extended warranty deferred costs are included in other assets (non-current) in the accompanying consolidated balance sheets. All other costs, such as costs of services performed under the contract, general and administrative expenses and advertising expenses are expensed as incurred.

The liability for extended warranty claims incurred is included in self-insurance liabilities in the accompanying consolidated balance sheets.  Changes in the liability for extended warranty claims are summarized as follows:

| (In millions) | | 2007 | | 2006 |
|---|---|---|---|---|
| Liability for extended warranty claims, beginning of period | $ | 10 | $ | - |
| Accrual for claims incurred | | 41 | | 17 |
| Claim payments | | (37) | | (7) |
| Liability for extended warranty claims, end of period | $ | 14 | $ | 10 |

**Cost of Sales and Selling, General and Administrative Expenses -** The following lists the primary costs classified in each major expense category:

| Cost of Sales | Selling, General and Administrative |
|---|---|
| ■  Total cost of products sold, including: <br> - Purchase costs, net of vendor funds; <br> - Freight expenses associated with moving merchandise inventories from vendors to retail stores; <br> - Costs associated with operating the Company's distribution network, including payroll and benefit costs and occupancy costs; <br> ■  Costs of installation services provided; <br> ■  Costs associated with delivery of products directly from vendors to customers by third parties; <br> ■  Costs associated with inventory shrinkage and obsolescence. | ■  Payroll and benefit costs for retail and corporate employees; <br> ■  Occupancy costs of retail and corporate facilities; <br> ■  Advertising; <br> ■  Costs associated with delivery of products from stores to customers; <br> ■  Third-party, in-store service costs; <br> ■  Tender costs, including bank charges, costs associated with credit card interchange fees, and amounts associated with accepting the Company's proprietary credit cards; <br> ■  Costs associated with self-insured plans, and premium costs for stop-loss coverage and fully insured plans; <br> ■  Long-lived asset impairment charges and gains/losses on disposal of assets; <br> ■  Other administrative costs, such as supplies, and travel and entertainment. |

**Vendor Funds** - The Company receives funds from vendors in the normal course of business principally as a result of purchase volumes, sales, early payments or promotions of vendors' products.  Based on the provisions of the vendor agreements in place, management develops accrual rates by estimating the point at which the Company will have completed its performance under the agreement and the amount agreed upon will be earned.  Due to the complexity and diversity of the individual vendor agreements, the Company performs analyses and reviews historical trends throughout the year to ensure the amounts earned are appropriately recorded.  As a part of these analyses, the Company validates its accrual rates based on actual purchase trends and applies those rates to actual purchase volumes to determine the amount of funds accrued by the Company and receivable from the vendor. Amounts accrued throughout the year could be impacted if actual purchase volumes differ from projected annual purchase volumes, especially in the case of programs that provide for increased funding when graduated purchase volumes are met.

Vendor funds are treated as a reduction of inventory cost, unless they represent a reimbursement of specific, incremental and identifiable costs incurred by the customer to sell the vendor's product. Substantially all of the vendor funds that the Company receives do not meet the specific, incremental and identifiable criteria. Therefore, the Company treats the majority of these funds as a reduction in the cost of inventory as the amounts are accrued, and recognizes these funds as a reduction of cost of sales when the inventory is sold.

**Advertising** - Costs associated with advertising are charged to expense as incurred.  Advertising expenses were $788 million, $873 million and $812 million in 2007, 2006 and 2005, respectively.  Cooperative advertising vendor funds are recorded as a reduction of these expenses with the net amount included in SG&A expense.  Cooperative advertising vendor funds were $5 million in 2007 but insignificant in both 2006 and 2005.

**Shipping and Handling Costs** - The Company includes shipping and handling costs relating to the delivery of products directly from vendors to customers by third parties in cost of sales.  Shipping and handling costs, which include salaries and vehicle operations expenses relating to the delivery of products from stores to customers, are classified as SG&A expense.  Shipping and handling costs included in SG&A expense were $307 million, $310 million and $312 million in 2007, 2006 and 2005, respectively.

**Store Opening Costs** - Costs of opening new or relocated retail stores, which include payroll and supply costs incurred prior to store opening and grand opening advertising costs, are charged to operations as incurred.

**Comprehensive Income** - The Company reports comprehensive income in its consolidated statements of shareholders' equity. Comprehensive income represents changes in shareholders' equity from non-owner sources and is comprised primarily of net earnings plus or minus unrealized gains or losses on available-for-sale securities, as well as foreign currency translation adjustments. Unrealized gains on available-for-sale securities classified in accumulated other comprehensive income on the accompanying consolidated balance sheets were $2 million at both February 1, 2008 and February 2, 2007. Foreign currency translation gains classified in accumulated other comprehensive income on the accompanying consolidated balance sheets were $6 million at February 1, 2008, and foreign currency translation losses were $1 million at February 2, 2007. The reclassification adjustments for gains/losses included in net earnings for 2007, 2006 and 2005 were insignificant.

**Recent Accounting Pronouncements** – In September 2006, the Financial Accounting Standards Board (FASB) issued Statement of Financial Accounting Standards (SFAS) No. 157, "Fair Value Measurements". SFAS No. 157 provides a single definition of fair value, together with a framework for measuring it, and requires additional disclosure about the use of fair value to measure assets and liabilities. SFAS No. 157 also emphasizes that fair value is a market-based measurement, not an entity-specific measurement, and sets out a fair value hierarchy with the highest priority being quoted prices in active markets. Under SFAS No. 157, fair value measurements are required to be disclosed by level within that hierarchy. SFAS No. 157 is effective for fiscal years beginning after November 15, 2007, and interim periods within those fiscal years. However, FASB Staff Position (FSP) No. FAS 157-2, "Effective Date of FASB Statement No. 157," issued in February 2008, delays the effective date of SFAS No. 157 for all nonfinancial assets and nonfinancial liabilities, except for items that are recognized or disclosed at fair value in the financial statements on a recurring basis, to fiscal years beginning after November 15, 2008, and interim periods within those fiscal years. The Company does not expect the adoption of SFAS No. 157 to have a material impact on its consolidated financial statements.

In February 2007, the FASB issued SFAS No. 159, "The Fair Value Option for Financial Assets and Financial Liabilities." SFAS No. 159 provides entities with an option to measure many financial instruments and certain other items at fair value, including available-for-sale securities previously accounted for under SFAS No. 115, "Accounting for Certain Investments in Debt and Equity Securities." Under SFAS No. 159, unrealized gains and losses on items for which the fair value option has been elected will be reported in earnings at each subsequent reporting period. SFAS No. 159 is effective for fiscal years beginning after November 15, 2007. The Company does not expect the adoption of SFAS No. 159 to have a material impact on its consolidated financial statements.

In June 2007, the Emerging Issues Task Force (EITF) reached a consensus on Issue No. 06-11, "Accounting for Income Tax Benefits of Dividends on Share-Based Payment Awards." EITF 06-11 states that an entity should recognize a realized tax benefit associated with dividends on nonvested equity shares, nonvested equity share units and outstanding equity share options charged to retained earnings as an increase in additional paid in capital. The amount recognized in additional paid in capital should be included in the pool of excess tax benefits available to absorb potential future tax deficiencies on share-based payment awards. EITF 06-11 should be applied prospectively to income tax benefits of dividends on equity-classified share-based payment awards that are declared in fiscal years beginning after December 15, 2007. The Company does not expect the adoption of EITF 06-11 to have a material impact on its consolidated financial statements.

In December 2007, the FASB issued SFAS No. 141(R), "Business Combinations" and SFAS No. 160, "Noncontrolling Interests in Consolidated Financial Statements – an amendment of ARB No. 51". SFAS No. 141(R) and SFAS No. 160 significantly change the accounting for and reporting of business combinations and noncontrolling interests in consolidated financial statements. Under SFAS No. 141(R), more assets and liabilities will be measured at fair value as of the acquisition date instead of the announcement date. Additionally, acquisition costs will be expensed as incurred. Under SFAS No. 160, noncontrolling interests will be classified as a separate component of equity. SFAS No. 141(R) and SFAS No. 160 should be applied prospectively for fiscal years beginning on or after December 15, 2008, with the exception of the presentation and disclosure requirements of SFAS No. 160, which should be applied retrospectively. The Company does not expect the adoption of SFAS No. 141(R) and SFAS No. 160 to have a material impact on its consolidated financial statements.

**Segment Information** – The Company's operating segments, representing the Company's home improvement retail stores, are aggregated within one reportable segment based on the way the Company manages its business. The Company's home improvement retail stores exhibit similar long-term economic characteristics, sell similar products and services, use similar processes to sell those products and services, and sell their products and services to similar classes of customers. The amount of long-lived assets and net sales outside the U.S. was not significant for any of the periods presented.

**Reclassifications** - Certain prior period amounts have been reclassified to conform to current classifications.

**NOTE 2 - Investments:**

The Company's investment securities are classified as available-for-sale. The amortized costs, gross unrealized holding gains and losses, and fair values of the investments at February 1, 2008, and February 2, 2007, were as follows:

| Type<br>(In millions) | | Amortized<br>Cost | | Gross<br>Unrealized<br>Gains | | Gross<br>Unrealized<br>Losses | | Fair<br>Value |
|---|---|---|---|---|---|---|---|---|
| | | | | February 1, 2008 | | | | |
| Municipal obligations | $ | 117 | $ | 1 | $ | - | $ | 118 |
| Money market funds | | 128 | | - | | - | | 128 |
| Certificates of deposit | | 3 | | - | | - | | 3 |
| **Classified as short-term** | | **248** | | **1** | | **-** | | **249** |
| | | | | | | | | |
| Municipal obligations | | 462 | | 5 | | - | | 467 |
| Mutual funds | | 42 | | 1 | | (1) | | 42 |
| **Classified as long-term** | | **504** | | **6** | | **(1)** | | **509** |
| | | | | | | | | |
| **Total** | $ | **752** | $ | **7** | $ | **(1)** | $ | **758** |

| Type<br>(In millions) | | Amortized<br>Cost | | Gross<br>Unrealized<br>Gains | | Gross<br>Unrealized<br>Losses | | Fair<br>Value |
|---|---|---|---|---|---|---|---|---|
| | | | | February 2, 2007 | | | | |
| Municipal obligations | $ | 258 | $ | - | $ | (1) | $ | 257 |
| Money market funds | | 148 | | - | | - | | 148 |
| Corporate notes | | 26 | | - | | - | | 26 |
| Certificates of deposit | | 1 | | - | | - | | 1 |
| **Classified as short-term** | | **433** | | **-** | | **(1)** | | **432** |
| | | | | | | | | |
| Municipal obligations | | 127 | | - | | - | | 127 |
| Mutual funds | | 35 | | 3 | | - | | 38 |
| **Classified as long-term** | | **162** | | **3** | | **-** | | **165** |
| | | | | | | | | |
| **Total** | $ | **595** | $ | **3** | $ | **(1)** | $ | **597** |

The proceeds from sales of available-for-sale securities were $1.2 billion, $412 million and $192 million for 2007, 2006 and 2005, respectively. Gross realized gains and losses on the sale of available-for-sale securities were not significant for any of the periods presented. The municipal obligations classified as long-term at February 1, 2008, will mature in one to 32 years, based on stated maturity dates.

Short-term and long-term investments include restricted balances pledged as collateral for letters of credit for the Company's extended warranty program and for a portion of the Company's casualty insurance and installed sales program liabilities. Restricted balances included in short-term investments were $167 million at February 1, 2008 and $248 million at February 2, 2007. Restricted balances included in long-term investments were $172 million at February 1, 2008 and $32 million at February 2, 2007.

**NOTE 3 - Property and Accumulated Depreciation:**

Property is summarized by major class in the following table:

| (In millions) | Estimated Depreciable Lives, In Years | February 1, 2008 | February 2, 2007 |
|---|---|---|---|
| Cost: | | | |
| Land | N/A | $ 5,566 | $ 4,807 |
| Buildings | 7-40 | 10,036 | 8,481 |
| Equipment | 3-15 | 8,118 | 7,036 |
| Leasehold improvements | 3-40 | 3,063 | 2,484 |
| Construction in progress | N/A | 2,053 | 2,296 |
| **Total cost** | | **28,836** | **25,104** |
| Accumulated depreciation | | (7,475) | (6,133) |
| **Property, less accumulated depreciation** | | **$ 21,361** | **$ 18,971** |

Included in net property are assets under capital lease of $523 million, less accumulated depreciation of $294 million, at February 1, 2008, and $533 million, less accumulated depreciation of $274 million, at February 2, 2007.

**NOTE 4 - Short-Term Borrowings and Lines of Credit:**

In June 2007, the Company entered into an Amended and Restated Credit Agreement (Amended Facility) to modify the senior credit facility by extending the maturity date to June 2012 and providing for borrowings of up to $1.75 billion. The Amended Facility supports the Company's commercial paper and revolving credit programs. Borrowings made are unsecured and are priced at a fixed rate based upon market conditions at the time of funding, in accordance with the terms of the Amended Facility. The Amended Facility contains certain restrictive covenants, which include maintenance of a debt leverage ratio as defined by the Amended Facility. The Company was in compliance with those covenants at February 1, 2008. Seventeen banking institutions are participating in the Amended Facility. As of February 1, 2008, there was $1.0 billion outstanding under the commercial paper program. The weighted-average interest rate on the outstanding commercial paper was 3.92%. As of February 2, 2007, there was $23 million of short-term borrowings outstanding under the senior credit facility, but no outstanding borrowings under the commercial paper program. The interest rate on the short-term borrowing was 5.41%.

In October 2007, the Company established a Canadian dollar (C$) denominated credit facility in the amount of C$50 million, which provides revolving credit support for the Company's Canadian operations. This uncommitted facility provides the Company with the ability to make unsecured borrowings, which are priced at a fixed rate based upon market conditions at the time of funding in accordance with the terms of the credit facility. As of February 1, 2008, there were no borrowings outstanding under the credit facility.

In January 2008, the Company entered into a C$ denominated credit agreement in the amount of C$200 million for the purpose of funding the build out of retail stores in Canada and for working capital and other general corporate purposes. Borrowings made are unsecured and are priced at a fixed rate based upon market conditions at the time of funding in accordance with the terms of the credit agreement. The credit agreement contains certain restrictive covenants, which include maintenance of a debt leverage ratio as defined by the credit agreement. The Company was in compliance with those covenants at February 1, 2008. Three banking institutions are participating in the credit agreement. As of February 1, 2008, there was C$60 million or the equivalent of $60 million outstanding under the credit facility. The interest rate on the short-term borrowing was 5.75%.

Five banks have extended lines of credit aggregating $789 million for the purpose of issuing documentary letters of credit and standby letters of credit. These lines do not have termination dates and are reviewed periodically. Commitment fees ranging from .225% to .50% per annum are paid on the standby letters of credit amounts outstanding. Outstanding letters of credit totaled $299 million as of February 1, 2008, and $346 million as of February 2, 2007.

**NOTE 5 - Long-Term Debt:**

| (In millions)<br>Debt Category | Interest Rates | Fiscal<br>Year<br>of Final<br>Maturity | February<br>1,<br>2008 | February<br>2,<br>2007 |
|---|---|---|---|---|
| **Secured debt:** [1] | | | | |
| Mortgage notes | 6.00 to 8.25% | 2028 | $    33 | $    30 |
| **Unsecured debt:** | | | | |
| Debentures | 6.50 to 6.88% | 2029 | 694 | 693 |
| Notes | 8.25% | 2010 | 499 | 498 |
| Medium-term notes - series A | 7.35 to 8.20% | 2023 | 20 | 27 |
| Medium-term notes - series B [2] | 7.11 to 7.61% | 2037 | 217 | 267 |
| Senior notes | 5.00 to 6.65% | 2037 | 3,271 | 1,980 |
| Convertible notes | 0.86 to 2.50% | 2021 | 511 | 518 |
| Capital leases and other | | 2030 | 371 | 400 |
| | | | | |
| **Total long-term debt** | | | **5,616** | **4,413** |
| Less current maturities | | | 40 | 88 |
| | | | | |
| **Long-term debt, excluding current maturities** | | | $    **5,576** | $    **4,325** |

[1]    *Real properties with an aggregate book value of $47 million were pledged as collateral at February 1, 2008, for secured debt.*

[2]    *Approximately 46% of these medium-term notes may be put at the option of the holder on the twentieth anniversary of the issue at par value.  The medium-term notes were issued in 1997.  None of these notes are currently putable.*

Debt maturities, exclusive of unamortized original issue discounts, capital leases and other, for the next five years and thereafter are as follows: 2008, $10 million; 2009, $10 million; 2010, $501 million; 2011, $1 million; 2012, $552 million; thereafter, $4.3 billion.

The Company's debentures, notes, medium-term notes, senior notes and convertible notes contain certain restrictive covenants.  The Company was in compliance with all covenants in these agreements at February 1, 2008.

*Senior Notes*

In September 2007, the Company issued $1.3 billion of unsecured senior notes, comprised of three tranches: $550 million of 5.60% senior notes maturing in September 2012, $250 million of 6.10% senior notes maturing in September 2017 and $500 million of 6.65% senior notes maturing in September 2037.  The 5.60%, 6.10% and 6.65% senior notes were issued at discounts of approximately $2.7 million, $1.3 million and $6.3 million, respectively.  Interest on the senior notes is payable semiannually in arrears in March and September of each year until maturity, beginning in March 2008.  The discount associated with the issuance is included in long-term debt and is being amortized over the respective terms of the senior notes.  The net proceeds of approximately $1.3 billion were used for general corporate purposes, including capital expenditures and working capital needs, and for repurchases of shares of the Company's common stock.

In October 2006, the Company issued $1.0 billion of unsecured senior notes, comprised of two tranches: $550 million of 5.40% senior notes maturing in October 2016 and $450 million of 5.80% senior notes maturing in October 2036.  The 5.40% senior notes and the 5.80% senior notes were each issued at a discount of approximately $4.4 million.  Interest on the senior notes is payable semiannually in arrears in April and October of each year until maturity, beginning in April 2007.  The discount associated with the issuance is included in long-term debt and is being amortized over the respective terms of the senior notes.  The net proceeds of approximately $991 million were used for general corporate general corporate purposes, including capital expenditures and working capital needs, and for repurchases of common stock.

In October 2005, the Company issued $1.0 billion of unsecured senior notes comprised of two $500 million tranches maturing in October 2015 and October 2035, respectively.  The first $500 million tranche of 5.0% senior notes was sold at a discount of $4 million.  The second $500 million tranche of 5.5% senior notes was sold at a discount of $8 million.  Interest on the senior notes is payable semiannually in arrears in April and October of each year until maturity, beginning in April 2006.  The discount associated with the issuance is included in long-term debt and is being amortized over the respective terms of the senior notes.  The net proceeds of approximately $988 million were used for the repayment of $600 million in outstanding notes due December 2005, for general corporate purposes, including capital expenditures and working capital needs, and for repurchases of common stock.

The senior notes issued in 2007, 2006 and 2005 may be redeemed by the Company at any time, in whole or in part, at a redemption price plus accrued interest to the date of redemption. The redemption price is equal to the greater of (1) 100% of the principal amount of the senior notes to be redeemed, or (2) the sum of the present values of the remaining scheduled payments of principal and interest thereon, discounted to the date of redemption on a semiannual basis at a specified rate. The indenture under which the 2007 senior notes were issued also contains a provision that allows the holders of the notes to require the Company to repurchase all or any part of their notes if a change in control triggering event occurs.  If elected under the change in control provisions, the repurchase of the notes will occur at a purchase price of 101% of the principal amount, plus accrued and unpaid interest, if any, on such notes to the date of purchase.   The indenture governing the senior notes does not limit the aggregate principal amount of debt securities that the Company may issue, nor is the Company required to maintain financial ratios or specified levels of net worth or liquidity. However, the indenture contains various restrictive covenants, none of which is expected to impact the Company's liquidity or capital resources.

Upon the issuance of each of the series of senior notes previously described, the Company evaluated the optionality features embedded in the notes and concluded that these features do not require bifurcation from the host contracts and separate accounting as derivative instruments.

*Convertible Notes*

The Company has $578.7 million aggregate principal, $497.1 million aggregate carrying amount, of senior convertible notes issued in October 2001 at an issue price of $861.03 per note. Cash interest payments on the notes ceased in October 2006. In October 2021 when the notes mature, a holder will receive $1,000 per note, representing a yield to maturity of approximately 1%. Holders of the notes had the right to require the Company to purchase all or a portion of their notes in October 2003 and October 2006, at a price of $861.03 per note plus accrued cash interest, if any, and will have the right in October 2011 to require the Company to purchase all or a portion of their notes at a price of $905.06 per note. The Company may choose to pay the purchase price of the notes in cash or common stock or a combination of cash and common stock. Holders of an insignificant number of notes exercised their right to require the Company to repurchase their notes during 2003 and 2006, all of which were purchased in cash. The Company may redeem for cash all or a portion of the notes at any time, at a price equal to the sum of the issue price plus accrued original issue discount on the redemption date.

Holders of the senior convertible notes may convert their notes into 34.424 shares of the Company's common stock only if: the sale price of the Company's common stock reaches specified thresholds, or the credit rating of the notes is below a specified level, or the notes are called for redemption, or specified corporate transactions representing a change in control have occurred. The conversion ratio of 34.424 shares per note is only adjusted based on normal antidilution provisions designed to protect the value of the conversion option.

The Company's closing share prices reached the specified threshold such that the senior convertible notes became convertible at the option of each holder into shares of common stock during specified quarters of 2006 and 2007. Holders of an insignificant number of senior convertible notes exercised their right to convert their notes into shares of the Company's common stock during 2007 and 2006. The senior convertible notes will not be convertible in the first quarter of 2008 because the Company's closing share prices did not reach the specified threshold during the fourth quarter of 2007.

The Company has $19.7 million aggregate principal, $13.8 million aggregate carrying amount, of convertible notes issued in February 2001 at an issue price of $608.41 per note. Interest will not be paid on the notes prior to maturity in February 2021, at which time the holders will receive $1,000 per note, representing a yield to maturity of 2.5%. Holders of the notes had the right to require the Company to purchase all or a portion of their notes in February 2004, at a price of $655.49 per note, and will have the right in February 2011 to require the Company to purchase all or a portion of their notes at a price of $780.01 per note. The Company may choose to pay the purchase price of the notes in cash or common stock, or a combination of cash and common stock. Holders of an insignificant number of notes exercised their right to require the Company to purchase their notes during 2004, all of which were purchased in cash.

Holders of the convertible notes issued in February 2001 may convert their notes at any time on or before the maturity date, unless the notes have been previously purchased or redeemed, into 32.896 shares of the Company's common stock per note. The conversion ratio of 32.896 shares per note is only adjusted based on normal antidilution provisions designed to protect the value of the conversion option. During 2007, holders of $18 million principal amount, $13 million carrying amount, of the Company's convertible notes issued in February 2001 exercised their right to convert their notes into 0.6 million shares of the Company's common stock at the rate of 32.896 shares per note. During 2006, holders of $118 million principal amount, $80 million carrying amount, of the Company's convertible notes issued in February 2001 exercised their right to convert their notes into 3.9 million shares of the Company's common stock.

Upon the issuance of each of the series of convertible notes previously described, the Company evaluated the optionality features embedded in the notes and concluded that these features do not require bifurcation from the host contracts and separate accounting as derivative instruments.

## NOTE 6 - Financial Instruments:

Cash and cash equivalents, accounts receivable, short-term borrowings, accounts payable and accrued liabilities are reflected in the financial statements at cost, which approximates fair value due to their short-term nature. Short- and long-term investments classified as available-for-sale securities, which include restricted balances, are reflected in the financial statements at fair value. Estimated fair values for long-term debt have been determined using available market information. For debt issues that are not quoted on an exchange, interest rates that are currently available to the Company for issuance of debt with similar terms and remaining maturities are used to estimate fair value. However, considerable judgment is required in interpreting market data to develop the estimates of fair value. Accordingly, the estimates presented herein are not necessarily indicative of the amounts that the Company could realize in a current market exchange. The use of different market assumptions and/or estimation methodologies may have a material effect on the estimated fair value amounts. The fair value of the Company's long-term debt, excluding capital leases and other, is as follows:

| (In millions) | February 1, 2008 | | February 2, 2007 | |
|---|---|---|---|---|
| | Carrying Amount | Fair Value | Carrying Amount | Fair Value |
| **Liabilities:** | | | | |
| Long-term debt (excluding capital leases and other) | $ 5,245 | $ 5,406 | $ 4,013 | $ 4,301 |

**NOTE 7 - Shareholders' Equity:**

Authorized shares of common stock were 5.6 billion ($.50 par value) at February 1, 2008 and February 2, 2007.

The Company has 5.0 million ($5 par value) authorized shares of preferred stock, none of which have been issued. The Board of Directors may issue the preferred stock (without action by shareholders) in one or more series, having such voting rights, dividend and liquidation preferences, and such conversion and other rights as may be designated by the Board of Directors at the time of issuance.

**NOTE 11 - Earnings Per Share:**

Basic earnings per share (EPS) excludes dilution and is computed by dividing the applicable net earnings by the weighted-average number of common shares outstanding for the period. Diluted earnings per share is calculated based on the weighted-average shares of common stock as adjusted for the potential dilutive effect of share-based awards and convertible notes as of the balance sheet date. The following table reconciles EPS for 2007, 2006 and 2005:

| (In millions, except per share data) | 2007 | 2006 | 2005 |
|---|---|---|---|
| **Basic earnings per share:** | | | |
| Net earnings | $ 2,809 | $ 3,105 | $ 2,765 |
| Weighted-average shares outstanding | 1,481 | 1,535 | 1,555 |
| Basic earnings per share | $ 1.90 | $ 2.02 | $ 1.78 |
| **Diluted earnings per share:** | | | |
| Net earnings | $ 2,809 | $ 3,105 | $ 2,765 |
| Net earnings adjustment for interest on convertible notes, net of tax | 4 | 4 | 11 |
| Net earnings, as adjusted | $ 2,813 | $ 3,109 | $ 2,776 |
| Weighted-average shares outstanding | 1,481 | 1,535 | 1,555 |
| Dilutive effect of share-based awards | 8 | 9 | 10 |
| Dilutive effect of convertible notes | 21 | 22 | 42 |
| Weighted-average shares, as adjusted | 1,510 | 1,566 | 1,607 |
| Diluted earnings per share | $ 1.86 | $ 1.99 | $ 1.73 |

Stock options to purchase 7.8 million, 6.8 million and 5.6 million shares of common stock for 2007, 2006 and 2005, respectively, were excluded from the computation of diluted earnings per share because their effect would have been antidilutive.

**NOTE 12 - Leases:**

The Company leases store facilities and land for certain store facilities under agreements with original terms generally of 20 years. For lease agreements that provide for escalating rent payments or free-rent occupancy periods, the Company recognizes rent expense on a straight-line basis over the non-cancelable lease term and any option renewal period where failure to exercise such option would result in an economic penalty in such amount that renewal appears, at the inception of the lease, to be reasonably assured. The lease term commences on the date that the Company takes possession of or controls the physical use of the property. The leases generally contain provisions for four to six renewal options of five years each.

Some agreements also provide for contingent rentals based on sales performance in excess of specified minimums. In 2007, 2006 and 2005, contingent rentals were insignificant.

The Company subleases certain properties that are no longer held for use in operations. Sublease income was not significant for any of the periods presented.

Certain equipment is also leased by the Company under agreements ranging from three to five years. These agreements typically contain renewal options providing for a renegotiation of the lease, at the Company's option, based on the fair market value at that time.

The future minimum rental payments required under capital and operating leases having initial or remaining non-cancelable lease terms in excess of one year are summarized as follows:

**NOTE 14 – Related Parties:**

A brother-in-law of the Company's Executive Vice President of Business Development is a senior officer of a vendor that provides millwork and other building products to the Company. In both 2007 and 2006, the Company purchased products in the amount of $101 million from this vendor, while in 2005 the Company purchased products in the amount of $84 million from this vendor. Amounts payable to this vendor were insignificant at February 1, 2008 and February 2, 2007.

**NOTE 15 - Other Information:**

Net interest expense is comprised of the following:

| (In millions) | | 2007 | | 2006 | | 2005 |
|---|---|---|---|---|---|---|
| Long-term debt | $ | 247 | $ | 183 | $ | 171 |
| Capitalized leases | | 32 | | 34 | | 39 |
| Interest income | | (45) | | (52) | | (45) |
| Interest capitalized | | (65) | | (32) | | (28) |
| Other | | 25 | | 21 | | 21 |
| **Net interest expense** | **$** | **194** | **$** | **154** | **$** | **158** |

Supplemental disclosures of cash flow information:

| (In millions) | | 2007 | | 2006 | | 2005 |
|---|---|---|---|---|---|---|
| Cash paid for interest, net of amount capitalized | $ | 198 | $ | 179 | $ | 173 |
| Cash paid for income taxes | $ | 1,725 | $ | 2,031 | $ | 1,593 |

Noncash investing and financing activities:

| | | 2007 | | 2006 | | 2005 |
|---|---|---|---|---|---|---|
| Noncash fixed asset acquisitions, including assets acquired under capital lease | $ | 99 | $ | 159 | $ | 175 |
| Conversions of long-term debt to equity | $ | 13 | $ | 82 | $ | 565 |

**Lowe's Companies, Inc.**
**Selected Financial Data (Unaudited)**

**Selected Statement of Earnings Data:**

| (In millions, except per share data) | 2007 | 2006 | 2005* | 2004 | 2003 |
|---|---|---|---|---|---|
| Net sales | $ 48,283 | $ 46,927 | $ 43,243 | $ 36,464 | $ 30,838 |
| Gross margin | 16,727 | 16,198 | 14,790 | 12,240 | 9,533 |
| Earnings from continuing operations | 2,809 | 3,105 | 2,765 | 2,167 | 1,807 |
| Earnings from discontinued operations, net of tax | - | - | - | - | 15 |
| Net earnings | 2,809 | 3,105 | 2,765 | 2,167 | 1,822 |
| Basic earnings per share - continuing operations | 1.90 | 2.02 | 1.78 | 1.39 | 1.15 |
| Basic earnings per share – discontinued operations | - | - | - | - | 0.01 |
| Basic earnings per share | 1.90 | 2.02 | 1.78 | 1.39 | 1.16 |
| Diluted earnings per share - continuing operations | 1.86 | 1.99 | 1.73 | 1.35 | 1.12 |
| Diluted earnings per share – discontinued operations | - | - | - | - | 0.01 |
| Diluted earnings per share | 1.86 | 1.99 | 1.73 | 1.35 | 1.13 |
| Dividends per share | $ 0.29 | $ 0.18 | $ 0.11 | $ 0.08 | $ 0.06 |

**Selected Balance Sheet Data:**

| | 2007 | 2006 | 2005* | 2004 | 2003 |
|---|---|---|---|---|---|
| Total assets | $ 30,869 | $ 27,767 | $ 24,639 | $ 21,101 | $ 18,667 |
| Long-term debt, excluding current maturities | $ 5,576 | $ 4,325 | $ 3,499 | $ 3,060 | $ 3,678 |

Note: The selected financial data has been adjusted to present the 2003 disposal of the Contractor Yards as a discontinued operation for all periods.
* Fiscal year 2005 contained 53 weeks, while all other years contained 52 weeks.

**Selected Quarterly Data:**

| (In millions, except per share data) | First | Second | Third | Fourth |
|---|---|---|---|---|
| **2007** | | | | |
| Net sales | $ 12,172 | $ 14,167 | $ 11,565 | $ 10,379 |
| Gross margin | 4,259 | 4,883 | 3,964 | 3,620 |
| Net earnings | 739 | 1,019 | 643 | 408 |
| Basic earnings per share | 0.49 | 0.68 | 0.44 | 0.28 |
| Diluted earnings per share | $ 0.48 | $ 0.67 | $ 0.43 | $ 0.28 |

| (In millions, except per share data) | First | Second | Third | Fourth |
|---|---|---|---|---|
| **2006** | | | | |
| Net sales | $ 11,921 | $ 13,389 | $ 11,211 | $ 10,406 |
| Gross margin | 4,169 | 4,478 | 3,865 | 3,687 |
| Net earnings | 841 | 935 | 716 | 613 |
| Basic earnings per share | 0.54 | 0.61 | 0.47 | 0.40 |
| Diluted earnings per share | $ 0.53 | $ 0.60 | $ 0.46 | $ 0.40 |

# TIME VALUE OF MONEY

## TIME VALUE OF MONEY

The time value of money is the idea that, quite simply, money received today is worth more than money to be received one year from today (or at any other future date), because it can be used to earn interest. If you invest $1,000 today at 10 percent, you will have $1,100 in one year. So $1,000 in one year is worth $100 less than $1,000 today because you lose the opportunity to earn the $100 in interest.

In some business situations, you will know the dollar amount of a cash flow that occurs in the future and will need to determine its value now. This type of situation is known as a present value problem. The opposite situation occurs when you know the dollar amount of a cash flow that occurs today and need to determine its value at some point in the future. These situations are called future value problems. The value of money changes over time because money can earn interest. The following table illustrates the basic difference between present value and future value problems:

|                | Now     | Future  |
|----------------|---------|---------|
| Present value  | ?       | $1,000  |
| Future value   | $1,000  | ?       |

Present and future value problems may involve two types of cash flow: a single payment or an annuity (which is the fancy word for a series of equal cash payments). Thus, you need to learn how to deal with four different situations related to the time value of money:

1. Future value of a single payment
2. Present value of a single payment
3. Future value of an annuity
4. Present value of an annuity

Most inexpensive handheld calculators and any spreadsheet program can perform the detailed arithmetic computations required to solve future value and present value problems. In later courses and in all business situations, you will probably use a calculator or computer to solve these problems. At this stage, we encourage you to solve problems using Tables C.1 through C.4 at the end of this appendix. We believe that using the tables will give you a better understanding of how and why present and future value concepts apply to business problems. The tables give the value of a $1 cash flow (single payment or annuity) for different periods ($n$) and at different interest rates ($i$). If a problem involves payments other than $1, it is necessary to multiply the value from the table by the amount of the payment.[1] In the final section of this appendix, we explain how to use Excel to compute present values.

## COMPUTING FUTURE AND PRESENT VALUES OF A SINGLE AMOUNT

### Future Value of a Single Amount

In future value of a single amount problems, you will be asked to calculate how much money you will have in the future as the result of investing a certain amount in the present. If you were to receive a gift of $10,000, for instance, you might decide to put it in a savings account and use the money as a down payment on a house after you graduate. The future value computation would tell you how much money will be available when you graduate.

To solve a future value problem, you need to know three items:

1. Amount to be invested.
2. Interest rate ($i$) the amount will earn.
3. Number of periods ($n$) in which the amount will earn interest.

---

[1] Present value and future value problems involve cash flows. The basic concepts are the same for cash inflows (receipts) and cash outflows (payments). No fundamental differences exist between present value and future value calculations for cash payments versus cash receipts.

The future value concept is based on compound interest, which simply means that interest is calculated on top of interest. Thus, the amount of interest for each period is calculated using the principal plus any interest not paid out in prior periods. Graphically, the calculation of the future value of $1 for three periods at an interest rate of 10 percent may be represented as follows:

Assume that on January 1, 2009, you deposit $1,000 in a savings account at 10 percent annual interest, compounded annually. At the end of three years, the $1,000 will have increased to $1,331 as follows:

| Year | Amount at Start of Year | + | Interest During the Year | = | Amount at End of Year |
|------|------------------------|---|--------------------------|---|-----------------------|
| 1 | $1,000 | + | $1,000 × 10% = $100 | = | $1,100 |
| 2 | 1,100 | + | 1,100 × 10% = 110 | = | 1,210 |
| 3 | 1,210 | + | 1,210 × 10% = 121 | = | 1,331 |

We can avoid the detailed arithmetic by referring to Table C.1, Future Value of $1, on page C14. For $i = 10\%$, $n = 3$, we find the value 1.3310. We then compute the balance at the end of year 3 as follows:

*From Table C.1, Interest rate = 10% n = 3*

$$\$1,000 \times 1.3310 = \$1,331$$

Note that the increase of $331 is due to the time value of money. It is interest revenue to the owner of the savings account and interest expense to the bank.

## Present Value of a Single Amount

The present value of a single amount is the worth to you today of receiving that amount some time in the future. For instance, you might be offered an opportunity to invest in a financial instrument that would pay you $1,000 in 3 years. Before you decided whether to invest, you would want to determine the present value of the instrument.

To compute the present value of an amount to be received in the future, we must discount (a procedure that is the opposite of compounding) at $i$ interest rate for $n$ periods. In discounting, the interest is subtracted rather than added, as it is in compounding. Graphically, the present value of $1 due at the end of the third period with an interest rate of 10 percent can be represented as follows:

Assume that today is January 1, 2009, and you have the opportunity to receive $1,000 cash on December 31, 2011. At an interest rate of 10 percent per year, how much is the $1,000 payment worth to you on January 1, 2009? You could discount the amount year by year,[2] but it is easier to use Table C.2, Present Value of $1, on pages C14–C15. For $i = 10\%$, $n = 3$, we find that the present value of $1 is 0.7513. The present value of $1,000 to be received at the end of three years can be computed as follows:

*From Table C.2, Interest rate = 10% n = 3*

$$\$1{,}000 \times 0.7513 = \$751.30$$

It is important to learn not only how to compute a present value but also to understand what it means. The $751.30 is the amount you would pay now to have the right to receive $1,000 at the end of three years, assuming an interest rate of 10 percent. Conceptually, you should be indifferent between having $751.30 today and receiving $1,000 in three years. If you had $751.30 today but wanted $1,000 in three years, you could simply deposit the money in a savings account that pays 10% interest and it would grow to $1,000 in three years. Alternatively, if you had a contract that promised you $1,000 in three years, you could sell it to an investor for $751.30 in cash today because it would permit the investor to earn the difference in interest.

What if you could only earn 6 percent during the three-year period from January 1, 2009, to December 31, 2011? What would be the present value on January 1, 2009, of receiving $1,000 on December 31, 2011? To answer this we would take the same approach, using Table C.2, except that the interest rate would change to $i = 6\%$. Referring to Table C.2, we see the present value factor for $i = 6\%$, $n = 3$, is 0.8396. Thus, the present value of $1,000 to be received at the end of three years, assuming a 6 percent interest rate, would be computed as $1,000 × 0.8396 = $839.60. Notice that when we assume a 6 percent interest rate the present value is greater than when we assumed a 10 percent interest rate. The reason for this difference is that, to reach $1,000 three years from now, you would need to deposit more money in a savings account now if it earns 6 percent interest than if it earns 10 percent interest.

**SELF-STUDY PRACTICE**

1. If the interest rate in a present value problem increases from 8 percent to 10 percent, will the present value increase or decrease?
2. What is the present value of $10,000 to be received 10 years from now if the interest rate is 5 percent, compounded annually?
3. If $10,000 is deposited now in a savings account that earns 5 percent interest compounded annually, how much will it be worth 10 years from now?

*After you have finished, check your answers with the solution at the bottom of the next page.*

## COMPUTING FUTURE AND PRESENT VALUES OF AN ANNUITY

Instead of a single payment, many business problems involve multiple cash payments over a number of periods. An **annuity** is a series of consecutive payments characterized by

1. An equal dollar amount each interest period.
2. Interest periods of equal length (year, half a year, quarter, or month).
3. An equal interest rate each interest period.

---

[2] The detailed discounting is as follows:

| Periods | Interest for the Year | Present Value* |
|---|---|---|
| 1 | $1,000 = ($1,000 × 1/1.10) = $90.91 | $1,000 − $90.91 = $909.09 |
| 2 | $909.09 = ($909.09 × 1/1.10) = $82.65 | $909.09 − $82.65 = $826.44 |
| 3 | $826.44 = ($826.44 × 1/1.10) = $75.14[†] | $826.44 − $75.14 = $751.30 |

*Verifiable in Table C.2.
[†]Adjusted for rounding

Examples of annuities include monthly payments on a car or house, yearly contributions to a savings account, and monthly pension benefits.

# Future Value of an Annuity

If you are saving money for some purpose, such as a new car or a trip, you might decide to deposit a fixed amount of money in a savings account each month. The future value of an annuity computation will tell you how much money will be in your savings account at some point in the future.

The future value of an annuity includes compound interest on each payment from the date of payment to the end of the term of the annuity. Each new payment accumulates less interest than prior payments, only because the number of periods remaining in which to accumulate interest decreases. The future value of an annuity of $1 for three periods at 10 percent may be represented graphically as

Future value
of an annuity
**$3.31**

Assume that each year for three years, you deposit $1,000 cash in a savings account at 10 percent interest per year. You make the first $1,000 deposit on December 31, 2009, the second one on December 31, 2010, and the third and last one on December 31, 2011. The first $1,000 deposit earns compound interest for two years (for a total principal and interest of $1,210); the second deposit earns interest for one year (for a total principal and interest of $1,100). The third deposit earns no interest because it was made on the day that the balance is computed. Thus, the total amount in the savings account at the end of three years is $3,310 ($1,210 + $1,100 + $1,000).

To calculate the future value of this annuity, we could compute the interest on each deposit, similar to what is described above. However, a faster way is to refer to Table C.3, Future Value of an Annuity of $1 for $i = 10\%$, $n = 3$ to find the value 3.3100. The future value of your three deposits of $1,000 each can be computed as follows:

> *From Table C.3,*
> *Interest rate = 10%*
> *n = 3*

$$\$1,000 \times 3.3100 = \$3,310$$

## The Power of Compounding

Compound interest is a remarkably powerful economic force. In fact, the ability to earn interest on interest is the key to building economic wealth. If you save $1,000 per year for the first 10 years of your career, you will have more money when you retire than you would if you had saved $15,000 per year for the last 10 years of your career. This surprising outcome occurs because the money you save early in your career will earn more interest than the money you save at the end of your career. If you start saving money now, the majority of your wealth will not be the money you saved but the interest your money was able to earn.

Solution to
Self-Study Practice

1. The present value will decrease.
2. $10,000 × 0.6139 = $6,139.
3. $10,000 × 1.6289 = $16,289.

**Effects of
Compound Interest**

- Deposits
- Deposits with interest

The chart in the margin illustrates the power of compounding over a brief 10-year period. If you deposit $1 each year in an account earning 10 percent interest, at the end of just 10 years, only 63 percent of your balance will be made up of money you have saved. The rest will be interest you have earned. After 20 years, only 35 percent of your balance will be from saved money. The lesson associated with compound interest is that even though saving money is hard, you should start now.

## Present Value of an Annuity

The present value of an annuity is the value now of a series of equal amounts to be received (or paid out) for some specified number of periods in the future. It is computed by discounting each of the equal periodic amounts. A good example of this type of problem is a retirement program that offers employees a monthly income after retirement. The present value of an annuity of $1 for three periods at 10 percent may be represented graphically as

Present value
of an annuity
**$2.49**

1   $1      2   $1      3   $1

Assume you are to receive $1,000 cash on each December 31, 2009, 2010, and 2011. How much would the sum of these three $1,000 future amounts be worth on January 1, 2009, assuming an interest rate of 10 percent per year? One way to determine this is to use Table C.2 to calculate the present value of each single amount as follows:

| | | FACTOR FROM TABLE C.2 | | |
|---|---|---|---|---|
| **Year** | **Amount** | **$i = 10\%$** | | **Present Value** |
| 1 | $1,000 | × | 0.9091 ($n = 1$) | = | $ 909.10 |
| 2 | $1,000 | × | 0.8264 ($n = 2$) | = | 826.40 |
| 3 | $1,000 | × | 0.7513 ($n = 3$) | = | 751.30 |
| | | | Total present value | = | $2,486.80 |

Alternatively, we can compute the present value of this annuity more easily by using Table C.4, as follows:

*From Table C.4,
Interest rate = 10%
n = 3*

**$1,000 × 2.4869 = $2,487 (rounded)**

## Interest Rates and Interest Periods

The preceding illustrations assumed annual periods for compounding and discounting. Although interest rates are almost always quoted on an annual basis, many compounding periods encountered in business are less than one year. When interest periods are less than a year, the values of $n$ and $i$ must be restated to be consistent with the length of the interest compounding period.

To illustrate, 12 percent interest compounded annually for five years requires the use of $n = 5$ and $i = 12\%$. If compounding is quarterly, however, there will be four interest periods per year (20 interest periods in five years), and the quarterly interest rate is one quarter of the annual rate (3 percent per quarter). Therefore, 12 percent interest compounded quarterly for five years requires use of $n = 20$ and $i = 3\%$.

# ACCOUNTING APPLICATIONS OF PRESENT VALUES

Many business transactions require the use of future and present value concepts. In finance classes, you will see how to apply future value concepts. In this section, we apply present value concepts to three common accounting cases.

## Case A—Present Value of a Single Amount

On January 1, 2009, General Mills bought some new delivery trucks. The company signed a note and agreed to pay $200,000 on December 31, 2010, an amount representing the cash equivalent price of the trucks plus interest for two years. The market interest rate for this note was 12 percent.

**1. How should the accountant record the purchase?**

**Answer:** This case requires the computation of the present value of a single amount. In conformity with the cost principle, the cost of the trucks is their current cash equivalent price, which is the present value of the future payment. The problem can be shown graphically as follows:

The present value of the $200,000 is computed as follows:

$$\$200{,}000 \times 0.7972 = \$159{,}440$$

*From Table C.2, Interest rate = 12% n = 2*

This transaction would be recorded with the journal entry shown below.

|  | Debit | Credit |
|---|---|---|
| Delivery Trucks (+A) | 159,440 |  |
| Note Payable (+L) |  | 159,440 |

| Assets | = | Liabilities | + Owners' Equity |
|---|---|---|---|
| Delivery Trucks    +159,440 |  | Note Payable    +159,440 |  |

**2. How should the effects of interest be reported at the end of 2009 and 2010?**

**Answer:** Interest expense would be calculated and recorded as follows:

<u>December 31, 2009</u>

Interest = Principal × Rate × Time
          = $159,440 × 12% × 12/12 = $19,132 (rounded)

**Coach's Tip**

The interest is recorded in the Note Payable account because it would be paid as part of the note at maturity.

|  | Debit | Credit |
|---|---|---|
| Interest Expense (+E, −OE) | 19,132 | |
| Note Payable (+L) | | 19,132 |

| Assets | = | Liabilities | + | Owners' Equity |
|---|---|---|---|---|
| | | Note Payable   +19,132 | | Interest Expense (+E)  −19,132 |

### December 31, 2010

Interest = Principal × Rate × Time
= ($159,440 + 19,132) × 12% × 12/12 = $21,428 (rounded)

|  | Debit | Credit |
|---|---|---|
| Interest Expense (+E, −OE) | 21,428 | |
| Note Payable (+L) | | 21,428 |

| Assets | = | Liabilities | + | Owners' Equity |
|---|---|---|---|---|
| | | Note Payable   +21,428 | | Interest Expense (+E)  −21,428 |

**Note Payable (L)**

| | |
|---|---|
| | 159,440  Jan. 1, 2009 |
| | 19,132  Interest 2009 |
| | 21,428  Interest 2010 |
| 200,000  Dec. 31, 2010 | |

3. **What is the effect of the $200,000 debt payment made on December 31, 2010?**

**Answer:**   At this date the amount to be paid is the balance in *Note Payable*, after it has been updated for interest pertaining to 2010, as shown in the T-account in the margin. Notice that, just prior to its repayment, the balance for the note on December 31, 2010 is the same as the maturity amount on the due date.

The debt payment would be recorded with the journal entry shown below.

|  | Debit | Credit |
|---|---|---|
| Note Payable (−L) | 200,000 | |
| Cash (−A) | | 200,000 |

| Assets | | = | Liabilities | | + | Owners' Equity |
|---|---|---|---|---|---|---|
| Cash | −200,000 | | Note Payable | −200,000 | | |

## Case B—Present Value of an Annuity

On January 1, 2009, General Mills bought new milling equipment. The company elected to finance the purchase with a note payable to be paid off in three years in annual installments of $163,686. Each installment includes principal plus interest on the unpaid balance at 11 percent per year. The annual installments are due on December 31, 2009, 2010, and 2011. This problem can be shown graphically as follows:

| 1/1/2009 | 12/31/2009 | 12/31/2010 | 12/31/2011 |
|---|---|---|---|
| ? | $163,686 | $163,686 | $163,686 |

1. **What is the amount of the note?**

**Answer:**    The note is the present value of each installment payment, $i = 11\%$ and $n = 3$. This is an annuity because the note repayment is made in three equal installments. The amount of the note is computed as follows:

> *From Table C.4,*
> *Interest rate = 11%*
> *$n = 3$*

$$\$163,686 \times 2.4437 = \$400,000$$

The acquisition on January 1, 2009, would be accounted for as follows:

|  | Debit | Credit |
|---|---|---|
| Milling Equipment (+A) | 400,000 | |
|     Note Payable (+L) | | 400,000 |

| Assets | = | Liabilities | + | Owners' Equity |
|---|---|---|---|---|
| Milling Equipment  +400,000 | | Note Payable  +400,000 | | |

2. **How should the payments made at the end of each year be accounted for?**

**Answer:**

**December 31, 2009**

Each payment includes both interest and principal. The interest part of the first payment is calculated as:

$$\text{Interest} = \text{Principal} \times \text{Rate} \times \text{Time}$$
$$= \$400,000 \times 11\% \times 12/12 = \$44,000$$

Now that we know the interest component, the principal portion of the first payment of $163,686 can be calculated ($163,686 − $44,000 = $119,686). Thus, the first payment on December 31, 2009, would be accounted for as:

|  | Debit | Credit |
|---|---|---|
| Interest Expense (+E, −OE) | 44,000 | |
| Note Payable (−L) ($163,686 − $44,000) | 119,686 | |
|     Cash (−A) | | 163,686 |

| Assets | = | Liabilities | + | Owners' Equity |
|---|---|---|---|---|
| Cash −163,686 | | Note Payable −119,686 | | Interest Expense (+E) −44,000 |

**December 31, 2010**

The interest portion of the second and third payments would be calculated in the same way, although notice that the principal balance in the Note Payable account changes after each payment.

$$\text{Interest} = \text{Principal} \times \text{Rate} \times \text{Time}$$
$$= [(\$400,000 − \$119,686) \times 11\% \times 12/12] = \$30,835$$
$$\text{Principal} = \text{Payment} − \text{Interest}$$
$$= \$163,686 − \$30,835 = \$132,851$$

|  | Debit | Credit |
|---|---|---|
| Interest Expense (+E, −OE) | 30,835 | |
| Note Payable (−L) | 132,851 | |
| Cash (−A) | | 163,686 |

| Assets | = | Liabilities | + | Owners' Equity |
|---|---|---|---|---|
| Cash −163,686 | | Note Payable  −132,851 | | Interest Expense (+E)  −30,835 |

### December 31, 2011

Interest = Principal × Rate × Time
= [($400,000 − $119,686 − $132,851) × 11% × 12/12]
= $16,223 (adjusted to accommodate rounding)

Principal = Payment − Interest
= $163,686 − $16,223 = $147,463

**Note Payable (L)**

|  |  |  |  |
|---|---|---|---|
| | | 400,000 | Jan.1, 2009 |
| Dec. 31, 2009 | 119,686 | | |
| Dec. 31, 2010 | 132,851 | | |
| Dec. 31, 2011 | 147,463 | | |
| | | 0 | Dec. 31, 2011 |

|  | Debit | Credit |
|---|---|---|
| Interest Expense (+E, −OE) | 16,223 | |
| Note Payable (−L) | 147,463 | |
| Cash (−A) | | 163,686 |

| Assets | = | Liabilities | + | Owners' Equity |
|---|---|---|---|---|
| Cash −163,686 | | Note Payable  −147,463 | | Interest Expense (+E) −16,223 |

## Case C—Present Value of a Single Amount and an Annuity

On January 1, 2009, General Mills issued 100 four-year, $1,000 bonds. The bonds pay interest annually at a rate of 6 percent of face value. What total amount would investors be willing to pay for the bonds if they require an annual return of: (*a*) 4 percent, (*b*) 6 percent, or (*c*) 8 percent?

**Answer:**   This case requires the computation of the present value of a single amount (the $100,000 face value paid at maturity) plus the present value of an annuity (the annual interest payments of $6,000). The problem can be shown graphically as follows:

**Coach's Tip**

Each interest payment of $6,000 is calculated as: $100,000 × 6% × 12/12.

### (a)  4 Percent Market Interest Rate

The present value of the $100,000 face value is computed as follows:

*From Table C.2, Interest rate = 4% n = 4*

$100,000 × 0.8548 = $85,480

The present value of the $6,000 annuity is computed as follows:

$6,000 × 3.6299 = $21,780*

> From Table C.4,
> Interest rate = 4%
> n = 4

*Adjusted to accommodate rounding in the present value factor.

The present value of the total bond payments, computed using the discount rate of 4 percent, is $107,260 (= $85,480 + $21,780).

## (b) 6 Percent Market Interest Rate

The present value of the $100,000 face value is computed as follows:

$100,000 × 0.7921 = $79,210

> From Table C.2,
> Interest rate = 6%
> n = 4

The present value of the $6,000 annuity is computed as follows:

$6,000 × 3.4651 = $20,790*

> From Table C.4,
> Interest rate = 6%
> n = 4

* Adjusted to accommodate rounding in the present value factor.

The present value of the total bond payments, computed using the discount rate of 6%, is $100,000 (= $79,210 + $20,790).

## (c) 8 Percent Market Interest Rate

The present value of the $100,000 face value is computed as follows:

$100,000 × 0.7350 = $73,503*

> From Table C.2,
> Interest rate = 8%
> n = 4

* Adjusted to accommodate rounding in the present value factor.

The present value of the $6,000 annuity is computed as follows:

$6,000 × 3.3121 = $19,873

> From Table C.4,
> Interest rate = 8%
> n = 4

**Coach's Tip**

The present values in a, b, and c demonstrate the calculation of the bond issue prices used in Chapter 14.

The present value of the total bond payments, computed using the discount rate of 8%, is $93,376 (= $73,503 + $19,873).

The following table summarizes these calculations:

|  | MARKET INTEREST RATES | | |
|---|---|---|---|
|  | 4% | 6% | 8% |
| Present value of $100,000 face value (principal) paid four years from now | $ 85,480 | $ 79,210 | $73,503 |
| Present value of $6,000 (interest) paid once a year for four years | 21,780 | 20,790 | 19,873 |
| Amount to pay | $107,260 | $100,000 | $93,376 |

Of course, these calculations are just the starting point for understanding how bond liabilities are determined and reported. You'll need to read Chapter 14 for information about how bond liabilities are accounted for.

# PRESENT VALUE COMPUTATIONS USING EXCEL

While the present value tables are useful for educational purposes, most present value problems in business are solved with calculators or Excel spreadsheets. Because of the widespread availability of Excel, we will show you how to solve present value problems using Excel. There are slightly different versions of Excel available, depending on the age of the computer. The illustrations in this text are based on Microsoft Office 2007.

## Present Value of a Single Payment

The calculation of a present value amount is based on a fairly simple mathematical formula:

$$PV = Payment/(1+i)^n$$

In this formula, *payment* is the cash payment made at some point in the future, $i$ is the interest rate each period, and $n$ is the number of periods in the problem. We could use this formula to solve all problems involving the present value of a single payment. It is, of course, easier to use a present value table (like the one at the end of this appendix) which is derived by solving the present value formula for various interest rates and numbers of periods. Unfortunately, a table that included all interest rates and numbers of periods actually encountered in business would be too large to work with. As a result, most accountants and analysts use Excel to compute a present value.

To compute the present value of a single payment in Excel, you enter the present value formula in a cell, using the format required by Excel. You should select a cell and enter the following formula:

$$= Payment/(1+i)\text{\textasciicircum}n$$

To illustrate, if you want to solve for the present value of a $100,000 payment to be made in five years with an interest rate of 10%, you would enter the following in the function field:

$$= 100000/(1.10)\text{\textasciicircum}5$$

Based on this entry, Excel would compute the present value of $62,092.13. This answer is slightly different from the answer you would have if you used the present value tables at the end of this appendix. The tables are rounded based on four digits. Excel does not round and, therefore, provides a more accurate computation.

## Present Value of an Annuity

The formula for computing the present value of an annuity is a little more complicated than the present value of a single payment. As a result, Excel has been programmed to include the formula so that you do not have to enter it yourself.

To compute the present value of an annuity in Excel, select a cell and click on the insert function button ($f_x$). The following dropdown box will appear:

Under the Select Category heading, you should pick "Financial," scroll down under "Select a Function," and click on PV. Then, click on "OK" and a new dropdown box will appear:

In this box, you should enter the interest rate, 10% in this example, under Rate. Notice that the rate must be entered as a decimal (i.e., 0.10). Enter the number of periods (20) under Nper. Excel has an unusual convention associated with the payment. It must be entered as a negative amount (−15000) under Pmt. Notice also that a comma should not be included in the amount you enter. When you click on OK, Excel will enter the present value in the cell you selected. In this example, the value determined by Excel is $127,703.46.

## Table C.1    Future Value of $1

| Periods | 2% | 3% | 3.75% | 4% | 4.25% | 5% | 6% | 7% | 8% |
|---|---|---|---|---|---|---|---|---|---|
| 0 | 1. | 1. | 1. | 1. | 1. | 1. | 1. | 1. | 1. |
| 1 | 1.02 | 1.03 | 1.0375 | 1.04 | 1.0425 | 1.05 | 1.06 | 1.07 | 1.08 |
| 2 | 1.0404 | 1.0609 | 1.0764 | 1.0816 | 1.0868 | 1.1025 | 1.1236 | 1.1449 | 1.1664 |
| 3 | 1.0612 | 1.0927 | 1.1168 | 1.1249 | 1.1330 | 1.1576 | 1.1910 | 1.2250 | 1.2597 |
| 4 | 1.0824 | 1.1255 | 1.1587 | 1.1699 | 1.1811 | 1.2155 | 1.2625 | 1.3108 | 1.3605 |
| 5 | 1.1041 | 1.1593 | 1.2021 | 1.2167 | 1.2313 | 1.2763 | 1.3382 | 1.4026 | 1.4693 |
| 6 | 1.1262 | 1.1941 | 1.2472 | 1.2653 | 1.2837 | 1.3401 | 1.4185 | 1.5007 | 1.5869 |
| 7 | 1.1487 | 1.2299 | 1.2939 | 1.3159 | 1.3382 | 1.4071 | 1.5036 | 1.6058 | 1.7138 |
| 8 | 1.1717 | 1.2668 | 1.3425 | 1.3686 | 1.3951 | 1.4775 | 1.5938 | 1.7182 | 1.8509 |
| 9 | 1.1951 | 1.3048 | 1.3928 | 1.4233 | 1.4544 | 1.5513 | 1.6895 | 1.8385 | 1.9990 |
| 10 | 1.2190 | 1.3439 | 1.4450 | 1.4802 | 1.5162 | 1.6289 | 1.7908 | 1.9672 | 2.1589 |
| 20 | 1.4859 | 1.8061 | 2.0882 | 2.1911 | 2.2989 | 2.6533 | 3.2071 | 3.8697 | 4.6610 |

| Periods | 9% | 10% | 11% | 12% | 13% | 14% | 15% | 20% | 25% |
|---|---|---|---|---|---|---|---|---|---|
| 0 | 1. | 1. | 1. | 1. | 1. | 1. | 1. | 1. | 1. |
| 1 | 1.09 | 1.10 | 1.11 | 1.12 | 1.13 | 1.14 | 1.15 | 1.20 | 1.25 |
| 2 | 1.1881 | 1.2100 | 1.2321 | 1.2544 | 1.2769 | 1.2996 | 1.3225 | 1.4400 | 1.5625 |
| 3 | 1.2950 | 1.3310 | 1.3676 | 1.4049 | 1.4429 | 1.4815 | 1.5209 | 1.7280 | 1.9531 |
| 4 | 1.4116 | 1.4641 | 1.5181 | 1.5735 | 1.6305 | 1.6890 | 1.7490 | 2.0736 | 2.4414 |
| 5 | 1.5386 | 1.6105 | 1.6851 | 1.7623 | 1.8424 | 1.9254 | 2.0114 | 2.4883 | 3.0518 |
| 6 | 1.6771 | 1.7716 | 1.8704 | 1.9738 | 2.0820 | 2.1950 | 2.3131 | 2.9860 | 3.8147 |
| 7 | 1.8280 | 1.9487 | 2.0762 | 2.2107 | 2.3526 | 2.5023 | 2.6600 | 3.5832 | 4.7684 |
| 8 | 1.9926 | 2.1436 | 2.3045 | 2.4760 | 2.6584 | 2.8526 | 3.0590 | 4.2998 | 5.9605 |
| 9 | 2.1719 | 2.3579 | 2.5580 | 2.7731 | 3.0040 | 3.2519 | 3.5179 | 5.1598 | 7.4506 |
| 10 | 2.3674 | 2.5937 | 2.8394 | 3.1058 | 3.3946 | 3.7072 | 4.0456 | 6.1917 | 9.3132 |
| 20 | 5.6044 | 6.7275 | 8.0623 | 9.6463 | 11.5231 | 13.7435 | 16.3665 | 38.3376 | 86.7362 |

## Table C.2    Present Value of $1

| Periods | 2% | 3% | 3.75% | 4% | 4.25% | 5% | 6% | 7% | 8% |
|---|---|---|---|---|---|---|---|---|---|
| 1 | 0.9804 | 0.9709 | 0.9639 | 0.9615 | 0.9592 | 0.9524 | 0.9434 | 0.9346 | 0.9259 |
| 2 | 0.9612 | 0.9426 | 0.9290 | 0.9246 | 0.9201 | 0.9070 | 0.8900 | 0.8734 | 0.8573 |
| 3 | 0.9423 | 0.9151 | 0.8954 | 0.8890 | 0.8826 | 0.8638 | 0.8396 | 0.8163 | 0.7938 |
| 4 | 0.9238 | 0.8885 | 0.8631 | 0.8548 | 0.8466 | 0.8227 | 0.7921 | 0.7629 | 0.7350 |
| 5 | 0.9057 | 0.8626 | 0.8319 | 0.8219 | 0.8121 | 0.7835 | 0.7473 | 0.7130 | 0.6806 |
| 6 | 0.8880 | 0.8375 | 0.8018 | 0.7903 | 0.7790 | 0.7462 | 0.7050 | 0.6663 | 0.6302 |
| 7 | 0.8706 | 0.8131 | 0.7728 | 0.7599 | 0.7473 | 0.7107 | 0.6651 | 0.6227 | 0.5835 |
| 8 | 0.8535 | 0.7894 | 0.7449 | 0.7307 | 0.7168 | 0.6768 | 0.6274 | 0.5820 | 0.5403 |
| 9 | 0.8368 | 0.7664 | 0.7180 | 0.7026 | 0.6876 | 0.6446 | 0.5919 | 0.5439 | 0.5002 |
| 10 | 0.8203 | 0.7441 | 0.6920 | 0.6756 | 0.6595 | 0.6139 | 0.5584 | 0.5083 | 0.4632 |
| 20 | 0.6730 | 0.5537 | 0.4789 | 0.4564 | 0.4350 | 0.3769 | 0.3118 | 0.2584 | 0.2145 |

## Table C.2    Present Value of $1 (*continued*)

| Periods | 9% | 10% | 11% | 12% | 13% | 14% | 15% | 20% | 25% |
|---|---|---|---|---|---|---|---|---|---|
| 1 | 0.9174 | 0.9091 | 0.9009 | 0.8929 | 0.8850 | 0.8772 | 0.8696 | 0.8333 | 0.8000 |
| 2 | 0.8417 | 0.8264 | 0.8116 | 0.7972 | 0.7831 | 0.7695 | 0.7561 | 0.6944 | 0.6400 |
| 3 | 0.7722 | 0.7513 | 0.7312 | 0.7118 | 0.6931 | 0.6750 | 0.6575 | 0.5787 | 0.5120 |
| 4 | 0.7084 | 0.6830 | 0.6587 | 0.6355 | 0.6133 | 0.5921 | 0.5718 | 0.4823 | 0.4096 |
| 5 | 0.6499 | 0.6209 | 0.5935 | 0.5674 | 0.5428 | 0.5194 | 0.4972 | 0.4019 | 0.3277 |
| 6 | 0.5963 | 0.5645 | 0.5346 | 0.5066 | 0.4803 | 0.4556 | 0.4323 | 0.3349 | 0.2621 |
| 7 | 0.5470 | 0.5132 | 0.4817 | 0.4523 | 0.4251 | 0.3996 | 0.3759 | 0.2791 | 0.2097 |
| 8 | 0.5019 | 0.4665 | 0.4339 | 0.4039 | 0.3762 | 0.3506 | 0.3269 | 0.2326 | 0.1678 |
| 9 | 0.4604 | 0.4241 | 0.3909 | 0.3606 | 0.3329 | 0.3075 | 0.2843 | 0.1938 | 0.1342 |
| 10 | 0.4224 | 0.3855 | 0.3522 | 0.3220 | 0.2946 | 0.2697 | 0.2472 | 0.1615 | 0.1074 |
| 20 | 0.1784 | 0.1486 | 0.1240 | 0.1037 | 0.0868 | 0.0728 | 0.0611 | 0.0261 | 0.0115 |

## Table C.3    Future Value of Annuity of $1

| Periods* | 2% | 3% | 3.75% | 4% | 4.25% | 5% | 6% | 7% | 8% |
|---|---|---|---|---|---|---|---|---|---|
| 1 | 1. | 1. | 1. | 1. | 1. | 1. | 1. | 1. | 1. |
| 2 | 2.02 | 2.03 | 2.0375 | 2.04 | 2.0425 | 2.05 | 2.06 | 2.07 | 2.08 |
| 3 | 3.0604 | 3.0909 | 3.1139 | 3.1216 | 3.1293 | 3.1525 | 3.1836 | 3.2149 | 3.2464 |
| 4 | 4.1216 | 4.1836 | 4.2307 | 4.2465 | 4.2623 | 4.3101 | 4.3746 | 4.4399 | 4.5061 |
| 5 | 5.2040 | 5.3091 | 5.3893 | 5.4163 | 5.4434 | 5.5256 | 5.6371 | 5.7507 | 5.8666 |
| 6 | 6.3081 | 6.4684 | 6.5914 | 6.6330 | 6.6748 | 6.8019 | 6.9753 | 7.1533 | 7.3359 |
| 7 | 7.4343 | 7.6625 | 7.8386 | 7.8983 | 7.9585 | 8.1420 | 8.3938 | 8.6540 | 8.9228 |
| 8 | 8.5830 | 8.8923 | 9.1326 | 9.2142 | 9.2967 | 9.5491 | 9.8975 | 10.2598 | 10.6366 |
| 9 | 9.7546 | 10.1591 | 10.4750 | 10.5828 | 10.6918 | 11.0266 | 11.4913 | 11.9780 | 12.4876 |
| 10 | 10.9497 | 11.4639 | 11.8678 | 12.0061 | 12.1462 | 12.5779 | 13.1808 | 13.8164 | 14.4866 |
| 20 | 24.2974 | 26.8704 | 29.0174 | 29.7781 | 30.5625 | 33.0660 | 36.7856 | 40.9955 | 45.7620 |

| Periods* | 9% | 10% | 11% | 12% | 13% | 14% | 15% | 20% | 25% |
|---|---|---|---|---|---|---|---|---|---|
| 1 | 1. | 1. | 1. | 1. | 1. | 1. | 1. | 1. | 1. |
| 2 | 2.09 | 2.10 | 2.11 | 2.12 | 2.13 | 2.14 | 2.15 | 2.20 | 2.25 |
| 3 | 3.2781 | 3.3100 | 3.3421 | 3.3744 | 3.4069 | 3.4396 | 3.4725 | 3.6400 | 3.8125 |
| 4 | 4.5731 | 4.6410 | 4.7097 | 4.7793 | 4.8498 | 4.9211 | 4.9934 | 5.3680 | 5.7656 |
| 5 | 5.9847 | 6.1051 | 6.2278 | 6.3528 | 6.4803 | 6.6101 | 6.7424 | 7.4416 | 8.2070 |
| 6 | 7.5233 | 7.7156 | 7.9129 | 8.1152 | 8.3227 | 8.5355 | 8.7537 | 9.9299 | 11.2588 |
| 7 | 9.2004 | 9.4872 | 9.7833 | 10.0890 | 10.4047 | 10.7305 | 11.0668 | 12.9159 | 15.0735 |
| 8 | 11.0285 | 11.4359 | 11.8594 | 12.2997 | 12.7573 | 13.2328 | 13.7268 | 16.4991 | 19.8419 |
| 9 | 13.0210 | 13.5975 | 14.1640 | 14.7757 | 15.4157 | 16.0853 | 16.7858 | 20.7989 | 25.8023 |
| 10 | 15.1929 | 15.9374 | 16.7220 | 17.5487 | 18.4197 | 19.3373 | 20.3037 | 25.9587 | 33.2529 |
| 20 | 51.1601 | 57.2750 | 64.2028 | 72.0524 | 80.9468 | 91.0249 | 102.4436 | 186.6880 | 342.9447 |

* There is one payment each period.

## Table C.4     Present Value of Annuity of $1

| Periods* | 2% | 3% | 3.75% | 4% | 4.25% | 5% | 6% | 7% | 8% |
|---|---|---|---|---|---|---|---|---|---|
| 1 | 0.9804 | 0.9709 | 0.9639 | 0.9615 | 0.9592 | 0.9524 | 0.9434 | 0.9346 | 0.9259 |
| 2 | 1.9416 | 1.9135 | 1.8929 | 1.8861 | 1.8794 | 1.8594 | 1.8334 | 1.8080 | 1.7833 |
| 3 | 2.8839 | 2.8286 | 2.7883 | 2.7751 | 2.7620 | 2.7232 | 2.6730 | 2.6243 | 2.5771 |
| 4 | 3.8077 | 3.7171 | 3.6514 | 3.6299 | 3.6086 | 3.5460 | 3.4651 | 3.3872 | 3.3121 |
| 5 | 4.7135 | 4.5797 | 4.4833 | 4.4518 | 4.4207 | 4.3295 | 4.2124 | 4.1002 | 3.9927 |
| 6 | 5.6014 | 5.4172 | 5.2851 | 5.2421 | 5.1997 | 5.0757 | 4.9173 | 4.7665 | 4.6229 |
| 7 | 6.4720 | 6.2303 | 6.0579 | 6.0021 | 5.9470 | 5.7864 | 5.5824 | 5.3893 | 5.2064 |
| 8 | 7.3255 | 7.0197 | 6.8028 | 6.7327 | 6.6638 | 6.4632 | 6.2098 | 5.9713 | 5.7466 |
| 9 | 8.1622 | 7.7861 | 7.5208 | 7.4353 | 7.3513 | 7.1078 | 6.8017 | 6.5152 | 6.2469 |
| 10 | 8.9826 | 8.5302 | 8.2128 | 8.1109 | 8.0109 | 7.7217 | 7.3601 | 7.0236 | 6.7101 |
| 20 | 16.3514 | 14.8775 | 13.8962 | 13.5903 | 13.2944 | 12.4622 | 11.4699 | 10.5940 | 9.8181 |

| Periods* | 9% | 10% | 11% | 12% | 13% | 14% | 15% | 20% | 25% |
|---|---|---|---|---|---|---|---|---|---|
| 1 | 0.9174 | 0.9091 | 0.9009 | 0.8929 | 0.8550 | 0.8772 | 0.8696 | 0.8333 | 0.8000 |
| 2 | 1.7591 | 1.7355 | 1.7125 | 1.6901 | 1.6681 | 1.6467 | 1.6257 | 1.5278 | 1.4400 |
| 3 | 2.5313 | 2.4869 | 2.4437 | 2.4018 | 2.3612 | 2.3216 | 2.2832 | 2.1065 | 1.9520 |
| 4 | 3.2397 | 3.1699 | 3.1024 | 3.0373 | 2.9745 | 2.9137 | 2.8550 | 2.5887 | 2.3616 |
| 5 | 3.8897 | 3.7908 | 3.6959 | 3.6048 | 3.5172 | 3.4331 | 3.3522 | 2.9906 | 2.6893 |
| 6 | 4.4859 | 4.3553 | 4.2305 | 4.1114 | 3.9975 | 3.8887 | 3.7845 | 3.3255 | 2.9514 |
| 7 | 5.0330 | 4.8684 | 4.7122 | 4.5638 | 4.4226 | 4.2883 | 4.1604 | 3.6046 | 3.1611 |
| 8 | 5.5348 | 5.3349 | 5.1461 | 4.9676 | 4.7988 | 4.6389 | 4.4873 | 3.8372 | 3.3289 |
| 9 | 5.9952 | 5.7590 | 5.5370 | 5.3282 | 5.1317 | 4.9464 | 4.7716 | 4.0310 | 3.4631 |
| 10 | 6.4177 | 6.1446 | 5.8892 | 5.6502 | 5.4262 | 5.2161 | 5.0188 | 4.1925 | 3.5705 |
| 20 | 9.1285 | 8.5136 | 7.9633 | 7.4694 | 7.0248 | 6.6231 | 6.2593 | 4.8696 | 3.9539 |

* There is one payment each period.

## Key Terms

Annuity (p. C4)                    Present Value (p. C2)                    Time Value of Money (p. C2)
Future Value (p. C2)

See complete glossary in back of text.

## Questions

1. Explain the concept of the time value of money.

2. Explain the basic difference between future value and present value.

3. If you deposited $10,000 in a savings account that earns 10 percent, how much would you have at the end of 10 years? Use a convenient format to display your computations.

4. If you hold a valid contract that will pay you $8,000 cash 10 years from now and the going rate of interest is 10 percent, what is its present value? Use a convenient format to display your computations.

5. What is an annuity?

6. Use tables C.1 to C.4 to complete the following schedule:

| | TABLE VALUES | | |
|---|---|---|---|
| | $i = 5\%, n = 4$ | $i = 10\%, n = 7$ | $i = 14\%, n = 10$ |
| FV of $1 | | | |
| PV of $1 | | | |
| FV of annuity of $1 | | | |
| PV of annuity of $1 | | | |

7. If you deposit $1,000 at the end of each period for 10 interest periods and you earn 8 percent interest, how much would you have at the end of period 10? Use a convenient format to display your computations.

# Multiple Choice

1.  You are saving up for a Porsche Carrera Cabriolet, which currently sells for nearly half a million dollars. Your plan is to deposit $15,000 at the end of each year for the next 10 years. You expect to earn 5 percent each year. How much will you have saved after 10 years, rounded to the nearest 10 dollars?

    a.  $150,000.
    b.  $188,670.
    c.  $495,990.
    d.  None of the above.

2.  Which of the following is a characteristic of an annuity?

    a.  An equal dollar amount each interest period.
    b.  Interest periods of equal length.
    c.  An equal interest rate each interest period.
    d.  All of the above are characteristics of an annuity.

3.  Which of the following is most likely to be an annuity?

    a.  Monthly payments on a credit card bill.
    b.  Monthly interest earned on a checking account.
    c.  Monthly payments on a home mortgage.
    d.  Monthly utility bill payments.

4.  Assume you bought a state of the art entertainment system, with no payments to be made until two years from now, when you must pay $6,000. If the going rate of interest on most loans is 5 percent, which table in this appendix would you use to calculate the system's equivalent cost if you were to pay for it today?

    a.  Table C.1 ( Future Value of $1)
    b.  Table C.2 (Present Value of $1)
    c.  Table C.3 (Future Value of Annuity of $1)
    d.  Table C.4 (Present Value of Annuity of $1)

5.  Assuming the facts in question 4, what is the system's equivalent cost if you were to pay for it today?

    a.  $5,442
    b.  $6,615
    c.  $11,100
    d.  $12,300

6.  Assume you bought a car using a loan that requires payments of $3,000 to be made at the end of every year for the next three years. The loan agreement indicates the annual interest rate is 6 percent. Which table in this appendix would you use to calculate the car's equivalent cost if you were to pay for it in full today?

    a.  Table C.1 (Future Value of $1)
    b.  Table C.2 (Present Value of $1)
    c.  Table C.3 (Future Value of Annuity of $1)
    d.  Table C.4 (Present Value of Annuity of $1)

7.  Assuming the facts in question 6, what is the car's equivalent cost if you were to pay for it today? Round to the nearest hundred dollars.

    a.  $2,600
    b.  $3,600
    c.  $8,000
    d.  $9,600

8.  Which of the following statements are true?

    a.  When the interest rate increases, the present value of a single amount decreases.
    b.  When the number of interest periods increase, the present value of a single amount increases.
    c.  When the interest rate increases, the present value of an annuity increases.
    d.  None of the above are true.

9.  Which of the following describes how to calculate a bond's issue price?

    | | Face Value | Interest Payments |
    |---|---|---|
    | a. | Present value of single amount. | Future value of annuity. |
    | b. | Future value of single amount. | Present value of annuity. |
    | c. | Present value of single amount. | Present value of annuity. |
    | d. | Future value of single amount. | Future value of annuity. |

10. If interest is compounded quarterly, rather than yearly, how do you adjust the number of years and annual interest rate when using the present value tables?

    | | Number of years | Annual interest rate |
    |---|---|---|
    | a. | Divide by 4 | Divide by 4 |
    | b. | Divide by 4 | Multiply by 4 |
    | c. | Multiply by 4 | Divide by 4 |
    | d. | Multiply by 4 | Multiply by 4 |

---

Solutions to Multiple-Choice Questions

1. b    2. d    3. c    4. b    5. a    6. d    7. c    8. a    9. c    10. c

---

# Mini Exercises

### MC-1 Computing the Present Value of a Single Payment
What is the present value of $500,000 to be paid in 10 years, with an interest rate of 8 percent?

### MC-2 Computing the Present Value of an Annuity
What is the present value of 10 equal payments of $15,000, with an interest rate of 10 percent?

### MC-3 Computing the Present Value of a Complex Contract
As a result of a slowdown in operations, Mercantile Stores is offering to employees who have been terminated a severance package of $100,000 cash; another $100,000 to be paid in one year; and an annuity of $30,000 to be paid each year for 20 years. What is the present value of the package, assuming an interest rate of 8 percent?

### MC-4 Computing the Future Value of an Annuity

You plan to retire in 20 years. Calculate whether it is better for you to save $25,000 a year for the last 10 years before retirement or $15,000 for each of the 20 years. Assume you are able to earn 10 percent interest on your investments.

## Exercises

### EC-1 Computing Growth in a Savings Account: A Single Amount

On January 1, 2009, you deposited $6,000 in a savings account. The account will earn 10 percent annual compound interest, which will be added to the fund balance at the end of each year.

*Required (round to the nearest dollar):*

1. What will be the balance in the savings account at the end of 10 years?
2. What is the interest for the 10 years?
3. How much interest revenue did the fund earn in 2009? 2010?

### EC-2 Computing Deposit Required and Accounting for a Single-Sum Savings Account

On January 1, 2009, Alan King decided to transfer an amount from his checking account into a savings account that later will provide $80,000 to send his son to college (four years from now). The savings account will earn 8 percent, which will be added to the fund each year-end.

*Required (show computations and round to the nearest dollar):*

1. How much must Alan deposit on January 1, 2009?
2. Give the journal entry that Alan should make on January 1, 2009 to record the transfer.
3. What is the interest for the four years?
4. Give the journal entry that Alan should make on (a) December 31, 2009, and (b) December 31, 2010.

### EC-3 Recording Growth in a Savings Account with Equal Periodic Payments

On each December 31, you plan to transfer $2,000 from your checking account into a savings account. The savings account will earn 9 percent annual interest, which will be added to the savings account balance at each year-end. The first deposit will be made December 31, 2009 (at the end of the period).

*Required (show computations and round to the nearest dollar):*

1. Give the required journal entry on December 31, 2009.
2. What will be the balance in the savings account at the end of the 10th year (i.e., 10 deposits)?
3. What is the total amount of interest earned on the 10 deposits?
4. How much interest revenue did the fund earn in 2010? 2011?
5. Give all required journal entries at the end of 2010 and 2011.

### EC-4 Computing Growth for a Savings Fund with Periodic Deposits

On January 1, 2009, you plan to take a trip around the world upon graduation four years from now. Your grandmother wants to deposit sufficient funds for this trip in a savings account for you. On the basis of a budget, you estimate that the trip currently would cost $15,000. Being the generous and sweet lady she is, your grandmother decided to deposit $3,500 in the fund at the end of each of the next four years, starting on December 31, 2009. The savings account will earn 6 percent annual interest, which will be added to the savings account at each year-end.

*Required (show computations and round to the nearest dollar):*

1. How much money will you have for the trip at the end of year 4 (i.e., after four deposits)?
2. What is the total amount of interest earned over the four years?
3. How much interest revenue did the fund earn in 2009, 2010, 2011, and 2012?

### EC-5 Computing Value of an Asset Based on Present Value

You have the chance to purchase an oil well. Your best estimate is that the oil well's net royalty income will average $25,000 per year for five years. There will be no residual value at that time. Assume that the cash inflow occurs at each year-end and that considering the uncertainty in your estimates, you expect to earn 15 percent per year on the investment.

*Required:*

What should you be willing to pay for this investment right now?

### EC-6 Comparing Options Using Present Value Concepts

After hearing a knock at your front door, you are surprised to see the Prize Patrol from a large, well-known magazine subscription company. It has arrived with the good news that you are the big winner, having won "$20 million." You discover that you have three options: (1) you can receive $1 million per year for the next 20 years, (2) you can have $8 million today, or (3) you can have $2 million today and receive $700,000 for each of the next 20 years. Your financial adviser tells you that it is reasonable to expect to earn 10 percent on investments.

**Required:**

Which option do you prefer? What factors influence your decision?

## Problem—Set A

### PAC-1 Comparing Options Using Present Value Concepts

After completing a long and successful career as senior vice president for a large bank, you are preparing for retirement. After visiting the human resources office, you have found that you have several retirement options: (1) you can receive an immediate cash payment of $1 million, (2) you can receive $60,000 per year for life (your remaining life expectancy is 20 years), or (3) you can receive $50,000 per year for 10 years and then $70,000 per year for life (this option is intended to give you some protection against inflation). You have determined that you can earn 8 percent on your investments. Which option do you prefer and why?

## Problem—Set B

### PBC-1 Comparing Options Using Present Value Concepts

After incurring a serious injury caused by a manufacturing defect, your friend has sued the manufacturer for damages. Your friend received three offers from the manufacturer to settle the lawsuit; (1) receive an immediate cash payment of $100,000, (2) receive $6,000 per year for life (your friend's remaining life expectancy is 20 years), or (3) receive $5,000 per year for 10 years and then $7,000 per year for life (this option is intended to compensate your friend for increased aggravation of the injury over time). Your friend can earn 8 percent interest and has asked you for advice. Which option would you recommend and why?

# INTERNATIONAL FINANCIAL REPORTING STANDARDS

It has become an old cliché but business really has gone global. Abercrombie is opening stores in Sweden, and Swedish companies like IKEA and H&M are opening stores throughout the United States. Similar trends are occurring in the investing world, where shares of foreign companies like Benetton and British Airways are traded on the New York Stock Exchange (NYSE). Until recently, investors struggled to compare the financial statements of companies like these because different countries used different accounting rules. All this is changing now, with the increasing acceptance of International Financial Reporting Standards (abbreviated IFRS, pronounced "eye-furs").

IFRS are developed by the International Accounting Standards Board (IASB), which is the international counterpart to the Financial Accounting Standards Board (FASB) in the United States. Over 100 different countries including Australia, China, the European Union, South Africa, and New Zealand currently require or permit the use of IFRS, or a local version of IFRS. This number is continuing to grow with IFRS becoming official in the near future in Brazil (2010), Canada (2011), India (2011), and other countries. Although the United States has not yet switched to IFRS, such a change is believed to be coming in the next six years or so. The Securities and Exchange Commission (SEC) has already begun moving in this direction by allowing foreign companies like Benetton and British Airways to issue stock in the United States without having to convert their IFRS-based accounting numbers to U.S. GAAP. The SEC plans to allow some U.S. companies to use IFRS in 2009, and aims to require IFRS starting in 2014. Many foreign-owned private companies in the United States, such as Mack Trucks and Dreyer's Ice Cream, already use IFRS to make it easy to combine their financial statements with their foreign owners' financial statements.

Although IFRS differ from the generally accepted accounting principles currently used in the United States, they do not dramatically alter what you have learned in this course. IFRS use the same system of analyzing, recording, and summarizing the results of business activities that you learned in Chapters 1–4. The most significant differences between IFRS and U.S. GAAP relate to technical issues that are typically taught in intermediate and advanced accounting courses. For the topics discussed in this course, differences between IFRS and U.S. GAAP are limited, which we summarize briefly in the table on the following page.

As we look to the future, it seems clear that U.S. GAAP and IFRS will converge as the FASB and IASB work together to remove differences between the two sets of accounting rules and to develop new rules through joint projects. One of the most exciting of these projects currently being worked on is the development of a new format for organizing items on the financial statements. Although it has not yet been finalized, a current proposal is to separately report the results of operating, investing, and financing activities in each of the financial statements similar to what is currently required for the statement of cash flows. Having learned the differences between typical financing and investing activities (in Chapter 2) and operating activities (in Chapter 3), you will be well-prepared to handle evolutions such as these as they arise during your career.

| Chapter Topic | U.S. GAAP | IFRS |
|---|---|---|
| 7: Inventories | • Allows 4 cost flow methods (p. 307)<br>• LCM rule bases market value on replacement cost (p. 313) | • Does not allow LIFO<br>• LCM bases market value on net realizable value (selling price less selling costs) |
| | • Inventory write-down required but reversal disallowed (p. 314) | • Both write-down and reversal required |
| 10: Long-Lived Tangible and Intangible Assets | • "Basket purchases" of assets are separated into components (p. 420)<br>• Do not revalue unless impaired (p. 430) | • Individual assets may be separated into significant components<br>• Regular revaluation at fair value permitted |
| 11: Current Liabilities and Payroll | • Contingent liabilities accrued if estimable and probable (p. 477) | • Contingent liabilities accrued if estimable and "more likely than not" |
| 13: Corporations | • Most preferred stock is reported as equity (p. 564) | • Most preferred stock is reported as debt |
| 16: Statement of Cash Flows | • Interest paid, interest received, and dividends received are classified as operating (p. 694) | • Interest paid can be either operating or financing; interest and dividends received can be either operating or investing |
| | • Dividends paid are classified as financing (p. 694) | • Dividends paid can be either operating or financing |

# Glossary

## A

**Account** p. 57 Individual record of both increases and decreases in a specific asset, liability, owner's equity, revenue, or expense.

**Account Receivable** p. 382 Amount owed on open account to a business by a customer.

**Accounting** p. 6 Information system designed to capture and communicate a business's financial condition and financial performance to decision makers inside and outside the organization.

**Accounting Cycle** p. 57 Activities during the accounting period: Analyze transactions, record the effects of the transactions in the journal, and post the effects to the ledger. Activities at the end of the accounting period: Take a trial balance, adjust the accounts, prepare financial statements, and close the records.

**Accounting Information System (AIS)** p. 204 Collects, classifies, summarizes, and reports the financial information about a business to interested parties.

**Accounting Rate of Return** p. 932 Estimated average return on investment that a project is expected to generate over its life cycle.

**Accounts Payable Subsidiary Ledger** p. 206 Used to collect and maintain all individual transactions with creditors that occurred on account.

**Accounts Receivable Subsidiary Ledger** p. 206 Used to collect and maintain all individual transactions with customers that occurred on account.

**Accrual Basis Accounting (accrual accounting)** p. 101 Principle that revenues are recorded when earned (i.e., the company performs the service or delivers goods to customers) and expenses are recorded when incurred to generate revenues in the same period.

**Accrued Expenses** p. 147 Expenses that are incurred but not recorded until the end of the period because cash is paid after the goods or services are used.

**Accrued Revenues** p. 147 Revenues earned but not recorded until the end of the period because cash is received after the services are performed or goods delivered.

**Active Investments** p. 643 Investments in stock of another business to influence or control that business; acquisition of 20 percent or more of the voting stock of a company is presumed to be an active investment.

**Activity Based Costing** p. 857 Product costing method used by companies that have diverse products to which indirect costs are assigned based on the underlying activities performed.

**Activity Cost Driver** p. 859 Underlying measure of activity used in activity based costing to assign the indirect cost to products and services.

**Actual Manufacturing Overhead** p. 806 Actual amount of indirect manufacturing costs incurred during the period.

**Adjusted Trial Balance** p. 160 Listing of all accounts and their balances after adjustments have been posted to the accounts to verify that debits equal credits.

**Adjusting Entries** p. 147 Entries necessary at the end of the accounting period to measure all revenues when earned and expenses when incurred during that period.

**Administrative Costs** p. 773 Costs associated with running the overall organization.

**Aging of Accounts Receivable Method** p. 386 Method that estimates the uncollectible accounts balance based on the age of each account receivable.

**Allocation Base** p. 804 Measurable item used to apply indirect overhead costs to products or services.

**Allowance for Doubtful Accounts** p. 383 Contra-asset containing the estimated portion of accounts receivable that will not be paid.

**Allowance Method** p. 383 Method of accounting that reduces accounts receivable (as well as net income) for an estimate of uncollectible accounts (bad debts).

**Amortization** p. 435 Name given to allocation of the cost of intangible assets over their limited useful lives.

**Amortized Cost** p. 644 Cost of bonds adjusted for the amortization of any bond discount or premium.

**Annual Rate of Return** p. 932 Estimated average return on investment that a project is expected to generate over its life cycle.

**Articles of Organization** p. 507 Document required in all states to form an LLC; provides important information about its operations and structure.

**Asset** p. 9 Measurable economic resource owned by the business that is likely to provide future benefits.

**Authorized Shares** p. 567 Shares of stock a corporation can issue as specified in the charter.

**Avoidable Cost** p. 922 Cost that can be avoided by choosing one decision option instead of another.

## B

**Bad Debt Expense** p. 383 Estimated expense for the period related to customers who will fail to pay.

**Balance Sheet** p. 51 Financial statement that reports the amount of a business's assets, liabilities, and owner's equity at a specific point in time.

**Balanced Scorecard** p. 1039 Comprehensive performance measurement system that translates an organization's vision and strategy into a set of operational performance metrics.

**Bank Reconciliation** p. 355 Internal accounting report that uses both the bank statement and the cash accounts of a business to determine the appropriate amount of cash in a bank account after considering delays or errors in processing cash transactions.

**Batch-Level Activities** p. 858 Activities performed for a group of units or customers all at once.

**Bonding** p. 347 Obtaining an insurance policy that partially reimburses the organization for losses caused by employee fraud.

**Bonds** p. 604 Financial instruments that outline future payments a company promises to make in exchange for receiving cash now.

**Book (or Carrying) Value** p. 424 Acquisition cost of an asset less accumulated depreciation (amount used in prior periods).

**Break-Even Analysis** p. 895 One application of cost-volume-profit analysis that determines the point at which fixed costs have been exactly covered and profit is zero.

**Break-Even Point** p. 895 Point at which total revenue equals total cost, resulting in zero profit; the point at which fixed costs exactly equal the contribution margin.

**Budget** p. 768 Quantification of the resources and expenditures that will be required during a given period of time to achieve a plan.

**Budget Slack** p. 961 Cushion that managers may try to build into their budget by understating expected sales or overstating budgeting expenses so that they are more likely to come in under budget for expenses and over budget for revenues.

**Budgeted Balance Sheet** p. 962 Balance sheet created from a combination of the financial budgets; shows expected balance of assets, liabilities, and owners' equity at the end of the budget period.

**Budgeted Cost of Goods Sold** p. 963 Budgeted manufacturing cost per unit multiplied by the number of units of expected sales.

**Budgeted Gross Margin** p. 964 Budgeted sales less budgeted cost of goods sold.

**Budgeted Income Statement** p. 962 Expectation of income after combining all operating budgets.

**Budgeted Manufacturing Cost per Unit** p. 963 Combination of all budgeted manufacturing costs.

## C

**Capital Budgeting** p. 920 Decision-making approach aimed at helping managers make decisions about investments in major capital assets.

**Capital Budgeting Decisions** p. 931 Long-term decisions regarding capital investments.

**Capital Deficiency** p. 531 Lack of sufficient capital in a partner's capital account to absorb losses resulting from the liquidation of the partnership.

**Capital Expenditure** p. 423 Amount paid to increase a long-lived asset's economic usefulness through increased efficiency, increased capacity, or longer life; capitalized as a cost of the asset.

**Capital Lease** p. 610 Similar to an operating lease, except that virtually all risks and rewards of owning the rented property transfer to the company that obtains the use of the property.

**Capitalize** p. 419 To record a cost as an asset rather than an expense.

**Carrying Value** p. 607 Amount at which an item is reported ("carried at") on the balance sheet after considering related contra-accounts.

**Cash Basis Accounting** p. 100 Concept that revenues are recorded when cash is received and expenses are recorded when cash is paid. Cash basis accounting is not a generally accepted accounting principle.

**Cash Budget** p. 964 Financial budget that provides information about budgeted cash receipts and disbursements.

**Cash Count Sheet** p. 350 Internal document on which a cashier records the amount of cash received from cash register sales and determines any cash shortage or overage.

**Cash Equivalent** p. 360 Amount of cash that a creditor would accept to settle a liability for a transaction or event immediately after it occurs.

**Cash-Equivalent Amount** p. 600 Amount of cash that would be accepted as full settlement of a liability the moment the liability is created.

**Cash Equivalents** p. 468 Short-term, highly liquid investments obtained within three months of maturity.

**Cash Equivalents** p. 682 Short-term, highly liquid investments that are both (1) readily convertible to known amounts of cash and (2) so near to maturity that there is little risk their value will change.

**Cash Flows from Financing Activities** p. 684 Cash inflows and outflows related to financing sources external to the company (owners and lenders).

**Cash Flows from Investing Activities** p. 684 Cash inflows and outflows related to the purchase or sale of investments and long-lived assets.

**Cash Flows from Operating Activities (Cash Flows from Operations)** p. 683 Cash inflows and outflows related to components of net income.

**Cash** p. 360 Money or any instrument that banks will accept for deposit and immediate credit to a bank account, such as a check, money order, or bank draft.

**Cash Payments Journal** p. 217 Used to record all transactions involving the payment of cash from a business.

**Cash Receipts Journal** p. 212 Used to record all cash receipts/collections in a business regardless of the reason for the receipt.

**Centralized Organization** p. 1028 Organization in which decision-making authority is kept at the very top level of the organization.

**Certified Public Accountant** p. 6 Individual who becomes a licensed accounting professional.

**Classified Balance Sheet** p. 68 Balance sheet separated into classifications: Current assets are listed separately from noncurrent assets; current liabilities are listed separately from noncurrent liabilities.

**Closing the Books** p. 164 Process of making all temporary accounts have a zero balance for the start of the next accounting period; the balances in the temporary accounts are transferred to owner's capital to update its balance.

**Code of Professional Conduct** p. 24 Rules established by the American Institute of Certified Public Accountants to govern the ethical performance of professional services by CPAs.

**Collude** p. 348 To work with another party to circumvent or avoid internal controls, rendering them ineffective.

**Common Stock** p. 561 Basic voting stock a corporation issues to stockholders.

**Comparable** p. 23 Characteristic of financial information stating that information is more useful when it can be compared against information for other companies.

**Computerized (Electronic) Accounting Information System** p. 204 Performs all steps in the accounting cycle electronically with the aid of general ledger software packages.

**Conservatism** p. 69 Accounting concept that, when doubt exists about the amount at which assets and liabilities should be reported, the least optimistic measurement should be used.

**Consistent** p. 23 Characteristic of financial information stating that information is more useful when it can be compared over time.

**Consolidated Financial Statements** p. 659 Single set of financial statements representing the combination of the operations of two or more companies.

**Construction in Progress** p. 419 Account used to accumulate construction costs for projects not yet complete.

**Contingent Liabilities** p. 476 Potential liabilities that arise as a result of past transactions or events and whose resolution depends (is "contingent") on a future event.

**Continuity Assumption** p. 74 Accounting concept that assumes a business will continue operating long enough to meet its contractual commitments and plan; it will continue to operate into the foreseeable future.

**Contra-account** p. 152 Account directly related to another but with an opposite balance.

**Contributed Capital** p. 562 Contributions made directly to a corporation by its owners (stockholders).

**Contribution Margin Income Statement** p. 892 Type of income statement that separates costs into variable or fixed costs; used to address many managerial problems.

**Contribution Margin** p. 893 Difference between sales revenue and variable costs.

**Contribution Margin Ratio** p. 893 Total contribution margin divided by total sales revenue; stated as a percentage of sales.

**Control Account** p. 206 Account in the general ledger that summarizes all transactions occurring in its related subsidiary ledger.

**Control** p. 768 One of the key functions of management; involves monitoring actual results to see whether the objectives set in the planning state are being made.

**Controllability Principle** p. 1030 Concept that managers should be held responsible for only those things that they can control.

**Conversion Cost** p. 772 Sum of direct labor and manufacturing overhead; total cost incurred to convert direct materials into a finished product.

**Copyright** p. 434 Form of protection provided to the original authors of literary, musical, artistic, dramatic, and other works of authorship.

**Corporation** p. 5 Legal and accounting entity that sells shares of stock to owners.

**Cost Behavior** p. 884 Describes how total costs change when some measure of activity level changes.

**Cost Center** p. 1030  Responsibility center in which manager has authority and responsibility for cost.

**Cost Driver** p. 857  Measure used to allocate or assign indirect costs to products.

**Cost Object** p. 770  Any item for which one wants to determine cost.

**Cost of Goods Completed** p. 811  Total amount of cost assigned to goods that were manufactured or completed during an accounting period.

**Cost of Goods Manufactured** p. 775  Total cost of all units completed during a given time period regardless of whether the units were sold during the current period or not.

**Cost of Goods Sold (CGS)** p. 270  Expense account including the total cost of inventory sold during the period.

**Cost of Goods Sold (COGS)** p. 806  Expense account including the total cost of jobs or units sold during the period.

**Cost of Goods Sold Equation** p. 306  BI + P − CGS = EI

**Cost** p. 769  Value given up in exchange for something else.

**Cost-Volume-Profit Analysis** p. 894  Analysis that focuses on a specific decision and determines how changes in volume will affect costs and profit.

**Credit** p. 58  Special accounting name for the right side of accounts.

**Crossfoot** p. 213  To verify that the total amounts of the Debit columns equal the total amounts of the Credit columns in a multicolumn special journal.

**Cumulative Dividend Preference** p. 571  Feature of preferred stock that requires dividends in arrears to be paid before current dividends.

**Current Assets** p. 68  Resources the business will use or turn into cash within one year.

**Current Dividend Preference** p. 570  Feature of preferred stock that grants priority to preferred dividends over dividends on common stock.

**Current Liabilities** p. 68  Short-term obligations that will be paid with current assets or settled by providing goods or services within the current operating cycle of the business or within one year of the balance sheet date, whichever is longer.

**Current Ratio** p. 469  Ratio measuring the extent to which current assets are sufficient to pay current liabilities; calculated by dividing current assets by current liabilities.

**Customer-Level Activities** p. 858  Activities performed for a specific customer.

**CVP Graph** p. 898  Graph that is useful for visualizing the relationship among unit sales volume, total revenue, total cost, and profit.

## D

**Debit** p. 58  Special accounting name for the left side of accounts.

**Debt-to-Assets Ratio** p. 611  Measures the extent of financing risk by indicating the proportion of total assets financed by liabilities.

**Decentralized Organization** p. 1028  Organization in which decision-making authority is spread throughout, and managers are responsible for deciding how to manage their particular area of responsibility.

**Declaration Date** p. 569  Date on which the board of directors officially approves a dividend.

**Declining-Balance Depreciation Method** p. 427  Method that assigns more depreciation to early years of an asset's life and less depreciation to later years.

**Dependent Variable** p. 889  Variable that depends on the level of X.

**Deposits in Transit** p. 357  Reconciling items on a bank reconciliation representing deposits made and recorded by the business but not yet shown on the bank statement.

**Depreciable Cost** p. 425  Portion of an asset's cost that will be used in generating revenue; calculated as asset cost minus residual value; allocated to depreciation expense throughout the asset's life.

**Depreciation** p. 152  Allocation of the cost of long-lived tangible assets over their estimated productive lives using a systematic and rational method.

**Differential Analysis** p. 921  See *Incremental Analysis*.

**Differential Cost** p. 922  Cost that differs between decision alternatives.

**Direct Costs** p. 770  Costs that can be directly attributed or traced to a specific cost object.

**Direct Labor Budget** p. 963  Budget indicating the amount of direct labor needed to meet expected production.

**Direct Labor Efficiency Variance** p. 997  Variance that calculates the portion of direct labor spending variance driven by the difference in the actual and the standard labor hours, noted as SR × (SH − AH).

**Direct Labor** p. 772  Costs for labor that can be physically and conveniently traced to the final product.

**Direct Labor Rate Variance** p. 997  Variance that calculates the portion of the direct labor spending variance that is driven by the difference in actual and standard labor rate, noted as AH × (SR − AR).

**Direct Labor Spending Variance** p. 997  Variance that represents the sum of the direct labor rate variance and the direct labor efficiency variances.

**Direct Labor Time Ticket** p. 803  Source document used to keep track of direct labor costs in a job order cost system.

**Direct Materials** p. 772  Primary material inputs that can be physically and conveniently traced to the final product.

**Direct Materials Price Variance** p. 995  Variance that calculates the portion of the direct materials spending variance driven by the difference in actual and standard price of direct materials, noted as AQ × (SP − AP).

**Direct Materials Quantity Variance** p. 995  Variance that calculates the portion of the direct materials spending variance driven by the difference in actual and standard quantity of direct materials, noted as SP × (SQ − AQ).

**Direct Materials Spending Variance** p. 996  Sum of the direct materials price variance and the direct materials quantity variances.

**Direct Method** p. 683  Method of presenting the Operating Activities section of the cash flow statement to report the components of cash flows from operating activities as gross receipts and gross payments.

**Direct Write-Off Method** p. 389  Method of accounting that records bad debt expense only when a company writes off specific accounts.

**Directing/Leading** p. 768  One of the key functions of management; involves all actions that managers must take to implement a plan.

**Discount** p. 605  Excess of a bond's face value over its issue price.

**Discounted Cash Flow Method** p. 932  Decision-making approach that incorporates the time value of money.

**Discounting** p. 601  Process of calculating the cash-equivalent "present value" of future payments by removing the interest component that is built into future payments.

**Dividends in Arrears** p. 571  Dividend rights from prior years that must be satisfied before dividends of the current year can be paid.

**Double-Declining-Balance Depreciation Method** p. 427  Type of declining-balance depreciation calculated using double the straight-line depreciation rate.

**DuPont Method** p. 1034  Formula developed by executives at DuPont in the early 1900s; shows that the return on investment is a function of profit margin and investment turnover.

## E

**Easily Attainable Standard** p. 988   Standard that can be met with relative ease.

**EBITDA** p. 439   Abbreviation for "earnings before interest, taxes, depreciation, and amortization," which is a measure of operating performance that some managers and analysts use in place of net income.

**Electronic Funds Transfer (EFT)** p. 351   Cash transferred into or out of a bank account using electronic means, such as the Internet or wire transfer.

**Employee Earnings Record** p. 480   Employer's internal record that indicates payroll computations for each employee for a particular pay period.

**Employee Payroll Taxes** p. 483   Amounts employers are legally required to pay in addition to salaries and wages; typically includes FICA taxes and state and federal unemployment taxes.

**Equity Method** p. 654   Active investments that are increased (decreased) by the investor's share of the investee's net income or loss (reported as income by the investor) and decreased by the investor's share of the dividends declared by the investee (not reported as income by the investor).

**Equivalent Unit** p. 851   Measure of the amount of work that occurred during the period.

**Ethics** p. 24   Standards of conduct for judging right from wrong, honest from dishonest, and fair from unfair.

**Expenses** p. 98   Dollar amount of resources an entity uses to earn revenues during a period.

**Extraordinary Repairs** p. 423   Expenditures that increase a tangible asset's economic usefulness in the future and are recorded as increases in asset accounts, not as expenses.

## F

**Face Value** p. 604   Amount a bond promises to pay on its maturity date.

**Facility-Level Activities** p. 858   Activities performed for the overall company.

**Favorable Variance** p. 989   Variance indicating that actual costs were less than budgeted or standard costs.

**Financial Accounting** p. 766   Area of accounting that prepares information used by external parties, such as investors, creditors, and regulators.

**Financial Accounting** p. 8   Accounting area focused on providing financial information to external users primarily to make investing and lending decisions.

**Financial Accounting Standards Board (FASB)** p. 23   Entity with the primary responsibility (as designated by the Securities and Exchange Commission) of setting underlying rules of accounting in the United States.

**Financial Budget** p. 962   Budget that focuses on the financial resources needed to support operations.

**Financing Activities** p. 18   Business activities involving borrowing from banks, repaying bank loans, receiving investments from owners, and distributing profits to owners (through withdrawals for proprietors and partnerships and through dividends to stockholders).

**Finished Goods Inventory** p. 775   Cost of all units that have been completed but have not yet been sold.

**First-In, First-Out (FIFO)** p. 307   Assumption that the oldest goods (the ones first in) are used first to calculate cost of goods sold.

**Fixed Assets** p. 418   Alternative name for long-lived tangible assets reflecting assets that are physically fixed in place.

**Fixed Costs** p. 771   Costs that remain the same, in total, regardless of activity level.

**Fixed Overhead Spending Variance** p. 1002   Variance that represents the difference in actual and budgeted fixed overhead costs.

**Fixed Overhead Volume Variance** p. 1002   Variance resulting from the difference between actual and budgeted production volume.

**Flexible Budget** p. 990   Budget showing how budgeted costs and revenues will change for different levels of sales.

**FOB Destination** p. 265   Sales term indicating that ownership changes when goods reach the buyer's premises and the seller pays the freight charges.

**FOB Shipping Point** p. 265   Sales term indicating that ownership changes when goods leave the seller's premises and the buyer pays the freight charges.

**Foot** p. 213   To add the dollar amounts in a column.

**Franchise** p. 434   Contractual right to sell certain products or services, use certain trademarks, or perform activities in a certain geographical region.

**Fundamental Accounting Equation** p. 9   Basic equation stating that assets equal liabilities plus owner's equity.

## G

**Generally Accepted Accounting Principles (GAAP)** p. 23   Accounting measurement and reporting rules to be applied by businesses.

**Goal Incongruence** p. 1038   Conflict between a manager and the organization that may cause managers to make decisions that are not in the best interest of the overall organization.

**Goods Available for Sale** p. 305   Sum of the beginning inventory and purchases of the period.

**Goodwill** p. 434   Premium a company pays to obtain the favorable reputation associated with another company.

**Gross Earnings** p. 478   Amounts employees earn as compensation for the work they provide.

**Gross Profit (or Gross Margin)** p. 276   Amount the company earned from selling goods over and above their cost.

**Gross Profit Percentage** p. 278   Percentage of profit earned on each dollar of sales after considering the cost of products sold.

## H

**High-Low Method** p. 890   Method of analyzing mixed costs using the two most extreme activity levels (X values) to estimate fixed and variable costs.

**Historical Cost** p. 9   Accounting principle stating that assets are initially measured at the total cost to acquire them.

**Horizontal (Trend) Analysis** p. 732   Comparison of individual financial statement items from year to year with the general goal of identifying significant sustained changes or trends.

**Hurdle Rate** p. 933   Minimum required rate of return for a project.

## I

**Ideal Standard** p. 988   Standard that can be achieved only under perfect or ideal conditions.

**Impairment** p. 430   Loss that occurs when the cash to be generated by an asset is estimated to be less than the carrying value of that asset.

**Imprest System** p. 352   System that acts as an internal control to restrict the amount paid to others by limiting the amount of money available to be paid; typically used for payroll and petty cash.

**Income Statement** p. 14   Financial statement that reports the performance of a business for a period of time.

**Income Summary** p. 164   Temporary account used only during the closing process; all revenues and expenses are closed to Income Summary and then Income Summary is closed to owner's capital.

**Incremental Analysis** p. 921   Short-term decision-making approach that focuses on the differential costs and benefits of alternate decision choices.

**Incremental Cost** p. 922  See *Differential Costs*.

**Independent Variable** p. 889  Variable that causes Y to change.

**Indirect Costs** p. 770  Costs that cannot be traced to a specific cost object or are not worth the effort to trace.

**Indirect Materials** p. 807  Materials that cannot be directly or conveniently traced to a specific unit and are therefore treated as manufacturing overhead.

**Indirect Method** p. 683  Method that starts with net income from the income statement and then adjusts it by removing items that do not involve cash but were included in net income and adding items that involved cash but were not yet included in net income.

**Intangible Assets** p. 418  Long-lived assets that lack physical substance.

**Interest Formula** p. 390  $I = P \times R \times T$ where $I$ = interest calculated, $P$ = principal, $R$ = annual interest rate, and $T$ = time period covered in the interest calculation (number of months out of 12).

**Internal Controls** p. 344  Methods an organization uses to protect against theft of assets, to enhance the reliability of accounting information, to promote efficient and effective operations, and to ensure compliance with applicable laws, regulations, and codes of ethical conduct.

**Internal Rate of Return** p. 935  Discount rate at which the present value of cash inflows exactly equals the cash outflows.

**Inventoriable Cost** p. 773  Cost that is counted as inventory on the balance sheet until the product is sold; another term for product cost.

**Inventory Budget** p. 963  Budget that shows how much finished goods, work in process, and raw materials inventory are planned at the beginning and end of each budget period.

**Investing Activities** p. 18  Business activities involving buying and selling productive resources with long lives.

**Investment Center** p. 1030  Responsibility center in which manager has authority and responsibility for profit (revenue – cost) and the investment of assets.

**Investment Turnover** p. 1034  Ratio of sales revenue to the investment base (assets).

**Investments for Significant Influence** p. 654  Investments in 20 percent or more of the voting stock of other companies to obtain significant influence or control over the financing and operating activities of those companies.

**Investments Held to Maturity** p. 654  Investments in bonds that management intends and has the ability to hold until the maturity date.

**Irrelevant Cost** p. 922  Cost that will not impact a particular decision.

**Issued Shares** p. 867  Shares of stock that have been sold or given to indicate ownership of a corporation.

## J

**Job Cost Sheet** p. 802  Document used to record all of the costs of producing a particular job or servicing a specific customer.

**Job Order Costing** p. 861  Costing system used by companies that make unique products or provide specialty services.

**Journal Entry** p. 58  Form used to record the effects of a transaction in the journal. Accounts to be debited are listed first with the amounts indicated in the left column; accounts to be credited are listed below the debited accounts with amounts indicated in the right column.

**Journal** p. 57  Chronological record of the effects of transactions on accounts.

## L

**Land Improvements** p. 419  Enhancements made to land that are expected to deteriorate over time.

**Last-In, First Out (LIFO)** p. 307  Assumption that the costs of the newest goods (the last ones in) are used first to calculate cost of goods sold.

**Ledger** p. 57  Record used to accumulate the effects of transactions on individual accounts.

**Liabilities** p. 9  Measurable and probable obligations that require the business to pay goods or services to others in the future.

**Licensing Right** p. 434  Limited permission to use property according to specific terms and conditions set out in a contract.

**Limited Liability Company (LLC)** p. 507  Business organizational form that offers its members limited liability protection and pass-through taxation.

**Line of Credit** p. 469  Preapproved loan that allows a business to borrow money (up to a predetermined limit) on an as-needed basis.

**Liquidity** p. 469  Measure of an organization's ability to pay amounts currently owed.

**Liquidity** p. 736  Ratio indicating the extent to which a company is able to pay its currently maturing obligations.

**Long-Lived Assets** p. 418  Resources owned by a business that enable it to produce the goods or services the business sells to customers.

**Long-Term Debt** p. 600  Liabilities requiring repayment over more than one year or if longer, the company's operating cycle.

**Long-Term Objective** p. 959  Specific goal that management wants to achieve over a long-term horizon of more than one year.

**Lower of Cost or Market (LCM)** p. 313  Process that writes inventory down to market value when the market value of inventory items falls below cost.

## M

**Managerial Accounting** p. 7  Accounting area focused on providing information to assist managers in making business decisions.

**Managerial Accounting** p. 766  Area of accounting that prepares information aimed at managers who are running the business; sometimes called internal reporting because it is used by individuals inside the company.

**Manual Accounting Information System** p. 204  Performs all steps in the accounting cycle by hand without the aid of a computerized program.

**Manufacturing Company** p. 262  Company that sells goods it has made itself.

**Manufacturing Costs** p. 772  Costs incurred to produce a physical product; generally classified as direct materials, direct labor, or manufacturing overhead.

**Manufacturing Firm** p. 773  Company that purchases raw materials and uses them to make a finished product to sell to wholesalers, retailers, or customers.

**Manufacturing Overhead Budget** p. 963  Budget that indicates overhead costs to be incurred to support budgeted production.

**Manufacturing Overhead** p. 772  All costs other than direct material and direct labor that must be incurred to manufacture a physical product.

**Margin of Safety** p. 896  Difference between actual or budgeted sales and the break-even point.

**Market Interest Rate** p. 606  Interest rate that the bond market ultimately obtains by purchasing a bond at a premium, a discount, or face value; represents a company's cost of borrowing.

**Market Value Method** p. 646  Adjust investments in available for sale and trading securities to market value at the end of each reporting period.

**Marketing or Selling Costs** p. 772  Costs incurred to sell a final product or service to the customer.

**Master Budget** p. 962  Integrated set of operating and financial budgets that reflects what management expects to achieve in a future accounting period.

**Matching Principle** p. 103 Principle that costs incurred to generate revenues should be recognized (recorded) in the same period to match the costs with benefits.

**Materials Requisition** p. 802 Document used to authorize the issuance of materials into production; details the cost and quantities of all materials needed to complete specific jobs.

**Maturity Date** p. 604 Date on which a bond's face value is scheduled to be paid to bondholders.

**Merchandising Company** p. 262 Company that sells goods (merchandise) obtained from a supplier.

**Merchandising Company** p. 773 Company that purchases goods (merchandise) from a supplier and sells them to other businesses or consumers.

**Merger** p. 659 Event that occurs when one company acquires the assets and liabilities of another company and the acquired company goes out of existence.

**Mixed Costs** p. 886 Costs that have both a fixed component and a variable component; also known as semivariable costs.

**Monetary Unit Assumption** p. 15 Theoretical concept stating that financial information is reported in the standard monetary denomination of the country in which the business operated.

## N

**Net Assets** p. 434 Shorthand term used to refer to assets minus liabilities.

**Net Book Value (also called book value or carrying value)** p. 152 Amount reported on the balance sheet (e.g., original cost of equipment minus accumulated depreciation).

**Net Income** p. 15 Positive difference between revenues earned during a period and the expenses that were incurred to generate the revenues during the period.

**Net Loss** p. 16 Result when expenses exceed revenues during a period.

**Net Present Value (NPV) Method** p. 934 Method that compares the present value of the future cash flows for a project to the original investment that is required at the start of the project.

**Net Profit Margin** p. 169 Ratio that measures how effective managers were at generating profit on every dollar of sales.

**Nondiscounting Methods** p. 932 Approaches to management decisions that do not consider the time value of money.

**Nonmanufacturing Costs** p. 772 Costs associated with running a business and selling a product as opposed to manufacturing a product; generally classified as marketing or selling costs or administrative costs.

**Nonvolume-Based Cost Drivers** p. 857 Allocation bases not directly related to the number of units produced.

**No-Par Value Stock** p. 563 Capital stock that has no par value specified in the corporate charter.

**Note Receivable** p. 382 Promise made in writing that requires another party to pay the business.

**Notes** p. 18 Additional information provided to accompany the basic financial statements to assist users in understanding amounts reported on the financial statements or other items that may affect their decisions.

**NSF (Not Sufficient Funds) Checks** p. 357 Checks written for an amount more than the funds available to cover them.

## O

**Operating (Cash-to-Cash) Cycle** p. 99 Process by which a company acquires and pays for goods and services and then sells goods and services to customers who pay cash to the company.

**Operating Activities** p. 18 Business activities directly related to earning profits.

**Operating Agreement** p. 507 Document recommended when an LLC is formed to address potential problem areas.

**Operating Budgets** p. 962 Budgets that cover the organization's planned operating activities for a particular period of time.

**Operating Lease** p. 610 Rental agreement that allows a company to obtain temporary use of property in exchange for future payments to the property's owner.

**Opportunity Cost** p. 770 Cost that occurs when you choose not to do something; a forgone benefit or lost opportunity in choosing one alternative instead of another.

**Ordinary Repairs and Maintenance** p. 423 Expenditures for routine operating upkeep of long-lived assets; recorded as expenses.

**Organizing** p. 768 One of the key functions of management; involves arranging the necessary resources to carry out the plan.

**Out-of-Pocket Costs** p. 790 Costs that involve an outlay of cash.

**Outstanding Check** p. 357 Reconciling item on a bank reconciliation representing checks written and recorded by the business but that have not yet cleared the bank.

**Outstanding Shares** p. 567 Issued shares currently held by stockholders, not the corporation itself.

**Over- or Underapplied Fixed Overhead** p. 1003 Sum of the fixed overhead spending variance and the fixed overhead volume variance.

**Overapplied Overhead** p. 812 Difference between actual and applied overhead when the overhead applied to Work in Process is higher than the actual overhead cost incurred during the period.

**Override** p. 348 To disarm or cancel internal controls, rendering them ineffective.

**Owner's Equity** p. 9 Difference between the assets the business owns and the liabilities the business owes. It represents the owner's stake in the business.

## P

**Par Value** p. 563 Value assigned to each share of capital stock as specified in the charter.

**Parent Company** p. 659 Company acquiring another for control.

**Participative Budgeting** p. 961 Method that allows employees throughout the organization to have input into the budget-setting process.

**Partner Return on Equity** p. 533 Ratio that measures a company's efficiency in generating profits from every dollar of equity invested in and retained by a partnership.

**Partner's Capital Statement** p. 516 Financial statement that replaces the owner's equity statement and shows all changes to capital for each partner in a partnership.

**Partnership** p. 506 An unincorporated business owned by two or more individuals.

**Partnership Agreement** p. 506 Recommended document when a partnership is formed to address potential problem areas.

**Partnership Dissolution** p. 517 When a partner is added, it causes the dissolution of the existing partnership (consisting of the old partners) and the creation of a new partnership (consisting of the new partners).

**Partnership Liquidation** p. 526 Process to terminate a partnership that involves selling the partnership assets, paying its liabilities, and distributing cash to partners.

**Passive Investments** p. 643 Investments in debt and stock instruments for the purpose of earning a return on the funds; acquisition of less than 20 percent of the voting stock of a company is presumed to be a passive investment.

**Pass-Through Taxation** p. 507 Taxation rule that allows profits from a business to flow directly through to the owners, avoiding taxation at the business level.

**Patent** p. 434 Right to exclude others from making, using, selling, or importing an invention.

**Payback Period** p. 933  Amount of time it takes to generate enough cash for a project to pay for its original investment.

**Payment Date** p. 569  Date on which a corporation pays a cash dividend to the stockholders of record.

**Payroll** p. 477  Process followed to pay employees for their work.

**Payroll Deductions** p. 478  Amounts subtracted from each employee's gross earnings so that they can be remitted to another organization or government agency on behalf of that employee.

**Payroll Register** p. 482  Internal record that accumulates payroll costs across all employees for a particular pay period; the basis for recording payroll journal entries.

**Percentage of Accounts Receivable Method** p. 386  Method that estimates the uncollectible accounts balance based on a single percentage of total accounts receivable that are likely to be uncollectible.

**Percentage of Credit Sales Method** p. 386  Method that estimates bad debt expense by multiplying the historical percentage of bad debt losses by the current year's credit sales.

**Period Cost** p. 773  Cost that is expensed as soon as it is incurred.

**Periodic Inventory System** p. 264  Inventory system that updates the inventory records "periodically," that is, at the end of the accounting period.

**Permanent Accounts** p. 164  Accounts that retain their balances from period to period (they are not closed); assets, liabilities, and owner's equity accounts are permanent.

**Perpetual Inventory System** p. 263  Inventory system that updates the inventory records "perpetually," that is, every time inventory is bought, sold, or returned.

**Petty Cash Fund** p. 353  Fund from which money is taken to reimburse employees for expenditures they have made on behalf of the organization.

**Planning** p. 768  Future-oriented aspect of the management process that involves setting long-term goals and objectives and short-term tactics necessary to achieve those goals.

**Predetermined Overhead Rate** p. 804  Rate estimated before the accounting period begins and used throughout the period to assign overhead costs to products based on actual values of an allocation base.

**Preference Decisions** p. 932  Decisions that require managers to choose from among a set of alternative capital investment opportunities.

**Preferred Stock** p. 561  Stock that has specified rights over common stock.

**Premium** p. 605  Excess of a bond's issue price over its face value.

**Prepaid Expenses** p. 147  Previously recorded assets that must be adjusted for the amount of expense incurred by using the asset during the period to generate revenues.

**Prime Cost** p. 772  Sum of direct materials and direct labor; represents the costs that can be directly traced to the end product.

**Private Accounting** p. 6  Sector of the accounting profession in which accountants are employed by a single business or non-profit organization.

**Private Companies** p. 560  Companies whose stock is bought and sold through private transactions.

**Process Costing** p. 800  Costing system used by companies that make very homogenous products or services.

**Product Costs** p. 773  Costs that become a part of the product that is being produced.

**Production Budget** p. 963  Budget that shows how many units need to be produced each period to meet projected sales.

**Production Report** p. 855  Essentially a summary of what occurred in the production process during the accounting period.

**Product-Level Activities** p. 858  Activities performed to support an overall product line.

**Profit Center** p. 1030  Responsibility center in which manager has authority and responsibility for profit (revenue − cost).

**Profit Margin** p. 1034  Ratio of operating profit to sales revenue.

**Profitability** p. 736  Profitability is the extent to which a company generates income.

**Promissory Note** p. 470  Written document outlining terms and conditions by which one individual or business will pay another.

**Public Accounting** p. 6  Sector of the accounting profession in which accountants charge fees for services to a variety of organizations.

**Public Companies** p. 560  Companies whose stock is bought and sold publicly on stock exchanges.

**Public Company Accounting Oversight Board (PCAOB)** p. 23  Entity that sets rules for auditors in the United States.

**Purchase Discount** p. 266  Cash discount received for prompt payment of a purchase on account.

**Purchase Return and Allowance** p. 266  Reduction in the cost of inventory purchases associated with unsatisfactory goods.

**Purchases Journal** p. 216  Used to record all purchases made or expenses incurred on account.

# R

**Raw Materials Inventory** p. 775  Cost of all materials purchased from suppliers that have not yet been used in production.

**Raw Materials Inventory Account** p. 785  Inventory account that includes the total cost of raw materials purchased but not yet issued to production.

**Raw Materials Purchases Budget** p. 963  Budget that indicates the quantity of raw materials that must be purchased to meet production and raw materials inventory needs.

**Record Date** p. 569  Date on which the corporation prepares the list of current stockholders; dividends are paid only to the stockholder who owns stock on this date.

**Regression Analysis** p. 890  Method of analyzing mixed costs by using a statistical package to calculate the "best-fitting" line using all available data points.

**Related-Party Transactions** p. 1040  Business transactions between units or divisions of the same company.

**Relevant Cost** p. 922  Cost that has the potential to influence a particular decision.

**Relevant** p. 23  Characteristic of financial information stating that information that is helpful in making decisions should be reported.

**Relevant Range** p. 884  Range of activity over which assumptions about cost behavior are expected to hold true.

**Reliable** p. 23  Characteristic of financial information stating that information is most useful when it is unbiased and verifiable.

**Remittance Advice** p. 351  Form that explains the reasons for a payment, often a tear-away attachment to a supplier's invoice or company check.

**Research and Development** p. 434  Expenditures that may some day lead to patents, copyrights, or other intangible assets but the uncertainty about their future benefits requires that they be expensed.

**Residual (or Salvage or Scrap) Value** p. 124  Estimated amount to be recovered at the end of the company's estimated useful life of an asset.

**Residual Income** p. 1036  Alternative measure for evaluating investment center performance; calculated as the difference between operating income and minimum profit needed to cover the required rate of return (hurdle rate).

**Responsibility Accounting** p. 1030  Area of accounting in which managers are given authority and responsibility over a particular area of the organization and are then evaluated based on the results of that area of responsibility.

**Responsibility Center** p. 1030  Area over which managers are given responsibility for specific operations of an organization.

**Retained Earnings** p. 563  Account used by corporations to accumulate the profits or losses generated each year (minus any dividends declared) since the corporation was first created.

**Return on Assets** p. 660  Ratio that measures how much the firm earned for each dollar invested in assets.

**Return on Investment (ROI)** p. 1034  Most common method of evaluating investment center performance; calculated as return (measured by operating profit) / investment (measured by average invested assets).

**Revenue Center** p. 1030  Responsibility center in which manager has authority and responsibility for revenue.

**Revenue Expenditure** p. 423  Amounts paid to maintain an asset's original operating capacity; matched to revenues as an expense in the period incurred.

**Revenue Journal** p. 209  Used to record services rendered to customers on account.

**Revenue Principle** p. 101  Concept that revenue should be recognized in the period earned (i.e., in which the company has performed a service or delivered goods to customers). Also known as the revenue recognition rule.

**Revenues** p. 10  Amounts earned when goods or services are delivered to customers.

# S

**Salaries** p. 477  Fixed amounts paid monthly, typically to managerial, sales, and administrative personnel.

**Sales Budget** p. 963  Estimate of the number of units to be sold and the total sales revenue to be generated in each budget period; also called the sales forecast.

**Sales Discount** p. 272  Discount given to customers for prompt payment of an account receivable.

**Sales Returns and Allowances** p. 271  Reductions in the amount owed by customers after goods have been found unsatisfactory.

**Sarbanes-Oxley (SOX) Act of 2002** p. 344  Act passed by Congress to restore investor confidence in and improve the quality of financial reporting by publicly traded companies in the United States.

**Scattergraph** p. 887  Graph of the relationship between total cost (Y) and activity level (X).

**S-Corporation** p. 508  Corporation that allows profits to pass through to the owners' personal income tax returns and provides owners limited liability.

**Screening Decisions** p. 931  Decisions made when managers evaluate a proposed capital investment to determine whether it meets some minimum criteria.

**Securities and Exchange Commission (SEC)** p. 23  Governmental agency that supervises the work of the Financial Accounting Standards Board and the Public Company Accounting Oversight Board.

**Securities Available for Sale** p. 646  Passive investments not actively traded; reported at market value as current and/or noncurrent assets, depending on management's intent; unrealized gains or losses are reported in stockholders' equity on the balance sheet.

**Segment Margin** p. 1032  Calculated as revenue minus all costs that are directly traceable to a particular business segment.

**Segmented Income Statement** p. 1032  Income statement that shows the profitability of individual business segments for a particular period of time.

**Segregation of Duties** p. 346  Internal control principle that involves separating employees' duties so that the work of one person can be used to check the work of another person.

**Selling and Administrative Expense Budget** p. 963  Budget of expected cost of selling and administration based on the planned level of sales.

**Separate Entity Assumption** p. 10  Assumption that activities of the business are reported separately from activities of its owners.

**Service Company** p. 262  Company that sells services rather than physical goods.

**Service Company** p. 773  Company that provides services to other businesses or consumers.

**Short-Term Objective** p. 959  Specific goal that management wants to achieve in the short-run; usually no longer than one year.

**Sole Proprietorship** p. 4  Business owned by one individual.

**Solvency** p. 736  Solvency is the ability to survive long enough to repay lenders when debt matures.

**Special Journal** p. 209  Used to record similar types of transactions in one convenient place.

**Specific Identification** p. 307  Inventory costing method that individually identifies and records the cost of each item sold.

**Spending Variances** p. 992  Variances calculated by comparing actual costs to the flexible budget cost.

**Standard Cost Card** p. 989  Form on which to record a summary of what it should cost to make a single unit of product based on expected production and sales for the upcoming period.

**Standard Cost System** p. 988  Cost system that records manufacturing costs at standard rather than actual amounts.

**Standard Unit Cost** p. 989  Expected cost to produce one unit based on standard prices and quantities.

**Stated Interest Rate** p. 604  Interest rate stated on the face of a bond certificate, which when multiplied by the face value indicates the dollar amount of interest paid each year.

**Statement of Cash Flows** p. 18  Financial statement that reports the business's cash inflows (receipts) and outflows (payments) by business activity (operating, investing, and financing) for a period of time.

**Statement of Owner's Equity** p. 16  Financial statement that reports the changes in owner's equity during the period.

**Static Budget** p. 990  Budget based on a single estimate of sales volume.

**Step Costs** p. 885  Costs that are fixed over some range of activity and then increase in a steplike fashion when a capacity limit is reached; can be treated as either step-variable or step-fixed costs.

**Step-Fixed Cost** p. 886  Step cost with relatively wide steps; typically treated as a fixed cost at least within a relevant range.

**Step-Variable Cost** p. 885  Step cost with relatively narrow steps; typically treated as a variable cost because multiple steps are encountered across the relevant range.

**Stock Dividend** p. 572  Distribution of additional shares of a corporation's own stock.

**Stock Split** p. 573  Increase in the total number of authorized and issued shares by a specified ratio; often is accompanied by a corresponding reduction in the per share value, resulting in no change to the stockholders' equity accounts.

**Stockholders** p. 560  Owners of a corporation who hold stock certificates indicating their share of ownership.

**Stockholders' Equity** p. 562  Category of the balance sheet that reports stockholders' claims on the resources of the corporation.

**Straight-Line Depreciation Method** p. 426  Method that allocates the depreciable cost of an asset in equal periodic amounts over its useful life.

**Strategic Plan** p. 959  Managers' vision of what they want the organization to achieve over a long-term horizon.

**Subsidiary Company** p. 659  Company acquired by another company gaining control.

**Subsidiary Ledger** p. 206  Group of accounts that share a common feature.

**Sunk Cost** p. 922  Cost incurred in the past; is not relevant to future decisions.

# T

**T-account** p. 61   Simplification of a page in the ledger, written in the form of a T with debit effects on the left of the T and credit effects on the right.

**Tactics** p. 959   Specific actions or mechanisms that management uses to achieve objectives.

**Tangible Assets** p. 418   Long-lived assets that have physical substance.

**Target Profit Analysis** p. 897   CVP analysis that determines the amount of sales necessary to earn a specific profit.

**Temporary Accounts** p. 164   Accounts that accumulated data for the current accounting period only (they are closed at the end of the period to owner's capital, a permanent account); revenues, expenses, and owner's drawing accounts are temporary.

**Time Period Assumption** p. 99   Assumption that, to measure income for a specific period of time, the long life of a company can be reported in shorter time periods.

**Times Interest Earned Ratio** p. 612   Measures the extent to which a company's income before the costs of financing and taxes are sufficient to cover interest expense.

**Top-Down Approach** p. 961   Method in which top management sets a budget and imposes it on lower levels of the organization.

**Trademark** p. 433   Special name, image, or slogan identified with a product or company.

**Trading Securities** p. 646   Investments in stocks and bonds that management actively trades; reported at market value in current assets section of balance sheet; unrealized gains or losses are reported on the income statement.

**Transactions** p. 68   Business activities that affect the accounting equation.

**Transfer Price** p. 1040   Amount charged when one division sells goods or services to another division of the same company.

**Treasury Stock** p. 565   Issued shares that the corporation has repurchased.

**Trial Balance** p. 65   List of individual accounts, usually in financial statement order, with their ending balances from the ledger (T-accounts) indicated in the appropriate column (debits on the left and credits on the right). Its purposes are to ensure that debits equal credits, summarize account balances, review and analyze necessary adjustments, and prepare financial statements.

# U

**Unadjusted Trial Balance** p. 112   List of individual accounts, usually in financial statement order, with their ending balances from the ledger (T-accounts) indicated in the appropriate column (debits on the left and credits on the right). The purpose is to check the accounting system to ensure that debits equal credits.

**Underapplied Overhead** p. 812   Difference in actual and applied overhead that occurs when the overhead applied to Work in Process Inventory is less than the actual overhead cost incurred during the period.

**Unearned Revenues** p. 147   Previously recorded liabilities, created when cash was received in advance of being earned, that need to be adjusted for the amount of revenue earned during the period.

**Unfavorable Variance** p. 990   Variance indicating that actual costs were more than budgeted or standard costs.

**Unit Contribution Margin** p. 893   Difference between sales revenue per unit and variable cost per unit; indicates how much each additional unit sold will contribute to fixed costs and profit.

**Unit-Level Activities** p. 858   Activities performed for each unit or customer (one at a time).

**Units-of-Production Depreciation Method** p. 426   Method that allocates the depreciable cost of an asset over its useful life based on the relationship of its periodic output to its total estimated output.

**Unrealized Holding Gains or Losses** p. 648   Temporary changes in the market value of passive investments.

**Useful Life** p. 424   Expected service life of an asset to the present owner.

# V

**Variable Costs** p. 771   Costs that change in total in direct proportion to changes in activity levels.

**Variable Overhead (VOH) Rate Variance** p. 999   Variance driven by the difference in actual and standard variable overhead rates.

**Variable Overhead Efficiency Variance** p. 987   Variance driven by the difference in actual amounts and standard amounts of a cost driver (e.g., direct labor hours) multiplied by the standard variable overhead rate.

**Variance** p. 987   Difference between actual costs and budgeted or standard costs.

**Vertical (Common Size) Analysis** p. 734   Analytic technique that expresses each line of the income statement (or balance sheet) as a percentage of total sales (or total assets).

**Visual Fit Method** p. 890   Method of analyzing mixed costs that involves "eyeballing" the data on a scattergraph.

**Volume Variance** p. 992   Variance driven by the difference in actual and budgeted sales volume.

**Volume-Based Allocation Measures** p. 857   Allocation bases traditionally used to assign indirect costs that are directly related to number of units produced.

**Voucher** p. 352   The accumulated documentation of each step in a voucher system.

**Voucher System** p. 352   Process for approving and documenting all purchases and payments made on account.

# W

**Wages** p. 477   Amounts paid based on a rate per hour or per unit of production, typically to clerks, factory workers, and part-time employees.

**Weighted Average** p. 307   Inventory costing method that uses the weighted average cost of goods available for sale as the unit cost for cost of goods sold and ending inventory.

**Work in Process Inventory** p. 775   Cost of units that have been started in the manufacturing operation but are incomplete at the end of an accounting period.

**Work in Process Inventory Account** p. 785   Inventory account that includes the total cost incurred to manufacture goods that are in process but not yet completed.

**Write Off** p. 384   To remove an uncollectible account and its corresponding allowance from the accounting records.